University Museum Monograph 112

TEPE GAWRA:
THE EVOLUTION OF
A SMALL, PREHISTORIC CENTER
IN NORTHERN IRAQ

Mitchell S. Rothman

with an Appendix by Brian Peasnall

UNIVERSITY OF PENNSYLVANIA
Museum of Archaeology and Anthropology
Philadelphia

Library of Congress Cataloging-in-Publication Data

Rothman, Mitchell S., 1952–
    The evolution of a small, prehistoric center in northern Iraq /
Mitchell S. Rothman; with an appendix by Brian Peasnall.
        p.   cm.
Includes bibliographical references and index.
    ISBN 0-924171-89-8 (alk. paper)
    1. Gawra, Tepe (Iraq)—History.   2. Excavations
(Archaeology)—Iraq—Gawra, Tepe.   I. Title.
DS70.5.G38 R67   2002
935—dc21   2001005767

Generous financial support from
the Hagop Kevorkian Fund
is gratefully acknowledged.

Preparation of this volume
was supported by National Endowment
for the Humanities Grant R0-21872-89.

This volume is dedicated to my wife, Leslie Mara Simon, and my
daughter, Dena Peri Simon Rothman. They have suffered
the many hours I was cloistered in my study preparing
this volume and have lovingly supported my efforts
throughout the entire project.

This volume is also dedicated to Charles Bache, the unsung
excavator of Tepe Gawra, without whose chits and
amazingly early, clear-headed understanding
of stratigraphy this re-analysis would
not have been possible.

Contents

Illustrations

Figures

Tables

Plates

Preface

A project as large as this re-analysis of Tepe Gawra is never the work of one person. I began this project in 1986 as a dissertation at the University of Pennsylvania. Dr. Robert H. Dyson, Jr., recommended that I focus on this site. I had actually talked with Dr. Dyson about doing a re-evaluation of the Gawra material in 1973 after writing a paper on Gawra seals and sealings for a course taught by Henry Wright at the University of Michigan, where I received my Bachelor of Arts degree. Between 1973 and 1986, another student had begun and then dropped this project. I had had dissertation projects curtailed by a revolution in Iran, a military takeover in Turkey, and a frustrated attempt to use ancient historical documents as the basis for a study of ancient agricultural decision-making. Dr. Dyson was right. This project is a gem.

My dissertation on Levels XI/XA-VIII (Rothman 1988) was the foundation for this expanded (and corrected) volume. In that effort, I received no end of help from Dr. Dyson and Dr. Richard Zettler. Dr. Dyson shared his expertise on ancient architecture, without which my redrawing of the town plans would not have been possible, and kept in check my youthful desire to speculate wildly. Richard Zettler was a deep pool of bibliographic knowledge and corrected many of my early misunderstandings of seals and sealings. Ward Goodenough had useful comments to make. His now-classic article on status and role (Goodenough 1965) was a critical one for me to put together a series of ideas about the evolution of organizations.

In my dissertation and beyond, I relied on the help of many members of the University of Pennsylvania Museum staff in doing the research for this book. As the data were mostly archival, I received no end of aid from Douglas Haller, then the Museum's Archivist, and his assistant, now Acting Archivist, Alessandro Pezzati. Maude de Schauensee and later Shannon White, keepers of the Near East Section, always had the key at the ready to the museum's deep dark sub-basement where Gawra artifacts are stored. Virginia Greene and Stuart Fleming, of Conservation and MASCA, respectively, have helped with the scientific studies that are reported here. Chrisso Boulis, now Registrar, was very considerate of a graduate student constantly looking through old registry cards. University Museum librarians Anita Fahringer and Jean Adelman were always available to help find a well-hidden book and to talk about this and that when fatigue set in. I thank Dr. Dyson and Dr. Jeremy Sabloff, past and current directors of the University of Pennsylvania Museum, for their support of this project. Dr. Sabloff arranged for a subsidy for this volume from the Kevorkian Foundation. Dr. Dyson helped to obtain the prepublication grant from the National Endowment for the Humanities, which underwrote preparation of the artwork and time for me to finish collecting data on Levels XII and XIAB. Associate Director of the Museum, Alan Waldt, and his assistant, Suzanne Clappier, helped me get through the maze of obtaining funds and reporting on progress to the NEH.

The publication process for this volume was a very long one from initial acceptance to final publication. I thank Karen Velucci, director of publications at the beginning phases and especially the current director of publications, Walda Metcalf, and her most able assistant, Helen Schenck, for bringing it to an end. Jennifer Smith and Jennifer Quick were helpful and capable facilitators later in the process.

The artwork for this volume was prepared by a number of people. Georgi Grentzenberg prepared the architectural plans and the schematic sections and drew all of the seals, sealings, and pottery. Jennifer Hook drew most of the other artifacts, except the lithics, which I drew, helped by my early training from Henry Wright in lithic illustration. My father, Carl Rothman, spent many hours with me in the uncomfortable sub-basement photographing all the seals and sealings from Gawra VIII-XII. A few of those photographs appear in Plate 64.

I thank the inventors of Adobe Photoshop and Quark Express and Steve Jobs of Apple for providing the tools I used to lay out the pottery drawings and the seals and sealing. I also could not have done any of the distribution maps without Adobe Illustrator. Anita Liebman and Joan Feinberg laid out the lithics, spindle whorl, metals, jewelry, ground stone, and clay objects plates. To all cited above, thank you most sincerely for your contributions and help.

Paul Zimansky and Elizabeth Stone were kind enough to inspect the Gawra seals and sealings they could find in the Iraq Museum and photograph the backs of sealings. I am very appreciative of their efforts.

A volume like this is also helped by those with less direct parts to play in the research, writing, illustration, and publication. I owe my wife, Leslie Simon, and my daughter, Dena Rothman, a gigantic debt of thanks.

There are also many friends, colleagues, and teachers who indirectly made this volume possible. In addition to Drs. Dyson, Zettler, and Goodenough, a number of teachers stand out in my training: Drs. Henry Wright, Kent Flannery, John Speth, and the late George Cameron of the University of Michigan, Greg Johnson, Susan Lees, and Daniel Bates of Hunter College, Bernard Wailes, Christopher Hamlin, Barry Eichler, Erle Leichty, and Åke Sjöberg of the University of Pennsylvania, Irene Winter now of Harvard, Richard Blanton now of Purdue University. Henry Wright has long had a master plan for explaining the origin of the state in ancient Mesopotamia. I have been honored and educated by being included as one of his unnamed research assistants. Each of the others has shown interest in me and shared a little of their deep knowledge and great insight into the ancient world or into the theoretical approaches needed to understand the greatest mystery, the nature of human beings in society.

I have made too many friends in the process of researching and writing this book to name them all. A few, however, stand out through discussions on the topic of this book and in many acts of kindness and help. They include Gil Stein of Northwestern University, Guillermo Algaze of the University of California San Diego, Holly Pittman of the University of Pennsylvania, Glenn Schwartz of Johns Hopkins, Mary Voigt of the College of William and Mary, Eleanor King of the University of Pennsylvania, Michael Rosenberg of the University of Delaware, Gary Feinman of the Field Museum, and T. Cuyler Young and Dan Rahimi of the Royal Ontario Museum. I thank Brian Peasnall for doing such a fine job on the graves of Gawra.

Thanks, too, to Widener University, who paid me during the period of this volume's production.

Despite all of the work, help, guidance, and friendship of those named above, do not blame any of them for my mistakes.

1

Introduction, Geographic and Cultural Background, and Analytical Goals

The seven hundred years from 4400 to 3700 BC[1] in Greater Mesopotamia set the stage for what Childe (1950) described as the second great revolution in human history: the rise of city life and the evolution of the economic and political organizations we know as states. It was in this Mesopotamian region, defined as the basins of the Tigris and Euphrates Rivers and their tributaries—the Khabur, Diyala, upper and lower Zab, Karkeh, Karun, and Ab-i Diz in modern Iraq, Syria, western Iran, and southeastern Turkey—where this revolution first occurred (see Figure 1.1, Rothman 1994c). This volume seeks to reconstruct the life of a small center, Tepe Gawra, in the northern Mesopotamian piedmont between the hills of western Iran and the steppes of northern Iraq during seven hundred years of this pre-state, pre-urban period. It is a tale of tradition and of change.

Goals

This volume has two separate but interrelated goals. The first is to place Levels XII–VIII at Tepe Gawra in the context of those radical transformations of the Greater Mesopotamian region over the span from the late fifth through the end of the fourth millennia B.C. The developments at Gawra relate directly to Algaze's application of World Systems Theory (Wallerstein 1974) to explain the North–South interaction, the Uruk Expansion (Algaze 1989, 1993, and in press).

That theory, outlined below, has become a paradigm for research concerning this region and this time period (e.g., Rothman, ed. in press; Stein, ed. 1999; Stein 1999; Postgate and Campbell in press).

Although, following a re-analysis by Gut (1995) and others, I now believe that Level VIII at Tepe Gawra burned or was burned at the beginning of the intensified interaction of northern and southern Mesopotamia in the mid-fourth millennium B.C., this site remains important. It is a linchpin for the chronology of northeastern Mesopotamia. Few other excavated sites have such a long, continuous sequence of levels through this period. Nearby Nineveh does not seem to have all the periods covered (see Rothman a in press; Gut 1995). In addition to chronology, Gawra is important for the study of evolutionary trends at the end of the fifth and the early fourth millennia. Tepe Gawra, as described in this volume, was enmeshed in many networks of cultural, economic, and political commonality and interaction out of which the sweeping local and regional changes of the later fourth millennium emerged. Because the excavators were able to dig unusually broad, horizontal exposures of the site, it offers us a unique view of the life of a small center before the rise of the state. Rarely can recent excavations retrieve as large a sample of each level as did the excavators of Gawra.

The second goal is as full a presentation of the basic data as is practical within the pages of this volume. The earlier publications by Speiser (1935a) and Tobler (1950) are incomplete and often inaccurate. The catalogue of those volumes lists only the illustrated objects, some 500 for Levels XII–VIII. The catalogue below includes almost 3,000 objects. Each of the records of these artifacts contains more information than one can glean from the earlier reports, especially as concerns their provenience. The catalogue in this volume is organized by level and by artifact type. Readers of this book can therefore reconstruct—if they want, challenge—my analysis and can conduct research on a given time period or a given artifact type on their own.

Because neither of the authors of the two earlier volumes actually spent much time on the mound during excavation (see Chapter 2) and the field architect for most of these levels, Mueller, did not draw the published architectural plans, many stratigraphic problems remain. As a result, there is still much confusion. For example, the otherwise noteworthy study of Gawra graves by Forest (1983) is simply unreliable. In the notes on graves, reviewed and corrected in the Appendix of this volume by Brian Peasnall, it is clear that some of Forest's reassignments of dates for particular tombs are simply impossible. Similarly, field notes contradict his reconstruction of town plans (see Chapter Three).

With these two interrelated goals in mind, I will now sketch out the cultural background for Greater Mesopotamia and the theoretical issues at the heart of my analysis.

The Cultural Landscape of Greater Mesopotamia in the Late Fifth and Fourth Millennia B.C.

The baseline for this transformation can be drawn at roughly 4400 BC. I say roughly, because as the reader will see, chronology presents one of the most seemingly intractable problems in approaching this material. According to the new C^{14} re-calibrations, the Late Ubaid/Early Uruk transition occurred after 4672 BC, not 4030, as earlier C^{14} dates indicated (Hole 1994: Table 1). For the sake of simplicity, however, I will continue to refer to the Late Chalcolithic or Uruk Period as the fourth millennium B.C. with the caveat that in calibrated years it extended back into the late fifth millennium.

Many chronological schemes are currently in use. Table 1.1 lists some of the ones mentioned in relationship to Gawra. They include the following chronologies: traditional southern Mesopotamian (see Porada 1965), the new SAR (School of American Research: see Rothman, ed. in press), Gut's northeastern Mesopotamian chronology (Gut 1995), the Amuq sequence (Braidwood and Braidwood 1960), calibrated dates, and the Chalcolithic sequence (Vértesalji 1987).

At this cultural baseline, many small networks of villages and towns dotted the landscape of Greater Mesopotamia. As scholars currently understand this period—Terminal Ubaid, Ubaid 4, Suse, Susa I or A,

and Late Farukh are some of its names—many of the larger settlements were the seats of newly institutionalized administrative organizations (chiefdoms in the step typology of Service 1962).

Members of these organizations had established their rank and promoted their well-being by extracting tribute in the form of staple goods and productive labor from subsidiary villages and camps, and by amassing specialized goods and exotic materials (Wright 1994; Stein 1994a). Among the strategies leaders used to maintain their authority and draw individuals into interacting with or living in these centers were performing religious rituals, sponsoring craft or food production, establishing trade connections and marketplaces, arranging food storage, organizing group social functions, and distributing symbolic tokens of membership in a privileged group (Hole 1983; Wright 1994).

In turn their acquisition of exotic goods to use as tokens of rank and of favor created functional interdependence among centers along routes of exchange, connecting local networks into loose regional networks. Rather than a formal trade organization, much of the exchange of exotic materials appears to have been handled through informal, down-the-line movements of goods.[2] To a lesser extent, the same sort of exchange had existed in the region since the Upper Paleolithic when hunter/gatherer bands traded dentalium shells from the Red Sea (Henry 1989:130).

For a region that was so loosely integrated economically, however, there was a surprising unity among its building and artifact styles. The relation between the spread of these cultural elements and the creation and elaboration of local administrative organizations determined the shape of societal evolution, locally and ultimately, regionally. The spread of cultural traditions has been interpreted in a number of ways. To some, it is a sign of a first political incorporation of areas in northern and eastern Mesopotamia by southern Mesopotamian societies (Porada 1965; Oates and Oates 1976:125f; Algaze 1993). To others, it represents newly established northern leadership organizations, which replicated the model of administrative organization and used the cultural symbols from elsewhere (Stein 1994a; Frangipane in press; see also Pollock 1983a, 1994). In the end, if we are to make cultural sense of remains recovered from the ground, one of our most critical task is to distinguish among these and other interpretations.

However, by the time the fourth millennium B.C. ended at the close of the Late Uruk, LC5, or Late Chalcolithic period, the region was deeply altered. The first states and the first true urban (city-based) systems were established on the southern alluvium of Mesopotamia, modern southern Iraq, and southwestern Iran (Adams 1981; Johnson 1973; Wright and Johnson 1975). Outside the highly developed southern alluvium, stronger, though still pre-state, networks of economic, administrative, and religious interdependence evolved in some

Table 1.1   Major Chronological Periods Mentioned in Text.

B.C.	SAR	Gut 1995	Southern Mesopotamia Traditional	Chalcolithic	Gawra
				Ninevite V	Tepe Gawra VII
3,000	LC5	Nineveh (Gut) Späturuk	Late Uruk	↑	
	late	Ninevite 4			
		L:31-20		Late	hiatus
3,400	LC4	Norduruk B	Late Middle	Chalcolithic	
		L:37-31	Uruk		
3,600					
	LC3	Norduruk A	Early Middle		Tepe Gawra VIII
		L:45-37	Uruk		
3800					Tepe Gawra IX–X
	late	Gawra B			
	LC2	L:59-45	Early		Tepe Gawra XI/XA
4000			Uruk		
	early	Gawra A			
					Tepe Gawra XIA/B
4200	LC1	hiatus?			Tepe Gawra XII
		L:60	'Ubaid transitional	↓	
	Term.		'Ubaid 4?	Middle	
4500	Ubaid			Chalcolithic	XIIA–XIII

sub-regions (Weiss 1986; Rothman 1988; Rothman et al. 1989; Rothman, ed. in press). Other sub-regions were abandoned or their settled population had adopted a pastoral nomadic or transhumant lifestyle, invisible to archaeologists (Mortensen 1976; Voigt 1989; Adams 1978).

Unlike the beginning of the millennium, the distribution of artifact styles, particularly pottery, at the end of the fourth millennium was far less homogeneous. The distribution of distinctive corpuses of style suggests that the region had been divided into two or three distinct interaction spheres, roughly corresponding to alluvial plain, open steppe, and foothills (south, north, and east-northeast) (see Roaf 1990:80). Strong local networks of exchange and influence emerged in each sub-region. At the same time the introduction of clearly southern Classic Uruk styles into northern and eastern networks can be interpreted as attempts to reorganize regional exchanges on a new basis. That new basis may represent "international," that is, large-scale intra-regional trade (Beale 1973), colonization (Algaze 1993), or emulation of symbols and replication of administrative structures (Stein 1990, 1999, in press). Again, alternative interpretations for artifact styles outside southern Mesopotamia

are possible (see the Local and Regional Context of Analysis below), but underlying all of them is the idea that relations among groups in the Mesopotamian region had changed radically over the span of the fourth millennium B.C. The effects of these changes were felt at the local, sub-regional, and regional level.[3]

This dynamic change has introduced a chronological conundrum. The term "Uruk" has been used as a name for a site, Uruk/Warka, in the southern alluvium, for the fourth millennium B.C. in general, and for styles of pottery and architecture associated with the southern reaches of modern-day Iraq and southwest Iran in the fourth millennium B.C. (Algaze 1993). The complexity of dealing with fine tuned relative chronology is complicated by this dichotomy of culturally defined versus purely chronologically defined units. For example, at Arslantepe the "Early Bronze IA" horizon appears to fit into the period of 3300 to 3100 B.C. chronologically (Alessio et al. 1983). Normally, that would be Late Uruk in date. Because VIA has a heavy component of Transcaucasian wares, usually associated with the Early Bronze I (EBI), its excavators place it chronologically in EBIA. However, the culturally Late Uruk palace fits the

VIA period. The "Late Chalcolithic," which can be anything from 4500 BC onward, is the phase of locally styled pottery carbon dated to the equivalent of the Middle Uruk Period or LC 3/4 (3700–3400 BC) at Arslantepe.

The context for the analysis of Tepe Gawra presented here is therefore the dynamics of the late fifth and fourth millennia B.C. Consequently, the evolutionary history of this site begins with its transitional late fifth millennium B.C. level, XII. It continues through five more architectural levels (XIA/B, XI/XA, X, IX, VIII) and seven sub-level phases (XIB, XIA, XI, XA, VIIIC, VIIIB, VIIIA) of its fourth millennium B.C. occupation. The fire that consumed Level VIII marks the end of the period of interest at Gawra. The site was not re-occupied until the third millennium.

If the context of Gawra's analysis is the transformation of the fourth millennium B.C., the initial goals of the analysis are to answer two deeper questions. First, what local processes of change are evident in the evolution of this one small town? Second, what is the connection between changes at Tepe Gawra and the transformation of the region as a whole during the late fifth and fourth millennia B.C.?

Questions and Theory

To accomplish the goals set out above I will ask specific questions about Gawra and its relation to the larger region. This section lists those questions and shows the theoretical connections between the description of each level and phase reported below and the interpretation of processes of local tradition and change and of regional development.

Specific Questions for Analysis

The evolutionary history of Tepe Gawra will be described in terms of three basic questions that define the analysis:

1. what are the economic, religious, or administrative activities performed by the residents on the mound during each identifiable segment of time (each level and sub-level phase); 2. how are these activities distributed throughout the site; and 3. how do the physical placements of these activities in or near buildings of distinctive architectural plan or size reflect a discoverable relationship between architectural forms and the functions they house?

Complexity

These three questions were chosen because to answer them is to define Gawra's place in its economic and social universe, to address issues relating to the evolution of complex societies, and to understand better the early social (pre-) history of Greater Mesopotamia. Their interpretive value lies in the concepts of complexity and centralization.

The concept of complexity in social structure, which informs the analysis of Tepe Gawra, states that a social transformation from less complex to more complex societies occurs when a new kind of economic, governmental, and religious interdependence evolves among people living in close contact in a multi-site society. At the heart of that interdependence is the functional "segregation (the amount of differentiation and specialization)" of the members of these networks and the necessary linkage among parts of these networks (Flannery 1972:409; also see Blanton et al. 1981:21–22; Rothman 1994c).

In this evolutionary process, each individual or group takes on one set of activities (e.g., making pottery, farming, governing) for more of their time than is needed to supply their family and immediate neighbors. They thereby become dependent on others for the products that they no longer have time to make or tasks to perform. Functional segregation is the first key to the organization that marks social complexity. Functional segregation reshuffles the deck of how groups identify themselves and interact. Often, status changes (social ranking or stratification) accompany increasing specialization and segregation.

The varying social identities are differently valued (see Goodenough 1965 for definitions of social identity, status, and role). This increased segregation changes the cognitive maps that people use to define their social identity and to interpret what institutions' actions, words, and other symbols mean. In short, it alters how people view their world and construct it symbolically.

The second key is leadership. Based on countless ethnographic and archaeological examples, functional segregation and interdependence leads to the development of formal leadership organizations (administrative or governmental specialists) to coordinate or regulate the various productive and service specialists. Coordination, on the one hand, involves "the mutual inter adjustment" of "the rates of activity of the members of an acting group" (Miller 1960:177). Regulation, on the other hand, involves the authority to create a plan defining the nature and goals of at least some activities, initiating action aimed at fulfilling those goals, and maintaining "the continuity of activities" by means of giving orders (Miller 1960:179). That authority, the hallmark of this next stage in complexity (the state), means not only having the ability to lay out the plan, and give orders, but also to enforce those orders using various means of coercion. The development of administrative forms of social organization (see Wallace 1971 for an explication of the term), typical of complex societies, occurs when kinship or community based societies are transformed into societies with many settlements "transcending local authority" (Carneiro 1981:37).

The economic foundation of leadership organizations at this level of societal complexity has been shown to affect the kinds of interactions among networks and the stability of local social structures. Such is the case when leaders are supported by the extraction of surplus foodstuffs or labor to produce foodstuffs for storage (staple finance) (D'Altroy and Earle 1985:188). It is similarly the case when leaders prosper through the procurement of exotic materials and production of specialized craft goods (wealth finance). In reality most leaders use some combination of wealth and staple finance. However, whichever of these alternative types of financing evolve, they determine the arrangements and relations of groups in local and regional networks. For example, wealth finance based on the importation of lapis lazuli and the manufacture of finished products creates larger networks along with greater political and economic instability.

Leaders must have local workers to produce goods desirable to exchange for exotic materials. At the same time competition among networks for such materials could cut off supplies precipitously. In the case of lapis lazuli, its favored route from Afghanistan into Mesopotamia near the end of Ubaid period appears to have gone through Gawra to Nineveh and then beyond. Near the end of the fourth millennium B.C. much of the trade in this material appears to have bypassed the piedmont by moving down the Western Zagros Mountains and through Susa (Hermann 1968). When the demand for locally produced goods for exchange along these routes change or other factors interrupt the flow of goods, leaders must have other economic strategies to guarantee loyalty or their authority wanes. Staple finance provides more stable, locally oriented, social relations, but because of the limits on surplus foodstuffs and storage facilities, the complexity of staple based polities, their degree of control, is limited (see Goodell 1980; Stein 1994a).

Leadership organizations, once established, can be based on differing goals (Rothman and Peasnall 1999, Blanton et al. 1996). Normally, one thinks of leaders in complex states as being self-aggrandizing. They are determined always to enhance their own power and wealth in comparison to those they rule. Another possibility, that they are motivated to promote the group as a whole, is also attested.

Centralization

Another way these functionally segregated and administratively specialized networks can be described is in terms of social and spatial centralization. Socially, centralization is "the degree of linkage between various sub-systems and the highest-order controls in society" (Flannery 1972:409), which is one element for defining the degree of coordination or regulation (Rothman 1988:9–10; Lloyd 1965:81–82). The other elements in defining the degree of centralization are the functions administered and organization of the control mechanisms.

Spatially, centralization means that one or a few sites, usually located the same travel time away from the other sites in the network, account for more of the flow of goods, people, information, and control functions than the majority of other sites (Kowalewski et al. 1983:35). That is to say, theoretically more of the specialized activities found in the network, or system, are performed at these central sites than elsewhere for the sake of efficiency (Blanton 1976; Johnson 1980a; 1980b; Christaller 1933). While the residents of villages and camps (satellite sites) depend on cities and towns (central sites) for the specialized goods and services (mass-produced and technically difficult to produce items, markets, temples, or governments), the cities and towns depend on villages and camps for labor, raw materials, and often foodstuffs. Again, this interdependence shapes networks.

Although this description of centralization is generally true for all complex societies, tremendous variation exists among complex networks ethnographically and historically. Sometimes, the centers of specialized activities are not highly populated, as Western central cities and towns tend to be. The *duka* trading centers of the Busoga of Africa are an example of small centers (Fallers 1965:56). Nor are all the specialized activities found in central sites. An example of this is metalworking among the Marghi and *ngkyaga* of West Africa (Vaughan 1973). From network to network, depending on factors such as the resources of their natural environment, technological sophistication, population size and area, specific functions and their social and spatial organization will vary. One measurement of that variation in functions and centralization is functional size (Blanton 1976:252). The role of each site in a network and the character of the network itself is dependent on the number, kind, and intensity of the activities (and the functions those activities represent) that are performed by the residents of each site, according to this measurement.

Therefore, the first question of the Tepe Gawra material listed above asks what Gawra's functional size is at each measurable point in time. The changes in functional size over the millennia provide the data for evolutionary analysis. The particular economic functions performed further define the probable kinds of organization and interaction.

By the same logic, more complex social and economic systems, like the one of which Gawra was a part

(Rothman 1988, 1989; Rothman and Blackman 1990), are marked by functional segregation within sites, especially central sites (Flannery 1972). The more institutionalized specialization becomes, the more likely it is for purposes of efficiency and control that the specialists of greatest importance would be physically segregated within sites. Network cohesion (integration) is thereby enhanced. This is the reason for the second question; how are activities distributed (and possibly put together) throughout the site.

Such segregation is never more clearly institutionalized than when architectural forms are developed to house specialized functions. We who live in the era with the most complex of state societies accept without questioning the idea that a bank, factory, church, government building, school, or house are readily identifiable by their architectural form. We understand intuitively that buildings are designed to provide spaces appropriate to their function; they communicate their cultural significance symbolically. We also are used to town plans in which these specialized functions (manufacturing, governance, residential) are divided into districts. However, in the world of ancient Mesopotamia the cultural code of architectural space and form and the sorts of town planning that existed remain, for the most part, to be discovered (Kubba 1987). Not only do researchers need to determine whether functions are associated with certain architectural forms, but which particular activities are segregated and which are associated in special function buildings or in particular parts of settlements. Such information is directly relevant to understanding interdependent networks.

The State

One of the reasons this period from 4500 to 3050 BC is of such interest is that at this time state-level society first evolved in the world. The debate over the use of the term, state, is quite fierce in anthropological circles at this time (e.g., Feinman and Neitzel 1984; Blanton et al. 1996; Wenke 1981; see Rothman and Peasnall 1999; Rothman 1994c). At the same time, even those that criticize the step typology of Service (1962) most intensely still use the term.

The importance of the use of the concept of the state for this study is to describe a kind of developmental threshold in societal complexity. It is a threshold that Gawra did not reach by Level VIII. However, elements of the evolutionary trajectory toward the state (Wright 1994) are evident and will be discussed below. The focus of that trajectory involves the control mechanisms and information-processing capabilities of administrative organizations (Johnson 1973, Wright 1977, 1984) and how these centralizing elements alter the functioning and cognitive maps of individuals and groups in their daily lives.

These increasingly complex and hierarchical levels of administration arose because of the challenges impelled by rapidly restructuring economic and political systems, growth in size, and attempts to integrate numerous smaller collectives into a larger polity. It involves issues of centralization and increasing segmentation of society, as discussed above.

For this volume, the concept of the state forms a kind of backdrop against which the analysis that follows is played out. The goal is not to label Gawra as a state or not a state, but rather to investigate the evolutionary trajectories that are common in the development of a state-level of complexity and its precursors worldwide.

Taken together, the three questions posed above regarding functional size, intra-site segregation of functions, and architectural correlates of that functional segregation relate to societal structure and function. By monitoring functional and architectural characteristics over approximately seven hundred years, processes of change and development—these are the dynamics of societal structure—can be discovered.

As the reader will see, Tepe Gawra through the late fifth and fourth millennium B.C. is a case against progressive ideas of cultural evolution. These progressive ideas are the ones expressed by early anthropologists like Tylor and Morgan (Voget 1975: Chapter 5). They thought that there was an inevitable ladder of development leading in one unilineal line to civilization. Although there is an over-all trend toward greater societal differentiation and segregation of functions (social complexity), and, as an earlier analysis documented, changes in the nature and extent to which administrators oversaw those activities (Rothman 1988), the trends do not follow a straight line of ascent. Rather, they sketch a line that twists and turns back on itself a number of times.

Impacts of Areas Outside the Locality

As stated above the evolutionary history of a site or a region is more than the structure and fate of its local network. Every site belongs to a number of possible networks, each having different elements and each based on differing kinds of interactions (economic, religious, linguistic, stylistic, governmental). Societies are not sharply bounded units, but strongly interdependent networks in which each node of the network is open to other networks as well. The fate of one local network can depend on the degree of integration of the regional networks and on its interaction with other networks in the region. Certainly, one network is affected by major changes in other networks with which it has relations. As Wolf (1982:3) states "the world of humankind constitutes a manifold, a totality of interconnected processes, and inquiries that disassemble this totality into bits and then fail to reassemble it falsify reality."

Centers can play a particularly important role in the interactions of local networks on a regional stage. Kowalewski et al. (1983) propose that perhaps the primary role for the central site in a local network (settlement system, polity, etc.) is to mediate interactions with other more distant networks.

Having said all this, a caution is necessary. Knowing a connection existed is not sufficient to define the nature of the connection or its effect on each node of interaction. The strength of interdependency is based on the kinds and extent of interactions. For example, the subsistence (and society) of Upper Paleolithic hunter/gatherer bands was unlikely to suffer collapse if dentalium shells were unavailable for a time. A modern industrial state cut off from sources of oil, coal, or gold is in a much more precarious position. In short, the nature and strength of the interaction must be specified.

The analysis of Tepe Gawra is based on these questions and theoretical tenets. The next section places Gawra in its sub-region and reviews differing interpretations of the fourth millennium B.C. regional situation and Tepe Gawra's place in it.

The Local and Regional Context of Analysis
The Place of Region in the Analysis of Local Sites

As the discussion above suggests, the reality of the ancient world, as of the modern one, is that no settlement exists in anything approaching total isolation. Each is part of a complex web of local and regional, sometimes interregional, relations or networks. To understand the region, however, the focus must be local. People and groups adapt first to their local resources and conditions. As previously stated, these conditions are affected by what was happening in the other sub-region(s) with which any sub-region or site had network connections.

Local Conditions in the Piedmont: Environmental and Productive Potentials

Tepe Gawra is situated within the Greater Mesopotamian region (see Figure 1.1) on the eastern

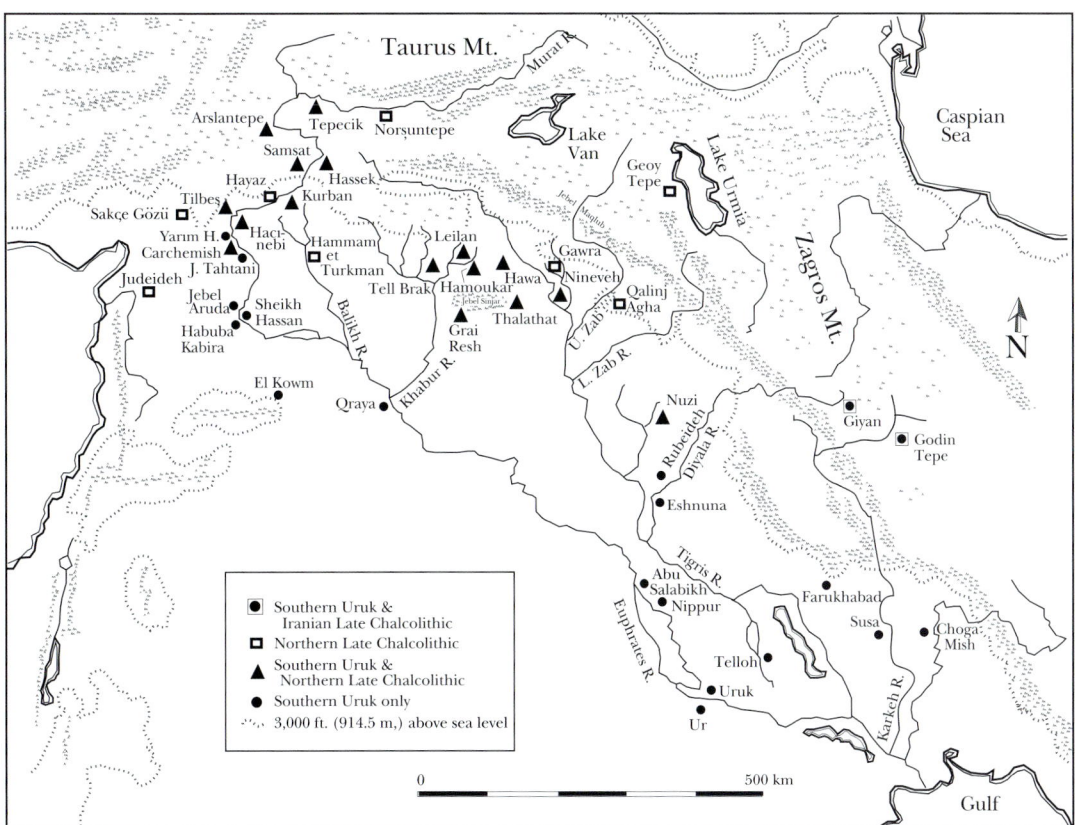

Figure 1.1   Map of Greater Mesopotamia in the late fifth through the end of the fourth millennium B.C. showing significant sites of the Uruk and Late Chalcolithic cultures.

flank of the piedmont of northern Mesopotamia, east of the Tigris River and north of the Greater Zab River. This is a zone of both rainfall and irrigation agriculture and of winter pasture for sheep and goat. It is probable—this is hardly a settled issue—that the same basic conditions existed in the fourth millennium B.C. as today. For example, Hubbard (1980:154) sees no significant change since 6000 B.C. Hole (1994) asserts to the contrary that radical change in sea level, climate, and the flow rates of the Tigris and Euphrates occurred between 5000 and 3800 B.C. in the Middle East. The northern part of the Mesopotamian region where Gawra is located was less affected than the southern alluvium, although it was a bit drier than present, according to Hole (1994). This stability in northern Mesopotamia contrasts with radical climatic, sea level, and cultural changes in southern Mesopotamia. However, as stated above, dramatic changes over a large part of a region will affect all social and economic networks throughout the region. In addition, even climatic stability does not imply a lack of change in the ecology of an area. In light of what happened in a sub-region like central Anatolia, cultural development and agriculture could have stripped away many of the deciduous trees in the area and thus changed its plant ecology by the end of the fourth millennium (see Miller 1985). Historically, the dense forests of earlier times are no longer evident in the Tigris piedmont.

Other Sites

Other fourth millennium B.C. sites in the piedmont (see Figure 1.2) include Nineveh (Mallowan 1933) and seven other sites in the same plain as Gawra (Abu al-Soof 1968), 104 in all in the Mosul *Liwa* or province, Qalinj Agha (Abu al-Soof 1967, 1969; Hijara 1973) and 46 other Uruk period sites in Erbil Liwa (Abu al-Soof 1968), 33 Uruk period sites in Sulaimaniyah Liwa (Abu al-Soof 1968), Yorgan Tepe/Nuzi (Starr 1939), 32 other Uruk sites in Kirkuk Liwa (Abu al-Soof 1968), and at least 15 in the area of the Mosul Dam survey, including a potentially huge Uruk period site, Tell al-Hawa (Ball et al. 1989, Wilkinson and Tucker 1995).

Sites in the earliest period, synchronous with Gawra Level XII and XIA/B were small, were placed in the most optimum locales for agricultural exploitation, and were already connected in a loose network of exchange. Lapis lazuli had appeared at Tepe Gawra, for example, in the Late Ubaid Period Level XIII. Worked copper objects are found for the first time in Level XIII, a single copper awl or pin, most likely hammered (Tobler 1950:212). Four crudely smelted copper objects appeared in Gawra XII (Pigott, personal communication). Obsidian also began to appear in Gawra XIII and increased through

Level XI. Salvage excavations at Shelgiyya on the Upper Tigris indicate that specialized production of fine pottery, specifically, sprig ware, may have already begun in the late fifth millennium, LC1 (Ball 1997). A concentration of sprig ware also was recovered from early Tell al-Hawa. This suggests that a far-flung network of exchange relations had already begun in the fifth millennium B.C. A neutron activation analysis study of sprig ware may indicate a specialized production center at Shelgiyya and at least a sub-regional exchange network (Blackman, personal communication).

In the Early Uruk period or LC2, an apparent increase in sites is notable. These sites seem to fill in the areas little occupied in LC1. For the so-called precontact (Stein 1999a, 1999b, in press) period before the expansion of southern Mesopotamian individuals and groups into northern Mesopotamia increased; this was a time of tremendous economic and political development. Tell al-Hawa grew to an extraordinary size at this time. "Concerning the possible introduction of urban concepts into the north by such southern implants, the investigations at Tell al-Hawa . . . suggest that the period of greater urban expansion was in the Earlier part of the Uruk period, while Southern Mesopotamian colonies are from the Later part" (Ball 1997:6).

Quite a number of sites of apparent importance were located in this Iraqi Jazira[4] sub-region, some away from the major river channels. In fact, Nineveh has yielded none of the wares typical of the early LC2 (Gawra XIA/B-XI, Gut's Gawra A). The settlement pattern data seems to indicate growth and the likelihood of evolving societal complexity, involving exploitation of the area's agricultural potential and increasing trade. This trend is not limited to the Jazira, however:

> Although larger in size (possibly owing to the greater availability of good quality agricultural land) and probably somewhat more integrated, the North Jazira [sub-] regional system exhibits the same highly centralized nature as that seen in the Karababa area. As with Samsat, the disproportionate size of Tell al-Hawa vis-à-vis surrounding settlements may be the result of its pre-eminent functional role and its participation in inter- [and intra-] regional exchange networks. Like Samsat in the Karababa area, Tell al-Hawa acted as the regional conduit between the North Jazira settlement system and the wider supra-local precontact period world that was characterized by wide-reaching interaction spheres. (Lupton 1996:26)

Gawra and other sites occupied contemporaneously—examples include Qalinj Agha near Erbil and

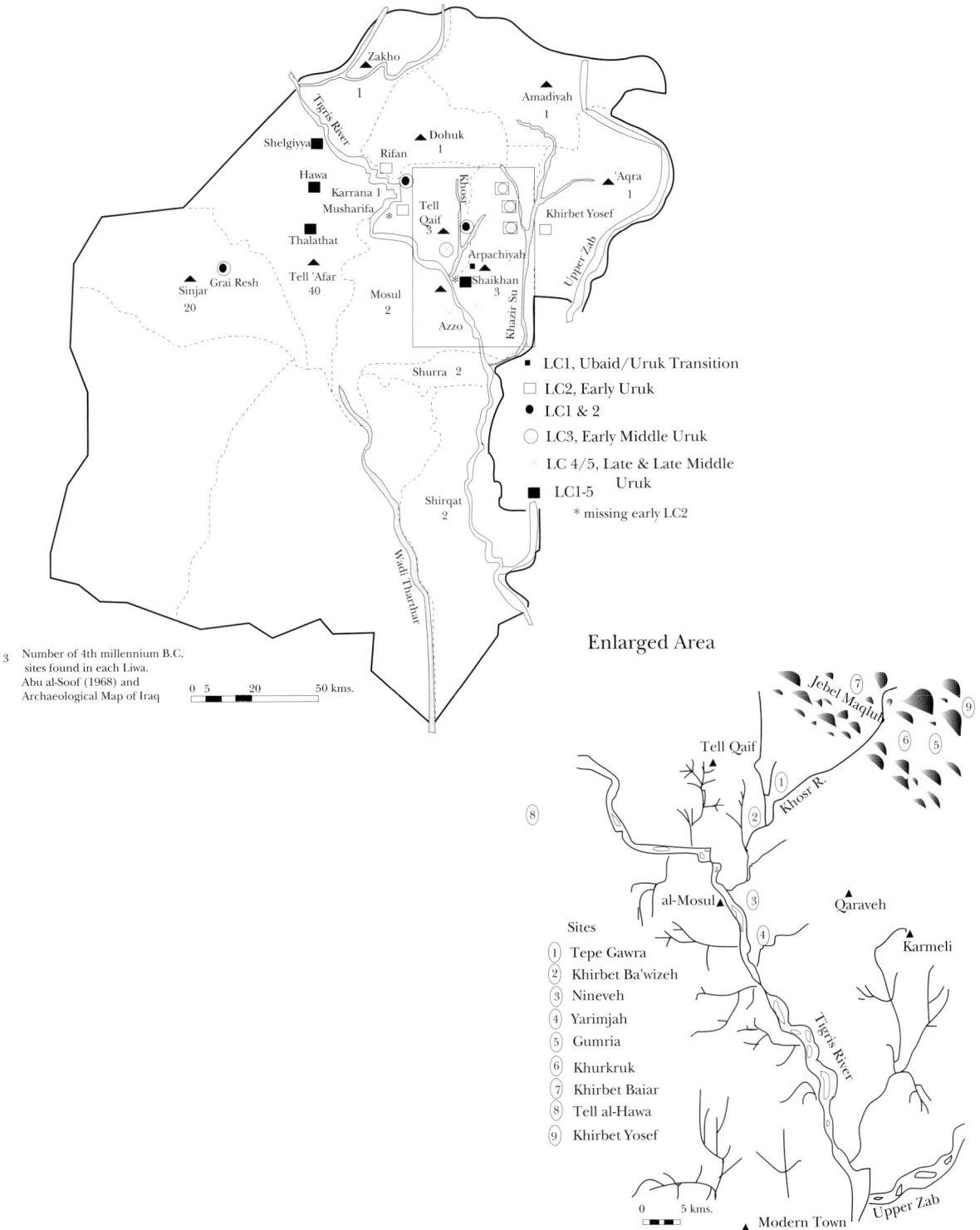

Figure 1.2   Map of the northeastern quadrant of Greater Mesopotamia, the Northern Jazira, and Iraqi piedmont zone.

Nuzi near Kirkuk—would have had more direct access to a number of raw materials and goods that might be important for larger networks of exchange.

The Early Middle Uruk or LC3 period was marked by the abandonment of Tepe Gawra and Grai Resh, Qalinj Agha, Musharifa, Rifan, and Khirbet Yosef somewhere early in the period (see Rothman a in press). Tell al-Hawa decreased in size although its central place in the North Jazira does not seem to have changed drastically (Lupton 1996:57–59). Nineveh was re-occupied and continued to grow. The Gawra mound was so narrow by the end of Level VIII that only fortresses and a

few special function buildings would be built on it afterwards.

The General Place of Gawra in the Region

Compared to large central sites like nearby Nineveh on the eastern bank of the Tigris River, Tell Brak, Habuba Kabira, Uruk/Warka, Ur, or Susa, Tepe Gawra at barely one hectare appears to have been a very small site during the fourth millennium B.C.[5] (see Figure 1.3). The site did not sit on one of the more obvious routes

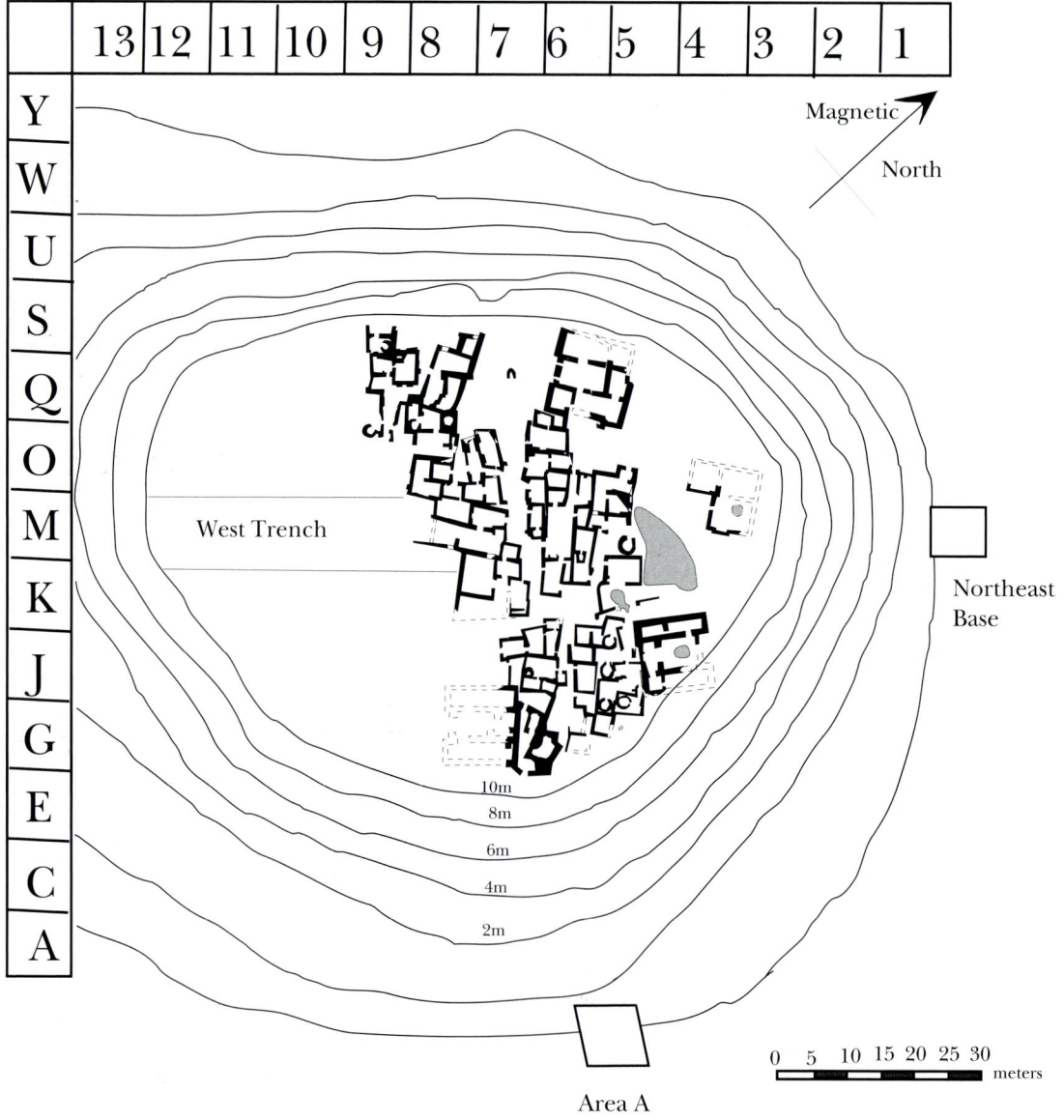

Figure 1.3   Topographic map of Tepe Gawra with town plan of Phase XI, Level XI/XA (topographic background after Speiser 1935a: plate I; town plan, drawing by author).

of trade and contact between northern and southern Mesopotamia. However, it is situated on a tributary of the Khosr River, a branch of the Tigris, by one of few natural passes through the Jebel Maqlub into the hills of the northern Zagros Mountains.

Both of these factors would seem to argue against Gawra being a significant center. However, in an earlier study of architectural Levels XI/XA to VIII (Rothman 1988), I argued and I continue to argue below that during this time Gawra was the center of a small, independent network or polity. That polity included the eastern piedmont plain north of the Greater Zab River and the first foothills of the Zagros.[6] Evidence for this proposal was of many types. For one thing, an extraordinarily large number of the seals and sealings used to control activities in late prehistoric Mesopotamia were found in these levels (see Rothman 1988, 1994a, 1994b). Further, these seals and sealings were recovered from all of the loci with specialized productive (cloth making, seal and bead cutting, wood working, stone tool making), storage, and religious activities. Those activities represented functions that seem more extensive than the estimated 150 to 200 residents of the site (Rothman 1988:272) would need.

At the same time, although the piedmont was a zone rich for rainfall agriculture, pastoralism, and hunting, few tools for agricultural or pastoral production were recovered from Levels XII–VIII. The sample of the site excavated (100 percent of Levels VIII to X and close to 70 percent of XI/XA) should have yielded many of these tools, if they were there. Further, a few graves and tombs sunk from later Levels X to VIII have unusually fine grave goods made of exotic materials like lapis lazuli, gold, silver, copper, and precious stones (Forest 1983; Robinson 1984; see Appendix below). Such differential wealth in grave goods has long been associated with the differential status typical of complex societies (Brown 1971; Pollock 1983). So, the activities present and absent suggest the sort of interdependence typical of the center of a complex society. Unfortunately, no complete survey of the surrounding area has ever been published (see Rothman 1993). Such a survey would give a better impression of Gawra's place in its immediate area.

Still, Gawra appears to have had important regional functions. Exotic materials like lapis lazuli (Hermann 1968; Caldwell 1976), obsidian (G. Wright 1969 and Chapters 4 and 5 below), and precious metals appear in sufficient quantity that they probably were transshipped through Gawra to other parts of Mesopotamia during the early fourth millennium B.C.

Such activity could mean that Gawra was a secondary center under the administrative control of another larger center. Nineveh, estimated at approximately twelve hectares during the mid- to late fourth millennium B.C. and located at a major river crossing of the Tigris, was the nearest and most likely primary center.

However, chemical characterization of sealing clays from Gawra, Nineveh, and Arpachiyah (Rothman and Blackman 1990) suggests that Gawra did not have a strong administrative dependence on Nineveh. Excavations at other piedmont sites, including Qalinj Agha south of the Greater Zab River near modern Erbil (Abu al-Soof 1969), and Yorgan Tepe (Nuzi) south of the Lesser Zab River near Kirkuk (Starr 1939), as well as a series of Eastern Turkish highland sites, Norşuntepe (Hauptmann 1976, 1982), and Tepecik (Esin 1976,1982) indicate that other small centers existed in this subregion. Greater stylistic similarity among these small centers than between them and the major riverine sites like Nineveh also suggests some significant social interaction or cultural identity among them.

Therefore, if Mesopotamian sites were classified into large centers ("cities"), small centers ("towns"), villages, and camps, Gawra appears to represent a small center.

As already stated, an understanding of the regional context of Mesopotamia to which the residents of Gawra and neighboring sites had to adapt is dependent on understanding the evolutionary trajectories and conditions in the region as a whole. Yet, the prehistory of Greater Mesopotamia illustrates the problems of making broad generalizations. Subregion to sub-region the conditions, both natural and human, were quite different, and the evidence to date indicates that the adaptations of people were equally different. Still, a picture showing some large-scale trends may be possible to draw. That picture will have three motifs: demographic change, elaboration of administrative organization, and regional exchange and integration toward the end the Late Chalcolithic or Late Uruk Period.

Summary of Demographic Trends in Other Greater Mesopotamian Sub-Regions

Southwestern Iran

An image of shifting population movements, and at times local population growth or decline, is evident from archaeological surveys and some excavated sites. A good case in point is the Susiana Plain, a geological extension of the southern alluvium of the Tigris and Euphrates Rivers. They constitute a relatively flat, open area with sufficient water from the Karkeh, Diz, and Karun Rivers for irrigation agriculture. Like most of Mesopotamia, during its most stylistically unified period in the Ubaid 1-3 periods (5300–4600 BC), Susiana was occupied by small villages (2 hectares or less). Presumably, these villagers subsisted through irrigation agriculture and animal husbandry (Dollfus 1985; Hole 1985). Not until the middle of this period did one site, Choga Mish, increase rapidly in size to 11 hectares. The site for which the area is named, Susa, had not been founded yet.

With the founding and rapid growth of Susa on the western edge of the Susa Plain at the onset of the Suse, Susa I (A) or Terminal Ubaid periods, a marked change occurred. Population grew at the time of the demographic explosion at Choga Mish and the founding of Susa. In the case of Susa, population increase probably represents a result of economic and political developments, rather than its cause. In pre-Suse times, every mountain valley in the southwest Iranian area was occupied. By Suse times, most valleys were abandoned, and population was concentrated on the Susa Plain (Wright and Johnson 1985:25–26). Emigration to take advantage of new economic opportunities seems a plausible interpretation.

The transition to the Early Uruk Period appears to have marked a decline in the power of Susa's administrators. The area occupied on the Susa mound declined. On the other hand, overall population as represented by mounded sites more than doubled in Susiana, and previously unoccupied areas of the plain where Choga Mish is located were settled (Johnson 1973: Figure 16). Three other sites dispersed throughout the plains grew to the size of Susa. The mountain valleys abandoned in the Suse Period were re-occupied (Wright and Johnson 1985:26). Seasonally occupied sites in those mountain areas suggest the possibility of transhumant or nomadic pastoral utilization.

The great florescence of organizational change and regional development occurred in the Middle Uruk period or LC4 in Susiana. This was accompanied not so much by an increase in population as by a restructuring of it (Johnson 1973: Figure 19). Choga Mish re-emerged as a large center. Susa and Abu Fanduweh south of Susa also grew. In the surrounding hills remains of seasonal pastoral encampments declined in number.

The Late Uruk Period on the Susiana Plains represents another change. The number of sites on the Susiana dropped dramatically, as did the size of Susa. Most notably, villages in the area north of Susa were abandoned. Johnson (1973:145–46) suggests that a buffer zone between the Susa and Choga Mish enclaves had been created.

Susiana in demographic terms shows an increase and then a decline in overall population size, with a restructuring of population toward agglomeration in the Suse and Late Uruk periods and dispersion in Early and Middle Uruk times.

Southern Alluvium

Although surprisingly little is known of the Uruk Period in the so-called heartland of cities (Adams 1981), the Late Uruk or LC5 period decline in settlement evident in Susiana does not seem to have occurred in the southern alluvium. Overall, the transition between Ubaid and Uruk Periods saw a marked increase in settled hectares in southern Mesopotamia (Adams 1981:60). This was not universally so. Adams asserts that settled hectares declined in the more northerly part of the alluvium north and east of Nippur (Adams 1981:61f.), and in the part southeast of Uruk/Warka near Eridu/Ur (Wright 1981). However, Pollock (in press) disagrees. Phenomenal growth is evidenced in and around the city of Uruk/Warka. From the Early-Middle to the Late Uruk Period the area occupied in the "environs of Uruk" city rose from 173.1 to 382.5 hectares (Adams 1981, Table 3). A survey of the city of Uruk revealed that the all of the center of the mound was occupied in the Late Uruk Period (Finkbeiner 1983). In looking at events and trends in this sub-region the fact that Uruk/Warka was of an order of magnitude greater than any other contemporaneous city is important to consider (Nissen in press). The largest Uruk period settlement in Susiana was 18 hectares. The site of Uruk/Warka reached almost 100 hectares during the Late Uruk Period (Nissen in press). Still, Johnson (1988/9) sees this seemingly dramatic growth as a possible result of normal, indigenous population growth, not large-scale migration. It is equally likely that many individuals migrated to the city of Uruk/Warka and its urban core from other areas of the southern alluvium. Such a possibility would be especially likely if Adams' hypothesis that one of the more northern channels of the Euphrates had gone out of use between the Early and Late Uruk Periods (Adams 1981:61f.).

Western Zagros

Moving up into the western Zagros Mountains, the Hulailan Valley of Luristan exhibits yet another demographic pattern (Mortensen 1976). In the Early Chalcolithic Period (Early Halaf into Ubaid), former hunter-gatherer populations moved down onto the best agricultural land on the flood plain. There they clustered into eleven very small villages (the largest 2 hectares). The Middle Chalcolithic, probably parallel to Late Suse Period in Susiana (therefore Gawra XIII), showed a decline in the size of sites, some abandonment, and wider dispersion of population. During the Uruk period (Mortensen's Late Chalcolithic) new hill sites were founded near Khorramabad. These new hillside encampments may be interpreted as a movement toward pastoral nomadism. After this earlier build-up of seasonal sites, virtually all permanent villages were abandoned for all of the Late Uruk and following Ninevite V or Jemdet Nasr Period. This abandonment may illustrate a strategy utilized to the present day of shifting from settled agriculture to pastoralism under uncertain political conditions (Adams 1978), or total migration.

The western Zagros was hardly homogeneous, however. Northeast of Hulailan in the Kangavar Valley, where Godin Tepe is located, a distinct jump in the number of sites from 23 to 39 occurred in the Late Chalcolithic after the Early and Middle Chalcolithic, in which a consistent number of smaller sites existed (Henrickson 1994: Table 1). North northwest of Hulailan and west of Kangavar in the Mahi Dasht Plain the numbers of sites plummeted from 150 in the Early-Middle Chalcolithic to 33 in the Late Chalcolithic (Henrickson 1994: Table 3). Population growth and site agglomeration in Kangavar appears to parallel population decline in neighboring valleys. Again, the real possibility of considerable population movement in the Late Chalcolithic is indicated.

Farther north in the Zagros, the Lake Urmia Basin was not densely settled in the fourth millennium (Voigt 1989). The southern part of this sub-region, Solduz-Ushnu, was settled early in the fourth millennium (Pisdeli period). Stylistically, close relations existed with Tepe Gawra and the Keban area of highland Eastern Anatolia for the late Ubaid-Uruk period transition (Gawra XIII–XII). After the Pisdeli, all sites in Solduz-Ushnu seem to have been abandoned, as happened in Hulailan and Mahi Dasht valleys. In the northwest part of this area two new sites were founded after the Pisdeli period, Gijlar and Geoy Tepe. These parallel Gawra XI/XA–IX, roughly the Early Uruk or LC2 period. However, occupation was sparse.

Jazira Steppes

To the west of Tepe Gawra across the Tigris River lies the open steppe, the North Jazira sub-region of Iraq (Ball et al. 1989, Wilkinson and Tucker 1995). This is part of the "granary of Mesopotamia" (Weiss 1986:40), where very productive wheat and barley crops are possible under rainfall agriculture conditions.[7] In terms of sheer numbers of fourth millennium sites (60 for just the Tell 'Afar and Sinjar provinces or liwas) this area was heavily occupied. In the Syrian Jezirah, larger sites like Tell Brak, Hamoukar, and Tell Leilan were occupied (see Wattenmaker and Stein 1989). Wilkinson and Tucker (1995:43f.) found a pattern of dispersed, small, probably agricultural sites in this sub-region. Sites like Grai Resh and Telul eth Thalathat represent some of the smaller, somewhat isolated sites of this period and place (see Figure 1.2). Exceptions like Tell al-Hawa and Tell Samir were larger sites, whose immediate hinterland was unoccupied, probably utilized for agricultural exploitation by its residents. Although the pattern of dispersion of sites was similar to that of the earlier Ubaid period, only 31 percent of Ubaid sites surveyed by Wilkinson and Tucker were re-occupied in the

fourth millennium. Interestingly, although population represented by site numbers seems to have risen somewhat from the Ubaid to Early Uruk period, site numbers declined markedly from the earlier to later Uruk period. Most sites were widely dispersed throughout the fifth and fourth millennia. Wilkinson and Tucker theorize that the pattern of shifting and dispersed village populations may represent land utilization. A pattern of very extensive land utilization with frequent movement was transformed into a pattern of shorter cropping intervals, which creates the appearance of massive site decline.

Another factor may lead to more stability and concentration. Early on, formal networks for transport and communication linked many of these sites. In the fourth millennium, a phenomenon of linear depressions, "hollow ways," marked the Northern Jazira (Wilkinson and Tucker 1995). Sites dominated by Classic Uruk pottery types clustered around these hollow ways, which Wilkinson and Tucker see as "well integrated into the Uruk distribution network" (Wilkinson and Tucker 1995:45). By the third millennium B.C., a formal road connected one of the largest mounds of the fourth and third millennia B.C., Tell al-Hawa, with the Tigris at modern Mosul to the southeast (on the opposite riverbank from Nineveh). This road continued toward Tell Leilan in the Khabur River Triangle to the west (Ball et al. 1989). Trade appears to have transformed this agriculturally self-sufficient sub-region toward the end of the fourth millennium. Butterlin (2000: Figure 3) proposes that the interaction sphere of this sub-region extended into the eastern Turkish highlands, especially the area of the Keban Dam near Elâzığ. The commonalities in pottery style support such a proposition (see Chapter 3), although the interaction sphere was probably much broader than just the highland area. Certainly, the Khabur sub-region also had many connections with the Iraqi Jazira.

Upper Euphrates

One sub-region where dramatic new settlement did occur in the Uruk Period, especially its later phases, was in the open plains of North Syria. Earlier settlement in this area is relatively sparse. Tell Sheikh Hassan on the eastern side of the Euphrates (Boesse 1986/7 1995) had a long sequence of fourth millennium levels, but most of the sites in the area were newly founded toward the end of the Middle Uruk, LC4, or the Late Uruk, LC5, period.

The most southerly of these new sites is Qraya, located where the Euphrates and its tributary, the Khabur River, meet (Reimer 1989, Simpson 1988). The site is small, and few other sites existed in its immediate area (Simpson 1988), but it has important economic functions (see below).

The size of some of the sites newly founded on the Upper Euphrates is significant. Habuba Kabira Süd is estimated to have been 18 hectares in size (Strommenger 1980:33). Habuba is part of an enclave of sites including the hilltop religious and public emplacement of Tell Qannas immediately above Habuba and Jebel Aruda (van Driel 1979), a hilltop site eight kilometers north of Habuba. All three sites are Southern Uruk cultural sites in all but location. McCorriston (1997) sees the importance of this area in its extensive pastureland, supporting an ever-increasing production of wool cloth. To others it was an area suited for transshipping goods. In any case, it was little occupied in the fifth millennium. In the period of greatest interaction between the alluvium and the hills, LC 3-5, numerous new sites were founded on its open plains. Almost all of those sites were abandoned at the end of the fourth millennium. Jebel Aruda was already in decline a few generations after it was founded (van Driel in press).

Farther up the Euphrates River, above the modern Syrian-Turkish border a significant number of early fourth millennium sites continued into the late fourth millennium B.C. Carchemish is a large complex mound right on the river crossing at the border. It is most notable for its later occupations, but was occupied at least from the Halaf Period through the Ubaid into the Uruk (Woolley 1952 Part III: 227f.). Unlike the Habuba Kabira/Qannas and Jebel Aruda enclave, at Carchemish locally made wares coexist with Southern types.

Within 20 km north of Carchemish, another enclave of five sites exists, all apparently founded in the Late Middle or Late Uruk LC4-5 period (Algaze et al. 1994). All but one was situated on the west bank of the Euphrates River. At the center of the enclave is a ridge top site called Şadı Tepe, on whose surface are many potsherds with distinctly southern shapes and decoration. The site is littered with flint debitage and flintknapping tools. The sites around it also appear from ceramic evidence to have been founded in the late fourth millennium. They vary in size from Tiladır (the only one of the set on the east side of the river) at 12 hectares to Yarım Höyük at perhaps .5 hectares (Rothman et al. 1998).

Just 15 km north of the Şadı Tepe enclave, but on the opposite side of the Euphrates River, lies Hacınebi (Stein 1994a, 1994b, 1999; Stein, ed. 1999). This site may eventually provide the best evidence of what was occurring during the so-called Contact period (Middle-Late Uruk LC3-4 period). Hacınebi, overlooking the Euphrates River on its east bank, appears to have been a town site from the early fourth millennium B.C.

By the late Middle Uruk or LC4 period, a distinct pattern developed in which buildings and trash pits with local wares existed in one area of the mound, buildings and trash pits with Classic Uruk southern wares in another. Probable emigration of actual Southerners may be indicated by the presence of foods typical of Southern diets and butchered according to Southern practices (Miller in Stein 1994b:171; Bigelow 1999).

The results of an advanced seminar at the School of American Research (SAR, Rothman, ed. in press) has shown that the so-called contact was a process that happened not over two-three hundred years, but five to six hundred, starting at about 3650 BC (Wright and Rupley in press). The earliest stage in the Early Middle or LC3 period saw increasing exchanges between northern and southern Mesopotamian societies. The LC4 seems to have seen the implantation of small trading posts of Southerners in Northern Mesopotamia. Hacınebi may be one, Nineveh another (Rothman b in press; Stein 1999).[8] Sheikh Hassan may be a fully Southern colony of this same period. The final stage, Late Uruk or LC5 period saw major cities implanted in the earlier under-populated Middle Euphrates sub-region (Habuba Kabira, Jebel Aruda, etc.). At this point the cultural interchange increased dramatically. At Hassek Höyük, for example, what originally had been seen as a small Southern trading site, now seems to be a site where local potters produced traditional Late Chalcolithic pottery and copies of Uruk pottery styles using local techniques (Helwing 1999).

Yet farther up the river, the pattern looks like the one at Carchemish. Earlier Late Chalcolithic sites with exclusively local wares continue into the late fourth millennium and their stylistic repertoire includes Southern Uruk types, often alongside local Late Chalcolithic types. The most striking of these sites are Samsat and Arslantepe (Özguç 1992; Frangipane and Palmieri 1983). Samsat sits at one of the best natural crossings of the Euphrates River and had been a major site for millennia. Arslantepe is a smaller site on the bend of the Upper Euphrates near modern Malatya. Other towns or villages excavated with modern techniques include Kurban Höyük, Lidar, Hassek Höyük, and on the Murat River tributary east of the Euphrates near Arslantepe, Tepecik, and Norşuntepe. All these sites were occupied in previous periods. Large increases in size and population are not observable in any of the areas of the Upper Euphrates. Butterlin (2000: Figure 3) proposes that the interaction sphere of this sub-region included the Amuq area to its west and the Khabur River basin to its south.

The Demographic Picture Regionally

Looked at regionally, Greater Mesopotamia through the fourth millennium B.C. shows areas of major population growth, often with a concomitant population decline in neighboring zones. This is the case in the southern alluvium at Late Uruk Period Uruk/Warka, near Godin Tepe in the Kangavar Valley of the Western Zagros, and to a lesser extent in the Susiana, the last mostly in the Susa A and Late Middle Uruk periods. These same sub-regions illustrate a trend toward agglomeration of population—probably part of an overall centralizing trend. On the Upper Euphrates in North Syria, an area little occupied in the previous periods, a sizable growth in large centers occurred in the Late Middle and Late Uruk or LC4-5 periods with populations showing strong cultural ties to southern Mesopotamia. Changes in population size in the area around Tepe Gawra and the piedmont and hills are harder to ascertain. Few high quality site surveys have been conducted there. What evidence we do have suggests an increase in population, although a relatively modest one.

The importance of the changing demography lies in two factors. Theoretically, bringing together large numbers of people in close proximity results from or result in changing economic and political structures. The changes in societal structure in each sub-region implied by (not necessarily impelled by) demographic changes should affect opportunities for production and exchange outside those sub-regions. Second, a more complex structure of leadership is necessary to confront these changes within each sub-region.

What did the changes, signaled by demographic change, look like across the region and how might they indicate changes in the web of interactions among sub-regions?

Organizational Changes

Organizationally, societies in Greater Mesopotamia appear to increase in complexity in the fourth millennium B.C., even in sub-regions where some demographic decline was evident.

Susiana

Organizationally, Ubaid 1-3 Susiana fits the model for the pre-Terminal Ubaid[9] period proposed by Stein (1994a). According to Stein, administrative forms of social organization were based on the mobilization of workers for the production and storage of staple foods (wheat and barley, mostly). The ideology of rule was based on fictive kinship ties. Therefore, symbols of status were kept to a minimum in graves, housing, and the public display of artifacts, especially artifacts made from exotic materials by full-time specialists. Some metals and imported materials have been found in Ubaid 1-3 Susiana sites,[10] but they have not been in contexts that would imply status differences (Hole 1985:21).

The Suse Period saw a radical change on the Susiana plains. At Susa, a massive platform with an administrative or religious building was constructed. A graveyard placed at the edge of the platform contained the graves of clearly high-ranking individual. These graves contained hordes of imported metal objects and finely made beakers. These beakers are proposed to have been tokens of rank within an administrative (leadership) organization (Hole 1983; Wright 1994). In terms of Stein's model (1994a), the staple finance that formed the basis of earlier Ubaid society was altered by the addition of a kind of wealth finance in which power and status were based on control of exotic materials, specialty crafts, and the like. This change resulted in competition among polities for trade goods and trade routes. Warfare ensued.[11] New symbols of status for public display—in Pollock's terms (1983a), these represent the "envaluation" of artifacts—were encoded in seal designs. These are the hallmarks of what anthropologists define as complex chiefdoms (see Wright 1994 for a complete explication of this time, place, and topic).

As the size of Susa declined in the Early Uruk or LC2 period, however, administrative organization was refined, as revealed in increasing numbers and complexity of seals and sealings (Johnson 1973:99–100). Seals were first evidenced as administrative tools in the Susiana d (Ubaid 3) and were common in the Suse, Susa A or LC 1 period. At this time, their numbers and information content swelled. In addition, leaders refocused their rule on staple finance. The construction of buildings in a new area of the Susa mound, possibly functioning as a staple (grain) storage depot suggests this (Wright and Johnson 1985:26).

The transition from the Early to Middle Uruk or LC3 periods is regarded as the one in which state levels of social organization evolved in this and the adjoining southern alluvial sub-regions of Mesopotamia (Wright and Johnson 1975; Wright 1977, 1981). Large industrial ceramic producing districts developed at the centers. Susa and Choga Mish leaders may also have taken on a new role in controlling the labor necessary to maintain irrigation water supplies to their satellite villages (Rothman 1987). Some specialized production is evident at smaller subsidiary sites like Sharafabad (Wright and Johnson 1985:27f.). At these same, small sites an increase in sealing use probably indicates direct control from center administrators. Mass-produced wares like the Beveled Rim Bowl (BRB, for short) appeared. Although the issue is still under debate, the BRB's in some contexts appear to have marked an organization of corvée labor and rations. Yet, contrary to these centralizing trends, most evidence of craft activity at this time suggests continued local manufacture. In the surrounding intermontane areas artifacts show the influence of Susiana style and possibly Susiana rulers' attempts at control.

The Late Uruk or LC5 period should, based on population theory, mark a rapid decline in administrative organization at Susa. If my analysis of Middle Uruk or LC 3-4 period Susiana is correct (Rothman 1987), controls at critical points on the irrigation systems were loosened, if not entirely lost by this following period. The only site that grew substantially was Choga Mish (Johnson 1973: Figure 32). However, at the same time as economic or political decline appears to typify Late Uruk period Susiana, a significant new complexity in the symbolic language of seal design and the first examples of written accounts appear at this time (Amiet 1979; Dittman 1986; Pittman 1993). Lapis lazuli by this period appears to be coming increasingly through Susa and to have declined in amount along the older piedmont routes (including Gawra and Nineveh). In general, what we may be seeing on the Susiana is not so much a decline as another re-orientation. This trend conforms to the theory of Kowalewski et al. (1983) that competition and re-orientation in an administered system requires restricting contacts with the outside, and at the same time imposing increasingly tight, direct control over a limited number of subsidiary sites by the center.

Uruk/Warka

Even at Uruk/Warka, whose excavated remains are preponderantly from the Late Uruk or LC5 period, the trajectory of its ascent to its pinnacle was hardly a straight upward curve. As Nissen (1993:128) points out, "from the well known Ubaid setting there is no continual, steady development to the setting of the latest phase of the Late Uruk period. Rather we have to count with phases of accelerated change." Very complex administrative systems and elaborate public buildings mark the Late Uruk period at Uruk/Warka. These administrative systems (Uruk IV in the Uruk/Warka dating system) include the earliest writing, almost exclusively used by administrators for accounting inputs and outflows of goods from centralized control systems (Nissen et al 1993; Nissen and Englund 1993). The possibility that the concept of kingship evolved at Uruk/Warka and possibly at Susa during the Late Uruk period is plausible (Pittman 1993, Schmandt-Besserat 1993). Certainly, those who write about intra-regional relations are correct in asserting the immense size and complexity of this site and its probable influence on its sub-region and region at the end of the fourth millennium.

Jazira and Steppe

The situation in the Jazira is far less clear. As stated above, some sites in this area grew in size and probably importance and became central places on the open steppe land of Mesopotamia. From all of the most potentially important of these sites for interpretation—Nineveh, Tell al-Hawa, Tell Brak, and Leilan—little of

their fourth millennium occupational area has been excavated or reported.[12] Most samples are from trial trenches or stratigraphic columns. They do have administrative hardware—seals and sealings—of increasing sophistication and are notable for the combination of local and Southern pottery styles recovered. Clearly, the new stylistic boundaries indicated by the appearance of classic Uruk pottery style do represent some cultural trend critical to understanding the evolution of the Mesopotamian region in the fourth millennium B.C. The full impact of information from these sites, however, awaits further excavation.

Upper Euphrates

Sites like Habuba Kabira (Strommenger 1980), Jebel Aruda (van Driel 1979), and Qraya (Reimer 1989) were established on the North Syrian stretch of the Euphrates River. As stated above, these sites are southern, culturally Uruk sites in all but location. Habuba Kabira is a densely packed city with a wall around its central district. A long series of docks lined its riverfront and a large administrative, and perhaps religious, building compound rested on a hill high above it. Qraya, as will be detailed below, is a small industrial complex that probably is a coordinated part of what is happening between northern and southern Mesopotamia, but not directly a part of the Habuba/Qannas-Jebel Aruda communities.

Arslantepe on a bend of the Euphrates in Turkey, far from the Habuba/Qannas-Jebel Aruda communities, provides the best evidence (aside from Gawra) for the operation of administrative systems outside southern Mesopotamia. This is especially true for Level VIA of the Late Uruk or LC5 period. Excavators recovered a series of very large public buildings, a palace and an attached temple (Frangipane and Palmieri 1983; Frangipane in press). The trash from these buildings includes a large number of sealings dumped in one abandoned room (206A), and sealings from locked storage rooms (particularly A340). Based on the way the sealings were found in room 206A, they were dumped in sets, probably from baskets where they were kept for auditing purposes.

A comparison of these two loci indicates that formal administrative procedures were used (Frangipane 1994). Goods that were brought into the palace as tribute or tax for the palace's use were brought in under seal. They were then placed in specific storerooms, which were opened by an authorized official who broke the door peg, clay lock. Receipts in the form of broken seals were placed in the corner of a room (in this case, A340), perhaps in a basket. Later, according to Frangipane (1994), after an audit, they were dumped together. This implies an administrative system as complex as that of Susa, for example. A central administration, with a top level of administration, would cause the material to be brought to the center. A lower level of administrators would actually account for the movement of goods and direct those responsible for extracting materials directly from producers. From what is known from southern Mesopotamia, this is the model of administrative structure practiced there. Although writing was not used, this seal-based system reflects the same underlying structure (see Rothman 1994a). According to Frangipane's analysis (Frangipane in press), newly instituted leadership organizations emerge from the households of earlier days. Depending on the modes of production, competition among households and the need to integrate various segments of society led to centralization. In this model, the responsibility of the central authorities becomes the provisioning of various segments of the population with food and with other goods to harness labor for integrative activities. However, because of a lower agricultural potential in Northern Mesopotamia, the potential for local centralization was always less than that of societies in southern Mesopotamia.

Western Zagros

As stated above, the Kangavar Valley in the middle of the western Zagros can be characterized demographically by growth and agglomeration. What appears to be the central place there, Godin Tepe, shows clear signs of the administrative elaboration found elsewhere toward the end of the fourth millennium. In this case, that administrative structure is represented by a walled oval at the top of the mound. Not only is this oval separated from the rest of the mound physically, its artifacts, particularly its pottery, is of the classic Southern Uruk style, while the rest of people in the contemporaneous levels used a local Late Chalcolithic pottery. This pattern led the original excavator to propose that the oval was a merchant colony (Young and Weiss 1975). Subsequent analysis (Badler 1989) questions that conclusion and suggests rather that it was a seat of a local (leadership?) elite, who based their power on wealth finance. Administrative tablets of Uruk IV type and sealings, as well as sling balls, stored food, and flint tools were found in the earliest phase of the Oval. A later phase saw a decline in administrative hardware, but an increase in flintknapping.

Regional Trends in Organization

For each sub-region of Greater Mesopotamia that is documented, the trend throughout the fourth millennium is of increased administrative sophistication and of increased centralization. A similar case could be proposed for Tell Brak, Tell Leilan, Nineveh, and Tell al-Hawa, but evidence is lacking. Where some centralization is not evident, population trends seem to indicate a significant decline in sites and overall population.

Regional Exchange and Integration

In looking at the regional background for the particular case of Tepe Gawra, the significant question is whether these centers and their sub-regions were economically integrated, and if so, how? This question is particularly significant if one factors in the new southern Mesopotamian enclaves of settlement on the Euphrates River and the presence of "foreign" stylistic types in northern Mesopotamia. This trend began at the time of Tepe Gawra VIII (and also, perhaps Level IX).

Colonial or World Systems Model

Our understanding of the regional organization of Greater Mesopotamia is predicated on the presence of southern Mesopotamian stylistic elements in northern Mesopotamia, especially in the LC3-5 period. Algaze (1993, in press) catalyzed research on this time and place by his theory of northern—southern Mesopotamian interaction. Algaze's theory argues that the presence of significant concentrations of Southern material in northern Mesopotamia represents a conscious attempt by Southern rulers to control trade routes or sites in the periphery where raw materials were extracted. The otherwise resource poor South reached out to control the flow of goods from its resource rich peripheries by placing physical colonies in the steppes of North Syria and the resource-rich hills of the Taurus and Zagros Mountains. They needed to do this in order to implement a new strategy of using wealth finance as one pillar of their status and authority. In fact, in Algaze's theory, this colonial expansion is a characteristic of state societies in general (Algaze in press).

The economic thrust from southern Mesopotamia constituted, according to Algaze, a peaceful, informal empire (Algaze 1989, 1993) or a "world system" (Wallerstein 1974). The underlying pattern of interactions was the same as the militarized empires of the Akkadian Period and later, but without military force. The model assumes that the societies of northern Mesopotamia (the periphery) were technically and culturally unsophisticated and were ripe for exploitation by the highly developed southern Mesopotamians (the core). Although the emphasis of Algaze's model is on the LC 4-5 periods, he also points to a continuous pattern of interchange from the Ubaid period (1993). His theory also assumes that all the possible settlements of southern Mesopotamians in northern Mesopotamia were under the direct control of southern leaders.

A number of researchers have argued that the necessary conditions for such a model are lacking (Stein 1990; 1999; Rothman 1993; Pollock 1994; Rothman, ed.b in press). Clearly, Mesopotamia was a unified region in the sense that established lines of communication existed, different groups knew of each other's existence and resources, and individuals and groups moved freely, though incredibly slowly,[13] throughout the region. The domestication of the donkey as a pack animal may have made such movement possible (Wright in press). However, little evidence exists for bulk "international" trade at this period. Unlike the late third millennium B.C. Early Dynastic III/Akkadian Period, when bronze importation to southern Mesopotamia was essential for the technology of war and commerce, no such essential goods are cited for fourth millennium B.C. trade.

As Wallerstein (1974:397) notes, "The distinction [between bulk trade in necessities and limited luxury trade] is crucial if we are not to fall in the trap of identifying every exchange activity as evidence of the existence of a system."

Also, a number of researchers (Frangipane 1993; Rothman 1993b, in press; Rothman and Peasnall 1999; Lupton 1996) assert, and Algaze accepts to a degree (Algaze in press), that many sub-regions of northern Mesopotamia developed administratively and economically before Classic Uruk styled artifacts appeared for the first time. This is one of the key points I will demonstrate in this volume.

There are a number of possible explanations of the presence of "foreign" artifacts in any sub-region. One is of actual colonies of people from those foreign cultures. Stein (1999) argues for a colony of immigrants from the southern alluvium at Hacınebi in the LC4 period. Another explanation involves the emulation or adoption of foreign styles. Stein (1994a) has argued for the Ubaid Period and Winter (1980) for the first millennium B.C. Neo-Assyrian Period that local cultures often adopt foreign artifact styles to denote special status or public identity. Often this adoption occurs without colonization or acculturation (public identity "is the perception and presentation of self in relation to the larger community . . . for example, group affiliation, hierarchical social status, and shared religious ideology," according to Stein 1991). Sites like Tell Brak, Leilan, Arslantepe, Godin Tepe, even Nineveh, may represent just such an adoption of foreign styles as high status markers of newly institutionalized leadership social identities without becoming colonized. Even if such artifacts do represent actual southern Mesopotamians, as the recent excavations at Hacınebi indicate (Stein 1994a, 1994b, 1999), there is little reason to assume that they are representatives of a southern administered trading system. Perhaps, as Johnson suggests (1988/89) and Stein implies, the new population was made up of immigrants.

Further, the assumption that southern Mesopotamia constitutes a core and the piedmont, steppe, and mountains a monolithic periphery ignores Mesopotamian prehistory. Demand for status goods at places like Susa and Uruk/Warka, created a new role for places like Gawra as suppliers, as did Tell Brak, Habuba Kabira/Qannas, Jebel Aruda, Arslantepe, etc. As outlined above, the region was at virtually the same organizational level during most of the Ubaid Period. Monumental building and administrative seal use, as well as evidence of metal smelting and metal molds (Esin 1982:109), were recovered from northern Mesopotamian sites at that earlier period.

However, even if the colonial or World Systems Theory is rejected in its current form, it is important not to ignore the connections that did exist in fourth millennium B.C. Greater Mesopotamia. Various sub-regions did exchange goods, critical ideas, and organizational models (see Algaze 1993: Chapter 4). Qraya, with over 40 fire emplacements, kilns, and ovens (Reimer 1989) was most likely serving northern and southern Mesopotamian sites. This exchange did affect local developments in each sub-region and at each site. A much more flexible and layered interpretation will help us to view each sub-region and the region as a whole in evolutionary perspective. Perhaps we need to see Mesopotamia, as Marfoe (1987:28) writes, as "a web of interlocking but discrete, individual links of enmeshed local systems."

Measuring Regional Interactions

How can the network of sub-regional interactions in Greater Mesopotamia be measured? What specifically can one point to as the basis of interconnection of residents of this site with any other site or sites?

As archaeologists, we are obviously limited in the components of the cultural picture we can reliably reconstruct. To some extent we can hope to understand shared symbolic—including religious—ideologies. To some extent we can understand ethnic movements. However, the most reliable axes of variability we can measure are economic. If we know what is produced or extracted locally for exchange outside the area of a site and we know where these sorts of products and raw materials ended up, we can hope to establish a network of interactions. This is the sort of approach I used to analyze the relations of Middle Uruk Susa and Choga Mish with their satellite sites by graphing the loci of production and exchange of certain pottery types in Susiana (Rothman 1987).

This approach should be helpful in the analysis that follows here. I will be especially careful to note:

1. the kinds of products manufactured in each level;
2. the probable scale of production; 3. whether raw materials used in production are easily extracted

locally or need to be imported; 4. where such products are most likely to go, and conversely; 5. what sort of products and raw materials are being imported to Gawra.

As Frangipane (in press) argues, the soundest approach to solving the problem of north-south relations in the Uruk or LC1–5 period is to view the phenomena also from northern Mesopotamia, not in terms of the degree to which the northern and southern Mesopotamian societies resembled each other or differed, but in terms of analyzing the features and processes which characterized the development of northern communities as well as the historical roots of their external relations.

In summary, the task remaining in this volume is to see how one small site functioned over the span of time from Terminal Ubaid, LC1, to the Early Middle Uruk, LC3 periods. In doing so, I will sketch out what kinds of connections that functioning implies, in other words, how the particular adaptation of people at this site reflects the larger region.

Remaining Chapters

Chapter 2 is a history of excavation indicating strengths and weaknesses in the data. Chapters 3 and 4 will discuss technical problems related to the analysis: excavation history, stratigraphy, and reconstruction of town plans, chronology, and the function of artifacts. Chapter 5 describes the evolutionary prehistory of the town. Chapter 6 concludes the volume and offers a synthesis of Tepe Gawra and of possible hypotheses to explain regional issues in Mesopotamia.

Notes

1. The appellation BC will appear in two formats. Following Hole (1994), I will use BC without periods for calibrated dates and B.C. for uncalibrated.

2. Typically, the quantity of goods exchanged in down-the-line trade decreased as they moved farther and farther from resource areas (see Renfrew 1977, Caldwell 1976 for descriptions of such trade).

3. The term region here covers the entire interaction sphere of Greater Mesopotamia. Although it is common to refer to, for example, the southern region or the Khabur region, as smaller subsets of the larger region, these are listed as sub-regions.

4. There is some confusion in the term Jazira, or alternatively Jazireh, or Jezirah. Some identify this area as the steppe lands west of the Euphrates and east of the Tigris. The British admiralty considered only the part of this steppe land in Iraq the "Jazira." I will by caveat refer to the Jazira as northeastern Iraq, and Jezirah as the larger area including the Syrian part encompassing the Khabur basin.

5. According to Algaze (1993:71–72) Gawra as excavated was only the acropolis of a larger site. He cites Gibson's trip to Gawra, and the "unexpected" complexity of such a small site. However, another observer on that same trip contradicts Gibson's observations (Rothman 1989:286). Also, none of the excavations off the mound yielded anything later than the Halaf Period of the seventh and sixth millennia B.C. (Tobler 1950). Although it strikes me as possible that a lower town could have existed, especially in Level VIII times, there is no evidence to support that conclusion, and no necessity logically to do so, either.

6. Contrary to Algaze (1993:72), I did not argue in 1988, nor will I here, that only semi-nomadic groups were part of the Gawran polity. I strongly suggest that such groups were present, but also villages occupied year round were part of the area Gawran leaders administered. In 1994 I suggested which of the sites from the Iraq survey were probably part of the Gawran network (see Figure 1.2).

7. Again, if Hole (1994) is correct, this area would have been drier and hotter in the Ubaid and Early Uruk Periods than earlier.

8. In the so-called colony at Hacınebi, the community of Southerners from the Uruk cultural tradition was marked by the use of southern technologies. These include Southern administrative systems, southern pottery, and also clay sickles. The traditional northern Mesopotamian flint sickles are readily available and are much more efficient than clay sickles. The presence of clay sickles at Hacınebi and also Nineveh (Mallowan 1933) in roughly the Late Middle Uruk or LC4 period may well indicate the physical presence of Southerners Rothman, in press b).

9. This Terminal Ubaid is also known as Suse, Susa I, Susa A, Ubaid 4 or LC1 period.

10. Theoretically, kinship systems are based on a relative equality of all persons. Although "leadership" in the form of Big Men, or low level "chiefs" exists, their leadership is not based on political authority, but on influence and moral persuasion.

11. At the end of contemporaneous Gawra XII fire and skeletons prone in the street with signs of violent death marked warfare.

12. The latest excavation project at Tell Brak may rectify this lack (Emberling et al. 1999, Oates and Oates 1997).

13. The itinerary of long distance traders 1,500 years later in the Old Assyrian Period records travel times in months (Larsen 1967).

Excavation History

Ephraim Speiser investigated Gawra in 1927 during a survey of the northern third of Iraq under the aegis of the University of Pennsylvania and the Baghdad School of ASOR (Barton 1927; Speiser 1929). Based on the discovery of prehistoric painted pottery at Susa and other "Aeneolithic" (Neolithic and Chalcolithic) sites, Speiser felt that he had found the oldest stratified site in northern Mesopotamia at Gawra (Speiser 1928). With $500 left of a grant obtained for the survey by Cyrus Adler of Dropsie College, Speiser and an architect named Wilenski spent fifteen working days over a three week period in October 1927 excavating a 5-meter-wide trench. This trench unusually started at the bottom and moved toward the top of the mound, a distance of approximately 20 meters (Barton 1927, 1928; Speiser 1929).

Speiser defined three "cultures" in the twenty architectural levels into which he divided the mound during the excavation. Gawra I was the "Aeneolithic painted pottery culture"—probably late Halaf and 'Ubaid (Speiser 1929:28–30). Gawra II was a "pre-bronze" society with unpainted, incised buff plainware—probably coterminous with the Uruk Period (Speiser 1929: 30–35). Gawra III was Bronze Age. It had Early Dynastic Period seals and pottery types known from the South in the lower parts of Gawra III. A Mittanian fort sat near the top of the Gawra III cultural horizon (Speiser 1929: 35–39).

In the fall of 1930, Speiser began to oversee excavations at nearby Tell Billa. During that year, numerous visits to Tepe Gawra resulted in the decision to excavate this site as well. A strategy designed to "dig the mound systematically by starting at the top and slicing off layer after layer" was devised (Speiser 1931c:5).

The first season of excavation at Gawra (G1) began on January 19, 1931 and ended six weeks later.

Dr. A. Saarisalo from the University of Helsinki and an architect named Detweiler assisted Speiser. During that season, Level I and varying portions of Levels II to IX were removed. The first season was followed by a second (G2) under Speiser's direction from October 12, 1931, to March 15, 1932. The remaining parts of Levels II to VI, all of VII, much of VIII, and two squares of IX were excavated in G2 (seasons are referred to hereafter alternatively by name or simply as G1 to G7). In that second season, Charles Bache of the University of Pennsylvania Museum and Cyrus Gordon then of the University of Pennsylvania joined the crew.

The plan of excavation, as mentioned above, was to strip architectural levels one after the other. The director divided the site into 10×10-meter squares. The site as a whole was divided into north and south halves, so that any two field supervisors could split the work gangs—"an average daily force of two hundred men" (Speiser 1932b: 566)—and each could concentrate on half the site. In fact, the halves were not dug at the same speed, so that parts of one level, for example Level V, were being excavated at the same time its antecedents, for example, Levels III and IV. During the course of removal, no bulks were kept for stratigraphic control and no sections were drawn.

Square designations were extremely confused. In 1927, the 5×5-meter squares had been numbered as follows in Table 2.1.

Each square moving up the slope had a unique letter designation. Within each square, strata were marked by numbers (for example, B4). When they reached an inward curve in mound at square J (the elevation of Level VIII), they expanded east and west, giving these squares lower case designations. Although it appears that this designation system was to be tried in the first season, it proved rather unacceptable when

Table 2.1   1927 Square Designations

```
                              N
                              M
                              L
                              K
  h g f e d c b a J   J a b c d e f g h
                              I
                              H
                              G
                              F
                              E
                              D
                              C
                              B
                              A
```

digging the entire surface of the mound. They therefore devised a new designation system, based on a designation of each square by its column and row. No written records exist to explain this system, but apparently the square designations worked as shown in Table 2.2 (see Rothman 1988 for method of decoding this system). Table 2.2 contrasts the first full season's square designations with the publication square designations of Speiser (1935a) and Tobler 1950.

As mentioned, each square was marked by a column capital letter and row lower case letter (for example, "Ma," which equals "8J" in the final publication).

In the second season (G2) a new numbering system had to be instituted because the area of the surface of the mound had expanded and the G1 designation system was no longer sufficient. This new G2 system, another modification of the 1927 trial trench system worked as shown in Table 2.3.

Each square was designated as the intersection of a row and column (for example, "Ma" in the registry book now equaled "7M" of the final publication). Evidence for the equivalence of G2 and publication numbers is found on an original architectural plan for phase VIIIA in the Archives of the University of Pennsylvania Museum.

Table 2.2   First Season Square Designation

Publication		10	9	8	7	6
	1st season registry	O	N	M	L	K
O	d					
M	c					
K	b					
J	a					

Recording during the first two seasons was done in registry books and provenience was based on the 10 × 10-meter grids into which the whole site was divided. Occasionally, when a special building, such as one of the buildings with buttressed exteriors in Level VIII, was discovered, the find spot of objects found in those numbered rooms was recorded. These buildings were assumed to be temples or shrines (see following chapters). No registry book had been kept for the 1927 trial trench. However, the first one hundred to one hundred and fifty numbers in the G1 registry appear copied from 1927 field notes. Artifacts from the first season were numbered 1150 forward, the second season 5001 forward. A last set of numbers, 6001 forward, appear to on objects added ex post facto from among unnumbered artifacts in the dig house at the beginning of the third (G3) season. Speiser included them in the first final report (1935a). A small daybook in Speiser's hand exists from the second season. His notes, however, are very sketchy and uninformative. For example, for October 19, Speiser wrote, "Stratum 3 being cleared. A stone mold for weapons in IL [Level] IV. Complete strainer in the same area." The registry books for G1 and part of the G2 are hardly more helpful. According to a letter of December 4, 1986, from Dr. Cyrus Gordon to me, the reason for the problems were inexperience and bad health.

I do know that the register of finds during 1931–32 was in grossly unsatisfactory hands under the first two recorders, until Stella Ben-Dor joined us and took over, to do a first-class job for the rest of the season in the expedition's "lab/museum" where the materials and records were kept and processed. Speiser was not in good health much of the time—which may account for some lacunae.

Of the artifacts actually recovered from the ground, a small, arbitrary sample of whole vessels, spectacular sherds, flint and obsidian objects, seals and seal impressions, spindle whorls, metal tools, figurines, and other objects were recorded. Of that sample, perhaps 75 percent were sent to the Iraq Museum or The University of Pennsylvania Museum for storage and future study.

On November 2, 1932, when much of Level VIII, phases A and B and small, though unrecognized parts of VIIIC had been exposed, Speiser's successor as field director, Charles Bache, began the third season (G3) of excavation, which ran to April 4, 1933. During this and the next three field seasons, E. Bartow Mueller handled the architectural detail. Bache's earlier experiences digging American Indian sites in the eastern United States (e.g., Bache and Satterthwaite 1930) appear to have made him a more careful excavator than Speiser had been. He continued to excavate Gawra by architectural layers, having one group of workers digging, for example, Level IX in one portion of the

Table 2.3   Second Season Square Designation

Publication		10	9	8	7	6	5	4
	2nd season registry	g	f/e	d/c	b/a	I	II	III
S								
Q	Q							
O	O/P							
M	M/N							
K	K/L							
J	J							
G	G							

mound while another was clearing Level X or even XI in the other portion (see Bache 1936a:5, Figure 1). However, Bache decreased the number of workers to an average of 100 (Bache 1933a:9), partly to save money and partly to gain more control over the recording of finds. In G3, Bache excavated the rest of Level VIII, all of Level IX and parts of Level X (see Tobler 1950:1 for crew make-up of the G3 to G7 seasons).

In order to reduce the confusion in recording experienced in the first two seasons, Bache again changed the designation of the squares as shown in Table 2.4.

Again, a row/column designation—for example, 8M—marked each square. The rows, however, were numbers. This system was used in the G3, G4, and G5 seasons.

In G3 Bache relied on the register for recording information on artifactual finds. Field object numbers from the third season to the end of excavation consist of the season number, a hyphen and an object number from 1 to whatever. For example 3-492 is item 492, a

small beaker from Level X, excavated in G3, the third season. In addition to the registries, Bache added small 4 × 6-inch cards to record information on graves, tombs and a very few features. He also added small object control cards for cataloguing objects as they came into the lab from the field. The control cards are 3.5 × 3-inch cards on which the field object number is first assigned (for example 3-492) and the excavation square and sometimes the object's dimensions are written. The object control cards were used at the division between the University of Pennsylvania Museum and the Iraqi government, at which time each artifact's final disposition was written on its card. Object control cards are preserved in the Archives of the University of Pennsylvania Museum for G3 and G4.

The fourth season (G4), again under Bache's direction, ran from November 7, 1934 to February 27, 1935. During that season "over one quarter of the mound, the 12th stratum from the top was uncovered, 10, 11 and sub-11 having been passed through, mapped and destroyed" (Bache 1935a:185). At this point, Bache

Table 2.4   3rd–5th Season Square Designation

Publication		11	10	9	8	7	6	5	4	3
	3rd 4th 5th season	G	H	J	K	L	M	N	P	R
S	7									
Q	8									
O	9									
M	10									
K	11									
J	12									
G	13									

thought that everything under X and above the newly discovered XI-A was in Level XI. Artifacts are accordingly catalogued.

Bache again improved his recording methods. First, he converted the 4 × 6-inch cards into preprinted 8.5 × 11-inch locus/grave forms and added what for this analysis is the most important new recording form: the "chit." A chit is a pre-numbered four by five-inch piece of notepad paper. Field supervisors carried them to the excavation and used them to record usually one, but sometimes two to four artifacts. Each chit consists of a 10 × 10-meter grid, on which the location of an object is marked as the object is excavated on the mound. Spaces are printed to record level, square, locus (if any special feature), date, and absolute elevation. Approximately 75 percent of all chits record object provenience to within a one by one-meter square. Perhaps, 50 percent give an absolute elevation for objects. Another 25 percent or so comment (in the margin) on the nature of the fill. Comments such as "on the floor of a room," "on a pavement," or "in ordinary red trash" are typical. Parenthetically, the term "pavement" initially appears to have been restricted to outdoor surfaces (streets, alleys, working spaces). In short order, however, it alternated arbitrarily with the term "floor." After objects were recorded in the dig house, the assigned field registry number was written on the chit.

Chits were used for a secondary purpose in G4. The masses of pottery sherds that were excavated were carried to the lab in baskets. Of the G4 chits 539 record the location and elevation of these baskets. However, few of these sherds from the baskets appear to have been saved. Of those found in the collections of the University of Pennsylvania Museum only a handful were marked with the chit number. Nor could notes be found in the Archives in which the differing wares in each basket were counted, weighed, or in any way recorded.

Not counting the pottery basket chits, approximately 4,000 chits exist from the G4, G5, and G7 seasons. These cover a small part of Level X, and much of Levels XI/XA to XX, with a drop off in Levels XIII to XVI, which Speiser excavated. The few chits that exist from G6 were used as locus sheets, mostly for grave goods. Perhaps 500 to 700 chits were destroyed by mildew when they were stored in a sub-basement of the University of Pennsylvania Museum during the 1940s and 1950s. Most importantly, Tobler apparently did not use the information on the chits in writing the second volume of the final report (Tobler 1950).

In the analysis that follows and in the catalogues this author will designate the sub-square information in the chits as shown in Table 2.5.

The designation works this way: a9, for example, designates a location inside the square at the "a" column and "9" row; a/b 9 designates a location on the

Table 2.5   Sub–square Designations

	a	b	c	d	e	f	g	h	i	j
1										
2										
3										
4										
5										
6										
7										
8										
9										
10										

line between "a" and "b" columns in the "9" row; a-c 8-9 indicates a provenience somewhere within the square encompassing columns "a", "b" and "c", rows "8" and "9."

Another improvement that Bache introduced in G4 was a redesign of the registry book. Instead of long columns, which accommodated up to 20 field numbered items, the registry was divided into four squares per sheet. This division permitted scale drawings of most registered objects. In addition to spaces for the field registry number, stratum, or level, elevation, disposal (that is, Philadelphia, Baghdad, or discarded), photograph number, drawing number, a space was printed for "field number." That field number is the chit number. Although G3 registries were of the 20 per page type, a G4 style registry exists in Philadelphia, redone by Bache at the end of G4. Bache apparently did many of the field registry drawings in the G3, G4, and G5 seasons.

The G5 season was again under the direction of Charles Bache. It lasted from October 31, 1935, to February 15, 1936. The excavators worked on what was thought to be Level XI to XIII. The workforce was increased to 180 men (Bache 1936b:6). As the crew dug under X in what excavators then called Level "XI" in the middle of the mound they discovered what was thought to be another intermediate level, called "XA" (for all sub-level phases the hyphen [e.g., X-A, VIII-C] will be dropped in this volume). Although XA deposits were apparently dug in G4, G5 was the first time the stratum was recognized. Below, it will be argued that XA is not a level distinct from XI, but a later rebuilding phase of the same level, XI/XA. Bache himself recognized this possibility. He wrote (1935B:14):

I have been referring to the new temple of 11. This may later prove not to be the case. There is some difficulty in this region as to stratification, and it will be some time before we shall be able to determine this definitively. It is entirely... possible that it belongs to an upper level ... The presence of walls of two, and occasionally three levels within the same area does not contribute much to the accuracy of observation.

It is important to note here, however, that the original excavators made no attempt to return to the G4 field notes and to distinguish artifacts belonging to the strata immediately under X (that is, XA) and the earlier building phase of the same level, designated as phase XI. As a result, based on absolute elevations, many artifacts appear mislabeled as to stratum, and the architectural plans published by Tobler (1950:Plates IV and V) appear in some respects confused. Suggested revisions of the plans appear later in the next chapter.

Recording methods in G5 remained as they were in G4, with the exception that the small object control cards seem to have been phased out.

The sixth season saw the return of E. A. Speiser as the director of field excavations. G6 lasted from October 12, 1936, to March 19, 1937. During this season, Speiser's crew excavated the Round House of XIA and deposits above it in XA and XI. Excavation was then extended from Level XII to XVI. Also, a trench into the unexcavated western half of the mound was begun.[1]

The return of Speiser was accompanied by a diminution in the quality of data recording. First, he returned to the 20 per page registry. Second, the Philadelphia artist, Alfred Bendiner, an excellent painter and sketch-artist, was a less precise object illustrator than Bache or his assistants had been. Third, Speiser all but eliminated the chit system of Bache, relying on the registry in the hands of an inexperienced registrar. There is again a small daybook in Speiser's hand. This notebook, which concentrates on burials, is not much more informative than the G2 book had been. It also contains notes written subsequently by Tobler questioning the accuracy of a few observations. Speiser again chose to change the designations of the excavation squares as illustrated in Table 2.6.

Bache continued this square designation system in the G7 season, and it is the designation system used by Tobler in the second final report (1950). It is also the designation scheme used in the first final publication (Speiser 1935a), differing only in that Speiser referred to squares by lettered row first, then column (e.g., M6 rather than 6M). To minimize confusion, this G6 square designation system, referring first to the numbered column, then lettered row, is the one used throughout the current volume. The other designation systems, including the designations for Level VIII in volume I (Speiser 1935a), I converted to that G6 system in the following pages and in the catalogue.

Bache returned to Gawra as field director November 1, 1937. G7, the last full season at Gawra, ended on

Table 2.6   Publication and This Volume Square Designation

	12	11	10	9	8	7	6	5	4	3	2
S											
Q											
O											
M											
K											
J											
G											

May 7, 1938 (with a break from December 15, 1937, to March 15, 1938 for work at Khafajeh). The western trench was continued to the elevation of XIIA, and excavations proceeded into the deepest strata of the mound proceeded. Virgin soil was never reached.

Bache retained the revised Speiser square designations and the compressed, 20 per page registry. He did revive the chit system of field notation to some extent, though not quite as completely as in G4 and G5.

In conclusion, the quality of record keeping varied from season to season. During the fourth, fifth, and seventh seasons, records were of sufficient quality that, for example, stratigraphically questionable assignments of artifacts could be corrected. Detailed analyses of artifacts in their original three-dimensional find spots could be done. In that, the excavators of those seasons were much more careful than many of their contemporaries. On the other hand, this excavation was not up to modern standards. Where three-dimensional provenience information was lacking, I have been forced to accept the original level assignment, even where I suspected it may have been wrong.

Excavators did not provide figures on the total sample of the artifacts recovered. Although field notes record the presence of ash lenses filled with animal bone, pots and rooms containing charred vegetable remains, and hearths with charcoal, none of these materials were saved. Modern techniques of screening and flotation were not known and therefore not utilized. The result is a virtual dearth of animal and plant remains and undoubtedly a general lack of the small finds that are recovered using screening or flotation. Also, site supervisors rarely recorded secondary and tertiary trash and fill deposits, if they noticed them at all. The ratio of site supervisors to hired excavators ranged from 1:40 to 1:100. The practical results of the quality of excavation on interpretation will be discussed in the following chapters.

An immediate problem arose when I compiled the catalogues. I was forced to use five separate sources, which neither were not nor could be entirely cross-referenced. The field catalogues are as complete as is possible, listing the catalogue number assigned in the field (what I call the field number, 1000, 5000, and G3–7) and a "field number" (the chit number). Perhaps 90 percent of all artifacts (except potsherds) appear to have been catalogued. At the University of Pennsylvania Museum, three-part museum numbers were penciled into the field catalogues and those sent to the Iraq Museum were marked "Baghdad," although some University of Pennsylvania Museum items were not given separate numbers. For a small number of sealings, I also have Iraq Museum (IM) numbers. The University of Pennsylvania Museum registrar's files list all the museum numbers and cross-list those with the field number and sometimes the chit number. Field numbers appear in the chits, but those items not catalogued are listed simply as "not cat." with no indication of where they were sent. The only direct information on the chit items not catalogued is if they were discarded in the field. Field locus pages sometimes indicate artifacts in situ, although some were never catalogued or seemingly noted in chits. In theory, some number of artifacts that do not appear in the field catalogues or in the chits exist in Baghdad, as they do in Philadelphia. However, my plans to include these artifacts and complete Iraq Museum numbers were put on permanent hold by the Gulf War of 1990. I had been scheduled to go to Baghdad in September 1990. However, based on

the material in Philadelphia from the original 50–50 division and on the number of sealings without original field numbers found by Elizabeth Stone and Paul Zimansky,[2] the percentage of the total corpus missing from the catalogues should be small. I estimate the loss at 1 percent of the total, but I cannot be sure. A few of these otherwise missing artifacts I found in the fourth source, the items included in the catalogues of the earlier Gawra reports (Speiser 1929, 1935a, and Tobler 1950).

In addition to the problem of missing artifacts, some much smaller number of artifacts that were not catalogued but were registered in chits may be listed twice in my catalogues. This number is, I think, very small.

The next chapter reconstructs the site plans based on chit and stratigraphic section information and attempts to date the various levels and sub-level phases.

Notes

1. The first appearance of artifacts from squares 9M, 10M and 11M of stratum XI in the G6 registry implies that Tobler (1950:2) mistakenly attributed the opening of the West Trench to G5.

2. Zimansky and Stone were kind enough to inspect the Gawra seals and sealings they could find in the Iraq Museum and photograph the backs of sealings. I am very appreciative of their efforts.

3

Site Stratigraphy and Chronology

In this chapter I discuss the vertical and horizontal relations of sets of buildings and open areas of the Gawra mound in an attempt to define their relative temporal position. I then assign a date for each Gawra level and sub-level phase relative to other Mesopotamian sites (virtually no reliable absolute dates exist for Tepe Gawra). As stated in Chapter 1, although this section speaks of distinct levels and sub-level phases,[1] all archaeological strata are like averages of continuous change in built environments, except where sites are leveled completely after long periods of abandonment and then rebuilt on a flat plane. Such comprehensive leveling did not happen from Levels XII to VIII.

Stratigraphy

Two major attempts have been made to define the stratigraphy of the levels called XII to VIII from the mound of Gawra. The first attempt was presented in the original site reports by Speiser (1935a) and Tobler (1950). Bache and Mueller were silent co-authors of the second report, although Tobler and Bendiner's additions and emendations to Bache's ideas are apparent when comparing Bache's preliminary site reports and Tobler's final publication. Speiser and Tobler saw the Gawra mound as a layer cake in which each layer, each architectural level, was a sealed record of contemporaneous town life (see Excavation History in Chapter 2). These discrete entities are the ones found in their publications.

The second attempt at a stratigraphic reconstruction (for Levels XIA to VIII only) was that of Jean-Daniel

Forest (1983). Forest's primary interest was burial practices in Mesopotamia from the fifth through the third millennia B.C. Specifically, his intent was to put the burial practices at his own excavation of Kheit Qasim in the Hamrin into a broader framework by comparing Kheit Qasim with Tepe Gawra and Ur. In order to understand the evolution of burial practice Forest felt it essential first to understand the relative stratigraphy of tombs and graves. Because he proposed that tombs were associated with major public buildings, especially those with religious functions, he sought to understand the stratigraphy of those buildings relative to the rest of the constructions on the mound. In doing his stratigraphic analysis, Forest's sole sources of information were Tobler and Speiser's volumes. He did not attempt to inspect any of the original field records, which are stored at the University of Pennsylvania Museum. Those records prove essential for understanding Gawra's stratigraphy. As the Appendix on mortuary practices demonstrates, using the original field notes produces a much different dating of tombs and graves than Forest proposes (see Forest's Reconstructions below).

New Stratigraphic Reconstruction and Critiques of Former Reconstructions

Sources

Although systematic stratigraphic notes were not made in the field, previously untapped stratigraphic information does exist for Tepe Gawra. Among the kinds of information recorded on chits (see Chapter 2) are details of stratigraphic significance. For example, one chit might note that an artifact was found in ordinary red trash in a specific 1 × 1-meter square and at such-and-such an elevation. It is therefore possible to map trashy fill to that stratigraphic space. Another chit might locate an artifact 20 centimeters above a floor. One can map the floor and assume some kind of secondary or tertiary trash fill at least 20 centimeters above it. In addition, the published architectural plans list elevations of floors and of the tops and bottoms of the remains of walls. This stratigraphic information is somewhat enhanced by wall elevations in Mueller's architectural notebooks and in the original pencil sketch plans Mueller drew for Levels XII, XIA, XI and VIIIA. These drawings are stored in the Archives of the University of Pennsylvania Museum.

To discover the stratigraphy some kind of stratigraphic section is needed. Using the stratigraphic information from chits and elevations in drawings of architecture, I drew what I call "schematic sections." Each of these sections covers the excavation from six to fifteen meters above plain level for each of 28 excavation squares (4J, 5J, 6J, 7J, 8J, 4K, 5K, 6K, 7K, 8K, 3M, 4M, 5M, 6M, 7M, 8M, 9M, 10M, 4O, 5O, 6O, 7O, 8O, 4Q, 5Q, 6Q, 7Q, 8Q). In Figures 3.1 to 3.5 these schematic sections are drawn in five east-to-west running sections (J, K, M, O, Q). Because there were no balks, I developed a different method of drawing sections. I drew an imaginary east-west line through the middle of each square. Any walls or features that would run parallel or perpendicular to this imaginary line were drawn in. Fortunately, it was rare that two parallel walls would run in the same square. These schematics are therefore a conflation, as if someone took the walls and features in any square and squashed them flat against an imaginary plane running east to west through the middle of each square. The identity of each wall that is drawn is identified in the schematic sections to help orient the reader.

These schematic sections do help to clarify many major stratigraphic questions. They certainly belie the layer cake idea of site stratigraphy, sometimes radically so. Their first contribution to understanding Gawra's fourth millennium B.C. stratigraphy is to define the stratigraphic position of Level XII in relation to its predecessors.

For those interested in following the detailed explanations of the stratigraphy and reconstruction of the town plans, I suggest copying Figures 3.1 to 3.15 and having them readily available for reference.

The Gawra mound was a high-sided mound with a gradual rise (Plate 1a).

Levels XIII to XII

The schematic sections show that Level XII, the earliest level discussed in this volume, is totally sepa-

rated in space and time from Ubaid 4 Period Level XIII. In a number of squares (e.g., 4M in Figure 3.3) walls of XIIA exist between Levels XIII and XII. Even where walls of XIIA do not appear between Level XIII and XII, fill of approximately one meter separates them (e.g. 4-5J, Figure 3.1). Such stratigraphy would imply that XIIA is a minor occupation after the buildings of XIII went out of use. The style of its pottery (see the Pottery Chronology of Tepe Gawra below) also implies a separation between two distinct levels.

Level XII (Figure 3.6) therefore represents a newly founded, dense, probably long-lived occupation of the site. Excavators uncovered a formally laid-out entrance road (spaces 53 and 59) at the northeast end of the mound. It is delimited on the east by rooms 51 and 52 and by a short wall in front of the large building with the white plastered walls, the "White Room" (room 42, see Plate 1b). Rooms 54 to 62 adjoin the road on the west. These and the large tripartite building flanking the southern end of that entrance road—the White Room, rooms 36 to 49—serve as the stratigraphic anchors for Level XII. To the immediate west of the rooms 54 to 62, a large open courtyard (63) separates rooms 54 to 62 from another small block of rooms (65 to 74). Actually, this courtyard is filled with low bins (Plate 2A). These bins are evident in field photographs, but were never drawn on the plans.

That XII was abandoned suddenly and replaced by the XIB phase of Level XIA/B is evident in the plan of XIB (Figure 3.7, the town plan of XIB, below). Where rooms of XII and XIB existed in the same square, the walls of XIA clearly overlie those of XII (see schematic sections, Figures 3.1 to 3.5). As Forest notes (1983: 27), "the superposition of the plans of XIA and XII do not reveal any striking coincidence."[2] However, Forest also indicates that there are a number of buildings in Tobler's XIA plan that do not directly overlie, but which resemble the plan of XII (Forest 1983: 27). Spaces 89 to 91 and 96 to 104 of XIA[B] (Square 5-6M, Figure 3.7 and 3.8) resemble spaces 84 to 89 of XII (Square 5M, Figure 3.6); spaces 105 and 106 (Square 5K), 109 and 110 of XIA[B] resemble spaces 95 to 101 of Level XII (Tobler 1950, Plate VIII). Added to Forest's list should be the small white-plastered tripartite building, rooms 39 to 48, of XIB (Squares 5J-K, Figure 3.7). Also included should be rooms 25 to 31 of XII (Square 4K, Figure 3.6), rooms 74 to 81 of XIB (Squares 5-6Q, Figure 3.7), and 37 to 45 of XII, the White Room building. From a stratigraphic point of view, Level XII's plan seems rebuilt in XIB with some clear changes.

The end of Level XII was probably the result of military attack. The White Room building and the surrounding buildings were burned. The recovery of bodies in the streets, one with a stone (sling missile?) in its back (Tobler 1950:25–26), suggests that the site

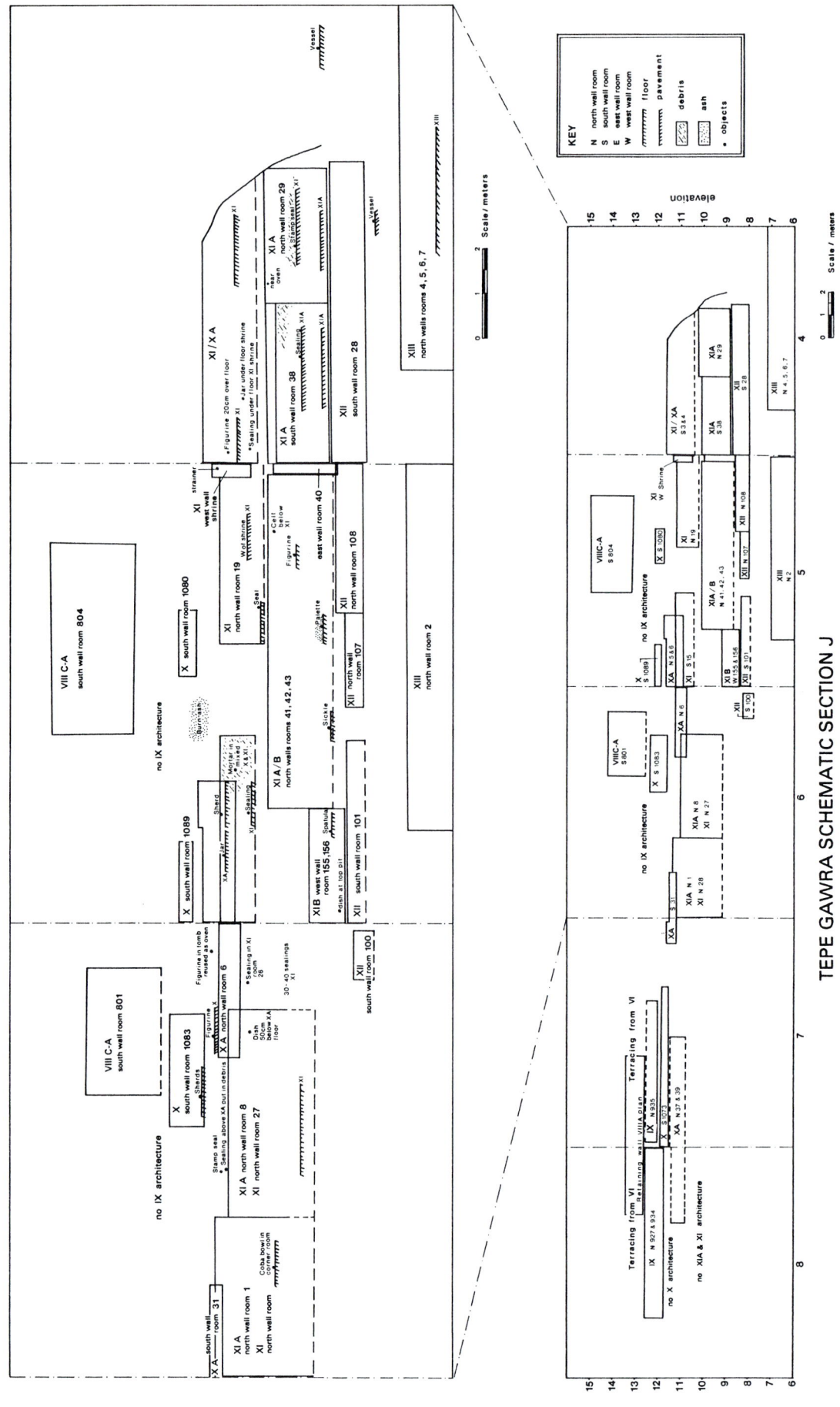

TEPE GAWRA SCHEMATIC SECTION J

Figure 3.1   Schematic section of the J transect at Tepe Gawra.

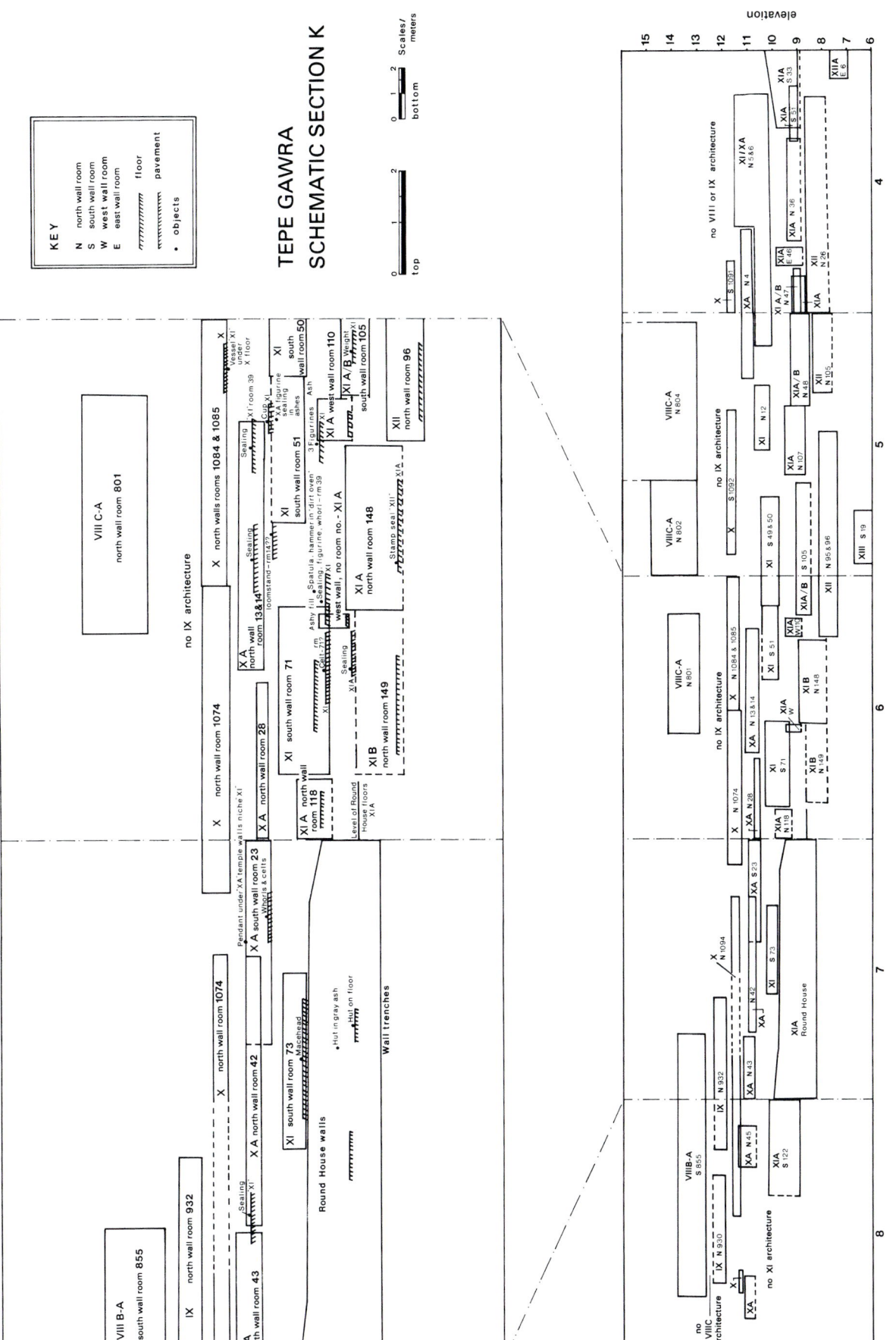

Figure 3.2   Schematic section of the K transect at Tepe Gawra.

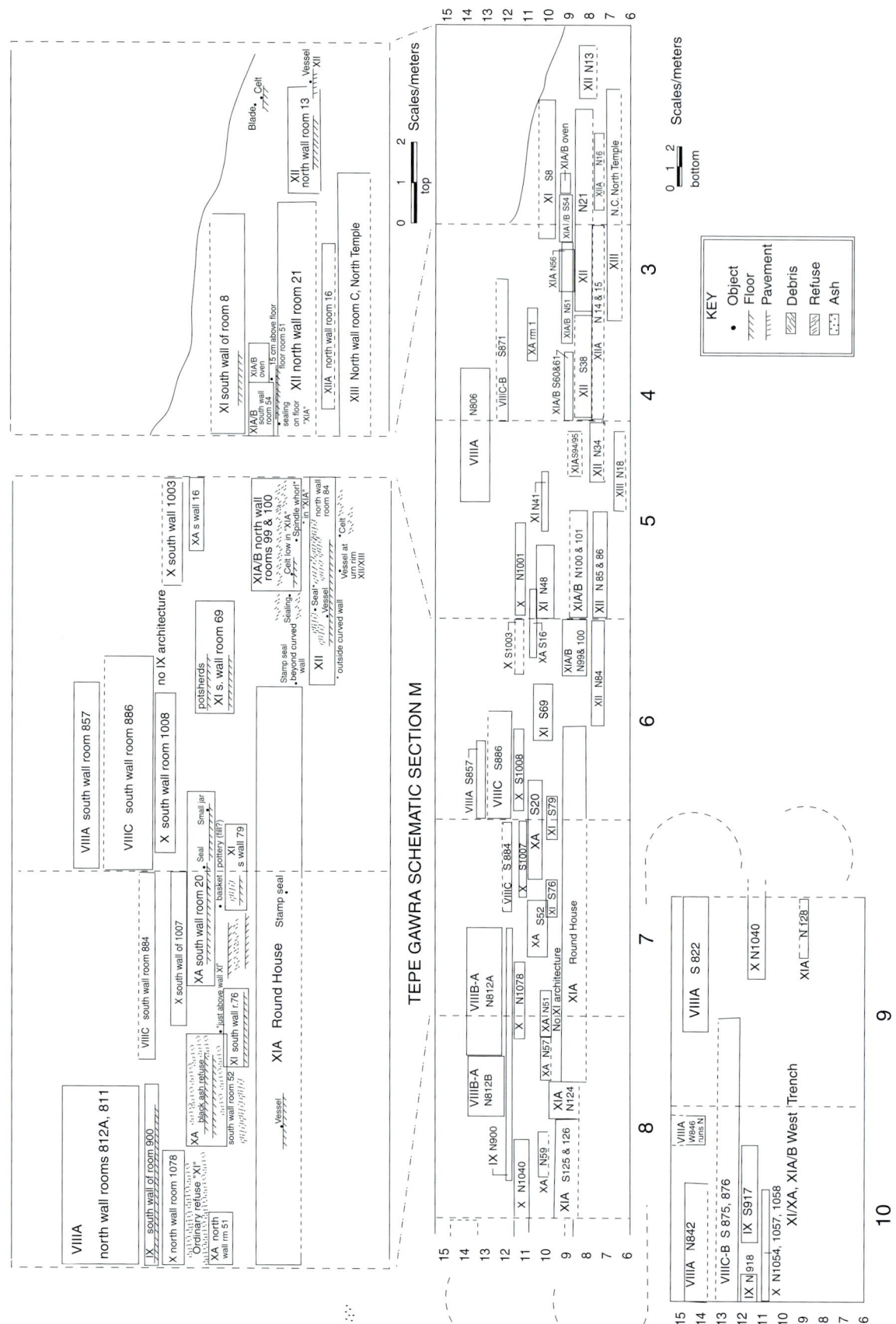

Figure 3.3   Schematic section of the M transect at Tepe Gawra.

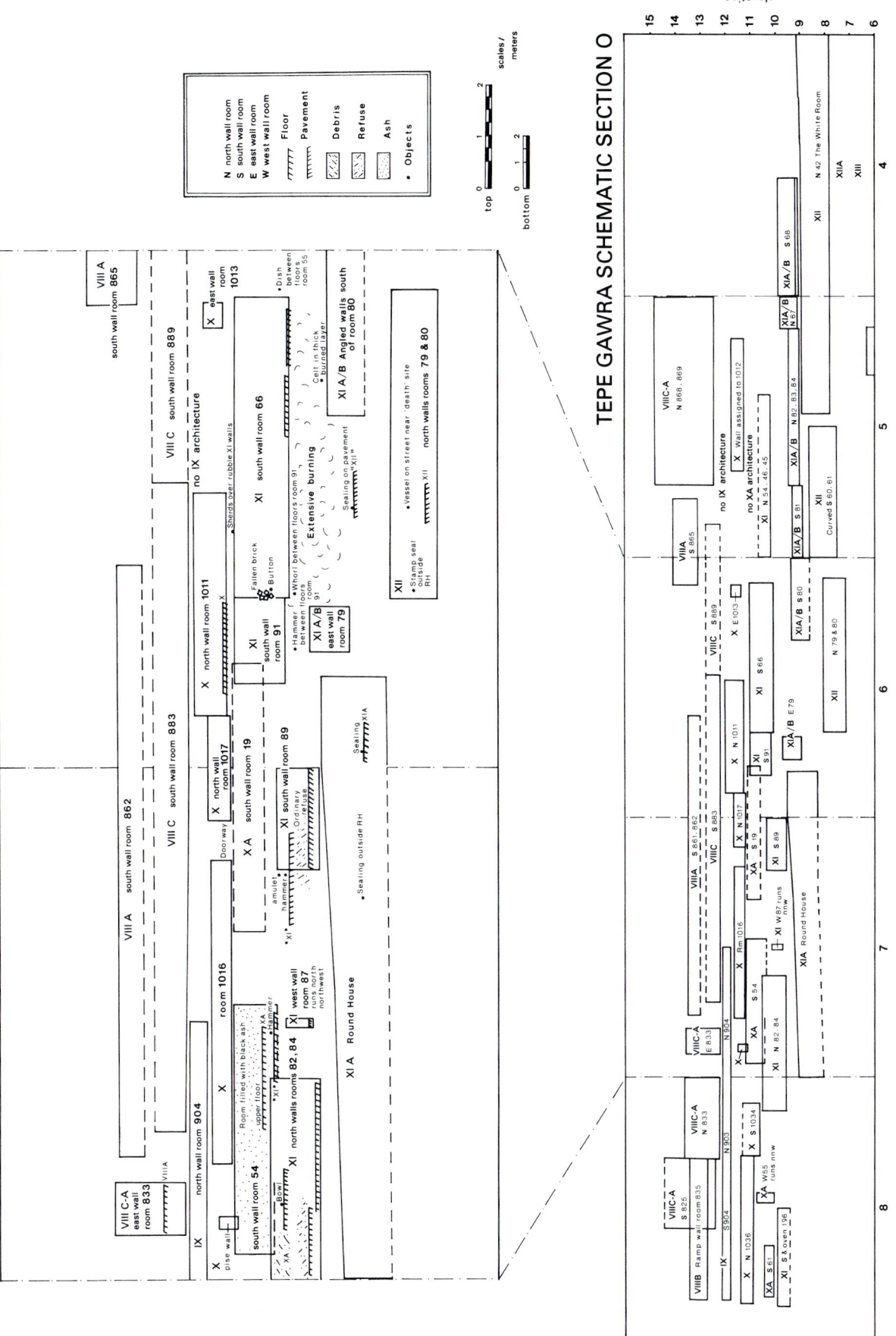

Figure 3.4   Schematic section of the O transect at Tepe Gawra.

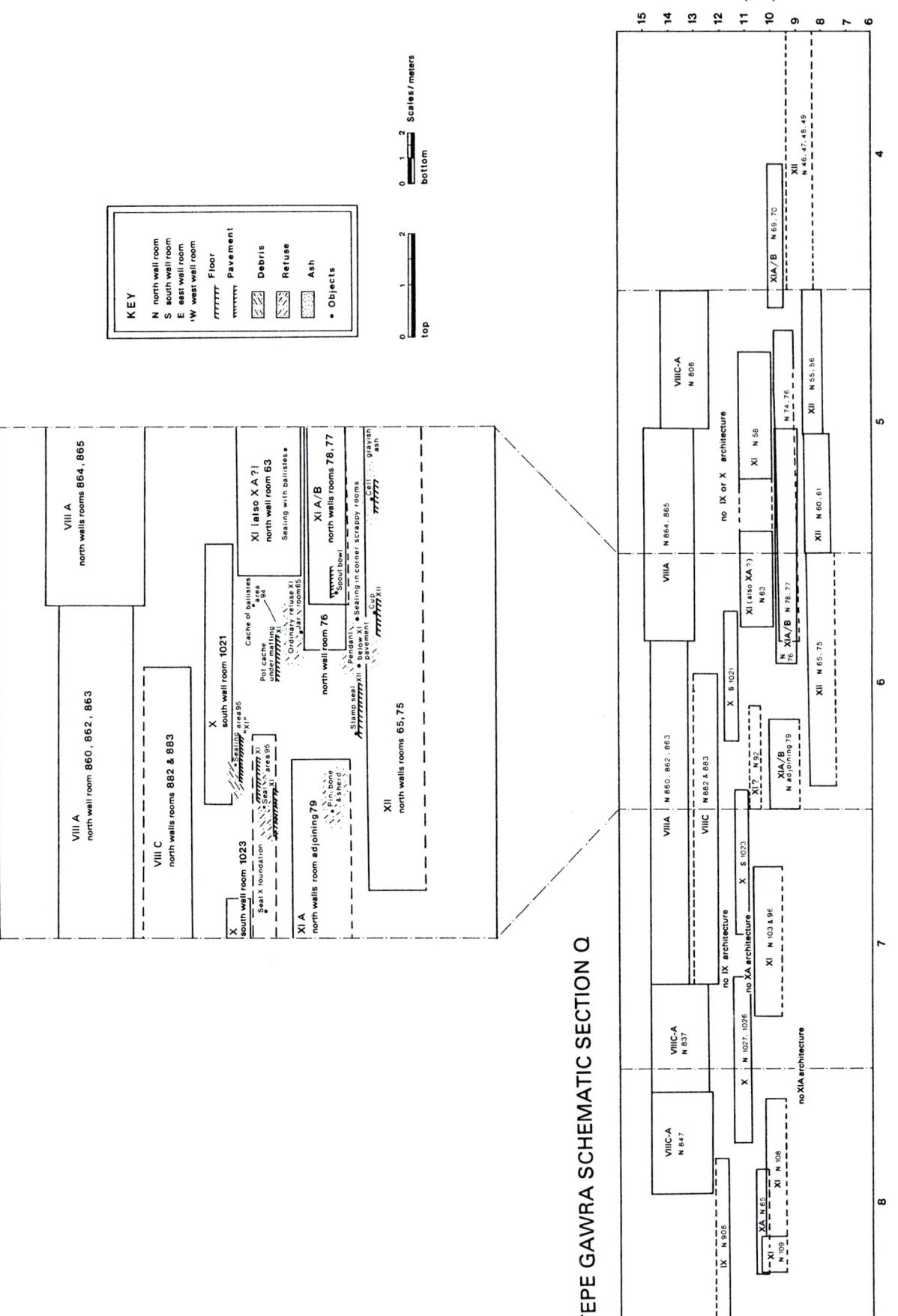

Figure 3.5   Schematic section of the Q transect at Tepe Gawra.

Figure 3.6   Reconstruction of Level XII.

was attacked. Again, the builders of XIA/B reproduced many elements of the XII plan.

Level XIA/B

Following this early stratigraphic and presumably very brief temporal gap, there is no evidence of a significant break in occupation or significant terracing of whole strata of the mound from Level XIA/B to IX. The evidence for the continuity of Levels XIA/B to IX lies in the continuity of some buildings from level to level. For example, although much of the southern portion of Phase XIA was burned, the building Tobler called the "watchtower" (rooms 4 to 10) of the published plan of XIA in Squares 6J and 6G (see Figure 3.8) continued into Phase XI (Figure 3.1), contrary to what Tobler and Mueller illustrate. Tobler notes the continuity of two "rooms" of this building yet asserts that the building as a whole was abandoned (1950:17). However, the schematic section of Square 6J (Figure 3.1) corroborates that room 1 (probably a room of a tripartite building (see Figure 3.9)) of Phase XIA is in fact space 28 of Level XI (Figure 3.9). Similarly, space 8 (probably an unroofed enclosure) of XIA is actually space 27 of XI. The thick walls of the "watchtower" in the published plan of XIA all appear to have existed during the life span of most of the surrounding buildings of XI. In fact, rooms and enclosures 4 to 7 and 12 of XIA/B may be limited to late XIA and XI. As Tobler writes, "Rooms 4–10 and 12 apparently having been added later, for the walls . . . are not bonded into the straight northwest to southeast walls of Rooms 1–3" (1950:19). This abutting kind of construction is typical of exterior walled courts added to established buildings in parts of the Middle East today (Dyson, personal communication). Further, the north wall of space 27 of their published plan of Level XI serves as the southern wall of room 30, in turn part of a tripartite building with a large central hall (room 32). Room 31 was presumably added after much of XIA was no longer in use. Room 31 is specifically mentioned in an unnumbered locus sheet (probably 156) as a "doorless, deep room" containing a two-necked pot and large storage jar with the "charred remains of wheat." Similarly, buildings, especially thick-walled, perhaps public ones, span two of Speiser and Bache's "architectural levels." Blocks of buildings first constructed near the end of the life of one architectural level, as defined by Speiser or Bache (the latter reported by Tobler), appear on the plan of a higher level during which the buildings were extensively used and sometimes remodeled.

Without doubt the most stratigraphically complex strata of fourth millennium B.C. Tepe Gawra are those designated by Tobler as XIA, XI, and XA. It is here that Tobler, Forest, and I disagree most sharply on the reconstruction of contemporaneous levels. Forest is certainly correct when he asserts that "the origin of those [stratigraphic] errors [at Gawra] reside without

doubt in a particularly rigid concept of levels: the excavators disassociated the central, highly elevated part of the mound (at XA) from that of its periphery (XI) in presenting certain reconstructions [representing] total change" (1983:27). Using the schematic sections (Figures 3.1 to 3.5), it is evident that there are more subtle problems than that.

The first buildings erected after the end of XII appear to be rooms 155 and 156 in Square 5J (Figure 3.7) and rooms 146 to 152 in Square 6K. These are among the rooms with the lowest wall bases and among the very few rooms whose wall bases are sunk to an elevation where the tops of Level XII walls still stood. Once you begin to look at how these rooms relate stratigraphically to the rest of the buildings assigned to XIA by Tobler and how the buildings of Tobler's XIA plan work together as functional spaces, one has to agree with Forest (1983:26) that the published plan of XIA is a "monstrosity."

For example, rooms 146 to 152, just described, do not abut the walls of the Round House in Square 6K (Figures 3.1 and 3.8). They appear to be cut off well before the thick walls of the Round House and to remain no higher than the lowest floor near the base of the wall trenches of that larger building. Similarly, the west angling wall of room 110 is shown abutting or interlocking at the junction of the south wall of room 148 and the east wall of room 152 in Square 6K on Tobler's plan (1950: Plate VI). The schematic section including Square 6K (Figure 3.2) indicates that the base of the wall of 110 is at the level of the top of room 148's north wall. The two do not meet at all. Other problems daunt the plan published by Tobler. In Square 5J (Figure 3.7 and 3.8), the walls of rooms 41 to 43 tower over the remains of rooms 23, 156, and 155, as does the thick wall cutting northwest to southeast across the southern side of room 23 (see Plate 2b). This latter wall seems to block the only entrance to room 23. Similarly, a jutting wall from room 34 blocks the only doorway to room 35 in Square 4J. Again, a lower wall appears to jut senselessly into room 29 of Square 4J in Tobler's plan (1950: Plate VI). No entrances or exits are evident in the court with an oven and adjoining room 25 and 27, also in Square 4J.

Similar problems mark the so-called watchtower (rooms 4 to 10) in Square 6G and 6J of Tobler's plan. In Mueller's original pencil plan he shows a large oven jutting from the east wall of room 8 and going over the eastern edge of Square 6J and the western edge of Square 5J, above rooms 155 and 156, the low lying rooms mentioned earlier. This oven is put onto Tobler's plan for XII (1950: Plate VII), where it is unconnected to any building or functional space. However, the chit for small jar 5-1492 of "XIA" places that vessel at sub square position a7/8 "by the oven." In short, the published plan of XIA appears to be the conflation of two phases in the life of a level referred to hereafter as XIA/B. Using the schematic sections and Mueller's

TEPE GAWRA LEVEL XIA/B,
PHASE XIB

Walls
Reconstructed walls
Elevations
Blocked doorway

0   5m   10m
Scale

Probable
building
complex

Figure 3.7   Reconstruction of Phase XIB, Level XIA/B.

Figure 3.8   Reconstruction of Phase XIA, Level XIA/B.

original pencil drawings from the Archives of the University of Pennsylvania Museum, the two phases were reconstructed.

Clearly, not all problems could be solved. Questions remain, especially for Square 4J, where small wall stubs were probably destroyed. However, by dividing the single "level" into two phases, the architectural plans not only make sense stratigraphically, but also functionally. That is to say, buildings have a flow of traffic typical of similar buildings in this level and other adjoining levels. Each has an entrance. Ovens are in probable unroofed courts adjoining small, probably roofed rooms, typical of modern and ancient building types. These proposed reconstructions were corroborated by the elevations of artifacts from these same squares, which fell into distinctly lower and higher elevations.

Although Tobler's Level XIA can be split into an earlier XIB and later XIA phases in the more southerly excavation squares, northern squares could not be easily divided stratigraphically. As the schematic section with Square 5O (Figure 3.4) illustrates, buildings were constructed right on top of the wall stubs of XII, presumably where the fire of XII was most destructive. Yet, one would expect the seemingly defensive tower by the entry complex to be associated with the Round House of XIA, not XIB, because in XIA construction seems to incorporate defense more than does XIB.

These stratigraphic reassignments affect the stratigraphic assessment of the most prominent XIA/B building, the Round House, on the western flank of XIA/B's excavated area. If rooms 146 to 152 of Square 6K are above Level XII and below the Round House, the Round House, despite the cutting of deep wall trenches (Tobler 1950:20), was built in Phase XIA of Level XIA/B. In the schematic section with Square 6M (Figure 3.3) the Round House is at the elevations of the walls of the complex with rooms 99 and 100. It therefore fits with other buildings occupied in late XIA/B, Phase XIA. Phase XIA might be "a fortified town rather than a peaceful agricultural and religious center," as Tobler (1950:18) proposed. Consistent with such an interpretation are the concurrent occupation of the Round House, Tobler's so-called watchtower (rooms 4 to 10), and a fortified gateway in Square 4M. If a compound had probably not eroded in Square 3K, as the pattern of erosion in other levels and the scattered walls and ovens suggest, Tobler's idea would be further supported. Building compounds would have been constructed to present a continuous line of house walls to the outside edge of the mound.

The stratigraphic evidence certainly contradicts Bache, Mueller, and Tobler's idea that the Round House might have been built during the occupation of Level XII houses, as indicated by drawings in the Archives. It is interesting to note that Qalinj Agha III, parallel in time to XIA/B-XI, had a piece of a round walled building similar to the Round House of Gawra XIA/B (Abu al-Soof 1969:7). This reinforces my theory that there were a series of small centers in each other major valley systems of the Jazira and piedmont (Rothman in press b).

Level XI/XA

The transition to the time when most of the buildings in the published plan of XI were occupied was probably a gradual one (although the Round House certainly ended in fire). However, the development of XI is somewhat confused by the clearest mistake of the original excavation, the creation of a separate "Level" XA.

The schematic section with Square 7M (Figure 3.3) shows that the walls of rooms 76 and 79 rest on the tops of the walls of the first floor of the Round House. Those overlying walls of rooms 76 and 79 do not, however, rest on top of interior Round House walls for their whole length and do not seem to have been walls of a second story of the Round House. Further, room 79 is directly connected with a series of rooms and unroofed enclosures, 80 to 89, in Square 7O, which extend beyond the area of the Round House. Walls of rooms 82, 84 and 89 in Square 7O sit on fill 10 to 20 centimeters thick over the first floor exterior walls of the Round House. In short, the Round House was not in use and its second story had already caved in or been pushed in when that series of rooms was built.

As mentioned above, the one major mistake the excavators made was to create a separate Level XA. Even if one fully accepted the idea that an archaeological mound was a layer cake of distinct architectural strata, one could not call XA such a separate stratum. The published plan of stratum XA (Tobler 1950: Plate IV) shows dense occupation in the middle of the mound (Squares 8-6,O-J). However, there is nothing in the periphery of the mound, where rooms 1 to 5, the enclosures with ovens, and the large tripartite buildings in Squares 7Q and 5-6Q of the published XI plan (Tobler 1950: Plate V) are situated.

This pattern might be coincidence but for the fact that "the elevation of Levels XA and XI are so complementary and concurrent as to give the impression of only one level that lasts a long time and has partial remodeling" (Forest 1983:25). The schematic section in Figure 3.2 illustrates this convergence. The north wall of room 5 of the published XA plan overlaps the south wall of room 15 in the published XI plan and, in fact, the walls abut in such a way as to indicate a remodeling of the enclosures with ovens early in the XA phase. This remodeling is also evident in a photograph (Plate 2c) in which an earlier upright bread oven (tanur) is knocked over and presumably buried, and a larger oven is built later. In the schematic section

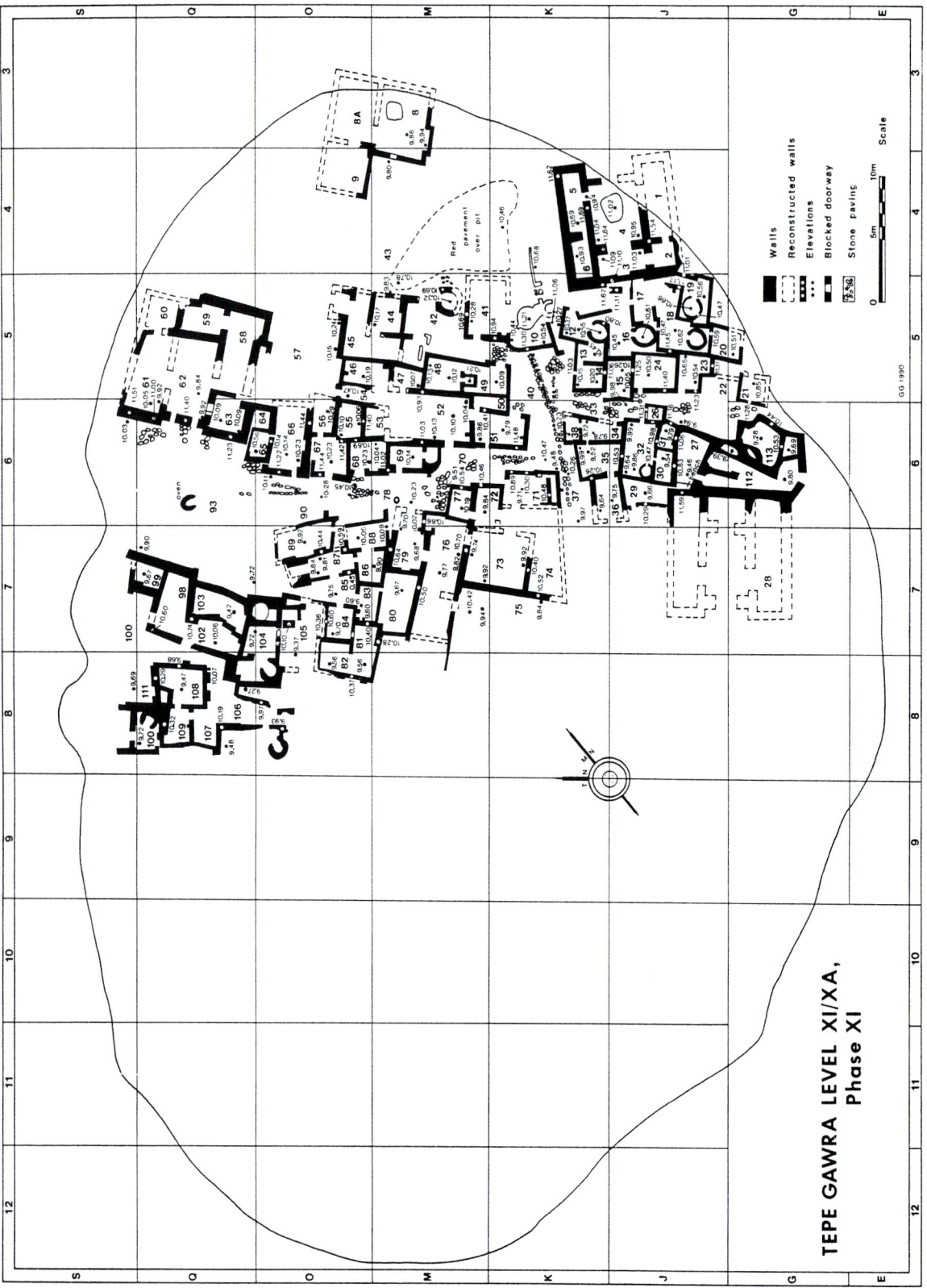

Figure 3.9 Reconstruction of Phase XI, Level XI/XA.

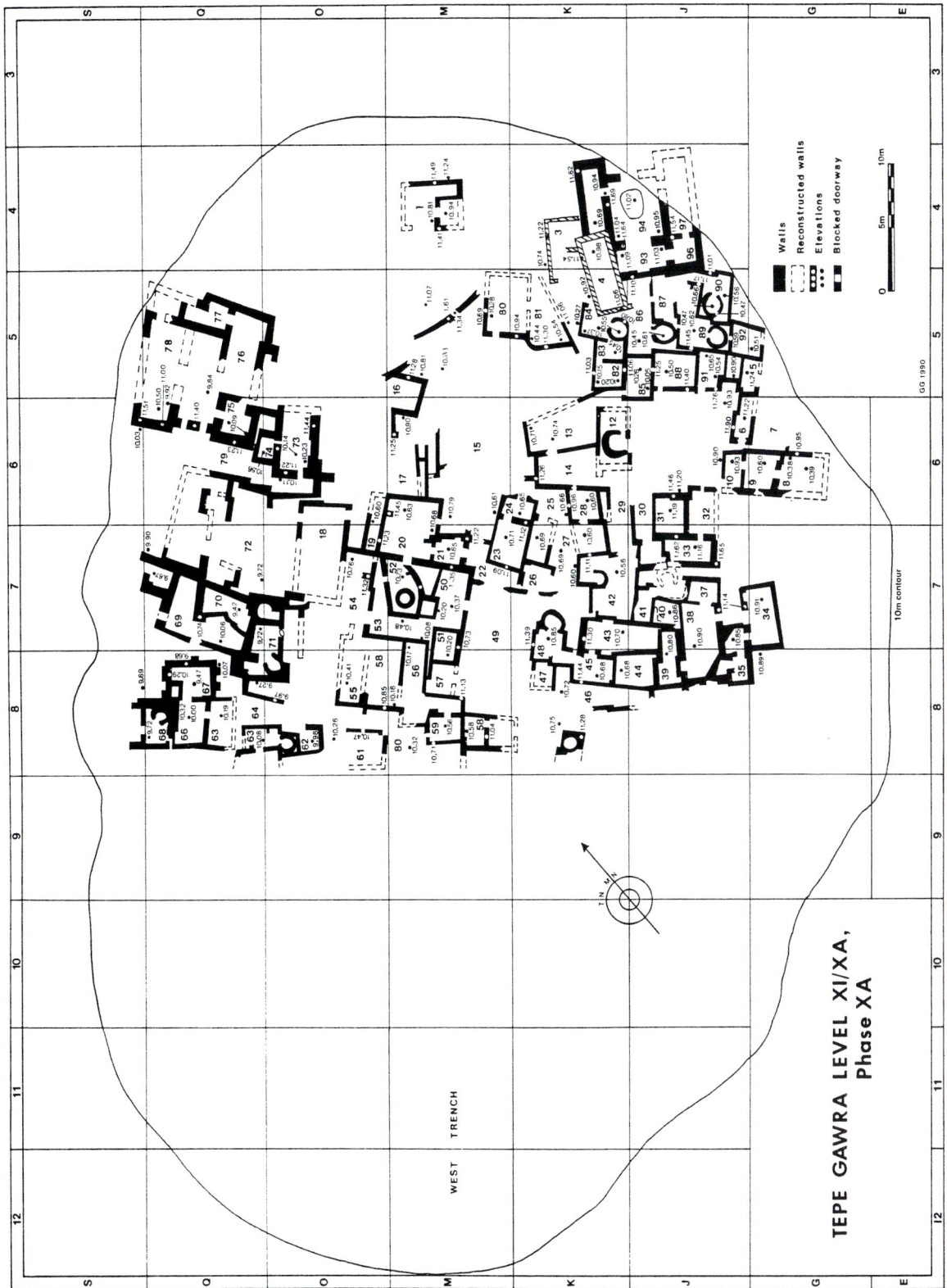

Figure 3.10   Reconstruction of Phase XA, Level XI/XA.

including Square 6Q (Figure 3.5), the north wall of the large, probably public building sits directly on a wall of XIA, rooms 77 and 78, and extends right up to the base of the overlying south wall of room 1021 in Level X. The convergence is also clear in Square 8O, where an oven on the published XI plan (Figure 3.9) is remodeled in the same exact spot on the published XA plan (Figure 3.10). Perhaps most critical is Tobler's idea (1950:17) that the "East Temple" (rooms 1 to 5 in Figure 3.9, 93 to 97 in Figure 3.10) was abandoned early in the XI phase. The pise walls of rooms 6 and 7 on the published XI plan (Tobler 1950: Plate V) cut the walls of rooms 3 and 5, and the oven rooms were built thereafter. This reconstruction is not borne out by stratigraphic analysis. The bottom of its walls (see Figure 3.1) sit at the elevation of the tops of Phase XIA walls and extend as high as 11.62 meters above plain level, as high as the remaining top of any other XA wall uncovered on the mound. In short, there is little doubt that XI and XA are one level (hereafter called XI/XA) in which XI and XA phases are different in those squares where small residential types of buildings are rebuilt. It is harder to distinguish in the periphery of the site where larger, possibly public buildings stood for a considerable length of time.

Forest's Reconstructions

Forest's reconstructions differ greatly from Tobler's or mine. The basis of the difference is that first Forest begins his analysis at the top of the most contentious strata XA, and works down, rather than building up from the bottom. Second, he relies on the height of floors. He assumes that the floors marked on the plan were not superimposed on a series of earlier floors. Third, he assumes that the large buildings on the periphery of Level XI/XA were in use only during the XA phase and not before in Phase XI. He therefore must project the buildings in the center of the XI mound downward, causing a massive reworking of XIA. As a result of this third assumption, his proposed Phase 3, the latest in time before Level X (Forest 1983: Plate 20) includes the buildings from the center of the mound in the published plan of Level XA (Tobler 1950: Plate IV). In addition, they include the three blocks of buildings from the periphery of the mound in the published plan of XI. This periphery includes the large tripartite buildings of the southeast and northeast (the "temple" and "fortress") and the seemingly connected compound of rooms 44 to 69 in Squares 5O, 6O, 5M, 6M, and 6K.

Although I agree with Forest that the large buildings on the periphery of the published plan fit the published "Level" XA plan and that the published XIA plan is inconsistent, our conclusions are quite different. A more detailed look at the reasons for the different results should clarify why one alternative appears more likely.

As Forest says (1983:25), "If one considers all aspects of the plan of Level XI, one notes that each section is a single unit, except in the East where a series of small rooms (12–24 in 5J) appear to pile up against the 'temple' (Squares 4J-K)." Given that the mound was not leveled into a flat plane, it is difficult to assess when each of the blocks of rooms were built in relation to one another or how long particular blocks remained in active use.

Forest proposes that the block of rooms, unroofed enclosures, and open courts (51 to 85) in the north of the site (Squares 6-4M, 5-4O, 4-3M) from the published plan of XIA were built after the Round House was no longer visible (consult Figures 3.8–3.10 here and Forest 1983: Figures 18 and 19). These would be contemporaneous with:

1. the block of rooms and enclosures 74 to 89 of XI overlying the Round House, 2. the series of rooms and enclosures by the southern entrance to the site (rooms and enclosures 27 to 38) in Squares 6J and 6K, 3. the rooms and enclosures with ovens in the southeast of the site (11 to 23) in Squares 5J and 5K, and 4. a small group of rooms and enclosures (106 to 111) in the northwest of the site in Square 8Q.

Rooms 1 to 5 Squares 4J and 4K he would have as a later construction during XA times.

The logic of his analysis is based on the height of floors and the existence of his Phase 1 (Forest 1983: Plate 18), in which only the Round House is standing: "A detailed examination of the elevations of the two units [rooms 1 to 5, rooms and enclosures 11 to 23] shows that the remains of the two units are incompatible: the elevation of the floors of rooms 12–24 are relatively high compared with that of the rest of the mound (10.50–10.60 m. as opposed to 10.10–10.20 m. in 5O, 6O, 5M, 6M, for example), but the block's perfect integration into the rest of the plan of the site and its dating leave no doubt. But the adjacent 'temple' is characterized by an altitude even more raised, its floor reaching 11.10 meters" (Forest 1983:25).

There are flaws in his reconstruction of the published plans. First, trying to match the absolute elevations of disconnected buildings, especially with only 20 or 30 centimeter differences, in order to judge contemporaneity is a dangerous procedure, requiring the assumption that the site was flat. As Rosen argues in describing mound development,

In reality, however, the stratigraphic build-up is rarely so orderly . . . a destroyed or abandoned [or rebuilt] town does not form a smooth plane, since buildings of different heights and mass collapse into small mounds of different sizes. With these factors considered, an abandoned [or even rebuilt] town should have an uneven, nonlinear surface, and unless succeeding inhabitants leveled the entire tell, the following town would inherit the topography of the previous settlement. (1986:9)

Given the large mass of the Round House and the small size of many buildings and the open spaces of the XIA and XII strata, the mound would not have been flat. Forest acknowledges this and contradicts his own implicit assumption in his remarks on the increased height of the middle of the mound in Squares 6-7M-K (Forest 1983:25, see quotation above). This area, not surprisingly, overlies the Round House.

Forest's assertion that rooms 1 to 5, the Temple in Squares 4J-K, post-date the adjoining rooms and enclosures with ovens based on floor heights is demonstrably incorrect. The schematic section with Square 4J (Figure 3.1) shows that there were a number of superimposed floors found in rooms 1 to 5, of which the 11.10 meter one was somewhere in the middle. All of the floors were found near the top or even above the remaining tops of the temple walls. All the floors over wall stubs are called "XI" floors in the chits, but lie above many of the wall stubs of XI buildings, implying they are associated with XA. However, the base of the wall of room 5 is almost a meter deeper. In the square, 5K, the base of the temple wall is approximately 10 centimeters below the base of the wall of enclosure 12, one of the "earlier" walls adjoining rooms 1 to 5 (Tobler 1950: Plate V). The remains of both sets of walls span the very same elevations. The floors discovered in the "oven rooms" were lower than the highest known floors of rooms 1 to 5. This might mean that rooms 1 to 5 were built before the enclosures with ovens or at about the same time. Rooms 1 to 5 may or may not have been actively used for a longer time than the enclosures with ovens, thus building up higher floors. The likelihood that rooms 1 to 5 had roofs to collapse and enclosures 11, 12, 13, 16, 17, 18, 19 probably did not, also affects the preservation of floors and therefore the interpretation of remains. So, too, does the fact that the oven room floors, without roofs, would have been pelted with rain. This would have accelerated their flattening.

In addition, the placement of rooms and enclosures 51 to 85 of the XIA plan in a new reconstruction contemporary with buildings of the published XI plan (Forest 1983: Plate 19) presents problems. The unpublished locus sheets speak of a wide area of intense burning in the northern and northeastern parts of the site. An unnumbered locus sheet, dated December 20, 1934, describes a large pavement of red clay over all of Squares 4K and 4M north of room 5. The sheet further reads "the area hereabouts (near rooms 1 to 5) is

underlain by a thick layer of Refuse (mostly ash), which may account for this remarkably thick pavement" (see Plate 3A for the deep pit). The red pavement is the top of the intrusive pit into XIA/B and XII. Locus sheet 132, drawn on the schematic section for Square 6O (Figure 3.4), describes a deep layer of ash filling the space from 9.28 to 10.03 meters in height over all of Squares 6O and 5O. According to the locus sheet, "the conflagration doubtless destroyed rooms in the surrounding squares (if not the entire mound)." If one then looks at the superposition of the walls (not floors) of rooms and enclosures 51 to 85 of XIA and the burned ash that fills and overlies it for a third of a meter, that building block appears firmly associated with the other buildings of XIA (including the Round House) and not Phase XI (see Figures 3.8 and 3.9).

In other words, I see little reason to change my initial reconstruction (Figure 3.8, 3.9, and 3.10), drawn before reading Forest's analysis, and to accept the radical reconstruction by Forest represented by his XI Phase 2 (Forest 1983: Plate 19). Forest's reconstruction does not appear to accommodate the available stratigraphic facts, nor does it have any consistent internal logic. Accepting his reconstruction would indeed create an incomprehensible "monstrosity," to use his words, of the XIA and XII "levels."

Not surprisingly, although Forest and I agree that the buildings on the periphery of the published plan of XI were occupied during Phase XA, we disagree on the reconstruction of what is for Forest Phase 3 and for me is the XA phase of Level XI/XA. Specifically, the two reconstructions differ in two aspects. First, Forest would have the building block made up of rooms and enclosures 42 to 68 of the published XI plan (Tobler 1950: Plate V) occur in the XA phase of XI/XA and not in the XI phase. Second, he argues that the rooms and enclosures with ovens (12 to 23 in the XI phase, 82 to 92 in this author's XA reconstruction, Figure 3.10) were in the XI Phase of XI/XA only. Tobler (1950:17) does speak of the high elevation of the floors of unroofed enclosures 48, 52 and 55 and the extraordinary meter and a half between them and the top of XIA wall deposits. These would imply a very late date.

However, the trouble with placing rooms and enclosures 42 to 68 in the XA phase is that there are already walls in the published XA plan which are clearly below X and at the elevation of XA. They are not remodeling walls, but perhaps windbreaks or enclosure walls for open courtyard 15. Forest resolves this problem simply by dismissing it, "the few walls of Squares 4M, 5M and 6M [in XA] appear to have little significance, if they exist at all" (1983:25). That, to my mind, is an unacceptable solution. Unless these walls are contemporaneous with the pise walls of rooms 3 and 4 in the published XA plan (apparently of a very late XA time, they represent a real change in site traffic patterns and utilization. A number of major buildings fell out of use and the settlement appears to have been re-planned in XA.

There are reasons to postulate such a change. The large north-south and east-west streets of the XI phase of XI/XA were disrupted in the XA phase by newly constructed enclosures 13 and 14 (see Figures 3.9 and 3.10). Also, access to the large, possibly public building in Squares 5Q and 6Q was limited by the construction of walls in the open court 93 of Phase XI, a practice used in XII to limit traffic to the White Room building. If the room and enclosure building block 42 to 68 were no longer in use and the newly created open space had been defined by new walls, perhaps as a pen, limiting access would make sense. Further access from the clearly new construction in Squares 7 and 8 O to J would be funneled through courtyard 64, eliminating the need for the direct north-south axis. In addition, the deep layer of ash described above as the result of a major burning of at least part of XIA may well account for the height of the floors and the depth of deposit between XI and XIA in the squares in question. As with the enclosures with ovens, exactly when the roofed rooms by the enclosures with ovens (rooms 82, 85, 88, 91, 92) were abandoned is very difficult to say. However, the newly constructed rooms 5, 6, 8, 9, and 10 on the published XA plan abut the walls and integrate into these rooms by the main north-south street of Phase XI. This pattern would suggest that the enclosures with ovens were not abandoned until sometime during XA.

One analytic problem raised by this confusion over XA and XI, as mentioned in Chapter 1, is assigning artifacts to the XA, XI, XIA, XIB and XII strata. XA was recognized in the fifth (G5) season, but was already dug in G4. The schematic section of Square 7M (Figure 3.3) illustrates this clearly. Within room 52, the chit locates an "XI" floor with black ash refuse above a "XA" floor. As mentioned above, no attempt was made to go back to the G4 field notes and change the stratum assignments. However, by determining a range of elevations for each phase of XI/XA in each square, and by more carefully noting the highest elevations of XIA, I re-assigned close to 100 artifacts to their adjoining phase or level. These reassignments better reflect the stratigraphic solutions suggested above (see the artifact catalogues below in which the original stratum assignment, new stratum assignment, and elevations are listed).

Before proceeding to Levels X, IX, and VIII, two further stratigraphic issues are noteworthy. The first is the reconstruction of the rooms in Squares 6G, 6J, 5G, and 5J of Phase XIA of XIA/B and Phase XI of XI/XA (see Figures 3.8 and 3.9, and Tobler 1950: Plate VI). This is the so-called "watchtower" complex. Below I will argue against that name and function for these buildings, but here I will explain the changes, especially as they affect the flow of traffic among rooms 8 and 7 of XIA and 27 and 112 of XI.

As originally presented by Tobler, room 8 was blocked off from 7. However, as Plate 3b illustrates (see upper left-hand corner), a door was carved in the adjoining wall through which individuals could pass. The thick walls of a possible tripartite building extending into Squares 7G and 7J can be seen in this plate. The door was apparently moved in Phase XI as Plate 4a shows. In Tobler's plan, room 15 seems blocked to the courtyard in all directions. Plate 4b indicates that the room was opened to the courtyard, and had doors to room 10 and a northern courtyard. Those doorways were sealed during a remodeling. The indentations in the floor in Plate 4b had held mortar stones, strange equipment for a watchtower.

The second issue regards the excavation of a western trench into Levels XA to XIIA. Tobler describes it as "prolific of small objects, and seals and impressions in particular, suggesting that it had been a sector where the inhabitants of the mound in Strata XA through XIIA had dumped accumulated debris from their settlements. Curiously enough, no walls or other building remains were found in the area explored by this trench" (Tobler 1950:3). Most of this western area is crowded with buildings in Levels VIII to X. The Level XI/XA to XII plans are warrens of dense building. Therefore, it seems very unlikely that no use was made of the whole western sector of the site. Only further excavation will reveal whether this area of hundreds of square meters was utilized. However, the chits imply that the story may be more complex than Tobler proposes. Chits speak of hard, prepared pavements in Squares 9M and 10M. Chit 2559 also locates an artifact on a pavement "near an old oven." An alternative suggestion to the "great trash pit" theory of Tobler is likely. A goodly part of this western section of the mound may have been a large open processing or manufacturing area along with the considerable trash that such activity would produce (see Chapter 5 below). The town plans of the overlying Levels X and IX suggest that a large public building may occupy the southwestern part of the mound. In short, it is most likely that in the rush of the last two seasons, excavators gave insufficient care to uncovering this part of the mound.

Levels X and IX

Levels X and IX present many fewer problems than Levels XII to XI/XA of the Tobler publication. Level X (Figure 3.11) contained two large public buildings: one in the center of the mound, whose remaining walls can be reconstructed. The other was an unique, large building in the southwest. The remaining architecture of the site is a hodge-podge of small houses divided into blocks by pebbled streets and alleys. Although there is some sense of planning, expansion and remodeling have obscured what that original plan might have been.

Level X appears to have developed out of XA. The most telling signs of a gradual evolution from Phase XA into Level X are the extent of construction into the northeast, and the walls of rooms and enclosures 1028 to 1032 and 1045 to 1047 (Squares 7–9 O-Q). Construction in X extends right up to Squares 5Q and 5O and there seems to stop. This was probably not coincidental. Considerable rubble of the large tripartite building in the northeast of XI/XA would be concentrated in those squares. A piece of the dividing walls in the court of that building of XA may have served as a back wall to the compound including room 1021. Further, the use of gray bricks typical of XI/XA (but atypical of X) in rooms and enclosures 1028 to 1032 and 1045 to 1047 and the superposition of those room blocks over XA reinforce this idea of gradual development. An undated and unnumbered locus card states that the northern wall of room 1032 was "definitely placed directly on a wall of 10A, so that it seemed to be one with it."

In general, from a stratigraphic and architectural point of view, Level X presents no real problems.

Level IX (Figure 3.12) also presents few stratigraphic dilemmas. The level appears very much to follow the X plan, although with seemingly fewer buildings. The temple building of IX (rooms 900 to 903 and probably unroofed enclosure 904) is better preserved and the plan more detailed than that of the X temple. Interestingly, the IX temple is not superimposed over the X temple but it is placed immediately north of it. This might be a practice of some duration. Tobler remarks:

> The builders of the Stratum X Temples, and the Stratum IX Temple, and the recessed courtyard southeast of the Stratum VIII Central Shrine selected closely adjoining [not superimposed] areas for these constructions, so that their walls would have been contiguous if all three had been simultaneously extant. This remarkable fact suggests that both the Central Shrine of VIII, and the Stratum IX Temple must have been constructed when at least the lower courses of the Strata IX and X Temples were visible above the floors of the new occupation levels (1950:7).

He means not the "lower" but the uppermost courses of brick. Also, the so-called "Central Shrine" was not a religious establishment (see Level VIII below). However, unlike Eridu, where temples were built one on top of another (Safar et al. 1981) this implies that the walls of the earlier buildings were standing at the time the later constructions were built.

The stratigraphic implication is that a long time did not pass between IX and VIII if some walls of the preceding buildings were standing, or at least the builders of VIII knew temple locations of both IX and X. Rather, Levels X and IX (and Phase XA) may have been intentionally cleaned out and dismantled in the rebuilding process. The unusually low wall remains of the X and IX temples and the fact that tombs associated with X and IX are built of bricks of the identical size and color (Bache 1935c:310) imply that temple bricks were used to build tombs. This supports the idea that parts of the preceding levels were intentionally dismantled and cleaned out. Excavators recovered many fewer artifacts from Levels X and IX than from the earlier levels. This, too, may indicate that ancient builders did some leveling.

Still, in rebuilding for Level IX, why would the builders leave the eastern quadrant of the site empty? Therefore, it is initially difficult to understand the emptiness of the north and northeastern quadrant on the published IX plan (Tobler 1950: Plate II). However, the stratigraphic schematics for Squares 7M, 6O, and 6Q (Figures 3.3, 3.4, and 3.5) resolve this quandary. The base of the walls of one building (rooms and enclosures 882 to 890) and the northern building of VIIIC (rooms and enclosures 808, 809 and 866) cut down to the level of the tops of Level X walls in Squares 6O and 6Q. In Square 7M, the bases of the VIIIC walls parallel the elevation of the back wall of the IX temple. Such large walls had not been built at Gawra since the Round House of XIA, and a similar down-cutting and destruction affected its underlying stratum, XIB. Most likely, the "missing" architecture of IX was present. Builders of Level VIII probably destroyed it.

Two of the earliest locus cards give some indication of what those missing buildings may have been. A locus card dated December 10, 1932 describes a greenish gray ware storage jar set into the floor by two walls at an elevation of 11.94 meters in the southeastern corner of Square 6Q of IX. On the stratigraphic schematic of this square (Figure 3.5), those walls would fit in the elevations between the tops of X walls and the base of walls of VIII, as one would expect IX wall stubs to do. In the drawing, the wall appears to be of a thickness typical of domiciles.

On the other hand, the pieces of the building described in locus cards 9 and 10 (November 2, 1932) are more monumental and quite mystifying. Those remains outline a broad room with a north window in Squares 5J and 6J. Attached to it are a set of three steps of one brick course apiece, the bottom one joined to a perpendicular bench. Locus card 9 describes this bench as being in 5K (it is so noted on the published plan of IX). However, if the orientation of the room in locus 10 (pointing to the 5K marker as being northwest of the window) is correct, the steps must be in 6J,

TEPE GAWRA LEVEL X

Figure 3.11   Reconstruction of Level X.

TEPE GAWRA LEVEL IX

Figure 3.12   Reconstruction of Level IX.

as they appear in Figure 3.12. Locus 9 questions whether the remains of this building are associated with VIIIC or IX. Unless it is a basement of rooms 801 to 804 of VIII, (like the strange basement tunnels of the Eye Temple of Tell Brak (Mallowan 1947)), its elevations are those of IX. The steps descend from an elevation of approximately 12.40 meters to 12.12 meters above the plain.

Those elevations fit in the space left open in Square 5J and Square 6J (in Figure 3.1, the area between the top of the known X wall stub and the unclear elevation of the base of the south wall, room 801 of VIII). The bench rose to 12.29 meters from that bottom level. Locus 1, a baby grave, apparently dug from room 801 of the East Temple or earlier, was found at an elevation of 12.39. The locus note for that grave states, "Either this is measured incorrectly or it is not a burial of 8, for it comes on the plan directly under a wall of the Eastern Temple! EBM" (EBM is the architect Mueller). Probably, the grave was measured a bit off laterally, as it was most likely from VIII. Stratigraphically, the grave's position is under VIII. However, one could not dig a grave into the existing basement of a building still in use. The steps must be under rooms 801 to 804 of VIII and the room filled in before overlying rooms 801 to 804 were actively in use. The steps and bench were covered with bitumen, as the liwan entrance and the ablution room (832) of rooms 801 to 804 of VIIIA had been. Perhaps in the case of these steps, the bitumen was mastic for stone paving. In general, the room behind the steps was quite large and led up to some utilized space at a higher level. The room was stuffed with discarded pottery, animal bone, and seed in "a rather hard yellow clay."

The two badly preserved buildings in the western part of the site also are problematic. Forest (1983:28) offers a logical and stratigraphically consistent reconstruction of the building in Squares 10 and 11, M to J. He correctly argues that the northwest to southeast running piece of wall in Squares 10 to 11M, attributed to VIIIC (Speiser 1935a: Plate XI), is actually at the elevation of IX. When placed on the IX plan, that wall and the remaining walls form the outline of a building (rooms and enclosures 1060 to 1071) of X. The two buildings do not share the same walls, but appear to have the same plan. The more northerly building also might be of the same form, although it is less easily reconstructed and appears to be a series of single or double rooms around a large unroofed court.

Another reconstruction of Forest's in Level IX appears less successful. This reconstruction relates to the southern building of VIIIC, rooms 925 to 936. Forest (1983: Plate 25) proposes that this building is part of two abutting tripartite buildings of Phase VIIIC of Level VIII. To make such a reconstruction Forest would include an intermediate series of walls first evident in the published VIIIB plan (Speiser 1935a: Plate X). This

would be necessary to tie the seemingly isolated wall running along the southern edge of Squares 7M and 8M of VIIIC into the plan of this newly reconstructed VIIIC building. The entire reconstruction is a rather torturous conglomeration of many pieces of buildings at seemingly different elevations.

It also presents some problems of internal consistency. First, there is no particular reason to reject Bache and Mueller's assessment of Level IX. The walls of the southern building are at the same elevation as the southern walls of the IX temple. The bricks are also of the same type and color as those of the IX tripartite building, as Forest (1983:29) admits. Further, the courtyard between the large tripartite building and the two entry doors is paved with two layers of what Tobler calls "libn" brick (one assumes this brick was unbaked, although Tobler seems to use the term libn for baked and unbaked mudbrick). Forest rejects this as a pavement, because he claims that unbaked brick exposed to inclement weather for a long time would disintegrate. That conclusion assumes, however, that there was not some kind of pebble or plaster coating, which covered the pavement or that the term libn had not been misused by Tobler to mean baked brick. The small tripartite building of VIIIB (Speiser 1935a: Plate X) rests directly on top of the pavement and the builders may have disturbed any surfacing material on the courtyard. However, perhaps most telling in favor of Forest's reconstruction would seem to be its ability to account for the large isolated niched wall in VIIIC, which seemingly serves no purpose. As will be explained in the reconstruction of VIIIC below, that wall was part of a paved area called the "hammam" in unpublished field notes. Thereafter, it was used as an alleyway for getting into the otherwise doorless storehouse of VIIIB and A. It therefore need not have been used in IX.

Level VIII

The first break in stratigraphy after the Level XII to XIA/B transition is that between IX and VIII. It is an exception to the continuity of buildings from Level XIA/B to IX. The three rebuilding phases of VIII, VIIIC to VIIIA (Figures 3.13, 3.14, 3.15), appear thoroughly planned before construction. Phase VIIIC does not reuse IX buildings. At the same time, the "hammam" of VIIIC does overlie the main hall of the temple of IX, implying that the stratigraphic continuity noted for Levels XII to IX would extend all the way to VIIIA.

The style of presentation of the plans in Speiser's volume (1935a, Plates IX, X, and XI) make the buildings look much more monumental than were those of preceding levels (Tobler 1950, Plates II to V). Actual floor area measurements indicate that, for example, the temple of VIII (rooms 801 to 804) at 86 m^2

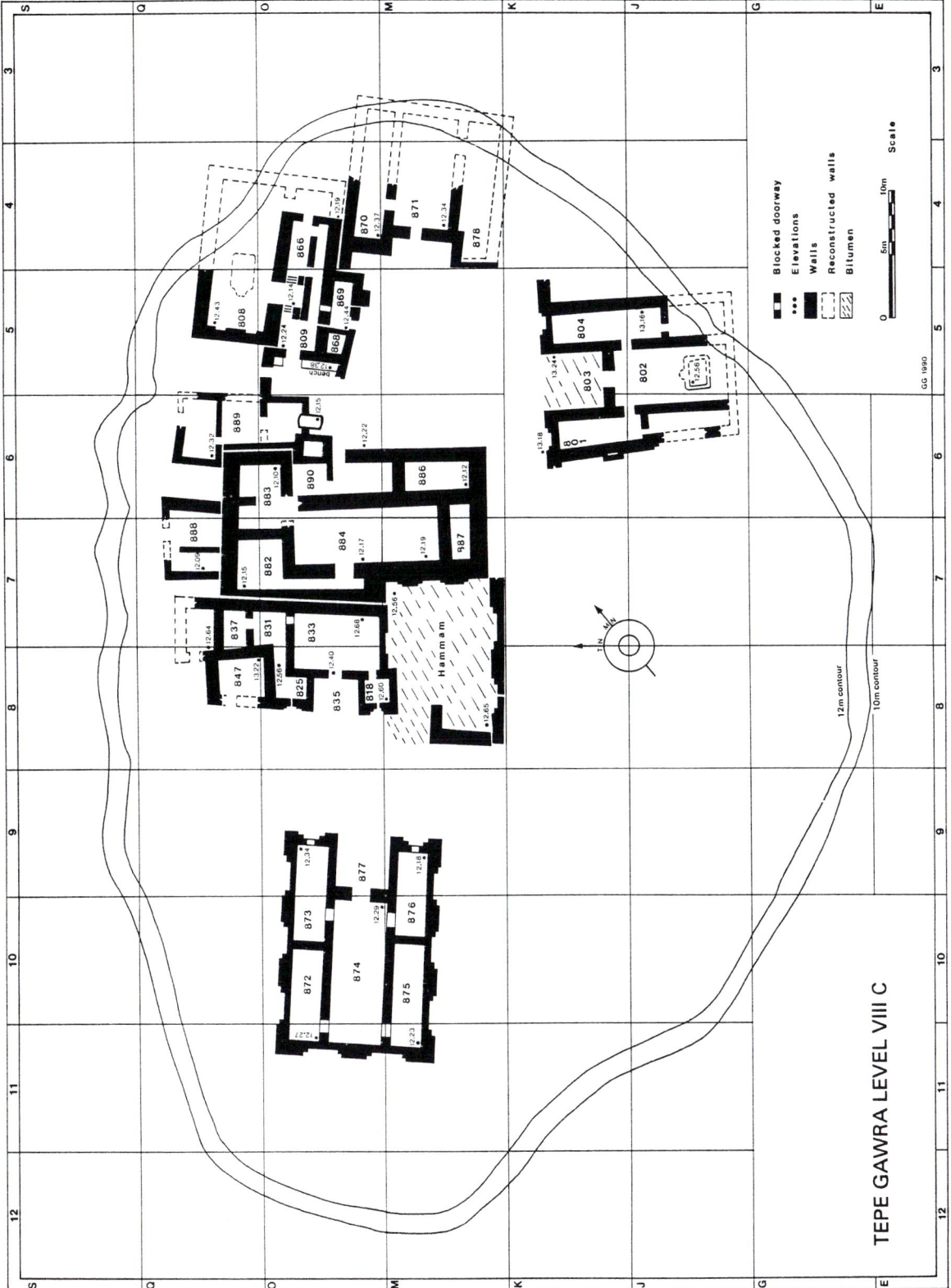

TEPE GAWRA LEVEL VIII C

Figure 3.13   Reconstruction of Phase VIIIC, Level VIII.

TEPE GAWRA LEVEL VIII B

Figure 3.14 Reconstruction of Phase VIIIB, Level VIII.

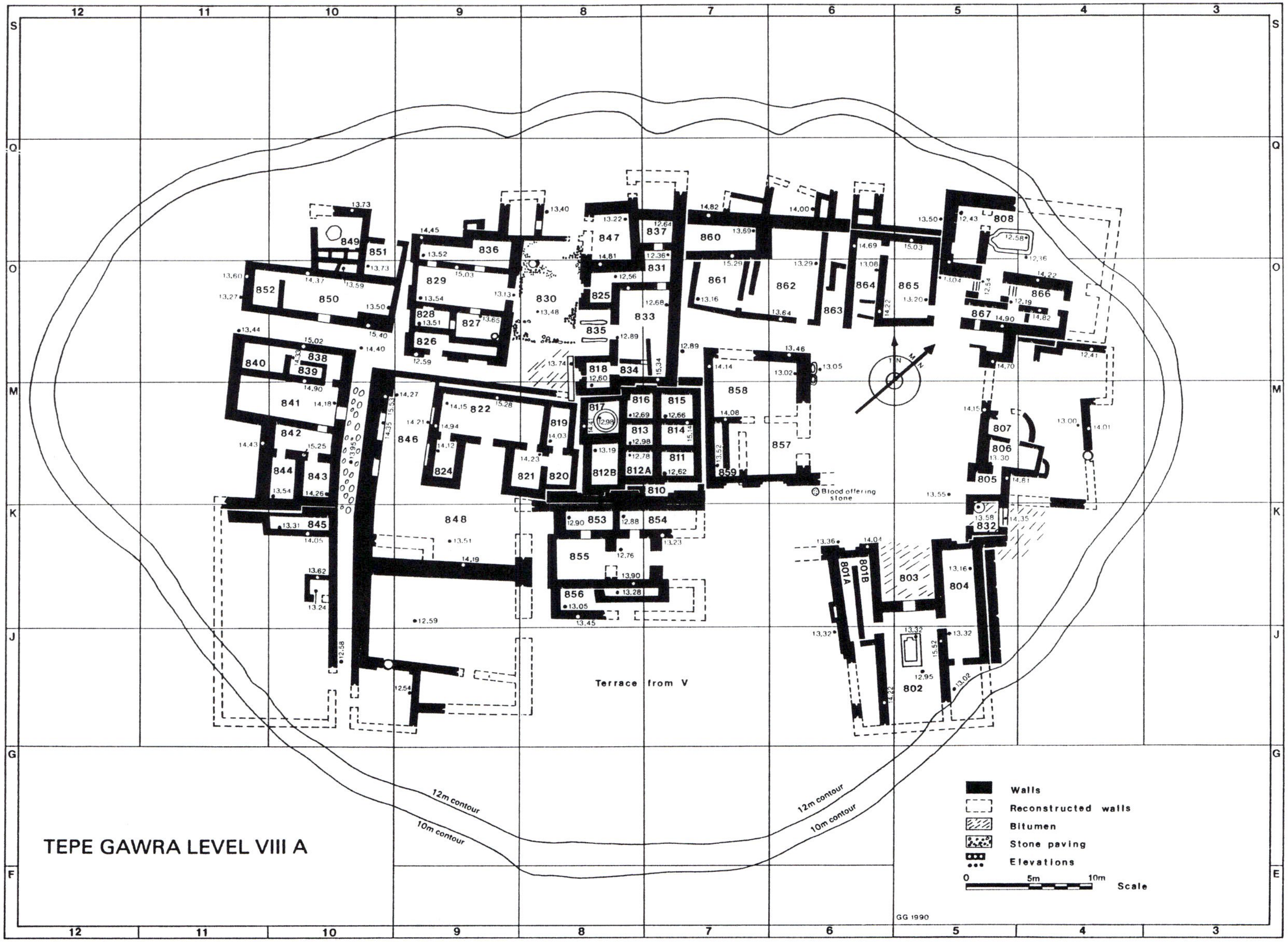

Figure 3.15   Reconstruction of Phase VIIIA, Level VIII.

(36.8 m^2 central hall) is comparable in size to the temple (rooms 900 to 903) of Level IX at 70 m^2 (central hall 34.2 m^2). It is also similar to the temple (rooms 1073 to 1075) of Level X at 85.9 m^2 (center hall 38.6 m^2).

There are few stratigraphic problems with VIII, because the last phase of Level VIII (VIIIA) was thoroughly burned and three buildings in the eastern and middle part of the VIII mound—rooms 801 to 804 (Speiser's "Eastern Temple"); 808 to 809, 866 to 869 (his "Northern Shrine"); and 818, 825, 831, 833, 837 (his "Central Shrine"—spanned the entire time VIII was occupied.

That said, there is one extremely important stratigraphic matter that relates to the dating of Level VIII (see below), namely, a massive disruption of the southern flank of the VIII mound by the builders of Level VI. The Gawra mound was uneven and sloped sharply after the fire consumed Phase VIIIA and apparently after some subsequent period of abandonment permitted large-scale erosion to take place (see Plate 1a). Therefore, the builders of VI cut a deep terrace into the underlying levels (as deep as IX) on the southern side of the mound. This terrace cut the bottom of rooms 802 and 804 in Squares 5J and 6J and the building in Square 9J (perhaps to 9K). As far as is possible to tell, Squares 7J and 8J were entirely disturbed. Squares 8K and 9K were partially affected. The builders of Level V actually constructed the stone retaining wall and building in the published plan of VIIIA (Speiser 1935a, Plate IX) and also the stone foundations of a well and rooms in Squares 6G and 7G of Level IX (Speiser 1935a: Plate VIII; Tobler 1950, Plate II). Those rooms are at the same elevation as the walls of VIIIA but are associated with Level VI of the late third millennium B.C. That this cut was made is further corroborated by the original pencil sketch of VIIIA, still in the Archives of the University of Pennsylvania, which reveals that the tops of the stone foundations of VI buildings from 4 to 10K were barely above the tops of the VIIIA wall remains. In short, in assessing the chronology of VIII, especially VIIIA, one has to factor in the massive disturbance in the southern flank caused by the builders of Level VI. Contained in these squares were a number of the pointed bowls and cups used to give VIIIA a post Uruk Period (Early Dynastic) date. The registry books acknowledge the unique problem of those southerly squares (especially 8J and 7J) by designating many artifacts from them "VIII sub-6."

In Summary

The study of Gawra's stratification discussed above concludes that there were significant problems with the presentation by Tobler (1950), especially with regard to the assigning of a separate "Level" XA. However, the general sequence of buildings from Level XIA to IX presented by Tobler is probably closer to the picture painted by the original field notes than are Forest's radical revisions (1983). The architectural plans for each of the levels and sub-level phases presented above conform as closely as possible to chit information, schematic sections, original architect's pencil drawings, and the final publications and notes, as well as a few ideas of Forest. The buildings make sense as functioning structures with ease of access and traffic flow.

The Chronological Framework

Based on the new plans, it is now possible to assess the chronology of the site from Level XII to VIII. As of 1997, the chronological terms used for the late fifth and fourth millennia B.C. in Mesopotamia included:

1. the Late Ubaid and Uruk (Early, Middle, Late), Protoliterate (Late Uruk into Jemdet Nasr) (Porada 1965; Porada et al. 1992), 2. the Gawran (Early, Middle, and Late) (Porada 1965; Perkins 1949), 3. Gawra A & B followed by Uruk A, B, C (Gut 1995), Northern Uruk (Oates and Oates 1996), or 4. the Late Chalcolithic Period.

The new SAR chronology adds LC 1-5 to this list (Rothman, ed. in press). This period lasted anywhere from 800 to 1400 years, depending on the calibration for C^{14} one uses. In addition, its length will vary depending on what markers are used for its beginning point and which sub-regions of Greater Mesopotamia one analyzes.

Aside from the multiplicity of nomenclatures, the greatest problem lies in the size and complexity of the region (Esin 2000). In the fourth millennium, three quite distinctive pottery-making traditions can be found: chaff-faced Amuq pottery, classic Uruk styles, other Late Chalcolithic forms, mostly plain but also painted in Ubaid like style. The chaff-faced tradition tends to occur in the western part of northern Mesopotamia, from the Khabur toward the Mediterranean coast. The classic Uruk tradition was localized in the southern alluvium until the Uruk expansion. The alternative plain and painted ware tradition existed in the Turkish highland and northeastern Mesopotamia, overlapping with the chaff-faced tradition at Brak.

Most relative chronologies are based on variability in artifact style over a more limited area. Gut (1995) argues that extending beyond local sub-regions for relative chronology always sacrifice specificity. This is true, but to look at regional developments one needs a regional chronology. In addition, it is less purely regional than it at first appears. Most pottery appears to have been locally made and should reflect some elements of local productive techniques. Even much of the classic

Uruk pottery types in northern Mesopotamia appear locally made (see Evins 1989 for Kurban Höyük and Helwing 1999 for Hassek Höyük). A number of scholars have published new attempts at sub-regional or regional chronologies (Oates and Oates 1994; Schwartz in press; Truffelli 1997, Rova 1999/2000; Gut 1995; Tsuneki and Miyake 1998). All suffer from some of the problems Esin highlights (see Rothman a in press, especially Table II, for summary and problems).

Using absolute C^{14} determinations in tandem with relative chronological dates should clarify the situation. The recent attempt to do so (Wright and Rupley in press) presents a convincingly different view of the periods than previously thought. It changes the basic framework. For example, the Beveled Rim Bowl had previously been dated to the Late Uruk or LC 5 period. Its appearance in northern Mesopotamia signaled the last two to three hundred years of the fourth millennium B.C. The new chronology based on radiocarbon dates places the first appearance of the Beveled Rim Bowl three to four hundred years earlier in the early Middle Uruk or LC 3 period. This framework is the one I will use.

Unfortunately, only one C^{14} date exists for Levels XII to VIII of Gawra, and an attempt to run bone dates failed.[3] Four C^{14} dates were run from the site of Tepe Gawra (Oates 1983:271). Using the Clark calibration, the samples from Level XII yielded a date of 3837 + 72 years B.C. (Oates 1983:271). Aurenche and Hours (1987:711), using another calibration, got dates of 4920–4450 B.C. for XII. The new Oxcal calibrations should yield a date of somewhere between 4700–4400 BC. Despite the lack of actual carbon dates for Gawra, the sites best correlated with Gawra, for example, Norşuntepe, might help. For levels matching Gawra -XI, the corresponding levels at Norşuntepe range in date from 4361 to 3985 at one standard deviation (di Nocera 2000: Table 2).

Before detailing the best current chronological scheme, it is good to ask how the older ones were determined.

The Analysis of Perkins and Porada

The current chronological understanding of Tepe Gawra was based on analyses of the material from Gawra by Perkins (1949) and Porada (1965, see also Porada et al. 1992). Gawra and the Nineveh deep sounding (Mallowan 1933, Gut 1995) are still the two sequences most often cited as reference points for the fourth millennium B.C. in northern Mesopotamia. Perkins coined the term "Gawran Period," because "the cultural divisions of the North do not coincide very well with those of the South" (Perkins 1949:162). In her chronological scheme, the Early Gawran Period begins in Level XIA after late Ubaid Level XII and ends in Phase VIIIB of Level VIII. She proposes that

VIIIA is synchronous in time to Ninevite V because of pointed base bowls and cups with incised bands. Although Perkins' analysis includes pottery, seal design, and architecture, her conclusions rely mainly on pottery typology. Porada's 1965 analysis of the Gawra sequence puts greater emphasis on seal design, especially in dating XA to VIIIC as Late Gawran (Porada 1965:147f.), parallel to the Late Uruk/Jemdet Nasr Period in the South. Porada differs from Perkins by including Gawra Level XII in the Early Gawran Period and VIIIA in a chronological position parallel to the Early Dynastic I period in the South. All those who have attempted to assess the chronology of Tepe Gawra (Abu al-Soof 1974a, Schwartz 1982, Forest 1983) have followed the general outline set by Perkins and Porada.

The Problem of the Dating of Level VIII

Of special importance in establishing the relative chronology of Tepe Gawra is the problem of placing the three phases of Level VIII in a proper time frame. Most scholars assume that there were no significant time gaps in the occupation at Gawra from Level XII to VIII. Most also see Level XII as a transitional phase between late Ubaid 4 and Early Uruk or Gawran Periods. Therefore, if you place VIIIA in the Ninevite V— this is what Perkins (1949:193), Porada (1965), Schwartz (1982: Table 12) and Forest (1983: Plate 2) do—two alternatives are possible. One must posit a very long life for IX (Schwartz 1982: Table 14) or stretch the whole sequence of XII to IX out, pushing XI to IX up into the Late Uruk Period (Forest 1983: Plate 2). Neither of those alternatives appears plausible. The new analyses by Gut (1995) and SAR (Rothman, ed. in press) challenge the premises of the Porada and Perkins analyses. As detailed above, there is basis for confusion if the results of excavation in the terrace from Level VI are mixed with the pottery from Level VIII.

Seal Design and Chronology

The two chronological studies have attempted to use seal design and shape to establish the relative chronology of Mesopotamia (Porada et al. 1992; von Wickede 1990). Both agree that the tête bêche style of portraying animals with three legs marks Levels VIII and IX as the latest fourth millennium level. Von Wickede (1990:152) attributes this style from Gawra IX and VIII to Uruk IV (Late Uruk). Porada relates the same characteristic of Gawra VIII to the gray layer of the Tell Brak Eye Temple, which is usually classified as Jemdet Nasr, or "Enduruk." It is now thought to be earlier. Porada uses the modeling, not the tête bêche style of portraying animals, to relate

Gawra Levels IX and VIII to Uruk IV. Porada et al. (1992) see a chronological relationship between the earlier Gawra levels, XIA-X, to Qalinj Agha, also in the piedmont, and to Susa, Level 25 of the excavation of DeMorgan's balk (the very end of the Ubaid or earliest Uruk). Von Wickede also argues for an early date for XII and XIA, associating them with Değirmentepe (Ubaid 4). Pittman (in press) agrees with Porada and von Wickede's dating of Gawra Levels XII to XI and the cultural connections they impute. However, she asserts that Levels IX and VIII of Gawra are not as late as the earlier researchers propose. She writes:

> In the region of the upper Tigris, there is precious little evidence for this early Middle Uruk phase. . . . It is, however, significant that Gawra VIII is dated to the Early Middle Uruk Period on the basis of ceramics. If this is indeed correct, there is a new composition introduced in this period which comes to be important in later Uruk glyptic that is strongly associated with the southern traditions. One of the compositions is cross-necked animals. The crossing of animal necks is common on seals from Uruk and Susa in the Late Uruk Period. It is very likely that this composition was developed in the last stages of the Ubaid stamp seal tradition seen at Gawra VIII and then borrowed by southern seal makers. Another composition that appears here for the first time is the tête bêche organization of animals. Finally, in Gawra VIII two fragments of what may be bone cylinders drilled with random patterns may be the northern version of the baggy style cylinder . . . Hacınebi Tepe Level B1 produced a small but interesting collection that displays connections to Gawra VIII, to Brak and to northern Anatolian glyptic styles.

The pottery relative chronology and the carbon dates of associated sites (Wright and Rupley in press) agree with Pittman.

The Pottery Chronology of Tepe Gawra Levels XII to VIII

Although at times equally confusing as the seal design, the pottery of Gawra may be a better source for relative chronology. The sample from which this chronology is built is approximately 325 whole pots and sherds from occupation levels (see Table 3.1). Specifically, those in the field registries, those in the publications (but not registered), and those at The University of Pennsylvania Museum can be adequately described. The vast majority of pottery sherds were discarded and not catalogued. The excavators did not

Table 3.1　Size of Sample for Relative Chronology

Level	Number of Items
XII	83
XIA/B	53
XI/XA	84
X	26
IX	25
VIII	54

draw or describe them. A good number of these appear in the catalogues below from chits or other field notes, but are not described in enough detail to use for chronology. It is also clear that Speiser and Bache saved mostly the painted or attractive sherds and whole pots. They simply did not have any concept of reliability sampling. In general, statistical analysis is impossible for Gawra chronology. I do not use ceramics from graves and tombs as their level of origin is still much debated (see Forest 1983 and the Appendix below).

Clearly, Tepe Gawra is a poor yardstick for chronology, even within the Iraqi Jazira. The following pottery seriation, using traditional matching techniques, should be good enough for general dating, but is still moot.

Ceramic Variation

The Gawra ceramic assemblage includes a considerable variety of shapes and decoration. There is significant conservatism in certain forms and decorative motifs, especially in sites like Gawra, which sit away from the main communication and travel routes (Helwing 2000:152). Some consistencies in color, temper, and ware are, however, notable. Late fifth and fourth millennium B.C. pottery can be classified into the following colors: buff, darker buff, creamy buff (in impressed wares only), green-gray, gray (to black), orange-red, red-brown, and a darker brown. Table 3.2 lists a variety of these colors with their Munsell values, so that it is possible to be more precise in relating my color names to a standard. Of these, buff, green-gray, and red-brown are the most common throughout the time from XII to VIII.

Tempers are also consistent. The most common are: (1) those with finely ground quartz and basalt grit (often with sand or a very little chaff), (2) fairly heavy chaff, usually with some quartz grit (giving a chaff faced look), or (3) heavy doses of larger basalt and quartz grit. In XII and a very few pieces in XI, a micaceous sand is common in the finer wares, which appears as a sparkle on the surface and interior when such a vessel is rotated toward a light. Type 1 fine grit tempering (often

Table 3.2   Pottery colors

Cat. No	Field No.	Level	Color	Munsell*
224	4-975	XII	gray	10YR 2/1
226	4-1038	XII	red-brown	10R 7/6
240	4-1215	XII	Orange-red	10R 5/6
267	5-1535	XII	brown	5YR 7/6
279	5-1621	XII	red-brown	2.5YR 6/3
280	5-1622	XII	red-brown	7.5YR 7/6
289	5-1713	XII	brown	7.5YR 7/6
307	6-120	XII	buff	10YR 8/3
320	6-588	XII	red-brown	7.5R 6/8
320	paint		dark brown	2.5YR 2.5/3
752	4-1022	XIAB	buff	2.5Y 8/3
759	4-1094	XIAB	buff	10YR 8/4
763	4-1110	XIAB	red-brown	2.5YR 5/3
767	4-1117	XIAB	gray buff	10YR 8/4
768	4-1118	XIAB	red-brown	10R 6/6
790	5-1411	XIAB	buff	10YR 8/2
798	5-1468	XIAB	buff	10YR 8/4
804	5-1489	XIAB	dark buff	10YR 7/3
807	5-1495	XIAB	brown	10YR 7/4
808	5-1505	XIAB	yellow buff	2.5Y 8/3
812	5-1525	XIAB	buff	10YR 8/4
822	5-1644	XIAB	gray	10YR 3/1
1368	5-1410	XI	buff	10YR 7/3
1398	4-670	XI	gray	10YR 5/1
1410	4-833	XI	brown	10YR 7/4
1415	4-898	XI	buff	10YR 7/4
1418	4-920	XI	buff	2.5Y 7/3
1440	5-1318	XI	red	10R 5/6
1441	5-1320	XI	buff	10YR 8/2
1450	5-1366	XI	orange-red	7.5R 6/8
1454	5-1403	XI	buff	2.5Y 8/3
1456	5-1430	XI	red-brown	10R 6/6
1459	5-1610	XI	buff	10YR 7/4
1460	5-1747	XI	buff	10YR 8/2
1460	paint	XI	dark brown	2.5Y 4/1
1477	6-557	XI	brown	7.5YR 7/6
1794	5-1271	XA	brown	2.5YR 3/2
1803	5-1559	XA	buff	10YR 8/4
1807	36-6-26	XA	gray	10R 3/6
1815	6-40	XA	pink buff	2.5Y 8/3
1936	3-353	X	buff	10YR 8/3
1937	3-355	X	brown	5YR 6/6
1944	3-370	X	buff	2.5Y 8/2
1945	3-379	X	buff	10YR 8/2
1946	3-395	X	buff	10YR 8/2
1950	3-494	X	red brown	5YR 7/6
1961	5-1267	X	buff	10YR 8/3
2221	32-21-526	IX	red-brown	2.5Y 8/2
2223	3-21	IX	buff	2.5Y 8/2
2225	3-366	IX	green gray	5Y 8/3
2238	3-212	IX	buff	5Y 8/3
2240	3-221	IX	gray	10YR 5/1
2243	3-248	IX	dark buff	5YR 6/6

(continued)

Table 3.2 (continued)

Cat. No	Field No.	Level	Color	Munsell*
2245	3-252	IX	brown	10YR 7/3
2247	3-277	IX	gray	2.5Y 7/3
2770	1117	VIII	buff	7.5YR 7/3
2774	1541	VIII	brown	2.5Y 8/4
2775	1665	VIII	buff	10YR 8/3
2778	5343	VIII	green gray	2.5Y 8/2
2781	5477	VIII	Brown	5YR 6/3
2783	5588	VIII	red brown	10R 4/6
2784	5598	VIII	buff	10YR 7/3
2787	5113	VIII	buff gray	2.5Y 7/2
2788	5623	VIII	buff	10YR 8/3
2789	5624	VIII	buff	2.5Y 8/4
2790	5626	VIII	red brown	7.5YR 7/3
2793	5631	VIII	green gray	2.5Y 8/3
2794	5636	VIII	brown	5Y 7/3
2803	5700	VIII	gray	2.5Y 7/2
2806	5725	VIII	green gray	2.5Y 8/4
2811	5751	VIII	green gray	2.5Y 8/4
2814	5808	VIII	buff	10YR 8/3
2820	5900	VIII	gray buff	2.5Y 8/3
2823	5956	VIII	brown	10YR 8/6
2850	3-67	VIII	gray	5YR 6/1

*Earth Colors (1997)

just quartz sand) occurs in the green-gray wares (especially in IX and VIII), as well as some gray wares, and the finer red and buff wares. This hard fired, wheel thrown green-gray ware is a key to dating IX and VIII.

As Gut (1995) asserts, consistent use of the wheel is typical of the early Middle Uruk period or LC 3. The type 2 chaff tempering occurs throughout mostly in the buff, orange-red, red-brown, and darker brown colors, although reddish buff wares like "sprig ware" have the micaceous sand temper, and some "gray wares"[4] have chaff. Type 3 temper occurs in gray wares, buff ware, red, and red-brown wares. Whether because of the tempering or the care given to these vessels, firing is usually high in the sand or fine grit tempered green-gray, gray, and buff wares, yielding a hard fabric, and lower temperature firing is evident in the chaff tempered buff, red-brown, brown, and gray wares.

The slow wheel (tournette) is already evident in XII, although a few pieces, like bowl 234 (Plate 7), look almost fast wheel made. By IX and VIII, the green-gray wares all appear to have been made using fast wheel technology. Throughout the late fifth and fourth millennium B.C., hand forming is the most common technique, especially among chaff tempered buff, red, and red-brown vessels.

Hand-made ceramics appear to dominate in XIA/B, although at least half of the ceramics I observed in each level appear to me to be handmade. Both coiling and slab techniques of hand forming are evident. Wide Flower Pots like their cousins the Beveled Rim Bowls are the crudest in shape and heaviest in chaff tempering, especially early in the sequence.

A number of shapes appear repeatedly throughout the late fifth and fourth millennium corpus. Most common of these I term "small jars." They are jars with rounded bases, round bodies (sometimes with a slight carination) and a gradually flaring line from the neck attachment to the rim. The neck and rim are approximately one quarter the height of the body. In height, they are less than 200 mm. Examples include 320 (Plate 7) and 240 (Plate 6) from XII, 804 (Plate 10) of XIB, 1460 (Plate 14) of XI, 1815 (Plate 16) of XA, 1936 (Plate 17) of X, 2788 (Plate 21) of VIII.

A crude, flat bottomed, flare-rimmed bowl with a fabric like the beveled rim bowl, the Wide Flower Pot, is also common throughout.[5] Examples include 303 (Plate 5) of XII, 821 (Plate 8) of XIA/B, 1406 (Plate 12) of XI, 1926a (Plate 18) of X, 2243 (Plate 19) of IX.

A third type is the globular jar with a shorter neck to rim length and where the maximum body width is closer to the top than small jars (in small jars it is near the middle of the body). Examples include 322 (Plate 7) of XII, 794 (Plate 11) of XIA/B, 1805 (Plate 16) of XA, 1927 (Plate 17) of X, 2231 (Plate 20) of IX, and 2835

(Plate 21) of VIII. Open bowls and hole mouth bowls (or open jars) with spouts are common although the placement and the shape of the spout is very variable from the straight open spout of XII 261 (Plate 6), to the flaring "cannon shaped" spouts of XIA/B (798, Plate 9) and XI (1453, Plate 12), to the straight spouts of XA (1807 Plate 15), X (1944, Plate 17), IX (2233, Plate 20) and VIII (2804, Plate 21).

Small hole mouthed bowls with bead rims reoccur throughout this time; e.g., in XIA/B (822, Plate 8), XI (1450, Plate 12), XA (1782, Plate 15), X (1950, Plate 17), and VIII (2804 with spout, Plate 21). Other types have shorter spans and will be discussed where chronologically important.

The details of ceramic correspondences, correlated with Wright and Rupley's radiocarbon dating (in press), sketch out the following relative chronology for Tepe Gawra. The types that form the basis of the relative chronology are as follows.

Stylistic Correspondences for Gawra XII to VIII Pottery

XII Parallels

Abu al-Soof (1974a:3) is essentially correct to write that "Gawra XII is best considered a transitional stage between Ubaid and Uruk periods." Much of the difficulty of dating the earliest period discussed in this book (see Table 3.3) is a conflation of two distinct levels, XIIA and XII. Level XIIA is a continuation of the Ubaid 4 period Level XIII, and XII, in which the first signs of the transition to the distinctive pottery of the fourth millennium began, fits within the LC1, Terminal Ubaid, or even Early Uruk Period. Levels XIIA and XII are clearly distinctive in stratigraphic terms. Figures 3.2 and 3.3, the schematic sections of K and M, show that after Level XIII a few architectural pieces of Level XIIA remain near the site's edges (see Tobler 1950, Plate X). Even where no architecture is present, a stratigraphically large gap existed between the top of XIII and the bottom of XII (Figure 3.1). Again, these are distinct architectural levels.

When pottery from the two strata are separated (Rothman a in press, Table III), it is clear that the pottery of XIIA is mostly painted, but the ceramics of XII have many fewer painted forms than XIIA and XIII. Typical painted pots of Gawra XIIA (223, 325, or 284, Plate 7) have good parallels with Hammam et Turkman IVD (Akkermans 1988, Figure 3.3, 3.5), which its excavator places in the last Ubaid period (Akkermans 1988). The problem of unrepresentative samples caused confusion. From Gawra, 85 percent of the Level XII sherds Speiser saved are painted. Among whole pots, however, 88 percent (n = 89) are unpainted, and 12 percent (n = 12) were painted (Rothman a in press). This trend toward plain pottery is

typical of the Late Chalcolithic Period and its southern Mesopotamian parallel, the early Uruk Period. The two exceptions in XII to the trend toward unpainted pottery are so-called sprig ware (321, 313, 256, 311, 324, 320 and 322, Plate 7), and the first appearance of cross-hatched triangles under the rim or neck (233, Plate 7). The latter type remains common across northern Mesopotamia for another 500 or 600 years (e.g., Leilan V, Schwartz 1988b, Figure 61, 12), and may be the model for Late Uruk period incised wares.

A chronologically sensitive type, the so-called Coba bowls, provide a way of distinguishing some of these earlier phases from later ones. Confusion of terminology—what fits into the category of Coba bowls and in another category of coarse chaff-faced wares, Wide Flower pots—obscures the distinction. I propose that there are four distinct types. The "true" Coba bowl is a high-sided flint-scraped bowl of the Late or Terminal Ubaid. It is found in the Euphrates Basin at sites like Değirmentepe and Hammam et Turkman IVD, but, as Rova (1999/2000) notes, not in the eastern steppe and piedmont. Mellart (1981: Figure 202) correctly places Coba bowls at the Ubaid/"Uruk" (LC1) boundary. However, there are three varieties of these open, chaff tempered, flint-scraped crude bowls at Gawra, which are chronologically sensitive. The first is an extended base variety, which ends after Gawra XII (258, 254, 289, 267, and 274, Plate 5). Clear parallels are found to Norşuntepe J/K 17 (Hauptmann 1982: Plate 36,1) and to Leilan VIb (Schwartz 1988: Figure 65, 4). These are, in effect, the eastern versions of the Coba bowl. The second variety is the Wide Flower Pot. These, too, are very crudely made, chaff-tempered bowls, in ware much like Beveled Rim Bowls, but not in their shape. They flare more than the earlier, extended base varieties. This second type appears earliest in XII (280, 239, 222, Plate 5) and continues at Gawra through Level XI (1406, Plate 12), in other words, LC1 to early LC2. The final variety in shape is identical to the previous forms of Wide Flower Pots, but is made with less chaff, and is smoothed, perhaps turned on a tournette (2230, 2243, Plate 19; 2853, 2863, and 2861, Plate 22). This third type is typical of Gawra IX and VIII, late LC2 into LC3. Wide Flower Pots appears also at Umm Qseir Late Chalcolithic II, Telul eth Thalathat VIIIa, Musharifa in the Eski Mosul area, in Arslantepe VII (Tsunneki and Miyake 1998: Figure 51, 2; Egami 1959: Figure 51, 2; Oguchi 1987: Figure 14, 16; and Frangipane 1993: Figure 9,10; respectively), as well as at Brak and other sites. The description of the Umm Qseir Flower Pot appears to link it chronologically to the latest Wide Flower Pots, although they do not detail the precise characteristics of the others illustrated.

The other pottery that argues for including Gawra XII in the transitional Ubaid to Uruk or even the Early Uruk is represented by many forms. For example, a hard fired, greenish-buff, stamped, and incised or appliqué ware (202, Plate 7) appeared first in XII and

Table 3.3   Relative Chronology of Tepe Gawra and Other Mesopotamian Sites.

B.C.		Southern Alluvium	Syria	Upper Euphrates	Western Iran	Tigris	Southern Mesopotamia
3,000	**LC 5** late	IVA Eanna IVB–V / Early 17 Susa *Acropole*	Sheik Hassan 4 / Habuba Kabira / Brak TW 11/12	Arslantepe VIA	Godin V	Mohamad Arab Late Uruk / Nineveh (Gut) Späturuk Ninevite 4	Late Uruk
3,400	**LC 4**	Eanna VI / Late 18 Susa / Eanna VII Early 18 Sharafabad	Sheikh Hassan 5–7 / Brak TW 13			L:31–20 Nordruk B / L:37–31	Late Middle Uruk
3,600	**LC 3**	Susa 19–22 / Eanna IX–VIII / hiatus?	Sheikh Hassan 8–10/13 / Brak TW 14–17 / Amuq F / Leilan IV	Tepecik / Arslantepe VII		Grai Resh / Nordruk A / L:45–37 / Tepe Gawra VIII	Early Middle Uruk
3,800	late 2		Brak CH 10/14 / Leilan V / Hammam Turkman VB			Tepe Gawra IX–X	
4,000	**LC 2** early 2	Eanna X–XIII	Brak TW 18–19 / hiatus?	IIIB Norşuntepe J/K 18/19	Geoy Tepe M	Qalinj Agha I–IV / Gawra B / L:59–45 Tepe Gawra XI/XA	Early Uruk
4,200	**LC 1**	Eanna XVI–XIV Susa Acropolis 23–27	Hammam Turkman VA / Brak CH 13/14 / Leilan late VIb / IVD	IIIA Norşun IIA J/K 17 / Arslantepe VIII / IIB–C		Gawra A / Tepe Gawra XIA/B / hiatus? Tepe Gawra XII / L:60 / XIIA–XIII	'Ubaid transitional 'Ubaid 4?
	Terminal Ubaid						

After Table 1.1, Rothman, ed. 2000

then increased in frequency in XIA/B and XI/XA. This ware, exhibiting the common rosette designs and characteristic firing bubbles, occurs in a Level XIII context at Tell Brak; that is, in the Early Uruk Period (Oates 1987: Plate 3,6). Similar pottery was found at Qalinj Agha Level III, also associated with the Early Uruk Period (Abu al-Soof 1969:22, 32).

At the same time as all these Uruk Period forms appear, other forms related to the Ubaid Period also existed at Gawra XII. Most striking of these are the sprig ware painted designs on finely made buff to red colored open bowls and small jars, mentioned above. These sprig ware forms have parallels in late Ubaid contexts at Tell Brak (Oates 1987:3–4) and Telul eth Thalathat IVb in Sinjar (Egami 1959: Figure 20:13–21). I would argue that this design on pottery begins in XII. A possible manufacturing center for sprig ware existed north of Gawra on the Tigris at Shelgiyya (Ball 1997). The one sprig ware pot Tobler assigned to Level XIII before XII (1950:CXXXVIII,184) was an unregistered pot with no known provenience and was probably assigned ex post facto. The parallels at Norşuntepe in southeastern Turkey cited by Porada et al (1992) parallel later versions of wares with a painted sprig between cross-hatched triangles (J/K 18/19). Another Late Ubaid type from Gawra XII is the pedestal footed bowl (292, 226, Plate 5). This form is paralleled in Telul eth Thalathat VIIb (Egami 1959: Plate 53,8) and at Madhur (Moon and Roaf 1984: Figure 21, 16). Interestingly, the complex painted design on the Madhur example is almost identical to the design on the outside of an open, ring-based bowl from Gawra XII (232, Plate 7). Excavators also recovered ring-based, carinated, open mouthed jars, reminiscent of Ubaid forms (e.g., 234, Plate 7; 307, Plate 5). This form continued into Gawra XIA/B (803, Plate 10), and was found in western Iran at Geoy Tepe, Level M (Burton-Brown 1951: Figure 4, 11, 31. 433). Geoy M is relatively dated to between Gawra Level XII and XI/XA.

Taken all in all, Gawra XII does appear to fit in some sort of transitional Ubaid to Uruk Period. Vertesalji (1987: Chronological Table 3) calls this phase Chalcolithic III B 1. In addition to the parallels in the Jazira, the Keban Dam areas of southeastern Turkey, and the rest of the piedmont zone—where most Gawra parallels are found—he finds parallels in time to terminal Susa A, Eridu Temple VI, Tell ʿUqair II, and Uruk-Warka Eanna XVI–XIII.

XIA/B Parallels

Gawra Level XIA/B represents a continuation and a change from XII. The ring base, slightly carinated hole-mouth bowls of XII continue. Both of the XIA/B examples are painted. Of the two, 803 (Plate 10) dates to the earlier XIB phase; the other cannot be assigned to one or the other phase. In other words, that form

may be a marker of the transition. Excavators recovered the ubiquitous small jar and Wide Flower Pots from XIA/B as they had from XII (small jars:788, 804, Plate 10; Wide Flower Pot:744, Plate 8). They also found many of the green buff and buff incised and appliqué design bowl sherds (725, 722, 733, 724, Plate 9). Characteristic of these sherds, the sides have bubbles, in part because of what looks to me like poor slab construction (see Vandiver 1985 for analysis of this technique). Possibly of note culturally, Vandiver found most of the slab made pots of the fifth and fourth millennium B.C. in the Zagros Mountains of western Iran. In addition to the ropes and appliqué rosettes of the XII example, impressed triangles and ladder-like designs were added (724, Plate 9). This triangle and ladder design establishes a parallel with Level J/K 18/19 at Norşuntepe (Hauptmann 1976: Plate 50, 3; Gülçur 2000: Plate 33), placing XIA/B firmly in the Early Uruk Period.

XIA/B also represents a change from XII. As many researchers have noticed (e.g., Abu al-Soof 1974a:4; Porada et al. 1992), the proportion of unpainted wares increased in XIA/B from XII (although the percentage of painted pottery in XII has been overestimated). In addition to a decline in painted pots, a number of new forms also came into use. One is a plainware bowl with a long flaring spout (cannonshaped). Three examples are illustrated below (767, 798, 720, Plate 9). These continued into Phase XI (1453, Plate 12) and are paralleled at Norşuntepe J/K 18/19 (Hauptmann 1982: Figure 39,4) and Qalinj Agha II (Abu al-Soof 1969: Plate XVII, 2). They are also cited as a typical Uruk (Chalcolithic IIIB2) type by Vertesalji (1987: Plate 3, 616) in the Uruk area of southern Iraq (for an even closer parallel, see Adams and Nissen 1972: Figure 52, 1). A large jar with short flaring rim is also new (794, Plate 10). Parallels to it are from Norşuntepe J/K 18-19 ((Hauptmann 1982: Plate 39,5) and Musharifa (Oguchi 1987: Figure 14, 25). Another distinctive, new type that marked XIA/B and continued throughout the remains of the fourth millennium B.C. is the double or channel rim bowl, often with holes on the inside rim to direct splashed liquids back into the bowl (790, 795,750, 723, Plate 9). Many of these were found in Level CH XIII at Tell Brak (Oates 1987: 194) and at Qalinj Agha II (Abu al-Soof 1969:15).

XIA/B certainly fits well into an early LC 2, Early Uruk time frame.

XI/XA Parallels

Like Level XIA/B before it, XI/XA pottery's predecessors are found in XIA/B and XII, but also some new forms were added. Like XIA/B, that pottery fits nicely into an early LC2 or Early Uruk time frame. Other sites in this period include Tell Brak and Telul eth Thalathat in the Jazira, Norşuntepe in Eastern Turkey, Qalinj Agha, Sakçe Gözü in Eastern Anatolia, Judeideh (Phase F) in the Amuq, and Madhur in the piedmont, Geoy Tepe near Lake Urmia in Iran, and Eridu in the South. The chaff-faced looking pottery like Amuq F (Braidwood and Braidwood 1960) are present, although the shapes are different and the chaff face was often partially smoothed.

Continuing into Phase XI from XIA/B were the plain bowls with cannon spout (1453, Plate 12), Wide Flower Pots (1406, Plate 12), double or channel rim bowls (1475, 1448, Plate 14), small jars, some painted (1403, 1440, 1460, 1478, 1477, Plate 14) and cream buff appliqué and impressed wares (1415, 1368, 1373, 1331, 1375, 1378, 1385, 1394, Plate 13). The Flower pots tie Gawra to Sakçe Gözü IVA, and Nuzi IX. Two ring base forms, one with the hatched triangle painted design, appear in XI (1402, Plate 12; 1472, Plate 14), although ring bases are rare. In Phase XI, impressed rosettes and rows of puncture holes, as if made with a comb, appear for the first time. These same impressed patterns are found in Early Uruk contexts at Tell Brak (Oates 1984: Plate XXXI,b), and at Norşuntepe J/K 18/19 (Hauptmann 1976: Figure 50, 1, 2). Impressed ladder designs are found at Sakçe Gözü IVC. Of the painted designs from Gawra, the bow tie of 1460, Plate 14) is found in the same context as impressed wares at Norşuntepe (Hauptmann 1976: Figure 50, 6,9; Gülçur 2000: Plate 48, 13). Another painted motif, cross-hatched triangles descending from the neck, also appears at Norşuntepe on the same kind of vessel (Gawra: 1472, Plate 14; Gülçur 2000: Plate 48, 7). Small bead rim hole mouth bowls (1450, Plate 12) and larger round bottom straight sided bowls (1398, 1418, Plate 12) also continued from XIA/B. Small, chaff-faced jars from XI (1403, Plate 14) are reminiscent of finds from Judeideh Amuq F, Yorgun Tepe (Nuzi) IX, and Telul eth Thalathat III, I/IV.

New to XI are two forms. They are the double-mouth jar with necks set more vertically and with better-formed rims than the Ubaid type (see Tobler 1950: CXXXI, 221; Moon and Roaf 1984: Figure 19: 7 for the Ubaid version). Tobler mistakenly presented this form as a "XIA" type (1444, Plate 14); Tobler 1950: Plate CXLIII, 356). The original register places this jar in "XA," although by elevation it appears to be from the XI phase. Other examples (1435, Plate 14) were also found in XI. Parallel jar types were found at Qalinj Agha, Level II (Abu al-Soof 1969: 15–16), Telul eth Thalathat XIV (Fukai et al 1974: Plate LXXV, 19) and VI/V (Egami 1959: Plate XIX,1, Figure 50,5), and "Early Uruk" Eridu (Abu al-Soof 1973: 18). Early Uruk Eridu parallels Uruk-Warka Eanna XII-VI (Lloyd 1948: 4) or XII-VIII (Vertesalji 1987: chart 3). Since Gawra XII parallels Uruk Eanna XVI–XIII, such a parallel for XI/XA makes some sense. Another new form from XI was a carinated cup with striations at the neck (1396, 1410,

1474, Plate 13). Tobler (1950: 156) proposed that the striations served for "a more secure grip." Similar cups come from Early Uruk levels at Brak (Oates 1987: Figure 3, 7) and Norşuntepe (Hauptmann 1976: Plate 50, 7).

Related to the cups are beakers, which have straighter though slightly flaring sides than cups (1416, 1455, Plate 13). Their function is probably the same, based on volumetric capacity and body diameter. The paste of both categories is mostly buff, although a green buff color is found on a number of beakers in XI/XA. The impressed and appliqué buff to cream buff wares were mostly beakers. These, too, are paralleled at Tell Brak (Oates 1984: Plate XXXI, b; Figure 2, 34) and Norşuntepe (Hauptmann 1976: Plate 50, 1,2, 3,6). Roaf recovered similar beakers from the "Ubaid Level 4, latest floor" at Madhur (Moon and Roaf 1984: Figure 16, 18), which I take to mean that there were LC2 or at least LC1 remains at Madhur.

Phase XA is a continuation of the other phase of XI/XA, but along with the older forms some new decoration and one important new forms originated in XA. Excavators found carinated cups (1775, 1780, Plate 15) and beakers (1791, Plate 15). However, 1780 also has an appliqué, thumb impressed band at the widest part of its body, and perhaps a small spout. The appliqué ropes and rosettes typical of XII and XIA/B—there are also found in XI—are absent in XA. Paint on a jar (1813, Plate 16) exactly matches a painted sherd from XIA/B (837, Plate 9). Another remainder from earlier times was a pedestal base cup (1817, Plate 15). This phase yielded small jars (1779, 1781, 1813, Plate 16), globular jars (1805, Plate 16), and a hole mouthed pot without the bead rim of earlier examples of this form (1799, Plate 15). Potter's marks typical of the LC2 and 3 in northern Mesopotamia appear in Phase XA (see Arslantepe VII example, Frangipane 1993, Figures 9 and 11).

Despite the strong similarity with the past, two new forms appeared in XA. The first is an open bowl with a in beveled rim and three blobs of paint on the rim (1816, 1819 (ring based) Plate 16). This form is found across a wide area, including Nineveh (mm 55, Gut 1995: Plate 53, 802), Geoy Tepe M (Burton Brown 1951: Figure 5), Qalinj Agha IV (Hijara 1973: Plate 15,13), Telul eth Thalathat III (Egami 1959: Figure 50, 4), Norşuntepe J/K 18/19 (Hauptmann 1972: Plate 71, 5), Tepecik (Esin 1972: Plate 114, 2), and possibly the hills of eastern Turkey (Russell 1980: type G). The other is a tall bottle (1821, Plate 16), reminiscent of the Late Uruk bottle neck jar, but whose neck is similar to a small jar. This is not the Classic Uruk bottle. A small spouted bowl with distinctive red slip and indentations (1807, Plate 15) was also found in CH 13/14 at Early Uruk LC 2 Tell Brak (Oates 1984: Plate XXXI, b4).

XI/XA is Early Uruk in date. Perhaps, most interesting, however, are a series of parallels to Madhur. Such correspondences are unexpected because Moon and Roaf (1984) claim that the site was occupied entirely in the Ubaid Period. Most of the parallels to Gawra are from strata they describe as "Latest Ubaid," suggesting they are really early Uruk Period. This conclusion is supported by a mid-fourth millennium B.C. C^{14} date from Late "Ubaid" Madhur (J. Oates 1983: Figure 9). These parallels must negate any assignment of XI/XA to the Late Uruk Period.

X Parallels

Unfortunately, little pottery from Level X was catalogued, described, or saved. Most of it has precursors in XI/XA tying it to the LC 2 or Early Uruk period sites. Among these types are Wide Flower Pots (1926, 1926a, Plate 18), carinated cups (1957, 1958, Plate 18), beakers (1949, 1955, Plate 18), small jars (1945, 1925, 1936, 1934, 1961, Plate 17), and globular jars (1927, 1932, 1937, Plate 17). Painted decoration returned to X in beakers and jars, while impressed and appliqué decoration disappeared. In particular, the cross hatched triangles descending from a band of paint and the abstract tree, reminiscent of sprig ware, were painted on globular jars (1932, 1942, Plate 17) and on beakers (1949, Plate 18). Also on 1949 were drawings of humans with upraised hands and animals. These painted designs are paralleled at Norşuntepe J/K 18/19 (Hauptmann 1976: Plate 50: 5, 12, 13, 14; 1982: Plate 38:5; Gülçur 2000: Plates 29 and 30). A small pedestal base bowl (1933, Plate 17) is reminiscent of earlier forms, but smaller (see Gülçur 2000: Plate 11, for a comparison).

However, Level X has some intimation of later Uruk forms. One of the beakers (1958, Plate 18) has a pointed base like the cups of VIII and a new beaker shape with a lower carination, pointed base, and painted "finger-paint" design developed in X (1924, Plate 18).[6] Cup 1924 appears to have been thrown on a fast wheel. Another new form is the crock—globular jars—with straight spouts (1943, 1944, Plate 17), Crock 1944 has a ring base, the others are round based. The closest parallel to 1943 is from Late Chalcolithic Tepecik in southeastern Turkey (Esin 1976: Plate 73:1). At Tepecik, this is the period just before the appearance of Beveled Rim Bowls, LC 3.

IX Parallels

In general, Level IX pottery shows parallels to both the LC 2, Early Uruk period and to the LC 3 or early Middle Uruk period. There is continuity from the earlier LC 2 levels. Wide Flower Pots (2230, 2243, Plate 19) continued to be made and used, as did double or channel rim bowls (2227, 2228, Plate 19). Excavators recovered at least one two necked jar (2251, Plate 20), a beaker (2226, Plate 19), and globular jars (2231, 2232, 2245, Plate 20), the last with a ring base. Globular jar

2245 matches an almost identical jar at Musharifa (Oguchi 1987: Figure 14,12). Narrower but otherwise very similar jars come from Sheikh Hassan, Middle Uruk (Boese 1995:270, Figure 13 bottom) and from Tell Brak TW 14 (Oates and Oates 1993: Figure 51, 29). Small jars, including two with the same triangle and sprig painting as in X were made (2242, 2234, Plate 20). This level yielded the last of the in-beveled rim bowls with three blobs of paint on the rim, first found in Phase XA, this time with a ring base (2236, Plate 19). Tying Gawra IX to X is another of the pointed base beakers with finger paint (field number 6081, not drawn but virtually identical to 1924, Plate 18) and a straight spouted globular jar (2233, Plate 20). A bead-rimmed, slightly band-rimmed bowl (2239, Plate 19) is paralleled at Hammam et Turkman Vb (Akkermans 1988: Figure 9, 149). Wright and Rupley (in press) report a range of 4220 to 3820 B.C. calibrated this level at Hammam et Turkman. It is a deep level. To me a date from 3900 to 3850 BC makes sense for Gawra IX.

What marks a new chronological stage for Level IX is the first of the wheel made green-gray ware, sand tempered pots, in this case a carinated ring base bowl with a bead rim (2255, Plate 19). This ware ties IX to Gawra VIII and the form is paralleled at Tell Brak TW 16 (Oates and Oates 1993: Plate 51, 29). As I wrote above, Gut (1995) sees the beginning of fast wheel technology as a marker of the beginning of the Middle Uruk or LC 3/4 period. Another late form is a tall footed bowl (2250, Plate 20). This is not the well-made version with triangular cutouts (see for Tepecik 3c, Esin 1982: Plate 72,33,34), but a cruder version like that found at Grai Resh II (Lloyd 1940, Figure 7:6).

Overall, the ceramic evidence from Gawra IX places it in the late LC2 or even earliest LC3 period.

VIII Parallels

The chronology of the three phases of Level VIII has proven one of the most troublesome, as stated above. I think that the level's chronology must first be viewed in terms of the whole 4th millennium B.C. The pottery from XI/XA provides little reason to agree with Forest (1983: Plate 2) that XI/XA was Late Uruk in date. Nor does Level IX exhibit the signs of remodeling that would support a long occupation there, as Schwartz's chronology suggests (1982: Table 14). If Gawra Level XII is LC 1, XIA/B and XI/XA are early LC 2, X and IX are late LC2 (X just merging into LC3, one would expect Level VIII to be LC3 or Early Middle Uruk in date. This assumes that there is no significant chronological break, for which there is no stratigraphic evidence.

The question, then, is what the pottery says about its chronology. One problem is that most of the pottery of Gawra VIII was not assigned to a particular phase by Speiser. No evidence exists for me to assign them, as I could for better recorded lower levels. However, looked at overall, the pottery of Gawra VIII continues styles of earlier levels but with something quite new added. The small jars (2787, 2788, 2849, 2862, 2856, Plate 21) of earlier times continued into VIII. Most are still buff ware and chaff faced. The one that is burnished red slipped ware (2783, Plate 21) is closely paralleled at Tell Brak (Oates 1984: Figure 2, 28). Jar 5623 (2787, Plate 21) is painted with the hatched triangle descending from a painted band at the neck, like jars going back to Level XII. On the other hand, jar 2777 (Plate 21) is of the green-gray sand tempered, wheel made types begun in Level IX. Gawra VIII yielded a number of other green-gray ware pieces (2819, 2834, 2779, 2852, Plate 21; 2806, 2828, 2793, 2827, 2829, Plate 22; 2785, 2812, 2811, 2850, 2838, 2820, 2791, Plate 23). Jar 2823 (Plate 21), the only one definitely from VIIIA differs from Gawra's earlier small jars because it has a flat base, but it is a brown basalt grit tempered ware like some earlier small jars. Wide Flower Pots continue as well (2853, 2861, 2863, Plate 22). Multiple spouted jars also continue, although with more than the older two mouths (2789, Plate 23).

Other pots represent new types. Bowl 2806 (Plate 22) with a ledge rim is very similar to one of Yorgun Tepe VIII (Starr 1939, vol II: Plate 50, C). The spouted crock of VIII (2804, Plate 21) is equated with similar crocks at Telul eth Thalathat I-IV (Porada et al 1992: Figure IV-4), and it is similar to the later variant from Nineveh with a folded rim (mm 35, Gut 1995: Plate 107, s67). The Gawra example may have been a model for this later type. Also from the VIIIA phase, a brown ware grooved pot (2774, Plate 23) with wet smoothed top is also found at Tell Brak (Oates 1984: Figure 2, 32), as well as at Hammam et Turkman VB (Akkermans 1988: Figure 9, 139) and at Umm Qseir (Tsuneki and Miyake 1998: Figure 63, 6). A number of small carinated, lip rimmed bowls (2790, 2830, Plate 23) match Phase II bowls from Hacinebi (Pollock and Coursey 1995, Figure 6, G,H), roughly LC 3 period B1 when Uruk-related pots begin to appear there. Three other types imply an LC 3 date for Gawra VIII. One is a wheel thrown, green-gray, flat bottomed bowl (2827, Plate 22) of Phase VIIIA which matches a bowl from Nineveh mm 41 (Gut 1995: Plate 54, 811). Another is a large flat-bottomed jar (2779, Plate 21) which has a parallel in Brak TW 16 (Oates and Oates 1993: Figure 52, 48). Pointed-base beakers or cups with incising represent a final connection of Gawra VIII to the LC3. These types (2811, Plate 23) appeared at the Leilan IV horizon (Schwartz 1982: Figure 42, 4, 5, 6).

Leilan IV is the period of Beveled Rim Bowls, which we now see as LC 3, not LC 5 or Late Uruk period.

Taken all in all, Gawra VIII's date is comfortably in the early LC 3. The pottery from that level contains types that clearly develop out of and continue LC2 northern Mesopotamia traditions. It also shows some significant changes, particularly in the percentage of fast wheel thrown ceramics.

Cultural Connections

One of the other points of interest in the distribution of pottery style zones represented by the networks of connections among sites. As Kramer (1977) warns, pots do not directly equal peoples. However, like dialects in language (Labov 1972), the more frequent the contact the more likely the creation of commonalities in style. The sphere of style for Gawrans was clearly that zone of resource availability highlighted by Algaze (1993). It encompassed the hilly country of northwestern Iran, eastern Turkey, and the Jazira steppes to the Khabur River. Amazingly, the connections apparently extended all the way into the Transcaucasus (Lyonnet 2000). As the evolutionary history of this small center is told, this factor should always be kept in mind.

Notes

1. I make a distinction between two kinds of strata. A level is a stratum with sets of buildings different from adjoining strata that also does not overlap the same elevations. Strata that share many buildings and common town plans and overlap each other stratigraphically I call sub-level phases. In one sense, sub-level phases XI and XIA should be united in one level as they share one large building complex, but overall they are quite distinctive in buildings, function, and town plan and do not overlap stratigraphically.

2. I have translated all of the Forest quotations from the French to be clear how I understand his reconstructions.

3. In 1999 the University of Pennsylvania Museum kindly allowed me to send a series of bone sample for dating to the NSF-Arizona Radiocarbon Lab. Unfortunately, the amount of collagen was too small for dating.

4. This gray-colored ware should not be confused with the gray wares of Tepe Hissar.

5. In the catalogue below, "dish" is synonymous with Wide Flower Pot. "Dishes" are those I have not actually seen, but all pots classified "dish" in the field registries have been Wide Flower Pots in shape and ware.

6. Contrary to his field registry books, Speiser published this cup as coming from IX (Speiser 1935a: Plate LXII, 15).

4

Artifact Characteristics and Functions

This chapter describes various classes of artifacts from Tepe Gawra Levels XII to VIII with special emphasis on exploring their functions. As noted in Chapter 1, "function" here is a term used to describe general categories of activity needed to maintain the residents of the site and service a local or more regional population. An evolutionary history of Tepe Gawra involves a retelling of what was happening on the site functionally and explaining how it was organized socially from level to level through time. Examples of such functions include agricultural and pastoral production, hunting, cloth, tool, pottery, and ceramic making, import and export exchange, running local exchange systems (market places if not marketing), food preparation, family living, resource extraction, building construction, military exercises, symbolic representations, religious and social ritual.

I will also note where appropriate the presence and use of raw materials exotic to this area. As discussed in Chapter 1, Gawra lies on the routes of exchange for many materials coming through the Jebel Maqlub into the alluvial areas of Mesopotamia in recent times. This same route was probably in use in the past. If the volume of exchange is as high as some hypothesize and trade itself as critical, signs of the movement of trade goods should be present in varying amounts throughout the late fifth and fourth millennia B.C. at Tepe Gawra.

Details of Analysis

In practical terms understanding the activities and functions of each phase of Gawra's existence means cataloging the artifacts found in each level and sub-level

phase and assessing as accurately as possible the activities in which they were used. In this way, some idea of the range of functions found at the site can be determined. An organized listing of functions is one level of analysis that will be utilized below.

Whenever possible, the distribution of artifacts in the building blocks and open spaces of the site provides a more powerful indication of function and, of course, the social organization of activities. As discussed in Chapter 1, the distribution of artifacts in space is a kind of social and political mapping of activities. Distribution maps of activities that occurred in buildings and open spaces will be discussed as a second level of analysis in Chapter 5.

The impossibility of drawing a truly comprehensive picture of all possible functions that occurred at the site in the past must be stated as a caveat. First, the artifacts recovered archaeologically represent only a small fraction of functional items originally used. Some of the original repertoire of tools and most raw materials were made of perishable materials and have disintegrated, or have been used off-site and lost. Some were refashioned for other uses. Others were discarded in a way that they are not recovered intact, or were intentionally taken from the site in antiquity. Second, the use for some artifacts cannot be fully understood today. Third, many artifacts do not remain in the provenience of their initial use at the site. At Tepe Gawra, whether in initial position or not, precise three-dimensional provenience is not available for most artifacts from Levels X to VIII. In VIII the field notes often do not specify whether artifacts are from the A, B, or C phases. Therefore, it is not always possible to know for certain whether artifacts in the same excavation square are actually associated through use or whether one was left in a primary context and others found their way to that provenience as secondary trash or in tertiary construction fill. Fourth, not every stratum is completely exposed, leaving the possibility that artifacts and physical areas where major activities were conducted remain mute and skew our understanding of site function. Ironically, the strata with the best provenience information, XII to XI/XA, are the ones that the excavators did not excavate completely.

With these goals and caveats in mind, the next sections of this and the following two chapters will assess the interpretation of artifact distributions to assess site functional size and organization.

Artifacts and Function

For each level and for the sub-level phases of XIA/B, XI/XA, and VIII summary tables of functional artifacts will be presented toward the end of this chapter. For convenience of presentation the summary tables for each phase and level are divided into craft tools and materials, domestic goods, ritual and symbolic, administrative and miscellaneous categories. Ritual and symbolic is a broad category, which includes items that appear to be used in religious rites at Gawra (e.g., censers) and items that may be used as symbols in ritual activities (e.g., figurines). Alternatively, "symbolic" artifacts may simply be pieces that are being classified as toys and games.

The "craft tools" section of the table includes tools used for agricultural production (sickles, grinding tools), for processing animal fibers and weaving (spindle whorls, pins, bobbins, loom weights and loom parts, perhaps blades/knives), for woodworking and building construction (celts, adzes, hammers), for pottery-making (burnishers, polishers, smoothers, and palettes for grinding pigments), and probably for hide tanning (scrapers, blades/knives). Added to these artifacts are kilns, ovens, and other architectural features that can be assigned to specific activities.

Most of the lithic tools from Levels XII, XIA/B, XI/XA, X, IX, and VIII are double edged, long blades (not microliths), with a few prepared scrapers. Knapped projectile points first appear in VIII. By level the numbers of lithics are 20 (XII), 19 (XIA/B), 30 (XI/XA), 5 (X), 64 (IX) and 189 (VIII). The dramatic increase in the numbers of blades in IX and VIII I interpret as both an increase in the knapping of obsidian blades for exchange, and an increase in activities using cutting tools. Large unexhausted cores in VIII indicate that raw blocks of obsidian were imported to the town for processing. Finished blades were not brought in.

The most critical evidence for the uses of these blades can be found by examining the condition and angle of the tools' working edges.[1] The following information is based on the total number of edges (all but one of the tools analyzed had two edges). For those that I was able to observe (well over two thirds of all lithics registered):

1. 17% (62) showed no signs of preparation (retouch) or use; 2. 21% (78) had little sign of wear; 3. 8% (31) had heavy use wear; 4. 2% (9) had sickle sheen; 5. 5% (19) had serrated, saw-like edges; 6. 30% (110) had striation marks emanating from their edges along the blade face (one or both sides); 7. 17% (64) had signs of original retouch (This retouch could be from use, but is more likely to be from edge preparation)

Obsidian does not show sickle sheen as clearly as flint does, so some of those marks may be for cutting grain. However, one would expect sickle blades to be hafted with bitumen. None of the obsidian blades I observed had bitumen traces; those that did were all flint (165, Plate 78, 170 from XII, 695 from XIA/B, 1769 from XA, 2168, 2171, 2205, and 2209 from IX, not illustrated).

Experimental work on edge wear indicates that the type of long striations found on many Gawra tools are often evidence for cutting vegetative parts (perhaps soft wood), raw wool or bovine hides (see Vaughan 1985). There is a non-random association of the angle of blade edges and the condition of the edge.[2] Unused blades had the lowest median angle; 56 percent fell within the range of 12 to 33 degrees. Among little-used blades the median was higher with 48 percent under 33 degrees. Of the frequently used tools, including those with sheen, striations, and serrated edges, the greatest number fell within the range of 38 to 42 degrees. None of the sickles (flints with sheen) had an edge angle less than 38 degrees. Therefore even among the cutting tools the optimal angle appears to be less than 50 degrees and greater that 38 degrees. The heavier the cutting job the greater the angle (under 50 degrees). Although 53.6 percent (59) of the blades with striations fall within the range of 34 to 48 degrees, 41.8 percent (46) are between 12 and 33 degrees. I interpret this pattern to mean that over 40 percent of blades with striations were used as knives for fine cutting of soft material and the remainder were used for work with wood, soft stone, or maybe bone.

All the prepared cores from XI/XA to IX were used to remove long narrow blades. Of the three obsidian cores recovered from stratum XI/XA plus one from a grave intrusive in XI, the three I could observe are all small and nearly exhausted. Only a couple of the blades found are narrow enough to be from these cores as they now exist. All three cores, including 4–760 from grave 109 (intrusive in XI), do show signs of secondary use as drills or burins. Core 1308 especially has surface striations like the blades and its tip is chipped through use or retouch.

Of the 327 lithic pieces recovered from Levels XII to VIII, 249 were obsidian, 77 are some form of flint or chert, one is a fine sandstone that was knapped, not ground. In terms of developments in the larger region, the volume of obsidian, especially in Level VIII, should mark it as a prime trade good.

What is most surprising then is the paucity of obsidian in many sites in the piedmont, the Western Zagros hills, and the alluvium. Eichmann (1986) does write of a cache of obsidian blades in the Riemchengebäude at Uruk-Warka, although much debitage from flint tool manufacture was also found there and it is much later than Gawra VIII is. Transtigridian sites like Rubeideh (Miller 1988:77), and also Farukhabad (Wright 1981: 275), and Abu Salabikh on the alluvium (Pollock 1990) yielded little, if any, obsidian.

A variety of other cutting tools were found at Tepe Gawra. Celts, hammers, and adzes are all of shapes and sizes typical for these artifacts (as shown in Tobler (1950: Plate XCV and CLXXVIII, Plates 65 to 69 below). Celts are usually used for woodworking of various kinds. The small size of many of them suggests that they were used for rather fine woodworking. Given the proximity of Gawra to the hills of Kurdistan, wood was undoubtedly available locally for fuel, for building materials, and for furniture or decorative detailing. The use for worked wood in looms is suggested below. All save the adzes are made of dense ground stone, a very fine basalt, limestone, granite, or marble. The hammers are mostly made of basalt. Two of the adzes from Level XI/XA (1315 from XI and 1770 from XA) are registered as bronze, but appear in later notes to be copper, perhaps hardened with a very small amount of arsenic.

The various stones used to manufacture these ground stone tools and seals must have been extracted from mountain sources. Basalt is a volcanic product, limiting its range of sources to the uppermost ranges of the Tigris River. Utilizing its passage into the Jebel Maqlub, Gawrans must have traded, extracted, or received them from satellite communities. The presence of similar materials elsewhere in the steppe and alluvium indicates exchange via the piedmont, Western Iranian Plateau, or southeastern Turkish hills. Until Gawra VIII, little evidence exists for on-site manufacture of stone tools.[3]

Based on the presence of tools for this activity, cloth making appears to have been an essential activity. The primary objects for use in processing animal fibers (wool) found at Gawra are spindle whorls (Plates 74–76). These small ball-shaped objects, pierced in the center, are placed near the base of a

stick to twirl combed wool into yarn. To process such yarn into cloth requires weaving in ancient times. Weaving activity is also indicated by the presence of what are listed under "bobbins/loom weights and loom parts." Examples of "bobbins/loom parts" for Level XI/XA include two loom base pieces in Locus 196 (1121, Tobler 1950: Plate LXXXVIIb) from area 39, 1120 from room 51. In addition, there are a set of loom weights ("ballistas"), 1131 (Tobler 1950: Plate 2LXXXVIIb) and 1112[4] (Tobler 1950: Plate LXXXXVIa7) from Square 6K, 1122 (Tobler 1950: Plate CLVII 69) and 1123 (Tobler 1950: Plate CLVII, 68) from Square 7Q, and 1733 from Square 4K.

The rest of the clay objects in the list below, according to Tobler, were used for "cultic" purposes. They are of two types. One is a clay object with a flat base and two projections (called "horns" by Tobler) with pierced holes along the base (1122 Tobler 1950: Plate CLVII, 69). The other is a smooth clay object with a flat base and a centrally placed knob on top, also pierced at the top of the knob and along the base (1123, Tobler 1950: Plate CLVII, 68). Tobler asserts that these items are cult objects presumably because a "horned" terra-cotta object with holes drilled through the base was found in situ by a door of the "altar" room of the Shrine (Rooms 801 to 804) of VIIIA (see Speiser 1929: Figures 16 and 89). A similar object was found on the Eye Temple platform of Jemdet Nasr Period Tell Brak (Mallowan 1947: Plate XXXIX). Object 1123 is so classified because it was found in primary context clearly associated with 1122. The assertion that all these objects are cultic is problematic for two reasons. First, the assumption that every item found in a building with ritual use (even in primary context) is cultic is not well founded. In the early historic Ur III period, a building in a clearly identified temple compound at Ur was a weaving shop (Forbes 1964, IV: 8). Rooms in the Temple Oval at Early Dynastic Khafaje included a stone grinding shop, copper workshop, bakery and so forth (Frankfort 1954:44). Second, even if the "horns" reported by Speiser in VIII are cultic in function, the objects in XI are different in size and shape. The set of terra-cotta "cultic" horns from Brak are much more like the Gawra VIII objects, just as a series of "horned" objects from Nuzi, identified by Starr as bases for vertical looms (Starr 1939, II: Plate 118, a2 and b2) are more like the XI clay items. The Nuzi and Gawra artifacts appear to share the same pattern of drilled holes with the Nuzi loom bases. Diamant and Rutter (1969) suggest that these and other similar objects were stands to hold up large pots, which could be ritual even if the objects themselves are not.

In fact, Bache proposed in locus sheet 196 that one of these "horned objects," the one found in area 39 (1121) with ballistas, was a loom stand. The shape of it and the holes do conform to one part of a horizontal loom, the base of the rod heddle (see Forbes 1964, Volume IV, Figure 32, A, 2). The rod heddle would sit between the projections as Forbes' example sits on two stones and the holes would be used to secure that immobile piece with thongs or string. The other cult object (1123) would also fit such a scheme, as a base for the breast-beam of the same type of loom (see Starr 1939, volume II, Plate 30,b for a horizontal loom of the 1930s with clay bases in action). Other objects found in association with the proposed loom bases in area 39 and room 51 of Square 6K of Phase XI support this interpretation. In area 39 a set of seven spindle whorls (all under field number (1555–1563) and the "ballistas" interpreted below as bobbins were recovered in primary context with the loom base. The proposed loom base in room 51 was found in good association with an object that the register lists as a crude hut statue, but which Tobler himself proposes is a loom weight (1112). As loom weights are most common on vertical looms, the presence of a vertical loom weight may suggest the presence of more than one loom in room 51. In fact, the set of artifacts found in primary context in area 39, room 51, and room 71 suggest the existence of weaving shops in that part of the mound (see Forbes 1964: Figure 27 for a model of an Egyptian weaving shop based on wall paintings, also below). A similar collection of items is found in Qalinj Agha III, room 8 (Abu al-Soof 1969:18, also Figure XI, 1 & 2); namely, a horned object, loom weight, pounders, celts, many obsidian scrapers and knives and a few figurines. These items at Gawra are therefore listed in the bobbins/loom weights category of Table 4.1.

The category "needles" includes objects what could serve in the production of clothing (e.g., 546, 2313, Plate 71). "Pins" in the adornment category could be needles, but are more likely to have been used to secure garments (e.g., 2730, 2750, Plate 77).

Another set of artifacts that Tobler (1950:173) saw as possible cult items are what the excavators called variously "dish molds," "mullers," or "weights." These items are large (237 mm in diameter) clay items (Tobler 1950: Plate LXXXIII,d) with "flat bases, solid hemispherical bodies, surmounted by flattened knobs." The one example from stratum IX in The University of Pennsylvania Museum (2056 Plate 81) is extremely heavy (far too heavy for a loom weight) and has a rough gritty bottom. How exactly these items would function as either dish molds (see Hodges 1976: Figure 2, 5 for dish mold) or cultic items is unclear. As grinders ("mullers"), however, they appear well suited for separating seeds from stalks or other course grinding tasks. Another point in favor of their being grinders is that their construction is much like the broken sherd, grit and clay "cement" used for querns in Level IX. Examples from XI/XA and IX are therefore counted as mullers under "grinding tools" in summary tables.

Palettes, flat ground stone objects with a slight flare on their long sides, certainly were used in pottery making or other clay items that are painted (for example, 614, Plate 66). Tobler (1950:207) notes the presence of flakes of paint on them when they were initially excavated, and grave 7–68 contained a palette, pottery smoothers, and burnishers (see Speiser 1939: Plate 10, 2). Illustrations of these tools and pottery molds can be found in Hodges (1976: Figure 2, no. 1, 2, and 5). At the same time, the possibility that some palettes were used to mix pigments for makeup should be left open. As illustrated, the most commonly recovered burnisher in the ancient Near East is a rounded sherd. Because the excavators saved only the most distinctive sherds, the number of smoothers recorded is probably smaller than the number that existed, if all sherds had been saved. The one pebble cited below as a smoother is of the right size and weight and is painted with dots, indicating some special function (if not as a polisher then perhaps as a toy). Excavators also unearthed bone burnishers or smoothers. They are in curved flattened pieces (e.g., 1, 4 (XII), 537 (XIA), Plate 70, XIA, 6–170 (545, 548 (XIA), 1098 (XI), 2318 (VIII), Plate 71). Potsherds are also ground too smooth to use for this purpose (e.g., 2353). The other most significant pottery tools are, of course, kilns, which excavators found (intact in Level IX).

The "domestic" section of the tables contains a mixed bag of categories. Under the heading "serving items" are ceramic vessels with fine paste and often elaborate surface decoration. These ceramics were probably used in serving food or drink. All cups and beakers are included in this category. Open and fine ware bowls are also included. The "serving" jars include double mouth jars (thought to be used to serve drinks with reed straws (see J. Oates 1982:207), small bottles, small-handled jars, bowls with spouts, stone jars, and generally very fine ware jars. Again, these vessels were probably for serving, although like the silver chalice in Catholic ritual or the beakers of Medieval European royal courts, they may have been used in ritual contexts. Open bowls of cruder wares, not counting Wide Flower Pots, have been separated out as "utilitarian bowls." This category has some justification in that such bowls have been found in contexts where serving bowls would be less likely to have been found. At the same time, it is not possible at this point to say with certitude what activity they were used for. Ladles, spoons, and scoops of ceramic and bone are also included under the heading of serving dishes (e.g., 14, 1106, Figure 80).

The food preparation and storage category includes cooking pots, strainers, and sieves, spatulas and large storage jars, an example of which was found in room 30 containing carbonized grain.[5] The crude, flare-sided Wide Flower Pot is placed between the two categories. The excavators called them "dishes" and they may have been used as such. However, the Wide Flower Pots appear to have a variety of uses. They are found as containers for baby burials, as lids on infant jar burials, and, in Level XII, as industrial mixing bowls with melted bitumen (e.g., 239, Plate 5). Proveniences other than burials include caches with other pottery (stacked up, in VIII in a room filled with grain off the main hall of the large western building of VIIIC and B), in open areas of the site, in domestic and public rooms. Their most intriguing provenience is described in locus sheet 123, referring to Square 7O, Phase XA: "dish . . . found inverted, covering a few stones and sherds, 2 small fragments of burnt animal bones and an animal tooth." This practice of placing bowls upside-down over magical items is known at Nippur (Zettler 1993). Whether Wide Flower Pots were ration bowls like the Classic Uruk-styled Beveled Rim Bowl or an all-purpose dish is unclear. They occur with some frequency, but from what can be gleaned Beveled Rim Bowls at Susa, Nineveh, or Uruk/Warka occur in much greater numbers. Also included in food preparation are grinding stones (e.g., 597, Plate 65, 613, Plate 66) and ovens.

Two other bowl types cross functional lines as well. One type is the double or channel rim bowl. Rysánek (1989) suggests that they are for making alcoholic beverages. On the other hand, such bowls are used to soak wool before processing it into yarn (Forbes 1964, IV). One was in fact found in street area 39 by weaving shop room 51 in Phase XI. However, the proveniences of others suggest an altogether different function as an ablution bowl. One, for example, was set into the floor or in the case of 1448 (Plate 14) into a bench. In the Phase VIIIA temple complex one is set in a bitumen-coated floor in room 832 and in VIIIC the same type is set in the court west of room 801. The inner wall of these vessels is pierced at the level of the channel (e.g., 795, Plate 9, 2227 Plate 19) to catch liquids before they overflow or to recycle splashes. As such, depending on their find context, I classify them as food preparation, manufacture, or ritual items.

The most ubiquitous jar type, the so-called small jar, also has a variety of purposes. Some of these jars are surely used for containing small personal items such as jewels, salves, or makeup. However, like Wide Flower Pots, these jars seem to have a variety of uses. Esin (1976, Plate 58,2) illustrates use of such a jar to transport Canaanite flint blades. A similar jar from Gawra Level XII contained gold beads. It may not be coincidental, therefore, that the circumferences of the necks of these jars appear to match that of a few of the more complete sealings from around the necks of jars. They are placed in the category "miscellaneous" (misc.), because they have a number of different functions.

The "adornment" sub-category of domestic includes buttons, beads, pendants and amulets, pins,

and rings, which presumably were items of personal ornamentation (Plates 72–73). In VIII, rings are added. Included as well will be makeup ("kohl") jars. Hooks and wires may be included here as well.

Among the materials from which these beads, pendants, and (in graves) rosettes are made include gold, silver, and lapis lazuli. All are again exotic to this area and all are found at Uruk-Warka (Algaze 1993:77), but in general are found in small amounts. The seemingly rich gold of Gawran tombs (see Appendix) and the small finds of it in the South would suggest not administered, but down-the-line trade (see Chapter 1, note 2).

The third set of categories includes "amusements, ritual, symbolic" and military." Under the category ritual are censers and bowl stands (or in VIII, braziers), because such items appear in seal designs showing some kind of ritual performance and in archaeological contexts in probable ritual contexts.

The use of the third ritual object, the so-called hut statue is still in question (see Plates 82–84). These artifacts have hollow, bell shaped bases (as if they were to be placed on staffs), indented bottoms (often with bitumen traces in the indent), or flat bases. All have double-voluted rings at the top. The two from tomb 31 are made of stone, but all the others are made of clay. Tobler counts a number of clay objects with a single or double hole, flat bottom, and more indefinite shape among this category. The name "hut statue" is derived from Andrae's theory that these items represent a Sumerian, reed hut idol, which he proposes is the model for the Ionian column (Speiser 1935a:99–100). Tobler (1950:171) rejects this theory because most are made of badly fired clay, because they are not found in buildings he defines as temples, and because they occur too frequently to be the major icon of the site. If they are connected to the Sumerians, why are none found in Early Dynastic levels in the South or after Level IX at Gawra? Rather, Tobler proposes that they are all loom weights. The irregularly shaped, square-bottomed objects (see Tobler 1950, Plate CLVII, 66, 67) and perhaps the stone "huts" in tomb 31 are most likely loom weights, as Tobler contends (one was even found in the context of a loom stand set on a floor of Square 6K).

However, like other categories of artifact, different shape or size may imply differing function, in this case a symbolic one, secular or divine. Evidence suggests that the regularly formed, hollow base hut statues may have been used by persons with ritual or administrative social identities. The symbol of the double voluted eyes occurs in a clearly religious-ritual context at Tell Brak in the Eye Temple. The walls of the Eye Temple were partially covered with copper sheeting impressed with eyes (Mallowan 1947:151). In and around the temple and its platform were literally thousands of "eye symbols" of stone and terra-cotta, including at least two "hut shaped" clay versions (Mallowan 1947: Plate XXV, 10 and 11). At Arslantepe stamped eyes decorate the walls of the Late Uruk or LC5 period (Frangipane 1997:64f.), and excavators recovered at least one example of a possible hut statue in culturally Late Chalcolithic Level VII (Frangipane 1993: Figure 7). In addition, a hollow based hut statue was found in the large, well-planned burnt building of Grai Resh II (Lloyd 1940), which was almost the same in plan as the tripartite house of Gawra X where a hut was also found. A hut-like clay item was found in Uruk levels at Tell Brak (Oates 1984), but the one illustrated has a square bottom and looks like the irregular "huts" designated as loom weights. Hollow-based huts are also found at Qalinj Agha (Abu Al-Soof 1969). They appear in Level II, room 12 with figurines (common at Gawra as well), with many obsidian blades, a celt, sealings and pounders. Excavators found another hut statue in room 16 with an animal figurine, loom weight, ladle, spindle whorls, ax and blades, etc., but if it is the one pictured (Abu Al-Soof 1969: Figure IX, 2), it is more likely a loom weight.

The image of the double-voluted object appears frequently in Uruk Period iconography. An Uruk seal impression from Tepe Sharafabad (Wright et al. 1980, Figure 6, 9) shows two men with staves drinking from a jar with straws, while another man looks at an object with two volutes very much in the shape of a hut statue. A seal impression from Gawra XI/XA (1578, Plate 43), found in the same square (6Q) as a hollow based hut statue and censers (incense burners) illustrates a single double voluted object. It has either four appendages or sits on a platform like a North Syrian stone carving of two double voluted images on a platform (Mallowan 1947: Plate XXVI, 1). This might explain the bitumen on the bases of indented versions. Another sealing from Gawra X (2023, Plate 52) illustrates a dog and two double voluted objects from a square due southeast of the main temple. An early Bronze Age wall painting from Tell Ghassul (Nunn 1988: Plate 49) draws the double volute as a mask for religious ritual of some kind.

The find spots of the Gawra hollow-based huts are not as random as Tobler implies. From Gawra Levels XI/XA to IX hut statues appear in ten excavation squares (5M, 6J, 6Q, 5O of Phase XI, 7K of Phase XA, 11K and 5J of X and 9O, 9M and 6O of Phase IX). In Squares 6J, 5O, and 7K more than one appears, but when the exact location is known, they are not in the same context. In Level IX, all three are found not in but close to the central temple. Their precise find spot is unknown, but they occur with figurines, game pieces, sealings with complex designs, weights and a variety of tools, especially obsidian blades. In Level X one was found in the large, seemingly public building in Square 11K with various domestic items (serving dishes, preparation pots, small jars). Registries cite

another in Square 5J of Level X in or near a very regularly planned tripartite house also associated with domestic items (cups, clay model, two spindle whorls), with numerous figurines, and with one of six concentrations of seals and sealings. The XA and XI phases of Level XI/XA contain the largest number of hut statues. Three huts are found in or near the large northern building called "the Fortress" in field notes. This building had a density of craft tools, serving items, and storage jars, as well as a censer and three concentrations of large military ballistas. In Square 6J, in or near the walled courts by the southern entrance to the site, hut statues were found in room 35 (by then a trash dump) along with figurines. In room 31 more were recovered with a serving jar and preparation pot, and yet another was buried in enclosure 27 among craft tools, a wash bowl, storage jar, and large collection of sealings. In Square 5M of XI, huts are found near an oven and a number of figurines, perhaps recently fired. The last place in XI/XA that excavators retrieved hut statues was in Square 7K of the XA phase. This appears to be a domestic or craft context with a spindle whorl, celt, pendant, beaker, and two naturalistic sealings. In Level XIA, two of the three hut statues appear in or near the Round House and the other in an open court near the eastern edge of the mound. The two illustrated as being from XII (Tobler 1950:LXXXVI) are probably both loom weights.

None of these lines of evidence can confirm a specifically ritual purpose for the hut statue. Objects used in ceremonies are among the most difficult to identify, because without some written evidence such ideological aspects of life are virtually unknowable. However, taken together, the find spots, characteristics, and associations appear to outline a circumstantial case for a symbolic meaning.

The "symbolic" half of the ritual and symbolic table includes figurines, models, and gaming pieces (Plates 80–84). A significant number of animal and human figurines were recovered from Levels XII to VIII at Tepe Gawra. Their exact function is unclear (see Voigt 1983:186–195). They may be used in apotropaic rituals, such as the first millennium B.C. namburbu (see Oppenheim 1977:210f.). They may just as easily have been toys. The same applies to miniature vessels and model axes or chariots, although their use as toys seems very likely. What are called "gaming pieces" in the literature are often counting tokens placed in hollow clay message balls called bullae (Schmandt-Besserat 1979). Although counting tokens were found at Gawra (a few are illustrated in Tobler 1950: Plate LXXXIV, a, second row, all from room K of the Round House, also b, XCVI, a)), most of the Gawra "gaming pieces" seem to be for games (e.g., 1188, Plate 66; 1899, Plate 67; 563a and b, Plate 80). A number of such pieces, crafted in human and animal shapes, was recovered (two of them together) from Level XV and XVI (Tobler 1950: Plate LXXXIV, b). As Tobler (1950:205) points out, most from Level XI/XA upward are made from lightweight, easily worked stones and are very standardized in shape and size. One such set was found in a child's hand in grave locus 181. The size of those in Levels XI to VIII and their shapes makes them unlikely candidates for tokens, because bullae (sealed clay envelopes) would have to be huge to accommodate them. It is also unlikely that carefully crafted stone tokens would be used regularly, as tokens are unlikely to be returned after a use. At the same time, these items might be small weights for balance scales. They are assigned as gaming pieces, but the alternate possibilities must be kept in mind.

The weapons section of the tables includes ballistas, mace heads, battle axes, a lance point, and arrowheads. Maceheads with hollowed centers appear to be symbolic or actual weapons e.g., 2429, Plate 69; Tobler 1950: Plate XCVIIa). Similar artifacts are commonly carried by rural dwellers in modern Iran to fend off dogs (Dyson, personal communication). The ones from XII to IX appear to be finished products. In VIII, most are partially finished (as are some hammers) in that their holes are not drilled through and edges polished, implying that they were being manufactured at Gawra.

Also included are so-called ballistas. These have been thought to be sling projectiles for warfare or hunting (Stout 1977). Many probably did serve this function. Another proposed function of small ballistas is children's toys (Jasim 1985:62). As with other artifact types, however, their range of use appears wider than that. Within the ballista artifact type are three kinds of clay and stone items. Two, the most common variety, are ovoid (like American footballs, e.g., 1897, Plate 67) and come in large (about 150 mm) and small (about 60 mm) varieties, and the others are cigar-shaped (Tobler 1950: Plate LXXXVII, a). The cigar-shaped ones would not, as Tobler (1950:174) notes, be useful for projectiles or even as clay nails.

The location of the ballistas seems the best guide to their function. One such function is as braces in firing and storing pottery. Locus sheet 148 from Square 4O of Level XIA describes a two-layer nest of pots (including Wide Flower Pots and simple round-bottomed bowls) with "ballistas [scattered] here and there, hither and thither." The implication is that whether these were drying or being pit-fired, the ballistas served to brace pottery vessels and separate them during production. It is tempting to impute a similar function to the large cache of cigar-shaped ballistas in Square 4M of Level XI, as they are near the set of ovens and the previously unpublished large kiln in Square 5M (see Chapter 3). On the other hand, the cigar shaped ones could be a convenient form for storing levigated clay (Dyson, personal communication).

Another use of small ballistas is as packing in construction. Locus sheet 120 illustrates the use of a nest of small ballistas to brace the side of libn tomb 45, intrusive in Square 6O of Level XI, against an adjoining wall. Yet one more use may be as some sort of bobbin (see Wulff 1966: Figure 268, lower right, for bobbins of the same approximate shape and size). The cache of small ovoid ballistas in Square 6K of Phase XI rest under what Bache interprets as the base of a horizontal loom stand. Since that square and room 51 in which they and the loom base were located are in a probable manufacturing or domestic room block in the middle of the site, their storage for defense seems unlikely. On the other hand, the large ballistas stored in rooms 63 and 62 of the large northern tripartite building of XI/XA and in room 66 of its adjoining building would be likely candidates for sling missiles. One of the ground stone ballistas from Level XI/XA (1174) is associated with those buildings. The small size of this stone ballista (56 mm) suggests it was not used as a weapon, although the important factor in ballista use may be shape and weight, in which case both the smaller stone and larger clay ballistas would be lethal weapons against animals or men. In short, the type "ballista" appears to contain weapons, pottery braces, construction materials, and bobbins, depending on their size, material, and shape. Counts of ballistas are distributed among the categories accordingly.

The last part of the tables, "miscellaneous," contains categories such as spheres, tokens, and weights. The spheres are found in both clay and ground stone. The ground stone spheres are roughly the same size (about 20 mm in diameter). Ancients carefully polished them to be evenly rounded. Whether they, too, are game pieces, weights or serve some other function is not obvious. Weights for scales or perhaps for looms are relatively rare at Gawra. Tobler (1950:206) did not find any convincing evidence of a standard system of weights among the "scale weights," although this does not preclude their use as such.

The last category of functional artifacts is the largest, that is, seals and sealings (Plates 24–64). These stone seals and clay sealings number in the hundreds and are clear indicators of the control of raw materials, finished products, and other restricted goods (see Rothman 1994a and b).

The foregoing describes the artifacts for which a reasonable function can be inferred (a very few additional categories will be added for Level VIII). A few clay items are recorded in the registers or chits for which no specific use is apparent to this author. Also, some potsherds cannot be classified as to their functions, although painted and impressed ones are counted among serving bowls below.

A last point concerns metalworking tools. So far, metalworking has not been mentioned as a category for craft tools. Some metal tools were recovered from

Gawra Levels XII to VIII. I found a hunk of what looked like copper ore in the storage room. However, there is no clear evidence for metal manufacturing on the Gawra mound until third millennium Gawra VI times. At sites with stylistic connections with Gawra, especially Norşuntepe (Hauptmann 1975) and Tepecik (Esin 1975), evidence of metallurgy in the form of slag and molds were found. Still, it is possible that among the hammers and other stone tools found at LC1–3 Gawra, some may have been used in metallurgy, especially for copper working (see copper-working tool kits in Wulff 1966:25f.).

As will be evident in Chapter 5, some activities cannot be revealed through a particular tool type, but are detectable through a combination of artifacts and structural features. For example, as noted above, finds of a set of unfinished mace heads suggest mace head manufacture, notes on finds of grain represent storage, etc.

Summaries and Interpretation

Tables 4.1 and 4.2 include raw counts and percentages of the various functional artifacts.[6] These are to be taken as somewhat impressionistic summaries of the activities on the Gawra mound during each level and phase of the fourth millennium B.C. They remain no more than impressionistic because, first, the sample of artifacts cannot be considered truly representative. As I wrote in Chapter 2, most workers were unsupervised and the excavators were not aware of modern recovery techniques.[7] Second, some of the criteria used to construct categories are open to debate. For example, the vessels listed under "storage jars" were those that were of larger size (usually 250 mm or more in height) and were undecorated. These criteria fit storage jars from sites where the contents of storerooms are well documented. However, some jars that field notes from Tepe Gawra list as having had stored grain are smaller than "storage jars" and sometimes decorated. Similarly, depending on how one chooses to do so, counts using potsherds can be done in a variety of ways. Although I attempt to be consistent in that case in separating out decorated bowls (serving vessels) from cups from cruder bowls, I suspect that each time I recount them there would be a small difference. With those limitations in mind, here are the raw counts.

Functional Size

Tables 4.1 and 4.2 sketch the functional size of Tepe Gawra from Levels XII to VIII. The total numbers of artifacts per level vary considerably XII = 484, XIA/B = 583, XI = 572, XA = 131, X = 168, IX = 217, and VIII = 571.[8] However, there are both marked similarities and differences in the functional size of each level and sub-level phase.

Not surprisingly, each level had a significant number of artifacts that signified domestic life, including items of personal adornment, games, toys, and food preparation items. In most levels food-serving artifacts constitute roughly 63 to 89 percent of food-related artifacts, and preparation artifacts constitute 11 to 36 percent.

In terms of craft production, every level under study here had remains of pottery making, cloth making, wood working, and flintknapping tools. In Levels XII, XIA/B, XI/XA and X cloth making tools are especially prominent. Levels IX and VIII show markedly fewer spindle whorls and other cloth related tools, in terms of both percent and raw counts, than the others. On the other hand, the number of pottery or ceramic making tools in Levels IX and VIII constitute a much larger percentage of the whole than in other levels. The same applies to woodworking. Levels IX and VIII both show evidence of considerable processing of obsidian and flint blades. Excavators recovered a lithic flaker in Level VIII. In Chapter 5 bead or seal cutting workshops will be proposed for Levels IX and VIII. A ground stone making craft is also evidenced by the many partially finished hammers and mace heads in VIII.

As noted in Chapter 1, few sickle blades are listed for any level. These figures on their own probably represent an underestimate of the importance of food production vis-a-vis other productive activities. It does, however, highlight that Gawra was more than a village during the entire time under investigation here.

Artifacts probably used in rituals of a religious or quasi-religious nature are listed for all levels. In fact, most levels have considerable numbers of ritual artifacts.[9] The lowest number of these items comes from Level XII. This may represent the fact that in other levels, formal temples were recovered, but not in XII. However, Level XIA/B without a formal temple still yielded many ritual items. The presence of large, formal temples in Levels XI/XA, X, IX, and VIII certainly speak of an audience for religious ritual greater than needed to service the numbers of people living on the exposed area of the mound (see Chapter 5 for estimates of population).

An activity not clearly evidenced in the tables of artifacts, but implied by the numbers of artifacts and by the raw materials from which they are made, is exchange or trade. The number of cloth-working tools as well as lithic blades and wood working tools does imply that these activities were more than domestic crafts. Again, this will be clearer in the following chapter, where the town plans are examined.

The question that is more daunting is how far away these exchange connections go. In terms of receiving raw materials, obsidians at Gawra come from as far away

Table 4.1 Artifacts by Function, Levels XII–VIII

		XII	XIAB	XI	XA	X	IX	VIII
Craft tools								
Farming	Sickles	2	1	1	0	0	4	1
Cloth making	Spindle whorls	96	122	101	3	16	10	46
	Bobbins	0	1	2*	1	1	1	14
	Loom parts	2	4	4	2	0	0	0
	Fine knives	5**	4	10**	1	2**	6	29****
	Needles	0	2	0	0	0	0	13
	Awls	5	1	4	0	2	1	4
	Utilitarian bowls	8	5	6	2	1	2	2
Wood working	Celts chisels	37	29	30	7	8	7	28
	Adzes	1	3	1	2	0	1	0
	Scrapers	0	1	2	0	0	0	0
	Hammers axes	6	9	9	2	2	11	6
	Heavy blades	9**	7	13**	3	2**	25	74****
Pottery makers	Smoother burnisher	0	1	1	1	0	6	10
	Palettes	3	1	1	0	1	2	1
	Kilns	?	2?	1	0	1	1	?
Lithic industry	Cores, flakers	8	3	3	0	1	3	4, 1
Domestic items								
Serving items	Cups/beakers	8	6	16	8	8	4	7
	Plates/bowls	56***	24	28	11	8	10	15
	Jars/spout jars	10	8	17	7	6	12	23
	Ladles/spoons	1	2	3	1	2	2	4
Food preparation	Cook pots	2	4	3	3	1	2	3
	Spatula	4	3	3	0	1	0	0
	Grinders	3	10	9	3	1	7	19
	Strainer	0	0	2	2	1	1	1
	Channel rim bowl	0	6	4	0	1	1	0
Storage	Jars	9	4	5	1	1	1	3
	Wide Flower Pot	12	20	6	4	2	8	9
	Small jars	10	8	18	3	5	5	5
Adornment	Pendants/amulets	17	15	19	3	6	10	22
	Beads	13*	9*	9*	6*	1	11*	22*
	Buttons/rings	3	4	5	0	0	3	6
	Wire hooks	0	0	0	0	0	0	2
	Kohl jar	2	1	0	0	0	0	0
	Pins	3	9	7	1	0	0	1
Games	Game pieces	3	11	11	1	1	6	1
	Models, pipes	3	2	2	1	1	1	8
Rituals	Censers	0	0	2	0	0	0	1
	Bowl stands	1	1	4	1	1	1	2
	Ablution bowls	0	0	1	1	0	2	4
	Hut statues	2	9	8	2	2	3	0
	Horns	0	0	0	1	0	2	2
	Altars	0	0	2	1	1	1	2
	Figurines	10	24	27	4	9	6	15
Administrative	Sealings	71	113	114	18	44	14	107
	Seals	46	58	26	11	20	11	19
	Weights	2	3	2	1	1	6	7
	Spheres, tokens	1	15	14	8	4	2	4

(*continued*)

Table 4.1   (*continued*)

		XII	XIAB	XI	XA	X	IX	VIII
Military	Maceheads, battle axes	8	4	4	2	2	4	10
	Sling missiles	2	14	11*	2	1	1	4
	Arrow heads	0	0	1	0	0	0	8
	Metal weapons	0	0	0	0	0	0	2
Totals	2726	484	583	572	131	168	217	571

*occurrences, not total count
**unclear edges divided equally among fine and heavy
***fine, painted assigned to this category
****unused not counted

as Central Anatolia (G. Wright 1969). As noted in Chapter 1, a cache of obsidian blades was found at Late Uruk or LC 5 period Uruk-Warka, although some likely recipients of Transtigridian trade, for example, Tell Rubeideh or Tepe Farukhabad lacked the material. Until trace analysis studies are done, we are left at best with a guess. My guess is that cloth making and such activities as religious ritual are probably restricted to a

Table 4.2   Summary of Artifacts by Function Tables

	XII	XIA/B	XI/XA	X	IX	VIII
Pottery	1.6*	2	1.9	5.4	1.1	4.74
making	3**	4	4	2	9	11
Cloth	63.7	71	63.8	59.4	32.5	46.5
making	116	139	136	22	20	108
Wood	29.1	25	32.4	32.4	55	46.5
working	53	49	69	12	44	108
Flint	4.4	1.5	1.4	2.7	3.75	1.7
knapping (cores)	8	3	3	1	3	4
Farming	1.2	0.5	0.5	0.0	3.75	0.4
(sickles)	2	1	1	0	4	1
Production summary	182	196	213	37	80	232
Serving	89	63.5	72	86	71.7	68
vessels	75	40	75	24	28	49
Food	11	36.5	28	14	28.3	32
preparation	9	23	29	4	11	23
Food	84	63	104	28	39	72
Ritual	10	15.2	21.8	15.8	31.2	15
items	13	34	54	13	15	26
Administrative	90	84.8	78.2	84.2	68.8	85
tools	120	189	194	69	33	148
Symbolic	133	223	248	82	48	174

*percentage
**raw count

local sphere of interaction. An earlier study of the sources of sealing clays from fourth millennium B.C. Tepe Gawra (Rothman and Blackman 1990) suggested that early on in the millennium, the size of the Gawran polity was small and the center, Gawra, tried to restrict access to other polities and other centers. This was in part determined by the universally local and homogeneous sources of sealing clay. This more "closed"[10] polity would have led Gawran leaders earlier in the millennium to emphasize locally exchanged products and services. Gawra may have served as a port for down-the-line trade, but was not actively encouraging more regional exchanges. Results of that same study suggest a more open system; that is, there is evidence in VIII a greater number of clay sources for sealing, many presumably non-local. The emphasis on easily transportable materials like obsidian blades, and ground stone mace heads or hammers (perhaps also seals) in those levels implies a more regional exchange network.

The large number and percentage of administrative hardware, seals, and sealings, in all levels implies that all these functions were formally, socially structured. In particular, some element of oversight must have been involved. Even if the seals represented individuals, the need socially to mark property and restrict access implies social organizations that are more complex than simple communal modes of action.

According to my earlier studies of sealing practice at Gawra (Rothman 1994a, 1994b, Rothman and Blackman 1990), the key productive and ritual activities were administered. I need to re-emphasize here that no claim is made that this site was part of a state. It is necessary to think of administration not as direct and tight control by leaders with coercive power. Various groups, some probably based on kinship ties, would have the ability through their contribution to activities to restrict access to their products. The structure of that administration appears to have been generalized in XI; that is, groups identifying themselves by the subject of seal design were coordinating religious/leadership and craft production activities respectively. By VIII, a more centralized control system, vested in the comptrollers of a central warehouse appears to have replaced the earlier structure. Again, the sort of change the evidence of seals and sealings suggests is one where contact with the larger region is likely. Probably commercial exchange was part of that contact, though not necessarily.

Mapping the Functions of Tepe Gawra

What is clearly missing in the listing of functional artifacts above is the information available through the association of artifacts with one another in the context of particular buildings or open spaces. In the following chapter, that mapping will be done. Much more information on the evolution of the site is then possible. Despite the questioning of some (Forest

1999:147), I argue that careful use of chits and other information makes accurate mapping of artifacts quite possible. If Forest's assessment were correct, all use of distribution data would be outside archaeology's reach, as most artifacts are from secondary contexts. Only burned buildings could be analyzed, and those only if one could prove that they were in no way disturbed.

Tables 4.1 and 4.2 include only those artifacts that could be assigned a function. In constructing the distribution maps, all those artifacts can be included. Anything that appears to be in primary context ("on the floor," "on the pavement") will be included, of course. In addition, artifacts in secondary context will be included. These are artifacts with a specific find spot that in all probability places an artifact in the building where it was used or in a context where its association with other artifacts is likely. For example, in Phase XI, a room was clearly filled with trash after it went out of primary use. The trash, however, appears to have been wasters from a nearby kiln. The trash can tell us nothing about the use of the room, but it can tell us about ceramic production. Tertiary trash fill or construction debris will not be included as it can tell us nothing of either the function of the space or the association of artifacts.

The discrimination of primary, secondary, and tertiary contexts, though far from easy, is certainly possible for Levels XII, XIA/B, XI/XA, and some of X. For XI/XA and X the reasons for assigning artifacts to primary or secondary contexts are based on information from the chits and the elevation of artifacts compared to the stratigraphic sections. Contexts for artifacts from Levels IX and VIII, and the parts of X excavated by Speiser, are particularly hard to determine, except where field notes specify particular contexts. Attempts will be made to do so (again, the rationale is explained in detail in Rothman 1988: Chapters 5 and 6). In general, full explanation will not be offered here for assigning each set of artifacts to primary, secondary, or tertiary contexts. Chit information will help explain my choices. The exceptions to this rule will be discussed in footnotes.

Notes

1. Some signs of seeming wear may result from the long-term storage and then moving of these tools in large open, metal trays.

2. Based on a Chi^2 statistic run on SPSSX. The crosstab was a 7×7 table with retouch, striations, serrated edges, sheen, heavy use, little use, and no use on the x axis and angles of 12–25, 26–30, 31–33, 34–37, 38–42, 43–48, and 49–75 degrees on the y axis. The breakpoints for edge angle categories were determined by inspection of a histogram of frequencies of all edge angles. Chi^2 = 89.89698, degrees of freedom = 36. There is a less than .0001 probability of random association.

3. That Gawra could have been involved in such trade is possible, although the greatest hole in the argument of those who see direct trade as evidence of an economic empire is their

inability to show what was received in exchange. Textiles or food have been proposed (Algaze 1993:74), but at Gawra XI specialized cloth manufacture is evidenced in XI (see Chapter 4) and food was readily available and difficult to transport.

4. Artifact 1112 is registered as a "hut statue," but Tobler thinks (and I agree) it is a loom weight.

5. This information is from locus sheet 156.

6. The numbers here vary somewhat from Rothman (1988) because my conception of which artifacts belong where has changed and because the catalogues have been both expanded and cleaned up. For example, "small jars" is a category limited both by size and shape. Many "small jars" I listed in 1988 are now in "jars and spouted bowls" under serving.

7. It is still amazing the number of clay sealings that were recovered. That recovery rate gives me optimism that the sample is still sufficient for drawing reliable conclusions.

8. These counts seem surprisingly different. However, the low counts in Levels IX and X represent the intentional planning of the subsequent levels and a partial terracing and cleaning to prepare for it. Levels XII, XIA/B, and VIII were burned over much of their surfaces sealing in artifactual remains. Level XA is difficult to assess, as it represents a second phase of XI/XA and a gradual transition to X. Perhaps, it should best be considered along with XI, as some of the artifacts marked XI may be from XA. However, I deemed it sufficiently distinct to treat separately. Some sherds and objects not identified by function are not included in the summary counts of Tables 4.1 And 4.2.

9. Again we assume that figurines are not toys.

10. See Rothman and Blackman (1990) and Rothman (1988, 1994a) for explication of closed and opened polities as they relate to Gawra.

5

The Evolutionary History
of Tepe Gawra

This chapter presents the evolutionary history of Tepe Gawra from Levels XII to VIII. As noted above, the evolutionary history of Tepe Gawra will be described along three axes of variability: functional size, complexity, and centralization. As described in Chapter 1, functional size measures the number, kind, and intensity of the activities (and the functions those activities represent) that are performed by the residents of each site (Blanton 1976:252). As also discussed above, I will give particular attention to the potential of functions to serve populations outside the circle of the Gawra's residents. This I will do by contrasting goods likely to have been produced or transshipped from Gawra to more distant sites and those that seem more likely to have been produced for local use. This is intended to measure the role of Gawra in various networks and to judge the character of the network itself. Similarly, I will note products that were likely to have been produced or extracted elsewhere and imported into Gawra. Complexity and centralization will be described in terms of the degree of specialization and of the administrative structure of the people living at the site.

In many cases, the conclusions of my analyses are based on the best fit of data. Some aspects remain speculative. If the overall pattern draws a reasonable picture, that is as much as one could hope for given the problems with data recovery at Gawra and the more general problem of analyzing archaeological remains. For example, population estimates are a way of suggesting the relative population size. I certainly would not want to claim that these are more than rough estimates.

Patterns of Function
and Interpretation

Functional spaces in late fifth and early fourth millennia B.C. Tepe Gawra fall into a limited number of categories: temples and religious shrines, secular public buildings, private residences, craft production areas, and open spaces.

Determining the nature of functional spaces requires analysis of both artifactual contents and architectural structure. As argued above in Chapter 1, making assumptions about the function of buildings based on their architectural plan alone often leads to questionable conclusions. At the same time, not keeping in mind the traffic pattern and nature of the spaces created in buildings—depending only on tool kits—is equally risky.

A case in point is religious temples. The criteria I use to define temples are as follows. In order to be a temple a building must have:

1. a tripartite plan with easy access from front of the building (often through double doors or an open courtyard); 2. a sacrificial platform in the central room; 3. niches, usually in the back wall of the main room, facing the front doors; 4. a large basin, often double rimmed, sunk in the floor of one of the adjoining rooms, usually one near the back wall with relatively open space; 5. carefully plastered and painted white or red walls

I developed these criteria based on Gawra buildings, but Jawad (1965) also cites the first three criteria as good indicators of religious temples from the Ubaid to historic periods in Mesopotamia. Kubba (1987) also concurs. All three of us would add another criterion: few domestic or craft artifacts may be present. Using a partial set of criteria leads to erroneous assignments of function. For example, Speiser (1935a) lists three temples in Level VIII: the "East," "Central," and "Western" Temples. As I will demonstrate below, two of these buildings could be temples by their architectural form, but cannot be based on content and other criteria.

Other categories I listed above that Jawad and Kubba also list include public secular buildings and private houses or domiciles. According to Jawad (quoted in Kubba 1987:112), secular public buildings "appear to be comparatively large, strategically located, possess a coherent plan and are oriented similarly to existing contemporary temples. They differ, however, from the latter in lacking podia, in the location of their entrance, in the irregularity of one or more of their portions, and in containing (although perhaps few in number) an abundant variety of utilitarian objects."

Jawad also specifies house and "ordinary building" types. Houses, that is, private domiciles can be defined as buildings with a limited number of rooms (2–5), usually only one entrance, a traffic pattern in which one enters the largest room, and the other rooms are reached through adjoining doors in the center of walls. Cooking and serving utensils, as well as items of personal adornment and perhaps toys or other clearly domestic artifacts, are found there. Craft activities can and are evidenced in houses. What distinguish houses from specialized craft production buildings are the presence in the latter of larger spaces, and where specialization is evident, usually multiple entryways and large storage rooms. Few domestic goods would be found in specialized craft areas. In their ethnographic studies, Watson (1979), Kramer (1982), and Horne (1994) show how complex the distribution of functions is in real villages. Kramer (1982:99) learned that the first room built in a new house is the kitchen with its oven. Next is the living room. This will be a key to counting houses. Specific room sizes listed by Watson (1979:294) are less useful, as the traditions of house construction change rather dramatically at Gawra. General proportions may be good guides to room function, however.

As to population size on each level and sub-level phase, I will offer estimates based on both Kramer's per house estimate (1982: Table 4.4) of 9.4–10.9 persons per house and Watson's estimate of 3.2 persons per room (Watson 1979:296).

Plazas are probably functional spaces if the town plan clearly creates these areas as open spaces and places them near buildings that perform public functions. A number of open plazas may well have been used as marketplaces, although this use is among the most difficult to verify.

For the levels that were completely exposed and, less reliably, for partially excavated levels, functional spaces in the categories mentioned above are structured into a limited number of configurations. In one configuration, temples are placed at the southeast quadrant of the mound, and their corners are oriented to cardinal points. This is the case in Levels VIII and XI/XA at Gawra. When the temple is in the southeast, a public building—perhaps a chief's house or something like a mudhif or community house—is placed in the northeast quadrant. As Jawad argues, the doors of the public secular buildings do not face the same direction as the doors of the contemporary temples. A second public building may exist in the west with this configuration, as in the case of VIIIB or VIIIA and as might be the case in Phase XI of Level XI/XA (see Chapter 3). Craft activities or larger scale storage facilities in this configuration are placed in the central area of the mound.

The other configuration, evident in IX and X, is to place the temple in the very center of the mound. A chiefly or public building then rests in the southwest quadrant. Craft activities are spread out in the north central and southern parts of the mound.

In XII, the pattern is quite different than any other. Tobler claims that there are no temples in XII (Tobler 1950:25f.). No building completely fits the definition of a temple, but there are ritual elements in some of the buildings on the eastern flank of the site. The religious elements of these buildings are much like the northeast building in VIII, which appears to have had a shrine on the first floor of a chiefly building. Usually, the building with the White Room is thought of as a chiefly house or community center, a mudhif, but part of the building may have served a religious function.

Level XIA/B has yet another configuration. Tobler (1950:23f.) suggests that the building in Squares 5O/Q and 6Q (rooms 72–77) is a temple, but by content and other characteristics, it does not fit the criteria for temples. The Round House that dominates the XIA phase of Level XIA/B does not fit any a model of any other building at Gawra at all, and I will argue below that it was built to serve as a fortress.

These differing patterns are important, I contend, because they represent an underlying social structuring of the roles the site played. What are emphasized through physical centrality are often the most critical functions of the time when the levels were occupied. The plans of XII and XIA/B suggest a transitional phase when the more formal patterns of Levels XI/XA to VIII had not yet been established.

Oates (1986:381) sees the time between Gawra XIII and Gawra XI/XA as a break in its building and town planning traditions, proposing that another major center was carrying on the traditions, and they were later re-introduced to the Gawrans. That no temple has been recovered at all from Level XII or XIA/B (see below) certainly had an effect on town plans. At the same time, Gawra XIII, with its large, well-planned public buildings, may indeed represent a break in the site's functional size, or more accurately, its functional focus.

Level by Level Analysis (Figure 5.1)

Level XII

Our understanding of Level XII comes from approximately 40 percent of the original surface of the mound at its elevation. That 40 percent gives one the impression of a bustling, small town.[1] Sickle blades were found, suggesting Gawra's residents farmed, but the number is surprisingly small, and none were found in primary or secondary contexts.

A visitor to the town of Tepe Gawra at the time when Level XII was occupied would probably enter the mound along the narrow curved street of the northeast mound in Square 4Q (Figure 3.6). From the excavators' vantage point we know that this was probably the route taken by whichever group attacked and destroyed the Level XII settlement. Evidence of the final days of Gawra XII include a skeleton of a child sprawled in the entry street with a stone in its back, other skeletons found sprawled face down or huddled in the corners of small rooms. All suggest death during a military attack (Tobler 1950:25–26), as does evidence of the large fires that burned much of the town. As Stein's theory (1994a) predicts, this is the first period in which wealth finance and chiefly rank based on the import of exotic materials is evident in the region. With this economic development came extended contacts beyond the site over a wide area and often violent competition for access to traded goods.

Functional Size

Along the street to the right as a visitor would have entered Gawra XII, a solid wall is all that would be visible. This wall obscured a series of small storerooms, workshops, or small houses (Figure 5.2). Stored objects, mostly ground stone tools (an ax, celts, and mace heads), filled these rooms.

The significance of these rooms may be better explained by what lay beyond their doors to the west. As Plate 2a illustrates, the courtyard was filled with clay bins, whose original height can only be guessed at. Unfortunately, little care was taken in collecting material from around the bins or even fully recording them. However, coupled with the contents of the small rooms

along the entry street, a visitor who managed to get around to the west side of these buildings would likely have seen an area where craft activities were carried out or large numbers of goods were sorted.

A large structure lay on the other side of the bins (Figure 5.3). Compared to the cramped quarters of entry road rooms, the building in Squares 6O and 6S (extending farther to the west) had multiple entryways and sizable rooms. Rather than tools and manufactured objects, this building's remains were primarily serving vessels, especially the functional equivalent of Beveled Rim Bowls, the Wide flower Pot. The function or functions of these crude vessels have been much debated (see Chapter 3), but their presence in numbers suggests either a workshop or storage facility, from which rations may have been distributed. Two sizable rooms in the building complex were possibly storerooms without ground level doors. This same kind of storeroom appears throughout Levels XII-VIII. They were probably entered through the roof. Little other evidence suggests that this building was a home, but it may well have served as a focal place for individuals working in the open courtyard with bins. No sealings were found here, but the seal found had the same pattern as one of the sealings from the small room complex to its east, suggesting a connection among those who used the larger building.

Certainly, the entry road functioned to shield visitors from the activities to the west of the road, but focused their attention on the building known as the White Room (Plate 1b) building because of its white plastered walls (Figures 5.4 and 5.5) in Squares 4O and 5O (Tobler 1950:27). A wall extending from the northwest corner of the building and shielding it from the wind and the remaining buildings created the only open plaza in the excavated portion of the Gawra XII town.

The White Room building proves a bit difficult to assess as a functional space, because it is unclear which artifacts are in primary context. The building was badly burned at the end of the Level XII occupation. In theory, all artifacts found were in close to primary context. However, on the floor, perhaps the lowest floor, were fewer artifactual remains (Figure 5.4 vs. 5.5). This distribution suggests at least two interpretations. One is that a few of the tripartite buildings along the eastern flank of the mound were of two stories. As Tobler (1950:29) notes, most of these buildings had thicker walls than comparable buildings in the later levels. The artifacts might have come from an upper story. Another possibility is that flattening out the surface to build Level XIA/B stirred up artifacts and deposited them out of context. I am persuaded by the chit information (see catalogue) that the former is more likely.

In its layout, the White Room Building had at least five of the characteristics of temples listed above. It had

Key to Symbols in Distribution Maps

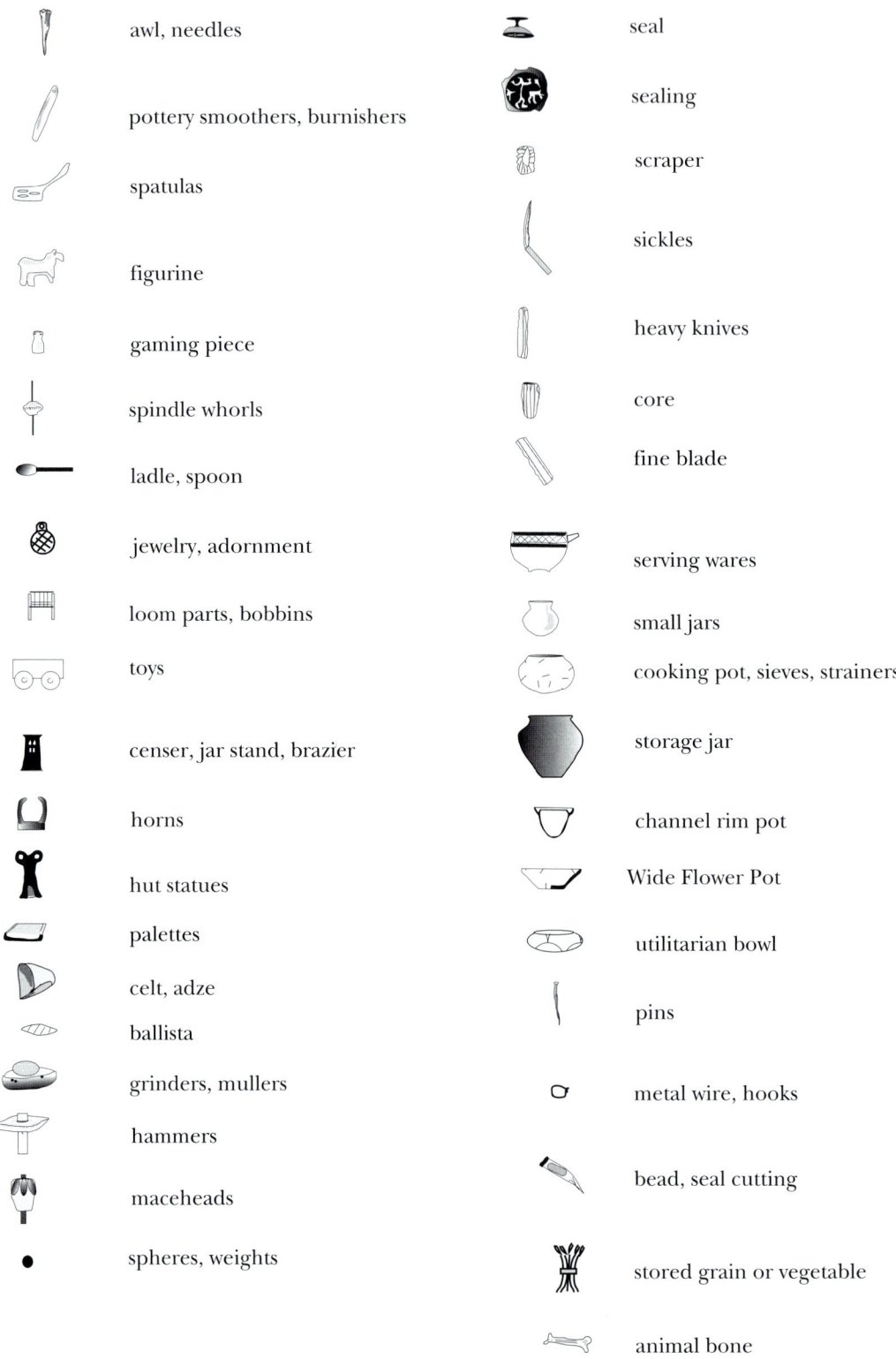

awl, needles		seal	
pottery smoothers, burnishers		sealing	
spatulas		scraper	
figurine		sickles	
gaming piece		heavy knives	
spindle whorls		core	
ladle, spoon		fine blade	
jewelry, adornment		serving wares	
loom parts, bobbins		small jars	
toys		cooking pot, sieves, strainers	
censer, jar stand, brazier		storage jar	
horns		channel rim pot	
hut statues		Wide Flower Pot	
palettes		utilitarian bowl	
celt, adze		pins	
ballista		metal wire, hooks	
grinders, mullers		bead, seal cutting	
hammers		stored grain or vegetable	
maceheads		animal bone	
spheres, weights			

Figure 5.1   Key to symbols in artifact distribution figures.

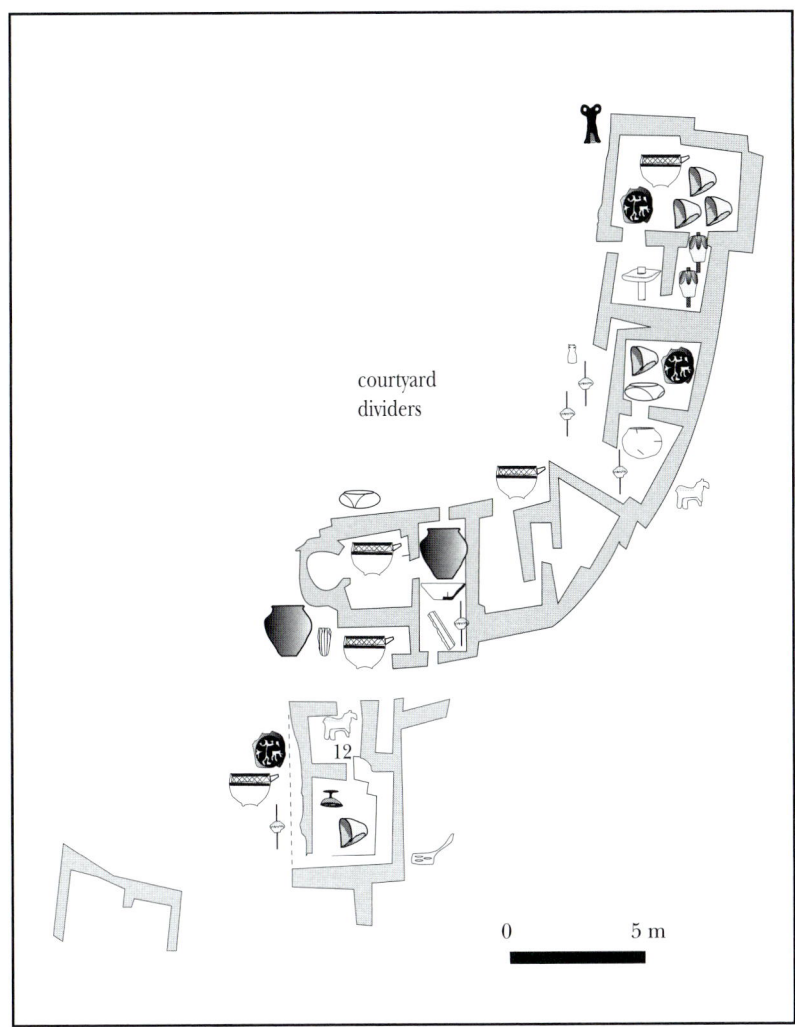

courtyard
dividers

0   5 m

Figure 5.2   Distribution of artifactual remains in situ in Level XII, small rooms
along entry road.

a clear tripartite plan, and its double doors opened off a plaza created by an angled wall. In addition, locus sheet 152 describes a channel rim bowl set in a bench in one of the side rooms. There were also niches in the back wall and a hut statue, which would not be out of place in a temple. However, there is no platform or altar, which should have been there if this room were preserved during the fire and, as Tobler notes (1950:27–28), many of the artifacts are not what one would expect to find in a temple. Excavators unearthed numerous small tools, including 16 spindle whorls for making yarn, a spatula, an obsidian core, and four small celts. Even in the distribution map with the best proveniences (Figure 5.5), two spindle whorls were found. In short, there were elements of religious ritual and of a domicile. The size and position on the mound of the building

makes it seem important. It is very much like the Northeast Building of VIII (Figure 5.65), except that building has a platform, which I will interpret below as the home of a leader with a shrine built on the first floor.

The small building to the south of the White Room in Square 4M (Figure 5.9) may be an extension of that larger building. It had a possible door into the White room itself. It yielded a number of domestic goods (a grinder and serving bowl), but also sealings, lithic cores, and other craft tools, suggesting a workshop function.

What perhaps explains the functions of the White Room building best are the remaining tripartite houses in Squares 4K (Figure 5.7), 3/4M (Figure 5.6), and 4/5J (Figure 5.8). In many respects, they share elements of the White Room building. Two of

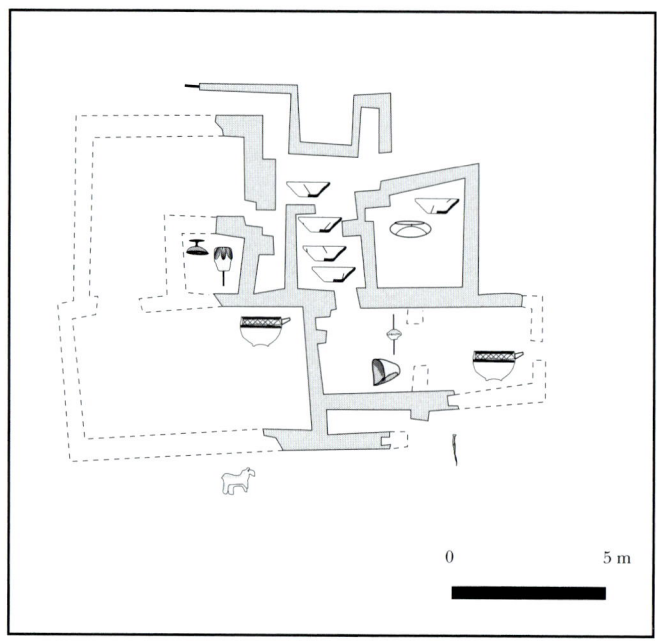

Figure 5.3   Distribution of artifactual remains in situ in Level XII, northeast building in squares 6Q/S.

them have niched back walls, double entrances toward the front, though not double doors on the front. Possible ritual items, for example, the two stands in rooms 25 and 26 of the Square 4K Building, and a piece of another channel rim jar (not in the best context) in the area of the Square 3/4M building suggest possible religious ritual (or other productive activities). When one compares the size of these buildings with domiciles in later levels, all are unusually large.

The size, possibly religious elements, and domestic artifacts suggest that these may have been extended family dwellings. Similar large multi-roomed buildings existed in the Trans-Tigridian area from the time of the Ubaid period. A building with many side rooms off a long, central hallway existed at Gawra in Ubaid period Levels XV and XIV (Tobler 1950: Plates XIV and XV). Such buildings also occurred at Tell Madhur in the Hamrin (Roaf 1984: Figure 7), and Tell Abada (Jasim 1985). The area of these buildings is enormous, whether there is a second floor, as Kubba (1987:126f.) suggests, or not (as Roaf claims). A pattern similar to these houses is evident in the traditional Western Anatolian house (Oliver 1987:135f.). This house has a central hall, like the ones in Gawra XII—it is called a salon in the Anatolian case—and then rooms are added, as more generations inhabit the house. Similar ideas of multi-family dwellings within one walled area are found among Yoruba cultivators in West Africa (Forde 1963:151f.) and among the house complexes of ancient Mesoamerica (Blanton et al. 1993:174f.).

The extraordinary number of burials under the floors of these Level XII buildings, especially of infants and children (Tobler 1950:28, 103f.), would also suggest an association of sizable families within these buildings over a long period of time.

Each of these house compounds appears to have had some craft activity. The compound in Square 4/5J (Figure 5.8) had the remains of a core and many blades, all obsidian. The Square 4K building (Figure 5.7) had cloth-making tools (two loom bases were found in Square 4K, although not in clear context), Square 3/4M building (large room 21, Figure 5.6) woodworking celts.

The two remaining buildings in Square 5/6K (Figure 5.11) and 5/6G (Figure 5.12) were considerably smaller than the three just mentioned or the White Room building. They have square central rooms with many, smaller adjoining rooms. The former, despite its differences from the tripartite planned buildings in overall floor area and shape, had their formal elements: a large central room, side room, and a storage room. It lacked the clearly domestic contents of the tripartite buildings. Its contents included a small jar with uncut seal and amulet and a blade and awl in adjoining areas. Somewhere in Square 5K was a set of 26 spindle whorls. In comparison

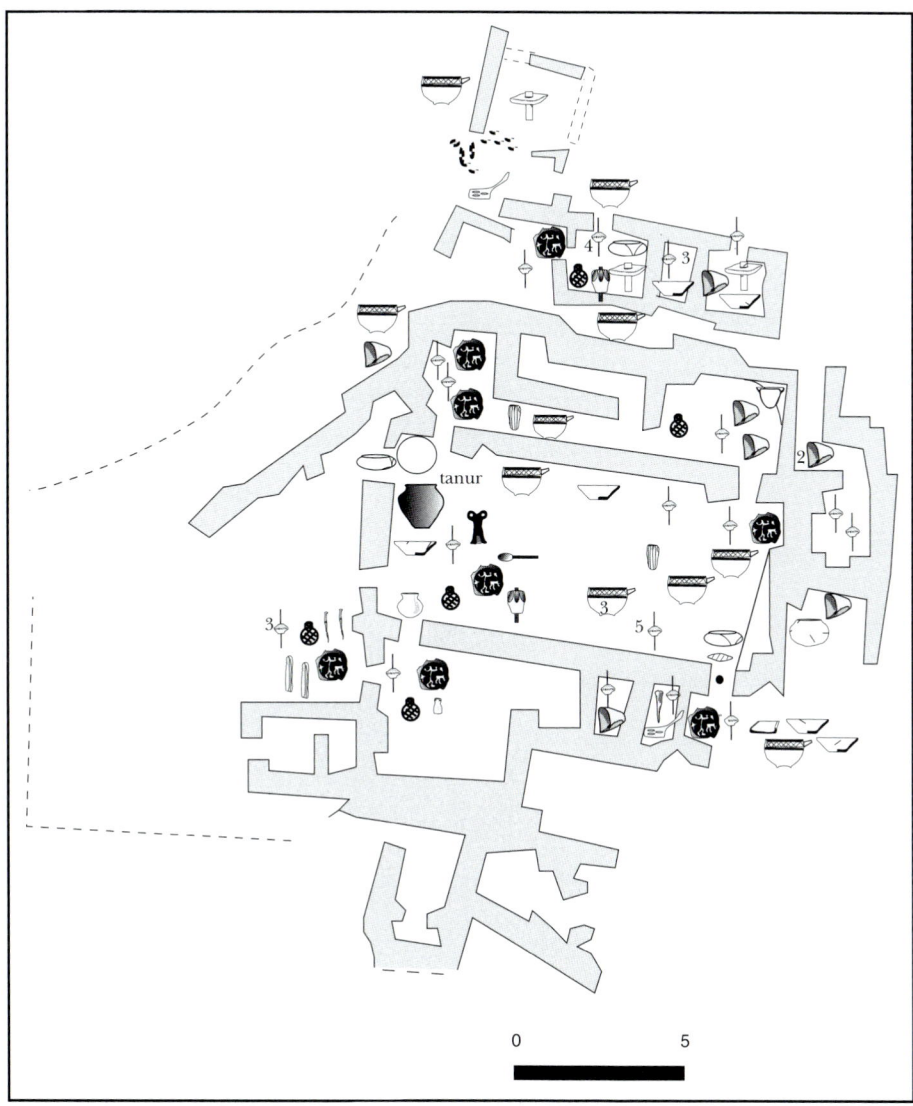

Figure 5.4   Distribution of artifactual remains in situ in Level XII, White Room building (the maximum possible artifacts).

to the weaving shop of Phase XI (Figure 5.28), this building lacks the clear evidence to assign it a function of a specialized shop, although the concentration of spindle whorls—again, not definitely in this building—and the blade and awl make it seem to have been a possible workshop. The three seals in it were mostly unfinished. The other building in the same figure yielded a toy, serving pot, and an obsidian core. All suggest a domicile. Neither building had the niches or other of the ritual remains of the tripartite buildings.

Based on Table 4.1 and 4.2, the craft activities represented most frequently in Level XII are cloth-making,

woodworking, and knapping tools. Most of the knapping is of obsidian, which must have been imported, and based on the number of cores recovered may have represented an exported item.

The last functional space to discuss is an unusually shaped structure in Square 5M (Figure 5.10). This structure consisted of a series of narrow, perhaps easily locked rooms off a very narrow central hallway. Unfortunately, few artifacts remained in good context. Of those that did, an unusual concentration of clay sealings is evident throughout the building. A storage jar, Wide flower Pot, and outside the door a grinding stone were found. The building most similar in form

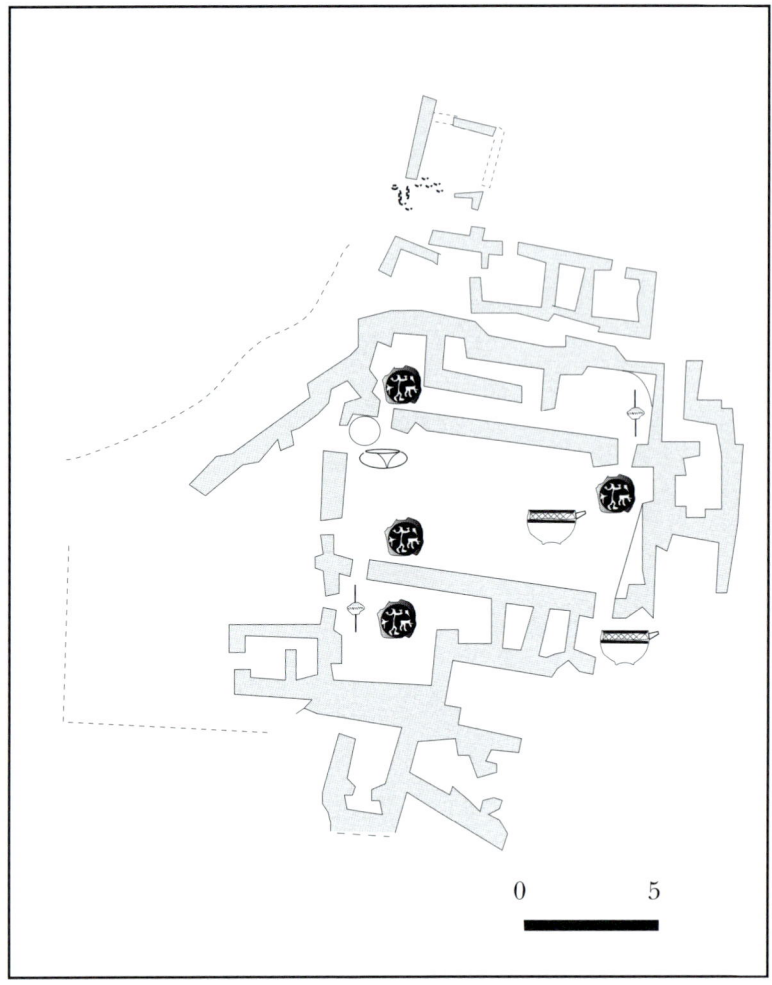

Figure 5.5   Distribution of artifactual remains in situ in Level XII, White
Room building (only artifacts in the securest primary proveniences).

was the storage area of the palace at Arslantepe (Frangipane 1993: Figure 2). As no production tools, household goods, or ritual items were found, these remains suggest that this was a storage house. Trümpelman (1989) argues that the Round House of Phase XIA was a silo. I argue against that, but the building in Figure 5.10 had many of the characteristics typical of that function.

As is evident below, the residents of Level XII shared many productive activities with the residents of later levels. Among the most prominent of these were cloth-making, woodworking, stone knapping, and some farming. Some activities were centralized at the site, although it is not completely clear whether they were production for local consumption or for exchange. Without the contents of the possible Square 5M storehouse (Figure 5.10) or a better understanding of what was happening in the clay bins

west of the small entryway rooms (Figure 5.2), it is hard to say which activity was more likely. Nonetheless, some centralization of functions appears to have occurred.

Contrary to that centralization, the dwellings of Level XII imply a far different picture of life in the transition to the Uruk period. The large tripartite buildings (Figures 5.4–5.8) seem to me to be best interpreted as extended family dwellings with the remains of domestic life, some craft production, and some religious ritual. Despite the larger size of the White Room Building and the wide variety of products or production tools found there, other indicators of status differences appear to be lacking. Tomb burial did not begin until the following XIA/B level, and graves were widely dispersed with few significant grave goods (Tobler 1950:103f.). Most graves were associated with the houses themselves.

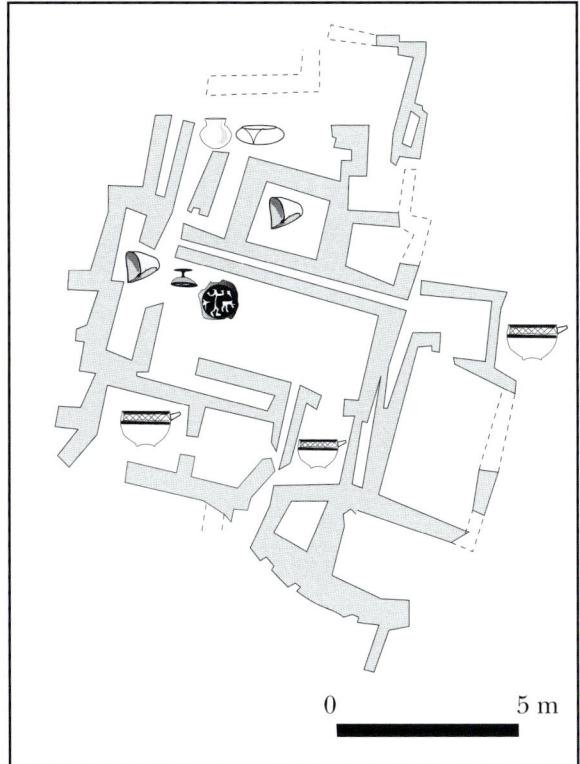

0   5 m

Figure 5.6   Distribution of artifactual remains in situ in Level XII, tripartite building in squares 3/4M.

Population

With the probably multi-story house compounds, and only 40 percent of the surface excavated, population estimates are particularly difficult for Level XII. Based on Kramer's method (see above), 76 people would live in the exposed part of the mound, and extrapolation over the whole surface would yield 190 people. This strikes me as being too low a number. Using Watson's method, 147 people would live in the excavated area, 325 on the mound as a whole. These are obvious crude estimates at best, but what they do say is that the amount of cloth and the products stored probably exceeded the needs of this community.

External Relations

Level XII had clear evidence of the presence of long distance exchange. Among the materials at Gawra from clearly "exotic" sources were gold and lapis lazuli (a small gold object outside the White Room (111, Figure 3.6)) and a gold and lapis pin, buried in a jar under the floor of a side room of the tripartite building in Square 4K (Figure 5.7). In addition, shell, alabaster, and obsidian were all

present in this level. For the first time, worked metal also appeared. Alabaster and copper ore are found in the hills to the north and west of Gawra in modern Turkey (G. Wright 1969:55). Copper smelting was already done in the late Ubaid Period in the hills of southeast Turkey (see Chapter 1) in an area with which Gawra shares its closest stylistic associations.

In other words, Gawra was a part of a far-flung network of exchange for materials coming from the hilly margins of Mesopotamia. It is very likely that, given the number of cores found, Gawra was also a transshipping point. Among the raw materials found, marble, granite and perhaps steatite were locally available. A seal of very Gawra-like style found in western Iran (Voigt 1989, Rothman a in press) suggests that Gawrans could have been manufacturers of seals. The blank seals in the possible workshop (Figure 5.11) affirm this possibility. That the small rooms in the northeast had remains of mace heads and celts of this material would indicate that these goods, too, were manufactured and might have been exported.

In this regard, the results of a neutron activation analysis James Blackman of the Smithsonian Institution and I did are relevant to this issue (Rothman and Blackman 1990). We were interested in some measure of the interaction of Gawra's residents and the outside world, measured by variables other than artifact style. Since sealed vessels, containers, or doors appear to have been the way goods were restricted to particular persons or offices, that is, ownership or administration (see Rothman 1994a), we hoped to find out whether the clay in Gawran sealings came from local or exotic sources. The analysis demonstrated that there was a very strong, homogeneous "Gawran" chemical signature for sealing clays. In Levels XI/XA to IX, only sealings with this chemical signature were found. In Level XII, excavators recovered one of two sealings that were not from that Gawran clay source. Admittedly, two sealings are too few to form a pattern, but given all the other indicators, Gawra at this time probably was engaged in the transshipping of various goods, and was part of an exchange network covering a significant portion of the Greater Mesopotamian region.

Administration

The primary source of information on the structure of administrative control comes from the remains of seals and sealings, particularly their distribution in relation to activities (functions) (see Rothman 1994a, 1994b). What do the distributions of seals and sealings tell us about which functions were controlled? Two assumptions are necessary to enable interpretation of the seals and sealings. First, seals

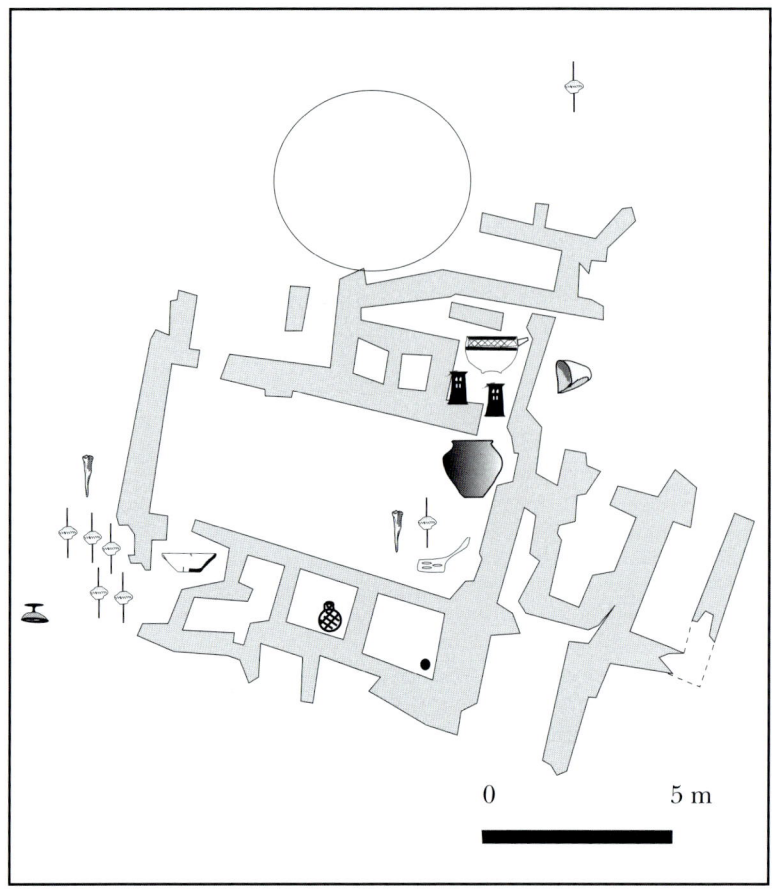

Figure 5.7   Distribution of artifactual remains in situ in Level XII, tripartite building in square 4K.

represent the owner or controlling authority. They may be used on the site where the containers (including doors) were sealed, or they may have been used at a production site away from the home base of the seal bearer to mark goods for shipment to that home site. The Old Babylonian šakinu inspector, for example, wrote his crop yield estimate and sealed his tablet at the fields or orchards themselves, although he was dispatched from a local capital (Cocquerillat 1967:212f.). A more direct example would be the goods transported in the Old Assyrian trade from Assur (Larsen 1967).

The second assumption is that the broken sealing represents a record, whether kept or discarded, of a legitimate owner or authority gaining access to restricted goods. These sealings may have been applied at another site (representing transport), at the same site (representing exchange of goods), or in the same building (representing storage). Because of this, they will tend to be discarded near where they were opened or where restricted items were sent within the site.

Although I feel that these assumptions are fair ones, the meaning given to seal design is very variable

from time to time and place to place (see Bregstein 1993, Rothman 1994b, and Chapter 1 for a comprehensive review). I also need to re-emphasize that the nature of the controlling authority varies over time and space. It is not possible to think always of a state agency, a king or mayor. We more likely are dealing with some sort of kinship based groupings. That there were so many seals and sealings, even if only a limited number were in good context, indicates a sense of property, and the necessity for controlling that property had begun to evolve in the LC1 period or earlier. The possibly centralized functions of the site—exchange and storage—were marked by such control mechanisms.

In later levels, the distribution of seals and sealings is a tight fit to the functional areas of the site. For XII, it is perhaps fitting that no clear pattern emerges, because everything else in the level speaks of a loosely, or at least not centrally administered site (Figure 5.13). Sealings were found in good context in all but one of the buildings, which I believe were for extended families. Most seals were applied to sealings on boxes, small jars, and baskets. Door lock sealings are a

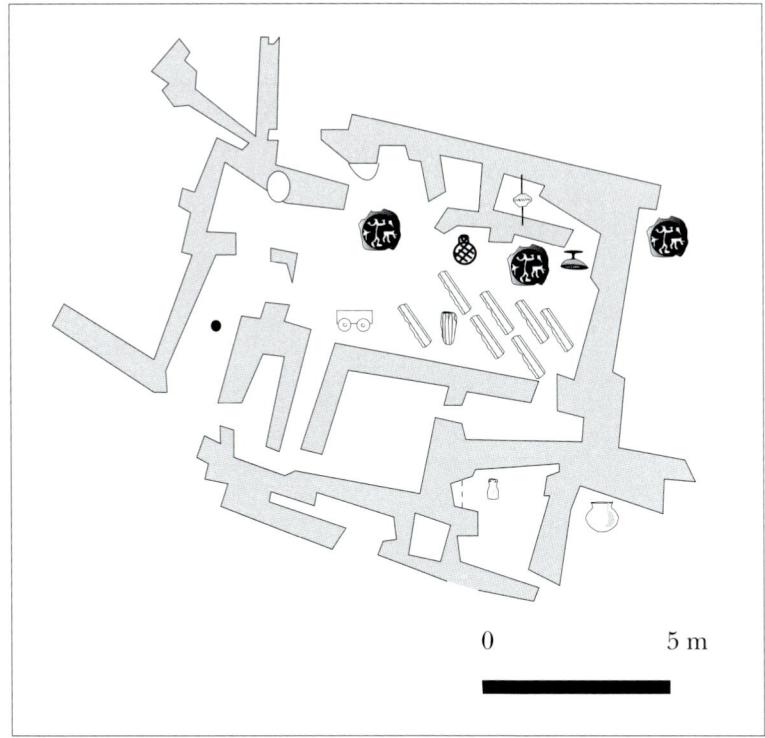

Figure 5.8   Distribution of artifactual remains in situ in Level XII, tripartite building in square 4/5J.

particular kind of evidence for control, as they may imply administrative control over larger scale of storage, as is evident at Arslantepe, or control by an owner if the storage area is small. The only two door lock

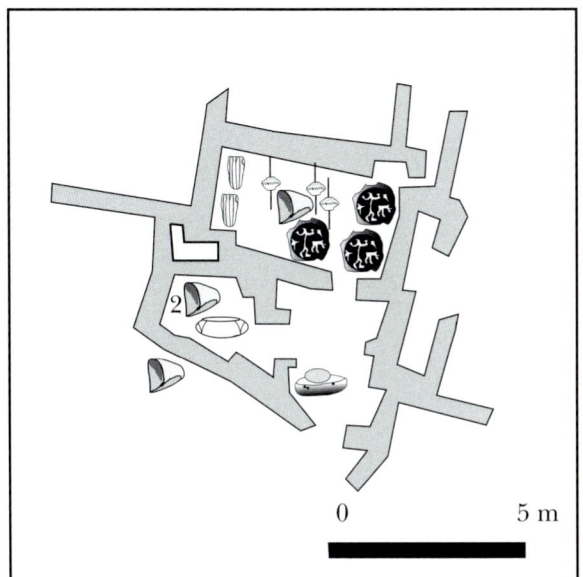

Figure 5.9   Distribution of artifactual remains in situ in Level XII, small building south of White Room.

sealings were both found in or near the White Room building. The three concentrations of sealings in XII were found in the southern part of the White Room complex and in the building of Square 5M that I suggested was a storeroom.

By contrast, Level XIII with its massive, public buildings, which contained a well filled with sealings, indicates that some level of administrative control was already evident in the Ubaid 4 period.

Level XIA/B

Shortly after the fire and attack that destroyed much of Gawra Level XII, construction of a new town was begun. The functional size and layout of this level suggest that major social changes had occurred.

As I argued above in Chapter 3, what Tobler saw as one unified level, and what Forest saw as a period of occupation followed by a singular fortress (the Round House), appear from field records to have been two phases of occupation. The earlier phase of occupation was largely residential, and the later phase of occupation, the one during which the Round House and, I suggest, the formal gate with its defensive tower and the southern thick-walled complex were built, retained many residential buildings, but developed a defensive posture. Tobler (1950:18f.)

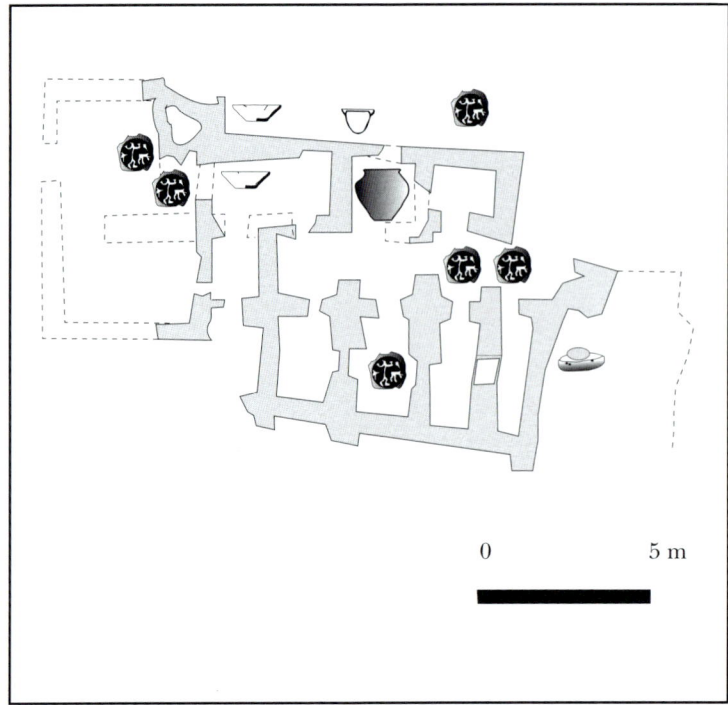

Figure 5.10   Distribution of artifactual remains in situ in Level XII, multi-room building in square 5M.

notes the defensive posture of the XIA mound, with a seemingly solid wall facing out on the world from the mound, but, again, if I am right, that defensive posture came late in the occupation of XIA/B, and presaged another level whose buildings ended in fire. One major problem in analyzing the two phases is that only the buildings in the southeast can be clearly separated and assigned to Phase XIB or XIA.

Functional Size

Tobler (1950:23f.) argues that whereas Level XII had no formal temple, XIA did have one. It was a tripartite building in Squares 5/6 Q (Figure 5.14). Although this building is one of two tripartite buildings of XIA/B and the entry room is one of few rooms sufficient for a congregation, this building does not meet the criteria of a temple. Access to the building, far from being easy and open was restricted. There was only one narrow doorway to the south of an open plaza. Perhaps, in Phase XIB, before the Gawrans built the gate tower, room 68 (Figure 5.15) would have been easier to access. However, it lacks a podium, niches in its back wall, a basin in an adjoining area, and any ritual contents at all. A hut statue was found north of it, but in rubble that might not be associated with the building or even that level.

What is clearly a trash deposit from this building (Figure 5.14) had no artifacts that would indicate a religious function.

On the other hand, this building does seem to have played what might be a specialized productive function. Many of the artifacts from the building or its trash represented cloth-making activities. Twelve spindle whorls, three bone needles, and a blade all were likely to be used in weaving, although no loom pieces were recovered, as they were in Phase XI. In the alcove near a large oven, a storehouse or production site was found. Chits describe it as a pottery cache with Wide Flower Pots mentioned. This might be an open pit, pottery firing site, as described below, or a storage site. Alternatively, given the proximity of a large oven, this might a place where food was cooked and distributed in the piles of bowls.

The building also had serving dishes and the remains of amulets or beads. It would seem that there were some living areas. One very real possibility is that we are seeing two phases of use conflated. In the earlier XIB phase, this building may have been an extended family dwelling like those in Level XII. The many alterations in its southern flank, as Tobler (1950:24) mentions, were all in the parts where productive activities were being performed. Therefore, its productive phase may have come after it was abandoned as a domicile. A similar situation may

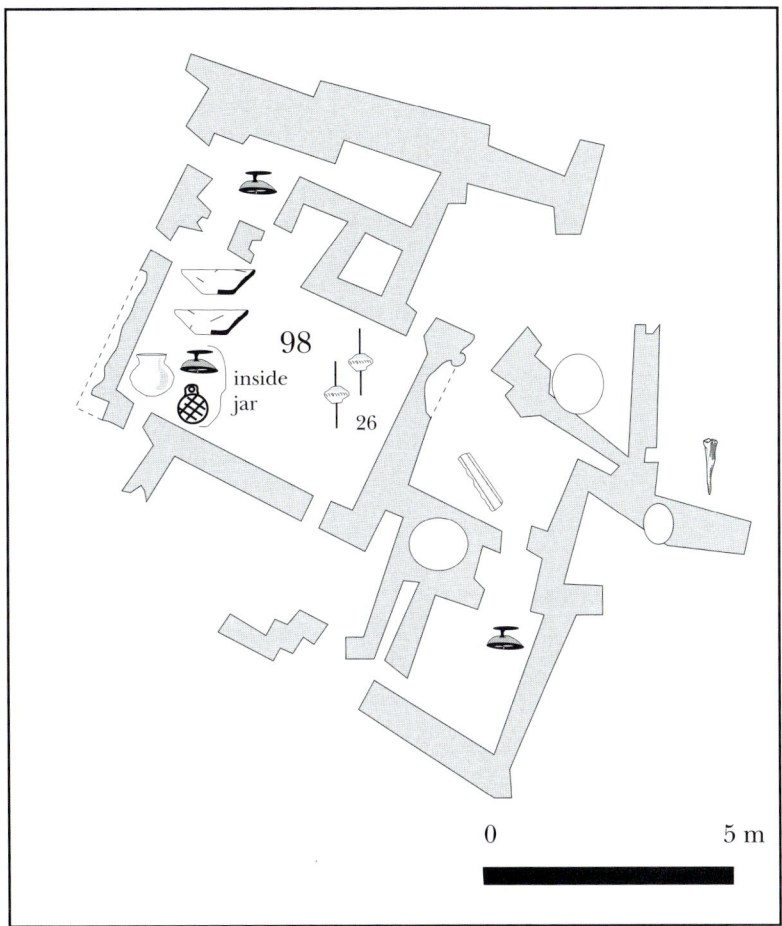

Figure 5.11   Distribution of artifactual remains in situ in Level XII, building
in square 5/6K (room 98).

have existed for the large western building of VIIIB
(Figure 5.73 below).

To the west of the building just discussed are the
remains of what appears to be another small tripartite
building (same figure). All that remains of the building were two serving vessels, a weight, and a set of clay
sealings. An interpretation of this building as a domicile is consistent with the evidence. It had elements of
a secular, public building as well. So little of the building is left, however, it is hard to offer an interpretation
supported by data.

The plaza of the large tripartite, perhaps craft,
building described above was probably affected by the
building of the tower, presumably in XIA (Figure 5.15).
The tower had double thick walls on the side facing
the mound's eastern edge, presumably the gate of the
settlement. The western face of the building was reinforced with two buttresses. Since there was no obvious
doorway, people may have entered the tower by ladder. The functions of the complex of rooms south of

the tower are hard to determine. Hammers, celts,
spindle whorls, a grinder, blades, and an obsidian core
were scattered throughout a set of small rooms surrounding the tower, which might suggest a craft working area. One function of the tower that is clear was
pottery making. A large pit had been dug and in it
were (presumably unbaked) pots in three layers. As
described in locus sheet 148, these were stacked with
clay ballistas strategically placed so that the pots would
not touch. This deposit matches descriptions of
pottery firing pits from various places. Again, we
might be seeing a conflation of the XIB and XIA, but
no stratigraphic evidence permits us to differentiate
them clearly.

The one area where the distinction of the XIB and
XIA phases of Tepe Gawra is clear is in the southeastern part of the mound. This and the area to its north
and west were where the residences of the XIA/B
mound were located. The first of the residential buildings was a small tripartite house built in Phase XIB in

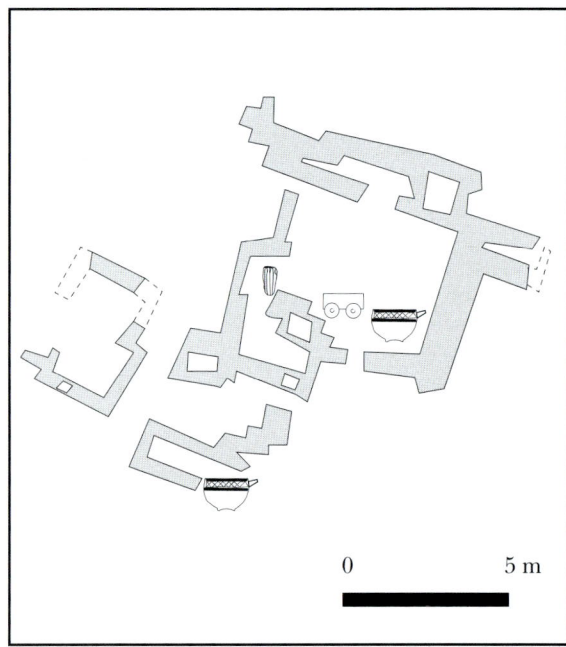

0   5 m

Figure 5.12   Distribution of artifactual remains in situ in Level XII, building in square 5/6G.

Squares 5 J/K (Figure 5.16). The only artifacts that remained from that earlier phase were a few clay sealings and a serving bowl. The remodeling of this building in XIA (Figure 5.17) clearly indicates a domestic function with a kohl (cosmetic) jar, model horse, and storage bowls. Two palettes for grinding pigments and two blades could indicate some domestic craft activity, but it is not clear which one(s). A small house adjoining this building also has a kohl jar, storage pot, a couple of Wide Flower utilitarian bowls, and a large kitchen.

In the XIB phase, just south of the tripartite building just discussed, excavators unearthed an unusually shaped compound with two ovens, two sets of deep storage pits or grain silos, a sickle, grinding stone, spatula, palette, celt and two bowls (Figure 5.18). A family, perhaps an extended family of farmers, probably lived there.

Two more sets of domiciles were located to the northwest and east of this building. In Square 5/6 K (Figure 5.19) a compound with two ovens and three sets of seemingly interlocking rooms (houses) were built. The artifacts found there were typical of residences: a spatula, grinding stone, channel-rimmed bowl, amulet, and a few spindle whorls.

The other set of individual, two or three room houses, each with a kitchen, was built on the southeastern flank of the mound, forming the wall that Tobler argues was to give the site a defensive perimeter (Figure 5.20). A set of artifacts—grinding stones, toys,

a gaming piece, storage bowl, some spindle whorls, knives and bowls—similar to the other houses mark these units.

At the same time as the tower was built (in XIA) in the northeast part of the mound, a thick-walled set of rooms was built in the south in an area where house compounds formerly existed (Figure 5.21). This building was re-used in Level XI/XA, where I interpret it as a series of workrooms. The few remains that can reliably be assigned to Phase XIA are of a domestic kind, but they remained in the northern part of the building and may not represent its function. The walls of this compound were thicker than most of the residences. What looks like a newel wall for a staircase runs between rooms 4 and 7 (Figure 3.8). Room 8 may be a small tower. Overall, this compound may have had a defensive purpose as one of its functions.

The one building that marks XIA most distinctly is the so-called Round House (Figures 5.22, 5.23). Based on stratigraphic sections (see Chapter 3), this building was constructed in Phase XIA. Most likely, the northeast tower (Figure 5.16) and southern complex (Figure 5.21) were built at the same time. Like the later round house at Tell Razuk (Gibson 1986), the most likely interpretation of the Round House is as a defensive fortress. The meter thick walls, the limited access through a steep ramp on its western side away from the edge of the mound, and the small narrow rooms all suggest a fortified emplacement. Alongside the other fortifications of XIA and the eventual burning of the Round House, this impression seems warranted. This does not mean that other interpretations have not been made. Trümpelmann (1989) suggests that the Round House was a very large grain silo. Because the traffic pattern seems directed toward the long central room with what looks like a long, low table, Speiser (1936a:12) interpreted this building as a "fortified" temple.

What, however, do the contents imply? Trümpelmann is correct in one regard. Part of the function of the Round House was to stockpile grain. Room G had clear indications of grain storage (Tobler 1950:23). The storage jar set into the wall of room E may also have contained grain. The room was remodeled to seal it and limit access to room G. On the other hand, there are no other indications that the primary function of the Round House was for storage of grain or any other goods. To the contrary, there are signs that the building had other uses. In the Round House room K a collection of gaming pieces were found together. Some, like Schmandt-Besserat (1979, 1992), want to interpret all small pieces as tokens for placing in bulla (administrative envelopes). Although there certainly were tokens at Gawra and elsewhere, these objects, by their size and shape, are ill suited as tokens and are, I argue, just

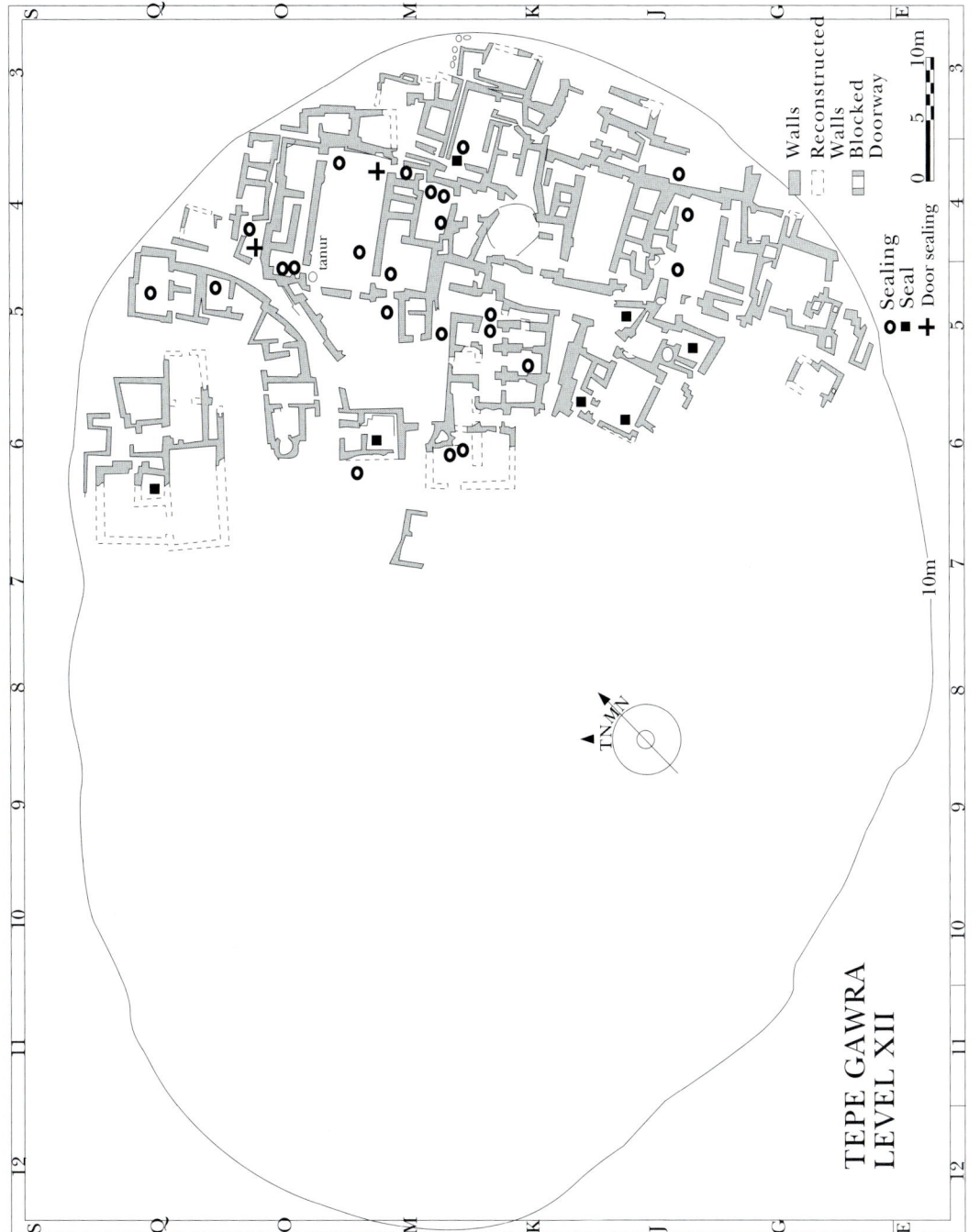

TEPE GAWRA
LEVEL XII

Figure 5.13 Distribution of seals and sealings in situ in Level XII.

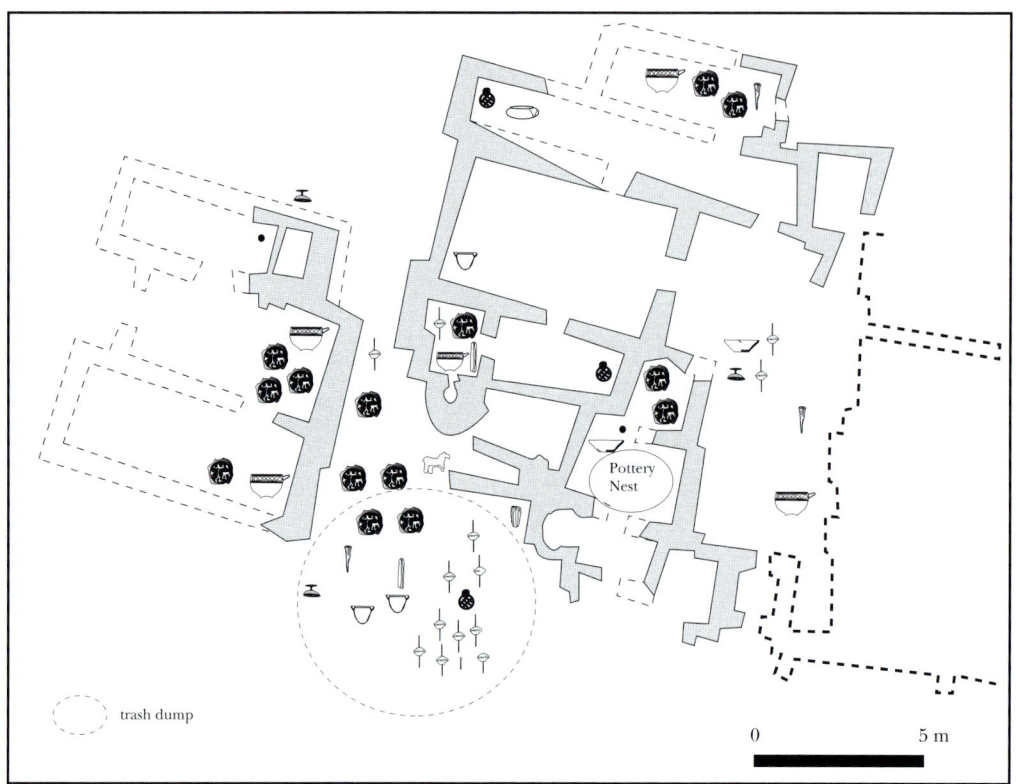

Figure 5.14   Distribution of artifactual remains in situ in Level XIA/B, buildings in squares 5/6Q.

what they were originally called: game pieces. Also, with the re-dating of Gawra, XIA/B is too early for bulla. Other artifacts, like a mace head and perhaps two hammers fit an interpretation of the Round House as a fortress well, as do, in a way, the game pieces, at least to anyone who has had to sit on guard duty for a long time. The presence of two stamp seals and sealings in the area of the storerooms also indicates something of the building's function (see below).

All in all, an interpretation of the Round House as a fortress fits the data. Other elements of the site that appear at about the same time are also defensive. Its construction, with meter thick walls, implies protection. Other examples of round buildings, although admittedly later, fulfill a similar function for defense.[2]

Margueron (1983) has attempted to construct an isometric plan of the Round House. Many of the details of that reconstruction seem warranted. There probably was an unroofed courtyard inside the wall and a parapet on a second floor. Some sort of upper level windows would be necessary to let light into the interior. He errs, in my estimation, in having some corner rooms, especially room G, open. A grain storage room opened to the air and elements would be a

rather ineffective storage space. An alternative construction is offered in Figure 5.23.

Another set of rooms included the ones surrounding the Round House. Because of ovens in them and their contents (Figure 5.22), they appear to be houses built up against the Round House. Based on schematic sections K and M (Figures 3.2 and 3.3), they do appear to be from the XIA phase. I am not sure why two of the larger of these rooms have no easy access.

Evolutionary Trends in Function and Organization, Level XIA/B

The occupation of Level XIA/B appears to represent considerable change from the time of Level XII. Early in its XIB phase, contrary to what Tobler sees, the occupation looks like a complex village. Some multifamily houses might have existed, the supposed temple being one. Smaller domestic units, however, started to appear in the XIB phase and were even more dominant in the XIA phase. One of the XIB houses in the southeastern part of the mound in Square 5G/J Room 23, can be interpreted as a farm family's house, complete with storage bins, which might have functioned much

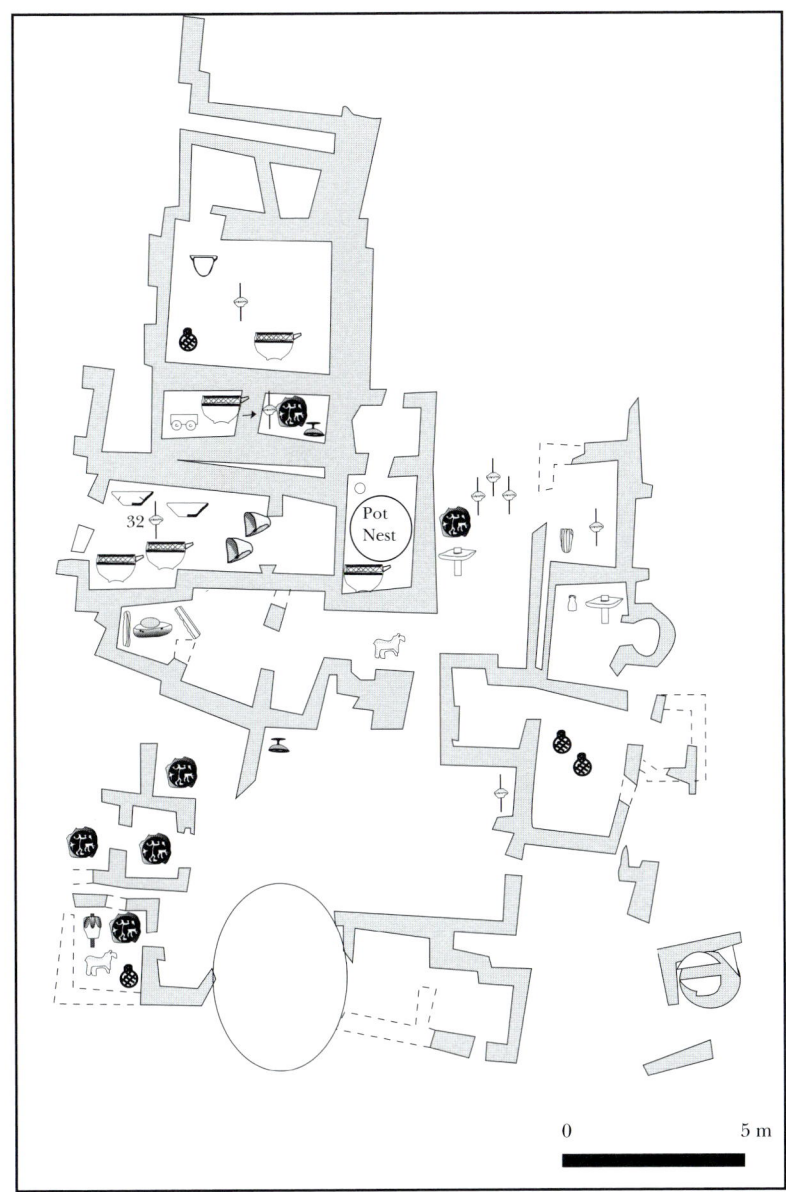

Figure 5.15   Distribution of artifactual remains in situ in Level XIA/B, gateway complex and associated rooms.

like grain storage bins do in modern Middle Eastern villages (e.g., see Kramer 1982: Figure 4.11).

The dramatic change appears to have happened between the village of XIB and the building of the Round House, northeastern tower, gate, and southern fortified structure with a possible tower in XIA. The Round House represented not only a major effort on the part of the residents of Gawra, but a coordinated attempt at self-defense. Stores of grain were brought from somewhere to heap up in one or two rooms, be they from the fields of residents or the

tribute of outlying villages. This effort certainly represents political centralization. To build, supply, and guard the fortress required an effort that a social system based on kinship or clan has traditionally had a hard time coordinating. It is noteworthy that, in contrast to XII, symbols of administrative authority, stamp seals, appeared in two higher-ranking graves (see Appendix). Both entomb adults, both were seals whose material is not the important variable, as it will be in later graves. Tomb burials with richer fittings, often burials of children, appeared in this level for

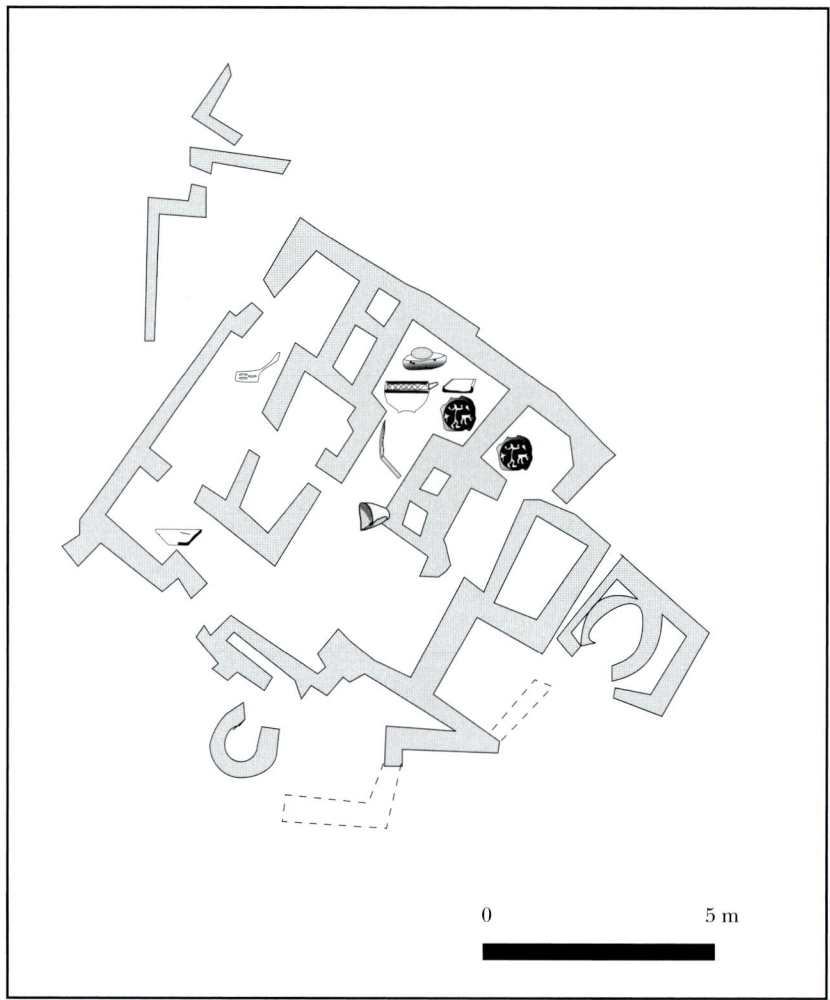

0   5 m

Figure 5.16   Distribution of artifactual remains in situ in Phase XIB, Level XIA/B, squares 5K/J tripartite building.

the first time. Archaeologists traditionally interpret graves with richer and less rich graves as a sign of increasing social differentiation.

As in Gawra XII, cloth-making and knapping were important, but the latter from the numbers seems less important (see Tables 4.1 and 4.2). The kind of intense family production evident in XII was not apparent in XIA/B, and the area where most production tool kits seem concentrated is far from the domiciles in the northern part of the mound. A pottery firing pit existed in that same area. An older building in the north of the mound appears to have been modified for craft production or exchange. In other words, craft production in Level XIA/B appears to have been more specialized, although we do not know what was in the western half of the mound from Levels XII to XI/XA.

Population

Based on either of the methods for calculating population described above, XIA/B represents a minor increase in the number of people living on the mound. The XIB phase, using Kramer's per-house measurement, had 227 people. Using Watson's figure per occupied room, it was 384. In the XIA phase, not counting the Round House as an occupation unit, the population was 370 using a per-house calculation, 364, using a per-occupied-room calculation.[3]

External Relations

As in Level XII, there is reason to see the residents of Gawra XIA/B as part of a network much larger than its immediate area. The reasons for building defensive

Figure 5.17 Distribution of artifactual remains in situ in Phase XIA, Level XIA/B, square 5K/J tripartite building.

systems in XIA were certainly related to larger con-flicts in the region. That the level ended in fire, as XII had, confirmed the fears that the residents of Gawra had, although the evidence of a final conflict is not as clear as in Level XII. As locus 132 reads, "Today layer of ashes found in these excavation pits, however, the conflagration doubtless destroyed rooms in the sur-rounding squares (if not the entire mound)." As re-flected in the schematic section for the squares of M (Figure 3.3), burned ash surrounded and covered the Round House.

In terms of exports and imports, the residents of Gawra continued to receive goods from the surround-ing highlands—obsidian, gold, alabaster—although gold appears only in a tomb and graves. No lapis lazuli was recovered in XIA/B catalogues. It is unclear what was being exported. Pottery was unlikely to have been much in demand, cloth may have been, although I would think of most cloth production would be for local

consumption. Perhaps some especially fine or rare cloth was exported.

In terms of the analysis of clays used in sealings, in a sample of eight, half were not from the Gawran source (Rothman and Blackman 1990).

This was also the period when nearby Nineveh may not have been occupied (see Chapter 3, Table 3.3), possibly enhancing Gawra's role in its sub-region.

Administration

Like Level XII, Level XIA/B had a very large num-ber of seals and sealings (171). The development of administration was clearly a priority. As described above, the residents, particularly of Phase XIA, were engaged with the larger world. Part of that engage-ment was bringing exotic goods in quantity to the site. Part of it was a competition for access, a competition that led to the level's demise, but also undoubtedly

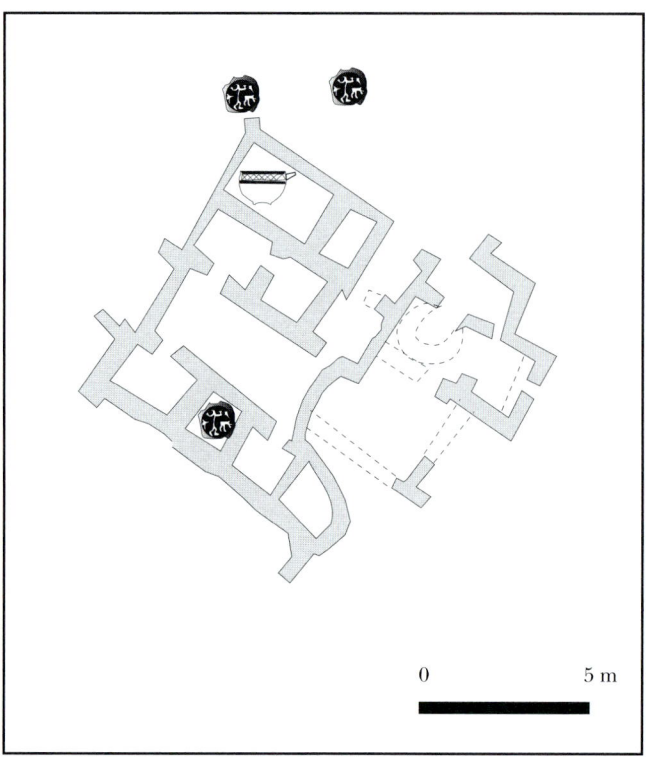

Figure 5.18   Distribution of artifactual remains in situ in Phase XIB, Level XIA/B, square 5G/J building.

caused the development of some kind of a control system for the coordinators of the Round House and probably the wider polity. Goods had to be brought in, as perhaps did fighters. Stored grain had to be collected and dispersed.

The distribution of XIB seals and sealings (Figure 5.24) shows a wide dispersion of sealings and a limited number of seals in good context. In contrast, the distribution of XIA seals and sealings (Figure 5.25) appears to have been more focused. Four sealings were recovered in the grain storage area of the Round House, as one would expect from its function. These sealings were on jars. A stamp seal was also found in what might be the living quarters or "offices" of that building. The area of the greatest concentration of sealings was by the large tripartite in the north of the site (Figure 5.14). That there should have been such a concentration makes eminent sense, because, this was the area where specialized production for export was most likely to have occurred, although I have not been able to define the specific goods and the nature of that production.

However, many of the houses had evidence of sealings and seals, so the system of control was not completely centralized. In that light, most of the sealings were from mobile media: jars, sacks, or baskets.

The results of the chemical characterization indicated that some sealed objects were coming from outside the immediate sphere of Gawra. This, too, makes sense.

The new level of complexity in XIA/B was reflected in a control system, but one that was still somewhat generalized. Again, this also was the period when Nineveh may not have been occupied, making the political role of Tepe Gawra as a center more achievable.

Level XI/XA, Phase XI

After the end of Level XIA/B, the building of Phase XI of Level XI/XA was begun, as a new settlement quickly arose after the destruction of Gawra XII. It is hard to say how long a period elapsed, but since the southern compound of XIA was reused in Phase XI, and since little deposition other than the ashes of XIA existed between them, a short period probably elapsed. I am persuaded that rebuilding was not immediate, however, if only because its successor was so very different from the preceding Level XIA/B. For one thing, the defensive posture of XIA was not reproduced in Phase XI. For another thing, the plan

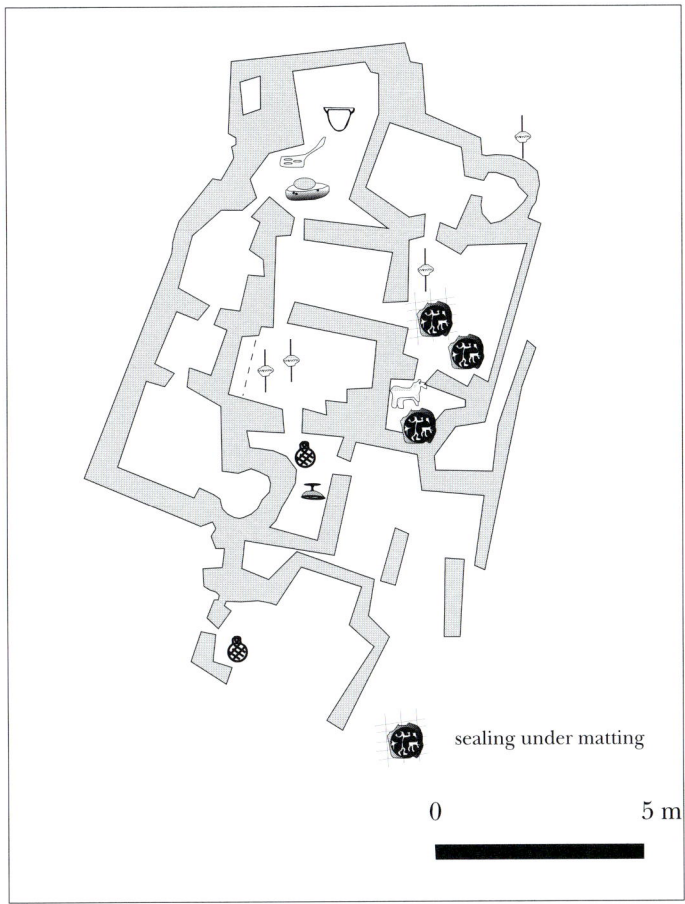

Figure 5.19   Distribution of artifactual remains in situ in Level XIA/B, square 5M building complex.

itself was of a completely different configuration, as discussed above. In the past, these differences would be used as the basis to argue for an intrusion of new "peoples." However, the continuity in stylistic repertoires for pottery, architecture, and seals and the continuity in the kinds of functions conducted by Gawrans, argue against such an intrusion.

Evolutionary Change in Function and Organization

The first noticeable change of XI/XA from XIA/B is the presence of a formal temple (Figure 5.26). This tripartite building met all the criteria for a temple. It had (1) thick walls, large rooms, (2) a liwan (recessed portico) entrance with a wide door, (3) a large hearth or podium, (4) a niche in the back wall facing the door, (5) a large pot set in the floor of an adjoining room, (6) signs of plaster, white and perhaps red, and (7) no clear domestic or craft artifacts, all set to the

cardinal points The large podium in the central hall had signs of burning. What makes this temple such a sharp contrast to XIA is that it had such easy access from the slope of the mound that was defended in XIA. The artifacts, too, fit the function. A fancy serving dish and a couple of small jars for holding ritual substances are consistent. A grinding stone is reminiscent of the braziers and phallic grinding stone of the temple of Level VIII.

Adjoining the back (west) wall of the temple of XI were a series of rooms (same figure). Four of the enclosures were equipped with ovens. Although Tobler speaks of "cooking and pottery ovens" (1950:16), he does not give any clue which is which, or why he thinks one is a kiln, another an oven. The only oven illustrated from the oven rooms is the one found in the northernmost room. If one can take the drawing of that oven in locus sheet 121 at face value, this construction does not appear to be a pottery kiln. It looks most like a short bread oven (see Wulff 1966: Figure 414). Plate 2c in Chapter 3 supports this conclusion

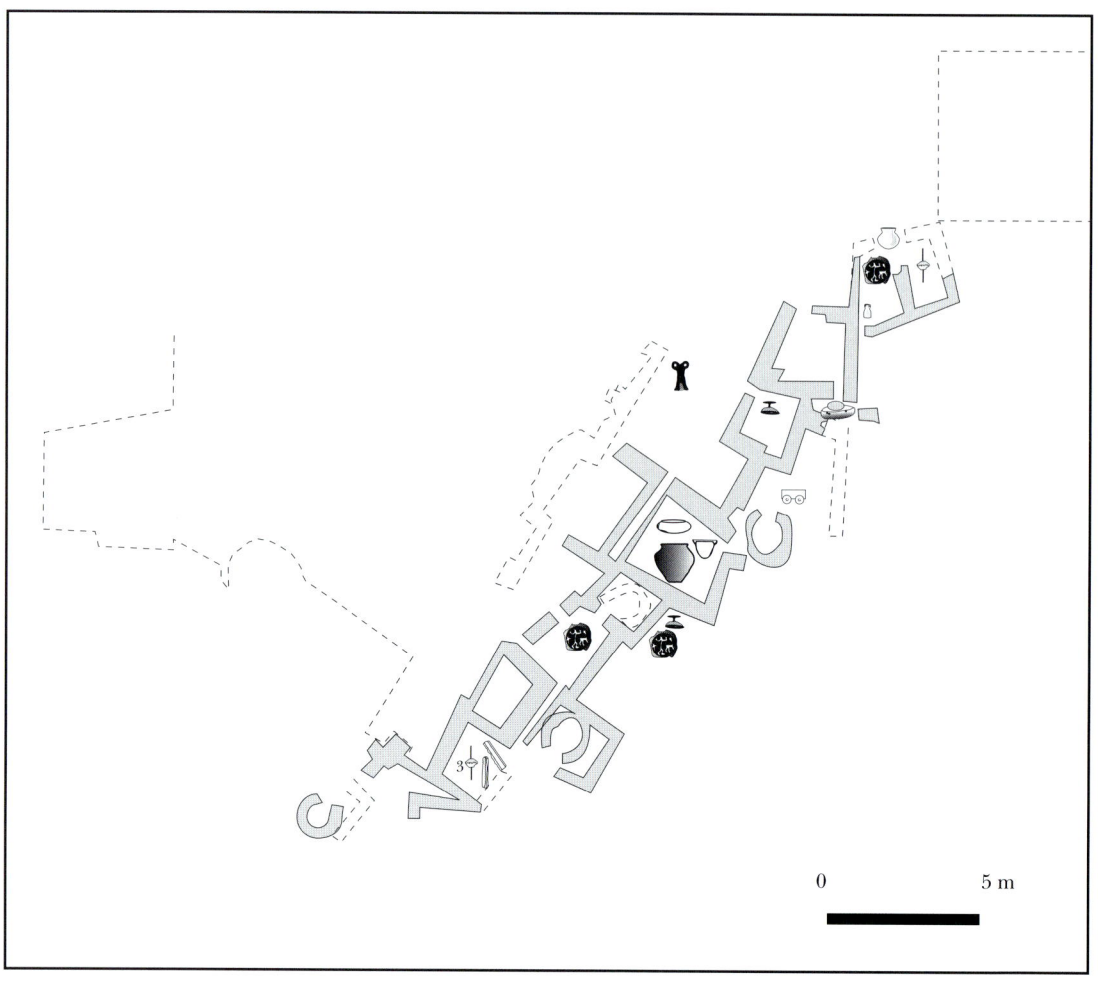

Figure 5.20   Distribution of artifactual remains in situ in Phase XIA, Level XIA/B, southeastern flank houses.

by showing how the new oven was built over a knocked down tanur, or traditional upright bread oven. An odd sort of cup was found in context next to the oven of this enclosure. Chits describe it as a "clay gadget." The cup looks like a ladle with its handle broken off. The other objects found in the enclosures include an animal figurine, a fine ware incised cup, and a small jar. From the number of ovens alone, it is possible to infer that this set of rooms had kitchens. The oven enclosures probably served a series of small houses to their west, although it is certainly likely that the southernmost oven room served the temple. All but one of the houses faced the main north-south street of the mound.

Whether the residents of these houses worked for or in the temple or not, what is striking about these and the other houses in Phase XI are their small size. Gone are the large, extended family residences of Levels XII and XIA/B. The one possible exception was the house in Square 7Q (Figure 5.30).

The temple and these rooms survived into the succeeding XA phase.

Another set of buildings, the large tripartite building at the northern end of the north-south street and the adjoining buildings, also remained standing and in use in XA (Figures 5.27 and 5.38). This large northern building was one of three tripartite buildings of the Phase XI mound (assuming the reconstruction of the southern one is correct). The walls of this building were at places a meter thick. The walls of the main hall were plastered, and the walls by the front door were painted red. The room north of the main room was covered with matting, and the western part of the southern room had a terrazzo sherd floor set into a wattle under-floor. Large military ballistas were found in two concentrations in the building or in an adjoining room. Because of the thickness of the walls and its position by the accessible northern slope of the mound, and

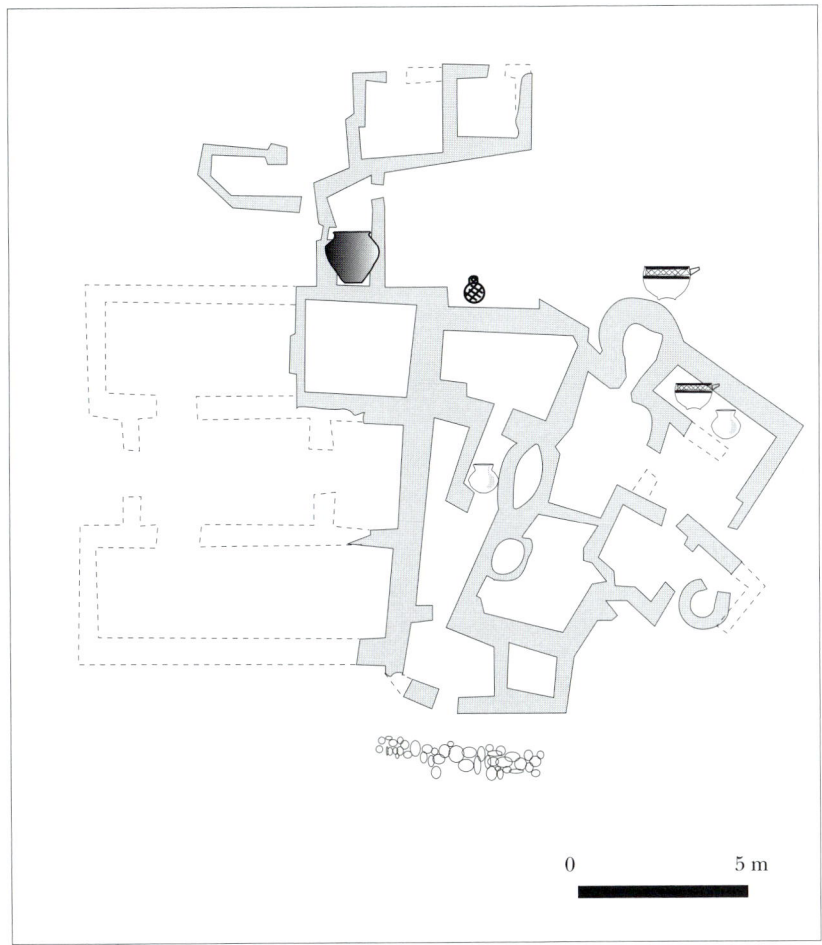

Figure 5.21 Distribution of artifactual remains in situ in Phase XIA, Level XIA/B, southern complex.

because of the ballistas, its excavators called this building the "Fortress."

Yet, the interpretation of the building's function also depends on the material found in an area in front of its doors. This is especially so in the case of this complex, because the small "u" of wall adjoining the south wall of building may have been part of a stairway to a second floor. If so, this building had a second floor like the large northeastern building of Level VIII (see below). The original contents of the second floor may have spilled out into the courtyards when the second floor finally collapsed. Some of the material out in the front courtyard or plaza—including cups, serving bowls, pendants, beads, and a Wide Flower Pot— reinforce the interpretation of a domestic function for the building.

However, other of the materials found in this courtyard suggest that the building may have housed many different functions. Two potsherds of double rim or channel jars were found in the southern flank

of the building. Vessels of this type are set in ante-rooms of temples or alternatively are used for dying cloth or fermenting beverages (see Chapter 4). The excavation crew discovered many spindle whorls in the debris of the open plaza. They along with the bowls suggest that this was a locale where cloth was being made. Two hammers and woodworking tools imply that considerable craft activity was taking place in the open court, associated with the tripartite building or one of the other buildings bordering that open area (see below).

That impression is reinforced by one of the odder finds in plaza, which was reported in locus sheet 105. Fifty small clay "ballistas," small jars, a hammer, two mortars and a pestle were found under a reed mat (the position of the mortars in chits is inconsistent with the locus sheet, placing them a couple meters away in the same square). The area in front of this building constituted one of two open plazas in the excavated area of XI. The houses to the west presented a

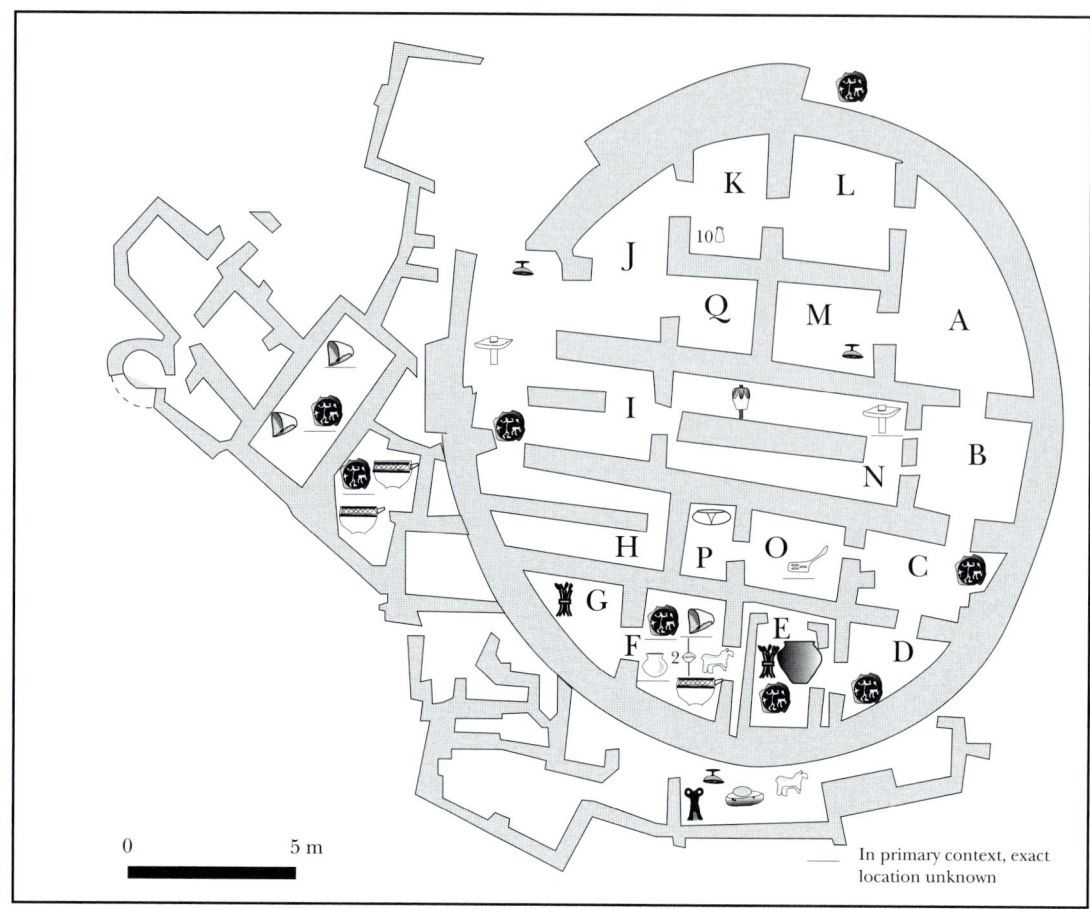

Figure 5.22   Distribution of artifactual remains in situ in Phase XIA, Level XIA/B, Round House.

solid wall to the plaza, which therefore directed people into the tripartite building.

By size, shape, orientation, and contents this was a secular public building. It had the formal tripartite plan with easily accessible double doors, and orientation to cardinal points that matches the characteristics of a temple. However, as defined by Jawad, it was oriented in a different direction from the temple. It also lacked the podium, niches, or contents of a temple. What is striking about its contents are two nests of military ballistas in a corner of the main room and in an adjoining room. Otherwise, the rooms of the building contained spheres, a miniature vessel, a sherd of a painted cup and a pendant, not to mention all the craft tools in the plaza. All of these are potentially domestic items, which could easily have been lost in building up floors during the XA phase. Yet, its functions did include preparation for defense. It may have served as well as a domicile for persons involved in the activities or perhaps, for individuals with chiefly rank.

South of the public building was a house (same figure), whose artifactual remains are notable because

another cache of military ballistas were found there (locus card 103). The latter building contained a cup, plate, and grinding stone, in other words, domestic activities. A palette was found in an alley room. It may have been from a store of goods, emptied later, or for grinding pigments for craft or cosmetics.

The two-room building at the southern end of the secular public building (Figure 5.27) contained domestic serving items: daisy cups, a small jar, serving plate and a lone spindle whorl on their floors, apparently in primary context. This may be the room with a terrazzo floor into which a mortar was set (locus sheet 133 does not specify which room of 6O contained this feature). It was clearly a small, family home on the main street of town.

The middle of the excavated mound contained, for the first time in the levels I am discussing, an area of clearly specialized production activities (Figure 5.28). In the southeast corner were two rooms badly cut by tombs 109 to 111, sunk from Level X. Just north of those disturbed rooms there was some indication of ceramic manufacture. The

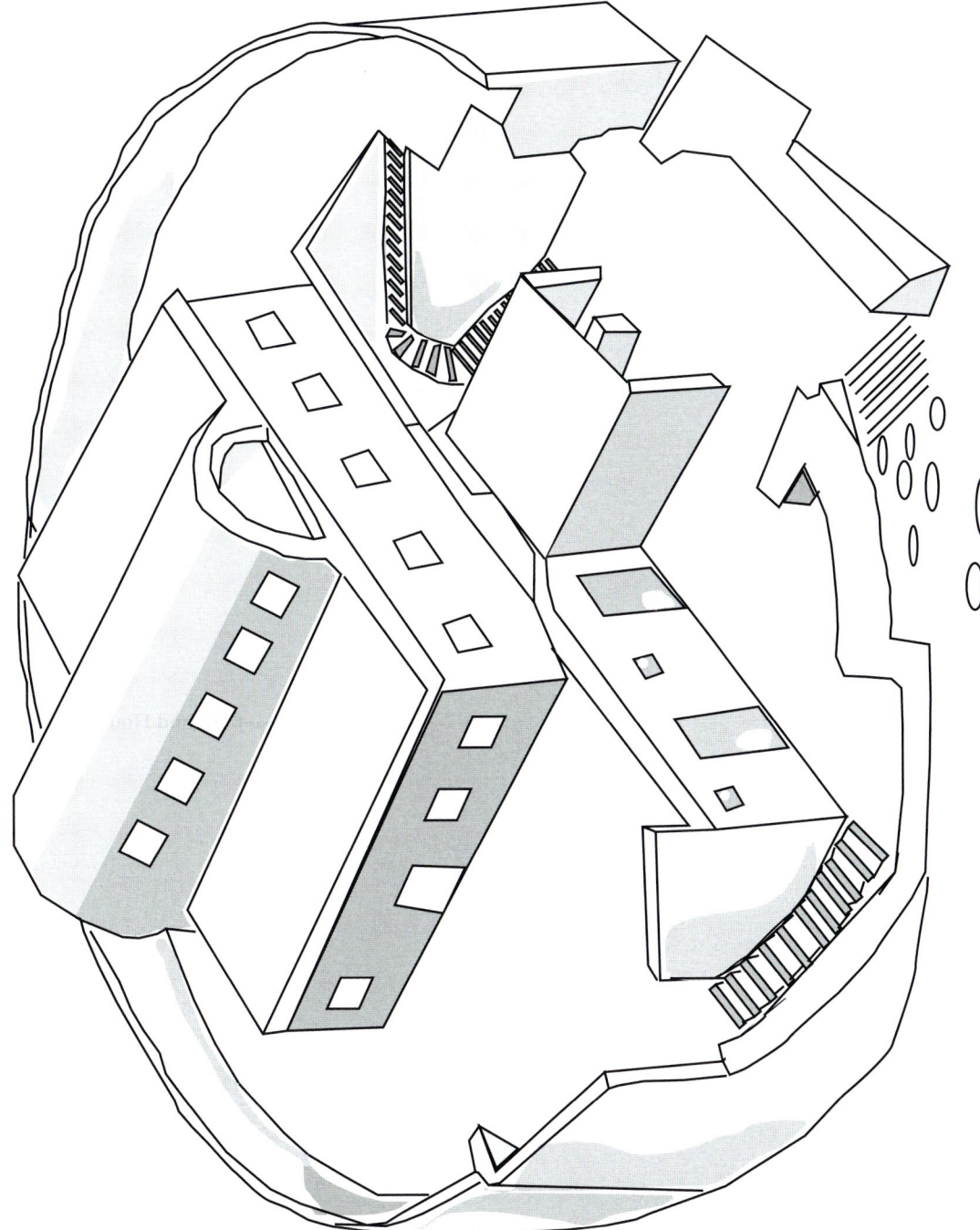

Figure 5.23   Three dimensional reconstruction of the Round House, Phase XIA, Level XIA/B.

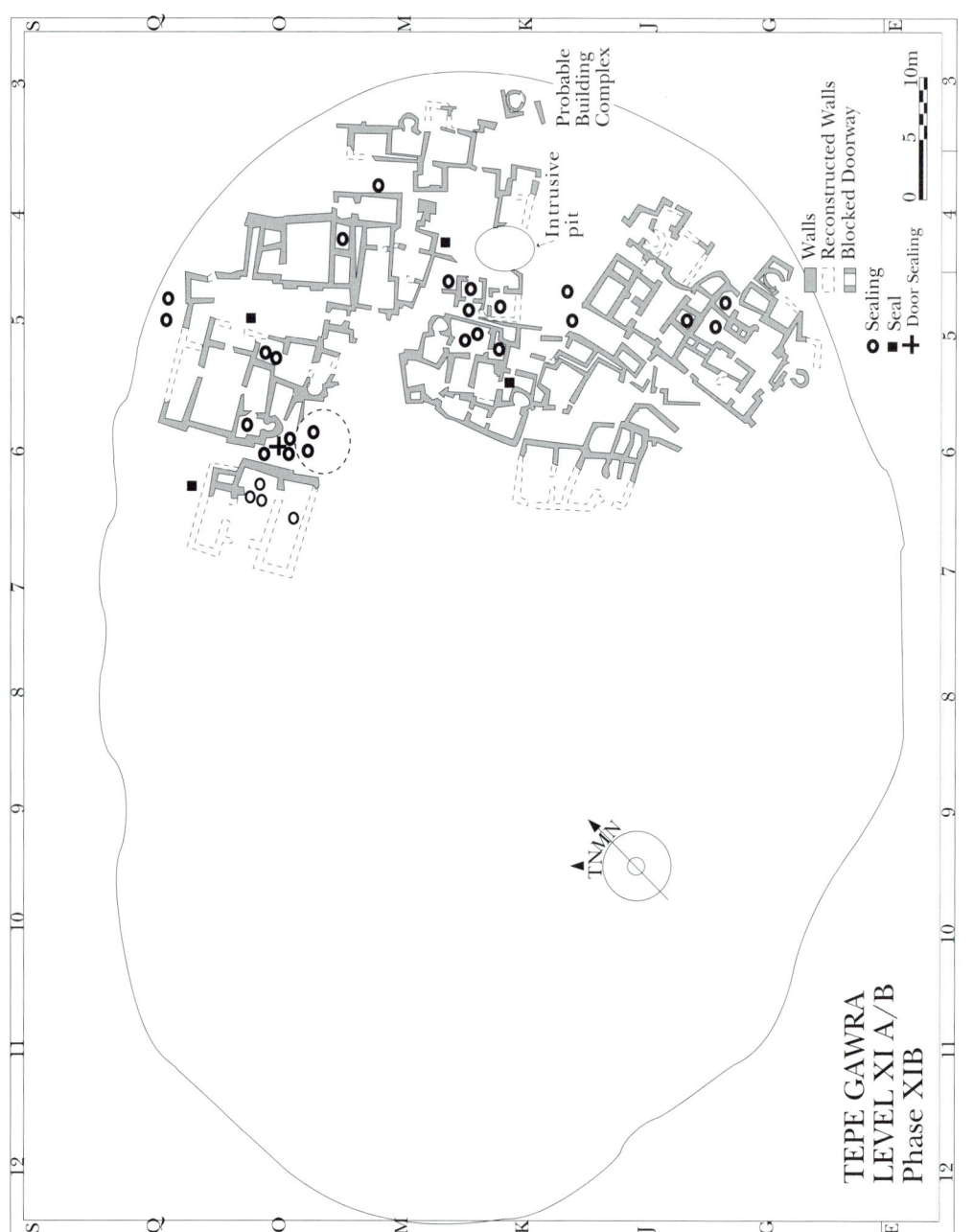

TEPE GAWRA
LEVEL XI A/B
Phase XIB

Probable Building Complex

Intrusive pit

Walls
Reconstructed Walls
Blocked Doorway

○ Sealing
■ Seal
+ Door Sealing

TN MN

0   5   10m

Figure 5.24   Distribution of seals and sealings in situ in Phase XIB, Level XIA/B.

Figure 5.25 Distribution of seals and sealings in situ in Phase XIA, Level XIA/B.

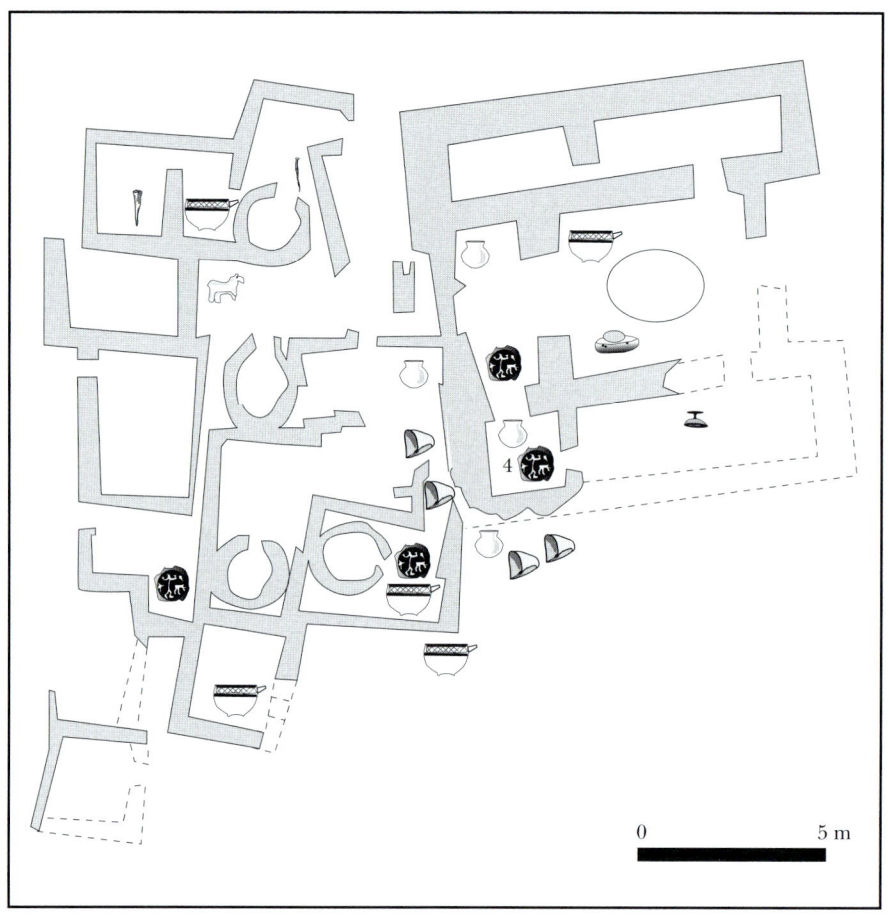

Figure 5.26   Distribution of artifactual remains in situ in Phase XI, Level XI/XA, temple and adjoining houses.

evidence for that activity includes the kiln in Square 5M, two large caches of cigar-shaped ballistas, and a hard packed red pavement in the area of Squares 5M, 4M, and 4K (see Figure 3.9). The oven cut by tomb 111 is drawn with a series of circles. These are not explained but look like the holes cut into the top of the firing chamber of a kiln, unlike the baking ovens described above. In a locus sheet of 20 December 1934 (unnumbered), the excavator speaks of a hard red clay pavement stretching from this area to the north wall of the temple. This floor was surely laid over a large trash pit to provide a hard smooth surface on the burned debris and fill over XIA. This is the only place where such care is taken. Such preparation would be useful in an area where ceramics were dried. The red color and hardness would certainly be enhanced if hot material was fired or dumped on it. In addition, the two large caches of cigar-shaped ballistas, which I argued in Chapter 4 were firing chips or stores of levigated clay, are found just south of tomb 109 (locus 104) and due east of the "kiln"

(locus 172) in Square 4M (just beyond the red pavement). Among the ballistas were a series of stones, whose size and function are unknown. Another minor support for the idea of a ceramic manufacturing area is the baked hut statue and unidentified figurine found near the oven. The other animal figurine near the hut statue was from a considerably lower elevation in XI. Its chit implies it laid on a floor under the floor on which the "kiln" sits (10.62 m. is presumably the top of the firing chamber, not of the whole oven) and over an earlier floor of XI. The third figurine could have been found anywhere in Square 5M. Given the location of the other hut statues, the placement of this one is best explained if it were just fired or, more accurately, misfired and dumped. On the other hand, as mentioned above, no cooking/bread ovens were found associated with the large tripartite building in the northeast or any of the series of rooms and enclosures on the eastern flank of the mound. In the end, therefore, a conclusion that pottery was being manufactured in this section of the

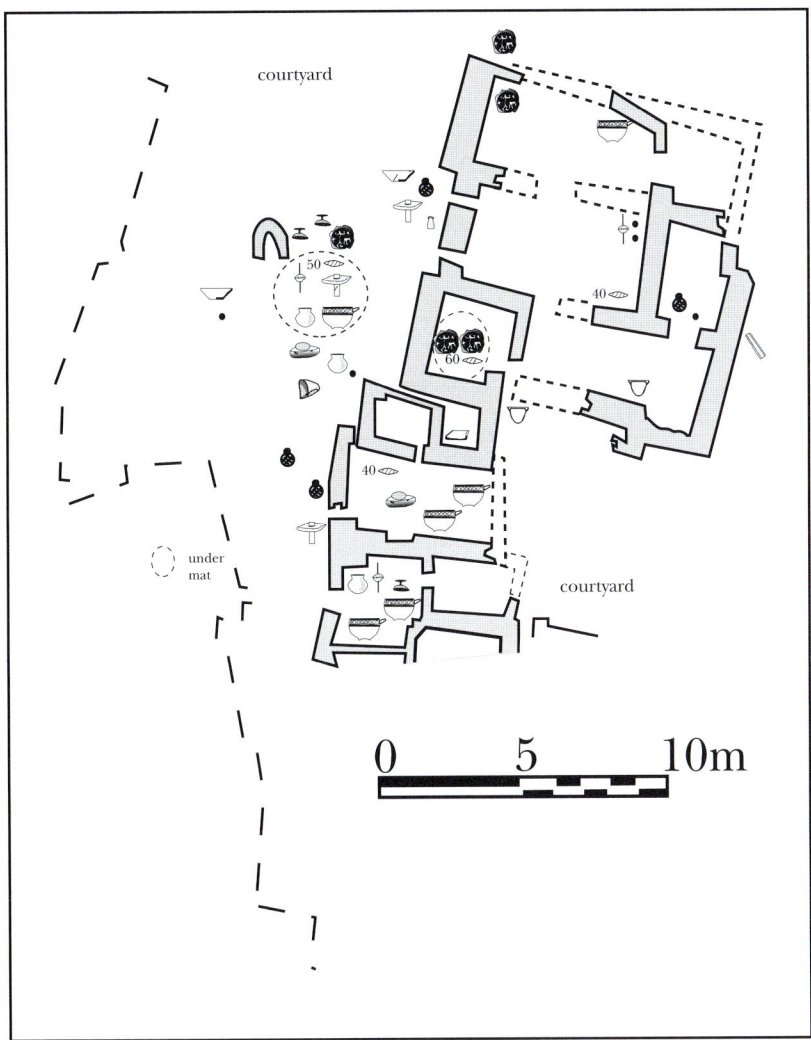

Figure 5.27   Distribution of artifactual remains in situ in Phase XI, Level XI/XA, secular public building and adjoining houses.

mound is certainly suggested, but the evidence is circumstantial.

To the west of the "kiln" (same figure) were the blocks of rooms (with rooms 44, 48, 69, and 52). The building with room 52 constituted a second specialized production site, in this case, a weaving shop and its storeroom. The first signs of this activity were the unusual concentration of spindle whorls (many in primary context), loom weights, and loom bases recovered in this area, including the street to its south. In the street excavators found a sherd of a double or channel rim jar. Without inferring too much for this find, a washbowl is a feature of dying or preparing wool for combing (Forbes 1964, volume IV). More directly, in no other part of Gawra during Phase XI was there an equal concentration of cloth making items

and, at the same time, such a lack of artifacts thought to be used in other activities. In no other part of the XI mound were there as many entrances from the street and other parts of the complex as for these rooms, implying a traffic pattern with much movement and little privacy. The doorless room near the northern door to this complex was, I suggest, a storeroom. That room yielded a Wide Flower Pot and a large storage jar buried between its floors.

The remaining buildings with rooms 44, 48, and 69 were by shape and content small private houses. Each had a cooking oven and domestic artifacts (the oven probably attached to house 44 was probably destroyed along with its eastern walls, assuming there was one).

On the other side of the main north-south street was a functional equivalent of the block just discussed

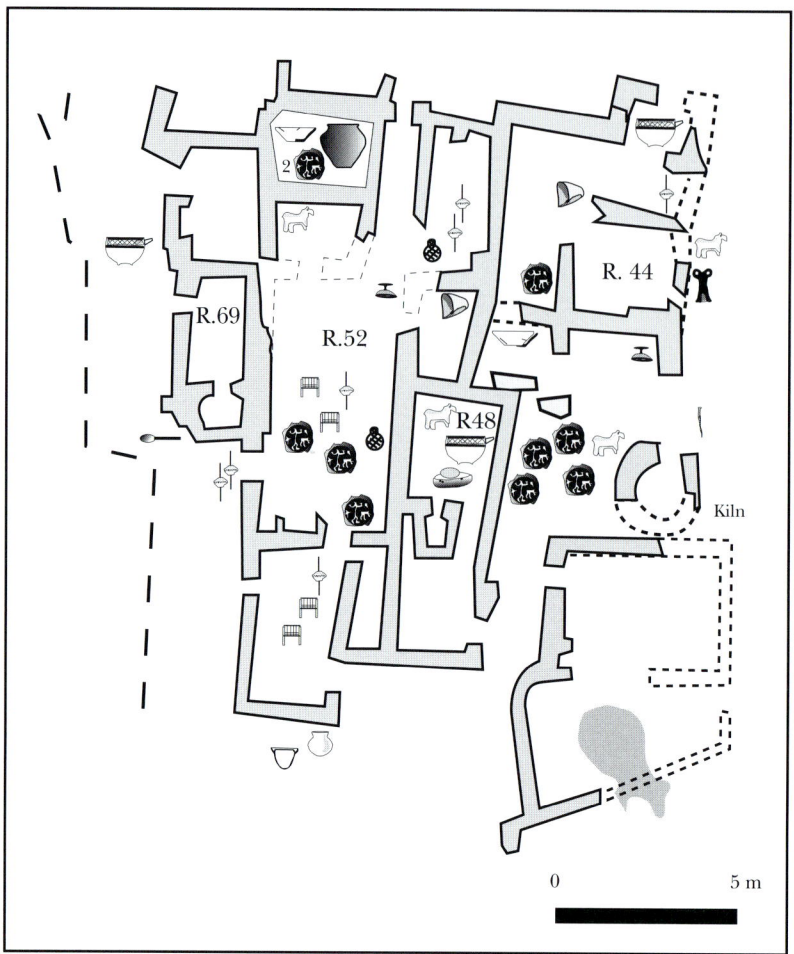

Figure 5.28   Distribution of artifactual remains in situ in Phase XI, Level XI/XA, weaving shop, kiln, and houses.

in that it includes specialized shops and houses. The block, illustrated in Figure 5.29, included buildings with rooms 73, 82, and 86). The first building (with room 73) yielded another set of spindle whorls, small ballistas (bobbins?) and loom parts. A small bin at its southeast corner, called a "dirt oven" in chits, yielded a hammer and bone spatula. Other rooms had celts on their floors. This area appears to house a spinning shop and a shop where small cutting tools and celts were used. From Chapter 4, in which celts were proposed to be wood-working tools, a woodworking area seems likely as well.

The two sets of rooms north of the shops and probably the sets of rooms north of that (Figure 5.30) were all dwellings, perhaps related to the shops, perhaps not. Unfortunately, the building complexes in Figure 5.30 were dug after Speiser returned as field director and the quality of recording and finds are consequently of lower reliability and quantity.

Two of the more unexpected finds in the large context illustrated in Figure 5.29 were a pair of cult stands or censers, one in Square 7M and one in the northwestern quadrant of Square 8M. Both were found in what is likely to be secondary, not primary contexts. The censer in Square 8M, a classic cult stand or censer with triangular cut-outs was found at a low elevation near an infant grave. Its relation to the grave, which had no grave goods, is unclear. The other censer was found much higher, either on a later floor or in room fill.

The area at the southern end of the north-south street in Squares 6K/J was made up of two sets of rooms (Figure 5.31). These were by structure and shape a house, including a kitchen with an oven, a main room, and two adjoining rooms. At the entrance to the last set of these rooms was an enclosure called the "fake oven" in various chits. Why it was "fake" is never specified, as a small enclosure for a hearth in the street would not be a bad use of space. The

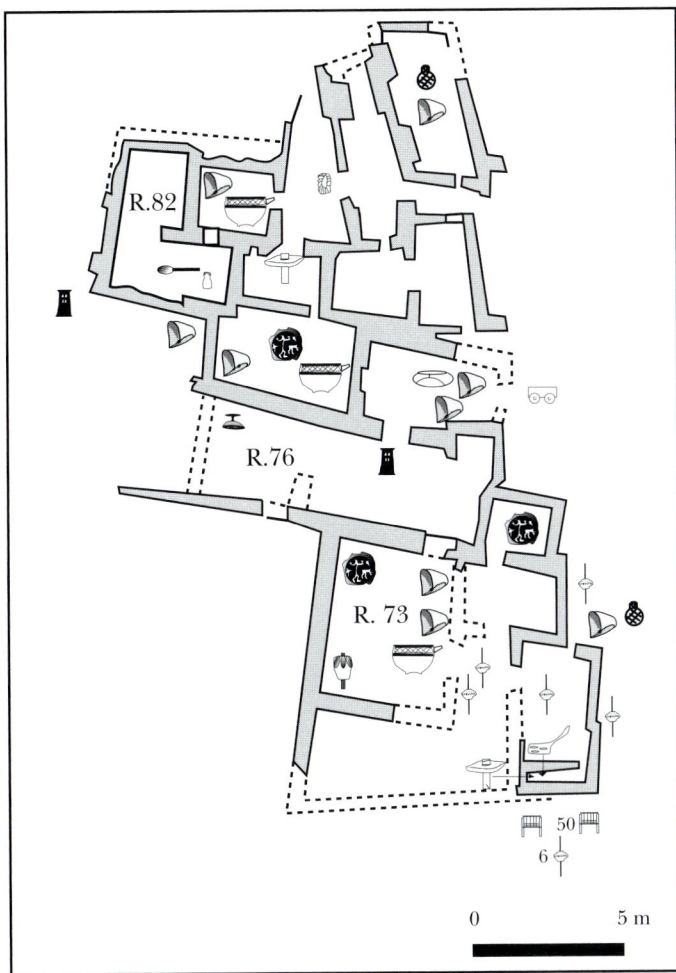

Figure 5.29   Distribution of artifactual remains in situ in Phase XI,
Level XI/XA, western shops and houses.

adjoining rooms to their south were apparently used as storage rooms. The main room had a two-mouth jar and a storage jar filled with carbonized grain (locus sheet 156?). The other room had a hut statue. A grinding stone and small hammer in the main room suggest a home as well. The semi-circular wall of the main room was probably a bin, much like ones in modern Middle Eastern homes (Kramer 1982: Figure 4.11).

At the end of Phase XI (same figure), the rooms to the north of the house just described were abandoned. Chits indicate that they had been converted into a dump. Many sealings and figurines and a hut statue were found "in a welter of ashes" in those rooms. Some of this trash may have come from the enclosures with ovens or more likely, the "kiln" (Figure 5.28). A plate and a small jar were found beneath the ash, implying that a domestic function may have typified this building when it was in active use.

The remains of the southern complex of XIA continued into XI, now numbered 27, 112 and 113 (Figure 3.9). They appear to have adjoined a third, reconstructed tripartite building. From photographs (see Plate 3b and Chapter 3) a doorway was cut into room 27. If a tower existed in XIA, it apparently was eliminated in XI. Enclosure 27, which is often called one of two "deep doorless rooms" in the field notes, was filled with sealings, a storage jar, a hut statue, and various workshop tools: a hammer, a mortar set in the floor, an awl, a washing bowl, and a dish (Figure 5.32). This enclosure must have served as a work area for the building to which it was attached (as no door was found, entry may have been from an open roof or second floor). Restricted (sealed) containers would have been opened for processing there and their sealings discarded. Room 112 of the complex contained a trough ("like a baby's bath"), a cup, two beakers (including a daisy impressed beaker), a

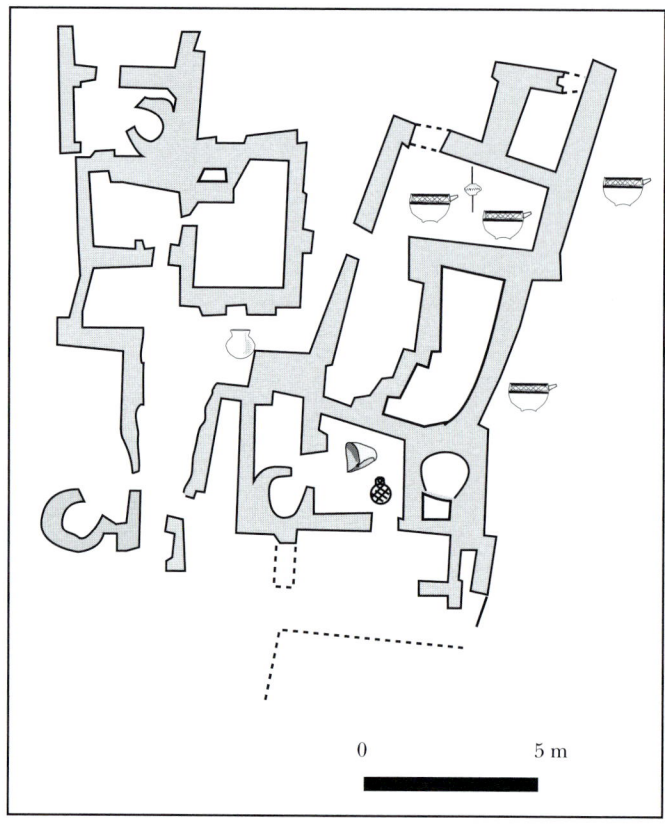

Figure 5.30   Distribution of artifactual remains in situ in Phase XI, Level XI/XA, northwest houses.

spouted bowl, and a small jar. The original suggestion that these "rooms" are a "watchtower" may have applied to Level XIA/B, but does not seem to fit XI. My own suggestion (Rothman 1988) that the southern part were sheep pens does not seem to fit the building when its XIA history is made clear. That earlier interpretation needs re-evaluation.

The placement of all three tripartite buildings by the edge of the mound may indicated a public purpose for the larger polity or they may be receiving stations for restricted goods coming onto the mound.

On the eastern edge of the mound, a few walls remained in Square 3/4 O/M (Figure 5.33). In addition, a podium from the building that once stood there and a niche in the wall were recovered. The exact function of this building is unclear. It has two of the elements of a temple, but appears not to have had any others. A jar stand was found in the building along with a cooking pot, weights, and a game piece. It is possible to speculate that it may have been a shrine, but it is otherwise impossible to verify.

The last part of the excavation of Phase XI was the trench through the unexcavated western part of the mound (Figure 5.34). The Phase XI floors of this trench were lower than much of the adjoining mound suggesting that no large scale building sat immediately below it. There was evidence that it was not merely a trash pit, however. The reference to "an old oven" in the chit for animal figurine 1165 suggests that some kind of work area existed there at some point in time. At the same time, the lower of the two XI floors in the West Trench was covered with ash debris. Squares 9M and 10M yielded a variety of stone and clay items: a Wide Flower Pot, two amulets, two metal pins, a bowl stand, two obsidian blades, two beads, and two celts. No single function can be assigned these assorted artifacts.

Functional Size

Phase XI of Level XI/XA contains a variety of functions and functional areas, each fairly specialized. There were defensive and storage areas, a temple, specialized cloth workshops, residences (some with evidence of craft activity), perhaps a ceramic production area and evidence of wood working in a specialized

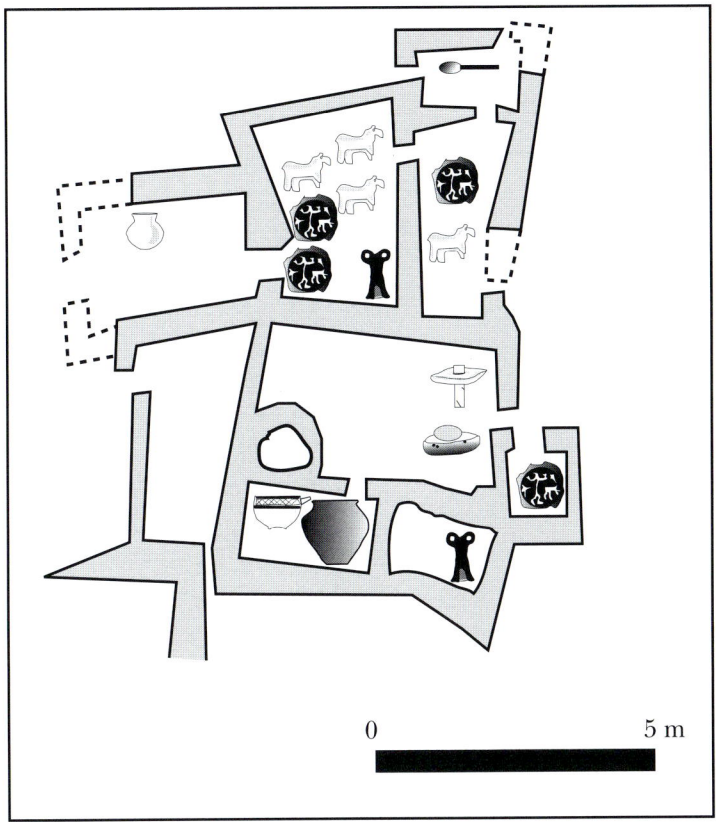

Figure 5.31   Distribution of artifactual remains in situ in Phase XI, Level XI/XA, southern houses by north-south street.

shop. One sickle blade was found, but out of context. In that, Gawra does not seem a village. The site does seem to have represented a quantum leap in centralization and complexity from Levels XII and XIA/B. The defensive posture of XIA/B was absent, as was an end in fire. The occupation of XI gradually evolved into Phase XA, where two of the major functions, represented by the temple and public administration building continued, while of the rest of the buildings decayed and were replaced.

Based on mortuary practice, the population of Gawra XI was divided into groups of two statuses (see Appendix). Those buried with finer material goods in libn or other built tombs constituted one group and those with few paltry remains, buried in pits or pots, were the second. There is no evidence of a third tier of status, as one would expect in more complex polity.

Population

Based on the method of counting people per house, the population of Phase XI rose to 414. By the per-room method, it equaled only 313. It is a function of the change in the structure of housing that, compared to XII and XIA/B, the "by-room" method fell short of the per-house method.

External Relations

In one sense Phase XI should have a greater role in regional exchange. All the imported products of earlier times—gold, alabaster, lapis lazuli, obsidian—continued, yet from the much expanded sample of clay sealings, a surprising result ensued (Rothman and Blackman 1990). All the clays used in sampled sealings on the XI mound were from the homogeneous, local source. Although the site was still receiving some of the same exotic goods, its products—cloth, and wood—seem more locally targeted. As Kowaleski et al. (1983) predicted, the focus was increasingly local. Gawrans made an attempt to centralize the focus of other local communities to the site of Gawra through religion and locally desirable goods, not through inclusion in broader geographical networks.

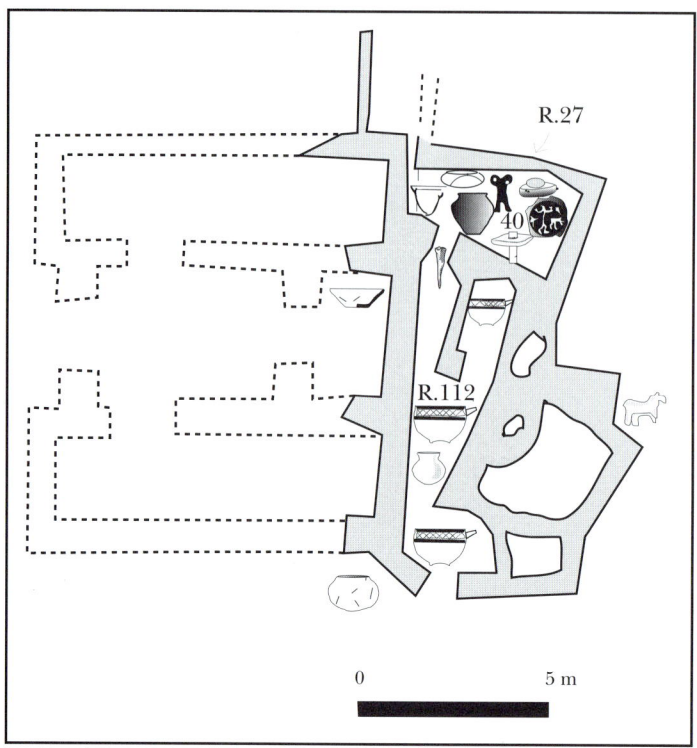

Figure 5.32   Distribution of artifactual remains in situ in Phase XI,
Level XI/XA, southern tripartite building and associated rooms.

Administration

Seals and sealings were found in most functional areas of the Phase XI mound. Overall, the seals and sealings of Phase XI of Level XI/XA created a pattern remarkably similar to the proposed functional map of the site (Figure 5.35). As stated above, religious ritual, chiefly or public functions, craft tools, and products were found in buildings and spaces other than domiciles. In fact, even counting seals and sealings in a secondary or tertiary context, the only control artifact found in any domestic room was a seal in a house in Square 6O northwest of the cloth workshop and south of the secular public building, and that seal was a blank. On the other hand, sealings were found in each specialized functional area on the mound. Seals were found in a limited subset of the specialized buildings. If my initial assumptions are correct, this means that a coordinating group controlled each of these specialized functions. Authorized individuals in those institutions were opening restricted items. Further, some seals must have been applied to sealings by seal-bearers for later storage or for transport to other sites in a very few of these locations (see Rothman 1988, 1994a).

What is particularly noteworthy about the pattern from Gawra XI is that these seal designs appear to have been a kind of symbolic representation of social identities and social groups because of the particular way they were distributed. Sealings with figural designs showing predation scenes appeared in the context of workshops, whereas sealings with figural designs of horned animals or herds of animals were found in the temple and secular public building (Rothman 1994b). Defining the offices or groups who used these designs seems to me all but impossible, but that the pattern existed strikes me as very significant, as the distinctions of administrative spheres of action may have reached a level where it was consciously symbolized. That there were two functioning weaving shops indicates that some cloth products were exported, but cloth, except exceptional kinds, would be more useful for local villagers or pastoral nomads passing through this area.

Phase XA, Level XI/XA

As described in detail in Chapter 3 above, XA represents a remodeling of XI (Figure 3.10). In a sense, the phase gradually faded out and was replaced by Level X. The transition to X was first apparent in Squares 8O and 8Q, as the only rooms that shared the gray brick of XI/XA in Level X are 1029 to 1032.

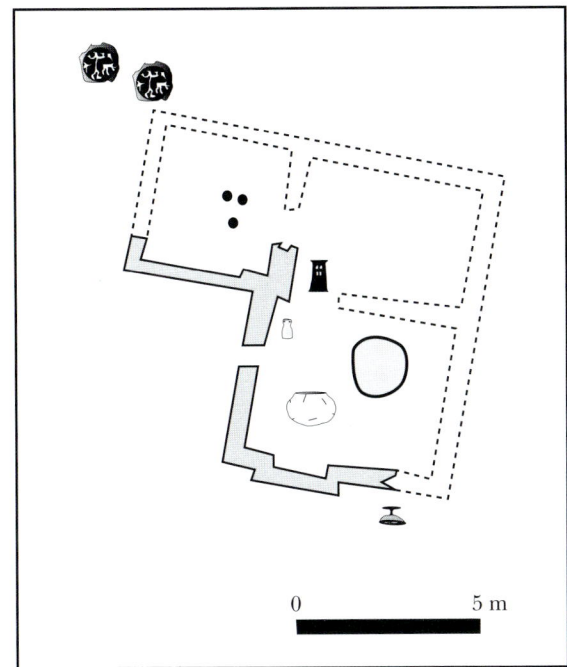

Figure 5.33   Distribution of artifactual remains in situ in Phase XI, Level XI/XA, possible eastern shrine.

Those buildings overlie the bottom part of room 71 and the open courtyard 54 and may have cut it (Figures 3.10 and 3.11). As such ancient Gawrans cleaned out some buildings, and the artifactual remains are less representative than from earlier levels. The number of artifacts is 25% less than Phase XI, Levels XII and XIA/B, and VIII. Although there are patterns worth observing, they may not be as significant as those found in other levels or sub-level phases.

Functional Size

The temple and area of houses to the west of it continued for some time (Figure 5.36), although they may have gone out of use before the end of XA (or more accurately, the time when XA and construction associated with Level X begin to merge). They retained their same character until near their end squatter-like rooms were built over decaying temple walls.

During the remodeling of XA, the traffic pattern of the site changed. The open court entrance in the north and the narrow path in the south were blocked. As a result, the open court 93 of XI was subdivided by new abutting walls, and new enclosures and rooms were created (Figures 3.9 and 3.10). Along the western side of the excavated part of the mound a new beehive of rooms was constructed. In the process two large open courtyards or areas were created in Phase XA: area 15 in Square 6M and 11 in Square 6J (Figure 3.10).

The new rooms in Square 6J (Figure 5.36) restricted access to the Square 6J court. Tobler feels this may be a new entranceway to the site (Tobler 1950:13). Easy access to the 6M court was blocked by a series of walls. Tombs 109, 110, 111, and 114 cut room 80 and enclosure 81. That these rooms were complete and were functioning is demonstrated by a feature noted in locus sheet 115 (not mentioned in Tobler's report). An almost complete hearth, cut by tomb 114, was found in Square 4K (room 80). The hearth was dug from a floor at the elevation of 10.90 meters. It was rectangular (50 × 35 cm., 24 cm. deep). Cooking ash filled it at the time of its discovery.

The new rooms in Square 6J abutted the older rooms adjoining the temple and defined the bottom of the entrance courtyard, according to Tobler (1950:13). Rooms in Square 6/7J (Figure 5.36), according to Tobler (1950:13), were guardrooms, because they had thick walls. Contrary to Tobler, they appear to have been used for food preparation and serving, perhaps hospitality or just domestic activities. The rooms lacked the ovens of most other private houses. In these rooms were found a small jar and a small bowl, a small jar, a clay muller, and two fine cups, a stone cup, preparation pot, Wide Flower Pot (all in primary context), and a weight (in unclear context). All of these are consistent with food preparation or serving. Although nothing was found in the courtyard, by its position on the mound, it would have been a natural public gathering place, perhaps for a periodic market.

North of the temple, the rooms in Square 6M and a curved wall in Square 5M defined another open court (Figures 3.10 and 5.37). This courtyard appears to have been a craft area from its contents. Quite distinct from the serving and preparation functions of the southern rooms, this courtyard (at the elevation of about 10.86 meters) was filled with cutting and hammering tools. Items of personal adornment like spheres, a pin, and a bead were found at a higher level (around 11.11m.), possibly in fill. This unusually dense collection of craft tools must indicate craft activities, perhaps woodworking.

Walls of a broken building (same figure) in the same relative position as the possible shrine of XI had a red ware basin, perhaps a double or channel rim jar, set in its floor (locus sheet 117). A piece of bitumen was found inside it. Whether this was related to the ritual in the temple is hard to say. It lacked the podium of its Phase XI counterpart, and unlike the small annex of the VIIIA temple with its separate room for a ritual bowl, this construction was ten meters from the entrance to the temple.

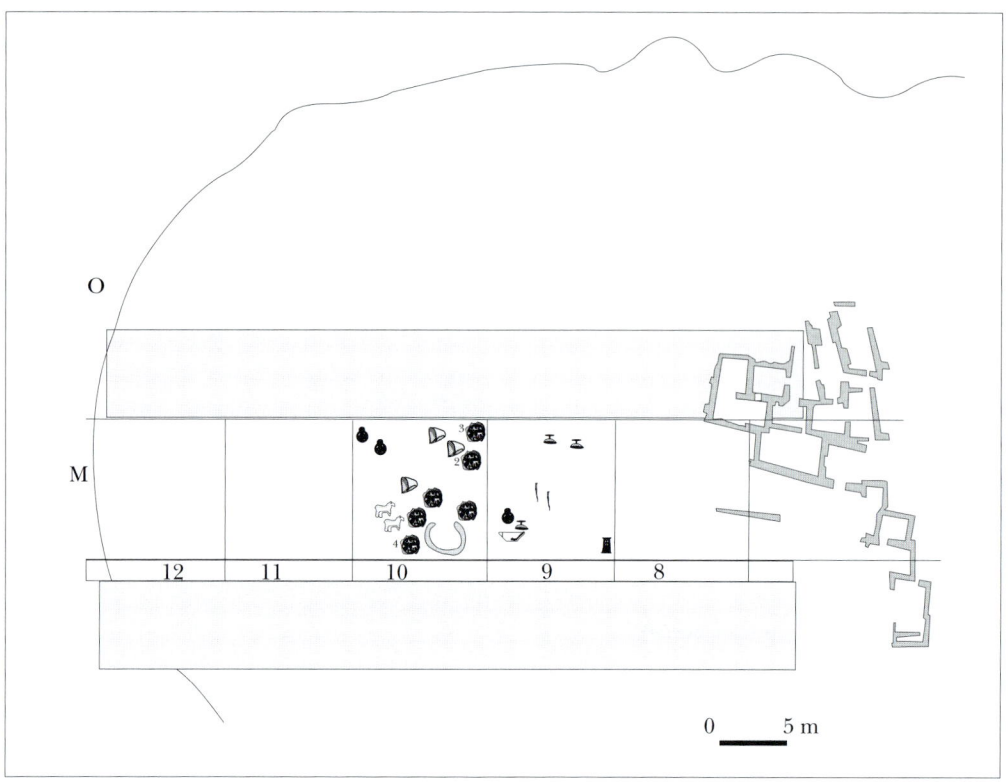

Figure 5.34   Distribution of artifactual remains in situ in Phase XI, Level XI/XA, West Trench.

The functions of the tripartite northern public building (Figure 5.38) have already been discussed. This large, perhaps two story building, continued from Phase XI to XA, although it probably did not last very long into XA. With the exception of some clay spheres and a mace head, no artifacts can be tied to the building in the XA phase. This probably means first that the building was cleaned out before it fell out of use and its second story fell in. There is no evidence that anything was built on top of it until the foundation of the room 808 of Phase VIIIC was laid, a full meter above the tops of its wall stubs. Construction in Level X extended right to the area of the northern tripartite building, where it stopped. Presumably, the mounded rubble of the building under discussion was not cleared away.

The room blocks in the southwest of the excavated area of XA (Figure 5.39) formed one of two areas of new construction in Phase XA. Together these complexes constituted the largest area of structured space in XA. They consisted of a series of medium and small rooms and four ovens. The contents of the complexes appear to be domestic, with some craft functions. With few exceptions, precise provenience is not provided for the artifacts in these buildings, so their function will be analyzed as a unit. Records do indicate that one room contained

two domestic items: a small plate and bowl. These fit the criteria for a block of small two or three room houses. All of these artifacts speak of domestic food storage, preparation, and serving. On the other hand, excavators recovered seven spindle whorls and a celt from room 23 in primary context, indicating some craft production. In addition to craft production, a hut statue was found nearby. Excavators unearthed a small gold and lapis bead in situ by a small niche just south of the room with the spindle whorls.

The other newly built room block was located in Squares 6M to 8M and 6O to 8O (Figure 5.40). At the center of attention in this room block was an unusually large, round oven, bracketed within the curved walls of what presumably was an open court (space 52). Enclosure 52 appears to have been set within the square walls of adjoining rooms with access to room 20, which Tobler (1950:14) cites as one of the only newly constructed rooms with a formal looking plan. As usual, no detail of the oven is available. The multiple entrances in this part of the complex reinforce the impression of specialized craft activities. What may be of most interest is the celt found here on the floor in "black ash refuse." Given the way the walls of room 52 were constructed, the oven must have been generating great heat.

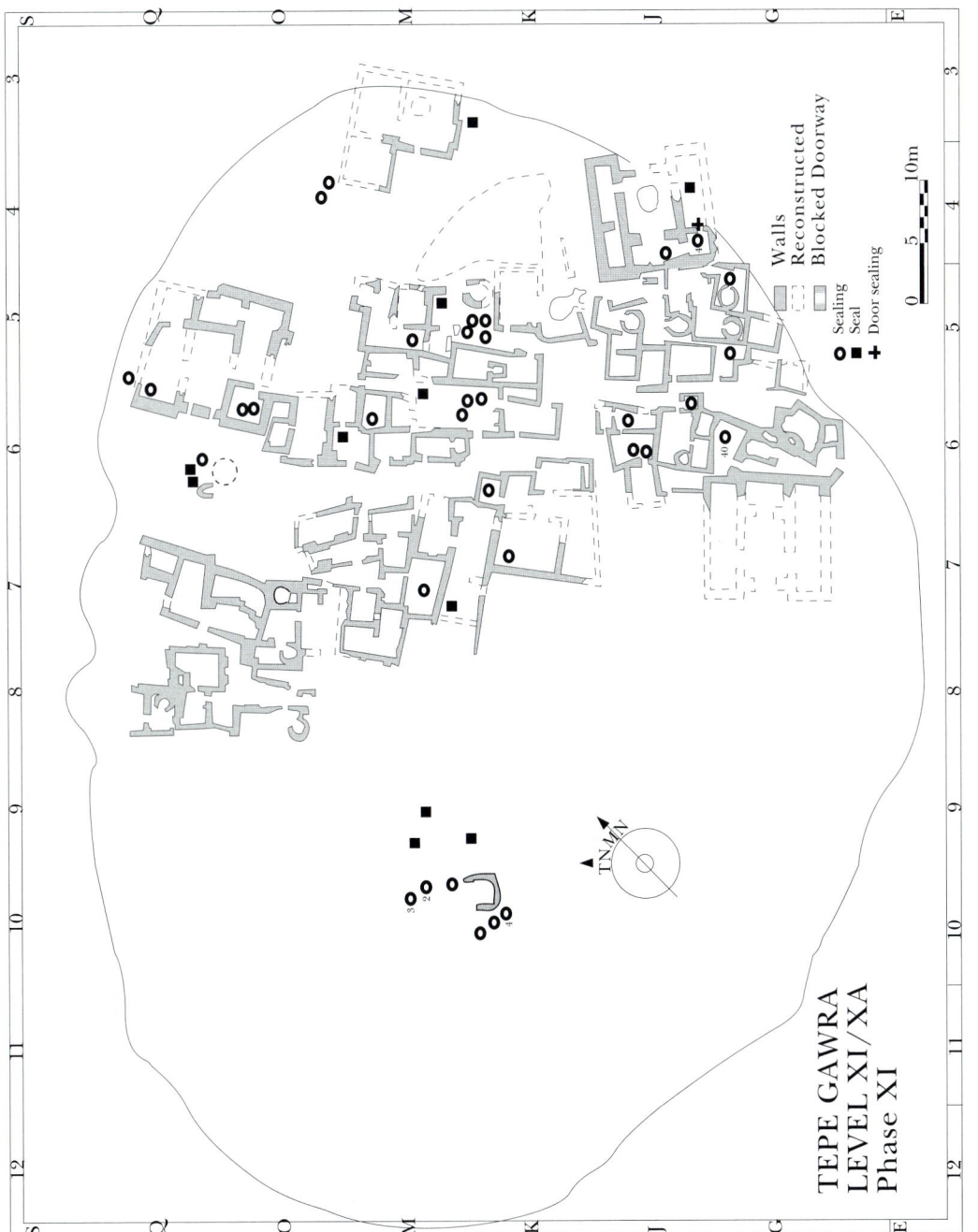

TEPE GAWRA
LEVEL XI/XA
Phase XI

Figure 5.35   Distribution of seals and sealings in situ in Phase XI, Level XI/XA.

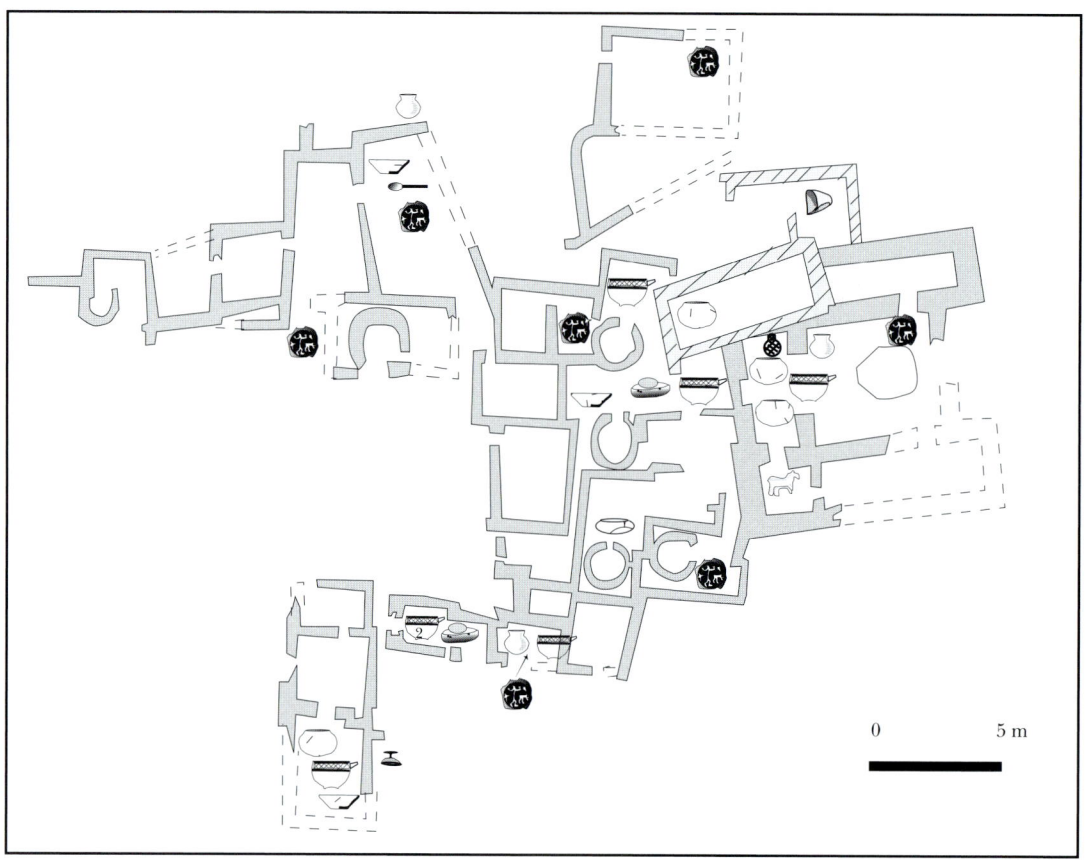

Figure 5.36   Distribution of artifactual remains in situ in Phase XA, Level XI/XA, temple and adjoining buildings.

Whether it was greater heat than is common for a baking oven is not possible to tell. However, one of the bowls (1803) has a thickened side as if were misfired. Alternatively, it could be a ladle with its handle broken off. Although this constitutes the most circumstantial of evidence, the oven in room 52 could have been a pottery kiln. An alternative interpretation is that this single large oven was used to cook and bake for all the residents of the compound, as opposed to the many smaller ovens of the southwest room block. All of these objects imply a domestic function with some possible craft activities. Two graves and two tombs of infants with simple beads were sunk from the floor of rooms 20 and its neighboring room, which like Gawra XII implies a family housing unit. A Wide Flower Pot, which was inverted, covering "stones, sherds, two fragments of burnt animal bone and an animal tooth" (locus sheet 123) was found just north of this complex. It is the only example at Gawra of a magical practice, referred to frequently in later written texts (see, for example, Oppenheimer and Reiner 1980:224, namburbū).

In what had been the large plaza in front of the northern public secular building Gawra residents built two large enclosures (Figure 5.41). These were very large and probably not roofed. They could have been a gateway structure, or perhaps the interior walls were destroyed, and their shape is therefore unclear. About all that was found in them were sherds of an incised cup.

The last area of XA to be discussed is the northwest, where two building complexes continued from Phase XI (Figure 5.42). Remodeling of the ovens and other parts of what had been houses indicates continued use. The few objects excavators recovered from there indicate that they remained domiciles.

Evolutionary Change in Function and Organization

During the XA Phase of Level XI/XA Gawra was less of a manufacturing center than it had been during the XI phase. The ritual specialization continued in the form of the temple. The residents of Gawra at this time were conducting craft activity. Some of it may have been specialized, especially in the open plaza (Figure 5.37) and in the large kiln in area 52.

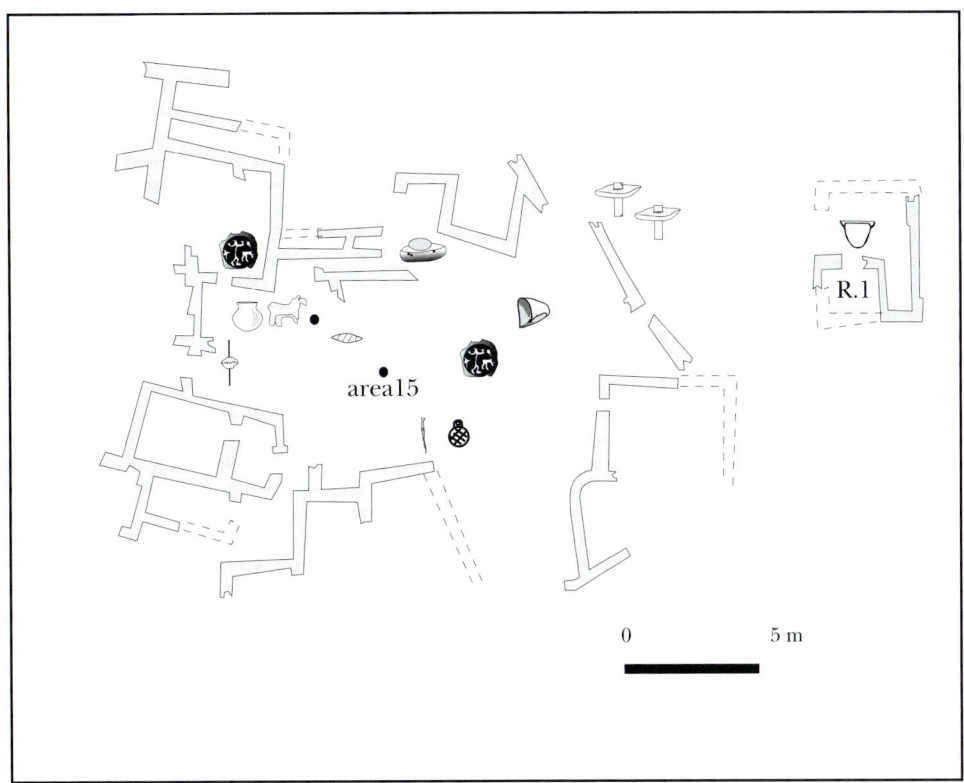

Figure 5.37 Distribution of artifactual remains in situ in Phase XA, Level XI/XA, open court 15.

However, the sense XI gives of functionally specialized cloth making workshops, concentrated in one area of the site does not continue, despite a collection of spindle whorls in room 23 and a piece of a loom found in Square 7O. Overall, then, one gets the impression of a decline in the economic fortunes of those living at Gawra and much more inward directed economic activity. The temple remained as the only major centralized functional area. The site of Gawra may well have served as a local focus for religion and some local exchange.

In contrast to XIA/B and XII, Level XI/XA remained at peace and the transition to the next level appears to have been somewhat gradual and without any intervention from the outside.

Population

Based on the by-house method, the population of Gawra XA was 327. By the per-room method, the population was 256.

External Relations

The kinds and number of imported goods had certainly declined from the XI phase. There were a very few obsidian blades and no cores of any kind. There was some gold and a piece of lapis on a pin, a few pieces of alabaster, but again in smaller numbers than before. However, as stated before, the sample seems arbitrarily low. Like Phase XI, all sampled sealing clays

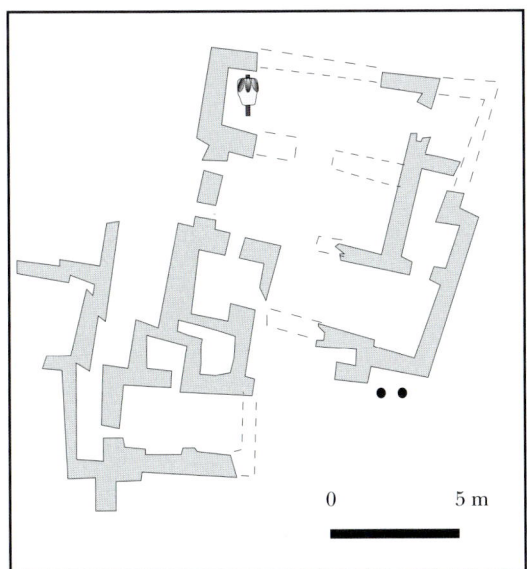

Figure 5.38 Distribution of artifactual remains in situ in Phase XA, Level XI/XA, public secular building.

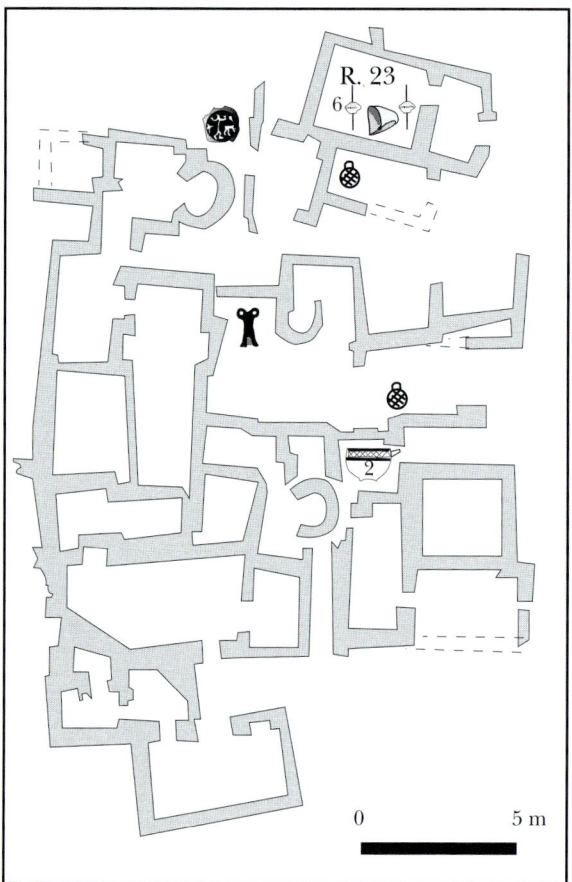

Figure 5.39   Distribution of artifactual remains in situ in Phase XA, Level XI/XA, southwest room block.

were from local sources (Rothman and Blackman 1990). In general, one gets the impression that XA represented a period of decline in the whole network, although confirming this decline would rely on finds from other local sites.

Administration

Sealings still seem to have been associated with the temple or productive areas: near the kiln in room 52, the plaza, the concentration of spindle whorls in room 23 (Figure 5.43). They seem to have been absent from purely domestic contexts, but whether that was a function of preservation or representative of a change is somewhat hard to say with any confidence.

Levels X and IX

The whole plan of X (Figure 3.11) seems to have been a rearrangement of elements of the earlier XI/XA plan. In Phase XI of Level XI/XA the largest

buildings were concentrated at the periphery of the site near the ends of the main streets. In Level X the temple building in Squares 7/8M (rooms 1073 to 1075) was placed not at the edge of the site, but at its center. The large, secular public building of the Level X (rooms 1054 to 1070) was situated in the mound's southwest corner in Squares 10/11 K/M, as opposed to the earlier apparently public tripartite building in the northeast quadrant of the mound. The following Level IX appears to have been a direct copy of the X plan in terms of the placement and architectural plans of major buildings. These two levels constituted a kind of cultural unit.

Considerable rebuilding and remodeling was evident in X, implying a long duration of occupation. Unlike X, IX exhibited less visible remodeling, and may have been occupied for a shorter time than X or XI/XA (Figure 3.9 and 3.10). However, this lack of remodeling and the small amount of domestic architecture noted by Tobler (1950:7) may be somewhat illusory, as the builders of VIII did more terracing and filling to flatten the mound than had any of the earlier occupants of Gawra. As proposed in Chapter 3, this terracing and filling surely obliterated any architecture that stood in the eastern third of the mound at the elevations of Level IX buildings.

The stratigraphic history of X and IX just reviewed has a very important corollary for the analysis that follows. That is, the buildings of X and IX, unlike the XI Phase of XI/XA, appear at least partially cleaned out. The number of artifacts, like XA, was surprisingly small compared to XI. The extent to which this factor skews the results of functional analysis can only be guessed. Certainly, items like spindle whorls, so important in XI would not be removed in large numbers, but fine ceramics, and certainly precious stones, metal, ground stone, and jewelry might have been taken away in antiquity. Certainly, the wealth of the burials in X and IX was not matched in the occupational contexts.

As critical for the functional analysis of X and IX is the fact that the chit system of recording, so essential for the analysis of XI/XA, was not instituted by Bache until most of Level X had been excavated. More than 80 percent of the artifacts from X and virtually all of those from IX remain poorly documented in terms of provenience. Whereas objects in the same square in XI could often be disassociated by the elevation of their find spots, no such analysis will be possible for later levels. Fortunately, the extensive terracing of the builders of VIII sealed the remaining artifacts into a much narrower stratum than had been the case between XIA and XI, XA and X (see schematic sections in Chapter 3). One result of this diminution in provenience detail will be much more of a focus on the contents of whole sets of rooms rather than individual rooms or loci to

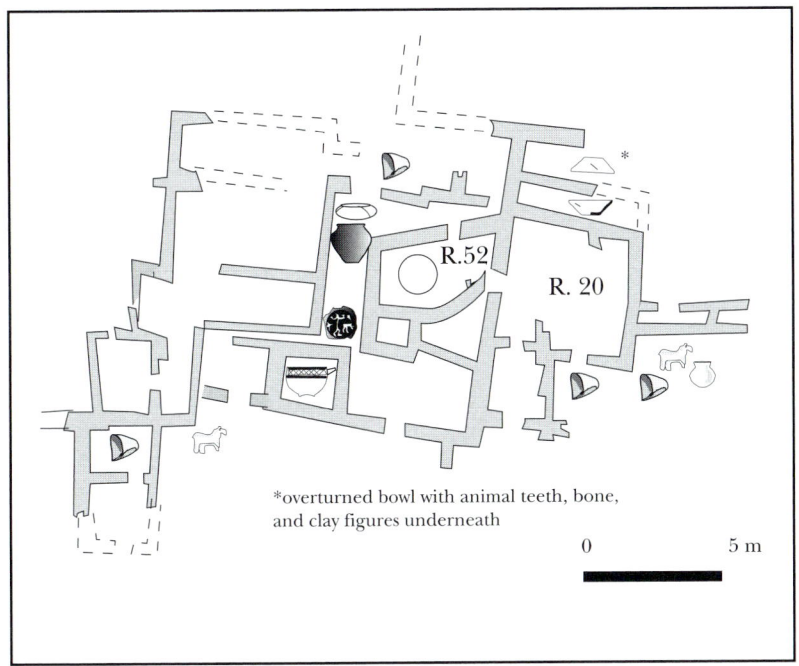

Figure 5.40   Distribution of artifactual remains in situ in Phase XA, Level XI/XA, west-central room block.

determine function. In short, the results here are that much more tentative than the already cautious conclusions of the analysis above.

Functional Size

Ironically, although Level X was the first where substantially the entire mound surface was excavated, it is harder to assess its functions, because it was excavated in part under the directorship of Speiser and during the earliest season under the direction of Bache.

The physical and functional heart of Level X was its temple (Figure 5.44). Because of the process of building and the modeling and remodeling of this level, the temple was in a very poor state of repair. The front entrance way and back wall disintegrated and much of the central room were destroyed. Despite my insistence that a temple must have all the criteria listed above, I feel that there is little doubt that this was a temple. It has the same identical dimensions and plan as the Level IX temple, and it sits in a central position with its doors open to a plaza. In the squares due south of the temple, excavators recovered a human figurine (male with erect phallus), and a celt, as well as a large proportion of the sealings from X.

For Level X, the secular public building, equivalent to the northeast tripartite building of XI/XA was the building complex with rooms and enclosures in

Squares 10/11 K/M (Figure 5.45). Again, according to Jawad's criteria, this building has a similar general shape to the temple, turned 90 degrees on its access. It has the double doors entered through what was originally an open plaza (a small three-room structure was built in front of it). The building lacks other of the markers of religious ritual. In fact, this building had unusually thick, niched and buttressed exterior walls, a coherent plan and unusually generous floor space (113.3 m^2 of floor space compared with 88.1 m^2 of floor space in the northeastern tripartite building of XI/XA). It had an addition, consisting of a southern flank of rooms.

Among the functional elements in or near that southern flank of the building were an oven and a cooking pot found in the southern flank. A locus card dated December 23, 1932 refers to a large scatter of charred barley in a room or on a pavement near the 10K marker; that is, just inside or just outside the oven room. A similar find was a large storage pot containing carbonized wheat in an adjoining room. The southern flank of the building was certainly a kitchen with storerooms for those using this building.

Inside the main part of the building excavators found two fine medium jars with lattice triangles and tree-of-life designs painted on them, two spouted crocks, three small jars, and a hut statue. The neighboring Square 10K (inside the building) yielded another

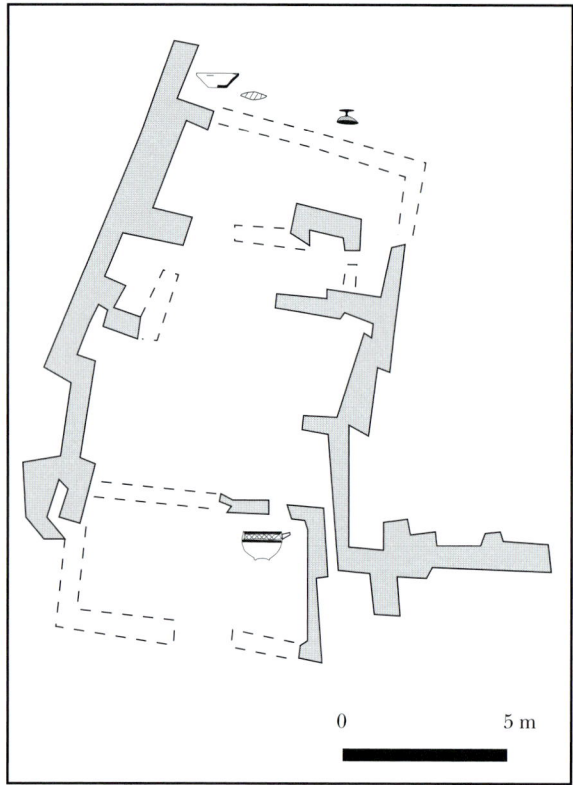

Figure 5.41   Distribution of artifactual remains in situ in Phase XA, Level XI/XA, enclosures in former courtyard 93.

days. Sadly, in the absence of concrete evidence, this line of inquiry must remain speculative.

The placement of a special shrine room (1003, Figure 5.47) over the tomb of an adult in this level of Tepe Gawra also suggests the sorts of social developments in which individuals might reach a high level of institutionalized status.

The rest of the buildings of Level X were domiciles. Unlike Level XI, there were no specialized craft shops at all. The function of this level is tied to those two poles of centralized religion and the social authority of centralized leadership, related to, if not dependent on religion.

One set of residences were located east of the temple along a open road that Tobler (1950:12) calls "Broadway." Tobler argues that they were built after the temple was abandoned, because he reconstructs the entrance to the temple facing eastward, an entrance they would have blocked. Contrary to that, an entrance facing westward, off "Centre Street," appears more plausible. The best evidence of a westward facing entrance is the temple building of Level lX (see Figures 3.12 and 5.54). If IX were a rebuilding of X, the orientation of the two buildings should be the same. Some corroboration of this assertion is provided by the fact that the temple of IX was placed immediately adjacent to that of Level X, suggesting that the modern practice of allowing religious buildings to collapse of their own accord was also common in the fourth millennium B.C. Unless the two

spouted crock, a fine ware small jar and bowl, and a slow wheel turned pointed base cup with buff slip and black "finger paint" design. In other words, present in the building were examples of all the finest ceramics from X, mostly in the categories of serving and cooking vessels. Present also was a symbol of an important social identity, the hut statue. Unlike the northeastern building of Level XI/XA, excavators recovered no craft tools or raw materials from this area of the Level X mound.

This building, then, appears to have been, without pushing the analysis beyond the data to support it, either the house of an extraordinarily important person or more likely the functional equivalent of the modern mudhif, a hospitality house, tied to rank in an extended kin group or an administrative hierarchy.

As was the case in earlier levels, the large open courtyard between the temple and the southwestern building was a plaza that could house gatherings, including an open air market. The added attraction of a ceremonial center is that it brings individuals physically to one place at regular times. Historical markets often take place in towns and cities with major churches or mosques, either on or just after religious

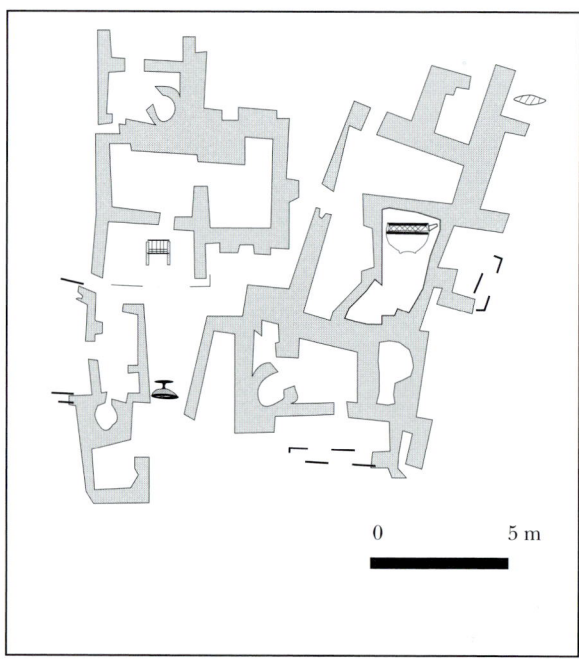

Figure 5.42   Distribution of artifactual remains in situ in Phase XA, Level XI/XA, northwest houses.

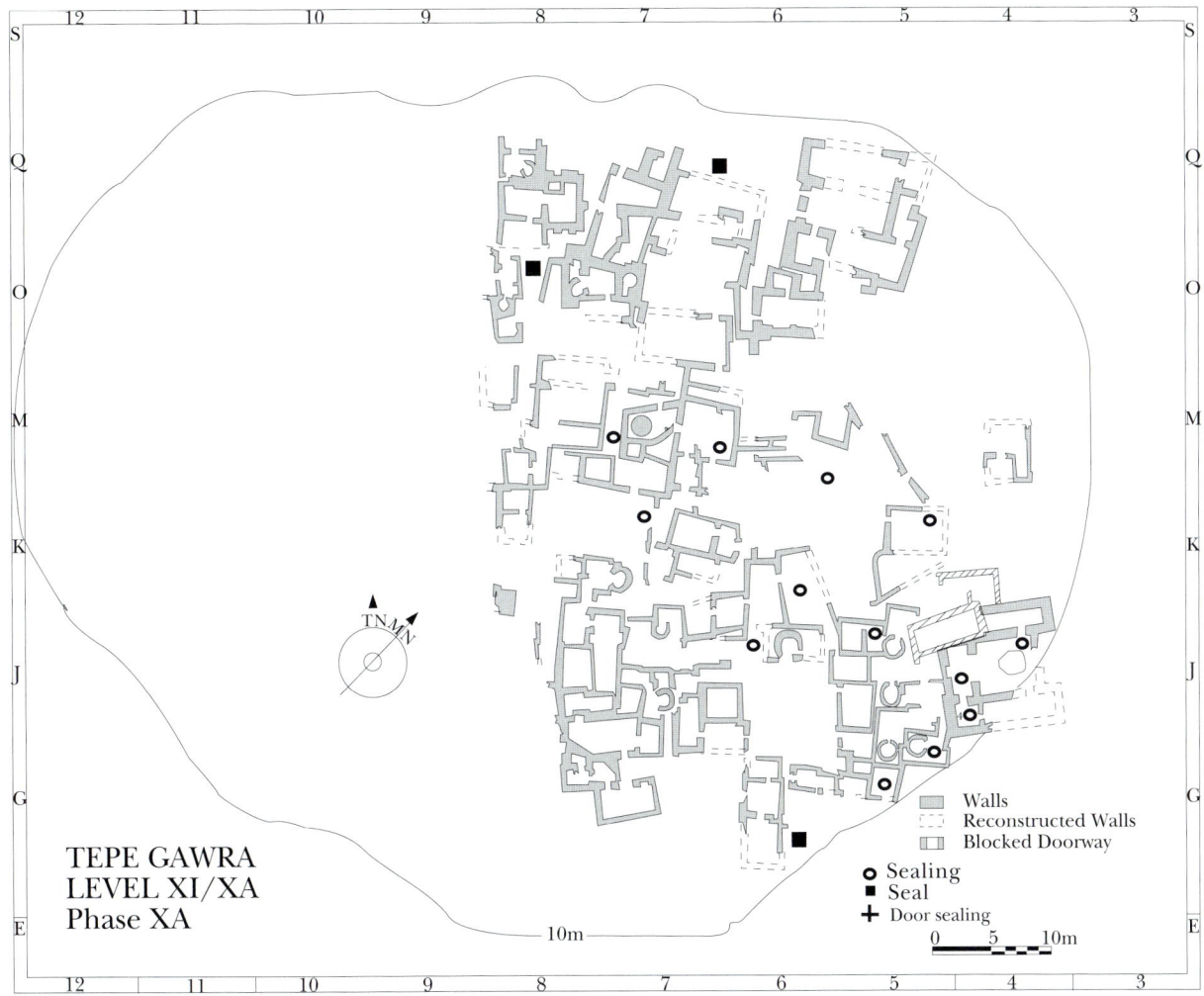

**TEPE GAWRA
LEVEL XI/XA
Phase XA**

Legend:
- Walls
- Reconstructed Walls
- Blocked Doorway
- o Sealing
- ■ Seal
- + Door sealing

Figure 5.43   Distribution of seals and sealings in situ in Phase XA, Level XI/XA.

buildings east of the temple were actually contemporary with it, they must have been contemporary with the Level X temple. The schematic sections support the conclusion of their contemporaneity with the temple and therefore, the reconstruction of its entrance.

In any case, the buildings in question (Figure 5.46) were modest sized structures. The building two buildings east of the temple, as Tobler (1950:12) points out, was a thin walled version of the northern half of the large secular public building in the southwest (Figure 5.45). It was also very reminiscent of the private houses of Habuba Kabira in Syria (see Strommenger 1979: Figures 3 and 4). Just north of the building was a clay ladle, supposedly found "below an oven," although no plans show an oven in that square or in the overlaying Level IX. The artifacts that were probably in the buildings, aside from seals and sealings, suggest a set of domiciles.

Other items found immediately south of the tripartite buildings in the court with "room" 1083 were three animal and one human (torso) figurines, assorted sherds, and a "spout". According to chit field records, "room" 1083 (marked "the kiln") was built up and used as a kiln. Presumably, the figurines were broken during firing or were of poor quality and thus discarded. So, too, were the sherds, found broken "some inside, some outside by the North Wall of Room 1083." They may well have been kiln wasters, but were discarded. The spout (1962) was set into the north wall of 1083 "15 to 20 centimeters off the floor," presumably as a peep hole for inspection during firing. This kiln is not the only one on Level X. Another kiln is illustrated in Tobler's report (1950: Plate XXXI), although its location is not mentioned in any of the preliminary or final reports or in the notes. The only round oven or kiln of the type illustrated is adjacent to

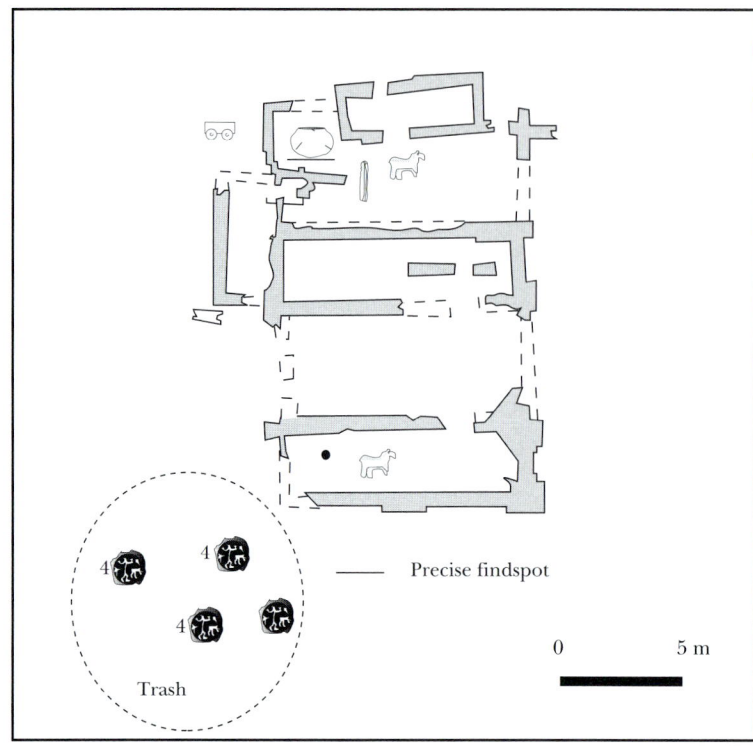

Figure 5.44   Distribution of artifactual remains in situ in Level X, temple.

the courtyard of the building to the east of the one just discussed. Other than a pottery kiln, two ground stone celts were found in Square 6J and 6G, one precisely spotted south of the set of three tiny rooms in Squares 6 J/G. Probably, these rooms were used for storage, as they are too small to be living spaces. A stone seal blank found in one of the rooms tends to support this conclusion. In sum, the rooms, enclosures, and open areas were parts of domiciles. They adjoined a ceramic kiln, which presumably was under the control of their inhabitants.

The set of rooms and the open court north of the ones just described are some of the most unusual in plan, and their contents corroborate a special function (Figure 5.47). Room 1003 appears to have been a shrine, resting over locus 107 (see Tobler 1950:12 and Appendix to this volume). Locus 107 was the libn tomb of an adult, partially robbed, in which seven alabaster spheres remained. The entrance wall on the eastern side contained a small niche, typical of the XI/XA, X and one of the VIII temples. On the outside of the opposite wall was a low bench under which a Wide Flower Pot and two cups were placed, one assumes intentionally. What is most unusual is that the floor was made up of a platform of libn bricks almost a meter in thickness, right to the top of tomb 107. In Square 5M, the one containing most of room 1003, other objects found included a stone

pendant (Tobler 1950: Plate XCI,b7) and the fine beaker with the painted tree of life and keeper of animals designs[4] (Tobler 1950: Plate CXLV, 398; color photograph in Safar et al. 1981: Plate 12,1). Two spindle whorls were also found, one four meters away (probably not in the same context). The rest of the rooms in this block contained a spindle whorl, a bone awl, obsidian blade, stone gaming piece, marble sphere, bead, ladle, and clay palette somewhere among the rooms. All of these artifacts appear have been used for domestic or minor craft activities. The other extraordinary find in this area was a collection of "several hundred" large oval ballistas filling in one room to "several decimeters." This cache is reminiscent of the piles of clay "ballistas" near the kiln in XI or those used in the pottery nest of XIA/B. The only mace head found on the site in X was from 7Q, but no obvious defensive function for these buildings is implied. In sum, this set of rooms combines domestic functions, minor craft activity, and an unusual shrine. The family that maintained the shrine may also have lived there, which accounts for the domestic remains.

The room block built around room 1010 in Squares 6/7 O (Figures 3.11 and 5.48) is very reminiscent of the tripartite house of XII. A kitchen was attached to its eastern side. Unfortunately, the room was cleaned out. The only artifact clearly associated with it

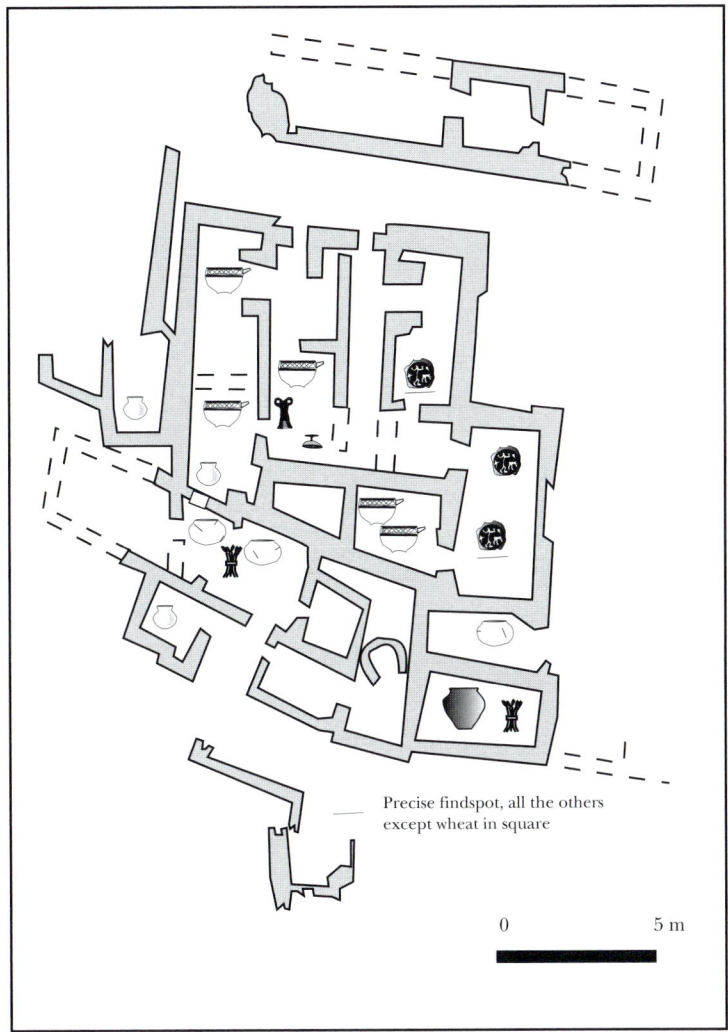

Precise findspot, all the others
except wheat in square

0   5 m

Figure 5.45   Distribution of artifactual remains in situ in Level X, public secular building.

was a single spindle whorl. As such, the assumption
that it was a domicile is based only on its floor area and
plan (similar to other houses and smaller than the
temple or southwest complex).

Immediately north and east of the building just
discussed were three sets of rooms and enclosures
along a set of east-west and north-south alleys in
Squares 6/7 Q (Figures 3.11 and 5.48). One of the
buildings was partially disturbed by tombs 45 and 34.
On their northeastern flanks, these rooms may have
used the rubble of the large tripartite building in the
northeast area of the XI/XA mound as a de facto
wall. In that rubble, excavators found a stone weight,
celt, a jar stand and stone sphere. Among these
items the stand certainly had nothing to do with the
adjoining buildings. A note on the stand indicates
that it "looks Assyrian." Its position "near the edge"

indicates it may have been in an area of slope wash.
The relation of the other objects to the room complex is unknown. A cache of pottery (locus 35) sat in
good primary context in one room. The focus of this
cache was a medium sized gray ware preparation pot
filled with vegetable matter, "apparently nuts" in its
chit. Leaned up against it were two stacked Wide
Flower Pots. Overturned on top of this pile (and
cracked as a result), there was a double or channel
rim wash bowl. A few centimeters away sat two small
green gray ware jars and a third Wide Flower Pot
sitting upright. An unidentified stone lay next to one
of the small jars. If not for the fact that the preparation pot contained nuts, one would assume that
some pottery making activity were being performed
in the nearby oven. However, no other artifacts in
association with the cache suggest a ceramic workshop.

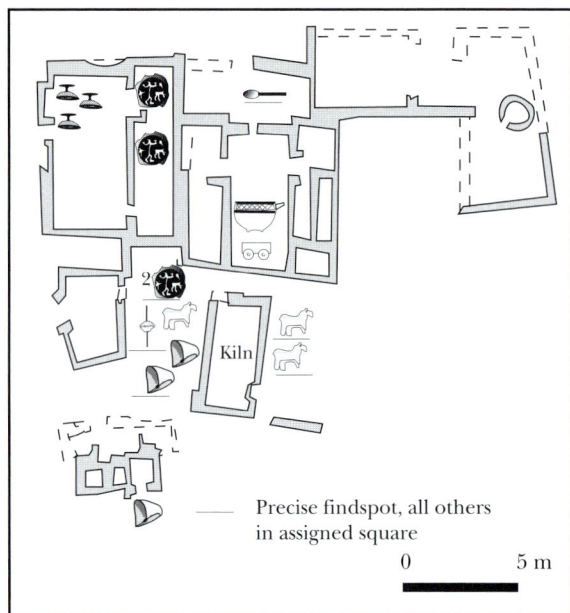

Figure 5.46   Distribution of artifactual remains in situ in Level X, tripartite buildings in the southeast and kiln.

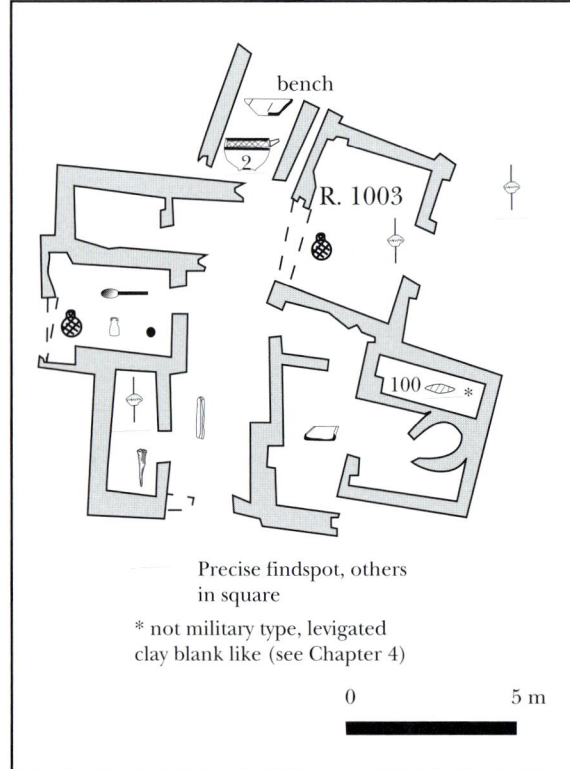

Figure 5.47   Distribution of artifactual remains in situ in Level X, shrine compound.

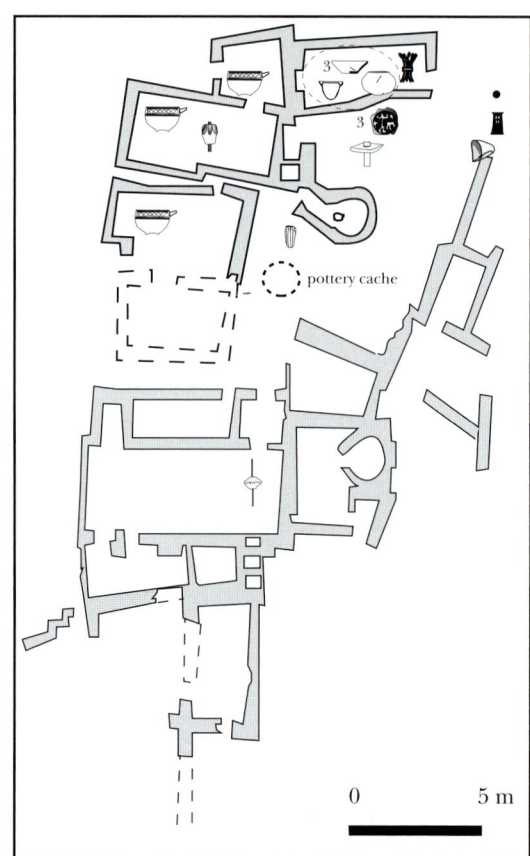

Figure 5.48   Distribution of artifactual remains in situ in Level X, northeastern tripartite building.

Other artifacts in the square with that oven included a hammer, obsidian core, and piece of unidentified copper in the oven. Somewhere in the adjoining rooms were three fine serving bowls (at least one painted bowl with an in beveled rim, ring base) and a stone mace head. All of these items suggest a domicile, perhaps with an informal guard function. The one odd thing found in this complex was under room 1022. A pot burial was sunk under the floor against the west wall. Such a burial containing a baby or infant is common at Gawra. In this case, the pot contained not a child, but the teeth of a donkey. In short, this set of rooms looks like another house with a central kitchen (and some poorly understood burial or ritual practices).

The sets of rooms and enclosures in Figure 5.50 had the same aspect of small domiciles as other sets of rooms so classified above. The rooms and enclosures look in plan very much like one of the other tripartite houses described above. Their oven enclosures ("kitchen") were set on their southern side to fit the crush of other dwellings. The objects found associated with these rooms included an animal figurine, spindle

Figure 5.49   Distribution of artifactual remains in situ in Level X, eastern portion of the mound.

whorls, and a celt. I surmise that they were private houses. The area cut by buildings of Level VIII also yielded some artifacts (Figure 5.49).

The set of rooms in Figure 5.51 joins the set of domiciles just described across a narrow alley and open court in Square 8O. These rooms contained domestic and minor craft items like their neighboring domiciles. The floor space of these rooms and courtyard were almost exactly double that of their neighboring houses, from which one might infer that these rooms constitute two houses. At the same time, there was no oven on the plan or in notes, although the excavators seem to have missed hearths occasionally. Excavators recovered an unusual plaster pot (no dimensions or further information is given and the object was discarded) and two small jars there. These would not be noteworthy, save for the concentrations of seal impressions discarded in this same area. What exactly was happening in this square is hard to say. It may have been that some kind of packing house or receiving depot existed there, as the north slope provides the easiest access route to the top of the mound. Alternatively, it could

have been the home of an agent of the leader of the local polity. One of the sealings found bears the same impression as one on a sealing associated with the temple. In sum, this complex had living space and some other function.

A last house sat in front of the temple with two ovens (Figure 5.52). This has been suggested as a cook's house for the temple (Tobler 1950). It is not clear what special functions it may have performed. From its shape and the few artifacts that it yielded, it was one (or two) house(s). They may be associated with the temple, or not.

Evolutionary Change in Function and Organization

Level X represents a new strategy for the residents of Gawra and a fertile new field for leaders to seek opportunities for control. Rather than manufacturing or transshipping, the primary function of Gawra Level X was religion. Leaders, as represented by the large building in the southwest, were more than ever in

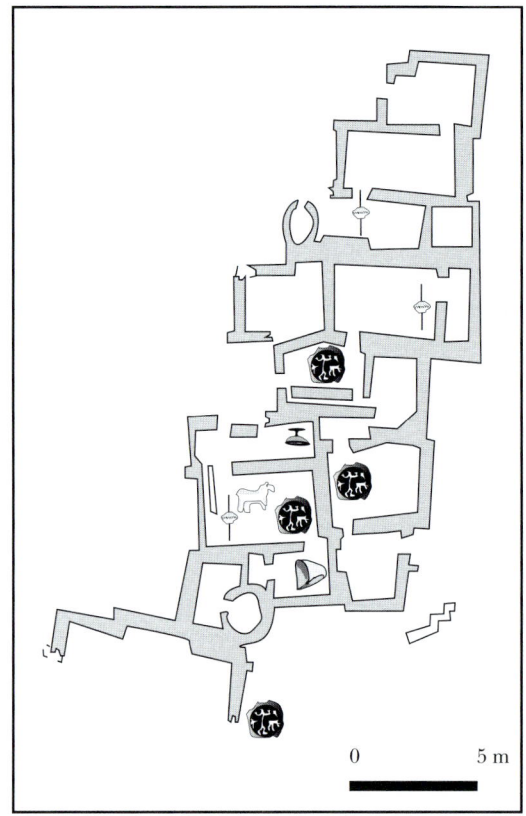

Figure 5.50   Distribution of artifactual remains in situ in Level X, north, central houses.

need of status to operate a system devoid of specialized flintknapping, wood-working, cloth-making, or any clear sign of agricultural production. Although Gawra functioned as a center, its craft production functions may have been taken up by satellite sites.

As such, a system of symbolizing the role of religious and secular leaders was essential. There appear to have been two mediums through which the symbols of this system of authority were displayed. One was mortuary practice. As Peasnall shows in the Appendix of this volume, it was this period when the spectacularly furnished tombs first appear at Gawra. In addition, a variety of traditional—in this case Ubaid-like styles—were associated with the room 1003 tomb and the secular public building. The cup referred to earlier portrayed the dancing people and natural scenery one associates with Ubaid iconography on seals and pottery. A white marble seal with a dancing man (2011, Plate 54) was unearthed somewhere near the bench of the shrine compound, although not in a clear context.

In terms of the control system, the clays used for sealing in Level X remained consistent with the Gawran clay source (Rothman and Blackman 1990).

Population

This is the first time when it is possible to extrapolate the population estimates over the whole of the mound. Based on the per-building method, 185 people lived in Gawra X. The by-room method yields

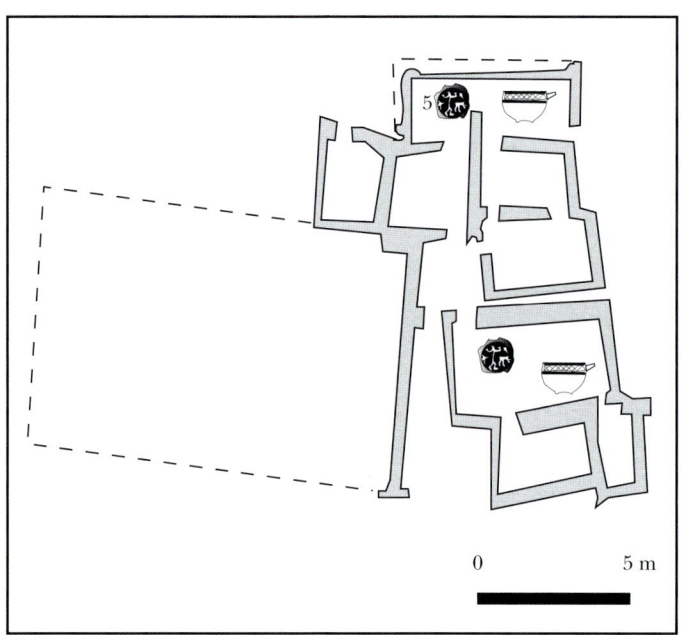

Figure 5.51   Distribution of artifactual remains in situ in Level X, north central west houses.

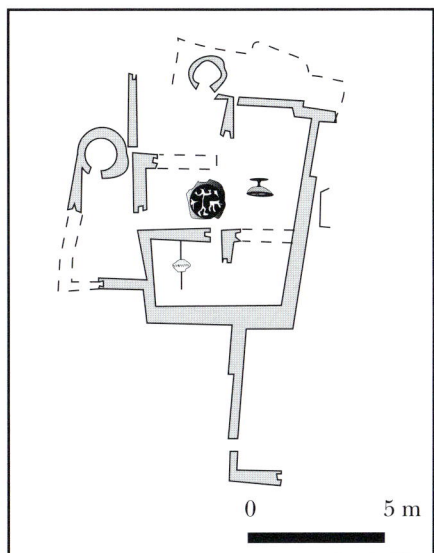

Figure 5.52   Distribution of artifactual remains in situ in Level X, "cooks'" house.

a number of 198. These lower numbers may imply that the estimates for the earlier levels are too high, but it is also true that the surface of the mound was considerably larger in earlier levels. They may reflect something more important for the evolution of the site. In earlier levels, Gawra was a functioning town with a great variety of activities being carried out by its residents. The kinds and number of functions had declined considerably, at the same time the signs of high status, especially in burials, rose dramatically.

Administration

As discussed above, there were specialized religious and social or chiefly buildings in Level X, but craft functions were scattered throughout buildings in which domestic artifacts were more numerous. The pattern of seal and sealing (Figure 5.53) finds correlates with that pattern as well. For example, seals and sealings were found in great numbers in an open trashy area directly south of the temple. Given the state of disrepair of the temple building, this trashy area was probably debris cleaned out of the temple before it was leveled and rebuilt in IX. A common seal design of two sheep and a structure was repeated in this temple trash and in the area of 9Q proposed as a receiving depot (2033, Plate 51). Excavators also recovered three sealings from the public building in the southwest corner of the mound, and a single seal from the kitchen and storage area on its southern flank. Unlike XI, however, both seals and sealings were scattered among the domiciles that also contained a limited number of craft tools.

Level IX

Level IX is in many ways a repetition of Level X. The one difference is that the total surface of the mound was considerably smaller, and the eastern third of the mound was virtually wiped clean by leveling for the construction of Gawra VIII buildings.

Functional Size

The temple of Level IX in Squares 7/8 M/O (Figure 5.54) dominated the mound. It is the most complete of the specialized ritual buildings so far discussed. However, it does not have the largest in floor space. Counting the adjoining rooms, the temple of Level X had 101 m^2 of space; its main hall was 38 m^2 (maybe a little less, depending on where the entry door is reconstructed). The temple of IX had 95 m^2 of floor space, although its central hall was only 34 m^2. On the other hand, a newel wall in room 902 suggests that the building had a second floor.

The remains of this building were in much better condition than the sanctuary of Level X had been. Its central podium or altar was still in place. So, too, an ablution bowl remained set in the floor in room 901. Contrary to Tobler's assertion, the blocking of the door between room 901, and 900 may not have been remodeling, but rather a common construction practice of stabilizing underlying walls to prevent uneven settling of the superimposed structure. The "hammam" of VIIIC rested over the central area of this building.

Excavators found many more artifacts in the temple of IX than in that of X. These included obsidian and gold (on copper wire) beads, a black stone pendant, and a hammer. They recovered a small jar with red slip, the jar with gazelles carved on its base (2229, Plate 20), a Wide Flower Pot, and stone counter (or more likely game piece or stone weight) in rooms 902, 901 or the courtyard outside the temple. This theme of herding sheep is similar to the seal designs associated with the temple and secular public building in Phase XI. Room 903A, according to a locus card, contained a small fine ware jar, two Wide Flower Pots, and a painted bowl with in-beveled rim and ring base. In rooms 903A or 904 the temple excavators recovered stone beads, an animal figurine, two hammers, and a spindle whorl. In rooms 903, 903A or enclosure 904 were a quartz pendant, a spouted crock, fine ware jar painted with lattice (and probably tree-of-life), two obsidian blades, and a hammer. Just north of these rooms, also presumably in fill or in a trash deposit from the temple (Square 7Q, Figure 5.58), were fine ware pots. They included a wheel-turned greenish gray ware bowl with bead rim and ring base and a painted bowl with an in-beveled rim and ring base, an animal figurine, miniature jar, and flint core. The pottery from the temple and surrounding trash

Figure 5.53   Distribution of seals and sealings in situ in Level X.

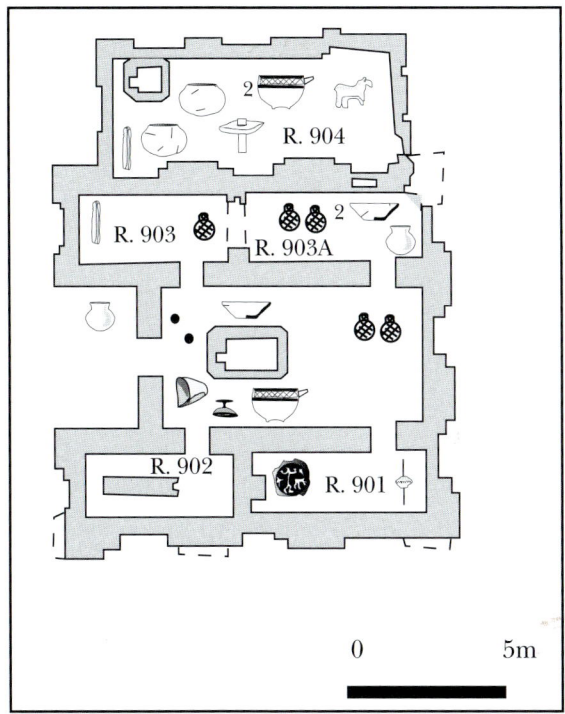

Figure 5.54   Distribution of artifactual remains in situ in Level IX, temple.

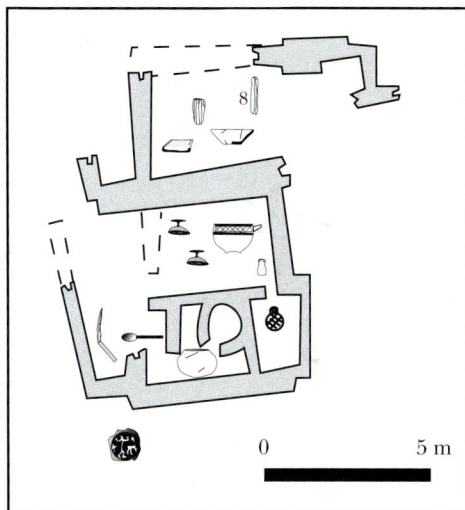

Figure 5.55   Distribution of artifactual remains in situ in Level IX, "priests'" house.

deposits is very reminiscent of that in the large southwestern building of Level X in overall quality and in functional types. These object are consistent with a temple's function and suggest that room 904 was a living space within the temple compound.

Very close to the temple in this open area was a building with two rooms and a small open enclosure with an oven (Figure 5.55). This building complex was in the same position to the temple as was the "cook's" house of Level X. The oven was one of the better-preserved examples of cook ovens from Gawra. It was beehive shaped in vertical cross section and horseshoe shaped in horizontal cross section. According to locus card 26, it "has a sloping floor of hard cement. The floor slopes toward the open part of the horseshoe and after leaving the latter it rises again into a conical hill built of the same hard cement. At the top of this small hill is an egg-shaped hole or cup, 14 cm. deep. At both sides of the structure were found fragments of pottery vessels smoked from fire and with quantities of ashes adhering."

This set of rooms yielded a ledge rim yellow storage bowl, Wide Flower Pot, ladle, small jar, gaming pieces, obsidian core, eight obsidian blades (one apparently with burin blow), two flint blades, a stone palette, and carnelian bead. The number of blades in association with an almost exhausted obsidian core certainly suggests the knapping of lithics. Based on the contents of the square, this activity could have been performed in

the open area north of the building where tomb 24 intruded into the occupation level. Still, an alternative interpretation of this activity area might be that it was for preparation of foods calling for much slicing and cutting. The oven was clearly for cooking and baking. This set of rooms, placed so close to the temple, but not, as Tobler would have it, blocking the entry court to that temple, may have been the residence for temple attendants or a large kitchen for the temple ritual (see the enclosures with ovens of Level XI/XA). As is discussed below, the presence of two seals in this room was quite unusual were it a simple residence.

The contents of the thick walled building south of the temple are hard to interpret (Figure 5.56). Tobler

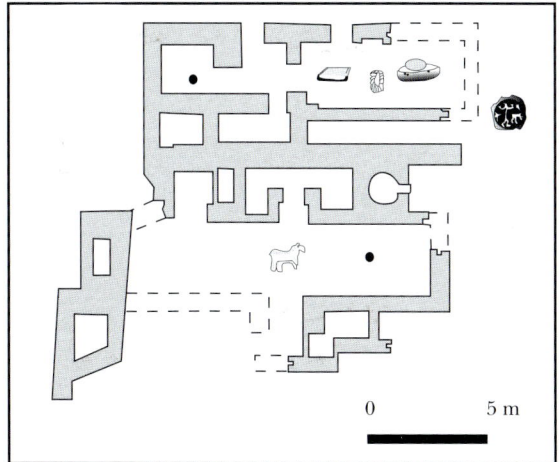

Figure 5.56   Distribution of artifactual remains in situ in Level IX, south building.

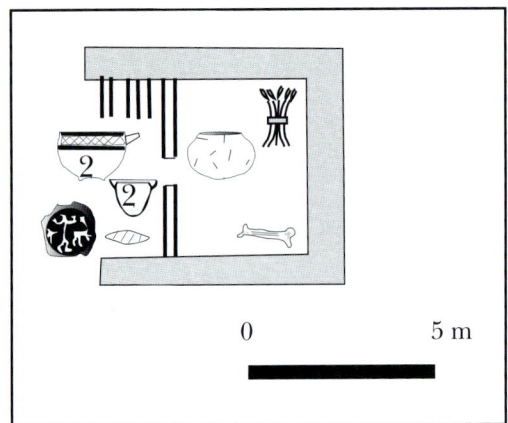

0   5 m

Figure 5.57   Distribution of artifactual remains in situ in Level IX, southeast building remains.

(1950:9) proposes that it was a house for "attendants of the temple and priests." In fact, associated with these rooms were a mortar, which is a domestic item, but also a marble object, classified as a weight, another weight, an obsidian scraper, and a pottery decorator. Excavators dug up a female figurine ("ishtarette") in Square 8 J. In short, save for the mortar, the artifacts do not lead one to an easy interpretation. A great number of alternatives are possible. The placement of the doors created an open circulation pattern from the building to the libn-paved courtyard and the large enclosed courtyard south of the temple. Such a circulation pattern suggests a public function (not a domestic one), but no definite function can be proposed or verified.

Another unusual functional space in Square 5/6 J (Figures 3.12 and 5.57) was an impressive scrap of what may have been a much larger building. The only reference to it is in locus cards 9 and 10 of November 5, 1932. As discussed in Chapter 3, there were two components of the structure. One component was a series of wide steps (the topmost 32 centimeters wide, then 27 centimeters, and finally 25 centimeters). The bottom step rested at an elevation of 12.12 meters. The steps were covered by thick bitumen. Running perpendicular to the steps was a bench at elevation 12.29 meters. A room stretched behind the steps and bench. This room sat directly under the altar of the VIIIC-A temple. The size of the room was smaller than that of the central room of the temple (19.4 m^2 as opposed to 34.2 m^2), but close in size to the largest room of the secular public building in the southwest (20.1 m^2).

According to the locus card, the room was filled with charred grain, animal bone and broken pottery in ashy conglomerated fill. Excavators found two double- or channel-rimmed bowls, a Wide Flower Pot, and a course red ware bottle inside. Other artifacts in

the same square and probably associated with this room were a stone ballista and a clay jar stopper (unsealed). Excavators unearthed a beaker with brown paint bands north of this room. The contents imply that it was a major storeroom for foodstuffs and was associated with other rooms with craft and domestic activities. Covering the steps with bitumen seems odd, unless the bitumen was a mastic for a stone covering, later removed (see Forbes 1964, volume 1, for this use of bitumen).

Another indication that the eastern part of the mound was occupied during Level IX was a greenish gray ware storage jar, 58 centimeters in diameter at the rim, referred to in a locus card of December 10, 1932 (see Figure 5.58). This object, according to the note, was set in the floor of a room in a corner up against the walls. Because no other walls or artifacts are reported, this single find gives little indication what the rest of the building entailed or for what purpose it was used.

Excavators also recovered a variety of artifacts east of the temple (Figure 5.58). Among these items were a metal adze, three spindle whorls, a ladle, hut statue, obsidian blade, stone beads, and a fragment of a stone (oolite) bowl. These artifacts combine domestic and craft tools. They might relate to activities carried on in the terraced-out eastern portion of the mound, or trash stirred up in construction.

Bordering the rooms just described was a collection of informally laid-out rooms and enclosures (Figure 5.59). Three tombs originating above Level IX cut into them. Associated with rooms 908 and 909 was a set of artifacts that suggests a bone and wood workshop. Primary among these artifacts were two pieces of bone carving (see Tobler 1950: Plate CLXXXII, 9 & 10 for illustration), one with traces of bitumen on it, as if it were attached to a chair or box. Also in Square 8Q were a bone awl, rubbing stone, stone celt, stone chisel, bone stamp seal, and a fine ware small jar (maybe serving jar) with painted latticework over a buff slip, and seven beads (one of bone and six of shell). In short, together there were the tools of woodworking and of bone-working, plus some of its actual products. The workers seem to have lived in the building. A mortar of sherd and pebble cement was set into the floor of one of the rooms. Nearby a preparation pot and a ring based storage jar sat near the floor. Also found in the environs were beads, a button, a pendant, spindle whorl, game piece, stone sphere, three stone stamp seals, and a celt. All in all, the building appears to have been the domicile and one if not two specialized workshops for craftsmen specializing in luxury goods. The placement of possible lithic manufacture associated with the temple may indicate that a florescence of small, specialty manufacturing under temple auspices had occurred, although it is hard to verify such a connection. Whether the clientele for

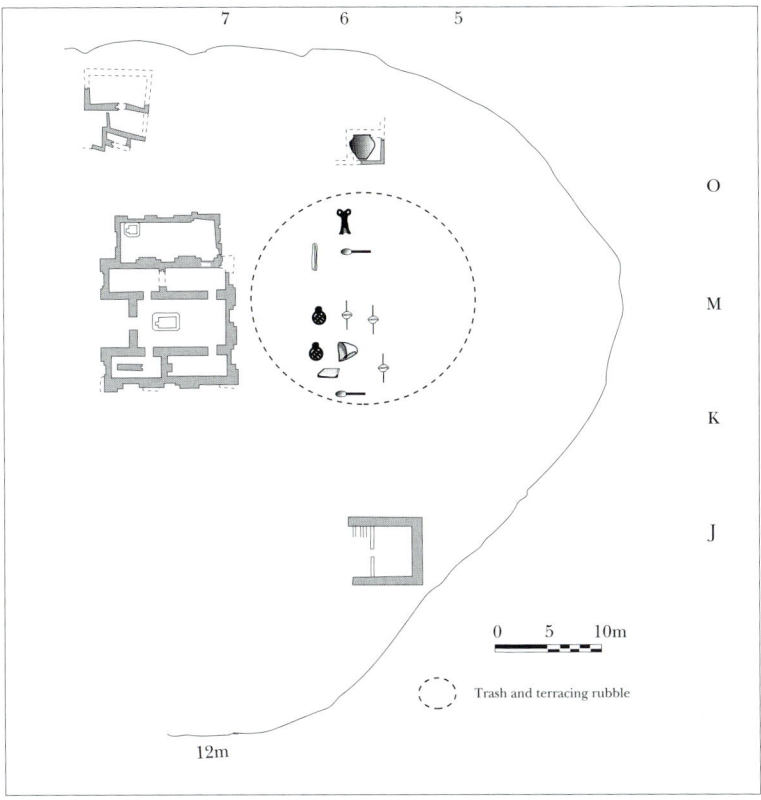

Figure 5.58   Distribution of artifactual remains in situ in Level IX, east section of mound.

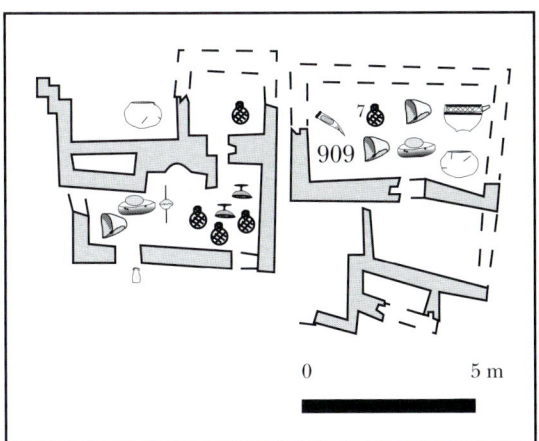

Figure 5.59   Distribution of artifactual remains in situ in Level IX, 908/909 buildings.

this craft activity extended beyond Tepe Gawra is also not possible to say.

In Squares 10/11 J/K/M a large reconstructed building (Figure 5.60) was excavated. The rest of what may have been the building was clearly scooped out or knocked down and filled in by the builders of VIII. Like the southwest building of Level X, it had a southern flank of rooms. However, there is no evidence of an oven among these rooms. There was a small oven on the slope due south of the flank in Square 11J. The major cooking oven for the complex may in this case have been north of the building in Squares 10M and 11M. The south flank of the IX building apparently did share a storage function with the X building. A 47 centimeter-wide storage pot was set in the floor of one room. Otherwise, the only other artifact found in Square 10K was a mace head. Square 11K, which covers the south and east flanks of the building, yielded a small gray ware jar, a pestle and the tall fruit stand (2250, Plate 20) of a kind characteristic of Northern Mesopotamian sites. Near the standing northern wall of the building, excavators found a tall sided bowl with painted lines and triangles, a Wide Flower Pot, miniature bowl, double mouth serving jar, alabaster beaker, clay sphere, and stone game piece. A unique feature of the central room of the southern flanking rooms was the treatment of its doorjamb. The doorsill was covered in thick reed matting and the jamb was covered with

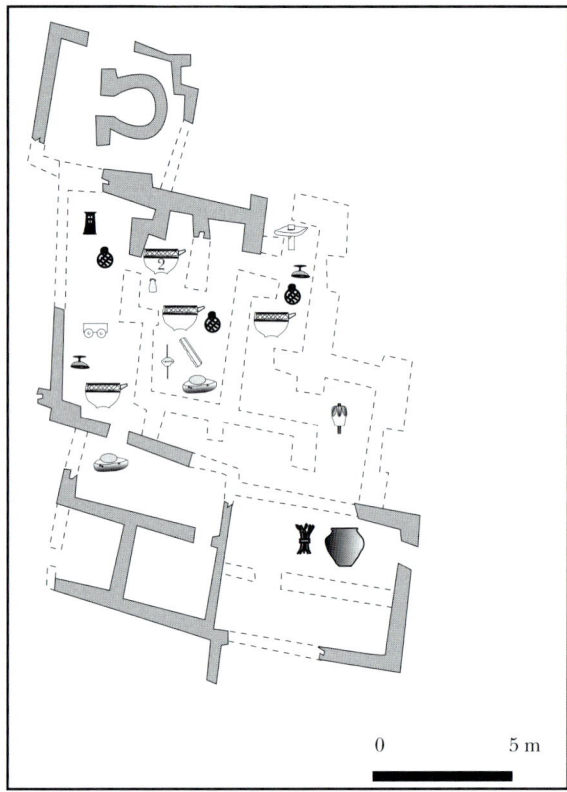

Figure 5.60   Distribution of artifactual remains in situ in Level IX, secular public building.

clay, stamped with the seal of a single stick figure with arms extended.

As the southwestern building was badly disturbed, its function is far less clear than that of the building of X immediately under it. The exquisite bowl stand, the mace head, and alabaster cup would indicate a special function, although the cup may not have been associated with that building. The mortar and storage pot indicate storage and cooking activities. If the tools in the court east of it indicate craft functions, those productive activities must have taken place in an otherwise grand residence or secular public building.

A further indication of some special function for this building may be the oven between this and the northern building on the west side of the mound (Figure 5.60). That oven was an unusually large version of the beehive oven described above. This southwestern building appears to have had some of the same functions as its predecessor. Like that other building, it was probably used by person of high rank. Unlike that earlier building, some craft activities may have been associated with it, although that, too, is far from certain.

The last of Level IX rooms were in the site's northwest corner (Figure 5.61). These appear to have been a series of houses around an open courtyard. The courtyard may, on the other hand, have represented nothing more than disruption from VIII above or decay. It had some superficial similarities to the southwest building. The southern rooms of this complex appear to parallel the southern flank rooms of the southwest buildings of both IX and X. Like the Level X building a beehive oven was located in that part of the complex. A concavity for a mortar existed somewhere in Square 10O and one of the large clay and grit mullers or grinding stones was also found in that square. Other artifacts found in the complex included an animal figurine, small black burnished jar, a white stone button, a flint blade, the bottom of a large pot with a dark red slip on the inside, a small black serving jar, and two beads (stone and bone). West of the southern rooms excavators found a complete basin or laver set into the cement floor of an apparently open courtyard. Except in the quality of some of the vessels, this complex seems only somewhat like the southwestern one. It appears to have been a series of domiciles.

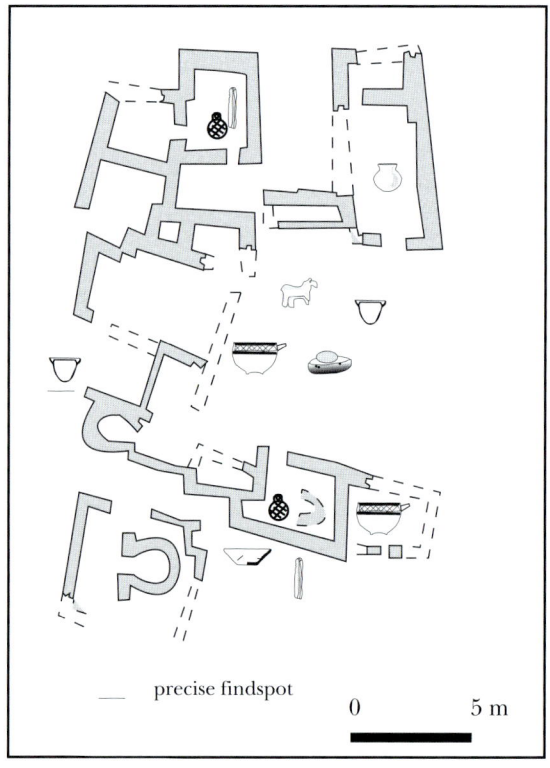

precise findspot

Figure 5.61   Distribution of artifactual remains in situ in Level IX, building block north of public building.

Evolutionary Change in Function and Organization

Level IX appears a shorter-lived, stripped-down version of Level X. A central temple and at least one large, coherently laid-out building dominated each level. A shrine of the kind found in X was not repeated, unless it was in the eastern sector of the IX mound, which was terraced into oblivion. Few houses were found in this level, although they may have been dense in the eastern flank. Evidence of the production of luxury goods—bone inlay and perhaps, wooden objects in which they were set, bone and stone beads and stamp seals—and possibly the knapping of lithics, and surely some pottery making (from the number of smoothers alone) do indicate the presence of craft activity. At the same time, there is no evidence that this production was on a large scale.

Population

This level has been so badly disturbed that estimating population is difficult at best. Even if the eastern section were as densely populated as the northern portion of Level X, the population still would be under 200. The trend started in Level X of a specialized center with a small population appears to have continued in Level IX.

External Relations

In effect the situation, as far as one can tell, was very much like Level X. The basic functional size was the same, with the exception of some craft production. In the Appendix to this volume, Peasnall does not separate the burials of IX and VIII, but many of the most spectacular tombs must have been sunk from Level IX.

The focus was local with a need for symbols of social status to be brought in to sanctify leaders and priests like Level X before it.

Administration

Level IX yielded the smallest number of seals and sealings from the levels of Gawra discussed here (Figure 5.62). In large part, that must be because whatever buildings had existed in the eastern part of the mound were destroyed by the builders of VIII, and material from that part of the mound was literally swept away.

This is the only level discussed in this volume in which seals in good context exceed sealings in number. Not counting the two seal blanks in the luxury workshop, seals and sealings were localized to the temple, possible priests' house, and secular public building. The only door lock was found associated with the temple.

Level VIII

Level VIII at Tepe Gawra was different than its predecessors in a number of respects. First, it was the deepest level; that is, the deepest deposit in which one or more of structures were utilized throughout three distinct phases (C to A). Second, VIII is the first level since XIII that appears to have been planned before construction to include more than one major religious sanctuary. Third, the number of artifacts recovered from the three phases of VIII exceeds all but Level XIA/B. Fourth, this is the first level since XIA/B whose occupation ended in fire. As Speiser notes (1935a: 23), "when it burned down, in a fire that almost turned the sun-dried bricks into baked ones, . . . the upper brick courses collapsed, filling the rooms to a considerable height. Rather than dig out the hard and often fused masses, subsequent occupants of the site allowed them to remain where they had fallen."

Theoretically, the end of VIIIA should represent a tremendous beginning for the functional analysis presented in this chapter. Speiser notes (1935a:23) that the fire sealed the artifactual remains of VIIIA into their original contexts. However, of the 571 objects reported in registry books, publications, field records, and University of Pennsylvania Museum registry cards for Phases VIIIC to VIIIA, 279 or 57 percent are listed simply as "VIII." There appears no way to determine the phase, certainly not by field number order. Perhaps, as reported in Chapter 2, this is because three registrars worked in season G2, allowing registering to back up. Perhaps, excavation squares were not dug as complete units. In any case, the result is that, for instance, in Square 11K artifact field number 5989 is listed as being from VIIIC, while 5992 is listed as being from VIIIA. Other clues for stratigraphic assignment, such as excavation date, absolute elevations, or even notes on the nature of fill are not available, because none of that information was recorded. In addition, with the exception of 51 objects specifically designated as being from one or another room, the only provenience information available for the remaining 440 artifacts is the excavation square from which they were recovered, if that. To further confuse the analysis, the terracing from Level VI in the southern part of the VIIIA phase at the site (certainly Squares 7J and 8J) eliminates the building and artifacts in those squares from serious analysis, although objects from those proveniences are included in the catalogue and counts. Further, evidence of intrusion from Level VI extends into Squares 8K and 9K.

The distribution maps presented below lack the 57 percent of artifacts whose phase is not specified in the catalogue. Where two of three phases is specified,

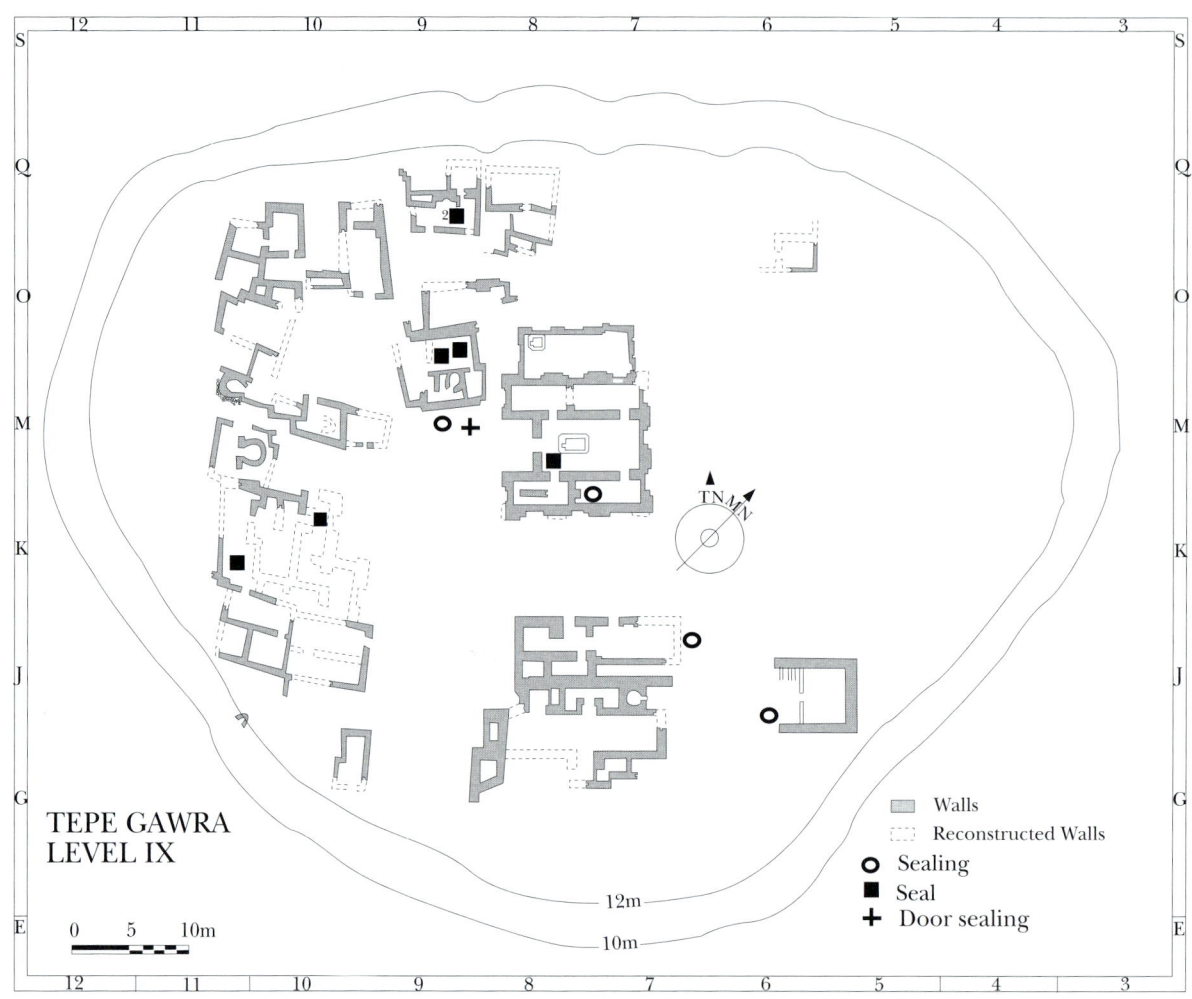

Figure 5.62   Distribution of seals and sealings in situ in Level IX.

the artifact is plotted on the maps for each phase. This leaves the considerable problem of how to deal with the majority of objects, which cannot be assigned to a phase. The method I use in this section is not to analyze each phase separately, but rather to follow individual buildings through their functional life. Artifacts clearly associated with some phase of that building's life are discussed with it. At the same time, those functional artifacts originally registered as "VIII" in the same squares as the building in question will be listed and their possible use in one or another phase will be probed. Where buildings' use ended short of three phases, the "VIII" only artifacts will be described and again, where feasible, a proposed association will be suggested.

Functional Size

Level VIII had, as its three previous levels did, a major temple (Figures 5.63 and 5.64). The temple is the

least changed building throughout the phases of Level VIII, and therefore represents a key and continuous function of Level VIII. This temple fits all the criteria for a temple, as discussed above. It had a coherent plan with large central hall, liwan entryway, niched and buttressed exterior walls. It contained a podium or altar with evidence of fire, and an ablution bowl was found in an adjoining area (the open courtyard near room 801 in VIIIC and probably B, a separate room in VIIIA). In the VIIIA phase the fire that destroyed the site sealed two basalt braziers or bowl stands, a phallus/pestle[5] (for illustration see Speiser 1935a:Plate XLVI,b), stone bowl/mortar, and a pair of clay horns in the central room (Figure 5.64). Excavators recovered many sheep knuckle bones in the adjoining room. Speiser and Tobler's differing style of plates make all the VIII buildings appear monumental compared to those of earlier levels. However, the floor area of the central hall in the southeastern

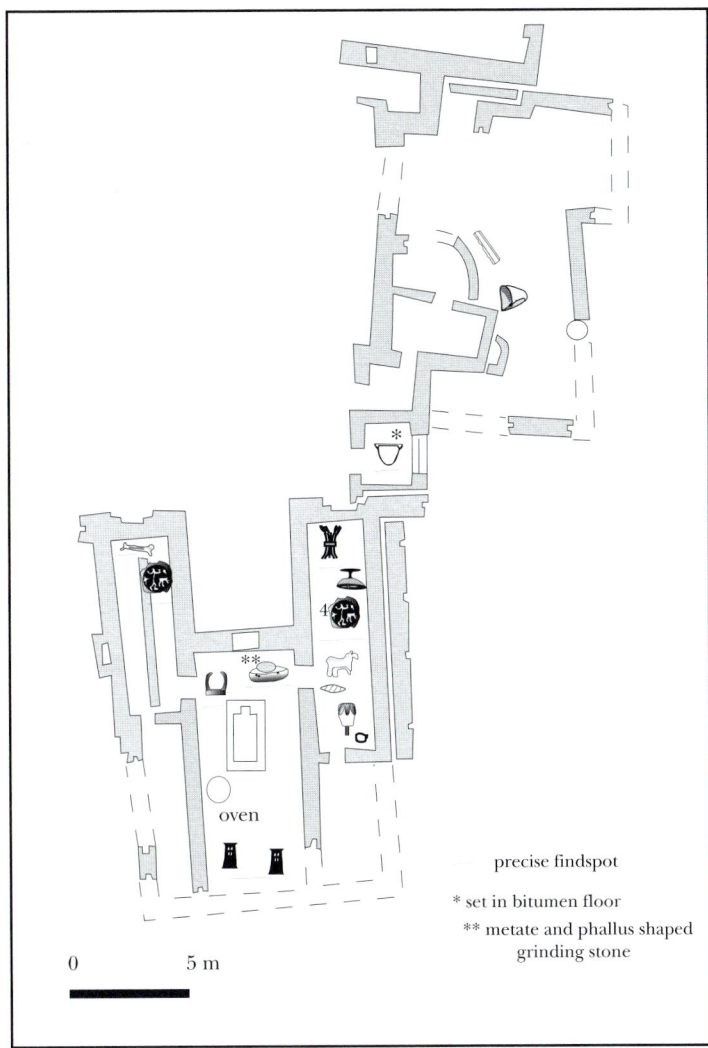

oven

precise findspot

* set in bitumen floor

** metate and phallus shaped
   grinding stone

0   5 m

Figure 5.63   Distribution of artifactual remains in situ in Level VIII,
Phase VIIIA temple.

tripartite building was smaller than that of the X temple and only slightly larger than that of the temple of IX. The rooms off the central hall were approximately twice as large as those of the X and IX temples. No unroofed enclosures were attached to it, as had been the case earlier.

Aside from wash basins mentioned above, two obsidian blades and one flint blade were found in or near the western room in VIIIC. In the VIIIA phase, room 804 contained an animal figurine, sherds of a painted beaker, a copper or arsenical bronze wire, a stone ballista, and a stone mace head. Just northeast of the southeastern tripartite building two small entry rooms and a large presumably unroofed enclosure were built onto the ablution room of the temple building during VIIIA (Figure 5.63).

Speiser (1935a:33) interpreted the enclosure as a holding pen for sacrificial animals. In favor of that interpretation is the evidence of butchered animals in the temple, the apparent trough on the exterior of the eastern wall of the enclosure and the way the walls were built as if to block free traffic to and from the enclosure. A base in an old doorway, thought to be for a pillar, on the eastern wall of the enclosure could have been placed to support an awning or half roof, typical in animal pens in modern times (Watson 1979, Plate 5.2). Alternatively, it could be for a strong gate device to permit herding animals into the pen from off the mound. Artifacts found in the area of the enclosure included an obsidian blade and a celt. These functional objects do not contradict nor particularly support Speiser's proposed function, unless the celt

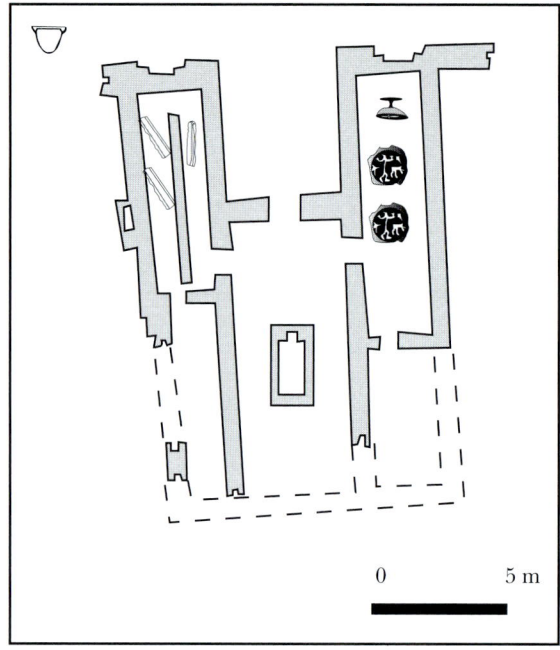

Figure 5.64   Distribution of artifactual remains in situ in Level VIII, Phase VIIIB temple.

was out of context. Whether the enclosure was an animal pen and whether it was specifically for use of the attendants of the temple will remain unresolved.

This thrice-remodeled temple offers one of the best glimpses into ancient ritual we are likely to find for this period.

Speiser interpreted the large northeast building (Figures 5.65 and 5.66) as a temple, because of its large hearth or altar. Facing that hearth were two niches on the front wall (back wall in Forest's reconstruction (Forest 1983: Plate 26). Unlike the building just described no buttresses or niches appeared on the exterior walls. The first two architectural elements certainly fit the criteria of an installation for ritual activity. The building was entered through a small doorway into the building's southern flank. A low bench of libn brick flanked the outside of the doorway. Entry into main room (the room with the large hearth) was gained by climbing two steps set inside a small "u"-shaped wall. People approached the other exit through a well-preserved doorway (Speiser 1935a:29) down two steps. A newel wall for a second floor stairway was found in the southwest corner of the building. In other words, the traffic pattern appears to be one where entry into the main

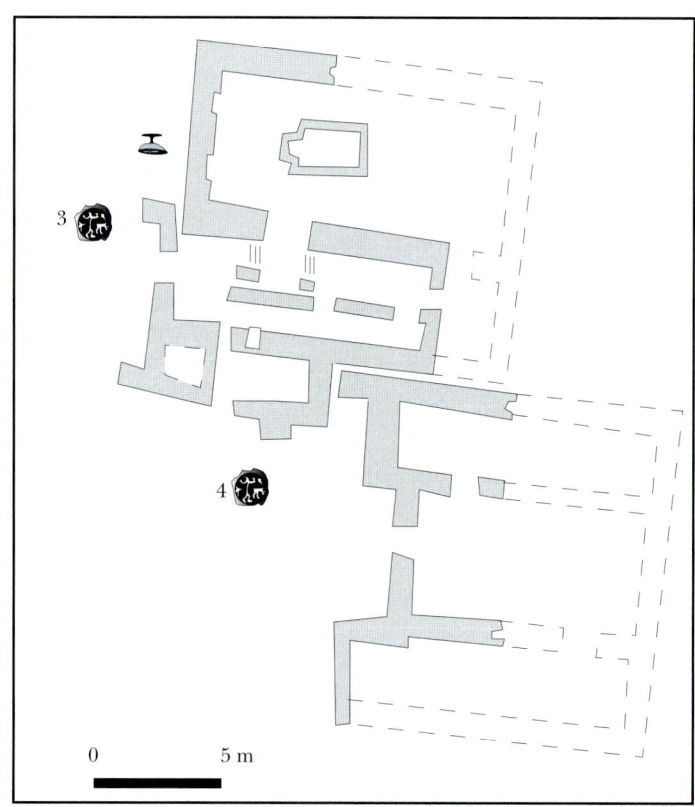

Figure 5.65   Distribution of artifactual remains in situ in Level VIII, Phase VIIIB shrine and public building.

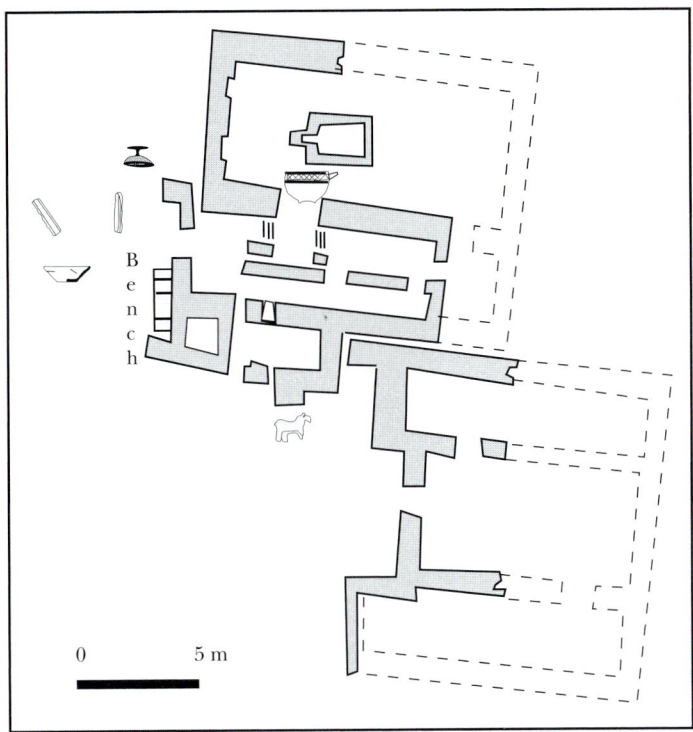

Figure 5.66   Distribution of artifactual remains in situ in Level VIII,
Phase VIIIC shrine and public building.

room of the building off the street was easy and direct, but entry to what may have been a second floor
was more restricted. This building fits Jawad's definition of both a temple and secular public building,
but its orientation (90° from the temple) favors a
secular function.

Was it a temple? All three phases of this building
had amazingly few artifacts assigned to them. A simple, round bottomed, handmade bowl with in-
beveled rim was found in Square 5O during VIIIB
(Figure 5.65). South of it an animal figurine was
found in the open court from Phases VIIIC or VIIIB.
An obsidian blade, celt, and Wide Flower Pot were
recovered west of the building in the same phases.
Parenthetically, the co-occurrence of blades and celts
in this northeastern building appears to have been
very common in Level VIII. In Chapter 4, artifacts
so classified were attributed to woodworking. That
conclusion fits the contexts in which "celts" were
found from XI/XA to IX, especially in association
with adzes, awls, and inlay in Level IX. However, one
wonders whether celts were being used in this context for another purpose.

In any case, in addition to the sparse artifact finds
associated with one or another phase of this building,
one of three or four large collections of functional artifacts listed as "VIII" were found in association with

this building. The Wide Flower Pot and oolite bowl,
found in Square 4O, are consistent with finds in other
ritual buildings of Levels XI/XA to IX. However, associated with the building in Square 5O were two flint
blades and an arrowhead, four celts, a pestle, hammer, metal nail, three spindle whorls, a bone and a
metal needle, a clay scoop, two pieces of a model
chariot, a mace head, an ivory plaque (see Speiser
1935a: Plate LV, a), shell and stone beads, a shell ring,
handmade bowl, herringbone, incised receptacle,
and a jar. All in all, these items seem very much like a
combination of domestic and workshop items. If a
possible second story of this building had collapsed in
during the fire, one would expect the artifactual debris to be scattered among the rooms at the slightly
lower elevation of the southern flank of the building.
Even if the central hall of the temple had been used
for a religious ritual as the podium and interior
niches imply, the rest of the space is likely to have
been a residence and workshop. In this regard, the
ivory plaque is significant. Seal impressions of a similarly large plaque with wavy border design were found
only in the same squares of the Level VIII mound as
this plaque. If seal quality and material equate with
status, the residents of this building must have been
persons with powerful leadership social identities. In
sum, the function of this building appears to have

combined a religious ritual and "secular," economic and leadership functions. The sanctification (see Chapter 1) of a new level of leadership, for which I argue below, would be expected.

In Phase VIIIA, a series of open courts and perhaps one or two rooms (860 to 862; 864 and 865) were built abutting the western side of the northeastern building just discussed (Figure 5.67). Excavators recovered an obsidian blade, spindle whorl and a thin walled greenish gray "candy dish" from these enclosures. Presumably, they served as domiciles with craft activity areas, perhaps with animal pens for those participating in the activities in the northeastern building. The southernmost wall appears from field records to have been unusually low indicating that it may have been an enclosure fence.

The third of the continuously used building is called the "Central Shrine" by Speiser (Figure 5.68). Its function as a shrine is suggested, according to Speiser, by the buttressing on its outside walls, an ablution bowl in the "hammam" of VIIIC and one in a room during VIIIA and perhaps VIIIB phases. Also, the two small rooms with buttressing had slit windows, their inside walls were smoked by fire, and their floors were covered with ash. Speiser does not think this ash was from the fire that ended VIIIA, but from burned sacrifices. However, excavators recovered no burned animal bones in the Central Shrine, as they had in the southeastern temple.

Certainly, the largest floor area in the building at 27.2 m^2 equals the central hall of the Level XI/XA temple in size. Still, the argument that this building had been a temple appears weak, as the contents do not seem those of a ritual establishment, nor are any of the other criteria for a temple met. In VIIIB or A the contents assigned to the building included a pestle,

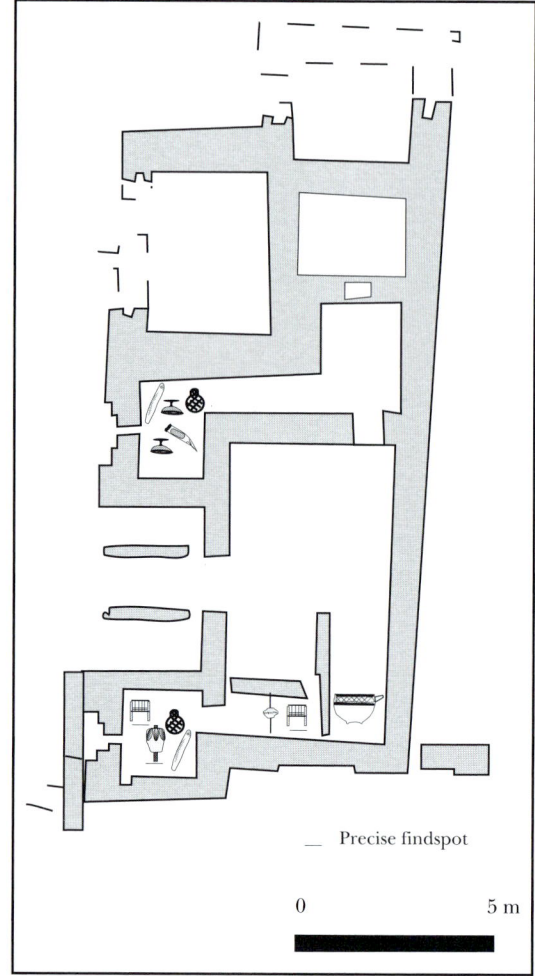

Figure 5.68   Distribution of artifactual remains in situ in Level VIII, Phase VIIIA central "temple."

mace head, and bead and (in VIIIA) a palette, spindle whorl, and loom weight or bobbin. Also, in one room of "VIII" are a preparation (cooking) pot, and a small jar with a side opening. Other "VIII" items associated with this building or courtyard 830 of VIIIA (that is from Squares 8O and 8Q) were a spool, mace head, burnisher, celt, flint arrowhead and core, two pottery smoothers, stone, paste and obsidian beads, a flint core, flint blade, bone spoon, bell-shaped jar with pierced top, a steatite cup, and a vertical sided, ribbed, greenish gray ware cup. Without a podium and considering all the craft tools and domestic artifacts, the role of this building as a shrine must be rejected. Perhaps, the most telling commentary is that Speiser himself thought it was a house during its excavation (Speiser 1932d). Unfinished cylinder seals may be the most telling finds. This building, like the luxury workshop of Level IX, had evidence of a variety of potentially

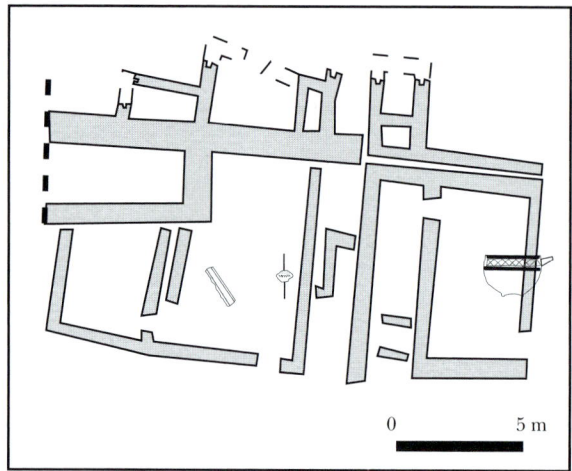

Figure 5.67   Distribution of artifactual remains in situ in Level VIII, Phase VIIIA houses 860–65.

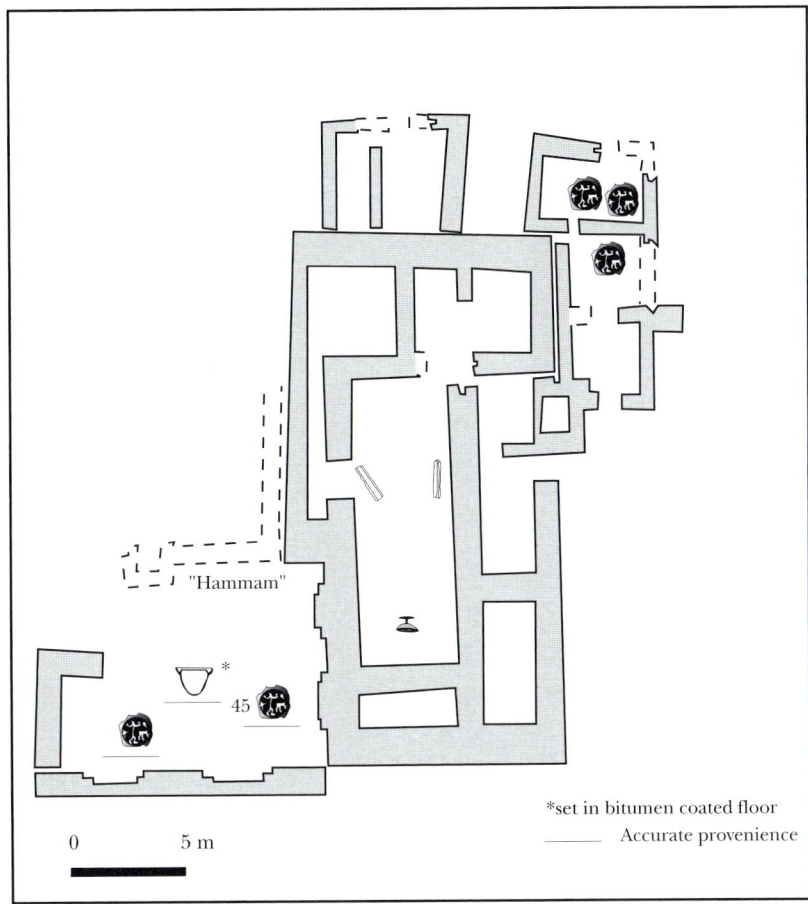

Figure 5.69   Distribution of artifactual remains in situ in Level VIII, Phase VIIIC central building.

high status materials and the tools to make them into finished products.

Immediately east of the building just described in VIIIC (Figure 5.69) was the only building of that phase not called a shrine or temple by Speiser (rooms and enclosures 882 to 889, Figure 3.13). The only artifacts definitely associated with these rooms and enclosures are two of the omnipresent obsidian blades. As the entry into the complex was narrow and restrictive, a suggestion that it was a storehouse is plausible, but unverified. It seems unlikely as a domicile.

Cradled between the central building and the building just described was the so-called "hammam" of VIIIC (Figure 5.69). If niches and buttresses are signs of a structure's importance, the three of the walls facing this area were so designed. However, the function and the association of the "hammam" with other buildings remains a mystery. Its only salient features were a three layer packed floor, apparently coated with bitumen (perhaps as a mastic) for stone paving and a large jar set in the floor. Its only

contents were 45 fragments of sealings with the impression of unidentifiable animals and 24 pieces of sealings with the impression of four well-modeled caprids.

During the VIIIB and A phase, the central storage function of Tepe Gawra appears to have been fulfilled by rooms 810 to 817 (Figures 5.70 and 5.71). These apparently doorless, small rooms (averaging 15 m^2) were filled with a variety of items. One contained a three-necked jar, two small jars, a Wide Flower Pot, model chariot wheel, loom weight or bobbin, bone bead, and celt. Excavators found three obsidian and two flint blades, a basalt pestle, basalt mace head, basalt celt, bone spindle whorl, obsidian pendant, stone and shell beads in another room. The rest of the set of rooms contained more bone and clay spindle whorls, hammers, beads, model chariot wheels, cups, and more blades. The rooms must have been entered by ladders placed in the alley to its south, thus restricting access to it. This formal warehouse was placed in the center of the town.

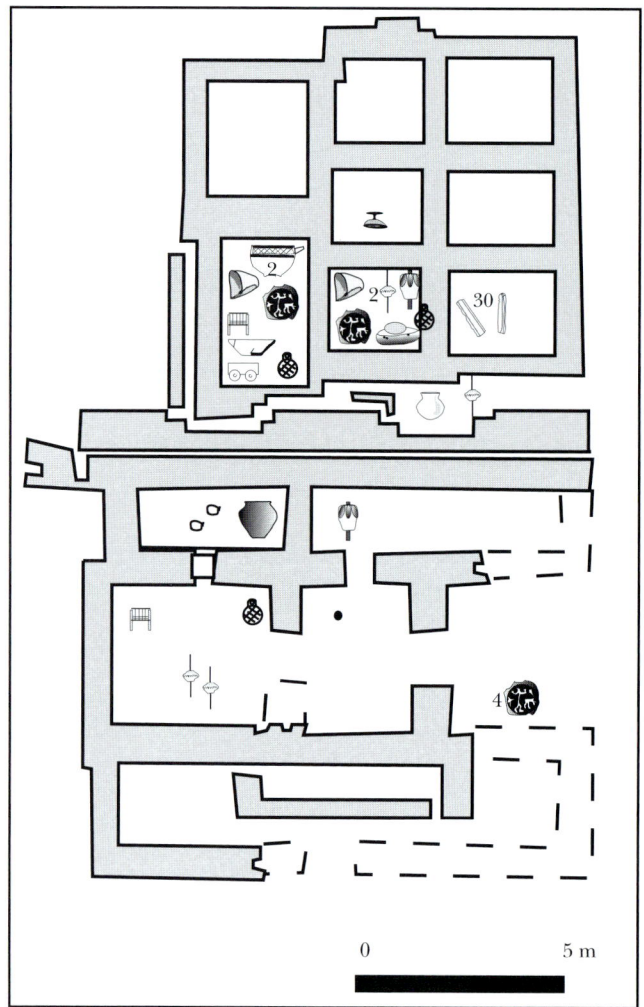

0   5 m

Figure 5.70   Distribution of artifactual remains in situ in Level VIII, Phase VIIIB central warehouse and adjoining tripartite building.

South of the warehouse in Phase VIIIB and A was the small tripartite building, rooms 853 to 856 (Figure 5.70). In the registry books, a structure near the south end of the building was called "the silo." This set of rooms was clearly affected by the terrace of Level VI. At least three different ceramic types found in Square 8K—a small open mouth jar with chevron design, a straight sided cup, and a square bodied bottle—are Early Dynastic III/Akkadian, not Late Chalcolithic types. Also, the "bronze" lance head, metal discs (bosses?), and metal hooks found in the silo are rather out of place at fourth millennium B.C. Gawra, where the common metal objects were needles, awls, nails, and flat adze blades (Tobler 1950:211f.). On the other hand, these items fit well into the inventory of Level VI metal artifacts. As will be even more apparent in the discussion of the buildings

of VIIIB and VIIIA in Square 9K, it is likely that these metal artifacts were associated with the VI terrace. The building itself was almost certainly associated with the Level VIII occupation. It contained spindle whorls and a storage jar (in VIIIA). Based on those artifacts with reasonably good Level VIII context, this building seems to have been a residence. The silo may have had a more public function, as it was probably entered from the outside of the building.

Another central building of VIIIA consisted of three rooms, 857 to 859 (Figure 5.72). Only their southern walls, facing the courtyard in front of the building just discussed, were buttressed. This building appears to have had a trough on its outside wall. Artifacts associated with it included the omnipresent blades, a metal needle, and perhaps one or two serving bowls. Their functions included those of a domicile,

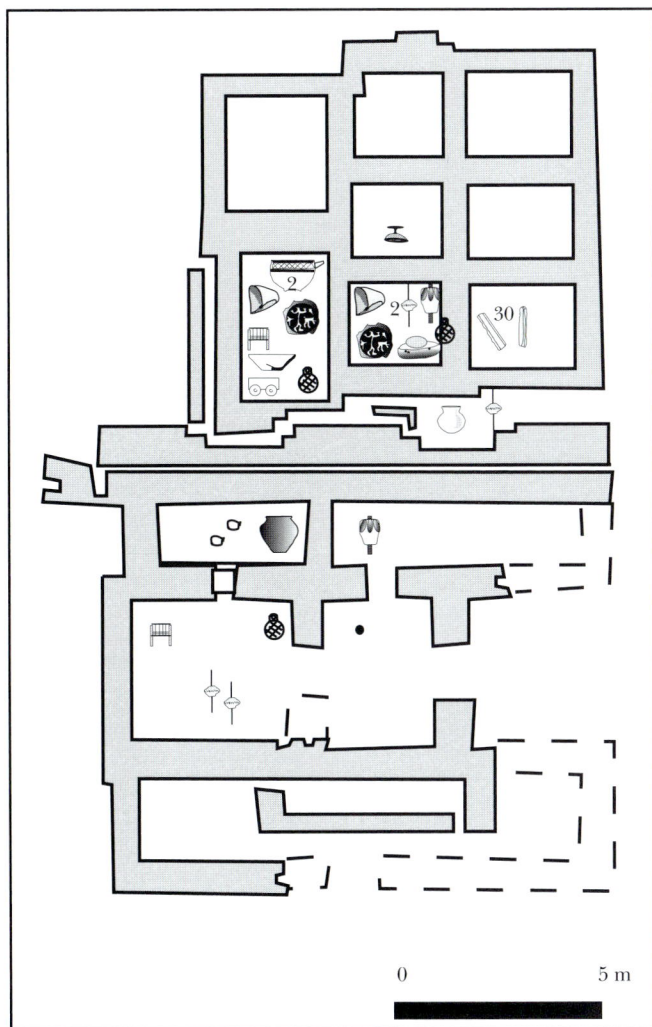

Figure 5.71   Distribution of artifactual remains in situ in Level VIII, Phase VIIIA central warehouse and adjoining tripartite building.

but what is odd about all the houses and other buildings in Level VIII is their absolute lack of ovens. What worked so well to define houses in earlier levels fails to do so here. This might point to a function different than a domicile.

The remaining buildings of Level VIII are those of the western third of the mound. In the planning of VIIIC, the builders of VIII laid out what would be the largest of the buildings at Tepe Gawra, the so-called Western Temple (Figure 5.73). This building had a central hall with floor area of 44 m^2. With its adjoining rooms, it had over 112 m^2 of floor space. The plan was perfectly symmetrical with buttressing on all outer walls. What is most interesting about this supposedly "classic" temple plan is that there is no evidence of a podium, of niches, or of ablution bowls, in

fact, of anything that marks it as a temple. It is oriented on the cardinal points, but opens in a different direction than the temple. The contents associated with it are not especially ritualistic. Included were nine flint and three obsidian blades, a flint core, gold and steatite pendants. In the southwest room six Wide Flower Pots were stacked up "in 5 cm. of charred grain," according to a note on a photograph. Given the extremely high percentage of flint and obsidian cores and blades in VIII, the presence of a core and numerous blades in this building suggest a productive function. In short, from the remains of the VIIIC level, the primary function of the western tripartite building was much more reminiscent of the northeastern tripartite building of Level XI/XA than of any of the temple buildings. It most likely had been a

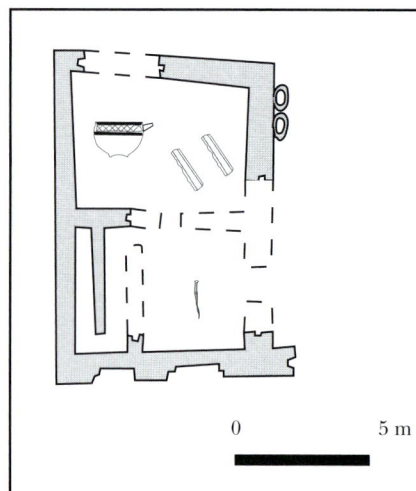

Figure 5.72   Distribution of artifactual remains in situ in Level VIII, small, Phase VIIIA house in squares 6/7 M/O.

secular, public building. The association of the Beveled Rim Bowl-like Wide Flower Pots, stacked up in a grain storeroom, is evocative of the ration function accorded to Beveled Rim Bowls in southern Mesopotamia and Iran and to a system of control based on corvée labor. Production may also be part of the building's function.

By the VIIIB phase, however, the central hall of this building had been at least partly sealed off and the central room not used in the same way as earlier

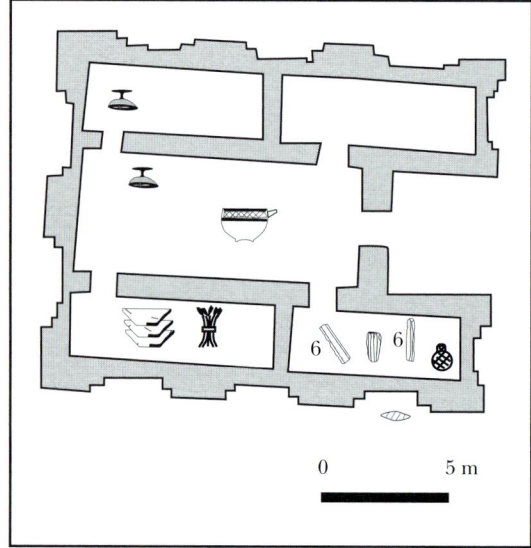

Figure 5.73   Distribution of artifactual remains in situ in Level VIII, Phase VIIIC western building.

(Figure 5.74). The ceiling of the central room may well have been too large to maintain. If the roof were intentionally brought down, it might have served as an interior unroofed courtyard. A tripartite building was also built abutting the northern wall of the older tripartite building (Figure 3.14). Some of its functional areas could have been moved to a new set of rooms, which were built around the front of the building.

Many of the same artifacts described for the VIIIC building (save the Wide Flower Pots and a couple blades) may have been deposited during the VIIIB phase. Added to those already listed functional artifacts (but from the VIIIB phase) were a storage jar, small jar, and handmade, round bottom bowl. The southernmost of the rooms newly added during VIIIB included a second room in VIIIB referred to as a "silo." It contained two metal chisels, a hematite weight, a metal needle, a straight-sided cup, and probably a metal sickle blade (the blade was from "VIII"). Again, these are not artifacts associated with religious ritual. The rooms seem to be domestic and craft activity areas with a shed for tools. However, chronologically disturbing are the presence in Square 9K of a small pot (2803), cup (2814), and similar cup (2802). The cups have exact parallels to cups in Level VI and cup 3–226. The latter was definitely from the Level VI terrace at the elevation of Levels VIII or IX. Pot 2802 is a common Gawra VI and Tell Taya VIII, late third millennium B.C. type. The "silo" in 9K may have postdated Level VIII, as did the silo in Square 8K.

The plan of this western tripartite building certainly conforms to that of a building that elsewhere had ritual functions, but its contents do not suggest any religious activity. This may be the case, because it was quickly abandoned as a temple or more likely because it never was one. The "Western Temple" seems to have been a secular public building where the collection and distribution of foodstuffs was coordinated in Level VIIIC and later was modified into smaller workshops and houses. There was a small set of rooms north of this building, which may have been one of these houses. However, excavators reported no artifacts from it.

By the time the buildings of VIIIB had begun to be replaced, the entire area of the Western Building and its modified structures was leveled to three courses of brick, filled in and raised for a series of rooms along two pebbled streets in VIIIA (Figures 5.75 to 5.77). Ramps were built, so that the central building could still be used. A formal court, 830 (Figure 5.75) was created to join that building to its new eastern neighbor, the central building. Despite some buttressing on the west and south walls of this building and a wash bowl set in the courtyard, the building seems to have had domestic and craft, not ritual, functions. It, too, had a

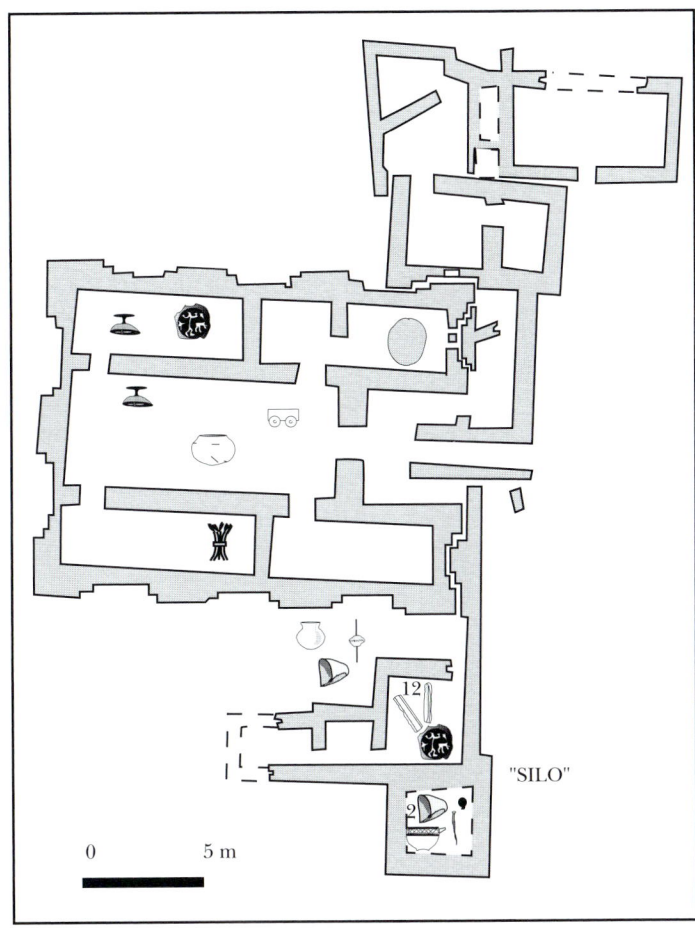

Figure 5.74   Distribution of artifactual remains in situ in Level VIII,
Phase VIIIB western building.

"silo" storeroom, which contained a metal dagger, metal needle, metal bracelet, a clay ring, and fancy small pot (2800). Speiser equated this pot with another, which is definitely from the VI terrace, but it is of a slightly different ware. Otherwise, the building contained two spindle whorls of VIII type, and a model or toy. Two bobbins or loom weights in the courtyard imply a cloth manufacturing function. A wash bowl set in the floor of the courtyard may have been associated with cloth manufacture as well (see Chapter 4). A toy in the building would suggest a domicile, but again no cooking ovens were recovered.

The large compound south of that building across the street contained a familiar constellation of objects (Figure 5.76). Among them were three obsidian blades and one flint sickle. The plan is very similar to the central building. The contents of this building are not especially domestic. With the vaulted court and open pen in front, an animal corral perhaps for a market place or for other use is possible but not verifiable.

West of the buildings just described and across the alley was another set of rooms, (Figure 5.77), one of which had a door to the alley, which was later blocked. These rooms contained five obsidian and one flint blades, a very large storage jar, (370 cm. in height, 465 cm diameter), and a small jar. It appears to have had some craft processing function.

The last building from Phase VIIIA to be discussed (Figure 5.78), was on the north side of the street from the building just described. Speiser proposed that the building was part of a suq or marketplace. The tiny stalls in it might conform to such a function. It was located on the northern slope, which earlier served as an entryway to the mound. On the other hand, the only artifacts possibly associated with it were three blades. Also, the "stalls" are only 7.5 m^2 in floor area, quite cramped for the major shop of a suq. In short, the theory is certainly an interesting one, and given the other activity, a marketplace for exchange is one likely function for VIIIA. More than

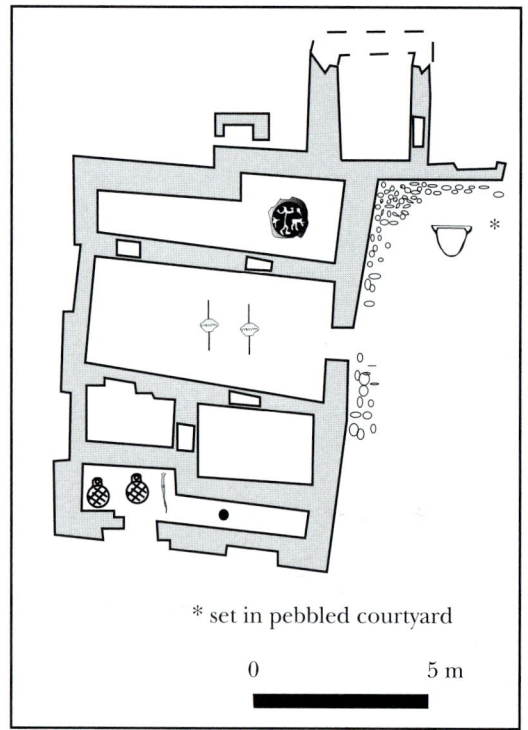

* set in pebbled courtyard

0   5 m

Figure 5.75   Distribution of artifactual remains in situ in Level VIII, Phase VIIIA northwest tripartite building.

Population

By any method it is hard to see that more than 50 people were living on the Gawra mound during any of the three phases of Level VIII, if that many. This is the one argument that favors Algaze's contention (1993) that there was a large, lower town, although again, there is no positive evidence of any occupation there after the sixth millennium B.C.

Evolutionary Change in Function and Organization

Level VIII, like the earlier levels of Gawra analyzed here, had many, different functions. One, perhaps most prominent in VIIIC, was religious. However, this religious function appears inextricably tied to its minor craft activity and probably marketing functions. Even more than in Levels X and IX, one senses that very few persons actually lived on the VIII mound, and those that did had some kind of specialized function as craftspersons, religious practitioners,

or coordinators. One indicator of the unusual nature of Level VIII was the lack of cooking ovens. Another odd part of the town plan of Phase VIIIA was the difficulty of moving from the eastern to the western half of the mound. No streets are evident and, in fact, any path across the two halves was blocked. The functions of the eastern half focused on public religious ritual and leadership. The western half's functions appear to have been economic. The dichotomy of religious/leadership and manufacturing evident in the seal designs of Phase XI took physical form in the plan of Level VIII.

What distinguishes VIII from all the previous levels is that Gawra VIII was not really a town with a sizable population and a few centralized functions. Gawra VIII was a center. It had little existence as a town outside its role in mediating relations within the polity encompassing its hinterland and with other, distant centers. Part of that mediation had to

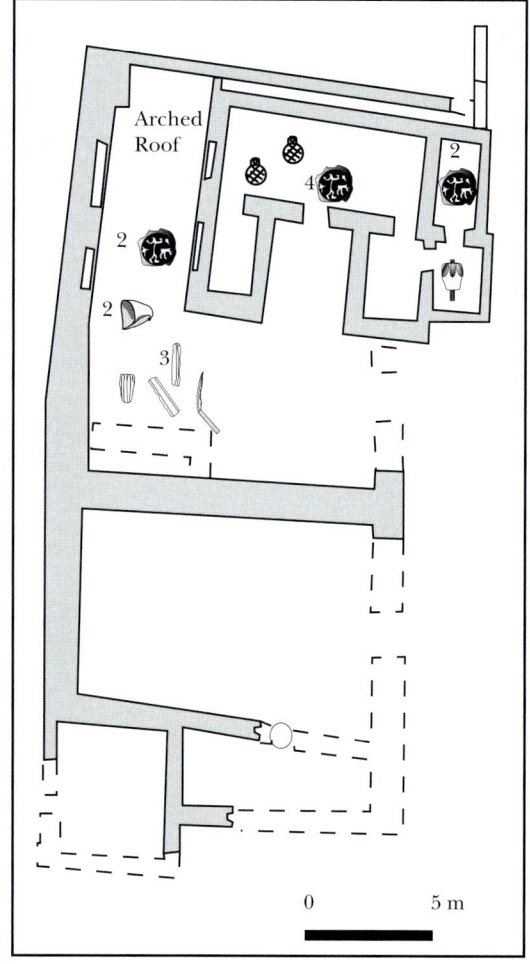

Figure 5.76   Distribution of artifactual remains in situ in Level VIII, Phase VIIIA square 9M building.

that, nothing can be offered to support or reject Speiser's contention.

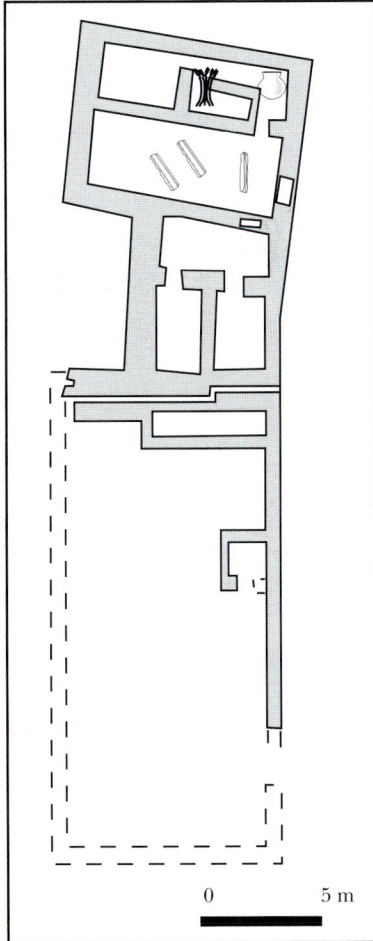

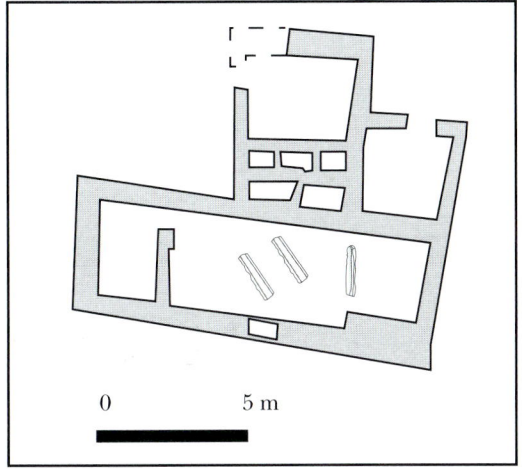

Figure 5.78 Distribution of artifactual remains in situ in Level VIII, far northwest building.

Figure 5.77   Distribution of artifactual remains in situ in Level VIII, VIIIA square 10M building.

do with the export or transshipment of obsidian. Much of it had to do with the larger changes in Mesopotamia. Those changes were reflected in the remains of Level VIII in two ways. For the first time since Level XIA/B, non-local clay sources were represented among sealings in Gawra VIII. In addition, new stylistic elements, more in seal design than in pottery, joined Gawra to the larger region (von Wickede 1990, Pittman in press). Even in pottery style, trends in production, tempering, firing, and shape are those that Gut (1995) attributes to the beginning of the Middle Uruk or LC 3 (her Uruk A) period. This is the time when many hypothesize a significant increase in exchange and contact with southern Mesopotamia. Certainly, the people of Tepe Gawra were aware of these regional changes and responding to them (see Chapter 6).

The individuals buried here exhibit a wide variety of social statuses, although the spectacular tombs[6]

were never more spectacular in terms of the variety of exotic materials buried in them. The importance of exotic materials, "wealth finance" (see Chapter 1), may be indicated by the kinds of seals buried with individuals. Whereas in Level XIA/B individuals were buried with seals of common materials, in VIII lapis lazuli seals were found in two tombs. The exotic material expresses something of the status of the individual.

External Relations

Gawra VIII had all of the elements of regional exchange exhibited in the other levels discussed, but more so. The amount of obsidian present in this level was by far the greatest of any Gawra level. Despite the claim that Gawrans and residents of other piedmont sites no longer controlled the transshipment of lapis (Hermann 1968), it was still available and present at Gawra.

In terms of the source of the sealing clay, although most were made from the Gawran source (Rothman and Blackman 1990), for the first time since Level XIA/B, a significant percentage of clays used in sealings were not from that source. All the levels with considerable sources of sealed goods outside the Gawran source area ended in fire. Perhaps, this is no coincidence. Although, unlike Level XII, there is no clear evidence that the fire that destroyed VIIIA was set by an enemy, each time when sealing clay sources suggest a wider sphere of interaction than the Gawran polity in exchange of goods, the settlement ended in fire. After the fire that burned Level VIII, only a few squatter buildings were built until almost a millennium later.

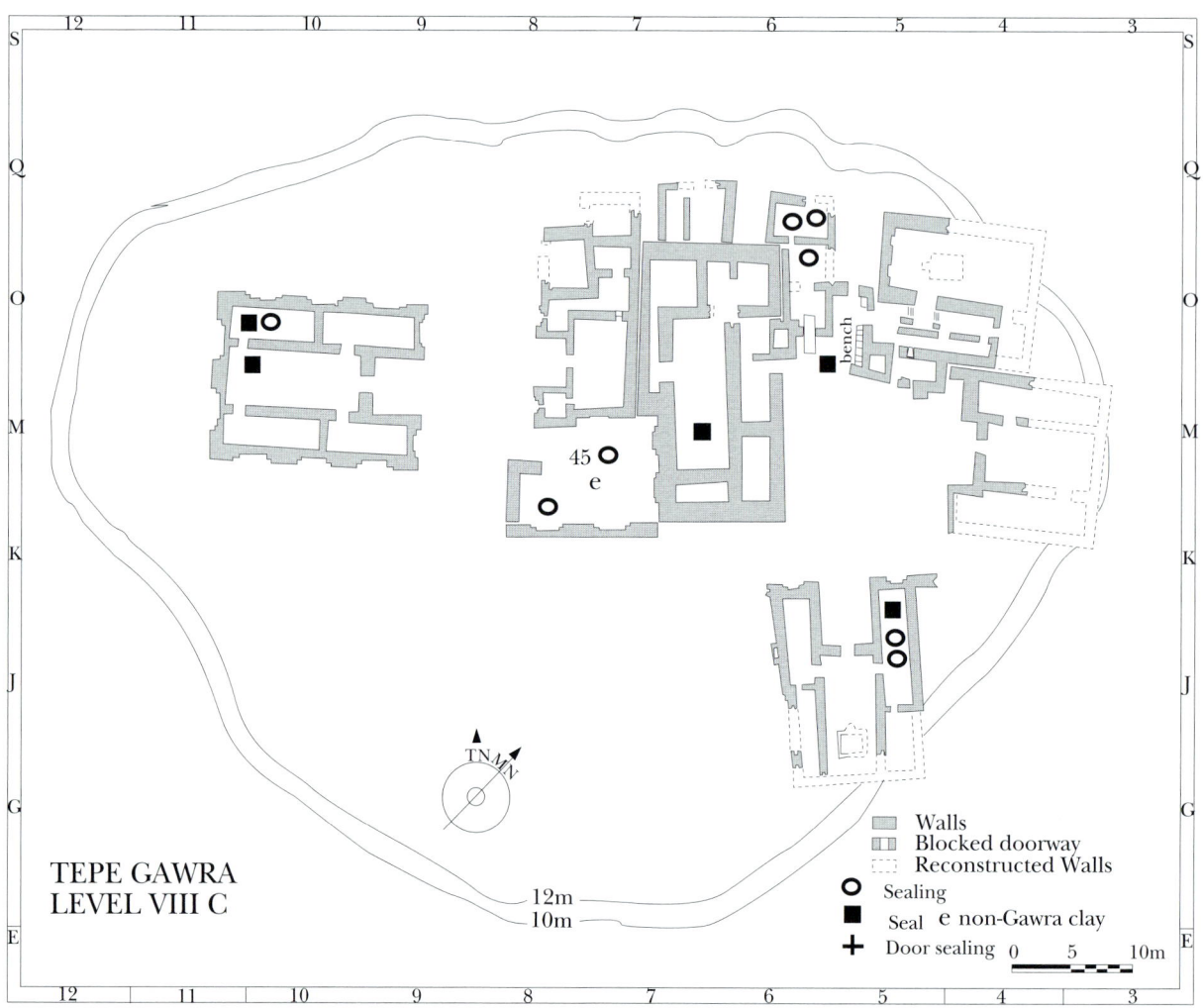

Figure 5.79 Distribution of seals and sealings in situ in Phase VIIIC, Level VIII.

Administration

Gawra VIII saw a marked increase in the number of seals and sealings recovered, especially compared to Level IX (Figures 5.79, 5.80, 5.81).

The only building dedicated solely to religious ritual in Level VIII was the southeastern temple. In its latest rebuilding, room 801 also yielded a sealing with a simple seal of a single horned animal (2926, Plate 60). In addition sealings 2920–2924 were found in room 804. These sealings from room 804 include images of a ram, dog, and fish (2929, Plate 59, also 2920), a bull, dog, and snake (image from 2939, Plate 58, also 2922, 2940–2942, 2944, 2945), and a spiky horned animal (2929, Plate 58, 2921).

These sealings are important not only because they were found in the temple, but because they lead to an understanding of changes in the administrative

structure of Level VIII. Seal designs 2920/2921 (field number 1660A and B) are from one sealing from the shoulders of a jar. Another seal of the same ram dog and fish (2929, field number 5612) was found in warehouse room 812 (A or B). That sealing was stamped with both seal impressions and joins 2920/21 precisely. These sealing are so plotted on Figure 5.80. As to the join of 2929 and 2920/21, one piece of the sealing was probably sent to the temple with the contents, while the other remained in the storeroom where the seal was broken. This indicates a system of administratively controlled goods flowing out of the central warehouse to other institutions. It represents a new technique, in effect using pieces of the sealing like the stub of a receipt.

The sealing dubbed 1660B1 (2939, Plate 58) had the so-called bull, dog, and snake seal impression, the most

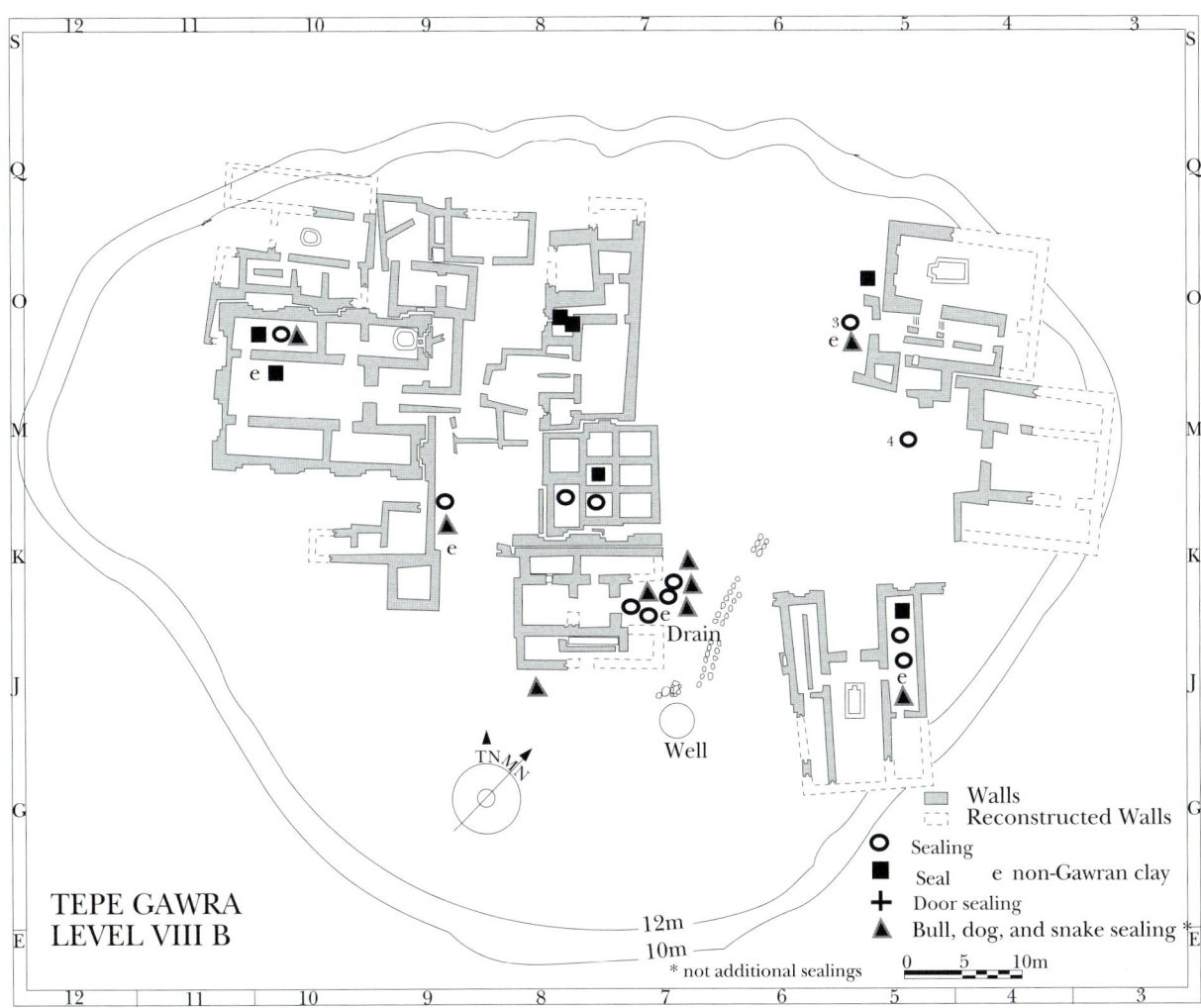

TEPE GAWRA
LEVEL VIII B

Walls
Reconstructed Walls

○ Sealing
■ Seal   e non-Gawran clay
+ Door sealing
▲ Bull, dog, and snake sealing *

12m
10m
* not additional sealings

0 5 10m

Figure 5.80   Distribution of seals and sealings in situ in Phase VIIIB, Level VIII.

common seal of VIIIB. Other impressions of this same seal on sealings from a variety of containers—sacks, baskets, and jars—were found throughout the institutions of Phase VIIIB. This sealing represents a new level in the vertical administrative structure of the site. All the major central institutions, the secular public building with a shrine, the temple, the western secular public building have pieces of sealings with the bull, dog and snake design from Phase VIIIB (Figure 5.80). The central warehouse also has copies, as does the tripartite building abutting the warehouse. What this seems to me to represent, certainly compared to Phase XI or Level X, is control of items passing to each major centralized institution through the mechanism of a central comptroller.

The comptroller, related to the highest level of leadership, controlled the other institutions by means of controlling their access to stored or transported goods.

Aside from the seals in the central building where they were probably produced, seals and the authority to control goods they represent (Rothman 1994a, 1994b) were associated with the temple, the public secular and shrine building in the northeast, and the western building from which rations may have been dispersed.

The level of control the overall pattern suggests is of the greatest vertical degree of any of the levels analyzed. Along with all the other information presented by remains from Level VIII, this to me says that the Gawran polity, of which Gawra is certainly now the controlling center, has developed a new set of relations with its hinterland and the wider region. That new set of relationships necessitated the development of new mechanisms of control, that is, new levels of complexity and centralization.

This administrative elaboration was happening at the beginning of the LC3 period when regional

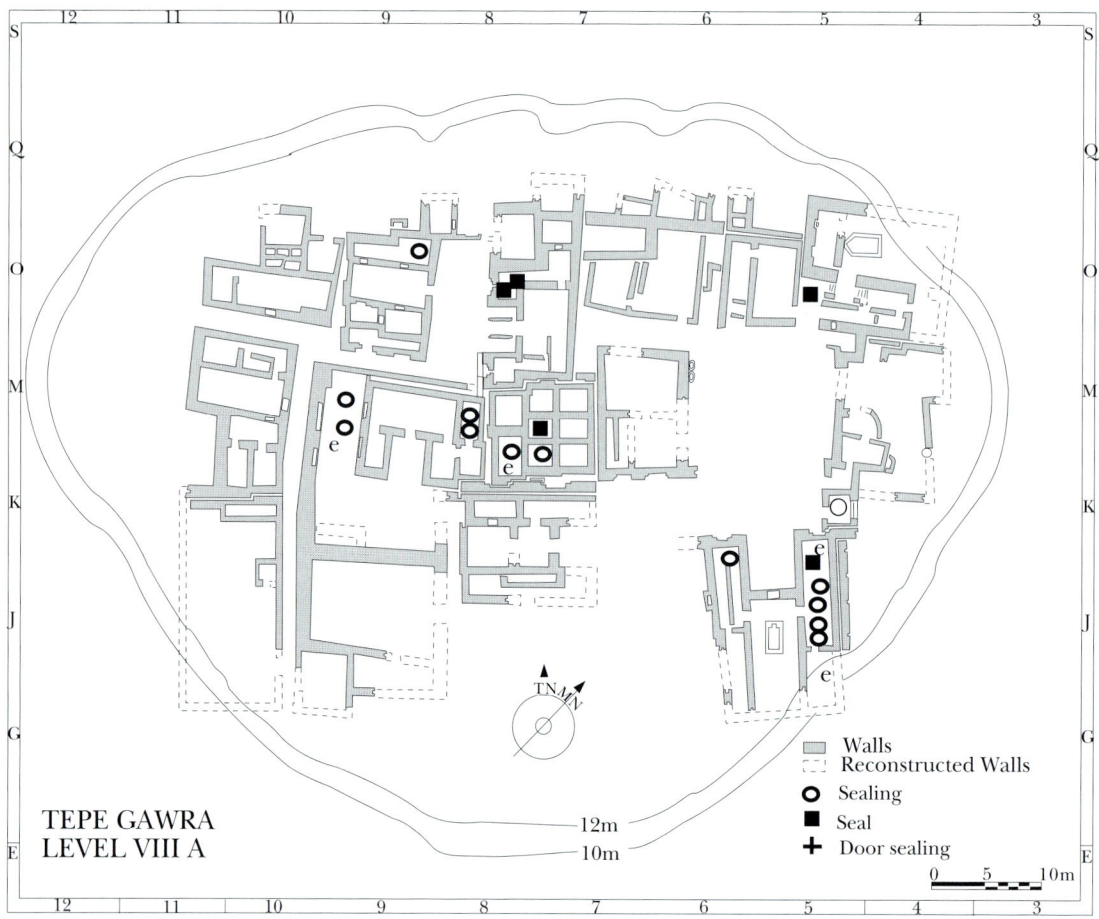

Figure 5.81   Distribution of seals and sealings in situ in Phase VIIIA, Level VIII.

networks are thought to be developing. In effect, it means that the larger world had changed the fate of the individuals living in this area of the Tigris piedmont. As will be argued in the concluding chapter, this also says something about the nature of the so-called Uruk Expansion, and what it meant for the wider region.

Notes

1. Again, the data from this and other levels can be considered at best generally representative. Inferences from negative evidence must be considered at best speculative, and evidence from positive data is more suggestive than fully validated.

2. In regard to the suggestion by Forest that the round enclosures at Kheit Qasim are good analogies to the various round houses, I agree with Gibson (1986:469) that they are not comparable, and cannot be used to explain Gawra's Round House. The enclosure at Kheit Qasim is an enclosure wall for a neighborhood, not a single building.

3. In XIA, 50 percent of the mound is accounted for by excavated area, as opposed to 40 percent for XII and XIB.

4. The similarity to themes in seal designs indicate that this is of signal importance. It is also one of the most Ubaid-like pots found at Gawra this late in time.

5. Based on other finds of grinding stones in earlier levels, I visited Dropsie to see if this too was a grinder. In fact the head of the phallus had clear pecking marks, typical of a pestle or grinder.

6. It is possible (see Appendix to this volume) that many of the "commoner" graves are associated with Level IX, or that, as at the Royal Cemetery of Ur, commoners placed graves near those of highest religious and political status.

6

Conclusion

At the beginning of this volume, I asked two questions. First, what is the evolutionary history of one particular site in the piedmont of northern Greater Mesopotamia, Tepe Gawra, during the time leading up to state formation, urban origins, and increasing intra-regional interactions. Second, how does the evolutionary history of this one particular site reflect changes in the larger region? In other words, how did developments at this site, whose occupation ended at the beginning of the so-called Uruk Expansion, presage the kinds of relations that would develop between southern and northern Mesopotamia near the end of the fourth millennium BC?

As Driessen (1992) asserts, one of the great methodological problems of all anthropological research, whether ethnographic or archaeological, is that our natural unit of analysis is the particular: the site, community, or cultural group. This unit is what we study to be capable of giving real texture, a sense of the individual players, to our analyses. However, in order to understand why our particular observations have a more general meaning, we have to understand the relationship of a site, or community, or cultural group to others in their widest context. The latter, by its very nature, must be less detailed and more generalized.

The contribution of Algaze (1993), and of Robert Adams before him, has been to remind us that the larger trends of time, process, and space are essential to our understanding. Larger regional trends must inform our understanding of the particular sites we analyze. Whether the theory of Uruk Expansion and informal empire or World Systems that Algaze (1993) proposes or Adams' (1981) theory that cites the centrality of urban growth to Mesopotamian culture prevail as key

models for explaining larger Mesopotamian trends remains moot. Similarly, the theories of state proposed by Wright (1977, 1984) are still being actively debated. However, whether these three are right is less important that they continue to be critical models. These models have framed the questions we are asking at a critical moment in the history of our discipline. The new approaches they propose spawned yet newer ideas and directed research into new areas. One of those areas is represented in the analytical orientation of this volume.

Therefore, this chapter has two parts. The first is a synthesis of the trends that have emerged in the particular case of Tepe Gawra in the late fifth and early fourth millennia B.C. The second is an analysis of what this case may say about the development of social complexity in this period, and what those developments imply for theories of state and, to a lesser extent, World Systems.

Evolutionary Trends at Tepe Gawra

As defined in Chapter 1, the evolution of Tepe Gawra and presumably its neighboring sites is one that exhibits a general trend toward greater complexity. That complexity, as Flannery (1972) defines it, involves a greater amount of differentiation and specialization in economic and political systems and increasing linkage in these sub-systems through greater sophistication in the mechanisms of control, greater centralization in the way leaders used those mechanisms. Increasing social complexity is not merely a top-down phenomenon. It has profound effects on the lives, activities, and beliefs of individuals and groups within the society in general. An evolutionary trajectory toward complexity also affects and is affected by the wider world.

Increasing Complexity

If my interpretations are correct, the beginning of the period under discussion in Level XII was still dominated by some sorts of extended family units, living in large, complex housing, ritual, and production units. These units may be part of a social structure that extends to those outside of the town, indicating the lineal or clan structures noted for later Mesopotamia (Adams 1966). At the same time, the number of seals and sealings certainly indicates that formal control of raw materials or products was an important social institution, one not usually necessary in a tribal or other predominantly kin-based societies.

As discussed in Chapter 1, one should not think of all administration as requiring powerful central governments with full-time, professional bureaucrats. Less centralized social organizations may require coordination of activities or access to goods or raw materials that are limited in quantity or difficult to obtain. As Nissen (2000) argues, stamp seals in many ways imply a smaller, partially kin-based audience, as opposed to cylinder seals. He writes (2000:212), "when stamp seals were used, protection was tied to the general familiarity with everyone that used the seal—and a high degree of familiarity is characteristics of small groups. In contrast, the new kind of protection [cylinder seals] was an impersonal one, and people who were not familiar with the seal code could at least determine whether the fastener was damaged or not" [because the cylinder seal's impression could easily cover the whole surface of the sealing].[1] Winter (1987) makes a similar point that variations in cylinder design during the Ur III period appear to encode various hierarchical ranks within a particular institution when face-to-face orders cannot be given practically.

There are other indications of social complexity, even if kinship remains a strong integrating force. The White Room building and its immediately adjoining buildings are not the secular public buildings of later Level X to VIII, but they do seem a precursor to those later public spaces because of their formal architectural features, position on the mound, and contents. The structure of the front doors and interior spaces of the White Room building is reminiscent of later temples, as are the niches in its back wall. However, its contents indicate domestic and minor craft production activities rather than public functions. The transformation of the extended kin household into the architectural expression of the household of the god (é.dingir) and then the household of the king (é.gal) may be one of the more significant markers of the evolution of ideological

systems. The fourth millennium concept of the gods as providers (Jacobsen 1976) makes some sense in this light.

Aside from the White Room, the bins and building to the west of the main entry road may indicate a coordinated trading function, whether transshipping of imported goods or processing of locally produced goods for export. This area of the XII mound suggests that a centralized economic function existed, making the residents of the White Room building seem more likely to be of higher rank. One concentration of sealings found in the southern area of the White Room complex, including the only door seal of XII, may indicate a special role for its residents, as the tripartite building with the bull, dog and snake seal did in VIIIB. The possible storehouse of Level XII in Square 5M further argues for centralized functions, although clearly not vertical integration of the kind evident in Level VIII. Unfortunately, the kinds of material stored in this storehouse remain unknown. There are a very few sickles for agriculture on the mound, and a grinding stone was found immediately outside it, which might imply that this could have been a grain storehouse, but that is not enough evidence to draw any firm conclusion.

To put this kind of increased complexity into perspective, the Susa A period occupation of the Acropole of Susa may indicate a similar trend (Pollock 1989). At that site a large platform built for some public function is bounded by a storehouse. What remains of the Susa storehouse looks much like the one in Square 5M at Gawra. This facility contained stored grain and small tools. Seals found in the area—their exact context is unclear—may indicate administration of the facilities, as broken sealings in better context at Gawra do. What is even more interesting is that Dollfus sees the Susa of that time as a series of villages with a central institution, represented by the platform (1985). Like Gawra XII, kinship and community remained integrating forces, even as administrative leadership groups were forming, based on some political or religious institutions that served the larger multi-site community.[2] Another instance of contemporaneous development, in this case economic, was discovered at Arslantepe, where excavators found evidence of mass-produced pottery and metallurgy early in the fourth millennium (Palmieri 1985).

For Gawrans living on the mound after the destruction of Level XII, there was some continuity in the organization and apparent complexity in the XIB phase. These continuities are evidenced in the buildings of that phase.

The buildings of Phase XIB in Squares 4/5J(K), clearly associated with the earlier phase of this level, have many of the elements of what I interpreted as extended family dwellings in XII. They have large, central, common rooms, exterior kitchens, and storage spaces. In the southern building, in which excavators found sickle blades, there were four deep bins or silos. However, these buildings do lack the niches in the back wall, or ritual objects, like the hut statue from the White Room. Excavators also recovered sealings from these buildings.

By the XIA phase of Level XIA/B a new level of social complexity is evident in Gawran society. The construction of the Round House fortress, gateway complex in the northeast and the southern complex—this may be a defensive structure as well—required significant input from the 360 or so people who lived on the mound and almost definitely from individuals living in nearby sites. Not only was it necessary to have central coordinators to plan the construction and recruit the labor necessary to build these buildings, but once built they needed to be manned and supplied. At the same time, the building to the west of the gateway complex, which existed in XIB times, was remodeled and apparently utilized as a specialized craft building. The new blocks of houses built on the southeastern flank of the mound and the area just west of the Round House were small, unlike the multi-family units of Level XII and Phase XIB. Gawrans clearly invested in their defense. Steponaitis (1991) distinguishes between warfare conducted by "guerrilla raids" and that in which many soldiers march together in formal military formations. He writes, "This larger-scale, organized warfare was conducted by centralized polities" (Steponaitis 1991:207). The Round House and the other constructions must evidence warfare of the latter kind. Also, craft production was physically segregated. These buildings and their functions describe a social arrangement in which administrative forms of social organization (see Chapter 1) were necessary and which permitted leaders to manipulate local systems.

In fact, the distribution of administrative hardware in this town indicates a greater degree of centralization than in the previous level and phase. The buildings that were potentially built under the auspices of centralized administrators are the ones where excavators found most of the seals and two of three concentrations of sealings from this phase. One of the sealings of non-Gawran clay was buried there (Rothman and Blackman 1990: Figure 9; Figure 5.80 in this volume). The implication of the exotic clay is that goods or raw materials were imported from some distance. All of the sealings in the Round House were of Gawran clay, and the places where seals were found outside the Round House were places where exotic clays in sealings were also found. Based on this pattern it appears that exotic goods or tribute were entering the mound, and then were re-sealed with local clay to provision the Round House. Such segregation of functions implies that a process of increased centralization was underway.

This process of segregation of functions and centralization increased in Level XI/XA. In Phase XI, a formal temple was placed at the southeast edge of the mound. Excavators found a secular public building at the opposite end of the main north-south street. In Squares 4-6K-O of the mound, the crew unearthed a specialized weaving shop, spinning and perhaps woodworking shop, and a kiln. Aside from the two house complexes in the northwest part of the excavated mound, the domiciles were clearly not big enough to house an extended family. They were small with one or two rooms, the second often a kitchen. At the same time that extended kin groups seem to have declined as an integrating mechanism, at least as shown by architectural form, the various specialized functions seem more directly controlled. Except for one seal—that probably out of place—all the seals and sealings were found in buildings with specialized functions, not in domiciles. Further, a study of seal design (see Rothman 1994b) indicates that the sealings found in association with craft production usually had among them images of predators attacking prey, whereas the designs associated with the temple and secular public building lacked predators and showed herds of domestic animals. The sealings associated with the temple of X also featured herd animals. This may imply a kind of horizontal segregation of authority, differentiating economic production from ideological and political leadership.

Although I have suggested an increasing degree of centralization and segregation, I do not mean to imply that the level of complexity in any of the levels is on a state level, although Level VIII gets as close as any (see below). Chiefly societies are organizationally capable of handling any of the activities so far suggested (Earle 1991). The division of ideological and craft activities in Phase XI would suggest a rather generalized and horizontally organized leadership, rather than the vertical leadership hierarchies of states. The lack of any marking of rank in mortuary ritual also fits the theory of Stein (1991), cited in Chapter 1. That the ideology of kinship needed to be maintained despite the increasing influence and rank of chiefs is evident in the graves of Levels XIA/B and XI/XA.

Level X provides a telling contrast to these earlier levels. With the exception of a kiln, gone are the most of the specialized craft production facilities of XI/XA, XIA/B, or XII. The temple, for the first time in the levels discussed here, is centrally located. A very large secular public building was also present. Some larger houses existed. For example, the house in Square 7O has many features of the buildings I thought might define extended family units in XII and XIA/B, although the walls would probably not hold a second floor. However, most of the houses of Level X were small, cramped buildings with a kitchen attached. A formal shrine room existed among one set of houses, and a possible depot was located north of the cluster of houses for receiving sealed goods. Most of the seal designs associated with the depot also were found in trash from the temple.

A large area of trashy remains associated with the temple yielded sealings presumably for provisioning the temple. The most common among them was a single seal design with sheep and a structure. Again, the same seal design appears among the sealings in the area I interpreted as a possible depot. Otherwise, excavators recovered seals in the following locations: the secular public building, buildings surrounding the temple, and in one of the rooms in the cluster of houses north of the temple. In my earlier analysis of Gawra X (Rothman 1988), I interpreted the evidence from Level X as indicating a diminution of centralization. Level X does represent a change in functional size, but I now think it represents a similar if not greater degree of centralization than Level XI/XA. What changed were the functions that were centralized.

If anything, Level IX is a repeat of Level X. Like X, it had as its major focus the temple in the center of the mound and a secular public building in its southwestern quadrant. A large, thick-walled building of indeterminate function rested in the south of the mound, bordering the terrace from Level VI. There was a luxury goods manufacturing shop in the north of the mound for carving seals, beads, bone inlay, and the like. None of the spinning, weaving, or woodworking emphasis of the levels before X existed. This was in no way a self-sustaining community from what is left. This is a center. The seals that excavators dug up were from the same functional spaces as they had been in Level X—the secular, public building, the temple, the building immediately in front of the temple. The seals from the carving shop were mostly uncut.

Level VIII represented a new stage in the process of centralization at Tepe Gawra. This level was undoubtedly a center. At most 50 people actually lived on the mound. Ovens of the kind that were common for more than 1,000 years before were not found. This is especially clear, because Speiser's crew dug the entire surface of the mound at VIII. The small houses of XIA to X were missing. The eastern half of the mound in which the temple and a public, secular building with a shrine were located was seemingly isolated from the west half in which economic enterprises were common by architecture that blocked any streets between the two halves. This represents the same dichotomy of functions that was evident in the seal design distributions of Phase XI. Luxury production in the central building mirrors the luxury workshop of Level IX. The exact range of economic activities evident in the western part of the mound are hard to document, but the extraordinary number of flint and obsidian cores (4) and blades (over 100), most not utilized, indicates that knapping, especially from imported obsidian, was one of the chief economic activities. In the VIIIC phase, the large secular public building may have had as one of its functions the distribution of grain rations. Presumably, this grain paid for workers on behalf of the central institutions.

Most telling in terms of the degree of centralization of the center in Level VIII was the appearance of a central warehouse. The distribution of seals and sealings confirm its function. The clearest evidence of increasing centralization consists of the distribution of the bull, dog, and snake seal (see Figure 5.80, Plate 58). As I wrote in Chapter 5, sealings from this seal were found in each of the major functional spaces on the mound: the temple, the secular public building with shrine, the warehouse, the tripartite building south of the warehouse (perhaps warehouse trash), and the large western building. The western building was probably a craft production area and, perhaps, a residence during in VIIIB. Similarly, among the sealings in each of these locations are one's of non-Gawra clay. The way the system worked may be best illustrated by matching pieces of the same sealing, one found in the warehouse, the other in the temple, as if each were a receipt for the goods that were opened and transported. In fact, those two pieces of this sealing were made from clay not from the Gawra source (Rothman and Blackman 1990). Not only does there seem to have been a central mechanism for provisioning various institutions, but that function seems to be vested in a single office (or official). Of the bull, dog, and snake sealings most were made of clay from the Gawran source, but one was from non-Gawran clay.[3] In Phase VIIIC, many of the 45 sealings in the "hammam" were also from non-Gawran clay sources. This all implies that Gawra was part of a far-flung network of exchange and interaction and was center of a coherent polity. Because Gawra VIII and perhaps IX were the only levels occupied during the beginning of the so-called Uruk Expansion, an expansion of the trade networks in which Gawrans were involved should not be surprising.

Compared to Levels XI–IX, the administration of Level VIII appears to have added a vertical, hierarchical step, approaching more closely the structure of a state than the complexity level typical of simple chiefdoms. Gawra nonetheless remained a chiefdom.

In general, then, one piece of the evolutionary history of Gawra was an increase in the complexity of the society's structures. These changes began at a time when kinship apparently was the major basis for social organization and cohesion. These structures evolved through a time when administrative forms of organization of a generalized kind held sway. By the time Gawra burned in Phase VIIIA, it exhibited administrative forms of organization with vertical and focused leadership extending into the countryside and becoming incorporated into larger regional exchange networks.

Social Differentiation

Most theories of the evolution of complexity cite a social aspect of the emergence of leadership organizations; namely, changes in social status that mark individuals in the leadership group. The study of the graves from Tepe Gawra in the appendix of this volume, one of the largest collections of interments from the fourth millennium, illustrates one clear set of markers of social differentiation. As Peasnall documents in the appendix, there are marked changes in the symbolic content of burials from Levels XIA/B to VIII. Those symbolic elements were encoded as much in the form or type and size of graves (loose, cist, pisè, sidewall, and tomb) as in burial goods. From XIA/B through XI/XA, distinctions among graves that could be interpreted as social ranking were evident. Some individuals, mostly those buried in built tombs, must have had ascribed status at birth, because children as well as adults were buried in higher ranking types of burials. However, as Peasnall writes, "in Levels XIA/B and XI/XA, some individuals were certainly set apart from the others in terms of mortuary practices, but these differences were never very great." Further, some of the exotic materials like gold and bone combs that were prominent in the later spectacular tombs appeared for the first time in XI/XA.

Why was the development of very broad differences in burial practice evident first in Level X? After the surprisingly early development of specialized craft centers in Phase XI and the military investment of Phase XIA, the scattered craft activity of Level X among a warren of domiciles would seem to predict a decline in societal complexity and status differences.

The explanations of these trends must lie in the particular trajectory of change through time in the Gawra area, especially as compared to other contemporaneous cases, such as that of the Susiana Plains of southwestern Iran.

Chiefdoms and States

As noted in Chapter 1, the level of complexity of evolving societies was a key issue in explaining the patterns observed from Gawra XII to VIII. In particular, issues regarding pre-state political formations are important for interpretation. In terms of the currently used nomenclature for describing socio-political organization, Gawra was chiefly. A chiefdom is a "socio-political entity in which overall social control activities are vested in a sub-system which is externally specialized vis-à-vis other activities, but not internally specialized in terms of control processes (e.g., observing, deciding, coercing); there is, in short, one generalized kind of political control" (Wright 1994:68). This is certainly a very good description of what was described for Gawra above. It certainly is appropriate to the situation in Phase XI, when economic specialization increased

dramatically, but the control mechanisms evidenced in seals and sealings remained largely generalized. At the baseline of our analysis, Level XII, the type of chiefdom fits Wright's description of simple chiefdoms. They are "those in which such control is exercised by figures drawn from an ascribed local elite subgroup; these chiefdoms have only one level of control hierarchy above the level of local community" (Wright ibid.) By the end of Gawra's fourth millennium BC occupation in Level VIII, Gawra fits Wright's description of complex chiefdoms. They are "those in which control is exercised by figures drawn from a class of people which cross-cuts many local sub-groups, a 'class' being defined as a ranked group whose members compete with each other for access to controlling positions and stand together in opposition to other people" (Wright ibid.).

Although the evolutionary level can be defined by the nomenclature of chiefdoms, that does not explain why Gawra took its particular developmental path. Gawra is clearly different in many ways from a contemporary complex chiefdom at Susa. Nothing even remotely similar to the construction of the massif at Susa can be found at Gawra. In certain respects Gawra also does not fit Wright's three features of complex chiefdom (Wright ibid.) Gawra did not become significantly larger through time. It did see changes in architectural plans for specialized functions, but little change was notable in residences, signifying differences in rank. As I wrote above, mortuary practice does indicate such differentiation in rank, however. This is Wright's third archaeological correlate.

Organizational change, however, can result from many different causes and can manifest itself in significantly different forms. The baseline assumption is that conditions to which the evolving societies were subjected generated a need for coordinated action and at the same time created opportunities for individuals or groups to become promoted to new, higher ranking, institutionalized social identities.

The conditions themselves may vary. Feinman (1994) cites as one of the major conditions for particular evolutionary trajectories that of scale. The very size of a polity or network may alter the nature of the resulting evolutionary response. As I alluded to above, the polity with Susa as its center encompassed a considerable geographical area. The open plains of the Susiana gave ample space for competing centers. Choga Mish was such a center, whose interactions with Susa varied over the course of the fourth millennium (Johnson 1973). Susa was also situated in an area rich in agricultural potential. Under irrigation, itself a condition of the Susa system and a potential tool for building new institutions (Rothman 1987, Adams 1981), the leaders of Susa could harness large surpluses of grain and considerable sources of settled labor, the latter especially in the non-agricultural seasons. The probable storehouses on the Susa A massif indicate storage was one chiefly function (Wright 1994:73–74) in a period parallel in time to Gawra XII and XIA/B.

The situation for Gawra in the piedmont was less prodigious. Although agriculture in its immediate environs would have been easy using only rainfall, the sites we do know of were small and quite scattered. As the map of the Gawra area (Figure 1.2) indicates, there were few other sites in its area, and many of those were in the hilly country immediately to the east. As I have argued elsewhere (Rothman 1988), the likelihood that pastoral nomads were part of the population that utilized the site is great, based on modern usage of this niche. Unlike Nineveh, which became a great and long-lived center and political capitol, river access would not have favored Gawra. It was in the center of a plain, as were Qalinj Agha and Nuzi south of the Greater and Lesser Zab Rivers, two small centers occupied at the same time as Gawra.

Gawra's potential for developing leadership organizations was limited. Those that did seek to establish themselves in higher-ranking social identities had two avenues, as the evidence from Gawra shows. One was what Potter (2000:296) calls allocative resources. These are material transfers. The specialized productive and goods storage functions found in Gawra XII, XIA/B, and XI/XA represent this type of resource for building authority and rank. The other type of resource is authoritative. "Authoritative resources, on the other hand, are primarily social in nature and encompass both structures of social reproduction, such as social organization and religious activities, and structures of biological reproduction, such as population size, density and organization" (Potter ibid.). Within authoritative resources, ritual is an essential element. As Potter (2000:297) writes, "First, access to the resources of ritual, such as the knowledge and meaning of symbols, may often be organized [in small-scale societies] more effectively than economic, or allocative resources.... Second, authority tends to be inherent in knowledge-based power and is thus more difficult to challenge directly than power based on allocative resources." This helps to explain the transformation to the temple as the central, specialized institution in Levels X and IX and its continuity into VIII as a major function of Gawra. To the religious ritual of the southeastern temple and the shrine of the northeastern building of VIII is added the allocative functions of the western part of the VIIIA mound, cut off from the eastern side, while still supplied by the central function of the warehouse.

Allocative Resources and Gawra's Relations with the World Outside the Mound

Clearly, allocative resources were what drew the residents of Gawra into larger networks of interaction outside the Gawran polity. There are a number of possible configurations of such networks. In other words, there are different kinds of exchange systems from down-the-line exchange to administered trade. Based on which resources were exchanged, where those resources were extracted, and how much processing of resources was done at each point in space, there were different ways in which Gawrans could fit into any one possible network configuration.

One theory that permits us to explore the role Tepe Gawra in larger networks is that of Kowalewski et al. (1983). In their construct, centers of polities tend to have two general kinds of relations with their own polity and with the world outside that polity. On the one hand, the polities are closed. That means that the center exerts strong influence on its own satellite sites in order to enhance its local role. Integration among satellite sites is discouraged, and all high order functions (like Great Tradition religion, markets, specialized craft production) flow through the center. The other alternative is that the system is open. In that circumstance, there is more integration among satellite sites, and the center's role, although potentially strong within its own polity, is more directed toward a role of mediating with areas outside the polity. In one sense, what Kowalewski et al. are describing is a situation in which a closed system is more likely to be based on staple finance, an open one on wealth finance (D'Altroy and Earle 1985). In addition to that, other high order functions may be important.

At Gawra, there were three times when the polity, of which Gawra is a part, was open: Levels XII, VIII, and probably XIA/B. All three ended in fire, although only the first was clearly set during military action. The openness of these levels is shown by the presence of sealings made of clays from non-Gawran sources. They are also marked as open by the productive or exchange activities that appear to define their economic structure.

In Level XII, the building and the area of bins west of the entry road must have been part of a formal exchange or transshipping system. Based on the contents of the rooms adjoining the bins, possible exports include finished tools, jewelry, and mace heads, some made of exotic materials. For Level VIII obsidian in unusually high numbers was present and perhaps was being transshipped as blades or cores. There is ample evidence that lithics were transported. At sites like Ubaid 4 period Değirmentepe, excavators found Canaanite blades in jars in which they were transported (Esin 1976, Plate 58,2), and a large cache of obsidian blades was found in the Riemchengebäude of Late Uruk, LC5 period Uruk-Warka (Eichmann 1986). Although the Riemchengebäude at Uruk-Warka was occupied long after Gawra was abandoned, the desirability of this imported material into the preeminent city of the Uruk period is clear. In the Uruk-Warka case, some debitage was also found, suggesting they obtained cores not blades. Export products from Level XIA/B are harder to specify. The probable craft building of the XIA phase was one where cloth and ceramics were possibly produced, not necessarily long distance export items, although all the functions of the building cannot be specified. At the same time, the military preparedness of the Gawrans of this level—preparedness that must have required labor or grain inputs from neighboring sites—indicates regular and unfriendly contact with others in the region.

The three unburned levels—XI/XA, X and IX—it seems, were directed more toward local control. The sealings were all made from this homogeneous Gawran clay source (Rothman and Blackman 1990). Level XI/XA continued the craft activity of the previous levels and, in fact, the functions were more clearly segregated into specialized shops or areas (or at least the archaeological evidence is clearer that they did). Very special cloth of the kind mentioned in the old Assyrian trading documents (Larsen 1967) can be an export item, as can pottery, but both of those products seem more logically directed toward the local consumption. The big change—again at least that is evidenced[4]—is the construction of a major religious institution, the first since the large emplacements of Ubaid 4 Level XIII. The focus of activity in Levels X and IX are the religious institutions, to the exclusion of craft production, which as I proposed above may be the ideal strategy for local control in small-scale societies. Among the few other excavated sites in the piedmont and open steppe west of the Tigris River, religious institutions of similar size existed (see Chapter 1), so the Gawran installations must have served a local population. These levels also have secular public buildings, which could be the centers of chiefly leadership or other community activities.

Thus, despite a general trend toward increased complexity, the functional size and functional focus of the late fifth and fourth millennium B.C. levels varied considerably. At the beginning of this period and at its end, the site was more engaged in exchange or conflict over a wider geographical sphere of interaction. The networks in which the residents were involved, hypothetically, were broader and more complex. As Feinman (1994) points out, the scale of political action and of cultural or exchange networks are often different.

In terms of the symbolization of rule (Pollock 1983a), tomb burials, particularly the first of the spectacularly fitted tombs of X (see the appendix) probably indicate an association of long distance trade and status (Helms 1988), but not a system-wide economic direction, or a high degree of wealth financing. The basis of authority and the social structure of the polity seem more clearly generated by ideological roles or controlling local production of some necessary goods.

The lack of sickle blades recovered from the occupational levels above XIA/B would suggest that the many staple goods, such as grains, were brought into the Gawran town as tribute or exchange, especially by Level VIII.

How can one measure the impact of the outside world on the people of Gawra and their lives? Chronologically, the two periods of openness, the end of the Ubaid/beginning of the Uruk period, LC 1-2, represented by Levels XII, XIA/B and the early Middle Uruk period, LC3, represented by VIII are certainly periods that, from everything we know, were times of population movement and regional change. In the LC3, the supposed expansion of southern Mesopotamian societies had begun. This was when economic opportunity was beginning to peak. The openness of Level VIII and the new degree of vertical administrative elaboration would only seem possible in the context of involvement with wider networks. This was surely a period of expanded contacts in the region. The LC1 to early LC2 also seems a period of population movement and newly formed networks, though of a different scale than later.

How else can involvement in other networks be measured? Artifact style, although more subjective and therefore more likely to produce a questionable interpretation, can provide at least some hypotheses (Frankel 1978, Plog 1980, Arnold 1985). As described in Chapter 1, there are clear style zones in northern Mesopotamia through the late fifth and fourth millennia. What else can these stylistic variations be but a symbolic drawing of a boundary separating the people of Gawra and especially their leaders from others in the region? As Cole and Wolf (1974:269) write, "the socio-cultural manifestations of the formation of new political groupings . . . is the result, not of ethnic groups disengaging themselves from one another, but of increased interaction among them. . . . It is a process by which a group . . . manipulates some customs, values, myths, symbols, and ceremonials from their cultural tradition in order to articulate an informal political organization, which is used as a weapon in that struggle."

The area Cole and Wolf are writing about, rural Tyrol, is a somewhat marginal agricultural and herding area of Central Europe like Gawra. The Ubaid-like pots found in the Early and Early Middle, LC2-3 periods were all from ritual or administrative contexts and may indicate a conscious reminder of a common past. Many of these same motifs re-emerge in the Ninevite V period when the Jazira and piedmont mark themselves as distinct from southern Mesopotamia, the western Zagros, and the Upper Euphrates basin. Pittman (in press) also sees shared and exchanged motifs in seal design with southern Mesopotamia, but only for Level VIII, when the increased interactions with other parts of the region began. Before then, stylistic variation tied Gawra to the rest of the pied-mont and to the hilly country of eastern Anatolia and northwestern Iran.

The major center in Gawra's immediate area was Nineveh. Algaze (1993) interprets Nineveh as an en-clave of southern Mesopotamian city-states. As such, it would have dominated Gawra. At the time Algaze wrote his analysis, most researchers, including me, thought that Gawra VIII was Late Middle or even Late Uruk, LC4-5, in date. Now we know that Gawra VIII was occupied earlier than the period when Nineveh might have had southern Mesopotamian settlers. Fur-ther, if Gut (1995) and I (Rothman in press) are cor-rect, Nineveh might not have been occupied at all dur-ing the 'open' period of Gawra XII and XIA/B. As part of our effort to map administered relations by sourcing sealing clay, Blackman and I (1990) were able to obtain some samples from Nineveh. None of those tested were within the population of the Gawran clay source or related to any other of the exotic clay sources. Although the sample was small, there is no positive evidence of any controlling connection be-tween the two sites.[5]

In short, despite Gawra's small size, all the current evidence supports the idea of its being a center of a small, somewhat remote center in the piedmont zone of northern Mesopotamia.

Gawra and Theories of the Uruk Expansion

Although Gawra's fourth millennium occupation ended at the beginning of the so-called Uruk Expansion in LC3, its evolution is relevant to that theory. Algaze's theory and some of its critics' views are summarized in Chapter 1. I have argued in detail in other publications (Rothman 1993, in press) why I have trouble accepting many of the tenets of Algaze's theory, which I will not repeat here.

However, the Gawra case is important for the theo-ries of interaction, such as those of the Uruk Expan-sion, for the following reasons. What the evolution of Gawra indicates is the complexity of the interaction among the local polities and the dynamics of networks of interaction at a more regional scale. Wallerstein's theory of World Systems implies that the unit of analy-sis is the whole trading network. It is predicated on the idea that, "A world-system is a social system, one that has boundaries, structures, member groups, rules of legitimation, and coherence" (1974:347), in particu-lar class society.

Clearly, Gawrans had already established many of the institutions and local adaptations before the in-creased opportunities of the LC3 or early contact pe-riod. These institutions were in many ways different from those at places like Susa. Barring military cataclysm

or total colonial domination, I believe it would be hard to argue that had Gawra survived into the LC4 or 5 periods, its response to the changes of ever-increasing contact and interaction would be the same as those of other polities. Although overarching theories like Algaze's must overlook some detail, I think that Gawra's particular evolution argues that perhaps ap-plying World Systems theory to such a diverse region simplifies too much.

In doing so, the overarching theory of World Sys-tems precludes looking at not only variable responses based on earlier evolutionary trajectories in various places, but also precludes looking at a number of al-ternative mechanisms for interaction. An example of such a mechanism is the "trading beach" (Bekker 1967:73). The idea of the trading beach is that goods are brought from areas where they are produced to the "beach" and natives take them to dispose of in their own areas. They later settle accounts with the traders at the beachhead. In such a system, sites like Habuba Kabira would not necessarily have been settled as a trading colony, but might have served as a beach front for northern Mesopotamian polities. Hassek Höyük may have become a trading beach closer to the extraction points. As Bekker writes (1967:73), "Even if geographical and physical limi-tations were less severe, social barriers were built around trade both by the local people and the foreign traders." Bekker's specific case, that of South-east Asia, may indicate one direction for future investi-gation of Mesopotamia. In that case, trade proceeded through trading beaches. Even though the cultural boundaries were maintained between trading cul-tures, cultural influences, particularly in decorative arts, like pottery, were common. As Bekker writes (1967:74), "If there was a particularly close link be-tween trade and the transmission of cultural influ-ences, it was perhaps due to the fact that early trade was in luxuries, and luxuries were part of the mate-rial culture of Southeast Asia which was most flexible and responsive to outside influences." In this case, as in the Mesopotamian case, it was not a world system. It was autonomy and a cultural conversation that laid the groundwork for a different kind of cultural ac-commodation, one accomplished by the organiza-tional and military advantage of the empire builders. A simpler conversation was probably going on in the late Ubaid/Early Uruk Period, when some cultural similarities are evident, in that case in religious archi-tecture and pottery style.

Final Thoughts

This volume has sketched the evolution of one small town and polity center in a rather marginal zone of Mesopotamia. Based on the patterns of change in complexity and function, its history is a complex one. As in much of the rest of the region, Tepe Gawra saw at times a gradual and at times a rapid increase in the degree of centralization. That centralization was not based on a lineal development in the function and role of the town. Gawra's functional size and functional focus changed through time. At the same time some structural elements, the dichotomy of craft production and leadership tied to religion, for example, remained.

Whether or not my interpretations stand the test of time, I hope this volume serves future researchers if only by presenting as comprehensive a presentation of the raw data as is practical, and by offering an analysis that illustrates how this data might be used for interpreting the past. In that way, others may confront and come to understand this most interesting place in a most critical time in the human story in their own way.

Notes

1. It would be interesting to catalogue all the sealings with repeated stamp seals; for example, 446 from Level XII (Plate 24).

2. Please note that in Chapter 1, Carneiro's definition of society beyond the tribal level (1981) fits my own description fairly exactly.

3. The non-Gawran clays do not have a single chemical composition, and so may be from many different sources.

4. It is possible that temples existed in the unexcavated parts of XII and XIA/B, although the areas of the mound in which temples were found from Levels XIII-VIII were uncovered.

5. In fact what we know of Nineveh from the Kuyunjik sounding is minimal.

References

Abu al-Soof, Behnam

1967   More Soundings at Tell Qalinj Agha (Erbil) *Sumer* 23:69–74.

1968   Distribution of Uruk, Jamdat Nasr and Ninevite V Pottery as Revealed by Field Survey in Iraq. *Iraq* 30:74–86.

1969   Excavations at Tell Qalinj Agha (Erbil), Summer 1968. *Sumer* 25:3–42.

1974a   Late Prehistoric Pottery at Nineveh, Gawra and the Neighboring Sites. *Sumer* 30:1–9.

1974b   Late Prehistoric Pottery at Tell 'Afar-Sinjar Region. *Sumer* 31:21–24.

Adams, Robert M.

1965   *Land Behind Baghdad.* Chicago: University of Chicago Press.

1966   *The Evolution of Urban Society.* Chicago: Aldine.

1978   Strategies of Maximization, Stability, and Resilience in Mesopotamian Society, Settlement, and Agriculture. *Proceedings of the American Philosophical Society* 122:329–335.

1981   *The Heartland of Cities.* Chicago: University of Chicago Press.

1984   Mesopotamian Social Evolution: Old Outlooks, New Goals. In *On the Evolution of Complex Societies.* T. Earle, ed. pp. 78–129. Malibu, CA: Undena.

Adams, Robert M., and Hans Nissen

1972   *The Uruk Countryside.* Chicago: University of Chicago Press.

Alessio, M., L. Allegri, C. Azzi, F. Bella, G. Calderoni, C. Cortesi, S. Improto, V. Petrone

1983 C^{14} Dating of Arslantepe. In *Perspectives on Protourbanization In Eastern Anatolia: Arslantepe (Malatya).* M. Frangipane and A. Palmieri, eds. Origini 12 (2 parte): 575–580.

Akkermans, Peter M. M. G.

1988a   The Period V Pottery. In *Hammam et-Turkman I.* M. van Loon, ed. pp. 287–350. Leiden: Nederlands Historisch-Archeologisch Instituut te Istanbul.

1988b   An Updated Chronology for the Northern Ubaid and Late Chalcolithic Periods in Syria. *Iraq* 50:109–45.

Algaze, Guillermo

1986a   *Mesopotamian Expansion and Its Consequences: Informal Empire in the Late Fourth Millennium B.C.* Ph.D. dissertation, University of Chicago.

1986b   Habuba on the Tigris: Archaic Nineveh Reconsidered. *Journal of Near East Studies* 45(2):125–137.

1989   The Uruk Expansion: Cross-cultural Exchange in the Early Mesopotamian Civilization. *Current Anthropology* 30(5):571–608.

1993   *The Uruk World System.* Chicago: University of Chicago Press.

In press The Prehistory of Imperialism: the Case of Uruk Period Mesopoamia. In *Uruk*

Mesopotamia and Its Neighbors: Cross-cultural Interactions in the Era of State Formation. M. Rothman, ed. Santa Fe: SAR Press.

Algaze, G., R. Breuninger, and J. Knudstad

1994   The Tigris-Euphrates Archaeological Reconnaisance Project: Final Report of the Birecik and Carchemish Dam Survey Areas. *Anatolica*: 1–96.

Amiet, Pierre

1979   Archaeological Discontinuity and Ethnic Duality in Elam. *Antiquity* 53(209):195–204.

1985   A propos de l'usage et de l'iconographie des scieux a Suse. *Paléorient* 11/2:37–38.

Andrae, Walter

1935   *Die Jüngeren Ischtar-Tempel in Assur.* Ausgrabungen der Deutschen Orientgesellschaft in Assur 58. Leipzig: J. C. Hinrichs Buchhandlung.

Anonymous

1931a   Tepe Gawra, a New Site. *Bulletin of The University Museum* 2(5):141–142.

1931b   The Expedition to Tell Billa and Tepe Gawra. *Bulletin of The University Museum* 3(2):59–66.

1932a   Developments at Tell Billa and Tepe Gawra. *Bulletin of The University Museum* 3(3/4):94–95.

1932b   Excavations at Tell Billa and Tepe Gawra. *Bulletin of The University Museum* 3(5):126–30.

1933a   Excavations at Tepe Gawra. *Bulletin of The University Museum* 4(2):36–40.

1933b   The Assyrian Expedition. *Bulletin of The University Museum* 4(4):102–103.

1935a   Tepe Gawra Excavations. *Bulletin of The University Museum* 5(5):34–36.

Arnold, D. E.

1975   Ceramic Ecology of the Ayacucho Basin, Peru. *Current Anthropology* 16:183–194.

1985   *Ceramic Theory and Cultural Process.* Cambridge: Cambridge University Press.

Aurenche, Olivier, Evin Jacques, and Francis Hours, eds.

1987   *Chronologies du Proche Orient/Chronologies in the Near East.* Oxford: BAR 379.

Bache, Charles

1933a   From Mr. Bache's First Report on the Joint Excavations at Tepe Gawra and Tell Billa, 1932–3. *BASOR* 49:8–14.

1933b   Work of the Baghdad School. *BASOR* 51:20–26.

1935a   Tepe Gawra 1934–35. *American Journal of Archaeology* 39:185–188.

1935b   A Report from Mr. Bache on the Tepe Gawra Expedition. *BASOR* 57:12–18.

1935c   Prehistoric Burials of Tepe Gawra. *Scientific American* 153(6):310–313.

1935d   The Joint Expedition: Letters from Mr. Bache. *BASOR* 58:5–9.

1936a   Report on the Joint Excavation of Tepe Gawra in Assyria. *BASOR* 61:5–10.

1936b   The Joint Assyrian Expedition. *BASOR* 62:6–14.

1936c   Gawra XII. *Bulletin of The University Museum* 6(4):93–97.

1936d   The Round House at Gawra. *Bulletin of The University Museum* 6(4):111–119.

Bache, C., and L. Satterthwaite

1930   Excavation on an Indian Mound of Beech Bottom. *Museum Journal* 21(1):133–188.

Badler, Virginia

1989   Social Structure Changes Suggested by Artifact Assembledges of Godin V and VI. *Paléorient* 15/1:288–89.

Ball, Warwick

1997   Tell Shelgiyya: An Early Uruk "Sprig Ware" Manufacturing and Exporting Centre on the Tigris. *Al-Rafidan* 18:93–101.

Ball, Warwick, David Tucker, and T. J. Wilkinson

1989   The Tell al-Hawa Project Archaeological Investigations in the North Jazira: 1986–87. *Iraq* LI:1–66.

Banton, Michael, ed.

1965   *Political Systems and the Distribution of Power.* AES Monograph 2. London: Tavistock.

1966   *The Social Anthropology of Complex Societies.* AES Monograph 4. London: Tavistock.

Barth, Frederick

1953   *Principles of Social Organization in Southern Kurdistan.* Oslo: Universitetets Etnografiske Museum Bulletin 7.

1969   *Ethnic Groups and Boundaries.* New York: Little, Brown.

Barton, George

1927   Report from the Director of the School in Baghdad. *BASOR* 28:12–18.

1928   Report from the Director of the School in Baghdad. *BASOR* 32:15–19.

Beale, Thomas

1973   Early Trade in Highland Iran: A View from a Source Area. *World Archaeology* 5(2):133–148.

1978   Bevelled Rim Bowls and Their Implications for Change and Economic Organization in the Later Fourth Millennium B.C. *Journal of Near East Studies* 37:289–313.

Behm-Blanke, M., M. Hoh, N. Karg, L. Masch, K. Parsche, L. Weiner, A. von Wickede, and G. Ziegelmayer

1984   Hassek Höyük: Vorläufiger Bericht über die Grabungen in den Jahren 1981–83. *Istanbuler Mitteilungen* 34:31–150.

Bekker, Konrad

1967   Historical Patterns of Culture Contact in Southern Asia. In *Beyond the Frontier.* P. Bohannon and F. Plog, eds. pp. 71–86. New York: American Museum of Natural History.

Bigelow, Lauren

1999   Zooarchaeological Investigations of Economic Organization and Ethnicity at Late Chalcolithic Hacınebi: a Preliminary Report. In The Uruk Expansion: Northern Perspectives from Hacınebi, Hassek Höyük, and Tepe Gawra. G. Stein, ed. *Paléorient* 25(1):83–90.

Billington, Ray

1967   The American Frontier. In *Beyond the Frontier.* P. Bohannon and F. Plog, eds. pp. 3–24. New York: American Museum of Natural History.

Blanton, Richard

1976   Anthropological Studies of Cities. *Annual Review of Anthropology* 5:249–64.

1978   *Monte Alban: Settlement Patterns at the Zapotec Capital.* New York: Academic Press.

Blanton, Richard, Gary Feinman, Stephen Kowalewski, and Peter Peregrine

1996   A Dual-Processual Theory for the Evolution of Mesoamerican Civilization. *Current Anthropology* 37(1):1–14.

Blanton, Richard, Stephen Kowalewski, Gary Feinman, and Jill Appel

1981   *Ancient Mesoamerica: A Comparison of Change in Three Regions.* Cambridge: Cambridge University Press.

1982   *Monte Alban's Hinterland, Part I: the Prehispanic Settlement Patterns of the Central and Southern Parts of the Valley of Oaxaca, Mexico.* Memoirs of the Museum of Anthropology 15. Ann Arbor: University of Michigan.

Blanton, Richard, Stephen Kowalewski, Gary Feinman, and Laura Finsten

1993   *Ancient Mesoamerica: A Comparison of Change in Three Regions,* 2nd ed. Cambridge: Cambridge University Press.

Boese, Johannes

1986/7   Excavations at Tell Sheikh Hassan, Preliminary Report on the 1987 Campaign. *Annales Archeologiques Arabes Syriennes* 26/27:67–100.

1995   *Ausgrabungen in Tell Sheikh Hassan: Vorläufige Berichte über die Grabungskampagnen 1984–1990 und 1992–1994.* Saarbrücken: Saarbrücker Druckerei und Verlag.

Bottéro, Jean

1967   The First Semitic Empire. In *The Near East: the Early Civilizations.* J. Bottéro, E. Cassin, and J. Vercoutter, eds. pp. 91–132. New York: Delacorte.

Braidwood, Robert, and Linda Braidwood

1960   *Excavations in the Plain of Antioch, the Early Assemblages.* Oriental Institute Publications 61. Chicago: University of Chicago Press.

Braidwood, Robert, and Bruce Howe

1960   *Prehistoric Investigations in Iraqi Kurdistan.* Studies in Ancient Oriental Civilization 31. Chicago: University of Chicago Press.

British Naval Intelligence Division

1944   *Iraq and the Persian Gulf.* Geographical Handbook Series. London: Naval Intelligence Division.

Bregstein, Linda

1993   *Seal Use in Fifth Century B.C. Nippur.* Ph.D. dissertation, University of Pennsylvania.

Brown, J. A.

1971   *Approaches to the Social Dimensions of Mortuary Practice.* Washington, DC: Memoir 25 of the the Society of American Archaeology.

Brown, T. Burton

1951   *Excavations in Azerbaijan, 1948.* London: John Murray.

Buccellati, Giorgio

1990   Salt at the Dawn of History: the Case of the Bevelled Rim Bowls. In *Resurrecting the Past: A Tribute to Adnan Bounni.* P. Matthiae, M. Van Loon, and H. Weiss, eds. pp. 17–40 Istanbul: Nederlands Historisch-Archaeologisch Instiuut te Istanbul.

Burney, Charles

1958   Eastern Anatolia in the Chalcolithic and Early Bronze Age. *Anatolian Studies* 8: 157–210.

Butterlin, Pascal

2000   La vallée de l'Euphrate et l'expansion urukéenne. In *Chronologies de Pays du Caucase et de L'Euphrate aux IVe–IIIe Millenaires.* Catherine Marro and Harald Hauptmann, eds. pp 23–52 Paris: De Boccard.

Caldwell, David

1976   The Early Glyptic of Gawra, Giyan, and Susa, and the Development of Long Distance Trade. *Orientalia* 45(3):227–250.

Campbell-Thompson R., and R. Hutchinson

1931   The Site of the Palace of Ashurbanipal at Nineveh Excavated in 1929–30 on Behalf of the British Museum. *Liverpool Annals of Archaeology and Anthropology* 18:81.

1932   The British Museum Excavations on the Temple of Ishtar at Nineveh. *Liverpool Annals of Archaeology and Anthropology* 19:78–79.

Carneiro, Robert

1981   The Chiefdom: Precursor to the State. In *The Transition to Statehood in the New World.* G. Jones and R. Kautz, eds. pp. 37–79. Cambridge: Cambridge University Press.

Carr, Christopher

1984   The Nature of Organization of Intrasite Archaeological Records and Spatial Analytical Approaches to Their Investigation. In *Advances in Archaeological Method and Theory.* M. Schiffer, ed. pp. 103–211. New York: Academic Press.

Childe, V. Gordon

1950   *The Urban Revolution.* Liverpool, Town Planning Review 21:3–17.

Christaller, Walter

1933   *Central Places in Southern Germany.* Englewood, NJ: Prentice-Hall.

Christian, William, Jr.

1972   *Person and God in a Spanish Valley.* New York: Seminar Press.

Cocquerillat, Denise

1967   Aperçus sur la Phéniciculture en Babylonie à l'Epoque de la I^{ére} Dynastie de Babylone. *Journal of the Economic and Social History of the Orient* 10:162–216.

Cole, John, and Eric Wolf

1974   *The Hidden Frontier.* New York: Academic Press.

Color Communications

1997   *Earth Colors: Soil Color Book.* Poughkeepsie, NY: Color Communications.

Colloques du C.N.R.S.

1980   *L'Archeologie de l'Iraq.* Paris: Editions du
         C.N.R.S.

D'Altroy, T., and T. Earle

1985   Staple Finance, Wealth Finance, and Stor-
         age in the Inka Political Economy. *Current
         Anthropology* 26(2):187–206.

Damerji, Muayad

1987   *The Development of the Architecture of Doors
         and Gates in Ancient Mesopotamia.* Trans. by
         Tomio Takase and Okada Yasuyoshi. Tokyo:
         Kokushikan University.

Davidson, T. E., and Hugh McKerrell

1976   Pottery Analysis and Halaf Period Trade in
         the Khabur Region. *Iraq* 38:45–56.

1980   The Neutron Activation Analysis of Halaf
         and 'Ubaid Pottery from Tell Arpachiyah
         and Tepe Gawra. *Iraq* 42:155–167.

Davis, Dave D.

1983   Investigating the Diffusion of Stylistic Inno-
         vations. In *Advances in Archaeological Method
         and Theory* 6. M. Schiffer, ed. pp. 53–89.
         New York: Academic Press.

Diamant, S., and J. Rutter

1969   Horned Objects in Anatolia and the Near
         East and possible Connections with the
         Minoan "Horns of Consecration." *Anatolian
         Studies* 19:147–177.

Di Nocera, Gian-Maria

2000   Radiocarbon Datings from Arslantepe and
         Norşuntepe. In *Chronologies de Pays du Cau-
         case et de L'Euphrate aux IVe–IIIe Millenaires.*
         Catherine Marro and Harald Hauptmann,
         eds. pp 73–96. Paris: De Boccard.

Dittman, Rene

1986   Thoughts on the Changing Pattern of Ad-
         ministrative Control from Late-Uruk to
         Proto-Elamite Period at Susa. In *Gemdet
         Nasr Period or Regional Style?* E. Finkbeiner
         and W. Röllig, eds. pp. 332–366. Tübingen:
         Beihefte zum Atlas.

Dollfus, Genvieve

1985   Le peuplement de la Susianae au cours du
         V^e millénaire. *Paléorient* 11/2:11–20.

Driessen, Henrik

1992   *On the Spanish-Moroccan Frontier.* New York:
         Berg.

Drennan, Richard

1976   Religion and Social Evolution in Formative
         Mesoamerica In *The Early Mesoamerican Vil-
         lage.* K. Flannery, ed. pp. 345–363. New
         York: Academic Press.

Earle, Timothy

1978   *Economic and Social Organization of a Com-
         plex Chiefdom: the Halelea District, Hawaii.*
         Anthropological Papers 63. Ann Arbor: the
         Museum of Anthropology, University of
         Michigan.

1987   Chiefdoms in Archaeological and Ethno-
         graphic Perspective. *Annual Review of An-
         thropology 16*:279–308.

1991   The Evolution of Chiefdoms, In *Chiefdoms,
         Power, Economy, and Ideology.* T. Earle, ed. pp.
         1-15. Cambridge: Cambridge University
         Press.

Edens, Christopher

1992   Dynamics of Trade in the Ancient
         Mesopotamian "World System." *American
         Anthropologist* 94(1):118–139.

Egami, Namio

1959   *Telul eth Thalathat, Report 1, the Excavation of
         Tell II 1956–57.* Tokyo: Yamakawa.

Eichmann, R.

1986   Die Steingeräte aus dem 'Riemchenge-
         bäude' in Uruk-Warka. *Baghdader Mitteilun-
         gen* 17:97–130.

Emberling, Geoff, Jack Cheng, Torben Larsen,
Holly Pittman, Tim Skulbquel, Jill Weber,
and Henry Wright

1999   Excavations at Tell Brak 1998: Preliminary
         Report. *Iraq* 61:1–41.

Esin, Ufik

1972   Tepecik Excavations, 1970. *Keban Project 1970 Activities.* Middle East Technical University 3:149–60. Ankara.

1975   Tepecik 1974. *Anatolian Studies* 25:46–49.

1976   Tepecik Excavations, 1973. *Keban Project 1973 Activities.* Middle East Technical University 6:97–112. Ankara.

1982   Tepecik Excavations, 1974. *Keban Project 1974–75 Activities.* Middle East Technical University 7:95–118. Ankara.

1985   Some Small Finds from the Chalcolithic Occupation at Değirmentepe (Malatya) in Eastern Turkey. *Studi di Palentologia in Onore di Salvatore Puglisi.* M. Liverani, A. Palmieri, and R. Peroni, eds. pp. 253–263. Rome: Università di Roma.

1986   Değirmentepe (Malatya-imamli Koyu) Kutarmakasizi *Kazi Sonuçlari Toplantisi* 8:95–137 (in Turkish).

2000   The Main Problems in Setting Up a Chronological Framework. in *Chronologies de Pays du Caucase et de L'Euphrate aux IVe–IIIe Millenaires.* Catherine Marro and Harald Hauptmann, eds. pp. 5–10. Paris: De Boccard.

Evins, Mary

1989   The Late Chalcolithic/Uruk Period in the Karababa Basin, Southeastern Turkey. In *Out of the Heartland: the Evolution of Complexity in Peripheral Mesopotamia during the Uruk Period.* M. Rothman, ed. *Paléorient* 15(1): 281–2.

Fallers, Lloyd

1965   *Bantu Bureaucracy.* Chicago: University of Chicago Press.

Feinman, Gary

1994   Social Boundaries and Political Change: A Comparative Perspective. In *Chiefdoms and Early States: The Organizational Dynamics of Complexity.* Gil Stein and Mitchell Rothman, eds. Madison, WI: Prehistory Press.

Feinman, Gary, and J. Neitzel

1984   Too Many Types: an Overview of Sedentary Prestate Societies in the Americas. In *Advances in Archaeological Method and Theory* 7. M. Schiffer ed. pp. 39–102. New York: Academic Press.

Ferioli, P., and E. Fiandra

1979   The Administrative Functions of Clay Sealings in Protohistorical Iran. In *Iranica.* G. Gnoli and A. Rossi, eds. pp. 307–312. Napoli: Instituto Universitario Orientale.

Ferioli, P., E. Fiandra, and S. Tusa

1975   Stamp Seals and the Functional Analysis of Their Sealings at Shahr-i-Sokhta II–III. In *South Asian Archaeology 1975.* J.E. Van Louhuizen-de Leeuw, eds. pp. 7–26.

Fernea, Robert

1970   *Shaykh and Effendi.* Cambridge, MA: Harvard University Press.

Fiandra, E.

1979   The Connection Between clay Sealings and Tablets in Administration In *South Asian Archaeology 1979.* H. Hartel, ed. pp. 29–43. Berlin: Dietrich Reimer Verlag.

Fielden, Kate

1981   A Late Uruk Pottery Group from Tell Brak, 1978. *Iraq* 43:157–66.

Finkbeiner, Uwe

1983   Uruk-Warka XXXV–XXXVI: Survey des Stadtgebietes von Uruk. *Sumer* 39(1/2): 195–211.

Finkbeiner, Uwe, and William Röllig

1986   *Gemdet Nasr: Period or Regional Style?* Wiesbaden: L. Reichert.

Finkelstein, Jacob

1953   Cuneiform Texts from Tell Billa. *Journal of Cuneiform Studies* 7:111–176.

Flannery, Kent V.

1972   The Cultural Evolution of Civilizations. *Annual Review of Ecology and Systematics* 3:399–426.

1976   *The Mesoamerican Village*. New York: Academic Press.

Forbes, R. J.

1964   *Studies in Ancient Technology*, 1–11. Leiden: Brill.

Forde, C. Daryll

1963   *Habitat, Economy, and Society*. New York: Dutton.

Forest, Jean-Daniel

1983   *Les pratiques funeraires en Mesopotamie du 5e millenaire au debut du 3e, etude de cas*. Memoire 19. Paris: Editions Recherche sur les civilisations.

1999   L'expansion Urukéenne: Notes d'un voyageur. In *The Uruk Expansion: Northern Perspectives from Hacınebi, Hassek Höyük, and Tepe Gawra*. Gil Stein, ed. *Paléorient* 25(1): 141–150.

Frangipane, Marcella

1993   Local Components in the Development of Centralized Societies in Syro-Anatolian Regions. In *Between the Rivers and over the Mountains*. M. Frangipane, H. Hauptmann, M. Liverani, P. Matthiae, and M. Mellink, eds. pp. 133–61. Rome: Universita di Roma "La Sapienza."

1994   The Record Function of Clay Sealings in Early Administrative Systems as seen from Arslantepe-Malatya." In *Archives Before Writing*. P. Ferioli, E. Fiandra, G. Fissore, and M. Frangipane, eds. pp. 125–37. Rome: Scriptorium.

1997   A 4th Millennium Temple/Palace Complex at Arslantepe-Malatya. *Paléorient* 23/1:45–73.

2000   The Late Chalcolithic/EB I Sequence at Arslantepe. In *Chronologies de Pays du Caucase et de L'Euphrate aux IVe–IIIe Millenaires*. Catherine Marro and Harald Hauptmann, eds. pp. 439–472. Paris: De Boccard.

In press   Centralization Processes in Greater Mesopotamia: Uruk "Expansion" as the Culmination of an Early System of Intra-regional Relations. In *Uruk Mesopotamia and Its Neighbors: Cross-cultural Interactions in the Era of State Formation*. M. Rothman, ed. Santa Fe, NM: SAR Press.

Frangipane, Marcella, and Alba Palmieri

1983   A Protourban Centre of the Late Uruk Period. *Origini* 12:287–454.

Frankel, David

1978   Pottery Decoration as an Indicator of Social Relationships a Prehistoric Cypriote Example. In *Art in Society: Studies in Style, Culture, and Aesthetics*. M. Greenhalgh and V. Megaw, eds. pp. 147–160. London: Duckworth.

Frankfort, Henri

1954   *The Art and Architecture of the Ancient Orient*. Harmondsworth: Penguin.

Fried, Morton

1967   *The Evolution of Political Society*. New York: Random House.

Fukai, S., K. Horiuchi, and T. Matsutani

1974   *Telul eth-Thalathat 3: The Excavation of Tell V*. Tokyo: Yamakawa.

Gearing, Fred

1962   *Priests and Warriors*. Memoir 93. Washington, DC: American Anthropological Association.

Gibson, McGuire

1981   *Uch Tepe I*. Chicago: University of Chicago Press.

1986   The Round Building at Razuk: Form and Function. In Colloques Internationaux C.N.R.S., *Préhistoire de al Mesopotamie*. pp. 467–474. Paris: Editions du C.N.R.S.

Goodell, Grace

1980   From Status to Contract: the Significance of Agrarian Relations of Production in the West, Japan, and in 'Asiatic' Persia. *Archives Europeannes de Sociologie* 21:285–325.

Goodenough, Ward

1965   Rethinking 'Status' and 'Role.' In *The Relevance of Models for Social Anthropology* M. Banton, ed. *A.S.A.* Monographs 1. pp. 1–24. London: Tavistock.

Gülçur, Sevil

2000   Norşuntepe: die Chalkolithische Keramik. In *Chronologies de Pays du Caucase et de L'Euphrate aux IVe–IIIe Millenaires.* Catherine Marro and Harald Hauptmann, eds. pp. 375–418. Paris: De Boccard.

Gut, Renate

1995   *Das Prähistorische Nineve.* Mainz: Verlag Philipp von Zabern.

Hauptmann, Harald

1972   Die Grabungen auf dem Norşun-Tepe, 1970. *Keban Project 1970 Activities.* Middle East Technical University 3:103–122. Ankara.

1975   Norşuntepe, 1974. *Anatolian Studies* 25: 35–38.

1976   Die Grabungen auf dem Norşun-Tepe, 1973. *Keban Project 1973 Activities.* Middle East Technical University 6:61–78. Ankara.

1982   Die Grabungen auf dem Norşun-Tepe, 1974. *Keban Project 1974–75 Activities.* Middle East Technical University 7:41–70. Ankara.

Helms, Mary

1988   *Ulysses' Sail.* Princeton, NJ: Princeton University Press.

Helwing, Barbara

1999   Cultural Interaction at Hassek Höyük, Turkey: New Evidence from Pottery Analysis. In *The Uruk Expansion: Northern Perspectives from Hacınebi, Hassek Höyük, and Tepe Gawra.* G. Stein, ed. *Paléorient* 25(1):91–100.

2000   Regional Variation in the Composition of Late Chalcolithic Pottery Assemblages. In *Chronologies de Pays du Caucase et de L'Euphrate aux IVe–IIIe Millenaires.* Catherine Marro and Harald Hauptmann, eds. pp 145–166. Paris: De Boccard.

Henrickson, Elizabeth

1994   The Outer Limits: Settlement and Economic Strategies in the Central Zagros During the Uruk Period. In *Chiefdoms and Early States in the Near East.* G. Stein and M. Rothman eds. pp. 85–102. Madison, WI: Prehistory Press.

Henry, Donald

1989   *From Foraging to Agriculture: The Levant at the End of the Ice Age.* Philadelphia: University of Pennsylvania Press.

Hermann, Georgina

1968   Lapis Lazuli: Early Phases of its Trade. *Iraq* 30(1):21–57.

Hijara, Ismail

1973   Excavations at Tell Qalinj Agha (Erbil), 4th Season. *Sumer* 29:13–35 (in Arabic).

Hodges, Henry

1976   *Artifacts.* London: John Baker.

Hole, Frank

1983   Symbols of Religion and Social Organization at Susa. In *Beyond the Hilly Flanks.* T. C. Young, P. Smith, P. Mortensen, eds., Studies in Ancient Oriental Civilization 36:315–344. Chicago: Oriental Institute.

1985   The Organization of Susiana Society, Periodization of Site Distributions. *Paléorient* 11/2:21–24.

1994   Environmental Instabilities and Urban Origins. In *Chiefdoms and Early States in the Near East.* G. Stein and M. Rothman, eds. pp. 121–152. Madison, WI: Prehistory Press.

Horne, Lee

1994   *Village Spaces: Settlement and Society in Northeast Iran.* Washington, DC: Smithsonian Institution Press.

Hubbard, N. L.

1980   Halafian Agriculture and Environment at Arpachiyah. *Iraq* 42(2):153–54.

Jacobsen, Thorkild

1976   *The Treasures of Darkness.* New Haven, CT: Yale University Press.

Jasim, Sabah

1985   *The Ubaid Period in Iraq.* BAR International Series 276.

Jawad, Abdul Jalil

1965   *The Advent of the Era of Townships in Northern Mesopotamia.* Leiden: Brill.

Johnson, Gregory

1973   *Local Exchange and State Development in Southwest Iran.* Anthropological Papers of the Museum of Anthropology 51. Ann Arbor: University of Michigan

1975   Locational Analysis and the Investigation of Uruk Local Exchange Systems. In *Ancient Civilization and Trade.* J. Sabloff and C. Lamberg-Karlovsky, eds. pp. 285–337. Albuquerque: University of New Mexico Press.

1978   Information Sources and the Development of Decision-making Organizations. In *Social Archaeology: Beyond Subsistence and Dating.* C. Redman, M. Berman, E. Curtis, W. Langhorne, N. Veraggi, and J. Wanser, eds. pp. 87–112. New York: Academic Press.

1980   Spatial Organization of Early Uruk Settlement Systems. In *L'Archeologie de l'Iraq.* Colloques internationaux du CNRS. pp. 233–263. Paris: Editions du C.N.R.S.

1988/89   Late Uruk in Greater Mesopotamia: Expansion or Collapse? *Origini* 14: 595–611.

Johnson, Jotham

1935a   The Great Mound of Tepe Gawra. *Scientific American* 153(4):178–79.

1935b   The Great Mound. *Bulletin of The University Museum* 5(6):63–70.

Kellersohn, Heinrich

1953   Die Landwirtschaft im Irak. *Erkunde* 7: 276–288.

Killick, Robert

1986   The Eski Mosul Region In *Gemdet Nasr: Period or Regional Style?* Uwe Finkbeiner and William Röllig eds. pp. 229–244. Wiesbaden: L. Reichert.

Kohl, Philip

1989   Comment on Algaze 1989. *Current Anthropology* 30(5):593–594.

1987   The Use and Abuse of World Systems Theory: The Case of the Pristine West Asian State. *Advances in Archaeological Method and Theory.* M. Schiffer, ed. 11:1–35. New York: Academic Press.

Kowalewski, Stephen, R. Blanton, Gary Feinman, and Laura Finsten

1983   Boundaries, Scale and Internal Organization. *Journal of Anthropological Archaeology* 2: 32–56.

Kramer, Carol

1977   Pots and People In *Mountains and Lowlands.* L. Levine and T. C. Young, eds. pp. 91–112. Malibu, CA: Undena.

1982   *Village Ethnoarchaeology.* New York: Academic Press.

1985   Ceramic Production and Specialization. *Paléorient* 11/2 (The Evolution of Complex Societies in Southwestern Iran): 117–120.

Kubba, Isamil

1987   *Mesopotamian Architecture and Town Planning.* Oxford: BAR International Series.

Larsen, M. T.

1967   *Old Assyrian Caravan Procedures.* Leiden: Uitg. v.h. Historisch-Archaeologische Institut te Istanbul 22.

Le Breton, Louis

1978   Le niveau 17B de l'Acropole de Suse. *Delegation Archeologique Francaise en Iran.* Cahiers 9: 57–154.

Lloyd, Peter

1965   The Political Structure of African Kingdoms. In *Political Systems and the Distribution of Power.* M. Banton, ed. pp. 63–112. London: Tavistock.

Lloyd, Seton

1938   Some Ancient Sites in the Sinjar Region. *Iraq* 5:124–142.

1940   Iraqi Government Soundings at Sinjar. *Iraq* 6:13–21.

1948   Uruk Pottery: A Comparative Study in Relation to Recent Finds at Eridu. *Sumer* 4: 39–51.

Lupton, Alan

1996   *Stability and Change: Socio-political Development in North Mesopotamia and South-east Anatolia 4000-2700 B.C.* Oxford: BAR International Series 627.

Lyonnet, Bertille

2000   Les Méstopotamie et le Caucase du Nord au IVe et au Deut du IIIe Millenaires. In *Chronologies de Pays du Caucase et de L' Euphrate aux IVe–IIIe Millenaires.* Catherine Marro and Harald Hauptmann, eds. pp. 299–320. Paris: De Boccard.

McAdam, E., and H. S. Mynors

1988   Chapter 3: Tell Rubeidheh, Pottery from the Uruk Mound. In *Tell Rubeidheh, an Uruk Village in the Jebel Hamrin.* R. Killick, ed. pp. 39–76. Baghdad: British School of Archaeology in Iraq.

Mallowan, Max

1933   The Prehistoric Sondage of Nineveh, 1931–32. *Annals of Archaeology and Anthropology* 20:127–77.

1947   Excavations at Tell Brak and Chagar Bazar. *Iraq* 9:1–259.

1970   The Development of Cities from Al 'Ubaid to the End of Uruk 5. *Cambridge Ancient History* I, 1:327–462.

Mallowan, Max, and Rose Cruikshank

1935   Excavations at Arpachiyah. *Iraq* 2:1–178.

Marfoe, Leon

1987   Cedar Forests to Silver Mountains: Social Change and the Development of Long-Distance Trade in Early Near Eastern Societies. In *Centre and Periphery in the Ancient World.* Michael Rowlands, Mogens Larsen, and Kristian Kristiansen, eds. pp. 25–35. Cambridge: Cambridge University Press.

Margueron, Jean

1983   La Maison Ronde de Tepe Gawra. Notes D'Archeologie et D'Architecture Orientales. *Syria* 60:1–24.

Matthers, John, ed.

1981   *The River Qoueiq, Northern Syria and Its Catchment* 1, 2. Oxford: BAR International Series 98.

McCorriston, Joy

1997   The Fiber Revolution. *Current Anthropology* 38(4):517–549.

Miller, Naomi

1985   Paleoethnobotanical Evidence for Deforestation in Ancient Iran. *Journal of Ethnobotany* 5(1):1–19.

1996   Plant Remains. In *Uruk Colonies and Anatolian Communities: An Interim Report on the 1992–93 Excavations at Hacınebi, Turkey.* G. Stein, R. Bernbeck, C. Coursey, A. McMahon, N. Miller, A. Mısır, J. Nicola, H. Pittman, S. Pollock, and H. Wright. *American Journal of Archaeology* 100:205–60.

Miller, Robert

1988   Chapter Four: Flaked Stone Technology from Tell Rubeidheh. In *Tell Rubeidheh, an Uruk Village in the Jebel Hamrin.* R. Killick, ed. pp. 71–97 Baghdad: British School of Archaeology in Iraq.

Miller, Walter

1960   A System for Describing and Analyzing the Regulation of Coordinated Activity. In *Men and Cultures.* A. F. C. Wallace ed. pp. 175–182. Philadelphia: University of Pennsylvania Press.

Moon, Jane, and Michael Roaf

1984   The Pottery from Tell Madhur. *Sumer* 43 (1/2):128–158.

Moorey, Roger

1976   The Late Prehistoric Administrative Building at Jamdat Nasr. *Iraq* 38(2):95–106.

Mortensen, Peder

1976   Chalcolithic Settlements in the Holailan Valley. In *Proceedings of the IVth Annual Symposium on Archaeological Research in Iran.* pp. 42–62. Tehran: Iranian Centre for Archaeological Research.

Muller, E. Bartow, and Charles Bache

1934   The Prehistoric Temple of Stratum IX at Tepe Gawra. *BASOR* 54:13–18.

Nelson, B. A.

1985   *Decoding Prehistoric Ceramics.* Carbondale, IL: Southern Illinois University Press.

Netting, Robert

1978   Sacred Power and Centralization. In *Population Growth.* B. Spooner, ed. pp. 219–44. Cambridge, MA: MIT Press.

Nicholas, Ilene

1980   *A Spatial/Functional Analysis of Late Fourth Millennium B.C. Occupation at the TUV Mound, Tal-e Malyan*, Iran. Ph.D. dissertation, University of Pennsylvania.

Nissen, Hans

In press   Cultural and Political Networks in the Ancient Near East During the Fourth and Third Millennia B.C. In *Uruk Mesopotamia and Its Neighbors: Cross-Cultural Interactions in the Era of State Formation.* M. Rothman, ed. Santa Fe, NM: SAR Press.

2000   A Mesopotamian Hierarchy in Action in Ancient Uruk. In *Hierarchies in Action, Cui Bono?* Michael Diehl, ed. pp. 210–220. Carbondale, IL: Center for Archaeological Investigation.

1993   The Early Uruk Period, A Sketch. In *Between the Rivers and Over the Mountains.* M. Frangipane, H. Hauptmann, M. Liverani, P. Matthiae, and M. Mellink, eds. pp. 123– 32. Rome: Università di Roma.

Nissen, Hans, Peter Damerow, and Robert Englund

1993   *Archaic Bookkeeping: Early Writing and Techniques of Economic Administration.* Chicago: University of Chicago Press.

Nissen, Hans, and Robert Englund

1993   *Die lexicalischen Liste der archaischen Texte aus Uruk.* Berlin: Gebr. Mann.

Nunn, Astrid

1988   *Die Wandmalerei und die glassierte Wandschmuck im Alten Orient.* Leiden: Brill.

Oates, David

1986   Different Traditions in Mesopotamian Temple Architecture in the Fourth Millennium B.C. In *Préhistoire de la Mesopotamie.* Colloques Internationaux C.N.R.S. pp. 379–383. Paris: Editions du C.N.R.S.

Oates, Joan

1982   Some Late Early Dynastic III Pottery from Tell Brak. *Iraq* XLIV (2):205–219.

1983   'Ubaid Mesopotamia Reconsidered. In *Beyond the Hilly Flanks.* T. C. Young, P. Smith, P. Mortensen, eds. pp. 251–282. Chicago: Oriental Institute.

1985   Tell Brak: Uruk Pottery from the 1984 Season. *Iraq* 47:175–186.

1987   A Note on 'Ubaid and Mitanni Pottery from Tell Brak. *Iraq* 49:193–98.

Oates, David, and Joan Oates

1976   Early Irrigation Agriculture in Mesopo-tamia. In *Problems In Economic and Social Archaeology.* G. Sieveking, I. Longworth, and K. Wilson, eds. pp. 109–135. London: Duckworth.

1991   Excavations at Tell Brak 1990–91. *Iraq* 53: 127–45.

1993   Excavations at Tell Brak 1992–93. *Iraq* 55: 155–199.

1994   Tell Brak: A Stratigraphic Summary 1976–1993. *Iraq* 56: 167–176.

Oates, Joan, and David Oates

1997   An Open Gate: Cities of the Fourth Millennium B.C. (Tell Brak 1997). *Cambridge Archaeological Journal* 7:287–307.

Oliver, Paul

1987   *Dwellings: the House Across the World.* Austin: University of Texas Press.

Oppenheim, A. Leo

1977   *Ancient Mesopotamia.* Chicago: University of Chicago Press.

Oppenheim, A. Leo, and Erica Reiner, eds.

1980   *The Assyrian Dictionary* 11, N. Chicago: University of Chicago Press.

Orthmann, W.

1979   Burial Customs of the Third Millennium B.C. in the Euphrates Valley. In *Le Moyen Euphrate*. J. Margueron, ed., pp. 97–105. Leiden: Brill.

Özdoğan, Mehmet

1977   *Lower Euphrates Basin 1977 Survey*. Ankara: Middle East Technical University.

Özguç, Nimet

1992   The Uruk Culture at Samsat. In *Von Uruk Nach Tuttul*. B. Hrouda, S. Kroll, and P. Spanos, eds. pp. 151–65. Munich: Profil Verlag.

Palmieri, A.

1981   Excavations at Arslantepe (Malatya). *Anatolian Studies* 31:101–120.

1985   Eastern Anatolia and Early Mesopotamian Urbanization. In *Studi di Paletnologia in Onore di Salvatore Puglisi*. M. Liverani, A. Palmieri, and P. Perone, eds. pp. 191–213. Rome: Università di Roma.

Perkins, Ann

1949   *The Comparative Archaeology of Ancient Mesopotamia*. Chicago: University of Chicago Press.

Pittman, Holly

In press   Intra-regional Relations Reflected through Glyptic Evidence. In *Uruk Mesopotamia and Its Neighbors: Cross-Cultural Interactions in the Era of State Formation*. M. Rothman, ed. Santa Fe, NM: SAR Press.

1993   Pictures of an Administration: The Late Uruk Scribe at Work. In *Between the Rivers and Over the Mountains*. M. Frangipane, H. Hauptmann, M. Liverani, P. Matthiae, and M. Mellink, eds. pp. 235–46. Rome: Università di Roma "La Sapienza."

Plog, Stephen

1980   *Stylistic Variation in Prehistoric Ceramics*. Cambridge: Cambridge University Press.

Pollock, Susan

In press   The Uruk Period in Southern Mesopotamia. In *Uruk Mesopotamia and Its Neighbors: Cross-Cultural Interactions and Their Consequences in the Era of State Formation*. M. Rothman, ed. Santa Fe, NM: SAR Press.

1994   Emergence of Civilization, Review of Algaze, *The Uruk World System. Science* 264 (3 June): 1481–1482

1990   Archaeological Investigations on the Uruk Mound, Abu Salabikh, Iraq. *Iraq* 52:85–93.

1989   Power Politics in the Susa A Period. In *Upon this Foundation: The 'Ubaid Reconsidered*. E. Henrickson and I. Thuessen, eds. pp. 281–292. Copenhagen: Carsten Niebuhr Institiute.

1983a   *The Symbolism of Prestige: An Archaeological Example from the Royal Cemetery of Ur*. Ph.D. dissertation, University of Michigan.

1983b   Style and Information. *Journal of Anthropological Archaeology* 2:354–390.

Pollock, Susan, and Cheryl Coursey

1995   Ceramics from Hacınebi Tepe: Chronology and Connections. *Anatolica* 21:101–141.

Porada, Edith

1965   The Relative Chronology of Mesopotamia. Part I. Seals and Trade (6,000–1,600 B.C.). In *Chronologies in Old World Archaeology*. Robert Ehrich, ed. pp. 133–181. Chicago: University of Chicago Press.

Porada, Edith, Donald Hansen, Sally Dunham, and S. Babcock

1992   Mesopotamian Chronologies, 7000–1600 B.C. In *Chronologies in Old World Archaeology*, 3rd ed. Robert W. Ehrich, ed. pp. 77–121. Chicago: University of Chicago Press.

Potter, James

2000   Ritual, Power, and Social Differentiation in Small-Scale Societies. In *Hierarchies in Action, Cui Bono?* Michael Diehl, ed. pp. 295–316. Carbondale, IL: Center for Archaeological Investigation.

Reade, Julian

1968   Tell Taya (1967): Summary Report. *Iraq* 30 (2):234–264.

Reimer, Stephen

1989   Tell Qraya on the Middle Euphrates. *Paléorient* 15/1:284.

Renfrew, C., J. E. Dixon, and J. R. Cann

1969   Further Analysis of Near Eastern Obsidians. *Proceedings of the Prehistoric Society* 34: 319–31.

Roaf, Michael

1984   The Stratigraphy and Architecture of Tell Madhur. *Sumer* 43(1/2):110–126.

Robinson, Lynda

1984   *Social Stratification and the State in Ancient Mesopotamia.* Ph.D. dissertation, University of Texas, Austin.

Rosen, Arlene

1986   *Cities of Clay.* Chicago: University of Chicago Press.

Rothman, Mitchell S.

a in press   Tepe Gawra: Chronology and Socio-Economic Change the Foothills of Northern Iraq in the Era of State Formation. In *Artefacts of Antiquity.* N. Postgate and S. Campbell, eds. Oxford: BAR.

b in press   The Tigris Piedmont and Eastern Jazira in the Fourth Millennium B.C. In *Uruk Mesopotamia and Its Neighbors: Cross-Cultural Interactions in the Era of State Formation.* M. Rothman, ed. Santa Fe, NM: SAR Press.

1994a   Seal and Sealing Findspots, Design, Audience and Function. In *Archives Before Writing.* P. Ferioli, E. Fiandra, G. Fisore, and M. Frangipane, eds. pp. 97–121. Università di Roma.

1994b   Sealings as a Control Mechanism in Prehistory: Tepe Gawra XI, X, and VIII. In *Chiefdoms and Early States in the Near East.* G. Stein and M. S. Rothman, eds. pp. 103–120. Madison, WI: Prehistory Press.

1994c   Introduction: Evolutionary Typologies and Cultural Complexity. In *Chiefdoms and Early States in the Near East.* G. Stein and M. Rothman, eds. pp. 1–10. Madison, WI: Prehistory Press.

1993   Another Look at the 'Uruk Expansion' from the Tigris Piedmont. In *Between the Rivers and Over the Mountains.* M. Frangipane, H. Hauptmann, M. Liverani, P. Matthiae, P., and M. Mellink, eds. pp. 163–77. Università di Roma.

1989   Re-Analysis of Fourth Millennium B.C. Tepe Gawra. *Paléorient* 15/1: 273–75.

1988   *Centralization, Administration, and Function at Fourth Millennium B.C. Tepe Gawra, Northern Iraq.* Ph.D. dissertation. University of Pennsylvania.

1987   Graph Theory and the Interpretation of Regional Survey Data. *Paléorient* 13/2: 73–92.

Rothman, Mitchell, ed.

In press   *Uruk Mesopotamia and Its Neighbors: Cross-Cultural Interactions in the Era of State Formation.* Santa Fe, NM: SAR Press.

Rothman, Mitchell S., and M. James Blackman

1990   Monitoring Administrative Spheres of Action in Late Prehistoric Northern Mesopotamia with the Aide of Chemical Characterization (INAA) of Clay Sealings. In *Economy and Settlement in the Near East.* N. Miller, ed. pp 19–45. MASCA Supplement, University Museum.

Rothman, Mitchell, and Brian Peasnall

1999   Societal Evolution of Small, Pre-State Ceneters and Polities: The example of Tepe Gawra in Northern Mesopotamia. In *The Uruk Expansion: Northern Perspectives from Hacınebi, Hassek Höyük, and Tepe Gawra.* G. Stein, ed. *Paléorient* 25(1):101–114.

Rova, Elena

1988   Report on the Late Uruk-Ninevite V Transition at Tell Karana III. Anthropology Colloquium. Philadelphia.

1999/ 2000   A Tentative Synchronization of the Local Late Chalcolithic Ceramic Horizons of Northern Syro-Mesopotamia. *Mesopotamia.* 34–35:175–196.

Rysánek, J.

1989   Estilacní Prístoj Ze Spisského Stvrtku. *Archeologicke Rozhledy* 41 (1):196–201.

Safar, Fuad, Mohammad ali Mustafa, and Seton Lloyd

1981   *Eridu.* Baghdad: State Organization of Antiquities.

Schmandt-Besserat, Denise

1979   An Archaic Recording System in the Uruk-Jemdet Nasr. *American Journal of Archaeology* 83:19–48.

1992   *Before Writing.* Austin: University of Texas Press.

1993   Images of Enship. In *Between the Rivers and Over the Mountains.* M. Frangipane, H. Hauptmann, M. Liverani, P. Matthiae, and M. Mellink, eds. pp. 201–220. Università di Roma.

Schwartz, Glenn

1982   *From Prehistory to History on the Habur Plains:* the Operation 1 Ceramic Periodization from Tell Leilan. Ph.D. dissertation, Yale University.

1988   *A Ceramic Chronology from Tell Leilan: Operation 1.* New Haven, CT: Yale University Press.

1985   The Ninevite V Period and Current Research. *Paléorient* 11/1:53–70.

1986   The Ninevite V Period and the Origins of Urbanization in Northern Mesopotamia. Lecture, University of Pennsylvania.

Service, Elman

1962   *Primitive Social Organization.* New York: Random House.

Simpson, Kay

1983   *Settlement Patterns on the Margins of Mesopotamia: Stability and Change along the Middle Euphrates, Syria.* Ph.D dissertation, University of Arizona.

1988   *Qraya Modular Reports 1:Early Soundings.* Malibu, CA: Undena Press.

Smith, Carol

1976   *Regional Analysis* 1,2. New York: Academic Press.

Smith, Michael E.

1986   The Role of Social Stratification in the Aztec Empire: a view from the Provinces. *American Anthropology* 88(1):70–91.

Solecki, Ralph, and Rose Solecki

1970   Grooved Stones from Zawi Chemi Shanidar, a Proto-Neolithic Site in Northern Iraq. *American Anthropologist* 72:831–841.

Southall, Aidan

1956   *Alur Society: A Study in Processes and Types of Domination.* Cambridge: Cambridge University Press.

1965   A Critique of the Typology of States and Political Systems. In *Political Systems and the Distribution of Power.* M. Banton, ed. pp. 113–140. ASA Monographs 2. London: Tavistock.

Speiser, Ephraim. A.

1928   Traces of the Oldest Cultures of Babylonia and Assyria. *Archiv für Orientschrift* 5: 161–64.

1929   Preliminary Excavations at Tepe Gawra. *AASOR* 9:17–94.

1931a   Letter of February 28 from Dr. Speiser to the President of Dropsie College and the Director of the American School at Baghdad. *BASOR* 42:10–12.

1931b   Tepe Gawra. *BASOR* 43:19–21.

1931c   The Excavation of Tepe Gawra. *BASOR* 44:5–8.

1932a   The Bearing of the Excavations at Tell Billa and at Tepe Gawra upon the Ethnic Problems of Ancient Mesopotamia. *American Journal of Archaeology* 36:29–35.

1932b   The Joint Excavation at Tepe Gawra. *American Journal of Archaeology* 36:564–568.

1932c   Reports from Professor Speiser on the Tell Billah and Tepe Gawra Excavations. *BASOR* 46:1–9.

1932d   The Joint Excavation at Tepe Gawra. *BASOR* 47:17–23.

1932e   The 'Chalice' Ware of Northern Mesopotamia and Its Historical Significance. *BASOR* 48:5–10.

1933   The Historical Significance of Tepe Gawra. *Annual Report of the Smithsonian Institution.* pp. 415–428.

1933b   The Pottery of Tella Billa. *Museum Journal* 23(3):249–308.

1934   Impression of a Cylinder Seal from Gawra VI. *BASOR* 55:2–3.

1935a   *Excavations at Tepe Gawra,* 1. Philadelphia: University of Pennsylvania Press.

1935b   The Season's Work at Tepe Gawra. *BASOR* 58:4–5.

1936a   On Some Recent Finds from Tepe Gawra. *BASOR* 62:10–14.

1936b   First Report of the Current Assyrian Campaign. *BASOR* 64:4–9.

1937a   Progress of the Joint Assyrian Expedition. *BASOR* 65:2–8.

1937b   Three Reports on the Joint Assyrian Expedition. *BASOR* 66:2–19.

1937c   Mesopotamian Miscellanea. *BASOR* 68:7–13.

1937d   New Discoveries at Tepe Gawra and Khafaje. American *Journal of Archaeology* 41:190–193.

1938   Progress of the Joint Expedition to Mesopotamia. *BASOR* 70:3–10.

1939   Closing the Gap at Tepe Gawra. *Annual Report of the Smithsonian Institution*. pp. 437–446.

Stafford, Howard

1963   The Functional Bases of Small Towns. *Economic Geography* 39:165–175.

Starr, Richard

1939   *Nuzi* 1,2. Cambridge, MA: Harvard University Press.

Stein, Gil

In press Indigenous Social Complexity at Hacınebi (Turkey) and the Organization of Colonial Contact in the Uruk Expansion. In *Uruk Mesopotamia and Its Neighbors: Cross-cultural Interactions in the Era of State Formation*. M. Rothman, ed. Santa Fe: SAR Press.

1999   *Rethinking World Systems: Diasporas, Colonies, and Interaction in Uruk Mesopotamia*. Tucson: University of Arizona Press.

1998   World Systems and Alternative Modes of Interaction in the Archaeology of Culture Contact. In *Studies in Culture Contact: Interaction, Culture Change, and Archaeology*. J. Cusik, ed. pp. 220–255. Carbondale, IL: Center for Archaeological Investigations.

1994a   Economy, Ritual, and Power in 'Ubaid Mesopotamia. In *Chiefdoms and Early States in the Near East*. G. Stein and M. S. Rothman, eds. pp. 47–66. Madison, WI: Prehistory Press.

1994b   Excavations at Hacınebi Tepe 1993. *16 Kazı Sonuçları Toplantısı*. pp. 121–147. Ankara: TC Ministry of Culture.

1991   Imported Ideologies and Local Identities: Northern Mesopotamia in the Fifth Millennium B.C. Society for American Archaeology meetings. New Orleans, April 26.

1990   On the Uruk Expansion. *Current Anthropology* 31(1):66–67.

Stein, Gil, and Mısır, Adnan

1994   Mesopotamian-Anatolian Interaction at Hacınebi, Turkey. Preliminary report on the 1992 excavations. *Anatolica* 20:145–189.

Stein, G., R. Bernbeck, C. Coursey, A. McMahon, N. Miller, A. Mısır, J. Nicola, H. Pittman, S. Pollock, and H. Wright

1996   Uruk Colonies and Anatolian Communities: An Interim Report on the 1992–93 Excavations at Hacınebi, Turkey. *American Journal of Archaeology* 100:205–60.

Stein, Gil, ed.

1999   The Uruk Expansion: Northern Perspectives from Hacınebi, Hassek Höyük, and Tepe Gawra. *Paléorient* 25 (1):91–100.

Steponaitis, Vince

1978   Location Theory and Complex Chiefdoms: A Mississippian Example. In *Mississippian Settlement Patterns*. B. Smith, ed. pp. 417–453. New York: Academic Press.

1981   Settlement Hierarchies and Political Complexity in Nonmarket Societies: The Formative Period of the Valley of Mexico. *American Anthropologist* 83:320–363.

1991   Contrasting Patterns of Mississippian Development. In *Chiefdoms: Power, Economy, and Ideology*. T. Earle, ed. pp. 193–228. Cambridge University Press.

Steward, Julian

1955a   *Theory of Culture Change*. Bloomington: University of Indiana Press.

1955b   *Irrigation Civilizations: A Comparative Study*. Washington, DC: Pan American Union.

Stout, Margret

1977   Clay Sling-Bullets from Tell Sweyhat. In Preliminary Report on Excavations at Tell es-Sweyhat, Syria 1975. Thomas Holland, ed. *Levant* 9:63–65.

Strommenger, Eva

1980   *Habuba Kabira: Eine Stadt vor 5000 Jahren.*
          Mainz: von Zabern.

Sürenhagen, Dietrich

1986   The Dry-Farming Belt: The Uruk Period and
          Subsequent Developments. In *The Origins of
          City in Dry-Farming Syria and Mesopotamia in
          the Third Millennium B.C.* H. Weiss, ed. pp.
          7–43, Guilford,CT: Four Quarters.

Taylor, J. du Plat, M.V. Seton Williams, and
J. Waechter

1950   The Excavations at Sakçe Gözü. *Iraq* 12:
          53–138.

Tobler, Arthur

1938   Progress of the Joint Expedition to Meso-
          potamia. *BASOR* 71:18–24.

1950   *Excavations at Tepe Gawra* 2. Philadelphia:
          University of Pennsylvania Press.

Trümpelmann, Leo

1989   Zum Frühgeschichtlichen Silobau im Alten
          Mesopotamien. In *Archaeologia Iranica et
          Orientalis.* L. DeMeyer and E. Haerinck,
          eds. pp. 67–83. Ghent: Peeters Press.

Trufelli, Franca

1997   Ceramic Correlations and Cultural Rela-
          tions in IVth Millennium Eastern Anatolia
          and Syro-Mesopotamia. *Studi Micenei de
          Egeo-Anatolici* 39:5–33.

Tsuneki, Akira, and Yutaka Miyake

1998   *Excavations at Tell Umm Qseir in Middle
          Khabur Valley, North Syria: Report of the 1996
          Season.* Tsukuba, Japan: Institute of History
          and Anthropology, University of Tsukuba.

Vandiver, Pamela

1985   *Sequential Slab Construction in Near Eastern
          Pottery Production Technology.* Ph.D. disserta-
          tion, Massachusetts Institute of Technology.

Van Driel, G.

In press   Jebel Aruda: Variations on a Late Uruk
           Domestic Theme. In *Artefacts of Antiquity.*

          N. Postgate and S. Campbell, eds. Oxford:
          BAR.

1983   Seals and Sealings from Jebel Aruda,
          1974–78. *Akkadica* 33:34–62.

1979   The Uruk Settlement on Jebel Aruda: a
          preliminary report. In *Le Moyen Euphrate.*
          J. Margueron, ed. pp. 75–93. Leiden:
          Brill.

Van Driel, G., and C. van Driel-Murray

1979   Jebel Aruda 1977–78. *Akkadica* 12:2–28.

1983   Jebel Aruda, the 1982 Season of Excava-
          tions. *Akkadica* 33:1–26.

Vaughan, James

1973   Ngkagu as Arstists in Marghi Society. In *The
          Traditional Artist in African Society.* Warren
          d'Azeredo, ed. pp. 162–193. Bloomington:
          Indiana University Press.

Vaughan, Patrick

1985   *Use-Wear Analysis of Flaked Stone Tools.* Tuc-
          son: University of Arizona Press.

Vértesalji, Peter

1987   The Chronology of the Chalcolithic in
          Mesopotamia (6200–3400 B.C.). In *Chrono-
          logies in the Near East.* Olivier Aurenche,
          Jacques Evin, Francis Hours, eds. pp.
          483–509. Oxford: BAR International
          Series.

Voget, Fred

1975   *A History of Ethnology.* New York: Holt,
          Rinehart, and Winston.

Voigt, Mary

1989   Northwest Iran in the Fourth Millennium
          B.C. *Paléorient* 15/1:286–87.

1983   *Hajji Firuz Tepe, Iran.* Philadelphia: Univer-
          sity of Pennsylvania Museum.

Voigt, Mary, and Robert H. Dyson, Jr.

1992   The Chronology of Iran, 8000 to 2000 B.C.
          In *Chronologies in Old World Archaeology.*
          R. Ehrich, ed. pp. 122–178. Chicago: Univer-
          sity of Chicago Press.

Von Loon, Maurits

1988   *Hammam et-Turkman.* Istanbul: Nederlands Historisch-Archeologisch Instituut.

Von Wickede, Alwo

1990   *Prähistorische Stempelglyptik in Vorderasien.* Munich: Profil Verlag.

Wallace, Anthony F. C.

1971   *Administrative Forms of Social Organization.* McCaleb Module in Anthropology 9. Reading, MA: Addison-Wesley.

Wallerstein, Immanuel

1974   *The Modern World-System I.* New York: Academic Press.

Watson, Patty Jo

1979   *Archaeological Ethnography in Western Iran.* New York: Viking Fund Publications in Anthropology 57.

Wattenmaker, Patricia, and Gil Stein

1989   Leilan 1987 Survey: Uruk Summary. *Paléorient* 15/1:283–84.

Webster, D.

1976   On Theocracies. *American Anthropologist* 78: 812–28.

Weiss, Harvey

1986   The Origins of Tell Leilan and Conquest of Space in the Third Millennium B.C. In *The Origins of Cities in Dry-farming Syria and Mesopotamia in the Third Millennium B.C.* H. Weiss, ed. pp. 71–108. Guilford, CT: Four Quarters.

Weiss, Harvey, and T. Cuyler Young

1975   The Merchants of Susa:Godin V and Plateau-Lowland Relations in the Late Fourth Millennium B.C. *Iran* 13:1–17.

Wenke, Robert

1981   Explaining the Evolution of Cultural Complexity: A Review. In *Advances in Archaeological*

Method and Theory 4. M. Schiffer, ed. pp 79–119. New York: Academic Press.

Whallon, Robert

1979   *An Archaeological Survey of the Keban Reservoir Area of East-Central Turkey.* Memoir 11 of the Museum of Anthropology. Ann Arbor: University of Michigan.

Whallon, Robert, and Sönmez Kantman

1969   Early Bronze Age Developments in the Keban Reservoir, East-Central Turkey. *Current Anthropology* 10(1):128–133.

Wilkinson, T. J., and D. J. Tucker

1995   *Settlement Development in the North Jazira, Iraq.* Baghdad: British School of Archaeology in Iraq.

Wilson, Karen

1988   The Middle and Late Uruk Ceramic Sequence from the Inanna Temple Sounding at Nippur. *Rencontre Assyriologique Internationale,* 11 July 1988. Philadelphia.

Winter, Irene

1987   Legitimation of Authority Through Image and Legend: Seals Belonging to Officials in the Administrative Bureaucracy of the Ur III State. In *The Organization of Power. Aspects of Bureaucracy in the Ancient Near East.* Studies in Ancient Oriental Civilization 46. M. Gibson, and R. Biggs, eds. pp. 69–116. Chicago: Oriental Institute.

1980   *A Decorated Breastplate from Hasanlu, Iran.* Philadelphia: University of Pennsylvania Museum.

Wolf, E.

1982   *Europe and the People without History.* Berkeley: University of California Press.

Woolley, Leonard

1934   Prehistoric Pottery of Carchemish. *Iraq* 1:146–162.

1952   *Carchemish, Report on Excavations at Djerabis 3.* London: British Museum.

Wright, Gary

1969   *Obsidian Analyses and Prehistoric Near Eastern Trade: 7500 to 3500 B.C.* Papers of the Museum of Anthropology 37. Ann Arbor: University of Michigan.

Wright, Henry

1969   *The Administration of Rural Production in an Early Mesopotamian Town.* Papers of the Museum of Anthropology 38. Ann Arbor: University of Michigan.

1972   A Consideration of Interregional Exchange in Greater Mesopotamia: 4,000–3,000 B.C. In *Social Exchange and Interaction.* E. Wilmsen, ed. Papers of the Museum of Anthropology 46. pp. 95–106. Ann Arbor: University of Michigan.

1977   Toward an Explanation of the Origin of the State. In *Explanation of Prehistoric Change.* J. Hill, ed. pp. 215–230. Albuquerque: University of New Mexico Press.

1981   *An Early Town on the Deh Luran Plain: Excavations at Tepe Farukhabad.* Memoirs of the Museum of Anthropology 13. Ann Arbor: University of Michigan.

1994   Prestate Political Formations. In *Chiefdoms and Early States in the Near East.* G. Stein and M. S. Rothman, eds. pp. 67–84. Madison, WI: Prehistory Press.

Wright, Henry, and Gregory Johnson

1975   Population, Exchange and Early State Formation in South Western Iran. *American Anthropologist* 77:267–291.

1985   Regional Perspectives on Southwest Iranian State Development *Paléorient* 11/2:25–30.

Wright, Henry, Naomi Miller, and Richard Redding

1980   Time and Process in an Uruk Rural Center. *In Colloques internationaux du C.N.R.S. L'Archeologie de L'Iraq.* pp. 265–284. Paris: Editions C.N.R.S.

Wright, Henry, and Eric Rupley

In press Calibrated Radiocarbon Age Determinations of Uruk Related Assemblies. In *Uruk Mesopotamia and Its Neighbors: Cross-cultural in the Era of State Formation.* M. Rothman, ed. Santa Fe: SAR Press.

Wulff, Hans

1966   *The Traditional Crafts of Persia.* Cambridge, MA: MIT Press.

Young, T. Cuyler

1975   An Archaeological Survey of the Kangavar Valley. In *Proceedings of the IIIrd Annual Symposium on Archaeological Research in Iran.* pp. 23–30. Tehran: Iranian Centre for Archaeological Research.

Zettler, Richard

1993   *Nippur.* Chicago: Oriental Institute.

Appendix

Burials From Tepe Gawra, Levels VIII to XIA/B

Brian L. Peasnall

The Interpretation of Mortuary Practices

Burials have long been recognized to be sensitive indicators of the social processes of the larger society acting at the time of interment. This is based on the premise that at least some of the social status attributed to an individual in life will be reflected in the treatment of the same individual in death (O'Shea 1984). In other words, the characteristics of mortuary practice reproduce the social values of the living culture at the time. Given this premise and given the large number of burials at Tepe Gawra (over 301 in Levels VIII to XIA/B), it is an ideal site for applying these types of data to derive information concerning the development of social organization in northern Mesopotamia during the late prehistoric period.

In spite of their potential importance, the mortuary data reflected in the publications of Speiser (1935) and Tobler (1950) are of very limited use. Therefore, the conclusions of those who rely solely on those publications are also questionable.

The excavators' perception of the site as a layer cake of sealed strata determined both the way in which the mound was excavated and the way in which the data were presented in the two monographs. For example, there was no attempt made in the field to trace the burials back to the strata from which they originated. Each burial was excavated along with the strata into which they intruded. Thus, with the exception of the chapters dealing specifically with the burials, most of the artifacts from the mortuary contexts are discussed with the other objects of the strata into which the burials intruded, not from which they came.

In the chapters dedicated to the graves and tombs, the attempt to place the burials according to their originating strata is almost wholly dependent on indirect evidence such as the placement of overlying walls or floors. Even this attempt, however, is weakened by certain a *priori* assumptions concerning the nature of the burials that often over-ruled sound archaeological principles of association. Perhaps, the most ubiquitous assumption is the attribution of many burials as being sacrificial in nature solely on the basis of their proximity to structures interpreted as having a religious function. A good example of this is Burial B, which was intrusive into Level X and crossed by the walls of a temple in Phase VIIIC of Level VIII outside of the area that had been terraced out. The logical inference regarding the level from which this burial originated would be that it was a stratum IX burial (an observation that Tobler himself makes (Tobler 1950:56 and Table A)). However, since Burial B contained the remains of an infant and was crossed by the walls of the Phase VIIIC temple, Tobler argues that this burial must be sacrificial. It must have been placed under the foundations of the temple "as a propitiatory or ritual gesture," thus making it a Phase VIIIC burial (Tobler 1950:56–57). However, other burials of adults and youths in similar contexts are interpreted differently. Another example is Burial 36–134, which Tobler assigns to Level XI on the basis of its location directly under the southeast corner of a Level XI temple in squares 4J and 4K (Tobler 1944). However, this burial lies more than 3 m. below the surface of Level XI. This seems to be an excessive depth compared to most of the other burials, which range from 1 to 2 m. under the surface from which they originated. Because of the attribution of sacrificial status to certain burials, the treatment of the data tends to be inconsistent.

The "layer cake" perception of the site also masked a very real problem presented by Levels VIII and IX. Rothman's analysis of the stratigraphy strongly suggests that most of the northeastern portion of Level IX had been terraced out by the builders of Level VIII. It is, therefore, difficult to distinguish those burials belonging to Level VIII from those belonging to Level IX. Phases XA and XI of Level XI/XA also present problems relevant to the stratigraphy of graves. Although some superimposed floor elevations of these two "levels" differ, many are the same. This suggests that rather than two distinct levels we have various phases of modification to the structures within a single level. Because of this, it is impossible to assign burials to either Phase XA or Phase XI as Tobler did (1950:100–102). Burials from these two phases should be seen as stratigraphically equivalent.

The nature of the questions that were important during the first half of the twentieth century has also determined the way in which the data were presented. Excavators were primarily interested in attributing specific periods of occupation to particular "ethnic" groups. However, this "ethnic question" was itself a part of the "Sumerian problem." As one of the earliest recorded civilizations in Mesopotamia, scholars were focused intensely on the origins of the Sumerian civilization (Tobler 1950:3; Speiser 1935:187).

Consequently, the data is presented in a descriptive manner from which comparisons are then drawn to other sites in terms of ethnic or cultural affinities. Additionally, by selecting only the portion of the data that were relevant to questions of interest at the time the volumes were published, it has made it difficult to draw new conclusions from the published data regarding questions of interest now. One can turn to the mortuary data for a good example of this limitation. Only 83 burials are mentioned in the catalogue of graves, although more than 400 (not including the "tombs" which are presented separately) were discovered at Gawra (Tobler 1950: Table D). In the text of the chapter concerning the graves, only a small number of burials are specifically discussed. The only real information that is given is the number of burials for each stratum and their vague locations. Only the "tombs" are listed in full (Tobler 1950:92–97). However, nowhere is there a complete listing of the grave furniture for either the tombs or the graves.

Clearly, then, a complete re-cataloguing and re-analysis of the mortuary data are necessary if these data are to contribute to our understanding of the social processes operating in northern Mesopotamia during the Late Chalcolithic, LC 2-3 periods. Several attempts at reanalyzing Gawra's mortuary data have been made in the past, but these have been less than successful. Their lack of success is due first to the failure to examine the original field notes (Forest 1983; Robinson 1984). Second, these studies make unwarranted assumptions concerning the meaning of the grave furniture and a heavy reliance on the loaded and often ambiguous concept of "wealth" based on subjectively assigned "wealth values" (Robinson 1984: 48–65).

Goals

The purpose of this Appendix is to present the mortuary data from the extant field notes so they can be used to their fullest potential. In order to do this the project has been broken down into several phases. The first phase consisted of compiling as accurately as possible a catalogue (see below) of all the artifacts that have come from mortuary contexts from Late Chalcolithic period Levels VIII to XIA/B. The second phase constituted the placement of each burial along with its associated grave furniture both vertically and horizontally to determine as accurately as possible the strata from which they had been dug. After the grave furniture were catalogued and the burials had been assigned to their most probable level, the burials were then compared to each other in order to observe differences in the treatment of the dead within and between levels.

The emphasis is on presentation of the data, and therefore this appendix will be primarily descriptive. However, some basic analysis of the data will also be presented in an attempt to identify major patterns and trends pertaining to the treatment of the dead and the mortuary ritual at Tepe Gawra during the late fifth and early fourth millennia B.C.

Cataloguing

In order to compile the catalogue, a number of sources were needed. As mentioned above, the monographs were incomplete and of little use. Consequently, they were used only to clarify questions that could not be resolved fully by the field notes. The field notes consist of several different recording systems. Some of these were used during the same season, and some reflect changes in recording systems from season to season. As Rothman writes (Chapter 2), the directorship of the excavations changed from season to season. Bache attempted to improve recording during the third to the fifth seasons. The various recording systems included the field registry, the locus sheets (for important features such as burials, caches of objects, interesting architectural details, and so on), burial recording forms, chits, maps, descriptive lists of loci, and notes.

While compiling the catalogue, I soon realized that the use of any particular recording form alone was not sufficient to provide complete detail of the burials and their associated artifacts. A large number of objects had been discarded in the field, and although some of these had been recorded in the field registry, others had not. Additionally, a number of locus sheets, which generally provided the most complete information, were lost or damaged. Furthermore, not all burials were recorded on the locus sheets, especially if they were not very spectacular. It is fortunate, however, that there is considerable overlap in the various recording systems regarding specific data, thus making it possible to compile a fairly accurate catalogue (see Table A.1).

In order to analyze the social processes reflected in the mortuary contexts, it is necessary to compile as complete a catalogue as is possible. Such data did not previously exist. It is for this reason that Forest's (1983) and Robinson's (1984) analyses of the mortuary data are unreliable, although in all fairness Robinson did utilize the field registry. However, since there are many other artifacts that had been excavated from the mortuary contexts at Tepe Gawra that were never entered into the registry, Robinson's analysis was doomed to fail even if her basic method of analysis had been sound.

A few words concerning the catalogue are now in order. All of the grave goods are grouped together by their burial location. Originally, most of the burials were given a locus number. However, some of the locus numbers also refer to other features, and some of the burials were not given locus numbers, especially during the first two seasons. For these reasons, the term "burial" has been substituted for "locus" following the convention set by Tobler in his discussion of the tombs (Tobler 1950:53, n.3). Some burials consisted of two or more individuals (Figure A.1). In those cases, an entry was made in the catalogue for each individual with the burial number appended with an upper-case letter. The provenience of the artifacts in such cases was detailed enough to attribute them to one or another individual. Underneath the burial number headings are listed the type of burial and the relative age of its occupant at death.

There were six basic types of burials at Gawra: libn, pisé, cist, sidewall, vessel, and loose. The libn burials represent the most complex form of internment. This type of burial consisted of a chamber made of sun-dried brick. It was often covered with wood, stone, or libn brick (Figures A.2 and A.3). In one case, the tomb roof appears to have been corbeled (Burial 36–032). Cist burials consisted of chambers lined with stone and usually covered with stone but occasionally covered with libn brick (Figure A.4). Sidewall burials generally consisted of a single libn brick wall parallel to the body of the deceased (Figure A.5). In two cases,

however, two walls were constructed, one on each side of the body (Burial 134 and 36-044). Pisé burials consisted of a low wall made of mud slabs that encircled the body of the deceased. Vessel burials were originally categorized as urn burials. Because the term urn is often used to refer to a particular type of pot, the general term 'vessel' has replaced it. This is perhaps a more accurate description, because this type of burial utilized a range of different vessel types. The most common were bowls, pots, and jars. A vessel burial involved the placement of the deceased (generally infants and children, but occasionally adults) into the vessel that was then buried (Figure A.6). Vessel burials were often covered with another vessel, most often with bowls, pots, and jars, but on occasion with goblets, plates, or sherds. Some of the vessel burials utilized vessels that had been broken before their use and for this reason those burials that were on large sherds have been lumped together into this category. The simplest form of internment was the loose burial in which the deceased was interned into a hole without any chamber or receptacle (Figure A.7). Where it is relevant, the type of cover used for each burial is included with the burial type.

Most of the skeletal remains were given relative ages in the field. Since there were no physical anthropologists on the site, it is difficult to assess the value of these relative ages. However, they are probably close enough to provide a rough estimate of differences in mortuary ritual due to age. In some cases, a more specific age is given (e.g., Burial 242), but it is probably best not to give too much weight to these specific ages. The relative ages are categorized as infant, child, youth, or adult. Frequently, there was some question in the field notes as to whether a particular burial should be labeled as infant or child. In such cases, these have been classified as infant/child. Additionally, some of the field records identify some skeletal remains as "tots." The term tot was occasionally used on one recording form whereas another type of form for the same burial expressed some uncertainty as to whether the remains were of an infant or child. All "tots" have therefore been classified as infant/child.

The next section for each burial is a list of the grave goods. This section is divided into four columns. The first column gives the field registry number. In some cases, there were several objects with the same field registry number. In others, especially for strung beads and pendants with a single field registry number, they have been divided according to various types, sizes, colors, and raw materials. For both of these cases, a lower case letter has been appended to the field registry number to make it easier to analyze and to describe these items individually.

In addition, all of the field registry numbers were originally prefixed with a "G." The "G" has been dropped as unnecessary. Those objects that were not

Table A.1   Sources Pertaining to the Late Chalcolithic Period Burials at Tepe Gawra.

Burial	Locus Sheet	Chit	Registry	Gawra Vol II	Locus List	Map
001	X				X	
002	X			Chap 2, 99	X	
003	X				X	
004	X				X	
005	X			Chap 2, 99	X	
006	X				X	
007	X				X	
009						
010			X			
011			X			
012	X		X			
013			X		X	
014	X		X	Chap 2	X	
016	X		X	Chap 2	X	
017	X				X	
018	X			Chap 2	X	
020	X			Chap 2	X	
024	X		X	Chap 2	X	
025	X		X	Chap 2	X	
029	X		X	Chap 2	X	
030	X			Chap 2	X	
031	X		X	Chap 2	X	
034	X		X	Chap 2	X	
037	X		X	Chap 2	X	
040	X		X		X	
045	X		X	Chap 2	X	
046	X		X	Chap 2	X	
047	X		X	99, 107, 116	X	
050	X				X	
051	X			110	X	
052	X			99	X	
053	X			Chap 2	X	
054	X			Chap 2	X	
055	X				X	
056	X				X	
057	X			Chap 2	X	
058	X				X	
059	X			Chap 2	X	
060	X			Chap 2	X	
061	X			Chap 2	X	
062	X			Chap 2	X	
063	X				X	
064	X			Chap 2	X	
065	X			Chap 2	X	
067	X				X	
068	X				X	
069	X				X	
070	X				X	
100	X	151	X	D	X	X
101	X				X	X
102	X	203	X	Chap 2	X	X
107	X	116	X	Chap 2	X	X
108	X	0117	X	Chap 2	X	

Burial	Locus Sheet	Chit	Registry	Gawra Vol II	Locus List	Map
109	X	121	X	Chap 2	X	X
110	X	122	X	Chap 2, 110	X	X
111	X	123	X	Chap 2	X	
113	X	322	X		X	X
114	X	127	X	Chap 2	X	X
119	X				X	
122	X				X	X
123		400	X		X	
124	X	404	X	Chap 2	X	
125	X				X	
126	X		X	D	X	X
127	X	374			X	
128	X	510	X		X	X
129	X				X	X
130	X				X	X
134	X			108, 109	X	
136	X				X	X
137	X	696			X	X
138	X	413			X	
140	X				X	
141	X				X	X
142	X	542	X	116, D	X	
144	X	801	X		X	X
145	X				X	X
146	X			108, 109, 110	X	
151	X				X	X
154	X	849			X	X
158	X	966			X	X
159	X	968			X	X
160	X				X	X
161	X				X	
163	X	985			X	X
164	X	794	X	D	X	
166	X	871			X	X
167	X	896		116	X	X
168	X	1451			X	
169	X	1087	X	Chap 2	X	
170	X	1091	X		X	
171	X			Chap 2	X	
175	X	1133	X	D	X	
176	X	1127			X	
177	X	1131	X		X	
178	X				X	
179	X				X	
180	X	1185	X	Chap 2	X	
181	X	1176	X	101, 116, D	X	
182	X				X	
183	X	1252			X	
184	X				X	
186	X				X	
187	X	216			X	
188	X	1223	X	101, 112	X	

(*continues*)

Burial	Locus Sheet	Chit	Registry	Gawra Vol II	Locus List	Map
189	X			109	X	
190	X	1305	X	D	X	
191	X			109	X	
192	X				X	
193	X	1264	X		X	
194	X	1230		102	X	
199	X	1018			X	
200	X			109	X	
201	X			100	X	
202	X		X	Chap 2, 99	X	
203	X		X		X	
204	X				X	
205	X	1024	X	D	X	
206	X	1026	X		X	
207	X				X	
208	X	1039	X		X	
209	X	1109	X	Chap 2	X	
210	X				X	
211	X				X	
212	X	1065	X		X	
213	X	1071	X	Chap 2	X	
214	X	1075	X		X	
215	X	1078	X		X	
216	X	1103	X		X	
217	X				X	
218	X				X	
219	X				X	
220	X			100	X	
221	X			109	X	
222	X			109	X	
223	X				X	
224	X	1311	X		X	
225	X	1242	X		X	
226	X	1270	X	Chap 2	X	
227	X				X	
228	X	1272			X	
229	X			100	X	
230	X	1360		D	X	
231	X	1360			X	
233	X				X	
234	X				X	
235	X	1364			X	
236	X	1366		D	X	X
237	X				X	X
238	X	1373	X	116	X	
239	X	1380		101	X	
241	X				X	
242	X	1386	X	100, 109	X	
243	X	1390			X	
244					X	X
245					X	X
246					X	X
247					X	X

Burial	Locus Sheet	Chit	Registry	Gawra Vol II	Locus List	Map
248					X	X
249	X			Chap 2	X	
250	X	1392		109, D	X	
251	X				X	
252	X				X	
253	X				X	
254	X	1408		D	X	
255	X	1410		D	X	
256	X	1411	X		X	
257	X				X	
258	X				X	
259	X	1287		D	X	
260					X	
261					X	X
263					X	X
265	X				X	
266	X	1269			X	
267						X
268	X			102	X	
269	X	1424			X	X
270					X	X
272					X	X
273	X	1429			X	
274	X				X	
275	X				X	
276	X				X	
278	X				X	
290-A	X				X	
315	X	1493			X	
318	X				X	
325	X	1556			X	
36-002	X	1612				
36-003	X					
36-004	X	1617				
36-005	X	1618				
36-006	X	1620	X			
36-007	X	1623				
36-008	X	1628		D		
36-009	X	1631		D		
36-010	X	1633		D		
36-011	X	1634				
36-013	X	1703	X			
36-014	X			Chap 2, 110		
36-015	X	1707				
36-016	X	1709				
36-017	X	1713		110		
36-019	X			102		
36-020	X	1716	X			
36-022	X					
36-026	X	1756		Chap 2		
36-027	X	1757		Chap 2, 100		
36-030	X			Chap 2		

(*continues*)

Burial	Locus Sheet	Chit	Registry	Gawra Vol II	Locus List	Map
36-031	X					
36-032	X	1777		Chap 2		
36-034	X	1780	X	Chap 2		
36-035	X					
36-036	X	1790	X	Chap 2		
36-037	X			112		
36-038	X	1794				
36-039	X			110, 112		
36-040	X	1798	X	Chap 2		
36-041	X	4104				
36-042	X			Chap 2		
36-043	X			Chap 2		
36-044	X			Chap 2		
36-046	X			Chap 2		
36-047	X					
36-048	X			Chap 2		
36-051	X	4123		D		
36-052	X					
36-057	X	4137		D		
36-058	X	4138				
36-060	X	4146	X	Chap 2		
36-068	X	1864	X	Chap 2		
36-074	X			Chap 2		
36-077	X	1877		D		
36-079	X					
36-080	X			110		
36-081	X			101, 110		
36-082	X	1885				
36-083	X					
36-084	X					
36-086	X			Chap 2		
36-087	X			110		
36-088	X	1888				
36-089	X	1890				
36-090	X	1892		Chap 2		
36-091	X					
36-100	X			Chap 2		
36-104	X	1908	X	Chap 2		
36-105	X	1909		Chap 2		
36-110	X	1918	X	Chap 2		
36-111	X	1924		Chap 2		
36-120	X			Chap 2		
36-122	X	1931		Chap 2		
36-129	X	1942	X	D		
36-134	X	4255	X	Chap 2		
36-135	X	4258	X	Chap 2		
36-137	X	4267		Chap 2		
36-144	X		X	Chap 2		
36-146	X	4286	X	Chap 2		
36-168	X					
36-171	X			116, D		X
7-001	X					
7-005	X	2511				

Table A.1   (continued)

Burial	Locus Sheet	Chit	Registry	Gawra Vol II	Locus List	Map
7-007	X			108		
7-009	X			Chap 2		
7-010	X					
7-012	X					
7-014	X					
7-015	X					
7-018	X					
7-023	X					
7-026	X					
7-028	X					
7-029	X					
7-030	X			103, 109		
A	X			Chap 2		
AA	X					
B	X			Chap 2		
BB	X					
C	X			Chap 2		
CC	X					
D	X			Chap 2		
DD	X			112		
E	X			Chap 2		
EE	X					
FF	X					
GG	X					
HH	X					
JJ	X					
KK	X					

recorded in the registry and thus have no registry number are designated as "none."

The next column refers to the present location of the artifacts. Those that went to Dropsie College or to Baghdad are designated as such. Those that went to the University of Pennsylvania Museum are given the accession number currently used by the museum. If the artifacts were discarded in the field, they are designated as "discard." If there is no record of where the objects went, they have been designated as "unrecorded." In most of the cases, those that are unrecorded were probably discarded in the field. In some cases, however, they may have gone to Baghdad. In cases where the particular object was listed as "none," the object or material was of a sort most likely recorded but not collected. This would include observations such as pigment, traces of reed matting, textiles, or animal bones. These things have been included in the catalogue, because some of these items, especially the pigment and textiles, may hold some symbolic value.

The next column refers to the number of artifacts of a particular class, type, or material from the burial.

In most cases, the number of items was tabulated from the field records. In some cases, however, no specific counts were recorded. If the item was in the University of Pennsylvania Museum, I was able to resolve this problem. In some cases, there were very large numbers of beads. When a very large string consisted of the same type and color of beads, the total length of the string was measured and then at five different points along the string the number of beads occupying a specific length was counted. The results were then averaged and an estimate was calculated for the whole string. Quantities for uncounted items that went to Dropsie or Baghdad, or were discarded in the field remain unresolved. For these items, no amount is given and only its presence is noted.

The last column is a list of the artifacts by size, color, shape, type of raw material, and class. In the case of ceramic vessels, the records are often vague. Frequently the same vessel might be referred to as a pot, jar, or bowl, depending on which recording form one is inspecting. Vessels that are not well described in the field records are classified as "ceramic vessel."

Figure A.1 Double libn tomb from Level VIII, Tepe Gawra. Reproduced by permission of the University of Pennsylvania Museum Archives.

Another place in which the catalogue is vague is in the category of beads, especially in reference to the raw materials from which they are made. Most problematical are the white beads that are often classified as paste or limestone, depending on which record one utilizes. A similar situation occurs with the black stone beads, where the same material might be classified as obsidian, black limestone, diorite, or serpentine.

In fact, with the small beads it is very hard to make a distinction between these raw materials. In such cases, they have been simply classified as white or black stone beads respectively. Some of the other raw materials from which beads are made also have contradictory descriptions in the records. For example, the records describe beads of turquoise, malachite, jadeite, green stone, beryl, and serpentine. Upon examination in the collection of the University of Pennsylvania Museum, all of these beads turned out to be turquoise, which grades from blue to green in color often on the same piece. Other types of beads in the field notes are those called shell barrel beads, white barrel beads, fluted barrel beads, or simply shell

beads. Upon examination, all of these were dentalium shells that have been strung in their natural form. This is important since there are barrel beads that are made of shell, paste, or stone. These latter beads are quite different from the natural dentalium shells.

As to the bead shapes, a number of classes have been defined: ring, cylinder, spherical, carinated, barrel, teardrop, plano-convex, triangular, flat square, sliced pebble, and roughed surface beads. For the most part these terms refer to the shape and are self-explanatory (Figure A.8). However, the last two bead types need more explanation. Sliced pebble beads, originally categorized as "irregular" in the field records, are beads that have been manufactured from a pebble. The craftsperson grinds away the sides but keeps the natural surface of the pebble around the bead, so the resulting product looks as if it had been sliced from a pebble. The roughed surface bead is a medium to large ring bead that has been pressure-flaked around its surface. Most roughed surface beads are made of obsidian but there is at least one made of carnelian (Burial 36-034).

Some of the items in the artifact column contain a superscript asterisk. This indicates that the object appears to have functioned as part of the burial rather than as a grave good. This includes those vessels that were used as receptacles for the deceased and their covers, as well as the reed mats and woven textiles, both of which were often wrapped around the body (Figures A.9 and A.10). However, these may also have carried some symbolic meaning. The fact that some bodies were completely unwrapped suggests that at the very least wrappings mark some difference in treatment after death. In the case of the reed matting and woven textiles, however, the problem of differential preservation must be kept in mind. These items must carry less weight in any analysis of mortuary variation. The apparent difference in function that these materials represent and also the fact that reed mats and woven textiles may have been more widely used than is observable archaeologically suggest this (see O'Shea 1984 for a discussion of this issue).

The last item included for some of the burial numbers is a short discussion giving a more precise description of the context in which the artifacts were found and an attempt, where possible, to state the actual function of specific artifacts such as necklaces, bracelets, ear ornaments, and headdresses. However, this specific type of information is very incomplete in the field records and so only a few burial numbers in the catalogue will contain this kind of detail.

Recreating the Burial Stratigraphy

Recreating the stratigraphy of burials proved to be a complex problem. There was no attempt in the field to trace the burials back to the levels from which they

Figure A.2   Libn brick tombs from Level X, Tepe Gawra. Reproduced by permission of the University of Pennsylvania Museum Archives.

had been dug. Therefore, their stratigraphic position had to be determined through less direct means, such as the presence of walls and floors lying over or under some of the burials. This problem was further complicated by Tobler's and the excavators' particular assumptions concerning the meaning of the burials of Tepe Gawra. As I mentioned above, the most ubiquitous assumption concerned the attribution of sacrificial status to many of the infant burials. Also, it was assumed that there was a close relationship between the

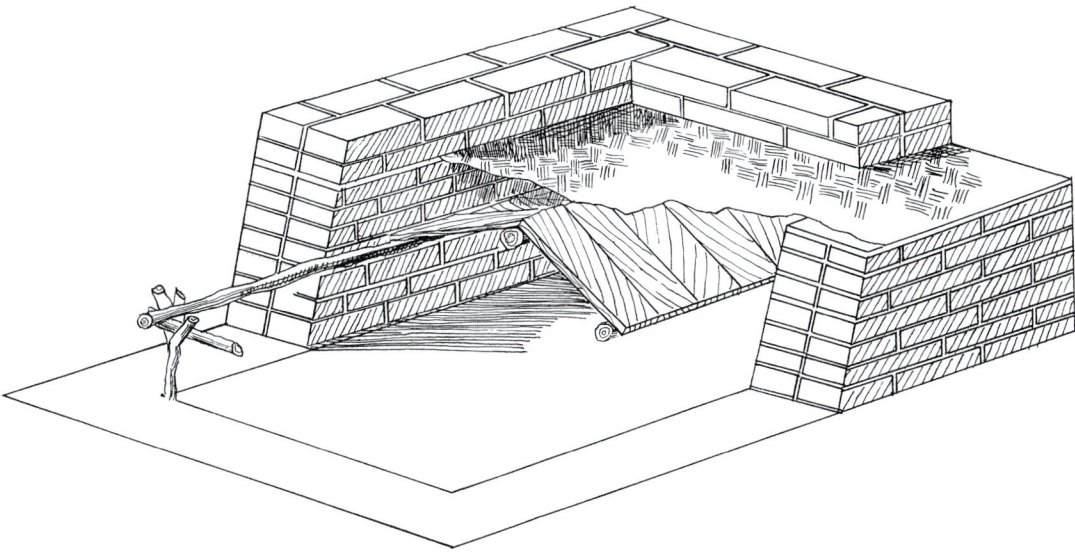

Figure A.3   Reconstruction of a libn tomb, Tepe Gawra. Reproduced by permission of the University of Pennsylvania Museum Archives.

Figure A.4   Cist grave, Tepe Gawra. Reproduced by permission of the University of Pennsylvania Museum Archives.

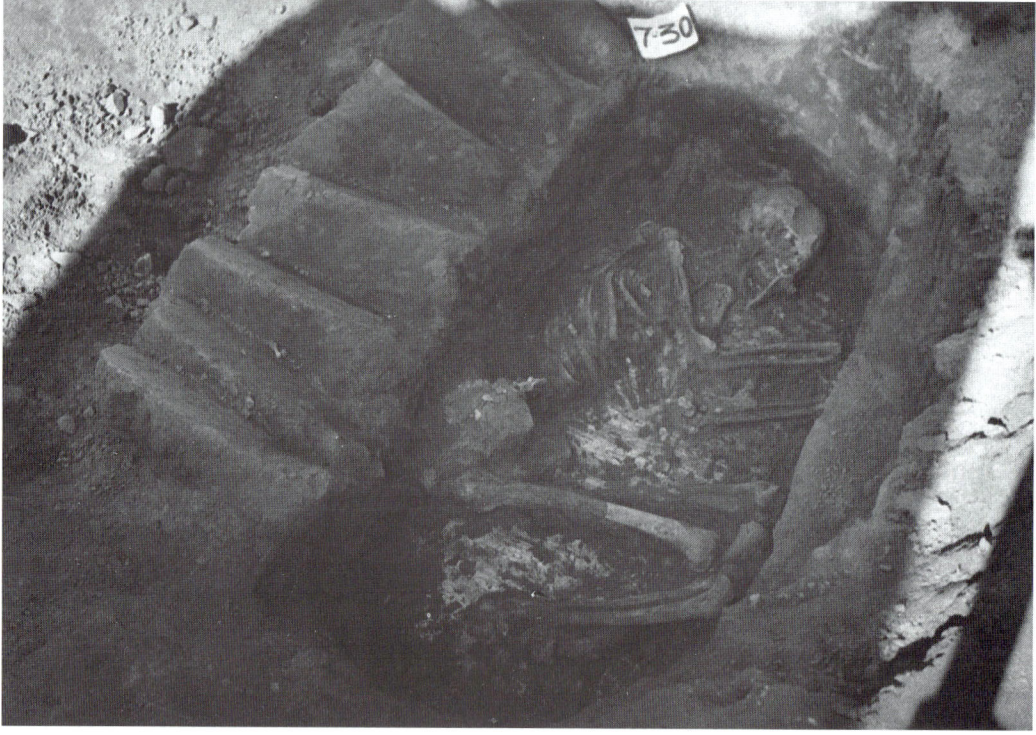

Figure A.5   Sidewall burial, Tepe Gawra. Reproduced by permission of the University of Pennsylvania Museum Archives.

Figure A.6 Infant pot burial, Tepe Gawra. Reproduced by permission of the University of Pennsylvania Museum Archives.

Figure A.7 Loose burial, Tepe Gawra. Reproduced by permission of the University of Pennsylvania Museum Archives.

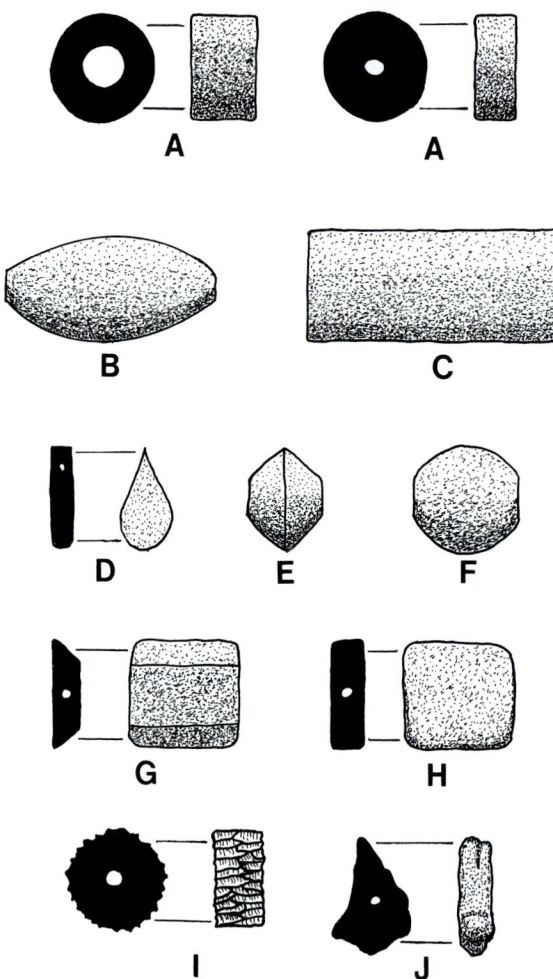

Figure A.8   Bead types from Tepe Gawra graves.

particular types of features or structures having some assumed ritual function. Once the stratigraphic relationships have been worked out, these other types of evidence can be investigated.

Another problem affecting the placement of burials, both horizontally and vertically, resulted from errors excavators made in recording and errors Tobler made while processing the data for publication. The majority of the errors made in the field concerned minor details such as whether the body had been laid on the left or right side during interment. These kinds of errors are of no consequence for determining the stratigraphic placement of the burials. However, in a small number of cases, locus numbers had been attributed to the wrong burials, and in other cases, burials were attributed to the wrong square. An example of this type of error concerns Burials 45 and 46. The field registry places Burial 45 in square 8O and Burial 46 in squares 6O/7O, while the locus sheets for these burials locate both burials in square 8O. Apparently, there had been some confusion in the field concerning the use of these locus numbers. This problem had been corrected on locus sheet 45 by a small note appended to it stating that the burial was in squares 6O/7O. The placement of Burial 45 in squares 6O/7O and Burial 46 in square 8O is verified by the illustrations used to place them on the locus sheets. However, this still leaves a discrepancy between the field registry and the locus sheets. It is most likely that the two burials had been confused with each other; therefore, the entry in the field registry for locus 45 is actually for locus 46, while the entry for 46 is actually for 45. This receives further confirmation by the fact that the field numbers for the artifacts found in Burial 45 and entered on locus sheet 45 are listed under burial 46 in the registry whereas those field numbers listed on locus sheet 46 are entered under locus 45 in the registry.

Errors in which burials were attributed to the wrong square directly impact their horizontal placement. In addition to completely changing their context in relationship to over- and underlying features, this error can potentially affect how the burials' vertical placement is viewed, because elevations change from square to square. A good example of this type of error relates to Burials 227 and 228. Both were intrusive into Level XIA/B. According to the locus sheet (both burials were put on the same locus sheet), both were in square 6Q. However, the illustrations used to locate these burials show that a mistake had been made. The original corner designations of the square had been crossed out and, in the same hand as the origin designations, corrections had been added placing these burials in square 5Q. Unfortunately, the entry for the square number was left unchanged. Such oversights often happen amid the flurry of activities during excavation. That these burials belong to square 5Q is

proximity of religious architecture and the placement of burials. These assumptions heavily influenced the placement of many of the burials into one or another level, sometimes to the detriment of sound judgment. Even Forest, who recognized the problems with some of the stratigraphic assignments made by Tobler, worked on the assumption that there was a relationship between certain types of structures and the placement of burials. Forest (1983:33) assumed that if burials were found in association with certain architectural features, such as the corners of walls or under the floors of buildings, it was justifiable to assign both the burials and the architecture to the same level. Unfortunately, given the density of structures from level to level throughout much of the mound, it is likely that many of the relationships between these features and burials were brought about by chance and were not purposeful.

Emphasis must be placed on the stratigraphic relationships rather than on the relationship of burials to

Figure A.9   Impression of reed matting from tomb, Tepe Gawra. Reproduced by permission of the University of Pennsylvania Museum Archives.

Figure A.10   Remains of textile from Tepe Gawra burial. Reproduced by permission of the University of Pennsylvania Museum Archives.

further supported by the fact that the locus sheet clearly states that Burial 227 cut into a wall. Square 5-Q is the only place that this burial could cut into a wall. If the error was not recognized the association between the wall and Burial 227 would be missed. Furthermore, the elevations for Level XIA/B in 6Q range from 8.61–8.78 m., while the elevation of 5Q in the vicinity of the burials was about 9.09 m.

In addition to affecting the horizontal and vertical placement of burials, these kinds of errors clearly show the importance of utilizing as many of the recording forms as possible to check, recheck, and confirm the data. The use of only one data source can lead to seriously flawed reconstructions of the site.

In addition to the errors made in the field by the excavators, there are those errors made by Tobler while processing the data for publication. For example, a comparison of the data from the locus sheets for Burials 1 and 70, both in square 6J, with Tobler's mapping of these burials (Tobler 1950) reveals a discrepancy in their horizontal placement. This discrepancy is easily explained for Burial 70. In most cases, the burials are located on the locus sheets by giving the distance from two corners of the square. In a few cases, Cartesian coordinates were used to place the burials, and in a few rare instances, the square was drawn to scale and the burials were plotted in. Burial 70 was plotted by use of measurements from the south and east corners. In placing this burial on the published map, Tobler accidentally transposed the measurements from these corners, thus placing the burial southwest of where it actually was located. The result of this error led to some confusion about the context of Burial 70. This confusion is evident in the note added to the locus sheet by Tobler stating that there were "no buildings or any other walls near this location!" However, the locus sheet is quite clear in stating that the burial was among walls, but that these walls did not seem to be part of a libn enclosure around the grave. Rather, the walls were most likely associated with the surrounding buildings. When the burial is plotted according to the measurements given in the locus sheet, it indeed sits among the walls of room 1083 of Level X. It is less clear as to why Tobler placed Burial 1 where he did. This burial is plotted in on the locus sheet by use of Cartesian coordinates that places the burial at 5.58 m. northwest from the east corner and 1.83 meters from the southwest. Tobler's placement is quite different, about 8.6 meters northwest of the east corner and then about 1.9 meters from the southwest. In all cases where there was a discrepancy between the field records and Tobler's treatment of the data, the field records proved to be more reliable. This reliability was borne out by the other details of the field records, as was the case with Burial 70.

Recreating the burial stratigraphy is further complicated by the fact that the overall site stratigraphy had to be revised (Rothman, this volume). The revision of the site stratigraphy, especially the stratigraphy involving Phases XA and XI, means that the original burial stratigraphy has to be modified accordingly. Accepting Tobler's published stratigraphic assignments without accounting for these recent revisions would lead to larger errors than those resulting from errors made in the field notes and those made during processing of the data for publication. For example, Burials 100, 101, and 113, all of which are in square 6O, were intrusive into Level XI according to the original stratigraphy. On this basis, they were assigned an origin from Phase XA. However, a comparison of the elevations from these burials with the revised surface elevations of Phases XA and XI shows that the original stratigraphy for these burials is no longer valid. Burial 100 is at an elevation of 10.87 m., Burial 101 is at an elevation of 10.53 m., and Burial 113 is at an elevation of 10.55 m. However, the lowest elevation of Phase XA is about 10.14 m. in the vicinity of Burials 100 and 101, and about 10.20 m. in the vicinity of Burial 113.

Given these problems, it was necessary to revise the locations of each burial from Levels VIII to XIA/B horizontally and vertically in order to make the data useful for any sort of analysis. Before this could be done, however, it was necessary to recreate Tobler's stratigraphic placement of the burials to create a comparative baseline from which to work. Originally, this proved to be a difficult task. Tobler did not fully publish his burial stratigraphy. In his chapter on the graves (Tobler 1950: chapter 3), he gives the number of burials for each level, the range of elevations for the burials by level, and the number of burials associated with particular squares and their relationship to particular types of structures. He then gives explicit detail concerning some of the more elaborate burials. Unfortunately, those burials he did not see as important went untreated. For example, Tobler mentions that there are 23 burials (not counting the 10 tombs) dug from Level X ranging in elevations from 9.83 to 11.17 m. He also mentions that three burials are associated with the Level X temple and that the rest of the burials formed two groups. One group consisted of five burials in squares 5J and 6G, while the other consisted of 15 burials in squares 8Q, 7Q, 8O, and 7O. With the exception of the three burials associated with the temple (Burials 201, 220, and 36-27), the burials remain unspecified. At the end of the chapter, Tobler discusses other aspects of the burials such as the types of burials and burial customs. These sections give a little more detail about his placement of the graves. Thus, in his discussion on pisé burials, Burial 36-14 is explicitly mentioned as a Level X burial, while in his discussion on burial customs, reference is made to another Level X burial (36-37). In his Table D, which gives some information on the grave furnishings of two more burials, 190 and 206, he refers to these as dug from Level X. Therefore, out of 23 burials only 7 are referred to explicitly.

I attempted to recreate Tobler's burial stratigraphy using the sparse detail in the publication. It soon became apparent that the accuracy of this recreated stratigraphy was highly uncertain owing to the considerable overlap in elevations for the levels across the site. Furthermore, hours of wading through the Tepe Gawra files at the University of Pennsylvania Museum failed to reveal the presence of any notes or lists detailing Tobler's stratigraphic division of the burials. However, a major breakthrough came while I was going through the burial sheets. Originally, there appeared to be no particular order to the way in which the burial sheets had been inserted into the file. However, I observed that at various places a slip of paper containing tallies of burial types and relative ages had been inserted into the stack of burial sheets. I found that the number of burial sheets in each group that had been separated by these slips of paper corresponded with the number of burials Tobler had cited for each level in his 1950 volume. Furthermore, the elevations and number of burials in each square for each level, grouped by these slips of paper, also matched Tobler's information for the burials. Although Tobler had made no list of his stratigraphic divisions for the burials, his burial stratigraphy had been preserved through the order in which he had placed the burial sheets in the file. It is fortunate that very few people had gone through these records and that no one was inclined to organize the burial sheets in a "more orderly" manner. A tabulation of the burial stratigraphy recreated from the published information with the more accurate burial stratigraphy compiled from the order of the burial sheets indicated that there was a 10–20 percent error for the various levels in the stratigraphy created if one used published information. Had I not noticed Tobler's stratigraphic divisions, dependence on the published information would have resulted in a significantly inaccurate recreation of his burial stratigraphy. That would have had an adverse impact on any later analysis of the burial data. Tobler's burial stratigraphy is presented in Table A.2.

Once I had reconstructed Tobler's stratigraphic divisions, they could then be compared to the site stratigraphy and, where necessary, revised. To do this, the burials were first plotted horizontally and vertically. For the most part, mapping the burials horizontally was a straightforward process involving nothing more than plotting them in place according to the measurements given in the burial sheets (Figure A.11). The only real problem concerned the inconsistency in the quality of the recording from season to season. Many of the burials excavated during the 1936 and

1937 seasons when Speiser returned as director were not plotted into their precise location. In fact, most of the burial sheets for these field seasons contained no provenience beyond square number and the level into which the burials intruded. In order to plot these burials, it was necessary to rely on the chits, which plotted the burials into 1 × 1-meter sub-squares. Speiser's team adopted these chits as locus sheets. Although it was impossible to get a precise location for many of these burials, it was possible to plot them within 1 m² of their original location. For some burials, there were no locus sheets. However, most of them had been located on chits. Therefore, their location could be plotted.

Once they had been plotted horizontally, the burials were then plotted vertically. This was accomplished by plotting the burials along the northeast-southwest axis of the square and then determining their elevation so as to get a picture of what the mound looked like in cross section (see Figures 3.1–3.5 in the main text). Once the burials were placed vertically, the horizontal maps were laid over the site plans in order to compare the position of the burials with over- and underlying architectural features. They were also compared with the surface elevations of the pertinent levels. The relevant features as well as the level surfaces were then transferred to the vertical map (Figure A.12). These vertical maps were then used to check Tobler's assignment of the burials to individual levels and to make the necessary adjustments resulting from the revised site stratigraphy. In cases where some architectural feature lay directly over a burial, it was assumed that the burial predated the feature. Changes to Tobler's original stratigraphy due to overlying features involve only a small number of burials. In a number of cases, however, the level assignments suggested exceptionally shallow or exceptionally deep interments. Although I did not assume what the proper depth of a burial had to be, some depths seem more probable than do others. For example, it seems highly unlikely that a body would be buried to a depth of only 10 centimeters. Nor does it seem likely that the effort would have been expended to dig a hole more than three meters deep for a relatively simple interment. In these cases, the burials were assigned either to the level above the original assignment for the shallow burials or to the level below the original assignment for the excessively deep elevations. This brought their depths into the same range as those burials on which both Tobler and I agreed (between 1 and 2 m. in depth for most of the burials). Only those burials that were excessive in the extreme were changed. Most of these kinds of changes resulted from the revision of the overall site stratigraphy by Rothman. These changes brought the burials back into the depth range they originally had under Tobler's scheme using the published site stratigraphy. In cases where my

Table A.2   Tobler's Original Stratigraphic Assignments For Burials.

Level VIII Burials

001	020*	051	202*
002*	024*	055	209*
003	025*	056	36-036*
004	029*	057*	A*
005*	030*	059*	AA
007	031*	060*	B*
014*	037*	061*	DD
016*	045*	063	
017	046*	064*	
018*	050	065*	

Level IX Burial

034*	069	211	E*
040	070	212	EE
047	124*	213*	FF
052	169*	214	GG
053*	171*	36-034*	HH
054*	199	36-040*	JJ
058	200	36-044*	KK
062*	203	C*	
067	204	CC	
068	205	D*	

Level X Burials

006	119	219	36-026*
102*	190	220	36-031
107*	193	256	36-037
108*	201	269	36-079
109*	206	36-013	7-001
110*	210	36-014*	7-005
111*	216	36-016	7-009*
114*	217	36-020	7-010

Level XA Burials

100	182	229	36-030*
101	186	242	36-035
113	207	249*	7-007
127	208	278	7-012
168	215	290A	7-014
177	226*	36-027*	

Level XI Burials

122	167	235	36-084
125	170	239	36-086*
128	175	252	36-088
129	176	253	36-089
130	178	258	36-090*
134	179	266	36-095*
136	180*	315	36-100*

Level XI Burials   (continued)

137	181	318	36-104*
138	184	36-032*	36-105*
140	187	36-038	36-110*
141	188	36-039	36-111*
142	189	36-041	36-120*
144	191	36-042*	36-122*
145	192	36-043*	36-129
146	218	36-046*	36-134*
151	221	36-047	36-135*
154	222	36-048*	36-137*
158	223	36-052	36-144*
159	224	36-060*	36-146*
160	225	36-068*	36-168
161	227	36-074*	7-015
163	228	36-080	7-018
164	233	36-081	7-023
166	234	36-083	

Level XIA/B Burials

183	257	36-006	36–077
194	259	36-007	36–082
230	265	36-008	36–087
231	268	36-009	36–091
236	273	36-010	36–150*
237	274	36-011	36–151*
238	275	36-015	36–155*
241	276	36-019	36–171
243	325	36-022	7–026
250	36-002	36-051	7–028
251	36-003	36-057	7–029
254	36-004	36-058	7–030
255	36-005	36-062	

Level XII Burials

294	329	36-092	36-133
295	36-001	36-093	36-136
296	36-017	36-094	36-138
297	36-021	36-096	36-139
298	36-023	36-097	36-140
299	36-024	36-098	36-141
300	36-025	36-099	36-142
301	36-029	36-101	36-143
302	36-045	36-102	36-145
303	36-049	36-106	36-147
304	36-050	36-107	36-154
305	36-053	36-108	36-156
306	36-054	36-109	36-164
307	36-055	36-112	36-170
308	36-059	36-113	36-173
309	36-061	36-114	7-008
310	36-063	36-115	7-034
311	36-064	36-116	7-036

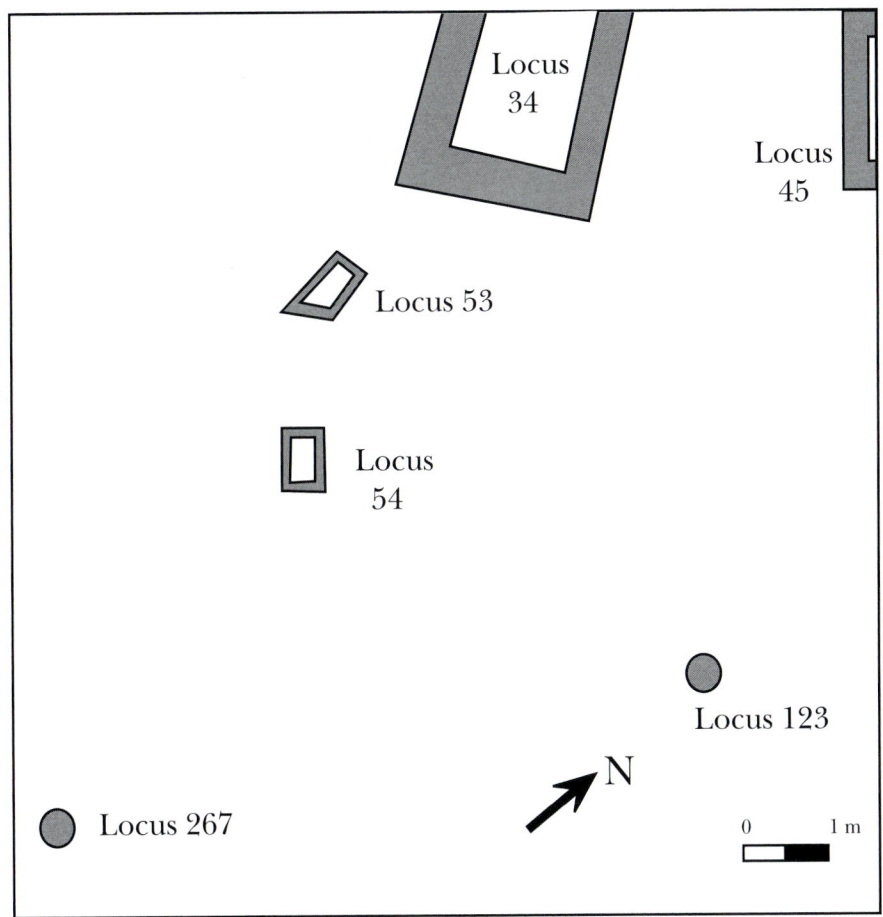

Figure A.11   Horizontal distribution of graves in Square 7O, Tepe Gawra.

stratigraphic assignments disagreed with Tobler's, but no strong argument could be made, I left Tobler's original assignment. The resulting revised burial stratigraphy is shown in Table A.3. The remaining disagreements along with the justifications for changing the level assignments between my burial stratigraphy and Tobler's are summed up in Table A.4.

Some explanation should be given to the stratigraphic units used in recreating the mortuary practices for levels XIA/B-VIII at Tepe Gawra. As Rothman points out, there were five levels (XIA/B, XI/XA, X, IX, and VIII) and seven sub-level phases (XIB, XIA, XI, XA, VIIIC, VIIIB, and VIIIA). Builders of later levels, especially VIII disturbed portions of underlying strata. Therefore, for example, in the northeastern portion of Level IX, it is impossible to make any distinction between those burials that had been dug from Level VIII and those from Level IX. In order to separate the burials into Level VIII burials and Level IX, a large portion of the mortuary data from these levels would have to be ignored. For this

reason, these two levels have been taken as a single stratigraphic unit in the following analyses. In some cases, it was possible to narrow down the stratigraphic relationships for some VIII/IX burials. Although all of Level VIII and IX burials are lumped together for the sake of analysis, more precise stratigraphic designations are provided in the catalogue and in the maps showing the relationship between burials and overlying structures (Figures A.14, A.16, A.18 and A.20). In addition, Figures A.13, A.15, A.17, A.19 show all VIII/IX burials in relation to the structures of Levels VIIIA, VIIIB, VIIIC, and IX. Combining all Level VIII and IX burials together for the sake of analysis will result in a loss of fine chronological control for understanding changes that occurred at Tepe Gawra during the period of 3900–3700 B.C. Nonetheless, we are able to preserve the full range of variation in mortuary forms. Therefore, the gains outweigh the losses. Some similar problems result from seeing XA and XI as part of one level and of Rothman's isolation of a XIB phase of Level XIA/B (see Chapter 3).

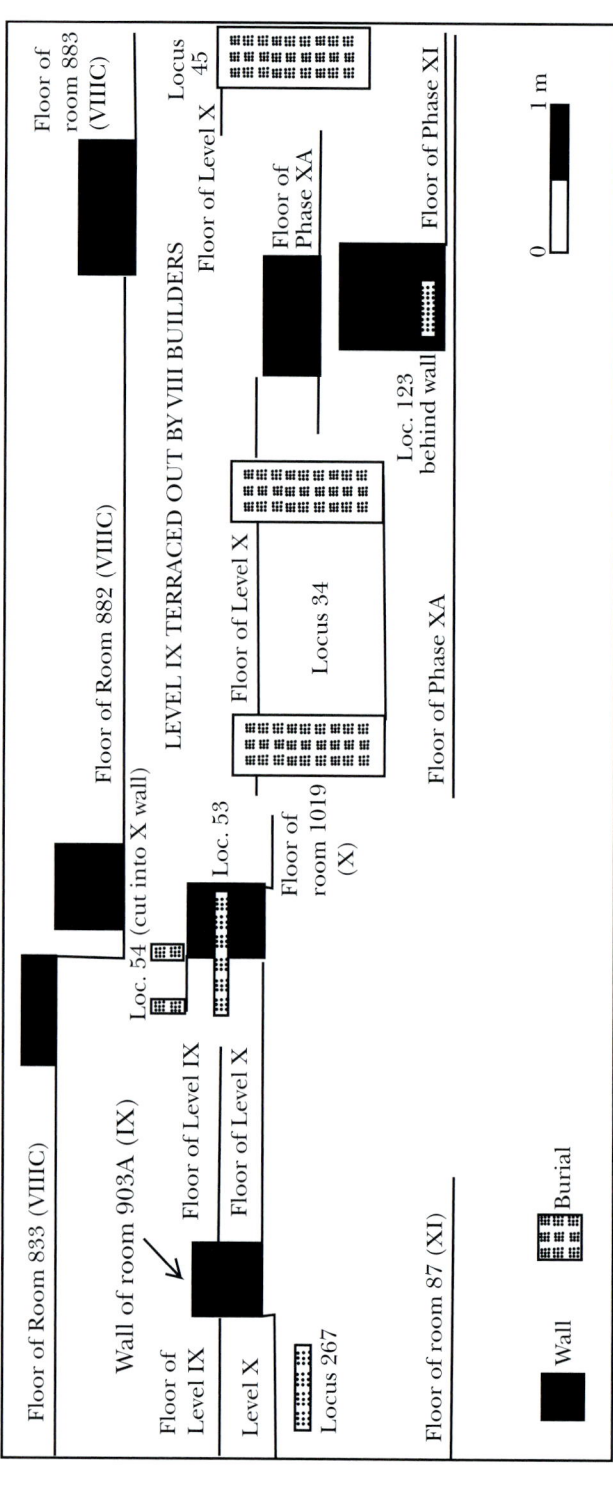

Figure A.12   Stratigraphic distribution of burials in Square 7O, Tepe Gawra.

Table A.3   Revised Burial Stratigraphy.

Level VIII/IX

001	030*	062*	267
002*	031*	063	36-036*
003	034*	064*	7-007
004	037*	065*	A*
005*	040	067	AA
007	045*	068	B*
009	046*	069	C*
010	047	070	CC
011	050	171*	D*
012	051	199	DD
013	052	200	E*
014*	053*	203	FF
016*	054*	204	GG
017	055	209*	HH
018*	056	211	JJ
020*	057*	212	KK
024*	058	213*	
025*	060*	214	
029*	061*	261	

Level X

006	119	210	36-031
059*	124*	216	36-034*
100	126	217	36-035
101	177	219	36-037
102*	182	220	36-040*
107*	190	256	36-044*
108*	201	269	36-047
109*	202*	36-013	36-079
110*	205	36-014*	7-001
111*	206	36-016	7-005
113	207	36-020	7-009*
114*	208	36-026*	EE

Level XA/XI

122	176	235	36-052
123	178	239	36-068*
125	179	242	36-080
127	180*	244	36-081
128	181	245	36-083
129	184	246	36-084
130	186	247	36-086*
134	187	249*	36-088
136	189	252	36-089
137	191	253	36-100*
138	192	258	36-104*
140	193	263	36-105*
141	215	266	36-110*
142	218	270	36-111*
144	221	278	36-129
145	222	290A	36-135*
146	223	315	36-137*

Level XA/XI   (continued)

151	224	318	36-144*
154	225	36-027*	36-146*
158	226*	36-030*	36-168
159	227	36-032*	7-010
160	228	36-038	7-012
163	229	36-039	7-014
164	230	36-041	7-015
168	231	36-042*	7-018
170	233	36-046*	7-023
175	234	36-048*	

Level XIA/B

161	255	36-007	36-077
162	257	36-008	36-082
166	259	36-009	36-087
167	265	36-010	36-090*
183	268	36-011	36-091
188	272	36-015	36-120*
194	273	36-017	36-122*
236	274	36-019	36-134*
237	275	36-022	36-171
238	276	36-043*	7-026
241	325	36-051	7-028
243	36-002	36-057	7-029
248	36-003	36-058	7-030
250	36-004	36-060*	
251	36-005	36-062	
254	36-006	36-074*	

* = Tobler's Libn Tombs

Changing Patterns in Mortuary Practices
Theoretical Underpinnings of Interpretation

Now that the burials, along with their associated grave furnishings, have been placed in their proper provenience, the basic trends concerning changing burial practices through time can be examined. The goal is to provide a basic interpretation of what these trends mean in terms of the sociopolitical processes occurring at Tepe Gawra during the late fifth and early fourth millennium B.C.

Although the study of mortuary data has long been an important aspect of archaeological inquiry, the basic methodological and theoretical approaches to the study of mortuary data were developed in the 1970's by Arthur Saxe (1970) and Lewis Binford (1971). Saxe, working with concepts developed by Ward Goodenough (1965) in the 1960's, argued that each member of a society has a number of social

Table A.4   Justification For New Level Assignment.

Burial	Change	Justification
059	VIII to X	Crossed by wall of Level X and above phase XA floor (grave dug before erection of level X wall.)
100	XA to X	Well above Phase XA floor. Burial is at about the same elevation as Burial 006, which Tobler assigns to Level X. Rothman's revised site stratigraphy necessitates shifting this burial from phase XA to X. Originally this burial was seen as intrusive into level XI, but the revised stratigraphy places this burial well above Level XI.
101	XA to X	Well above Phase XA floor. Burial is at about the same elevation as Burial 006, which Tobler assigns to Level X. Rothman's revised site stratigraphy necessitates shifting this burial from Phase XA to X. Originally this burial was seen as intrusive into level XI, but the revised stratigraphy places this burial well above Level XI.
113	XA to X	Well above Phase XA floor. Burial is at about the same elevation as Burial 006, which Tobler assigns to Level X. Rothman's revised site stratigraphy necessitates shifting this burial from phase XA to X. Originally this burial was seen as intrusive into Level XI, but the revised stratigraphy places this burial well above Level XI.
124	IX to X	Cut into wall of XI and is too far below Level IX. Burial is at about the same elevation as Burial 107, which Tobler associates with level X.
126	XA to X	Crossed by wall of Level X and above phase XA floor (grave dug before erection of level X wall.)
161	XI to XIAB	Crossed by wall of XIAB (grave dug before erection of level XIAB wall.)
166	XI to XIAB	Crossed by wall of XI and below floor of XIAB.
167	XI to XIAB	Crossed by walls of levels XI and XIAB and above floor of Level XII (?).
169	Deleted	This does not seem to be a real burial.
177	XA to X	At 10.15 m., just under the floor of Phase XA (c. 10.40 m.), too shallow (only 25 cm. deep). If this grave originates from Level X (c. 11.80 m.) would be 1.65 m. deep.
182	XA to X	This burial is at an elevation of 10.57 and is only 10 cm under floor of phase XA (10.67), too shallow. If it originated from level X (c. 11.78 m.) it would be about 1.21 m. deep.
188	XI to XIAB	Crossed by wall of Level XIAB and cuts into wall of Level XII (grave dug before erection of Level XIAB wall.)
193	X to XA/XI	Crossed by wall of Phase XA and well above level XIAB surface.
202	VIII to X	Crossed by wall of Level IX and intrusive into phase XA.
205	IX to X	On floor of phase XA and partly under level X wall (grave dug before erection of level X wall.)
207	XA to X	Just above floor of Phase XA, too high to be a phase XA burial.
208	XA to X	Crossed by wall of level X and cut into Phase XI wall and above floor of phase XA (grave dug before erection of level X wall.)
230	XIAB to XA/XI	This burial is at most 59 cm. below the surface of Level XIAB (c. 9.03 m.), too shallow. If it originated from phase XI/XA (10.00 m.) it would have a more realistic depth of about 1.56 m. Associated with Burial 231.
231	XIAB to XA/XI	Too shallow. Associated with burial 230 and the same argument, used for reassigning Burial 230, is also valid for this burial.
36-017	XII to XIAB	This burial was found at the foot of Burial 36-019 (originating from level XIAB) suggesting that both had originated from the same level.
36-034	IX to X	Originally cited as a level X burial on the burial sheet, this burial is intrusive into Phase XI, which has an elevation of about 9.90 to 10.56 m. The walls of

Burial	Change	Justification
		this tomb were 45 cm. Assuming the whole tomb was within Phase XI (implied by the burial sheet) the bottom of the burial would have been at about 10.11 m. or deeper (9.84 m.). If this burial had originated from level IX (at about 11.98 m.), it would have been about 1.87 to 2.14 m. deep. Although it is possible, it seems that if an origin in Level X (c. 11.49 m.) would have been more likely for a depth of 1.38–1.65 m. This along with the original attribution to level X in the burial sheet argues in favor of a Level X source.
36-035	XA to X	According to the burial sheet, this burial is next to and at about the same elevation as Burial 36-034, suggesting that both originated from the same level. Also, if this had originated from phase XA as suggested by Tobler, it would have been 72 cm deep at most, again not impossible but unlikely. A depth of 1.38–1.65 m. is more probable.
36-040	IX to X	The surface of Level VIIIC/IX ranges from 12.15 to 12.09 m. This burial was intrusive into Level XIAB which ranges from about 9.72 at its top to about 8.80 m. at its bottom giving a depth 2.37–3.29 m. for Tobler's placement. Too far below Level IX.
36-043	XI to XIAB	This burial is intrusive into Level XIIA and so would have been below 7.97 m. (surface elevation of XII). The burial sheet gives the height of the tomb walls as 40 cm. and so the bottom of the tomb would have been at about 7.57 m. or deeper. Tobler's assignation of this tomb to Phase XI (c. 10.50 m.) puts it at 2.93 m. deep or deeper below the surface of origination. If this burial had originated from the surface of Level XIAB (ranging from 9.15–9.38 m.) it would have had a depth of about 1.58–1.81 m.
36-044	IX to X	This burial is fairly close to Burial 36–040 and the same argument used for reassigning 36–040 of Level X also applies here. However, in this case the burial sheet mentions that the tomb walls were 52 cm. in height. If this had been a level IX burial, it would have been at least 2.43 m. deep and perhaps as much as 3.29 m. deep. Too far below Level IX. This burial was also originally attributed to level X in the burial notes.
36-047	XI to X	Burial below surface of XI in Level XIAB. As a phase XI burial, it would have been a shallow burial (ca. 70 cm.). The burial sheet also places this burial close to and at about the same level as 36–044, suggesting that both originated from the same level.
36-060	XI to XIAB	This burial is intrusive into Level XIIA (below 7.42 m.). If this burial had originated from Phase XI (10.12 m.) it would have a depth of more than 2.7 m. By placing it as a Level XIAB (8.85 m.) burial, we get a more realistic depth of 1.43 m.
36-090	XI to XIAB	This burial is intrusive into Level XIIA (below 7.44 m.). If this burial had originated from phase XI (10.20 m.) it would have a depth of more than 2.76 m. Too deep. By placing it as a Level XIAB (8.91 m.) burial, we get a more realistic depth of a little more than 1.47 m.
36-074	XI to XIAB	This burial is 1 meter below the surface of Level XII. The surface of Level XII is at about 7.78 m. making the elevation of the burial 6.78 m. If this burial had originated from Phase XI (surface elevations range from 10.15 to 10.45 m.) the depth of the burial would have been at least 3.37 m. or as deep as 3.67 m. This is much too deep. If it had been dug from Phase XIB (no elevations exist for the immediate area, but a good estimate would probably be 8.6 m. or somewhat lower) the depth would be about 1.82 m.
36-095	XI to XII	This burial is well below Level XII. The burial sheet explicitly states that it was under a wall of Level XII and so can not be from Level XI.

(continues)

Burial	Change	Justification
36-120	XI to XIAB	This burial is intrusive into Level XIIA (below 8.09 m.). If this burial had originated from Phase XI (surface elevation ranges from 10.54 to 10.65 m.) it would have a depth of more than 2.45–2.56 m. Too deep. By placing it as a Level XIAB (surface elevation ranges from 9.28 to 9.38 m.) this burial would be somewhat deeper than 1.19–1.29 m. deep.
36-122	XI to XIAB	This burial is intrusive into Level XIIA (below 8.14 m.). If this burial had originated from Phase XI (surface elevation ranges from 10.56 to 10.62 m.) it would have a depth of more than 2.42 to 2.48 m. Too deep. Although there are no surface elevations given for level XIAB in this area, the elevation of its surface is something above 9 m. (perhaps as high as 9.4 m., judging from the surrounding elevations). If this was a Level XIAB burial, it would be within a more reasonable depth of about 1.26 m.
36-134	XI to XIAB	This burial is intrusive into Level XIIA (below 8.00 m.). Tobler attempts to correlate this burial with the Phase XI temple since it lies directly below the southeast corner of the temple. The surface of phase XI is at about 11.00 m. If the burial originated at Phase XI it would have been more than 3.00 m. deep. If it originates from level XIAB (c. 9.50 m.), it would be a little deeper than 1.50 m. Its location under the temple is coincidental.
36-150	XIAB to XII	This burial intrudes into level XIII. Although there are no elevations in the immediate area of the burial for Level XIIA or XIII, elevations from adjacent squares suggest that if a Level XIAB burial had been dug down into this level, it would have been over 3.00 m. deep, too deep.
36-151	XIAB to XII	This burial was below the surface of Level XIII. As with burial 36-150, an origin from level XIAB would make this burial too deep (in fact it would be deeper than 36-150).
36-155	XIAB to XII	This burial was below Level XIII. As with burial 36-151, an origin from level XIAB would make this burial excessively deep.
7-007	XA to VIII/IX	Wall of Level X cut into by burial.
7-010	X to XA/XI	Crossed by wall of Phase XI and above surface of XIAB (?) (this grave was dug before erection of Phase XI wall.)
EE	IX to X	Crossed by wall of Level X and above phase XA floor (?) (this grave was dug before erection of Level X wall.)

Also, there were notes on a number of burials that Tobler did not include. Speiser (1935) had published some of these burials; Tobler understandably ignored them. Others, however, were from later seasons, and the reason Tobler left them out is unclear. The field notes on these burials seem to be accurate, and so I have included them.

From Tepe Gawra, volume 1 (Speiser 1935a).

Burial 009
Burial 010
Burial 011
Burial 012
Burial 013

Burials not previously published

Burial 123	XI/XA	Burial 247	XI/XA
Burial 162	XIAB	Burial 248	XIAB
Burial 165	XI/XA	Burial 262	XIAB
Burial 244	XI/XA	Burial 267	VIII/IX
Burial 245	XI/XA	Burial 270	XI/XA
Burial 246	XI/XA	Burial 272	XIAB

identities depending on the social context. A person's role is the sum of all their social identities. An individual might be a father, a husband, a great hunter, and a storyteller. However, not all of the social identities held by an individual will be equally applicable to all social interactions. Depending on the context of a particular social interaction, each individual must choose which social identities to express. Goodenough calls this expression of various social identities in a given social context the "social persona." The manner and degree to which various social personae can be expressed will differ depending on how a society's social system is organized. Therefore, observing how social roles are expressed will provide insight into the organizing principles of a society (Saxe 1970:7).

The number and degree of social identities that can be expressed in any particular society will vary, depending on its level of social complexity. Thus, in an egalitarian society, infants are limited to the social identity of their tribal affiliation. Adults may accumulate additional social identities depending on their experiences and accomplishments. By contrast, a society in which some infants display social identities of higher rank than some adults is indicative of a socially differentiated society in which there is social ranking from birth (Saxe 1970:8).

These principles form the theoretical and methodological basis for developing social inferences from mortuary data. The use of these principles in the analysis of mortuary data is dependent on the assumption that the social identities held by an individual in life will be reflected in some way in the treatment of that individual after death (O'Shea 1984). These underlying assumptions have been tested ethnographically and found to be essentially sound (Binford 1971). However, the one error that is most often made in the use of mortuary data to draw inferences about social processes is the primacy of burial goods as the primary indicator of status differences to the exclusion of most other aspects of mortuary practices. Tainter (1978) has argued that mortuary practices are much more complex in nature and involve far more than just differences in burial goods. Of particular importance are aspects of mortuary practices that include the treatment of the corpse, the time and energy expended on the mortuary ritual, and the time and labor expended on the construction of the burial facilities, in addition to differences in burial goods. Furthermore, mortuary practices may become very complex resulting in patterns that are not readily apparent. In fact, burial ritual can become so complex that it results in patterns that contradict a society's ideology. This is what Tainter refers to as the "archaeologist's nightmare." It is important, therefore, to find redundant features in all these aspects of mortuary practice.

For Tepe Gawra, I considered observable patterns for several aspects of mortuary practice and then compared them to each other in order to show how these patterns were related and how the relationships between them changed over time. Tainter suggests a number of ways in which patterns observed in mortuary contexts can be quantified for use in comparing differences between individuals. For the most part, however, the emphasis of the study of the mortuary contexts in the Late Chalcolithic period (only LC 2-3 in this case) at Tepe Gawra has been on documenting two interrelated factors. The first was the presence of differences in these patterns. The second were the changes in these patterns over time, rather than on developing a precise measure of these differences. Ideally, an attempt could be made to correlate these patterns and the differences between them to the various ways in which social roles are assigned. Differences in the treatment of individuals in death are not based solely on social rank, but can depend on factors such as gender and age (Chapman and Randsborg 1981). Unfortunately, the data from Tepe Gawra do not permit those variables to be measured fully, because none of the burials were sexed and the ages given are only rough estimates. However, the possibility of differences occurring for reasons other than status position must be kept in mind. Ultimately, the purpose of this study is to document the basic nature of the mortuary practices at Tepe Gawra, changes in these practices, and the nature of these changes. The study aims to provide some explanation of these changes. The patterns observed in the mortuary data can then be compared to patterns occurring in other archaeological contexts from the site, analyzed by Rothman in the main text.

Before looking at the trends occurring in the mortuary contexts at Tepe Gawra, some caveats must be offered. First, it seems highly unlikely that the 301 burials recovered from the Late Chalcolithic period strata represent the entire population that had lived and died at Tepe Gawra. The number of burials would certainly have been larger had all of the Late Chalcolithic levels been entirely excavated. Given the relatively small number of burials from Levels VIII to X, the levels which had been completely excavated, the burials from these levels must represent only a portion of the total Late Chalcolithic population. This is particularly true of Level X, because as Rothman writes in Chapter 5, the actual population size of Levels IX and VIII was small. I concur with Tobler (1950:121) that there must be another burial location somewhere off of the mound. This must certainly be the case for the periods post-dating Level VIII, since none of these levels (I–VII) contained any burials. If this is the case for the Late Chalcolithic burials, then it is quite possible that the total range of variation in burial types has not been recovered. Secondly, only a portion of Levels XI/XA and XIA/B were excavated. Therefore, there is also the possibility that data from these two levels are not entirely representative of the full range of mortuary practices that occurred during their occupation. However, the correlation between various aspects of mortuary practices and the presence of trends that continue into Levels VIII, IX, and X suggest that this may not be a real problem.

Horizontal Distribution of the Burials

There are 301 burials from the four stratigraphic units that make up the Early Uruk and Early Middle Uruk or LC 2-3 periods at Tepe Gawra. Each level displays different patterns in terms of the spatial distribution of the burials. These patterns are briefly discussed below.

Levels VIII/IX

There are 78 burials belonging to Levels VIII/IX (Figures A.13–A.20). These burials form two major

concentrations across the site. One concentration occurs on the eastern side of the mound within squares 5K, 5J, 6G, 6J, and 7J. All of these burials are relatively small. It seems likely that most of the burials in this concentration make up a single group associated with the structure consisting of rooms 801–804, the southeast temple, in Level VIII. However, several of the burials (Burials 005, 007, and 204) are crossed by the remnants of walls that belonged to a Level IX structure (room 937).

The second concentration occurs throughout the western half of the mound in squares 6M to 6Q, 7M to 7Q, 8M to 8Q, 9M to 9Q, 10K to 10Q, and 11K to 11M. The northwest half of this area contains mostly libn tomb burials. It is in this area that excavators unearthed the largest libn tombs. Most of the burials in the southwestern portion of this area tend to be relatively small and display a larger variation in burial

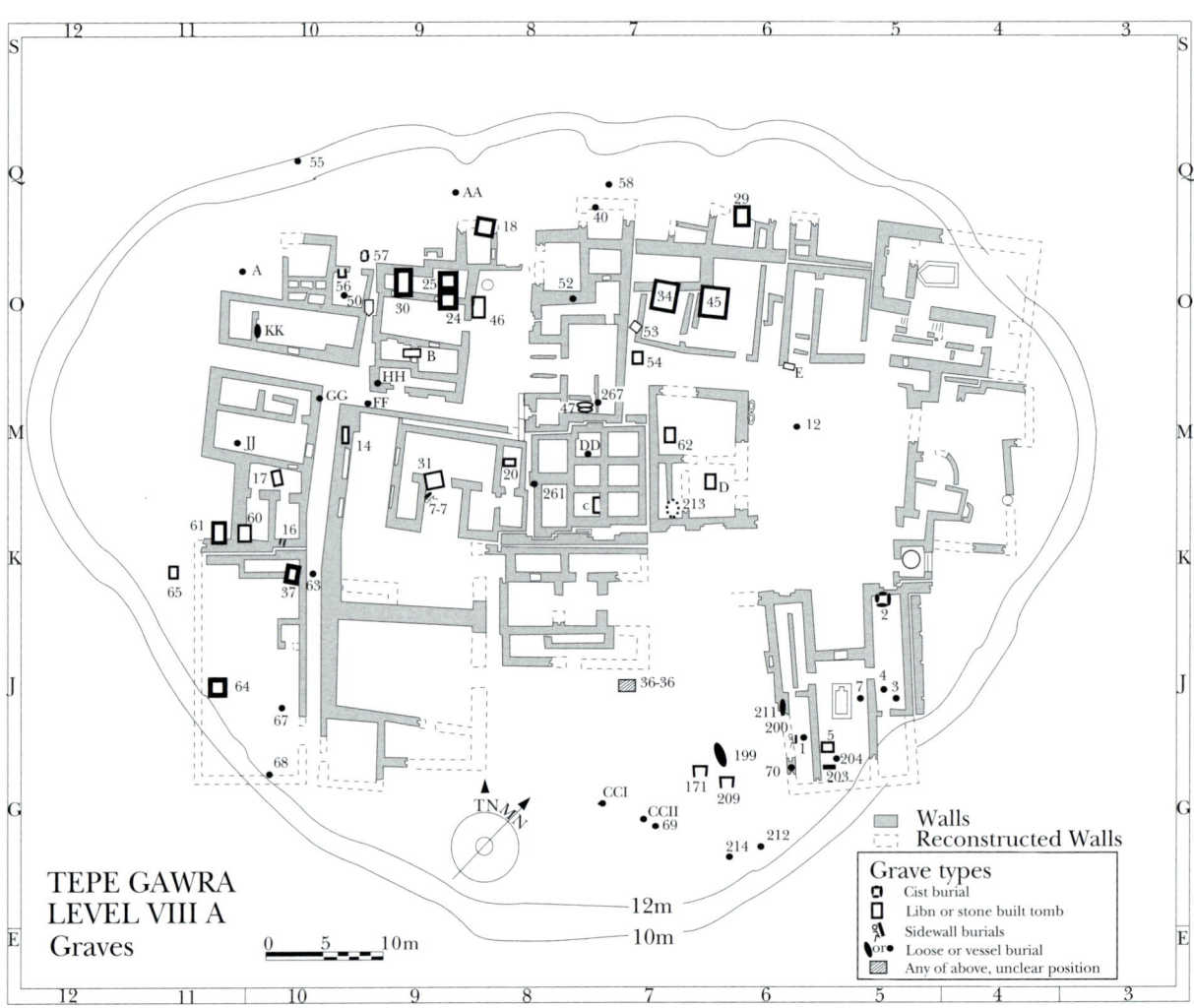

Figure A.13   Grave distribution, Phase VIIIA, Level VIII, Tepe Gawra (the maximum possible number of graves in this level).

Figure A.14   Grave distribution, Phase VIIIA, Level VIII, Tepe Gawra (the minimal possible number of graves in this level).

types. It seems likely that this concentration constitutes two different sub-groups with one group associated with the structure containing rooms 872–877 in Phases VIIIB and VIIIC, the western administrative building, and the other associated with the structure made up of rooms 900–904, the central temple, in Level IX.

Level X

There are 51 burials belonging to Level X (Figure A.21). These burials form three major concentrations across the site. The first concentration occurs on the northeast portion of the mound in squares 6M, 5K to 5O, and 4K to 4M. This concentration consists solely of the largest libn tombs arranged in two distinct groups. The first group is made up of Burials 109, 110, 111, and 114. The second group is located west of the first group and consists of Burials 102, 107, and 124.

The remaining two concentrations form two groups of burials distributed below the various buildings of Level X. One group is located throughout the northeast quarter of the mound, whereas the other is distributed throughout the western half of the site. The burials of these two groups tend to be relatively small and display a range of burial types.

Level XI/XA

There are 108 burials originating from Level XI/XA (Figures A.22 and A.23). No major concentrations or groupings can be discerned in this level, the burials being distributed throughout most of the excavated portions of the mound. Furthermore, the many finds of burials in the southwest half of the site from the "West Trench" indicate that interments may have been distributed across the whole site at this level.

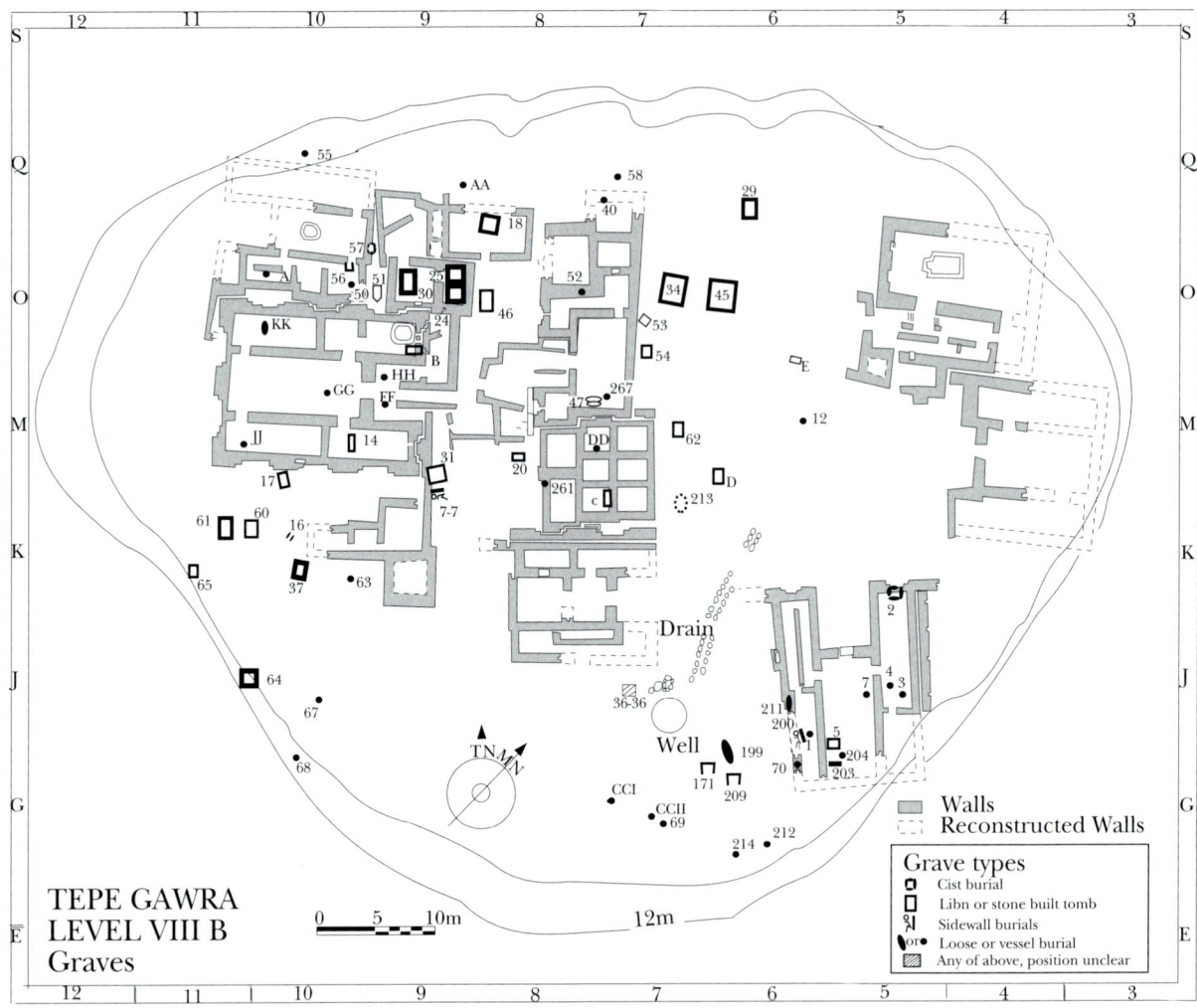

Figure A.15   Grave distribution, Phase VIIIB, Level VIII, Tepe Gawra (the maximum possible number of graves in this level).

Level XIA/B

There are 64 burials associated with Level XIA/B (Figures A.24 and A.25). These burials form two major groups. The first group occurs at the northwestern edge of the mound in squares 6S, 6Q, 5Q, and 4Q. The largest number of burials in this group (22 percent of all Level XIA/B burials) are found in square 5Q below the structure made up of rooms 71–76, a building with a potentially specialized productive or trade function (not a temple, see Chapter 5).

The second group of burials occurs in the northeast quarter of the mound in squares 6K, 5J, 5K, 5M, 4J, 4K, and 3M. The largest number of burials in this group (23 percent of all Level XIA/B burials) were located in square 5M below the structure consisting of rooms 89–104, a series of domiciles (see Chapter 5).

Another group of burials also occurs in this level from squares 6/7M, 8M, and 9M. Unlike the first two groups, this group is relatively minor, having only four burials. These burials appear to be associated with the Round House in Phase XIA.

Patterns in the Horizontal Distribution of Burials

With the exception of Level XI/XA, the burials in each level tend to be concentrated into various groups. However, the location and patterning of the burial groups changed from level to level. In a number of cases, it appears that these burial groups were associated with particular structures, some of which represented a religious or other special purpose. Thus, the clustering of burials into distinct groups may reflect a

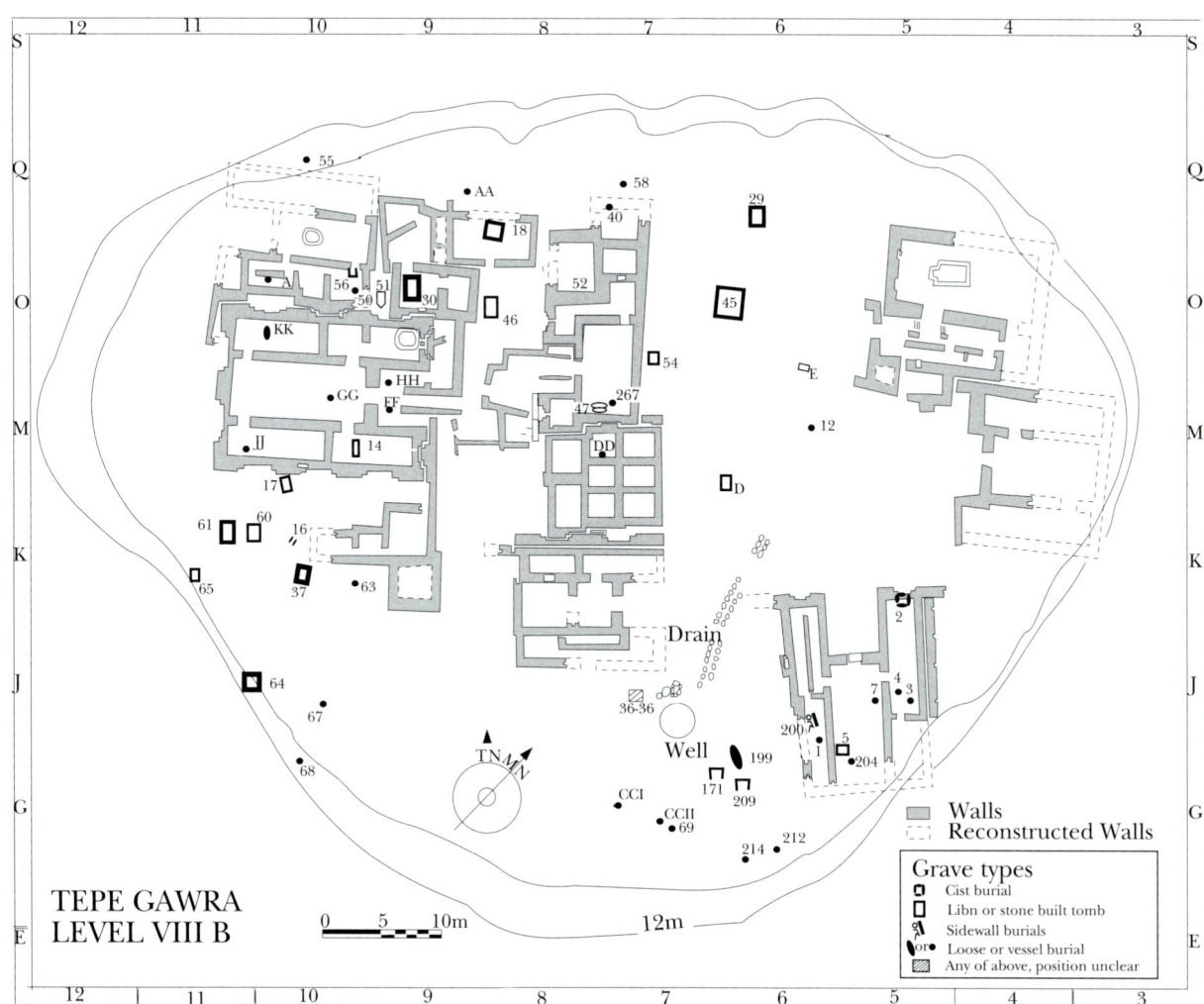

Figure A.16   Grave distribution, Phase VIIIB, Level VIII, Tepe Gawra (the minimal possible number of graves in this level).

particular focus upon these particular buildings in each level. The failure of any observable burial concentrations in Level XI/XA may be partly due to the decrease in the size of the horizontal exposure at this level.

Distribution of Burial Types

As mentioned in the overview to the catalogue, the 301 burials originating from Levels XIA/B to VIII at Tepe Gawra can be divided into six basic types: loose, vessel, sidewall, pisé, cist, and libn tomb burials. Of these burial types, loose, vessel, and libn tomb burials are the most frequent types, whereas sidewall, pisé, and cist burials are rare (see Table A.5 for the number of each burial type represented in

each level, Figure A.26 for the percentage of the totals for each burial type across strata, and Figure A.27 for the percentage of burial types within each stratum).

The overall distribution for each burial type (Figure A.26) was calculated by counting the total number of each type of burial for all four stratigraphic units (Table A.5). The number of each type in each level was then enumerated and expressed in terms of the percent of the total number of each burial type (Figure A.26). For example, there are 85 loose burials in Levels VIII to XIA/B. Of these, 17 (20 percent) originated from Levels VIII/IX, 17 (20 percent) originated from Level X, 36 (42 percent) originated from Level XI/XA, and 15 (18 percent) originated from Level XIA/B. The distribution of each type of burial is summarized below:

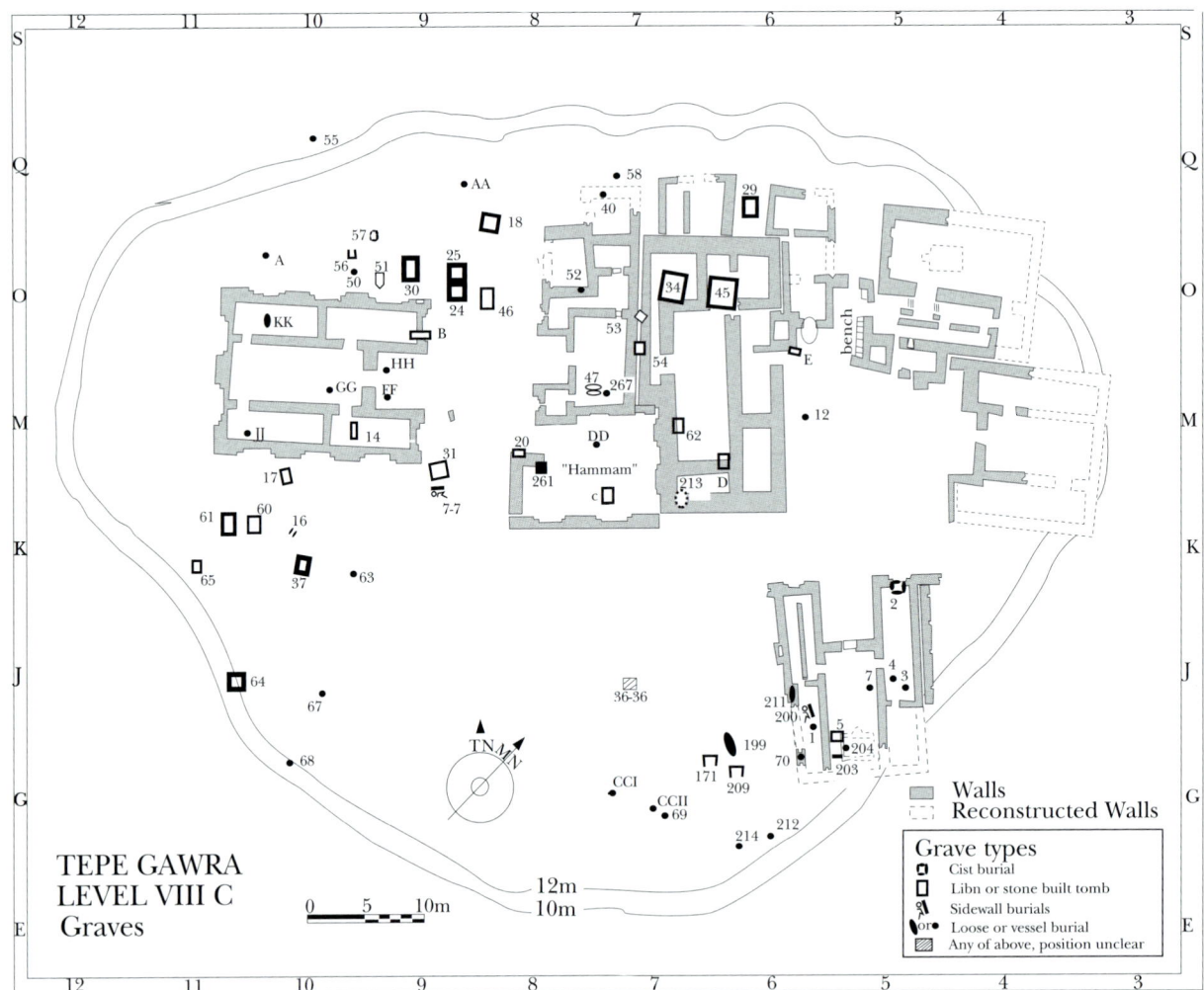

Figure A.17   Grave distribution, Phase VIIIC, Level VIII, Tepe Gawra (the maximum possible number of graves in this level).

Loose Burials

Excavators unearthed 85 loose interments for the four strata. The majority of this burial type originated from Level XI/XA with about 42 percent of all loose burials. The remainder of the loose burials are more or less evenly distributed among Levels VIII/IX, X, and XIA/B.

Vessel Burials

Excavators recovered 108 vessel burials for all four levels. The majority of vessel burials occur in burials originating from Levels XI/XA with 38 percent of all vessel burials and XIA/B with 32 percent of all

vessel burials. The smallest percentage is associated with Level X.

Sidewall Burials

The mound yielded 14 sidewall burials for all four strata. The greatest percentage, 43 percent of all sidewall burials originated from Level XI/XA. Level X had 29 percent of all sidewall burials, while Levels VIII/IX and XIA/B each had 14 percent.

Pisé Burials

Excavators found eight pisé burials for all four strata. Half of them originated from Level XI/XA.

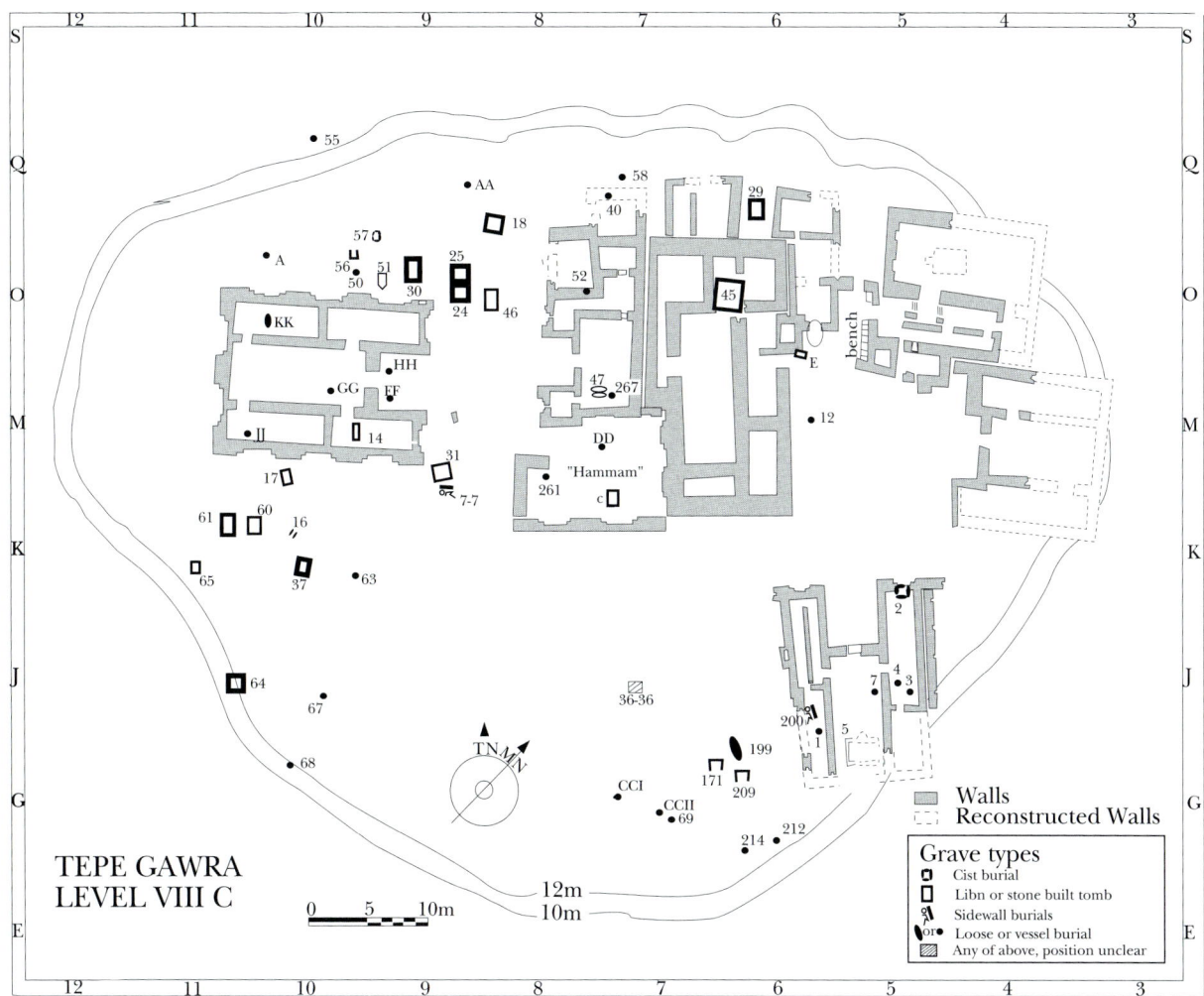

Figure A.18   Grave distribution, Phase VIIIC, Level VIII, Tepe Gawra (the minimal possible number of graves in this level).

The remaining pisé burials are evenly split among Levels X and XIA/B. There are no burials of this type associated with Levels VIII/IX.

Cist Burials

Excavators found eight cist burials from all strata analyzed. The majority of this burial type originated from Levels VIII/IX and X, each with three cist burials—38 percent for each level. Levels XI/XA and XIA/B each contained 1 cist burial or 12 percent for each level.

Libn Tomb Burials

There were 78 libn tomb burials total for all four strata. However, the actual number of tombs is only 69.

The reason for this discrepancy is that a number of libn tombs contained two or three individuals. Therefore, these statistics refer to the number of individuals interred in this type of burial rather than the number of libn tombs. The majority of this burial type originated from Levels VIII/IX, which had 43 percent of all libn tomb burials. The next highest percentage of this burial type originated in Level XI/XA with 26 percent. 18 percent of the libn tomb burials originated from Level X and 13 percent from Level XIA/B.

Patterns in the Distribution of Burial Types

By looking at the distribution of each individual burial type in four strata, patterns emerge that might

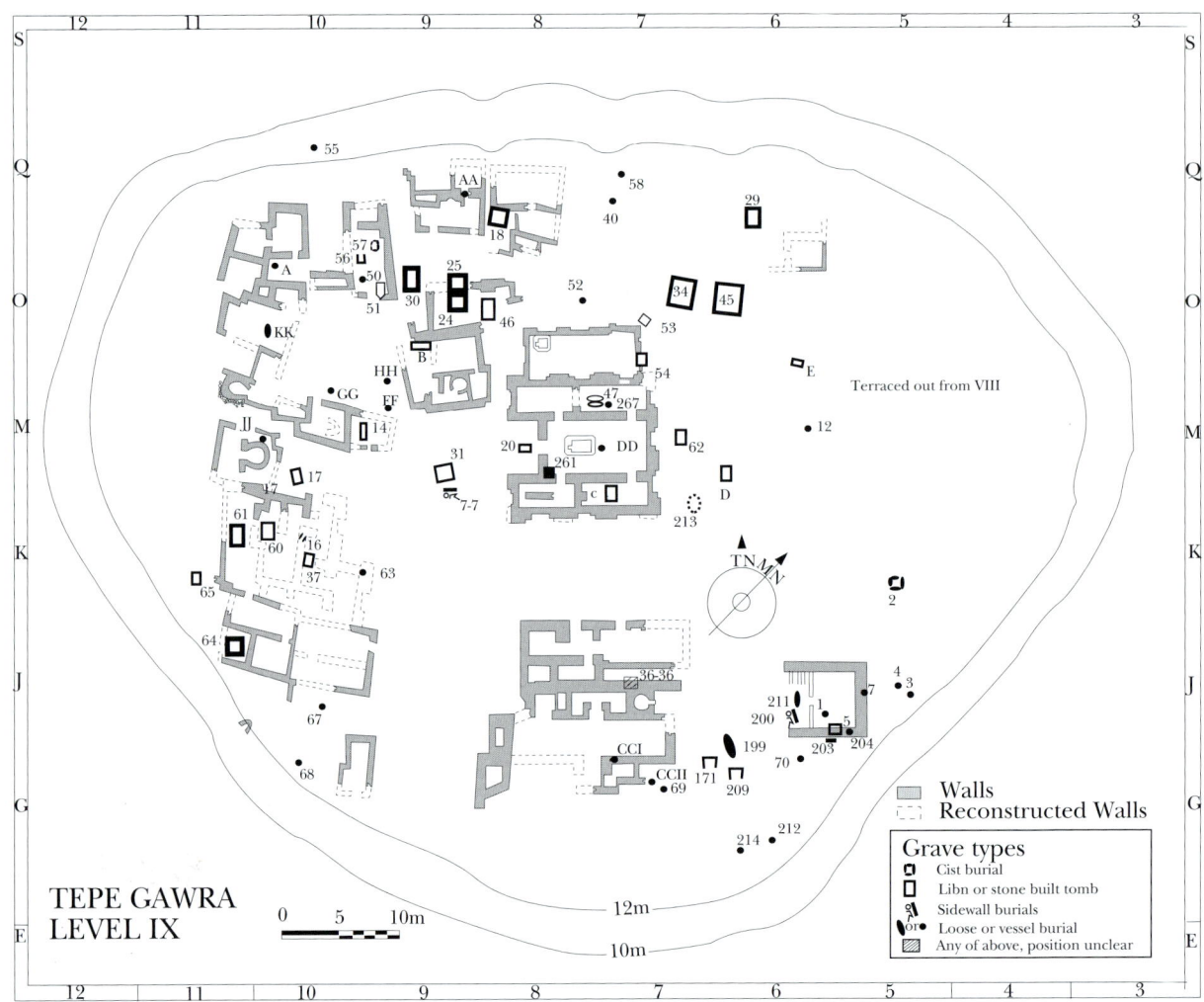

Figure A.19   Grave distribution, Level IX, Tepe Gawra (the maximum possible number of graves in this level).

explain the social ideas lying behind burial practice. The greatest number of burials is associated with Level XI/XA. However, the majority of the cist and libn tomb burials originated from Levels VIII/IX (Figure A.26), whereas a relatively small percentage of the libn tombs originated Level X (Figure A.26). This is especially interesting since there are more large libn tombs associated with Level X than with any other level. Cist burials are a small percentage of burials in any stratum.

The distribution of each burial type throughout the strata of Tepe Gawra reveals important trends concerning the point at which the various types were used most. However, the most important details concerning changing trends in the use of the various burial types over time are those involving a comparison of each burial type to all of the other types for each level (Figure A.27). The proportion of burial types in each level was calculated by counting the total number of burials in each level. Then, the number of each burial type

that originated from each level was counted and expressed in terms of a percentage. For example, there are 78 burials in Levels VIII/IX. Of these burials, three are cist burials (4 percent), 17 are loose burials (22 percent), two are sidewall burials (2 percent), 34 are libn tomb burials (44 percent), and 22 are vessel burials (28 percent). The proportion of burial types for each level is presented in Figure A.27.

For all levels, pisé, sidewall, and cist burials constitute the smallest proportion of the burial types. Furthermore, the percentage of these burial types in relation to the other types remains relatively constant over time with only a slight increase in the proportion of sidewall burials in Levels X and XI/XA and cist burials in Levels VIII/IX and X and the discontinued use of pisé burials in Levels VIII/IX. By comparison, loose, vessel, and libn tomb burials were by far the most numerous forms of burial throughout the Late Chalcolithic period at Tepe Gawra. The loose burials account

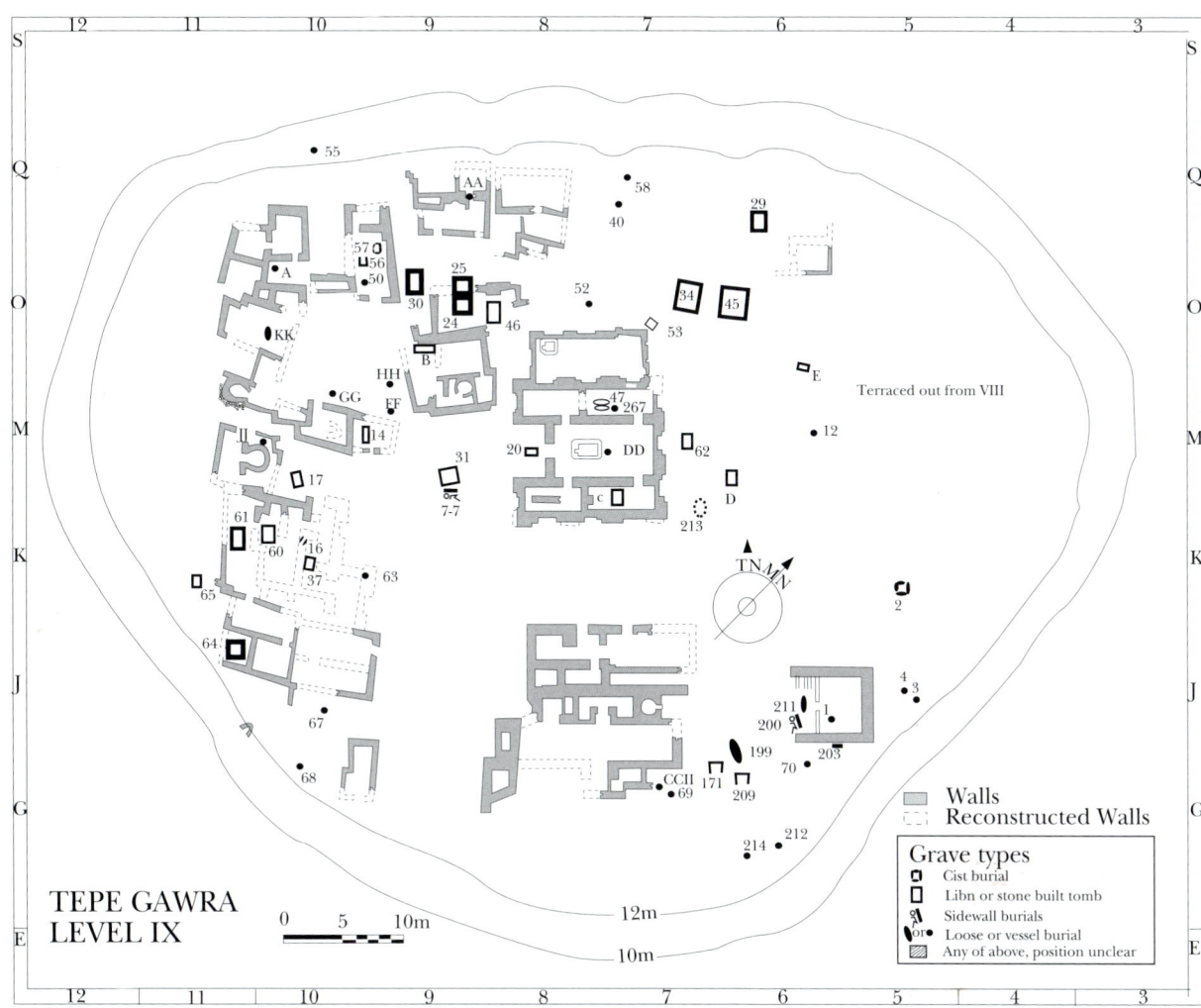

Figure A.20   Grave distribution, Level IX, Tepe Gawra (the minimal possible number of graves in this level).

for a little less than a quarter of the burial forms used during Level XIA/B. In Levels XI/XA and X, loose burials became somewhat more popular, accounting for one-third of the burials for these levels. During Levels VIII/IX, loose burials return to the same proportion as seen in Level XIA/B. Perhaps the most important trend can be seen in the differences between vessel burials and libn tomb burials throughout the four levels. Over time, vessel burials decrease in use from 53 percent of the total burial forms in Level XIA/B to 28 percent in Levels VIII/IX, while libn tomb burials increase over time from 16 percent in Level XIA/B to 44 percent in Levels VIII/IX. By Levels VIII/IX, more individuals, including a larger number of children and infants, are being buried in libn tombs. However, by this level, there is also a greater range in the size and quality of the libn tombs.

In the earlier levels, the limited use of this burial type may reflect limited access to this type of treatment based on people's status differences. Fewer people qualified for this type of interment. The later increase in the proportion of libn tombs may reflect the extension of the use of this burial type to a greater range of individuals as new ways of displaying status fit new, more hierarchical social identities. Alternatively, it may reflect a change in the overall status or functions of the site or of the people occupying the mound in later times. As Rothman points out above, the population of Levels VIII and IX was lower than in earlier levels and the proportion of buildings that represent specialized functions increased.

Relationship Between Relative Age Categories and Burial Types

Other important trends can be observed by comparing the relationships between the various burial

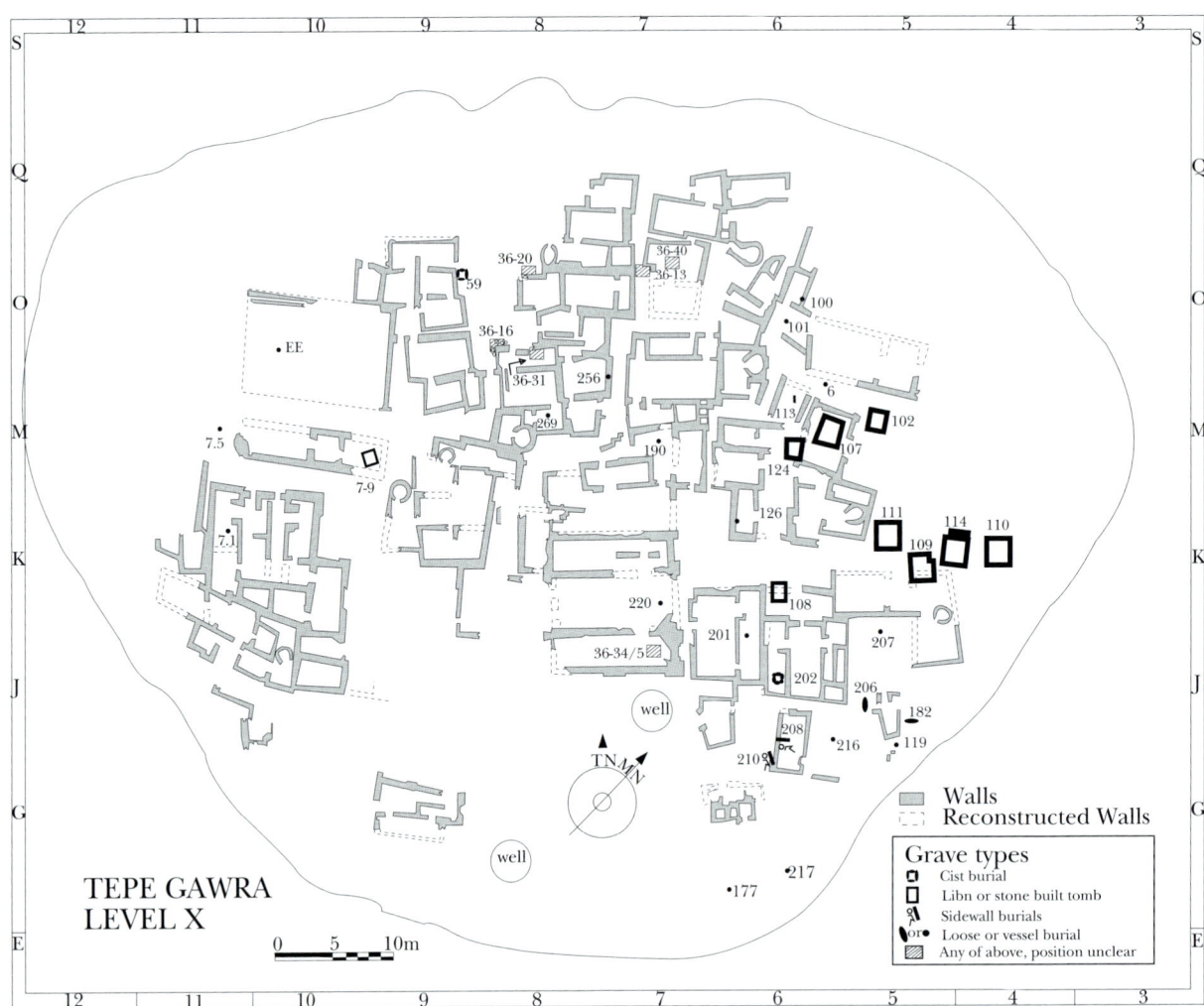

Figure A.21   Grave distribution, Level X, Tepe Gawra.

types and the relative age groups associated with them. Two major issues are involved in these relationships. The first entails the way in which each of the burial types was used. The second involves how each of the relative age categories was treated in terms of mortuary practices.

On the basis of the field notes, five relative age categories were defined: infants, infants/children, children, youths, and adults. The category of infant/child is based on the indecision as to whether an individual was a child or an infant in some of the field notes and on the fact that many of these are referred to elsewhere as "tots." When each relative age category is compared to the other age categories in each level, we see that the proportion of each age category is not entirely consistent from level to level (Figure A.28), although they are distributed within a narrow range.

To some extent, the inconsistencies in the proportion of each age group relative to the other age groups may be a result of the intermediate categories of youth and infant/child. Both of these categories refer to the point in an individual's life where quick growth occurs. For the individuals in these two categories, it is difficult to make a distinction when a person is no longer a toddler but a child, or no longer an adolescent but an adult. There is a good chance that these two age categories are actually mixed categories with "youth" consisting of older children and younger adults, and "child/infant" consisting of infants and children. This is further suggested by the inconsistent results given for these two categories in the analysis of how the burial types were used and the analysis of the association of the age groups with the various burial types (Tables A.6 and A.7). For this reason, the statistics for all five age groups will be given in the tables and graphs, but discussion will concern only the three primary age categories of adult, child, and infant.

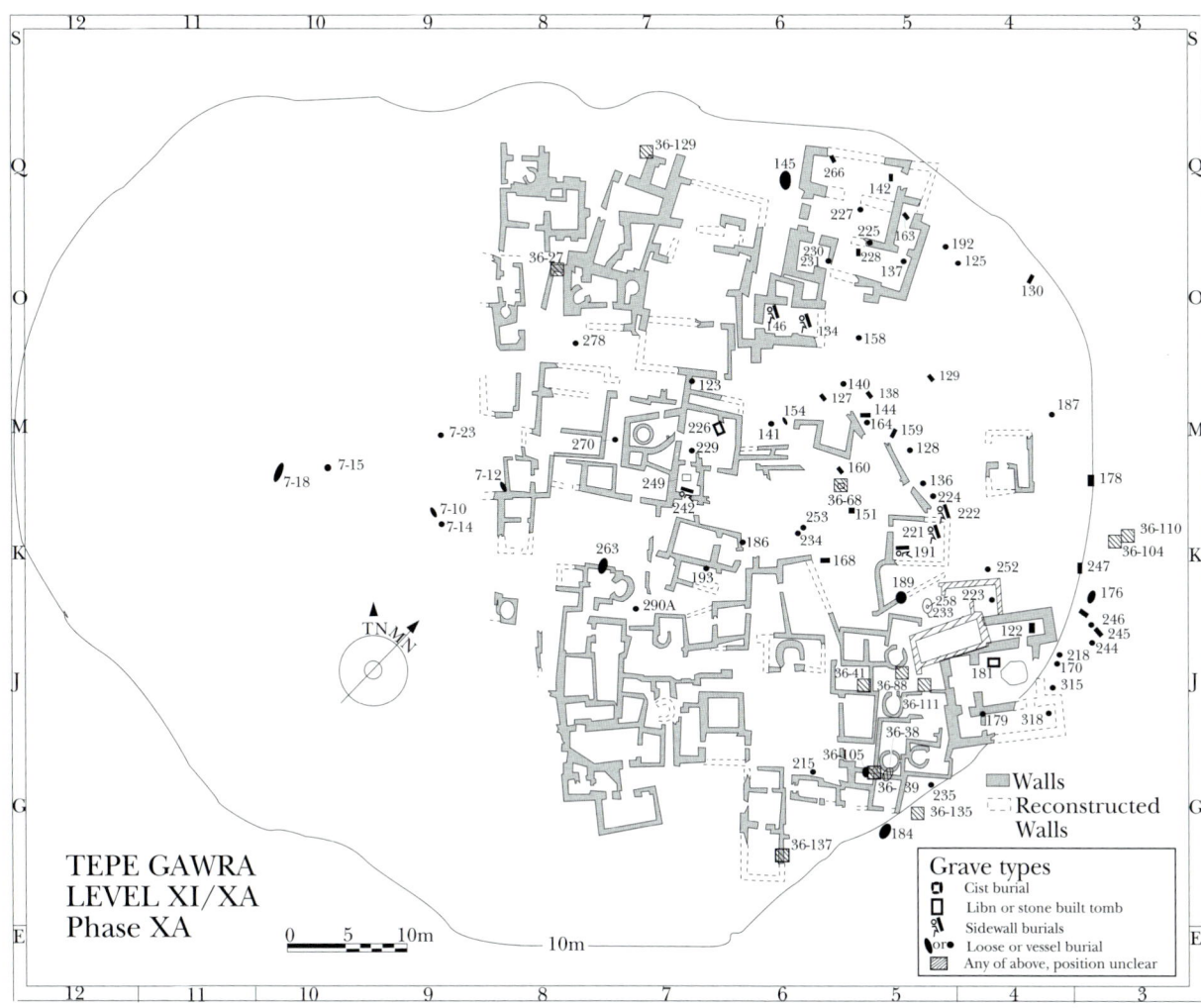

Figure A.22   Grave distribution, Phase XA, Level XI/XA, Tepe Gawra.

The way in which the burial types were used was calculated by counting the number of each burial type in each of the four stratigraphic units and then counting the number of occurrences of each relative age group for the various burial types. For example, 36 loose burials originated from Levels VIII/IX. Of these, there are 3 adults, 3 youths, 14 children, 1 infant/child, and 15 infants. These were then converted into percentages and are presented in Table A.6 and A.7 and in Figures A.29–A.32. A number of trends concerning changes in the use of burial types over time occur.

Loose Burials

The use of loose burials appears to be somewhat variable from level to level (Table A.6, Figures A.29–A.31). However, in all but Level XI/XA, this type of burial was

used mostly for children, followed by the incidence of use for infants. In Level XI/XA, this burial type was used mostly for infants. In addition, a sizable number of loose burials were used for adults in all four strata.

Vessel Burials

Vessel burials were used primarily for infants and children (Table A.6, Figures A.29–A.31). Vessel burial for infants was the largest group. Relatively few vessel burials were used for adults, and then only in Levels XI/XA and XIA/B.

Sidewall Burials

In Level XIA/B, sidewall burials were used only for adults (Table A.6, Figure A.29–31). By Level XI/XA, adults are no longer buried in sidewall tombs, and the

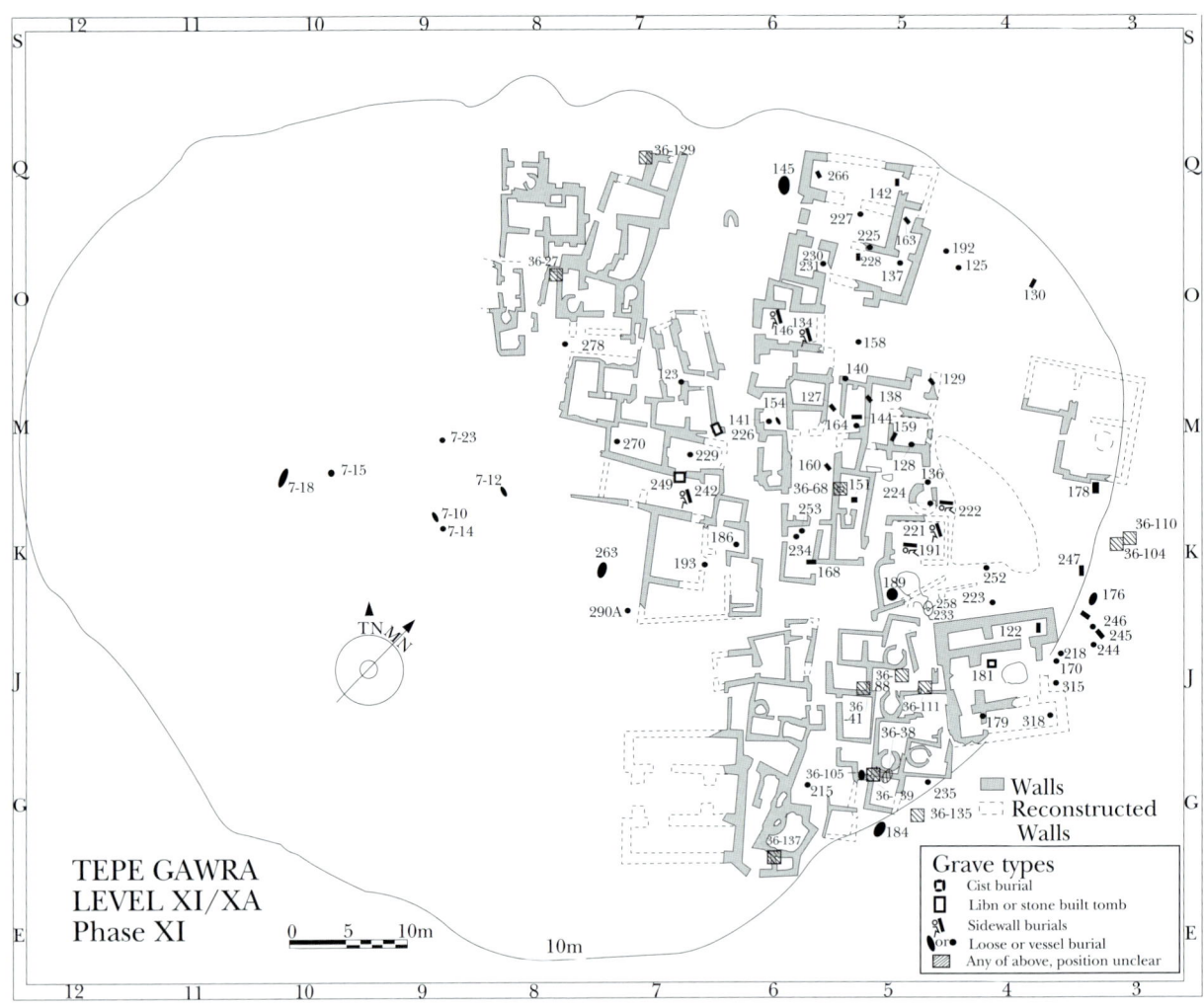

Figure A.23.   Grave distribution, Phase XI, Level XI/XA, Tepe Gawra.

use of this burial type was extended to children and infants.

Pisé Burials

Like sidewall burials, pisé burials were used only for adults in Level XIA/B (Table A.6, Figures A.29–A.32). Beginning with Level XI/XA, the use of pisé tombs for adults decreased, and children were buried in this type. By Level X children were the only age group for which this burial type was utilized. By Levels VIII/IX, this burial type was no longer in use at all.

Cist Burials

Throughout all four stratigraphic units, cist burials were used only to inter children (Table A.6, Figures A.29–A.31).

Libn Tombs

Libn tombs were used for all three major age categories throughout the four stratigraphic units (Table A.6, Figures A.29–A.32). However, in Level XIA/B, the majority of libn tombs were used for adults.

The major trend through time in respect to this burial type is toward an equal proportion in the use of libn tombs for all three age groups. This entails a decreasing percentage of libn tombs used for adults and an increasing percentage used for both children and infants. For the most part this trend is evident in Table A.6. The major exception to this trend was in Level XI/XA, during whose occupation a greater percentage of children were buried in libn tomb than were adults. This level is somewhat problematic, since there are more libn tombs for those whose relative age fits the category of uncertain age than those whose age is known. Therefore, the relatively high

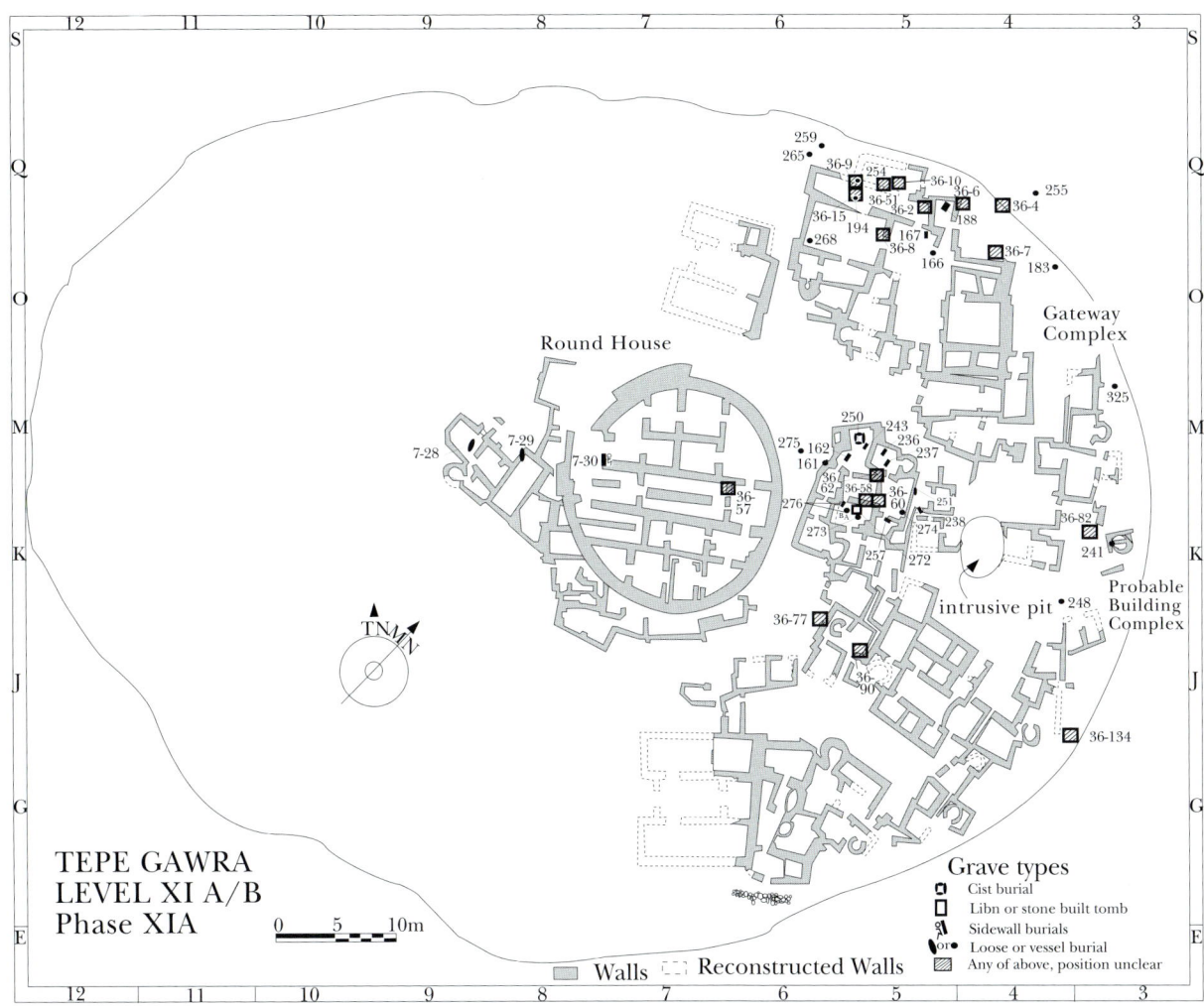

Figure A.24   Grave distribution, Phase XIA, Level XIA/B, Tepe Gawra.

percentage of child and infant libn tombs and the low percentage of adult libn tombs cannot be determined accurately.

Patterns in the Relationship Between Age and Burial Type

The major changes in terms of the uses of the burial types involve primarily the sidewall, pisé, and libn tomb types. It is likely that in Level XIA/B sidewall and pisé burials were reserved for individuals of a particular status, however that status position was assigned. Infants and children who were buried in tombs may have been of high status, because the amount of labor required for tomb construction would have been greater than that required for the construction of sidewall and pisé burials. Therefore, sidewall and pisé burials may have indicated a lower ranking position for adults than tombs and a higher status position than loose or vessel burials. For the group with this status, its younger members may have been interred in either vessels or loose burials.

The extension of sidewall and pisé burials to younger age groups and the decrease in the use of these burial types for adults in Level XI/XA occurs at the point in which a greater number of adults are buried in libn tombs (Table A.6). At the same time, the percentage of libn tombs used for adults declined. This apparent contradiction was the result of a general increase in the use of libn tombs for all three major age groups. Therefore, although a greater number of adults were buried in libn tombs, more libn tombs were also used for infant and child burials. This resulted in a decrease in the percentage of libn tombs used for adults and an increase in the percentage used for children and infants.

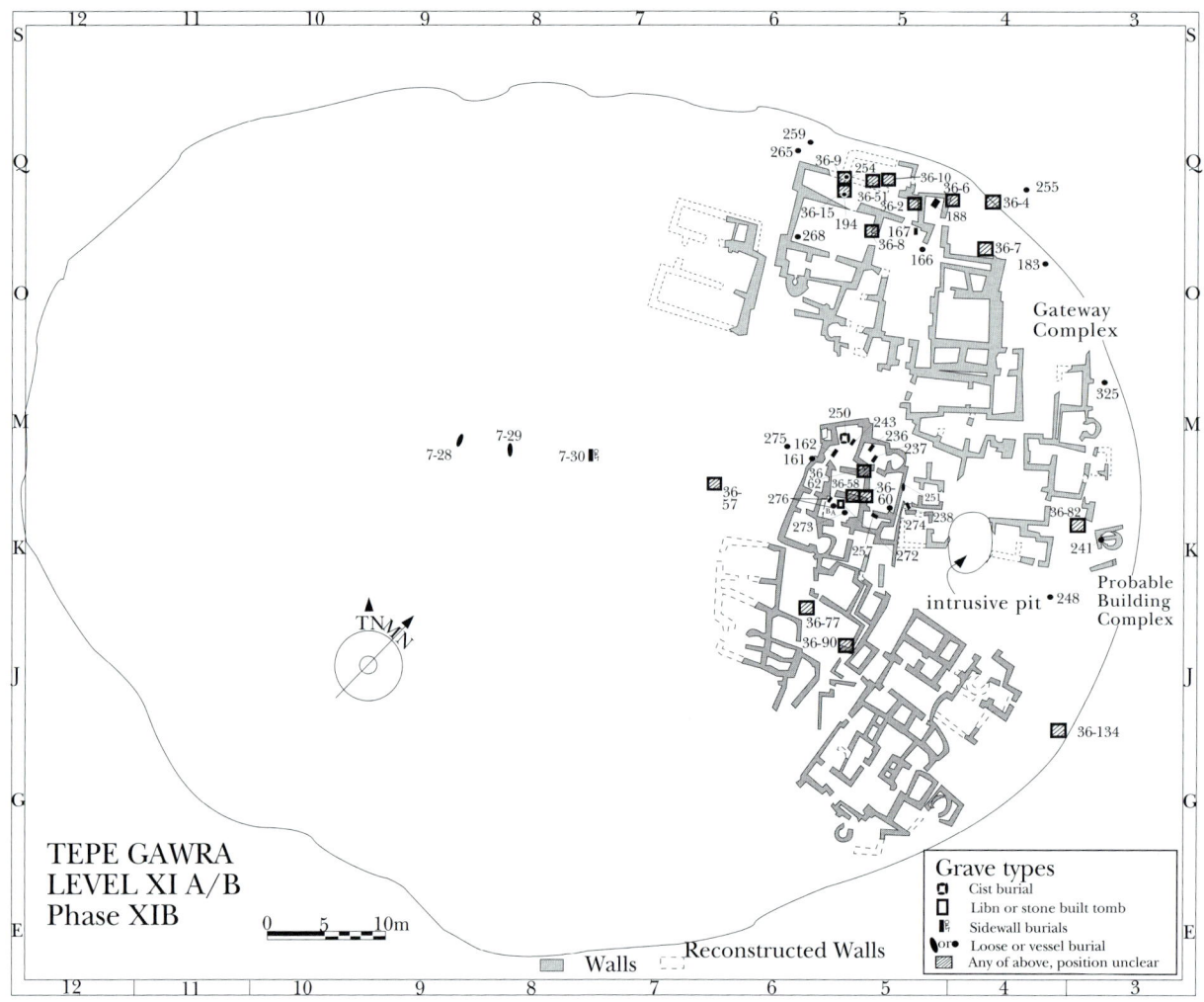

Figure A.25   Grave distribution, Phase XIB, Level XIA/B, Tepe Gawra.

These shifts occur at the same time that there are increasing differences in the use of burial goods among burials in general (see below). It seems likely that, as new ways of signifying status became available, the older symbols of status became available to members of lower ranking groups. This may also explain the similar proportion of libn tombs used by all three age groups in Levels VIII/IX as material symbols of

prestige became more important for indicating the status of the deceased.

Treatment by Relative Age Group

By looking at the relationship among burial types and the relative age categories in a slightly different

Table A.5   Number of Each Burial Types, VIII/IX to XIA/B.

Levels	Libn Tomb	Pisé	Cist	Side-wall	Vessel	Loose	Total
VIII/IX	34	0	3	2	22	17	78
X	14	2	3	4	11	17	51
XI/XA	20	4	1	6	41	36	108
XIAB	10	2	1	2	34	15	64
Total	78	8	8	14	108	85	301

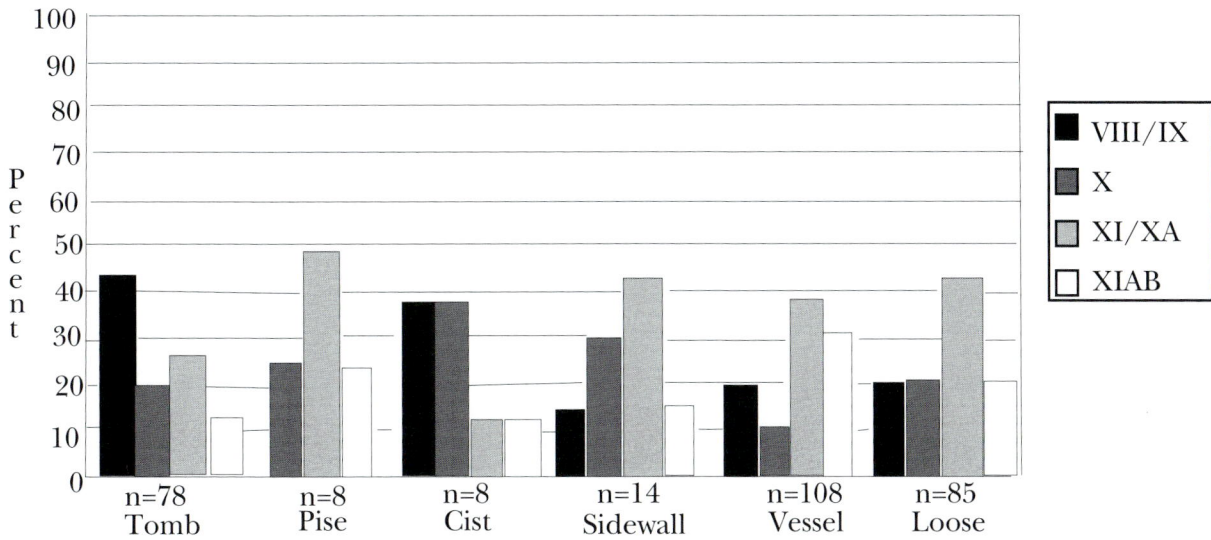

Figure A.26   Histogram of the distribution of burial types, Tepe Gawra.

way, other trends in the mortuary practices at Tepe Gawra can be discovered. In this case, we are interested in changes concerning the treatment of individuals according to their relative ages. In other words, who is buried where? In order to observe these changes, the number of individuals for each age group was counted for each level, followed by the number of individuals from each age group occurring in the various burial types. For example, there are 11 adults in Levels VIII/IX. Of these, two were interred in loose burials and 9 in libn tombs. These were then converted into percentages and are presented in Table A.7. The trends concerning the

change in treatment of the relative age groups are summarized below.

Adults

A major change in the way adults are treated occurs in Level X. In the lower levels, adults were interred in all burial types with the exception of cist graves, which were used only for children. By Level X adult burials are limited to loose and libn tomb burials. Furthermore, a much larger percentage of the adults in Level X are buried in libn tombs than in either Level XIA/B or Level XI/XA.

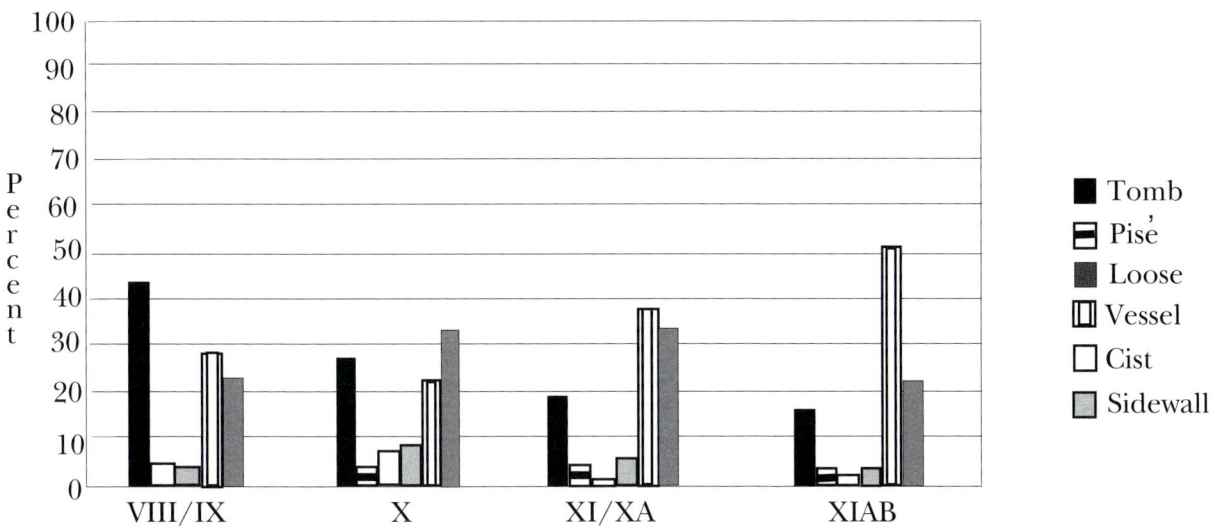

Figure A.27   Histogram of the changes in percentage of burial types through time, Tepe Gawra.

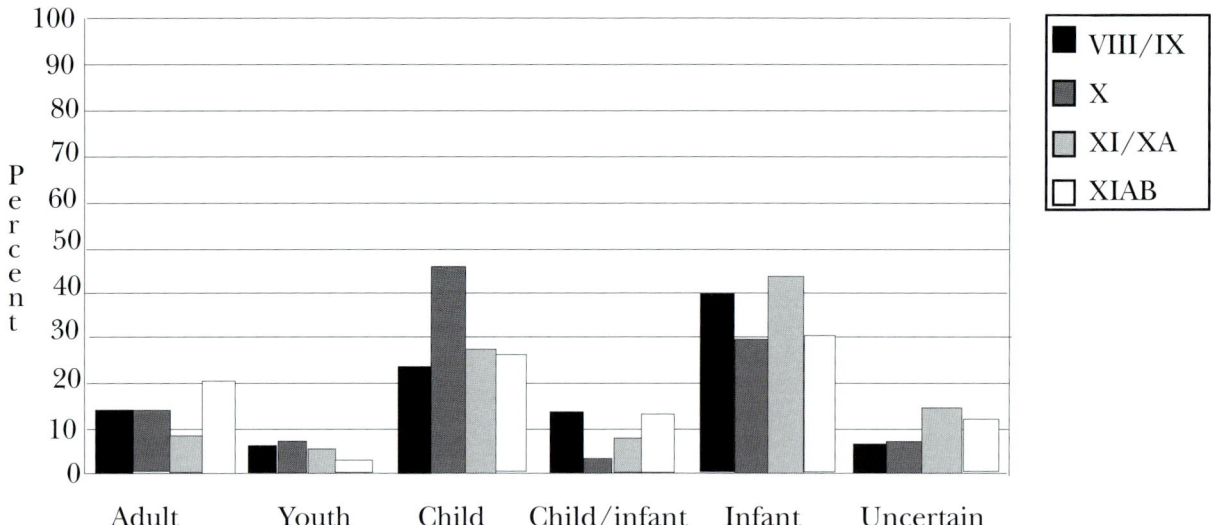

Figure A.28   Histogram of the changes of relative age categories through time, Tepe Gawra.

Children

We begin to see a small change in the way children are treated in Level X. A smaller percentage of children were interred in loose burials and more buried in cist graves. However, a major change occurs between Levels X and VIII/IX. At that time a large increase in the percentage of children buried in libn tomb occurred. Throughout all four strata children are buried in cist burials.

Infants

Changes in the treatment of infants over time are a bit more complex than the changes for adults and children. The first change occurred between Levels XIA/B and XI/XA with a decrease in the percentage of infants interred in vessel burials. Throughout Levels XI/XA and X, the percentages remain relatively stable. Another change occurs between Levels X and VIII/IX with a significant increase in the percentage of infants buried in libn tombs.

Patterns in the Treatment of the Relative Age Groups

The most noticeable change involves the libn tombs. There was a large jump in the percentages of adults who were buried this way in Level X. This increase was followed by an increase in the percentages of children and infants buried in libn tombs in Levels VIII/IX. These changes occur at a point in time when a greater range in the sizes of libn tombs is evident and when a small number of these tombs display a much greater variety of burial goods (see Burial Goods and the Analysis of Status below). Again, this suggests that a change in the way prestige was displayed paralleled changes in the treatment of the various age groups measured by the percentage of burial types utilized.

Tomb Size

Another important change that occurred over time involves the size of the enclosed burials (pisé, cist, and libn tomb burials). For the purpose of analysis, tomb size was calculated in terms of the inside area of each of the enclosed burial types (Table A.8). The inside area was used, because in many cases no details concerning the outside measurements of the tombs were recorded. In addition, several tomb measurements were missing, making it impossible to calculate tomb size for some enclosed burials. In most cases, there were only a small number of tombs without measurement data, and many of these were probably small burials, judging from the burial sheets. However, for Level XI/XA there were six tombs whose size could not be calculated. This may account for the relatively small mean displayed for this level.

After the area was calculated for each enclosed burial, the mean and median areas were calculated for each stratum. The overall mean area was also calculated for the enclosed burials from all four levels. This came out to .77 m^2. The levels were then compared to each other in terms of their respective means and medians. Each stratum was compared in terms of the percentage of enclosed burials that lay above and below the overall mean of .77 square meters (Figure A.34). The levels were then graphed according to both the number and percentage of enclosed burials at each square meter

Table A.6   Percentage of Each Type of Burial Used by Age Groups.

	Adult	Youth	Child	Child/Inf	Infant
Loose					
VIII/IX	11.8	11.8	23.5	29.4	23.5
X	6.7	0.0	60.0	6.7	26.6
XI/XA	8.3	8.3	38.9	2.8	41.7
XIAB	15.0	5.0	35.0	35.0	10.0
Vessel					
VIII/IX	0.0	0.0	4.5	18.2	77.3
X	0.0	0.0	18.2	0.0	81.8
XI/XA	2.6	0.0	10.3	15.4	71.7
XIAB	8.3	0.0	29.2	0.0	62.5
Sidewall					
VIII/IX	0.0	0.0	50.0	0.0	50.0
X	0.0	0.0	100.0	0.0	0.0
XI/XA	0.0	16.7	66.6	0.0	16.7
XIAB	100.0	0.0	0.0	0.0	0.0
Pisé					
VIII/IX	0.0	0.0	0.0	0.0	0.0
X	0.0	0.0	100.0	0.0	0.0
XI/XA	25.0	25.0	50.0	0.0	0.0
XIAB	100.0	0.0	0.0	0.0	0.0
Cist					
VIII/IX	0.0	0.0	100.0	0.0	0.0
X	0.0	0.0	100.0	0.0	0.0
XI/XA	0.0	0.0	100.0	0.0	0.0
XIAB	0.0	0.0	100.0	0.0	0.0
Libn					
VIII/IX	30.0	6.7	30.0	3.3	30.0
X	46.2	23.1	23.1	0.0	7.6
XI/XA	33.3	0.0	44.4	0.0	22.3
XIAB	50.0	0.0	12.5	12.5	25.0

interval from 0 to 4 square meters (Figures A.35 and A.36). Finally, the range in tomb area was calculated for each level by subtracting the area of the smallest tomb from the area of the largest tomb.

For strata VIII/IX, X, and XI/XA, the percentage of enclosed burials above each level's mean is relatively constant, ranging from 32 percent to 35 percent. For Level XIA/B, the mean and the median are almost identical and so 50 percent of the tombs are above the mean for this level. A major change in tomb size occurs in Level X (Figures A.33–A.36 and Table A.8). The area of the enclosed burials increased dramatically at this point as a comparison of its mean of 1.26 m^2 with the means of Level XI/XA (.42 m^2) and Level XIA/B (.51 m^2) demonstrates. The occurrence of larger tombs continued into Levels VIII/IX, although with a lower mean tomb size of .82 m^2. This abrupt change between Level X and those levels underlying it is also documented by the ranges between

the smaller and larger tombs for each level. In Levels XIA/B and XI/XA, the ranges are .39 m^2 and 1.13 m^2 respectively. In Level X, this range suddenly jumps to 3.08 m^2, more than twice the range size in Level XI/XA. This range increases further in Levels VIII/IX to 3.16 m^2. Comparing each of the levels in terms of the percentages of tombs that lay above and below the total mean area for all four strata can also illustrate this change. In this case, all of the enclosed burials in Level XIA/B and about 95 percent of the burials in Level XI/XA lie below this overall mean. From Level XI/XA to Level X, the percentage of enclosed burials rises above the overall mean from about 5 percent to 53 percent.

The largest of all the enclosed burials (Burial 045) originated from Levels VIII/IX with an area of 3.3 m^2. However, the largest burials overall and the largest number of large burials occurs in Level X. This is very apparent no matter what statistic is used: mean,

Table A.7   Percentage of Each Relative Age Buried in Each Type of Burial.

	Libn Tomb	Cist	Pise	Sidewall	Vessel	Loose
Adults						
VIII/IX	81.8	0.0	0.0	0.0	0.0	18.2
X	85.7	0.0	0.0	0.0	0.0	14.3
XI/XA	37.5	0.0	12.5	0.0	12.5	37.5
XIAB	30.7	0.0	15.4	15.4	15.4	23.1
Youths						
VIII/IX	50.0	0.0	0.0	0.0	0.0	50.0
X	100.0	0.0	0.0	0.0	0.0	0.0
XI/XA	0.0	0.0	20.0	20.0	0.0	60.0
XIAB	0.0	0.0	0.0	0.0	0.0	100.0
Children						
VIII/IX	50.0	16.7	0.0	5.5	5.5	22.3
X	13.0	13.0	8.7	17.4	8.7	39.2
XI/XA	13.8	3.4	6.9	13.8	13.8	48.3
XIAB	6.3	6.3	0.0	0.0	43.7	43.7
Children/Infants						
VIII/IX	10.0	0.0	0.0	0.0	40.0	50.0
X	0.0	0.0	0.0	0.0	0.0	100.0
XI/XA	0.0	0.0	0.0	0.0	85.7	14.3
XIAB	12.5	0.0	0.0	0.0	0.0	87.5
Infants						
VIII/IX	29.0	0.0	0.0	3.3	54.8	12.9
X	7.1	0.0	0.0	0.0	64.3	28.6
XI/XA	4.3	0.0	0.0	2.2	60.9	32.6
XIAB	10.5	0.0	0.0	0.0	79.0	10.5

median, percentage above overall mean, percentage of enclosed burials appearing in the 2–4 m^2 range, or raw numbers of enclosed burials in the 2–4 m^2 range. This is even more interesting, because there were many fewer enclosed burials in general and fewer libn tombs in particular in Level X, compared with Levels VIII/IX. This dramatic increase in tomb size co-occurred with the changes in the use of different burial types for individual age groups, described above.

Burial Orientation

Important differences between burials can often be seen in the way the burials are oriented. Orientation is often expressed in one of two ways, both of which often occur together. First, the body may be oriented towards a particular direction such as south and north. Second, individuals may be consistently laid on either their right or left sides. At times, when the orientation of the body is an important part of the mortuary practice, the rules for orientation may become complex (Tainter 1978:108). For instance, important individuals may be oriented to face an important structure in the community. Working out the

orientation in such cases is more difficult. However, in those cases where orientation was an important aspect of burial ritual, there should be some recognizable pattern that can be found if one looks hard enough for it. In terms of the burials at Tepe Gawra, few such patterns are observable (Table A.9).

Generally, the lack of observable patterns in orientation may be a reflection of differences in the quality of field recording from season to season and from excavator to excavator. In many cases, the orientation of the burial is not recorded in the field notes. In cases where explicit information about orientation was missing, but sketches or photos were available, the orientation could be worked out. In other cases, only partial information was recorded. If enough data were available, the missing information could be reconstructed. For example, a particular burial sheet might mention that the individual's head was at the southeast, and his feet were at the northwest and that he was facing southwest, but give no detail about the side on which the corpse lay. Extrapolating from the known to the unknown in this case, one can discover that the person must have been laid on his left side. Although many of the omissions in orientation were corrected for, many others lacked this information. The presence of so

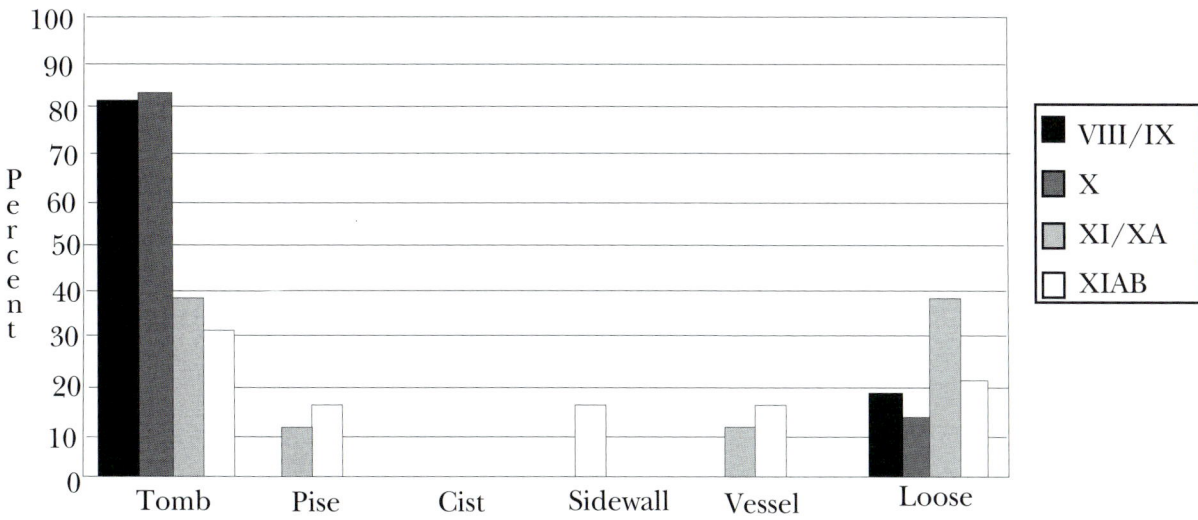

Figure A.29   Histogram of the distribution of burial types among adults, Tepe Gawra.

many gaps in this part of the data may mask whatever patterns had existed.

Another problem concerns the presence of inconsistencies in the orientation data that are available. One excavator in particular seems to have been slightly dyslexic. He consistently confused right and left. At times, someone else caught these mistakes, and some sort of insulting note would be appended to the burial sheet. Too often, however, this mistake went unnoticed. Again, where there was enough data, these errors could be corrected. For this reason, all burial orientation was examined in terms of its internal consistency and, where necessary, corrections were made.

To make these problems even more complicated, there was a tendency to use both magnetic north and grid north without identifying which orientation system was being used. Where possible this was corrected for by using magnetic north as the reference (all compass directions in this appendix are based on magnetic north). It may be for this reason that there are few northwest to southeast or northeast to southwest-oriented burials in Level XIA/B. Unfortunately, Speiser's crew did not draw many sketch illustrations of the burials, nor did they attempt to pinpoint the burials accurately on site plans. Thus, it is impossible to check these burials for accuracy. Because of this, Tobler's (1950:77) suggestion that a change in mortuary

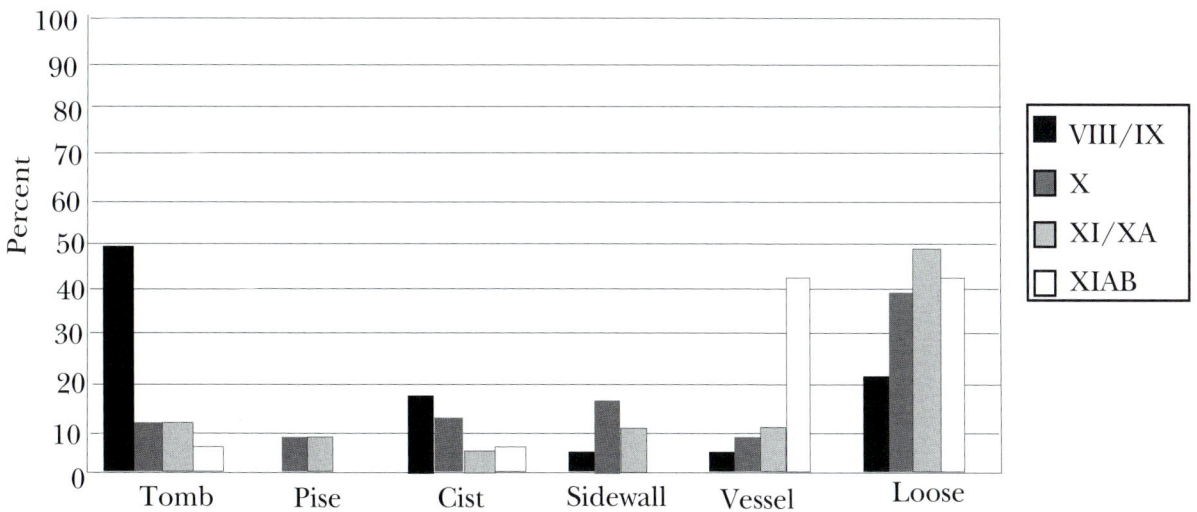

Figure A.30   Histogram of the distribution of burial types among children, Tepe Gawra.

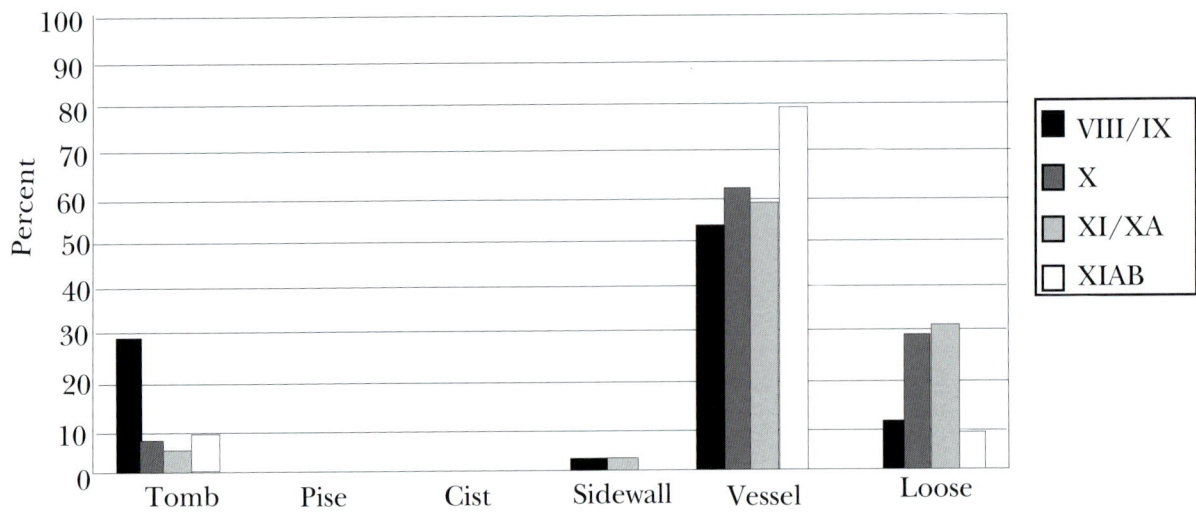

Figure A.31   Histogram of the distribution of burial types among infants, Tepe Gawra.

ritual had occurred in "Level" XA on the basis of the change in the orientation of libn tombs from a north-south orientation to a northwest-southeast orientation is not reliable.

In attempting to locate patterns of orientation, the data were entered onto a spread sheet and sorted according to criteria such as age, burial type, burial size, location and so on. Very few significant patterns emerged. Overall, a northwest-southeast orientation prevailed, although a northeast-southwest orientation was also common. Less common for Levels VIII/IX and Level X is a north-south or east-west orientation. In Levels XI/XA and XIA/B, most burials were oriented either north-south or east-west. However, as

mentioned above, the orientation data for these levels may be unreliable. In terms of whether the body was laid on the right or left side, both seem to have been equally customary for all levels.

The only real pattern that emerged was in relation to the largest enclosed burials for each level (Table A.9). Those in strata VIII/IX and X were all oriented northwest-southeast (with either the head or the feet at the northwest), and all but one corpse was laid on the left side. In Level XI/XA, the largest enclosed burials were oriented either northwest-southeast or north-south, and all those bodies were left-sided burials. In Level XIA/B, all the largest enclosed burials were recorded as being oriented south-north and all

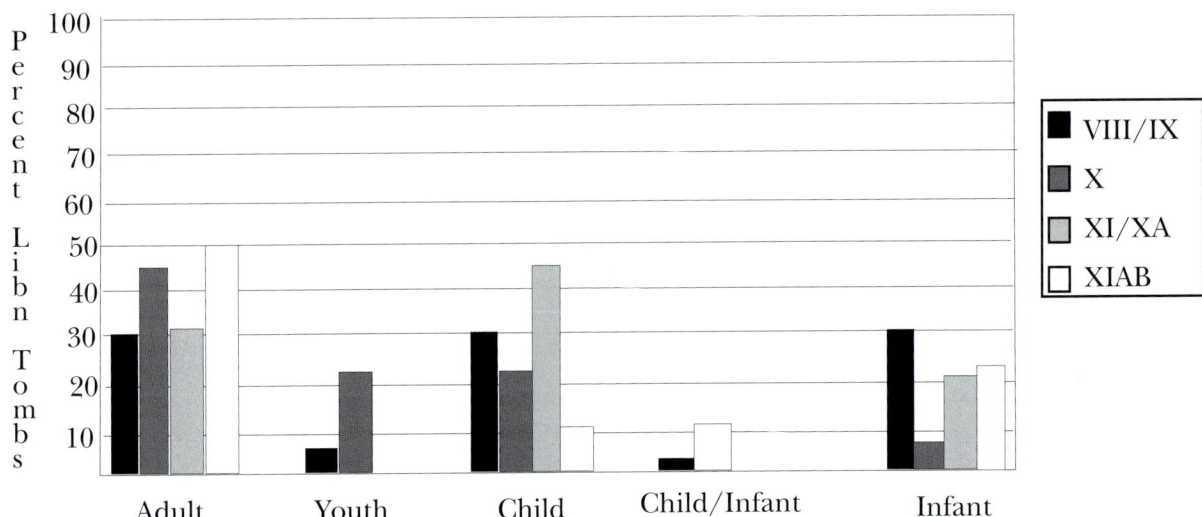

Figure A.32   Histogram of the changes in the percentage of libn tombs for each age group, Tepe Gawra.

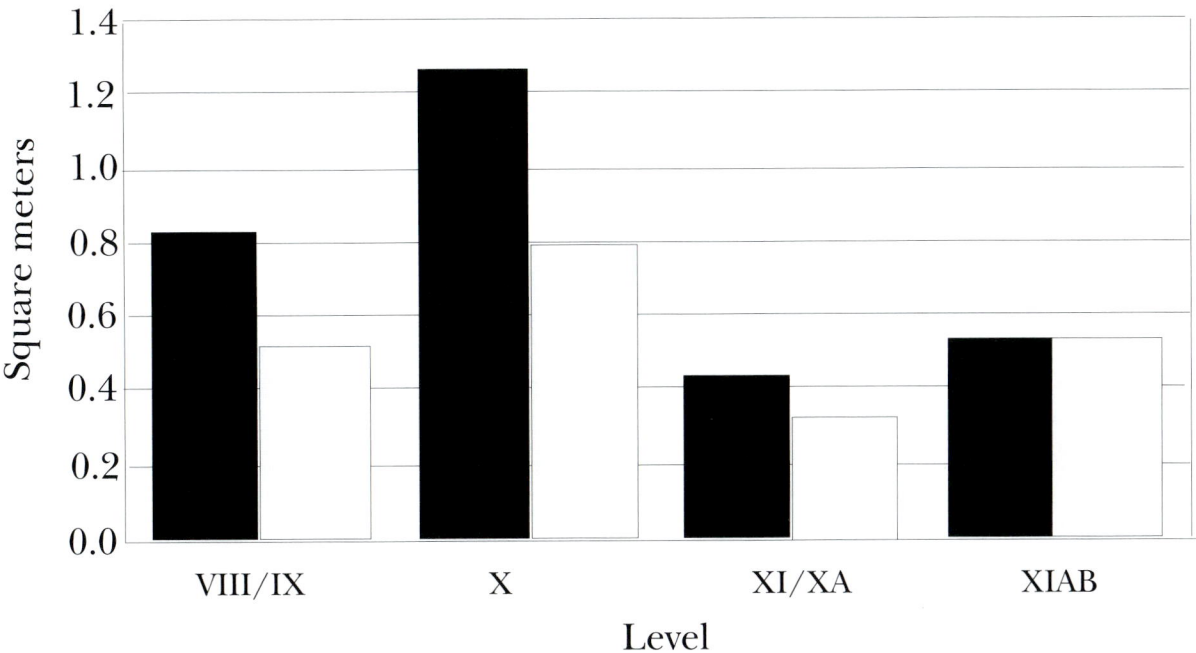

Figure A.33   Mean (black) and median (white) distribution of enclosed burials for each level, Tepe Gawra.

of these were laid on the left side. In Level X, the pattern of northwest-southeast orientation is extended to the majority of the libn tombs with all but one laid on the left side (Table A.9). However, this pattern disappears in Levels VIII/IX. Tobler (1950:77) originally suggested that the left-side position was characteristic

of libn tomb burials. However, in some cases, the data were used uncritically, and a number of errors in the field records were missed. After correcting for these errors, a somewhat different picture emerges. It is only in Level X and, to a lesser extent, in Level XI/XA that left-sided burials show any obvious predominance

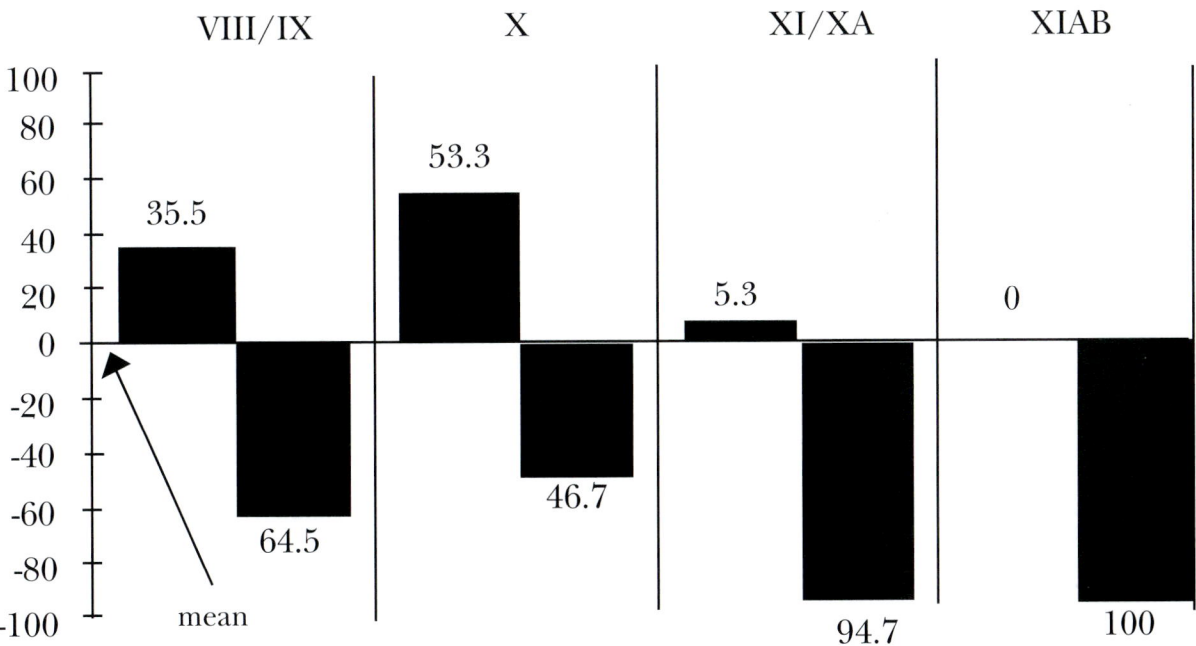

Figure A.34   Histogram of the percentage of enclosed burials above and below the mean in size, Tepe Gawra.

Table A.8   Inside Area and Other Factors For Enclosed Burials.

Burial	Level	Square	Type	Age	Head	Feet	Side	Face	Length	Width	Area
45	VIII/IX	6-O/7-O	Libn	?	?	?	?	?	2.05	1.60	3.28
34	VIII/IX	7-O	Libn	Adult	SE	NW	L	SW	2.27	1.25	2.84
46	VIII/IX	8-O	Libn	Adult	N	S	L	E	1.75	1.05	1.84
29-A	VIII/IX	6-Q	Libn	Youth	SE	NW	L	SW	1.45	0.98	1.42
30-A	VIII/IX	9-O/9-Q	Libn	Adult	NW	SE	L	NE	1.52	0.92	1.40
31	VIII/IX	9-M	Libn	Adult	SE	NW	L	SW	1.31	1.05	1.38
18	VIII/IX	8-Q	Libn	Adult	?	?	?	?	1.25	1.10	1.38
24	VIII/IX	9-O	Libn	Adult	SE	NW	L	SW	1.32	0.98	1.29
25-A	VIII/IX	9-Q	Libn	Adult	NE	SW	L	SE	1.30	0.98	1.27
47	VIII/IX	8-O	Libn	Child	?	?	L	?	0.95	0.87	0.83
B	VIII/IX	9-O	Libn	?	NE	SW	L	SE	1.30	0.63	0.82
2	VIII/IX	5-K	Cist	Child	SE	NW	?	?	1.05	0.70	0.74
64	VIII/IX	11-K	Libn	Infant	NE	SW	R	NW	0.86	0.75	0.65
62	VIII/IX	7-M	Libn	Child	?	?	?	?	0.97	0.63	0.61
36-036	VIII/IX	7-J	Libn	Infant	E	W	L	S	0.77	0.77	0.59
213	VIII/IX	7-M	Cist	Child	?	?	?	?	0.92	0.55	0.51
171	VIII/IX	6-J	Libn	Youth	E	W	R	NW	0.75	0.65	0.49
D	VIII/IX	6-M	Libn	?	?	?	?	?	0.93	0.50	0.47
57	VIII/IX	9-Q	Cist	Child	W	E	R	S	0.84	0.55	0.46
37	VIII/IX	10-K	Libn	Child	?	?	?	?	0.79	0.55	0.43
20	VIII/IX	8-M	Libn	Child	?	?	?	?	0.79	0.45	0.36
60	VIII/IX	10-M/11-M	Libn	Infant	SE	NW	R	NE	0.82	0.40	0.33
E	VIII/IX	6-O	Libn	?	?	?	?	?	0.65	0.50	0.33
C	VIII/IX	7-M	Libn	Infant	?	?	?	?	0.80	0.40	0.32
5	VIII/IX	5-J/6-J	Libn	Child	NE	SW	?	?	0.72	0.37	0.27
65	VIII/IX	11-K	Libn	Child	W	E	R	S	0.55	0.40	0.22
209	VIII/IX	6-J	Libn	Child	NW	SE	L	E	0.67	0.32	0.21
53	VIII/IX	7-O	Libn	Infant	E	W	R	N	0.55	0.30	0.17
54	VIII/IX	7-O	Libn	Infant	NW	SE	R	SE	0.55	0.30	0.17
14	VIII/IX	10-M	Libn	Child	NW	SE	R	SW	0.60	0.22	0.13
51	VIII/IX	9-O	Libn	Infant	NW	SE	R	SW	0.64	0.20	0.13
12	VIII/IX	10-M	Libn	Inf/Ch	?	?	?	?	0.00	0.00	0.00
61	VIII/IX	11-M	Libn	Infant	NW	SE	L	NE	0.00	0.00	0.00
A	VIII/IX	10-Q	Libn	Infant	?	?	?	?	0.00	0.00	0.00

| | | | | | | | | | **Avg. Area** | **VIII/IX** | 0.82 |
| | | | | | | | | | **Median Area** | **VIII/IX** | 0.51 |

111	X	5-M	Libn	Adult	NE	SW	L	SSE	2.06	1.55	3.19
114	X	4-K/4-M	Libn	Adult	SE	NW	R	NE	1.90	1.50	2.85
110	X	4-K/4-M	Libn	Youth	SE	NW	L	SW	1.85	1.40	2.59
109	X	5-K	Libn	Adult	SE	NW	L	SW	1.85	1.25	2.31
107	X	5-M/6-M	Libn	Adult	SE	NW	L	W	1.94	1.17	2.27
124	X	6-M	Libn	?	S	N	?	?	1.10	1.10	1.21
102	X	5-O	Libn	Youth	NW	SE	L	NE	1.10	0.93	1.02
108	X	6-K	Libn	Child	NW	SE	L	NE	0.92	0.86	0.79
36-026	X	8-O	Cist	Child	W	E	L	N	0.76	0.76	0.58
36-034	X	7-K	Libn	Child	E	W	L	S	0.82	0.65	0.53
59	X	9-O/9-Q	Cist	Child	SE	NW	L	SW	0.85	0.56	0.48
202	X	6-J	Cist	Child	N	S	L	E	0.95	0.47	0.45
7-009	X	9-M	Libn	Child	NW	SE	L	NE	0.68	0.50	0.34
36-014	X	8-Q	Pise	Child	W	E	B	S	0.64	0.35	0.22
36-013	X	7-Q	Libn	Youth	W	E	L	N	0.56	0.21	0.12
36-035	X	7-K	Pise	Child	S	N	R	?	0.00	0.00	0.00
36-040	X	7-Q	Libn	Infant	N	S	L	E	0.00	0.00	0.00

| | | | | | | | | | **Avg. Area** | **Level X** | 1.26 |
| | | | | | | | | | **Median Area** | **Level X** | 0.79 |

Burial	Level	Square	Type	Age	Head	Feet	Side	Face	Length	Width	Area
36-104	XA/XI	3-K/3-M	Libn	Adult	N	S	L	E	1.30	1.00	1.30
36-081	XA/XI	4-J	Pise	Adult	SE	NW	L	W	1.10	0.70	0.77
36-111	XA/XI	5-J	Libn	?	NW	SE	L	E	1.09	0.65	0.71
36-110	XA/XI	3-M	Libn	Adult	?	?	?	?	1.20	0.58	0.70
36-086	XA/XI	4-J	Libn	?	E	W	L	S	0.90	0.62	0.56
36-068	XA/XI	5-M	Libn	?	?	?	?	?	1.05	0.45	0.47
36-137	XA/XI	6-G	Libn	?	E	W	L	S	0.85	0.45	0.38
36-105	XA/XI	5-J	Libn	?	N	S	R	W	0.90	0.40	0.36
249	XA/XI	7-M	Libn	Child	SE	NW	L	W	0.79	0.45	0.36
36-046	XA/XI	5-J	Libn	?	S	N	L	W	0.80	0.40	0.32
36-146	XA/XI	4-G	Libn	?	NW	SE	R	S	0.73	0.37	0.27
36-042	XA/XI	5-J	Libn	?	S	N	R	E	0.65	0.41	0.27
36-144	XA/XI	6-J	Libn	?	W	E	L	N	0.70	0.38	0.27
36-135	XA/XI	5-G	Libn	Adult	N	S	L	E	0.70	0.37	0.26
36-027	XA/XI	8-Q	Libn	Child	NW	SE	R	S	0.74	0.34	0.25
36-048	XA/XI	5-J	Cist	Child	S	N	R	E	0.70	0.35	0.25
36-032	XA/XI	4-J	Libn	Infant	E	W	R	N	0.55	0.40	0.22
36-030	XA/XI	8-O	Libn	?	NW	SE	L	E	0.60	0.30	0.18
36-100	XA/XI	4-K	Libn	?	SSE	NNW	L	?	0.42	0.41	0.17
180	XA/XI	4-J	Libn	Child	W	E	L	N	0.00	0.00	0.00
181	XA/XI	4-K	Libn	Child	W	E	L	N	0.00	0.00	0.00
226	XA/XI	6-M	Libn	Infant	SE	NW	L	W	0.00	0.00	0.00
36-039A	XA/XI	5-J	Pise	Youth	S	N	R	E	0.00	0.00	0.00
36-039B	XA/XI	5-J	Pise	Child	N	S	L	E	0.00	0.00	0.00
36-080	XA/XI	4-K	Pise	Child	N	S	R	W	0.00	0.00	0.00

								Avg. Area	**Level XI/XA**	0.42
								Median Area	**Level XI/XA**	0.32

Burial	Level	Square	Type	Age	Head	Feet	Side	Face	Length	Width	Area
36-122A	XIAB	5-J	Libn	Adult	?	?	?	?	1.15	0.62	0.71
36-087	XIAB	3-O	Pise	Adult	S	N	L	W	1.25	0.55	0.69
36-017	XIAB	5-Q	Pise	Adult	S	N	L	W	1.10	0.60	0.66
36-090	XIAB	5-K	Libn	?	S	N	L	W	0.75	0.75	0.56
36-043	XIAB	5-J	Libn	?	S	N	L	W	0.80	0.60	0.48
36-074	XIAB	5-K	Libn	Adult	E	W	R	SW	0.82	0.42	0.34
36-134	XIAB	4-J	Libn	Adult	N	S	R	W	0.80	0.42	0.34
36-060	XIAB	5-M	Libn	Child	?	?	?	?	0.80	0.40	0.32
272	XIAB	5-M	Libn	Inf/Ch	N	S	L	SE	0.00	0.00	0.00
36-120	XIAB	5-J	Libn	Adult	S	N	R	E	0.00	0.00	0.00

								Avg. Area	**Level XIAB**	0.51
								Median Area	**Level XIAB**	0.52

Sum of All Enclosed Burial Areas for VIII/IX	25.3
Sum of All Enclosed Burial Areas for X	18.95
Sum of All Enclosed Burial Areas for XI/XA	8.05
Sum of All Enclosed Burial Areas for XIAB	4.10
Sum of All Enclosed Burial Areas for All Strata	56.41
Overall Average Area of Enclosed Burials	0.77

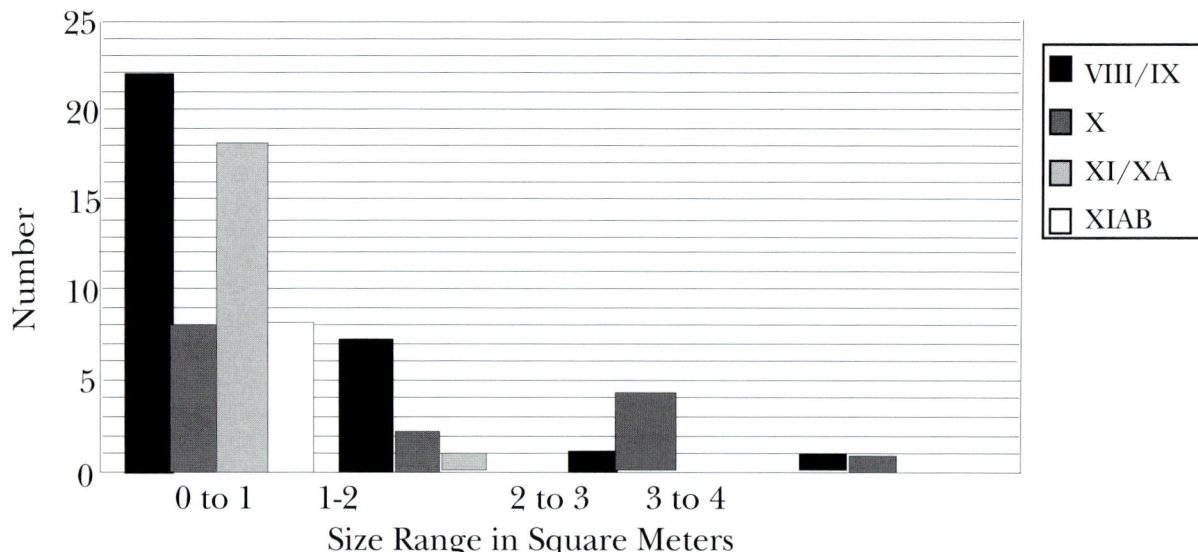

Figure A.35   Histogram of the number of enclosed burials in each one-meter-square interval, Tepe Gawra.

(Table A.9). In strata VIII/IX and XIA/B, both right-sided and left-sided libn tomb burials are common, with the only pattern showing up in reference to the largest tombs. However, in both of these levels, there was also a high percentage of the libn tomb burials for which there is no orientation data. Given the lack of any real consistency in orientation overall, it is likely that the northwest-southeast orientation observed for the larger strata VIII/IX and X enclosed burials may have been dictated by the general orientation of the

architectural features rather than on ideological or cosmological factors (Figures A.13–A.25).

Burial Goods and Analysis of Social Status

One of the most important symbolic ways of signifying status differences is the inclusion of objects in graves. The catalogue of the grave goods

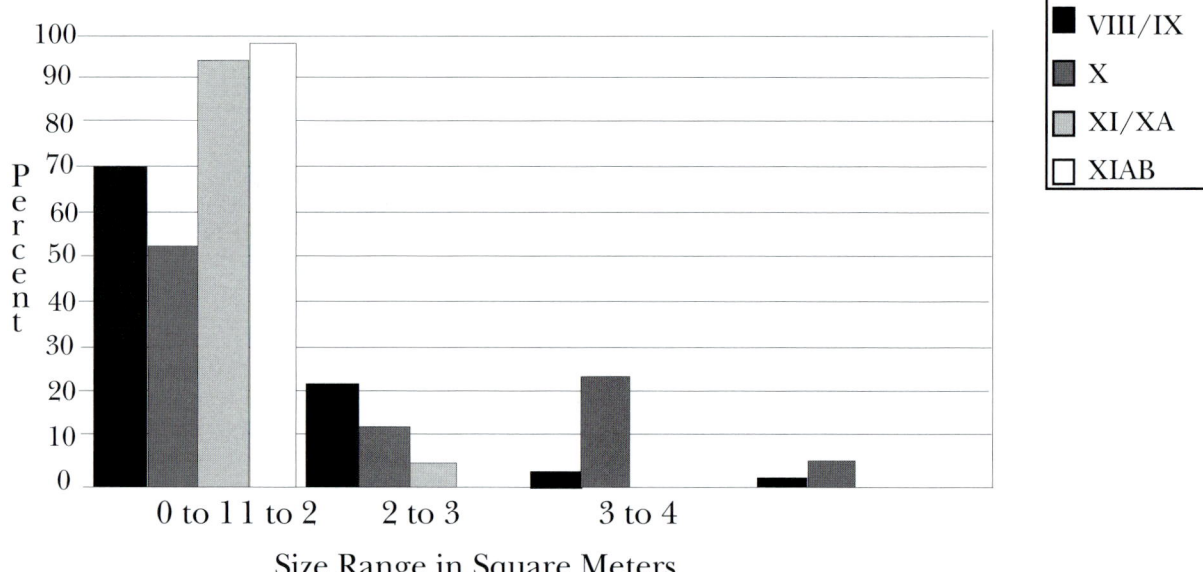

Figure A.36   Histogram of the percentage of enclosed burials in each one-meter-square interval, Tepe Gawra.

Table A.9   Burial Orientation.

Burial	Level	Square	Type	Age	Head	Feet	Face	Side
001	VIII/IX	6J	Loose	Infant	SW	NE?	NW	L
002	VIII/IX	5K	Cist	Child	SE	NW	?	?
003	VIII/IX	5J	Loose	Infant	NE	SW?	S	L
004	VIII/IX	5J	Loose	Infant	SE	NW?	N	R
005	VIII/IX	5J/6J	Libn	Child	NE	SW	?	?
007	VIII/IX	5J	Vessel	Infant	?	?	?	?
009	VIII/IX	10K	Loose	Inf/Child	?	?	?	?
010	VIII/IX	10M	Loose	Inf/Child	?	?	?	?
011	VIII/IX	10M	Loose	Inf/Child	?	?	?	?
012	VIII/IX	10M	Libn	Inf/Child	?	?	?	?
013	VIII/IX	11O	Loose	Infant	?	?	?	?
014	VIII/IX	10M	Libn	Child	NW	SE	SW	R
016	VIII/IX	10M	Loose	Inf/Child	SSW	NNE?	NW	L
017	VIII/IX	10M	Loose	Youth	SE	NW	NE	R
018	VIII/IX	8Q	Libn	Adult	?	?	?	?
020	VIII/IX	8M	Libn	Child	?	?	?	?
024	VIII/IX	9O	Libn	Adult	SE	NW	SW	L
025A	VIII/IX	9Q	Libn	Adult	NE	SW	SE	L
025B	VIII/IX	9Q	Libn	Adult	NE	SW	NW	R
029A	VIII/IX	6Q	Libn	Youth	SE	NW	SW	L
029B	VIII/IX	6Q	Libn	Adult	SE	NW	NE	R
030A	VIII/IX	9O/9Q	Libn	Adult	NW	SE	NE	L
030B	VIII/IX	9O/9Q	Libn	Child	SW	NE	SE	R
031	VIII/IX	9M	Libn	Adult	SE	NW	SW	L
034	VIII/IX	7O	Libn	Adult	SE	NW	SW	L
037	VIII/IX	10K	Libn	Child	?	?	?	?
040	VIII/IX	7Q	Vessel	Infant	?	?	?	?
045	VIII/IX	6O/7O	Libn	?	?	?	?	?
046	VIII/IX	8O	Libn	Adult	N	S	E	L
047	VIII/IX	8O	Libn	Child	?	?	?	L
050	VIII/IX	10O	Vessel	Infant	NE	SW	SW	R
051	VIII/IX	9O	Libn	Infant	NW	SE	SW	R
052	VIII/IX	8O	Vessel	Infant	NE	SW	NW	R
053	VIII/IX	7O	Libn	Infant	E	W	N	R
054	VIII/IX	7O	Libn	Infant	NW	SE	SE	R
055	VIII/IX	10S	Vessel	Infant	?	?	?	?
056	VIII/IX	10Q	Vessel	Infant	?	?	?	?
057	VIII/IX	9Q	Cist	Child	W	E	S	R
058	VIII/IX	7Q	Vessel	Infant	?	?	?	?
060	VIII/IX	10M/11M	Libn	Infant	SE	NW	NE	R
061	VIII/IX	11M	Libn	Infant	NW	SE	NE	L
062	VIII/IX	7M	Libn	Child	?	?	?	?
063	VIII/IX	10K	Vessel	Infant	N	?	SW	R
064	VIII/IX	11K	Libn	Infant	NE	SW	NW	R
065	VIII/IX	11K	Libn	Child	W	E	S	R
067	VIII/IX	10J	Vessel	Infant	?	?	?	?
068	VIII/IX	10J	Vessel	Infant	SE	W	SW	L
069	VIII/IX	7J	Vessel	Infant	SE	NW	W	L
070	VIII/IX	6J	Loose	Adult	SE	NW	NE	R
171	VIII/IX	6J	Libn	Youth	E	W	NW	R
199	VIII/IX	6J	Loose	Youth	SE	NW	N	R
200	VIII/IX	6J	Sidewall	Child	SE	NW	SW	L

(*continues*)

Burial	Level	Square	Type	Age	Head	Feet	Face	Side
203	VIII/IX	5J/6J	Loose	Child	SSW	NNE	N	L
204	VIII/IX	5J/6J	Vessel	Infant	SE	NW	NE	R
209	VIII/IX	6J	Libn	Child	NW	SE	E	L
211	VIII/IX	6J	Loose	Child	NW	SE	E	L
212	VIII/IX	6G	Loose	Child	NE	SW	SE	L
213	VIII/IX	7M	Cist	Child	?	?	?	?
214	VIII/IX	6G	Vessel	Infant	?	?	?	?
261	VIII/IX	8M	Loose	Inf/Child	?	?	?	?
267	VIII/IX	7O	Vessel	Inf/Child	?	?	?	?
36-036	VIII/IX	7J	Libn	Infant	E	W	S	L
7-007	VIII/IX	9M	Sidewall	Infant	SW	NE	E	R
A	VIII/IX	10Q	Libn	Infant	?	?	?	?
AA I	VIII/IX	9Q	Vessel	Infant	N	S	W	R
AA II	VIII/IX	9Q	Vessel	Infant	N	S	W	R
B	VIII/IX	9O	Libn	?	NE	SW	SE	L
C	VIII/IX	7M	Libn	Infant	?	?	?	?
CC I	VIII/IX	7J	Vessel	Infant	?	?	?	?
CC II	VIII/IX	7J	Vessel	Infant	?	?	?	?
D	VIII/IX	6M	Libn	?	?	?	?	?
DD	VIII/IX	7M	Loose	Adult	?	?	?	?
E	VIII/IX	6O	Libn	?	?	?	?	?
FF	VIII/IX	9O	Vessel	Inf/Child	?	?	?	?
GG	VIII/IX	10O	Vessel	Inf/Child	?	?	?	?
HH	VIII/IX	9O	Vessel	Inf/Child	?	?	?	?
JJ	VIII/IX	10M	Vessel	Child	?	?	?	?
KK	VIII/IX	10O	Loose	Child	SE	NW	SW	L
006	X	6O	Vessel	Infant	?	?	?	?
059	X	9O/9Q	Cist	Child	SE	NW	SW	L
100	X	6O	Vessel	Infant	NE	SE	S	L
101	X	6O	Loose	Child	NE	SW	S	L
102	X	5O	Libn	Youth	NW	SE	NE	L
107	X	5M/6M	Libn	Adult	SE	NW	W	L
108	X	6K	Libn	Child	NW	SE	NE	L
109	X	5K	Libn	Adult	SE	NW	SW	L
110	X	4K/4M	Libn	Youth	SE	NW	SW	L
111A	X	5M	Libn	Adult	NE	SW	SSE	L
111B	X	5M	Libn	Adult	SE	NW	W	L
111C	X	5M	Libn	Adult	SE	NW	W	L
113	X	6O	Loose	Child	SE	SW	N	R
114	X	4K/4M	Libn	Adult	SE	NW	NE	R
119	X	5J	Loose	Infant	SW	NE	?	?
124	X	6M	Libn	?	S	N	?	?
126	X	6M	Vessel	Child	?	?	?	?
177	X	6G	Loose	Child	E	NW	?	?
182	X	5J	Loose	Infant	SW	NE	N	L
190	X	7M	Vessel	Infant	?	?	?	?
201	X	6K	Vessel	Infant	?	?	?	?
202	X	6J	Cist	Child	N	S	E	L
205	X	6J	Loose	Child	E	W	S	L
206	X	5J	Loose	Child	NW	SE	S	R
207	X	5K	Vessel	Infant	?	?	?	?
208	X	6J	Sidewall	Child	SW	NE	N	L
210	X	6J	Sidewall	Child	S	N	E	R

Burial	Level	Square	Type	Age	Head	Feet	Face	Side
216	X	5J	Vessel	Infant	?	?	?	?
217	X	6G	Vessel	Infant	?	?	?	?
219	X	7M	Sidewall	Child	NW	SE	SW	R
220	X	7K	Loose	Infant	?	?	?	?
256	X	7O	Loose	Child	NW	SE	NE	L
269	X	8M	Vessel	Infant	?	?	?	?
36-013	X	7Q	Libn	Youth	W	E	N	L
36-014	X	8Q	Pise	Child	W	E	S	B
36-016	X	8O	Loose	Child	NW	SE	SW	R
36-020	X	8Q	Loose	Child	S	N	E	R
36-026	X	8O	Cist	Child	W	E	N	L
36-031	X	8O	Loose	Inf/Child	NW	SE	S	R
36-034	X	7K	Libn	Child	E	W	S	L
36-035	X	7K	Pise	Child	S	N	?	R
36-037A	X	8K	Loose	?	N	S	E	L
36-037B	X	8K	Loose	?	N	S	W	R
36-040	X	7Q	Libn	Infant	N	S	E	L
36-044	X	7Q	Sidewall	Child	W	E	N	L
36-047	X	7Q	Loose	Infant	E	W	S	L
36-079	X	7Q	Vessel	Infant	N	S	W	R
7-001	X	11M	Loose	Adult	W	E	S	R
7-005	X	11M	Vessel	Child	?	?	?	?
7-009	X	9M	Libn	Child	NW	SE	NE	L
EE	X	10O	Loose	Child	?	?	?	?
122	XI/XA	4K	Loose	Infant	W	E	S	R
123	XI/XA	7O	Vessel	?	?	?	?	?
125	XI/XA	4Q	Vessel	Infant	?	?	?	?
127	XI/XA	5O	Loose	Infant	NW	SE	?	?
128	XI/XA	5M	Vessel	Infant	?	?	?	?
129	XI/XA	5O	Loose	Child	W	E	N	L
130	XI/XA	4Q	Loose	Infant	S	N	E	R
134	XI/XA	6O	Sidewall	Infant	NW	SE	S	R
136	XI/XA	5M	Loose	Infant	NE	SW	SE	L
137	XI/XA	5Q	Vessel	Infant	E	W	NNW	R
138	XI/XA	5O	Loose	Infant	NW	SE	E	L
140	XI/XA	5O	Vessel	Infant	E	W	N	R
141	XI/XA	6M	Vessel	Infant	W	E	S	R
142	XI/XA	5Q	Loose	Youth	SE	NW	SW	L
144	XI/XA	5M	Loose	Child	N	S	E	L
145	XI/XA	6Q	Loose	Adult	SE	NW	W	L
146	XI/XA	6O	Sidewall	Child	NW	SE	NE	L
151	XI/XA	5M	Loose	Infant	?	?	?	?
154	XI/XA	6M	Loose	Child	NW	SE	NE	L
158	XI/XA	5O	Vessel	Infant	?	?	?	?
159	XI/XA	5M	Loose	Infant	NW	SE	NE	L
160	XI/XA	5M	Loose	Child	SE	NW	SW	L
163	XI/XA	5Q	Loose	Child	E	W	N	R
164	XI/XA	5M	Vessel	Infant	?	?	?	?
168	XI/XA	6K	Loose	Child	NE	SW	SE	L
170	XI/XA	4K	Vessel	Infant	?	?	?	?
175	XI/XA	4J	Vessel	Infant	?	?	?	?
176	XI/XA	3K	Loose	Child	N	S	E	L

(continues)

Burial	Level	Square	Type	Age	Head	Feet	Face	Side
178	XI/XA	3M	Loose	Infant	NW	SE	?	?
179	XI/XA	4J	Vessel	Infant	?	?	UP	B
180	XI/XA	4J	Libn	Child	W	E	N	L
181	XI/XA	4K	Libn	Child	W	E	N	L
184	XI/XA	5G	Loose	Youth	S	N	NW	L
186	XI/XA	6K	Vessel	Inf/Child	?	?	?	?
187	XI/XA	3O	Vessel	Infant	?	?	?	?
189	XI/XA	5K	Loose	Infant	?	?	?	?
191	XI/XA	5K	Sidewall	Child	NE	SW	SE	L
192	XI/XA	5Q	Vessel	Infant	?	?	?	?
193	XI/XA	7K	Vessel	Infant	?	?	?	?
215	XI/XA	6J	Vessel	Infant	?	?	?	?
218	XI/XA	4K	Vessel	Infant	?	?	?	?
221	XI/XA	5M	Sidewall	Youth	NW	SE	SW	R
222	XI/XA	5M	Sidewall	Child	SW	NE	SE	R
223	XI/XA	4K	Vessel	Infant	?	?	?	?
224	XI/XA	5M	Vessel	Infant	?	?	?	?
225	XI/XA	5Q	Vessel	Infant	?	?	?	?
226	XI/XA	6M	Libn	Infant	SE	NW	W	L
227	XI/XA	6Q	Vessel	Child	?	?	?	?
228	XI/XA	6Q	Loose	Child	SE	NW	UP	B
229	XI/XA	7M	Loose	Child	SE	NW	SW	L
230	XI/XA	6Q	Vessel	Inf/Child	?	?	?	?
231	XI/XA	6Q	Vessel	Inf/Child	?	?	?	?
233	XI/XA	5K	Loose	Adult	SE	NW	NE	R
234	XI/XA	6M	Vessel	Infant	?	?	?	?
235	XI/XA	5J	Vessel	Infant	?	?	?	?
239	XI/XA	3K	Loose	Child	E	W	S	L
242	XI/XA	7M	Sidewall	Child	NW	SE	E	L
244	XI/XA	3K	Vessel	Infant	?	?	?	?
245	XI/XA	3K	Loose	Inf/Child	?	?	?	?
246	XI/XA	3K	Vessel	Inf/Child	?	?	?	?
247	XI/XA	3K	Loose	Infant	?	?	?	?
249	XI/XA	7M	Libn	Child	SE	NW	W	L
252	XI/XA	4K	Loose	Infant	?	?	?	?
253	XI/XA	6M	Vessel	Infant	?	?	?	?
258	XI/XA	5K	Loose	Infant	?	?	?	?
263	XI/XA	7K	Vessel	Inf/Child	?	?	?	?
266	XI/XA	5S	Loose	Child	NW	SE	E	L
270	XI/XA	7M	Vessel	Inf/Child	?	?	?	?
278	XI/XA	8O	Loose	Infant	?	?	?	?
290A	XI/XA	7K	Vessel	Child	?	?	?	?
315	XI/XA	4J	Vessel	Infant	?	?	?	?
318	XI/XA	4J	Loose	Infant	?	?	?	?
36-027	XI/XA	8Q	Libn	Child	NW	SE	S	R
36-030	XI/XA	8O	Libn	?	NW	SE	E	L
36-032	XI/XA	4J	Libn	Infant	E	W	N	R
36-038	XI/XA	5J	Vessel	Infant	?	?	?	?
36-039A	XI/XA	5J	Pise	Youth	S	N	E	R
36-039B	XI/XA	5J	Pise	Child	N	S	E	L
36-041	XI/XA	5J	Vessel	Infant	?	?	?	?
36-042	XI/XA	5J	Libn	?	S	N	E	R
36-046	XI/XA	5J	Libn	?	S	N	W	L

Burial	Level	Square	Type	Age	Head	Feet	Face	Side
36-048	XI/XA	5J	Cist	Child	S	N	E	R
36-052	XI/XA	5J	Vessel	Infant	?	?	?	?
36-068	XI/XA	5M	Libn	?	?	?	?	?
36-080	XI/XA	4K	Pise	Child	N	S	W	R
36-081	XI/XA	4J	Pise	Adult	SE	NW	W	L
36-083	XI/XA	4J	Vessel	Child	E	W	N	R
36-084	XI/XA	5K	Vessel	Child	?	?	?	?
36-086	XI/XA	4J	Libn	?	E	W	S	L
36-088	XI/XA	5J	Vessel	Infant	?	?	?	?
36-089	XI/XA	5J	Vessel	?	?	?	?	?
36-100	XI/XA	4K	Libn	?	SSE	NNW	?	L
36-104	XI/XA	3K/3M	Libn	Adult	N	S	E	L
36-105	XI/XA	5J	Libn	?	N	S	W	R
36-110	XI/XA	3M	Libn	Adult	?	?	?	?
36-111	XI/XA	5J	Libn	?	NW	SE	E	L
36-129	XI/XA	7S	Vessel	Adult	?	?	?	?
36-135	XI/XA	5G	Libn	Adult	N	S	E	L
36-137	XI/XA	6G	Libn	?	E	W	S	L
36-144	XI/XA	6J	Libn	?	W	E	N	L
36-146	XI/XA	4G	Libn	?	NW	SE	S	R
36-168	XI/XA	11M	Loose	Infant	?	?	?	?
7-010	XI/XA	9M	Loose	Child	SW	NE	SE	R
7-012	XI/XA	8M	Loose	Child	WNW	ESE	S	R
7-014	XI/XA	9M	Loose	Child	NW	SE	NE	L
7-015	XI/XA	10M	Loose	Adult	S	N	E	R
7-018	XI/XA	11M	Loose	Youth	SW	NE	NE	R
7-023	XI/XA	9M	Vessel	Infant	?	?	?	?
161	XIAB	6M	Loose	Child	NW	SE	NE	L
166	XIAB	5Q	Vessel	Child	NE	SW	S	L
167	XIAB	5Q	Loose	Child	E	W	W	L
183	XIAB	4Q	Vessel	Child	?	?	?	?
188A	XIAB	5Q	Loose	Adult	E	W	S	L
188B	XIAB	5Q	Loose	Adult	E	W	S	L
194	XIAB	5Q	Vessel	Infant	?	?	?	?
236	XIAB	5M	Loose	Infant	?	?	?	?
237	XIAB	5M	Loose	Infant	?	?	?	?
238	XIAB	5M	Loose	Youth	NW	SE	E	L
241	XIAB	3M	Vessel	Inf/Child	?	?	?	?
243	XIAB	5M	Loose	Child	SW	NE	E	R
248	XIAB	3K	Vessel	Infant	?	?	?	?
250	XIAB	5M	Cist	Child	SE	NW	SW	B
251	XIAB	5M	Loose	Child	NW	SE	SW	R
254	XIAB	5Q	Vessel	Inf/Child	?	?	?	?
255	XIAB	4Q	Vessel	Child	?	?	?	?
257	XIAB	5M	Loose	Child	SW	NE	NW	L
259	XIAB	6S	Vessel	Inf/Child	?	?	?	?
265	XIAB	6S	Vessel	Adult	?	?	?	?
268	XIAB	6Q	Loose	Adult	?	?	?	?
272	XIAB	5M	Libn	Inf/Child	N	S	SE	L
273	XIAB	5M	Vessel	Inf/Child	?	?	?	?
274	XIAB	5M	Vessel	Inf/Child	?	?	?	?
275	XIAB	6M	Loose	Child	?	?	?	?

(*continues*)

Table A.9   (continued)

Burial	Level	Square	Type	Age	Head	Feet	Face	Side
276A	XIAB	5M	Vessel	Inf/Child	?	?	?	?
276B	XIAB	5M	Loose	?	?	?	?	?
325	XIAB	3O	Vessel	Inf/Child	?	?	?	?
36-002	XIAB	5Q	Vessel	Child	?	?	?	?
36-003	XIAB	5O	Vessel	Infant	?	?	?	?
36-004	XIAB	4Q	Vessel	Infant	?	?	?	?
36-005	XIAB	4S	Vessel	Child	?	?	?	?
36-006	XIAB	4Q	Vessel	Infant	?	?	?	?
36-007	XIAB	4Q	Vessel	Infant	?	?	?	?
36-008	XIAB	5Q	Vessel	Infant	?	?	?	?
36-009	XIAB	5Q	Vessel	?	?	?	?	?
36-010	XIAB	5Q	Vessel	?	?	?	?	?
36-011	XIAB	4S	Vessel	Infant	?	?	?	?
36-015	XIAB	5Q	Vessel	Infant	?	?	?	?
36-017	XIAB	5Q	Pise	Adult	S	N	W	L
36-019	XIAB	5Q	Vessel	Adult	?	?	?	?
36-022	XIAB	5M	Loose	?	E	W	N	R
36-043	XIAB	5J	Libn	?	S	N	W	L
36-051	XIAB	5Q	Vessel	Infant	?	?	?	?
36-057	XIAB	6M	Vessel	Infant	?	?	?	?
36-058	XIAB	3M	Vessel	Infant	?	?	?	?
36-060	XIAB	5M	Libn	Child	?	?	?	?
36-062	XIAB	5M	Vessel	Infant	?	?	?	?
36-074	XIAB	5K	Libn	Adult	E	W	SW	R
36-077	XIAB	6K	Vessel	Infant	?	?	?	?
36-082	XIAB	3M	Vessel	?	?	?	?	?
36-087	XIAB	3O	Pise	Adult	S	N	W	L
36-090	XIAB	5K	Libn	?	S	N	W	L
36-091	XIAB	3M	Vessel	Child	?	?	?	?
36-120	XIAB	5J	Libn	Adult	S	N	E	R
36-122A	XIAB	5J	Libn	Adult	?	?	?	?
36-122B	XIAB	5J	Libn	Infant	?	?	?	?
36-122C	XIAB	5J	Libn	Infant	?	?	?	?
36-134	XIAB	4J	Libn	Adult	N	S	W	R
36-171	XIAB	11M	Vessel	Child	?	?	?	?
7-026	XIAB	8M	Sidewall	Adult	SE	NW	?	R
7-028	XIAB	9M	Vessel	Infant	S	N	NE	R
7-029	XIAB	8M	Loose	Child	E	W	SW	L
7-030	XIAB	8M	Sidewall	Adult	NW	SE	NE	L

suggests that this was indeed an important aspect of the mortuary practice at Tepe Gawra. It is quite evident that some graves contain more items than do other graves. However, the mere fact that one grave has a greater number of objects than the others is not enough on its own to signify a major difference in status. It is necessary to factor in the nature and types of objects included in the burials. In fact, the number of different types of objects seems to be more significant than the total number of items.

To interpret grave goods as symbols of status we must keep in mind that an ancient value system is certainly quite different from our modern one. We must be very careful not to impose our value system upon the one we are studying (Renfrew 1986; Hodder 1987). It is all too easy to assume that certain items, such as gold ornaments, carry more value than do other items, but the logic in the ancient case may be very different. We might, as Robinson (1984) does, assume that gold was much more limited in supply than other items and so access to them would make it an ideal symbol of prestige. In the historically attested case of ancient Panama, however, the value of gold was established by its malleability, not its rarity. As Helms (1979:79) writes, "this point is evidenced in the reprimand reportedly given the Spaniards by the son of the *quevi* Comogre, who, perplexed by the conquistador's melting of artistic pieces into ingots, is said to have pointed out that rough gold had no more value than a lump of clay."

Choices about how much weight to give to various types of raw materials can be quite difficult when more than one type is in limited supply. For example, how does one assess the value of an ornament made of gold leaf in contrast to the value of an elaborate carved bead made of lapis lazuli or carnelian? Another factor to consider is the amount of workmanship involved in the crafting of the material objects of status. We must also decide what kind of value is to be attributed to the objects.

In too many cases, the value attributed to the grave goods of long-dead cultures involves researchers' imposition of their preconceptions about wealth (see Robinson 1984:55 for an example of this problem). This implies that the meaning behind the material remains interred with the deceased was economic in nature. Although status and prestige are often related to economic issues, status and economics are not always the same thing. Thus, the assignation of arbitrary wealth values, or any other type of value for that matter, to the grave furniture will most likely tell us more about the researcher than about the burials under study.

To minimize these potential biases, a number of statistical tools have been devised that can help to draw meaning from the data while at the same time limiting the amount of subjective judgment on the part of the researcher. Various types of univariate, bivariate, multivariate, nearest neighbor, and other statistical procedures have been used successfully to gain insight from mortuary data on the social, political, and economic processes occurring in the past (Shennan 1975; Peebles and Kus 1977; Chapman and Randsborg 1981; Pollock 1983).

A particularly useful tool for finding patterns in mortuary data has been the use of nearest neighbor analysis, which is often referred to as cluster analysis. Cluster analysis is a technique whereby a number of entities are sorted and grouped together so that all members of the group contain certain attributes that make them more similar to one another than to the entities of other groups. In other words, it is a tool used to discover the structure within a body of data being analyzed when that structure is not readily visible (Anderberg 1973:4).

The primary problem with cluster analysis is that, unlike many other statistical applications, the results are always somewhat ambiguous. There is no level where the resulting clusters are more significant.

Although the actual procedure is mechanical once the units to be clustered have been chosen, the attributes of these units defined, and the clustering criteria set, the results themselves are devoid of any inherent truth or validity (Anderberg 1973:176). The analyst must take an active role in interpreting the results. In many ways, subjecting the data to one of several clustering algorithms results in a summary descriptive statistic much like the mean, median, and variance. On their own, these clusters mean relatively little, but put in context and interpreted by the analyst, these can provide a good deal of information.

Ultimately, the primary goal of clustering data is to produce a set of clusters that are highly differentiated (Anderberg 1973:14–15). The fact remains, however, that there is a certain amount of subjectivity involved in this statistical technique. Such factors as what attributes are to be used to form the clusters, which units should be included and which should be excluded, and defining which clusters are significant remains unspecified by the technique. Therefore, cluster analysis is probably best used as an exploratory tool for teasing out the nature of the data structure under study (Anderberg 1973:19).

I applied cluster analysis to the mortuary data from Tepe Gawra in an attempt to gain some understanding about how the burials differed from one another for each level and to develop some means for grouping the burials into more or less natural groups. The successful clustering of the burials into groups does not necessarily imply the presence of differential status. All we end up with are a number of groups that may or may not make sense when compared to the other forms of mortuary data. These groups only provide the material for formulating hypotheses about the possible meaning underlying the use of these objects in the mortuary ritual, which must then be tested against other forms of data.

Once the burials had been grouped, the burials were then subjected to a simple and straightforward analysis of the differences between burials in terms of burial goods. The results of this analysis were then compared with the results from the cluster analysis in order to draw out the primary trends occurring in relation to the burial goods through time. Certainly, more sophisticated forms of statistical analysis could have been applied to the data. The primary aim of this Appendix, however, is to present the data in as complete a form as possible and to tease out some of the primary trends occurring in the late fifth and fourth millennium levels of Tepe Gawra. Therefore, the analyses of the mortuary data only involved relatively simple analytical procedures, most of which are presented in terms of descriptive statistics.

The units to be clustered were the burials themselves, using the grave goods. Burials that had no grave goods were omitted from the analysis. These are treated as a separate and distinct cluster for each level by virtue of the absence of grave goods. Furthermore, not all burials with grave goods were included in the analysis. Vessel burials with no grave goods were excluded from the analysis. Further, in those vessel burials where other grave goods were present, only these other items were treated as attributes and the burial vessel was excluded. Also excluded from analysis were the majority of the graves that had been disturbed or robbed. This in particular affected the analysis of Levels VIII/IX where many of the large libn tombs had been robbed. In a couple of cases, burials that had been disturbed and partly robbed were included in the analysis. These two cases were Burials 034 and 046. They were included in the analysis because, although they had been robbed, there seemed to be enough burial goods remaining to be roughly representative of the original range of burial types. In fact, the analysis had been run several times both with and without these burials with only relatively little change in the burial clusters. All the other robbed burials had too lit-

tle material in them. After the analysis had been run, it was possible to place some of the robbed tombs into one of the resulting clusters on the basis of what objects remained in them.

Depending the choices of units to cluster, attributes to use for defining the clusters, how these attributes are to be expressed, what clustering algorithm is used, and what level used to define the clusters, the results will differ. In the case of the material from Tepe Gawra, the attributes and level of analysis was adjusted after each run in order to reduce the number of units that ended up as residue (i.e., did not sort into any group) and to develop the best well-defined clusters. The problem here is in choosing those attributes that will create unique groups while holding enough units together so that each unit does not form its own cluster. The burial goods used as attributes in the analysis are shown in Table A.10. Because, in many cases, the actual number of items was missing (this is especially the case for those items that were left in Baghdad), the burial goods were entered on the basis of whether they

Table A.10 Grave Good Types by Level.

Level XIAB	Black Beads	Gold Ornaments	Stamp Seals
	White Beads	Bone Ornaments	Mace Heads
	Shell Beads	Paste Rosettes	Ceramic Vessels
Total n = 9			
Level XI/XA	Black Beads	Turquoise Beads	Natural Shells
	White Beads	Carved Beads	Gold Rosettes
	Grey Beads	Gold Beads	Stamp Seals
	Carnelian Beads	Copper Beads	Mace Heads
	Lapis Beads	Gold Ornaments	Ceramic Vessels
	Shell Beads	Copper Ornaments	Tokens
Total n = 18			
Level X	Black Beads	Carved Beads	Combs
	White Beads	Gold Beads	Ointment Vessels
	Grey Beads	Electrum Beads	Stamp Seals
	Carnelian Beads	Gold Ornaments	Mace Heads
	Lapis Beads	Lapis Ornaments	Stone Vessels
	Shell Beads	Bone Ornaments	Ceramic Vessels
	Turquoise Beads	Natural Shells	Tokens
	Green Stone Beads	Gold Rosettes	Honing Stones
	Brown Paste Beads	Hair Ornaments	
Total n = 26			
Level VIII/IX	Black Beads	Green Stone Beads	Natural Shells
	White Beads	Brown Paste Beads	Gold Rosettes
	Grey Beads	Carved Beads	Hair Ornaments
	Carnelian Beads	Gold Beads	Combs
	Quartz Beads	Copper Beads	Ointment Vessels
	Lapis Beads	Gold Ornaments	Stamp Seals
	Shell Beads	Bone Ornaments	
	Turquoise Beads	Copper Ornaments	
Total n = 22			

were present or absent in the burial. Although the number of individual items is an important aspect used to differentiate one individual from another, the presence of particular items may be more important than the mere quantity of goods. In particular, the presence of a greater variety in the types of burial goods may be more indicative of higher rank than the quantity of any one particular item. Each level was analyzed separately, using the Jaccard matching coefficient to cluster the data (see Anderberg 1973:88–90 for a discussion on matching coefficients). The results are summarized in Table A.11.

Once the burials had been clustered, the burials were then analyzed in terms of how they ranked on the basis of differences in burial goods. The rank of each burial was calculated within each stratum by comparing the occurrence of each type of burial good with the occurrence of other types of burial goods. From this, the average number of different burial goods that occurred in the burials having the specified type was calculated and the resulting figure was taken as a ranking index for that particular category of burial goods. For example, the calculation of the ranking index for ceramic vessels in Level X is based on the occurrence

Table A.11   Clusters of Graves by Grave Good.

Group	#	Type Characterized by the Presence of
		Level XIAB
1	6	common white and black beads. One burial contains a rosette ornament made of paste.
2	6	ceramic vessels
3	2	stamp seals
4	1	a bone spacer bead and a stone mace head
		Level XI/XA*
1	4	turquoise and carved beads and the absence of white beads.
2	10	white beads along with beads made of exotic material such as lapis, carnelian, green stone, turquoise quartzite and shell as well as gold rosettes and ornaments. One burial contained a stone mace head
3	8	white beads only
4	6	ceramic vessels in all burials. In addition, 2 burials contained stamp seals
5	1	gold beads, rosettes, and ornaments. Although this burial came out as a residue, it seems to be an unique burial and probably constitutes a separate cluster
		Level X*
1	4	white beads only
2	8	white, black, and carnelian beads as well as beads made of other exotic material
3	4	elaborate ornaments such as gold rosettes, gold ornaments of various types, grooming tools (combs, ointment vessels, hair ornaments), weapon-related items (hone, obsidian blades, mace) and administrative items (stamp seals and tokens).
4	4	ceramic vessels only.
		Stratum VIII/IX
1	10	gold and copper ornaments and all types of stone beads except those made of lapis.
2	7	very similar to group 1 except in the absence of metal ornaments and in the presence of lapis beads.
3	2	similar to group 4, but lacks the more elaborate ornaments and grooming tools. It is characterized by exotic stone beads, gold beads and ornaments, carved beads and an ivory comb.
4***	3	elaborate gold rosettes and ornaments, grooming tools, and administrative items
5	3	white beads only with the exception of one burial, burial JJ, which also had a copper bead.

*One of the residual burials, burial 181, is unique in character and is probably best viewed as a distinct group containing only a single member:

**Any attempt to reduce the number of residual burials either resulted in clusters that did not make sense or in no change. One of these, burial 102, is close in character to group 3 but with just enough difference to set it apart from all other burials. This is further supported by the analysis of its ranked position in terms of the burial goods for this burial presented further on in this study.

***This group is very similar to group 3 for level X.

of these vessels in six burials. The total number of burial good types in these burials is 18:

1. Burial 102 8 types of burial goods
2. Burial 111-A 1 type of burial good
3. Burial 111-B 1 type of burial good
4. Burial 111-C 6 types of burial goods
5. Burial 205 1 type of burial good
6. Burial 206 1 type of burial good

By dividing the number of burial good types by the number of burials containing the ceramic vessels, a social status index of 3.00 is obtained. Because the associations between burial goods changed slightly from level to level, the ranking index for particular objects may also differ from level to level. By applying this procedure for each type of burial good, a series of social status indices was developed for all the types that occurred in each level. These indices are presented in Tables A.12–A.15. The ranking indices for the various burial types were then added together for each burial to provide a burial ranking score (Tables A.16–A.19). On the basis of the burial ranking scores, the burials from each level could then be ordered relative to one another.

This method of calculating social rank is dependent on a number of underlying assumptions. As mentioned above, the first assumption is that, although differences in the number of items in a particular burial may indicate differential status, the number of different types may be even more important. Thus, the presence of 1 lapis seal, 2 gold rosettes, and 4 gold eye ornaments is probably indicative of higher social rank than a burial having only 500 white beads. Therefore, the greater the number of other burial good types occurring with a specific object, the greater the ranking index. Furthermore, this procedure allows for the fact that certain types of goods will occur in relatively few burials, because access to this particular good is limited. Therefore, if it occurs with a large number of other types of burial goods an item that occurs in only one burial will have a relatively high ranking index. It is also self-correcting, because it allows for the fact that

Table A.12   Ranking Indices for Level XIA/B.

Burial Good Type	Ranking Index
Stamp Seals	1.00
Ceramic Vessels	1.29
White Beads	1.83
Bone Ornaments	2.00
Gold Ornaments	2.00
Mace Heads	2.00
Black Beads	3.00
Paste Rosettes	3.00
Shell Beads	3.00

Table A.13   Ranking Indices for Level XI/XA.

Burial Good Type	Ranking Index
Carved Beads	1.00
Ceramic Vessels	1.67
Stamp Seals	2.00
Turquoise Beads	2.00
White Beads	2.21
Natural Shells	2.75
Copper Ornaments	3.00
Black Beads	3.50
Gold Ornaments	3.50
Lapis Beads	3.80
Carnelian Beads	4.00
Grey Beads	4.00
Copper Beads	5.00
Mace Heads	5.00
Gold Rosettes	5.50
Gold Beads	6.00
Shell Beads	6.00
Tokens	6.00

the occurrence of some types of goods may be relatively rare for reasons other than limited access. For example, a particular type of good that occurs in only two burials where one of the burials has a total of 17 different burial good types and the other has 23 different types will have a ranking index of 20.00. By contrast, another type of burial good that occurs in two burials where each burial has only two different types of goods will have a ranking index of 2.00.

This procedure for calculating social status can never give a precise equivalent for what the individual items meant for the occupants of Tepe Gawra. It does, however, give a more or less empirical means for ranking the burials in each level relative to one another in terms of differences in burial goods. In this way, it is possible to avoid subjective ways of assigning value to the objects. By using this procedure, and by understanding the assumptions underlying it, it is possible to get some idea of the trends that occurred in the Late Chalcolithic period at Tepe Gawra in terms of the material expression of status differences.

The results of the social status analysis were then compared to the groups of burials that resulted from the clustering of the burial data (Tables A.16–A.19).

Level XIA/B

The comparison of the 4 groups with the ranked order of burials for this level shows a tight correlation between the clusters and their position along the scale of burial ranking scores (Table A.16). The range between the highest and lowest ranking burial is small

Table A.14   Ranking Indices for Level X.

Burial Good Type	Ranking Index
Green Stone Beads	2.00
Brown Paste Beads	3.00
Ceramic Vessels	3.00
White Beads	4.21
Black Beads	4.25
Natural Shells	4.33
Grey Beads	4.50
Carnelian Beads	7.50
Turquoise Beads	8.60
Shell Beads	9.20
Gold Beads	10.20
Mace Heads	10.67
Stone Vessels	11.67
Gold Ornaments	11.75
Lapis Beads	11.75
Tokens	12.25
Combs	13.50
Gold Rosettes	13.67
Stamp Seals	13.67
Bone Ornaments	14.00
Honing Stones	14.00
Electrum Beads	15.50
Hair Ornaments	15.50
Carved Beads	17.00
Lapis Ornaments	17.00
Ointment Vessels	17.00

Table A.15   Ranking Indices for Levels VIII/IX.

Burial Good Type	Ranking Index
Copper Beads	2.00
Brown Paste Beads	4.00
White Beads	4.13
Black Beads	4.59
Quartz Beads	5.43
Natural Shells	5.50
Carnelian Beads	5.56
Shell Beads	5.58
Grey Beads	5.67
Green Stone Beads	6.20
Carved Beads	6.33
Copper Ornaments	6.67
Lapis Beads	7.60
Bone Ornaments	8.00
Turquoise Beads	8.00
Gold Beads	9.00
Combs	9.50
Hair Ornaments	9.50
Gold Rosettes	10.00
Gold Ornaments	10.33
Ointment Vessels	12.00
Stamp Seals	12.00

is that this group contained only one type of item—white beads—and so all group 3 burials have the same burial ranking score. Group 2 burials align at the upper end of the scale. Although burial 138 is a residual unit from the cluster analysis, it probably best fits

Table A.16   Burial Ranking Scores for Level XIA/B.

Burial	Group	Index of Highest Ranking Type in Burial	Ranking Burial
			Score
36-134	3	1.00	1.00
7-026	3	1.00	1.00
250	2	1.29	1.29
36-022	2	1.29	1.29
255	2	1.29	1.29
188-B	2	1.29	1.29
236	2	1.29	1.29
36-090	2	1.29	1.29
36-077	1	1.83	1.83
36-082	1	1.83	1.83
36-006	1	1.83	1.83
167	1	2.00	3.83
238	4	2.00	4.00
36-060	1	3.00	6.12
243	1	3.00	7.83

(6.83). The highest-ranking burials (243 and 36-060) were of children: a loose grave and a libn tomb burial. The two burials containing stamp seals were those of adults. Only nine different types of burial goods were used in this level. Of these, all the beads were of the common white and black variety. There were no beads made of exotic stones, and gold items were very rare (only 1 gold ornament from a group 1 burial (Table A.11). Although a rosette occurred in this level, it was made of paste rather than gold. The differences between these burials are relatively small compared to the later periods, and it is most likely that these four groups represent the same status. Therefore, there are probably two primary status levels represented in this stratigraphic unit: those with burial goods and those without.

Level XI/XA

The comparison of the five groups from this level with the ranked order of burials shows that groups 1 and 4 were mixed throughout the lower end of the ranked scale (Table A.17). Group 3 interments are clumped in the middle at the level of 2.21. The reason

Table A.17 Burial Ranking Scores for Level XI/XA.

Burial	Group	Index of Highest Ranking Type in Burial	Ranking Burial
			Score
137	1	1.00	1.00
318	1	1.00	1.00
36-146	4	1.67	1.67
36-105	4	1.67	1.67
36-111	4	1.67	1.67
122	1	2.00	2.00
154	3	2.21	2.21
159	3	2.21	2.21
36-100	3	2.21	2.21
36-144	3	2.21	2.21
128	3	2.21	2.21
140	3	2.21	2.21
228	3	2.21	2.21
36-137	3	2.21	2.21
130	1	3.50	3.50
36-129	4	2.00	3.67
36-110	4	2.00	3.67
193	2	2.75	4.96
127	2	2.75	4.96
138	2	3.50	5.71
144	2	3.80	6.01
163	2	3.80	8.01
36-135	4	3.50	8.17
36-027	2	4.00	8.96
242	2	4.00	9.71
226	2	4.00	9.71
180	2	4.00	12.76
142	2	5.50	19.01
266	2	5.00	19.51
181	5	6.00	31.00

group 2. Furthermore, the robbed tomb excluded from analysis (36–140) is probably also a group 2 burial. The single group 5 burial is the highest-ranking burial in this level. The range between the lowest and highest ranking burials at 30.00 is greater than the range in Level XIA/B. However, this difference is still relatively small. There may be two primary status groups: those burials with no burial goods and those that make up groups 1, 2, 3, and 4. Group 5 may represent a new stage beginning to emerge. There are twice as many types of burial goods used in this level than in the earlier level. Many of the items that would eventually adorn the more spectacular burials of Level X and VIII/IX appeared in XI/XA. As in Level XIA/B, stamp seals were restricted to adult burials. Those burials equipped with ceramic vessels were also restricted to adults. The highest-ranking burial in this level was a child interred in a libn tomb.

Level X

The comparison of the four groups from this level with the ranked order of burials shows a clear distinction between each of the groups according to their burial ranking score (Table A.18). Group 4 burials displayed the lowest set of burial ranking scores, followed by group 1 and then group 2 burials. Group 3 burials rank at the extreme upper end of the ranking scale. The range between group 1, 2, and 4 burials is rather small, showing a relatively steady increase in ranking number. A major jump in the burial ranking scores occurs between group 2 and group 3 burials. This suggests a very real difference between group 3 burials and all of the other burials in this level in terms of the social standing of the individuals interred in these burials. This is further supported by the fact that all of the group 3 burials consist of the largest libn tombs in this level.

Although there are differences in the burial ranking scores for group 1, 2, and 4 burials, it is probably best to view these burials as different components of individuals of the same status. The primary differences between these groups are in the presence of exotic versus common white beads, or of ceramic vessels.

Table A.18 Burial Ranking Scores for Level X.

Burial	Group	Index of Highest Ranking Type in Burial	Ranking Burial
			Score
111-A	4	3.00	3.00
111-B	4	3.00	3.00
206	4	3.00	3.00
205	4	3.00	3.00
36-016	1	4.21	4.21
36-026	1	4.21	4.21
7-009	1	4.21	4.21
100	1	4.21	6.21
113	2	4.25	8.46
36-013	residual	9.20	9.20
256	2	4.25	11.46
36-040	residual	4.33	11.55
269	2	4.50	12.96
108	2	8.60	16.10
208	2	7.50	20.30
202	2	8.60	24.56
36-020	2	10.20	26.16
36-034	2	9.20	34.00
111-C	3	11.75	52.80
102	3	12.25	62.75
110	3	13.67	116.62
114	3	15.50	168.25
109	3	17.00	209.96

It is very likely that these differences point to some aspect of status ascription other than prestige. Group 3 burials, on the other hand, are different enough to assign them to a higher ranking, more prestigious group. The primary symbols of prestige appear to be gold rosettes and ornaments, grooming implements, and administrative tools. Therefore, there are three primary levels of status in this level: those interments with no burial goods, those with various types of beads or ceramic vessels, and those of high rank, containing gold ornaments of various types, grooming implements, and administrative items.

A number of burials had been excluded from the cluster and rank order analyses, because they appeared to have been robbed at some point in the past. The most important of these are Burials 107 and 124. Burials 107 and 124 were libn tombs similar in size to the other large tombs in Level X. On the basis of what remained in these burials when they were excavated, it seems most likely that these two burials should also be assigned to group 3. Although Burial 102 was a residual burial during the clustering procedure, it, too, is probably a group 3 burial. The failure of this burial to cluster with the other group 3 burials may be due to its having been disturbed in the past, although no evidence for this is cited in the field notes.

A primary difference between this level and the lower levels is the dramatic jump in the range between the lowest and highest burial ranking scores. Furthermore, there is a dramatic increase in the number of burial good types, from 18 to 26, between Levels XI/XA and X. Unlike Levels XIA/B and XI/XA, all of the highest-ranking burials in Level X were of adults and youths. Infants were rare in all four burial groups.

Levels VIII/IX

The comparison of the five groups from this level with the ranked order of burials shows a clear distinction between the group 5 burials and all other groups (Table A.19). All burials from this group are distributed at the lowest end of the ranking scale. Group 1 and 2 burials are mixed along the middle range of the scale. Similarly, group 3 and 4 burials are mixed along the upper range of the burial ranking scores. However, there seems to be some problems with the clustering of the burials from this level. In particular, Burial 013, which clustered as a group 1 burial, has a very high rank. Burial 013's assignation to cluster 1 is based on the absence of lapis beads. Beads of this material are present in all group 3 burials. However, in other aspects, such as the presence of gold ornaments, this burial is quite similar to Burial 012. Therefore, Burial 013 is probably best seen as a group 3 burial along with Burials 012 and 034. Furthermore, burials C and 060 failed to cluster with any group. Both of these burials are somewhat unique. Burial 060 differs from group 1

Table A.19   Burial Ranking Scores
for Levels VIII/IX.

Burial	Group	Index of Highest Ranking Type in Burial	Ranking Burial
			Score
KK	5	4.13	4.13
213	5	4.13	4.13
JJ	5	4.13	6.13
203	2	5.56	9.69
009	1	5.58	10.17
C	residual	6.33	11.76
060	residual	6.20	11.76
061	2	5.67	14.38
001	1	5.56	15.58
212	1	5.58	15.60
A	1	5.58	15.73
037	1	6.67	16.84
002	2	7.60	17.29
016	2	5.50	18.21
004	1	5.58	19.73
209	2	5.56	19.78
014	1	5.58	19.86
214	2	5.67	19.88
36–036	2	6.20	20.48
010	1	8.00	27.86
011	1	8.00	33.29
034	3	9.50	48.83
047	4	9.50	52.53
046	4	10.00	56.11
013	1	10.33	62.23
012	3	10.33	63.54
031	4	12.00	104.51

burials in the absence of copper ornaments and from group 2 burials in the absence of lapis lazuli beads. Although it differs from groups 1 and 2 in these aspects, it is similar to both in other aspects and is, therefore, associated with individuals of the same status. Burial C, on the other, hand defies any attempt to cluster it with any of the five groups. Based on the four elaborately carved lapis beads, It seems to constitute a unique group. However, this interment appears to be of the same status as those of groups 1 and 2.

Given the burial ranking scores of burial groups 1 and 2, these burials probably represent different aspects of individuals of the same status. Furthermore, because there is not a great difference between the group 5 burials and those of groups 1 and 2 in terms of the burial ranking scores, these, too, probably represent another aspect of this same status. If the apparently aberrant assignment of Burial 013 to group 1 were ignored, group 3 and 4 burials would appear to constitute two different aspects of higher-ranking burials.

The interpretation of group 3 and 4 burials as higher-ranking is based on the larger gap between the highest-ranking group 1 burial (ignoring Burial 013), Burial 011, and the low-ranking group 3 Burial 034. This gap is smaller than the gap between the higher and lower rankings in Level X. The smaller gap between the two differently ranked groups in Levels VIII/IX is somewhat deceptive. Although Burial 034 was included in the analyses, it is, nevertheless, a disturbed burial and would have had a much higher social status rank had it not been robbed. In fact, Burial 034 may have originally ranked as high as, if not higher than, Burial 031. As in Level X, a number of important burials (024, 025, 029, 030, and 045) had to be excluded from analysis, because they were too disturbed. However, on the basis of what remained in these burials, they, too, are most likely group 3 or 4 burials. The exclusion of so many burials from analysis may account for the narrower range between the lowest and highest ranking burials than among burials of Level X. Like Level X, the highest-ranking burials consist of the largest libn tombs. However, these graves contain children as well as adults. Also, there are a great many more infants in the burials from Levels VIII/IX analyzed. Furthermore, the same types of burial goods are used to display high rank as were used in Level X. There is a smaller number of burial good types used in Levels VIII/IX (22 types) than in X. However, this may also be due to the exclusion of a large number of important burials from analysis for this level. Therefore, Levels VIII/IX are roughly comparable to Level X.

Conclusions

The general pattern of social, political, and economic development is relatively well understood for Mesopotamia as a whole. However, in terms of the specific nature of these changes, the processes occurring in northern Mesopotamia are only recently becoming understood for the Late Chalcolithic or LC 1-5 periods.

The mortuary data from Tepe Gawra suggest that the Late Chalcolithic period was a time in which important social, political, and economic changes occurred. By Level XIA/B Tepe Gawra had already attained a significant level of social complexity. This is most evident in the fact that, while some adults were given relatively simple forms of burial, some children and infants were interred in more substantial burial types, such as tombs, which required more attention, time, and labor to construct. Based on the development in the use of this form from Level XIA/B to Levels VIII/IX, its symbolic importance is clear. Therefore, social rank was already ascribed for some individuals at birth.

This level of complexity should not be surprising, however, since there had been a continuous development in social complexity ever since the establishment of the first sedentary villages in Mesopotamia. Further important changes began to emerge early on in the Late Chalcolithic period, as the main text of this volume illustrates. During Levels XIA/B and XI/XA, changes in the way individuals of the three primary age groups were treated can be observed in the abandonment of the use of sidewall and pisé burials for adults and the extension of these burial types to children and infants. Also, beginning in Level XI/XA the percentage of infants buried in vessels decreased. This decrease in the percentage of vessel burials marked the emergence of a trend that continues through all four stratigraphic units, the decrease in the percentage of vessel burials in each level and a concomitant increase in the percentage of libn tomb burials. The end result of this trend is a proportionate number of infants, children, and adults buried in libn tombs. It is also in Level XI/XA that we begin to see the use of exotic materials, such as lapis lazuli, green stone, turquoise, and carnelian for beads. Previously, almost all stone beads had been made of common material, primarily limestone or paste, and in a few cases diorite (this is the term used most often in the field notes although the actual composition of the material has not been analyzed). Level XI/XA is also the level in which certain material items that would later appear only in the more elaborate burials (gold ornaments and grooming implements) come into use as mortuary offerings for the first time.

Although these changes begin to appear in Levels XIA/B and XI/XA, it is not until Level X that they become pronounced. The differences between this level and the lower levels are nothing short of dramatic. In Levels XIA/B and XI/XA, some individuals are certainly set apart from the others in terms of mortuary practices, but these differences are never very great. Even the libn tombs, which are more substantial than the other forms of constructed mortuary features tend to be small and are only slightly more substantial then the other types in Levels XI/XA and XIA/B.

Differences in terms of the burial goods are also relatively small and, in many ways, seem to be of only minor importance in terms of differentiating individuals from one another. With Level X, all adults are buried in either loose burials or libn tombs—all other forms of burial were abandoned for this age group—resulting in a larger percentage of adults interred in libn tombs than had been in Levels XIA/B and XI/XA. These changes in the use of burial types and the way in which the various age groups were treated is paralleled by a change in the degree to which certain individuals were set apart from the majority of the others in terms of the various aspects of the mortuary practice. During the occupation of Level X, there was a dramatic jump in the size of libn tombs overall, whereas at the same time the range between the smallest and largest libn tombs increased to almost three times the tomb size range in Level XI/XA.

It is also during this time that there was an increase in the number of different types of objects included in the burials. This was paralleled by a dramatic increase in the disparity between individuals in terms of the burial goods. This disparity is manifest both in the number of different types of burial goods and in the sheer number of objects included in a small number of burials. In every case, the burials that were richest in terms of the burial goods consisted of the largest libn tomb burials. These large, well-endowed tombs are further differentiated from the other burials, because they are set apart from the others spatially. The majority of large libn tombs also provide evidence that the individuals buried in them were distinguished from other individuals in terms of more complex treatment of the body. This complex treatment of the deceased is suggested by the presence of red, green, or blue pigment found in these burials and nowhere else. The changes in mortuary practices that distinguishes Level X from the underlying levels continued into Levels VIII/IX.

In summary, the four stratigraphic units that constitute the LC 2-3 span of the Late Chalcolithic period document major changes in social relationships among individuals at Tepe Gawra. However, not until Level X were these changes fully expressed in the mortuary data. There seems to have been a change in ideology concerning the way in which status was displayed underlying these changes.

This change in ideology most likely reflected the changes in social structure described in Chapter 5. In Levels XIA/B and XI/XA, individuals were differentiated from each other primarily in terms of burial types, and although some differences can be observed in terms of burial goods, material objects play only a minor role. By Level X, those forms of burial indicative of higher rank in the lower levels are increasingly available to a larger segment of the population. At the same time, there was a greater degree of difference in terms of the material objects included in the mortuary contexts. Therefore, a shift towards the use of material items for displaying status differences is evidenced. However, material objects were not the only way in which status was displayed in Levels X and VIII/IX. At the same time that a larger segment of the population was buried in libn tombs, the tombs containing the higher-ranking individuals became much larger and more complex with some of them containing wooden floors and, possibly, roofs (Figure A.3). These tombs were also set apart from the others spatially. Thus, differences in burial form continued to be an important aspect of status display.

Status display seems to have been expressed in most observable aspects of the mortuary practices at Tepe Gawra by Level X. The high-ranking burials are differentiated from the other burials in terms of differences in the amount of labor expended in the construction of the burials, more complex treatment of the body of the deceased, the spatial placement of the tombs, and the inclusion of a greater number and more elaborate forms of burial goods. Therefore, it seems likely that the change in social relationships among individuals was also paralleled by changes in the economic and political systems at Tepe Gawra.

Acknowledgments

Although the interpretations and conclusions drawn from the Tepe Gawra mortuary data are my own, the compilation and analysis of the burial goods could not have been done without the help and support of a number of people working behind the scenes.

Above all, I would like to thank Dr. Mitchell Rothman for giving me the opportunity to be a part of this project. His constructive comments and suggestions contributed greatly to the outcome of this appendix.

I have also incurred a great debt to Dr. Robert H. Dyson, Jr., for instilling in me the importance of conducting archival research in order to answer new questions from sites excavated long before such questions were ever asked. I am especially thankful that he took time out of an already full schedule as Director of the University of Pennsylvania Museum of Archaeology and Anthropology to conduct an independent study of Near Eastern research with me. The insights gained from this time of instruction have proven invaluable for this analysis of the Tepe Gawra burial contexts.

I would also like to thank Dr. Richard Zettler and Ms. Maude de Schauensee of the University of Pennsylvania Museum for providing me with access to the collections from Tepe Gawra. Access to this material proved to be of the utmost importance for resolving various issues concerning the burial goods.

I also owe a great debt of gratitude to Mr. Douglas M. Haller, former Museum Archivist, and to Mr. Alessandro Pezzati, the current Acting Archivist, both of the University of Pennsylvania Museum, for putting up with me and with my incessant demands for hours on end. Additionally, Alex put in a good deal of time photocopying many of the field notes for me.

A great deal of thanks is also owed to Mr. Charles Kline, Photographic Archivist at the University of Pennsylvania Museum, for providing me with access to the original negatives from the Tepe Gawra excavations.

I would also like to thank Drs. Guillermo Algaze, Gil Stein, and Michael Rosenberg for the conversations we shared on the Late Chalcolithic period. Most of these conversations occurred at the ARIT hostel in Ankara and in a number of taxi cabs while commuting to and from the various sessions of the International Symposium of Excavations, Surveys, and Archaeometry held each year in Turkey. These conversations contributed greatly to my own general understanding of the social processes occurring during the LC 2-5 period throughout northern and southern Mesopotamia.

And last, but by no means least, I am indebted to my wife, Mary, and my son, Sean, both of whom were a great encouragement to me throughout this project. Mary read most of the text, and in spite of my stubborn resistance to changing parts of the text, her suggestions have improved the text in significant ways. Sean accepted my absence from play time.

To each of them I offer my sincere and heartfelt gratitude.

References

Anderberg, Michael R.

1973   *Cluster Analysis for Applications.* New York: Academic Press.

Bache, Charles

1933   From Mr. Bache's First Report on the Joint Excavations at Tepe Gawra and Tell Billah, 1932–3. *Bulletin of the American Schools of Oriental Research* 49: 8–14.

Binford, Lewis R.

1971   Mortuary Practices: Their Study and Potential. In *Approaches to the Social Dimensions of Mortuary Practices.* J. A. Brown, ed. pp. 6–29. Washington, DC: Memoirs of the Society for American Archaeology, No. 25.

Chapman, Robert W., and Klavs Randsborg

1981   Approaches to the Archaeology of Death. In *The Archaeology of Death.* R. Chapman, I. Kinnes, and Klaus Randsborg, eds. pp. 1–24. Cambridge: Cambridge University Press.

Forest, Jean-Daniel

1983   *Les pratiques funéraires en Mésopotamie du 5ᵉ millénaire au début du 3ᵉ, étude de cas.* Paris: Editions Recherche sur les civilisations.

Goodenough, W. H.

1965   Rethinking "Status" and "Role": Toward a General Model of the Cultural Organization of Social Relationships. In *The Relevance of Models for Social Anthropology.* M. Banton, ed. pp. 1–24. *A.S.A. Monographs,* No. 1. London: Tavistock.

Helms, Mary

1979   *Ancient Panama: Chiefs in Search of Power.* Austin: University of Texas Press.

Hodder, Ian

1987   The Contextual Analysis of Symbolic Meanings. In *The Archaeology of Contextual Meanings.* Ian Hodder, ed. pp. 1–10. Cambridge: Cambridge University Press.

O'Shea, John M.

1984   *Mortuary Variability: An Archaeological Investigation.* Orlando: Academic Press.

Peebles, Christopher S., and Susan M. Kus

1977   Some Archaeological Correlates of Ranked Societies. *American Antiquity* 42:421–448.

Pollock, Susan

1983   *The Symbols of Prestige: An Archaeological Example from the Royal Cemetery of Ur.* Ph.D. dissertation, University of Michigan.

Renfrew, Colin

1986   Varna and the Emergence of Wealth in Prehistoric Europe. In *The Social Life of Things: Commodities in Cultural Perspective.* Arjun Appadurai, ed. pp. 141–168. Cambridge: Cambridge University Press.

Robinson, Lynda S.

1984   *Social Stratification and the State in Ancient Mesopotamia.* Ph.D. dissertation, University of Texas at Austin.

Rosen, Arlene M.

1986   *Cities of Clay: The Geoarchaeology of Tells.* Chicago: University of Chicago Press.

Rothman, Mitchell S.

1988   *Centralization, Administration, and Function at Fourth-Millennium B.C. Tepe Gawra, Northern Iraq.* Ph.D. dissertation, University of Pennsylvania.

Saxe, A. A.

1970   *Social Dimensions of Mortuary Practices.* Ph.D. dissertation, University of Michigan.

Shennan, S.

1975   The Social Organization at Branc. *Antiquity* 49: 279–288.

Speiser, Ephraim A.

1935   *Excavations at Tepe Gawra* 1. Philadelphia: University of Pennsylvania Press.

Tainter, J. A.

1978   Mortuary Practices and the Study of Prehistoric Social Systems. In *Advances in Archaeological Method and Theory* 1. Michael B. Schiffer, ed. pp. 105–141. New York: Academic Press.

Tobler, Arthur J.

1944   Note penciled on Locus Sheet 36–134, initialed by Tobler and dated Jan. 18, 1944

1950   *Excavations at Tepe Gawra 2.* Philadelphia: University Museum.

Concordance of Object Numbers

Over the 60 plus years since the excavation of Tepe Gawra, a multiplicity of numbers have been associated with objects from the excavation. These include the field number, chit number, catalogue number for this volume, catalogue number for other Gawra publications, especially Speiser (1935a) and Tobler (1950), and museum accession numbers. It was my hope to use the field number as the unique referent, but that proved very cumbersome. I hope people who refer to objects use the field number (1000-, 5000-, 6000-, 3-xxx, 4-xxx, 5-xxx, 6-xxx, 7-xxx) number in addition to whatever other number they cite. If any future researcher wants to re-inspect the field notes in the Archives of the University of Pennsylvania Museum, they will need the field number. To find the object itself in the University of Pennsylvania Museum, a researcher needs the Museum accession number. This concordance relates the catalogue numbers here to the field number, museum accession number (33-3-xxx, 35-10-xxx, 36-6-xxx, 37-16-xxxx, 38-13-xxx) or its current location if it is not in Philadelphia, all organized by the object's level/phase of origin. A listing of references to Tobler's (1950) and Speiser's (1935) illustration numbers follows this concordance.

Concordance   Concordance   (continued)

Field Number	Catalogue Number	Location	Level/ Phase	Field Number	Catalogue Number	Location	Level/ Phase
4-0644	0418	35-10-260	XII	4-1156	0043	Discarded	XII
4-0667	0419	35-10-261	XII	4-1158	0427	35-10-249	XII
4-0674	0334	35-10-230	XII	4-1160	0044	Baghdad	XII
4-0676	0335	Baghdad	XII	4-1161	0109	philano#	XII
4-0677	0336	Baghdad	XII	4-1164	0111	Baghdad	XII
4-0679	1135	Baghdad	XII	4-1167	0175	35-10-246	XII
4-0685	0219	35-10-232	XII	4-1168	0112	35-10-255	XII
4-0686	0220	35-10-197	XII	4-1170	0155	Baghdad	XII
4-0694	0221	Baghdad	XII	4-1171	0428	35-10-250	XII
4-0712	0337	Baghdad	XII	4-1172	0345	35-10-241	XII
4-0713	0222	Baghdad	XII	4-1173	0045	Baghdad	XII
4-0714	0039	Baghdad	XII	4-1174	0046	Baghdad	XII
4-0715	0040	Baghdad	XII	4-1175	0235	35-10-189	XII
4-0903	0041	Baghdad	XII	4-1176	0429	35-10-253	XII
4-0919	0223	35-10-215	XII	4-1178	0047	35-10-236	XII
4-0929	0177	35-10-213	XII	4-1180	0346	35-10-226	XII
4-0948	0151	35-10-360	XII	4-1181	0430	IM24594	XII
4-0949	0338	Baghdad	XII	4-1183	0236	Baghdad	XII
4-0950	0339	Baghdad	XII	4-1184	0048	35-10-235	XII
4-0951	0340	35-10-227	XII	4-1185	0237	Baghdad	XII
4-0966	0107	Baghdad	XII	4-1186	0238	Baghdad	XII
4-0976	0341	35-10-223	XII	4-1187	0179	Baghdad	XII
4-0978	0420	IM24978	XII	4-1188	0239	35-10-196	XII
4-0979	0421	35-10-266	XII	4-1189	0001	35-10-245	XII
4-0994	0178	35-10-105	XII	4-1190	0431	35-10-269	XII
4-0995	0224	35-10-192	XII	4-1191	0432	IM25000	XII
4-1012	0152	Baghdad	XII	4-1192	0433	35-10-259	XII
4-1023	0225	35-10-193	XII	4-1193	0434	35-10-270	XII
4-1038	0226	35-10-142	XII	4-1194	0435	35-10-271	XII
4-1084	0227	Baghdad	XII	4-1195	0436	IM25002	XII
4-1098	0228	phila?	XII	4-1197	0347	35-10-221	XII
4-1124	0014	35-10-194	XII	4-1198	0437	35-10-272	XII
4-1132	0422	IM25007	XII	4-1199	0438	IM25039	XII
4-1133	0423	IM24979	XII	4-1200	0439	35-10-257	XII
4-1135	0968	Baghdad	XII	4-1201	0440	35-10-273	XII
4-1136	0042	35-10-242	XII	4-1202	0441	35-10-274	XII
4-1137	0153	Baghdad	XII	4-1203	0442	35-10-275	XII
4-1138	0108	35-10-248	XII	4-1204	0443	IM24980	XII
4-1139	0174	Baghdad	XII	4-1205	0444	IM24972	XII
4-1140	0229	35-10-195	XII	4-1207	0445	35-10-276	XII
4-1141	0230	Baghdad	XII	4-1208	0446	35-10-277	XII
4-1143	0231	35-10-188	XII	4-1209	0447	35-10-278	XII
4-1144	0232	Baghdad	XII	4-1211	0448	35-10-280	XII
4-1145	0233	35-10-199	XII	4-1213	0449	IM25037	XII
4-1146	0424	IM24963	XII	4-1214	0450	IM24973	XII
4-1147	0425	IM24962	XII	4-1215	0240	35-10-190	XII
4-1147c	0342	35-10-225	XII	4-1216	0451	IM25009	XII
4-1150	0154	35-10-243	XII	4-1219	0452	Baghdad	XII
4-1151	0343	Baghdad	XII	4-1222	0105	philano#	XII
4-1152	0344	35-10-224	XII	4-1223	0049	35-10-240	XII
4-1153	0015	35-10-218	XII	4-1224	0016	Baghdad	XII
4-1154	0426	35-10-252	XII	4-1225	0453	35-10-281	XII

Concordance (continued)

Field Number	Catalogue Number	Location	Level/Phase
4-1226	0002	35-10-244	XII
4-none	0017	unknown	XII
4-none	0018	unknown	XII
4-none	0019	unknown	XII
4-none	0020	unknown	XII
4-none	0025	unknown	XII
4-none	0026	unknown	XII
4-none	0028	discarded	XII
4-none	0029	unknown	XII
4-none	0050	36-6-274	XII
4-none	0051	unknown	XII
4-none	0113	36-6-302	XII
4-none	0114	discarded	XII
4-none	0115	discarded	XII
4-none	0116	discarded	XII
4-none	0117	unknown	XII
4-none	0118	unknown	XII
4-none	0119	unknown	XII
4-none	0120	unknown	XII
4-none	0121	unknown	XII
4-none	0172	Discarded	XII
4-none	0180	35-10-200	XII
4-none	0181	35-10-201	XII
4-none	0182	35-10-203	XII
4-none	0183	35-10-204	XII
4-none	0184	35-10-206	XII
4-none	0185	35-10-207	XII
4-none	0186	35-10-208	XII
4-none	0187	35-10-209	XII
4-none	0188	35-10-210	XII
4-none	0189	35-10-211	XII
4-none	0190	35-10-212	XII
4-none	0191	35-10-214	XII
4-none	0193	unknown	XII
4-none	0194	unknown	XII
4-none	0211	unknown	XII
4-none	0212	unknown	XII
4-none	0241	discarded	XII
4-none	0242	discarded	XII
4-none	0243	unknown	XII
4-none	0244	unknown	XII
4-none	0245	unknown	XII
4-none	0246	unknown	XII
4-none	0247	unknown	XII
4-none	0248	unknown	XII
4-none	0249	unknown	XII
4-none	0250	unknown	XII
4-none	0349	35-10-219	XII
4-none	0350	35-10-231	XII
4-none	0351	35-10-379	XII
4-none	0352	35-10-384	XII
4-none	0353	Baghdad	XII

Concordance (continued)

Field Number	Catalogue Number	Location	Level/Phase
4-none	0354	discarded	XII
4-none	0355	unknown	XII
4-none	0356	unknown	XII
4-none	0357	unknown	XII
4-none	0358	unknown	XII
4-none	0359	unknown	XII
4-none	0360	unknown	XII
4-none	0361	unknown	XII
4-none	0362	unknown	XII
4-none	0363	unknown	XII
4-none	0364	unknown	XII
4-none	0365	unknown	XII
4-none	0366	unknown	XII
4-none	0367	unknown	XII
4-none	0368	unknown	XII
4-none	0369	unknown	XII
4-none	0370	unknown	XII
4-none	0371	unknown	XII
4-none	0372	unknown	XII
4-none	0373	unknown	XII
4-none	0374	unknown	XII
4-none	0375	unknown	XII
4-none	0376	unknown	XII
4-none	0377	unknown	XII
4-none	0379	unknown	XII
4-none	0380	unknown	XII
4-none	0381	unknown	XII
4-none	0454	discarded	XII
4-none	0455	discarded	XII
4-none	0456	35-10-258	XII
5-1233	0385	36-6-255	XII
5-1235	0252	36-6-259	XII
5-1236	0253	Baghdad	XII
5-1237	0457	36-6-306	XII
5-1238	0458	IM27044	XII
5-1239	0459	36-6-305	XII
5-1240	0460	36-6-313	XII
5-1241	0254	36-6-235	XII
5-1242	0461	IM26965	XII
5-1243	0993	Baghdad	XII
5-1244	0462	IM26995	XII
5-1246	0463	36-6-308	XII
5-1247	0464	36-6-310	XII
5-1279?	0255	unknown	XII
5-1388	0256	Baghdad	XII
5-1406	0465	36-6-311	XII
5-1407	0466	36-6-293	XII
5-1408	0106	Baghdad	XII
5-1436	0257	36-6-241	XII
5-1437	0467	IM27043	XII
5-1450	0054	36-6-183	XII
5-1453	0055	Baghdad	XII

(continues)

Concordance   (continued)

Concordance   (continued)

Field Number	Catalogue Number	Location	Level/ Phase	Field Number	Catalogue Number	Location	Level/ Phase
5-1461	0056	Baghdad	XII	5-1640	0477	36-6-297	XII
5-1462	0057	Baghdad	XII	5-1641	0478	36-6-298	XII
5-1478	0058	36-6-271	XII	5-1642	0123	Baghdad	XII
5-1497	0059	36-6-188	XII	5-1646	0038	Baghdad	XII
5-1498	0003	36-6-195	XII	5-1647	0005	Baghdad	XII
5-1499	0259	36-6-166	XII	5-1648	0479	IM26962	XII
5-1501	0260	36-6-133	XII	5-1654	0070	Baghdad	XII
5-1503	0261	Baghdad	XII	5-1655	0071	36-6-270	XII
5-1510	0030	36-6-242a	XII	5-1663	0286	Baghdad	XII
5-1514	0468	36-6-307	XII	5-1664	0072	36-6-263	XII
5-1515	0060	36-6-272	XII	5-1672	0006	36-6-280	XII
5-1520	0469	36-6-294	XII	5-1687	0287	Baghdad	XII
5-1522	0061	Baghdad	XII	5-1699	0480	IM26988	XII
5-1523	0262	36-6-365	XII	5-1707	0073	36-6-268	XII
5-1526	0263	Baghdad	XII	5-1712	0288	36-6-238	XII
5-1529	0264	Baghdad	XII	5-1724	0074	Baghdad	XII
5-1531	0265	Baghdad	XII	5-1739	0124	Baghdad	XII
5-1534	0266	Baghdad	XII	5-1740	0290	Baghdad	XII
5-1535	0267	36-6-226	XII	5-1741	0075	Baghdad	XII
5-1537	0268	Baghdad	XII	5-1755	0291	36-6-143	XII
5-1547	0470	IM26977	XII	5-1758	0292	Discarded	XII
5-1554	0062	Baghdad	XII	5-1760	0481	36-6-299	XII
5-1558	0269	36-6-220	XII	5-none	0007	unknown	XII
5-1560	0004	36-6-281a	XII	5-none	0032	36-6-254	XII
5-1561	0270	36-6-218	XII	5-none	0033	unknown	XII
5-1562	0063	Baghdad	XII	5-none	0076	36-6-267	XII
5-1563	0064	Baghdad	XII	5-none	0077	36-6-275	XII
5-1566	0031	Baghdad	XII	5-none	0078	36-6-277	XII
5-1568	0271	Baghdad	XII	5-none	0079	unknown	XII
5-1579	0065	Baghdad	XII	5-none	0080	unknown	XII
5-1580	0386	36-6-256	XII	5-none	0081	unknown	XII
5-1581	0066	36-6-266	XII	5-none	0125	36-6-278	XII
5-1582	0067	36-6-262	XII	5-none	0126	36-6-282	XII
5-1586	0272	Baghdad	XII	5-none	0127	36-6-283	XII
5-1589	0068	36-6-264	XII	5-none	0128	36-6-284	XII
5-1590	0273	36-6-240	XII	5-none	0129	36-6-285	XII
5-1593	0274	36-6-225	XII	5-none	0130	36-6-286	XII
5-1595	0472	36-6-309	XII	5-none	0131	36-6-290	XII
5-1596	0387	Baghdad	XII	5-none	0132	36-6-292	XII
5-1599	0275	Baghdad	XII	5-none	0157	36-6-276	XII
5-1600	0473	IM27005	XII	5-none	0192	36-6-414	XII
5-1601	0474	IM26972	XII	5-none	0195	36-6-244	XII
5-1605	0276	Baghdad	XII	5-none	0196	36-6-245	XII
5-1606	0277	36-6-221	XII	5-none	0197	36-6-248	XII
5-1615	0069	Baghdad	XII	5-none	0199	36-6-252	XII
5-1618	0278	36-6-222	XII	5-none	0200	36-6-401	XII
5-1621	0279	36-6-236	XII	5-none	0201	36-6-404	XII
5-1622	0280	36-6-228	XII	5-none	0202	36-6-408	XII
5-1623	0281	Baghdad	XII	5-none	0203	36-6-417	XII
5-1629	0282	Baghdad	XII	5-none	0204	36-6-424	XII
5-1636	0283	36-6-234	XII	5-none	0205	36-6-425	XII
5-1637	0284	36-6-223	XII	5-none	0206	36-6-426	XII

Concordance   (continued)

Field Number	Catalogue Number	Location	Level/ Phase
5-none	0207	36-6-427	XII
5-none	0208	unknown	XII
5-none	0213	36-6-250	XII
5-none	0214	discarded	XII
5-none	0215	unknown	XII
5-none	0293	36-6-246	XII
5-none	0294	36-6-247	XII
5-none	0388	36-6-258	XII
5-none	0389	unknown	XII
5-none	0482	36-6-287	XII
5-none	0483	36-6-288	XII
5-none	0484	36-6-289	XII
5-none	0485	36-6-291	XII
5-none	0486	36-6-300	XII
5-none	0487	36-6-301	XII
5-none	0488	36-6-303	XII
5-none	0489	36-6-304	XII
5-none	0491	unknown	XII
5-none	0492	unknown	XII
5-none	0493	unknown	XII
6-002	0296	Baghdad	XII
6-003	0034	37-16-142	XII
6-004	0390	Baghdad	XII
6-005	0297	Baghdad	XII
6-006	0298	unknown	XII
6-008	0299	unknown	XII
6-010	0158	Baghdad	XII
6-013	0082	Baghdad	XII
6-014	0083	Baghdad	XII
6-016	0300	Discarded	XII
6-021	0008	37-16-188	XII
6-022	0084	Baghdad	XII
6-023	0085	37-16-173	XII
6-031	0035	Baghdad	XII
6-066	0301	37-16-066	XII
6-074	0022	37-16-053	XII
6-081	0494	IM32625	XII
6-088	0303	unknown	XII
6-089	0495	37-16-216	XII
6-096	0496	Baghdad	XII
6-098	0133	Baghdad	XII
6-099	0134	Baghdad	XII
6-100	0304	Baghdad	XII
6-108	0498	unknown	XII
6-109	0013	37-16-189	XII
6-110	0305	37-16-115	XII
6-116	0135	37-16-206	XII
6-117	0136	37-16-206	XII
6-119	0306	unknown	XII
6-120	0307	37-16-107	XII
6-143	0137	Baghdad	XII
6-144	0086	unknown	XII

Concordance   (continued)

Field Number	Catalogue Number	Location	Level/ Phase
6-146	0023	lost	XII
6-150	0308	Baghdad	XII
6-151	0499	37-16-208	XII
6-152	0500	Baghdad	XII
6-154	0309	37-16-171	XII
6-160	0138	Baghdad	XII
6-161	0501	37-16-215	XII
6-163	0139	unknown	XII
6-167	0502	Baghdad	XII
6-175	0310	discarded	XII
6-195	0140	unknown	XII
6-201	0311	Baghdad	XII
6-202	0141	37-16-195	XII
6-203	0503	37-16-205	XII
6-204	0166	37-16-183	XII
6-204	0167	37-16-184	XII
6-204a	0159	Baghdad	XII
6-204b	0160	37-26-182	XII
6-205	0312	37-16-113	XII
6-213	0313	37-16-108	XII
6-219	0161	37-16-185	XII
6-239	0087	Baghdad	XII
6-241	0162	Baghdad	XII
6-246	0314	unknown	XII
6-250	0504	37-16-211	XII
6-257	0505	37-16-209	XII
6-258	0315	Baghdad	XII
6-262	0009	37-16-187	XII
6-264	0316	37-16-114	XII
6-265	0088	Baghdad	XII
6-272	0089	Baghdad	XII
6-280	0024	Discarded	XII
6-298	0142	Baghdad	XII
6-303	0506	37-16-207	XII
6-304	0163	37-16-181	XII
6-312	0090	37-16-069	XII
6-313	0317	Baghdad	XII
6-318	0318	unknown	XII
6-366	0507	Baghdad	XII
6-406	0319	37-16-222	XII
6-581	0509	Baghdad	XII
6-594	0322	37-16-117	XII
6-595	0091	37-16-186	XII
6-611	0510	37-16-212	XII
6-616	0144	37-16-202	XII
6-622	0325	37-16-104	XII
6-none	0010	37-16-190	XII
6-none	0011	unknown	XII
6-none	0012	unknown	XII
6-none	0036	37-16-141	XII
6-none	0037	unknown	XII
6-none	0093	37-16-175	XII

(*continues*)

Concordance   (continued)

Field Number	Catalogue Number	Location	Level/ Phase
6-none	0094	37-16-176	XII
6-none	0095	37-16-174	XII
6-none	0097	unknown	XII
6-none	0098	unknown	XII
6-none	0099	unknown	XII
6-none	0100	unknown	XII
6-none	0145	37-16-194	XII
6-none	0146	unknown	XII
6-none	0165	37-16-180	XII
6-none	0169	unknown	XII
6-none	0170	unknown	XII
6-none	0173	unknown	XII
6-none	0209	37-16-125	XII
6-none	0216	37-16-119	XII
6-none	0217	37-16-137	XII
6-none	0391	37-16-143	XII
6-none	0393	37-16-145	XII
6-none	0394	37-16-146	XII
6-none	0395	37-16-147	XII
6-none	0396	37-16-148	XII
6-none	0397	37-16-149	XII
6-none	0398	37-16-150	XII
6-none	0399	37-16-151	XII
6-none	0400	37-16-152	XII
6-none	0401	37-16-153	XII
6-none	0402	37-16-154	XII
6-none	0403	37-16-155	XII
6-none	0404	37-16-156	XII
6-none	0405	37-16-157	XII
6-none	0406	37-16-158	XII
6-none	0407	37-16-159	XII
6-none	0408	37-16-160	XII
6-none	0409	37-16-161	XII
6-none	0410	37-16-162	XII
6-none	0411	37-16-163	XII
6-none	0412	37-16-164	XII
6-none	0413	37-16-165	XII
6-none	0414	37-16-166	XII
6-none	0415	37-16-167	XII
6-none	0416	37-16-168	XII
6-none	0417	37-16-169	XII
6-none	0511	IM32830	XII
7-055	0331	38-13-032	XII
7-056	0518	38-13-050	XII
7-154	0332	discarded	XII
7-194	0101	Baghdad	XII
7-206	0519	38-13-029	XII
7-209	0520	IM42359	XII
7-211	0521	IM42660	XII
7-212	0522	Baghdad	XII
7-212A	0523	38-13-051	XII
7-228	0524	38-13-046	XII

Concordance   (continued)

Field Number	Catalogue Number	Location	Level/ Phase
7-230	0102	38-13-036	XII
7-231	0525	Baghdad	XII
7-235b	0528	38-13-044b	XII
7-251	0526	38-13-043	XII
7-252	0147	38-13-041	XII
7-253	0527	38-13-044	XII
7-255	0529	IM42264	XII
7-257	0530	38-13-045	XII
7-258	0148	38-13-040	XII
7-261	0103	38-13-509	XII
7-262	0104	Baghdad	XII
7-264	0149	38-13-039	XII
7-267	0531	38-13-047	XII
7-272	0218	38-13-033	XII
7-274	0532	38-13-042	XII
7-480	0533	38-13-028	XII
7-481	0534	Baghdad	XII
7-none	0150	unknown	XII
7-none	0171	38-13-037	XII
7-none	0210	discarded	XII
7-none	0328	unknown	XII
7-none	0329	unknown	XII
7-none	0333	38-13-035	XII
7-none	0512	discarded	XII
7-none	0513	unknown	XII
7-none	0514	unknown	XII
7-none	0515	unknown	XII
7-none	0516	unknown	XII
7-none	0517	unknown	XII
4-0970	0027	35-10-216	XII?
4-1149	0234	35-10-198	XII?
4-1163	0110	Baghdad	XII?
4-none	0021	unknown	XII?
4-none	0052	unknown	XII?
4-none	0053	unknown	XII?
4-none	0156	unknown	XII?
4-none	0251	unknown	XII?
4-none	0348	35-10-160	XII?
4-none	0378	unknown	XII?
4-none	0382	unknown	XII?
4-none	0383	unknown	XII?
4-none	0384	unknown	XII?
5-1490	0258	Baghdad	XII?
5-1555	0122	Baghdad	XII?
5-1588	0471	36-6-296	XII?
5-1630	0475	IM27027	XII?
5-1631	0476	Baghdad	XII?
5-1643	0285	Baghdad	XII?
5-1713	0289	36-6-230	XII?
5-none	0198	36-6-249	XII?
5-none	0295	unknown	XII?
5-none	0490	Discarded	XII?

Concordance (continued)

Field Number	Catalogue Number	Location	Level/ Phase
6-085	0302	unknown	XII?
6-107	0497	37-16-214	XII?
6-579	0508	37-16-215	XII?
6-587	0143	Baghdad	XII?
6-588	0320	37-16-094	XII?
6-589	0321	Baghdad	XII?
6-601	0323	Baghdad	XII?
6-602	0092	37-16-179	XII?
6-603	0164	Baghdad	XII?
6-618	0324	Baghdad	XII?
6-623	0326	Baghdad	XII?
6-none	0096	unknown	XII?
6-none	0168	unknown	XII?
6-none	0327	37-16-092	XII?
6-none	0330	unknown	XII?
6-none	0392	37-16-144	XII?
7-271	0176	38-13-038	XII?
4-0710	0535	Baghdad	XIA
4-0762	0841	Baghdad	XIA
4-0838	0536	Baghdad	XIA
4-0907	0919	IM25042	XIA
4-0939	0922	IM24977	XIA
4-1015	0935	phila no#	XIA
4-1016	0936	IM25004	XIA
4-1017	0937	IM24976	XIA
4-1030	0597	35-10-234	XIA
4-1035	0940	35-10-181	XIA
4-1051	0691	Baghdad	XIA
4-1052	0943	IM24572	XIA
4-1053	0944	Baghdad	XIA
4-1062	0572	Baghdad	XIA
4-1076	0957	Baghdad	XIA
4-1101	0599	Baghdad	XIA
4-1102	0852	35-10-158	XIA
4-1148	0969	35-10-176	XIA
4-1166	0600	35-10-233	XIA
4-none	0555	unknown	XIA
4-none	0604	discarded	XIA
4-none	0778	discarded	XIA
4-none	0857	35-10-152	XIA
4-none	0861	35-10-229	XIA
4-none	0865	35-10-380	XIA
4-none	0875	unknown	XIA
4-none	0876	unknown	XIA
4-none	0877	unknown	XIA
4-none	0976	unknown	XIA
4-none	0977	unknown	XIA
4-none	0980	discarded	XIA
5-1328	0995	36-6-112	XIA
5-1376	0997	36-6-216	XIA
5-1377	0998	Discarded	XIA
5-1378	0999	IM26980	XIA

Concordance (continued)

Field Number	Catalogue Number	Location	Level/ Phase
5-1385	1001	IM27032	XIA
5-1393	0786	Baghdad	XIA
5-1399	1005	36-6-213	XIA
5-1399B	1006	IM26979	XIA
5-1422	0615	phila no#	XIA
5-1423	0792	discarded	XIA
5-1424	1007	36-6-200	XIA
5-1444	0795	Baghdad	XIA
5-1457	0797	Baghdad	XIA
5-1488	1017	36-6-209	XIA
5-1549	0816	Baghdad	XIA
5-1550	0817	36-6-141	XIA
5-1557	1019	IM26989	XIA
5-1594	1023	36-6-121	XIA
5-1624	1025	IM26996	XIA
5-1626	1027	IM26963	XIA
5-1627	1028	IM26968	XIA
5-1628	1029	IM26994	XIA
5-1638	1030	36-6-204	XIA
5-1650	1032	IM26974	XIA
5-1651	1033	36-6-210	XIA
5-1668	1034	36-6-207	XIA
5-none	0547	unknown	XIA
5-none	0585	36-6-164	XIA
5-none	0739	unknown	XIA
5-none	0740	unknown	XIA
5-none	0826	unknown	XIA
5-none	0906	unknown	XIA
5-none	0907	unknown	XIA
5-none	1038	discarded	XIA
5-none	1039	discarded	XIA
5-none	1042	dicarded	XIA
5-none	1043	discarded	XIA
5-none	1044	discarded	XIA
5-none	1046	unknown	XIA
6-065	0642	37-16-067	XIA
7-254	1087	Baghdad	XIA
4-0695	0839	Baghdad	XIAB
4-0696	0840	35-10-351	XIAB
4-0733	0743	35-10-140	XIAB
4-0795	0684	Baghdad	XIAB
4-0901	0685	35-10-243	XIAB
4-0921	0744	Discarded	XIAB
4-0925	0745	Discarded	XIAB
4-0930	0842	Baghdad	XIAB
4-0934	0592	Baghdad	XIAB
4-0935	0746	discarded	XIAB
4-0936	0920	35-10-178	XIAB
4-0938	0921	35-10-179	XIAB
4-0946	0593	35-10-238	XIAB
4-0947	0923	Baghdad	XIAB
4-0952	0843	Baghdad	XIAB

(continues)

Concordance   (continued)

Concordance   (continued)

Field Number	Catalogue Number	Location	Level/ Phase	Field Number	Catalogue Number	Location	Level/ Phase
4-0953	0924	35-10-177	XIAB	4-1059	0757	Baghdad	XIAB
4-0955	0925	35-10-263	XIAB	4-1061	0948	IM24998	XIAB
4-0957	0926	35-10-264	XIAB	4-1063	0758	Baghdad	XIAB
4-0958	0927	35-10-265	XIAB	4-1065	0949	35-10-182	XIAB
4-0961	0654	phila?	XIAB	4-1066	0950	35-10-175	XIAB
4-0963	0655	Baghdad	XIAB	4-1067	0951	IM24976	XIAB
4-0965	0686	phila?	XIAB	4-1068	0952	IM25069	XIAB
4-0967	0687	Baghdad	XIAB	4-1069	0953	IM24964	XIAB
4-0968	0928	35-10-256	XIAB	4-1070	0954	35-10-174	XIAB
4-0972	0656	35-10-247	XIAB	4-1074	0955	IM25049	XIAB
4-0973	0594	35-10-237	XIAB	4-1075	0956	IM25050	XIAB
4-0977	0929	IM25040	XIAB	4-1078	0958	Discarded	XIAB
4-0980	0650	discarded	XIAB	4-1079	0959	35-10-183	XIAB
4-0981	0930	35-10-137	XIAB	4-1080	0960	35-10-184	XIAB
4-0982	0595	35-10-355	XIAB	4-1081	0961	35-10-185	XIAB
4-0983	0688	35-10-095	XIAB	4-1085	0851	Baghdad	XIAB
4-0985	0689	35-10-359	XIAB	4-1087	0658	Baghdad	XIAB
4-0987	0596	35-10-239	XIAB	4-1089	0962	IM24600	XIAB
4-0988	0552	Baghdad	XIAB	4-1094	0759	35-10-139	XIAB
4-0989	0931	IM25001	XIAB	4-1095	0760	35-10-032	XIAB
4-0991	0844	35-10-229	XIAB	4-1096	0651	discarded	XIAB
4-0997	0747	35-10-187	XIAB	4-1105	0573	Baghdad	XIAB
4-0998	0932	35-10-267	XIAB	4-1106	0538	Baghdad	XIAB
4-0999	0748	Baghdad	XIAB	4-1108	0761	phila?	XIAB
4-1000	0749	philano#	XIAB	4-1109	0762	Baghdad	XIAB
4-1004	0933	IM25051	XIAB	4-1110	0763	35-10-374	XIAB
4-1005	0845	35-10-161	XIAB	4-1111	0764	discarded	XIAB
4-1005	0846	35-10-162	XIAB	4-1112	0708	Discarded	XIAB
4-1005	0847	35-10-163	XIAB	4-1113	0709	Baghdad	XIAB
4-1005	0848	35-10-164	XIAB	4-1114	0710	Discarded	XIAB
4-1005	0849	35-10-165	XIAB	4-1115	0765	Discarded	XIAB
4-1007	0934	35-10-180	XIAB	4-1116	0766	Baghdad	XIAB
4-1008	0750	35-10-144	XIAB	4-1117	0767	35-10-145	XIAB
4-1018	0657	Baghdad	XIAB	4-1118	0768	35-10-372	XIAB
4-1019	0690	Baghdad	XIAB	4-1118	0769	35-10-373	XIAB
4-1020	0751	35-10-166	XIAB	4-1119	0770	Discarded	XIAB
4-1022	0752	35-10-144	XIAB	4-1120	0771	phila?	XIAB
4-1024	0753	discarded	XIAB	4-1121	0772	unknown	XIAB
4-1025	0938	Baghdad	XIAB	4-1126	0963	IM24958	XIAB
4-1027	0537	35-10-170	XIAB	4-1127	0964	IM25003	XIAB
4-1028	0571	35-10-146	XIAB	4-1129	0965	IM25038	XIAB
4-1031	0754	Baghdad	XIAB	4-1130	0966	IM24975	XIAB
4-1032	0755	Baghdad	XIAB	4-1131	0967	IM24966	XIAB
4-1033	0756	Baghdad	XIAB	4-1159	0574	35-10-217	XIAB
4-1034	0939	35-10-173	XIAB	4-1165	0775	35-10-138	XIAB
4-1036	0941	IM24969	XIAB	4-1179	0575	Baghdad	XIAB
4-1037	0942	IM25043	XIAB	4-1206	0971	35-10-186	XIAB
4-1049	0850	35-10-150	XIAB	4-1210	0972	35-10-279	XIAB
4-1050	0598	35-10-167	XIAB	4-1217	0659	Baghdad	XIAB
4-1054	0945	IM24967	XIAB	4-1218	0854	35-10-220	XIAB
4-1055	0946	IM24605	XIAB	4-1220	0974	IM24583	XIAB
4-1058	0947	35-10-172	XIAB	4-1221	0975	35-10-251	XIAB

Concordance   (continued)

Concordance   (continued)

Field Number	Catalogue Number	Location	Level/ Phase	Field Number	Catalogue Number	Location	Level/ Phase
4-none	0539	unknown	XIAB	4-none	0783	unknown	XIAB
4-none	0553	discarded	XIAB	4-none	0784	unknown	XIAB
4-none	0554	discarded	XIAB	4-none	0855	35-10-148	XIAB
4-none	0556	unknown	XIAB	4-none	0856	35-10-149	XIAB
4-none	0557	unknown	XIAB	4-none	0858	35-10-153	XIAB
4-none	0558	unknown	XIAB	4-none	0859	35-10-154	XIAB
4-none	0567	unknown	XIAB	4-none	0860	35-10-159	XIAB
4-none	0568	unknown	XIAB	4-none	0862	35-10-376	XIAB
4-none	0569	unknown	XIAB	4-none	0863	35-10-377	XIAB
4-none	0576	discarded	XIAB	4-none	0864	35-10-378	XIAB
4-none	0577	unknown	XIAB	4-none	0866	35-10-381	XIAB
4-none	0578	unknown	XIAB	4-none	0867	discarded	XIAB
4-none	0579	unknown	XIAB	4-none	0868	discarded	XIAB
4-none	0601	35-10-168	XIAB	4-none	0869	discarded	XIAB
4-none	0602	35-10-168	XIAB	4-none	0870	unknown	XIAB
4-none	0603	35-10-169	XIAB	4-none	0871	unknown	XIAB
4-none	0605	discarded	XIAB	4-none	0872	unknown	XIAB
4-none	0606	unknown	XIAB	4-none	0873	unknown	XIAB
4-none	0607	unknown	XIAB	4-none	0874	unknown	XIAB
4-none	0608	unknown	XIAB	4-none	0878	unknown	XIAB
4-none	0609	unknown	XIAB	4-none	0879	unknown	XIAB
4-none	0652	discarded	XIAB	4-none	0880	unknown	XIAB
4-none	0653	unknown	XIAB	4-none	0881	unknown	XIAB
4-none	0660	discarded	XIAB	4-none	0882	unknown	XIAB
4-none	0661	unknown	XIAB	4-none	0883	unknown	XIAB
4-none	0662	unknown	XIAB	4-none	0884	unknown	XIAB
4-none	0663	unknown	XIAB	4-none	0885	unknown	XIAB
4-none	0664	unknown	XIAB	4-none	0886	unknown	XIAB
4-none	0665	unknown	XIAB	4-none	0887	unknown	XIAB
4-none	0666	unknown	XIAB	4-none	0888	unknown	XIAB
4-none	0667	unknown	XIAB	4-none	0889	unknown	XIAB
4-none	0693	unknown	XIAB	4-none	0890	unknown	XIAB
4-none	0703	unknown	XIAB	4-none	0891	unknown	XIAB
4-none	0704	unknown	XIAB	4-none	0892	unknown	XIAB
4-none	0711	35-10-143	XIAB	4-none	0893	unknown	XIAB
4-none	0712	unknown	XIAB	4-none	0894	unknown	XIAB
4-none	0713	unknown	XIAB	4-none	0895	unknown	XIAB
4-none	0714	unknown	XIAB	4-none	0896	unknown	XIAB
4-none	0715	unknown	XIAB	4-none	0897	unknown	XIAB
4-none	0716	unknown	XIAB	4-none	0978	unknown	XIAB
4-none	0717	unknown	XIAB	4-none	0981	discarded	XIAB
4-none	0718	unknown	XIAB	4-none	0982	discarded	XIAB
4-none	0719	unknown	XIAB	4-none	0983	discarded	XIAB
4-none	0734	unknown	XIAB	4-none	0984	discarded	XIAB
4-none	0735	unknown	XIAB	4-none	0985	discarded	XIAB
4-none	0736	unknown	XIAB	4-none	0986	discarded	XIAB
4-none	0737	unknown	XIAB	4-none	0987	discarded	XIAB
4-none	0777	discarded	XIAB	4-none	0988	discarded	XIAB
4-none	0779	discarded	XIAB	4-none	0989	discarded	XIAB
4-none	0780	unknown	XIAB	4-none	0990	unknown	XIAB
4-none	0781	unknown	XIAB	4-none	0991	unknown	XIAB
4-none	0782	unknown	XIAB	4-none	0992	unknown	XIAB

(*continues*)

Concordance   (continued)   Concordance   (continued)

Field Number	Catalogue Number	Location	Level/ Phase	Field Number	Catalogue Number	Location	Level/ Phase
5-1245	0994	IM26997	XIAB	5-1524	0583	Baghdad	XIAB
5-1329	0610	36-6-099	XIAB	5-1525	0812	36-6-139	XIAB
5-1330	0611	Baghdad	XIAB	5-1530	0898	36-6-167A	XIAB
5-1337	0570	Baghdad	XIAB	5-1530	0899	36-6-167B	XIAB
5-1367	0996	Baghdad	XIAB	5-1530	0900	36-6-167C	XIAB
5-1379	1000	IM27006	XIAB	5-1533	0813	36-6-136	XIAB
5-1382	0612	36-6-185	XIAB	5-1539	0621	Baghdad	XIAB
5-1383	0668	36-6-109	XIAB	5-1541	0622	Baghdad	XIAB
5-1384	0580	Baghdad	XIAB	5-1542	0623	Baghdad	XIAB
5-1387	0581	36-6-146	XIAB	5-1545	0815	Baghdad	XIAB
5-1389	1002	Baghdad	XIAB	5-1548	1018	IM26976	XIAB
5-1391	0785	Baghdad	XIAB	5-1556	0584	36-6-147	XIAB
5-1392	1003	Baghdad	XIAB	5-1565	0624	36-6-178	XIAB
5-1395	0787	Baghdad	XIAB	5-1571	0818	Discarded	XIAB
5-1396	1004	36-6-205	XIAB	5-1574	1022	IM26990	XIAB
5-1397	0788	36-6-144	XIAB	5-1578	0625	Baghdad	XIAB
5-1398	0789	Baghdad	XIAB	5-1585	0819	Baghdad	XIAB
5-1411	0790	36-6-149	XIAB	5-1598	0626	36-6-181	XIAB
5-1415	0791	discarded	XIAB	5-1602	0820	Baghdad	XIAB
5-1416	0613	36-6-172	XIAB	5-1612	1024	36-6-397	XIAB
5-1421	0614	36-6-174	XIAB	5-1625	1026	36-6-206	XIAB
5-1428	1008	IM26983	XIAB	5-1634	0545	36-6-196	XIAB
5-1429	1009	36-6-212	XIAB	5-1635	0670	phila?	XIAB
5-1431	0540	Baghdad	XIAB	5-1639	1031	Baghdad	XIAB
5-1432	0793	Baghdad	XIAB	5-1644	0822	36-6-135	XIAB
5-1433	0694	36-6-176	XIAB	5-1645	0823	36-6-148	XIAB
5-1434	0616	Baghdad	XIAB	5-1652	0627	36-6-182	XIAB
5-1438	1011	36-6-391	XIAB	5-1669	0628	Baghdad	XIAB
5-1442	0794	discarded	XIAB	5-none	0546	36-6-279	XIAB
5-1446	0796	Baghdad	XIAB	5-none	0559	unknown	XIAB
5-1447	0541	Baghdad	XIAB	5-none	0586	36-6-165	XIAB
5-1448	0695	phila?	XIAB	5-none	0587	36-6-253	XIAB
5-1449	0696	Baghdad	XIAB	5-none	0588	unknown	XIAB
5-1454	0617	Baghdad	XIAB	5-none	0589	unknown	XIAB
5-1455	0618	36-6-173	XIAB	5-none	0629	36-6-180	XIAB
5-1459	0619	Baghdad	XIAB	5-none	0630	36-6-183	XIAB
5-1460	0582	36-6-163	XIAB	5-none	0631	36-6-186	XIAB
5-1465	1012	Baghdad	XIAB	5-none	0632	36-6-187	XIAB
5-1468	0798	36-6-138	XIAB	5-none	0633	36-6-189	XIAB
5-1469	1013	Baghdad	XIAB	5-none	0634	36-6-190	XIAB
5-1471	1014	IM27039	XIAB	5-none	0635	36-6-191	XIAB
5-1475	0799	Baghdad	XIAB	5-none	0636	36-6-091	XIAB
5-1476	1015	IM27037	XIAB	5-none	0637	unknown	XIAB
5-1482	0800	36-6-138	XIAB	5-none	0638	unknown	XIAB
5-1483	1016	36-6-203	XIAB	5-none	0639	unknown	XIAB
5-1484	0542	36-6-193	XIAB	5-none	0640	unknown	XIAB
5-1484	0543	36-6-194	XIAB	5-none	0641	unknown	XIAB
5-1492	0805	Baghdad	XIAB	5-none	0697	unknown	XIAB
5-1494	0806	discarded	XIAB	5-none	0698	unknown	XIAB
5-1495	0807	36-6-137	XIAB	5-none	0705	unknown	XIAB
5-1505	0808	36-6-134	XIAB	5-none	0720	36-6-243	XIAB
5-1516	0810	discarded	XIAB	5-none	0721	36-6-244	XIAB

Concordance   (continued)

Field Number	Catalogue Number	Location	Level/Phase
5-none	0722	36-6-421	XIAB
5-none	0723	36-6-150	XIAB
5-none	0724	36-6-154	XIAB
5-none	0725	36-6-015?	XIAB
5-none	0726	36-6-156	XIAB
5-none	0727	36-6-157	XIAB
5-none	0728	36-6-158	XIAB
5-none	0729	36-6-159	XIAB
5-none	0730	36-6-160	XIAB
5-none	0731	36-6-161	XIAB
5-none	0732	36-6-162	XIAB
5-none	0733	36-6-412	XIAB
5-none	0741	unknown	XIAB
5-none	0824	36-6-145	XIAB
5-none	0825	discarded	XIAB
5-none	0827	unknown	XIAB
5-none	0901	36-6-151	XIAB
5-none	0902	36-6-155	XIAB
5-none	0903	36-6-168	XIAB
5-none	0904	36-6-169	XIAB
5-none	0905	36-6-170	XIAB
5-none	1036	36-6-201	XIAB
5-none	1037	36-6-202	XIAB
5-none	1040	discarded	XIAB
5-none	1041	discarded	XIAB
5-none	1045	unknown	XIAB
5-none	1047	unknown	XIAB
5-none	1048	unknown	XIAB
5-none	1049	unknown	XIAB
6-068	0671	37-16-072	XIAB
6-071	0828	Baghdad	XIAB
6-073	1050	IM32503	XIAB
6-075	0643	37-16-068	XIAB
6-076	1051	37-16-078	XIAB
6-077	1052	37-16-087	XIAB
6-078	0560	37-16-052	XIAB
6-079	1053	Baghdad	XIAB
6-080	1054	IM32542	XIAB
6-082	0644	Baghdad	XIAB
6-084	1055	37-16-086	XIAB
6-086	1056	37-16-075	XIAB
6-087	0829	37-16-050	XIAB
6-089	1057	37-16-216	XIAB
6-090	1058	37-16-083	XIAB
6-091	0699	37-16-071	XIAB
6-092	1059	37-16-074	XIAB
6-093	1060	unknown	XIAB
6-095	0672	unknown	XIAB
6-097	0645	Baghdad	XIAB
6-101	1061	IM32857	XIAB
6-104	0561	unknown	XIAB
6-106	0831	Baghdad	XIAB

Concordance   (continued)

Field Number	Catalogue Number	Location	Level/Phase
6-115	0832	Baghdad	XIAB
6-127	0673	37-16-079	XIAB
6-128	0833	Baghdad	XIAB
6-130	0700	Baghdad	XIAB
6-131	0590	discarded	XIAB
6-133	1062	37-16-076	XIAB
6-134	1063	IM32567	XIAB
6-135	1064	Baghdad	XIAB
6-136	0674	37-16-085	XIAB
6-137	1065	Baghdad	XIAB
6-139	1066	Baghdad	XIAB
6-141	0706	unknown	XIAB
6-142	0675	unknown	XIAB
6-145	0676	37-16-080	XIAB
6-156	0834	Baghdad	XIAB
6-173	0835	unknown	XIAB
6-200	0677	37-16-081	XIAB
6-208	0707	unknown	XIAB
6-214	1067	37-16-077	XIAB
6-216	0678	Baghdad	XIAB
6-266	1068	37-16-088	XIAB
6-315	0646	Baghdad	XIAB
6-317	0836	unknown	XIAB
6-340	1069	37-16-082	XIAB
6-606	0837	37-16-051	XIAB
6-none	0548	37-16-065	XIAB
6-none	0701	37-16-070	XIAB
6-none	0742	unknown	XIAB
6-none	0908	37-16-054	XIAB
6-none	0909	37-16-055	XIAB
6-none	0910	37-16-056	XIAB
6-none	0911	37-16-057	XIAB
6-none	0912	37-16-058	XIAB
6-none	0913	37-16-059	XIAB
6-none	0914	37-16-060	XIAB
6-none	0915	37-16-061	XIAB
6-none	0916	37-16-062	XIAB
6-none	0917	37-16-063	XIAB
6-none	0918	37-16-064	XIAB
7-0054	0681	38-13-009	XIAB
7-053	0591	Baghdad	XIAB
7-057	1076	IM42678	XIAB
7-058	1077	IM42626	XIAB
7-116	0562	38-13-007	XIAB
7-133	1078	IM42372	XIAB
7-134A	1079	IM42676	XIAB
7-134B	1080	38-13-031	XIAB
7-143	1081	IM42670	XIAB
7-144	1082	IM42672	XIAB
7-145	1083	IM42672	XIAB
7-150	0648	Baghdad	XIAB
7-179	1084	38-13-030	XIAB

(continues)

Concordance   (continued)

Field Number	Catalogue Number	Location	Level/ Phase
7-215	0563	38-13-023	XIAB
7-216	0564	38-13-024	XIAB
7-217	0565	38-13-025	XIAB
7-232	1085	38-13-048	XIAB
7-236	1086	Baghdad	XIAB
7-none	0549	unknown	XIAB
7-none	0550	unknown	XIAB
7-none	0551	38-13-027	XIAB
7-none	0566	unknown	XIAB
7-none	0647	unknown	XIAB
7-none	0649	38-13-026	XIAB
7-none	0679	unknown	XIAB
7-none	0680	unknown	XIAB
7-none	0682	unknown	XIAB
7-none	0683	unknown	XIAB
7-none	0702	unknown	XIAB
7-none	0838	unknown	XIAB
7-none	1070	unknown	XIAB
7-none	1071	unknown	XIAB
7-none	1072	unknown	XIAB
7-none	1073	unknown	XIAB
7-none	1074	unknown	XIAB
7-none	1075	unknown	XIAB
7-none	1088	Discarded	XIAB
7-none	1089	Discarded	XIAB
7-none	1090	unknown	XIAB
4-1104	0853	Baghdad	XIB
4-1122	0773	Baghdad	XIB
4-1123	0774	discarded	XIB
4-1155	0692	Baghdad	XIB
4-1157	0970	35-10-254	XIB
4-1169	0776	Baghdad	XIB
4-1212	0973	IM25011	XIB
4-none	0979	discarded	XIB
5-1435	1010	36-6-215	XIB
5-1466	0669	Baghdad	XIB
5-1485	0801	36-6-171	XIB
5-1486	0802	Baghdad	XIB
5-1487	0803	Baghdad	XIB
5-1489	0804	36-6-140	XIB
5-1493	0620	36-6-184	XIB
5-1506	0809	Baghdad	XIB
5-1517	0811	36-6-281b	XIB
5-1518	0544	36-6-281B	XIB
5-1536	0814	Baghdad	XIB
5-1564	1020	36-6-295	XIB
5-1573	1021	36-6-208	XIB
5-1620	0821	Baghdad	XIB
5-1710	1035	36-6-199	XIB
5-none	0738	unknown	XIB
6-094	0830	unknown	XIB
1046	1168	31-52-395	XI

Concordance   (continued)

Field Number	Catalogue Number	Location	Level/ Phase
1099c	1291	31-52-444	XI
1109	1169	31-52-446	XI
1109	1292	31-52-445	XI
1109a	1293	31-52-444	XI
1110	1391	31-52-441	XI
1112	1170	31-52-448	XI
1115	1132	31-52-447	XI
1202	1392	31-52-442	XI
1203	1171	31-52-442	XI
3-0482	1294	Baghdad	XI
3-0486	1577	Baghdad	XI
3-none	1128	unknown	XI
4-0603	1486	Baghdad	XI
4-0604	1487	Baghdad	XI
4-0604	1488	Baghdad	XI
4-0611	1489	35-10-002	XI
4-0612	1101	Baghdad	XI
4-0613	1490	35-10-067	XI
4-0614	1491	Baghdad	XI
4-0615	1492	Phila no#	XI
4-0617	1172	Baghdad	XI
4-0619	1493	Baghdad	XI
4-0621	1393	Baghdad	XI
4-0622	1173	Baghdad	XI
4-0625	1174	35-10-88	XI
4-0627	1394	35-10-025	XI
4-0628	1395	Baghdad	XI
4-0629	1133	Baghdad	XI
4-0630	1134	35-10-035	XI
4-0631	1167	Phila no #	XI
4-0632	1396	Baghdad	XI
4-0641	1578	35-10-119	XI
4-0642	1579	IM24961	XI
4-0643	1580	IM25046	XI
4-0645	1581	IM24968	XI
4-0649	1582	35-10-113	XI
4-0650	1397	Baghdad	XI
4-0655	1255	Baghdad	XI
4-0656	1102	35-10-052	XI
4-0657	1494	35-10-072	XI
4-0658	1495	35-10-070	XI
4-0659	1496	Baghdad	XI
4-0660	1497	discarded	XI
4-0663	1498	discarded	XI
4-0664	1583	IM25044	XI
4-0665	1103	Baghdad	XI
4-0666	1584	35-10-124	XI
4-0669	1499	35-10-347	XI
4-0670	1398	35-10-028	XI
4-0671	1256	35-10-111	XI
4-0675	1175	Baghdad	XI
4-0682	1257	phila no#	XI

Concordance   (continued)

Field Number	Catalogue Number	Location	Level/ Phase
4-0683	1585	IM24578	XI
4-0687	1500	Baghdad	XI
4-0688	1176	Baghdad	XI
4-0689	1399	Baghdad	XI
4-0690	1400	discarded	XI
4-0695	1501	Baghdad	XI
4-0698	1177	Baghdad	XI
4-0700	1401	discarded	XI
4-0701	1502	Baghdad	XI
4-0702	1503	discarded	XI
4-0705	1504	Baghdad	XI
4-0706	1178	Baghdad	XI
4-0707	1586	IM24603	XI
4-0708	1136	discarded	XI
4-0711	1505	Baghdad	XI
4-0716	1506	35-10-073	XI
4-0718	1507	Baghdad	XI
4-0719	1508	35-10-066	XI
4-0728	1509	Baghdad	XI
4-0728B	1510	Baghdad	XI
4-0731	1511	Baghdad	XI
4-0732	1402	discarded	XI
4-0734	1403	Baghdad	XI
4-0735	1404	discarded	XI
4-0763	1512	discarded	XI
4-0764	1405	Baghdad	XI
4-0776	1513	35-10-064	XI
4-0777	1587	35-10-110	XI
4-0778	1514	Baghdad	XI
4-0781	1588	IM24985	XI
4-0781A	1589	35-10-137	XI
4-0784	1137	Baghdad	XI
4-0787	1091	Baghdad	XI
4-0790	1179	35-10-093	XI
4-0791	1180	35-10-294	XI
4-0804	1406	discarded	XI
4-0805	1407	Baghdad	XI
4-0807	1590	IM24988	XI
4-0808	1591	35-10-105	XI
4-0809	1408	35-10-030	XI
4-0810	1409	Baghdad	XI
4-0812	1181	35-10-094	XI
4-0813	1515	discarded	XI
4-0814	1516	35-10-354	XI
4-0816	1138	35-10-054	XI
4-0818	1517	35-10-056	XI
4-0819	1314	Baghdad	XI
4-0820	1592	IM24584	XI
4-0833	1410	35-10-029	XI
4-0834	1518	35-10-076	XI
4-0836	1258	Baghdad	XI
4-0837	1259	35-10-104	XI

Concordance   (continued)

Field Number	Catalogue Number	Location	Level/ Phase
4-0839	1182	Baghdad	XI
4-0841	1260	35-10-331	XI
4-0842	1593	35-10-107	XI
4-0843	1594	35-10-117	XI
4-0844	1139	35-10-036	XI
4-0845	1183	Baghdad	XI
4-0848A	1595	35-10-122	XI
4-0848C	1597	IM24991	XI
4-0849	1598	35-10-128	XI
4-0850	1599	35-10-130	XI
4-0851	1600	IM24971	XI
4-0854	1411	Baghdad	XI
4-0855	1519	35-10-074	XI
4-0856	1520	35-10-059	XI
4-0857	1521	Baghdad	XI
4-0858	1522	35-10-069	XI
4-0859	1523	35-10-090	XI
4-0860	1412	Baghdad	XI
4-0861	1601	IM24989	XI
4-0862	1184	Baghdad	XI
4-0865	1140	Baghdad	XI
4-0866	1524	discarded	XI
4-0867	1295	Baghdad	XI
4-0869	1413	35-10-027	XI
4-0870	1602	35-10-125	XI
4-0873	1603	35-10-132	XI
4-0874	1604	IM24981	XI
4-0876	1185	Baghdad	XI
4-0879	1329	35-10-038	XI
4-0881	1605	IM24990	XI
4-0882	1606	IM24986	XI
4-0883	1261	Baghdad	XI
4-0884	1607	IM24994	XI
4-0885	1186	Baghdad	XI
4-0886	1608	Phila no#	XI
4-0887	1609	IM24983	XI
4-0888	1610	35-10-124	XI
4-0889	1611	35-10-126	XI
4-0890	1612	35-10-134	XI
4-0891	1613	35-10-121	XI
4-0892	1141	Baghdad	XI
4-0893	1614	35-10-123	XI
4-0894	1254	discarded	XI
4-0895	1615	IM24984	XI
4-0896	1616	35-10-106	XI
4-0897	1617	IM24987	XI
4-0898	1414	35-10-026	XI
4-0899	1415	Baghdad	XI
4-0900	1416	Baghdad	XI
4-0904	1618	IM24602	XI
4-0905	1142	35-10-147	XI
4-0906	1417	35-10-031	XI

(*continues*)

Concordance   (continued)

Concordance   (continued)

Field Number	Catalogue Number	Location	Level/ Phase	Field Number	Catalogue Number	Location	Level/ Phase
4-0908	1525	35-10-222	XI	4-1077	1629	35-10-127	XI
4-0910	1526	Baghdad	XI	4-1082	1630	35-10-116	XI
4-0911	1187	Baghdad	XI	4-1083	1631	IM24999	XI
4-0912	1330	discarded	XI	4-1086	1197	35-10-078	XI
4-0914	1262	Baghdad	XI	4-1088	1632	35-10-115	XI
4-0915	1263	Baghdad	XI	4-1090	1270	Baghdad	XI
4-0916	1188	35-10-099	XI	4-1091	1333	Baghdad	XI
4-0917	1619	35-10-109	XI	4-1092	1633	35-10-120	XI
4-0918	1189	35-10-084	XI	4-1093	1198	phila?	XI
4-0918	1190	35-10-085	XI	4-1095	1423	35-10-032	XI
4-0918A	1191	35-10-081	XI	4-1099	1634	IM25012	XI
4-0918B	1192	Baghdad	XI	4-1103	1529	Baghdad	XI
4-0920	1418	35-10-033	XI	4-1107	1092	Baghdad	XI
4-0922	1296	35-10-100	XI	4-1125	1424	Baghdad	XI
4-0923	1297	Baghdad	XI	4-1128	1635	IM24965	XI
4-0924	1298	Baghdad	XI	4-1134	1636	IM25005	XI
4-0927	1193	Baghdad	XI	4-848B	1596	35-10-122	XI
4-0928	1194	Baghdad	XI	4-none	1109	unknown	XI
4-0929	1195	35-10-086	XI	4-none	1110	unknown	XI
4-0931	1299	35-10-098	XI	4-none	1111	unknown	XI
4-0932	1300	35-10-096	XI	4-none	1129	unknown	XI
4-0933	1301	35-10-097	XI	4-none	1130	unknown	XI
4-0937	1620	IM24995	XI	4-none	1143	discarded	XI
4-0940	1621	IM25008	XI	4-none	1144	unknown	XI
4-0942	1622	philanono	XI	4-none	1199	35-10-394	XI
4-0944	1302	35-10-099	XI	4-none	1200	35-10-396	XI
4-0945	1264	35-10-102	XI	4-none	1201	35-10-080	XI
4-0964	1265	Baghdad	XI	4-none	1202	discarded	XI
4-0971	1104	Baghdad	XI	4-none	1203	unknown	XI
4-0974	1196	35-10-079	XI	4-none	1204	unknown	XI
4-0975	1105	35-10-055	XI	4-none	1205	unknown	XI
4-0986	1623	IM25041	XI	4-none	1206	unknown	XI
4-0989	1315	35-10-101	XI	4-none	1207	unknown	XI
4-0990	1624	35-10-136	XI	4-none	1208	unknown	XI
4-0992	1419	discarded	XI	4-none	1271	unknown	XI
4-0993	1331	35-10-051	XI	4-none	1272	unknown	XI
4-1001	1106	35-10-034	XI	4-none	1273	unknown	XI
4-1002	1266	Baghdad	XI	4-none	1274	unknown	XI
4-1003	1267	35-10-108	XI	4-none	1275	unknown	XI
4-1009	1107	Baghdad	XI	4-none	1303	unknown	XI
4-1010	1420	Baghdad	XI	4-none	1304	unknown	XI
4-1011	1421	Baghdad	XI	4-none	1316	discarded	XI
4-1014	1332	discarded	XI	4-none	1317	unknown	XI
4-1021	1422	discarded	XI	4-none	1327	unknown	XI
4-1026	1108	Baghdad	XI	4-none	1334	unknown	XI
4-1029	1626	IM24960	XI	4-none	1335	unknown	XI
4-1041	1527	discarded	XI	4-none	1336	35-10-39	XI
4-1046	1528	discarded	XI	4-none	1337	35-10-41	XI
4-1056	1268	Baghdad	XI	4-none	1338	35-10-042	XI
4-1057	1269	35-10-103	XI	4-none	1339	35-10-043	XI
4-1060	1627	IM25006	XI	4-none	1340	35-10-044	XI
4-1064	1628	35-10-133	XI	4-none	1341	35-10-045	XI

Concordance   (continued)

Field Number	Catalogue Number	Location	Level/ Phase
4-none	1342	35-10-046	XI
4-none	1343	35-10-047	XI
4-none	1344	35-10-048	XI
4-none	1345	35-10-049	XI
4-none	1346	35-10-050	XI
4-none	1347	unknown	XI
4-none	1348	unknown	XI
4-none	1349	unknown	XI
4-none	1350	unknown	XI
4-none	1351	unknown	XI
4-none	1352	unknown	XI
4-none	1353	unknown	XI
4-none	1354	unknown	XI
4-none	1355	unknown	XI
4-none	1356	unknown	XI
4-none	1357	unknown	XI
4-none	1358	unknown	XI
4-none	1359	unknown	XI
4-none	1360	unknown	XI
4-none	1361	unknown	XI
4-none	1362	unknown	XI
4-none	1363	unknown	XI
4-none	1364	unknown	XI
4-none	1386	unknown	XI
4-none	1387	unknown	XI
4-none	1388	unknown	XI
4-none	1425	discarded	XI
4-none	1426	discarded	XI
4-none	1427	unknown	XI
4-none	1428	unknown	XI
4-none	1429	unknown	XI
4-none	1430	unknown	XI
4-none	1431	unknown	XI
4-none	1432	unknown	XI
4-none	1433	unknown	XI
4-none	1530	35-10-157	XI
4-none	1531	35-10-057	XI
4-none	1532	35-10-058	XI
4-none	1533	35-10-060	XI
4-none	1534	35-10-061	XI
4-none	1535	35-10-062	XI
4-none	1536	35-10-063	XI
4-none	1537	35-10-065	XI
4-none	1538	35-10-068	XI
4-none	1539	35-10-071	XI
4-none	1540	35-10-075	XI
4-none	1541	35-10-077	XI
4-none	1542	unknown	XI
4-none	1543	unknown	XI
4-none	1544	unknown	XI
4-none	1545	unknown	XI
4-none	1546	unknown	XI

Concordance   (continued)

Field Number	Catalogue Number	Location	Level/ Phase
4-none	1547	unknown	XI
4-none	1548	unknown	XI
4-none	1549	unknown	XI
4-none	1550	unknown	XI
4-none	1551	unknown	XI
4-none	1552	unknown	XI
4-none	1553	unknown	XI
4-none	1554	unknown	XI
5-1234	1276	36-6-107	XI
5-1250	1145	36-6-006	XI
5-1253	1555	36-6-010	XI
5-1253	1556	36-6-010	XI
5-1253	1557	36-6-011	XI
5-1253	1558	36-6-011	XI
5-1253	1559	36-6-012	XI
5-1253	1560	36-6-013	XI
5-1253	1561	36-6-014	XI
5-1253	1562	36-6-014	XI
5-1253	1563	36-6-009	XI
5-1261	1434	36-6-055	XI
5-1262	1365	36-6-057	XI
5-1263	1637	discarded	XI
5-1268	1638	36-6-123	XI
5-1270	1366	Baghdad	XI
5-1279	1639	36-6-132	XI
5-1284	1640	discarded	XI
5-1285	1641	IM26998	XI
5-1286	1435	36-6-054	XI
5-1288	1146	36-6-065	XI
5-1289A	1642	36-6-126	XI
5-1289B	1643	IM26961	XI
5-1290	1209	36-6-095	XI
5-1292	1210	Baghdad	XI
5-1293	1147	Baghdad	XI
5-1294	1112	Baghdad	XI
5-1296	1211	Baghdad	XI
5-1297	1436	Baghdad	XI
5-1300A	1644	36-6-115	XI
5-1300B	1645	36-6-122	XI
5-1300C	1646	36-6-124	XI
5-1300D	1647	IM26775	XI
5-1300E	1648	IM26999	XI
5-1300F	1649	IM27000	XI
5-1300G	1650	IM27001	XI
5-1301A	1651	36-6-127	XI
5-1301B	1652	IM27002	XI
5-1301C	1653	36-6-211	XI
5-1301D	1654	IM27008	XI
5-1303A	1655	36-6-117	XI
5-1303B	1656	IM26986	XI
5-1303C	1657	IM27004	XI
5-1303D	1658	36-6-118	XI

(continues)

Concordance   (continued)

Concordance   (continued)

Field Number	Catalogue Number	Location	Level/ Phase	Field Number	Catalogue Number	Location	Level/ Phase
5-1303E	1659	IM26992	XI	5-1370	1670	36-6-130	XI
5-1304	1437	Baghdad	XI	5-1371	1671	36-6-113	XI
5-1305	1290	36-6-016	XI	5-1372	1672	36-6-111	XI
5-1306A	1148	Baghdad	XI	5-1373	1451	discarded	XI
5-1306B	1149	36-6-007	XI	5-1374	1155	Baghdad	XI
5-1306C	1150	Baghdad	XI	5-1375	1218	36-6-097	XI
5-1307A	1151	36-6-067	XI	5-1380	1452	Baghdad	XI
5-1307B	1152	36-6-068	XI	5-1381	1219	Baghdad	XI
5-1307C	1153	36-6-069	XI	5-1394	1569	Baghdad	XI
5-1310a	1660	36-6-043	XI	5-1400	1453	36-6-056	XI
5-1310b	1661	36-6-041	XI	5-1401	1114	Baghdad	XI
5-1310b	1662	36-6-41b	XI	5-1403	1454	36-6-049	XI
5-1310c	1663	IM26991	XI	5-1404	1455	Baghdad	XI
5-1312	1367	Baghdad	XI	5-1405	1673	36-6-214	XI
5-1313	1438	discarded	XI	5-1409	1220	Baghdad	XI
5-1314	1212	Baghdad	XI	5-1410	1368	36-6-059	XI
5-1315	1439	Baghdad	XI	5-1417	1156	Baghdad	XI
5-1316	1564	Baghdad	XI	5-1425	1674	IM26967	XI
5-1318	1440	36-6-023	XI	5-1426	1675	IM26971	XI
5-1320	1441	36-6-050	XI	5-1427	1280	36-6-198	XI
5-1325	1664	36-6-120	XI	5-1430	1456	36-6-142	XI
5-1326	1665	36-6-119	XI	5-1458	1095	Baghdad	XI
5-1333	1666	36-6-128	XI	5-1477	1221	36-6-036	XI
5-1335	1667	36-6-125	XI	5-1480	1457	36-6-030	XI
5-1337	1113	Baghdad	XI	5-1491	1115	36-6-066A	XI
5-1338	1442	36-6-047	XI	5-1491	1116	Baghdad	XI
5-1339	1443	Baghdad	XI	5-1496	1222	Baghdad	XI
5-1340	1444	Baghdad	XI	5-1502	1458	Baghdad	XI
5-1341	1445	36-6-052	XI	5-1508	1223	36-6-096	XI
5-1342	1565	Baghdad	XI	5-1509	1224	Baghdad	XI
5-1343	1446	36-6-025	XI	5-1511	1225	36-6-087	XI
5-1346	1447	unclear	XI	5-1512	1096	Baghdad	XI
5-1347	1093	36-6-197	XI	5-1513	1226	Baghdad	XI
5-1348	1448	Baghdad	XI	5-1544	1281	36-6-367	XI
5-1349	1668	36-6-114	XI	5-1592	1676	36-6-110	XI
5-1350	1213	36-6-086	XI	5-1597	1227	Baghdad	XI
5-1351	1214	36-6-098	XI	5-1603	1228	Baghdad	XI
5-1352	1094	Baghdad	XI	5-1610	1459	36-6-048	XI
5-1353	1449	36-6-192	XI	5-1614	1282	Baghdad	XI
5-1354	1566	36-6-032	XI	5-1616	1117	Baghdad	XI
5-1354	1567	36-6-033	XI	5-1619	1677	IM26984	XI
5-1355	1215	36-6-092	XI	5-1700s	1229	unknown	XI
5-1356	1216	Baghdad	XI	5-1708	1570	36-6-175	XI
5-1357	1669	IM26973	XI	5-1744	1097	Baghdad	XI
5-1359	1277	36-6-108	XI	5-1747	1460	36-6-051	XI
5-1361	1154	Baghdad	XI	5-none	1118	36-6-080	XI
5-1362	1568	36-6-078	XI	5-none	1119	36-6-081	XI
5-1363	1278	36-6-372	XI	5-none	1120	unknown	XI
5-1364	1217	Baghdad	XI	5-none	1121	Loc196	XI
5-1365	1318	Baghdad	XI	5-none	1131	unknown	XI
5-1366	1450	36-6-045	XI	5-none	1157	36-6-131	XI
5-1368	1279	36-6-106	XI	5-none	1158	36-6-063	XI

Concordance (continued)

Field Number	Catalogue Number	Location	Level/Phase
5-none	1159	36-6-064	XI
5-none	1230	36-6-100	XI
5-none	1231	36-6-101	XI
5-none	1232	36-6-102	XI
5-none	1233	36-6-103	XI
5-none	1234	36-6-104	XI
5-none	1235	36-6-105	XI
5-none	1236	36-6-034	XI
5-none	1237	36-6-088	XI
5-none	1238	36-6-089	XI
5-none	1239	36-6-090	XI
5-none	1240	36-6-091	XI
5-none	1241	36-6-093	XI
5-none	1242	36-6-094	XI
5-none	1243	unknown	XI
5-none	1244	unknown	XI
5-none	1305	36-6-082	XI
5-none	1306	36-6-083	XI
5-none	1307	36-6-083	XI
5-none	1308	36-6-084	XI
5-none	1319	unknown	XI
5-none	1320	Baghdad	XI
5-none	1369	36-6-402	XI
5-none	1370	36-6-403	XI
5-none	1371	36-6-406	XI
5-none	1372	36-6-408	XI
5-none	1373	36-6-409	XI
5-none	1374	36-6-410	XI
5-none	1375	36-6-411	XI
5-none	1376	36-6-418	XI
5-none	1377	36-6-419	XI
5-none	1378	36-6-420	XI
5-none	1379	36-6-060	XI
5-none	1380	36-6-061	XI
5-none	1381	36-6-062	XI
5-none	1382	unknown	XI
5-none	1390	unknown	XI
5-none	1461	36-6-058	XI
5-none	1462	unknown	XI
5-none	1463	unknown	XI
5-none	1464	unknown	XI
5-none	1465	unknown	XI
5-none	1466	unknown	XI
5-none	1467	unknown	XI
5-none	1468	unknown	XI
5-none	1571	36-6-070	XI
5-none	1572	36-6-075	XI
5-none	1573	36-6-076	XI
5-none	1574	36-6-077	XI
5-none	1575	36-6-079	XI
5-none	1576	37-16-035	XI
5-none	1678	discarded	XI

Concordance (continued)

Field Number	Catalogue Number	Location	Level/Phase
5-none	1679	unknown	XI
6-009	1328	Baghdad	XI
6-0103	1680	IM32626	XI
6-015	1469	Baghdad	XI
6-032	1470	Baghdad	XI
6-049	1245	Baghdad	XI
6-050	1160	37-16-034	XI
6-052	1471	37-16-036	XI
6-054	1321	Baghdad	XI
6-058	1472	Baghdad	XI
6-059	1122	Baghdad	XI
6-0594	1681	Baghdad	XI
6-0610	1682	Baghdad	XI
6-105	1123	Baghdad	XI
6-140	1473	Baghdad	XI
6-149	1309	Baghdad	XI
6-157	1161	37-16-038	XI
6-158	1474	Baghdad	XI
6-165	1475	discarded	XI
6-170	1098	unknown	XI
6-274	1246	Baghdad	XI
6-379	1283	unknown	XI
6-394	1476	Baghdad	XI
6-557	1477	37-16-032	XI
6-593	1478	Baghdad	XI
6-614	1284	Baghdad	XI
6-none	1099	37-16-043	XI
6-none	1100	37-16-044	XI
6-none	1162	Plate82	XI
6-none	1163	unknown	XI
6-none	1247	37-16-039	XI
6-none	1248	37-16-040	XI
6-none	1249	unknown	XI
6-none	1310	37-16-041	XI
6-none	1383	37-16-033	XI
6-none	1389	unknown	XI
6-none	1479	unknown	XI
6-none	1480	unknown	XI
6-none	1481	unknown	XI
6-none	1482	unknown	XI
6-none	1683	IM32900	XI
6-none	1684	unknown	XI
6-none	1685	unknown	XI
7-0018	1285	38-13-331	XI
7-0036	1686	Baghdad	XI
7-0052	1483	discarded	XI
7-0053	1164	Baghdad	XI
7-0054	1286	38-13-009	XI
7-0059	1165	discarded	XI
7-0060	1687	IM42679	XI
7-0062A	1688	IM42680	XI
7-0062B	1689	discarded	XI

(continues)

Concordance   (continued)

Concordance   (continued)

Field Number	Catalogue Number	Location	Level/Phase	Field Number	Catalogue Number	Location	Level/Phase
7-0064	1690	38-13-015	XI	4-1013	1625	Baghdad	XI?
7-0065A	1691	IM42693	XI	4-0601	1733	Baghdad	XA
7-0065B	1692	Baghdad	XI	4-0651	1734	35-10-037	XA
7-0065C	1693	38-13-016	XI	4-0661	1834	35-10-112	XA
7-0066	1484	Baghdad	XI	4-0678	1735	phila?	XA
7-0068	1694	Baghdad	XI	4-0680	1778	philano#	XA
7-0073	1250	Baghdad	XI	4-0691	1736	Baghdad	XA
7-0075	1323	Baghdad	XI	4-0692	1835	35-10-131	XA
7-0078	1251	38-13-008	XI	4-0697	1718	35-10-087	XA
7-0082A	1695	IM42682	XI	4-0697B	1719	Baghdad	XA
7-0082A	1696	IM42682	XI	4-0717	1737	Baghdad	XA
7-0083	1697	Baghdad	XI	4-0730	1836	IM24591	XA
7-0083	1698	Baghdad	XI	4-0780	1738	35-10-091	XA
7-0084	1699	38-13-021	XI	4-0782	1837	discarded	XA
7-0085	1700	discarded	XI	4-0786	1779	Baghdad	XA
7-0086	1701	38-13-014	XI	4-0788	1739	Baghdad	XA
7-0087	1702	IM42684	XI	4-0789	1727	phila?	XA
7-0088	1703	38-13-017	XI	4-0793	1771	Baghdad	XA
7-0090	1312	Baghdad	XI	4-0797	1838	35-10-118	XA
7-0091	1287	Baghdad	XI	4-0811	1780	Baghdad	XA
7-0092	1704	38-13-019	XI	4-0815	1839	35-10-262	XA
7-0093	1705	38-13-018	XI	4-0835	1840	35-10-114	XA
7-0094	1706	38-13-020	XI	4-0840	1841	IM24992	XA
7-0095	1707	38-13-022	XI	4-0846	1781	Baghdad	XA
7-0096	1708	38-13-013	XI	4-0847	1740	Baghdad	XA
7-0097	1709	IM42685	XI	4-0863	1741	35-10-396	XA
7-0101	1710	IM42686	XI	4-0864	1782	Baghdad	XA
7-0114	1711	38-13-010	XI	4-0868	1783	Baghdad	XA
7-0129	1712	IM42674	XI	4-0871	1742	Baghdad	XA
7-0130	1713	IM42675	XI	4-0872	1842	35-10-129	XA
7-0132	1714	38-13-012	XI	4-0877	1764	phila?	XA
7-0140	1324	discarded	XI	4-0926	1754	35-10-101	XA
7-0153	1715	38-13-011	XI	4-0956	1843	IM25048	XA
7-none	1124	unknown	XI	4-0969	1728	Baghdad	XA
7-none	1125	unknown	XI	4-1006	1755	discarded	XA
7-none	1126	unknown	XI	4-none	1720	unknown	XA
7-none	1127	38-13-006	XI	4-none	1726	unknown	XA
7-none	1166	unknown	XI	4-none	1772	unknown	XA
7-none	1288	unknown	XI	4-none	1774	unknown	XA
7-none	1289	unknown	XI	4-none	1784	unknown	XA
7-none	1311	unknown	XI	4-none	1785	unknown	XA
7-none	1313	unknown	XI	4-none	1786	unknown	XA
7-none	1322	unknown	XI	4-none	1787	unknown	XA
7-none	1325	unknown	XI	4-none	1788	unknown	XA
7-none	1326	unknown	XI	4-none	1789	unknown	XA
7-none	1384	discarded	XI	4-none	1831	unknown	XA
7-none	1385	38-13-005	XI	5-1248	1844	IM26987	XA
7-none	1485	unknown	XI	5-1251	1721	36-6-004	XA
7-none	1716	discarded	XI	5-1252	1790	Baghdad	XA
7-none	1717	unknown	XI	5-1254	1845	36-6-044	XA
none	1252	unknown	XI	5-1256	1743	Baghdad	XA
none	1253	discarded	XI	5-1258	1846	36-6-040	XA

Concordance   (continued)

Field Number	Catalogue Number	Location	Level/ Phase
5-1260	1744	Baghdad	XA
5-1264	1791	36-6-001	XA
5-1265	1792	Baghdad	XA
5-1266	1793	36-6-003	XA
5-1271	1794	36-6-024	XA
5-1272	1795	Baghdad	XA
5-1274	1796	36-6-021	XA
5-1277	1797	36-6-020	XA
5-1281	1745	36-6-386	XA
5-1308	1798	Baghdad	XA
5-1311	1746	Baghdad	XA
5-1319	1775	36-6-022	XA
5-1327	1747	36-6-035	XA
5-1331	1832	Baghdad	XA
5-1332	1833	36-6-31	XA
5-1336	1756	Baghdad	XA
5-1344	1847	36-6-039	XA
5-1345	1848	Baghdad	XA
5-1369	1799	lost	XA
5-1451	1849	36-6-038	XA
5-1456	1757	Baghdad	XA
5-1472	1800	discarded	XA
5-1474	1748	Baghdad	XA
5-1527	1801	36-6-053	XA
5-1528	1802	Baghdad	XA
5-1538	1749	Baghdad	XA
5-1546	1850	36-6-129	XA
5-1552	1851	36-6-042	XA
5-1559	1803	36-6-046	XA
5-1567	1852	36-6-116	XA
5-1570	1804	discarded	XA
5-1607	1758	36-6-037	XA
5-1613	1805	Baghdad	XA
5-1617	1806	Baghdad	XA
5-none	1722	unknown	XA
5-none	1729	unknown	XA
5-none	1750	36-6-085	XA
5-none	1765	unknown	XA
5-none	1776	36-6-028	XA
5-none	1807	36-6-026	XA
5-none	1808	36-6-027	XA
5-none	1809	unknown	XA
5-none	1810	unknown	XA
5-none	1811	unknown	XA
5-none	1812	unknown	XA
5-none	1860	discarded	XA
5-none	1862	discarded	XA
6-033	1813	Baghdad	XA
6-039	1814	37-16-022	XA
6-040	1815	37-16-020	XA
6-042	1853	IM32499	XA
6-044	1816	Baghdad	XA

Concordance   (continued)

Field Number	Catalogue Number	Location	Level/ Phase
6-046	1854	37-16-031	XA
6-047	1759	Baghdad	XA
6-053	1723	Baghdad	XA
6-055	1817	Baghdad	XA
6-056	1818	37-16-037	XA
6-057	1760	37-16-028	XA
6-060	1819	Baghdad	XA
6-063	1855	IM32624	XA
6-067A	1730	37-16-023	XA
6-067B	1731	Baghdad	XA
6-069	1766	Baghdad	XA
6-070	1820	Baghdad	XA
6-114	1821	Baghdad	XA
6-129A	1822	discarded	XA
6-129B	1823	discarded	XA
6-166	1724	Discarded	XA
6-172	1824	Baghdad	XA
6-180	1725	Baghdad	XA
6-181	1761	Baghdad	XA
6-182A	1856	37-16-030	XA
6-182B	1857	IM32610	XA
6-194	1773	Baghdad	XA
6-196	1732	Baghdad	XA
6-273	1858	37-16-029	XA
6-none	1751	37-16-021	XA
6-none	1752	unknown	XA
6-none	1762	unknown	XA
6-none	1767	37-16-025	XA
6-none	1768	37-16-026	XA
6-none	1769	37-16-027	XA
6-none	1825	37-16-21	XA
6-none	1826	unknown	XA
6-none	1827	unknown	XA
6-none	1828	unknown	XA
6-none	1829	unknown	XA
6-none	1861	discarded	XA
7-0008	1763	38-13-003	XA
7-0012	1753	Baghdad	XA
7-002	1859	38-13-004	XA
7-none	1770	38-13-002	XA
7-none	1777	38-13-001	XA
none	1830	unknown	XA
1027	1980	31-52-408	X
1087	1866	31-52-431	X
1088	1884	31-52-433	X
1090	1863	31-52-438	X
1137	1914	31-52-435	X
1158	1885	31-52-437	X
1162	1886	31-52-434	X
1163	1887	31-52-432	X
1189	1922	31-52-428	X
1193	1906	31-52-440	X

(*continues*)

Concordance   (continued)

Field Number	Catalogue Number	Location	Level/ Phase
3-0605	2011	Baghdad	X
3-263	1925	33-3-128	X
3-316	1926	33-3-153	X
3-318	1927	Baghdad	X
3-323	1920	Discarded	X
3-332	1981	33-3-158	X
3-333	1888	Baghdad	X
3-336	1928	Baghdad	X
3-337	1929	discarded	X
3-338	1930	discarded	X
3-339	1931	Baghdad	X
3-341	1964	Baghdad	X
3-342	1913	discarded	X
3-343	1889	33-3-161	X
3-344	1932	33-3-162	X
3-346	1933	Baghdad	X
3-347	1934	33-3-164	X
3-348	1982	Baghdad	X
3-352	1935	33-3-167	X
3-353	1936	33-3-168	X
3-355	1937	33-3-170	X
3-357	1938	33-3-172	X
3-359	1939	discarded	X
3-360	1872	33-3-174	X
3-361	1940	33-3-175	X
3-362	1983	33-3-176	X
3-363	1864	33-3-177	X
3-364	1941	33-3-178	X
3-365	1890	33-3-179	X
3-368	1942	Baghdad	X
3-369	1943	33-3-182	X
3-370	1944	33-3-183	X
3-371	1891	33-3-184	X
3-372	1892	Baghdad	X
3-376A	1984	33-3-186	X
3-376B	1985	33-3-186	X
3-379	1945	33-3-188	X
3-395	1946	33-3-196	X
3-397	1986	Baghdad	X
3-398	1987	33-3-198	X
3-399	1988	33-3-199	X
3-406	1915	Baghdad	X
3-408	1989	Baghdad	X
3-409	1990	33-3-203	X
3-413	1991	IM15977	X
3-415	1965	33-3-208	X
3-416	1893	Baghdad	X
3-419	1873	33-3-211	X
3-421	1867	33-3-212	X
3-428	1992	33-3-216	X
3-429	1947	33-3-217	X
3-433	1993	Baghdad	X

Concordance   (continued)

Field Number	Catalogue Number	Location	Level/ Phase
3-434	1994	IM26897	X
3-435	1995	33-3-220	X
3-436	1874	33-3-221	X
3-438	1996	35-10-016	X
3-440	1997	Baghdad	X
3-441	1894	discarded	X
3-444	1918	35-10-363	X
3-445	1948	discarded	X
3-446	1895	Baghdad	X
3-480	1896	35-10-020	X
3-481	1999	35-10-020	X
3-483	1875	Baghdad	X
3-485A	2001	Phila?	X
3-485B	2000	35-10-258	X
3-492	1949	IM20855	X
3-493	1876	Baghdad	X
3-494	1950	Phila no#	X
3-495A	2002	IM25075	X
3-495BC	2003	35-10-018A	X
3-495D	2004	35-10-018B	X
3-496A	2005	35-10-019	X
3-496B	2006	IM24566	X
3-497	2007	IM25109	X
3-498	2008	35-10-023	X
3-499	2009	35-10-021	X
3-500	2010	IM24568	X
3-502	1951	Baghdad	X
3-none	1868	unknown	X
3-none	1897	33-3-256	X
3-none	1898	33-3-277	X
3-none	1899	33-3-286	X
3-none	1907	33-3-261	X
3-none	1921	33-3-230	X
3-none	1952	33-3-273	X
3-none	1953	unknown	X
3-none	1954	unknown	X
3-none	2039	33-3-238	X
3-none	2040	33-3-238	X
3-none	2041	33-3-245	X
3-none	2042	33-3-238	X
3-none	2043	33-3-237	X
4-0602	1900	35-10-010	X
4-0609	2012	35-10-015	X
4-0618	1966	discarded	X
4-0620	1967	Baghdad	X
4-0626	1869	Baghdad	X
4-0647	2013	IM24997	X
4-0652	1901	Baghdad	X
4-0668	2014	35-10-024	X
4-0703	1955	Baghdad	X
4-0704	1956	35-10-003	X
4-0721	2015	IM24607	X

Concordance   (continued)   Concordance   (continued)

Field Number	Catalogue Number	Location	Level/Phase	Field Number	Catalogue Number	Location	Level/Phase
4-0722	2016	IM25045	X	6-026	1904	37-16-013	X
4-0723	2017	IM24993	X	6-029	2030	37-16-017	X
4-0724	2018	35-10-022	X	6-043	2031	IM32623	X
4-0725	2019	IM25047	X	6-079	1883	Baghdad	X
4-0726	1908	35-10-012	X	6-184	1905	37-16-012	X
4-0727	1909	Baghdad	X	6-210	2032	IM32897	X
4-0729	1968	35-10-008	X	6-210A	2033	37-16-015	X
4-0779	2020	35-10-017	X	6-210B	2034	IM32620	X
4-0796	1877	35-10-053	X	6-210B2	2035	37-16-15b	X
4-0798	1957	35-10-001	X	6-210C	2036	37-16-016	X
4-0799	1958	Baghdad	X	6-none	1919	unknown	X
4-0800	1969	35-10-007	X	6-none	2037	IM32896	X
4-0801	1902	Baghdad	X	6-none	2038	IM32899	X
4-0803	1959	Baghdad	X	6087	1924	Baghdad	X
4-0852	2021	Baghdad	X	3-449	1998	IM24567	X?
4-0853	1910	35-10-013	X	1002	2218	Baghdad	IX
4-0875	1911	Baghdad	X	1020	2219	31-52-416	IX
4-0902	1916	Baghdad	X	1051	2078	31-52-418	IX
4-1039	1970	Phila no#	X	1052	2049	31-52-417	IX
4-1040	1971	33-3-258	X	1053	2044	31-52-424	IX
4-1042	1972	discarded	X	1054	2125	31-52-425	IX
4-1043	1973	Baghdad	X	1073	2079	Baghdad	IX
4-1044	1974	Baghdad	X	1085	2220	31-52-421	IX
4-1047	1975	Baghdad	X	1086a	2149	31-52-423	IX
4-1048	2022	IM24996	X	1086b	2150	31-52-423	IX
4-none	1912	unknown	X	1086c	2151	31-52-423	IX
4-none	1960	unknown	X	1086d	2152	31-52-423	IX
4-none	1976	unknown	X	1086e	2153	31-52-423	IX
4-none	1977	unknown	X	1086f	2154	31-52-423	IX
5-1249	1878	36-6-008	X	1091	2155	31-52-422	IX
5-1255	2023	IM26985	X	1091	2156	31-52-422	IX
5-1257	1879	Baghdad	X	1091	2157	31-52-422	IX
5-1259	2024	36-6-019	X	1091	2158	31-52-422	IX
5-1267	1961	36-6-002	X	1091	2159	31-52-422	IX
5-1273	1962	Baghdad	X	1091	2160	31-52-422	IX
5-1276	2025	36-6-396	X	1091	2161	31-52-422	IX
5-1282	1903	36-6-017	X	1091	2162	31-52-422	IX
5-1283A	1880	Baghdad	X	1091	2163	31-52-422	IX
5-1283B	1881	36-6-005	X	1091	2164	31-52-422	IX
5-1287	2026	IM27030	X	1091a	2165	31-52-422	IX
5-1291	2027	36-6-018	X	1092	2080	31-52-420	IX
5-none	1870	35-10-005	X	1093	2081	31-52-419	IX
5-none	1871	discarded	X	2-none	2050	32-21-528	IX
5-none	1882	35-10-004	X	2-none	2051	32-21-529	IX
5-none	1963	unknown	X	2-none	2082	32-21-533	IX
5-none	1978	35-10-006	X	2-none	2083	32-21-534	IX
5-none	1979	35-10-009	X	2-none	2084	32-21-535	IX
5-none	2028	unknown	X	2-none	2126	32-21-536	IX
5004	1923	32-21-548	X	2-none	2166	32-21-539	IX
6-020	2029	37-16-019	X	2-none	2217	32-21-527	IX
6-024	1917	Baghdad	X	2-none	2221	32-21-526	IX
6-025	1865	37-16-011	X	2-none	2272	32-21-530	IX

(*continues*)

Concordance   (continued)

Field Number	Catalogue Number	Location	Level/ Phase
2-none	2273	32-21-531	IX
2none a	2167	32-21-537	IX
2none b	2168	32-21-537	IX
2none b	2169	32-21-538	IX
2none b	2170	32-21-538	IX
2none c	2171	32-21-537	IX
2none c	2172	32-21-538	IX
2none c	2173	32-21-538	IX
2none d	2174	32-21-538	IX
2none e	2175	32-21-538	IX
2none g	2176	32-21-538	IX
2none i	2177	32-21-538	IX
2none j	2178	32-21-538	IX
2none k	2179	32-21-538	IX
2none l	2180	32-21-538	IX
2none m	2181	32-21-538	IX
2none n	2182	32-21-538	IX
2none o	2183	32-21-538	IX
2none p	2184	32-21-538	IX
2none q	2185	32-21-538	IX
2none s	2186	32-21-538	IX
2none t	2187	32-21-538	IX
2none u	2188	32-21-538	IX
2none v	2189	32-21-538	IX
2none w	2190	32-21-538	IX
2none x	2191	32-21-538	IX
2none x	2192	32-21-538	IX
3-011	2127	Baghdad	IX
3-015	2085	33-3-008	IX
3-016	2086	Baghdad	IX
3-017	2087	Baghdad	IX
3-020	2222	33-3-009	IX
3-021	2223	33-3-010	IX
3-022	2052	Baghdad	IX
3-025	2193	Baghdad	IX
3-027	2274	Baghdad	IX
3-028	2088	33-3-013	IX
3-029	2089	Baghdad	IX
3-030	2090	33-3-014	IX
3-031	2091	Baghdad	IX
3-034	2128	Baghdad	IX
3-035	2224	unknown	IX
3-037	2129	33-3-016	IX
3-038	2225	discarded	IX
3-041	2226	Baghdad	IX
3-042	2275	Baghdad	IX
3-043	2130	discarded	IX
3-044A	2276	Baghdad	IX
3-044B	2277	33-3-018	IX
3-051	2194	33-3-024	IX
3-071	2227	33-3-036	IX
3-072	2228	Baghdad	IX

Concordance   (continued)

Field Number	Catalogue Number	Location	Level/ Phase
3-077	2069	Baghdad	IX
3-080	2282	IM15844	IX
3-082	2053	discarded	IX
3-083	2195	Baghdad	IX
3-087	2092	33-3-212	IX
3-089	2196	Baghdad	IX
3-095	2093	33-3-045	IX
3-096	2094	Baghdad	IX
3-097	2070	Baghdad	IX
3-098	2131	Baghdad	IX
3-099	2095	33-3-046	IX
3-100	2071	Baghdad	IX
3-101	2229	Baghdad	IX
3-103	2096	Baghdad	IX
3-104	2230	33-3-052	IX
3-105	2054	33-3-048	IX
3-106	2097	33-3-049	IX
3-108	2197	Baghdad	IX
3-110	2283	Baghdad	IX
3-113	2045	Baghdad	IX
3-114	2055	Baghdad	IX
3-133	2231	Baghdad	IX
3-134	2232	33-3-067	IX
3-137	2233	33-3-063	IX
3-146	2056	33-3-069	IX
3-153A	2046	Baghdad	IX
3-153B	2047	Baghdad	IX
3-154	2234	33-3-072	IX
3-155	2235	discarded	IX
3-157	2098	Baghdad	IX
3-158	2198	Baghdad	IX
3-159	2199	Baghdad	IX
3-160	2132	Baghdad	IX
3-161	2057	Baghdad	IX
3-164	2278	33-3-074	IX
3-165	2099	Baghdad	IX
3-166	2200	33-3-075	IX
3-167	2100	Baghdad	IX
3-168	2101	Baghdad	IX
3-169	2133	33-3-076	IX
3-170	2236	33-3-077	IX
3-172	2058	33-3-079	IX
3-173	2284	33-3-080	IX
3-177	2059	Baghdad	IX
3-178	2102	33-3-083	IX
3-179	2285	33-3-084	IX
3-183	2072	33-3-086	IX
3-185	2134	Baghdad	IX
3-189	2289	IM15979	IX
3-189a	2286	33-3-089	IX
3-189b	2287	33-3-089	IX
3-189c	2288	33-3-089	IX

Concordance   (continued)

Field Number	Catalogue Number	Location	Level/ Phase
3-190	2135	Baghdad	IX
3-191	2201	discarded	IX
3-194	2103	Baghdad	IX
3-195	2290	33-3-091	IX
3-196	2291	33-3-092	IX
3-197	2292	33-3-093	IX
3-198	2237	33-3-094	IX
3-200	2293	33-3-095	IX
3-201	2202	33-3-097	IX
3-202	2136	Baghdad	IX
3-203	2073	33-3-098	IX
3-204	2074	33-3-099	IX
3-205	2137	Baghdad	IX
3-207	2294	Baghdad	IX
3-208	2060	33-3-100	IX
3-208	2203	33-3-100	IX
3-209	2295	33-3-101	IX
3-211	2061	33-3-103	IX
3-212	2238	33-3-104	IX
3-213	2062	33-3-105	IX
3-214	2104	Baghdad	IX
3-215	2063	Baghdad	IX
3-219	2204	33-3-107	IX
3-220	2296	33-3-108	IX
3-221	2105	33-3-109	IX
3-223	2106	33-3-110	IX
3-224	2239	Baghdad	IX
3-227	2240	33-3-112	IX
3-228	2241	33-3-113	IX
3-229	2242	33-2-114	IX
3-233	2138	Baghdad	IX
3-234	2205	Baghdad	IX
3-235	2297	IM15933	IX
3-236	2206	33-3-117	IX
3-237	2139	33-3-118	IX
3-238	2107	33-3-259	IX
3-239	2140	Baghdad	IX
3-240	2298	33-3-119	IX
3-243	2299	IM15845	IX
3-245	2300	33-3-120	IX
3-246	2207	Baghdad	IX
3-247	2208	33-3-121	IX
3-248	2243	33-3-122	IX
3-251	2244	discarded	IX
3-252	2245	33-3-124	IX
3-254	2213	33-3-125	IX
3-255	2141	33-3-126	IX
3-256	2108	Baghdad	IX
3-257	2246	Baghdad	IX
3-259	2142	Baghdad	IX
3-260	2064	Baghdad	IX
3-261	2065	discarded	IX

Concordance   (continued)

Field Number	Catalogue Number	Location	Level/ Phase
3-262	2109	Baghdad	IX
3-264	2301	33-3-129	IX
3-267	2302	IM15929	IX
3-269	2066	discarded	IX
3-271	2143	33-3-132	IX
3-272	2110	Baghdad	IX
3-274	2214	discarded	IX
3-275	2075	33-3-134	IX
3-276	2209	33-3-135	IX
3-277	2247	33-3-136	IX
3-278	2248	discarded	IX
3-291	2303	IM15846	IX
3-297	2304	IM15931	IX
3-298	2305	IM15928	IX
3-301	2215	Baghdad	IX
3-302	2249	Baghdad	IX
3-303	2111	Baghdad	IX
3-304	2279	33-3-144	IX
3-305	2144	33-3-145	IX
3-306	2067	33-3-146	IX
3-307	2068	discarded	IX
3-308	2112	Baghdad	IX
3-310	2210	33-3-148	IX
3-311	2145	33-3-149	IX
3-312	2146	Baghdad	IX
3-313	2250	33-3-150	IX
3-314	2076	33-3-151	IX
3-315	2306	33-3-152	IX
3-319	2147	33-3-154	IX
3-320	2251	Baghdad	IX
3-321	2216	33-3-155	IX
3-322	2252	discarded	IX
3-324	2280	Baghdad	IX
3-325	2113	Baghdad	IX
3-326	2114	Baghdad	IX
3-329	2148	33-3-157	IX
3-330	2115	Baghdad	IX
3-331	2048	Baghdad	IX
3-334	2281	33-3-159	IX
3-335	2077	33-3-160	IX
3-340	2253	Baghdad	IX
3-351	2116	Baghdad	IX
3-354	2254	33-3-169	IX
3-366	2255	33-3-180	IX
3-367	2256	33-3-181	IX
3-386	2257	discarded	IX
3-389	2258	discarded	IX
3-487	2259	35-10-343	IX
3-490	2211	Baghdad	IX
3-491	2212	Baghdad	IX
3-none	2117	33-3-254	IX
3-none	2118	33-3-275	IX

(continues)

Concordance   (continued)   Concordance   (continued)

Field Number	Catalogue Number	Location	Level/Phase	Field Number	Catalogue Number	Location	Level/Phase
3-none	2119	33-3-278	IX	1018	2769	31-52-405	VIII
3-none	2120	33-3-279	IX	1019a	2563	31-52-392	VIII
3-none	2121	33-3-284	IX	1019b	2562	31-52-392	VIII
3-none	2122	33-3-285	IX	1019c	2564	31-52-392	VIII
3-none	2123	unknown	IX	1019d	2565	31-52-392	VIII
3-none	2260	33-3-021	IX	1019e	2566	31-52-392	VIII
3-none	2261	33-3-228	IX	1019f	2567	31-52-392	VIII
3-none	2262	33-3-228	IX	1023	2388	31-52-406	VIII
3-none	2263	33-3-228	IX	1024	2389	31-52-402	VIII
3-none	2264	33-3-255	IX	1025	2482	31-52-413	VIII
3-none	2265	unknown	IX	1028	2483	31-52-372	VIII
3-none	2266	unknown	IX	1048	2390	31-52-397	VIII
3-none	2267	unknown	IX	1049	2871	31-52-379	VIII
3-none	2268	unknown	IX	1055	2391	31-52-396	VIII
3-none	2269	unknown	IX	1056a	2568	31-52-392	VIII
3-none	2270	33-3-155	IX	1056b	2569	31-52-392	VIII
6084	2124	Dropsie	IX	1056c	2570	31-52-392	VIII
6086	2271	unknown	IX	1056d	2571	31-52-392	VIII
1094	2394	31-52-040	VIII	1056e	2572	31-52-392	VIII
1-none	2534	31-52-390	VIII	1056f	2573	31-52-392	VIII
1-none	2535	31-52-393	VIII	1056g	2574	31-52-392	VIII
1-none	2536	31-52-392	VIII	1056h	2575	31-52-392	VIII
1-none	2537	31-52-392	VIII	1063	2484	31-52-409	VIII
1-none	2538	31-52-392	VIII	1072	2918	31-52-384	VIII
1-none	2539	31-52-392	VIII	1076	2392	31-52-403	VIII
1-none	2540	31-52-392	VIII	1082	2485	31-52-410	VIII
1-none	2541	31-52-392	VIII	1084	2320	31-52-099	VIII
1-none	2542	31-52-392	VIII	1099	2919	31-52-385	VIII
1-none	2543	31-52-392	VIII	1106	2486	31-52-285	VIII
1-none	2544	31-52-392	VIII	1113	2393	31-52-394	VIII
1-none	2545	31-52-392	VIII	1114	2321	31-52-381	VIII
1-none	2546	31-52-392	VIII	1117	2770	31-52-374	VIII
1-none	2547	31-52-392	VIII	1119	2322	Baghdad	VIII
1-none	2548	31-52-392	VIII	1123	2307	31-52-439	VIII
1-none	2549	31-52-392	VIII	1133	2771	31-52-373	VIII
1008	2917	31-52-383	VIII	1135	2772	31-52-376	VIII
1010a	2550	31-52-392	VIII	1146	2487	31-52-411	VIII
1010b	2551	31-52-392	VIII	1147a	2576	31-52-392	VIII
1010c	2552	31-52-392	VIII	1147b	2577	31-52-392	VIII
1010d	2553	31-52-392	VIII	1147c	2578	31-52-392	VIII
1010e	2554	31-52-392	VIII	1147d	2579	31-52-392	VIII
1010f	2555	31-52-392	VIII	1147e	2580	31-52-392	VIII
1010g	2556	31-52-392	VIII	1147f	2581	31-52-392	VIII
1011	2869	31-52-380	VIII	1198	2773	31-52-377	VIII
1012	2870	31-52-378	VIII	1199	2395	31-52-401	VIII
1013	2386	31-52-399	VIII	1225	2582	31-52-389	VIII
1014	2387	31-52-398	VIII	1225	2583	31-52-391	VIII
1016a	2557	31-52-392	VIII	1655	2775	31-52-375	VIII
1016b	2558	31-52-392	VIII	1660B1	2922	31-52-386	VIII
1016c	2559	31-52-392	VIII	1667	2776	unknown	VIII
1016d	2560	31-52-392	VIII	2-none	2353	32-21-349	VIII
1016e	2561	31-52-392	VIII	2-none	2354	32-21-352	VIII

Concordance   (continued)

Field Number	Catalogue Number	Location	Level/ Phase
2-none	2374	32-21-313	VIII
2-none	2468	32-21-456	VIII
2-none	2685	32-21-403	VIII
2-none	2686	32-21-423	VIII
2-none	2843	32-21-352	VIII
2-none	2844	32-21-469	VIII
2-none	2912	32-21-343	VIII
2-none	2913	32-21-344	VIII
2-none	2914	32-21-345	VIII
2-none	2970	32-21-518	VIII
2-none	2971	32-21-520	VIII
2-none	2972	32-21-521	VIII
2-none	2973	32-21-523	VIII
2-none b	2586	32-21-404	VIII
2none	2584	32-21-404	VIII
2none a	2687	32-21-426	VIII
2none b	2688	32-21-426	VIII
2none b	2689	32-21-426	VIII
2none c	2690	32-21-426	VIII
2none d	2691	32-21-426	VIII
2none e	2692	32-21-426	VIII
2none e	2693	32-21-426	VIII
2none f	2694	32-21-426	VIII
2none g	2695	32-21-426	VIII
2none i	2696	32-21-426	VIII
2none j	2697	32-21-426	VIII
2none k	2698	32-21-426	VIII
2none l	2699	32-21-426	VIII
2none l	2700	32-21-426	VIII
2none m	2701	32-21-426	VIII
2none n	2702	32-21-426	VIII
2none p	2703	32-21-426	VIII
2none q	2704	32-21-426	VIII
2none s	2705	32-21-426	VIII
2none u	2707	32-21-426	VIII
2none v	2708	32-21-426	VIII
2none w	2709	32-21-426	VIII
2none x	2710	32-21-426	VIII
2none y	2711	32-21-426	VIII
2none z	2712	32-21-426	VIII
2none d	2587	32-21-404	VIII
2none e	2588	32-21-404	VIII
2none f	2589	32-21-404	VIII
2none g	2590	32-21-404	VIII
2none i	2592	32-21-404	VIII
2none j	2593	32-21-404	VIII
2none l	2595	32-21-404	VIII
3-003	2974	Baghdad	VIII
3-005	2975	33-3-002	VIII
3-007	2977	33-3-003	VIII
3-008	2520	Baghdad	VIII
3-012	2375	33-3-006	VIII

Concordance   (continued)

Field Number	Catalogue Number	Location	Level/ Phase
3-013	2521	33-3-007	VIII
3-014	2522	Baghdad	VIII
3-018	2376	discarded	VIII
3-019	2845	Baghdad	VIII
3-021	2846	33-3-010	VIII
3-023	2713	Baghdad	VIII
3-024	2714	33-3-011	VIII
3-026	2978	33-3-012	VIII
3-033	2523	discarded	VIII
3-036	2469	33-3-015	VIII
3-039	2847	33-3-017	VIII
3-040	2848	discarded	VIII
3-045	2915	33-3-019	VIII
3-046	2377	33-3-020	VIII
3-047	2849	33-3-021	VIII
3-048	2378	33-3-022	VIII
3-049	2524	33-3-023	VIII
3-050	2525	Baghdad	VIII
3-052	2379	Baghdad	VIII
3-055	2470	33-3-025	VIII
3-056	2471	Baghdad	VIII
3-057	2715	Baghdad	VIII
3-058	2716	33-3-026	VIII
3-059	2355	33-3-096	VIII
3-061	2526	33-3-028	VIII
3-062	2980	33-3-029	VIII
3-063	2981	33-3-030	VIII
3-064	2982	33-3-031	VII!
3-065	2472	Baghdad	VIII
3-066	2473	Baghdad	VIII
3-067	2850	33-3-032	VIII
3-068	2717	33-3-033	VIII
3-069	2916	33-3-034	VIII
3-070	2527	33-3-035	VIII
3-073	2851	33-3-037	VIII
3-075	2718	Baghdad	VIII
3-076	2528	33-3-088	VIII
3-078	2719	33-3-039	VIII
3-079	2474	Baghdad	VIII
3-081	2475	Baghdad	VIII
3-084	2852	33-3-040	VIII
3-085	2853	33-3-041	VIII
3-088	2758	Baghdad	VIII
3-090	2854	33-3-043	VIII
3-092	2316	Baghdad	VIII
3-093	2476	Baghdad	VIII
3-102	2380	33-3-047	VIII
3-109	2477	Baghdad	VIII
3-111	2317	33-3-050	VIII
3-112	2318	33-3-051	VIII
3-115	2983	33-3-053	VIII
3-116	2720	Baghdad	VIII

(*continues*)

Concordance   (continued)   Concordance   (continued)

Field Number	Catalogue Number	Location	Level/ Phase	Field Number	Catalogue Number	Location	Level/ Phase
3-119	2721	Baghdad	VIII	5490	2760	Baghdad	VIII
3-120	2529	Baghdad	VIII	5491	2761	32-21-350	VIII
3-121	2984	Baghdad	VIII	5492	2401	32-21-442	VIII
3-122	2381	Baghdad	VIII	5493	2878	Baghdad	VIII
3-123	2356	Baghdad	VIII	5494	2402	32-21-444	VIII
3-125	2855	33-3-055	VIII	5576	2927	Baghdad	VIII
3-126	2985	33-3-056	VIII	5577	2928	Baghdad	VIII
3-127	2357	33-3-057	VIII	5582	2489	Baghdad	VIII
3-127	2986	33-3-057	VIII	5585	2491	32-21-474	VIII
3-130	2358	33-3-059	VIII	5594	2762	Baghdad	VIII
3-131	2988	Baghdad	VIII	5595	2405	Baghdad	VIII
3-135	2478	33-3-061	VIII	5596	2492	32-21-471	VIII
3-136	2856	33-3-062	VIII	5597	2879	32-21-327	VIII
3-138	2857	discarded	VIII	5603	2880	32-21-328	VIII
3-139	2858	discarded	VIII	5604	2881	32-21-329	VIII
3-140	2859	33-3-064	VIII	5606	2786	Baghdad	VIII
3-143	2861	discarded	VIII	5613	2787	32-21-301	VIII
3-144	2862	33-3-068	VIII	5614	2327	32-21-354	VIII
3-145	2863	discarded	VIII	5615	2328	Baghdad	VIII
3-147	2864	discarded	VIII	5623	2788	32-21-302	VIII
3-162	2359	discarded	VIII	5625	2408	32-21-446	VIII
3-163	2360	33-3-073	VIII	5626	2790	32-21-291	VIII
3-186	2532	Baghdad	VIII	5627	2329	32-21-556	VIII
3-187	2533	Baghdad	VIII	5628	2791	32-21-292	VIII
3-230	2865	33-3-115	VIII	5629	2792	Baghdad	VIII
3-231	2866	discarded	VIII	5630	2613	32-21-389	VIII
3-279	2361	discarded	VIII	5631	2793	32-21-288	VIII
3-none	2479	33-3-280	VIII	5636	2794	32-21-293	VIII
3-none	2480	33-3-281	VIII	5637	2614	32-21-383	VIII
3-none	2481	33-3-282	VIII	5638	2795	32-21-304	VIII
3-none	2767	33-3-227	VIII	5639	2796	unknown	VIII
5286	2872	Baghdad	VIII	5644	2798	32-21-284	VIII
5330	2777	32-21-298	VIII	5648	2410	32-21-447	VIII
5343	2778	32-21-285	VIII	5650	2331	32-21-312	VIII
5362	2875	Baghdad	VIII	5652	2615	Baghdad	VIII
5363	2876	Dropsie	VIII	5653	2411	32-21-437	VIII
5364	2877	32-21-326	VIII	5654	2412	32-21-429	VIII
5365	2366	Baghdad	VIII	5655	2413	32-21-430	VIII
5371	2601	Baghdad	VIII	5656	2414	Baghdad	VIII
5377	2602	Baghdad	VIII	5658	2308	unknown	VIII
5380	2325	Baghdad	VIII	5659	2729	Baghdad	VIII
5381	2398	Baghdad	VIII	5660	2496	Baghdad	VIII
5426	2779	unknown	VIII	5661	2730	32-21-361	VIII
5439	2326	32-21-320	VIII	5666	2415	32-21-457	VIII
5458	2780	32-21-466	VIII	5669	2618	32-21-384	VIII
5479	2488	Baghdad	VIII	5670	2416	32-21-454	VIII
5480	2925	Baghdad	VIII	5671	2417	32-21-455	VIII
5481	2759	Dropsie	VIII	5672	2418	Baghdad	VIII
5484	2603	32-21-405	VIII	5673	2333	Baghdad	VIII
5485	2782	Baghdad	VIII	5674	2497	Baghdad	VIII
5488	2604	32-21-386	VIII	5676	2367	32-21-314	VIII
5489	2605	32-21-388	VIII	5677	2800	32-21-308	VIII

Concordance   (continued)

Concordance   (continued)

Field Number	Catalogue Number	Location	Level/ Phase	Field Number	Catalogue Number	Location	Level/ Phase
5678	2364	unknown	VIII	5769	2812	32-21-309	VIII
5679	2334	Baghdad	VIII	5771	2502	Dropsie	VIII
5680	2886	32-21-378	VIII	5772	2503	32-21-479	VIII
5681	2887	32-21-331	VIII	5773	2341	32-21-561	VIII
5682	2419	32-21-431	VIII	5774	2342	Baghdad	VIII
5683	2420	Baghdad	VIII	5777	2934	32-21-497	VIII
5684	2421	32-21-448	VIII	5778	2504	32-21-480	VIII
5685	2619	Baghdad	VIII	5780	2363	32-21-319	VIII
5686	2763	Baghdad	VIII	5781	2370	Baghdad	VIII
5687	2801	unknown	VIII	5782	2343	unknown	VIII
5688	2888	32-21-332	VIII	5783	2439	Baghdad	VIII
5689	2362	Baghdad	VIII	5785	2893	32-21-379	VIII
5690	2731	Baghdad	VIII	5786	2631	32-21-394	VIII
5691	2802	32-21-294	VIII	5787	2894	32-21-380	VIII
5700	2803	32-21-055	VIII	5788	2895	32-21-381	VIII
5703	2804	Baghdad	VIII	5789	2936	32-21-499	VIII
5705	2620	32-21-392	VIII	5790	2937	32-21-500	VIII
5706	2805	32-21-287	VIII	5792	2310	Baghdad	VIII
5708	2335	32-21-558	VIII	5793	2344	32-21-351	VIII
5709	2336	Baghdad	VIII	5797	2632	32-21-412	VIII
5710	2889	Baghdad	VIII	5801	2507	32-21-481	VIII
5713	2932	Baghdad	VIII	5802	2633	Baghdad	VIII
5722	2368	32-21-068	VIII	5805	2345	32-21-321	VIII
5725	2806	32-21-289	VIII	5806	2897	Baghdad	VIII
5736	2429	32-21-441	VIII	5807	2813	32-21-290	VIII
5737	2498	Baghdad	VIII	5809	2508	Baghdad	VIII
5738	2430	Baghdad	VIII	5810	2440	Baghdad	VIII
5739	2622	Baghdad	VIII	5811	2938	Baghdad	VIII
5740	2891	32-21-333	VIII	5812	2441	32-21-464	VIII
5741	2810	Baghdad	VIII	5813	2898	Baghdad	VIII
5743	2623	32-21-410	VIII	5814	2899	32-21-334	VIII
5746	2742	Baghdad	VIII	5815	2634	Baghdad	VIII
5747	2624	Baghdad	VIII	5817	2900	32-21-335	VIII
5748	2625	32-21-411	VIII	5818	2442	Baghdad	VIII
5749	2499	32-21-443	VIII	5819	2815	Baghdad	VIII
5750	2431	32-21-450	VIII	5824	2943	Baghdad	VIII
5751	2811	32-21-295	VIII	5825	2635	Baghdad	VIII
5752	2743	Dropsie	VIII	5826	2346	32-21-347	VIII
5753	2744	32-21-363	VIII	5828	2747	Baghdad	VIII
5755	2432	Baghdad	VIII	5829	2443	Baghdad	VIII
5757	2433	32-21-432	VIII	5831	2636	32-21-413	VIII
5758	2501	Baghdad	VIII	5834	2901	32-21-336	VIII
5759	2745	Baghdad	VIII	5835	2444	Baghdad	VIII
5760	2626	32-21-393	VIII	5836	2445	Baghdad	VIII
5760b	2627	32-21-393	VIII	5838	2446	Baghdad	VIII
5760c	2628	32-21-393	VIII	5843	2637	32-21-395	VIII
5761	2434	32-21-462	VIII	5844	2638	Baghdad	VIII
5762	2435	32-21-451	VIII	5845	2347	32-21-562	VIII
5763	2436	Baghdad	VIII	5846	2817	Baghdad	VIII
5764	2437	Baghdad	VIII	5847	2348	32-21-318	VIII
5766	2629	unknown	VIII	5850	2447	Baghdad	VIII
5767	2630	Baghdad	VIII	5851	2904	Baghdad	VIII

(*continues*)

Concordance   (continued)

Field Number	Catalogue Number	Location	Level/ Phase
5853	2905	Baghdad	VIII
5859	2946	Baghdad	VIII
5860	2640	32-21-414	VIII
5863	2947	32-21-506	VIII
5885	2953	32-21-512	VIII
5889	2752	Baghdad	VIII
5899	2452	32-21-452	VIII
5909	2312	32-21-546	VIII
5913A	2512	32-21-483	VIII
5913B	2513	Baghdad	VIII
5917	2958	32-21-525	VIII
5920	2514	32-21-487	VIII
5923	2313	32-21-377	VIII
5934	2314	32-21-547	VIII
5936	2454	Baghdad	VIII
5996	2756	unknown	VIII
6003	2681	32-21-428	VIII
6015	2831	Baghdad	VIII
6016	2832	Baghdad	VIII
6024	2839	Baghdad	VIII
6066	2840	Baghdad	VIII
6071	2765	32-21-353	VIII
6072	2352	32-21-306	VIII
6074	2373	32-21-317	VIII
6077	2966	32-21-522	VIII
6078	2967	32-21-524	VIII
6079	2968	32-21-519	VIII
6083	2465	32-21-438	VIII
6096	2969	Baghdad	VIII
3-001	2757	33-3-001	VIII?
3-006	2976	Baghdad	VIII?
3-128	2987	Baghdad	VIII?
3-129	2530	33-3-058	VIII?
3-148	2531	33-3-070	VIII?
5756	2500	Baghdad	VIII?
0850	2382	Dropsie	VIIIA
0853	2383	Dropsie	VIIIA
1-none	2319	1929:89	VIIIA
1-none	2365	unknown	VIIIA
1-none	2384	Dropsie?	VIIIA
1-none	2385	1929:	VIIIA
1541	2774	31-52-317	VIIIA
1656	2396	Dropsie	VIIIA
1657	2397	Dropsie	VIIIA
1658	2768	unknown	VIIIA
1659	2722	31-52-407	VIIIA
1660A	2920	31-52-386	VIIIA
1660B	2921	Baghdad	VIIIA
1661	2923	31-52-387	VIIIA
1662	2924	Dropsie	VIIIA
3-004	2315	Baghdad	VIIIA
5473	2399	Baghdad	VIIIA

Concordance   (continued)

Field Number	Catalogue Number	Location	Level/ Phase
5477	2781	32-21-299	VIIIA
5495	2926	32-21-492	VIIIA
5593	2611	32-21-409	VIIIA
5619	2723	Baghdad	VIIIA
5634	2726	32-21-356	VIIIA
5641	2330	32-21-346	VIIIA
5642	2930	32-21-494	VIIIA
5645	2727	Baghdad	VIIIA
5693	2733	Baghdad	VIIIA
5712	2338	32-21-559	VIIIA
5714	2425	Dropsie	VIIIA
5715	2426	Baghdad	VIIIA
5716	2621	Dropsie	VIIIA
5717	2738	Baghdad	VIIIA
5718	2739	32-21-132	VIIIA
5719	2764	Baghdad	VIIIA
5723	2369	32-21-069	VIIIA
5724	2890	Baghdad	VIIIA
5726	2807	32-21-061	VIIIA
5727	2808	32-21-062	VIIIA
5728	2809	Baghdad	VIIIA
5733	2740	Baghdad	VIIIA
5744	2340	32-21-560	VIIIA
5745	2892	Baghdad	VIIIA
5765	2438	Baghdad	VIIIA
5779	2505	Baghdad	VIIIA
5803	2896	Baghdad	VIIIA
5832	2816	Baghdad	VIIIA
5833	2371	Baghdad	VIIIA
5837	2748	Baghdad	VIIIA
5839	2749	Baghdad	VIIIA
5857	2509	32-21-371	VIIIA
5858	2311	32-21-376	VIIIA
5861	2641	32-21-415	VIIIA
5862	2908	32-21-340	VIIIA
5864	2350	32-21-348	VIIIA
5865	2909	32-21-341	VIIIA
5866	2642	Baghdad	VIIIA
5921	2515	Baghdad	VIIIA
5938	2664	Baghdad	VIIIA
5939	2665	Baghdad	VIIIA
5943	2960	32-21-515	VIIIA
5944	2961	32-21-564	VIIIA
5945	2962	Baghdad	VIIIA
5946	2457	unknown	VIIIA
5949	2666	32-21-419	VIIIA
5952	2517	32-21-475	VIIIA
5953	2753	unknown	VIIIA
5954A–D	2963	32-21-516	VIIIA
5955	2964	Baghdad	VIIIA
5956	2823	32-21-305	VIIIA
5957	2824	Baghdad	VIIIA

Concordance   (continued)

Concordance   (continued)

Field Number	Catalogue Number	Location	Level/Phase	Field Number	Catalogue Number	Location	Level/Phase
5958	2754	unknown	VIIIA	5611	2612	Baghdad	VIIIAB
5959	2668	Dropsie	VIIIA	5612	2929	32-21-493	VIIIAB
5960	2669	unknown	VIIIA	5618	2406	32-21-445	VIIIAB
5961	2670	32-21-421	VIIIA	5622	2407	32-21-440	VIIIAB
5962	2671	unknown	VIIIA	5624	2789	32-21-303	VIIIAB
5963	2672	32-21-422	VIIIA	5632	2724	32-21-367	VIIIAB
5964	2673	32-21-385	VIIIA	5633	2725	32-21-368	VIIIAB
5965	2674	unknown	VIIIA	5635	2409	Baghdad	VIIIAB
5966	2676	unknown	VIIIA	5640	2797	Baghdad	VIIIAB
5967	2677	32-21-424	VIIIA	5643	2931	32-21-495	VIIIAB
5968	2675	32-21-425	VIIIA	5651	2495	32-21-477	VIIIAB
5969	2678	unknown	VIIIA	5657	2728	32-21-357	VIIIAB
5971	2459	32-21-453	VIIIA	5662	2332	32-21-557	VIIIAB
5975	2463	unknown	VIIIA	5663	2883	Baghdad	VIIIAB
5991	2965	32-21-490	VIIIA	5664	2884	Dropsie	VIIIAB
5992	2519	32-21-473	VIIIA	5665	2885	32-21-330	VIIIAB
6011	2827	Baghdad	VIIIA	5667	2616	32-21-390	VIIIAB
6012	2828	Baghdad	VIIIA	5668	2617	32-21-391	VIIIAB
6014	2830	Baghdad	VIIIA	5675	2799	Baghdad	VIIIAB
6022	2837	Baghdad	VIIIA	5694	2422	Baghdad	VIIIAB
6023	2838	Baghdad	VIIIA	5697	2424	32-21-461	VIIIAB
6092	2682	unknown	VIIIA	5698	2309	Baghdad	VIIIAB
6093	2683	unknown	VIIIA	5701	2736	32-21-369	VIIIAB
6095	2466	32-21-470	VIIIA	5702	2737	Baghdad	VIIIAB
6097	2467	Baghdad	VIIIA	5711	2337	Baghdad	VIIIAB
6098	2684	unknown	VIIIA	5721	2427	32-21-449	VIIIAB
unknown	2841	unknown	VIIIA	5730	2428	32-21-468	VIIIAB
5264	2596	Baghdad	VIIIA?	5731	2339	Baghdad	VIIIAB
5265	2597	Baghdad	VIIIA?	5734	2741	Baghdad	VIIIAB
5266	2598	Baghdad	VIIIA?	5800	2506	Baghdad	VIIIAB
5267	2599	32-21-407	VIIIA?	5840	2750	32-21-366	VIIIAB
5268	2600	Baghdad	VIIIA?	5841	2902	Baghdad	VIIIAB
5285	2323	32-21-322	VIIIA?	5842	2903	32-21-337	VIIIAB
5287	2873	32-21-325	VIIIA?	5852	2639	Baghdad	VIIIAB
5292	2324	32-21-555	VIIIA?	5854	2906	32-21-338	VIIIAB
5307	2874	Baghdad	VIIIA?	5855	2349	32-21-324	VIIIAB
5598	2784	32-21-307	VIIIA?	5856	2907	32-21-339	VIIIAB
5602	2785	Baghdad	VIIIA?	5896	2654	Baghdad	VIIIAB
2-none	2842	unknown	VIIIAB	3-032	2979	IM15643	VIIIB
5486	2400	Baghdad	VIIIAB	5776	2933	32-21-496	VIIIB
5581	2403	Baghdad	VIIIAB	5784	2935	32-21-498	VIIIB
5583	2490	32-21-472	VIIIAB	5820	2939	32-21-501	VIIIB
5584	2404	32-21-439	VIIIAB	5821	2940	32-21-502	VIIIB
5587	2606	32-21-387	VIIIAB	5822	2941	32-21-503	VIIIB
5588	2783	32-21-300	VIIIAB	5823	2942	32-21-517	VIIIB
5589	2607	Baghdad	VIIIAB	5830	2944	32-21-504	VIIIB
5590	2608	Baghdad	VIIIAB	5848	2945	32-21-505	VIIIB
5591	2609	32-21-408	VIIIAB	5901	2657	32-21-401	VIIIB
5592	2610	Baghdad	VIIIAB	6009	2825	Baghdad	VIIIB
5601	2493	32-21-476	VIIIAB	6013	2829	Baghdad	VIIIB
5608	2494	Baghdad	VIIIAB	6018	2833	Baghdad	VIIIB
5610	2882	32-21-382	VIIIAB	6019	2834	Baghdad	VIIIB

(*continues*)

Concordance   (continued)

Field Number	Catalogue Number	Location	Level/ Phase
6020	2835	Baghdad	VIIIB
6021	2836	Baghdad	VIIIB
5692	2732	Baghdad	VIIIB?
5695	2734	32-21-362	VIIIB?
5696	2423	32-21-459	VIIIB?
5699	2735	32-21-359	VIIIB?
5791	2746	Baghdad	VIIIB?
5808	2814	32-21-296	VIIIB?
2none t	2706	32-21-426	VIIIBC
2none a	2585	32-21-404	VIIIBC
2none h	2591	32-21-404	VIIIBC
2none k	2594	32-21-404	VIIIBC
5867	2818	32-21-311	VIIIBC
5868	2510	32-21-375	VIIIBC
5869	2511	Baghdad	VIIIBC
5870	2751	32-21-358	VIIIBC
5871	2643	Baghdad	VIIIBC
5872	2644	32-21-396	VIIIBC
5873	2645	32-21-427	VIIIBC
5874	2948	32-21-507	VIIIBC
5875	2646	32-21-397	VIIIBC
5876	2647	32-21-416	VIIIBC
5877	2648	32-21-417	VIIIBC
5878	2372	32-21-315	VIIIBC
5879	2819	32-21-310	VIIIBC
5880	2949	32-21-508	VIIIBC
5881	2950	32-21-509	VIIIBC
5882	2951	32-21-510	VIIIBC
5883	2952	32-21-511	VIIIBC
5884	2448	Baghdad	VIIIBC
5886	2649	Baghdad	VIIIBC
5887	2650	Baghdad	VIIIBC
5888	2651	32-21-398	VIIIBC
5890	2449	32-21-433	VIIIBC
5891	2351	32-21-322	VIIIBC
5892	2652	32-21-399	VIIIBC
5893	2653	32-21-400	VIIIBC
5894	2450	Baghdad	VIIIBC
5895	2451	32-21-465	VIIIBC
5897	2655	Baghdad	VIIIBC
5898	2656	Baghdad	VIIIBC
5900	2820	32-21-297	VIIIBC

Concordance   (continued)

Field Number	Catalogue Number	Location	Level/ Phase
5902	2658	32-21-402	VIIIBC
5903	2453	32-21-434	VIIIBC
5904	2659	32-21-418	VIIIBC
5905	2910	Baghdad	VIIIBC
5906	2911	32-21-342	VIIIBC
5907	2954	32-21-513	VIIIBC
5908	2955	32-21-514	VIIIBC
5911	2956	32-21-563	VIIIBC
5911	2957	Baghdad	VIIIBC
5922	2821	Baghdad	VIIIBC
5924	2959	32-21-491	VIIIBC
5928	2660	Baghdad	VIIIBC
5929	2661	32-21-420	VIIIBC
5930	2662	Baghdad	VIIIBC
5937	2663	32-21-406	VIIIBC
5940	2516	Baghdad	VIIIBC
5941	2455	32-21-460	VIIIBC
5942	2456	32-21-435	VIIIBC
5948	2822	Baghdad	VIIIBC
5950	2667	Baghdad	VIIIBC
5951	2458	unknown	VIIIBC
5970	2679	unknown	VIIIBC
3-141	2860	33-3-065	VIIIC
3-188	2989	33-3-088	VIIIC
3-188	2990	33-3-088	VIIIC
3-188	2991	33-3-088	VIIIC
3-188	2992	33-3-088	VIIIC
3-250	2766	33-3-123	VIIIC
3-250	2867	33-3-124	VIIIC
5972	2460	unknown	VIIIC
5973	2461	unknown	VIIIC
5974	2462	32-21-463	VIIIC
5978	2464	32-21-436	VIIIC
5989	2755	unknown	VIIIC
5990	2518	unknown	VIIIC
5995	2680	unknown	VIIIC
6010	2826	Baghdad	VIIIC
3-none	2868	unknown	VIIIC?
3-none	2993	33-3-239	VIIIC?
3-none	2994	33-3-239	VIIIC?
3-none	2995	33-3-239	VIIIC?

Other Illustrations
and Museum Archives
Negative Numbers

This listing is provided for two reasons. First, many early writers about Gawra cited objects in the two earlier Gawra publications (Speiser 1935a, Tobler 1950) by their illustration numbers; for example, alabaster model vase 219 in this volume (field number 4-685) might be cited as Tobler 70. The multiplicity of numbers for objects undoubtedly causes problems. Also, not every object illustrated in the earlier volumes could be illustrated here. For technical reasons, this information could not be included in the catalogue of this volume. Therefore, I include this listing for comparative reasons. I hope those who cite this volume will include the one consistent number, the field number (1000-, 5000-, 3-xx, 4-xxx, 5-xxx, 6-xxx, 7-xxx), in addition to any illustration number. Secondly, the Archives of the University of Pennsylvania

Museum houses many negatives of object photographs from the excavation. I include the negative number in case a reader may want a photograph. This listing is based on registry books. Many of these negatives still exist, although some have deteriorated and are no longer printable. Inquiries should be directed to the Archives. The third column of numbers are the Museum's accession numbers (36-6-xxx, 37-16-xxx, 38-13-xxx). Those along with the negative number are the ones to use in referring to a specific negative.

[1 = Speiser 1935, 2 = Tobler 1950, Sp 29 = Speiser 1929, 5 digits starting with '4' University of Pennsylvania Photographic Archives accession number Column 1 = catalogue number, 2 = field no., 3 = location, 4 = illustration or negative].

1	2	3	4	1	2	3	4
8.	6-021	37-16-188	2CLXXXII, 14	226.	4-1038	35-10-142	2CXLV1, 401
9.	6-262	37-16-187	2CLXXXII, 12	227.	4-1084	Baghdad	44147
13.	6-109	37-16-189	44922	229.	4-1140	35-10-195	2CXXXIII, 237
16.	4-1224	Baghdad	44214	230.	4-1141	Baghdad	44224
30.	5-1510	36-6-242a	2LXXXVI, a5	232.	4-1144	Baghdad	2CXXXIV, 251
35.	6-031	Baghdad	2CLIV, 19	233.	4-1145	35-10-199	2CXXXIX, 307
39.	4-0714	Baghdad	2XCVI, b2	239.	4-1188	35-10-196	44220
41.	4-0903	Baghdad	44586	243.	4-none	unknown	2CLXXXI 8
54.	5-1450	36-6-183	44733	252.	5-1235	36-6-259	2CLXXX 64
55.	5-1453	Baghdad	44799	253.	5-1236	Baghdad	44667
56.	5-1461	Baghdad	44733	254.	5-1241	36-6-235	2CXXXIV 261
58.	5-1478	36-6-271	46430	256.	5-1388	Baghdad	2CXXXIII 245
60.	5-1515	36-6-272	44740	257.	5-1436	36-6-241	2CXL 327
62.	5-1554	Baghdad	44739	258.	5-1490	Baghdad	2CXLI 332
63.	5-1562	Baghdad	44740	261.	5-1503	Baghdad	2CXLI 342
64.	5-1563	Baghdad	44740	266.	5-1534	Baghdad	44736
66.	5-1581	36-6-266	44740 46428	267.	5-1535	36-6-226	44735
67.	5-1582	36-6-262	44739	269.	5-1558	36-6-220	44741
68.	5-1589	36-6-264	46420	270.	5-1561	36-6-218	2LXXIX f
70.	5-1654	Baghdad	44760	271.	5-1568	Baghdad	2CXXXV 272
71.	5-1655	36-6-270	44760	277.	5-1606	36-6-221	44785
74.	5-1724	Baghdad	44802	278.	5-1618	36-6-222	2CXXXV 267
82.	6-013	Baghdad	2CLXXVII, 24	281.	5-1623	Baghdad	2CXL 312
83.	6-014	Baghdad	44926	286.	5-1663	Baghdad	2CXXXIII 242
84.	6-022	Baghdad	44926	287.	5-1687	Baghdad	none
86.	6-144	unknown	2CLXXIX, 57	288.	5-1712	36-6-238	46449
87.	6-239	Baghdad	2CLXXVII, 30	290.	5-1740	Baghdad	2CXXXIII 240
89.	6-272	Baghdad	2CLXXVII, 31	292.	5-1758	Discarded	2CXXXV 271
91.	6-595	37-16-186	2XCVII, b9	301.	6-066	37-16-66	2CLXXX 65
101.	7-194	Baghdad	2XCV, d	303.	6-088	unknown	2CXLIII 366
102.	7-230	38-13-36	45103	304.	6-100	Baghdad	2CXLII 353
104.	7-262	Baghdad	45103	307.	6-120	37-16-107	2CXXXIV 258
106.	5-1408	Baghdad	44733	308.	6-150	Baghdad	2CLXXX 68
110.	4-1163	Baghdad	44645	309.	6-154	37-16-171	2CLXXX 67
133.	6-098	Baghdad	44831	311.	6-201	Baghdad	2CXXXIX 310
134.	6-099	Baghdad	2CLXXII, 27	312.	6-205	37-16-113	2CXL 324
137.	6-143	Baghdad	2CLXXVI, 17	313.	6-213	37-16-108	2CXXXIII 244
138.	6-160	Baghdad	44837	320.	6-588	37-16-94	2CXXXIX 311
139.	6-163	unknown	2CLXXIII, 44	321.	6-589	Baghdad	2CXXXIII 243
140.	6-195	unknown	44829 44837	322.	6-594	37-16-117	2CXXXVII 294
141.	6-202	37-16-195	2XCI a	324.	6-618	Baghdad	2CXXXVII 295
142.	6-298	Baghdad	2CLXXII, 23	334.	4-0674	35-10-230	2LXXXV 6
143.	6-587	Baghdad	2CLXXI, 10	336.	4-0677	Baghdad	2CLV 34-37
147.	7-252	38-13-41	2XCII, b7	340.	4-0951	35-10-227	2LXXXV 8
148.	7-258	38-13-40	2CLXXIII, 47	341.	4-0976	35-10-223	2LXXXV 1
158.	6-010	Baghdad	2CLXXVI, 2	344.	4-1152	35-10-224	2LXXXV 3
159.	6-204a	Baghdad	2CLXXVI, 3, 5	346.	4-1180	35-10-226	2LXXXV 4
160.	6-204b	37-26-182-	2CLXXVI, 4, 6	347.	4-1197	35-10-221	2LXXXV 2
163.	6-304	37-16-181	2CLXXVI, 10	385.	5-1233	36-6-255	2LXXXV 12
164.	6-603	Baghdad	2CLXXVI, 15	386.	5-1580	36-6-256	2LXXXV 9
176.	7-271	38-13-38	2XCVIII, a2	387.	5-1596	Baghdad	2CLV 38
218.	7-272	38-13-33	2CXXXIII, 252	390.	6-004	Baghdad	2CLV 33
219.	4-0685	35-10-232	2CLXXX, 70	418.	4-0644	35-10-260	44536/37
222.	4-0713	Baghdad	2CXXXIV, 260	427.	4-1158	35-10-249	44646 48095
225.	4-1023	35-10-193	44152	428.	4-1171	35-10-250	2CLVIII 8

1	2	3	4	1	2	3	4
429.	4-1176	35-10-253	2CLIX 24	537.	4-1027	35-10-170	44136
430.	4-1181	IM24594	2CLX 40	560.	6-078	37-16-52	2CXLIII, 364
431.	4-1190	35-10-269	44542	561.	6-104	unknown	2CXLIII, 363
432.	4-1191	IM25000	2CLXIII 90	563.	7-215	38-13-23	2LXXXIV, a1-6
433.	4-1192	35-10-259	4655 44533	564.	7-216	38-13-24	2LXXXIV, a9
434.	4-1193	35-10-270	2CLXIV 99	565.	7-217	38-13-25	2LXXIV, a 7 8
435.	4-1194	35-10-271	44531 44532	571.	4-1028	35-10-146	46459
442.	4-1203	35-10-275	2CLXX, 182	572.	4-1062	Baghdad	2CLIV, 20
446.	4-1208	35-10-277	2CLVIII, 17	573.	4-1105	Baghdad	2CLIV, 22
447.	4-1209	35-10-278	2CLXVI, 122	574.	4-1159	35-10-217	2LXXXIII, c
453.	4-1225	35-10-281	2CLVIII, 6	581.	5-1387	36-6-146	2LXXXVI, a4
457.	5-1237	36-6-306	2CLXVI, 126	583.	5-1524	Baghdad	2LXXXVI, a9
458.	5-1238	IM27044	44761	584.	5-1556	36-6-147	2LXXXVI, a1
459.	5-1239	36-6-305	2CLXX, 179	588.	5-none	unknown	44652
460.	5-1240	36-6-313	2CLXVII, 138	590.	6-131	Discarded	2CLIII, 11
461.	5-1242	IM26965	44312	593.	4-0946	35-10-238	44095
464.	5-1247	36-6-310	44286	594.	4-0973	35-10-237	46421
465.	5-1406	36-6-311	2CLXVI, 128	596.	4-0987	35-10-239	46420 44097
466.	5-1407	36-6-293	44761 48106	597.	4-1030	35-10-234	44141
467.	5-1437	IM27043	44761	611.	5-1330	Baghdad	44657
468.	5-1514	36-6-307	2CLXII, 67	612.	5-1382	36-6-185	44733
471.	5-1588	36-6-296	2CLX, 35	613.	5-1416	36-6-172	2XCVII d2
472.	5-1595	36-6-309	2CLXII, 78	616.	5-1434	Baghdad	44740
475.	5-1630	IM27027	2CLXII, 75	619.	5-1459	Baghdad	44731
477.	5-1640	36-6-297	2CLXI,I 76	621.	5-1539	Baghdad	44740
478.	5-1641	36-6-298	2CLIX, 25	623.	5-1542	Baghdad	44740
479.	5-1648	IM26962	2CLXI, 63	625.	5-1578	Baghdad	44740
485.	5-none	36-6-291	48103 48105	627.	5-1652	36-6-182	44802
496.	6-096	Baghdad	2CLXV, 107	628.	5-1669	Baghdad	no plate
499.	6-151	37-16-208	2CLXV, 111	645.	6-097	Baghdad	2CLXXVI 18
500.	6-152	Baghdad	44829	646.	6-315	Baghdad	2CLXXVIII 47
501.	6-161	37-16-215	44933	648.	7-150	Baghdad	45103
502.	6-167	Baghdad	44933	655.	4-0963	Baghdad	2CLXXIX 48
503.	6-203	37-16-205	44849	656.	4-0972	35-10-247	2XCII a8
504.	6-250	37-16-211	44932	657.	4-1018	Baghdad	2CLXXIV 59
505.	6-257	37-16-209	2CLXX, 176	658.	4-1087	Baghdad	44645
506.	6-303	37-16-207	44837	671.	6-068	37-16-72	2XCI b9
507.	6-366	Baghdad	2CLVIII, 14	673.	6-127	37-16-79	44850
509.	6-581	Baghdad	44933	674.	6-136	37-16-85	44917 44918
518.	7-056	38-13-50	44972	676.	6-145	37-16-80	44895 48108
519.	7-206	38-13-29	45025	677.	6-200	37-16-81	44830
520.	7-209	IM42359	2CLXII, 68	678.	6-216	Baghdad	44895
522.	7-212	Baghdad	2CLXI, 71	685.	4-0901	35-10-243	44587
524.	7-228	38-13-46	2CLCVII, 139	695.	5-1448	phila ?	2CLXXV 16
525.	7-231	Baghdad	45092	696.	5-1449	Baghdad	no plate
526.	7-251	38-13-43	2CLIX, 27	697.	5-none	35-10-155	no plate
527.	7-253	38-13-44	45022	698.	5-none	unknown	no plate
528.	7-235b	38-13-44b	45022	699.	6-091	37-16-71	2CLXXV 12
529.	7-255	IM42264	45022	700.	6-130	Baghdad	2CLXXVI 11
530.	7-257	38-13-45	2CLXVII, 132	709.	4-1113	Baghdad	44225
532.	7-274	38-13-42	2CLXI, 57	744.	4-0921	Discarded	2CXLI 330
533.	7-480	38-13-28	45062	747.	4-0997	35-10-187	44146
534.	7-481	Baghdad	45062	749.	4-1000	phila no#	44222
535.	4-0710	Baghdad	44137	754.	4-1031	Baghdad	44225
536.	4-0838	Baghdad	44136	755.	4-1032	Baghdad	44223

(*continues*)

1	2	3	4	1	2	3	4
756.	4-1033	Baghdad	44223	946.	4-1055	IM24605	2CLIX, 30
759.	4-1094	35-10-139	2CXLII 352	947.	4-1058	35-10-172	44646
762.	4-1109	Baghdad	44224	949.	4-1065	35-10-182	44534
763.	4-1110	35-10-374	44222	950.	4-1066	35-10-175	44535
767.	4-1117	35-10-145	2CXLI 340	957.	4-1076	Baghdad	44646
768.	4-1118	35-10-372	44227	962.	4-1089	IM24600	2CLXV, 109
769.	4-none	unknown	2CXLI, 335	971.	4-1206	35-10-186	2CLVIII, 18
770.	4-1119	Discarded	44227	975.	4-1221	35-10-251	2LXXXVIII, a9
771.	4-1120	phila ?	44228	993.	5-1243	Baghdad	2CLXIV, 93
772.	4-1121	unknown	44219	995.	5-1328	36-6-112	2CLIX, 28
773.	4-1122	Baghdad	44627	996.	5-1367	Baghdad	2CLXIV, 106
775.	4-1165	35-10-138	2CXLII 344	997.	5-1376	36-6-216	2CLXV, 114
786.	5-1393	Baghdad	44663	999.	5-1378	IM26980	2CLXI, 53
787.	5-1395	Baghdad	44663	1000.	5-1379	IM27006	44755
788.	5-1397	36-6-144	2CXLIII 362	1001.	5-1385	IM27032	2CLX, 33
789.	5-1398	Baghdad	44666 44664	1003.	5-1392	Baghdad	2CLXX, 183
792.	5-1423	Discarded	2CXLII 351	1005.	5-1399	36-6-213	2CLXIII, 85
794.	5-1442	Discarded	2CXLII 349	1008.	5-1428	IM26983	2CLXVII, 143
795.	5-1444	Baghdad	2CXLII 346	1010.	5-1435	36-6-215	44297 44755
796.	5-1446	Baghdad	2CXLIII 357	1012.	5-1465	Baghdad	44761
797.	5-1457	Baghdad	2CLXXX 66	1014.	5-1471	IM27039	2CLVIII, 10
798.	5-1468	36-6-138	2CXLI 341	1015.	5-1476	IM27037	44761
799.	5-1475	Baghdad	2CXLII 345	1016.	5-1483	36-6-203	44761 48101
800.	5-1482	36-6-138	2CXLIII 359	1017.	5-1488	36-6-209	44309 44755
802.	5-1486	Baghdad	2CXLI 333	1019.	5-1557	IM26989	2CLXIII, 89
803.	5-1487	Baghdad	2CXLI 339	1020.	5-1564	36-6-295	44761
804.	5-1489	36-6-140	44736	1021.	5-1573	36-6-208	2CLXVIII, 156
807.	5-1495	36-6-137	2CXLI, 338	1022.	5-1574	IM26990	2CLXVIII, 155
808.	5-1505	36-6-134	CXLI, 336	1023.	5-1594	36-6-121	2CLXIX, 161
810.	5-1516	Discarded	2CXLIII, 365	1025.	5-1624	IM26996	2CLXIX, 166
812.	5-1525	36-6-139	2CXLII, 354	1026.	5-1625	36-6-206	2CLXIV, 97
813.	5-1533	36-6-136	44735	1030.	5-1638	36-6-204	2CLXVI, 127
815.	5-1545	Baghdad	44783	1032.	5-1650	IM26974	46421
816.	5-1549	Baghdad	2CXLI, 337	1033.	5-1651	36-6-210	2CLXVIII, 154
817.	5-1550	36-6-141	44784	1034.	5-1668	36-6-207	2CLXIX, 169
818.	5-1571	Discarded	2CXLII, 350	1050.	6-073	IM32503	2CLX, 32
819.	5-1585	Baghdad	44784	1051.	6-076	37-16-78	44830
820.	5-1602	Baghdad	44785	1053.	6-079	Baghdad	44831
821.	5-1620	Baghdad	2CXLI, 328	1054.	6-080	IM32542	44850
822.	5-1644	36-6-135	2CXLI, 331	1055.	6-084	37-16-86	2CLX 45
823.	5-1645	36-6-148	2CLVI, 48	1056.	6-086	37-16-75	2CLXII66
828.	6-071	Baghdad	2CLXXXII, 7	1058.	6-090	37-16-83	2CLXI 60
829.	6-087	37-16-50	2CXLIII, 355	1059.	6-092	37-16-74	2CLX 31
830.	6-094	unknown	2CXLII, 348	1060.	6-093	unknown	44850 44830
831.	6-106	Baghdad	2CXLI, 334	1061.	6-101	IM32857	2CLXIII 82
832.	6-115	Baghdad	2CXLI, 329	1062.	6-133	37-16-76	2CLXIII 83
836.	6-317	unknown	2CXLIII, 358	1063.	6-134	IM32567	2CLXV 113
844.	4-0991	35-10-229	2LXXXV, 10	1064.	6-135	Baghdad	2CLX 36
850.	4-1049	35-10-150	2CLV, 39	1065.	6-137	Baghdad	44828
854.	4-1218	35-10-220	2LXXXV, 5	1066.	6-139	Baghdad	44850
930.	4-0981	35-10-137	44171	1067.	6-214	37-16-77	2CLXV 115
931.	4-0989	IM25001	44188	1068.	6-266	37-16-88	2CLXX 174
932.	4-0998	35-10-267	2CLXIII, 83	1069.	6-340	37-16-82	2CLXXI 9
938.	4-1025	Baghdad	2CLXX, 181	1076.	7-057	IM42678	45003 44973
943.	4-1052	IM24572	2CLXI, 73	1077.	7-058	IM42626	2CLXIII 86

1	2	3	4	1	2	3	4
1078.	7-133	IM42372	44996	1191.	4-0918A	35-10-81	12230
1079.	7-134A	IM42676	2CLXII 79	1192.	4-0918B	Baghdad	12230
1081.	7-143	IM42670	44993 94	1197.	4-1086	35-10-78	44543 44128
1082.	7-144	IM42672	2CLXVI 129	1210.	5-1292	Baghdad	44312
1084.	7-179	38-13-30	48117	1212.	5-1314	Baghdad	2XCVII, d1
1085.	7-232	38-13-48	2CLXI 50	1214.	5-1351	36-6-98	44657 46433
1086.	7-236	Baghdad	45022	1216.	5-1356	Baghdad	44657
1087.	7-254	Baghdad	45021	1217.	5-1364	Baghdad	44733
1091.	4-0787	Baghdad	2CLXXXII8	1218.	5-1375	36-6-97	44657
1095.	5-1458	Baghdad	2CLXXXII6	1219.	5-1381	Baghdad	44733
1104.	4-0971	Baghdad	44645	1220.	5-1409	Baghdad	44733
1107.	4-1009	Baghdad	2CXLVIII 438	1221.	5-1477	36-6-36	44733 46418
1108.	4-1026	Baghdad	44192	1222.	5-1496	Baghdad	44802
1112.	5-1294	Baghdad	2LXXXVI a7	1223.	5-1508	36-6-96	46419
1114.	5-1401	Baghdad	44672	1225.	5-1511	36-6-87	44740
1115.	5-1491	36-6-66A	2LXXXVII	1226.	5-1513	Baghdad	44740
1116.	5-1491	Baghdad	2LXXXVII	1236.	5-none	36-6-34	46418
1117.	5-1616	Baghdad	2CXLVIII 439	1245.	6-049	Baghdad	44926
1121.	5-none	unknown	2LXXXVII b	1246.	6-274	Baghdad	2CLXXIX, 52
1122.	6-059	Baghdad	2CLVII 69	1250.	7-0073	Baghdad	45102
1123.	6-105	Baghdad	2CLVII 68	1251.	7-0078	38-13-8	45159
1131.	5-none	unknown	2LXXXVII	1253.	none	unknown	2XCVI a1
1133.	4-0629	Baghdad	2CLVII 62	1255.	4-0655	Baghdad	44645
1134.	4-0630	35-10-35	44578	1258.	4-0836	Baghdad	2CLXXIX, 49
1139.	4-0844	35-10-36	44142	1260.	4-0841	35-10-331	44590
1140.	4-0865	Baghdad	44143	1261.	4-0883	Baghdad	2CLXXI, 11
1142.	4-0905	35-10-147	44101	1262.	4-0914	Baghdad	44645
1145.	5-1250	36-6-6	2LXXXIIc4	1264.	4-0945	35-10-102	2CLVIII, 6
1146.	5-1288	36-6-65	2LXXXVI 48	1266.	4-1002	Baghdad	44645
1147.	5-1293	Baghdad	2LXXXVI a3	1270.	4-1090	Baghdad	44653
1148.	5-1306A	Baghdad	2LXXXIIc1	1276.	5-1234	36-6-107	2CLXXIII, 42
1149.	5-1306B	36-6-7	44653	1277.	5-1359	36-6-108	2CLXXV, 64
1150.	5-1306C	Baghdad	44653	1279.	5-1368	36-6-106	2XCI, b6
1151.	5-1307A	36-6-67	2LXXXIIc3	1282.	5-1614	Baghdad	2CLXXII, 21
1152.	5-1307B	36-6-68	44653	1285.	7-0018	38-13-331	2CLXXI, 1
1153.	5-1307C	36-6-69	44653	1286.	7-0054	38-13-9	2CLXXII I, 43
1155.	5-1374	Baghdad	2LXXXVI a2	1287.	7-0091	Baghdad	2CLXXIV, 58
1160.	6-050	37-16-34	2CLIV 21	1295.	4-0867	Baghdad	44227 44587
1161.	6-157	37-16-38	2CLXXIV 62	1309.	6-149	Baghdad	2CLXXVI, 7-9
1162.	6-none	Baghdad	2LXXXIIc5	1314.	4-0819	Baghdad	2CLXXXII, 3
1170.	1112	31-52-448	1XLIII b	1323.	7-0075	Baghdad	2XCVIII, a1
1174.	4-0625	35-10-88	2CLXXI 95	1325.	7-none	unknown	45100
1175.	4-0675	Baghdad	44586	1331.	4-0993	35-10-51	2CLII, 518
1176.	4-0688	Baghdad	44144	1332.	4-1014	discarded	44656
1177.	4-0698	Baghdad	2XCVI b1	1333.	4-1091	Baghdad	2CLII, 522
1181.	4-0812	35-10-94	2CLXXVIII 43	1365.	5-1262	36-6-57	2LXXX, a
1182.	4-0839	Baghdad	44613	1368.	5-1410	36-6-59	2LXXIX, a2
1183.	4-0845	Baghdad	44144	1391.	1110	31-52-441	1LXII, 1
1184.	4-0862	Baghdad	44586	1392.	1202	31-52-442	1LXII 16
1185.	4-0876	Baghdad	44586	1393.	4-0621	Baghdad	44145
1186.	4-0885	Baghdad	44645	1394.	4-0627	35-10-25	2CLII, 519
1187.	4-0911	Baghdad	44096 44586	1396.	4-0632	Baghdad	2CXLV, 388
1188.	4-0916	35-10-19	2XCVII, b6	1398.	4-0670	35-10-28	2CXLIV, 373
1189.	4-0918	35-10-84	12230	1399.	4-0689	Baghdad	44102
1190.	4-0918	35-10-85	12230	1402.	4-0732	discarded	2XLIV, 382

(continues)

1	2	3	4	1	2	3	4
1403.	4-0734	Baghdad	2CXLVII, 423	1526.	4-0910	Baghdad	44123
1405.	4-0764	Baghdad	2CXLIV 372	1556.	5-1253	36-6-10	44656
1406.	4-0804	discarded	2CXLIV 369	1558.	5-1253	36-6-11	44656
1409.	4-0810	Baghdad	44189	1559.	5-1253	36-6-12	44659
1410.	4-0833	35-10-29	2CXLV 385	1560.	5-1253	36-6-13	44656
1411.	4-0854	Baghdad	2CXLV 390	1562.	5-1253	36-6-14	44656
1413.	4-0869	35-10-27	2CXLVII 426	1563.	5-1253	36-6-9	44656
1414.	4-0899	Baghdad	44150	1564.	5-1316	Baghdad	2CLV 41
1415.	4-0898	35-10-26	2LXXXIX d	1565.	5-1342B	35-10-156	2CLV 40
1416.	4-0900	Baghdad	2CXLV 393	1566.	5-1354	36-6-32	2CLV 45
1418.	4-0920	35-10-33	44190	1567.	5-1354	36-6-33	2CLV 45
1420.	4-1010	Baghdad	44194	1569.	5-1394	Baghdad	44655
1421.	4-1011	Baghdad	2CXLVIII 442	1577.	3-0486	Baghdad	2CLXI, 56
1422.	4-1021	discarded	44148	1579.	4-0642	IM24961	44199
1423.	4-1095	35-10-32	44158	1582.	4-0649	35-10-113	2LXXXVIII, 11
1435.	5-1286	36-6-54	2CXLVIII 434	1590.	4-0807	IM24988	44175
1436.	5-1297	Baghdad	no plate	1591.	4-0808	35-10-105	2CLX, 42
1437.	5-1304	Baghdad	2CXLVIII 440	1592.	4-0820	IM24584	44589
1439.	5-1315	Baghdad	2CXLVIII 436	1593.	4-0842	35-10-107	44175
1440.	5-1318	36-6-23	2CXLVIII 430	1595.	4-0848A	35-10-122	44159
1442.	5-1338	36-6-47	44674	1596.	4-848B	35-10-122	44159
1443.	5-1339	Baghdad	2CXLIII 360	1597.	4-0848C	IM24991	44159
1444.	5-1340	Baghdad	2CXLIII 356	1599.	4-0850	35-10-130	44168
1449.	5-1353	36-6-192	2CLXXXII 2	1600.	4-0851	IM24971	44178
1450.	5-1366	36-6-45	2CXLIV 379	1602.	4-0870	35-10-125	44170
1451.	5-1373	discarded	2CXLVII 414	1604.	4-0874	IM24981	44166
1452.	5-1380	Baghdad	44666	1605.	4-0881	IM24990	44181
1454.	5-1403	36-6-49	44663	1606.	4-0882	IM24986	44160
1472.	6-058	Baghdad	2CXLVI 408	1607.	4-0884	IM24994	44162
1473.	6-140	Baghdad	2CXLVIII 437	1608.	4-0886	phila no#	44180
				1609.	4-0887	IM24983	44183
1474.	6-158	Baghdad	2CXLV 386	1611.	4-0889	35-10-126	44544 44174
1475.	6-165	discarded	2CXLVI 405	1613.	4-0891	35-10-121	44173
1476.	6-394	Baghdad	2CLXXXI 92	1614.	4-0893	35-10-123	44165 44536
1477.	6-557	37-16-32	2CXLVII 419	1616.	4-0896	35-10-106	2CLXV, 112
1478.	6-593	Baghdad	2CXLVIII 443	1617.	4-0897	IM24987	44185
1484.	7-0066	Baghdad	2CXLVIII 435	1618.	4-0904	IM24602	44656
1494.	4-0657	35-10-72	46461	1621.	4-0940	IM25008	44184
1495.	4-0658	35-10-70	46462	1623.	4-0986	IM25041	44169
1497.	4-0660	discarded	44579	1628.	4-1064	35-10-133	44536 48094
1498.	4-0663	discarded	44113	1630.	4-1082	35-10-116	48092 48093
1499.	4-0669	35-10-347	44123 46473	1632.	4-1088 .	35-10-115	2LXXXVIII, 4
1500.	4-0687	Baghdad	44579	1639.	5-1279	36-6-132	45239
1503.	4-0702	discarded	44112	1641.	5-1285	IM26998	44756
1504.	4-0705	Baghdad	44108	1642.	5-1289A	36-6-126	44650
1505.	4-0711	Baghdad	44104	1643.	5-1289B	IM26961	44650
1506.	4-0716	35-10-73	2CLV 42	1644.	5-1300A	36-6-115	44724
1508.	4-0719	35-10-66	46461	1645.	5-1300B	36-6-122	44724
1509.	4-0728	Baghdad	44104	1646.	5-1300C	36-6-124	44724
1510.	4-0728B	Baghdad	44104	1647.	5-1300D	IM26775	44724?
1513.	4-0776	35-10-64	44119 44579	1648.	5-1300E	IM26999	44724?
1517.	4-0818	35-10-56	44122 46462	1649.	5-1300F	IM27000	44724?
1518.	4-0834	35-10-76	44116 44579	1650.	5-1300G	IM27001	44724?
1522.	4-0858	35-10-69	44115	1651.	5-1301A	36-6-127	44650 44304
1523.	4-0859	35-10-90	46432	1652.	5-1301B	IM27002	44304 44311

1	2	3	4	1	2	3	4
1653.	5-1301C	36-6-211	44311 44650	1734.	4-0651	35-10-37	2XCVI b4
1654.	5-1301D	IM27008	44304 44650	1735.	4-0678	phila?	2XCVI b3
1655.	5-1303A	36-6-117	44650 44724	1736.	4-0691	Baghdad	2XCVI
1656.	5-1303B	IM26986	44310 44302	1738.	4-0780	35-10-91	44586 46432
1657.	5-1303C	IM27004	44650 44302	1740.	4-0847	Baghdad	44613
1658.	5-1303D	36-6-118	44310 44724	1742.	4-0871	Baghdad	44645
1659.	5-1303E	IM26992	44724 44650	1744.	5-1260	Baghdad	2XCVI a6
1661.	5-1310b	36-6-41	2CLXIX, 164	1745.	5-1281	36-6-386	2XCVI a13
1662.	5-1310b	36-6-41b	44650	1746.	5-1311	Baghdad	2CLXXVII 32
1663.	5-1310c	IM26991	44295	1747.	5-1327	36-6-35	44733
1664.	5-1325	36-6-120	48099 48100	1748.	5-1474	Baghdad	44733 ?
1665.	5-1326	36-6-119	45237 44291	1749.	5-1538	Baghdad	44760 44740
1666.	5-1333	36-6-128	44756	1753.	7-0012	Baghdad	2XCVII a3
1668.	5-1349	36-6-114	2CLXII, 72	1756.	5-1336	Baghdad	2CLXXI 2
1670.	5-1370	36-6-130	44756 44557	1757.	5-1456	Baghdad	2CLXXV 66
1672.	5-1372	36-6-111	44756 44761	1761.	6-181	Baghdad	44917/18
1674.	5-1425	IM26967	2CLXII, 87	1766.	6-069	Baghdad	2CLXXVI 13
1675.	5-1426	IM26971	44755 44298	1775.	5-1319	36-6-22	2CXLV 387
1676.	5-1592	36-6-110	44761 48097	1779.	4-0786	Baghdad	2CXLVI 418
1677.	5-1619	IM26984	2CLXIX, 163	1780.	4-0811	Baghdad	2CXLV 391
1680.	6-0103	IM32626	44937	1781.	4-0846	Baghdad	2CXLVII 420
1681.	6-0594	Baghdad	2CLXVII 135	1782.	4-0864	Baghdad	2CXLIV 376
1687.	7-0060	IM42679	45003 44972	1783.	4-0868	Baghdad	44190
1688.	7-0062A	IM42680	45003 44972	1790.	5-1252	Baghdad	2CLII 516
1689.	7-0062B	discarded	45003?	1791.	5-1264	36-6-1	2CXLV 394
1690.	7-0064	38-13-15	45002 44973	1793.	5-1266	36-6-3	44662
1691.	7-0065A	IM42693	45001 44973	1794.	5-1271	36-6-24	44662
1692.	7-0065B	Baghdad	45001 44973	1795.	5-1272	Baghdad	2CXLIV 380
1693.	7-0065C	38-13-16	45001 44973	1796.	5-1274	36-6-21	44664
1694.	7-0068	Baghdad	44996	1798.	5-1308	Baghdad	2CLXXXI 90
1695.	7-0082A	IM42682	45002 44990	1799.	5-1369	lost	2CXLVI, 402
1696.	7-0082A	IM42682	45003 44990	1804.	5-1570	discarded	2CXLVII, 413
1697.	7-0083	Baghdad	44991 45003	1805.	5-1613	Baghdad	2CXLVII, 412
1698.	7-0083	Baghdad	44991	1813.	6-033	Baghdad	2CXLVIII, 433
1699.	7-0084	38-13-21	45001 44988	1814.	6-039	37-16-22	2CLII, 515
1701.	7-0086	38-13-14	44979	1816.	6-044	Baghdad	2CXLIV, 375
1702.	7-0087	IM42684	44988	1817.	6-055	Baghdad	2CXLVI, 399
1703.	7-0088	38-13-17	44991/2	1818.	6-056	37-16-37	2CLXXXI, 91
1704.	7-0092	38-13-19	44988	1819.	6-060	Baghdad	2CXLIV, 383
1705.	7-0093	38-13-18	44990 45003	1821.	6-114	Baghdad	2CXLVIII, 432
1706.	7-0094	38-13-20	44979	1833.	5-1332	36-6-31	2CLV 46
1708.	7-0096	38-13-13	2CLXIX 159	1838.	4-0797	35-10-118	44164 44536
1709.	7-0097	IM42685	44991/2	1839.	4-0815	35-10-262	44176
1710.	7-0101	IM42686	44979 45003	1840.	4-0835	35-10-114	44589
1711.	7-0114	38-13-10	2CLXII 77	1841.	4-0840	IM24992	44198 44161
1712.	7-0129	IM42674	44990	1842.	4-0872	35-10-129	44179
1713.	7-0130	IM42675	44979	1843.	4-0956	IM25048	2CLXIII, 91
1714.	7-0132	38-13-12	44985	1844.	5-1248	IM26987	44756
1715.	7-0153	38-13-11	2CLIX 23	1846.	5-1258	36-6-40	45240
1724.	6-166	Discarded	2CLVI 60	1847.	5-1344	36-6-39	2CLVIII, 13
1727.	4-0789	phila ?	44140	1848.	5-1345	Baghdad	2CLIX, 22
1728.	4-0969	Baghdad	44101	1849.	5-1451	36-6-38	2CLVIII, 7
1730.	6-067A	37-16-23	2CLVI 61	1850.	5-1546	36-6-129	45238 44757
1731.	6-067B	Baghdad	2CLVI 61	1852.	5-1567	36-6-116	45245 44288
1733.	4-0601	Baghdad	2CLVII 66	1853.	6-042	IM32499	2CLXIX, 160

(*continues*)

1	2	3	4	1	2	3	4
1856.	6-182A	37-16-30	44932	2003.	3-495BC	35-10-18A	2CLXVIII 149
1868.	6-273	37-16-29	2CLXVIII, 145	2004.	3-495D	35-10-18B	2CLXVIII 149
1859.	7-002	38-13-4	44996	2005.	3-496A	35-10-19	44527
1865.	6-025	37-16-11	44922	2006.	3-496B	IM24566	44527
1869.	4-0626	Baghdad	44191	2012.	4-0609	35-10-15	2CLXVIII 148
1878.	5-1249	36-6-8	44653	2015.	4-0721	IM24607	2CLXV 108
1880.	5-1283A	Baghdad	2LXXXII, c6	2020.	4-0779	35-10-17	2CLX 41
1881.	5-1283B	36-6-5	44652	2024.	5-1259	36-6-19	2CLXVI 116
1883.	6-079	Baghdad	2CLIII 10	2026.	5-1287	IM27030	44650
1885.	1158	31-52-437	44445 44446	2033.	6-210A	37-16-15	2CLXVIII 150
1888.	3-333	Baghdad	44076	2034.	6-210B	IM32620	2CLCVIII 150
1893.	3-416	Baghdad	44084	2035.	6-210B2	37-16-15b	2CLCVIII 150
1899.	3-none	33-3-286	2XCVII, b7	2036.	6-210C	37-16-16	2CLXVIII 150
1900.	4-0602	35-10-10	2CLXXVII, 40	2039.	3-none	33-3-238	2LXXXIX a
1901.	4-0652	Baghdad	44613	2045.	3-113	Baghdad	2CLXXII 5
1902.	4-0801	Baghdad	44586	2046.	3-153A	Baghdad	2CLXXXII 9
1903.	5-1282	36-6-17	44733	2047.	3-153B	Baghdad	2CLXXXII 10
1904.	6-026	37-16-13	44922	2052.	3-022	Baghdad	43911
1905.	6-184	37-16-12	2CLXXVII, 28	2053.	3-082	discarded	43968
1908.	4-0726	35-10-12	2XCI, b7	2054.	3-105	33-3-48	43922
1911.	4-0875	Baghdad	2CLXXIII, 37	2055.	3-114	Baghdad	43906
1915.	3-406	Baghdad	44063	2056.	3-146	33-3-69	2LXXXIII d
1924.	6087	Baghdad	1LXII, 15	2057.	3-161	Baghdad	43990
1927.	3-318	Baghdad	2CXLVII, 425	2058.	3-172	33-3-79	43968
1928.	3-336	Baghdad	2CXLIV, 384	2060.	3-208	33-3-100	43959
1931.	3-339	Baghdad	44046	2061.	3-211	33-3-103	43989
1932.	3-344	33-3-162	2CLII, 523	2062.	3-213	33-3-105	44001
1933.	3-346	Baghdad	44039 44040	2063.	3-215	Baghdad	43990
1937.	3-355	33-3-170	2CXLVII, 424	2064.	3-260	Baghdad	44064
1942.	3-368	Baghdad	2CLII, 525	2067.	3-306	33-3-146	43978
1943.	3-369	33-3-182	44020	2068.	3-307	discarded	2LXXX b
1944.	3-370	33-3-183	2CXLVI, 410	2069.	3-077	Baghdad	2CLVII 64
1946.	3-395	33-3-196	44037	2070.	3-097	Baghdad	2CLVI 59
1949.	3-492	IM20855	2CXLV, 398	2071.	3-100	Baghdad	43938
1950.	3-494	phila no#	2CXLVII, 415	2072.	3-183	33-3-86	43952
1955.	4-0703	Baghdad	2CXLV, 397	2073.	3-203	33-3-98	45307
1956.	4-0704	35-10-3	44154	2074.	3-204	33-3-99	45307
1957.	4-0798	35-10-1	2CXLV, 389	2077.	3-335	33-3-160	44028
1958.	4-0799	Baghdad	44189	2079.	1073	Baghdad	1XLIV c
1959.	4-0803	Baghdad	2CXLV, 395	2080.	1092	31-52-420	44448
1961.	5-1267	36-6-2	44662	2085.	3-015	33-3-8	2XCVII b5
1964.	3-341	Baghdad	44065	2086.	3-016	Baghdad	43886
1969.	4-0800	35-10-7	44579 44119	2087.	3-017	Baghdad	43886 44068
1980.	1027	31-52-408	1LVI 2	2088.	3-028	33-3-13	43885
1981.	3-332	33-3-158	2LXXXVIII 2	2089.	3-029	Baghdad	44083 43885
1984.	3-376A	33-3-186	2CLXX 184	2090.	3-030	33-3-14	2XCIV a
1986.	3-397	Baghdad	2CLXXI 12	2091.	3-031	Baghdad	44082
1989.	3-408	Baghdad	2CLXVI 125	2092.	3-087	33-3-212	2CLXXIX 59
1991.	3-413	IM15977	2CLXI 54	2093.	3-095	33-3-45	43979
1994.	3-434	IM26897	2CLXVII 137	2094.	3-096	Baghdad	43933
1996.	3-438	35-10-16	2CLXVII 136	2095.	3-099	33-3-46	43936
1999.	3-481	35-10-20	2CLXX 178	2096.	3-103	Baghdad	43936
2000.	3-485B	35-10-258	44525/26	2097.	3-106	33-3-49	2XCVII, b2
2001.	3-485A	phila ?	44525/6	2098.	3-157	Baghdad	43960
2002.	3-495A	IM25075	44528/29	2099.	3-165	Baghdad	43958

1	2	3	4	1	2	3	4
2100.	3-167	Baghdad	44075 43982	2224.	3-035	unknown	43912
2101.	3-168	Baghdad	43982 44072	2225.	3-038	discarded	43878
2102.	3-178	33-3-83	43998	2226.	3-041	Baghdad	2CXLV, 396
2103.	3-194	Baghdad	43982 44071	2227.	3-071	33-3-36	2CXLVI, 406
2104.	3-214	Baghdad	43987	2228.	3-072	Baghdad	44012
2105.	3-221	33-3-109	43960	2229.	3-101	Baghdad	2CXLVII 428
2106.	3-223	33-3-110	43989	2230.	3-104	33-3-52	2CXLIV 368
2107.	3-238	33-3-259	43979	2231.	3-133	Baghdad	2CXLVII 427
2108.	3-256	Baghdad	43976	2232.	3-134	33-3-67	2CXLVII 416
2109.	3-262	Baghdad	44067 43983	2233.	3-137	33-3-63	2CXLVII 411
2110.	3-272	Baghdad	2CLXXVIII, 41	2234.	3-154	33-3-72	2CLII 521
2112.	3-308	Baghdad	44007	2237.	3-198	33-3-94	2CXLVIII 441
2115.	3-330	Baghdad	2CLXXVII, 35	2238.	3-212	33-3-104	43966
2116.	3-351	Baghdad	44070	2239.	3-224	Baghdad	2CXLIV 378
2122.	3-none	33-3-285	2XCVII, b1	2240.	3-227	33-3-112	2CXLVII 422
2127.	3-011	Baghdad	43924	2242.	3-229	33-2-114	2CLII 524
2128.	3-034	Baghdad	43876	2243.	3-248	33-3-122	2CXLIV 371
2129.	3-037	33-3-16	2XCI, b4	2244.	3-251	discarded	2CXLIV 374
2130.	3-043	discarded	43910	2245.	3-252	33-3-124	2CXLVI 409
2132.	3-160	Baghdad	44088	2246.	3-257	Baghdad	44047
2133.	3-169	33-3-76	2XCII, a2	2247.	3-277	33-3-136	44021
2134.	3-185	Baghdad	43971	2249.	3-302	Baghdad	44050
2135.	3-190	Baghdad	44090	2250.	3-313	33-3-150	2CXLVI 400
2136.	3-202	Baghdad	44495	2253.	3-340	Baghdad	2LXXX c
2137.	3-205	Baghdad	43990	2255.	3-366	33-3-180	2CXLIV 381
2138.	3-233	Baghdad	43997	2271.	6086	unknown	1LXII 5
2139.	3-237	33-3-118	44000	2274.	3-027	Baghdad	2CLV 43
2140.	3-239	Baghdad	44000	2275.	3-042	Baghdad	43884
2141.	3-255	33-3-126	2XCI, b8	2276.	3-044A	33-3-18	43884
2142.	3-259	Baghdad	43974	2277.	3-044B	33-3-18	43884
2143.	3-271	33-3-132	44002	2278.	3-164	33-3-74	43958
2144.	3-305	33-3-145	43975	2279.	3-304	33-3-144	2CLV 44
2145.	3-311	33-3-149	2XCI,b5	2280.	3-324	Baghdad	44065
2146.	3-312	Baghdad	2CLXXIV, 57	2283.	3-110	Baghdad	43998
2193.	3-025	Baghdad	44080	2284.	3-173	33-3-80	44014
2194.	3-051	33-3-24	43916	2285.	3-179	33-3-84	43954
2195.	3-083	Baghdad	44080	2286.	3-189a	33-3-89	2CLXIX 165
2196.	3-089	Baghdad	44080	2287.	3-189b	33-3-89	2CLXIX 165
2197.	3-108	Baghdad	43916	2288.	3-189c	33-3-89	2CLXIX 165
2198.	3-158	Baghdad	43930	2289.	3-189	IM15979	2CLXIX 165
2199.	3-159	Baghdad	43930	2293.	3-200	33-3-95	2CLXVI 118
2200.	3-166	33-3-75	43986	2294.	3-207	Baghdad	2CLXVI 117
2201.	3-191	discarded	43920	2295.	3-209	33-3-101	43955
2202.	3-201	33-3-97	43980	2296.	3-220	33-3-108	2CLXII 74
2204.	3-219	33-3-107	43986	2297.	3-235	IM15933	44010
2205.	3-234	Baghdad	2XCIV, b	2298.	3-240	33-3-119	44000
2207.	3-246	Baghdad	2CLXXVI, 14	2299.	3-243	IM15845	44005
2208.	3-247	33-3-121	46417	2300.	3-245	33-3-120	44004
2209.	3-276	33-3-135	43985	2302.	3-267	IM15929	44013
2213.	3-254	33-3-125	44496	2306.	3-315	33-3-152	2CLX 44
2215.	3-301	Baghdad	44031	2307.	1123	31-52-439	46413
2218.	1002	Baghdad	1LXII, 14	2309.	5698	Baghdad	1LXXXII 15
2220.	1085	31-52-421	44445 44446	2311.	5858	32-21-376	1LII a
2222.	3-020	33-3-9	43927	2312.	5909	32-21-546	46413
2223.	3-021	33-3-10	2CXLVII, 421	2314.	5934	32-21-547	46413

(continues)

1	2	3	4	1	2	3	4
2315.	3-004	Baghdad	43888	2420.	5683	Baghdad	1XXXIX, a9
2316.	3-092	Baghdad	44012	2427.	5721	32-21-449	1XL, b6
2317.	3-111	33-3-50	43902	2428.	5730	32-21-468	no plate
2318.	3-112	33-3-51	43906	2429.	5736	32-21-441	1XL, a6
2319.	1-none	unknown	Sp 1929:89	2430.	5738	Baghdad	1XXXIX, a6
2320.	1084	31-52-99	1LXXIX 7	2431.	5750	32-21-450	1XLII, 15
2322.	1119	Baghdad	1LXXIX 11	2436.	5763	Baghdad	1XL, b11
2328.	5615	Baghdad	1XXXIV c3	2439.	5783	Baghdad	1XL, b10
2329.	5627	32-21-556	1XXXVII c9	2441.	5812	32-21-464	1XLII, 9
2331.	5650	32-21-312	1XXXI b3	2443.	5829	Baghdad	1XXXIX, a12
2334.	5679	Baghdad	1LXXX 4	2444.	5835	Baghdad	1XL, a2
2335.	5708	32-21-558	1XXXVII c14	2445.	5836	Baghdad	1XL, b7
2342.	5774	Baghdad	1LXXX 1	2453.	5903	32-21-434	1XXXIX, a11
2347.	5845	32-21-562	1XXXVII c11	2455.	5941	32-21-460	1XLIII, 6
2352.	6072	32-21-306	1XXXI b1	2456.	5942	32-21-435	1XXXIX, a8
2355.	3-059	33-3-96	43946	2462.	5974	32-21-463	1XLI, b2
2356.	3-123	Baghdad	43915	2465.	6083	32-21-438	1XLI, a5
2358.	3-130	33-3-59	43922	2466.	6095	32-21-470	1XLII, 11
2360.	3-163	33-3-73	43959	2467.	6097	Baghdad	1XL, b8
2363.	5780	32-21-319	1XXXIV, c1	2469.	3-036	33-3-15	43925
2365.	1-none	unknown	Sp 29:92	2470.	3-055	33-3-25	43886
2366.	5365	Baghdad	1XXXIV, c9	2471.	3-056	Baghdad	43886
2367.	5676	32-21-314	1XXXIV, c10	2472.	3-065	Baghdad	43883
2368.	5722	32-21-68	44393	2473.	3-066	Baghdad	44066
2369.	5723	32-21-69	44393	2474.	3-079	Baghdad	44081 43939
2370.	5781	Baghdad	1XXXIV, c6	2475.	3-081	Baghdad	43886
2372.	5878	32-21-315	1XXXIV, c8	2476.	3-093	Baghdad	43961
2373.	6074	32-21-317	1XXXVI, 7	2477.	3-109	Baghdad	43938
2376.	3-018	discarded	43878	2478.	3-135	33-3-61	43941
2377.	3-046	33-3-20	43945	2482.	1025	31-52-413	1LXXXIII 2
2378.	3-048	33-3-22	43890	2483.	1028	31-52-372	1LXXXV 9
2379.	3-052	Baghdad	43890	2484.	1063	31-52-409	1LXXXIV 16
2380.	3-102	33-3-47	43932	2485.	1082	31-52-410	no plate
2381.	3-122	Baghdad	43940	2486.	1106	31-52-285	1LXXXIII 4&7
2382.	0850	Dropsie	1LXXVI, 17	2489.	5582	Baghdad	1LXXXIII 5
2383.	0853	Dropsie	1XLVI, b	2491.	5585	32-21-474	1LIV c1
2388	1023	31-52-406	44445 44446	2493.	5601	32-21-476	1LIII a8
2394.	1094	31-52-400	1XLI, a6	2494.	5608	Baghdad	44369
2395.	1199	31-52-401	46283 46286	2495.	5651	32-21-477	1LXXXIII 3
2396.	1656	Dropsie	Sp 29:93	2497.	5674	Baghdad	1LXXXIV 1
2398.	5381	Baghdad	1LXXVI, 18	2500.	5756	Baghdad	1LXXXIV 3
2399.	5473	Baghdad	1XL, b3	2501.	5758	Baghdad	1LXXXIV 6
2400.	5486	Baghdad	1XXXIX, a10	2502.	5771	Dropsie	1LXXXIV 4
2401.	5492	32-21-442	1XL, a4	2503.	5772	32-21-479	1LXXXIII8-11
2403.	5581	Baghdad	44368	2504.	5778	32-21-480	1LXXXIII 6
2404.	5584	32-21-439	1XL, a7	2512.	5913A	32-21-483	1LIII a5
2405.	5595	Baghdad	1XL, b9	2513.	5913B	Baghdad	1LIII a5
2407.	5622	32-21-440	1XL, a3	2514.	5920	32-21-487	1LIII a9
2409.	5635	Baghdad	1XL, a1	2517.	5952	32-21-475	1LIV c2
2411.	5653	32-21-437	1XXXIX, a4	2519.	5992	32-21-473	1LXXXIV 5
2412.	5654	32-21-429	44368	2520.	3-008	Baghdad	43883
2413.	5655	32-21-430	44368	2521.	3-013	33-3-7	43883
2416.	5670	32-21-454	1XXXI, a1	2522.	3-014	Baghdad	43883
2418.	5672	Baghdad	44383	2523.	3-033	discarded	43883
2419.	5682	32-21-431	1XXXIX, a3	2524.	3-049	33-3-23	2XCII a10

1	2	3	4	1	2	3	4
2525.	3-050	Baghdad	43883	2765.	6071	32-21-353	1XXXI, a3
2526.	3-061	33-3-28	43883	2774.	1541	31-52-317	1XXVII, b2
2527.	3-070	33-3-35	43883	2776.	1667	unknown	1LXIV, 50
2528.	3-076	33-3-88	43883	2777.	5330	32-21-298	1XXVII, b4
2529.	3-120	Baghdad	44090	2780.	5458	32-21-466	1LXXVI, 20
2530.	3-129	33-3-58	43998	2783.	5588	32-21-300	1LXIV, 43
2531.	3-148	33-3-70	43990	2785.	5602	Baghdad	1LXIII, 38
2532.	3-186	Baghdad	44089	2787.	5613	32-21-301	1LXIV, 42
2533.	3-187	Baghdad	43990	2788.	5623	32-21-302	1LXIV, 40
2535.	1-none	31-52-393	46391	2789.	5624	32-21-303	1XXVII, b7
2596.	5264	Baghdad	44368	2790.	5626	32-21-291	1LXIII, 30
2597.	5265	Baghdad	44368	2791.	5628	32-21-292	1XXVII, b9
2601.	5371	Baghdad	1XXXVIII b2	2793.	5631	32-21-288	1XXVII, b3
2603.	5484	32-21-405	1XXXIX b3	2794.	5636	32-21-293	1XXVII, b6
2604.	5488	32-21-386	1XXXVIII a5	2800.	5677	32-21-308	44372
2611.	5593	32-21-409	1XXXVIII b9	2802.	5691	32-21-294	44371
2613.	5630	32-21-389	1XXXVIII a9	2804.	5703	Baghdad	1XXVIII, b5
2614.	5637	32-21-383	44368	2806.	5725	32-21-289	1LXIII, 37
2620.	5705	32-21-392	1XXXVIII a11	2809.	5728	Baghdad	1LXIV, 45
2626.	5760	32-21-393	1XXXVIII a6	2811.	5751	32-21-295	1XXVII, b5
2627.	5760 b	32-21-393	1XXXVIII a6	2812.	5769	32-21-309	1LXIII, 29
2628.	5760 c	32-21-393	1XXXVIII a6	2813.	5807	32-21-290	1LXIII, 27
2629.	5766	unknown	1XXXVIII b10	2818.	5867	32-21-311	1LXXVI, 15
2631.	5786	32-21-394	1XXXVIII a10	2823.	5956	32-21-305	1XXVII, b8
2632.	5797	32-21-412	1XXXVIII b6	2825.	6009	Baghdad	1LXIII, 20
2640.	5860	32-21-414	1XXXVIII b14	2826.	6010	Baghdad	1LXIII, 21
2644.	5872	32-21-396	1XXXVIII a7	2827.	6011	Baghdad	1LXIII, 23
2645.	5873	32-21-427	1XXXVIII b1	2828.	6012	Baghdad	1LXIII, 24/25
2647.	5876	32-21-416	1XXXVIII b13	2829.	6013	Baghdad	1LXIII, 26
2655.	5897	Baghdad	1XXXVIII b12	2830.	6014	Baghdad	1LXIII, 28
2657.	5901	32-21-401	1LXXXI 9	2831.	6015	Baghdad	1LXIII, 36
2660.	5928	Baghdad	1XXXVIII b4	2832.	6016	Baghdad	1LXIII, 32
2663.	5937	32-21-406	1XXXIX b7	2833.	6018	Baghdad	1LXIII, 22
2664.	5938	Baghdad	1XXXVIII b15	2834.	6019	Baghdad	1LXIV, 41
2667.	5950	Baghdad	1XXXVIII b8	2835.	6020	Baghdad	1LXIV,44
2668.	5959	Dropsie	1XXXVIII, a12	2836.	6021	Baghdad	1LXIV, 46
2672.	5963	32-21-422	1XXXVIII, b10	2837.	6022	Baghdad	1LXIV, 48
2673.	5964	32-21-385	1XXXVIII, b3	2838.	6023	Baghdad	1LXIV, 49
2681.	6003	32-21-428	1XXXIX, b2	2839.	6024	Baghdad	1LXIV, 51
2682.	6092	unknown	1XXXVIII, b5	2840.	6066	Baghdad	1LXXV, 217
2683.	6093	unknown	1XXXVIII, b7	2845.	3-019	Baghdad	44048
2684.	6098	unknown	1LXXXI, 8	2846.	3-021	33-3-10	43899
2713.	3-023	Baghdad	44080	2847.	3-039	33-3-17	43900
2714.	3-024	33-3-11	43896	2848.	3-040	discarded	43904
2715.	3-057	Baghdad	43881	2850.	3-067	33-3-32	43889
2716.	3-058	33-3-26	43881	2851.	3-073	33-3-37	43909
2717.	3-068	33-3-33	43882	2852.	3-084	33-3-40	43891
2718.	3-075	Baghdad	43881	2853.	3-085	33-3-41	43879
2719.	3-078	33-3-39	43882	2854.	3-090	33-3-43	43912
2720.	3-116	Baghdad	43934	2855.	3-125	33-3-55	43951
2721.	3-119	Baghdad	43939	2856.	3-136	33-3-62	43880
2752.	5889	Baghdad	1LXXXII, 28	2857.	3-138	discarded	44024
2757.	3-001	33-3-1	43888	2858.	3-139	discarded	44025
2758.	3-088	Baghdad	43987	2860.	3-141	33-3-65	43873
2761.	5491	32-21-350	1XXXI, 42	2862.	3-144	33-3-68	43962

(continues)

1	2	3	4	1	2	3	4
2881.	5604	32-21-329	1XXXVII c5	2955.	5908	32-21-514	1LVII 19
2886.	5680	32-21-378	1LII b7	2956.	5911	32-21-563	1LVII 28
2910.	5905	Baghdad	1XXXVII c1	2957.	5911	Baghdad	1LVII 28
2915.	3-045	33-3-19	43884	2958.	5917	32-21-525	1LVII 29
2916.	3-069	33-3-34	43884	2960.	5943	32-21-515	1LVIII 41
2918.	1072	31-52-384	1LVII 17	2961.	5944	32-21-564	1LVIII 31
2919.	1099	31-52-385	1LVI 9	2962.	5945	Baghdad	1LVII 20
2921.	1660B	Baghdad	1LVII 23	2963.	5954	32-21-516	1LVIII 38
2922.	1660B1	31-52-386	1LVII 24	2964.	5955	Baghdad	1LVIII 34
2923.	1661	31-52-387	1LVIII 32	2966.	6077	32-21-522	1LVII 27
2924.	1662	Dropsie	1LVIII 37	2967.	6078	32-21-524	1LVII 26
2925.	5480	Baghdad	1LVI 5	2968.	6079	32-21-519	1LVII 15
2926.	5495	32-21-492	1LVI 12	2969.	6096	Baghdad	1LVI 10
2927.	5576	Baghdad	1LVIII 36	2973.	2-none	32-21-523	1LVII 28
2928.	5577	Baghdad	1LVIII 35	2974.	3-003	Baghdad	43943 43874
2929.	5612	32-21-493	1LVI 11	2975.	3-005	33-3-2	43957
2930.	5642	32-21-494	1LVIII 33	2976.	3-006	Baghdad	43942 43872
2931.	5643	32-21-495	ILVII 22	2977.	3-007	33-3-3	43950
2934.	5777	32-21-497	1LVIII 39	2978.	3-026	33-3-12	43919
2935.	5784	32-21-498	1LVII 24	2979.	3-032	IM15643	43926
2936.	5789	32-21-499	1LVIII 40	2984.	3-121	Baghdad	43955 44061
2938.	5811	Baghdad	1LVIII 42	2987.	3-128	Baghdad	44090
2940.	5821	32-21-502	44384	2988.	3-131	Baghdad	44010
2941.	5822	32-21-503	44384	2989.	3-188	33-3-88	44017
2943.	5824	Baghdad	1LVI 8	2990.	3-188	33-3-88	44017
2946.	5859	Baghdad	1LVI 4	2991.	3-188	33-3-88	44017
2947.	5863	32-21-506	1LVII 18	2992.	3-188	33-3-88	44017
2954.	5907	32-21-513	1LVI 13				

Catalogue of Grave Goods From Tepe Gawra

Burial 001: Levels VIII/IX (VIII A–C, IX) Square 6J
  Burial Type: Loose burial
  Relative Age: Infant

  Grave Goods:

3-2-a	Baghdad		black stone beads
3-2-b	Baghdad	1	carnelian bead
3-2-c	Baghdad	6	crystal ring beads
3-2-d	Baghdad	1	quartz cylinder beads

  Discussion:

Beads were found near the chest of the skeleton, some of which seem to have been strung together and hung around the neck.

Burial 002 Levels VIII/IX (VIIIA–C, IX) Square 5K
  Burial Type: Cist burial with stone cover
  Relative Ave: Child

  Grave Goods:

3-10-a	33-3-5		limestone beads
3-10-b	33-3-5	32	carnelian beads
3-10-c	33-3-5	10	lapis beads
none	unrecorded	1	conical jar spout
none	none		traces of copper oxide on bones
none	none		reed matting*

  Discussion:

The beads were found near the chest of the skeleton. White and black beads were originally strung into separate strings.

Burial 003 Levels VIII/IX (VIIIA–C, IX) Square 5J
  Burial Type: Loose burial
  Relative Age: Infant

  Grave Goods:

none	none	reed matting*

Burial 004 Levels VIII/IX (VIIIA–C, IX) Square 5J
  Burial Type: Loose burial
  Relative Age: Infant

  Grave Goods:

3-9-a	33-3-4	202	white stone beads
3-9-b	33-3-4	212	mother of pearl beads
3-9-c	33-3-4	115	black stone beads
3-9-d	33-3-4	4	quartz beads
none	none		reed matting*

  Discussion:

Beads were found near the hips and above the chest of the skeleton.

Burial 005 Levels VIII/IX (VIIIA–C) Square 5J/6J
  Burial Type: Libn burial
  Relative Ave: Child

  Grave Goods:

none	none	reed matting*

Burial 006 Level X Square 6O
  Burial Type: Vessel burial with vessel cover
  Relative Age: Infant

Grave Goods:

none	unrecorded		1 ceramic open mouth jar*
none	unrecorded		1 ceramic bowl*

Burial 007 Levels VIII/IX (VIIIA–C) Square 5-J
Burial Type: Vessel burial in libn enclosure
Relative Age: Infant

Grave Goods:

none	unrecorded		1 ceramic vessel*

Burial 009 Levels VIII/IX (VIIIA–C, IX) Square 10K
Burial Type: Loose burial
Relative Age: Infant/Child

Grave Goods:

5977-a	unrecorded	18	shell barrel beads
5977-b	unrecorded		ring beads
5977-c	unrecorded	2	pink stone ring beads
5977-d	unrecorded		obsidian beads

No locus number exists for this burial, but since it correlates with burial number 9 in *Excavations at Tepe Gawra* vol. I, p. 141, I have decided to refer to it as Burial 009.

Burial 010 Levels VIII/IX (VIIIA–C, IX) Square 10M
Burial Type: Loose burial
Relative Age: Infant/Child

Grave Goods:

5919-a	32-21-486	378	small white ring beads
5919-b	32-21-486	110	white shell ring beads
5919-c	32-21-486	1	white shell barrel bead
5919-d	32-21-486	454	black stone ring beads
5919-e	32-21-486	4	carnelian ring beads
5919-f	32-21-486	15	turquoise ring beads

Burial 011 Levels VIII/IX (VIIIA–C, IX) Square 10-M
Burial Type: Loose burial
Relative Age: Infant/Child

Grave Goods:

5987-a	Dropsie		white stone ring beads
5987-b	Dropsie		white shell ring beads
5987-c	Dropsie		black stone ring beads
5987-d	Dropsie		black stone wheel beads
5987-e	Dropsie	1	carnelian flat bead
5987-f	Dropsie		turquoise beads
5987-g	Dropsie		crystal ring beads
5987-h	Dropsie	1	rose quartz pendant
5987-i	Dropsie	1	shell fluted bead

Burial 012 Levels VIII/IX (VIIIA–C, IX) Square 10M
Burial Type: Libn burial
Relative Age: Infant/Child

Grave Goods:

5925	Baghdad	1	gold over bitumen core ornament
5926	32-21-372	1	gold over bitumen core ornament
5927	Baghdad	1	gold over bitumen core ornament
6081-a	32-21-488	242	small white beads
6081-b	32-21-488	37	turquoise ring beads
6081-c	32-21-488	1	turquoise pendant
3-54-a	Baghdad	10	lapis beads
3-54-b	Baghdad	1	black stone bead
3-54-c	Baghdad	2	lapis bird figurines
3-54-d	Baghdad	1	ivory irregular pendant
3-54-e	Baghdad	4	gold beads
3-54-f	Baghdad		white paste beads
3-54-g	Baghdad	28	carnelian beads
3-54-h	Baghdad	1	carnelian pendant
none	unrecorded	1	lump of iron

Burial 013 Levels VIII/IX (VIIIA–C, IX) Square 11O
Burial Type: Loose burial
Relative Age: Infant

Grave Goods:

5912A-a	Baghdad		white stone ring beads
5912A-b	Baghdad		shell ring beads
5912A-c	Baghdad		black stone ring beads
5912B-a	32-21-482	186	white ring beads
5912B-b	32-21-842	5	white shell barrel beads
5912B-c	32-21-482	175	black stone ring beads
5912B-d	32-21-482	1	turquoise ring bead
5914	32-21-370	1	bronze flat band ring
5915	Baghdad	1	bronze flat band ring
5916	Dropsie	2	bronze flat band rings
5918A-a	Baghdad		white shell ring beads
5918A-b	Baghdad		white shell spherical beads
5918A-c	Baghdad		black stone ring beads
5918A-d	Baghdad		green stone ring beads
5918B-a	32-21-484	89	white ring beads
5918B-b	32-21-484	85	black stone ring beads
5918B-c	32-21-484	2	gray stone ring beads
5918B-d	32-21-484	3	carnelian ring beads
5918B-e	32-21-484	14	turquoise ring beads
5918B-f	32-21-484	1	turquoise triangular bead
5918B-g	32-21-484	12	red and white variegated stone ring beads

5918C-a	32-21-485	29	white spherical beads
5918C-b	32-21-485	81	black stone ring beads
5918C-c	32-21-485	1	amethyst irregular bead
5918C-d	32-21-485	1	cowrie shell
5931	Baghdad	1	gold ornament
5932	32-21-373	1	gold ornament
5933	32-21-374	1	gold ornament

Burial 014 Levels VIII/IX (VIIIB–C, IX) Square 10M
Burial Type: Libn burial
Relative Ave: Child

Grave Goods:

3-91-a	33-3-44	8	white ring beads
3-91-b	33-3-44	2	shell barrel beads
3-91-c	33-3-44	530	black stone ring beads
3-91-d	33-3-44	1	carnelian carinated bead

Burial 016 Levels VIII/IX (VIIIB–C, IX) Square 10M
Burial Type: Loose burial
Relative Age: Infant/Child

Grave Goods:

3-132-a	33-3-60	c.1245	small white ring beads
3-132-b	33-3-60	c.692	black stone ring beads
3-132-c	33-3-60	c.360	small brown paste barrel beads
3-132-d	33-3-60	23	dentalia shells
none	none		reed matting*

Discussion:
Beads formed a bracelet on the right wrist of the skeleton.

Burial 017 Levels VIII/IX (VIIIA–C, IX) Square 10M
Burial Type: Loose burial
Relative Age: Youth

Grave Goods:

none	none	reed matting*

Burial 018 Levels VIII/IX (VIIIA–C) Square 8Q
Burial Type: Libn burial
Relative Age: Possible Adult

Grave Goods:

no grave goods

Discussion:
This is a disturbed burial.

Burial 020 Levels VIII/IX (IX) Square 8M
Burial Type: Libn burial
Relative Ave: Child

Grave Goods:

none	none	reed matting*

Discussion:
This is a disturbed burial.

Burial 024 Level VIII/XI (VIIIC, IX) Square 9O
Burial Type: Libn burial
Relative Age: Adult

Grave Goods:

3-151	33-3-71	1	bone comb with traces of blue pigment
3-152	Baghdad	1	bone, lapis, turquoise, and gold hair ornament
3-232	33-3-116	1	oolite ointment jar
none	none		traces of blue and green pigment on chest

Discussion:
The comb was found in the right hand of the skeleton, held out in front of the face. The hair ornament and ointment jar were placed near the comb.

Burial 025-A and -B Levels VIII/IX (VIIIC, IX) Square 9Q
Burial Type: Libn burial
Relative Age: Adult (two)

Grave Goods:

3-171	33-3-78	1	red-brown slipped red-buff ware jar
3-174	Baghdad	1	gold discoid pendant
3-175	33-3-81	1	turquoise pendant

Discussion:
There is not enough detail in the notes to attribute the grave furniture to one or the other skeleton and so they are listed as one burial.

Burial 029-A Levels VIII/IX (VIIIA–C, IX) Square 6Q
Burial Type: Libn burial
Relative Age: Youth

Grave Goods:

3-199A	Baghdad	1	gold ribbon-rosette ornament
3-199B	Baghdad	1	gold rosette ornament
3-241	Baghdad	1	bone hemisphere button
3-242	Baghdad	1	obsidian blade
3-420	Baghdad	1	limestone footed mortar
none	none		traces of green, blue and red pigment on chest
none	none		reed matting*

Discussion:
This locus is a double burial with all of the grave goods were near the heel of skeleton 29-A. Skeleton 29-B (see below) had no grave goods associated with it.

Burial 029-B Levels VIII/IX (VIIIA–C, IX) Square 6Q
  Burial Type: Libn burial
  Relative Age: Adult

  Grave Goods:

none none   reed matting*

Burial 030-A Levels VIII/IX (VIIIB–C, IX)
Square 9O/9Q
  Burial Type: Libn burial
  Relative Age: Adult

  Grave Goods:

none none   traces of blue-green pigment on
              and around head
none none   reed matting*

Discussion:

This locus is a double burial made up of skeletons 30-A and 30-B (see below). Skeleton 30-A had traces of blue-green pigment on and around the head. The skull was blackened by the decay of some sort of organic material that may have formed a head covering of 30-A.

Burial 030-B Levels VIII/I X (VIIIB–C, IX)
Square 9O/9Q
  Burial Type: Libn burial
  Relative Ave: Child

  Grave Goods:

none none   reed matting*

Burial 031 Levels VIII/IX (VIIIC, IX) Square 9M
  Burial Type: Libn burial
  Relative Age: Adult

  Grave Goods:

3-282-a	33-3-137	32	white shell beads
3-282-b	33-3-137	57	carnelian beads
3-282-c	33-3-137	1	pink carnelian pendant
3-282-d	33-3-137	29	lapis beads
3-282-e	33-3-137	120	turquoise beads
3-282-f	33-3-137	2	crystal beads
3-282-g	33-3-137	16	gold spherical beads
3-283	Baghdad	1	alabaster ointment vase
3-284	33-3-138	1	bone zigzag hair ornament
3-285	Baghdad	1	translucent serpentine ointment dish
3-286	Baghdad	1	gold foil ribbon-rosette ornament
3-287	Baghdad	11	gold over bitumen core hemisphere studs
3-288	33-3-139	1	oolite ointment vessel
3-289	33-3-140	1	ivory or bone plaque seal
3-290	Baghdad	256	beads

3-292	Baghdad	1	Mosul marble double ointment dish
3-293	Baghdad	1	Mosul marble eye or hut idol
3-294	33-3-141	1	Mosul marble eye or hut idol
3-295	Baghdad	1	bone comb
3-296	Baghdad	1	bone comb
none	none		traces of green pigment on chest
none	none		animal bones with traces of green pigment
none	none		reed matting*

Discussion:

Gold, lapis and carnelian beads were found around the skull. Remains of gold foil which may have been the cover for some ornament was found on the nose of the skull. Mother of pearl beads were found near the left hand and may have formed a bracelet(?). Also near the left hand were a comb, a plaque seal, a stone cup, a stone hut idol, and a white cylinder bead. The animal bones were found at the feet of the skeleton.

Burial 034 Levels VIII/IX (VIIIC, IX) Square 7O
  Burial Type: Libn burial
  Relative Age: Adult

  Grave Goods:

3-380	33-3-189	1	bone comb
3-390	Baghdad	1	limestone macehead
3-391-a	33-3-194	4	large shell ring beads
3-391-b	33-3-194	1	black stone ring bead
3-391-c	33-3-194	1	carnelian ring bead
3-391-d	33-3-194	1	carnelian carinated bead
3-391-e	33-3-194	2	small lapis ring beads
3-391-f	33-3-194	27	turquoise ring beads
3-392	Baghdad	1	bone spatula
none	none		reed matting*
none	none		traces of woven textile*

Discussion:

This burial appears to have been robbed as evidenced by broken and disarrayed grave furniture and disturbed bones.

Burial 037 Levels VIII/IX (VIIIB–C, IX) Square 10K
  Burial Type: Libn burial
  Relative Ave: Child

  Grave Goods:

3-327	33-3-156	1	copper pin
3-328	discard	1	copper pin
3-329-a	33-3-157	1	white shell ring bead
3-329-b	33-3-157	1	white shell barrel bead
3-329-c	33-3-157	4	white shell spherical beads

| 3-329-d | 33-3-157 | 8 | black stone ring beads |
| 3-329-e | 33-3-157 | 1 | black stone spherical bead |

Burial 040 Levels VIII/IX (VIIIA–C, IX) Square 7-Q
Burial Type: Vessel burial with vessel cover
Relative Age: Infant

Grave Goods:

3-356	33-3-171	1	red ware bowl*
3-358	33-3-173	1	red ware stand
3-387	discard	1	red ware bowl*

Discussion:
The bones were burnt.

Burial 045 Levels VIII/IX (VIIIC, IX) Square 6O/7O
Burial Type: Libn burial
Relative Age: Uncertain

Grave Goods:

3-424	Baghdad	1	green serpentine bowl
3-425	33-3-214	1	marble lugged jar
3-426	33-3-215	1	alabaster globular jar
none	none		reed matting*

Discussion:
This burial had been robbed as evidenced by the broken grave furniture and missing bones.

Burial 046 Levels VIII/IX (VIIIB–C, IX) Square 8O
Burial Type: Libn burial
Relative Age: Youth/Adult

Grave Goods:

3-423	33-3-213	1	gold foil rosette ornament
3-427-a	Baghdad	6	shell ring beads
3-427-b	Baghdad	11	carnelian beads
3-427-c	Baghdad	48	green stone ring beads
3-427-d	Baghdad	24	blue stone ring beads
3-427-e	Baghdad	8	rose quartz ring beads
3-427-f	Baghdad	1	gold bead
3-427-g	Baghdad	1	stone frog shaped bead
none	none		traces of blue pigment on head
none	none		reed matting*

Discussion:
The gold foil rosette was found at the head of the skeleton and was probably part of a head dress. Burial had been disturbed and robbed.

Burial 047 Levels VIII/IX (VIIIA–C, IX) Square 8O
Burial Type: Libn burial with stone cover
Relative Ave: Child

Grave Goods:

3-430	Baghdad	1	gold head band
3-431-a	33-3-218	21	carnelian carinated beads
3-431-c	33-3-218	2	lapis beads
3-431-d	33-3-218	26	green stone beads
3-431-f	33-3-218	1	blue stone bead
3-431-b	33-3-218	15	gold spherical beads
3-431-e	33-3-218	2	bronze beads

Discussion:
The gold foil head band was found in situ around the skull.

Burial 050 Levels VIII/IX (VIIIB–C, IX) Square 10O
Burial Type: Vessel burial
Relative Age: Infant

Grave Goods:

| 3-225 | discard | 1 | ceramic buff ware bowl* |

Burial 051 Levels VIII/IX (VIIIB–C) Square 9O
Burial Type: Libn burial with libn cover
Relative Age: Infant

Grave Goods:
no grave goods

Burial 052 Levels VIII/IX (VIIIB–C, IX) Square 8O
Burial Type: Vessel burial
Relative Age: Infant

Grave Goods:

| 3-388 | discard | 1 | gray ware jar* |
| none | unrecorded | 1 | ceramic ballista |

Burial 053 Levels VIII/IX (IX) Square 7O
Burial Type: Libn burial with stone cover
Relative Age: Infant

Grave Goods:

| none | none | | reed matting* |

Burial 054 Levels VIII/IX (VIIIA–B) Square 7O
Burial Type: Libn burial
Relative Age: Infant

Grave Goods:
no grave goods

Burial 055 Levels VIII/IX (VIIIA–C, IX) Square 10S
Burial Type: Vessel burial with vessel cover
Relative Age: Infant

Grave Goods:

| none | unrecorded | 1 | ceramic dish* |
| none | unrecorded | 1 | ceramic dish* |

Burial 056 Levels VIII/IX (VIIIA–C, IX) Square 10Q
Burial Type: Vessel burial in libn enclosure
Relative Age: Infant

Grave Goods:

| 3-258 | 33-3-127 | 1 ceramic w/interior burnishing red ware bowl* |

Burial 057 Levels VIII/IX (VIIIC, IX) Square 9Q
Burial Type: Cist with libn end walls
Relative Ave: Child

Grave Goods:
no grave goods

Discussion:
This is a disturbed burial.

Burial 058 Levels VIII/IX (VIIIA–C, IX) Square 7Q
Burial Type: Vessel burial
Relative Age: Infant

Grave Goods:

| 3-381 | 33-3-190 | 1 ceramic with greenish slip red ware bowl* |

Burial 059 Level X Square 9O/9Q
Burial Type: Cist burial with stone cover
Relative Ave: Child

Grave Goods:

| none | unrecorded | 1 stone hammer |
| none | none | reed matting* |

Burial 060 Levels VIII/IX (VIIIB–C, IX) Square 10M/11M
Burial Type: Libn burial
Relative Age: Infant

Grave Goods:

none	unrecorded	1 carnelian bead
none	unrecorded	2 green stone beads
none	none	charred barley grains
none	none	reed matting*

Discussion:
Barley was found near the hands and knees of the skeleton.

Burial 061 Levels VIII/IX (VIIIB–C, IX) Square 11M
Burial Type: Libn burial with libn and poured mud cover
Relative Age: Infant

Grave Goods:

| none | unrecorded | black stone beads |
| none | unrecorded | numerous tiny white beads |

Discussion:
All of the beads were found near the chest of the skeleton suggesting that they may have formed a necklace.

Burial 062 Levels VIII/IX (IX) Square 7-M
Burial Type: Libn burial with stone cover
Relative Ave: Child

Grave Goods:

| none | none | charred wheat |

Discussion:
This burial had been robbed as evidenced by disturbed bones and the out of place cover.

Burial 063 Levels VIII/IX (VIIIA–C, IX) Square 10K
Burial Type: Vessel burial
Relative Age: Infant

Grave Goods:

| none | unrecorded | 1 ceramic vessel* |

Burial 064 Levels VIII/IX (VIIIA–C, IX) Square 11K
Burial Type: Libn burial
Relative Age: Infant

Grave Goods:

| none | none | reed matting* |

Burial 065 Levels VIII/IX (VIIIA–C, IX) Square 11K
Burial Type: Libn burial
Relative Ave: Child

Grave Goods:

| none | none | ceramic sherds under matting |
| none | none | reed matting* |

Burial 067 Levels VIII/IX (VIIIA–C, IX) Square 10J
Burial Type: Vessel burial
Relative Age: Infant

Grave Goods:

| none | unrecorded | 1 bottom portion of ceramic jar* |

Burial 068 Levels VIII/IX (VIIIA–C, IX) Square 10J
Burial Type: Vessel burial
Relative Age: Infant

Grave Goods:

| none | unrecorded | 1 ceramic vessel* |

Burial 069 Levels VIII/IX (VIIIA–C, IX) Square 7J
Burial Type: Vessel burial
Relative Age: Infant

Grave Goods:

| none | unrecorded | 1 large red ware sherd* |

Burial 070 Levels VIII/IX (IX) Square 6J
Burial Type: Loose burial
Relative Age: Adult

Grave Goods:

no grave goods

Burial 100 Level X Square 6O
Burial Type: Vessel burial
Relative Age: Infant

Grave Goods:

4-633	Baghdad	1	coarse red-brown ware bowl*
4-681-a	35-10-286	1	green stone pendant
4-681-b	discard	1	tiny white paste bead

Discussion:

The tiny white bead was found in the bowl and the green stone pendant was found just outside of it.

Burial 101 Level X Square 6O
Burial Type: Loose burial
Relative Ave: Child

Grave Goods:

| none | none | reed matting* |

Burial 102 Level X Square 5O
Burial Type: Libn burial
Relative Age: Youth

Grave Goods:

4-634	Baghdad	1	obsidian spouted pot
4-635	35-10-287	1	obsidian spouted bowl
4-636	Baghdad	1	marble macehead
4-637-a	35-10-289	7	marble spheres
4-637-b	35-10-290	2	marble discs
4-637-c	35-10-291	3	marble stones
4-638-a	35-10-288	204	shell ring beads
4-638-b	35-10-288	56	carnelian carinated and ring beads
4-639-a	35-10-292	24067	white ring beads
4-639-b	35-10-292	1125	obsidian ring beads
4-640	discard	1	red ware bowl

Burial 107 Level X Square 5M/6M
Burial Type: Libn burial
Relative Age: Adult

Grave Goods:

| 4-699 | 35-10-293 | 6 | alabaster spheres |
| none | none | | reed matting* |

Burial 108 Level X Square 6K
Burial Type: Libn burial with stone cover
Relative Ave: Child

Grave Goods:

| 4-709-a | Baghdad | 1 | carnelian bead |
| 4-709-b | Baghdad | 1 | turquoise bead |

Discussion:

Both beads were found in front of the face of the skeleton.

Burial 109 Level X Square 5K
Burial Type: Libn burial with wood coffin
Relative Age: Adult

Grave Goods:

4-736	Baghdad	1	marble jar
4-737	35-10-295	1	oolite bowl
4-738	35-10-296	1	alabaster bowl
4-739	Baghdad	1	gold rosette ornament
4-740	Baghdad	21	turquoise beads
4-741	35-10-306	1	gold ribbon-rosette ornament
4-742	35-10-307	2	gold rosette ornaments
4-743	35-10-308	1	gold rosette ornament
4-744	25-10-309	50	gold studs
4-745	35-10-314	3	gold ornaments
4-746	35-10-311	3	gold ornaments
4-747	Baghdad	1	gold ferrule
4-748	35-10-312	20	gold crescent ornaments
4-749	35-10-310	3	gold and lapis eye shape ornaments
4-750	35-10-313	90	gold bangles
4-751-a	35-10-301	125	gold beads
4-751-b	35-10-301	34	large electrum beads
4-751-c	35-10-301	76	small electrum beads
4-752	35-10-299	366	lapis beads
4-753-a	35-10-304	1	lapis stamp seal
4-753	35-10-303	1	large lapis carved bead
4-753	see memo	15	various shaped lapis beads
4-754-a	35-10-300	432	carnelian beads
4-754-b	35-10-300	390	turquoise beads
4-755-a	35-10-302	3	white carinated beads
4-755-b	35-10-302	5	carnelian ring beads
4-755-c	35-10-302	11	carnelian carinated beads
4-755-d	35-10-302	52	lapis ring beads
4-755-e	35-10-302	3	lapis carinated beads
4-755-f	35-10-302	5	lapis cylinder beads
4-755-g	35-10-302	3	lapis irregular beads
4-755-h	35-10-302	5	turquoise carinated beads
4-755-i	35-10-302	5	turquoise teardrop beads
4-755-j	35-10-302	2	turquoise flat square beads
4-755-k	35-10-302	23	turquoise natural pebble beads
4-755-l	35-10-302	2	electrum spherical beads
4-756-a	Baghdad	3	carnelian beads

4-756-b	Baghdad	28	lapis beads
4-756-c	Baghdad	24	turquoise beads
4-756-d	Baghdad	2	gold beads
4-756-e	Baghdad	9	electrum beads
4-757	35-10-297	2	obsidian blades
4-758	Baghdad	1	unidentified ceramic object
4-759	Baghdad	1	gold and lapis fly figurine
4-761	Baghdad	1	bone comb
4-762	Baghdad	145	shell beads
4-791	35-10-294	1	ceramic sphere
none	unrecorded	1	bone, gold, lapis, and turquoise hair ornament
none	none		traces of blue pigment on head, chest and forearms

Discussion:

Comb was held in front of face with one hand. One of the stone vessels was placed near the comb. Gold crescents, beads and bangles were in the other hand. Large electrum and lapis beads were found near the wrist of the hand holding the gold crescents. Carved lapis beads and turquoise beads were at the top of the head while the head itself was covered with beads. An oolite and alabaster bowl as well as a hair ornament were found at the feet of the skeleton.

Burial 110 Level X Square 4K/4M
Burial Type: Libn burial with stone cover
Relative Age: Youth

Grave Goods:

4-765	35-10-319	3	gold rosette ornaments
4-766	35-10-320	2	gold rosette ornaments
4-767	unrecorded	1	gold ribbon-rosette ornament
4-768	35-10-321	2	eye ornaments
4-769	35-10-323	1	lapis stamp seal
4-770	35-10-316	6	brown marble spheres
4-771	35-10-317	2	marble mace heads
4-772	unrecorded	1	serpentine cup
4-773	35-10-315	1	serpentine cup
4-774-a	35-10-318	2	stone beads
4-774-b	35-10-318	198	carnelian spherical beads
4-774-c	35-10-318	3	lapis beads
4-774-d	35-10-318	18	gold cylindrical beads
4-775	35-10-322	1	bone comb
none	none		traces of blue and green pigment on chest and femora

Discussion:

Rosettes were found at the top of the skull. Beads were found near the chest. The comb was found in front and above the skull. One macehead and the marble spheres were placed near the comb.

Burial 111-A Level X Square 5M
Burial Type: Libn burial
Relative Age: Adult

Grave Goods:

4-802	35-10-324	1	green ware jar

Discussion:

The jar was located near the head of the skeleton.

Burial 111-B Level X Square 5-M
Burial Type: Libn burial
Relative Age: Adult

Grave Goods:

none	discard	1	ceramic vessel

Discussion:

The jar was located near the feet of the skeleton.

Burial 111-C Level X Square 5M
Burial Type: Libn burial
Relative Age: Adult

Grave Goods:

4-794-a	Baghdad	1	stone bead
4-794-b	Baghdad	19	carnelian beads
4-794-c	Baghdad	2	lapis beads
4-794-d	Baghdad	40	turquoise beads
4-794-e	Baghdad	4	gold beads
4-794-f	Baghdad	1	gold hoof pendant
4-794-g	Baghdad	1	gold spatula pendant
4-794-h	Baghdad	1	gold spiral ornament
none	discard	1	ceramic jar

Discussion:

The jar was located near the feet of the skeleton. All beads and pendants were located near the fingers of the skeleton, which were raised above the skull.

Burial 113 Level X Square 6O
Burial Type: Loose burial
Relative Ave: Child

Grave Goods:

4-806-a	Baghdad	100	small white and yellow beads
4-806-b	Baghdad	1	black stone bead

Burial 114 Level X Square 4K/4M
Burial Type: Libn burial with wood cover
Relative Age: Adult

Grave Goods:

4-821-a	Baghdad	1	electrum wolf head figurine
4-821-b	Baghdad	8	lapis beads
4-821-c	Baghdad	1	turquoise bead
4-822	Baghdad	1	stone with gold band honing stone
4-823	35-10-325	1	hematite macehead
4-824	35-10-326	1	alabaster macehead
4-825	35-10-327	6	red jasper stones
4-826	Baghdad	1	bone with gold bands hair ornament
4-827	35-10-330	3	bone ornaments
4-828-a	35-10-328	40	lapis beads
4-828-b	35-10-328	24	turquoise beads
4-828-c	35-10-328	33	gold beads
4-829-a	35-10-329	55	carnelian beads
4-829-b	35-10-329	230	lapis beads
4-829-c	35-10-329	374	turquoise beads
4-829-d	35-10-329	29	gold beads
4-830	Baghdad	1	gold rosette ornament with lapis center
4-831	Baghdad	1	lapis stamp seal
4-832-a	Baghdad	45	shell beads
4-832-b	Baghdad	33	carnelian beads
4-832-c	Baghdad	4	lapis beads
4-832-d	Baghdad	2	gold beads

Discussion:

The hair ornament and gold beads were found near the chest of the skeleton. The hone and beads of shell and carnelian were located near the abdomen. No other details are given in respect to the location of the other beads. A rosette was located at the top of the head as was the electrum wolf head. The red jasper stones were placed near the northwest wall of the tomb and arranged in two rows of three.

Burial 119 Level X Square 5J
    Burial Type: Loose burial
    Relative Age: Infant

Grave Goods:

no grave goods

Burial 122 Level XI/XA Square 4K
    Burial Type: Loose burial
    Relative Age: Infant

Grave Goods:

none	unrecorded	1	blue cylindrical bead

Discussion:

The bead was found in front of the face of the skeleton.

Burial 123 Level XI/XA Square 7O
    Burial Type: Vessel burial with vessel cover
    Relative Age: Uncertain

Grave Goods:

4-959	discard	1	ceramic dish*
4-960	Baghdad	1	ceramic bowl*

Burial 124 Level X Square 6-M
    Burial Type: Libn burial with stone lined walls, floor and stone cover
    Relative Age: Uncertain

Grave Goods:

4-909-a	35-10-333	1	gold ribbon rosette ornament
4-909-b	35-10-332	1	turquoise flat, square bead
4-996	discard	1	ceramic dish
none	none		barley grains

Discussion:

This burial may have been disturbed.

Burial 125 Level XI/XA Square 4Q
    Burial Type: Vessel burial
    Relative Age: Infant

Grave Goods:

none	unrecorded	1	ceramic pot*

Burial 126 Level X Square 6-M
    Burial Type: Vessel burial
    Relative Ave: Child

Grave Goods:

4-941	discard	1	ceramic vessel*

Burial 127 Level XI/XA Square 5-O
    Burial Type: Loose burial
    Relative Age: Infant

Grave Goods:

none	discard	27	small white beads
none	discard	1	shell

Burial 128 Level XI/XA Square 5M
    Burial Type: Vessel burial
    Relative Age: Infant

Grave Goods:

4-954	Baghdad	1	ceramic bowl*
none	unrecorded	1	small white bead

Burial 129 Level XI/XA Square 5O
    Burial Type: Loose burial
    Relative Ave: Child

Grave Goods:

no grave goods

Burial 130 Level XI/XA Square 4Q
    Burial Type: Loose burial
    Relative Age: Infant

Grave Goods:

none   discard   1 bitumen core of some
                     ornament
none   none   reed matting*

Burial 134 Level XI/XA Square 6O
Burial Type: Double sidewall burial
Relative Ave: Child

Grave Goods:

none   none   reed matting*

Burial 136 Level XI/XA Square 5M
Burial Type: Loose burial with sherd cover
Relative Age: Infant

Grave Goods:

none   unrecorded   1 ceramic sherd*

Burial 137 Level XI/XA Square 5Q
Burial Type: Vessel burial
Relative Age: Infant

Grave Goods:

4-1018   Baghdad   1 stone acorn
none   unrecorded   1 ceramic vessel*

Burial 138 Level XI/XA Square 5O
Burial Type: Loose burial
Relative Age: Infant

Grave Goods:

4-961-a   Baghdad   small white ring beads
4-961-b   Baghdad   1 gold disc ornament

Burial 140 Level XI/XA Square 5O
Burial Type: Vessel burial
Relative Age: Infant

Grave Goods:

none   unrecorded   1 white bead
none   unrecorded   1 ceramic vessel*

Burial 141 Level XI/XA Square 6M
Burial Type: Vessel burial with vessel cover
Relative Age: Infant

Grave Goods:

none   unrecorded   1 ceramic vessel*
none   unrecorded   1 ceramic dish*

Burial 142 Level XI/XA Square 5Q
Burial Type: Loose burial
Relative Ave: Child/Youth

Grave Goods:

4-1071   35-10-334   1348 tiny white ring beads
4-1071   35-10-334   129 small white carinated
                            beads
4-1071   35-10-334   733 small black stone ring
                            beads
4-1071   35-10-334   1   carnelian ring bead
4-1071   35-10-334   1   lapis grooved bead
4-1072   35-10-335   1   gold rosette ornament
4-1097   Baghdad   1   slate axe head

Discussion:
The gold rosette (or disc) was located on the left
temple of the skull.

Burial 144 Level XI/XA Square 5M
Burial Type: Loose burial
Relative Ave: Child

Grave Goods:

4-1071   35-10-334   tiny white ring beads
                                 (locus 144 and 142
                                 beads were accidentally
                                 strung together)
none   unrecorded   1 mother of pearl
                         ornament
none   unrecorded   1 decomposed orange-
                         brown ornament
none   none   reed matting*

Discussion:
The beads and mother of pearl ornament formed a
necklace. The decomposed orange-brown ornament
was located near the lower part of the skeleton's chest.

Burial 145 Level XI/XA Square 6Q
Burial Type: Loose burial
Relative Age: Adult

Grave Goods:

none   none   reed matting*

Burial 146 Level XI/XA Square 6-O
Burial Type: Sidewall burial with libn cover
Relative Ave: Child

Grave Goods:

none   none   reed matting*

Burial 151 Level XI/XA Square 5M
Burial Type: Loose burial
Relative Age: Infant

Grave Goods:

no grave goods

Burial 154 Level XI/XA Square 6M
Burial Type: Loose burial
Relative Ave: Child

Grave Goods:

none   unrecorded   2 white stone beads
none   none   reed matting*

Discussion:
The beads were found near neck of the skeleton.

Burial 158 Level XI/XA Square 5O
Burial Type: Vessel burial
Relative Age: Infant

Grave Goods:
none   discard   1 ceramic vessel*

Burial 159 Level XI/XA Square 5M
Burial Type: Loose burial
Relative Age: Infant

Grave Goods:
4-1196 unrecorded   tiny white beads
none   none   reed matting*

Discussion:
The beads formed a bracelet around each wrist.

Burial 160 Level XI/XA Square 5M
Burial Type: Loose burial
Relative Ave: Child

Grave Goods:
none   none   reed matting*

Burial 161 Level XIA/B Square 6M
Burial Type: Loose burial
Relative Ave: Child

Grave Goods:
none   none   reed matting*

Burial 163 Level XI/XA Square 5Q
Burial Type: Loose burial
Relative Ave: Child

Grave Goods:
none   36-6-349   2 lapis ring beads
none   36-6-349   2 turquoise natural pebble
                       beads
none   36-6-349   1 buff natural pebble bead

Discussion:
Two of the beads were found on the head.

Burial 164 Level XI/XA Square 5M
Burial Type: Vessel burial with vessel cover
Relative Age: Infant

Grave Goods:
4-1227-a Baghdad   1 ceramic pot*
4-1227-b Baghdad   1 red ware plate*

Burial 166 Level XIA/B Square 5Q
Burial Type: Vessel burial with vessel cover
Relative Ave: Child

Grave Goods:
none   unrecorded   1 ceramic cooking pot*
4-1228 unrecorded   1 ceramic dish*

Burial 167 Level XIA/B Square 5Q
Burial Type: Loose burial
Relative Ave: Child

Grave Goods:
4-1232-a 35-10-366   tiny white beads
4-1232-b 35-10-366   1 gold foil over bitumen
                         core ear ornament

Discussion:
The white beads were located at the neck of
the skeleton and probably formed a necklace. The
gold ornament was found at the left ear of the
skeleton.

Burial 168 Level XI/XA Square 6K
Burial Type: Loose burial
Relative Ave: Child

Grave Goods:
none   none   reed matting*

Burial 170 Level XI/XA Square 4K
Burial Type: Vessel burial with vessel cover
Relative Age: Infant

Grave Goods:
5-1358 Baghdad   1 painted ceramic
                     bowl*
none   unrecorded   1 ceramic vessel*

Burial 171 Levels VIII/IX (VIIIA–C, IX) Square 6J
Burial Type: Libn burial
Relative Ave: Child/Youth

Grave Goods:
none   none   reed matting*

Burial 175 Level XI/XA Square 4J
Burial Type: Vessel burial with possible libn cover
Relative Age: Infant

Grave Goods:
5-1443 discard   1 spouted burnished red
                     slipped gray ware pot*

Burial 176 Level XI/XA Square 3K
Burial Type: Loose burial
Relative Ave: Child

Grave Goods:
5-1395 Baghdad   1 ceramic vessel
5-1418 Baghdad   beads

Burial 177 Level X Square 6-G
  Burial Type: Loose burial
  Relative Ave: Child

  Grave Goods:
  5-1402   Baghdad   35 stone beads

  Discussion:
  The beads were found at the pelvis of the skeleton
  and may have formed part of a girdle or belt.

Burial 178 Level XI/XA Square 3M
  Burial Type: Loose burial
  Relative Age: Infant

  Grave Goods:
  no grave goods

Burial 179 Level XI/XA Square 4J
  Burial Type: Vessel burial
  Relative Age: Infant

  Grave Goods:
  none   unrecorded   1 ceramic bowl*

Burial 180 Level XI/XA Square 4J
  Burial Type: Libn burial with libn cover
  Relative Ave: Child

  Grave Goods:

5-1439-a	Baghdad		various types of large beads
5-1439-b	Baghdad	1	lapis pendant
5-1440-a	36-6-350	320	small white ring beads
5-1440-b	36-6-350	378	small white carinated beads
5-1440-c	36-6-350	1	white stone irregular bead
5-1440-d	36-6-350	29	carnelian ring beads
5-1440-e	36-6-350	10	carnelian carinated beads
5-1440-f	36-6-350	1	lapis cylinder bead
5-1440-g	36-6-350	20	dentalia shells
5-1445	Baghdad		various types of beads

  Discussion:
  Some of the large beads and the lapis pendant
  formed a necklace.

Burial 181 Level XI/XA Square 4K
  Burial Type: Libn burial
  Relative Ave: Child

  Grave Goods:

5-1412	36-6-351	2 alabaster stone objects
5-1413-a	36-6-353A	1 alabaster sphere
5-1413-b	36-6-353B	1 marble sphere
5-1413-c	Baghdad	1 marble sphere

5-1413-d	Baghdad	1 alabaster sphere
5-1414-a	36-6-351	1 alabaster hemisphere
5-1414-b	36-6-352	2 alabaster hemispheres
5-1419	26-6-354	1 gold rosette ornament
5-1420	Baghdad	1 gold disc ornament
5-1441-a	Baghdad	shell beads
5-1441-b	Baghdad	carnelian beads
5-1441-c	Baghdad	gold beads

Burial 182 Level X Square 5J
  Burial Type: Loose burial
  Relative Age: Infant

  Grave Goods:
  no grave goods

Burial 183 Level XIA/B Square 4Q
  Burial Type: Vessel burial with vessel cover
  Relative Ave: Child

  Grave Goods:
  5-1463 discard   1 large ceramic pot*
  none   discard   1 incomplete ceramic
                        vessel*

Burial 184 Level XI/XA Square 5G
  Burial Type: Loose burial
  Relative Age: Youth

  Grave Goods:
  none   none   reed matting*

Burial 186 Level XI/XA Square 6K
  Burial Type: Vessel burial
  Relative Age: Infant/Child

  Grave Goods:
  none   unrecorded   1 ceramic vessel*

Burial 187 Level XI/XA Square 3O
  Burial Type: Vessel burial
  Relative Age: Infant

  Grave Goods:
  none   discard   1 ceramic vessel*

Burial 188-A Level XIA/B Square 5Q
  Burial Type: Loose burial
  Relative Age: Adult

  Grave Goods:
  5-1467 Baghdad   beads
  none   unrecorded   ceramic sherds

  Discussion:
  Burial 188 was a double burial consisting of skeletons 188-A and 188-B (see below) each about 40 cm.
  apart. Beads located at the neck of 188-A formed a
  necklace.

Burial 188-B Level XIA/B Square 5Q
    Burial Type: Loose burial
    Relative Age: Adult

    Grave Goods:
    5-1470   discard   1 ceramic pot

    Discussion:
    The bowl was located at the feet of skeleton 188-B.

Burial 189 Level XI/XA Square 5K
    Burial Type: Loose burial
    Relative Age: Infant

    Grave Goods:
    no grave goods

Burial 190 Level X Square 7M
    Burial Type: Vessel burial with sherd cover
    Relative Age: Infant

    Grave Goods:
    5-1473   discard   1 coarse cream slipped
                           red-brown ware jar*
    none   discard   1 ceramic sherd*

Burial 191 Level XI/XA Square 5K
    Burial Type: Sidewall burial
    Relative Ave: Child

    Grave Goods:
    no grave goods

Burial 192 Level XI/XA Square 5Q
    Burial Type: Vessel burial
    Relative Age: Infant

    Grave Goods:
    none   unrecorded   1 ceramic vessel*

Burial 193 Level XI/XA Square 7K
    Burial Type: Vessel burial with vessel cover
    Relative Age: Infant

    Grave Goods:
    5-1479-a   36-6-355   167   small white ring
                                   beads
    5-1479-b   36-6-355   6   spherical beads
    5-1479-c   36-6-355   1   plano convex bead
    5-1479-d   36-6-355   1   dentalium shell
    none   unrecorded 1   ceramic vessel*
    none   unrecorded 1   ceramic vessel*

Burial 194 Level XIA/B Square 5Q
    Burial Type: Vessel burial
    Relative Age: Infant

    Grave Goods:
    5-1481   36-6-356   1 ceramic pot*

Burial 199 Levels VIII/IX (VIIIA–C, IX) Square 6J
    Burial Type: Loose burial
    Relative Age: Youth

    Grave Goods:
    no grave goods

Burial 200 Levels VIII/IX (VIIIA–C, IX) Square 6J
    Burial Type: Sidewall burial
    Relative Ave: Child

    Grave Goods:
    no grave goods

Burial 201 Level X Square 6K
    Burial Type: Vessel burial
    Relative Age: Infant

    Grave Goods:
    none   unrecorded   1 ceramic sherd*

Burial 202 Level X Square 6J
    Burial Type: Cist burial with stone cover
    Relative Ave: Child

    Grave Goods:
    5-1280-a   36-6-357   354   small white ring
                                   beads
    5-1280-b   36-6-357   62   small white carinated
                                   beads
    5-1280-c   36-6-357   22   obsidian carinated
                                   beads
    5-1280-d   36-6-357   1   carnelian ring bead
    5-1280-e   36-6-357   1   turquoise natural
                                   pebble bead

Burial 203 Levels VIII/IX (IX) Square 5J/6J
    Burial Type: Loose burial
    Relative Ave: Child (c. 6 years old)

    Grave Goods:
    5-1278-a   Baghdad   white stone beads
    5-1278-b   Baghdad   carnelian beads
    none   none   reed matting*

    Discussion:
    Beads formed a bracelet.

Burial 204 Levels VIII/IX (VIIIA–B) Square 5J/6J
    Burial Type: Vessel burial
    Relative Age: Infant

    Grave Goods:
    none   unrecorded   1 ceramic dish*

Burial 205 Level X Square 6J
    Burial Type: Loose burial
    Relative Ave: Child

Grave Goods:

5-1269	Baghdad	1	ceramic vessel
none	none		reed matting*

Burial 206 Level X Square 5J
Burial Type: Loose burial
Relative Ave: Child

Grave Goods:

5-1299	discard	1	wet-smoothed green ware jar

Discussion:

Jar was located at the feet of the skeleton.

Burial 207 Level X Square 5K
Burial Type: Vessel burial
Relative Age: Infant

Grave Goods:

none	unrecorded	1	ceramic jar base*

Burial 208 Level X Square 6J
Burial Type: Sidewall burial
Relative Ave: Child

Grave Goods:

5-1295-a	36-6-358	1084	white ring beads
5-1295-b	36-6-358	2	black stone ring beads
5-1295-c	36-6-358	2	obsidian ring beads
5-1295-d	36-6-358	1	carnelian ring bead
5-1295-e	36-6-258	1	large thick carnelian ring bead
5-1295-f	36-6-358	24	dentalia shells

Discussion:

Cylindrical and medium sized white beads formed a bracelet. Tiny white beads formed a necklace. The 3 carnelian beads were located at the chin of the skeleton. A large number of beads were located at the knees of the skeleton.

Burial 209 Levels VIII/IX (VIIIA–C, IX) Square 6J
Burial Type: Libn burial
Relative Ave: Child

Grave Goods:

5-1298-a	36-6-359	14	white ring beads
5-1298-b	36-6-359	381	small black stone ring beads
5-1298-c	36-6-359	3	small yellow carnelian ring beads
5-1298-d	36-6-359	40	dentalia shells
none	none		reed matting*

Discussion:

All of the beads were located at the top of the head of the skeleton.

Burial 210 Level X Square 6J
Burial Type: Sidewall burial
Relative Ave: Child

Grave Goods:

none	none	reed matting*

Burial 211 Levels VIII/IX (IX) Square 6J
Burial Type: Loose burial
Relative Ave: Child

Grave Goods:

no grave goods

Burial 212 Levels VIII/IX (VIIIA–C, IX) Square 6G
Burial Type: Loose burial
Relative Ave: Child

Grave Goods:

5-1309-a	Baghdad	30	shell cylinder beads
5-1309-b	Baghdad	c.90	black stone ring beads
5-1309-c	Baghdad	79	quartz ring beads
none	none		reed matting*

Discussion:

The quartz beads were all strung together at one wrist forming a bracelet. The white shell and black stone beads were strung together in a pattern of 3 black and 1 white to form a bracelet at the other wrist. The number of white shell beads are given in the registry, but the number of black beads are not recorded. I have estimated the number of black beads to be about 90 from the pattern of 3 black to 1 white bead recorded in the locus sheet for this burial.

Burial 213 Levels VIII/IX (IX) Square 7M
Burial Type: Cist burial with stone cover
Relative Ave: Child

Grave Goods:

5-1317	36-6-360	18	small white ring beads
none	none		reed matting*

Discussion:

The beads formed a bracelet.

Burial 214 Levels VIII/IX (VIIIA–C, IX) Square 6G
Burial Type: Vessel burial inside of another vessel
Relative Age: Infant

Grave Goods:

5-1321-a	36-6-361	282	small white carinated beads
5-1321-b	36-6-362	71	white carinated beads
5-1321-c	36-6-362	3	white barrel beads

5-1321-d	36-6-362	107	obsidian ring beads
5-1321-e	36-6-362	113	grey stone ring beads
5-1321-f	36-6-362	1	large grey stone ring bead
5-1321-g	36-6-362	1	grey stone barrel bead
5-1321-h	36-6-362	18	dentalia shells
5-1324	discard	1	ceramic bowl*
none	unrecorded	1	ceramic vessel*

Burial 215 Level XI/Xa Square 6J
Burial Type: Vessel burial with vessel cover
Relative Age: Infant

Grave Goods:

| 5-1322 | discard | 1 | ceramic bowl* |
| 5-1323 | discard | 1 | incomplete wet-smoothed buff ware pot* |

Burial 216 Level X Square 5J
Burial Type: Vessel burial
Relative Age: Infant

Grave Goods:

| 5-1334 | Baghdad | 1 | ceramic bowl* |

Burial 217 Level X Square 6-G
Burial Type: Vessel burial
Relative Age: Infant

Grave Goods:

| none | unrecorded | 1 | ceramic dish* |

Burial 218 Level XI/XA Square 4K
Burial Type: Vessel burial
Relative Age: Infant

Grave Goods:

| none | unrecorded | 1 | ceramic vessel* |

Burial 219 Level X Square 7M
Burial Type: Sidewall burial
Relative Ave: Child

Grave Goods:

no grave goods

Burial 220 Level X Square 7K
Burial Type: Loose burial
Relative Age: Infant

Grave Goods:

| none | none | | reed matting* |

Burial 221 Level XI/XA Square 5M
Burial Type: Sidewall burial
Relative Age: Youth

Grave Goods:

| none | unrecorded | 1 | obsidian blade |

Discussion:
The blade was found at the ribs of the skeleton.

Burial 222 Level XI/XA Square 5M
Burial Type: Sidewall burial
Relative Ave: Child

Grave Goods:

| none | none | | reed matting* |

Burial 223 Level XI/XA Square 4K
Burial Type: Vessel burial
Relative Age: Infant

Grave Goods:

| none | unrecorded | 1 | ceramic vessel* |

Burial 224 Level XI/XA Square 5M
Burial Type: Vessel burial
Relative Age: Infant

Grave Goods:

| 5-1500 | Baghdad | 1 | spouted ceramic pot* |

Burial 225 Level XI/XA Square 5Q
Burial Type: Vessel burial with sherd cover
Relative Age: Infant

Grave Goods:

| 5-1519-a | 36-6-363 | 1 | spouted ceramic jar* |
| 5-1519-b | 36-6-363 | 1 | incomplete ceramic bowl* |

Burial 226 Level XI/XA Square 6M
Burial Type: Libn burial
Relative Age: Infant

Grave Goods:

5-1504-a	36-6-364	c.3290	tiny white paste carinated and ring beads
5-1504-b	36-6-364	1	white paste ring bead
5-1504-c	36-6-364	1	white paste incised plano convex bead
5-1504-d	36-6-364	1	black stone rectangular bead
5-1504-e	36-6-364	2	carnelian ring beads
5-1504-f	36-6-364	1	carnelian cylinder bead

Discussion:
The beads were at the ankles of the skeleton.

Burial 227 Level XI/XA Square 6Q
Burial Type: Vessel burial
Relative Ave: Child

Grave Goods:

none   unrecorded   1 ceramic jar base*

Burial 228 Level XI/XA Square 6Q
   Burial Type: Loose burial
   Relative Ave: Child (3–4 years old)

Grave Goods:

5-1521   36-6-375   c.740 small white carinated,
                                 ring, and cylinder
                                 beads
none   none   reed matting*

Burial 229 Level XI/XA Square 7M
   Burial Type: Loose burial
   Relative Ave: Child

Grave Goods:

no grave goods

Burial 230 Level XI/XA Square 6Q
   Burial Type: Vessel burial with vessel cover
   Relative Age: Infant/Child

Grave Goods:

5-1569   discard   1 brown ware jar*
none   discard   1 coarse ceramic plate

Burial 231 Level XI/XA Square 6Q
   Burial Type: Vessel burial
   Relative Age: Infant/Child

Grave Goods:

none   discard   1 ceramic vessel*

Burial 233 Level XI/XA Square 5K
   Burial Type: Loose burial
   Relative Age: Adult

Grave Goods:

none   none   reed matting*

Burial 234 Level XI/XA Square 6M
   Burial Type: Vessel burial
   Relative Age: Infant

Grave Goods:

none   unrecorded   1 ceramic cooking pot*

Burial 235 Level XI/XA Square 5J
   Burial Type: Vessel burial
   Relative Age: Infant

Grave Goods:

none   discard   1 ceramic cooking pot*

Burial 236 Level XIA/B Square 5M
   Burial Type: Loose burial
   Relative Age: Infant

Grave Goods:

5-1523   36-6-365   1 brown ware bottle

Burial 237 Level XIA/B Square 5M
   Burial Type: Loose burial
   Relative Age: Infant

Grave Goods:

no grave goods

Burial 238 Level XIA/B Square 5M
   Burial Type: Loose burial
   Relative Age: Youth

Grave Goods:

5-1532-a   36-6-366   1 oolite mace head
5-1532-b   unrecorded   1 bone bead spreader

Discussion:
The macehead was held in one of the hands and
was positioned near the left shoulder.

Burial 239 Level XI/XA Square 3K
   Burial Type: Loose burial
   Relative Ave: Child (c. 12 years old)

Grave Goods:

no grave goods

Burial 241 Level XIA/B Square 3M
   Burial Type: Vessel burial
   Relative Age: Infant/Child

Grave Goods:

none   unrecorded   1 ceramic vessel*

Burial 242 Level XI/XA Square 7M
   Burial Type: Sidewall burial
   Relative Ave: Child (3–4 years old)

Grave Goods:

5-1543-a   Baghdad   25 white stone beads
5-1543-b   Baghdad   26 gray stone beads
5-1544-a   36-6-367   79 white ring beads
5-1544-b   36-6-367   19 obsidian ring beads
5-1544-c   36-6-367   1 obsidian roughed
                            surface bead
5-1544-d   36-6-367   3 gray stone ring beads

Discussion:
The obsidian and some of the white beads were located at the waist of the skeleton and seem to have
formed a girdle. Gray and white beads formed a
bracelet at the right wrist of the skeleton.

Burial 243 Level XIA/B Square 5M
   Burial Type: Loose burial
   Relative Ave: Child

Grave Goods:

5-1551-a	36-6-368	511	small white ring beads
5-1551-b	36-6-368	1	shell ring bead
5-1551-c	36-6-369	588	tiny white ring beads
5-1551-d	36-6-369	605	small obsidian ring beads
none	none		reed matting*

Discussion:

The small obsidian beads grade in color from black to a brownish red. There are 78 definitely red beads and 527 beads tending more towards black, most of which are definitely black but with some being hard to distinguish exactly. The beads were found at the chest of the skeleton.

Burial 244 Level XI/XA Square 3K
    Burial Type: Vessel burial
    Relative Age: Infant

Grave Goods:

none   unrecorded   1 ceramic vessel*

Burial 245 Level XI/XA Square 3K
    Burial Type: Loose burial
    Relative Age: Infant/Child

Grave Goods:

records missing

Burial 246 Level XI/XA Square 3K
    Burial Type: Vessel burial
    Relative Age: Infant/Child

Grave Goods:

none   unrecorded   1 ceramic vessel*

Burial 247 Level XI/XA Square 3K
    Burial Type: Loose burial
    Relative Age: Infant

Grave Goods:

records missing

Burial 248 Level XIA/B Square 4K
    Burial Type: Vessel burial
    Relative Age: Infant

Grave Goods:

none   unrecorded   1 ceramic vessel*

Burial 249 Level XI/XA Square 7M
    Burial Type: Libn burial
    Relative Ave: Child

Grave Goods:

none   none   reed matting*

Burial 250 Level XIA/B Square 5M
    Burial Type: Cist burial
    Relative Ave: Child (5–6 years old)

Grave Goods:

5-1553   36-6-370   1 small brown ware jar

Burial 251 Level XIA/B Square 5M
    Burial Type: Loose burial
    Relative Ave: Child

Grave Goods:

none   none   reed matting*

Burial 252 Level XI/XA Square 4K
    Burial Type: Loose burial
    Relative Age: Infant

Grave Goods:

no grave goods

Burial 253 Level XI/XA Square 6M
    Burial Type: Vessel burial
    Relative Age: Infant

Grave Goods:

none   unrecorded   1 ceramic jar base*

Burial 254 Level XIA/B Square 5Q
    Burial Type: Vessel burial
    Relative Age: Infant/Child

Grave Goods:

5-1572   36-6-371   1 brown ware pot*

Burial 255 Level XIA/B Square 4Q
    Burial Type: Vessel burial with vessel cover
    Relative Ave: Child

Grave Goods:

5-1584	Baghdad	1	painted green ware cup
none	unrecorded	1	large ceramic vessel*
none	unrecorded	1	broken ceramic vessel*

Discussion:

The cup was located at the chest and near the right shoulder of the skeleton.

Burial 256 Level X Square 7O
    Burial Type: Loose burial
    Relative Ave: Child

Grave Goods:

5-1587-a	36-6-372	985	tiny white paste carinated beads
5-1587-b	36-6-372	4	small black stone ring beads
5-1587-c	36-6-372	346	tiny brown paste barrel beads

Discussion:
The small white carinated paste beads show very faint traces of a blue coating that once covered the beads but has since deteriorated. The beads were found at the wrist and ankle of the skeleton.

Burial 257 Level XIA/B Square 5M
Burial Type: Loose burial
Relative Ave: Child (7–10 years old)

Grave Goods:
no grave goods

Burial 258 Level XI/XA Square 5K
Burial Type: Loose burial
Relative Age: Infant

Grave Goods:
no grave goods

Burial 259 Level XIA/B Square 6S
Burial Type: Vessel burial
Relative Age: Infant/Child

Grave Goods:
5-1611   36-6-373   1 incomplete spouted burnished red slipped black ware pot*

Burial 261 Levels VIII/IX (VIIIC) Square 8M
Burial Type: Loose burial
Relative Age: Infant/Child

Grave Goods:
records missing

Burial 263 Level XI/XA Square 7K
Burial Type: Vessel burial
Relative Age: Infant/Child

Grave Goods:
none   unrecorded   1 ceramic vessel*

Burial 265 Level XIA/B Square 6Q
Burial Type: Vessel burial
Relative Age: Adult

Grave Goods:
none   unrecorded   1 ceramic vessel*

Burial 266 Level XI/XA Square 5S
Burial Type: Loose burial
Relative Ave: Child (2–3 years old)

Grave Goods:
5-1608   Phila.   1 macehead
5-1609-a Baghdad   white beads
5-1609-b Baghdad   lapis beads
5-1609-c Baghdad   copper beads

5-1609-d Baghdad   1 gold ear ring
none   none   reed matting*

Discussion:
The beads were found around the left wrist of the skeleton. The macehead was held at the chest by one hand.

Burial 267 Levels VIII/IX (VIIIB–C, IX) Square 7O
Burial Type: Vessel burial
Relative Age: Infant/Child

Grave Goods:
none   unrecorded   1 ceramic vessel*

Burial 268 Level XIA/B Square 6Q
Burial Type: Loose burial
Relative Age: Adult

Grave Goods:
no grave goods

Burial 269 Level X Square 8M
Burial Type: Vessel burial
Relative Age: Infant

Grave Goods:
5-1632   unrecorded   1   ceramic dish*
5-1633-a 36-6-374   38 white stone ring beads
5-1633-b 36-6-374   7   obsidian ring beads
5-1633-c 36-6-374   54 gray stone ring beads

Burial 270 Level XI/XA Square 7M
Burial Type: Vessel burial
Relative Age: Infant/Child

Grave Goods:
none   unrecorded   1 ceramic vessel*

Burial 272 Level XIA/B Square 5M
Burial Type: Loose burial
Relative Age: Infant/Child

Grave Goods:
records missing

Burial 273 Level XIA/B Square 5M
Burial Type: Vessel burial
Relative Age: Infant/Child

Grave Goods:
5-1666   unrecorded   1 painted ceramic pot*

Burial 274 Level XIA/B Square 5M
Burial Type: Vessel burial with vessel cover
Relative Age: Infant/Child

Grave Goods:
none   unrecorded   1 spouted ceramic pot*
none   unrecorded   1 incomplete cooking pot*

Burial 275 Level XIA/B Square 6M
  Burial Type: Loose burial
  Relative Ave: Child (ca. 2 years old)

  Grave Goods:
  no grave goods

Burial 276-A Level XIA/B Square 5M
  Burial Type: Vessel burial
  Relative Age: Infant/Child

  Grave Goods:
  none   unrecorded   1 ceramic vessel*

Burial 276-B Level XIA/B Square 5M
  Burial Type: Loose burial
  Relative Age: Infant/Child

  Grave Goods:
  no grave goods

Burial 278 Level XI/XA Square 8O
  Burial Type: Loose burial
  Relative Age: Infant

  Grave Goods:
  no grave goods

Burial 290-A Level XI/XA Square 7K
  Burial Type: Vessel burial
  Relative Ave: Child

  Grave Goods:
  none   unrecorded   1 large ceramic jar sherd*

Burial 315 Level XI/XA Square 4J
  Burial Type: Vessel burial with vessel cover
  Relative Age: Infant

  Grave Goods:
  5-1756   unrecorded   1 ceramic bowl*
  none   discard   1 ceramic dish*
  none   discard   beads

Burial 318 Level XI/XA Square 4J
  Burial Type: Loose burial
  Relative Age: Infant

  Grave Goods:
  none   unrecorded   1 small stone acorn

Burial 325 Level XIA/B Square 3O
  Burial Type: Vessel burial
  Relative Age: Infant/Child

  Grave Goods:
  5-1766   Baghdad   1 ceramic vessel*

Burial 36-002 Level XIA/B Square 5Q
  Burial Type: Vessel burial with stone cover
  Relative Age: Child

  Grave Goods:
  6-17   unrecorded   1 painted ceramic jar*

Burial 36-003 Level XIA/B Square
  Burial Type: Vessel burial with vessel cover
  Relative Age: Infant

  Grave Goods:
  none   unrecorded   1 ceramic vessel*
  none   unrecorded   1 ceramic vessel*

Burial 36-004 Level XIA/B Square 4Q
  Burial Type: Vessel burial
  Relative Age: Infant

  Grave Goods:
  6-61   unrecorded   1 ceramic vessel*

Burial 36-005 Level XIA/B Square 4S
  Burial Type: Vessel burial
  Relative Age: Infant

  Grave Goods:
  6-41   unrecorded   1 ceramic jar*

Burial 36-006 Level XIA/B Square 4Q
  Burial Type: Unrecorded
  Relative Age: Infant

  Grave Goods:
  6-28   37-16-193   186 small white ring beads

Burial 36-007 Level XIA/B Square 4Q
  Burial Type: Vessel burial with vessel cover
  Relative Age: Infant (c. 1 year old)

  Grave Goods:
  6-18-a   discard   1 ceramic vessel*
  6-18-b   37-16-112   1 painted red ware vessel*

Burial 36-008 Level XIA/B Square 5Q
  Burial Type: Vessel burial with vessel cover
  Relative Age: Infant

  Grave Goods:
  6-19   unrecorded   1 ceramic jar*
  6-38   Baghdad   1 spouted brown ware pot*

Burial 36-009 Level XIA/B Square 5Q
  Burial Type: Vessel burial with vessel cover
  Relative Age: Possible Child

  Grave Goods:
  6-37   unrecorded   1 ceramic jar*
  6-45   Baghdad   1 mottled black and brown
                          slipped black ware pot*

Burial 36-010 Level XIA/B Square 5Q
  Burial Type: Vessel burial with sherd cover
  Relative Age: Uncertain

Grave Goods:

6-34	unrecorded	1	ceramic sherd*
6-35	37-16-109	1	green ware bowl*

Burial 36-011 Level XIA/B Square 4S
Burial Type: Vessel burial
Relative Age: Infant

Grave Goods:

none   discard   1 red ware jar*

Burial 36-013 Level X Square 7Q
Burial Type: Libn burial with libn cover
Relative Age: Youth/Adult

Grave Goods:

6-48-a	37-16-14	1	mother of pearl triangular pendant
6-48-b	unrecorded	1	bead
none	none		reed matting*

Discussion:

The bead and pendant were found at the neck of the skeleton.

Burial 36-014 Level X Square 8Q
Burial Type: Libn and pisé burial with pisé cover
Relative Ave: Child

Grave Goods:

none   none   reed matting*

Burial 36-015 Level XIA/B Square 5Q
Burial Type: Vessel burial with vessel cover
Relative Age: Infant

Grave Goods:

6-62	unrecorded	1	green-gray ware vessel*
none	discard	1	ceramic vessel*

Burial 36-016 Level X Square 8O
Burial Type: Loose burial
Relative Ave: Child (3–4 years old)

Grave Goods:

6-57   37-16-28   56 white paste ring beads

Discussion:

The beads were found at the neck of the skeleton.

Burial 36-017 Level XIA/B Square 5Q
Burial Type: Pisé burial
Relative Age: Adult

Grave Goods:

no grave goods

Burial 36-019 Level XIA/B Square 5Q
Burial Type: Vessel burial
Relative Age: Adult

Grave Goods:

none   unrecorded   1 ceramic vessel*

Burial 36-020 Level X Square 8Q
Burial Type: Loose burial
Relative Ave: Child (c. 6 years old)

Grave Goods:

6-64-a	Baghdad		white beads
6-64-b	Baghdad		black stone beads
6-64A-a	unrecorded	1	carnelian bead
6-64A-b	unrecorded	1	gold bead

Discussion:

The white and black beads were found at the ankles and wrists of the skeleton. The gold and carnelian beads were located at the neck.

Burial 36-022 Level XIA/B Square 5M
Burial Type: Loose burial
Relative Age: Uncertain

Grave Goods:

none   unrecorded   1 ceramic bowl

Discussion:

The bowl was in the right hand and held at the chest.

Burial 36-026 Level X Square 8O
Burial Type: Cist with stone cover
Relative Ave: Child

Grave Goods:

none	unrecorded	1	marble bead
none	none		reed matting*

Discussion:

The bead was found on the chest of the skeleton.

Burial 36-027 Level XI/XA Square 8Q
Burial Type: Libn and stone burial with libn cover
Relative Ave: Child

Grave Goods:

6-147-a	unrecorded		white paste beads
6-147-b	unrecorded	1	carnelian bead
6-148-a	37-16-49	2	white ring beads
6-148-b	37-16-49	960	cowrie shells

Burial 36-030 Level XI/XA Square 8O
Burial Type: Libn burial
Relative Age: Infant or Child

Grave Goods:

none   none   reed matting*

Burial 36-031 Level X Square 8O
Burial Type: Loose burial
Relative Age: Infant/Child

Grave Goods:

no grave goods

Burial 36-032 Level XI/XA Square 4J
Burial Type: Libn burial with corbeled libn cover
Relative Age: Infant

Grave Goods:

no grave goods

Burial 36-034 Level X Square 7K
Burial Type: Libn burial with wood floor or coffin
and pisé cover
Relative Ave: Child

Grave Goods:

6-193-a	Baghdad	c.5046	ring and cylinder beads
6-193-b	37-16-46	267	small white paste carinated beads
6-193-c	37-16-46	11	white shell barrel beads
6-193-d	37-16-46	202	obsidian ring beads
6-193-e	37-16-46	14	obsidian carinated beads
6-193-f	37-16-46	14	obsidian roughed surface beads
6-193-g	37-16-46	47	grey stone ring beads
6-193-h	37-16-46	1	carnelian roughed surface bead
6-193-i	37-16-46	48	dentalia shells
6-193-j	37-16-47	c.900	white and black paste ring beads
6-193-k	37-16-48	c.2000	ring beads

Discussion:

The small white paste carinated beads (6-193-b)
show faint traces of a blue coat that has since worn
away. The beads were found at the head, neck,
wrists, fingers and waist of the skeleton. The beads
from the area of the waist formed a herringbone
pattern.

Burial 36-035 Level X Square 7K
Burial Type: Pisé burial
Relative Ave: Child

Grave Goods:

none	none	reed matting*

Burial 36-036 Levels VIII/IX (VIIIA–C) Square 7J
Burial Type: Libn burial with wood cover
Relative Age: Infant

Grave Goods:

6-192-g	lost	white limestone cylinder beads

6-192-c	lost		black stone beads
6-192-a	lost	1	black stone pendant
6-192-b	lost		carnelian beads
6-192-d	lost		jadeite beads
6-192-f	lost		white marble beads
6-192-e	lost		pink stone beads
none	none		woven textile*
none	none		reed matting*

Burial 36-037-A Level X Square 8K
Burial Type: Loose burial
Relative Age: Uncertain

Grave Goods:

no grave goods

Burial 36-037-B Level X Square 8K
Burial Type: Loose burial
Relative Age: Uncertain

Grave Goods:

no grave goods

Burial 36-038 Level XI/XA Square 5J
Burial Type: Vessel burial
Relative Age: Infant

Grave Goods:

none	lost	1	red ware jar*

Burial 36-039-A Level XI/XA Square 5J
Burial Type: Pisé burial with libn cover
Relative Age: Youth

Grave Goods:

no grave goods

Burial 36-039-B Level XI/XA Square 5J
Burial Type: Pisé burial with libn cover
Relative Ave: Child

Grave Goods:

no grave goods

Burial 36-040 Level X Square 7Q
Burial Type: Libn burial
Relative Age: Infant

Grave Goods:

6-197-a	37-16-45	130	small white ring beads
6-197-b	37-16-45	46	small brown paste barrel beads
6-197-c	37-16-45	1	dentalium shell
none	none		woven textile*

Discussion:

The beads were found at one of the wrists of the the
skeleton.

Burial 36-041 Level XI/XA Square 5J
  Burial Type: Vessel burial
  Relative Age: Infant

Grave Goods:

| none | unrecorded | 12 | beads |
| none | unrecorded | 1 | incomplete ceramic pot* |

Burial 36-042 Level XI/XA Square 5J
  Burial Type: Libn burial
  Relative Age: Infant or Child

Grave Goods:

no grave goods

Burial 36-043 Level XIA/B Square 5J
  Burial Type: Libn burial
  Relative Age: Infant or Child

Grave Goods:

no grave goods

Burial 36-044 Level X Square 7Q
  Burial Type: Double sidewall burial with libn cover
  Relative Ave: Child

Grave Goods:

| none | none | woven textile* |

Burial 36-046 Level XI/XA Square 5J
  Burial Type: Libn burial
  Relative Age: Infant or Child

Grave Goods:

| none | none | reed matting* |

Burial 36-047 Level X Square 7Q
  Burial Type: Loose burial with libn cover
  Relative Age: Infant

Grave Goods:

| none | none | reed matting* |

Burial 36-048 Level XI/XA Square 5J
  Burial Type: Cist with pisé and sherd cover
  Relative Ave: Child

Grave Goods:

no grave goods

Burial 36-051 Level XIA/B Square 5Q
  Burial Type: Vessel burial
  Relative Age: Possible Infant

Grave Goods:

| 6-235 | Baghdad | 1 | green slipped brown ware pot* |

Burial 36-052 Level XI/XA Square 5J
  Burial Type: Vessel burial
  Relative Age: Infant

Grave Goods:

| none | unrecorded | 1 | ceramic vessel* |

Burial 36-057 Level XIA/B Square 6M
  Burial Type: Vessel burial
  Relative Age: Possible Infant

Grave Goods:

| 6-254 | Baghdad | 1 | wet-smoothed buff ware jar |

Burial 36-058 Level XIA/B Square 5M
  Burial Type: Vessel burial with vessel cover
  Relative Age: Infant

Grave Goods:

| none | unrecorded | 1 | ceramic vessel* |
| none | unrecorded | 1 | ceramic bowl* |

Burial 36-060 Level XIA/B Square 5M
  Burial Type: Libn and stone burial with libn cover
  Relative Ave: Child

Grave Goods:

6-258	Baghdad	1	small brown ware jar
6-330A	Baghdad	3075	beads
6-330B-a	37-16-191	3300	ring beads
6-330B-b	37-16-191	1	yellow paste rosette pendant
6-330C	37-16-192	1	ivory rosette ornament
none	none		reed matting*

Discussion:

The jar was held in both hands and located above the head of the skeleton. The beads were found at the neck and wrists of the skeleton.

Burial 36-062 Level XIA/B Square 5M
  Burial Type: Vessel burial with vessel cover
  Relative Age: possible infant

Grave Goods:

| 6-251 | 37-16-110 | 1 | green slipped red ware pot* |
| 6-260 | unrecorded | 1 | ceramic vessel* |

Burial 36-068 Level XI/XA Square 5M
  Burial Type: Libn burial
  Relative Age: Uncertain

Grave Goods:

| 6-267 | Baghdad | 1 | brown ware pot |

Discussion:
This burial seems to have been disturbed and robbed as evidenced by the broken and scattered nature of the pot.

Burial 36-074 Level XIA/B Square 5K
    Burial Type: Libn burial
    Relative Age: Adult

    Grave Goods:
    no grave goods

Burial 36-077 Level XIA/B Square 6K
    Burial Type: Vessel burial
    Relative Age: Infant

    Grave Goods:
    6-279   Baghdad   1 red slipped brown
                                     ware jar*
    none   unrecorded   beads

Burial 36-079 Level X Square 7Q
    Burial Type: Vessel burial
    Relative Age: Infant

    Grave Goods:
    none   unrecorded   1 ceramic vessel*

Burial 36-080 Level XI/XA Square 4K
    Burial Type: Pisé burial
    Relative Ave: Child

    Grave Goods:
    no grave goods

    Discussion:
    This is a disturbed burial.

Burial 36-081 Level XI/XA Square 4J
    Burial Type: Pisé burial
    Relative Age: Adult

    Grave Goods:
    no grave goods

Burial 36-082 Level XIA/B Square 3M
    Burial Type: Vessel burial
    Relative Age: Infant

    Grave Goods:
    none   Unrecorded   4 Beads
    6-290   unrecorded   1 large ceramic jar*

Burial 36-083 Level XI/XA Square 4J
    Burial Type: Vessel burial with vessel cover
    Relative Ave: Child

    Grave Goods:
    none   unrecorded   1 ceramic vessel*
    none   unrecorded   1 ceramic vessel*

Burial 36-084 Level XI/XA Square 5K
    Burial Type: Vessel burial with vessel cover
    Relative Ave: Child

    Grave Goods:
    none   unrecorded   1 ceramic vessel*
    none   unrecorded   1 ceramic vessel*

Burial 36-086 Level XI/XA Square 4J
    Burial Type: Semi circular libn burial with stone
    cover
    Relative Age: Child

    Grave Goods:
    no grave goods

Burial 36-087 Level XIA/B Square 3O
    Burial Type: Pisé burial
    Relative Age: Adult

    Grave Goods:
    no grave goods

Burial 36-088 Level XI/XA Square 5J
    Burial Type: Vessel burial with vessel cover
    Relative Age: Infant

    Grave Goods:
    none   unrecorded   beads
    none   unrecorded   1 ceramic vessel*
    none   unrecorded   1 ceramic vessel*

Burial 36-089 Level XI/XA Square 5J
    Burial Type: Vessel burial
    Relative Age: Infant

    Grave Goods:
    none   unrecorded   1 ceramic vessel*

Burial 36-090 Level XIA/B Square 5K
    Burial Type: Libn burial
    Relative Age: Uncertain

    Grave Goods:
    6-277   unrecorded   1 ceramic bowl

Burial 36-091 Level XIA/B Square 3M
    Burial Type: Vessel burial
    Relative Age: Child

    Grave Goods:
    none   discard   1 large green ware jar*

Burial 36-100 Level XI/XA Square 4K
  Burial Type: Libn burial
  Relative Age: Child

  Grave Goods:

  none   unrecorded   paste beads

  Discussion:

  The beads were found in the right hand of the skeleton.

Burial 36-104 Level XI/XA Square 3K/3M
  Burial Type: Libn burial
  Relative Age: Adult

  Grave Goods:

  none   unrecorded   1 bead
  6-281   Baghdad   1 painted wet-smoothed
                             green ware pot
  6-284   37-16-217   1 brown slipped grey ware
                             bowl

  Discussion:

  This burial had been disturbed and robbed as evidenced by the broken and scattered nature of the vessels. It appears as if the vessels were originally placed in front of the face of the skeleton.

Burial 36-105 Level XI/XA Square 5J
  Burial Type: Libn burial
  Relative Age: Uncertain

  Grave Goods:

  none   unrecorded   1 ceramic bowl

  Discussion:

  The bowl was located at the feet of the skeleton.

Burial 36-110 Level XI/XA Square 3M
  Burial Type: Libn burial
  Relative Age: Adult

  Grave Goods:

  6-297   Baghdad   1 gray-black steatite stamp
                             seal
  6-307   37-16-95   1 small buff ware jar

Burial 36-111 Level XI/XA Square 5J
  Burial Type: Libn burial
  Relative Age: Probably an adult

  Grave Goods:

  none unrecorded   1 small buff ware bowl

Burial 36-120 Level XIA/B Square 5J
  Burial Type: Libn burial
  Relative Age: Adult

  Grave Goods:

  no grave goods

Burial 36-122 Level XIA/B Square 5J
  Burial Type: Libn burial
  Relative Age: Adult

  Grave Goods:

  no grave goods

Burial 36-129 Level XI/XA Square 7S
  Burial Type: Vessel burial
  Relative Age: Adult (old age)

  Grave Goods:

  6-326   Baghdad   1 small double rimmed
                             gray slipped brown ware
                             pot
  none   unrecorded   1 ceramic vessel*
  none   unrecorded   1 black stamp (seal or
                             sealing?)

Burial 36-134 Level XIA/B Square 4J
  Burial Type: Libn burial
  Relative Age: Adult

  Grave Goods:

  6-363   Baghdad   1 white paste stamp seal

  Discussion:

  The stamp seal was found at the left shoulder of the skeleton.

Burial 36-135 Level XI/XA Square 5G
  Burial Type: Libn burial
  Relative Age: Adult

  Grave Goods:

  6-376   unrecorded   1 copper double spiral
                             pendant
  6-377   37-16-199   1 obsidian discoid
                             pendant
  none   unrecorded   1 gray ware vessel

  Discussion:

  The bronze and obsidian pendants were found at the throat of the skeleton. The vessel was located near the hip.

Burial 36-137 Level XI/XA Square 6G
  Burial Type: Libn burial
  Relative Age: Child

  Grave Goods:

  none   unrecorded paste beads

  Discussion:

  The beads were found at the wrists of the skeleton.

Burial 36-144 Level XI/XA Square 6J
  Burial Type: Libn burial
  Relative Age: Child

Grave Goods:

6-370   Baghdad   650 hard white paste ring
                          beads

Discussion:

The beads were found near the left hand of the skeleton.

Burial 36-146 Level XI/XA Square 4G
    Burial Type: Libn burial
    Relative Age: Uncertain

    Grave Goods:
    6-620   Baghdad   1 wet smoothed brown ware
                            bowl

Burial 36-168 Level XI/XA Square 11M
    Burial Type: Loose burial
    Relative Age: Infant

    Grave Goods:
    none   unrecorded   very small beads

Burial 36-171 Level XIA/B Square 11M
    Burial Type: Vessel burial with vessel cover
    Relative Age: Child

    Grave Goods:
    6-590   Baghdad   1 bone pipe or whistle
    none   unrecorded   1 ceramic vessel*
    none   unrecorded   1 ceramic vessel*

Burial 7-001 Level X Square 11M
    Burial Type: Loose burial
    Relative Age: Adult

    Grave Goods:
    no grave goods

Burial 7-005 Level X Square 11M
    Burial Type: Vessel burial
    Relative Ave: Child (3–4 years old)

    Grave Goods:
    none   unrecorded   1 rough brown ware bowl*

Burial 7-007 Levels VIII/IX (VIIIC, IX) Square 9M
    Burial Type: Sidewall burial
    Relative Age: Infant

    Grave Goods:
    no grave goods

Burial 7-009 Level X Square 9M
    Burial Type: Libn burial
    Relative Ave: Child (4–5 years old)

    Grave Goods:
    none   unrecorded   4 small white paste beads
    none   none   reed matting*

Burial 7-010 Level XI/XA Square 9M
    Burial Type: Loose burial
    Relative Ave: Child (4–5 years old)

    Grave Goods:
    none   none   reed matting*

Burial 7-012 Level XI/XA Square 8M
    Burial Type: Loose burial
    Relative Ave: Child (1–2 years old)

    Grave Goods:
    none   none   reed matting*

Burial 7-014 Level XI/XA Square 9M
    Burial Type: Loose burial
    Relative Age: Child (5–6 years old)

    Grave Goods:
    none   none   reed matting*

Burial 7-015 Level XI/XA Square 10M
    Burial Type: Loose burial
    Relative Age: Adult (young age)

    Grave Goods:
    none   none   reed matting*

Burial 7-018 Level XI/XA Square 11-M
    Burial Type: Loose burial
    Relative Age: Youth (14–15 years old)

    Grave Goods:
    none   none   reed matting*

Burial 7-023 Level XI/XA Square 9M
    Burial Type: Vessel burial
    Relative Age: Infant

    Grave Goods:
    none   unrecorded   1 ceramic vessel*

Burial 7-026 Level XIA/B Square 8M
    Burial Type: Sidewall burial
    Relative Age: Adult

    Grave Goods:
    none   unrecorded   1 paste seal

Burial 7-028 Level XIA/B Square 9M
    Burial Type: Vessel burial with sherd cover
    Relative Age: Infant

    Grave Goods:
    none   unrecorded   1 broken ceramic vessel*
    none   unrecorded   ceramic sherds*

Burial 7-029 Level XIA/B Square 8M
    Burial Type: Loose burial
    Relative Age: Child

Grave Goods:

no grave goods

Burial 7-030 Level XIA/B Square 8M
    Burial Type: Sidewall burial
    Relative Age: Adult

    Grave Goods:

    no grave goods

Burial A Levels VIII/IX (VIIIA–C, IX) Square 10Q
    Burial Type: Libn burial
    Relative Age: Infant

    Grave Goods:

    none   unrecorded   shell beads
    none   unrecorded   black stone beads
    none   unrecorded   carnelian beads

Burial AA I Levels VIII/IX (VIIIA–C, IX) Square 9Q
    Burial Type: Vessel burial with vessel cover
    Relative Age: Infant

    Grave Goods:

    none   unrecorded   1 flat gray ware bowl*
    none   unrecorded   1 ceramic vessel*
    none   unrecorded   1 obsidian blade

Burial AA II Levels VIII/IX (VIIIA–C, IX) Square 9Q
    Burial Type: Vessel burial with vessel cover
    Relative Age: Infant

    Grave Goods:

    none   unrecorded   1 bowl*
    none   unrecorded   1 ceramic vessel*
    none   unrecorded   1 ceramic vessel*
    none   unrecorded   1 ceramic spindle whorl
    none   unrecorded   1 small copper fragment

Burial B Levels VIII/IX (IX) Square 9O
    Burial Type: Libn burial
    Relative Age: Uncertain

    Grave Goods:

    none   unrecorded   1 alabaster jar

Burial C Levels VIII/IX (VIIIC, IX) Square 7M
    Burial Type: Libn burial
    Relative Age: Infant

    Grave Goods:

    3-432-a   33-3-219   1 lapis acorn bead
    3-432-b   33-3-219   1 lapis animal bead
    3-432-c   33-3-219   1 lapis square bead
    3-432-d   33-3-219   1 crystal ring bead

Burial CC I Levels VIII/IX (VIIIA–C) Square 7J
    Burial Type: Vessel burial
    Relative Age: Infant

    Grave Goods:

    none   unrecorded   1 ceramic vessel*

Burial CC II Levels VIII/IX (VIIIA–C, IX) Square 7J
    Burial Type: Vessel burial
    Relative Age: Infant

    Grave Goods:

    none   unrecorded   1 ceramic vessel*

Burial D Levels VIII/IX (IX) Square 6-M
    Burial Type: Libn burial
    Relative Age: Uncertain

    Grave Goods:

    no grave goods

Burial E Levels VIII/IX (VIIIA–C, IX) Square 6O
    Burial Type: Libn burial
    Relative Age: Uncertain

    Grave Goods:

    no grave goods

Burial EE Level X Square 10O
    Burial Type: Loose burial
    Relative Ave: Child

    Grave Goods:

    no grave goods

Burial FF Levels VIII/IX (VIIIA–C, IX) Square 9O
    Burial Type: Vessel burial
    Relative Age: Infant/Child

    Grave Goods:

    none   unrecorded   1 large ceramic sherd*

Burial GG Levels VIII/IX (VIIIB–C, IX) Square 10O
    Burial Type: Vessel burial
    Relative Age: Infant/Child

    Grave Goods:

    none   unrecorded   1 ceramic bowl*
    none   unrecorded   beads

Burial HH Levels VIII/IX (VIIIB–C, IX) Square 9O
    Burial Type: Vessel burial
    Relative Age: Infant/Child

    Grave Goods:

    none   unrecorded   1 ceramic vessel*

Burial JJ Levels VIII/IX (VIIIA–C, IX) Square 10M
  Burial Type: Vessel burial
  Relative Ave: Child

  Grave Goods:
  none   unrecorded   limestone beads
  none   unrecorded   other types of stone
                         beads
  none   unrecorded   1 copper bead
  none   unrecorded   1 ceramic vessel*

Burial KK Levels VIII/IX (VIIIA–C, IX) Square 10O
  Burial Type: Loose burial
  Relative Ave: Child

  Grave Goods:
  none   unrecorded   small white cylindrical
                         beads
  none   none   reed matting*

Catalogue Key

Artifacts from Occupation Levels XII-VIII

Column	Content
1	Catalogue number
2	Field registry number (1-5000, 3-, 4-, 5-, 6-, 7- x-none means season x, no field designation)
3	Location (Baghdad and IM ####, Iraq Museum, 31-52-###, 32-21-###, 33-3-###, 35-10-###, 36-6-###, 37-16-####, phila no#, University of Pennsylvania Museum; Dropsie = Center for Judaic and Ancient Near Eastern Studies, University of Pennsylvania, Discarded.)
4	Chit number (not applicable to level VIII)
5	Level (for levels XII, XIAB, XI/XA, left number is original assignment from registry, the right is my level assignment (see chapter 3)
6	Artifact type
7	Material
8	Square assignment from registry books
9	Square of object according to the standard square nomenclature of Tobler 1950.
10	Sub-square designation (see chapter 2).
11–13	Measurements (L = length, W = width, T = thickness, D = diameter, H = height, RD = rim diameter, BD = base diameter, D = body diameter, SP = spout length.
14	Elevation from mound base.
15	Chit information ("MR"- additional information, unknown = no information).
16–20	Extra information (for pottery, HM = handmade, WM = wheelmade, painted designs; TM = tournette finished); Seal = seal design dimensions as opposed to the remaining sealing's or seal's dimensions, function (seal or what the sealing was pressed on), seal design, where they are seals, seal shape; for lithics left edge, right edge, numbers are edge angles.

Note: in Plates seals are drawn in box, sealings not.

Level XII

1	2	3	4	5	6	7	8	9	10	11	12
	Bone	item									
1.	4-1189	35-10-245	0796	XII XII	spatula	bone	10P	4M	f2	L208	W30
2.	4-1226	35-10-244	0887	XII XII	awl	bone	10P	4M	f1	L75	W12
3.	5-1498	36-6-1951	0237	XIA XII	awl	bone	8N	5Q	c8	L65	W16
4.	5-1560	36-6-281a	1397	XII XII	spatula	bone	11P	4K	f 8/9	L228	W20
5.	5-1647	Baghdad	1456	XII XII	spatula	bone	9M	6O	i9	L141	W23
6.	5-1672	36-6-280	1515	XII XII	awl	bone	9N	5O	i2	L106	ina
7.	5-none	unknown	1261	XIA XII	spatula	bone	8N	5Q	i/j7/8	none	none
8.	6-021	37-16-188	1621	XII XII	flute	bone	5Q	5Q	h8	L105	W25
9.	6-262	37-16-187	1873	XII XII	pipe	bone	4J	4J	d9	L106	W22
10.	6-none	37-16-190	none	XII XII	handle	bone	5K	5K	none	L125	W20
11.	6-none	unknown	1758	XII XII	awl	bone	5K	5K	c5/6	none	none
12.	6-none	unknown	1680	XII XII	needle	bone	5K	5K	g4	none	none
13.	6-109	37-16-189	1738	XII XII	awl	bone	4K	4K	f8	L128	D19
		Clay	item								
14.	4-1124	35-10-194	0835	XII XII	ladle	clay	9P	4O	c6	L130	W155
15.	4-1153	35-10-218	0772	XII XII	none	clay	10P	4M	a/b1/2	L63	W48
16.	4-1224	Baghdad	0881	XII XII	spout	clay	10P	4M	j5	none	none
17.	4-none	unknown	0893	XII XII	wall nail	clay	10P ?	4M	i4	none	none
18.	4-none	unknown	0888	XII XII	object	clay	10N	5M	i4	none	none
19.	4-none	unknown	0999	XII XII	wall nail	clay	9N	5O	d9	none	none
20.	4-none	unknown	0996	XII XII	game piece	clay	8N	5Q	d4	none	none
21.	4-none	unknown	0884	XII XII	knuckle	clay	9M	6O	d9	none	none
22.	6-074	37-16-53	none	XII XII	loom	clay	4K	4K	none	H102	W72
23.	6-146	lost	none	XII XII	loom base	clay	4K	4K	none	H147	W260
24.	6-280	Discarded	1883	XII XII	peg	green ware	3K	3K	e6	L161	D85
25.	4-none	unknown	0854	XII XII	game pieces	clay	9N	5O	c8	none	none
26.	4-none	unknown	0963	XII XII	game pieces	unknown	9P	4O	a10	none	none
27.	4-0970	35-10-216	0592	XII XII	hut statue	ceramic	9N	5O	j5	H80	BD65
28.	4-none	Discarded	0902	XII XII	unknown	clay ?	10M	6M	h/i 1	none	none
29.	4-none	unknown	0587	XII XII	quadruped	clay ?	8M	6Q	none	none	none
30.	5-1510	36-6-242a	1355	XII XII	hut statue	ceramic	7N	5S	d/e8/9	W160	T30
31.	5-1566	Baghdad	1405	XII XII	human	terracotta	8M	6Q	e8	H52	none
32.	5-none	36-6-254	none	XII XII	animal	clay	9M	6O	none	H29	L40
33.	5-none	unknown	1437	XII XII	animal	none	9M	6O	e/f5/6	none	none
34.	6-003	37-16-142	1603	XII XII	animal	clay	5Q	5Q	h8	L50	H35
35.	6-031	Baghdad	1636	XII XII	animal	terracotta	5S	5S	g4	L37	H20
36.	6-none	37-16-141	none	XII XII	ram	clay	5K	5K	none	H39	L56
37.	6-none	unknown	4135	XII XII	animal	clay	5K	5K	a10	none	none
38.	5-1646	Baghdad	1427	XII XII	foot	stone	7M	6S	e/f 7	L240	W102
		Ground	stone								
39.	4-0714	Baghdad	0294	XIA XII	hammer	limestone	8P	4Q	h8	L70	none
40.	4-0715	Baghdad	0295	XIA XII	door socket	stone	8P	4Q	h8	D200	T90
41.	4-0903	Baghdad	0406	XII XII	celt	stone	9P	4O	i2	L32	D65
42.	4-1136	35-10-242	0839	XII XII	macehead	red stone	9P	4O	g/h10	none	none
43.	4-1156	Discarded	0955	XII XII	celt	stone	10P	4M	d1	none	none
44.	4-1160	Baghdad	0758	XII XII	implement	stone	9P	4O	c10	none	none
45.	4-1173	Baghdad	0978	XII XII	celt	stone	10P	4M	c8	none	none
46.	4-1174	Baghdad	0975	XII XII	celt	stone	10P	4M	g6	none	none
47.	4-1178	35-10-236	0974	XII XII	celt	stone	9N	5O	e7	L38	W40
48.	4-1184	35-10-235	0857	XII XII	celt	stone	10P	4M	b6	L51	W45
49.	4-1223	35-10-240	0886	XII XII	celt	stone	10P	4M	none	L45	W26
50.	4-none	36-6-274	0848	XII XII	ballista	white marble	9P	4O	h10	D19	none
51	4-none	unknown	0366	XII XII	hammer	stone	8P	4Q	f10	none	none
52.	4-none	unknown	0234	XIA XII	mortar	stone	8N	4Q	i 9/10	none	none
53.	4-none	unknown	0558	XII XII	weight	stone	8N	5Q	b2	none	none
54.	5-1450	36-6-183	1215	XIA XII	celt	stone	8N	5Q	i2	L54	W36
55.	5-1453	Baghdad	1217	XIA XII	hammer	steatite	8N	5Q	i/j 3	L115	W49
56.	5-1461	Baghdad	1222	XIA XII	small celt	stone	7N	5S	none	L34	W26
57.	5-1462	Baghdad	1222	XIA XII	palette	stone	7N	5S	none	L79	W57
58.	5-1478	36-6-271	1229	XII ? XII	celt	stone	8N	5Q	b 3/4	L42	W42
59.	5-1497	36-6-188	1238	XIA XII	grinding	stone	8N	5Q	a8	L50	W26
60.	5-1515	36-6-272	1250	XIIX II	celt	stone	8N	5Q	f/g 5	L47	W11
61.	5-1522	Baghdad	1274	XII XII	palette	stone	11P	4K	h4	L104	W77
62.	5-1554	Baghdad	1394	XII XII	macehead	stone	8P	4Q	e6	H46	D58
63.	5-1562	Baghdad	1400	XII XII	celt	stone	8M	6Q	i3	L50	W36

·

13	14	15	16	17	18	19
T3.5	7.90	unknown				
T6	8.50	unknown				
ina	8.78	on pavement in ordinary refuse				
ina	8.30	E corner on pavement				
		White Room II				
ina	7.50	unknown				
ina	7.90	from a wall of XII				
none	8.73	other side of wall from grave 192				
ina	0.00	in dirt				
T14	0.00	unknown				
ina	0.00	unknown				
none	0.00	unknown				
none	0.00	on floor				
ina	0.00	unknown				
T26	8.20	in White Room debris				
T5	8.48	unknown				
none	8.50	strange context				
none	7.90	unknown				
ina	7.90	unknown		incised		
none	7.93	unknown				
none	8.47	unknown				
none	8.50	unknown				
ina	0.00	in "cult door" under XIA		cult object ?		
ina	0.00	unknown		like 6-59		
ina	0.00	unknown				
none	7.96	unknown				
none	8.43	unknown				
ina	8.91	unknown				
none	0.00	unknown				
none	8.36	under XI				
ina	8.48	on pavement near edge of tepe				
ina	8.24	unknown				
ina	0.00	unknown				
none	7.40	unknown				
ina	0.00	unknown				
ina	7.70	unknown				
ina	0.00	unknown				
none	0.00	unknown				
T147	7.97	below surface near wall				
ina	8.51	unknown				
ina	8.51	unknown				
ina	8.20	unknown				
none	7.93	in east door of White Room				
none	7.83	unknown				
none	8.42	room 37 south of White Room				
none	8.50	unknown				
none	8.80	unknown				
T18	8.00	unknown				
T21	8.57	unknown				
T11	8.90	unknown				
ina	7.93	White Room outside east door				
none	8.53	unknown				
none	9.20	40 cm above floor				
none	9.14	unknown				
ina	8.25	on pavement in corner of room				
none	8.25	on pavement in corner of room				
T14	8.39	unknown				
T13	8.39	unknown				
T13	7.99	in dark ash bearing deposit				
T14	8.78	on pavement no walls nearby				
T13	8.12	from pavement apparently XII				
T15	8.55	between two walls				
ina	8.38	under floor in small room near	White Room			
T17	8.44	on pavement in grayish refuse				

(*continues*)

Level XII   (continued)

1	2	3	4	5	6	7	8	9	10	11	12
64.	5-1563	Baghdad	1401	XII XII	celt	stone	9N	5O	h/i2/3	L37	W34
65.	5-1579	Baghdad	1413	XII XII	celt	stone	9N	4O	i 2/3	L28	W25
66.	5-1581	36-6-266	1414	XII XII	celt	stone	8N	5Q	i2	L41	W38
67.	5-1582	36-6-262	1414	XII XII	macehead	stone	8N	5Q	i2	H40	D60
68.	5-1589	36-6-264	1281	XII XII	celt	stone	9N	5O	g1	L83	W60
69.	5-1615	Baghdad	1337	XII XII	macehead	stone	7M	6S	c7	L36	D57
70.	5-1654	Baghdad	1441	XII XII	celt	stone	9R	3O	a/b3/4	L23	W31
71.	5-1655	36-6-270	1501	XII XII	celt	stone	11P	4K	i3	L35	W35
72.	5-1664	36-6-263	1459	XII XII	palette	stone	10P	4M	h2	L125	W79
73.	5-1707	36-6-268	1534	XII XII	celt	stone	11R	3K	a/b 10	L30	W25
74.	5-1724	Baghdad	1487	XII XII	hammer	stone	8N	5Q	j3	L66	W52
75.	5-1741	Baghdad	1544	XII XII	celt	stone	10R	3M	a 3/4	L46	W48
76.	5-none	36-6-267	1414	XII XII	celt	granite	8N	5Q	i2	L118	W42
77.	5-none	36-6-275	none	XII XII	ballista	gray marble	none	none	none	D23	none
78.	5-none	36-6-277	none	XII XII	game piece	white marble	8N	5Q	none	D23	T4
79.	5-none	unknown	1554	XII XII	celt	stone	9R	3O	c8	none	none
80.	5-none	unknown	1513	XII XII	large celt	stone	8P	4Q	none	none	none
81.	5-none	unknown	1439	XII XII	hammer	stone	8P	4Q	e/f 9	none	none
82.	6-013	Baghdad	1611	XII XII	celt	basalt	5Q	5Q	f4	L34	W34
83.	6-014	Baghdad	1611	XII XII	celt	basalt	5Q	5Q	f4	L34	W20
84.	6-022	Baghdad	1619	XII XII	celt	basalt	6O	6O	f 8/9	L63	W56
85.	6-023	37-16-173	1622	XII XII	celt	basalt	4Q	4Q	j8	L42	W25
86.	6-144	unknown	none	XII XII	palette	marble	5M	5M	none	L60	D94
87.	6-239	Baghdad	4131	XII XII	macehead	limestone	4J	4J	f2	H37	D55
88.	6-265	Baghdad	none	XII XII	macehead	marble	5K	5K	none	H35	D50
89.	6-272	Baghdad	none	XII XII	macehead	marble	5J	5J	none	H31	D60
90.	6-312	37-16-69	1929	XIA XII	macehead	marble	6J	6J	i9	H47	D53
91.	6-595	37-16-186	none	XII XII	weight	haematite	3J	3J	none	H14	D14
92.	6-602	37-16-179	none	XII XII	palette	red sandstone	11M	11M	none	L153	W45
93.	6-none	37-16-175	none	XII XII	celt	green granite	5K	5K	none	L51	W40
94.	6-none	37-16-176	none	XII XII	celt	green stone	4K	4K	none	L59	W71
95.	6-none	37-16-174	none	XII XII	celt	haemetite	5J	5J	none	L31	W40
96.	6-none	unknown	3161	XII XII	celts 3	stone	11M	11M	f1	none	none
97.	6-none	unknown	4299	XII ? XII	cylinder	stone	3J	3J	a10	none	none
98.	6-none	unknown	1884	XII XII	object	stone	4J	4J	e9	none	none
99.	6-none	unknown	1774	XII XII	slab	slate	4K	4K	d9	none	none
100.	6-none	unknown	1863	XII XII	sphere	alabaster	5J	5J	e5	none	none
101.	7-194	Baghdad	1846	XIA XII	kohl jar	steatite	8M	8M	g2	H42	W19
102.	7-230	38-13-36	2152	XII XII	celt	gray stone	8M	8M	d 1/2	L50	W26
103.	7-261	38-13-509	2058	XII XII	celt	gray stone	8M	8M	e/f 5/6	L30	W17
104.	7-262	Baghdad	2055	XII XII	celt	stone	9M	9M	e/f 7	L42	W33
105.	4-1222	phila no#	0874	XII XII	pestle	limestone	10P	4M	d8	none	none
106.	5-1408	Baghdad	1174	XII XII	celt	stone	11R	3K	b3	L45	W33

Jewelry

1	2	3	4	5	6	7	8	9	10	11	12
107.	4-0966	Baghdad	0582	XII XII	pear-shaped	stone	10P	4M	c5	none	none
108.	4-1138	35-10-248	0837	XII XII	pendant	steatite	9P	4O	c8	L15	W15
109.	4-1161	phila no#	0770	XII XII	pin/needle	bone	9N	5O	e/f6/7	none	none
110.	4-1163	Baghdad	0775	XII XII	button	stone	none	none	none	none	none
111.	4-1164	Baghdad	0774	XII XII	object	gold	9N	5O	i/j 9	none	none
112.	4-1168	35-10-255	0967	XII XII	button	stone	10P	4M	f6	L13	W11
113.	4-none	36-6-302	0957	XII XII	pendant	gray marble	10P	4M	d1	D16	T4
114.	4-none	Discarded	0858	XII XII	pin	copper	9N	5O	d10	none	none
115.	4-none	Discarded	0879	XII XII	pin	copper	9M	6O	f5	none	none
116.	4-none	Discarded	0520	XIA XII	cut gem	rock crystal	8M	6Q	j8	none	none
117.	4-none	unknown	0659	XII XII	bead	black stone	9P	4O	g2	none	none
118.	4-none	unknown	0551	XII XII	pendant	unknown	8P	4Q	d8	none	none
119.	4-none	unknown	0995	XII XII	bead	stone	9N	5O	b7	none	none
120.	4-none	unknown	0852	XII XII	pendant	stone	9N	5O	f4	none	none
121.	4-none	unknown	0853	XII XII	button	stone	9N	5O	d10	none	none
122.	5-1555	Baghdad	1276	XII XII	amulet	stone	11R	3K	b2	L15	W12
123.	5-1642	Baghdad	1434	XII XII	beads	stone	9P	4O	c 4/5	none	none
124.	5-1739	Baghdad	1542	XII XII	pendant	stone	12P	4J	j3	L22	D12
125.	5-none	36-6-278	none	XII XII	pin	steatite	7N	5S	none	L17	D8
126.	5-none	36-6-282	none	XII XII	pendant	steatite	none	none	none	L17	W12
127.	5-none	36-6-283	none	XII XII	bead	steatite	none	none	none	H10	L15

13	14	15	16	17	18	19
T16	7.92	unknown				
T12	7.90	on pavement XII outside				
		White Room				
T10	8.03	on pavement of small room				
ina	8.03	on pavement of small room				
T8	0.00	outside White Room complex				
ina	8.34	in debris inside outer wall of tepe				
T12	7.80	unknown				
T11	8.10	unknown				
T15	0.00	from base of White Room walls				
T10	8.82	unknown				
T29	0.00	immediately below wall near grave				
T16	8.81	unknown				
ina	8.03	on pavement of small room				
ina	0.00	unknown				
ina	0.00	unknown				
none	7.83	unknown				
none	7.80	unknown				
none	7.95	on floor under NW wall				
		White Room				
T13	0.00	in fill				
T14	0.00	loose in fill				
T23	0.00	unknown				
T13	0.00	unknown				
ina	0.00	unknown				
ina	0.00	unknown				
ina	0.00	unknown				
ina	0.00	unknown				
ina	0.00	unknown				
ina	0.00	unknown				
T20	0.00	unknown				
none	0.00	unknown				
T20	0.00	unknown				
none	0.00	unknown				
none	0.00	unknown				
none	0.00	found on edge 3J marker				
none	0.00	unknown	with bored hole			
none	0.00	unknown				
none	0.00	unknown				
none	8.00	at base of Round House				
T13	8.00	unknown				
ina	8.00	in black refuse				
ina	7.80	in black refuse				
none	7.90	unknown				
T9	8.481	a little above floor				
none	8.91	well below XI structures				
T4	7.93	on floor White Room				
none	8.48 2/	2 m outside SW wall of White Room				
none	0.002/	unknown				
none	7.90	outside south door of White Room				
T6	8.33	unknown				
ina	7.83	unknown				
none	8.50	unknown				
none	8.50	unknown				
none	8.421	unknown				
none	8.19	unknown				
none	8.42	unknown				
none	8.00	unknown				
none	7.93	unknown				
none	8.50	unknown				
T7	7.96	on floor of small room with celt				
none	7.85	just under NW wall of White Room				
ina	8.06	unknown				
ina	0.00	unknown	D at head			
ina	0.00	unknown				
ina	0.00	unknown	duck shaped			

(*continues*)

Level XII   (continued)

1	2	3	4	5	6	7	8	9	10	11	12
128.	5-none	36-6-284	none	XII XII	beads 5	obsidian	none	none	none	none	none
129.	5-none	36-6-285	none	XII XII	beads 6	paste shell	none	none	none	D7	to
130.	5-none	36-6-286	none	XII XII	spreader	shell	none	none	none	L18	W8
131.	5-none	36-6-290	none	XII XII	amulet	gray marble	none	none	none	D13	T7
132.	5-none	36-6-292	none	XII XII	amulet	agate	none	none	none	H9	W19
133.	6-098	Baghdad	1735	XII XII	bead	bitumen	4J	4J	c3	H10	D21
134.	6-099	Baghdad	1733	XII XII	amulet	diorite ?	none	none	none	L28	W20
135.	6-116	37-16-206	1745	XII XII	beads 11	1 stone & paste	4J	4J	d1	44850	D13
136.	6-117	37-16-206	1747	XII XII	amulet	limestone	3J	3J	c1	L22	W15
137.	6-143	Baghdad	1762	XII XII	spatulate	mother pearl	8Q	8Q	d8	L15	W9
138.	6-160	Baghdad	1763	XII XII	amulet	unclear	6J	6J	e4	H6	D13
139.	6-163	unknown	1692	XII XII	amulet	steatite	6K	6K	a/b5/6		W9
140.	6-195	unknown	1700	XII XII	bead	haemetite	6J	6J	e 5/6	D14	H8
141.	6-202	37-16-195	4107	XII XII	beads	gold	lapis+	5K	e9		none
142.	6-298	Baghdad	none	XII XII	pendant	steatite	dump	dump	dump	L21	W12
143.	6-587	Baghdad	none	XII XII	bead	serpentine	11M	11M	none	L21	W15
144.	6-616	37-16-202	none	XII XII	amulet	amethyst	5H/G	5H/G	none	D18	none
145.	6-none	37-16-194	none	XII XII	beads 62	paste	5M	5M	none	D2	to
146.	6-none	unknown	4140	XII XII	button	black stone	5M	5M	j1	none	none
147.	7-252	38-13-41	2033	XII XII	pendant	steatite	9M	9M	a10	L19	D12
148.	7-258	38-13-40	2061	XII XII	amulet	serpentine	11M	11M	e/f 8	L10	W19
149.	7-264	38-13-39	2035	XII XII	amulet	serpentine	none	none	none	none	none
150.	7-none	unknown	2070	XII XII	pendant	black stone	8M	8M	i8	none	none
		Lithics									
151.	4-0948	35-10-360	0578	XII ? ?XII	blade	obsidian	8P	4Q	f9	L71	W10
152.	4-1012	Baghdad	0672	XII XII	core	obsidian	9P	4O	c2	none	none
153.	4-1137	Baghdad	0844	XII XII	knife	flint	9N	5O	a2	none	none
154.	4-1150	35-10-243	0779	XII XII	cores 2	obsidian	10P	4M	b/c2/3	L113	W77
155.	4-1170	Baghdad	0982	XII XII	blades 2	obsidian	9N	5O	d9	none	none
156.	4-none	unknown	0232	XIA XII	core ?	obsidian	9M	6O	h 3/4	none	none
157.	5-none	36-6-276	none	XII XII	core	obsidian	9P	4O	none	H117	W35
158.	6-010	Baghdad	1609	XII XII	blade	obsidian	5Q	5Q	a4	L63	W11
159.	6-204a	Baghdad	none	XII XII	obsidian	microliths	4J	4J	none	L30	W6
160.	6-204b	37-26-182	184	XII XII	obsidian	microliths	4J	4J	none	L39	W8
161.	6-219	37-16-185	none	XII XII	core	obsidian	4J	4J	none	L83	D21
162.	6-241	Baghdad	4130	XII XII	core	obsidian	5H/G	5H/G	g4	L115	D48
163.	6-304	37-16-181	1925	XII XII	blade	obsidian	6J	6J	h10	L125	W22
164.	6-603	Baghdad	none	XII XII	blade	flint	11M	11M	none	L62	W25
165.	6-none	37-16-180	none	XII XII	blade	flint	8J	8J	none	L80	W18
166.	6-204	37-16-183	none	XII XII	blade	obsidian	4J	4J	none	L33	W5
167.	6-204	37-16-184	none	XII XII	blade	obsidian	4J	4J	none	L23	W9
168.	6-none	unknown	1722	XIA ? XII	blade	obsidian	4J	4J	g2	none	none
169.	6-none	unknown	1746	XII XII	blade	none	5J	5J	b1	none	none
170.	6-none	unknown	1639	XII XII	blade	flint	8Q	8Q	i9	none	none
171.	7-none	38-13-37	none	XII XII	blade	obsidian	7M	7M	none	L80	W21
172.	4-none	Discarded	0908	XII XII	hunk	obsidian	10P ?	4M	none	none	none
173.	6-none	unknown	4133	XII XII	unknown	salt ?	5M	5M	c3	none	none
		Metal	**item**								
174.	4-1139	Baghdad	0761	XII XII	chisel	metal	10P	4M	e-f 2	none	none
175.	4-1167	35-10-246	0447	XII XII	adze	metal	10P	4M	e-f 3	L73	W45
176.	7-271	38-13-38	2155	XII XII	axe	metal	11M	11M	f2	L73	W32
		Potsherd									
177.	4-0929	35-10-213	513	XII XII	none	ceramic	none	none	none	none	none
178.	4-0994	35-10-105	0591	XII XII	sprig bowl	ceramic	8P	4Q	a3	none	none
179.	4-1187	Baghdad	0790	XII XII	dish	ceramic	10N	5M	a4	none	none
180.	4-none	35-10-200	0504	XII XII	painted	ceramic	8P	4Q	none	none	none
181.	4-none	35-10-201	none	XII XII	painted	ceramic	9P	4O	none	none	none
182.	4-none	35-10-203	none	XII XII	painted	orange redware	9P	4O	none	none	none
183.	4-none	35-10-204	none	XII XII	painted jar	orange redware	none	none	none	none	none
184.	4-none	35-10-206	none	XII XII	painted	buffware	9N	5O	none	none	none
185.	4-none	35-10-207	none	XII XII	painted	ceramic	none	none	none	none	none
186.	4-none	35-10-208	none	XII XII	2 rim bowl	buffware	10P	4M	none	none	none
187.	4-none	35-10-209	none	XII XII	painted	ceramic	9N	5O	none	none	none
188.	4-none	35-10-210	none	XII XII	painted	ceramic	10N	5M	none	none	none
189.	4-none	35-10-211	none	XII XII	painted	buffware	9P	4O	none	none	none
190.	4-none	35-10-212	none	XII XII	painted	buffware	10P	4M	none	none	none
191.	4-none	35-10-214	none	XII XII	painted	ceramic	10P	4M	none	none	none

13	14	15	16	17	18	19
none	0.00	unknown	steatite shell			
D16	0.00	unknown	and stone			
ina	0.00	unknown				
ina	0.00	unknown				
ina	0.00	unknown				
ina	0.00	unknown				
ina	0.00	in new dirt (surface ?)				
ina	0.00	unknown				
T7	0.00	unknown	incised design			
ina	0.00	unknown				
ina	0.00	unknown				
ina	0.00		in shape of claw			
ina	0.00	unknown				
none	none	at base under floor in jar				
ina	0.00	unknown				
T6	0.00	unknown				
ina	0.00	unknown				
D3	0.00	unknown				
none	0.00	unknown				
ina	8.00	in black refuse in west trench				
ina	7.75	in black refuse				
ina	0.00	unknown				
none	7.50	in brown ash refuse				
T3	8.40	found near edge of tepe	striations 43 & 32			
none	8.29	unknown				
none	8.00	outside door NW wall White Room				
T45	7.80	in room southeast of White Room	backed stria 93			
none	7.95	unknown				
none	8.65	unknown				
T19	0.00	unknown	4 mm wide blades			
ina	0.00	next to vessel 6-008				
ina	0.00	seven found in oblong room				
ina	0.00	seven found in oblong room	striations 52	break 94		
none	0.00	in oblong room	missing from storage			
ina	0.00	unknown				
ina	0.00	unknown				
T15	0.00	unknown				
T4.5	0.00	unknown	bitumen serrated 34			
T2.2	0.00	unknown	striations 46 ridge 41			
T2.4	0.00	unknown	a few striations 41 & 39			
none	0.00	under XIA	translucent			
none	0.00	unknown				
none	0.00	unknown	with bitumen			
ina	0.00	unknown	minor striations 34 & 36			
none	0.00	30 cm above floor of White Room				
none	0.00	unknown				
none	8.66	outside White Room				
T10	7.94	on XII pavement				
T9	0.00	by edge of tepe				
ina	0.00	unknown				
ina	8.80	close to edge of tepe				
none	7.82	unknown				
ina	0.00	unknown	gift to English museum			
ina	0.00	unknown				
ina	0.00	unknown	buff slip	painted	quartz & basalt grit	HM
ina	0.00	unknown	quartz & basalt	HM		
ina	0.00	unknown	micaceous & basalt grit	HM		
ina	0.00	unknown				
ina	0.00	unknown	painted quartz grit &	chaff	HM	
ina	0.00	unknown	donated to the American	Museum of Natural	History	
ina	0.00	unknown	donated to English	museum		
ina	0.00	unknown	quartz & chaff	HM		
ina	0.00	unknown	hatched design quartz	chaff	HM	
ina	0.00	unknown				

(*continues*)

Level XII   (continued)

1	2	3	4	5		6	7	8	9	10	11	12
192.	5-none	36-6-414	0880	XII	XII	moulded	ceramic	10P	4M	c7	none	none
193.	4-none	unknown	0614	XII	XII	rim	ceramic	8P	4Q	b/c 7	none	none
194.	4-none	unknown	0883	XII	XII	painted	ceramic	10N	5M	i4	none	none
195.	5-none	36-6-244	none	XII	XII	impressed	green buffware	10N	5M	none	none	none
196.	5-none	36-6-245	none	XII	XII	bowl	sprig ware	7M	6S	none	D85	T5.5
197.	5-none	36-6-248	none	XII	XII	jar	ceramic	7M	6S	none	none	none
198.	5-none	36-6-249	none	XII	XII	painted jar	buffware	9R	3O	none	none	none
199.	5-none	36-6-252	none	XII	XII	painted bowl	ceramic	10M	6M	none	none	none
200.	5-none	36-6-401	none	XII	XII	painted jar	brown ware	10P	4M	none	H110	none
201.	5-none	36-6-404	none	XII	XII	painted rim	green grayware	9N	5O	none	none	none
202.	5-none	36-6-408	757	XII	XII	bowl	green grayware	9N	5O	none	L55	W59
203.	5-none	36-6-417	none	XII	XII	impressed	green buffware	9N	5O	none	none	none
204.	5-none	36-6-424	none	XII	XII	painted rim	ceramic	10P	4M	none	none	none
205.	5-none	36-6-425	none	XII	XII	painted	buffware	10P	4M	none	none	none
206.	5-none	36-6-426	none	XII	XII	painted	ceramic	9P	4O	none	none	none
207.	5-none	36-6-427	none	XII	XII	painted	ceramic	9N	5O	none	none	none
208.	5-none	unknown	1233	XIA	XII	paint bowl	ceramic	8N	5Q	h3	none	none
209.	6-none	37-16-125	none	XII	XII	painted	ceramic	none	none	none	none	none
210.	7-none	Discarded	4263	XII	XII	foot	ceramic	6G	6G	none	none	none
211.	4-none	unknown	0439	XII	XII	painted	ceramic	10P	4M	h-i 9	none	none
212.	4-none	unknown	0293	?	XII	unknown	ceramic	8P	4Q	h8	none	none
213.	5-none	36-6-250	1459	XII	XII	painted	ceramic	10P	4M	h2	none	none
214.	5-none	Discarded	1537	XII	XII	painted	ceramic	7N	5S	i9	none	none
215.	5-none	unknown	1257	XIA	XII	decorated	ceramic	10R	3M	d 1/2	none	none
216.	6-none	37-16-119	none	XII	XII	painted	red brownware	6G	6G	none	ina	ina
217.	6-none	37-16-137	none	XII	XII	painted	buffware	none	none	none	none	none
218.	7-272	38-13-33	2069	XII	XII	painted	ceramic	7M	7M	j1	none	none
		Vessels										
219.	4-0685	35-10-232	0113	XIA	XII	model jar	alabaster	8P	4Q	i6	H20	RD18
220.	4-0686	35-10-197	0114	XIA	XII	small jar	buffware	8P	4Q	i6	H86	RD46
221.	4-0694	Baghdad	0275	XII ?	XII	goblet	ceramic	8P	4Q	i6	H121	RD76
222.	4-0713	Baghdad	0292	XII ?	XII	Wide flower	ceramic	8P	4Q	h8	H64	RD200
223.	4-0919	35-10-215	0365	XII	XII	painted bowl	ceramic	8P	4Q	f10	H80	RD130
224.	4-0995	35-10-192	0581	XII	XII	bowl	grayware	8P	4Q	f9	H66	W40
225.	4-1023	35-10-193	0728	XII	XII	bowl	red brownware	8P	4Q	b/c7/8	H138	RD218
226.	4-1038	35-10-142	0536	XIA	XII	chalice	red brownware	9N	5O	none	H60	D97
227.	4-1084	Baghdad	0438	XII	XII	jar	ceramic	9N	5O	g 3-4	H296	RD168
228.	4-1098	discarded	0441	XII	XII	urn	ceramic	8P	4O	b 8/9	H268	RD216
229.	4-1140	35-10-195	0841	XII	XII	bowl	orange redware	9P	4O	f7	H80	RD174
230.	4-1141	Baghdad	0842	XII	XII	dish	ceramic	9P	4O	plan	none	none
231.	4-1143	35-10-188	0762	XII	XII	finger bowl	ceramic	9P	4O	d2	H24	RD68
232.	4-1144	Baghdad	0756	XII	XII	bowl	ceramic	9N	5O	g/h3/4	H62	RD240
233.	4-1145	35-10-199	0838	XII	XII	large jar	ceramic	9N	5O	h1	H384	RD228
234.	4-1149	35-10-198	0759	XII	XII	painted bowl	buffware	9N	5O	h10	`	D108
235.	4-1175	35-10-189	0963	XII	XII	small jar	brownware	9N	5O	f8	H103	RD64
236.	4-1183	Baghdad	0856	XII	XII	model cup	ceramic	10P	4M	d4	H26	RD42
237.	4-1185	Baghdad	0793	XII	XII	paint bowl	ceramic	10P	4M	e/f7/8	H48	RD105
238.	4-1186	Baghdad	0862	XII	XII	small jar	ceramic	10P	4M	d6	H124	RD74
239.	4-1188	35-10-196	0450	XII	XII	2 Wide flower	brownware	10P	4M	i-j 3	H70	D215
240.	4-1215	35-10-190	0866	XII	XII	small jar	orange redware	10P	4M	g5	H96	RD72
241.	4-none	Discarded	0642	XII	XII	unknown	ceramic	8P	4Q	f9	none	none
242.	4-none	Discarded	0983	XII	XII	pot	ceramic	8N	5Q	e7	none	none
243.	4-none	unknown	0827	XII	XII	bowl	stone	9R	3O	a8	H44	D110
244.	4-none	unknown	0754	XII	XII	large jar	ceramic	9P	4O	loc152	none	none
245.	4-none	unknown	0662	XII	XII	unknown	ceramic	8P	4Q	d8	none	none
246.	4-none	unknown	0641	XII	XII	dish	ceramic	8P	4Q	f9	none	none
247.	4-none	unknown	0638	XII	XII	bowl	ceramic	8P	4Q	f9	none	none
248.	4-none	unknown	0953	XII	XII	container	unbaked clay	10N	5M	j1	none	none
249.	4-none	unknown	0956	XII	XII	container	ceramic	10N	5M	j1	none	none
250.	4-none	unknown	0719	XII	XII	crude	ceramic	9N	5O	i5	none	none
251.	4-none	unknown	0430	XIA	XII	jar	ceramic	8N	5Q	c4	none	none
252.	5-1235	36-6-259	0906	XII	XII	model jar	steatite	10P	4M	none	H28	RD17
253.	5-1236	Baghdad	0907	XII	XII	painted jar	ceramic	10P	4M	none	H72	RD86
254.	5-1241	36-6-235	0905	XII	XII	bowl	orange redware	10P	4M	none	H59	RD148
255.	5-1279 ?	unknown	1279	XII	XII	juglet	ceramic	8M	6Q	j3	none	none
256.	5-1388	Baghdad	1143	XII	XII	sprig bowl	ceramic	11P	4K	h/i 3	H44	RD105

13	14	15	16	17	18	19
ina	8.00	unknown				
none	8.69	near edge of tepe				
none	7.90	unknown				
ina	0.00	unknown	circles triangles & rope	sand temper	HM	
ina	0.00	unknown	like 36-6-156 XIAB	micaceous grit	WM	
ina	0.00	unknown	donated to Peabody	Museum	check & ladder	
ina	0.00	unknown	hatched triangles off line	quartz & chaff	HM	
ina	0.00	unknown	bird design			
none	0.00	unknown				
ina	0.00	unknown	bistre paint			
ina	7.94	with 4-1147 seal impression	cream slip			
ina	0.00	unknown	rosettes	sand temper	HM	
ina	0.00	unknown				
ina	0.00	unknown	squiggle bird design	quartz & basalt grit	HM	
ina	0.00	unknown				
ina	0.00	unknown				
ina	8.98	on top of wall				
ina	0.00	unknown				
none	0.00	unknown				
ina	9.00	unknown				
ina	8.51	unknown				
ina	0.00	from base of White Room walls				
ina	8.11	unknown				
ina	8.29	unknown				
ina	0.00	unknown	crosshatch triangle	quartz & basalt grit	HM	
ina	0.00	unknown	sand & chaff	HM		
none	8.00	under walls of Round House				
BD10	8.50	unknown				
BD17	8.50	unknown	2 beads inside	basalt grit	HM	
BD43	0.00	seems XII				
D78	8.51	unknown				
BD72	8.47	unknown	XIIA ?	running triangles	lines at rim	
T3.8	8.37	near edge	burnished fine quartz grit	HM		
BD78	8.47	unknown	micaceous grit	HM		
ina	8.86	unknown	burnished footed	quartz & chaff	HM	
D328	8.26	in west corner of White Room				
D244	0.00	in lens of ash and sherds				
D184	7.93	2 m from northeast wall of White Room		quartz & chaff	HM	
none	7.93	on floor of White Room	Wide flower pot ?			
BD46	7.90	just outside and SE of White Room	painted	sprigs		
BD46	8.60	unknown	ring base	painted exterior		
D384	8.42	unknown	Paint	cross-hatched	triangles	
BD42	8.96	just outside White Room east door	ring base painted	dark core sand temper	TM	cross hatch
D128	8.50	in layer of ashes and animal bones	quartz & chaff	HM		
BD32	8.61	unknown				
BD38	7.87	unknown	ring base painted	Cross hatch		
D154	7.95	unknown				
ina	7.90	outside and East of White Room	chaff temper	HM		
D118	7.95	unknown	quartz & chaff	HM		
none	8.37	near edge				
none	8.54	unknown				
none	8.70	unknown				
none	7.90	on raised platform in corner of	room 43 ?			
none	8.38	near edge of tepe				
none	8.37	near edge of tepe	Wide flower ?			
none	8.37	near edge of tepe				
none	7.78	unknown				
none	7.78	unknown				
none	8.21	on floor big plastered room				
none	8.90	in libn refuse				
D18	0.00	close to floor of White Room	carved running v's			
D101	0.00	30 cm off floor of White Room	cross hatch	triangles		
BD92	0.00	near White Room	chaff temper	HM	Extended base	
none	7.97	unknown	Maltese cross design			
BD43	8.631	in debris	burnished			

(continues)

Level XII   (continued)

1	2	3	4	5	6	7	8	9	10	11	12
257.	5-1436	36-6-241	1199	XII XII	small bowl	Buff ware	9P	4O	i 7/8	H27	RD63
258.	5-1490	Baghdad	1317	XIA XII	bowl	ceramic	7M	6S	h/i8	H52	RD142
259.	5-1499	36-6-166	1243	XIA XII	foot	ceramic	8N	5Q	e/f5/6	H34	BD55
260.	5-1501	36-6-133	1235	XIA XII	bowl	buffware	7M	6S	i5	H57	RD146
261.	5-1503	Baghdad	1245	XIA XII	spouted bowl	ceramic	8N	5Q	c8	H83	RD137
262.	5-1523	36-6-365	1366	XII XII	bottle	brownware	10N	5M	c3	H104	RD43
263.	5-1526	Baghdad	1358	XII XII	trumpet vase	ceramic	8N	5Q	e/f 9	H180	RD170
264.	5-1529	Baghdad	1361	XII XII	jar sherds	ceramic	10R	3M	e/f7/8	H59	RD42
265.	5-1531	Baghdad	1374	XII XII	dish	ceramic	11R	3K	f/g 3	H40	RD90
266.	5-1534	Baghdad	1365	XII XII	jar	ceramic	10N	5M	a4	H102	RD81
267.	5-1535	36-6-226	1367	XII XII	bowl	brownware	10R	3M	i/j6/7	H91	D190
268.	5-1537	Baghdad	1375	XII XII	cup	ceramic	10R	3M	c10	H35	RD40
269.	5-1558	36-6-220	1275	XII XII	paint jar	buffware	11P	3K	i4	H197	RD101
270.	5-1561	36-6-218	1399	XII XII	painted bowl	buffware	10P	4M	g/h 10	H88	RD124
271.	5-1568	Baghdad	1398	XII XII	cup	ceramic	8M	6Q	g10	H104	RD136
272.	5-1586	Baghdad	1416	XII XII	Wide flower	ceramic	11P	4K	a/b 9	H62	RD148
273.	5-1590	36-6-240	1272	XII XII	model jar	grayware	8M	6Q	?	H21	RD21
274.	5-1593	36-6-225	1285	XII XII	bowl	orange redware	9P	4O	none	H71	RD68
275.	5-1599	Baghdad	1289	XII XII	jar	ceramic	10N	5M	b 5/6	H191	RD102
276.	5-1605	Baghdad	1325	XII XII	dish	brown warw	10M	6M	f/g4/5	H82	RD201
277.	5-1606	36-6-221	1335	XII XII	jar	ceramic	8N	5Q	a10	H92	RD67
278.	5-1618	36-6-222	1340	XII XII	jar	ceramic	9M	6O	e/f3	H174	RD147
279.	5-1621	36-6-236	1343	XII XII	Wide flower	red brownware	11M	6K	g6	H78	RD210
280.	5-1622	36-6-228	1342	XII XII	Wide flower	red brownware	11M	6K	g/h7/8	H61	RD206
281.	5-1623	Baghdad	1343	XII XII	small jar	red ware	11M	6K	g6	H137	RD97
282.	5-1629	Baghdad	1422	XII XII	Wide flower	ceramic	7M	6S	i8	H62	RD136
283.	5-1636	36-6-234	1427	XII XII	Wide flower	ceramic	7M	6S	e/f 7	H57	RD139
284.	5-1637	36-6-223	1430	XII XII	painted bowl	buffware	10N	5M	h 8/9	H64	RD85
285.	5-1643	Baghdad	1440	XII XII	Wide flower	ceramic	10N	5M	j2	H68	RD205
286.	5-1663	Baghdad	1459	XII XII	low bowl	red ware	10P	4M	h2	H40	RD196
287.	5-1687	Baghdad	1470	XII XII	bowl	ceramic	10N	5M	g/h 9	H86	RD196
288.	5-1712	36-6-238	1476	XII XII	stand	brown ware	7M	6S	e/f5/6	H112	D114
289.	5-1713	36-6-230	1536	XII XII	bowl	brownware	10N	5M	e7	H63	D140
290.	5-1740	Baghdad	1543	XII XII	painted bowl	buffware	12P	4J	J3	H54	RD178
291.	5-1755	36-6-143	1553	XIA XII	small jar	brownware	11N	5K	e/f8/9	H45	D50
292.	5-1758	Discarded	1563	XII XII	jar stand	red ware	11P	4K	g/h 3	H65	RD146
293.	5-none	36-6-246	none	XII XII	painted bowl	ceramic	10M	6M	none	none	ina
294.	5-none	36-6-247	1295	XII XII	2 Wide flower	ceramic	7M	6S	e9	none	ina
295.	5-none	unknown	1407	XII XII	dish	ceramic	9M	6O	i3	none	none
296.	6-002	Baghdad	1607	XII XII	painted bowl	brown ware	6S	6S	g7	H54	RD121
297.	6-005	Baghdad	1601	XII XII	small jar	green ware	6Q	6Q	j9	H75	RD54
298.	6-006	unknown	1604	XII XII	bowl	brown ware	5Q	5Q	f6	H75	BD55
299.	6-008	unknown	1608	XII XII	bowl	brown ware	5O	5O	a4	H57	D158
300.	6-016	Discarded	1615	XII XII	cup	buff green ware	5Q	5Q	a 2/3	H72	RD70
301.	6-066	37-16-66	1720	XII XII	kohl bottle	steatite	4K	4K	none	H56	RD9
302.	6-085	unknown	1670	XIA XII	small bowl	brown ware	5M	5M	f10	H32	D82
303.	6-088	unknown	none	XII XII	Wide flower	brownware	4J	4J	none	H42	RD114
304.	6-100	Baghdad	none	XII XII	storage jar	brownware	4K	4K	none	H163	RD105
305.	6-110	37-16-115	1732	XII XII	small jar	red brownware	4J	4J	e10	H32	RD21
306.	6-119	unknown	none	XII XII	bowl	brownware	5O	5O	none	L22	W15
307.	6-120	37-16-107	none	XII XII	bowl	buffware	5O	5O	none	H130	RD145
308.	6-150	Baghdad	none	XII XII	model jar	serpentine	4K	4K	none	H29	RD30
309.	6-154	37-16-171	1769	XII XII	model bowl	basalt	5G	5G	g4	H11	RD17
310.	6-175	discarded	none	XII XII	spouted bowl	buffware	4K	4K	none	H270	D350
311.	6-201	Baghdad	4107	XII XII	sprig pot	brownware	5K	5K	e9	H96	RD66
312.	6-205	37-16-113	4106	XII XII	model jar	grayware	5M	5M	e/f 9	H35	RD20
313.	6-213	37-16-108	4116	XII XII	sprig bowl	brownware	5G	5G	d9	H28	D64
314.	6-246	unknown	none	XII XII	small jar	greenware	4J	4J	none	none	none
315.	6-258	Baghdad	none	XII XII	small jar	brown greenware	5M	5M	none	H107	D114
316.	6-264	37-16-114	1866	XII XII	model jar	brown ware	4J	4J	b 5/6	H34	RD26
317.	6-313	Baghdad	1929	XIA XII	cup	blackware	6J	6J	i9	H42	RD71
318.	6-318	unknown	none	XII XII	small jar	brownware	5J	5J	none	H102	RD68
319.	6-406	37-16-222	none	XII XII	bowl	green grayware	6G	6G	none	H100	D133
320.	6-588	37-16-94	none	XII XII	sprig pot	red brownware	11M	11M	h1	H96	RD78
321.	6-589	Baghdad	none	XII XII	sprig bowl	ceramic	11M	11M	none	H40	RD84

13	14	15	16	17	18	19
BD21	8.11	under floor	at back of White Room	paint		
BD87	8.81	against or set in wall	Extended base			
ina	8.40	refuse below XI walls				
D145	8.08	on pavement near wall	quartz grit & chaff	HM		
D160	8.60	on pavement	spout L141	applique on spout		
BD82	7.63	on top of baby grave 236	quartz grit & chaff	HM		
ina	8.10	unknown	fragmentary			
BD65	8.79	found in ballista deposit				
ina	8.45	on pavement in ordinary refuse	Wide flower ?			
BD122	7.67	in ordinary refuse				
ina	7.91	on pavement of large room	quartz & chaff	HM		
ina	8.57	in black ash refuse				
D203	8.37	by side wall next to baby grave pot	quartz & chaff	HM	cross hatch	
D148	8.14	on pavement in ordinary refuse	quartz & chaff	HM	bands cross hatch	
BD14	8.38	on pavement				
BD88	8.50	unknown	same as 5-1490			
D37	7.97	unknown	basalt grit	HM		
D87	0.00	on floor at north corner of White Room	quartz grit & chaff	HM		
D205	0.00	from oven	not quite to floor			
BD100	7.61	from debris above floor	Wide flower ?			
D103	8.00	on pavement				
BD69	7.80	on floor or street near 'death site'				
BD85	0.00	in hole in corner of room	chaff temper	HM		
BD89	0.00	in debris	chaff temper	HM		
D158	0.00	in hole at corner of room	pebble burnished			
BD102	0.00	near edge of tepe definitely XII				
BD63	7.97	below tell surface near wall				
D112	8.50	from top of XII wall stub	chaff & quartz HM			
BD80	7.35	in dark black ash				
BD90	0.00	From base White Room walls	Wide flower ?			
BD86	7.80	in mortar in the floor of room	grave ?	ring base		
ina	0.00	unknown				
ina	7.38	unknown	quartz & chaff	HM		
BD80	8.51	unknown	cross hatch, bands			
ina	8.50	under floor near leaning wall of Pisa	quartz & basalt	HM		
BD100	0.00	on floor lamp ?				
ina	0.00	unknown	stitched design			
ina	0.00	unknown				
none	8.50	in dark gray refuse				
BD61	0.00	just below walls	ring base	cross hatch		
D84	0.00	at foundation level	pointed base			
D190	0.00	in wall	extended base			
BD75	0.00	next to 6-009				
D98	0.00	unknown				
D16	0.00	unknown	listed as XIA in vol 2	incised sprig		
ina	0.00	above XII walls below level XIA	HM			
BD46	0.00	unknown	funnel ?			
D182	0.00	under XIA near "cult" door	buff slip	black paint on rim		
D37	0.00	unknown	sand temper	HM		
T7	0.00	unknown	ring based			
D187	0.00	unknown	ring based quartz & chaff	HM		
D34	0.00	unknown				
D20	0.00	unknown				
none	0.00	unknown				
D103	0.00	against stone				
D33	0.00	unknown	sand temper	HM		
RD58	0.00	unknown	gritty temper			
none	0.00	in oblong room				
ina	0.00	unknown				
BD37	0.00	unknown				
BD28	0.00	unknown				
D104	0.00	unknown				
ina	0.00	unknown	fine basalt grit	WM		
D125	0.00	unknown	quartz & chaff	HM		
BD46	0.00	unknown				

(continues)

Level XII   (continued)

1	2	3	4	5		6	7	8	9	10	11	12
322.	6-594	37-16-117	none	XII	XII	sprig bowl	red brownware	4S	4S	none	H72	RD153
323.	6-601	Baghdad	none	XII ?	XII	painted bowl	ceramic	none	none	none	H134+	D266
324.	6-618	Baghdad	none	XII	XII	sprig bowl	buffware	11M	11M	none	H270	RD190
325.	6-622	37-16-104	none	XII	XII	painted bowl	green grayware	5G	5G	quad c	H50	D88
326.	6-623	Baghdad	none	XII ?	XII	bowl	ceramic	none	none	none	H150	D150
327.	6-none	37-16-92	none	XII	XII	painted bowl	green grayware	11M	11M	none	none	none
328.	7-none	unknown	4127	XII	XII	kohl jar	alabaster	3M	3M	d4	none	none
329.	7-none	unknown	1614	XII	XII	jar	ceramic	5S	5S	c4	none	none
330.	7-none	unknown	4256	XII ?	XII	spouted jar	ceramic	6J	6J	e8	none	none
331.	7-055	38-13-32	none	XII	XII	small jar	red brownware	none	none	none	H56	RD39
332.	7-154	discarded	2009	XIA	XII	jar	brown ware	8M	8M	h3	H100	RD79
333.	7-none	38-13-35	none	XII	XII	bowl	green grayware	7M	7M	none	none	ina
		Spindle	**whorl**									
334.	4-0674	35-10-230	0271	XII ?	XII	whorl	clay	8P	4Q	i6	H11	D24
335.	4-0676	Baghdad	0111	XII ?	XII	whorl	stone	8P	4Q	i6	none	none
336.	4-0677	Baghdad	0110	XII ?	XII	whorls 7	clay	8P	4Q	i6	H19	D33
337.	4-0712	Baghdad	0290	XIA	XII	whorl	clay	8P	4Q	g8	none	none
338.	4-0949	Baghdad	0552	XII	XII	whorl	clay	8P	4Q	d8	H23	D33
339.	4-0950	Baghdad	0556	XII	XII	whorl	clay	9P	4O	j5	H12	D27
340.	4-0951	35-10-227	0567	XII	XII	whorl	clay	8P	4Q	f9	H21	D34
341.	4-0976	35-10-223	0597	XII	XII	whorl	clay	8P	4Q	d9	H25	D40
342.	4-1147c	35-10-225	0757	XII	XII	whorl	clay	9N	5O	plan	H25	D36
343.	4-1151	Baghdad	0954	XII	XII	whorl	clay	9N	5O	d4	H22	D31
344.	4-1152	35-10-224	0771	XII	XII	whorl	clay	8N	5Q	e/f7/8	H20	D39
345.	4-1172	35-10-241	0972	XII	XII	whorl	clay	8N	5Q	g8	none	none
346.	4-1180	35-10-226	0448	XII	XII	whorl	clay	10P	4M	d 3/4	H24	D25
347.	4-1197	35-10-221	1000	XII	XII	whorl	clay	9N	5O	d8	H28	D44
348.	4-none	35-10-160	0734	XIA	XII	whorls	clay	9N	5O	c3	H15	D30
349.	4-none	35-10-219	716	XII	XII	whorl	clay	8N	5Q	g8	D40	T26
350.	4-none	35-10-231	0874	XII	XII	whorl	clay	9M	6O	d8	H14	D20
351.	4-none	35-10-379	0573	XII	XII	whorls	clay	9P	4O	j6	H21	D31
352.	4-none	35-10-384	0712	XII	XII	whorl	clay	9P	4O	a2	H19	D36
353.	4-none	Baghdad	0844	XII	XII	whorl	clay	9N	5O	a2	none	none
354.	4-none	Discarded	0903	XII	XII	whorl	clay	9R	3O	h3	none	none
355.	4-none	unknown	0991	XII	XII	whorl	clay	10P	4M	h2	none	none
356.	4-none	unknown	0994	XII	XII	whorl	clay	10P	4M	d2	none	none
357.	4-none	unknown	0997	XII	XII	whorl	clay	10P	4M	g8	none	none
358.	4-none	unknown	0986	XII	XII	whorl	clay	10P	4M	f7	none	none
359.	4-none	unknown	0859	XII	XII	whorl	clay	10P	4M	g5	none	none
360.	4-none	unknown	0785	XII	XII	whorl	clay	10P	4M	i/j 3	none	none
361.	4-none	unknown	0787	XII	XII	whorl	clay	10P	4M	d/e3/4	none	none
362.	4-none	unknown	0780	XII	XII	whorl	clay	10P	4M	e/f 1	none	none
363.	4-none	unknown	0765	XII	XII	whorl	clay	10P	4M	c/d2/3	none	none
364.	4-none	unknown	0449	XII	XII	whorl	clay	10P	4M	i3	none	none
365.	4-none	unknown	0602	XII	XII	whorl	clay	9P	4O	c4	none	none
366.	4-none	unknown	0990	XII	XII	whorl	clay	9P	4O	e/f 9	none	none
367.	4-none	unknown	0760	XII	XII	whorls 5	clay	9P	4O	e10	none	none
368.	4-none	unknown	0418	XII	XII	whorl	clay	9P	4O	g5	none	none
369.	4-none	unknown	0574	XII	XII	whorl	clay	8P	4Q	f9	none	none
370.	4-none	unknown	0575	XII	XII	whorls 2	clay	8P	4Q	f9	none	none
371.	4-none	unknown	0564	XII	XII	whorl	clay	8P	4Q	f9	none	none
372.	4-none	unknown	0403	XII	XII	whorl	clay	8P	4Q	g/h 6	none	none
373.	4-none	unknown	0390	XII	XII	whorl	clay	8P	4Q	g10	none	none
374.	4-none	unknown	0291	?	XII	whorl	clay	8P	4Q	h8	none	none
375.	4-none	unknown	0272	?	XII	whorl	clay	8P	4Q	i6	none	none
376.	4-none	unknown	0604	XII	XII	whorl	clay	9N	5O	i4	none	none
377.	4-none	unknown	0992	XII	XII	whorl	clay	9N	5O	b8	none	none
378.	4-none	unknown	0976	XII	XII	whorl	clay	9N	5O	b5	none	none
379.	4-none	unknown	0895	XII	XII	whorl	clay	9N	5O	b8	none	none
380.	4-none	unknown	0843	XII	XII	whorl	clay	9N	5O	h/i8	none	none
381.	4-none	unknown	0777	XII	XII	whorl	clay	9N	5O	e/f 10	none	none
382.	4-none	unknown	0731	XIA	XII	whorl	clay	9N	5O	b1	none	none
383.	4-none	unknown	0594	XII	XII	whorl	clay	8P	5Q	b2	none	none
384.	4-none	unknown	0753	XII	XII	whorl	clay	8M	6Q	none	none	none
385.	5-1233	36-6-255	0904	XII	XII	whorls 2	clay	10P	4M	none	H25	D42
386.	5-1580	36-6-256	1415	XII	XII	whorl	clay	8M	6Q	i/j 2	H22	D38

13	14	15	16	17	18	19
BD113	0.00	unknown	micaceous	HM		
RD160	0.00	room 160 ?				
D320	0.00	unknown				
ina	0.00	unknown	basalt & chaff	HM		
ina	0.00	unknown				
ina	0.00	unknown				
none	0.00	found in wall				
none	0.00	burial ?				
none	0.00	unknown				
D71	0.00	unknown	quartz & chaff	HM		
D105	8.10	next to Round House				
ina	0.00	unknown	carinated herringbone	incised design		
ina	8.50	from edge tepe below XII				
none	8.50	unknown				
ina	8.50	at edge of tepe				
none	8.51	unknown				
ina	8.42	unknown				
ina	8.71	found below XI structure				
ina	8.40	near edge of tepe				
ina	8.42	unknown				
ina	7.94	unknown				
ina	8.58	unknown				
ina	8.68	on pavement				
none	8.64	unknown				
ina	7.90	unknown				
ina	7.98	unknown				
ina	8.90	unknown				
ina	9.33	near top of XII				
ina	8.30	unknown				
ina	8.71	unknown				
ina	8.62	unknown				
none	8.00	NW wall White Room behind mortar				
none	0.00	jst NE of White Room in room 43				
none	7.95	unknown				
none	7.97	unknown				
none	7.97	unknown				
none	8.52	unknown				
none	8.12	unknown				
none	7.90	unknown				
none	7.90	unknown				
none	7.90	unknown				
none	8.41	narrow room outside White Room				
none	7.90	unknown				
none	8.11	unknown				
none	8.25	unknown				
none	7.97	unknown				
none	8.90	from White Room				
none	8.40	near edge of tepe				
none	8.40	near edge of tepe				
none	8.40	unknown				
none	8.76	unknown				
none	8.98	at edge of tepe				
none	8.51	unknown				
none	8.50	unknown				
none	8.83	unknown				
none	8.46	unknown				
none	7.80	unknown				
none	7.95	unknown				
none	7.93	south door SE wall of White Room				
none	8.05	unknown				
none	8.90	unknown				
none	9.00	unknown				
none	8.88	on pavement below Fortress				
ina	0.00	area of White Room				
ina	8.50	unknown				

(*continues*)

Level XII   (continued)

1	2	3	4	5	6	7	8	9	10	11	12
387.	5-1596	Baghdad	1290	XII XII	whorl	clay	12P	4J	c/d1/2	H18	D36
388.	5-none	36-6-258	0904	XII XII	whorl	clay	10P	4M	none	H21	D42
389.	5-none	unknown	1391	XII XII	whorl	clay ?	11P	4K	g7	none	none
390.	6-004	Baghdad	1602	XII XII	whorl	clay	5Q	5Q	a4	H25	D40
391.	6-none	37-16-143	none	XII XII	whorls	clay	5K ??	5K ??	none	H22	D34
392.	6-none	37-16-144	none	XII XII	whorl	clay	5K ?	5K ?	none	H23	D38
393.	6-none	37-16-145	none	XII XII	whorl	clay	5K ?	5K ?	none	H23	D37
394.	6-none	37-16-146	none	XII XII	whorl	clay	5K ?	5K ?	none	H22	D40
395.	6-none	37-16-147	none	XII XII	whorl	clay	5K ?	5K ?	none	H15	D37
396.	6-none	37-16-148	none	XII XII	whorl	clay	5K ?	5K ?	none	H24	D38
397.	6-none	37-16-149	none	XII XII	whorl	clay	5K ?	5K ?	none	H15	D28
398.	6-none	37-16-150	none	XII XII	whorl	clay	5K ?	5K ?	none	H14	D28
399.	6-none	37-16-151	none	XII XII	whorl	clay	5K ?	5K ?	none	H16	D31
400.	6-none	37-16-152	none	XII XII	whorl	clay	5K ?	5K ?	none	H19	D23
401.	6-none	37-16-153	none	XII XII	whorl	clay	5K ?	5K ?	none	H23	D31
402.	6-none	37-16-154	none	XII XII	whorl	clay	5K ?	5K ?	none	H25	D45
403.	6-none	37-16-155	none	XII XII	whorl	clay	5K ?	5K ?	none	H25	D42
404.	6-none	37-16-156	none	XII XII	whorl	clay	5K ?	5K ?	none	H25	D40
405.	6-none	37-16-157	none	XII XII	whorl	clay	5K ?	5K ?	none	H20	D35
406.	6-none	37-16-158	none	XII XII	whorl	clay	5K ?	5K ?	none	H20	D37
407.	6-none	37-16-159	none	XII XII	whorl	none	5K ?	5K ?	none	H22	D38
408.	6-none	37-16-160	none	XII XII	whorl	none	5K ?	5K ?	none	H24	D40
409.	6-none	37-16-161	none	XII XII	whorl	clay	5K ?	5K ?	none	H21	D36
410.	6-none	37-16-162	none	XII XII	whorl	clay	5K ?	5K ?	none	H22	D33
411.	6-none	37-16-163	none	XII XII	whorl	clay	5K ?	5K ?	none	H17	D35
412.	6-none	37-16-164	none	XII XII	whorl	clay	5K ?	5K ?	none	H25	D45
413.	6-none	37-16-165	none	XII XII	whorl	clay	5K ?	5K ?	none	H18	D35
414.	6-none	37-16-166	none	XII XII	whorl	clay	5K ?	5K ?	none	H22	D36
415.	6-none	37-16-167	none	XII XII	whorl	clay	5K ?	5K ?	none	H22	D40
416.	6-none	37-16-168	none	XII XII	whorl	clay	5K ?	5K ?	none	H21	D35
417.	6-none	37-16-169	none	XII XII	whorl	clay	5K ?	5K ?	none	H22	D33
		Seals	**sealing**								
418.	4-0644	35-10-260	0008	XII XII	impression	clay	9N	5O	none	L39	W38
419.	4-0667	35-10-261	0205	XII XII	impression	clay	9N	5O	none	L16	W29
420.	4-0978	IM24978	0595	XII XII	impression	clay	8P	4Q	a3	none	none
421.	4-0979	35-10-266	0596	XII XII	impression	clay	8P	4Q	d9	L22	W33
422.	4-1132	IM25007	0248	XII XII	impression	clay	9P	4O	b2	L29	W24
423.	4-1133	IM24979	0249	XII XII	impression	clay	9P	4O	none	L28	W25
424.	4-1146	IM24963	0846	XII XII	impression	clay	9N	5O	a 8/9	L35	W38
425.	4-1147	IM24962	0757	XII XII	impression	clay	9N	5O	h/i9	none	none
426.	4-1154	35-10-252	0958	XII XII	stamp	steatite	10P	4M	d1	D15	none
427.	4-1158	35-10-249	0959	XII XII	stamp	steatite	10P	4M	d2	D25	none
428.	4-1171	35-10-250	0973	XII XII	stamp	bone	9N	5O	e7	L18	W21
429.	4-1176	35-10-253	0962	XII XII	stamp	steatite	9N	5O	c6	D16	T4
430.	4-1181	IM24594	0784	XII XII	stamp	steatite	9N	5O	b9	S22	T4
431.	4-1190	35-10-269	0783	XII XII	impression	clay	9P	4O	b/c 9	L27	W27
432.	4-1191	IM25000	0795	XII XII	impression	clay	10P	4M	h/i6/7	L48	W46
433.	4-1192	35-10-259	0788	XII XII	impression	clay	10P	4M	f/g3/4 4	L32	W30
434.	4-1193	35-10-270	0781	XII XII	impression	clay	10P	4M	h 1/2	L43	W45
435.	4-1194	35-10-271	0965	XII XII	impression	clay	9N	5O	d10	L33	W31
436.	4-1195	IM25002	0851	XII XII	impression	clay	9N	5O	c8	L28	W36
437.	4-1198	35-10-272	0776	XII XII	impression	clay	none	none	none	L26	W54
438.	4-1199	IM25039	0960	XII XII	impression	clay	9N	5O	e9	L29	W26
439.	4-1200	35-10-257	0782	XII XII	impression	clay	10P	4M	e1	+L27	W25
440.	4-1201	35-10-273	0792	XII XII	impression	clay	9N	5O	d9	L48	W32
441.	4-1202	35-10-274	0791	XII XII	impression	clay	10P	4M	f/g3/4	L40	W22
442.	4-1203	35-10-275	0847	XII XII	impression	clay	9P	4O	h/i6	L40	W38
443.	4-1204	IM24980	0855	XII XII	impression	clay	9N	5O	d10	none	none
444.	4-1205	IM24972	0977	XII XII	impression	clay	10P	4M	d3	D28	none
445.	4-1207	35-10-276	0998	XII XII	impression	clay	9N	5O	c9	L25	W17
446.	4-1208	35-10-277	0755	XII XII	impression	clay	9P	4O	plan	L52	W48
447.	4-1209	35-10-278	0979	XII XII	impression	clay	9N	5O	d10	L61	W42
448.	4-1211	35-10-280	0860	XII XII	impression	clay	9N	5O	a7	W17	T11
449.	4-1213	IM25037	0789	XII XII	impression	clay	10P	4M	d/e3/4	L37	W29
450.	4-1214	IM24973	0786	XII XII	impression	clay	10P	4M	g2	L34	W23
451.	4-1216	IM25009	0863	XII XII	impression	clay	10N	5M	e1	L33	W35
452.	4-1219	Baghdad	0868	XIA XII	stamp	paste	9M	6O	d/e 9	D15	T5

13	14	15	16	17	18	19
ina	8.40	unknown				
ina	0.00	area of White Room				
none	8.50	unknown				
ina	0.00	under wall	applique design			
ina	0.00	unknown				
ina	0.00	unknown				
ina	0.00	unknown	incised design			
ina	0.00	unknown	incised design			
ina	0.00	unknown				
ina	0.00	unknown				
ina	0.00	unknown	incised design			
ina	0.00	unknown				
ina	0.00	unknown				
ina	0.00	unknown				
ina	0.00	unknown				
ina	0.00	unknown				
ina	0.00	unknown	incised design			
ina	0.00	unknown				
ina	0.00	unknown	incised design			
ina	0.00	unknown				
ina	0.00	unknown	scratches			
ina	0.00	unknown	punctate design			
ina	0.00	unknown	incised design			
ina	0.00	unknown				
ina	0.00	unknown				
ina	0.00	unknown	incised design			
ina	0.00	unknown	incised design			
ina	0.00	unknown	incised design			
ina	0.00	unknown	incised design			
ina	0.00	unknown	incised design			
T13	0.00	unknown	Seal 15×10	sack or wall plate	Quadruped ?	horned
T10	0.00	unknown	Seal 11+×15+	too broken to know	quadruped	
none	8.80	near edge of tepe	none	unknown	obscure	
T21	8.42	unknown	Seal 20+×17+	door peg	stick man ?	
none	0.00	in 'usta' dump	Seal 29+×12+	unknown	snake	
none	0.00	unknown	Seal 26+×14+	unknown	animal & plant	
none	8.15	over & outside corner White Room	Seal 17 dia	unknown	quadruped	
none	7.98	just outside SE door White Room	none	with other junk	unknown	netting
ina	7.83	unknown	Seal 15 dia	seal	starburst	hemispheroid ?
ina	8.50	unknown	Seal 25 dia	seal	abstract lines	hemispheroid
T8	8.00	unknown	Seal 18×21	Seal	triangle criss cross	flat hemisphere
ina	8.20	unknown	Seal 16 dia	seal	cruciform	hemispheroid
ina	8.42	in heavy ash layer	Seal 22 dia	seal	lines off vertical	lentoid
T14	7.90	see note	Seal 15 diam	on top container	2 animals	hemispheroid
none	8.61	unknown	Seal 20 dia	3 people dance		
T13	7.90	see note	Seal 16×20	on jar shoulder	stick figure hunter	
T21	7.90	see note	Seal 23×22+	on sack peg tie	bearded man	leads herd
T15	8.00	unknown	Seal 28+×25+	over basket cover	circling quadrupeds	
none	7.96	unknown	Seal 28+×36+	unknown	dancing man	animals
T25	0.00	unknown	Seal 19+×24+	in jar mouth ?	big quadruped filler	
none	7.90	unknown	Seal 17+dia	unknown	animal with plumes	
T10	7.90	see note	Seal 22+×25	on basket cover	long necked animal	
T21	8.10	in thick layer of refuse	Seal 17 diam	on jar shoulder	quadruped plumes	
T14	7.90	unknown	Seal 17 diam	same as 4-1025	on top container	starburst
T11	7.93	in White Room niche east wall	Seal 21×18+	wall tag ?	scorpion	
none	8.50	unknown	none	same as 4-888 XI ?	unknown	horns gazelle
ina	7.90	unknown	Seal 18 dia	same as 4-1202	unknown	starburst
T12	8.10	unknown	Seal 17 diam	in jar mouth ?	crude quadruped	
T20	7.93	in White Room	Seal 11 diam	on basket cover	cruciform	
T24	7.90	unknown	Seal 21 diam	on jar shoulder	long horn gazelle	
ina	7.96	unknown	Seal 12 diam L32	in jar mouth	cruciform	
none	7.90	see note		mat impression	leaf skeleton	
none	7.90	see note	Seal 17 dia	unknown	lozenge	
none	7.95	unknown	Seal 28+×24	unknown	abstraction:	animal ?
ina	8.16	in west trench	Seal 15 dia	seal	lozenges	hemispheroid

(continues)

Level XII   (continued)

1	2	3	4	5	6	7	8	9	10	11	12
453.	4-1225	35-10-281	0867	XII XII	impression	clay	10P	4M	c/d3/4	L32	W22
454.	4-none	Discarded	0870	XII XII	impression	clay	10P	4M	f4	none	none
455.	4-none	Discarded	0861	XII XII	impression	clay	9N	5O	c7	none	none
456.	4-none	35-10-258	0901	XII XII	impression	clay	9N	5O	i/j2	L22	W27
457.	5-1237	36-6-306	0911	XII XII	impression	clay	10P	4M	none	L40	W41
458.	5-1238	IM27044	0911	XII XII	stamp	steatite	10P	4M	none	D29	T13
459.	5-1239	36-6-305	0911	XII XII	impression	clay	10P	4M	none	L21	W72
460.	5-1240	36-6-313	0911	XII XII	impression	clay	10P	4M	none	L44	W34
461.	5-1242	IM26965	0829	XII XII	impression	clay	9M	6O	j10	D20	none
462.	5-1244	IM26995	0889	XII XII	impression	clay	8M	6Q	j8	D22	none
463.	5-1246	36-6-308	0890	XII XII	impression	clay	9N	5O	a7	L50	W36
464.	5-1247	36-6-310	0909	XII XII	impression	clay	8N	5Q	a7	L43	W29
465.	5-1406	36-6-311	1192	XII XII	impression	clay	8N	5Q	j10	L41	W24
466.	5-1407	36-6-293	1174	XII XII	stamp	stone	11R	3K	b3	D20	none
467.	5-1437	IM27043	1212	XII XII	stamp	marble	9R	3O	c/d8/9	none	none
468.	5-1514	36-6-307	1249	XII XII	impression	clay	10P	4M	i 5/6	L41	W42
469.	5-1520	36-6-294	1249	XII XII	stamp	steatite	10P	4M	i 5/6	D12	T6
470.	5-1547	IM26977	1388	XII XII	impression	clay	10M	6M	g 1/2	none	none
471.	5-1588	36-6-296	1419	XII XII	stamp	stone	8M	6Q	d/e 2	D17	T8
472.	5-1595	36-6-309	1284	XII XII	impression	clay	8N	5Q	h 6/7	L35	W49
473.	5-1600	IM27005	1291	XII XII	impression	clay	10M	6M	e6	none	none
474.	5-1601	IM26972	1291	XII XII	impression	clay	10M	6M	e6	none	none
475.	5-1630	IM27027	1426	XII XII	stamp	stone	11M	6K	e/f5/6	D21	T8
476.	5-1631	Baghdad	1432	XII XII	stamp	steatite	9N	5O	a 7/8	D13	T7
477.	5-1640	36-6-297	1435	XII XII	stamp	stone	9M	6O	c8	D21	T9
478.	5-1641	36-6-298	1455	XII XII	stamp	serpentine	9M	6O	d8	L18	W14
479.	5-1648	IM26962	1447	XII XII	impression	clay	9M	6O	e/f7/8	D24	none
480.	5-1699	IM26988	1473	XII XII	impression	clay	10P	4M	none	D21	none
481.	5-1760	36-6-299	1557	XII XII	stamp	stone	9R	3O	c9	D16	T8
482.	5-none	36-6-287	none	XII XII	stamp	white marble	none	none	none	D22	T7
483.	5-none	36-6-288	none	XII XII	stamp	steatite	none	none	none	D22	T6
484.	5-none	36-6-289	none	XII XII	stamp	steatite	none	none	none	D23	T9
485.	5-none	36-6-291	none	XII XII	stamp	agate	none	none	none	L14	W11
486.	5-none	36-6-300	none	XII XII	stamp	steatite	10N	5M	none	D25	T9
487.	5-none	36-6-301	none	XII XII	stamp	steatite	8N	5Q	none	D22	T6
488.	5-none	36-6-303	1359	XII XII	stamp	alabaster	10N	5M	d 2/3	D27	T10
489.	5-none	36-6-304	none	XII XII	stamp	paste	10P	4M	none	D17	T8
490.	5-none	Discarded	1480	XII XII	impression	clay	10N	5M	e/f8/9	none	none
491.	5-none	unknown	1379	XII XII	stamp	unknown	10R	3M	g3	none	none
492.	5-none	unknown	1454	XII XII	stamp	unknown	9P	4O	none	none	none
493.	5-none	unknown	1439	XII XII	stamp	unknown	8P	4Q	e/f 9	none	none
494.	6-081	IM32625	none	XII XII	impression	clay	5M	5M	none	L21	W28
495.	6-089	37-16-216	none	XII XII	impression	clay	5K	5K	none	L58	W62
496.	6-096	Baghdad	1744	XII XII	impression	clay	4J	4J	i2	L96	W49
497.	6-107	37-16-214	none	XIA XII	impression	clay	4J	4J	none	L52	W29
498.	6-108	unknown	1740	XII XII	impression	clay	4J	4J	none	none	none
499.	6-151	37-16-208	1776	XII XII	stamp	serpentine	5J	5J	e1	D22	T9
500.	6-152	Baghdad	1773	XII XII	stamp	steatite	4J	4J	e2	D16	T8
501.	6-161	37-16-215	1763	XII XII	impression	clay	6J	6J	e4	L42	W40
502.	6-167	Baghdad	none	XII XII	impression	clay	6K	6K	none	L28	W41
503.	6-203	37-16-205	4107	XII XII	stamp	limestone	5K	5K	e9	D47	none
504.	6-250	37-16-211	none	XII XII	impression	clay	5K	5K	none	L34	W42
505.	6-257	37-16-209	1861	XII XII	stamp	steatite	5J	5J	h3	D22	T10
506.	6-303	37-16-207	1926	XII XII	stamp	steatite	6G	6G	h3	D24	none
507.	6-366	Baghdad	none	XII XII	stamp	limestone	6G	6G	none	D21	T9
508.	6-579	37-16-215	none	XII XII	impression	black clay	11M	11M	none	L37	W31
509.	6-581	Baghdad	none	XII XII	impression	black clay	11M	11M	quad a	none	none
510.	6-611	37-16-212	none	XII XII	impression	clay	5M	5M	quad a	L74	W60
511.	6-none	IM32830	none	XII XII	impression	clay	3J	3J	none	L38	W37
512.	7-none	Discarded	1862	XII XII	impression	clay	5J	5J	h3	none	none
513.	7-none	unknown	1752	XII XII	stamp	unknown	5K	5K	c8	none	none
514.	7-none	unknown	1698	XII XII	impression	clay	5K	5K	b9	none	none

13	14	15	16	17	18	19
T11	7.90	unknown	Seal 17 diam	same as 4-1028	on jar shoulder	cruciform
none	7.95	unknown	none	unknown	unknown	
none	7.93	unknown	none	unknown	unknown	
none	0.00	in NW door White Room	Seal 19+×22+	unknown		
T29	0.00	70 cm over floor near White Room	Seal 28+×30+	on door or box	animals in	branches
ina	0.00	70 cm over floor near White Room	Seal 29 dia	seal	horns or abstracts	hemispheroid
T15	0.00	70 cm over floor near White Room	Seal 21+×47	on basket cover	snakes	
T20	0.00	70 cm over floor near White Room	Seal 17+×17	sack tie ?	animal with plumes	
ina	0.00	in debris just above floor	Seal 20 dia	unknown	dismembered	horns
ina	0.00	found below XIA floor	Seal 22 dia	unknown	cruciform	vegetation
T17	7.95	unknown	Seal 35+×17+	flat tab	animal	
T15	0.00	under west wall of 'deep room'	Seal 16 diam	sack tie ?	starburst	
T14	8.20	on floor of room	Seal 19+×21+	on basket cover	stick horned animal	
ina	8.48	a little above floor and celt	Seal 20 dia	seal	abstract burst	stem handled
none	8.27	on pavement	none	seal	unknown	hemispheroid
T16	8.20	just above pavement in largish room	Seal 18+×10+	on sack tie	lozenges	
ina	8.20	just above pavement in largish room	Seal 12 dia	seal	lines in 4 quadrants	hemispheroid
none	8.00	in black refuse outside curved wall	Seal 26 dia	unknown	fish quadruped	
ina	8.75	on pavement of XII near edge of tepe	Seal 17 dia	seal	starburst	
T16	0.00	unknown	Seal 26+×29	on jar shoulder	triangle body man	
none	0.00	outside below Round House walls	none	unknown	unknown	
none	0.00	outside below Round House walls	none	unknown	unknown	
ina	8.11	unknown	Seal 21 dia	seal	dots	lentoid
ina	7.80	in black ash refuse near White Room	Seal 13 dia	seal	unknown	
ina	7.41	in black refuse	Seal 21 dia	seal	bird headed man	hemispheroid
T10	7.70	just outside of Round House	Seal 18×14	seal	abstract criss cross	conoid
ina	7.50	pavement of XII north of Round House	Seal 24 dia	unknown	cruciform in	lozenge
ina	7.50	unknown	Seal 21 dia	unknown	horn animal &legs ?	
ina	7.76	alongside grave	Seal 16 dia	seal	cruciform	hemispheroid
ina	0.00	unknown	Seal 22 dia	seal	2 verticals & filler	hemispheroid
ina	0.00	unknown	Seal 22 dia	seal	abstract lines	hemispheroid
ina	0.00	unknown	Seal 23 dia	seal	abstract lines	hemispheroid
T8	0.00	unknown	Seal 14×11	seal	x- cross diamond	hemispheroid
ina	0.00	unknown	Seal 25 dia	seal	crude cross	hemispheroid
ina	0.00	unknown	Seal 22 dia	seal	2 crude lozenges	flat cylinder
ina	8.36	on top of XII wall	uncut	seal	uncut	hemispheroid
ina	0.00	unknown	Seal 17 dia	seal	rosette ?	hemispheroid
none	7.35	on floor near 5-1713	none	unknown	unknown	
none	7.98	from pavement near edge of tepe	none	seal	unknown	
none	7.90	in w wall room N of Round House seal	none	unknown		
none	7.95	on floor under NW wall of White Room	none	seal	unknown	
none	0.00	unknown	Seal 16+×16+	unknown	quadruped	
none	0.00	unknown	Seal 20 dia	unclear	horned animal	
none	0.00	unknown	Seal 23×15	unknown	horn animal &	sphere
T14	ina	unknown	Seal 22 diam	curved tab	obscure	
none	0.00	in large room with bone bead	none	unknown	unknown	
ina	0.00	unknown	Seal 22 dia	seal	gazelle	hemispheroid
ina	0.00	unknown	Seal 16 dia	seal	criss cross	
T30	0.00	unknown	Seal 26+×27+	in jar mouth	large animal	
none	0.00	unknown	Seal 20+×29	unknown	dogs ibex snake	
ina	0.00	found in pot with necklace	uncut	seal	eroded	hemispheroid
T22	0.00	unknown	Seal 15+×21+	in jar mouth ?	2 horned animals	
ina	0.00	unknown	Seal 22 dia	seal	3 fish	hemispheroid
ina	0.00	unknown	Seal 24 dia	seal	bird head man legs	hemispheroid
ina	0.00	unknown	Seal 21 dia	seal	rosette ?	hemispheroid
T19	0.00	unknown	Seal 22+ ×24	on top container	many animals	
none	0.00	unknown	Seal 29×25+	unknown	unclear	
T20	0.00	unknown	Seal 27+×25	in jar mouth ??	overlapped horn	animal
T14	0.00n	under XIA	Seal 15×10	on jar shoulder	horned animal	
none	0.00	unknown	none	unknown	unknown	
none	0.00	unknown	none	seal	unknown	
none	0.00	unknown	none	unknown	unknown	

(continues)

Level XII (continued)

1	2	3	4	5		6	7	8	9	10	11	12
515.	7-none	unknown	4136	XII	XII	impression	clay	5M	5M	b10	none	none
516.	7-none	unknown	1751	XII	XII	impression	clay	5O	5O	none	none	none
517.	7-none	unknown	1771	XII	XII	impression	clay	6K	6K	b 9/10	none	none
518.	7-056	38-13-50	none	XII	XII	impression	clay	none	none	none	L34	W32
519.	7-206	38-13-29	1984	XIA	XII	stamp	steatite	8M	8M	none	L16	W13
520.	7-209	IM42359	1987	XII	XII	stamp	paste	7M	7M	c5	D24	T6
521.	7-211	IM42660	1988	XII	XII	impression	clay	7M	7M	a4	none	none
522.	7-212	Baghdad	1988	XII	XII	impression	clay	7M	7M	a4	none	none
523.	7-212A	38-13-51	1988	XII	XII	impression	clay	7M	7M	a4	L54	W45
524.	7-228	38-13-46	2000	XII	XII	stamp	obsidian	8M	8M	none	D18	T13
525.	7-231	Baghdad	2152	XII	XII	impression	clay	8M	8M	d 1/2	none	none
526.	7-251	38-13-43	2030	XII	XII	stamp	paste	6M	6M	none	D22	T10
527.	7-253	38-13-44	2032	XII	XII	stamp	steatite	7M	7M	h/i 3	D22	T8
528.	7-235b	38-13-44b	2032	XII	XII	stamp	steatite	7M	7M	h/i 3	D19	T8
529.	7-255	IM42264	2034	XII	XII	stamp	steatite	8M	8M	none	D20	T8
530.	7-257	38-13-45	2063	XII	XII	stamp	serpentine	11M	11M	e/f 9	D21	T11
531.	7-267	38-13-47	2064	XII	XII	stamp	steatite	10M	10M	e/f 3	D13	T6
532.	7-274	38-13-42	2060	XII	XII	stamp	white paste	7M	7M	e/f5/6	D25	T7
533.	7-480	38-13-28	1986	XI A	XII	stamp	marble	8M	8M	none	D24	T10
534.	7-481	Baghdad	1986	XIA	XII	stamp	stone	8M	8M	none	D21	T10

13	14	15	16	17	18	19
none	0.00	unknown	none	unknown	unknown	
none	0.00	unknown	none	unknown	unknown	
none	0.00	unknown	none	unknown	animal	
T25	0.00	unknown	Seal 25+×17+	rope marks	man horned animal	
T5	8.00	black ash refuse	Seal 16×13	seal	man and ladders	tabloid
ina	0.00	under Round House	Seal 24 dia	seal	circled cross	hemispheroid
ina	0.0	under Round House 2 m west of 7-209	Seal 14 dia	unknown	quadruped	
none	0.00	under Round House 2 m west of 7-209	Seal 13 dia	cloth impressions	2 parallel lozenges	
T22	0.00	under Round House 2 m west of 7-209	Seal 13 diam	on cloth ??	lost	geometric
ina	8.00	in black debris	Seal 18 dia	seal	animal fish?arrow ?	hemispheroid
none	8.00	unknown	Seal 24 dia	unknown	quadrupeds	
ina	0.00	unknown	Seal 22 dia	seal	4 quadrants of lines	hemispheroid
ina	8.00	in black refuse under Round House	Seal 22 dia	seal	gazelle	hemispheroid
ina	8.00	in black refuse under Round House	Seal 19 dia	seal	gazelle	
ina	0.00	unknown	Seal 20 dia	seal	crude animal	
ina	7.75	in black refuse	Seal 21 dia	seal	horn head animal	hemispheroid
ina	8.00	in black refuse in west trench	Seal 13 dia	seal	cruciform	hemispheroid
ina	8.00	under the Round House	Seal 25 dia	seal	3 sets herringbone	hemispheroid
none	8.00	in west trench	Seal 24 dia	seal	abstract lines	hemispheroid
none	8.00	in west trench	Seal 21 dia	seal	2 hatched verticals	lentoid

Level XIAB

1	2	3	4	5	6	7	8	9	10	11	12	13	14
		Bone	**item**										
535.	4-0710	Baghdad	0118	XII XIA	spatula	bone	10N	5M	a 2/3	L170	T21	ina	9.15
536.	4-0838	Baghdad	0329	XIA XIA	spatula	bone	9M	6O	j7	none	none	none	10.08
537.	4-1027	35-10-170	0726	XIA XIAB	spatula	bone	9N	5O	b8	L84	W22	T3.5	9.11
538.	4-1106	Baghdad	0243	XIA XIAB	needle	bone	8N	5Q	j10	none	none	none	9.15
539.	4-none	unknown	0952	XIA XIAB	awl	bone	9M	6O	e4	none	none	none	8.78
540.	5-1431	Baghdad	1094	XII XIAB	spatula	bone	8N	5Q	h/i4/5	L127	W16	ina	9.41
541.	5-1447	Baghdad	1100	XIA XIAB	spatula	bone	12N	5J	c4	L310	W21	ina	8.76
542.	5-1484	36-6-193	1266	XIA XIAB	scraper	bone	12N	5J	i2	L120	W17	ina	0.00
543.	5-1484	36-6-194	1266	XIA XIAB	scraper	bone	12N	5J	i2	L145	W15	ina	0.00
544.	5-1518	36-6-281B	1354	XII XIB	spatula	bone	10N	5M	a3	L117	W18	T3	8.52
545.	5-1634	36-6-196	1453	XIA XIAB	spatula	bone	10L	7M	none	L192	W19	ina	0.00
546.	5-none	36-6-279	1278	XII XIAB	awl	bone	10M	6M	e/f 2	L98	W11	ina	8.19
547.	5-none	unknown	1496	XI XIA	blade	bone	11N	5K	e 9/10	none	none	none	7.16
548.	6-none	37-16-65	none	XIA XIAB	spatula	bone	7O	7O	none	L126	W21	none	0.00
549.	7-none	unknown	4113	XIA XIAB	implement	bone	7O	7O	e2	none	none	none	0.00
550.	7-none	unknown	4111	XIA XIAB	implement	bone	7Q	7Q	i9	none	none	none	0.00
551.	7-none	38-13-27	none	XIA XIAB	chisel	bone	7M	7M	none	L173	W23	ina	0.00
		Clay	**item**										
552.	4-0988	Baghdad	0603	XII XIAB	unknown	ceramic	9P	4O	i9	none	none	none	9.24
553.	4-none	Discarded	0387	XII XIAB	unknown	ceramic	9P	4O	a5	none	none	none	9.30
554.	4-none	Discarded	0245	XIA XIAB	small ball	clay	9P	4O	d7	none	none	none	8.80
555.	4-none	unknown	0392	XIA XIA	small ball	unknown	10N	5M	b7	none	none	none	9.93
556.	4-none	unknown	0289	XI XIAB	unknown	clay	9N	5O	g10	none	none	none	9.25
557.	4-none	unknown	0695	XIA XIAB	game piece	vessel	8N	5Q	b7	none	none	none	9.36
558.	4-none	unknown	0808	XIA XIAB	nail	clay	9M	6O	d7	none	none	none	9.53
559.	5-none	unknown	1172	XIA XIAB	semicircle	clay	12P	4J	none	none	none	none	9.64
560.	6-078	37-16-52	none	XIA XIAB	lamp ?	green ware	5K	5K	none	L86	W52	ina	0.00
561.	6-104	unknown	none	XIA XIAB	tube	clay	5J	5J	none	L213	D182	ina	0.00
562.	7-116	38-13-7	1965	XIA XIAB	tube	clay	10M	10M	none	L54	D25	ina	0.00
563.	7-215	38-13-23	2024	XIA XIAB	6 game pieces	terra cotta	7M	7M	plan	H31	D16	ina	8.55
564.	7-216	38-13-24	2024	XIA XIAB	2 game pieces	ceramic	7M	7M	plan	H12	D18	ina	8.55
565.	7-217	38-13-25	2024	XIA XIAB	2 game pieces	ceramic	7M	7M	plan	H19	D23	ina	8.55
566.	7-none	unknown	1979	XIA XIAB	game piece	ceramic	11M	11M	b3	none	none	none	0.00
567.	4-none	unknown	0820	XIA XIAB	game piece	unknown	10M	6M	f4	none	none	none	8.85
568.	4-none	unknown	0736	XIA XIAB	game piece	unknown	10M	6M	g4	none	none	none	9.55
569.	4-none	unknown	0666	XIA XIAB	cone base	unknown	9M	6O	i2	none	none	none	9.61
570.	5-1337	Baghdad	1154	? XIAB	ladle	ceramic	11P	4K	f9	none	none	none	9.16
		Figurine											
571.	4-1028	35-10-146	0723	XIA XIAB	animal	ceramic	9M	6O	g3	L52	H43	none	9.92
572.	4-1062	Baghdad	0223	XIA XIA	animal	ceramic	10N	5M	d 8/9	L46	H38	ina	8.86
573.	4-1105	Baghdad	0829	XIA XIAB	animal	ceramic	7M	6S	j10	L49	H58	ina	9.63
574.	4-1159	35-10-217	0764	XII XIAB	animal	ceramic	10P	4M	f/g3/4	L43	H39	T20	9.03
575.	4-1179	Baghdad	0969	XIA XIAB	animal head	clay	10M	6M	h6	none	none	none	9.26
576.	4-none	Discarded	0806	XIA XIAB	quadruped	clay ?	8N	5Q	g2	none	none	none	9.44
577.	4-none	unknown	0706	XIA XIAB	animal	clay	10P	4M	f3	none	none	none	9.42
578.	4-none	unknown	0385	XII XIAB	wheel	clay	9P	4O	a5	none	none	none	9.30
579.	4-none	unknown	0865	XIA XIAB	unknown	clay ?	10M	6M	h3	none	none	none	9.10
580.	5-1384	Baghdad	1168	XIA XIAB	animal	ceramic	12P	4J	i3	L60	H37	ina	9.35
581.	5-1387	36-6-146	1122	XIA XIAB	hut statue	ceramic	11P	4K	f10	H172	D85	none	8.89
582.	5-1460	36-6-163	1225	XIA XIAB	animal	ceramic	10N	5M	g/h8/9	H45	L51	ina	8.78
583.	5-1524	Baghdad	1368	XIA XIAB	hut statue	ceramic	11L	7K	e/f3/4	H124	D19	ina	9.30
584.	5-1556	36-6-147	1277	XIA ?XIAB	hut statue	clay	11L	7K	f8	H125	W115	ina	8.95
585.	5-none	36-6-164	1096	XIA XIA	animal	clay	12N	5J	h/i3/4	L40	H40	ina	9.53
586.	5-none	36-6-165	1339	XIA XIAB	animal	clay ?	9L	7O	h9	H37	L48	ina	8.70
587.	5-none	36-6-253	1278	XII XIAB	animal	clay ?	10M	6M	e/f 2	H27	L43	ina	8.19
588.	5-none	unknown	1137	XIA XIAB	animal	clay	11P	4K	a/b 10	none	none	none	9.27
589.	5-none	unknown	1220	XIA XIAB	hut	clay	8M	6Q	e/f 1	none	none	none	9.52
590.	6-131	Discarded	none	XIA ? XIAB	foot	clay	3K	3K	none	L242	W111	ina	0.00
591.	7-053	Baghdad	2540	XI XIAB	sheep	clay	10M	10M	f8	L75	H57	T24	9.34
		Ground	**stone**										
592.	4-0934	Baghdad	0378	XII ? XIAB	hammer	stone	9P	4O	h8	none	none	none	9.50
593.	4-0946	35-10-238	0568	XII XIAB	celt	stone	9P	4O	a7	L53	W34	T15	9.31
594.	4-0973	35-10-237	0588	XII XIAB	celt	stone	9M	6O	h4	L35	W43	T21	9.54
595.	4-0982	35-10-355	0526	XIA XIAB	sphere	marble	9P	4O	c7	D20	ina	ina	9.22
596.	4-0987	35-10-239	0524	XII XIAB	celt	stone	9P	4O	d3	L58	W38	T15	9.27
597.	4-1030	35-10-234	0705	XII XIA	grinding	limestone	10N	5M	h3	L300	W165	T50	9.51

15	16	17	18	19	20
found below floor tomb 107					
30 cm below XI floor	MR- burn zone				
unknown					
unknown					
unknown					
under wall XIA					
on floor in corner of room					
on floor of room					
on floor of room					
on pavement near no wall					
in Round House					
outside curved wall					
in crevice of libn walls					
unknown					
unknown					
unknown					
unknown					
unknown					
unknown					
unknown					
unknown					
below floor of XI					
unknown					
at level of top of wall					
unknown					
unknown					
with cloth wrapping marks					
room K Round House					
room K Round House					
room K Round House					
in west trench					
unknown					
unknown					
unknown					
2m below temple wall in sherd & ash					
unknown					
below floor					
in debris just above floor					
possibly XI	painted				
unknown					
unknown					
unknown					
unknown					
unknown					
near edge of tepe					
unknown					
in debris under tombs 109	111				
dark refuse with some ash					
on floor					
on pavement in black ash refuse					
just outside great wall					
outside curved wall					
in debris above floor					
near edge tepe in ordinary refuse					
unknown					
in west trench					
unknown					
unknown					
in thick burned layer					
room lower XI	sherds of XI type				
under foundation XIA wall					
unknown					

(*continues*)

Level XIAB   (continued)

1	2	3	4	5	6	7	8	9	10	11	12	13	14
598.	4-1050	35-10-167	0741	XIA XIAB	celt	stone	9N	5O	c9	L35	W35	T14	9.01
599.	4-1101	Baghdad	237	XIA ? XIA	celt	steatite	10P	4M	i8	none	none	none	8.90
600.	4-1166	35-10-233	0980	XII XIA	handmortar	stone	10N	5M	b3	none	none	none	9.00
601.	4-none	35-10-168	0246	XIA XIAB	celt	gray marble	9P	4O	d7	L80	W32	ina	8.88
602.	4-none	35-10-168	none	XIA XIAB	celt	black stone	11M	6K	none	L47	W25	ina	0.00
603.	4-none	35-10-169	0658	XIA XIAB	game piece	limestone	9N	5O	i8	D20	ina	ina	9.11
604.	4-none	Discarded	0691	XIA XIA	hammer	stone	10N	5M	i5	none	none	none	9.21
605.	4-none	Discarded	0720	XIA XIAB	weight	stone	9N	5O	c2	none	none	none	9.30
606.	4-none	unknown	0700	XII XIAB	celt	stone	9P	4O	a10	none	none	none	9.12
607.	4-none	unknown	0361	XII XIAB	celt	stone ?	9P	4O	d7	none	none	none	8.23
608.	4-none	unknown	0735	XIA XIAB	nail	stone	9N	5O	d9	none	none	none	9.50
609.	4-none	unknown	0737	XIA XIAB	pyramid	stone	9M	6O	e3	none	none	none	9.30
610.	5-1329	36-6-99	1102	XI XIAB	game piece	stone	10R	3M	none	D25	T7	ina	8.91
611.	5-1330	Baghdad	1102	XI XIAB	hammer	stone	10R	3M	b2	L63	W58	ina	8.91
612.	5-1382	36-6-185	1169	XIA XIAB	celt	stone	10R	3M	i5	L32	W29	T13	9.28
613.	5-1416	36-6-172	1180	XIA XIAB	mortar	stone	12P	4J	i1	D197	T86	ina	9.23
614.	5-1421	36-6-174	1184	XIA XIAB	palette	stone	12N	5J	j4	L74	W62	T10	0.00
615.	5-1422	phila no#	1189	XIA XIA	palette	stone	12N	5J	g1	L150	W127	T16	8.92
616.	5-1434	Baghdad	1207	XIA XIAB	celt	stone	8M	6Q	b-c 1	L29	W35	T13	9.48
617.	5-1454	Baghdad	1213	XIA XIAB	pestle	stone	12N	5J	e-f6-7	L248	W77	ina	8.77
618.	5-1455	36-6-173	1213	XIA XIAB	palette	stone	12N	5J	e-f6-7	L103	W83	T21	8.77
619.	5-1459	Baghdad	1225	XIA XIAB	macehead	stone	10N	5M	g/h8/9	H42	W44	BD44	8.78
620.	5-1493	36-6-184	1269	XIA XIB	celt	stone	12N	5J	none	L54	W20	T9	0.00
621.	5-1539	Baghdad	1381	XII XIAB	large celt	stone	11R	3K	e/f 2	L81	W57	T29	8.95
622.	5-1541	Baghdad	1383	XII XIAB	game piece	stone	11R	3K	a8	D26	T12	ina	8.90
623.	5-1542	Baghdad	1384	XII XIAB	scraper	stone	11R	3K	d4	L58	W22	T10	9.50
624.	5-1565	36-6-178	1404	XIA XIAB	macehead	stone	10L	7M	g/h6/7	H39	D56	ina	9.00
625.	5-1578	Baghdad	1418	XI XIAB	celt	stone	11L	7K	d 3/4	L37	W18	T12	9.01
626.	5-1598	36-6-181	1292	XII ? XIAB	hammer	stone	10L	7M	none	L95	W53	T31	0.00
627.	5-1652	36-6-182	1442	XIA XIAB	hammer	stone	10K	8M	plan	L84	W75	T29	8.82
628.	5-1669	Baghdad	1516	XIA XIAB	grinding	stone	11L	7K	e/f5/6	L53	T25	ina	9.50
629.	5-none	36-6-180	none	XIA XIAB	hammer	brown marble	8N	5Q	none	L75	W55	ina	0.00
630.	5-none	36-6-183	none	XIA XIAB	celt	stone	8M	6Q	none	L53	W49	T18	0.00
631.	5-none	36-6-186	none	XIA XIAB	celt	green stone	10R	3M	none	L34	W25	ina	0.00
632.	5-none	36-6-187	none	XIA XIAB	celt	green stone	7N	5S	none	L41	W29	ina	0.00
633.	5-none	36-6-189	none	XIA XIAB	celt	black stone	13N	5G	none	L55	W48	ina	0.00
634.	5-none	36-6-190	none	XIA XIAB	ballista	marble	12N	5J	none	D20	none	ina	0.00
635.	5-none	36-6-191	none	XIA XIAB	ballista	marble	10N	5M	none	D21	ina	ina	0.00
636.	5-none	36-6-91	none	XIA XIAB	ballista	marble	10N	5M	none	D21	none	ina	0.00
637.	5-none	unknown	1378	XII XIAB	celt	stone	11P	4K	i/j 4	none	none	none	8.90
638.	5-none	unknown	1233	XIA XIAB	celt	stone?	10M	6M	h 3/4	none	none	none	8.53
639.	5-none	unknown	1300	XIA XIAB	hammer	stone	10L	7M	plan	none	none	none	0.00
640.	5-none	unknown	1425	XIA XIAB	celt	stone	10L	7M	plan	none	none	none	8.72
641.	5-none	unknown	1458	XIA XIAB	celt	stone	11K	8K	e/f1/2	none	none	none	9.40
642.	6-065	37-16-67	1662	XIA XIA	macehead	pink marble	5K	5K	f9	H50	D57	ina	9.25
643.	6-075	37-16-68	1667	XII XIAB	macehead	marble	5K	5K	a/b 7	H43	D58	ina	0.00
644.	6-082	Baghdad	none	XIA XIAB	piece	porphyry	5K	5K	none	D21	T7	ina	0.00
645.	6-097	Baghdad	1739	XIA XIAB	handle	limestone	5J	5J	a10	L127	W30	ina	0.00
646.	6-315	Baghdad	none	XIA XIAB	grinding	basalt	6J	6J	none	L141	W45	T31	0.00
647.	7-none	unknown	1736	XIA XIAB	celt	stone	4J	4J	d8	none	none	none	0.00
648.	7-150	Baghdad	2566	XIA XIAB	celt	steatite	10M ?	10M	none	L29	W22	T9	0.00
649.	7-none	38-13-26	none	XIA XIAB	gamepiece2	alabaster	none	none	none	L15	D12	ina	0.00
		Misc.	**imprint**										
650.	4-0980	discarded	0585	XII XIAB	rope	clay	8N	5Q	c9	none	none	none	9.69
651.	4-1096	discarded	0721	XIA XIAB	reed mat	clay	9M	6O	g3	none	none	none	9.92
652.	4-none	Discarded	0814	XIA XIAB	unknown	bitumen	8M	6Q	c8	none	none	none	8.95
653.	4-none	unknown	0606	XIA XIAB	unknown	clay	9P	4O	j9	none	none	none	0.00
		Jewelry											
654.	4-0961	phila ?	0413	? XIAB	beads	shell	9N	5O	none	none	none	none	9.88
655.	4-0963	Baghdad	0580	XII XIAB	button	stone	8N	5Q	b2	D28	T13	ina	9.24
656.	4-0972	35-10-247	0583	XII XIAB	pendant	stone	9P	4O	b3	L45	W27	T8	9.11
657.	4-1018	Baghdad	0696	XIA XIAB	acorn	stone	8N	5Q	c9	H30	D15	ina	9.42
658.	4-1087	Baghdad	0436	XI XIAB	pendant	obsidian	8M	6Q	f10	none	none	none	8.66
659.	4-1217	Baghdad	0865	XIA XIAB	button	stone	10M	6M	b3	none	none	none	9.10
660.	4-none	Discarded	0872	XII XIAB	toggle pin	unknown	9M	6O	g5	none	none	none	8.60

15	16	17	18	19	20
unknown					
unknown					
unknown					
unknown					
unknown					
unknown	ballista ?				
below floor of XI					
unknown					
on floor of XII room					
unknown					
unknown					
unknown					
on pavement near to wall with seal					
on pavement next to wall with seal					
on floor					
in corner of room					
on floor of room					
on floor in ashes					
in ash debris below floor above walls					
unknown					
unknown					
n debris under tombs 109	111				
in corner room at tops of bins					
40 cm above floor next to wall					
in ordinary refuse					
in ordinary refuse at top of XII walls					
on pavement of circular structure					
on pavement of Round House room					
on floor of central room	in Round House				
in room L of Round House					
outside and East of Round House					
unknown					
unknown					
unknown					
unknown	hammer?				
unknown					
unknown					
unknown					
unknown					
from pavement deep in XIA					
in refuse					
30 cm off floor in Round House					
from Round House					
just back of Round House					
inside or against wall					
at floor level XIA or just below					
unknown					
unknown					
unknown					
unknown					
from west trench					
under pavement of Round House					
unknown					
unknown	container ?				
unknown					
above room with white plaster					
unknown					
below foundations of XI building					
from room under XI structures					
near grave 137					
in ordinary refuse below					
XI pavement					
with spindle whorls	figurines	sherds			
unknown					

(*continues*)

Level XIAB   (continued)

1	2	3	4	5	6	7	8	9	10	11	12	13	14
661.	4-none	unknown	0569	XII XIAB	button	potsherd	10P	4M	j9	none	none	none	9.10
662.	4-none	unknown	0865	XIA XIAB	button	none	10M	6M	h3	none	none	none	9.10
663.	4-none	unknown	0804	XIA XIAB	pendant	black stone	10M	6M	h6	none	none	none	9.74
664.	4-none	unknown	0733	XIA XIAB	pendant	obsidian	9M	6O	g4	none	none	none	9.60
665.	4-none	unknown	0538	XI XIAB	pendants	none	8M	6Q	j 2/3	none	none	none	8.89
666.	4-none	unknown	0878	XII XIAB	ring	clay	8M	6Q	h8	none	none	none	9.00
667.	4-none	unknown	0873	XII XIAB	pin	copper	9M	6O	h8	none	none	none	8.60
668.	5-1383	36-6-109	1165	XI XIAB	amulet	stone	10R	3M	b4	L11	W4	ina	9.03
669.	5-1466	Baghdad	1307	XIA XIB	pendant	stone	11N	5K	i2	L18	W12	none	8.63
670.	5-1635	phila ?	1453	XIA XIAB	2 sets beads	stone	10L	7M	none	none	none	none	0.00
671.	6-068	37-16-72	none	XIA XIAB	pendant	steatite	7J	7J	none	L40	W21	ina	0.00
672.	6-095	unknown	1734	XIA XIAB	bead	clay	5M	5M	g9	L30	W22	T10	0.00
673.	6-127	37-16-79	none	XIA XIAB	bead	serpentine	3K	3K	none	D16	T7	ina	0.00
674.	6-136	37-16-85	1684	XIA XIAB	amulet	paste	6K	6K	h/i 6	D10	T5	ina	0.00
675.	6-142	unknown	none	XIA XIAB	bead	agate	6J	6J	none	none	none	none	0.00
676.	6-145	37-16-80	1688	XIA XIAB	bead	limestone	6K	6K	i9	L18	D14	T10	0.00
677.	6-200	37-16-81	4109	XIA XIAB	amulet	black steatite	7O	7O	none	H7	D14	ina	0.00
678.	6-216	Baghdad	4114	XIA XIAB	bead	paste	6O	6O	b8	D12	T6	ina	0.00
679.	7-none	unknown	1683	XIA XIAB	amulet	none	5M	5M	a10	none	none	none	0.00
680.	7-none	unknown	1799	XIA XIAB	pendant	stone	7Q	7Q	c3	none	none	none	0.00
681.	7-054	38-13-9	2538	XI XIAB	pendant	granite	9M	9M	b8	L23	W11	T8	9.21
682.	7-none	unknown	1978	XIA XIAB	pendant	black steatite	10M	10M	b/c7/8	none	none	none	0.00
683.	7-none	unknown	1960	XIA XIAB	beads 2	steatite	9M	9M	c9	none	none	none	0.00
		Lithics											
684.	4-0795	Baghdad	0065	? XIAB	blade	obsidian	10N	5M	c/d6/7	none	none	none	0.00
685.	4-0901	35-10-243	0405	XII XIAB	blade	obsidian	10M	6M	h/i 2	L172	W13	T3.7	9.50
686.	4-0965	phila ?	0589	XII ? XIAB	blade	obsidian	8P	4Q	b9	none	none	none	9.87
687.	4-0967	Baghdad	0590	XIA XIAB	blade	obsidian	8M	6Q	h9	none	none	none	9.76
688.	4-0983	35-10-95	0608	XIA XIAB	core	obsidian	9P	4O	j9	L101	W23	T18.4	9.68
689.	4-0985	35-10-359	0528	XIA XIAB	blade	Obsidian	9M	6O	f5	L93	W23	T10	9.28
690.	4-1019	Baghdad	0701	XII XIAB	core	obsidian	9N	5O	i2	none	none	none	9.12
691.	4-1051	Baghdad	0740	XIA XIA	blades 2	obsidian	10N	5M	h3	none	none	none	9.26
692.	4-1155	Baghdad	0951	XIA XIB	blade	obsidian	10N	5M	c4	none	none	none	8.63
693.	4-none	unknown	0232	XI XIAB	core	obsidian	9M	6O	h 3/4	none	none	none	8.65
694.	5-1433	36-6-176	1095	XIA XIAB	blade	obsidian	10R	3M	h/i3/4	L132	W22	T3.4	9.53
695.	5-1448	phila ?	1251	XIA XIAB	sickle	flint	12N	5J	e6	none	none	none	8.71
696.	5-1449	Baghdad	1219	XIA XIAB	blade	obsidian	12N	5J	b3	L115	W11	T3	9.53
697.	5-none	35-10-155	1093	XIA XIAB	saw	chert	12P	4J	b 8/9	none	none	none	9.33
698.	5-none	unknown	1093	XIA XIAB	knife	obsidian	12P	4J	b 8/9	none	none	none	9.33
699.	6-091	37-16-71	none	XIA XIAB	blade	obsidian	4J	4J	none	L129	W15	T3	0.00
700.	6-130	Baghdad	none	XIA XIAB	blade	obsidian	4J	4J	none	L113	W15	none	0.00
701.	6-none	37-16-70	none	XIA XIAB	blade	flint	none	none	none	L70	W18	none	0.00
702.	7-none	unknown	1632	XIA XIAB	disc	flint	6Q	6Q	a 5/6	none	none	none	0.00
		Metal	**item**										
703.	4-none	unknown	0586	XII XIAB	needle	copper	8N	5Q	b2	none	none	none	9.24
704.	4-none	unknown	0970	XIA XIAB	fibula	copper	10M	6M	j4	none	none	none	8.84
705.	5-none	unknown	1362	XII XIAB	nail	copper	9M	6O	e5	none	none	none	9.20
706.	6-141	unknown	1679	XIA XIAB	adze blade	metal	5J	5J	c9	L73	W33	T9	0.00
707.	6-208	unknown	4110	XIA XIAB	chisel	copper	7O	7O	j5	L73	W8	T7	0.00
		Potsherd											
708.	4-1112	Discarded	235	XIA XIAB	rim	clay	9P	4O	c7	none	none	none	8.80
709.	4-1113	Baghdad	235	XIA XIAB	rim	clay	9P	4O	c7	none	none	none	8.80
710.	4-1114	Discarded	235	XIA XIAB	rim	clay	9P	4O	c7	none	none	none	8.80
711.	4-none	35-10-143	none	XIA XIAB	painted	ceramic	10N	5M	none	none	none	ina	0.00
712.	4-none	unknown	0663	XIA XIAB	none	brown ware	9P	4O	a9	none	none	none	9.35
713.	4-none	unknown	0635	XII XIAB	carinated	clay	9P	4O	b3	none	none	none	9.11
714.	4-none	unknown	0368	XII XIAB	daisy	clay	9N	5O	i10	none	none	none	9.52
715.	4-none	unknown	0616	XIA XIAB	rim	green ware	8N	5Q	b/c 2	none	none	none	9.27
716.	4-none	unknown	0612	XIA XIAB	2 rim bowl	clay	9M	6O	h9	none	none	none	9.19
717.	4-none	unknown	0826	XIA XIAB	2 rim bowl	clay	9M	6O	i10	none	none	none	9.43
718.	4-none	unknown	0828	XIA XIAB	carinated	clay	8M	6Q	c9	none	none	none	9.13
719.	4-none	unknown	0825	XIA XIAB	rim	clay	none	none	none	none	none	none	9.33
720.	5-none	36-6-243	none	XIA XIAB	spout bowl	green buffware	10N	5M	none	L99	W84	SP53	0.00
721.	5-none	36-6-244	none	XIA XIAB	bowl	buffware	10N	5M	none	none	none	ina	0.00
722.	5-none	36-6-421	none	XIA XIAB	bowl	buffware	9N	5O	none	L57	W57	T4	0.00
723.	5-none	36-6-150	none	XIA XIAB	2 rim bowl	orange redware	7M	6S	none	none	none	ina	0.00

15	16	17	18	19	20
near edge of tepe					
unknown					
unknown					
unknown					
unknown					
unknown					
15 cm above floor in corner					
unknown					
in Round House					
wall of well					
unknown	incised				
unknown					
unknown					
unknown					
unknown					
unknown	incised star				
unknown					
unknown					
unknown					
with obsidian blade					
in west trench					
unknown					
in libn brick in wall					
below stone floor locus 124	unused 33 used 45				
in wall of XIA					
unknown					
just above White Room	5 to 7 mm blades				
unknown	striations under	50 & 39			
unknown					
unknown					
unknown					
unknown	minor striations 26	& 26			
on floor of room	bitumen on edge	missing			
in debris above pavement					
in small white plastered room					
by wall					
in wall small white plastered room					
unknown	striations 29 & 29				
unknown					
unknown	serrated				
on floor of room 79A					
near edge of tepe					
unknown					
unmistakably in XII	MR-elevation of	XIAB			
50 cm over floor					
unknown					
pottery nest- locus 148					
pottery nest- locus 148					
pottery nest- locus 148					
unknown					
unknown					
unknown					
unknown					
unknown					
unknown					
unknown					
unknown					
unknown					
unknown	sand temper	HM			
unknown	impressed ware				
unknown	applique rosettes				
unknown	quartz & basalt grit	HM			

(continues)

Level XIAB　　(continued)

1	2	3	4	5	6	7	8	9	10	11	12	13	14
724.	5-none	36-6-154	1124	XIA XIAB	incised	ceramic	11R	3K	a/b4/5	none	none	ina	9.41
725.	5-none	36-6-15 ?	none	XIAXIXIAB	impressed	ceramic	10P	4M	none	none	none	ina	0.00
726.	5-none	36-6-156	none	XIA XIAB	sprig ware	brownware	8N	5Q	none	none	none	ina	0.00
727.	5-none	36-6-157	none	XIA XIAB	sprig ware	ceramic	8M	6Q	none	none	none	ina	0.00
728.	5-none	36-6-158	none	XIA XIAB	painted	buffware	8N	5Q	none	none	none	ina	0.00
729.	5-none	36-6-159	none	XIA XIAB	painted	ceramic	10N	5M	none	none	none	ina	0.00
730.	5-none	36-6-160	none	XIA XIAB	painted	ceramic	12P	4J	none	none	none	ina	0.00
731.	5-none	36-6-161	none	XIA XIAB	painted	ceramic	8N	5Q	none	none	none	ina	0.00
732.	5-none	36-6-162	none	XIA XIAB	painted	buffware	12P	4J	none	none	none	ina	0.00
733.	5-none	36-6-412	0460	XIA XIAB	impressed	ceramic	10N	5M	none	none	none	ina	0.00
734.	4-none	Discarded	0615	XII XIAB	open dish	clay	9P	4O	c3	none	none	none	9.30
735.	4-none	unknown	0648	XIA XIAB	incised	clay	9N	5O	i7	none	none	none	9.11
736.	4-none	unknown	0865	XIA XIAB	incised	clay	10M	6M	h3	none	none	none	9.10
737.	4-none	unknown	0613	XIA XIAB	spouted	clay	9M	6O	c2	none	none	none	9.27
738.	5-none	unknown	1130	XI XIB	incised	clay	11P	4K	c/d 9	none	none	none	8.85
739.	5-none	unknown	1302	XIA XIA	painted	clay	12N	5J	c5	none	none	none	9.42
740.	5-none	unknown	1255	XIA XIA	mixed	clay	12N	5J	c8	none	none	none	9.42
741.	5-none	unknown	1200	XIA XIAB	painted	clay	7N	5S	h10	none	none	none	8.91
742.	7-none	unknown	1724	XIA XIAB	unknown	clay	5J	5J	none	none	none	none	0.00
		Vessels											
743.	4-0733	35-10-140	0306	XIA XIAB	bowl	red brownware	7N	5S	none	H60	RD192	BD48	0.00
744.	4-0921	discarded	0369	? XIAB	Wide flower	ceramic	9N	5O	h/i8/9	H112	RD316	ina	9.50
745.	4-0925	Discarded	0509	XII XIAB	bowl	ceramic	8N	5Q	j 7/8	H74	RD98	BD40	9.02
746.	4-0935	discarded	0381	XIA ? XIAB	Wide flower	ceramic	8P	4Q	c9	H66	RD196	BD86	9.50
747.	4-0997	35-10-187	0419	XII XIAB	trumpet vase	brown ware	9R	3O	d-f 7	H428	RD192	BD72	8.75
748.	4-0999	Baghdad	0416	XII XIAB	vase	ceramic	9R	3O	a7	H324	RD204	BD68	8.75
749.	4-1000	phila no#	0523	XII XIAB	dish	ceramic	9P	4O	none	none	none	none	9.07
750.	4-1008	35-10-144	0649	XIA XIAB	2 rim bowl	red brownware	8M	6Q	g7	L73	W46	T12	9.51
751.	4-1020	35-10-166	0708	XIA XIAB	jar	stone	8M	6Q	j2	L36	W43	T5	9.60
752.	4-1022	35-10-144	0425	XIA XIAB	bowl	buffware	9P	4O	d-e 9	H42	RD154	BD26	9.13
753.	4-1024	discarded	0725	XIA XIAB	bowl	ceramic	8N	5Q	c3	H111	W64	T7	9.70
754.	4-1031	Baghdad	0427	XIA XIAB	Wide flower	ceramic	9N	5O	c2	H70	RD210	BD88	8.96
755.	4-1032	Baghdad	0427	XIA XIAB	bowl	ceramic	9N	5O	c2	none	none	none	8.96
756.	4-1033	Baghdad	0427	XIA XIAB	bowl	ceramic	9N	5O	c2	none	none	none	8.96
757.	4-1059	Baghdad	0751	XIA XIAB	not listed	stone	8N	5Q	e2	none	none	none	9.43
758.	4-1063	Baghdad	0224	XIA XIAB	spouted bowl	ceramic	8M	6Q	rm 78	L111	T6	SP68	9.19
759.	4-1094	35-10-139	0452	XIA XIAB	small jar	buffware	8M	6Q	b3	H69	RD46	D84	9.94
760.	4-1095	35-10-32	0434	XI XIAB	trumpet vase	brownware	9N	5O	a6	H300	RD149	BD84	9.09
761.	4-1108	phila ?	0235	XIA XIAB	Wide flower	ceramic	9P	4O	c7	none	none	none	8.80
762.	4-1109	Baghdad	0235	XIA XIAB	Wide flower	ceramic	9P	4O	c7	none	none	none	8.80
763.	4-1110	35-10-374	0235	XIA XIAB	Wide flower	red brownware	9P	4O	c7	none	none	none	8.80
764.	4-1111	Discarded	0235	XIA XIAB	bowl	ceramic	9P	4O	c7	H27	RD79	D85	8.80
765.	4-1115	Discarded	0235	XIA XIAB	dish	ceramic	9P	4O	c7	none	none	none	8.80
766.	4-1116	Baghdad	0244	XIA XIAB	bowl	ceramic	9P	4O	c7	H41	RD78	D91	8.30
767.	4-1117	35-10-145	0244	XIA XIAB	spouted bowl	gray buff	9P	4O	c7	H45	RD69	SP24	8.30
768.	4-1118	35-10-372	0244	XIA XIAB	Wide flower	red br ware	9P	4O	c7	H66	D220	ina	8.30
769.	4-none	unknown	none	XIA XIAB	bowl	buff ware	7M	7M	none	H140	D300	none	0.00
770.	4-1119	Discarded	0241	XIA XIAB	dish	ceramic	9P	4O	c7	none	none	none	8.45
771.	4-1120	phila ?	241	XIA XIAB	dish	ceramic	9P	4O	c7	none	none	none	8.45
772.	4-1121	unknown	000	XIA XIAB	unknown	ceramic	9P	4O	c7	none	none	none	8.45
773.	4-1122	Baghdad	0247	? XIB	spouted bowl	ceramic	10N	5M	c/d 4	H39	RD49	D59	8.53
774.	4-1123	discarded	0247	? XIB	dish	ceramic	10N	5M	c/d 4	none	none	none	8.53
775.	4-1165	35-10-138	778	XIA XIAB	pot	brown ware	10N	5M	loc 157	H154	RD120	D220	8.52
776.	4-1169	Baghdad	0767	XIA XIB	bowl	ceramic	10N	5M	d/e5/6	none	none	none	8.56
777.	4-none	Discarded	0639	XIA XIAB	dish	ceramic	8P	4Q	e10	none	none	none	9.22
778.	4-none	Discarded	0984	XIA XIA	2 rim bowl	ceramic	10N	5M	a3	none	none	none	8.64
779.	4-none	Discarded	0729	XII XIAB	dish	ceramic	8N	5Q	h10	none	none	none	9.23
780.	4-none	unknown	0634	XII XIAB	2 rim bowl	ceramic	9P	4O	b3	none	none	none	9.11
781.	4-none	unknown	0563	XII XIAB	tiny cup	ceramic	9P	4O	c5	none	none	none	9.12
782.	4-none	unknown	0244	XIA XIAB	pots	ceramic	9P	4O	c7	none	none	none	8.30
783.	4-none	unknown	0412	XII XIAB	jar top	ceramic	9N	5O	f7	none	none	none	8.98
784.	4-none	unknown	0690	XIA XIAB	unknown	unbaked clay	9M	6O	g3	none	none	none	10.0
785.	5-1391	Baghdad	1134	XIA XIAB	spouted bowl	potsherd	11P	4K	i4	none	none	none	9.24
786.	5-1393	Baghdad	1145	XIA XIA	small jar	ceramic	12P	4J	a1	H77	RD59	D105	9.17
787.	5-1395	Baghdad	1127	XIA XIA	small jar	ceramic	11R	3K	a5	H90	none	none	9.05
788.	5-1397	36-6-144	1129	XIA XIAB	model jar	red brownware	11P	4K	h3	H44	RD31	D44	9.49

15	16	17	18	19	20
in fill					
unknown	comb impressed				
unknown	micaceous grit	HM			
unknown					
unknown	quartz grit & chaff	HM			
unknown					
unknown	donated to Louvre				
unknown					
unknown	cross-hatching				
unknown	impressed rosette				
unknown					
unknown					
unknown					
unknown	with potter's mark				
in rubbish below temple wall					
in little room					
on floor of room					
unknown					
on floor					
unknown	quartz grit & chaff	HM			
a few cm above floor against wall	size in Tobler	different here from	registry		
unknown	thick sided				
below this one 7 others found					
east of the door					
at door of room					
unknown					
unknown	quartz grit & chaff	HM			
unknown					
from floor of room	green slip	bubbled sand &	vegetable temper	HM	
unknown	hole mouth	beaded rim			
in pottery cache					
in pottery cache					
in pottery cache					
on pavement near edge of tepe					
just below floor	with cannon spout				
MR- fill	sand & chaff	HM			
in wall of XIA/B					
pottery nest- locus 148					
pottery nest- locus 148					
pottery nest- locus 148	chaff temper	HM			
pottery nest- locus 148	carinated				
Pottery nest- locus 148	fragmentary	Wide flower ?			
pottery nest- locus 148					
pottery nest- locus 148	quartz grit & chaff				
pottery nest- locus 148	chaff temper	HM			
Round House	wet smoothed		HM		
pottery nest 2nd level- locus 148	fragmentary Wide	flower ?			
pottery nest 2nd level- locus 148					
pottery nest- locus 148					
over floor	upturned spout				
over floor	Wide flower ?				
by small oven in corner of room	faintly burnished				
on floor corner of room					
under mats					
unknown					
unknown					
on XII floor					
unknown					
unknown					
locus 148 nest of pots					
next to wall of XII					
below floor of					
in fill over walls					
in corner of room by wall					
unknown					
open area of rubbishy fill	quartz grit & chaff	HM			

(continues)

Level XIAB   (continued)

1	2	3	4	5		6	7	8	9	10	11	12	13	14
789.	5-1398	Baghdad	1132	XIA	XIAB	WideFlower	red ware	11P	4K	a/b 9	H84	RD277	none	9.84
790.	5-1411	36-6-149	1171	XIA	XIAB	2 rim bowl	buffware	12P	4J	e/f4/5	L29	RD154	none	10.1
791.	5-1415	discarded	1173	XIA	XIAB	bowl	ceramic	12P	4J	none	H106	RD184	D208	8.98
792.	5-1423	discarded	1148	XIA	XIA	large jar	ceramic	12P	4J	d4	H320	RD210	D320	0.00
793.	5-1432	Baghdad	1197	XIA	XIAB	footed pot	ceramic	7N	5S	h/i 9	H39	LB44	W31	9.33
794.	5-1442	discarded	1208	XIA	XIAB	large jar	red ware	11N	5K	g/h8/9	H350	RD235	D412	8.78
795.	5-1444	Baghdad	1210	XIA	XIA	2 rim bowl	ceramic	12N	5J	e/f10	H228	RD332	D480	9.64
796.	5-1446	Baghdad	1251	XIA	XIAB	paint jar	gray green	12N	5J	e6	H100	RD45	D75	8.71
797.	5-1457	Baghdad	1226	XIA	XIA	kohl jar	stone	11M	6K	j10	H40	RD16	D22	9.01
798.	5-1468	36-6-138	1227	XIA	XIAB	spout bowl	buffware	7M	6S	e/f8/9	H104	RD157	D161	9.19
799.	5-1475	Baghdad	1259	XIA	XIAB	painted jar	gray green	7N	5S	c9	H168	RD172	BD92	9.00
800.	5-1482	36-6-138	1231	XIA	XIAB	small jar	brown ware	8N	5Q	c8	H108	RD77	BD125	0.00
801.	5-1485	36-6-171	1315	XIA	XIB	cup	marble	10N	5M	f 9/10	H51	RD88	D97	8.60
802.	5-1486	Baghdad	1310	XIA	XIB	bowl	light red	11N	5K	g4	H122	RD190	D206	8.58
803.	5-1487	Baghdad	1310	XIA	XIB	painted bowl	buff ware	11N	5K	f/g 5	H100	RD160	BD66	8.58
804.	5-1489	36-6-140	1314	XIA	XIB	jar	dark buffware	11P	4K	f/g6/7	H105	RD74	D99	8.75
805.	5-1492	Baghdad	1267	XIA	XIAB	small jar	ceramic	12N	5J	a7/8	H66	RD46	D66	0.00
806.	5-1494	discarded	1258	XIA	XIAB	large jar	ceramic	12M	6J	b/c 4	none	RD620	none	9.47
807.	5-1495	36-6-137	1234	XIA	XIAB	bowl	ple brownware	11P	4K	h 3/4	H90	RD118	BD64	9.23
808.	5-1505	36-6-134	1271	XIA	XIAB	bowl	yellow buff	7N	5S	d 4/5	H45	RD89	D95	8.63
809.	5-1506	Baghdad	1273	XIA	XIB	dish	ceramic	12N	5J	a10	H78	RD224	none	8.57
810.	5-1516	discarded	1316	XIA	XIAB	jar stand	red ware	11P	4K	b10	H120	RD264	BD392	8.93
811.	5-1517	36-6-281b	1354	XII	XIB	spouted bowl	ceramic	10N	5M	a3	H109	RD185	none	8.52
812.	5-1525	36-6-139	1368	XIA	XIAB	small jar	buffware	11L	7K	e/f3/4	H133	RD107	D140	9.30
813.	5-1533	36-6-136	1368	XIA	XIAB	bowl	buffware	11L	7K	e/f3/4	H78	RD151	D187	9.30
814.	5-1536	Baghdad	1369	XII	XIB	small jar	ceramic	10N	5M	g/h3/4	H105	RD77	BD115	8.80
815.	5-1545	Baghdad	1385	XII	XIAB	painted bowl	ceramic	11R	3K	a/b1/2	H57	RD151	BD58	9.00
816.	5-1549	Baghdad	1370	XIA	XIA	bowl	buffware	11N	5K	c10	H88	RD202	D194	9.10
817.	5-1550	36-6-141	1370	XIA	XIA	jar	brownware	11N	5K	c10	H177	RD104	D185	9.10
818.	5-1571	Discarded	1389	XIA	XIAB	storage jar	ceramic	11L	7K	h-i3/4	H480	RD194	D464	9.40
819.	5-1585	Baghdad	1417	XI	XIAB	bowl	ceramic	10L	7M	a 7/8	H99	RD107	D147	8.85
820.	5-1602	Baghdad	1421	XIA	XIAB	jar	ceramic	11L	7K	plan	H95	RD60	D120	9.01
821.	5-1620	Baghdad	1344	XIA	XIB	Wide flower	ceramic	10N	5M	c/d3/4	H51	RD168	BD71	8.37
822.	5-1644	36-6-135	1436	XIA	XIAB	bowl	grayware	10K	8M	plan	H64	RD130	D148	9.21
823.	5-1645	36-6-148	1436	XIA	XIAB	"v" cup	ceramic	10K	8M	plan	H130	RD55	BD3	9.21
824.	5-none	36-6-145	none	XIA	XIAB	funnel	brown ware	12N	5J	none	H128	D62	ina	0.00
825.	5-none	Discarded	1190	XIA	XIAB	dish	ceramic	10M	6M	c7	none	none	none	9.49
826.	5-none	unknown	1209	XIA	XIA	trumpet vase	ceramic	11N	5K	e/f 9	none	none	none	9.16
827.	5-none	unknown	1409	XIA	XIAB	jar	ceramic	10L	7M	d7	none	none	none	8.84
828.	6-071	Baghdad	1719	XIA	XIAB	kohl jar	bone	5J	5J	h2	H80	RD7	BD9	0.00
829.	6-087	37-16-50	1729	XIA	XIAB	small jar	green buffware	4J	4J	none	H90	RD64	D103	0.00
830.	6-094	unknown	1672	XIA	XIB	pot	green buffware	4J	4J	a/b 3	H113	RD130	D162	0.00
831.	6-106	Baghdad	none	XIA	XIAB	bowl	brown ware	4J	4J	none	H56	RD100	D102	0.00
832.	6-115	Baghdad	none	XIA	XIAB	large bowl	brown ware	4J	4J	none	H220	D365	ina	0.00
833.	6-128	Baghdad	1755	XIA	XIAB	bowl	brown ware	5J	5J	c8	D95	BD34	ina	0.00
834.	6-156	Baghdad	none	XIA	XIAB	painted bowl	ceramic	6K	6K	none	H62	RD178	BD73	0.00
835.	6-173	unknown	1690	XIA	XIAB	bowl	basalt	5G	5G	none	none	none	none	0.00
836.	6-317	unknown	1917	XIA	XIAB	small jar	green grayware	6J	6J	f10	H102	D132	ina	0.00
837.	6-606	37-16-51	none	XIA	XIAB	painted jar	green grayware	4K	4K	none	H105	none	ina	0.00
838.	7-none	unknown	1675	XIA	XIAB	dishes 2	ceramic	5K	5K	a/b 3	none	none	none	0.00
839.	4-0695	Baghdad **Spindle**	0257 **whorl**	XII ?	XIAB	whorl	clay	9P	4O	g2	H18	D26	ina	9.51
840.	4-0696	35-10-351	0262	XII ?	XIAB	whorl	clay	9P	4O	g2	none	none	ina	9.51
841.	4-0762	Baghdad	0147	XI	XIA	whorl	clay	10N	5M	e-f2-3	H23	D39	ina	9.19
842.	4-0930	Baghdad	0379	XII	XIAB	whorl	clay	9N	5O	g1	H17	D33	ina	9.66
843.	4-0952	Baghdad	0557	XIA	XIAB	whorl	clay	8N	5Q	b2	H16	D34	ina	9.14
844.	4-0991	35-10-229	0609	XII	XIAB	whorl	clay	9R	3O	b8	H24	D39	ina	8.80
845.	4-1005	35-10-161	0656	XIA	XIAB	whorls 9	clay	9N	5O	i7	H20	D38	ina	9.11
846.	4-1005	35-10-162	0656	XIA	XIAB	whorls 9	clay	9N	5O	i7	H21	D36	ina	9.11
847.	4-1005	35-10-163	0656	XIA	XIAB	whorl	clay	9N	5O	i7	H20	D38	ina	9.11
848.	4-1005	35-10-164	0656	XIA	XIAB	whorls 9	clay	9N	5O	i7	H17	D35	ina	9.11
849.	4-1005	35-10-165	0656	XIA	XIAB	whorls 9	clay	9N	5O	i7	H17	D33	ina	9.11
850.	4-1049	35-10-150	0738	XIA	XIAB	whorl	clay	9M	6O	h6	H21	D40	ina	9.40
851.	4-1085	Baghdad	0817	XIA	XIAB	whorl	clay	9M	6O	j6	H19	D31	ina	8.90
852.	4-1102	35-10-158	0830	XIA	XIA	whorl	clay	10N	5M	b7	H23	D36	ina	8.90

15	16	17	18	19	20
unknown					
above walls near oven	painted quartz grit	& chaff	HM		
on floor					
pot grave on shelf above floor	Wet smoothed				
found directly over walls					
under layer of black ashy refuse	MR-fill	wet smoothed			
next to wall near another jar	wet smoothed				
on floor of room	Neck 30	circles & bands			
on pavement	BD13	Incised cross hatch			
outside wall	spout 50 quartz	& chaff	HM		
unknown	ring base	cross hatch			
directly below wall	quartz grit	burning			
on pavement					
under floor in refuse at east corner					
under floor in refuse at east corner	ring base	bands			
in ordinary refuse near no walls					
by oven					
on floor					
from top of stubby wall	maybe door	sand & chaff	WM	ring base	
near edge tepe among stones	sand & chaff	HM			
at top of deep pit in corner	Wide flower pot ?				
of room					
on pavement of small room	burnished				
in pieces					
on pavement near no wall					
in dark refuse with some ash	quartz & basalt grit	HM			
in dark refuse with some ash	sand & chaff	HM			
from top of wall					
unknown	cross hatch				
under paving in corner of room	by oven	Red slip			
under paving in corner of room	by oven	fine quartz & basalt	HM		
set into wall 10cm off pavement					
unknown					
on pavement					
unknown					
outside Round House wall	burnished quartz	grit	HM		
outside Round House wall					
unknown	white grit temper				
unknown					
on pavement wide end in wall					
on pavement of room of Round	House				
unknown					
unknown					
unknown					
unknown					
unknown					
unknown					
unknown	painted scallop				
at bottom of well at foundation					
unknown					
unknown	fine quartz &	basalt grit	HM		
unknown					
unknown	applique blobs				
unknown					
on pavement	incised edge				
found under plaster of XI wall	punctate design				
below XI structure	incised edge				
unknown	punctate design				
unknown	incised edge				
unknown	thumb print on	edge			
unknown	incised edge				
unknown					
unknown					
unknown					
unclear	punctate design				
unknown	incised circles	on top			

(*continues*)

Level XIAB   (continued)

1	2	3	4	5	6	7	8	9	10	11	12	13	14
853.	4-1104	Baghdad	0832	XII XIB	whorl	clay	10N ?	5M ?	d4	none	none	none	8.60
854.	4-1218	35-10-220	0869	XII XIAB	whorl	clay	8N	5Q	h8	H16	D32	ina	9.33
855.	4-none	35-10-148	0537	XIA XIAB	whorl	clay	9M	6O	none	H17	D37	ina	0.00
856.	4-none	35-10-149	none	XIA XIAB	whorl	clay	none	none	none	H21	D35	ina	0.00
857.	4-none	35-10-152	734	XIA XIA	whorl	clay	9N	5O	c3	H18	D30	ina	8.90
858.	4-none	35-10-153	none	XIA XIAB	whorl	clay	10N	5M	none	H22	D28	ina	0.00
859.	4-none	35-10-154	none	XIA XIAB	whorl	clay	10M	6M	none	H25	D35	ina	0.00
860.	4-none	35-10-159	none	XIA XIAB	whorl	clay	11N	5K	none	H20	D34	ina	0.00
861.	4-none	35-10-229	0409	XII XIA	whorl	clay	10N	5M	d 5/6	H20	D34	ina	9.43
862.	4-none	35-10-376	none	XIA XIAB	whorl	clay	9M	6O	none	H21	D35	ina	0.00
863.	4-none	35-10-377	none	XIA XIAB	whorl	clay	9N	5O	none	H20	D36	ina	0.00
864.	4-none	35-10-378	0363	XIA XIAB	whorl	clay	9P	4O	h9	H19	D33	ina	9.82
865.	4-none	35-10-380	0730	XIA XIA	whorls 2	clay	10N	5M	h3	H19	D40	ina	9.13
866.	4-none	35-10-381	0231	XIA XIAB	whorl	clay	10P	4M	h/i 7	H22	D41	ina	9.30
867.	4-none	Discarded	0650	XIA XIAB	whorls 2	clay	9P	4O	e8	none	none	none	9.36
868.	4-none	Discarded	0657	XIA XIAB	whorls 3	clay	9N	5O	i8	none	none	none	9.11
869.	4-none	Discarded	0670	XIA XIAB	whorl	clay	9M	6O	i3	none	none	none	9.65
870.	4-none	unknown	0605	XII XIAB	whorl	clay	9P	4O	c3	none	none	none	9.30
871.	4-none	unknown	0607	XIA XIAB	whorl	clay	9P	4O	j9	none	none	none	9.68
872.	4-none	unknown	0570	XII XIAB	whorl	clay	9P	4O	h3	none	none	none	9.39
873.	4-none	unknown	0565	XII XIAB	whorl	clay	9P	4O	c5	none	none	none	9.12
874.	4-none	unknown	0407	XII XIAB	whorl	clay	8P	4Q	c9	none	none	none	9.03
875.	4-none	unknown	0693	XIA XIA	whorl	clay	10N	5M	h5	none	none	none	9.21
876.	4-none	unknown	0571	XII XIA	whorl	clay	10N	5M	b8	none	none	none	9.71
877.	4-none	unknown	0572	XII XIA	whorl	clay	10N	5M	h3	none	none	none	9.22
878.	4-none	unknown	0647	XIA XIAB	whorls 2	clay	9N	5O	i7	none	none	none	9.11
879.	4-none	unknown	0716	XII XIAB	whorl	clay	8N	5Q	g8	none	none	none	9.33
880.	4-none	unknown	0668	XIA XIAB	whorls 2	clay	8N	5Q	e7	none	none	none	9.78
881.	4-none	unknown	0593	XIA XIAB	whorl	clay	8N	5Q	b1	none	none	none	9.27
882.	4-none	unknown	0981	XIA XIAB	whorl	clay	7N	5S	b9	none	none	none	10.0
883.	4-none	unknown	0987	XIA XIAB	whorl	clay	10M	6M	h8	none	none	none	9.12
884.	4-none	unknown	0988	XIA XIAB	whorl	clay	10M	6M	j9	none	none	none	8.50
885.	4-none	unknown	0989	XIA XIAB	whorl	clay	10M	6M	h9	none	none	none	9.20
886.	4-none	unknown	0865	XIA XIAB	whorl	clay	10M	6M	h3	none	none	none	9.10
887.	4-none	unknown	0736	XIA XIAB	whorl	clay	10M	6M	g4	none	none	none	9.55
888.	4-none	unknown	0697	XIA XIAB	whorl	clay	9M	6O	e1	none	none	none	9.32
889.	4-none	unknown	0601	XIA XIAB	whorls 2	clay	9M	6O	g4	none	none	none	9.29
890.	4-none	unknown	0952	XIA XIAB	whorl	clay	9M	6O	e4	none	none	none	8.78
891.	4-none	unknown	0805	XIA XIAB	whorl	clay	9M	6O	j6	none	none	none	9.20
892.	4-none	unknown	0810	XIA XIAB	whorl	clay	9M	6O	i8	none	none	none	9.06
893.	4-none	unknown	0766	XIA XIAB	whorl	clay	9M	6O	g10	none	none	none	8.93
894.	4-none	unknown	0713	XIA XIAB	whorl	clay	8M	6Q	g8	none	none	none	9.31
895.	4-none	unknown	0714	XIA XIAB	whorl	clay	8M	6Q	c4	none	none	none	9.80
896.	4-none	unknown	0664	XIA XIAB	whorl	clay	8M	6Q	h8	none	none	none	9.45
897.	4-none	unknown	0553	XIA XIAB	whorl	clay	8M	6Q	i1	none	none	none	9.64
898.	5-1530	36-6-167A	1363	XIA XIAB	whorls 3	clay	11L	7K	e/f 4	H19	D37	ina	9.20
899.	5-1530	36-6-167B	1363	XIA XIAB	whorl	clay	11L	7K	e/f 4	H17	D36	ina	9.20
900.	5-1530	36-6-167C	1363	XIA XIAB	whorl	clay	11L	7K	e/f 4	H21	D37	ina	9.20
901.	5-none	36-6-151	1140	XIA XIAB	whorl	clay	11R	3K	d5	H23	D35	ina	9.35
902.	5-none	36-6-155	1093	XIA XIAB	whorls 3	clay	12P	4J	b 8/9	H19	D37	ina	9.33
903.	5-none	36-6-168	none	XIA XIAB	whorl	clay	12N	5J	none	H22	D44	ina	0.00
904.	5-none	36-6-169	none	XIA XIAB	whorl	clay	12N	5J	none	H25	D47	ina	0.00
905.	5-none	36-6-170	none	XIA XIAB	whorl	clay	10R	3M	none	H30	D42	ina	0.00
906.	5-none	unknown	1496	XI XIA	whorl	clay	11N	5K	e9	none	none	none	9.16
907.	5-none	unknown	1496	XI XIA	whorl	clay	11N	5K	e 9/10	none	none	none	7.16
908.	6-none	37-16-54	none	XIA XIAB	whorl	clay	5K	5K	none	H25	D40	ina	0.00
909.	6-none	37-16-55	none	XIA XIAB	whorl	clay	5K	5K	none	H27	D40	ina	0.00
910.	6-none	37-16-56	none	XIA XIAB	whorl	clay	5K	5K	none	H21	D44	ina	0.00
911.	6-none	37-16-57	none	XIA XIAB	whorl	clay	5K	5K	none	H24	D40	ina	0.00
912.	6-none	37-16-58	none	XIA XIAB	whorl	clay	5K	5K	none	H20	D33	ina	0.00
913.	6-none	37-16-59	none	XIA XIAB	whorl	clay	5K	5K	none	H23	D42	ina	0.00
914.	6-none	37-16-60	none	XIA XIAB	whorl	clay	5K	5K	none	H29	D43	ina	0.00
915.	6-none	37-16-61	none	XIA XIAB	whorl	clay	5K	5K	none	H19	D39	ina	0.00
916.	6-none	37-16-62	none	XIA XIAB	whorl	clay	5K	5K	none	H19	D37	ina	0.00
917.	6-none	37-16-63	none	XIA XIAB	whorl	clay	5K	5K	none	H20	D33	ina	0.00
918.	6-none	37-16-64	none	XIA XIAB	whorl	clay	5K	5K	none	H27	D44	ina	0.00

15	16	17	18	19	20
unknown					
unknown	punctate bottom	incised edges			
unknown	incised				
unknown	incised edge				
unknown					
unknown					
unknown	punctate design				
unknown	incised				
unknown					
unknown	incised				
unknown					
unknown	incised				
unknown					
unknown					
unknown					
unknown					
unknown					
unknown					
above room with white plaster					
unknown					
unknown					
on pavement					
below floor of XI					
unknown					
unknown					
unknown					
unknown					
unknown					
unknown					
in lower phase XIA					
in lower phase XIA					
unknown					
unknown					
unknown					
unknown					
unknown					
unknown					
unknown					
on pavement					
unknown					
unknown	potsherd used as				
unknown					
unknown					
unknown					
unknown					
unknown					
on pavement near no walls	upper surface	incised			
by wall in small white plastered room	incised edges				
unknown					
unknown	incised				
unknown	applique blobs				
in wall crevice					
in crevice of libn walls					
unknown					
unknown	applique knobs				
unknown	grooves				
unknown					
unknown	knob shaped				
unknown	incised				
unknown	incised				
unknown	incised				
unknown	incised				
unknown	incised				
unknown	deeply incised				

(continues)

Level XIAB   (continued)

1	2	3	4	5	6	7	8	9	10	11	12	13	14
		Seal	sealing										
919.	4-0907	IM25042	0409	XII XIA	impression	clay	10N	5M	d 5/6	L43	W30	none	9.43
920.	4-0936	35-10-178	0391	XIA XIAB	impression	clay	8N	5Q	f1	L30	W24	T15	9.80
921.	4-0938	35-10-179	0388	XIA XIAB	impression	clay	8N	5Q	f1	L44	W32	T21	9.80
922.	4-0939	IM24977	0514	XIA XIA	impression	clay	10N	5M	d/e7/8	L39	W28	T11	9.57
923.	4-0947	Baghdad	0566	XIA XIAB	stamp	steatite	8N	5Q	b2	D13	T5	ina	9.00
924.	4-0953	35-10-177	0518	XIA XIAB	impression	clay	8N	5Q	none	L28	W34	T14	9.27
925.	4-0955	35-10-263	0577	XII XIAB	impression	clay	9P	4O	g4	L105	W62	T34	9.32
926.	4-0957	35-10-264	0576	XII XIAB	impression	clay	8N	5Q	c10	L24	W26	T19	9.73
927.	4-0958	35-10-265	0576	XII XIAB	impression	clay	8N	5Q	c10	L32	W38	T15	9.73
928.	4-0968	35-10-256	0415	XII XIAB	stamp	steatite	9M	6O	i1	none	none	none	9.66
929.	4-0977	IM25040	0579	XII XIAB	impression	clay	8N	5Q	d10	L56	W27	T12	9.63
930.	4-0981	35-10-137	0585	XII XIAB	impression	clay	8N	5Q	c9	L32	W18	T8	9.69
931.	4-0989	IM25001	0527	XIA XIAB	impression	clay	9M	6O	g7	L45	W31	T9	9.28
932.	4-0998	35-10-267	0584	XII XIAB	impression	clay	8N	5Q	c8	L38	W38	T17	9.32
933.	4-1004	IM25051	0653	XI XIAB	impression	clay	9P	4O	none	L18	W20	ina	9.23
934.	4-1007	35-10-180	0660	XIA XIAB	impression	clay	9M	6O	j1	L22	W32	T17	9.73
935.	4-1015	phila no#	0667	XIA XIA	impression	clay	10N	5M	b3	L19	W14	none	9.64
936.	4-1016	IM25004	0671	XII XIA	impression	clay	10N	5M	i5	L43	W31	none	9.67
937.	4-1017	IM24976	0671	XII XIA	impression	clay	10N	5M	i5	L33	W28	none	9.67
938.	4-1025	Baghdad	0428	XI XIAB	stamp	obsidian	9P	4O	c/d6/7	D13	T9	ina	9.17
939.	4-1034	35-10-173	0433	XIA XIAB	stamp	stone	8N	5Q	f10	L15	W13	none	9.06
940.	4-1035	35-10-181	0727	XIA XIA	impression	clay	10N	5M	g7	L39	W32	T13	9.29
941.	4-1036	IM24969	0724	XIA XIAB	impression	clay	9M	5O	f8	L33	W26	T11	9.30
942.	4-1037	IM25043	0718	XIA XIAB	impression	clay	9N	5O	a8	L36	W27	none	9.72
943.	4-1052	IM24572	0543	XIA-XI XIA	stamp	paste	10M	6M	none	D16	T7	ina	9.61
944.	4-1053	Baghdad	0750	XIA-XI XIA	stamp	stone	10M	6M	g3	D8	none	ina	9.60
945.	4-1054	IM24967	0584	XII XIAB	impression	clay	8N	5Q	c8	L47	W71	none	9.32
946.	4-1055	IM24605	0745	XIA XIAB	stamp	steatite	9M	6O	i5	D15	T7	ina	9.11
947.	4-1058	35-10-172	0802	XIA XIAB	stamp	steatite	9N	5O	c8	D24	T12	ina	9.08
948.	4-1061	IM24998	0739	XIAXIXIAB	impression	clay	8M	6Q	d9	L27	W14	none	9.97
949.	4-1065	35-10-182	0546	XIA XIAB	impression	clay	9M	6O	c9		W23	T11	9.71
950.	4-1066	35-10-175	0803	XIA XIAB	impression	clay	9M	6O	d7	L20	W41	T13	9.53
951.	4-1067	IM24976	0807	XIA XIAB	impression	clay	8N	5Q	g2	L27	W14	none	9.44
952.	4-1068	IM25069	0747	XIA XIAB	impression	clay	8N	5Q	e3	L27	W26	T17	9.59
953.	4-1069	IM24964	0747	XIA XIAB	impression	clay	8N	5Q	e3	L29	W53	none	9.59
954.	4-1070	35-10-174	0732	XIA XIAB	impression	clay	9M	6O	g4	L72	W34	T16	9.60
955.	4-1074	IM25049	0366	XIA XIAB	impression	clay	8M	6Q	f10	L55	W19	none	0.00
956.	4-1075	IM25050	0823	XIA XIAB	impression	clay	9M	6O	e2	L48	W20	none	9.15
957.	4-1076	Baghdad	0811	XIA XIA	stamp	terracotta	10M	6M	f8	L17	W18	T14	9.50
958.	4-1078	Discarded	0809	XIA XIAB	impression	clay	9M	6O	c9	L26	W22	none	9.56
959.	4-1079	35-10-183	0812	XIA XIAB	impression	clay	9M	6O	i8	L26	W18	T8	9.06
960.	4-1080	35-10-184	0812	XIA XIAB	impression	clay	9M	6O	i8	L33	W24	none	9.06
961.	4-1081	35-10-185	0821	XIA XIAB	impression	clay	9M	6O	e2	L30	W21	T15	9.15
962.	4-1089	IM24600	0445	XII XIAB	stamp	steatite	9M	6O	c/d 9	D24	none	ina	8.77
963.	4-1126	IM24958	0226	XIA XIAB	impression	clay	7M	6S	h/i 9	L42	W52	none	9.63
964.	4-1127	IM25003	0236	XIA XIAB	impression	clay	7N	5S	b9	L42	W52	none	9.70
965.	4-1129	IM25038	0225	XIA XIAB	impression	clay	7N	5S	e9	L37	W41	none	9.55
966.	4-1130	IM24975	0228	XIA XIAB	impression	clay	10P	4M	i 6/7	L15	W27	T8	9.30
967.	4-1131	IM24966	0250	XIA XIAB	impression	clay	9P	4O	d7	L18	W18	none	8.80
968.	4-1135	Baghdad	0836	XII XII	stamp	stone	9N	5O	f2	none	none	none	7.93
969.	4-1148	35-10-176	0840	XIA XIA	impression	clay	10M	6M	j 4/5	L21	W35	none	9.65
970.	4-1157	35-10-254	0773	XII XIB	stamp	steatite	10N	5M	c3	D19	none	ina	8.63
971.	4-1206	35-10-186	0850	XIA XIAB	impression	clay	9M	6O	c4	L60	W29	T25	8.78
972.	4-1210	35-10-279	0763	XII XIAB	impression	clay	9M	6O	f/g 10	L32	W33	T25	8.93
973.	4-1212	IM25011	0768	XIA XIB	impression	clay	10N	5M	d/e5/6	L36	W23	none	8.56
974.	4-1220	IM24583	0885	XII XIAB	stamp	steatite	9M	6O	j3	none	none	none	8.90
975.	4-1221	35-10-251	0875	XII XIAB	stamp	shell	10P	4M	j6	D17	T10	ina	9.00
976.	4-none	unknown	0698	XIA XIA	impression	clay	10N	5M	d9	none	none	none	9.90
977.	4-none	unknown	0692	XIA XIA	impression	clay	10N	5M	g9	none	none	none	9.83
978.	4-none	unknown	0699	XII XIAB	impression	clay	9N	5O	i2	none	none	none	9.12
979.	4-none	Discarded	0245	XIA XIB	impression	clay	9P	4O	d7	none	none	none	8.80
980.	4-none	Discarded	0694	XIA XIA	impression	clay	10N	5M	i5	none	none	none	9.21
981.	4-none	Discarded	0909	XIA XIAB	impression	clay	10N	5M	none	none	none	none	0.00
982.	4-none	Discarded	0707	XII XIAB	impression	clay	9N	5O	i2	none	none	none	9.00

15	16	17	18	19	20
unknown	Seal 12+ dia	unknown	abstract animal		
unknown	Seal 19+×17+	on jar shoulder	longhorn beast	stick	
near edge unclear strata	Seal 18 diam	like 4-936	on jar shoulder	longhorn	beast stick
unknown	Seal 28+ dia	on jar shoulder	sheep & 2 animals		
below XI structure with spindle whorl	Seal 13 dia	seal	blank ?	hemispheroid	
unknown	Seal 20+×19+	top of container	buck	snake and ?	
unknown	Seal 25+×31+	wall tag ?	stick figure & snake		
unknown	Seal 14+×19+	sack or basket tie	stickman ?		
unknown	Seal 25+×18+	sack tie	too obscure		
in ordinary refuse	none	(missing)	seal	hemispheroid	
found below . . . of XI in XII	Seal 10 dia	on jar shoulder	sheep ?		
unknown	Seal 17+×11+	(same as 4-1035 ?)	knot over hide ?	double horn	head
unknown	Seal 41 dia	on jar shoulder	animals in nature		
unknown	Seal 25+×38+	in jar mouth ?	man hut arrow		
unknown	Seal 18+×20+	string tag	animal		
unknown	Seal 22+×20+	on jar shoulder	2 animals (lion ?)		
unknown	Seal 19+×14+	(same as 4-1058)	unknown	animal	
unknown	Seal 31×18+	unknown	abstract animal		
unknown	Seal 28×22	unknown	horned quadruped		
unknown	Seal 13 dia	seal	plant stalk	hemispheroid	
on pavement	Seal 15×13	seal	cruciform	hemispheroid	
unknown	Seal 19+×19	(same as 4-981)	on sack or jar	horned head	double
unknown	Seal 8 dia	sack tie ?	quadruped		
unknown	Seal 23+×17+	too broken to know	horned animals		
unknown	Seal 16 dia	seal	ladder motif ?	carinated	hemisphere
unknown	Seal 8 dia	seal	unknown	hemispheroid	
found with 4-998	Seal 29+×50	unknown	man animal	balloon ?	
unknown	Seal 15 dia	seal	cruciform	hemispheroid	
unknown	Seal 24 dia	seal	stick animal	hemispheroid	
unknown	Seal 7×10+	on top container	fish ?		
unknown	Seal 22+×13+ L26	on jar at handle	crude horned	animal	
unknown	Seal 20+×28	jar shoulder	horned animal	plants	
unknown	Seal 27+×28+	too broken to know	horned animal	river ?	
unknown	Seal 26×19+	jar or sack tie	animals		
unknown	Seal 21+×16+	sack tie ?	thongs	perky animals	
unknown	Seal 13×13	(missing)	unknown	starburst	
unknown	Seal 16+×15+	on jar shoulder	quadruped		
unknown	Seal 27+×19+	too broken to know	2 animals		
unknown	Seal 17×18	seal	netting		
unknown	Seal 17+dia	unknown	quadruped		
unknown	Seal 26×18+	(missing)	unknown	saluki dog	
unknown	Seal 33+×19+	(missing)	unknown	saluki dog	
unknown	Seal 16+×13+	on jar shoulder	intertwined snakes		
unknown	Seal 24 dia	seal	long horn animal	hemispheroid	
very near edge of tepe	Seal 20 dia	on basket cover	tooth ??		
unknown	Seal 17 dia	sack tie ? thongs	swirl in lozenge		
very near edge of tepe	Seal 28+×18+	wall tag ??	animal		
unknown	Seal 15+dia	too broken to know	scorpion ?		
near locus 114 ? grave	Seal 10+dia	too broken to know	sheep ? and ?		
on floor of White Room	none	seal	unknown		
over well XII	Seal 21 dia	sack tie	legs of quadruped		
unknown	Seal 19 dia	seal	uncut	scratches	hemisphere
unknown	Seal 15×13	'x' with hatching			
on pavement	Seal 22+×19+	horn beast snake ?			
on floor in corner room under mats	Seal 23+×20+	sheep			
unknown	none	seal	unknown	hemispheroid	
unknown	Seal 17 dia	seal	lines off vertical	hemisphere	
under floor main part of phase XI	none	unknown	unknown		
below floor of XI	none	unknown	unknown		
unknown	none	unknown	unknown		
unknown	none	unknown	unknown		
below floor of XI	none	unknown	unknown		
by ? west wall of "deep room"	none	unknown	unknown		
unknown	none	unknown	unknown		

(*continues*)

Level XIAB   (continued)

1	2	3	4	5	6	7	8	9	10	11	12	13	14
983.	4-none	Discarded	0242	XIA XIAB	impression	clay	8N	5Q	j10	none	none	none	9.18
984.	4-none	Discarded	0864	XIA XIAB	impression	clay	10M	6M	h3	none	none	none	9.10
985.	4-none	Discarded	0891	XII XIAB	impression	clay	9M	6O	j3	none	none	none	8.90
986.	4-none	Discarded	0746	XIA XIAB	impression	clay	9M	6O	i5	none	none	none	9.11
987.	4-none	Discarded	0432	XIA XIAB	impression	clay	9M	6O	g 5/6	none	none	none	9.78
988.	4-none	Discarded	0877	XII XIAB	impression	clay	8M	6Q	h8	none	none	none	9.00
989.	4-none	Discarded	0822	XIA XIAB	impression	clay	8M	6Q	h3	none	none	none	8.95
990.	4-none	none	0384	XIA ? XIAB	stamp	unknown	7N	5S	e10	none	none	none	10.0
991.	4-none	unknown	0053	XIA XIAB	stamp	unknown	8P	4Q	none	none	none	none	9.65
992.	4-none	unknown	0742	XIA XIAB	impression	clay	9M	6O	j5	none	none	none	9.25
993.	5-1243	Baghdad	0912	XII XII	impression	clay	9M	6O	none	L37	W27	none	0.00
994.	5-1245	IM26997		? XIAB	impression	clay	9P	4O	none	L25	W14	none	0.00
995.	5-1328	36-6-112	1102	XI XIA	stamp	steatite	10R	3M	b2	D18	T7	ina	8.91
996.	5-1367	Baghdad	1116	XI XIAB	stamp	bone	11P	4K	e6	D21	T6	ina	9.15
997.	5-1376	36-6-216	1166	XIA XIA	impression	clay	11P	4K	a7	none	none	none	9.23
998.	5-1377	Discarded	1167	XIA XIA	impression	clay	12P	4J	e/f 4	none	none	none	9.36
999.	5-1378	IM26980	1120	XIA XIA	impression	clay	11R	3K	c/d 7	L54	W38	T22	9.33
1000	5-1379	IM27006	1121	XIA XIAB	impression	clay	10R	3M	a4	D26	T8	ina	8.90
1001.	5-1385	IM27032	1123	XIA XIA	stamp	limestone	12P	4J	h2	D20	T8	ina	9.48
1002.	5-1389	Baghdad	1092	XIA XIAB	stamp	stone	7P	4S	a10	D13	T8	ina	0.00
1003.	5-1392	Baghdad	1147	XIA XIAB	stamp	stone	12P	4J	b3	D20	T10	ina	0.00
1004.	5-1396	36-6-205	1136	XIA XIAB	stamp	steatite	11P	4K	d3	D24	T7	ina	9.35
1005.	5-1399	36-6-213	1139	XIA XIA	impression	clay	12P	4J	d5	L43	W31	T16	9.99
1006.	5-1399B	IM26979	1139	XIA XIA	impression	clay	12P	4J	d5	L56	W38	T15	9.99
1007.	5-1424	36-6-200	1150	XIA XIA	stamp	limestone	10M	6M	b/c 7	D12	T5	ina	8.90
1008.	5-1428	IM26983	1138	XIA XIAB	impression	clay	10P	4M	e9	L23	W33	T15	9.33
1009.	5-1429	36-6-212	1138	XIA XIAB	impression	clay	10P	4M	e9	L29	W51	T19	9.33
1010.	5-1435	36-6-215	1198	XIA XIB	impression	clay	12N	5J	g/h5/6	L31	W28	T21	8.90
1011.	5-1438	36-6-391	1211	XIIXI XIAB	stamp	stone	dump	dump	none	D17	T32	ina	0.00
1012.	5-1465	Baghdad	1301	XIA XIAB	stamp	steatite	11P	4K	a/b 7	D17	T6	ina	8.97
1013.	5-1469	Baghdad	1227	XIA XIAB	stamp	stone	7M	6S	e/f8/9	D25	T21	ina	9.19
1014.	5-1471	IM27039	1254	XIA XIAB	stamp	stone	11N	5K	i5	L20	W15	T8	8.85
1015.	5-1476	IM27037	1259	XIA XIAB	stamp	paste	7N	5S	c9	D20	T7	ina	9.00
1016.	5-1483	36-6-203	1232	XIA XIAB	stamp	stone	7N	5S	d7	D24	T12	ina	0.00
1017.	5-1488	36-6-209	1312	XIA XIA	impression	clay	11M	6K	d9	L65	W55	T29	8.91
1018.	5-1548	IM26976	1377	XIA XIAB	impression	clay	8M	6Q	f/g4/5	L37	W26	none	8.72
1019.	5-1557	IM26989	1393	XIA XIA	impression	clay	11M	6K	a3	L56	W34	T32	9.20
1020.	5-1564	36-6-295	1403	XII XIB	stamp	steatite	10M	6M	f/g 8	L24	W19	T9	8.42
1021.	5-1573	36-6-208	1268	XIA XIB	impression	clay	12N	5J	none	L34	W45	T14	0.00
1022.	5-1574	IM26990	1228	XIA XIAB	impression	clay	10P	4M	b/c8/9	L88	W43	none	9.15
1023.	5-1594	36-6-121	1282	XIA XIA	impression	clay	11L	7K	none	L52	W37	T25	0.00
1024.	5-1612	36-6-397	none	XIIXI XIAB	impression	clay	dump	dump	none	none	none	none	0.00
1025.	5-1624	IM26996	1420	XIA XIA	impression	clay	10M	6M	b9	L128	W98	none	0.00
1026.	5-1625	36-6-206	1336	XIA XIAB	impression	clay	9M	6O	a10	L51	W57	T23	8.73
1027.	5-1626	IM26963	1299	XIAXII XIA	impression	clay	9L	7O	note	L47	W29	T23	8.73
1028.	5-1627	IM26968	1338	XIA XIA	impression	clay	9L	7O	h9	L49	W39	T32	8.72
1029.	5-1628	IM26994	1298	XIAXII XIA	impression	clay	11L	7K	note	L43	W24	T7	8.90
1030.	5-1638	36-6-204	1438	XIA XIA	stamp	limestone	10L	7M	i 3/4	D23	T8	ina	8.82
1031.	5-1639	Baghdad	none	XIAXII XIAB	impression	clay	dump	dump	none	L19	W27	none	0.00
1032.	5-1650	IM26974	1448	XIAXII XIA	impression	clay	dump	dump	none	L32	W29	T6	0.00
1033.	5-1651	36-6-210	1445	XIA XIA	impression	clay	10L	7M	plan	L52	W33	T20	8.85
1034.	5-1668	36-6-207	1516	XIA XIA	impression	clay	11L	7K	e/f5/6	L34	W35	T15	9.50
1035.	5-1710	36-6-199	1533	XIA ? XIB	stamp	gray marble	10K	8M	i2	L33	W22	T6	0.00
1036.	5-none	36-6-201	1260	XIA XIAB	stamp	paste	11N	5K	i3	D10	T5	none	8.90
1037.	5-none	36-6-202	none	XIA XIAB	stamp	steatite	12N	5J	none	D20	T8	none	0.00
1038.	5-none	Discarded	1246	XII XIA	impression	clay	10R	3M	c8	none	none	none	10.00
1039.	5-none	Discarded	1146	XIA XIA	impression	clay	122P	4J	a/b7/8	none	none	none	9.32
1040.	5-none	Discarded	1149	XIA XIAB	impression	clay	12P	4J	c8	none	none	none	0.00
1041.	5-none	Discarded	1308	XIA XIAB	impression	clay	11P	4K	b 3/4	none	none	none	0.00
1042.	5-none	Discarded	1190	XIA XIA	impression	clay	10M	6M	c7	none	none	none	9.49
1043.	5-none	Discarded	1406	XIA XIA	impression	clay	11L	7K	none	none	none	none	10.0
1044.	5-none	Discarded	1341	XIA XIA	impression	clay	9L	7O	h9	none	none	none	8.71
1045.	5-none	unknown	1309	XIA XIAB	stamp	unknown	8N	5Q	c/d 1	none	none	none	0.00
1046.	5-none	unknown	1135	XIA XIA	stamp	unknown	12P	4J	c/d7/8	none	none	none	10.0
1047.	5-none	unknown	1288	XIA XIAB	impression	clay	8P	4Q	d9	none	none	none	0.00
1048.	5-none	unknown	1313	XIA XIAB	impression	clay	10M	6M	g/h5/6	none	none	none	8.64

15	16	17	18	19	20
unknown	none	unknown	unknown		
unknown	none	unknown	unknown		
unknown	none	unknown	unknown		
unknown	none	unknown	unknown		
in debris	none	unknown	unknown		
unknown	none	unknown	unknown		
unknown	none	unknown	unknown		
unknown	none	seal	unknown		
unknown	none	seal	unknown		
unknown	none	unknown	unknown		
unknown	Seal 37+×27+	unknown	procession of	persons	
unknown	Seal 25+×14+	unknown	crab legs ??		
on pavement next to wall	Seal 18 dia	seal	cruciform	hemispheroid	
found on pavement in debris	Seal 21 dia	seal	gazelle in foliage	doubleconvex	disk
south of tomb 114	Seal 10 dia	on jar shoulder	stick man & plant		
below floor Temple over walls of XIA	none	unknown	unknown		
on floor near edge of tepe	Seal 22 dia	on jar shoulder	parallel plant stalks		
on floor of room	Seal 26+ dia	string tag	animals lions ?		
in room	Seal 20 dia	seal	iron cross	hemispheroid	
on surface	Seal 13 dia	seal	unknown		
debris outside tomb	Seal 20 dia	seal	scorpion fish ?	hemispheroid	high
on floor	Seal 24 dia	seal	horned gazelle ?	hemispheroid	
in debris half a meter from floor	Seal 33+×29+	on jar shoulder	man house animals		
in debris half a meter from floor	Seal 30+×32	on jar shoulder ?	man & beast by	house	
on floor of room	Seal 12 dia	seal	cross	item missing	
one of sealings on floor	Seal 33 dia	on basket cover	2 balls & filler		
one of sealings on floor	Seal 24+×23	on jar cover	animals in nature		
unknown	Seal 19+×20+	rope traces	2 animals		
unknown	Seal 17 dia	seal	criss cross	conoid	
in debris near floor	Seal 17 dia	seal	unknown		
outside wall	Seal 25 dia	seal	unknown		
in general area of dirt	Seal 20×15	seal	double netting	hemispheroid	
unknown	Seal 16 dia	seal	unknown	hemispheroid	
ordinary refuse at edge of the tell	Seal 24 dia	seal	abstract lines	grooved flat	hemisphere
on pavement of XIA	Seal 34 ×22+	in jar mouth	dogs chase horn	beast	
in corner of tiny scrappy rooms	Seal 33+×18+	leather bag tie	herd of horned	animals	
unknown	Seal 24+×22+	in jar ? on basket ?	hunters birds		
just behind circular structure	Seal 24×19	seal	2 hatched verticals	hemispheroid	
in corner of room at top of bins	Seal 25+×27+	string tag	herd animals		
in ordinary refuse	Seal 53×28	sack ties ??	herd of sheep/goat		
in Round House	Seal 28×28	in jar mouth	herd of pigs		
unknown	Seal 24 dia	too broken to know	horned animals		
Round House room C or D	Seal 29 dia	unknown	animals snakes		
on floor just inside curved wall	Seal 20+×22+	door ? peg & thong	dancing man		
in Round House	Seal 24 dia	on jar shoulder	sheep		
outside great wall with figurines	Seal 15+×16+	on jar shoulder	snake		
in Round House	Seal 23+×12+	on jar shoulder	abstract figure ?		
on pavement room of Round House	Seal 23 dia	seal	feather horn	gazelle	Hemisphere
dump	Seal 19+×27+	unknown	bird horn beast &		
Round House fill	Seal 21×23+	string tag	2 woolly horn beats		
room M of Round House	Seal 20 ×12+	on jar shoulder	baby & mom	quadruped	
outside east of Round House	Seal 28+×27+	in jar mouth	birds		
from under ramp of Round House	Seal 33×22	seal	animal	missing	
unknown	Seal 10 dia	seal	cross	carinated	hemisphere
unknown	Seal 20 dia	seal	uncut	hemispheroid	
from top of XII wall	none	unknown	scorpion		
on floor near wall	none	unknown	dog		
on floor	none	unknown	unknown		
unknown	none	dog			
unknown	none	unknown	unknown		
unknown	none	unknown	unknown		
just outside great wall	none	unknown	unknown		
on floor near edge tepe	none	seal	unknown		
on setback in wall	none	seal	unknown		
unknown	none	unknown	unknown		
in ordinary refuse	none	unknown	unknown		

(continues)

Level XIAB   (continued)

1	2	3	4	5		6	7	8	9	10	11	12	13	14
1049.	5-none	unknown	1239	XIA	XIAB	impression	clay	7M	6S	h5	none	none	none	8.08
1050.	6-073	IM32503	1673	XIA	XIAB	stamp	paste	5J	5J	i8	D25	T7	ina	0.00
1051.	6-076	37-16-78	1668	XIA	XIAB	stamp	steatite	5K	5K	b2	D20	T7	ina	0.00
1052.	6-077	37-16-87	1668	XIA	XIAB	impression	clay	5K	5K	d7	L36	W25	T14	0.00
1053.	6-079	Baghdad	1726	XIA	XIAB	stamp	bitumen	5K	5K	b8	D21	T8	ina	0.00
1054.	6-080	IM32542	1674	XIA	XIAB	stamp	bitumen	4J	4J	h/i 8	D15	T8	ina	0.00
1055.	6-084	37-16-86	1730	XIA	XIAB	stamp	paste	4J	4J	none	D11	T9	ina	0.00
1056.	6-086	37-16-75	1677	XIA	XIAB	stamp	steatite	5K	5K	f/g10	D31	T12	ina	0.00
1057.	6-089	37-16-216	1676	XIA	XIAB	impression	clay	5K	5K	g/h1/2	L61	W67	T24	0.00
1058.	6-090	37-16-83	1725	XIA	XIAB	stamp	paste	5K	5K	b7	D18	T4	ina	0.00
1059.	6-092	37-16-74	1742	XIA	XIAB	stamp	marble	5M	5M	d10	D35	T12	ina	0.00
1060.	6-093	unknown	1743	XIA ?	XIAB	stamp	unknown	dump	dump	dump	D13	T5	ina	0.00
1061.	6-101	IM32857	1728	XIA	XIAB	impression	clay	5T ?	5O ?	b3	L52	W33	T17	0.00
1062.	6-133	37-16-76	1685	XIA	XIAB	stamp	granite	6J	6J	i7	L27	W22	T12	0.00
1063.	6-134	IM32567	1687	XIA	XIAB	stamp	serpentine	6K	6K	h/i 3	L26	W25	T10	0.00
1064.	6-135	Baghdad	1681	XIA	XIAB	stamp	haematite	5G	5G	j 1/2	L17	W14	T8	0.00
1065.	6-137	Baghdad	1686	XIA	XIAB	stamp	steatite	5J	5J	b3	none	none	none	0.00
1066.	6-139	Baghdad	1760	XIA	XIAB	stamp	unknown	4M	4M	d5	D10	T6	ina	0.00
1067.	6-214	37-16-77	none	XIA	XIAB	stamp	steatite	6O	6O	c8	D25	T9	ina	0.00
1068.	6-266	37-16-88	1870	XIA	XIAB	impression	black clay	dump	dump	dump	L32	W30	T9	0.00
1069.	6-340	37-16-82	none	XIA	XIAB	stamp	black stone	7S	7S	none	L25	W20	none	0.00
1070.	7-none	unknown	4129	XIA	XIAB	stamp	black stone	7Q	7Q	i8	none	none	none	0.00
1071.	7-none	unknown	1721	XIA	XIAB	impression	clay	4J	4J	g4	none	none	none	0.00
1072.	7-none	unknown	1678	XIA	XIAB	impression	clay	5J	5J	a3	none	none	none	0.00
1073.	7-none	unknown	1759	XIA	XIAB	impression	clay	5K	5K	i6	none	none	none	0.00
1074.	7-none	unknown	1770	XIA	XIAB	impression	clay	6K	6K	e/f 2	none	none	none	0.00
1075.	7-none	unknown	4122	XIA	XIAB	2 impression	clay	7Q	7Q	j1	none	none	none	0.00
1076.	7-057	IM42678	1956	XI	XIAB	impression	clay	9M	9M	none	L58	W21	none	9.14
1077.	7-058	IM42626	1975	XIA	XIAB	impression	paste	9M	9M	d9	none	none	none	0.00
1078.	7-133	IM42372	1977	XIA	XIAB	stamp	paste	10M	10M	d9	D14	T5	ina	0.00
1079.	7-134A	IM42676	1980	XIA	XIAB	impression	clay	9M	9M	g 8/9	L33	W29	none	0.00
1080.	7-134B	38-13-31	1980	XIA	XIAB	impression	clay	9M	9M	g 8/9	L32	W18	T13	0.00
1081.	7-143	IM42670	1981	XIA	XIAB	impression	clay	10M	10M	f 3/4	L27	W32	none	0.00
1082.	7-144	IM42672	1981	XIA	XIAB	impression	clay	10M	10M	f 3/4	L46	W35	T9	0.00
1083.	7-145	IM42672	2007	XIA	XIAB	impression	clay	10M	10M	none	L37	W33	T12	0.00
1084.	7-179	38-13-30	1833	XIA	XIAB	impression	clay	9M	9M	c6	L67	W46	T36	0.00
1085.	7-232	38-13-48	1998	XII	XIAB	stamp	steatite	8M	8M	i 8/9	D15	T5	ina	8.40
1086.	7-236	Baghdad	1997	XII	XIAB	stamp	steatite	8M	8M	none	D14	T7	ina	8.40
1087.	7-254	Baghdad	2031	XIA	XIA	stamp	obsidian	7M	7M	j1	D11	T9	ina	8.40
1088.	7-none	Discarded	2539	XI	XIAB	impression	clay	9M	9M	a8	none	none	none	9.21
1089.	7-none	Discarded	2539	XIA	XIAB	impression	clay	9M	9M	a8	none	none	none	9.21
1090.	7-none	unknown	1960	XIA	XIAB	stamp	steatite	9M	9M	c9	none	none	none	0.00

15	16	17	18	19	20
on floor near wall in refuse	none	unknown	geometric		
unknown	Seal 25 dia	seal	cruciform	hemispheroid	
unknown	Seal 20 dia	seal	stick horn animal	low	hemisphere
unknown	Seal 15×17	too small to know	obscure		
unknown	Seal 21 dia	seal	cruciform	hemispheroid	
unknown	Seal 15 dia	seal	stick horn animal	high	hemisphere
unknown	Seal 11 dia	seal	circles off vertical	high	hemisphere
unknown	Seal 31 dia	seal	cruciform	hemispheroid	
unknown	Seal 20 diam	in jar mouth ??	quadruped		
unknown	Seal 18 dia	seal	triangle of lozenges	convex disk	
unknown	Seal 35 dia	seal	filled in 'x'	hemispheroid	
dump	Seal 13 dia	seal	cross with hatching	hemispheroid	
unknown	Seal 33+×17+	door lock ?	man by building		
unknown	Seal 27×22	seal	kneeling bird man	flattened	cylinder
unknown	Seal 26×25	seal	gazelle in nature	grooved	hemisphere
unknown	Seal 17×14	seal	starburst		
unknown	none	seal	unknown		
unknown	Seal 10 dia	seal	crosshatch		
unknown	Seal 25 dia	seal	gazelle	hemispheroid	
dump	Seal 21×24+	on top container	man & horned	animal	
unknown	Seal 25×20	seal	abstract stalks	flattened	cylinder
unknown	none	seal	unknown		
under XIA	none	unknown	unknown		
unknown	none	unknown	unknown		
unknown	none	unknown	unknown		
unknown	none	unknown	animal		
unknown	none	unknown	unknown		
unknown	Seal 15×22	leather bag tie	radiating 'x'		
in west trench	Seal 29 dia	unknown	sexual intercourse		
in west trench	Seal 14 dia	seal	filled in cross	hemispheroid	
in west trench	Seal 19 dia	on basket cover	bird headed man		
in west trench	Seal 13+×18	on basket cover	bird headed man		
in west trench	Seal 25+×16+	on jar shoulder	animal		
in west trench	Seal 17 dia	in jar mouth	quadruped in	nature	
in west trench	Seal 25+×27+	in jar mouth	2 preditory animals		
in west trench	Seal 32+×33+	rope marks	parts 3 horn beasts		
in black refuse	Seal 15 dia	seal	abstract	hemispheroid	
in black refuse	Seal 14 dia	seal	horned animal	hemispheroid	
at base of wall	Seal 11 dia	N of Round House	seal	2 fish ?	hemisphere
unknown	none	animals			
unknown	none	unknown			
in west trench	none	abstract lines			

Level XI/XA

1	2	3	4	5		6	7	8	9	10	11	12	13
		Bone	**item**										
1091.	4-0787	Baghdad	314	XI	XI	tube	bone	12P	4J	h1	H69	RD18	BD11
1092.	4-1107	Baghdad	0239	XIA	XI	spatula	bone	7M	6S	b10	none	none	none
1093.	5-1347	36-6-197	1156	XIA	XI	spatula	bone	11M	6K	none	L171	W16	ina
1094.	5-1352	Baghdad	1160	XI	XI	spatula	bone	11M	6K	e5	L119	W22	ina
1095.	5-1458	Baghdad	1253	XI	XI	ferrule	bone	12N	5J	c10	L56	W15	D15
1096.	5-1512	Baghdad	1244	XI	XI	scraper	bone	9L	7O	e/f7/8	L204	W24	ina
1097.	5-1744	Baghdad	1495	XI	XI	awl	bone	12P	4J	b/c9	L112	W12	T6
1098.	6-170	unknown	1768	XI	XI	implement	bone	8S	8S	c2	L142	W22	T10
1099.	6-none	37-16-43	1748	XI	XI	burin ?	bone	7O	7O	none	L145	T17	ina
1100.	6-none	37-16-44	none	XI	XI	awl	bone	7Q	7Q	none	L70	W23	ina
		Clay	**item**										
1101.	4-0612	Baghdad	4	XI	XI	game piece	ceramic	9P	4O	none	H16	D11	ina
1102.	4-0656	35-10-52	192	XI	XI	ballistas	clay	8M	6Q	none	L150	D75	ina
1103.	4-0665	Baghdad	43	XI	XI	weight	ceramic	8M	6Q	f8	H26	BD23	RD12
1104.	4-0971	Baghdad	598	XI	XI	disc	clay	10M	6M	c7	none	none	none
1105.	4-0975	35-10-55	421	XI	XI	disc	clay	10M	6M	d/e7/8	none	none	none
1106.	4-1001	35-10-34	651	XI	XI	ladle	ceramic	10M	6M	none	none	none	none
1107.	4-1009	Baghdad	655	XI	XI	drain pipe	ceramic	9P	4O	none	H300	RD184	BD92
1108.	4-1026	Baghdad	711	XI	XI	ladle	ceramic	10M	6M	d5	none	none	none
1109.	4-none	unknown	252	XI	XI	ballistas	clay	10P	4M	g8	none	none	none
1110.	4-none	unknown	289	XI	XI	object	clay	9N	5O	f10	none	none	none
1111.	4-none	unknown	none	XI	XI	ballistas	clay	8M	6Q	e6	L54	D31	ina
1112.	5-1294	Baghdad	1036	XI	XI	loomweight	ceramic	11M	6K	i3	H172	D95	ina
1113.	5-1337	Baghdad	1154	XI	XI	ladle	ceramic	11P	4K	f9	L177	ina	ina
1114.	5-1401	Baghdad	1141	XI	XI	trough	ceramic	13M	6G	c/d4	H96	none	none
1115.	5-1491	36-6-66A	none	XI	XI	4 ballistas	clay	11N	5K	loc172a	L115	D27	ina
1116.	5-1491	Baghdad	none	XI	XI	3 ballistas	clay	11N	5K	loc172a	L115	D27	ina
1117.	5-1616	Baghdad	1345	XA	XI	ladle	ceramic	9L	7O	b9	H87	R145	B100
1118.	5-none	36-6-80	none	XI	XI	disc	buffware	8M	6Q	none	D20	T6	ina
1119.	5-none	36-6-81	none	XI	XI	ball	pottery	9M	6O	none	D17	ina	ina
1120.	5-none	unknown	1036	XI	XI	loom base	ceramic	11M	6K	i3	none	none	none
1121.	5-none	unknown	Loc.196	XI	XI	loom base	clay	11M	6K	d7	none	none	none
1122.	6-059	Baghdad	1704	XI	XI	loom base	unbaked clay	7Q	7Q	b1	H173	D245	ina
1123.	6-105	Baghdad	none	XI	XI	loom part ?	ceramic	7Q	7Q	none	H200	D300	BD135
1124.	7-none	unknown	1959	XI	XI	ballista	clay	9M	9M	g8	none	none	none
1125.	7-none	unknown	1959	XI	XI	ballista	clay	9M	9M	g8	none	none	none
1126.	7-none	unknown	1959	XI	XI	ballista	clay	9M	9M	g8	none	none	none
1127.	7-none	38-13-6	none	XI	XI	ballista	ceramic	9M	9M	none	L62	D38	ina
1128.	3-none	unknown	none	XI	XI	ballistas	clay	8N	5Q	none	none	none	none
1129.	4-none	unknown	610	XI	XI	spheres	clay	8M	6Q	b7	none	none	none
1130.	4-none	unknown	none	XI	XI	ballistas	clay	9M	6O	none	none	none	none
1131.	5-none	unknown	none	XI	XI	ballistas	clay	11M	6K	d7	none	none	none
		Figurines											
1132.	1115	31-52-447	none	XI	XI	animal	white stone	Mn2	5M	none	L14	W12	T8
1133.	4-0629	Baghdad	185	XI	XI	hut statue	ceramic	9N	5O	none	H104	W64	ina
1134.	4-0630	35-10-35	188	XI	XI	hut statue	ceramic	9N	5O	none	H111	W64	ina
1135.	4-0679	Baghdad	253	XI-X II ?		animal	ceramic	dump	dump	none	L23	W18	ina
1136.	4-0708	discarded	59	XI	XI	animal	ceramic	10N	5M	b5	none	none	none
1137.	4-0784	Baghdad	210	XI	XI	animal	stone	11P	4K	b4	L49	W29	ina
1138.	4-0816	35-10-54	219	XI	XI	animal	clay	10N	5M	i/j3/4	L45	W40	ina
1139.	4-0844	35-10-36	67	XI	XI	hut statue	ceramic	8M	6Q	f1	H100	W60	T38
1140.	4-0865	Baghdad	335	XI	XI	hut statue	ceramic	10N	5M	i4	none	none	none
1141.	4-0892	Baghdad	83	XI	XI	animal	clay	10P	4M	none	none	none	none
1142.	4-0905	35-10-147	96	XI	XI	human	ceramic	10N	5M	none	L31	W37	T13
1143.	4-none	discarded	308	XI	XI	unknown	unknown	10N	5M	h6	none	one	none
1144.	4-none	unknown	149	XI	XI	animal	unknown	9M	6O	i-j7-8	none	none	none
1145.	5-1250	36-6-6	1056	XA	XI	animal	clay	12N	5J	ef1	L56	W43	ina
1146.	5-1288	36-6-65	1042	XI	XI	hut statue	ceramic	12M	6J	e/f1	H135	W127	ina
1147.	5-1293	Baghdad	1043	XI	XI	hut statue	ceramic	12M	6J	h/i5	H130	BD119	RD124
1148.	5-1306A	Baghdad	1068	XA	XI	animal	ceramic	11M	6K	g/h10	L66	H36	ina
1149.	5-1306B	36-6-7	1068	XA	XI	animal	ceramic	11M	6K	gh10	L33	H28	ina
1150.	5-1306C	Baghdad	1068	XA	XI	animal	ceramic	11M	6K	gh10	L26	H21	ina
1151.	5-1307A	36-6-67	1048	XI	XI	animal	ceramic	11M	6K	g9	L58	W49	T24
1152.	5-1307B	36-6-68	1048	XI	XI	animal	ceramic	11M	6K	g9	L47	W33	none
1153.	5-1307C	36-6-69	1048	XI	XI	animal	ceramic	11M	6K	g9	L38	W25	none
1154.	5-1361	Baghdad	1088	XI	XI	human	sandstone	13M	6G	h/i5	H90	W92	T30

14	15	16	17	18	19
10.71	in mixed libn & sherd debris	at edge			
10.05	at edge of tepe				
10.67	unknown				
9.76	dirt of oven with hammerstone				
0.00	unknown				
0.00	unknown				
0.00	on floor with celt & painted pot				
0.00	unknown				
0.00	in dirt				
0.00	unknown	articulation used	as butt		
0.00	unknown				
0.00	50-60 in room 63 locus 103				
10.38	unknown				
10.07	unknown	with knobs in relief			
10.07	unknown				
10.39	unknown				
9.34	unknown				
10.16	unknown				
10.46	cache 50-60 cigar-shaped	in locus 104			
9.26	unknown				
10.4	50 under mats with pestle vessel				
10.0	in room 51 with loom base				
9.16	2m below temple wall in ash trash				
9.74	on floor near wall	like kid's bathtub			
0.00	in nest of ballistas	cigar shaped			
0.00	in nest of ballistas	cigar shaped			
10.20	unknown				
0.00	unknown				
0.00	unknown				
10.06	with loom weight 5-1294	called "horned cult"	figurine		
10.62	with ballistas & spindle whorls	area 39			
0.00	unknown				
0.00	found with 6-59				
9.99	unknown				
9.99	unknown				
9.99	unknown				
0.00	unknown				
0.00	50 along south wall room 62				
9.97	unknown				
10.58	40 on floor of room 66				
10.62	50 under loom stand on floor of	area 39			
0.00	trial trench				
10.54	found with 4-630				
10.54	found with 4-629				
0.00	dump				
0.00	unknown				
10.93	on floor .4 cm from north wall				
0.001	below [between] floor				
10.67	southwest of temple				
9.93	on floor of room				
10.0	unknown				
9.50	unknown				
10.20	unknown				
10.07	unknown				
10.47	unknown				
10.70	within walls near grave 202				
9.85	in room 31 near fake oven				
10.52	in welter of ashes with sealing				
10.52	in welter of ashes with sealing				
10.52	in welter of ashes with sealing				
9.64	in ashy lens above floor	20cm from wall			
9.64	in ashy lens above floor	20cm from wall			
9.64	in ashy lens above floor	20cm from wall			
9.24	from pavement				

(continues)

Level XI/XA   (continued)

1	2	3	4	5	6	7	8	9	10	11	12	13
1155.	5-1374	Baghdad	1205	XI XI	hut statue	ceramic	12M	6J	loc174	H157	RD150	BD97
1156.	5-1417	Baghdad	1182	XI XI	animal	ceramic	12N	5J	none	H50	L64	W21
1157.	5-none	36-6-131	none	XI XI	animal	ceramic	11M	6K	none	D28	none	ina
1158.	5-none	36-6-63	none	XI XI	sheep	gray ware	11P	12K	none	L50	H34	ina
1159.	5-none	36-6-64	none	XI XI	hut statue	ceramic	10L	7M	none	L96	W96	none
1160.	6-050	37-16-34	1706	XI XI	animal	buffware	8Q	8Q	h1	W27	T14	L57
1161.	6-157	37-16-38	1778	XI XI	dog	white marble	8O	8O	c8	L26	H21	T5
1162.	6-none	Baghdad	none	XI XI	animal	terracotta	6K	6K	none	L46	H35	ina
1163.	6-none	unknown	1876	XI XI	unknown	unknown	8K	8K	d5	none	none	none
		Ground	**stone**									
1170.	1112	31-52-448	none	XI XI	tablet	diorite	M13	13M	none	L39	W26	T9
1171.	1203	31-52-442	none	XI XI	celt	gray stone	none	none	none	L42	W33	none
1172.	4-0617	Baghdad	163	XI XI	sphere	stone	9M	6O	none	D15	ina	ina
1173.	4-0622	Baghdad	193	XI XI	hand mortar	stone	8M	6Q	none	L163	W102	T30
1174.	4-0625	35-10-88	22	XI XI	ballista	limestone	9N	5O	none	L56	W36	T28
1175.	4-0675	Baghdad	260	XI XI	celt	green steatite	9N	5O	e10	L45	none	ina
1176.	4-0688	Baghdad	191	XI XI	hammer	limestone	9M	6O	none	L142	W114	T48
1177.	4-0698	Baghdad	255	XI XI	hammer	limestone	8M	6Q	f6	L55	W54	T34
1178.	4-0706	Baghdad	57	XI XI	celt	stone	10M	6M	c8	none	none	ina
1179.	4-0790	35-10-93	62	XI XI	celt	stone	8M	6Q	c/d10	L48	W25	T10
1180.	4-0791	35-10-294	126	XI XI	sphere	stone	11N	5K	h/i1	D22	ina	ina
1181.	4-0812	35-10-94	216	XI XI	hammer	stone	9M	6O	c4	L86	W57	T23
1182.	4-0839	Baghdad	328	XI XI	macehead	stone	12N	5J	h9	none	none	none
1183.	4-0845	Baghdad	333	XI XI	mortar	limestone	8M	6Q	d8	none	none	none
1184.	4-0862	Baghdad	138	XI XI	celt	stone	10N	5M	c/d2/3	none	none	none
1185.	4-0876	Baghdad	350	XI XI	celt	stone	12N	5J	i6	L62	W24	24
1186.	4-0885	Baghdad	80	XI XI	game piece	stone	10P	4M	i/j2	none	none	none
1187.	4-0911	Baghdad	92	XI XI	celt	stone	8P	4Q	d8	none	none	none
1188.	4-0916	35-10-19	355	XI XI	weight	stone	9P	4O	j7	H21	L35	W29
1189.	4-0918	35-10-84	none	XI XI	game piece	alabaster	9P	4O	none	H22	D17	ina
1190.	4-0918	35-10-85	none	XI XI	game piece	alabaster	9P	4O	none	H21	D15	ina
1191.	4-0918A	35-10-81	356	XI ? XI	spheres	alabaster	9P	4O	j7	D25	ina	ina
1192.	4-0918B	Baghdad	356	XI ? XI	spheres 5	alabaster	9P	4O	j7	none	ina	ina
1193.	4-0927	Baghdad	507	XI XI	sphere	stone	8N	5Q	d/e4/5	none	none	none
1194.	4-0928	Baghdad	371	XI XI	sphere	stone	8N	5Q	e4	none	none	none
1195.	4-0929	35-10-86	513	XI XI	sphere	agate	8N	5Q	g8	none	ina	ina
1196.	4-0974	35-10-79	599	XI XI	pestle	stone	10M	6M	c7	none	none	none
1197.	4-1086	35-10-78	437	XIXIA XI	palette	stone	9P	4O	e/f5/6	none	none	none
1198.	4-1093	phila ?	816	XI XI	mortar	limestone	10N	5M	b8	none	none	none
1199.	4-none	35-10-394	none	XI XI	mortar	stone	10N	5M	none	none	ina	ina
1200.	4-none	35-10-396	none	XI XI	mortar	limestone	10N	5M	none	L61	W34	none
1201.	4-none	35-10-80	none	XI XI	ballista	marble	8M	6Q	none	D19	ina	ina
1202.	4-none	discarded	627	XI XI	crushing	stone	12N	4J	d2	none	none	none
1203.	4-none	unknown	138	XI XI	stones	stone	10P	4M	e-f7-8	none	none	none
1204.	4-none	unknown	332	XI XI	rubbing	stone	12N	5J	f9	none	none	none
1205.	4-none	unknown	338	XI XI	mortars	stone	12N	5J	d7	none	none	none
1206.	4-none	unknown	339	XI XI	weight 2	stone	12N	5J	d7	none	none	none
1207.	4-none	unknown	389	XI XI	weight	stone	8N	5Q	g1	none	none	none
1208.	4-none	unknown	128	XI XI	hammer	stone	8M	6Q	f/g3	none	none	none
1209.	5-1290	36-6-95	none	XI XI	macehead	stone	12M	6J	none	L55	W48	ina
1210.	5-1292	Baghdad	1045	XI XI	burin ?	stone	12M	6J	h8	L43	W21	T12
1211.	5-1296	Baghdad	1038	XI XI	grooved	stone	12M	6J	h3	L80	W38	T12
1212.	5-1314	Baghdad	1074	XI XI	mortar	stone	12M	6J	e/f6/7	D209	H74	ina
1213.	5-1350	36-6-86	1085	XI XI	celt	stone	11M	6K	c-e1-2	L36	W38	T14
1214.	5-1351	36-6-98	1160	XI XI	hammer	stone	11M	6K	e5	L86	W60	T29
1215.	5-1355	36-6-92	1114	XI XI	celt	green stone	11P	4K	d/e8	L24	W15	T8
1216.	5-1356	Baghdad	1112	XA XI	rubbing	limestone	11P	4K	h8	H63	W44	T35
1217.	5-1364	Baghdad	1201	XI XI	celt	stone	11P	4K	c/d6/7	L39	W30	T14
1218.	5-1375	36-6-97	1205	XI XI	hammer	serpentine ?	12M	6J	loc174	L93	W72	T35
1219.	5-1381	Baghdad	1206	XI XI	celt	stone	12P	4J	c6	L34	W30	T9
1220.	5-1409	Baghdad	1188	XI XI	celt	stone	12N	5J	i5/6	L30	W28	T10
1221.	5-1477	36-6-36	1265	XA XI	celt	stone	10L	7M	j 2/3	L109	W73	T30
1222.	5-1496	Baghdad	none	XI XI	hammer	stone	11L	7K	none	L85	W53	T32
1223.	5-1508	36-6-96	1352	XI XI	macehead	haematite	11L	7K	f/g3/4	none	none	none
1224.	5-1509	Baghdad	1353	XI XI	hammer	stone	9L	7O	h/i6/7	L58	BD30	ina
1225.	5-1511	36-6-87	1356	XI XI	celt	stone	10L	7M	g/h10	L29	W41	T13
1226.	5-1513	Baghdad	1247	XI XI	celt	stone	10L	7M	g/h10	L52	W40	T12

14	15	16	17	18	19
9.63	from deep room with matting	& objects			
10.241	50cm east of grave 182				
0.00	unknown				
0.00	unknown				
0.00	unknown	fragmentary			
0.00	unknown	painted decoration			
0.00	unknown				
0.00	unknown				
0.00	trial trench				
0.00	trial trench	incised carving			
0.00	trial trench				
0.00	unknown				
0.00	unknown				
10.85	unknown				
10.15	unknown				
0.001	unknown				
10.88	oc105: cache of ballistas				
0.00	with spindle whorl				
10.84	on pavement of room				
10.75	between loc 109 & 111 tombs				
10.11	between floors in corner area 93	socketed			
10.78	1.5 m from edge with sherds				
10.75	in debris with XI sherds				
10.27	in refuse with pot and adze				
10.61	on pavement west of East Shrine				
10.87	unknown				
9.24	with 4-970 spindle whorls				
9.87	unknown				
0.00	unknown				
0.00	unknown				
9.87	unknown	also 35-10-82 83 84	85		
9.87	unknown				
10.0	unknown				
10.0	unknown				
9.99	unknown				
10.0	unknown				
9.31	above White Room	below pavement of XI			
10.19	unknown				
0.00	unknown	given to donor			
0.00	unknown				
0.00	unknown				
10.2	unknown				
10.13	with ballistas				
10.86	in mixed context of XI and later				
10.87	mixed XI and X context				
10.87	mixed XI and X context				
9.50	unknown				
10.7	unknown				
0.00	unknown				
10.44	near fake oven	with 5-1293 hut statue			
10.56	near fake oven				
9.52	above the pavement	in deep doorless room			
9.64	on pavement				
9.76	in/near/by "dirt oven"				
0.00	unknown				
9.49	near edge of tepe				
9.94	in gray fill NW of XI "Temple"				
0.00	matting & objects in deep room				
0.00	in open area no walls	at edge of tepe			
10.0	below floor XI /XA	above wall XIA			
10.6	unknown				
9.93	unknown				
9.99	on pavement				
10.2	on pavement				
10.2	on pavement of large room				
10.1	30cm above pavement	near wall in refuse			

(*continues*)

Level XI/XA (continued)

1	2	3	4	5		6	7	8	9	10	11	12	13
1227.	5-1597	Baghdad	1294	XI	XI	celt	stone	9L	7O	h5	L38	W21	T12
1228.	5-1603	Baghdad	1319	XI	XI	macehead	stone	10L	7M	d9	H41	D51	ina
1229.	5-1700s	unknown	?	XI	XI	celt	stone	12P	4J	c8	none	none	none
1230.	5-none	36-6-100	none	XI	XI	game piece	marble	10N	5M	none	D18	T4	ina
1231.	5-none	36-6-101	none	XI	XI	game piece	marble	10N	5M	none	D16	T4	ina
1232.	5-none	36-6-102	none	XI	XI	game piece	marble	10N	5M	none	D17	T2	ina
1233.	5-none	36-6-103	none	XI	XI	game piece	marble	10N	5M	none	D18	ina	ina
1234.	5-none	36-6-104	none	XI	XI	game piece	marble	10N	5M	none	D16	ina	ina
1235.	5-none	36-6-105	none	XI	XI	ball	stone	10N	5M	none	D15	ina	ina
1236.	5-none	36-6-34	1330	XA	XI	celt	limestone	10K	8M	g/h3	none	none	none
1237.	5-none	36-6-88	1495	XI	XI	celt	stone	12P	4J	b/c9	L45	W44	none
1238.	5-none	36-6-89	1248	XI	XI	celt	limestone	10L	7M	j4	L63	W44	ina
1239.	5-none	36-6-90	1327	XI	XI	celt	gray stone	10L	7M	d/e3/4	L56	W34	ina
1240.	5-none	36-6-91	1324	XI	XI	celt ?	purple stone	9L	7O	d7	L41	W21	ina
1241.	5-none	36-6-93	none	XI	XI	adze	limestone	11P	4K	none	L82	W46	none
1242.	5-none	36-6-94	none	XI	XI	celt	limestone	11P	4O	none	L103	W70	none
1243.	5-none	unknown	1495	XI	XI	celt	stone	12P	4J	none	none	none	none
1244.	5-none	unknown	1322	XI	XI	pointed	marble	9L	7O	e9	none	none	none
1245.	6-049	Baghdad	1705	XI	XI	celt	jadeite	8Q	8Q	i1	L41	W27	T14
1246.	6-274	Baghdad	1881	XI	XI	game piece	serpentine	7J	7J	h6	D25	T5	ina
1247.	6-none	37-16-39	none	XI	XI	polishing	limestone	7Q	7Q	none	H37	W39	T20
1248.	6-none	37-16-40	none	XI	XI	celt	granite	8Q	8Q	none	L91	W50	T20
1249.	7-none	unknown	1682	XI	XI	celt	stone	7Q	7Q	a/b9	none	none	none
1250.	7-0073	Baghdad	2563	XI	XI	celt	serpentine	10M	10M	d/e8	L42	W34	T14
1251.	7-0078	38-13-8	2004	XI	XI	hammer	basalt	8-11M	10M	none	L94	W75	ina
1252.	none	unknown	none	XI	XI	mortar	unknown	9M	6O	none	L300	W300	T120
1253.	none	unknown	none	XI	XI	game piece	alabaster	none	4O	none	D22	ina	ina
		Impressed											
1254.	4-0894	discarded	86	XI	XI	rope	clay	10N	5M	g5	none	none	none
		Jewelry											
1255.	4-0655	Baghdad	10	XI	XI	pendant	stone	8M	6Q	none	none	none	none
1256.	4-0671	35-10-111	278	XI	XI	bead	stone	9N	5O	none	L16	W16	T9
1257.	4-0682	phila no#	279	XI	XI	pendant	steatite	11M	6K	e2	D28	T11	ina
1258.	4-0836	Baghdad	331	XI	XI	button	steatite	9M	6O	d4	L31	W21	T13
1259.	4-0837	35-10-104	327	XI	XI	pendant	stone	8L	7Q	b10	L18	W11	ina
1260.	4-0841	35-10-331	72	XI	XI	beads 131	stone shell	9L	7O	none	ina	ina	ina
1261.	4-0883	Baghdad	451	XI	XI	bead	marble	9P	4O	i9	L24	W15	ina
1262.	4-0914	Baghdad	100	XI	XI	pendant	specked stone	10N	5M	b/c1	none	none	none
1263.	4-0915	Baghdad	353	XI	XI	pendant	paste	9P	4O	h7	none	none	none
1264.	4-0945	35-10-102	516	XI	XI	pendant	stone	8N	5Q	h7	L24	W15	T15
1265.	4-0964	Baghdad	420	XI	XI	pin	gold	8M	6Q	c3	none	none	none
1266.	4-1002	Baghdad	645	XI	XI	button	stone	8M	6Q	i3	none	none	none
1267.	4-1003	35-10-108	646	XI	XI	button	steatite	10M	6M	c3	none	none	none
1268.	4-1056	Baghdad	547	XI	XI	pendant	stone	8M	6Q	b/c2	none	none	none
1269.	4-1057	35-10-103	539	XI	XI	pendant	stone	9M	6O	d/e3	none	none	none
1270.	4-1090	Baghdad	819	XI	XI	pendant	steatite	10M	6M	i7	none	none	none
1271.	4-none	unknown	0521	XIA	XI	bead	stone	8M	6Q	c2	none	none	none
1272.	4-none	unknown	180	XI	XI	bead	unknown	9P	4O	none	none	none	none
1273.	4-none	unknown	154	XI	XI	bead	white paste	9N	5O	none	none	none	none
1274.	4-none	unknown	164	XI	XI	bead	stone	9M	6O	none	none	none	none
1275.	4-none	unknown	562	XI	XI	button	shell	9M	6O	b2	none	none	none
1276.	5-1234	36-6-107	none	XI	XI	pendant	mother of pearl	none	none	none	H13	W9	ina
1277.	5-1359	36-6-108	1090	XI	XI	amulet	marble	13M	6G	h/i6/7	L23	W12	ina
1278.	5-1363	36-6-372	none	XI	XI	amulet	stone	dump	dump	none	L22	W14	T6
1279.	5-1368	36-6-106	1116	XI	XI	amulet	stone	11P	4K	e6	L28	W18	ina
1280.	5-1427	36-6-198	1097	XIA	XI	pendant	stone	10M	6M	c/d7/8	H53	W30	T4
1281.	5-1544	36-6-367	1386	XI	XI	beads 103	stone	10L	7M	none	ina	ina	ina
1282.	5-1614	Baghdad	1423	XI	XI	pendant	stone	9L	7O	h/i4	L16	W10	T7
1283.	6-379	unknown	4265	XI ?	XI	pendant	black stone	7Q	7Q	f1	L34	W22	T9
1284.	6-614	Baghdad	none	XI	XI	amulet	serpentine	7Sa	7Sa	none	D19	H9	ina
1285.	7-0018	38-13-331	2557	XI	XI	bead	carnelian	10M	10M	a/b2/3	L25	W20	T6
1286.	7-0054	38-13-9	2538	XI	XI	pendant	black granite	9M	9M	b8	L23	W8	T11
1287.	7-0091	Baghdad	2565	XI	XI	pendant	marble	10M	10M	none	L19	W14	T4
1288.	7-none	unknown	1954	XI	XI	pin	copper	9M	9M	e7	none	none	none
1289.	7-none	unknown	1954	XI	XI	pin	copper	9M	9M	e7	none	none	none
		Lithics											
1290.	5-1305	36-6-16	1063	XA	XI	knife	obsidian	11L	7K	J2	L82	W15	T04
1291.	1099c	31-52-444	none	XI	XI	blade	obsidian	none	none	none	L34	W14	none

14	15	16	17	18	19
10.20	on floor	amulet ?			
9.491	found in wall				
0.00	on floor with pot 5-1747 &	tool 5-1744			
0.00	unknown	disc			
0.00	unknown	disc			
0.00	unknown	disc			
0.00	unknown	ball			
0.00	unknown				
0.00	unknown				
10.47	unknown				
0.00	on floor with 5-1744 spoon	& 5-1747 pot			
10.04	on pavement with debris				
10.26	found in debris				
9.84	unknown				
0.00	unknown				
0.00	unknown				
0.00	on floor with pot 5-1744	& spoon 5-1747			
10.51	found on floor				
0.00	unknown				
0.00	unknown				
0.00	unknown				
0.00	unknown	triangular green			
0.00	unknown	chipped			
9.20	in black ash debris with 2 sealings				
0.00	trench				
10.73	set in floor of red clay & sherds				
0.00	unknown				
9.60	unknown				
0.00	unknown				
9.38	unknown				
10.77	unknown				
10.61	found in fallen brick				
10.84	in debris stones libn 1m from edge				
10.45	unknown				
0.001	unknown				
10.05	unknown				
9.85	in debris . . . types . . XI				
9.70	unknown				
9.43	in bone & sherd refuse				
9.66	unknown				
10.3	unknown				
10.1	unknown				
9.29	unknown				
10.1	unknown				
10.1	unknown				
0.00	unknown				
10.3	unknown				
0.00	unknown				
10.25	unknown				
0.00	unknown				
9.87	in undifferentiated dirt				
0.00	dump				
9.15	on pavement in debris with seal				
9.99	on pavement of room				
10.11	unknown				
10.40	above pavement				
0.001	unknown				
0.00	unknown				
10.00	on second pavement in trench				
9.21	found with obsidian blade				
9.00	in black ash debris over pavement	with other objects			
9.64	unknown				
9.64	unknown				
10.61	with sphere on pavement	E corner of room			
0.00	trial trench	little used 37 & 35			

(*continues*)

Level XI/XA   (continued)

1	2	3	4	5		6	7	8	9	10	11	12	13
1292.	1109	31-52-445	none	XI	XI	blade	brown flint	none	none	none	L52	W11	T3
1293.	1109a	31-52-444	none	XI	XI	Blade	obsidian	none	none	none	L42	W22	T5.5
1294.	3-0482	Baghdad	none	XI	XI	core	obsidian	9N	5O	none	L103	W43	T28
1295.	4-0867	Baghdad	137	XI	XI	core	obsidian	10P	4M	none	L130	W21	ina
1296.	4-0922	35-10-100	none	XI	XI	knife	obsidian	none	none	none	L73	W15	T4
1297.	4-0923	Baghdad	none	XI	XI	knife	obsidian	none	none	none	none	none	none
1298.	4-0924	Baghdad	none	XI	XI	knife	obsidian	none	none	none	none	none	none
1299.	4-0931	35-10-98	385	XI	XI	knife	obsidian	8N	5Q	h8	L91	W11	T2.9
1300.	4-0932	35-10-96	515	XI	XI	scraper	obsidian	10M	6M	b6	L78	W20	T5
1301.	4-0933	35-10-97	lost	XI	XI	knife	obsidian	8P	4Q	none	L137	W17	T9.6
1302.	4-0944	35-10-99	560	XI	XI	knife	obsidian	10M	6M	c4	L94	W17	T4
1303.	4-none	unknown	264	XI	XI	knife	obsidian	9P	4O	g2	none	none	none
1304.	4-none	unknown	282	XI	XI	knife	obsidian	10N	5M	c8	none	none	none
1305.	5-none	36-6-82	none	XI	XI	blade	tan flint	none	none	none	L86	W14	T3.4
1306.	5-none	36-6-83	none	XI	XI	sickle	flint	none	none	none	L70	W22	ina
1307.	5-none	36-6-83	none	XI	XI	blade	flint	none	none	none	L65	W16	T5.3
1308.	5-none	36-6-84	none	XI	XI	core	obsidian	none	none	none	L98	W24	T14
1309.	6-149	Baghdad	none	XI	XI	blades 3	obsidian	5H	5H	none	L60	ina	ina
1310.	6-none	37-16-41	none	XI	XI	blade	obsidian	7Q	7Q	none	L68	W18	T6
1311.	7-none	unknown	1954	XI	XI	knife	obsidian	9M	9M	e7	none	none	none
1312.	7-0090	Baghdad	2565	XI	XI	knife	obsidian	10M	10M	a1	L125	W20	ina
1313.	7-none	unknown	1954	XI	XI	blade	obsidian	9M	9M	e7	none	none	none
		Metal	**items**										
1314.	4-0819	Baghdad	none	XI	XI	adze	copper	8M	6Q	none	L142	W21	T9
1315.	4-0989	35-10-101	522	XI	XI	adze	bronze	9M	6O	none	none	none	none
1316.	4-none	discarded	174	XI	XI	pin	copper	8M	6Q	none	none	none	none
1317.	4-none	unknown	717	XI	XI	pin	copper	10N	5M	i7	none	none	none
1318.	5-1365	Baghdad	1118	XI	XI	nail	copper	11R	3K	a4	L80	ina	ina
1319.	5-none	unknown	1161	XI	XI	unclear	copper	11N	5K	none	none	none	none
1320.	5-none	unknown	1179	XI	XI	needle	copper	11N	5K	b10	none	none	none
1321.	6-054	Baghdad	1660	XA-X	XI	point	copper	8Q	8Q	c4	L45	T05	ina
1322.	7-none	unknown	1954	XI	XI	pin	copper	9M	9M	e7	none	none	none
1323.	7-0075	Baghdad	2562	XI	XI	celt	copper	10M	10M	i2	L61	W35	T7
1324.	7-0140	discarded	1971	XI	XI	pin	copper	5S	5S	none	L96	ina	ina
1325.	7-none	unknown	2558	XI	XI	pin	copper	8M	8M	a4	none	none	none
1326.	7-none	unknown	2533	XI	XI	pin	copper	9M	9M	c/d2/3	none	none	none
		Misc	**item**										
1327.	4-none	unknown	506	XIA	XI	cone	stone	8M	6Q	i2	none	none	none
1328.	6-009	Baghdad	none	XI	XI	ring	white marble	7Q	7Q	none	D35	T15	none
		Potsherd											
1329.	4-0879	35-10-38	348	XI	XI	incised	brownware	9M	6O	d/e6/7	L166	W100	T12
1330.	4-0912	discarded	143	XI	XI	bowl ?	ceramic	9M	6O	g-j3-5	H57	RD273	T5
1331.	4-0993	35-10-51	417	XI	XI	beaker	green buff	9P	4O	g5	L84	W108	T6
1332.	4-1014	discarded	532	XI	XI	dish	ceramic	8M	6Q	none	L111	W34	T7
1333.	4-1091	Baghdad	none	XI	XI	painted	ceramic	10M	6M	none	L53	W60	none
1334.	4-none	unknown	0824	XIA	XI	rim	clay	10N	5M	h/i 9	none	none	none
1335.	4-none	unknown	0824	XIA	XI	carinated	clay	10N	5M	h/i 9	none	none	none
1336.	4-none	35-10-39	none	XI	XI	none	ceramic	9M	6O	none	none	none	none
1337.	4-none	35-10-41	none	XI	XI	none	ceramic	11M	6K	none	none	none	none
1338.	4-none	35-10-42	none	XI	XI	jar	ceramic	9M	6O	none	none	none	none
1339.	4-none	35-10-43	none	XI	XI	none	ceramic	none	none	none	none	none	none
1340.	4-none	35-10-44	none	XI	XI	small jar	buffware	8M	6Q	none	none	none	none
1341.	4-none	35-10-45	none	XI	XI	none	Buffware	9M	6O	none	none	none	none
1342.	4-none	35-10-46	none	XI	XI	none	ceramic	9N	5O	none	none	none	none
1343.	4-none	35-10-47	none	XI	XI	none	buffware	8M	6Q	none	none	none	none
1344.	4-none	35-10-48	none	XI	XI	bowl	ceramic	10N	5M	none	none	none	none
1345.	4-none	35-10-49	none	XI	XI	jar	ceramic	10N	5M	none	none	none	none
1346.	4-none	35-10-50	none	XI	XI	bowl	ceramic	8M	6Q	none	none	none	none
1347.	4-none	unknown	622	XI	XI	flaring rim	ceramic	11P	4K	j3	none	none	none
1348.	4-none	unknown	623	XI	XI	flaring rim	ceramic	8M	6Q	b6	none	none	none
1349.	4-none	unknown	168	XI	XI	jar	ceramic	10P	4M	h/i5/6	none	none	none
1350.	4-none	unknown	644	XI	XI	double rim	ceramic	11M	6K	g5	none	none	none
1351.	4-none	unknown	632	XI	XI	rim & spout	ceramic	8M	6Q	g2	none	none	none
1352.	4-none	unknown	630	XI	XI	rim	ceramic	9R	3O	a9	none	none	none
1353.	4-none	unknown	628	XI	XI	rim & spout	ceramic	11P	4K	j3	none	none	none
1354.	4-none	unknown	678	XI	XI	painted	ceramic	11P	4K	d5	none	none	none
1355.	4-none	unknown	626	XI	XI	unknown	ceramic	10P	4M	b6	none	none	none

14	15	16	17	18	19
0.00	trial trench	little used 29 & 38			
0.00	trial trench	striations wear 42	& 38		
0.00	unknown				
10.51	found in situ in flat plate				
0.00	unknown	minor use 35 & 36			
0.00	unknown				
0.00	unknown				
9.00	below foundations [of X ?	striations 32 none 31			
10.13	unknown	working edge 49			
9.41	unknown	retouch 59	striations 42		
10.61	pure XI context	minor striations	29 & 31		
9.71	unknown				
10.48	unknown				
0.00	unknown	pointed end 30 & 34			
0.00	unknown	sheen on blade			
0.00	unknown	retouch 35 sheen 48			
0.00	unknown	tip borer ? striations 40			
0.00	unknown				
0.00	unknown	retouch 40 unused 24			
9.64	unknown				
9.00	in black ash- over whole square				
9.64	unknown	with copper pin			
10.20	unknown				
10.02	unknown				
0.001	unknown				
9.39	unknown				
9.77	unknown				
0.00	immediately over oven near Temple				
0.00	with pieces of sealing				
9.90	on floor of room				
9.64	with obsidian blade				
9.20	in black ash debris with 2 sealings				
0.00	edge tepe				
10.00	definitely out of XI pavement				
0.00	unknown				
10.04	on floor of room W Round House				
0.00	unknown				
10.50	unknown	incised lines rosettes	quartz grit	HM	
10.19	unknown				
9.62	above walls of White Room	sand	HM		
10.09	unknown				
0.00	unknown				
10.05	unknown				
10.05	unknown				
0.00	unknown	brown paint			
0.00	unknown	painted tree pattern			
0.00	unknown	grooved neck			
0.00	unknown	orange criss-x paint			
0.00	unknown	bistre paint	quartz grit & chaff	HM	
0.00	unknown	bistre paint	fine quartz	& basalt grit	HM
0.00	unknown	brown painted design			
0.00	unknown	sepia paint	quartz grit & chaff	HM	
0.00	unknown	bistre painted			
0.00	unknown	dark red paint			
0.00	unknown	bistre painted			
10.98	edge tepe	carinated shoulder			
0.001	unknown	carinated shoulder			
0.001	edge of tepe				
10.83	unknown				
10.11	unknown				
10.73	edge of tepe				
10.98	unknown				
10.95	unknown				
10.15	unknown				

(continues)

Level XI/XA   (continued)

1	2	3	4	5	6	7	8	9	10	11	12	13
1356.	4-none	unknown	625	XI XI	2 rim bowl	ceramic	9N	5O	a1	none	none	none
1357.	4-none	unknown	633	XI XI	daisy cup	ceramic	9N	5O	h8	none	none	none
1358.	4-none	unknown	675	XI XI	2 rim bowl	ceramic	8N	5Q	d9	none	none	none
1359.	4-none	unknown	682	XI XI	painted	ceramic	8N	5Q	d1	none	none	none
1360.	4-none	unknown	620	XI XI	rim	ceramic	10M	6M	i8	none	none	none
1361.	4-none	unknown	674	XI XI	rim	ceramic	10M	6M	h9	none	none	none
1362.	4-none	unknown	677	XI XI	decorated	ceramic	10M	6M	d2	none	none	none
1363.	4-none	unknown	679	XI XI	painted	ceramic	8L	7Q	f9	none	none	none
1364.	4-none	unknown	680	XI XI	rim	ceramic	8M	7Q	c6	none	none	none
1365.	5-1262	36-6-57	none	XI XI	incised	green buffware	12N	5J	none	L45	W31	ina
1366.	5-1270	Baghdad	1163	XI XI	beaker	ceramic	12N	5J	f10	L121	W82	ina
1367.	5-1312	Baghdad	1072	XI XI	2mouth jar	ceramic	12M	6J	e/f5/6	none	RW284	ina
1368.	5-1410	36-6-59	1194	XI XI	daisy	buffware	13M	6G	d6	L104	W129	T4.5
1369.	5-none	36-6-402	none	XI XI	bowl	ceramic	10M	6M	none	none	none	none
1370.	5-none	36-6-403	none	XI XI	rim	green buffware	9N	5O	none	none	none	none
1371.	5-none	36-6-406	380	XI XI	cup	ceramic	8N	5Q	g10	none	none	none
1372.	5-none	36-6-408	757	XI XI	bowl	green buffware	8N ?	5Q ?	none	L63	W75	T6
1373.	5-none	36-6-409	none	XI ? XI	none	ceramic	10M	6M	none	L43	W52	T4
1374.	5-none	36-6-410	none	XI ? XI	none	ceramic	10P	4M	none	none	none	none
1375.	5-none	36-6-411	none	XI XI	impressed	brown ware	10N	5M	none	L45	W53	T9
1376.	5-none	36-6-418	none	XI XI	none	ceramic	11R	3K	none	none	none	none
1377.	5-none	36-6-419	71	XI XI	none	buffware	11P	4K	none	none	none	ina
1378.	5-none	36-6-420	377	XI XI	jar	ceramic	10M	6M	none	L61	W63	T6
1379.	5-none	36-6-60	1204	XI XI	bowl	ceramic	11N	5K	a8/9	none	none	none
1380.	5-none	36-6-61	none	XI XI	none	buffware	12N	6J	none	L71	none	ina
1381.	5-none	36-6-62	none	XI XI	none	buff ware	11P	4K	none	L58	none	ina
1382.	5-none	unknown	1130	XI XI	incised	ceramic	11P	4K	c/d9	none	none	none
1383.	6-none	37-16-33	none	XI XI	unknown	grayware	8Q	8Q	none	none	none	none
1384.	7-none	Discarded	1655	XI-X XI	cup	green buffware	7Q	7Q	f5	none	none	none
1385.	7-none	38-13-5	none	XI XI	bowl	green buffware	9-11M	10M	none	none	none	none
1386.	4-none	unknown	399	XI XI	unclear	ceramic	12P	4J	none	none	none	none
1387.	4-none	unknown	394	XI XI	2 spouted	ceramic	9M	6O	d7	none	none	none
1388.	4-none	unknown	230	XI XI	painted	ceramic	8M	6Q	b/c1/2	none	none	none
1389.	6-none	unknown	1649	XI XI	painted jar	ceramic	8Q	8Q	h8	none	none	none
1390.	5-none	unknown	1144	XI XI	2 unknown	ceramic	10M	6M	b3	none	none	none
		Vessel										
1391.	1110	31-52-441	none	XI XI	saucer	green grayware	M13	13M	none	H24	D107	ina
1392.	1202	31-52-442	none	? XI	bowl	brownware	M13	13M	none	H92	RD102	ina
1393.	4-0621	Baghdad	175	XI XI	bowl	ceramic	9M	6O	none	H68	RD175	T12
1394.	4-0627	35-10-25	156	XI XI	beaker	buffware	9N	6O	none	L100	W122	ina
1395.	4-0628	Baghdad	178	XI XI	bowl	ceramic	8M	6Q	none	L72	W50	T4
1396.	4-0632	Baghdad	189	XI XI	cup	buffware	9N	5O	none	H93	RD114	BD60
1397.	4-0650	Baghdad	173	XI XI	unclear	steatite	10R	3M	none	none	none	none
1398.	4-0670	35-10-28	42	XI XI	bowl	gray ware	8M	6Q	a2	H91	RD191	BD62
1399.	4-0689	Baghdad	258	XI XI	bowl	ceramic	9P	4O	g2	H76	RD200	BD18
1400.	4-0690	discarded	169	XI XI	stand	ceramic	8M	6Q	none	H180	BD96	RD126
1401.	4-0700	discarded	26	XI XI	beaker	ceramic	8M	6Q	d9	none	none	none
1402.	4-0732	discarded	285	XI XI	dish	green gray ware	10N	5M	c8	H80	RD184	BD44
1403.	4-0734	Baghdad	305	XI XI	small jar	buff ware	9M	6O	e5	H90	RD58	BD56
1404.	4-0735	discarded	288	XI XI	dish	ceramic	9N	5O	none	H68	RD296	BD116
1405.	4-0764	Baghdad	90	XI XI	bowl	ceramic	10M	6M	b2	H144	RD280	BD108
1406.	4-0804	discarded	218	XI XI	dish	ceramic	9M	6O	h/i7/8	H108	RD332	BD120
1407.	4-0805	Baghdad	218	XI XI	jar	ceramic	9M	6O	h/i7/8	H76	RD144	ina
1408.	4-0809	35-10-30	324	XI XI	jar	ceramic	8M	6Q	e5	H77	RD46	BD20
1409.	4-0810	Baghdad	324	XI XI	jar	ceramic	8M	6Q	e5	H56	RD40	BD22
1410.	4-0833	35-10-29	325	XI XI	beaker	brownware	8M	6Q	e5	H90	RD128	BD58
1411.	4-0854	Baghdad	75	XI XI	cup	ceramic	8L	7Q	h/i3	H76	RD80	BD30
1412.	4-0860	Baghdad	76	XI XI	plate	ceramic	9M	6O	none	H40	RD140	BD42
1413.	4-0869	35-10-27	343	XI XI	small jar	brown ware	12P	4J	b6	H114	RD62	BD24
1414.	4-0899	Baghdad	145	XI XI	bowl	ceramic	9M	6O	g-i2-4	H90	RD94	BD90
1415.	4-0898	35-10-26	141	XI XI	daisy cup	buffware	9M	6O	f-i3-5	H62	RD116	BD32
1416.	4-0900	Baghdad	150	XI XI	beaker	ceramic	9M	6O	f-i2-5	H98	RD136	BD36
1417.	4-0906	35-10-31	94	XI XI	model bowl	red brownware	8N	5Q	none	H38	RD44	BD30
1418.	4-0920	35-10-33	370	XI XI	jar stand	buffware	9Q	3O	b10	H122	RD160	BD154
1419.	4-0992	discarded	624	XI XI	Wide flower	ceramic	10N	5M	d3	H80	RD276	BD140
1420.	4-1010	Baghdad	531	XI XI	jar	ceramic	9M	6O	none	H75	RD48	BD19
1421.	4-1011	Baghdad	423	XI XI	small jar	ceramic	8M	6Q	e/f10	H50	RD20	BD10

14	15	16	17	18	19
10.60	unknown				
9.661	unknown	daisy impressed			
10.06	near edge				
9.74	near edge				
10.20	unknown				
10.24	unknown				
10.35	unknown				
10.39	unknown				
10.38	unknown				
0.00	unknown	sand temper	HM		
9.93	with 5-1320 by walls	daisy impressed			
9.5	unknown				
10.04	within 3m of edge	fine quartz	& basalt grit	HM	
0.00	unknown	ring base			
0.00	unknown				
0.00	in the wall ??	painted			
0.00	unknown	applique rosettes			
0.00	unknown	fork incised			
0.00	unknown	incised design			
0.00	unknown	wide triangle design	quartz grit		HM
11.04	unknown	impressed			
0.00	unknown	impressed rosettes	sand temper	HM	
0.00	unknown	impressed triangles	and squares		
9.69	with alabaster bowl	painted brown design			
0.00	unknown	painted			
0.00	unknown	painted			
8.85	in rubbish below temple wall				
0.00	unknown	green slip & painted	quartz & basalt grit		HM
0.00	blackened on floor	flaring rim	incised & applique		
0.00	unknown	& temper			HM
10.28	unknown	triangle impressed			
10.78	unknown	double false spout			
0.00	edge of tepe				
0.00	unknown				
10.32	unknown				
0.00	trial trench	sand temper HM			
0.00	trial trench	quartz grit & chaff	HM	tripod	
10.61	unknown				
10.72	unknown	punctate lines at rim			
0.00	unknown	painted wide bands			
0.00	unknown				
0.00	near edge of tepe				
10.56	unknown				
9.51	unknown	flint scraped base			
0.00	unknown				
10.90	unknown				
10.48	unknown	ring base			
10.87	unknown	cream slip	traces red paint		
0.001	on floor of XI	Wide flower ?			
0.00	unknown				
10.37	between floors of XI next to wall	Wide flower ?			
10.37	between floors of XI with 4-804	neck only			
10.43	on floor sherds ballistas matting	pointed base			
10.43	on Locus 105 floor with sherds	ballista & matting	pointed base		
10.43	from Loc 105 pot cache on floor	incised fine	quartz & basalt	TM ?	
10.50	unknown	top distorted			
10.26	unknown	plate ?			
10.78	found under floor of shrine	at edge	red slip		
10.19	unknown				
10.19	on pavement of room	sand temper	HM		
10.19	with sherds	punctate lines			
9.91	unknown	quartz grit	HM		
10.14	unknown	sand temper	HM		
9.60	found next to Locus 102 tomb				
9.43	unknown				
9.95	in ordinary refuse				

(continues)

Level XI/XA (continued)

1	2	3	4	5	6	7	8	9	10	11	12	13
1422.	4-1021	discarded	703	XI XI	Wide flower	brown ware	10P	4M	g7	none	none	none
1423.	4-1095	35-10-32	434	XI XI	trumpet vase	buffware	9N	5O	j7	H300	RD149	BD84
1424.	4-1125	Baghdad	0238	XIA XI	oval bowl	ceramic	8M	6Q	a/b1/2	none	none	none
1425.	4-none	discarded	144	XI XI	sherds	ceramic	9M	6O	f-i7-8	none	none	none
1426.	4-none	discarded	142	XI XI	potsherds	ceramic	9M	6O	g-i2-5	none	none	none
1427.	4-none	unknown	159	XI XI	ball	clay	9N	5O	none	none	none	none
1428.	4-none	unknown	636	XI XI	bowl	ceramic	9M	6O	g8	none	none	none
1429.	4-none	unknown	398	XI XI	clay sieve	ceramic	10R	3M	c5	none	none	none
1430.	4-none	unknown	184	XI XI	pot tube	ceramic	9N	5O	none	none	none	none
1431.	4-none	unknown	283	XI XI	Wide flower	ceramic	10M	6M	g6	none	none	none
1432.	4-none	unknown	395	XI XI	pot	ceramic	10M	6M	d8	none	none	none
1433.	4-none	unknown	187	XI XI	bowl	ceramic	9M	6O	none	none	none	T4
1434.	5-1261	36-6-55	1030	XI XI	cup	ceramic	11N	5K	e/f9	H40	RD38	T4
1435.	5-1286	36-6-54	1002	XI XI	2 mouth jar	brownware	12N	5J	i9	L136	W224	RD108
1436.	5-1297	Baghdad	1046	XI XI	jar	ceramic	12M	6J	none	L104	RD64	BW112
1437.	5-1304	Baghdad	1067	XI XI	bowl	ceramic	12M	6J	h8	H28	RD80	BD25
1438.	5-1313	discarded	1073	XI XI	jar or cup	ceramic	11M	6K	h/i6/7	RD94	BD163	ina
1439.	5-1315	Baghdad	1066	XI XI	bowl	red buffware	12M	6J	h5	H124	RD300	BD108
1440.	5-1318	36-6-23	1080	XA XI	small jar	buff ware	11M	6K	b9/10	H85	RD52	BD84
1441.	5-1320	36-6-50	1163	XI XI	small jar	orange buff	12M	6J	f10	H92	RD71	BD108
1442.	5-1338	36-6-47	1152	XA XI	beaker	green grayware	13M	6G	c5	H134	RD 170	T4
1443.	5-1339	Baghdad	1153	XIA XI	strainer	buff ware	13M	6G	c4	H336	D222	ina
1444.	5-1340	Baghdad	1151	XA XI	2 neck jar	ceramic	10L	7M	none	H196	RD88	ina
1445.	5-1341	36-6-52	1157	XI XI	jar	ceramic	11M	6K	i5	H65	RD60	BD28
1446.	5-1343	36-6-25	1152	XA XI	jar	ceramic	13M	6G	c5	H79	RD52	BD48
1447.	5-1346	unclear	1159	XA XI	strainer	ceramic	13M	6G	b7	D205	ina	ina
1448.	5-1348	Baghdad	1084	XI XI	2 rim bowl	gray ware	12M	6J	d 5/6	H213	RD210	BD84
1449.	5-1353	36-6-192	1086	XI XI	vase	copper	11P	4K	a10	H65	RD25	BD16
1450.	5-1366	36-6-45	1203	XI XI	bowl	orange redware	11R	3K	a9	H95	RD125	BD160
1451.	5-1373	Discarded	1205	XI XI	storage jar	ceramic	12M	6J	loc174	H745	RD725	BD680
1452.	5-1380	Baghdad	1126	XI XI	Wide flower	ceramic	12M	6J	c8/9	H80	RD277	none
1453.	5-1400	36-6-56	1142	XI XI	spouted bowl	buffware	13M	6G	d2	L72	W106	SP48
1454.	5-1403	36-6-49	1183	XI XI	jar	pink buffware	12N	5J	j4	H67	RD57	BD73
1455.	5-1404	Baghdad	1193	XI XI	beaker	yellow ware	10L	7M	I/j9	H189	RD95	BD74
1456.	5-1430	36-6-142	1099	XIA XI	small jar	red brownware	10M	6M	b/c7/8	H65	D75	ina
1457.	5-1480	36-6-30	1263	XA XI	fire stand	ceramic	10L	7M	fg 5/6	H129	RD117	D176
1458.	5-1502	Baghdad	1240	XI XI	bowl	ceramic	9L	7O	g/h7/8	H85	RD123	BD36
1459.	5-1610	36-6-48	1326	XI XI	bowl	buffware	9L	7O	c/d8	H91	RD121	ina
1460.	5-1747	36-6-51	1495	XI XI	jar	buffware	12P	4J	a/b9	H95	RD86	BD146
1461.	5-none	36-6-58	none	XI XI	cup	ceramic	10L	7M	none	L75	none	none
1462.	5-none	unknown	1113	XI XI	spout	ceramic	11R	3K	a10	none	none	none
1463.	5-none	unknown	1204	XI XI	bowl	alabaster	11R	3K	a8/9	none	none	none
1464.	5-none	unknown	1070	XI XI	jar	ceramic	12M	6J	g-i5-6	med	none	none
1465.	5-none	unknown	1293	XI XI	2 mouth	ceramic	10L	7M	f2	none	none	none
1466.	5-none	unknown	1329	XA XI	tiny bowl	ceramic	9L	7O	b10	none	none	none
1467.	5-none	unknown	none	XI XI	large jar	clay	12M	6J	f5	none	none	none
1468.	5-none	unknown	1431	XI XI	spouted jar	clay	10L	7M	none	none	none	none
1469.	6-015	Baghdad	1613	XI XI	jar	yellow ware	7Q	7Q	h10	H121	D130	ina
1470.	6-032	Baghdad	1641	XI XI	jar	green grayware	7Q	7Q	c8/9	H101	D120	ina
1471.	6-052	37-16-36	1712	XI ? XI	model bowl	grayware	8Q	8Q	i10	H19	D40	ina
1472.	6-058	Baghdad	none	XI XI	painted jar	ceramic	6K	6K	none	H157	D250	ina
1473.	6-140	Baghdad	none	XI XI	funnel	green ware	8Q	8Q	none	RD266	BD125	0.00
1474.	6-158	Baghdad	1694	XI-XA XI	cup	redware	8O	8O	e5/6	H86	D112	ina
1475.	6-165	discarded	none	XI XI	2 rim bowl	brown ware	8Q	8Q	none	H365	D535	ina
1476.	6-394	Baghdad	none	XI XI	bowl	marble	7K	7K	none	H41	D99	ina
1477.	6-557	37-16-32	3145	XI XI	small jar	brownware	11M	11M	j9	H85	D96	ina
1478.	6-593	Baghdad	none	XI XI	jar	brownware	6Q	6Q	none	D54	ina	0.00
1479.	6-none	unknown	1656	XI XI	cups	redware	7Q	7Q	none	none	none	none
1480.	6-none	unknown	1654	XIXA XI	2 hole cup	ceramic	7Q	7Q	f5	none	none	none
1481.	6-none	unknown	1701	XI XI	jar	ceramic	7Q	7Q	e/f9	none	small	ina
1482.	6-none	unknown	1650	XI XI	jar	ceramic	8Q	8Q	i7	none	none	none
1483.	7-0052	Discarded	2531	XI XI	stand	clay	9M	9M	h/i8/9	H205	RD205	BD190
1484.	7-0066	Baghdad	2525	XI XI	censer	brown ware	8M	8M	a/b3	H710	RD390	BD435
1485.	7-none	unknown	2541	XI XI	bowl	rough ware	9M	9M	c8	none	none	none
		Spindle	**whorl**									
1486.	4-0603	Baghdad	160	XI XI	whorl	ceramic	9P	4O	none	D34	T21	ina
1487.	4-0604	Baghdad	0162	XII XI	whorl	ceramic	9P	4O	none	none	none	none

14	15	16	17	18	19
10.00	unknown				
9.09	found in wall of XI				
10.07	at edge				
10.24	from floor of room				
10.19	unknown				
10.05	unknown				
10.06	unknown				
10.27	unknown				
0.00	unknown				
10.81	unknown				
10.42	unknown				
0.00	unknown				
10.55	next to oven				
0.00	in oven room on floor	quartz grit	HM		
10.08	unknown	with double handle	neck & shoulder		
10.60	50cm below floor of XA				
10.65	from pavement				
9.85	unknown				
10.63	no surrounding except dirt	red slip			
9.93	with 5-1271 within walls	buff slip	basalt grit & chaff	HM	
10.39	on floor 1m below Locus 214	with amulet			
10.39	15cm above floor near	edge of tepe			
10.65	questionable provenience	red slip			
9.92	under stones in "y" on floor	with sherds			
10.39	on floor with amulet	1m below Locus 214	badly broken		
10.39	next to well near edge of tepe	same as 5-1559 ?			
9.40	in room with buttress on bench	in SE	red slip		
10.63	unknown				
9.69	at edge surely XI	painted rim	fine basalt & quartz	TM	
9.40	on bench in deep room 1127	with matting & objects			
10.01	in corner public room with figurine				
9.31	found on floor	quartz grit & chaff	HM	fragment	
9.87	in area of ashes	bubbled vegetable	& fine quartz grit	HM	
10.71	complex of walls				
9.96	on pavement of room	quartz grit & chaff	HM		
10.65	unknown				
0.00	40cm above pavement	in ordinary refuse			
9.84	found in debris above floor				
0.00	on floor with celt & eating awl	fine quartz & basalt	HM		
0.00	unknown	fork impressed			
9.97	unknown				
9.69	with 5-1366	painted sherds			
9.85	with 5-1315 and lots of sealings				
10.40	just above walls				
10.33	on floor				
9.52	in deep room 31	charred wheat inside			
10.50	in eroding refuse				
0.00	loose				
0.00	unknown				
0.00	unknown	quartz grit	HM		
0.00	unknown	gritty	gray slip	cross hatch lines	
	incised inbeveled rim				
0.00	unknown	incised shoulder			
0.00	unknown	gritty			
0.00	unknown				
0.00	unknown	quartz grit			
0.00	unknown				
0.00	on floor of room				
0.00	inside room				
0.00	unknown				
9.84	unknown				
9.33	1 oc 7-13 at level XI walls				
9.21	unknown				
0.00	unknown				
10.1	unknown				

(*continues*)

Level XI/XA   (continued)

1	2	3	4	5	6	7	8	9	10	11	12	13
1488.	4-0604	Baghdad	0162	XII XI	whorl	ceramic	9P	4O	none	none	none	none
1489.	4-0611	35-10-228	0161	XII XI	whorl	ceramic	9N	5O	none	H27	D33	ina
1490.	4-0613	35-10-67	177	XI XI	whorl	ceramic	8M	6Q	none	D37	T21	ina
1491.	4-0614	Baghdad	157	XI XI	whorl	ceramic	9N	5O	none	D28	T18	ina
1492.	4-0615	phila no#	199	XI XI	whorl	ceramic	8M	6Q	none	D34	T21	ina
1493.	4-0619	Baghdad	183	XI XI	whorl	ceramic	9N	5O	none	D34	T18	ina
1494.	4-0657	35-10-72	166	XI XI	whorl	ceramic	9M	6O	none	D34	T18	ina
1495.	4-0658	35-10-70	155	XI XI	whorl	ceramic	9M	6O	none	D31	T18	ina
1496.	4-0659	Baghdad	176	XI XI	whorl	ceramic	8M	6Q	none	D24	T13	ina
1497.	4-0660	discarded	179	XI XI	whorl	ceramic	9P	4O	none	D36	T12	ina
1498.	4-0663	discarded	47	XI XI	whorl	ceramic	10M	6M	i6	D39	T21	ina
1499.	4-0669	35-10-347	207	XI ? XI	whorl	ceramic	8M	6Q	none	D34	T23	ina
1500.	4-0687	Baghdad	261	XI XI	whorl	ceramic	9P	4O	g2	D30	T22	ina
1501.	4-0695	Baghdad	257	XI XI	whorl	ceramic	9P	4O	g2	D26	T19	ina
1502.	4-0701	Baghdad	281	XI XI	whorl	ceramic	8M	6Q	e6	D33	T17	ina
1503.	4-0702	discarded	284	XI XI	whorl	ceramic	9N	5O	h10	D39	T21	ina
1504.	4-0705	Baghdad	56	XI XI	whorl	ceramic	10M	6M	c8	D32	T21	ina
1505.	4-0711	Baghdad	119	XI XI	whorl	Ceramic	11M	6K	none	D28	T14	ina
1506.	4-0716	35-10-73	296	XI XI	whorl	ceramic	10M	6M	f7	D34	T22	ina
1507.	4-0718	Baghdad	299	XI XI	whorl	ceramic	11N	5K	d1	D37	T21	ina
1508.	4-0719	35-10-66	300	XI XI	whorl	ceramic	10N	5M	a7	D31	T16	ina
1509.	4-0728	Baghdad	120	XI XI	whorls 2	ceramic	10N	5M	b2	D36	T18	ina
1510.	4-0728B	Baghdad	120	XI XI	whorl	stone	10N	5M	b2	D20	T13	ina
1511.	4-0731	Baghdad	304	XI XI	whorl	ceramic	11M	6K	b2	D36	T22	ina
1512.	4-0763	discarded	146	XI XI	whorl	ceramic	9M	6O	g-i6-8	none	none	none
1513.	4-0776	35-10-64	307	XI XI	whorl	ceramic	11M	6K	f5	D35	T22	ina
1514.	4-0778	Baghdad	311	XI XI	whorl	ceramic	11M	6K	b3	D36	T20	ina
1515.	4-0813	discarded	217	XI XI	whorl	ceramic	9M	6O	d4	none	none	none
1516.	4-0814	35-10-354	66	XI XI	whorl	Ceramic	12N	5J	j8	D37	T19	ina
1517.	4-0818	35-10-56	none	XI XI	whorl	ceramic	8M	6Q	none	D36	T22	ina
1518.	4-0834	35-10-76	330	XI XI	whorl	ceramic	8L	7Q	j10	D29	T18	ina
1519.	4-0855	35-10-74	none	XI XI	whorl	ceramic	8L	7Q	none	D38	T20	ina
1520.	4-0856	35-10-59	79	XI XI	whorl	ceramic	8L	7Q	e3	D33	T19	ina
1521.	4-0857	Baghdad	none	XI XI	whorl	ceramic	11N	5K	none	D34	T13	ina
1522.	4-0858	35-10-69	none	XI XI	whorl	ceramic	11P	4K	none	D27	T24	ina
1523.	4-0859	35-10-90	none	XI XI	whorl	stone	8N	5Q	none	D48	H15	ina
1524.	4-0866	discarded	none	XI XI	whorl	ceramic	10M	6M	none	D39	T22	ina
1525.	4-0908	35-10-222	0410	XII XI	whorl	ceramic	10M	6M	e8	H23	D37	ina
1526.	4-0910	Baghdad	402	XI XI	whorls 9	ceramic	8P	4Q	d8	D36	T22	ina
1527.	4-1041	discarded	none	XI XI	whorl	ceramic	8N	5Q	none	none	none	none
1528.	4-1046	discarded	none	XI XI	whorl	ceramic	9H	9O	none	none	none	none
1529.	4-1103	Baghdad	833	XI XI	whorl	ceramic	7M	6S	d9	D35	T21	ina
1530.	4-none	35-10-157	0722	XIA XI	whorls 2	ceramic	10M	6M	d7	H28	D45	none
1531.	4-none	35-10-57	358	XI XI	whorl	unknown	10M	6M	c5	H22	D37	none
1532.	4-none	35-10-58	533	XI XI	whorl	ceramic	10N	5M	none	none	none	none
1533.	4-none	35-10-60	631	XI XI	whorl	unknown	9P	4O	c8	H25	D33	ina
1534.	4-none	35-10-61	749	XI XI	whorl	unknown	10P	4M	h6	H20	D37	ina
1535.	4-none	35-10-62	none	XI XI	whorl	ceramic	8L	7Q	none	H20	D35	ina
1536.	4-none	35-10-63	none	XI XI	whorl	ceramic	10N	5M	none	H20	D35	ina
1537.	4-none	35-10-65	993	XI XI	whorl	ceramic	7M	6S	c9	H21	D35	ina
1538.	4-none	35-10-68	none	XI XI	whorl	ceramic	8L	7Q	none	H19	D33	none
1539.	4-none	35-10-71	none	XI XI	whorl	ceramic	10-	-M	none	H15	D36	ina
1540.	4-none	35-10-75	376	XI XI	whorl	ceramic	10M	6M	none	H22	D30	ina
1541.	4-none	35-10-77	372	XI XI	whorl	ceramic	10M	6M	g10	H10	D24	ina
1542.	4-none	unknown	172	XI XI	whorl	unknown	9R	3O	none	none	none	none
1543.	4-none	unknown	629	XI XI	whorl	unknown	11P	4K	j3	none	none	none
1544.	4-none	unknown	354	XI XI	whorl	unknown	10P	4M	g4	none	none	none
1545.	4-none	unknown	748	XI XI	whorl	unknown	10P	4M	h6	none	none	none
1546.	4-none	unknown	359	XI XI	whorl	unknown	9P	4O	i7	none	none	none
1547.	4-none	unknown	403	XI XI	whorl	unknown	8P	4Q	g/h6	none	none	none
1548.	4-none	unknown	182	XI XI	whorl	unknown	9N	5O	none	none	none	none
1549.	4-none	unknown	181	XI XI	whorl	unknown	9N	5O	none	none	none	none
1550.	4-none	unknown	408	XI XI	whorl	unknown	8N	5Q	d4	none	none	none
1551.	4-none	unknown	297	XI XI	whorl	unknown	10M	6M	f7	none	none	none
1552.	4-none	unknown	196	XI XI	whorl	unknown	8M	6Q	none	none	none	none
1553.	4-none	unknown	198	XI XI	whorl	unknown	8M	6Q	none	none	none	none
1554.	4-none	unknown	229	XI XI	whorl	unknown	7M	6S	c10	none	none	none

14	15	16	17	18	19
10.15	unknown				
10.57	unknown				
0.001	unknown				
10.51	unknown				
0.001	unknown				
0.001	unknown				
0.00	unknown				
10.3	unknown				
0.00	unknown				
0.00	unknown				
10.2	unknown				
0.00	unknown				
9.51	unknown				
9.51	near edge of tepe				
10.3	unknown				
10.00	unknown				
0.001	unknown				
10.71	beneath pavement of X	on pavement of XI			
10.84	unknown				
10.77	unknown				
10.27	unknown				
9.501	alongside Locus 107 tomb				
9.50	alongside Locus 107 tomb				
10.75	unknown				
10.24	unknown				
10.80	unknown				
10.61	unknown				
10.1	between floors in corner	of room 1013			
0.00	under tepe surface	at edge with stones			
0.00	unknown				
10.17	on floor 3m from edge of tepe				
0.00	unknown				
10.55	with "Uruk ring" sherds				
0.00	unknown				
0.00	unknown				
10.06	unknown				
0.00	unknown				
10.64	in ordinary refuse				
9.24	unknown				
0.00	unknown G3 season				
0.00	unknown G3 season				
9.90	unknown				
9.88	unknown	punctate design			
10.60	unknown	incised design			
0.00	unknown	pellet applique			
10.52	unknown	incised design			
9.32	unknown				
0.00	unknown	incised & pellets			
0.00	unknown	incised			
9.90	unknown	incised design			
0.00	unknown	punctate design			
0.00	unknown	incised 'x'			
10.79	unknown	conoid top			
10.64	unknown				
0.00	near edge of tepe				
10.98	unknown				
10.28	unknown				
9.32	unknown				
9.85	unknown				
8.76	unknown				
0.00	unknown				
0.00	unknown				
9.92	west of "fortress"				
10.84	unknown				
0.00	unknown				
0.00	unknown				
10.12	near edge tepe				

(continues)

Level XI/XA   (continued)

1	2	3	4	5	6	7	8	9	10	11	12	13
1555.	5-1253	36-6-10	1028	XA XI	whorl	ceramic	11M	6K	d7	D29	T10	ina
1556.	5-1253	36-6-10	1028	XA XI	whorl	ceramic	11M	6K	d7	D29	T16	ina
1557.	5-1253	36-6-11	1028	XA XI	whorl	ceramic	11M	6K	d7	D31	T16	ina
1558.	5-1253	36-6-11	1028	XA XI	whorl	ceramic	11M	6K	d7	D31	T16	ina
1559.	5-1253	36-6-12	1028	XA XI	whorl	ceramic	11M	6K	d7	D28	T11	ina
1560.	5-1253	36-6-13	1028	XA XI	whorl	ceramic	11M	6K	d7	D32	T20	ina
1561.	5-1253	36-6-14	1028	XA XI	whorl	ceramic	11M	6K	d7	D28	T10	ina
1562.	5-1253	36-6-14	1028	XA XI	whorl	gray ware	11M	6K	d7	D28	T10	ina
1563.	5-1253	36-6-9	1028	XA XI	whorl	ceramic	11M	6K	d7	D31	T20	ina
1564.	5-1316	Baghdad	1050	XI XI	whorl	ceramic	11M	6K	e2	D36	T15	ina
1565.	5-1342B	35-10-156	1156	XIA XI	whorl	ceramic	11M	6K	none	D35	T23	ina
1566.	5-1354	36-6-32	1110	XA XI	whorl	ceramic	13M	6G	d6	D28	T15	ina
1567.	5-1354	36-6-33	1110	XA XI	whorl	ceramic	13M	6G	d6	D32	T15	ina
1568.	5-1362	36-6-78	1089	XI XI	whorl	ceramic	13M	6G	h/i6/7	D39	T21	ina
1569.	5-1394	Baghdad	none	XI XI	whorl	ceramic	11P	4K	none	D36	T17	ina
1570.	5-1708	36-6-175	1530	XIA XI	whorl	ceramic	9L	7O	note	D28	T20	ina
1571.	5-none	36-6-70	1083	XI XI	whorl	gray ware	11M	6K	none	D28	T18	none
1572.	5-none	36-6-75	none	XI XI	whorl	ceramic	none	none	none	D34	T21	ina
1573.	5-none	36-6-76	none	XI XI	whorl	ceramic	13M	6G	none	D38	T22	ina
1574.	5-none	36-6-77	none	XI XI	whorl	ceramic	13M	6G	none	D34	T19	ina
1575.	5-none	36-6-79	1083	XI XI	whorl	ceramic	11M	6K	none	D30	T10	none
1576.	5-none	37-16-35	none	XI XI	whorl	yellow ware	5K	5K	none	D40	T20	ina
	Seal		**sealing**									
1577.	3-0486	Baghdad	none	XI XI	stamp	granite	8N	5Q	none	L17	W16	T5
1578.	4-0641	35-10-119	171	XI XI	impression	clay	8M	6Q	none	L41	W35	T26
1579.	4-0642	IM24961	39	XI XI	impression	clay	8M	6Q	j7	L75	W63	ina
1580.	4-0643	IM25046	9	XI XI	impression	clay	8M	6Q	none	L36	W34	ina
1581.	4-0645	IM24968	5	XI XI	impression	clay	9N	5O	none	L22	W25	ina
1582.	4-0649	35-10-113	1	XI XI	stamp	steatite	10M	6M	g2	D12	none	ina
1583.	4-0664	IM25044	41	XI XI	impression	clay	8N	5Q	a1	L52	W49	none
1584.	4-0666	35-10-124	40	XI XI	impression	clay	8M	6Q	none	L33	W42	T20
1585.	4-0683	IM24578	277	XI XI	stamp	steatite	9N	5O	none	D10	none	ina
1586.	4-0707	IM24603	58	XI XI	stamp	steatite	11N	5K	f2	D15	none	ina
1587.	4-0777	35-10-110	309	XI XI	stamp	steatite	9M	6O	e8	L18	W7	ina
1588.	4-0781	IM24985	315	XI XI	impression	clay	10N	5M	c4	L45	W58	none
1589.	4-0781A	35-10-137	315	XI XI	impression	clay	10N	5M	c4	none	none	none
1590.	4-0807	IM24988	321	XI XI	impression	clay	11P	4K	c4	L25	W33	ina
1591.	4-0808	35-10-105	323	XI XI	stamp	stone	9M	6O	f6	D22	T13	ina
1592.	4-0820	IM24584	220	XIA XI	stamp	stone	8M	6Q	h4	D14	none	ina
1593.	4-0842	35-10-107	130	XI XI	stamp	steatite	8M	6Q	c3	D26	T10	ina
1594.	4-0843	35-10-117	334	XI XI	stamp	limestone	8M	6Q	none	D13	T6	ina
1595.	4-0848A	35-10-122	63	XI XI	2 impression	clay	12P	4J	a5	L73	W28	T28
1596.	4-848B	35-10-122	63	XI XI	impression	clay	12P	4J	a5	L34	W40	ina
1597.	4-0848C	IM24991	63	XI XI	2 impression	clay	12P	4J	a5	L36	W40	ina
1598.	4-0849	35-10-128	63	XI XI	impression	clay	12P	4J	a5	L32	W38	ina
1599.	4-0850	35-10-130	63	XI XI	impression	clay	12P	4J	a5	L19	W18	T22
1600.	4-0851	IM24971	63	XI XI	impression	clay	12P	4J	a5	L32	W22	ina
1601.	4-0861	IM24989	134	XI XI	impression	clay	10N	5M	e/f2	none	none	none
1602.	4-0870	35-10-125	344	XI XI	impression	clay	10P	4M	h7	L29	W25	T11
1603.	4-0873	35-10-132	345	XI XI	impression	clay	12P	4J	b5	L18	W44	T13
1604.	4-0874	IM24981	349	XI XI	impression	clay	12N	5J	j9	L44	W43	ina
1605.	4-0881	IM24990	none	XI XI	impression	clay	12N	5J	none	L17	W33	ina
1606.	4-0882	IM24986	401	XI XI	impression	clay	9P	4O	e/f2	L36	W29	ina
1607.	4-0884	IM24994	81	XI XI	impression	clay	9P	4O	e/f2	L32	W30	ina
1608.	4-0886	phila no#	139	XIA XI	impression	clay	10N	5M	none	L20	W50	ina
1609.	4-0887	IM24983	139	XIA XI	impression	clay	10N	5M	none	L28	W25	ina
1610.	4-0888	35-10-124	139	XIA XI	impression	clay	10N	5M	none	L44	W38	T20
1611.	4-0889	35-10-126	139	XIA XI	impression	clay	10N	5M	none	L30	W25	T12
1612.	4-0890	35-10-134	139	XIA XI	impression	clay	10N	5M	none	L36	W38	T14
1613.	4-0891	35-10-121	82	XI XI	impression	clay	9P	4O	none	L40	W45	T24
1614.	4-0893	35-10-123	84	XI XI	impression	clay	10P	4M	none	L22	W30	T8
1615.	4-0895	IM24984	89	XII XI	impression	clay	10P	4M	none	L34	W22	none
1616.	4-0896	35-10-106	140	XI XI	stamp	steatite	10R	3M	c8	D20	T9	ina
1617.	4-0897	IM24987	148	XI XI	impression	clay	10N	5M	e-f5-7	L26	W35	ina
1618.	4-0904	IM24602	95	XIA XI	stamp	steatite	10N	5M	none	L22	W17	T9
1619.	4-0917	35-10-109	362	XI XI	stamp	steatite	11M	6K	d1	D13	T5	ina
1620.	4-0937	IM24995	383	XI XI	impression	clay	8M	6Q	j7	L25	W34	ina

14	15	16	17	18	19
10.68	with ballistas	loom parts in area 39			
10.68	with ballistas	loom parts in area 39			
10.68	with ballistas	loom parts in area 39			
10.68	with ballistas	loom parts in area 39			
10.68	with ballistas	loom parts in area 39			
10.68	with bobbins	loom parts in area 39			
10.68	with ballistas	loom parts in area 39			
10.68	with ballistas	loom parts in area 39	edge incised		
10.68	with ballistas	loom parts in area 39			
9.64	10 cm above floor in ash	near 4-1037			
10.67	unknown	incised & punctate			
10.38	three whorls near top of wall of XI	perforated			
10.38	three whorls near top of wall of XI	incised top			
9.87	on pavement apparently XI				
0.00	unknown				
9.70	from top of wall of Round House				
9.52	unknown	incised underside			
0.00	unknown	incised lines			
0.00	unknown	edge incised			
0.00	unknown				
9.52	unknown	punctate design			
0.00	unknown				
0.00	unknown	Seal 17×16	seal	lozenges × cross	hemispheroid
0.00	unknown	Seal 20+ ×18	on jar shoulder	hut on stand ?	
10.25	oc103: room with ballista nest	Seal 26×22	unknown	6 rows of	wedges
0.00	unknown	Seal 21×26	on jar shoulder	standing goat	sheep
0.00	unknown	Seal 18+×22+	broken:from jar	horned goat	by bush
10.85	unknown	Seal 12 dia	seal	cross of stalks	hemispheroid
10.33	unknown	Seal 20×23+	unclear	1 horned animal	
10.40	unknown	Seal 20 ×10+	basket/jar mouth	snake	
9.38	unknown	Seal 10 dia	seal	lines off cross	hemispheroid
0.00	unknown	Seal 15 dia	seal	not clear	
11.18	unknown	Seal 18×7+	seal	not clear	hemispheroid
10.10	on floor of room	Seal 14×10	bulla	2 arrows animal	
10.10	on floor of room	Seal 14×10	too broken to know	arrowhead	
10.80	in burned debris in level XI room	Seal 16+×25	bulla ? on sack ?	back to back	animals
10.42	ashes above the floor of a room	Seal 22 dia	seal	leaf skeleton	reel shaped
0.00	under or between XI floor(s)	Seal 14 dia	seal	leaf skeleton	"button"
10.70	20 cm above pavement in refuse	Seal 26 dia	seal	horned animal	hemispheroid
10.69	just under X foundations	Seal 13 dia	seal	starburst	hemispheroid
0.00	outside Temple on floor of a room	Seal 25×30 L73	on jar cover	4 sheep	2 with horns
0.00	outside temple on floor of room	Seal 31 dia	Type T door lock	4 sheep	2 with horns
0.00	near edge on floor of Temple room	Seal 22+×31+	unclear	4 sheep	2 with horns
0.00	loc 112: on floor in temple room	Seal 26×17	unknown	an animal	
0.00	loc 112: on floor in temple room	Seal 19+×17+	jar neck	horned animal	
0.00	loc 112: on floor in temple room	Seal 12×17+	on sack	horned animal	
0.00	loose earth in ?	same 4-781	a wall	unknown	arrowhead
10.43	north of & adjoining ballista nest	Seal 21×18	on basket cover	2 rams heads	
10.64	25 cm under floor of East Shrine	Seal 12+×16+	reed on back: ??	one animal	
9.61	below East Shrine foundations	Seal 18 dia	on jar shoulder ?	horn beast &	legs
10.87	unknown	Seal 9+×18+	too broken to know	horned ? &	sheep ?
10.41	at edge of tepe not in structure	Seal 30+ dia	bale tag ?	circlng sheep 2	horn
10.40	unknown	Seal 26+ dia	too broken to know	2 intertwined	snakes
9.75	in ordinary refuse w/4-887 to 890	Seal 20+×50	unknown	2 dogs ? & snake	
9.75	in ordinary refuse with 4-886 888-90	Seal 28+×22+	bale tag	3 sheep	
9.75	in ordinary refuse with 4-886/7/8	Seal 11 diam	on jar shoulder	horned animal	
9.75	in ordinary refuse with 4-886-890	Seal 12×8	on basket tag	2 fish	
9.75	in ordinary refuse with 4-886-888	Seal 20+×18+	too broken to know	horned ?	
9.77	unknown	Seal 14+ ×32	on jar shoulder	2 animals ?	
9.74	unknown	Seal 9+×26+	on jar shoulder	dog chase horn	beast
10.46	in fill levels XIA to XI	Seal 22×15+	unknown	animal & plant ?	
9.82	close to edge of tepe next to wall	Seal 21 dia	seal	horned stag	carinated hemisphere
9.59	unknown	Seal 17 dia	on sack	horned animal ?	
9.50	unknown	Seal 22×17	seal	cross dots lines	carinated hemisphere
10.78	unknown	Seal 13 dia	seal	lines off midline	
10.03	below floor ?	Seal 20+×21+	twist of grass: ?	lozenges in ?	

(continues)

Level XI/XA   (continued)

1	2	3	4	5	6	7	8	9	10	11	12	13
1621.	4-0940	IM25008	377	XI XI	impression	clay	10M	6M	d4	L35	W40	ina
1622.	4-0942	phila no#	561	XI XI	stamp	steatite	8M	6Q	a9	D18	T7	ina
1623.	4-0986	IM25041	519	XIA XI	impression	clay	8M	6Q	none	L34	W39	ina
1624.	4-0990	35-10-136	529	XI XI	impression	clay	10M	6M	c8	L17	W25	T18
1625.	4-1013	Baghdad	669	XI-XIA ?	impression	clay	dump	dump	ina	L33	W37	ina
1626.	4-1029	IM24960	535	XI XI	impression	clay	9M	6O	i/j9	L46	W49	ina
1627.	4-1060	IM25006	752	XI XI	impression	clay	9M	6O	g8	L27	W33	ina
1628.	4-1064	35-10-133	744	XI XI	impression	clay	8M	6Q	f1	L43	W48	T22
1629.	4-1077	35-10-127	818	XI XI	impression	clay	10M	6M	j8	L40	W28	T21
1630.	4-1082	35-10-116	435	XI XI	stamp	stone	10M	6M	none	L16	W23	T8
1631.	4-1083	IM24999	435	XI XI	impression	clay	10M	6M	none	L18	W31	ina
1632.	4-1088	35-10-115	444	XI XI	stamp	steatite	10P	4M	i4	D15	T4	ina
1633.	4-1092	35-10-120	440	XI XI	impression	clay	9N	5O	j 4/5	L70	W58	T26
1634.	4-1099	IM25012	227	XI ? XI	impression	clay	7M	6S	i/j 9	L12	W22	ina
1635.	4-1128	IM24965	240	XI XI	impression	clay	7M	6S	b/c1/2	L20	W24	ina
1636.	4-1134	IM25005	831	XI XI	impression	clay	7N	5S	e9	L32	W44	ina
1637.	5-1263	discarded	1015	XA XI	impression	clay	11M	6K	c8	none	none	none
1638.	5-1268	36-6-123	1031	XI XI	impression	clay	11N	5K	b4	L24	W22	T16
1639.	5-1279	36-6-132	1003	XI XI	impression	clay	12N	5J	i 7/8	L27	W28	T15
1640.	5-1284	discarded	1037	XI XI	impression	clay	12M	6J	i4	none	none	none
1641.	5-1285	IM26998	1040	XI XI	impression	clay	12M	6J	g 5/6	L25	W18	none
1642.	5-1289A	36-6-126	1044	XI XI	impression	clay	12M	6J	g/h7	L26	W28	T11
1643.	5-1289B	IM26961	1044	XI XI	impression	clay	12M	6J	g/h7	L26	W39	T10
1644.	5-1300A	36-6-115	1044	XI XI	impression	clay	12M	6J	g/h7	L34	W38	T20
1645.	5-1300B	36-6-122	1044	XI XI	impression	clay	12M	6J	g/h7	L39	W32	T12
1646.	5-1300C	36-6-124	1044	XI XI	impression	clay	12M	6J	g/h7	L26+	W24	T11
1647.	5-1300D	IM26775	1044	XI XI	impression	clay	12M	6J	g/h7	L47	W39	ina
1648.	5-1300E	IM26999	1044	XI XI	impression	clay	12M	6J	g/h7	L33	W25	ina
1649.	5-1300F	IM27000	1044	XI XI	impression	clay	12M	6J	g/h7	L40	W18	ina
1650.	5-1300G	IM27001	1044	XI XI	impression	clay	12M	6J	g/h7	L55	W39	ina
1651.	5-1301A	36-6-127	1047	XI XI	impression	clay	12M	6J	f7	L31	W21	T9
1652.	5-1301B	IM27002	1047	XI XI	impression	clay	12M	6J	f7	D17	ina	ina
1653.	5-1301C	36-6-211	1047	XI XI	impression	clay	12M	6J	f7	L23	W22	T7
1654.	5-1301D	IM27008	1047	XI XI	impression	clay	12M	6J	f7	D17	none	ina
1655.	5-1303A	36-6-117	1044	XI XI	impression	clay	12M	6J	f7	L32	W56	T17
1656.	5-1303B	IM26986	1044	XI XI	impression	clay	12M	6J	f7	L18	W24	ina
1657.	5-1303C	IM27004	1044	XI XI	impression	clay	12M	6J	f7	L18	W24	ina
1658.	5-1303D	36-6-118	1044	XI XI	impression	clay	12M	6J	f7	L56	W30	T16
1659.	5-1303E	IM26992	1044	XI XI	impression	clay	12M	6J	f7	L18	W21	none
1660.	5-1310a	36-6-43	1068	XA XI	impression	clay	11M	6K	g/h10 a	none	none	none
1661.	5-1310b	36-6-41	1068	XA XI	impression	clay	11M	6K	g/h10	L22	W26	T28
1662.	5-1310b	36-6-41b	1068	XI XI	impression	clay	11M	6K	g/h10	L45	W26	T14
1663.	5-1310c	IM26991	1068	XA XI	impression	clay	11M	6K	g/h10	none	none	none
1664.	5-1325	36-6-120	1044	XI XI	impression	clay	12M	6J	f7	L57	W35	T21
1665.	5-1326	36-6-119	1044	XI XI	impression	clay	12M	6J	f7	L27	W22	ina
1666.	5-1333	36-6-128	1050	XI XI	impression	clay	11M	6K	e 2/3	L43	W41	T16
1667.	5-1335	36-6-125	1158	XI XI	impression	clay	12N	5J	c8	L15	W20	ina
1668.	5-1349	36-6-114	1162	XI XI	stamp	ceramic	12N	5J	g8	D16	T7	ina
1669.	5-1357	IM26973	1111	XA XI	impression	clay	13N	5G	a/b3/4	L38	W23	T13
1670.	5-1370	36-6-130	1202	XI XI	impression	clay	11M	6K	h 5/6	L40	W34	T18
1671.	5-1371	36-6-113	1117	XI XI	stamp	steatite	12P	4J	e/f 6	D14	T4	ina
1672.	5-1372	36-6-111	1119	XI XI	stamp	stone	11P	4K	f/g3/4	D20	T12	ina
1673.	5-1405	36-6-214	1175	XIA XI	impression	clay	11N	5K	c 5/6	L33	W12	T17
1674.	5-1425	IM26967	1170	XIA XI	impression	clay	12P	4J	b5	L72	W63	none
1675.	5-1426	IM26971	1196	XI XI	impression	clay	11N	5K	e 3/4	none	none	none
1676.	5-1592	36-6-110	1283	XI XI	stamp	steatite	10L	7M	c6	D25	T9	ina
1677.	5-1619	IM26984	1333	XI XI	impression	clay	10L	7M	d/e2	none	none	none
1678.	5-none	discarded	1029	XI XI	impression	clay	12M	6J	i 6/7	none	none	none
1679.	5-none	unknown	1181	XI XI	stamp	unknown	12N	5J	i1	none	none	none
1680.	6-0103	IM32626	none	XI XI	impression	clay	5J	5J	none	L72	W51	none
1681.	6-0594	Baghdad	none	XI XI	stamp	obsidian	6K	6K	a ?	T10	L22	W20
1682.	6-0610	Baghdad	none	XI XI	impression	clay	7K	7K	none	D24	ina	ina
1683.	6-none	IM32900	none	XI XI	impression	clay	7K	7K	none	L45	W39	ina
1684.	6-none	unknown	1785	XI XI	impression	clay	7K	7K	h8	none	none	none
1685.	6-none	unknown	1960	XI XI	stamp	steatite	9M	9M	c9	none	none	none
1686.	7-0036	Baghdad	2523	XI XI	stamp	steatite	9M	9M	e/f 1	D16	T6	ina
1687.	7-0060	IM42679	2532	XI XI	impression	clay	10M	10M	i2	L56	W41	T17

14	15	16	17	18	19
10.50	unknown	Seal 25+×21+	bale tag	animal	
10.67	in soil around X foundation	Seal 18 dia	seal	abstract animal	hemispheroid
10.17	in pit with sherds like those XIA-X	Seal 20×21+	sack	animal on river	
10.37	pure XI context	Seal 14+ ×9+ L17	on jar shoulder	dogs chase	sheep
0.00	dump	Seal 9+×21	on jar shoulder	horn beast eat	stalk
9.51	unknown	Seal 36 dia	unknown	dogs chase	animals
9.48	unknown	Seal 19+×15+	on door	animal	
10.24	unknown	Seal 17+×21+	tab: in jar mouth ?	horn animal	& other
10.19	unknown	Seal 40+ ×18	on flat tab	animal	
9.86	with sealing 4-1083	Seal 16×23	seal	cross & lines	gable
9.86	with 4-1082	Seal 13+×23+	bale tag ?	crab like legs	
9.61	on pavement of XI	Seal 15 dia	seal	cross & wedges	low hemispheroid
8.91	in well found at White Room level	Seal 32 diam	in jar mouth ?	city plan	w rivers ?
9.60	edge of tepe at XIA	Seal 12 dia	on sack	multi line cross	
10.07	unknown	Seal 12+×15+	bale tag	animal	
9.40	near edge of tepe	Seal 11 dia	unknown	lines off cross	
0.0	below X walls	none	unknown	unknown	
10.65	unknown	Seal 19+×16+	tab ?:jar shoulder ?	dog and	ram horn
0.00	on floor of oven room	Seal 17 ×12+	bale tag	running dog & ?	
10.67	from "fake oven" room	none	unknown	unclear	
10.70	north & 50 cm under loc 208 grave	Seal 17 dia	bale tag	2 back to back	dogs
9.85	with 30–40 sealings and macehead	Seal 19+×17+	on hide cover	2 animals & ?	
9.85	with 30–40 sealings and macehead	Seal 26 dia	on sack	two animals & ?	
9.85	with 30–40 sealings and macehead	Seal 13+× 26	on jar shoulder	2 horned	animals & ?
9.85	with 30–40 sealings and macehead	Seal 12+×20	on jar shoulder	2 horned	animals & ?
9.85	with 30–40 sealings and macehead	Seal 20+×18+	on jar shoulder	2 horned	animals & ?
9.85	with 30–40 sealings and macehead	Seal 21×23	on jar shoulder	2 horned	animals & ?
9.85	with 30–40 sealings and macehead	Seal 21×23	on jar shoulder	2 horned	animals & ?
9.85	with 30–40 sealings and macehead	Seal 21×23	on jar shoulder	2 horned	animals & ?
9.73	unknown	Seal 17 diam	on sm jar shoulder	2 horned	animals & ?
9.73	unknown	Seal 17 dia	on sack	2 back to back	dogs
9.73	unknown	Seal 16+ ×17 L23	on jar cover	2 back to back	dogs
9.73	unknown	Seal 17 dia	on sack	2 horned	animals & ?
9.85	with 30–40 sealings and nacehead	Seal 22+×32+ L32	on jar shoulder	2 horned	animals & ?
9.85	with 30–40 sealings and macehead	Seal 21×25 * L18	on jar shoulder	2 horned	animals & ?
9.85	with 30–40 sealings and macehead	Seal 21×25 * L18	on jar shoulder	2 horned	animals & ?
9.85	with 30–40 sealings and macehead	Seal 16 ×24+ L56	on jar shoulder	2 horned	animals & ?
9.85	with 30–40 sealings and macehead	Seal 21×25 * L18	on jar shoulder	2 horned	animals & ?
10.52	with 3 figurines in welter of ashes	lost	bale tag	animal	wavy line
10.52	with 3 figurines in welter of ashes	Seal 14+×28+ L22	on sack tie	dogs chase	sheep
0.00	with 3 figurines in welter of ashes	Seal 31+×14+	on tie sack	dogs chase	sheep
10.52	with 3 figurines in welter of ashes	Seal 29 dia	on jar shoulder ?	dogs chase sheep	
9.85	with 30–40 sealings and macehead	Seal 23+×28	on jar shoulder	3 salukhis &	snake ?
9.85	with 30–40 sealings and macehead	Seal 23+×28	bundle tag ??	3 salukhis &	snake ?
9.64	10cm above floor in ashy fill	Seal 26×22	on jar top	drilled holes loop	
10.53	on floor in corner of room	Seal 14+×18+ L15	unknown	3 dismembered	horns
10.31	in corner of room	Seal 16 dia	seal	lozenges	hemispheroid
10.29	at edge of tepe	Seal 15×16	tag on basket	human and ?	
10.72	with ballista & bicornicopia	Seal 17 diam L40	on jar cover	lozenges	triangle
9.55	on pavement in debris	Seal 14 dia	seal	lines off cross	hemispheroid
9.53	in debris above floor near wall	Seal 20 dia	seal	strutting bird & ?	high hemispheroid
9.92	unknown	Seal 24+×15	in jar mouth	walking birdhead	man
10.15	just above wall XIA: under floor ?	Seal 32 dia	flat chaff: door ?	birdman lovers	snake
10.00	unknown	Seal 28 dia	unknown like tablet	horned animals	& ?
0.00	on floor	Seal 25 dia	seal	scratched star	lentoid
10.60	just under X walls	Seal 38 dia	unknown	dogs chase	antelopes
0.00	unknown	none	unknown	unknown	
10.12	unknown	none	unknown	unknown	
0.00	unknown	Seal 23×26	unclear	2 crossed lions	
0.00	unknown	Seal 22×20	seal	goat on leash	gable
0.00	unknown	Seal 24 dia	unknown	unclear	
0.00	unknown	Seal 31+×26+ L45	on sack	2 dogs ?	
0.00	unknown	none	unknown	unknown	
0.00	unknown	none	seal	unknown	
10.00	unknown	Seal 15 dia	seal	starburst	
9.34	unknown	Seal 22×26	on jar shoulder	dogs chase	antelope

(continues)

Level XI/XA   (continued)

1	2	3	4	5		6	7	8	9	10	11	12	13
1688.	7-0062A	IM42680	1955	XI	XI	impression	clay	10M	10M	j5	L57	W35	none
1689.	7-0062B	discarded	1955	XI	XI	impression	clay	10M	10M	j5	none	none	none
1690.	7-0064	38-13-15	2542	XI	XI	impression	clay	10M	10M	g/h8	L34	W55	T23
1691.	7-0065A	IM42693	2543	XI	XI	impression	clay	10M	10M	f9/10	L52	W35	none
1692.	7-0065B	Baghdad	2543	XI	XI	impression	clay	10M	10M	f9/10	none	none	none
1693.	7-0065C	38-13-16	2543	XI	XI	impression	clay	10M	10M	f9/10	L67	W54	T32
1694.	7-0068	Baghdad	2559	XI	XI	stamp	steatite	10M	10M	g/h8	D20	T7	ina
1695.	7-0082A	IM42682	2559	XI	XI	impression	clay	10M	10M	g/h8	L44	W30	none
1696.	7-0082A	IM42682	2559	XI	XI	impression	clay	10M	10M	g/h8	D19	ina	ina
1697.	7-0083	Baghdad	1819	XI	XI	impression	clay	10M	10M	none	L53	W31	T11
1698.	7-0083	Baghdad	1819	XI	XI	impression	clay	10M	10M	none	L53	W31	T11
1699.	7-0084	38-13-21	1819	XI	XI	impression	clay	10M	10M	none	L35	W26	T16
1700.	7-0085	discarded	1819	XI	XI	impression	clay	10M	10M	none	none	none	none
1701.	7-0086	38-13-14	1819	XI	XI	impression	clay	10M	10M	none	L30	W22	T12
1702.	7-0087	IM42684	1819	XI	XI	impression	clay	10M	10M	none	L48	W31	none
1703.	7-0088	38-13-17	1819	XI	XI	impression	clay	10M	10M	none	L29	W40	T20
1704.	7-0092	38-13-19	2565	XI	XI	impression	clay	10M	10M	none	L34	W25	T13
1705.	7-0093	38-13-18	2565	XI	XI	impression	clay	10M	10M	none	none	none	none
1706.	7-0094	38-13-20	none	XI	XI	impression	clay	10M	10M	none	L47	W24	T13
1707.	7-0095	38-13-22	none	XI	XI	impression	clay	10M	10M	none	L23	W14	T7
1708.	7-0096	38-13-13	2562	XI	XI	impression	clay	10M	10M	i2	L54	W50	T21
1709.	7-0097	IM42685	2562	XI	XI	impression	clay	10M	10M	i2	L32	W20	ina
1710.	7-0101	IM42686	2005	XI	XI	impression	clay	10M	10M	none	L38	W34	T18
1711.	7-0114	38-13-10	1964	XIA	XI	stamp	steatite	10M	10M	i9	D28	T10	ina
1712.	7-0129	IM42674	2547	XI	XI	impression	clay	10M	10M	g9	L29	W37	T16
1713.	7-0130	IM42675	2549	XI	XI	impression	clay	10M	10M	h9	L30	W19	T8
1714.	7-0132	38-13-12	none	XI	XI	impression	clay	10M	10M	none	W45	T28	0.00
1715.	7-0153	38-13-11	2010	XI	XI	stamp	steatite	9M	9M	j 2/3	D17	T7	ina
1716.	7-none	discarded	2545	XI	XI	stamp	unknown	10M	10M	h/i6/7	none	none	none
1717.	7-none	unknown	2544	XI	XI	impression	clay	10M	10M	e/f 9	none	none	none
		Clay	**items**										
1718.	4-0697	35-10-87	251	XI	XA	spheres 3	clay	9N	5O	f2 i10	none	ina	ina
1719.	4-0697B	Baghdad	251	XI	XA	spheres 3	clay	9N	5O	f2 i10	none	none	none
1720.	4-none	unknown	340	XI	XA	model axe	clay	10R	3M	b4	none	none	none
1721.	5-1251	36-6-4	1027	X	XA	ladle	clay	11M	6K	j 5/6	L222	ina	ina
1722.	5-none	unknown	1064	XA	XA	muller	clay	12M	6J	e/f 10	none	none	none
1723.	6-053	Baghdad	1711	XA	XA	loom base ?	ceramic	8O	8O	b2	h64	w40	ina
1724.	6-166	Discarded	1696	XA	XA	loom part	ceramic	8Q	8Q	c7	H78	D65	ina
1725.	6-180	Baghdad	1792	XA	XA	burnisher	ceramic	8J	8J	d5	L40	W21	ina
1726.	4-none	unknown	312	XI	XA	ball	clay	10M	6M	e6	none	none	none
		Figurines											
1727.	4-0789	phila ?	319	XI	XA	boat	ceramic	12P	4J	a4	L114	W58	T17
1728.	4-0969	Baghdad	414	XI	XA	human	ceramic	10M	6M	a5/6	none	none	none
1729.	5-none	unknown	1342	XA	XA	animal	clay	10K	8M	g8	none	none	none
1730.	6-067A	37-16-23	1665	XA	XA	hut statue	ceramic	7K	7K	j10	H165	W122	ina
1731.	6-067B	Baghdad	1665	XA	XA	hut statue	ceramic	7K	7K	j10	H160	W120	ina
1732.	6-196	Baghdad	1788	XA	XA	bukranium	copper	7H	7G	e3	L38	W32	T19
1733.	4-0601	Baghdad	3	XI	XA	loomweight	mineral ?	11P	4K	none	H115	W105	T40
		Ground	**stone**										
1734.	4-0651	35-10-37	30	XI	XA	rubbing	limestone	10M	6M	i3	none	none	none
1735.	4-0678	phila ?	38	XI	XA	hammer	limestone	10N	5M	i3	L62	W60	ina
1736.	4-0691	Baghdad	36	XI	XA	hammer	stone	10N	5M	i3	b6	L62	W52
1737.	4-0717	Baghdad	298	XI	XA	ballista	limestone	10M	6M	f7	L70	T39	ina
1738.	4-0780	35-10-91	310	XI	XA	celt	gray marble	11P	4K	d4	L67	W46	T15
1739.	4-0788	Baghdad	318	XI	XA	implement	stone	7M	6S	j10	L69	W56	ina
1740.	4-0847	Baghdad	131	XI	XA	grinding	limestone	12N	5J	none	none	none	none
1741.	4-0863	35-10-396	132	XI	XA	ballista	stone	8L	7Q	h1	none	none	none
1742.	4-0871	Baghdad	351	XI	XA	game piece	stone	12N	5J	e7	H19	BD13	RD7
1743.	5-1256	Baghdad	1053	XI	XA	weight	stone	13M	6G	e/f6/7	L27	W15	ina
1744.	5-1260	Baghdad	1032	XI	XA	sphere	marble	10M	6M	h8/9	D19	ina	ina
1745.	5-1281	36-6-386	1016	XA	XA	sphere	white marble	12N	5J	b3	D21	ina	ina
1746.	5-1311	Baghdad	1049	X	XA	macehead	marble	13M	6G	f3	D50	H47	ina
1747.	5-1327	36-6-35	1105	XA	XA	celt	stone	11L	7K	i/j1/2	L57	W217	T15
1748.	5-1474	Baghdad	1262	XA	XA	celt	stone	10L	7M	j 5/6	L56	W32	T16
1749.	5-1538	Baghdad	1376	XA	XA	celt	stone	9L	7O	d/e 6	L26	W20	T06

14	15	16	17	18	19
9.23	unknown	Seal 17+×22	on jar shoulder	lovers	
9.23	unknown	none	unknown	unknown	
9.25	unknown	Seal 20+×16	on reeds: door ?	stag & horned head	
9.17	unknown	Seal 34×26	on jar shoulder	15 wild rams horns	
9.17	unknown	Seal 34×26	on jar shoulder	15 wild rams horns	
9.17	unknown	Seal 37×21	on jar shoulder	15 wild rams horns	
0.00	on pavement in ash debris	Seal 20 dia	seal	spider's web	hemispheroid
0.00	from pavement near old oven	1. Seal 19 d L44	on sack	1.lovers 2.cruciform	
0.00	from pavement near old oven	2.Seal 18 d	on sack	1.lovers 2.cruciform	
9.18	8 sealings in the same provenience	1.Seal12+×18	on jar shoulder	1.stag 2. snakes	
9.18	8 sealings in the same provenience	2. Seal 10 d	on jar shoulder	1. stag 2. snakes	
9.18	8 sealings in the same provenience	Seal 13 ×13+	on jar by handle	lozenges triangle	
9.18	8 sealings in the same provenience	none	unknown	obscured	
9.18	unknown	Seal 21+×17+	on jar shoulder ??	2 animals & snake	
9.18	unknown	Seal 23+×13+	on jar shoulder	6 rows wedges	
9.18	with 8 sealings	Seal 25+×22	on sack tie ?	5 wild rams horns	
9.00	in black ash over pavement	Seal 22 diam	on string hide: ?	man holds snake & ?	
9.00	in burnt ash over pavement	Seal 36×29+	on door	bird head man w/club	
0.00	unknown	Seal 18+×17	on sack tie	stag & horned head	
0.00	unknown	Seal 19+×7+	on jar cover	two animals	
9.20	in black ash debris with celt	Seal 29×27	on jar shoulder	dogs chase animals	
9.20	in black ash debris with celt	Seal 25+×22	on sack	5 horns same 7-88	
0.00	unknown	Seal 19+×23+	on jar shoulder	2 dogs & ?	
0.00	unknown	Seal 28 dia	seal	man club & shield	hemispheroid
0.00	unknown	Seal 15×14	on jar shoulder	man worships ?	?
0.00	unknown	Seal 22 dia	bale tag	2 running animals	
no date	flat rounded clay	Seal 23+×32 L98	2 animals (sheep ?)		
10.00	above walls XIA	Seal 17 dia	seal	broken circles	hemispheroid
0.00	unknown	none	unknown	unknown	
9.17	unknown	none	unknown	unknown	
11.33	unknown				
11.33	unknown				
10.79	near edge of tepe				
11.05	with pottery object & half sealing				
11.22	on floor of room 6				
0.00	unknown	stand ?			
0.00	unknown	weight ?	base ?		
0.00	unknown				
10.91	unknown				
11.12	20 cm over floor of room edge tepe				
11.02	unknown				
10.42	unknown				
10.88	on floor near round hunk of clay				
10.88	on floor near round hunk of clay				
0.00	unknown				
11.07	edge of tepe				
10.86	unknown				
10.86	unknown				
ina	11/17/34 unknown				
10.84	unknown				
11.51	below X walls in rubbish	10cm above XI floor			
11.28	20cm above XI floor in dirt near	Loc 105			
11.70	near sealing 4-840 SW of Temple				
10.90	near edge on pavement	ordinary refuse			
11.30	unknown				
10.86	30cm below surface tepe at edge				
10.86	unknown				
0.00	unknown				
10.55	on floor	"very fine"			
10.70	on pavement near center of room				
10.79	with fragment of small pot				
10.75	upper pavement of room black ash				

(continues)

Level XI/XA   (continued)

1	2	3	4	5		6	7	8	9	10	11	12	13
1750.	5-none	36-6-85	1412	XI	XA	celt	purple stone	9L	7O	c8	L48	W46	ina
1751.	6-none	37-16-21	none	XA	XA	celt	green marble	5M	5M	none	L40	W27	T8
1752.	6-none	unknown	1645	XA	XA	celt	green stone	8M	8M	c8	none	none	none
1753.	7-0012	Baghdad	2551	XA	XA	macehead	white marble	10M	10M	h/i 9	H46	D55	ina
		Jewelry											
1754.	4-0926	35-10-101	508	XI	XA	pin	copper	10M	6M	i10	none	none	none
1755.	4-1006	discarded	665	XI	XA	bead	paste	10M	6M	j10	D34	T19	ina
1756.	5-1336	Baghdad	1155	XI	XA	amulet	stone	11P	4K	a10	L42	W31	T8
1757.	5-1456	Baghdad	1221	XI	XA	pendant	gold lapis	11L	7K	h/i2/3	L23	W9	T6
1758.	5-1607	36-6-37	1323	XA	XA	beads	stone	11K	8K	none	none	none	none
1759.	6-047	Baghdad	1702	XA	XA	pendant	diorite	8K	8K	b9	L30	W19	T05
1760.	6-057	37-16-28	none	XA	XA	56 beads	white paste	8O	8O	none	D03	ina	ina
1761.	6-181	Baghdad	1699	XA	XA	bead	gold on bitu	7G	7G	i 2/3	L17	W10	T02
1762.	6-none	unknown	1643	XA	XA	bead	unknown	7K	7K	j10	none	none	none
1763.	7-0008	38-13-3	2506	XA	XA	bead	gray marble	10M	10M	d4	D15	T6	ina
		Lithics											
1764.	4-0877	phila ?	346	XI	XA	knife	obsidian	13N	5G	c2	L111	W22	ina
1765.	5-none	unknown	1321	XI	XA	knife	obsidian	9L	7O	e9	none	none	none
1766.	6-069	Baghdad	1666	XA	XA	blade	obsidian	6K	6K	a10	L136	W27	ina
1767.	6-none	37-16-25	none	XA	XA	blade	flint	5M	5M	none	L93	W15	T4.2
1768.	6-none	37-16-26	none	XA	XA	blade frag	flint	5M	5M	none	L61	W19	T5.5
1769.	6-none	37-16-27	none	XA	XA	blade	red sandstone	5M	5M	none	L56	W21	ina
1770.	7-none	38-13-2	none	XA	XA	blade	obsidian	10M	10M	none	L75	W10	T2.5
		Metal	**item**										
1771.	4-0793	Baghdad	60	XI	XA	adze	copper	10N	5M	c8	none	none	none
1772.	4-none	unknown	195	XI	XA	nail	copper	9R	3O	none	none	none	none
1773.	6-194	Baghdad	1779	XA	XA	adze blade	copper	8K	8K	c9	L51	W24	ina
		Potsherd											
1774.	4-none	unknown	673	XI	XA	2 mouth jar	ceramic	11N	5K	g9	none	none	none
1775.	5-1319	36-6-22	1077	XA	XA	cup	buffware	10M	7M	a5	H35	BD60	ina
1776.	5-none	36-6-28	none	XA	XA	none	buffware	11L	7K	none	L67	none	ina
1777.	7-none	38-13-1	none	XA	XA	none	brownware	10M	10M	none	none	none	none
		Vessel											
1778.	4-0680	phila no#	112	XI	XA	double jar	ceramic	11M	6K	i/j1/2	H37	RD23	BD22
1779.	4-0786	Baghdad	208	XI	XA	jar	brownware	11P	4K	c9	H106	RD56	BD40
1780.	4-0811	Baghdad	214	XI	XA	cup	light redware	12P	4J	none	H80	RD116	BD52
1781.	4-0846	Baghdad	222	XI	XA	jar	red brownware	9L	7O	i/j6	H104	RD84	BD48
1782.	4-0864	Baghdad	336	XI	XA	bowl	buff ware	12P	4J	a2	H102	RD140	BD52
1783.	4-0868	Baghdad	347	XI-XXA		jar stand	ceramic	10R	3M	b3	none	none	none
1784.	4-none	unknown	684	XI	XA	strainer	ceramic	12P	4J	b3	none	none	none
1785.	4-none	unknown	685	XI	XA	strainer	ceramic	12N	5J	none	none	none	none
1786.	4-none	unknown	136	XA	XA	sherds	ceramic	12N	5J	g1	none	none	none
1787.	4-none	unknown	46	XI	XA	Wide flower	course ware	11M	6K	j3	none	none	none
1788.	4-none	unknown	373	XI	XA	potsherds	ceramic	10M	6M	e6	none	none	none
1789.	4-none	unknown	?299	XI	XA	Wide flower	red ware	9L	7O	i8	D280	H80	ina
1790.	5-1252	Baghdad	1051	XA	XA	daisy sherd	gray buffware	12N	5J	c9	L86	W36	ina
1791.	5-1264	36-6-1	1033	XA	XA	cup	buffware	13M	6G	ij 1/2	H66	RD89	ina
1792.	5-1265	Baghdad	1033	XA	XA	cup	ceramic	13M	6G	ij 1/2	H90	none	none
1793.	5-1266	36-6-3	1025	X	XA	small jar	buffware	13M	6G	none	H108	RD68	BD125
1794.	5-1271	36-6-24	1011	XA	XA	jar	brownware	12N	5J	b10	H79	BD89	RD73
1795.	5-1272	Baghdad	1012	XA	XA	bowl	brownware	13N	5G	b1	H62	RD136	none
1796.	5-1274	36-6-21	1054	XA	XA	Wide flower	orang redware	12N	5J	ef 1	H77	D272	ina
1797.	5-1277	36-6-20	1014	XA	XA	daisy sherd	ceramic	11M	6K	c5	L20	W15	ina
1798.	5-1308	Baghdad	1069	XI	XA	cup	stone	13M	6G	e/f3/4	H45	RD68	BD31
1799.	5-1369	lost	1164	XI	XA	cooking pot	buffware	11N	5K	i/j10	H267	RD200	BD335
1800.	5-1472	Discarded	1303	X	XA	jar ?	ceramic	10L	7M	g/h 3	H316	RD150	none
1801.	5-1527	36-6-53	1357	XI	XA	model bowl	grayware	10L	7M	d9	H34	BD37	ina
1802.	5-1528	Baghdad	1357	XI	XA	cup	ceramic	10L	7M	none	H24	BD38	ina
1803.	5-1559	36-6-46	1395	XI	XA	bowl	buffware	10L	7M	none	H78	RD114	ina
1804.	5-1570	discarded	1402	XI	XA	bowl	brownware	10L	7M	b/c1/2	H252	RD308	ina
1805.	5-1613	Baghdad	1332	XA	XA	jar	buffware	9L	7O	b 7/8	H128	RD134	D187
1806.	5-1617	Baghdad	1297	XA	XA	bowl	buffware	10L	7M	none	H90	RD96	BD132
1807.	5-none	36-6-26	none	XA	XA	spout bowl	red brown	13M	6G	none	L42	W76	SP16
1808.	5-none	36-6-27	1082	XA	XA	sherds	buffware	9L	7O	j 3/4	none	none	none
1809.	5-none	unknown	1104	XA	XA	small jar	ceramic	10M	6M	a-c5	none	none	none

14	15	16	17	18	19
10.85	on pavement just below X walls				
0.00	unknown				
0.00	unknown				
10.40	pavement just below X near	2 lines stone			
10.91	unknown				
11.11	found under X wall				
11.31	15cm above floor back room Temple				
11.13	under walls of temple X niche XA				
11.02	in burned ??? just below top level				
0.00	unknown				
0.00	unknown				
0.00	unknown				
0.00	unknown				
0.00	unknown				
11.25	at edge X foundation 20cm	above XI floor			
10.79	unknown				
0.00	cm above floor				
0.00	unknown	minor use 39 & 38			
0.0	unknown	retouch 39 & 48		fragment	
0.00	unknown	bitumen on right	sideused 34	unused 44 fragment	
0.00	unknown	retouch 24 & 52			
10.73	unknown				
11.91	unknown				
0.00	unknown				
11.15	unknown				
10.92	with incised sherd	sand & vegetable	HM		
0.00	unknown	sand temper	HM	impressed	
0.00	unknown	green slip	pellets		
11.49	just below pavement of X				
11.17	on floor under walls of X	6cm from walls	slipped		
11.12	assoc with temple near edge [XI]				
10.94	under floor of X	gray slip			
11.19	common XI type				
10.51	2m from edge tepe post XI				
11.22	from East Shrine				
11.21	from East Shrine				
11.45	next to wall	painted			
11.31	unknown	VIII to XI type			
10.90	by ? wall of oven floor of XI				
11.04	covering stones	sherds	animal bones		
11.22	north of 5-1272 10cm above floor				
11.32	found with 5-1265				
11.32	found with 5-1264 (cup)				
0.00	right side up (in situ ?) w/5-1271	quartz & basalt	HM		
11.1	on floor level	open end against wall	chaff & quartz		HM
0.00	upside down .1 cm above floor				
11.72	in burned ash above door of XI room	chaff temper	HM		
0.00	with spindle whorl below X a little				
10.85	30 cm below surface tepe				
11.01	in place above cowel of the	back wall of Temple			
11.03	found inside wall				
10.90	in black ash refuse on pavement	quartz grit	HM		
10.90	in black ash refuse on pavement				
11.00	in ordinary red refuse with 5-1567	chaff & sand	HM		
11.00	with small cup				
10.40	debris just below X	painted dots on body "sherba"			
0.00	unknown				
0.00	unknown	indents red brown slip	quartz grit	HM	
11.31	near wall	incised	sand temper	HM	
10.711	on floor				

(continues)

Level XI/XA   (continued)

1	2	3	4	5	6	7	8	9	10	11	12	13
1810.	5-none	unknown	1081	XA XA	large bowl	ceramic	9L	7O	j 3/4	none	none	none
1811.	5-none	unknown	1060	X XA	cooking pot	brownware	13M	6G	e/f 4	none	none	none
1812.	5-none	unknown	1060	X XA	Wide flower	brownware	13M	6G	e/f 4	none	none	none
1813.	6-033	Baghdad	1651	XA XA	painted jar	red brownware	8M	8M	c10	H150	D175	ina
1814.	6-039	37-16-22	1642	XA XA	sherd	buffware	7K	7K	j10	L77	W76	ina
1815.	6-040	37-16-20	1652	XA XA	small jar	pink buffware	8M	8M	c/d10	H105	D120	ina
1816.	6-044	Baghdad	1653	XA XA	bowl	ceramic	8M	8M	c/d10	H89	D261	ina
1817.	6-055	Baghdad	1659	XI XA	stand	brown ware	8S	8S	h10	H64	D86	ina
1818.	6-056	37-16-37	1659	XI XA	bowl	granite	8S	8S	h10	H61	D155	ina
1819.	6-060	Baghdad	1646	XA XA	bowl	ceramic	8M	8M	b7	H150	D355	ina
1820.	6-070	Baghdad	none	XA XA	pot	brownware	8K	8K	none	H175	D210	ina
1821.	6-114	Baghdad	1663	XA XA	tall jar	redware	8K	8K	j9	H530	D250	ina
1822.	6-129A	discarded	none	XA XA	large bowl	ceramic	7J	7J	none	H105	D420	ina
1823.	6-129B	discarded	none	XA XA	large bowl	ceramic	7J	7J	none	H120	D420	ina
1824.	6-172	Baghdad	1697	XA XA	spouted pot	buffware	8Q	8Q	c8	H47	D81	SP20
1825.	6-none	37-16-21	1664	XA XA	open bowl	grayware	7J	7J	i2	none	none	none
1826.	6-none	unknown	1661	XA XA	small plate	gray ware	7J	7J	h2	H104	RD121	none
1827.	6-none	unknown	1671	XA XA	wheel	ceramic	7J	7J	j1	none	none	none
1828.	6-none	unknown	1710	XA XA	cup	greenware	8K	8K	ab9/10	none	none	none
1829.	6-none	unknown	1644	XA XA	small pot	ceramic	8Q	8Q	d9	none	none	none
1830.	none	unknown	Loc 117	XA XA	2 rim bowl ?	red ware	10P	4M	none	D920	H700	ina
		Spindle	**whorl**									
1831.	4-none	unknwon	375	XI XA	whorl	unknown	10M	6M	b8	none	none	none
1832.	5-1331	Baghdad	1107	XA XA	whorl	ceramic	11L	7K	i 1/2	D31	T21	ina
1833.	5-1332	36-6-31	1107	XA XA	whorl	ceramic	11L	7K	i 1/2	D32	T21	ina
		Seal	**sealing**									
1834.	4-0661	35-10-112	45	XI XA	stamp	steatite	10N	5M	h3	D14	none	ina
1835.	4-0692	35-10-131	107	XI XA	impression	clay	10N	5M	c10	L39	W17	T14
1836.	4-0730	IM24591	303	XI XA	stamp	steatite	8M	6Q	d3	D14	none	ina
1837.	4-0782	discarded	none	XI XA	stamp	paste	11P	4K	none	L18	W11	none
1838.	4-0797	35-10-118	61	XI XA	impression	clay	11P	4K	loc112	L98	W99	T58
1839.	4-0815	35-10-262	320	edge XA	impression	clay	12N	5J	i8	S18	L22	W25
1840.	4-0835	35-10-114	326	XI XA	stamp	steatite	8M	6Q	d3	L22	W17	none
1841.	4-0840	IM24992	67	XI XA	impression	clay	12N	5J	f1	L31	W34	none
1842.	4-0872	35-10-129	337	XI XA	impression	clay	11M	6K	h5	L44	W39	T14
1843.	4-0956	IM25048	555	XI ? XA	impression	clay	10R	3M	a10	L60	W54	ina
1844.	5-1248	IM26987	1057	XI XA	impression	clay	11M	6K	f/g8	L27	W34	ina
1845.	5-1254	36-6-44	1013	XA XA	impression	clay	12N	5J	a-c 10	L71	W43	T26
1846.	5-1258	36-6-40	1052	XA XA	impression	clay	12M	6J	e 3/4	L35	W36	T13
1847.	5-1344	36-6-39	1108	XA XA	stamp	steatite	11P	4K	c7	D13	T06	ina
1848.	5-1345	Baghdad	1109	XA XA	stamp	steatite	13M	6G	g/h 7	D15	T05	ina
1849.	5-1451	36-6-38	1214	XA XA	stamp	steatite	10M	6M	a3	d15	t07	ina
1850.	5-1546	36-6-129	1372	XI XA	impression	clay	11L	7K	c1	L39	W35	T16
1851.	5-1552	36-6-42	1371	XA XA	impression	clay	9L	7O	d-e5-6	L32	W34	T10
1852.	5-1567	36-6-116	1396	XI XA	impression	clay	10L	7M	a 5/6	L49	W58	T24
1853.	6-042	IM32499	none	XA XA	stamp	bone	8O	8O	none	L38	w32	h11
1854.	6-046	37-16-31	none	XA XA	impression	clay	8K	8K	none	L42	W41	T28
1855.	6-063	IM32624	none	XA XA	impression	clay	7K	7K	none	L36	W40	none
1856.	6-182A	37-16-30	none	XA XA	impression	clay	8K	8K	none	L17	W22	T6
1857.	6-182B	IM32610	none	XA XA	impression	clay	8K	8K	none	L40	W30	none
1868.	6-273	37-16-29	none	XA XA	stamp	serpentine	6H	6G	none	D24	T10	ina
1859.	7-002	38-13-4	1810	XA XA	stamp	serpentine	9M	9M	i 1/2	D13	T07	ina
1860.	5-none	discarded	1017	XA XA	impression	clay	11M	6K	c 8/9	none	none	none
1861.	6-none	discarded	1784	XA XA	impression	clay	8K	8Q	none	none	none	none
1862.	5-none	discarded	1331	XA XA	stamp	unknown	9L	7O	a/b 8	none	none	none

14	15	16	17	18	19
11.31	60 cm above floor of XA				
11.44	next to wall				
11.44	with cooking pot next to wall				
0.00	unknown	buff slip	cross hatch		
0.00	unknown	impressd rosette lines	sand temper	HM	
0.00	on floor	incised 'X' at base	chaff & sand	HM	
0.00	on floor same room as 6-40	blob paint	In turned rim		
10.16	in room at edge of tepe				
10.16	in room at edge of tepe				
0.00	found upside down	blob paint	inturned rim		
0.00	unknown				
0.00	on floor of room				
0.00	unknown	Wide flower ?			
0.00	unknown	Wide flower ?			
0.00	unknown	quartz grit	cannon spout		
10.80	above floor near chit 1661	quartz & chaff	HM	burnish	
10.85	next to wall near well near chit 1664				
0.00	discoid!	punctured			
0.00	unknown				
0.00	unknown				
10.92	set in floor of room 1 ?	bitumen inside			
11.09	unknown				
10.70	seven whorls & celt 5-1327	on pavement			
10.70	seven whorls & celt 5-1327	on pavement			
11.01	unknown	Seal 14 dia	seal	starburst	hemispheroid
10.95	XA floor 30cm below base X walls	Seal 32+×13+	bale tag/jar mouth	fish snake other	
11.50	unknown	Seal 8+×14	seal	angled lines off line	
11.04	no date	Seal 17×10+		seal	filled lozenges
11.31	near podium on floor of temple	Seal 28 diam	in jar mouth	vulture attacks stag	
11.15	in mixed debris 2m from edge tepe	Seal 17+×14+	bale tag or cover	2 animals	
11.41	10 cm above floor in mixed debris	Seal 22 ×17	seal	filled lozenges	lentoid
11.71	southwest of Temple	Seal 17 dia	on sack	floating ram heads	
10.94	on floor of XI room	Seal 17×17	unclear	2 horned heads & ?	
11.07	under stone matting near edge tepe	Seal 23×28	on jar shoulder	2 men stirring vat	
10.96	on pavement	Seal 26+×34+	in jar mouth	intertwined snakes	
0.00	10 cm above floor	Seal 21×22	on jar shoulder	lion ? and dog	
11.14	above pavement in debris	Seal 12+×13+	on hide:jar neck	lion attacking buck	
10.52	debris of wall above XI Temple	Seal 13 dia	seal	cruciform	hemispheroid
10.04	on floor near wall under surface	Seal 15 dia	seal	cross in cut circles	hemispheroid
10.85	in door of room on pavement edge	Seal 15 dia	seal	criss cross lattice	hemispheroid
11.00	on pavement	Seal 23+×23	unknown	fish dog and ?	
0.00	on floor in ash filled room under X	Seal 16×17+	on string bag	horned animal & heart	
11.00	in ordinary reddish refuse	Seal 21×22+	on door ??	horned sheep dog & ?	
0.00	unknown	Seal 30+×28+	seal	stag escaping 2 dogs	gable
0.00	unknown	Seal 22+×29	sack or jar tie	2 animals	
0.00	unknown	Seal 27+×19+	on jar rim	intertwined snakes	
0.00	unknown	Seal 16+×22+	unknown	4 animals: boar ?	
0.00	unknown	Seal 25×16	unknown	vulture & 2 dogs ?	
0.00	unknown	Seal 24 dia	seal	dog chases stag	hemispheroid
10.50	unknown	Seal 13 dia	seal	angled lines off line	hemisheroid
0.00	below level X on floor	none	unknown	unknown	
0.00	unknown	none	unknown	unknown	
10.35	in debris	none	unknown	unknown	

Level X

1	2	3	4	5	6	7	8	9	10	11	12
		Bone	**item**								
1863.	1090	31-52-438	none	X	spatula	bone	none	none	none	L114	W28
1864.	3-363	33-3-177	none	X	awl	bone	10M	6M	none	L108	W16
1865.	6-025	37-16-11	1626	X	awl	bone	8M	8M	h6	L106	W14
		Clay	**item**								
1866.	1087	31-52-431	none	X	wall knob	buffware	none	none	none	L110	D55
1867.	3-421	33-3-212	none	X	palette	redware	10M	6M	none	H20	D105
1868.	3-none	unknown	none	X	ballistas	clay	10N	5M ?	Rm1001	none	none
1869.	4-0626	Baghdad	194	X	ladle handle	ceramic	10M	6M	none	L200	W112
1870.	5-none	35-10-5	none	X	disc	clay	11G	11K	none	D103	T15
1871.	5-none	discarded	1035	X	ladle	ceramic	11M	6K	j 6/7	none	none
		Figurine									
1872.	3-360	33-3-174	none	X	hut statue	buffware	11G	11K	Loc39	H14	W15
1873.	3-419	33-3-211	none	X	animal	buffware	9K	8O	none	H80	L80
1874.	3-436	33-3-221	none	X	animal	redware	10L	7M	none	H118	L31 ?
1875.	3-483	Baghdad	none	X	hut statue	redware	12N	5J	none	L107	W86
1876.	3-493	Baghdad	none	X	animal	ceramic	8H	10Q	none	none	none
1877.	4-0796	35-10-53	64	X	animal	ceramic	11M	6K	i1	L54	H40
1878.	5-1249	36-6-8	none	X	human	ceramic	12M	6J	none	H28	W26
1879.	5-1257	Baghdad	1055	X	animal	clay	12M	6J	g 5/6	L50	W39
1880.	5-1283A	Baghdad	1061	X	animal	ceramic	12M	6J	i/j4/5	L63	H31
1881.	5-1283B	36-6-5	1061	X	animal	clay	12M	6J	i/j4/5	L71	H52
1882.	5-none	35-10-4	none	X	hut statue	ceramic	9L	7O	none	H122	W94
1883.	6-079	Baghdad	1796	X	human male	brown ware	8J	8J	b5	H57	ina
		Ground	**stone**								
1884.	1088	31-52-433	none	X	hone	blue gray stone	none	none	none	L123	W18
1885.	1158	31-52-437	none	X	mortar	marble	none	none	none	L43	D68
1886.	1162	31-52-434	none	X	celt	haemetite	none	none	none	L43	W29
1887.	1163	31-52-432	none	X	pick	green stone	none	none	none	L55	none
1888.	3-333	Baghdad	none	X	ballista	crystal gypsum	9G	11O	none	none	none
1889.	3-343	33-3-161	none	X	macehead	granite	8L	7Q	none	L109	W65
1890.	3-365	33-3-179	none	X	game piece	white stone	10M	6M	none	D20	T4
1891.	3-371	33-3-184	none	X	sphere	white marble	10M	6M	none	D16	ina
1892.	3-372	Baghdad	none	X	sphere	black stone	11K	8K	none	D20	ina
1893.	3-416	Baghdad	none	X	hammer	limestone	dump	dump	ina	H26	L60
1894.	3-441	discarded	none	X	sphere	green stone	8N	5Q	none	D17	ina
1895.	3-446	Baghdad	none	X	celt	gray limestone	8N	5Q	none	L39	none
1896.	3-480	35-10-20	none	X	celt	green steatite	12M	6J	none	W40	L38
1897.	3-none	33-3-256	none	X	ballista	marble	12K	8J	none	L70	D36
1898.	3-none	33-3-277	none	X	battle ax	basalt	11G ?	11K ?	none	L90	W60
1899.	3-none	33-3-286	none	X	weight	basalt/marble	8N	5Q	none	H28	D22
1900.	4-0602	35-10-10	153	X	hammer	limestone	8M	6Q	none	L120	W96
1901.	4-0652	Baghdad	28	X	celt	stone	10M	6M	i2	none	none
1902.	4-0801	Baghdad	none	X	celt	stone	12N	5J	none	none	none
1903.	5-1282	36-6-17	1062	X	celt	steatite	13M	6G	b/c2/3	L26	W25
1904.	6-026	37-16-13	1626	X	celt	marble	8M	8M	h6	L45	W36
1905.	6-184	37-16-12	1789	X	celt	green granite	7H	7H	b2	L40	W23
		Jewelry									
1906.	1193	31-52-440	none	X	pendant	gray stone	none	none	none	L22	W17
1907.	3-none	33-3-261	none	X	amulet	white marble		9P	4O	none	none
1908.	4-0726	35-10-12	none	X	pendant	stone	10N	5M	none	L28	W17
1909.	4-0727	Baghdad	none	X	bead	shell	10M	6M	none	none	none
1910.	4-0853	35-10-13	78	X	pendant	stone	10R	3M	a4	L19	W13
1911.	4-0875	Baghdad	342	X	pendant	stone	9H	10O	none	H15	W08
1912.	4-none	unknown	167	X	pendant	ceramic	10P	4M	none	none	none
		Lithics									
1913.	3-342	discarded	none	X	blade	obsidian	9H	10O	none	L125	W15
1914.	1137	31-52-435	none	X	blade	tan flint	none	none	none	L132	W22
1915.	3-406	Baghdad	none	X	core	obsidian	8M	6Q	none	H235	ina
1916.	4-0902	Baghdad	98	X	blade	obsidian	10M	6M	none	none	none
1917.	6-024	Baghdad	1626	X	blade	obsidian	8M	8M	h6	L85	W15
		Metal	**item**								
1918.	3-444	35-10-363	none	X	nail	copper	8H	10O	none	L5	W06
1919.	6-none	unknown	1638	X	unknown	copper	8M	8M	d8	none	none
		Potsherds									
1920.	3-323	Discarded	none	X	2 rim	buff redslip	8M	6Q	Loc 35	none	none
1921.	3-none	33-3-230	none	X	vessel	green grayware	10L	4M	none	L63	W37

13	14	15	16	17	18	19
ina	0.00	trial trench				
T09	0.00	unknown				
ina	0.00	unknown				
none	0.00	trial trench				
ina	0.00	unknown				
none	0.00	cache oval type on floor	room 1001 ?			
ina	11.26	unknown				
ina	0.00	unknown				
none	11.86	30cm below base of oven				
ina	0.00	vessel cache				
ina	0.00	unknown				
ina	0.00	unknown				
ina	0.00	unknown				
none	0.00	unknown				
ina	0.00	on pavement				
ina	0.00	unknown				
ina	11.41	on pavement				
ina	11.52	in a tomb reused	as an oven intra XA			
ina	11.52	in tomb reused as an oven	intra XA			
ina	0.00	unknown	loomweight ?			
ina	0.00	unknown				
ina	0.00					
ina	0.00	trial trench				
ina	0.00	trial trench				
ina	0.00	trial trench				
none	0.00	unknown				
T40	0.00	unknown				
ina	0.00	unknown				
ina	0.00	unknown				
ina	0.00	unknown				
ina	0.00	unknown				
ina	0.00	unknown				
none	0.00	unknown				
T16	0.00	unknown				
none	0.00	unknown				
T30	0.00	unknown				
ina	0.00	unknown				
T36	0.00	unknown				
none	11.45	unknown				
none	0.00	unknown				
T11	11.44	near surface opposite wall	near chit 1060			
T15	0.00	unknown				
T11	0.00	unknown				
ina	0.00	trial trench				
none	0.00	unknown				
T08	0.00	unknown				
none	0.00	unknown				
T8	11.32	near edge of tepe				
T02	0.00	on west part tepe				
none	0.00	unknown				
T04	0.00	unknown				
T5.5	0.00	trail trench				
ina	0.00	unknown				
none	0.00	unknown				
T04	0.00	unknown				
T05	0.00	near edge of tepe				
none	0.00	unknown				
none	11.37	in cache with 3-263 316 318	see 3-71 IX			
T6.7	0.00	unknown				

(continues)

Level X   (continued)

1	2	3	4	5	6	7	8	9	10	11	12
		Vessel									
1922.	1189	31-52-428	none	X	saucer	grayware	none	none	none	H29	D45
1923.	5004	32-21-548	none	X	strainer	buffware	none	none	none	D32	none
1924.	6087	Baghdad	none	X	cup	buffware	10M	10M	none	H99	D120
1925.	3-263	33-3-128	none	X	small jar	buffware	8M	6Q	Loc35	H56	BD65
1926.	3-316	33-3-153	none	X	2 Wide flower	brownware	8M	6Q	Loc35	H75	RD290
1927.	3-318	Baghdad	none	X	small jar	green buffware	8M	6Q	Loc 35	H120	RD90
1928.	3-336	Baghdad	none	X	bowl	redware	8L	7Q	none	H12	D32
1929.	3-337	discarded	none	X	bowl	redware	8L	7Q	none	D32	H14
1930.	3-338	discarded	none	X	bowl	redware	8L	7Q	none	D38	none
1931.	3-339	Baghdad	none	X	bowl	redware	11H	10K	none	H7	D19
1932.	3-344	33-3-162	none	X	jar top	green grayware	11G	11K	none	none	RD106
1933.	3-346	Baghdad	none	X	footed bowl ?	redware	11G	11K	none	H15	RD18
1934.	3-347	33-3-164	none	X	small jar	brownware	11G	11K	none	H83	RD59
1935.	3-352	33-3-167	none	X	jar	red brownware	11G	11K	none	H65	D100
1936.	3-353	33-3-168	none	X	small jar	buffware	8J	9Q	none	H11	RD12
1937.	3-355	33-3-170	none	X	small jar	brownware	11G	11K	none	H9	D11
1938.	3-357	33-3-172	none	X	jar	brownware	8J	9Q	none	H9	RD7
1939.	3-359	discarded	none	X	container	white plaster	8J	9Q	none	none	none
1940.	3-361	33-3-175	none	X	jar	redware	11H	10K	none	H10	RD8
1941.	3-364	33-3-178	none	X	model bowl	grayware	10K	8M	none	H3	D3
1942.	3-368	Baghdad	none	X	jar	red ware	11G	11K	none	none	RD14
1943.	3-369	33-3-182	none	X	crock	brownware	11G	11K	none	H93	RD13
1944.	3-370	33-3-183	none	X	crock	buffware	11G	11K	none	H16	RD17
1945.	3-379	33-3-188	none	X	small jar	buffware	9G	11O	none	H10	RD8
1946.	3-395	33-3-196	none	X	crock	buffware	11H	10K	none	H58	D93
1947.	3-429	33-3-217	none	X	bowl ? pot	green gritty	9J	9O	none	H83	RD81
1948.	3-445	discarded	none	X	jar stand	ceramic	8N	5Q	none	H132	none
1949.	3-492	IM20855	none	X	beaker	buffware	10N	5M	none	H18	RD20
1950.	3-494	phila no#	none	X	bowl	red brownware	12N	5J	none	H9	RD9
1951.	3-502	Baghdad	none	X	beaker	ceramic	12N	5J	none	H10	RD11
1952.	3-none	33-3-273	none	X	cup	buffware	8H	10Q	none	L61	W82
1953.	3-none	unknown	none	X	cookng pot	ceramic	10K	8M	d/e 8	H350	BD540
1954.	3-none	unknown	none	X	jar	gray ware	8M	6Q	Loc 35	none	none
1955.	4-0703	Baghdad	108	X	beaker	green grayware	9M	6O	i/j 10	H112	RD148
1956.	4-0704	35-10-3	109	X	beaker	ceramic	9M	6O	i/j 10	H152	RD168
1957.	4-0798	35-10-1	213	X	cup	green buffware	12N	5J	none	H65	RD80
1958.	4-0799	Baghdad	212	X	cup	ceramic	12N	5J	none	H56	RD60
1959.	4-0803	Baghdad	211	X	storage jar	buffware	12H	10J	d8	H212	RD256
1960.	4-none	unknown	none	X	Wide flower	crude ware	9M	6O	i/j 10	none	none
1961.	5-1267	36-6-2	1019	X	small jar	buffware	12M	6J	e1	H85	RD69
1962.	5-1273	Baghdad	1004	X	spout	ceramic	12M	6J	i 5/6	L108	D08
1963.	5-none	unknown	1009	X	sherds	ceramic	12M	6J	Rm1083	none	none
		Spindle	**whorl**								
1964.	3-341	Baghdad	none	X	whorl	clay	8L	7Q	none	D33	T20
1965.	3-415	33-3-208	none	X	whorl	stone	dump	dump	none	none	none
1966.	4-0618	discarded	165	X	whorl	clay	10N	5M	none	37	18
1967.	4-0620	Baghdad	158	X	whorl	clay	8K	8Q	none	40	21
1968.	4-0729	35-10-8	302	X	whorl	clay	10M	6M	c7	D12	ina
1969.	4-0800	35-10-7	none	X	whorl	clay	12N	5J	none	D30	T34
1970.	4-1039	phila no#	none	X	whorl	clay	9H	10O	none	D36	T40
1971.	4-1040	33-3-258	none	X	whorl	clay	9H	10O	none	D36	T12
1972.	4-1042	discarded	none	X	whorl	clay	9L	7O	none	D22	T22
1973.	4-1043	Baghdad	none	X	whorl	clay	9G	11O	none	none	none
1974.	4-1044	Baghdad	none	X	whorl	clay	10J	9M	none	D34	T34
1975.	4-1047	Baghdad	none	X	whorl	clay	12N	5J	none	D22	T22
1976.	4-none	unknown	24	X	whorl	unknown	10N	5M	h3	none	none
1977.	4-none	unknown	197	X	whorl	unknown	9P	4O	none	none	none
1978.	5-none	35-10-6	none	X	whorl	clay	9P	4O	none	H20	D35
1979.	5-none	35-10-9	none	X	whorl	clay	12N	5J	none	H13	D28
		Seal	**sealing**								
1980.	1027	31-52-408	none	X	stamp	black stone	k	12M	none	L22	W13
1981.	3-332	33-3-158	none	X	stamp	black stone	11G	11K	none	D18	T8
1982.	3-348	Baghdad	none	X	stamp	stone	dump	dump	none	D16	H06
1983.	3-362	33-3-176	none	X	impression	clay	9J	9O	none	L48	W36
1984.	3-376A	33-3-186	none	X	impression	clay	9K	8O	none	L49	W25
1985.	3-376B	33-3-186	none	X	impression	clay	9K	8O	none	L49	W25

13	14	15	16	17	18	19
ina	0.00	trial trench	basalt and quartz grit			
ina	0.00	unknown				
ina	0.00	unknown				
RD47	11.37	in cache with 3-316 318 323	basalt grit & vegetable	HM		
BD140	11.37	in cache w/ 3-263 318 323				
BD140	11.37	in cache with 3-316 263 323				
ina	0.00	unknown	gray slip			
ina	0.00	unknown	gray slip			
none	0.00	unknown	red paint on rim			
ina	0.00	unknown				
ina	0.00	unknown	fine quartz grit	sprig paint	WM	
BD31	0.00	unknown				
BD54	0.00	unknown	basalt & quartz grit			
ina	0.00	unknown	basalt & quartz grit			
ina	0.00	unknown	quartz grit & chaff HM			
ina	0.00	unknown	basalt & quartz grit HM			
BD10	0.00	unknown	smoke marks on bottom			
none	0.00	unknown				
BD11	0.00	unknown	same type as 3-144			
ina	0.00	unknown	basalt grit HM			
ina	0.00	unknown	sprig-like painted design			
SP 40	0.00	unknown	with spout	fine & coarse	quartz grit	HM
ina	0.00	unknown	fine quartz & chaff	HM		
BD12	0.00	unknown	same type as 3-357	chaff & quartz grit	HM	
ina	0.00	unknown	fine quartz & basalt grit	HM		
BD72	0.00	unknown	lattice & lozenge design			
none	0.00	edge of tepe				
ina	0.00	unknown	keeper of animals			
BD12	0.00	unknown	bead rim hole mouth	fine quartz grit	WM	
BD9	0.00	unknown				
T5	0.00	unknown painted	like IX 32-21-526	fine & coarse	quartz grit	WM
none	0.00	in room 1077 ash	with fowl bones lithics			
none	11.37	in cache	contained nuts	like 3-368		
BD140	0.00	sherds under bench	outside Rm 1003			
BD78	0.00	under bench outside Rm 1003				
BD52	0.00	unknown				
BD32	0.00	unknown				
BD160	10.53	unknown	carbomized wheat	brown paint		
none	0.00	with cups under bench	outside Rm 1003			
BD94	0.00	below/outside SE wall	Rm 1080	chaff and quartz	grit HM	
ina	0.00	in NE wall of room 1083	15-30 cm over	floor		
none	11.67	on floor near NE wall inside	& outside wall			
ina	0.00	unknown				
none	0.00	unknown	missing from storage			
ina	0.00	unknown				
ina	0.00	unknown				
ina	11.60	unknown				
ina	0.00	unknown				
ina	0.00	unknown	from G3 season			
ina	0.00	unknown	from G3 season			
ina	0.00	unknown	from G3 season			
none	0.00	unknown	from G3 season			
ina	0.00	unknown	from G3 season			
ina	0.00	unknown	from G3 season			
none	0.00	unknown				
none	0.00	unknown				
ina	0.00	unknown				
none	0.00	unknown				
T20.5	0.00	near surface of excavation	Seal 22×13	seal	horned animal	hemisphere
ina	0.00	unknown	Seal 17 dia	seal	ellipse off 2 lines	hemispheroid
ina	0.00	unknown	Seal 16 dia	seal	star	hemisphere
T17	0.00	unknown	Seal 19×19	on jar shoulder	crude animal	
T13	0.00	unknown	Seal 17+×18+	on jar shoulder	scorpion	
T13	0.00	unknown	Seal 17+×18+	on jar shoulder ?	goat ??	

(*continues*)

Level X   (continued)

1	2	3	4	5	6	7	8	9	10	11	12
1986.	3-397	Baghdad	none	X	stamp	black stone	9P	4O	none	L29	W13
1987.	3-398	33-3-198	none	X	impression	clay	9P	4O	none	L22	W33
1988.	3-399	33-3-199	none	X	impression	clay	9N	5O	none	L25	W26
1989.	3-408	Baghdad	none	X	stamp	steatite	9P	4O	none	D20	none
1990.	3-409	33-3-203	none	X	stamp	steatite	9P	4O	none	none	none
1991.	3-413	IM15977	none	X	impression	clay	8M	6Q	none	L20	W15
1992.	3-428	33-3-216	none	X	impression	clay	10J	9M	none	L23	W37
1993.	3-433	Baghdad	none	X	stamp	steatite	9K	8O	none	D18	H11
1994.	3-434	IM26897	none	X	impression	clay	9K	8O	none	L38	W20 ?
1995.	3-435	33-3-220	none	X	stamp	brown stone	8J	9Q	none	D8	T6
1996.	3-438	35-10-16	none	X	stamp	marble	10J	9M	none	L21	W18
1997.	3-440	Baghdad	none	X	stamp	stone	8N	5Q	none	D15	ina
1998.	3-449	IM24567	none	X ?	impression	clay	7N	5S	none	L24	W21
1999.	3-481	35-10-20	none	X	impression	clay	11M	6K	none	L60	W37
2000.	3-485B	35-10-258	none	X	impression	clay	11M	6K	none	S20	L35
2001.	3-485A	phila ?	none	X	impression	clay	11M	6K	none	L39	W30
2002.	3-495A	IM25075	none	X	4 impression	clay	8J	9Q	none	L63	W49
2003.	3-495BC	35-10-18A	none	X	2 impression	clay	8J	9Q	none	L57	W49
2004.	3-495D	35-10-18B	none	X	3 impression	clay	8J	9Q	none	L55	W44
2005.	3-496A	35-10-19	none	X	impression	clay	8J	9Q	none	L55	W29
2006.	3-496B	IM24566	none	X	impression	clay	8J	9Q	none	L41	W29
2007.	3-497	IM25109	none	X	impression	clay	12K	8J	none	L45	W30
2008.	3-498	35-10-23	none	X	impression	clay	12K	8J	none	L25	W42
2009.	3-499	35-10-21	none	X	impression	clay	12K	8J	none	L38	W54
2010.	3-500	IM24568	none	X	stamp	black stone	11O	6K	none	L22	W17
2011.	3-0605	Baghdad	7	X	stamp	white marble	9M	6O	none	L31	W26
2012.	4-0609	35-10-15	12	X	stamp	steatite	9P	4O	none	L15	W19
2013.	4-0647	IM24997	6	X	impression	clay	11H	10K	Rm1060	L32	W20
2014.	4-0668	35-10-24	206	X	impression	clay	11H	10K	Rm1058	L30	W20
2015.	4-0721	IM24607	none	X	stamp	steatite	12N	5J	none	D20	none
2016.	4-0722	IM25045	none	X	impression	clay	12K	8J	none	L43	W32
2017.	4-0723	IM24993	none	X	impression	clay	12K	8J	none	L41	W50
2018.	4-0724	35-10-22	none	X	impression	clay	12K	8J	none	L36	W25
2019.	4-0725	IM25047	none	X	impression	clay	8N	5Q	none	L35	W28
2020.	4-0779	35-10-17	none	X	stamp	white paste	12N	5J	none	D12	T6
2021.	4-0852	Baghdad	77	X	stamp	stone	10P	4M	e/f 2	L16	W10
2022.	4-1048	IM24996	none	X	impression	clay	12K	8J	none	L20	W17
2023.	5-1255	IM26985	1023	X	impression	clay	12M	6J	i/j8/9	L22	W27
2024.	5-1259	36-6-19	1020	X	impression	clay	12M	6J	e1	L55	W50
2025.	5-1276	36-6-396	none	at X	impression	clay	dump	dump	none	L34	W38
2026.	5-1287	IM27030	1041	X	stamp	soapstone	12M	6J	e2	D18	ina
2027.	5-1291	36-6-18	1058	X	stamp	stone	13M	6G	b2	D27	T14
2028.	5-none	unknown	1010	X	stamp	"crappy"	11M	6K	b/c2/3	none	none
2029.	6-020	37-16-19	none	X	stamp	serpentine	6K	6K	none	D9	T5
2030.	6-029	37-16-17	none	X	impression	clay	8M	8M	none	L26	W35
2031.	6-043	IM32623	none	X	impression	clay	10K	10K	none	L47	W43
2032.	6-210	IM32897	none	X	impression	clay	8J	8J	none	none	none
2033.	6-210A	37-16-15	none	X	impression	clay	8J	8J	none	L88	W50
2034.	6-210B	IM32620	none	X	impression	clay	8J	8J	none	L22	W19
2035.	6-210B2	37-16-15b	none	X	impression	clay	8J	8J	none	L43	W27
2036.	6-210C	37-16-16	none	X	impression	clay	8J	8J	none	S34+	L35
2037.	6-none	IM32896	none	X	impression	clay	8J	8J	none	L45	W34
2038.	6-none	IM32899	none	X	impression	clay	8J	8J	none	L36	W28
2039.	3-none	33-3-238	none	X	impression	clay	9M	6O	none	L38	W32
2040.	3-none	33-3-238	none	X	impression	clay	9M	6O	none	L38	W32
2041.	3-none	33-3-245	none	X	impression	clay	9M	6O	none	L80	W53
2042.	3-none	33-3-238	none	X	impression	clay	9M	6O	none	L35	W33
2043.	3-none	33-3-237	none	X	impression	clay	9M	6O	none	L40	W25

13	14	15	16	17	18	19
T7	0.00	unknown	Seal 28×11	seal cruciform	bone shaped	hemisphere
T13	0.00	unknown	Seal 16+×19+	too broken to know	horned animal	wings
T14	0.00	unknown	Seal 16+×17+	on basket cover	abstract horned	head
ina	0.00	unknown	Seal 20 dia	seal	Irr. antler beast	hemispheroid
none	0.00	unknown	none	unknown	unknown	
ina	0.00	unknown	Seal 18×14	unknown	3 rows wedges	
T12	0.00	unknown	Seal 20×20	hide thong: tag ?	2 small horned	animal
ina	0.00	unknown	Seal 18 dia	seal	abstract ?	high hemispheroid
ina	0.00	unknown	Seal 24+×10+	on sack	cross-hatch bear	
ina	0.00	unknown	Seal 8 dia	seal	unknown	missing
T9	0.00	unknown	Seal 21×18	seal	antelope	hemisphere
ina	0.00	unknown	Seal 15 dia	seal	star in circles	ovoid
none	0.00	unknown	Seal 21+×16+	bale tag ??	abstract ?	
T31	0.00	unknown	Seal 19×19	on sack tie	intertwined snakes	
T25	0.00	unknown	Seal 20 dia	corner string:door	longhorn goat	
none	0.00	unknown	Seal 39+×30+	on sack	circling horned	beasts
ina	0.00	unknown	Seal 24×20	bale tags	2 sheep & structure	
T29	0.00	unknown	Seal 22+×19	on jar shoulder	2 sheep & structure	
T21	0.00	unknown	Seal 23+×27+	on hide string	lion and stag	
T11	0.00	unknown	Seal 32+×20+	on hide cover ?	crude animal	
ina	0.00	unknown	Seal 32+×24+	on matted fur: ?	crude animal	
ina	0.00	unknown	Seal 32+×26+	on jar shoulder ??	leaping stag	
T19	0.00	unknown	Seal 18+×33+	ion jar cover	3 dogs	
T26	0.00	unknown	Seal 33+×24+	on jar shoulder	2 sheep heads	
none	0.00	unknown	Seal 22×17	seal	animal: bovid ?	tabloid
T12	0.00	unknown	Seal 30×24	seal	dancing man beast	hemispheroid
T09	0.00	unknown	Seal 14×18	seal	2 dogs	tabloid
ina	0.00	Room 1060	Seal 25+×20+	in NW wall window	on sack	animal in circle
T15	0.00	in room 1058	Seal 15×13	on jar shoulder ?	antelope ?	
ina	0.00	unknown	Seal 20 dia	seal	big horn stag	hemisphere
ina	0.00	unknown	Seal 23×17	bale tag	2 sheep & structure	
ina	0.00	unknown	Seal 27+×29+	unknown	deer and bird	
T27	0.00	unknown	Seal 16+×14	on jar shoulder ??	2 sheep & structure	
ina	0.00	unknown	Seal 24+×13+	on sack	animal eating bush	
ina	0.00	unknown	Seal 12 dia	seal	leaf skeleton	hemispheroid
T10	11.00	unknown	Seal 16×10	seal	criss cross	pyramid
ina	0.00	unknown	Seal 16 dia		bale tag ??	animal ?
ina	0.00	10 cm above top of wall	Seal 21+×22+	unknown	dog & huts	
T14	0.00	outside SE wall of room 1080	Seal 16×17	in jar mouth	horned animal	
none	0.00	dump	Seal 20×21	on basket cover	2 salukhis	
ina	11.24	74cm southeast grave 202	Seal 18 dia	seal	2 people & dogs	hemispheroid
ina	11.83	unknown	uncut	seal	none	high hemispheroid
none	0.00	unknown	none	seal	unknown	none
ina	0.00	unknown	Seal 9 dia	seal	criss cross grid	hemispheroid
T12	0.00	unknown	Seal 20+×20+	on hide thong	animal	
T23	0.00	unknown	Seal 27+×28+	on knot	dogs chase	antelope
none	0.00	unknown	none	too broken to know	2 sheep & structure	
T16	0.00	in cache of sealings	Seal 19+×17	too broken to know	2 sheep & structure	
ina	0.00	in cache of sealings	Seal 19+×17	on jar shoulder	4 animals	
T17	0.00	in cache of sealings	Seal 19+ ×17	on jar shoulder	2 sheep & structure	
W31	0.00	in cache of sealings	Seal 19+×17	too broken to know	2 sheep & structure	
ina	0.00	unknown	Seal 28+×16+	bulla	horned animal	heart
ina	0.00	unknown	Seal 33+×28+	too broken to know	line of horned	sheep
T17	0.00	unknown	Seal 10×14	bale tag	animal with spiked	horn
T16.5	0.00	unknown	Seal28+×24+	bale tag ?	back to back	animals
ina	0.00	unknown	Seal 27×15+	(missing)	on jar shoulder	animal
T14	0.00	unknown	Seal 32+×33+	bale tag ?	2 bulls	man & horn
none	0.00	none	Seal 29+×17+	unclear	quadruped heart	

Level IX

1	2	3	4	5	6	7	8	9	10	11	12	13	14
		Bone	**item**										
2044.	1053	31-52-424	none	IX	tool	bone	m	6K ?	none	L101	none	ina	0.00
2045.	3-113	Baghdad	none	IX	unknown	bone	9L	7O	none	L61	W21	T7	0.00
2046.	3-153A	Baghdad	none	IX	carved	bone	8K	8Q	none	H55	W19	T12	0.00
2047.	3-153B	Baghdad	none	IX	inlay	bone bitumen	8K	8Q	none	H38	W12	T10	0.00
2048.	3-331	Baghdad	none	IX	awl	bone	8J	8Q	none	L78	D18	ina	0.00
		Clay	**item**										
2049.	1052	31-52-417	none	IX	stoppers	brown ware	m	6K ?	none	H42	D26	ina	0.00
2050.	2-none	32-21-528	none	IX	horns	brown ware	Mg	10M	none	H55	W77	ina	0.00
2051.	2-none	32-21-529	none	IX	horns	buffware	Mg	10M	none	H77	W67	ina	0.00
2052.	3-022	Baghdad	none	IX	jarstopper	clay	12M	6J	none	D41	T26	ina	0.00
2053.	3-082	discarded	none	IX	ladle	redware	9M	6O	none	L245	W100	T32	0.00
2054.	3-105	33-3-48	none	IX	jarstopper	fine ware	10J	9M	none	L56	W51	T38	0.00
2055.	3-114	Baghdad	none	IX	smoother	red ware	11J	9K	none	L99	W26	T15	0.00
2056.	3-146	33-3-69	none	IX	muller	redware	9H	10O	none	D237	H147	ina	0.00
2057.	3-161	Baghdad	none	IX	ring	baked clay	8J	9Q	none	D12	L11	ina	0.00
2058.	3-172	33-3-79	none	IX	ladle	buffware	9J	9O	none	L175	W76	T31	0.00
2059.	3-177	Baghdad	none	IX	smoother	grayware	11L	7K	none	L44	W16	T04	0.00
2060.	3-208	33-3-100	none	IX	decorator	red buffware	10L	7M	none	L53	W28	T08	0.00
2061.	3-211	33-3-103	none	IX	game piece	brown buffware	10J	9M	none	none	none	none	0.01
2062.	3-213	33-3-105	none	IX	game piece	grayish ware	9J	9O	none	D19	H5	ina	0.00
2063.	3-215	Baghdad	none	IX	ring	red buffware	8J	9Q	none	D18	T5	ina	0.00
2064.	3-260	Baghdad	none	IX	weight	red brown ware	12L	7J	none	D34	H16	ina	0.00
2065.	3-261	discarded	none	IX	game piece	yellow ware	10J	9M	none	D20	H3	ina	0.00
2066.	3-269	discarded	none	IX	wall peg	brown-buff ware	10H	10M	none	L70	D40	D08	0.00
2067.	3-306	33-3-146	none	IX	sphere	buffware	10H	10M	none	D21	ina	ina	0.00
2068.	3-307	discarded	none	IX	horn ?	greenware	8G	11Q	none	L136	T38	W41	0.00
		Figurine											
2069.	3-077	Baghdad	none	IX	hut statue	clay	9J	9O	none	W124	W112+	ina	0.00
2070.	3-097	Baghdad	none	IX	hut statue	redware	10J	9M	none	H124	W106	T92	0.00
2071.	3-100	Baghdad	none	IX	animal	clay	11J	9K	none	L27	H24	T07	0.00
2072.	3-183	33-3-86	none	IX	animal	brown ware	9J	9O	none	L41	W36	T10	0.00
2073.	3-203	33-3-98	none	IX	animal	brown buffware	8L	7Q	none	L46	H35	W16	0.00
2074.	3-204	33-3-99	none	IX	animal	brown buffware	9L	7O	none	L57	H38	W21	0.00
2075.	3-275	33-3-134	none	IX	animal	brown ware	9H	10O	none	L35	H25	W11	0.00
2076.	3-314	33-3-51	none	IX	hut ?statue	redware	9M	6O	none	L100	W97	ina	0.00
2077.	3-335	33-3-160	none	IX	female	yellow clay	12K	8J	none	H40	W46	T25	0.00
		Ground	**stone**										
2078.	1051	31-52-418	none	IX	celt	blue stone	m	12M ?	none	L76	W43	none	0.00
2079.	1073	Baghdad	none	IX	loomweight	gray marble	11M	11M	none	H145	D98	none	0.00
2080.	1092	31-52-420	none	IX	hone	brown stone	l2	7G ?	none	L122	W44	none	0.00
2081.	1093	31-52-419	none	IX	polisher	brown stone	l2	7G ?	none	L109	W24	none	0.00
2082.	2-none	32-21-533	none	IX	hammer	gray stone	Ke	9K	none	L90	none	ina	0.00
2083.	2-none	32-21-534	none	IX	weight	haemetite	Ke	9K	none	L28	D19	ina	0.00
2084.	2-none	32-21-535	none	IX	weight	blue stone	Ke	9K	none	L28	D13	ina	0.00
2085.	3-015	33-3-8	none	IX	game piece	obsidian	10P	4M	none	D13	T12	ina	0.00
2086.	3-016	Baghdad	none	IX	celt	stone	12M	6J	none	L36	W33	T14	0.00
2087.	3-017	Baghdad	none	IX	celt	granite	10L	7M	none	W31	T17	L49	0.00
2088.	3-028	33-3-13	none	IX	hammer	limestone	none	none	none	D69	T39	ina	0.00
2089.	3-029	Baghdad	none	IX	hammer	limestone	none	none	none	D81	T37	ina	0.00
2090.	3-030	33-3-14	none	IX	hammer	limestone	none	none	none	L70	T30	BW82	0.00
2091.	3-031	Baghdad	none	IX	palette	stone	10M	6M	none	D90	T18	ina	0.00
2092.	3-087	33-3-212	none	IX	mortar	gray stone	11K	8K	none	H58	RD155	BD155	0.00
2093.	3-095	33-3-45	none	IX	hammer	stone	10H	10M	none	L87	W58	T39	0.00
2094.	3-096	Baghdad	none	IX	grinder	stone	10H	10M	none	H72	W62	T56	0.00
2095.	3-099	33-3-46	none	IX	hammer	gray stone	9K	8O	none	L94	W65	T35	0.00
2096.	3-103	Baghdad	none	IX	hammer	gray stone	9L	7O	none	L100	W65	T29	0.00
2097.	3-106	33-3-49	none	IX	weight	white marble	10J	9M	none	D35	T25	ina	0.00
2098.	3-157	Baghdad	none	IX	ballista	limestone	12M	6J	nonc	L59	D35	ina	0.00
2099.	3-165	Baghdad	none	IX	counter	sandstone	10K	8M	none	D26	H14	ina	0.00
2100.	3-167	Baghdad	none	IX	celt	stone	8J	9Q	none	L102	W37	none	0.00
2101.	3-168	Baghdad	none	IX	celt	slate	8K	8Q	none	L41	W34	none	0.00
2102.	3-178	33-3-83	none	IX	ring	gray stone	9L	7O	none	D23	Hol10	T4	0.00
2103.	3-194	Baghdad	none	IX	celt	green stone	10K	8M	none	L59	W26	T17	0.00
2104.	3-214	Baghdad	none	IX	decorator	gray stone	11L	7K	none	none	none	none	0.00
2105.	3-221	33-3-109	none	IX	hammer	mottled stone	9L	7O	none	L52	D72	ina	0.00
2106.	3-223	33-3-110	none	IX	sphere	white stone	8J	9Q	none	D20	ina	ina	0.00

15	16	17	18	19
trial trench				
unknown				
unknown				
unknown				
unknown				
trial trench				
unknown	figurine ? like 5847			
unknown	figurine ? like 5847			
unknown				
unknown				
unknown				
unknown				
unknown				
unknown				
unknown				
unknown				
unknown				
unknown				
unknown				
unknown				
unknown				
unknown				
unknown				
unknown				
unknown				
unknown				
unknown				
unknown				
unknown				
on top of wall				
unknown				
unknown				
trial trench				
unknown				
trial trench				
trial trench				
unknown	perforated			
unknown				
unknown	elliptical			
unknown				
unknown				
unknown				
unknown				
unknown				
unknown				
unknown				
unknown				
unknown				
unknown				
unknown				
unknown				
unknown				
unknown				
unknown				
unknown				
unknown				
unknown	for vessel			
unknown				
unknown				

(*continues*)

Level IX   (continued)

1	2	3	4	5	6	7	8	9	10	11	12	13	14
2107.	3-238	33-3-259	none	IX	hammer	basalt	none	none	none	L86	W69	br18	0.00
2108.	3-256	Baghdad	none	IX	rubbing	black stone	8K	8Q	none	L90	H61	T51	0.00
2109.	3-262	Baghdad	none	IX	rubbing	porous stone	10J	9M	none	L63	W57	T25	0.00
2110.	3-272	Baghdad	none	IX	hammer	gray stone	10L	7M	none	W59	T32	0.00	
2111.	3-303	Baghdad	none	IX	palette	black stone	9J	9O	none	L135	T24	W81	0.00
2112.	3-308	Baghdad	none	IX	chisel	green stone	8K	8Q	none	L70	H20	T11	0.00
2113.	3-325	Baghdad	none	IX	game piece	buff stone	10H	10M	none	D26	H4	ina	0.00
2114.	3-326	Baghdad	none	IX	game piece	green stone	8J	9Q	none	D17	H4	ina	0.00
2115.	3-330	Baghdad	none	IX	macehead	limestone	11H	10K	none	L52	D52	none	0.00
2116.	3-351	Baghdad	none	IX	rubbing	porous stone	11G	11K	none	H82	W76	T38	0.00
2117.	3-none	33-3-254	none	IX	weight	basalt	9K	8O	none	L68	D37	ina	0.00
2118.	3-none	33-3-275	none	IX	macehead	granite	10J	9M	none	L40	D67	ina	0.00
2119.	3-none	33-3-278	none	IX	battle ax	stone	8K	11J	none	L70	W52	T27	0.00
2120.	3-none	33-3-279	none	IX	battle ax	basalt	11G	11K	none	L85	W62	T32	0.00
2121.	3-none	33-3-284	none	IX	pestle	basalt	10H	10M	none	L60	W62	T41	0.00
2122.	3-none	33-3-285	none	IX	weight	marble	11K	8K	none	H35	D40	ina	0.00
2123.	3-none	unknown	none	IX	mortar	stone	8J	9Q	h/i 5	none	none	none	0.00
2124.	6084	Dropsie	none	IX	hammer	diorite	10M	6M	none	L93	W82	T37	0.00
		Jewelry											
2125.	1054	31-52-425	none	IX	beads	shell stone	none	none	none	none	none	none	0.00
2126.	2-none	32-21-536	none	IX	pendant	white stone	IM	6M	none	L59	none	ina	0.00
2127.	3-011	Baghdad	none	IX	pendant	obsidian	10L	7M	none	L29	D11	ina	0.00
2128.	3-034	Baghdad	none	IX	beads	limestone shell	10M	6M	none	none	none	none	0.00
2129.	3-037	33-3-16	none	IX	pendant	diorite	9L	7O	none	T8	W17	H23	
2130.	3-043	discarded	none	IX	pendant	stone	9L	7O	none	L28	none	ina	0.00
2131.	3-098	Baghdad	none	IX	bead	carnelian	9J	9O	none	T9	W11	L27	0.00
2132.	3-160	Baghdad	none	IX	pendant	stone	11J	9K	none	L26	W24	T6	0.00
2133.	3-169	33-3-76	none	IX	bead	stone	8J	9Q	none	L30	W23	T5	0.00
2134.	3-185	Baghdad	none	IX	beads 16	white marble	10M	6M	none	none	none	none	0.00
2135.	3-190	Baghdad	none	IX	pendant	quartz	9K	8O	none	H19	W17	T6	0.00
2136.	3-202	Baghdad	none	IX	bead	gold	10L	7M	none	L5	D5	ina	0.00
2137.	3-205	Baghdad	none	IX	button	paste	8J	9Q	none	D17	T4	ina	0.00
2138.	3-233	Baghdad	none	IX	pendant	black stone	10L	7M	none	L24	D8	ina	0.00
2139.	3-237	33-3-118	none	IX	amulet	green stone	dump	dump	dump	L29	W12	T4	0.00
2140.	3-239	Baghdad	none	IX	bead	lapis lazuli	dump	dump	ina	none	none	none	0.00
2141.	3-255	33-3-126	none	IX	pendant	green stone	10J	9M	none	L28	W10	T7	0.00
2142.	3-259	Baghdad	none	IX	beads 7	bone/6 shell	8K	8Q	none	none	none	none	0.00
2143.	3-271	33-3-132	none	IX	bead	bone	10H	10M	none	L41	W15	H12	0.00
2144.	3-305	33-3-145	none	IX	bead	gray stone	10H	10M	none	L28	D9	ina	0.00
2145.	3-311	33-3-149	none	IX	pendant	gray stone	11G	11K	none	L20	W9	T2	0.00
2146.	3-312	Baghdad	none	IX	pendant	black stone	8J	9Q	none	L30	W8	T6	0.00
2147.	3-319	33-3-154	none	IX	button	white stone	8G	11Q	none	D17	T5	ina	0.00
2148.	3-329	33-3-157	none	IX	beads 15	stone	10G	11M	none	none	none	none	0.00
		Lithics											
2149.	1086a	31-52-423	none	IX	blade	obsidian	m	12M ?	none	L35	W13	T3.6	0.00
2150.	1086b	31-52-423	none	IX	blade	flint	m	12M ?	none	L30	W19	T4.4	0.00
2151.	1086c	31-52-423	none	IX	blade	black flint	m	12M ?	none	L44	W18	T4.7	0.00
2152.	1086d	31-52-423	none	IX	blade	black flint	m	12M ?	none	L61	W17	T3.6	0.00
2153.	1086e	31-52-423	none	IX	blade	black flint	m	12M ?	none	L45	W17	T4	0.00
2154.	1086f	31-52-423	none	IX	blade	black flint	m	12M ?	none	L33	W13	T3.3	0.00
2155.	1091	31-52-422	none	IX	blade	obsidian	l2	7G ?	none	L53	W20	T2.8	0.00
2156.	1091	31-52-422	none	IX	blade	obsidian	l2	7G ?	none	L83	W14	T4.4	0.00
2157.	1091	31-52-422	none	IX	blade	obsidian	l2	7G ?	none	L35	W9	T2.3	0.00
2158.	1091	31-52-422	none	IX	blade	obsidian	l2	7G ?	none	L60	W16	T5.3	0.00
2159.	1091	31-52-422	none	IX	blade	obsidian	l2	7G ?	none	L50	W14	T4.1	0.00
2160.	1091	31-52-422	none	IX	blade	obsidian	l2	7G ?	none	L53	W9	T3.6	0.00
2161.	1091	31-52-422	none	IX	blade	obsidian	l2	7G ?	none	L52	W18	T4	0.00
2162.	1091	31-52-422	none	IX	blade	obsidian	l2	7G ?	none	L38	W16	T3.2	0.00
2163.	1091	31-52-422	none	IX	blade	obsidian	l2	7G ?	none	L51	W9	T2	0.00
2164.	1091	31-52-422	none	IX	blade	obsidian	l2	7G ?	none	L45	W9	T3.5	0.00
2165.	1091a	31-52-422	none	IX	blade	obsidian	l2	7G ?	none	L38	W11	T3.8	0.00
2166.	2-none	32-21-539	none	IX	blade	obsidian	Ke	9K	none	L48	W27	T7.2	0.00
2167.	2-none a	32-21-537	none	IX	blade	tan flint	Me	9M	none	L55	W23	T4	0.00
2168.	2-none b	32-21-537	none	IX	blade	tan flint	none	none	none	L62	W19	T5	0.00
2169.	2-none b	32-21-538	none	IX	blade	obsidian	none	none	none	L35	W14	T4.2	0.00
2170.	2-none b	32-21-538	none	IX	blade	obsidian	Ke	9K	none	L43	W9	T2.2	0.00
2171.	2-none c	32-21-537	none	IX	blade	tan flint	none	Ke	none	L61	W17	T3.3	0.00

15	16	17	18	19
unknown				
unknown				
unknown				
unknown				
unknown				
unknown				
unknown				
unknown				
unknown				
unknown				
unknown				
unknown	canoe shaped			
unknown				
unknown				
unknown				
set in terrazo floor	in room 909A			
unknown				
trial trench				
unknown				
unknown				
unknown	53 limestone 9 shell			
unknown				
unknown				
unknown				
unknown				
unknown				
unknown				
unknown				
unknown	on copper wire			
near edge of tepe				
unknown				
dump	fish or fir tree			
unknown				
unknown				
unknown				
unknown				
unknown				
unknown				
unknown				
unknown	5 white 9 gray 1 gypsum			
trial trench	sheen 52 retouch 29			
trial trench	unused 36 34			
trial trench	unused 29 33			
trial trench	unused 47 serrated 43			
trial trench	unused 46 43			
trial trench	unused backed 31 29			
trial trench	striations 38 retouch 40			
trial trench	striations 33 unused 34			
trial trench	striations 30 & 24			
trial trench	striations 35 pointed 47			
trial trench	little used 29 31			
trial trench	little used 55 40			
trial trench	striations 53 used 30			
trial trench	little used 32 34			
trial trench	ununsed 15 27			
trial trench	little used 43, 37			
trial trench	retouch 48 51 point			
unknown	striations 47 retouch 35			
unknown	sheen retouch 46	sheen 41		
unknown	bitumen 43 sheen 44			
unknown	heavy retouch 52 53			
unknown	little striations 35 & 47			
unknown	bitumen 33 sheen 39			

(*continues*)

Level IX (continued)

1	2	3	4	5	6	7	8	9	10	11	12	13	14
2172.	2-none c	32-21-538	none	IX	blade	obsidian	K ?	9K ?	none	L66	W10	T3.2	0.00
2173.	2-none c	32-21-538	none	IX	blade	obsidian	Ke	9K	none	L45	W10	T2.7	0.00
2174.	2-none d	32-21-538	none	IX	blade	obsidian	Ke	9K	none	L82	W22	T5.7	0.00
2175.	2-none e	32-21-538	none	IX	blade	obsidian	Ke	9K	none	L52	W13	T3.7	0.00
2176.	2-none g	32-21-538	none	IX	blade	obsidian	Me	9M	none	L47	W11	T2.9	0.00
2177.	2-none i	32-21-538	none	IX	blade	obsidian	IIk	5K	none	L64	W17	T2.5	0.00
2178.	2-none j	32-21-538	none	IX	blade	obsidian	Ke	9K	none	L65	W13	T3.7	0.00
2179.	2-none k	32-21-538	none	IX	blade	obsidian	Ke	9K	none	L55	W23	T7	0.00
2180.	2-none l	32-21-538	none	IX	blade	obsidian	none	none	none	L50	W12	T3.5	0.00
2181.	2-none m	32-21-538	none	IX	blade	obsidian	none	none	none	L63	W14	T4.9	0.00
2182.	2-none n	32-21-538	none	IX	blade	obsidian	Ke	9K	none	L53	W15	T2.2	0.00
2183.	2-none o	32-21-538	none	IX	blade	obsidian	Ke	9K	none	L48	W17	T3.1	0.00
2184.	2-none p	32-21-538	none	IX	blade	obsidian	K ?	9K ?	none	L43	W8	T2.1	0.00
2185.	2-none q	32-21-538	none	IX	blade	obsidian	Kg	10K	none	L72	W16	T4.7	0.00
2186.	2-none s	32-21-538	none	IX	blade	obsidian	Ke	9K	none	L43	W17	T4.4	0.00
2187.	2-none t	32-21-538	none	IX	blade	obsidian	Ke	9K	none	L52	W13	T3	0.00
2188.	2-none u	32-21-538	none	IX	blade	obsidian	IIIg	4G	none	L30	W26	T6.2	0.00
2189.	2-none v	32-21-538	none	IX	blade	obsidian	IIIg	4G	none	L51	W12	T3.7	0.00
2190.	2-none w	32-21-538	none	IX	blade	obsidian	Ke	9K	none	L45	W12	T2.8	0.00
2191.	2-none x	32-21-538	none	IX	blade	obsidian	Kg	10K	none	L83	W18	T5.5	0.00
2192.	2-none x	32-21-538	none	IX	blade	obsidian	Ke	9K	none	L47	W11	T3.4	0.00
2193.	3-025	Baghdad	none	IX	knife	obsidian	9N	5O	none	L102	W15	T4	0.00
2194.	3-051	33-3-24	none	IX	knife frag	obsidian	12J	9J	none	L80	W19	T3	0.00
2195.	3-083	Baghdad	none	IX	knife	obsidian	9M	6O	none	L121	W21	T5	0.00
2196.	3-089	Baghdad	none	IX	knife	obsidian	10H	10M	none	L95	W16	T4	0.00
2197.	3-108	Baghdad	none	IX	knife	obsidian	11J	9K	none	L113	W23	T4	0.00
2198.	3-158	Baghdad	none	IX	knife	obsidian	9J	9O	none	L55	W17	T3	0.00
2199.	3-159	Baghdad	none	IX	scraper	obsidian	11L	7K	none	L61	W11	T3	0.00
2200.	3-166	33-3-75	none	IX	knife	obsidian	9K	8O	none	L54	W12	T2	0.00
2201.	3-191	discarded	none	IX	knives 6	obsidian	9J	9O	none	none	none	none	0.00
2202.	3-201	33-3-97	none	IX	knife	obsidian	9J	9O	none	none	none	none	0.00
2203.	3-208	33-3-100	none	IX	blade	obsidian	10L	7M	none	L54	W28	ina	0.00
2204.	3-219	33-3-107	none	IX	knife	obsidian	9K	8O	none	L56	W3	T2	0.00
2205.	3-234	Baghdad	none	IX	core	flint	8L	7Q	none	H100	none	none	0.00
2206.	3-236	33-3-117	none	IX	core	obsidian	8L	7Q	none	L131	D52	T45	0.00
2207.	3-246	Baghdad	none	IX	blade	flint	9J	9O	none	L105	W16	T5	0.00
2208.	3-247	33-3-121	none	IX	blade	flint	8H	10Q	none	L54	W13	T5.5	0.00
2209.	3-276	33-3-135	none	IX	sickle	flint	9J	9O	none	L124	W22	T4	0.00
2210.	3-310	33-3-148	none	IX	core	obsidian	9J	9O	none	L81	W26	T21	0.00
2211.	3-490	Baghdad	none	IX	knife	obsidian	12J	9J	none	L77	W20	ina	0.00
2212.	3-491	Baghdad	none	IX	knife	obsidian	9J	9O	none	L79	W20	none	0.00
		Metal	**item**										
2213.	3-254	33-3-125	none	IX	nail	copper	10H	10M	none	L49	D5	ina	0.00
2214.	3-274	discarded	none	IX	implement	copper	10J	9M	none	none	none	none	0.00
2215.	3-301	Baghdad	none	IX	chisel	copper	10M	6M	none	L83	W38	T7	11.73
		Potsherd											
2216.	3-321	33-3-155	none	IX	small jar	buffware	10K	8M	none	L58	W57	T8	0.00
2217.	2-none	32-21-527	none	IX	none	buffware	Ie	9J	none	none	none	none	0.00
		Vessel											
2218.	1002	Baghdad	none	IX	bowl	brown ware	j	10M	none	H90	D135	ina	0.00
2219.	1020	31-52-416	none	IX	deep bowl	green grayware	l	11M ?	none	none	none	none	0.00
2220.	1085	31-52-421	none	IX	saucer	gray stone	h	5J	none	H19	D47	none	0.00
2221.	2-none	32-21-526	none	IX	cup	red brownware	none	none	none	H99	D120	ina	0.00
2222.	3-020	33-3-9	none	IX	pot	red brownware	12M	6J	none	H88	D1035	BD58	0.00
2223.	3-021	33-3-10	none	IX	small jar	buffware	9L	7O	none	H12	D13	RD100	0.00
2224.	3-035	unknown	none	IX	bowl	oolite	10M	6M	none	H52	RD60	BD50	0.00
2225.	3-038	discarded	none	IX	Wide flower	buffware	12M	6J	none	H75	RD265	BD125	0.00
2226.	3-041	Baghdad	none	IX	beaker	buffware	11M	6K	none	H110	RD143	BD132	0.00
2227.	3-071	33-3-36	none	IX	channel rim jar	Grayware	12M	6J	none	H470	RD541	ina	0.00
2228.	3-072	Baghdad	none	IX	channel rim jar	grayware	12M	6J	none	H52	RD83	ina	0.00
2229.	3-101	Baghdad	none	IX	jar	green grayware	10K	8M	none	D121	H77	ina	0.00
2230.	3-104	33-3-52	none	IX	Wide flower	red brownware	10H	10M	none	H81	RD257	BD108	0.00
2231.	3-133	Baghdad	none	IX	jar	blackware	9H	10O	none	H101	RD121	ina	0.00
2232.	3-134	33-3-67	none	IX	pot	buffware	8J	9Q	none	H123	RD120	BD75	0.00
2233.	3-137	33-3-63	none	IX	crock	red brownware	9K	8O	none	H303	RD380	ina	0.00
2234.	3-154	33-3-72	none	IX	jar fragment	orange redware	8K	8Q	none	ina	RD100	ina	0.00
2235.	3-155	discarded	none	IX	dish	redware	10K	8M	none	none	none	none	0.00

15	16	17	18	19
unknown	retouch 43 40			
unknown	striations retouch 24 31			
unknown	striations 50 grinding 48			
unknown	striations 28 retouch 37			
unknown	striations 36 retouch 39			
unknown	minor striations 35 & 24			
unknown	retouch 32 & 39			
unknown	striations 39 used 39			
unknown	minor striations 38 & 34			
unknown	striations 36 retouch 44			
unknown	striations 34 & 36			
unknown	striations retouch 28 31			
unknown	striations 41 unused 19			
unknown	striations 48 retouch 34			
unknown	striations 44 retouch 34			
unknown	unused 23 32			
unknown	striations 47 retouch 47			
unknown	little retouch 45 & 35			
unknown	little used 34 & 25			
unknown	heavy retouch 44 & 49			
unknown	unused 32 28			
base of wall of VIII				
unknown	fragmentary			
unknown				
unknown				
unknown				
unknown				
unknown				
unknown	missing from storage			
unknown				
unknown	missing from storage			
unknown				
unknown	unused 41 & 37			
unknown	traces of bitumen	scraper ?		
unknown	10 to 15 mm blades			
unknown	curved and pointed			
unknown	retouch 49 serrated 45			
unknown	bitumen retouch 29	none 55		
unknown	5 to 8 mm blades			
unknown				
unknown				
unknown				
in front of temple				
unknown				
unknown	red slip			
unknown				
unknown				
trial trench				
trial trench				
unknown	buff slip	quartz grit and sand	black paint band	WM
dumped in room with other	garbage	chaff & grit	HM	
on floor room 903A	chaff & quartz grit	HM		
unknown				
dumped in room	with other garbage			
unknown	brown paint lines			
dumped in room	with other garbage	burn marks		
dumped in room	with other garbage			
unknown	incised gazelles on base			
unknown				
unknown				
unknown	fine quartz & basalt grit	paint dot inside rim	WM	hole drilled in side
unknown	straight spout			
unknown	sand & vegetable temper	buff slip red paint	HM	
unknown				

(continues)

Level IX   (continued)

1	2	3	4	5	6	7	8	9	10	11	12	13	14
2236.	3-170	33-3-77	none	IX	bowl	green grayware	9L	7O	none	D21	H81	ina	0.00
2237.	3-198	33-3-94	none	IX	model bowl	buffware	10H	10M	none	H27	D45	ina	0.00
2238.	3-212	33-3-104	none	IX	strainer	buffware	9J	9O	none	H74	W105	T74	0.00
2239.	3-224	Baghdad	none	IX	bowl	buffware	9J	9O	none	H255	RD470	ina	0.00
2240.	3-227	33-3-112	none	IX	small jar	grayware	8H	10Q	none	H103	D125	ina	0.00
2241.	3-228	33-3-113	none	IX	jar	buffware	9J	9O	none	H95	D105	ina	0.00
2242.	3-229	33-2-114	none	IX	jar fragment	buffware	9K	8O	none	none	none	none	0.00
2243.	3-248	33-3-122	none	IX	Wide flower	buffware	9J	9O	none	H88	D252	ina	0.00
2244.	3-251	discarded	none	IX	bowl	brownware	7H	10S	none	H84	RD260	BD80	0.00
2245.	3-252	33-3-124	none	IX	jar	brownware	8J	9Q	none	H185	D163	ina	0.00
2246.	3-257	Baghdad	none	IX	cup	alabaster	10H	10M	none	H75	D61	ina	0.00
2247.	3-277	33-3-136	none	IX	Wide flower	grayware	11J	9K	none	H69	RD237	BD120	0.00
2248.	3-278	discarded	none	IX	jar fragment	redware	9H	10O	none	H22	D30	ina	0.00
2249.	3-302	Baghdad	none	IX	jar	grayware	11G	11K	none	H66	RD60	BD80	0.00
2250.	3-313	33-3-150	none	IX	stand	orange redware	11G	11K	none	H18	D19	ina	0.00
2251.	3-320	Baghdad	none	IX	2 mouth jar	red buffware	10H	10M	none	RD160	D180	none	0.00
2252.	3-322	discarded	none	IX	jar rim	buff ware	10H	10M	none	RD19	none	none	0.00
2253.	3-340	Baghdad	none	IX	bowl	redware	8J	9Q	loc 33	H9	D26	ina	0.00
2254.	3-354	33-3-169	none	IX	small jar	brownware	8L	7Q	none	H10	RD6	D12	0.00
2255.	3-366	33-3-180	none	IX	bowl	green grayware	8L-K	7Q	none	H92	RD162	BD52	0.00
2256.	3-367	33-3-181	none	IX	bowl	grayware	8L-K	7Q	none	H129	D310	ina	0.00
2257.	3-386	discarded	none	IX	Wide flower	buffware	12J	9J	none	none	none	none	0.00
2258.	3-389	discarded	none	IX	trough	buffware	12L	7J	none	none	none	none	0.00
2259.	3-487	35-10-343	none	IX	cup	red brownware	12N	5J	none	H50	RD68	BD49	0.00
2260.	3-none	33-3-21	none	IX	jar	buffware	none	none	none	L49	W35	T5	0.00
2261.	3-none	33-3-228	none	IX	jar	green grayware	12K	8J	none	L32	W73	T3.9	0.00
2262.	3-none	33-3-228	none	IX	jar	buffware	11G	10K	none	L60	W108	T5.8	0.00
2263.	3-none	33-3-228	none	IX	bowl	buffware	KIII	4K	none	L48	W69	T6.4	0.00
2264.	3-none	33-3-255	none	IX	Wide flower	buffware	10L	7M	none	H70	D205	ina	0.00
2265.	3-none	unknown	none	IX	store jar	buff ware	11H	10K	i9	H315	BD470	RD450	11.28
2266.	3-none	unknown	none	IX	laver	ceramic	8J	9Q	i5	H160	BD250	none	11.14
2267.	3-none	unknown	none	IX	bowl	green grayware	8M	6Q	ij9/10	H270	BD580	none	11.94
2268.	3-none	unknown	none	IX	2 rim jar ?	gray ware	10L	7M	d 6/7	none	none	none	11.60
2269.	3-none	unknown	none	IX	Wide flower	brownware	9L	7O	none	none	none	none	0.00
2270.	3-none	33-3-155	none	IX	small jar	buffware	none	none	none	RD91	none	ina	0.00
2271.	6086	unknown	none	IX	bowl	redware	J7	9S	none	H150	D295	ina	0.00
		Spindle	**whorl**										
2272.	2-none	32-21-530	none	IX	whorl	clay	Ke	9K	none	H22	D36	ina	0.00
2273.	2-none	32-21-531	none	IX	whorl	clay	IM	6M	none	H19	D33	ina	0.00
2274.	3-027	Baghdad	none	IX	whorl	clay	9L	7O	none	D36	T18	ina	0.00
2275.	3-042	Baghdad	none	IX	whorl	clay	10M	6M	none	H26	T30	ina	0.00
2276.	3-044A	33-3-18	none	IX	whorl	stone	10M	6M	none	H24	D38	ina	0.00
2277.	3-044B	33-3-18	none	IX	whorl	clay	10M	6M	none	D34	none	ina	0.00
2278.	3-164	33-3-74	none	IX	whorl	clay	10K	8M	none	D32	W20	ina	0.00
2279.	3-304	33-3-144	none	IX	whorl	clay	10H	10M	none	D31	H19	ina	0.00
2280.	3-324	Baghdad	none	IX	whorl	stone	8J	9Q	none	D28	H22	ina	0.00
2281.	3-334	33-3-159	none	IX	whorl	clay	12J	9J	none	D35	H26	ina	0.00
		Seal	**sealing**										
2282.	3-080	IM15844	none	IX	impression	clay	10K	8M	none	H35	W45	T20	0.00
2283.	3-110	Baghdad	none	IX	amulet	steatite	10H	10M	none	W95	H09	T04	0.00
2284.	3-173	33-3-80	none	IX	impression	clay	12M	6J	none	L38	W19	T17	0.00
2285.	3-179	33-3-84	none	IX	stamp	gray stone	10K	8M	none	D16	T08	ina	0.00
2286.	3-189a	33-3-89	none	IX	impression	clay	10K	8M	Rm902	L71	W43	T19	12.20
2287.	3-189b	33-3-89	none	IX	impression	clay	10K	8M	Loc 22	L62	W53	T3	12.20
2288.	3-189c	33-3-89	none	IX	impression	clay	10K	8M	Loc 22	L33	W34	T25	12.20
2289.	3-189	IM15979	none	IX	impression	clay	10K	8M	Loc 22	none	none	ina	12.20
2290.	3-195	33-3-91	none	IX	impression	clay	10K	8M	none	L28	W16	T11	0.00
2291.	3-196	33-3-92	none	IX	impression	clay	10K	8M	none	L36	W31	T21	0.00
2292.	3-197	33-3-93	none	IX	impression	clay	10K	8M	none	L50	W51	T32	0.00
2293.	3-200	33-3-95	none	IX	impression	clay	10K	8M	none	L52	W36	T19	0.00
2294.	3-207	Baghdad	none	IX	stamp	steatite	8J	9Q	none	D22	T09	ina	0.00
2295.	3-209	33-3-101	none	IX	stamp	black stone	9J	9O	none	D19	H17	ina	0.00
2296.	3-220	33-3-108	none	IX	stamp	soft stone	9J	9O	none	D11	H06	ina	0.00
2297.	3-235	IM15933	none	IX	stamp	brown stone	none	none	none	D10	T06	ina	0.00
2298.	3-240	33-3-119	none	IX	amulet	stone	8L	7Q	none	D15	T04	ina	0.00
2299.	3-243	IM15845	none	IX	impression	clay	9K	8O	none	L34	W35	ina	0.00
2300.	3-245	33-3-120	none	IX	impression	clay	10L	7M	none	L35+	W24	T20	0.00

15	16	17	18	19
room 903A on floor	basalt & quartz ring base	inbeveled rim	blob paint HM	
unknown	quartz & basalt grit	HM		
unknown	chaff & quartz grit	HM		
unknown	black core			
unknown	traces of burnishing			
unknown				
unknown	cross hatch			
unknown	chaff temper	HM		
unknown				
unknown	chaff & quartz ring base	HM		
unknown				
unknown	buff slip	chaff & quartz grit	HM	
unknown	see 3-71			
unknown				
unknown	buff slip	quartz grit & vegetable	HM	
unknown				
on top of wall	high relief animals			
unknown	smoked black	quartz grit & chaff	HM	
unknown	sand temper ring base	WM		
unknown	basalt grit	blob paint rim ring base	inbevel rim	
unknown				
unknown	basalt grit	WM		
unknown	fine basalt and quartz grit	red paint overall	HM	
unknown	sand temper cross hatch	WM		
unknown	buff slip	chaff and quartz HM	paint crosshatch	
unknown	painted crosshatch	& tree		
unknown	chaff & quartz grit HM			
set on floor by wall	room 923			
set in floor room 909A				
set in floor by walls				
set in floor SE corner	room 901			
in room 903A on floor				
unknown	gray paint grit & chaff	WM		
unknown				
unknown				
unknown				
unknown				
unknown				
unknown				
unknown				
unknown				
unknown				
unknown				
unknown	Seal 12×10	on jar shoulder	procession of sheep	
unknown	none	seal	unclear	lentoid
unknown	Seal 31+×21+	on jar shoulder	2 men shear sheep	
unknown	Seal 16 dia	seal	cruciform	hemispheroid
sealings corner door	Seal 32×32	Loc 22: cache	ram sheep and fish	
cache in a corner of rm 902	Seal 32×32	door	ram sheep and fish	
in corner of room 902	Seal 32×32	wall tag	ram sheep and fish	
door	Seal 32×32	ram sheep and fish		
from the "pig"?= locus 22	Seal 15+×13+	on jar cover ?	animal: lion ? ox ?	
from the "pig"?=locus 22	Seal 14×14	bale tag	animal and structure	
from the "pig"?=locus 22	Seal 25×23+	Type T door lock ?	abstract animal	
from the "pig"?= locus 22	Seal 20×22	on jar cover	crude horned animal	
unknown	Seal 22 dia	seal	antelope and fillers	hemispheroid
unknown	Seal 13×15	seal	snake ? and fillers	hemispheroid
unknown	Seal 11 dia	seal	5 drilled holes	high hemispheroid
unknown	Seal 10 dia	seal	petals off center	dot ovoid
unknown	Seal 15 dia	seal	three stars 1 in box	lentoid
unknown	Seal 34+×32+	on jar shoulder	ox and animal ?	
unknown	Seal 32+×23+	on jar shoulder	3 cats ? animals	

(*continues*)

Level IX   (continued)

1	2	3	4	5	6	7	8	9	10	11	12	13	14
2301.	3-264	33-3-129	none	IX	impression	clay	9H	10O	none	L23	W18	T11	0.00
2302.	3-267	IM15929	none	IX	stamp	bone	8J	9Q	none	D17	H04	ina	0.00
2303.	3-291	IM15846	none	IX	impression	clay	10J	9M	none	L36	W42	none	0.00
2304.	3-297	IM15931	none	IX	stamp	green stone	8L	7Q	none	D13	T07	ina	0.00
2305.	3-298	IM15928	none	IX	stamp	paste	11G	11K	none	D18	T11	ina	0.00
2306.	3-315	33-3-152	none	IX	stamp	paste	8L	7Q	none	D12	H04	ina	0.00

15	16	17	18	19
unknown	Seal 12+×11+	too broken to know	starburst	
unknown	Seal 17 dia	seal	stalks of grain ?	hemispheroid
unknown	Seal 33+×40+	on jar shoulder ?	lion ? attacks cow ?	
unknown	Seal 13 dia	seal	cruciform	hemisphere
unknown	Seal 10×12	seal	4 drilled dots	high hemispheroid
unknown	Seal 12 dia	seal	petals off stalk ?	lentoid

Level VIII

1	2	3	4	5	6	7	8	9	11	12	13
	Bone	**item**									
2307.	1123	31-52-439	none	VIII	needle	bone	h3?	5J?	L100	none	ina
2308.	5658	unknown	none	VIII	needle	bone	IIO	5O	L84	D4	ina
2309.	5698	Baghdad	none	VIIIAB	pin needle	bone	Ke	9K	L111	none	ina
2310.	5792	Baghdad	none	VIII	needle	bone	Me	9M	L37	ina	ina
2311.	5858	32-21-376	none	VIIIA	object	bone	none	9O	L111	W24	ina
2312.	5909	32-21-546	none	VIII	needle	bone	well	none	L97	none	ina
2313.	5923	32-21-377	none	VIII	needle	bone	Me	9M	L71	none	ina
2314.	5934	32-21-547	none	VIII	needle	bone	none	none	L111	none	ina
2315.	3-004	Baghdad	none	VIIIA	awl	bone	12N	5J	L93	W22	ina
2316.	3-092	Baghdad	none	VIII	spoon	bone	8K	8Q	L51	W34	T6
2317.	3-111	33-3-50	none	VIII	smoother ?	bone	12J	9J	L129	W30	T34
2318.	3-112	33-3-51	none	VIII	flaker ?	bone	12J	9J	L87	W21	T11
	Clay	**item**									
2319.	1-none	unknown	none	VIIIA	clay horns	clay	JI	6J	H210	D220	T180
2320.	1084	31-52-99	none	VIII	bobbin	buffware	h	10M ?	L66	ina	ina
2321.	1114	31-52-381	none	VIII	rings 7	buff ware	O2	10K	D23	H9	ina
2322.	1119	Baghdad	none	VIII	bobbin	buffware	g2	9M	L75	none	ina
2323.	5285	32-21-322	none	VIII A ?	loomweight	green grayware	Of	10O	L74	none	ina
2324.	5292	32-21-555	none	VIII A ?	loomweight	buffware	Of	9M	L55	none	ina
2325.	5380	Baghdad	none	VIII	toy wheel	green grayware	Mc	8M	D58	ina	ina
2326.	5439	32-21-320	none	VIII	toy wheel	green grayware	Mc	8M	D32	ina	ina
2327.	5614	32-21-354	none	VIII	scoop	gray ware	IIO	5O	L67	W39	ina
2328.	5615	Baghdad	none	VIII	chariot	green grayware	IIO	5O	L72	W32	T37
2329.	5627	32-21-556	none	VIII	loomweight	gray ware	none	none	L58	T25	ina
2330.	5641	32-21-346	none	VIIIA	ring	red buffware	none	9O	D29	T13	ina
2331.	5650	32-21-312	none	VIII	ladle	red ware	Qa	7Q	L180	D115	T65
2332.	5662	32-21-557	none	VIIIAB	loomweight	redware	Kc	8K	L74	none	ina
2333.	5673	Baghdad	none	VIII	bobbin	buffware	Kc	8K	L68	none	ina
2334.	5679	Baghdad	none	VIII	loomweight	unbaked clay	IIO	5O	H113	W155	ina
2335.	5708	32-21-558	none	VIII	loomweight	green grayware	Ke	9K	L75	none	ina
2336.	5709	Baghdad	none	VIII	toy wheel	buffware	Ke	9K	D51	ina	ina
2337.	5711	Baghdad	none	VIIIAB	loomweight	gray ware	Ma ?	8M	L64	none	ina
2338.	5712	32-21-559	none	VIIIA	loomweight	buffware	none	8O	L67	none	ina
2339.	5731	Baghdad	none	VIIIAB	toy wheel	gray ware	Ma ?	8M	D45	ina	ina
2340.	5744	32-21-560	none	VIIIA	loomweight	buffware	none	8O	L76	ina	ina
2341.	5773	32-21-561	none	VIII	loomweight	green grayware	IIM	5M	L62	ina	ina
2342.	5774	Baghdad	none	VIII	spool	brown ware	Oc	8O	L50	W63	ina
2343.	5782	unknown	none	VIII	palette	gray ware	IM	6M	D63	T26	ina
2344.	5793	32-21-351	none	VIII	smoother	green grayware	Me	9M	L49	W20	T5
2345.	5805	32-21-321	none	VIII	toy wheel	redware	IK	6K	D42	ina	ina
2346.	5826	32-21-347	none	VIII	ring	buffware	IIIM	4M	D17	T8	ina
2347.	5845	32-21-562	none	VIII	loomweight	buffware	Kc	8K	L60	W35	ina
2348.	5847	32-21-318	none	VIII	horns	ceramic	IQ	6Q	H80	W106	ina
2349.	5855	32-21-324	none	VIIIAB	loomweight	green grayware	Ja	7J	L52	ina	ina
2350.	5864	32-21-348	none	VIIIA	ring	ceramic	Ja	7J	D29	T10	ina
2351.	5891	32-21-322	none	VIIIBC	toy wheel	gray ware	Me	9M	D75	ina	ina
2352.	6072	32-21-306	none	VIII	ladle	buffware	Q6	6Q	L250	D180	ina
2353.	2-none	32-21-349	none	VIII	ring	buff ware	IO	6O	H10	D21	ina
2354.	2-none	32-21-352	none	VIII	smoother	gry-buffware	IIO	5O	L57	none	none
2355.	3-059	33-3-96	none	VIII	censer	gry buffware	10H	10M	H77	BD106	ina
2356.	3-123	Baghdad	none	VIII	ballista	brown ware	12L	7J	L49	T30	ina
2357.	3-127	33-3-57	none	VIII	geometric	clay	12K	8J	L26	W23	T8
2358.	3-130	33-3-59	none	VIII	sphere	brown ware	12K	8J	D25	ina	ina
2359.	3-162	discarded	none	VIII	lug	gray ware	12K	8J	none	none	none
2360.	3-163	33-3-73	none	VIII	game piece	gray ware	11L	7K	D38	T11	ina
2361.	3-279	discarded	none	VIII	tube	buffware	8M	6Q	L45	D11	ina
2362.	5689	Baghdad	none	VIII	toy wheel	buffware	IIO	5O	D44	ina	ina
2363.	5780	32-21-319	none	VIII	toy body	green grayware	Jc	8J	L90	W87	ina
2364.	5678	unknown	none	VIII	horns	ceramic	Kc	8K	D200	T185	ina
		Figurine									
2365.	1-none	unknown	none	VIIIA	animal	gray clay	J2	5J	L80	H67.5	none
2366.	5365	Baghdad	none	VIII	animal	clay	Mb	8M	L46	H42	ina
2367.	5676	32-21-314	none	VIII	animal	gray ware	IO	6O	L43	H29	T18
2368.	5722	32-21-68	none	VIII 6-sub ?	animal	buffware	Ja	7J	L83	W41	ina
2369.	5723	32-21-69	none	VIIIA 6-sub ?	animal	buffware	Ja	7J	L83	T62	ina
2370.	5781	Baghdad	none	VIII	bull head	gray ware	IO	6O	L55	W57	ina

15	16	17	18	19
unknown				
unknown	polished			
unknown	incised			
unknown				
room 826	inlaid with lapis ?			
well				
unknown	grooved			
well				
near wall of burial	from leg bone of animal			
unknown	crudely made			
unknown				
unknown				
in room 802 in door 801	elevation 13.26m	called "cultic" horns		
unknown	fastener ?			
trial trench	rectangular cross	section		
unknown	fastener			
between 9M and 10M				
unknown	like 5007			
unknown	for chariot			
unknown	for chariot			
unknown				
unknown	body of chariot			
unknown				
Room 826				
unknown	thickness of bowl			
unknown	traces of burning	like 5074		
unknown				
unknown	semi circles 2 holes			
unknown	like 5074			
unknown	for chariot			
room 812B	narrow center groove			
Room 830	like 5005			
room 812B	for chariot	like 5439		
Room 834	like 5074			
unknown				
unknown				
unknown	broken & repaired			
context				
unknown	for chariot			
unknown				
unknown				
unknown	signs of attachment	figurine ?		
unknown				
unknown				
unknown	for chariot			
unknown				
unknown				
unknown				
unknown	bitumen on one side			
unknown				
unknown	incised not stamped			
unknown				
unknown	like 3-97 of IX			
unknown				
unknown				
unknown	for chariot			
unknown	for chariot			
unknown				
in room 804 ?				
unknown	traces of burning			
unknown				
unknown				
unknown				
unknown				

(continues)

Level VIII   (continued)

1	2	3	4	5	6	7	8	9	11	12	13
2371.	5833	Baghdad	none	VIIIA	animal	buffware	Ja	7J	L73	T43	ina
2372.	5878	32-21-315	none	VIIIBC	animal	ceramic	IIM	5M	L53	T40	ina
2373.	6074	32-21-317	none	VIII	animalhead	green grayware	O6	6O	L61	ina	ina
2374.	2-none	32-21-313	none	VIII	goat	green grayware	IO	6O	L83	H45	T25
2375.	3-012	33-3-6	none	VIII	animal	ceramic	9M	6O	L70	W50	T35
2376.	3-018	discarded	none	VIII	hand ?	clay	11L	7K	L92	W54	T38
2377.	3-046	33-3-20	none	VIII	animal	buffware	12J	9J	L31	W28	ina
2378.	3-048	33-3-22	none	VIII	snake head	clay	10M	6M	L21	ina	ina
2379.	3-052	Baghdad	none	VIII	animal ?	clay	12J	9J	L25	W20	T22
2380.	3-102	33-3-47	none	VIII	sheep	buffware	11L	7K	L71	W55	T43
2381.	3-122	Baghdad	none	VIII	animal	gray ware	11K	8K	L52	W34	T14
	Ground	**stone**									
2382.	0850	Dropsie	none	VIIIA	bowl stand	basalt	JII	5J	H305	D360	ina
2383.	0853	Dropsie	none	VIIIA	phallus	limestone	JII	5J	L120	D51	ina
2384.	1-none	Dropsie ?	none	VIIIA	bowl stand	basalt	JII	5J	none	none	none
2385.	1-none	unknown	none	VIIIA	bowl	stone	JII	5K	none	none	none
2386.	1013	31-52-399	none	VIII	polisher	gray stone	m	6K ?	L95	none	ina
2387.	1014	31-52-398	none	VIII	polisher	gray stone	m	6K ?	L59	none	ina
2388.	1023	31-52-406	none	VIII	palette	marble	l	6K ?	D66	H29	none
2389.	1024	31-52-402	none	VIII	rubbing	basalt	l	6K ?	H76	D47	none
2390.	1048	31-52-397	none	VIII	pick	green stone	k	6K ?	L59	none	ina
2391.	1055	31-52-396	none	VIII	celt	green stone	m	7K ?	L46	W27	ina
2392.	1076	31-52-403	none	VIII	rubbing	basalt	g	5J ?	H57	D59	none
2393.	1113	31-52-394	none	VIII	blade	serpentine	O2	5O ?	L142	W45	none
2394.	1094	31-52-400	none	VII	smoother	calcine shale	g2	10M	L49	W11	ina
2395.	1199	31-52-401	none	VIII	drill bit	blue stone	Mk4	8Q ?	L77	none	ina
2396.	1656	Dropsie	none	VIIIA	macehead	stone	J2	5K	H55	D60	ina
2397.	1657	Dropsie	none	VIIIA	ballista	stone	J2	5K	L80	D38	ina
2398.	5381	Baghdad	none	VIII	mortar	basalt	Me	9M	H65	B104	ina
2399.	5473	Baghdad	none	VIIIA	rubbing	basalt	Oa	7O	L69	T52	ina
2400.	5486	Baghdad	none	VIIIAB	celt	green stone	Ka	7K	T36	L55	ina
2401.	5492	32-21-442	none	VIII	macehead ?	stone	IIO	5O	L36	T41	ina
2402.	5494	32-21-444	none	VIII	rubbing	basalt	IIM	5M	L80	T46	ina
2403.	5581	Baghdad	none	VIIIAB	celt	basalt	Ma	7M	L51	T42	ina
2404.	5584	32-21-439	none	VIIIAB	macehead	basalt	Ma	7M	L54	T49	ina
2405.	5595	Baghdad	none	VIII	weight	basalt	Ma	7M	L76	none	ina
2406.	5618	32-21-445	none	VIIIAB	rubbing	basalt	Ma	7M	T44	D47	ina
2407.	5622	32-21-440	none	VIIIAB	macehead	limestone	none	8O	T45	D58	ina
2408.	5625	32-21-446	none	VIII	rubbing	stone	none	none	T47	D68	ina
2409.	5635	Baghdad	none	VIIIAB	macehead	gray stone	Ma	7M	L52	T59	T32
2410.	5648	32-21-447	none	VIII	rubbing	basalt	Kc	8K	L71	T55	ina
2411.	5653	32-21-437	none	VIII	celt	green stone	IIO	5O	L39	W43	ina
2412.	5654	32-21-429	none	VIII	celt	blue gray stone	IIO	5O	L46	W36	ina
2413.	5655	32-21-430	none	VIII	celt	black stone	IIO	5O	L48	W28	ina
2414.	5656	Baghdad	none	VIII	hammer ?	gray stone	IIO	5O	L55	T13	ina
2415.	5666	32-21-457	none	VIII	hammer	basalt	Kc	8K	L99	T54	ina
2416.	5670	32-21-454	none	VIII	smoother	gray stone	Oc	8O	L46	W18	none
2417.	5671	32-21-455	none	VIII	smoother	gray stone	Kc	8K	L60	W14	ina
2418.	5672	Baghdad	none	VIII	ballista	stone	Ma	7M	L66	D37	D26
2419.	5682	32-21-431	none	VIII	celt	green stone	Ma ?	8M	L42	W26	ina
2420.	5683	Baghdad	none	VIII	celt	green stone	Kc	8K	L37	T32	ina
2421.	5684	32-21-448	none	VIII	rubbing	basalt	IIO	5O	L57	D56	D43
2422.	5694	Baghdad	none	VIIIAB	rubbing	basalt	none	8O	L83	T55	ina
2423.	5696	32-21-459	none	VIIIB ?	weight ?	haematite	Ke	9K	L18	T9	ina
2424.	5697	32-21-461	none	VIIIAB	disc	haemetite	Ke	9K	D18	T12	ina
2425.	5714	Dropsie	none	VIIIA6-sub ?	celt	diorite	Jc	8J	L54	W32	ina
2426.	5715	Baghdad	none	VIIIA6-sub ?	celt	gray stone	Jc	8J	L3	W22	ina
2427.	5721	32-21-449	none	VIIIAB	rubbing	basalt	Ma	7M	L91	T64	ina
2428.	5730	32-21-468	none	VIIIAB	lid	sandstone	Ma	7M	D79	T22	ina
2429.	5736	32-21-441	none	VIII	macehead	limestone	Oc	8O	L55	D55	ina
2430.	5738	Baghdad	none	VIII	celt	stone	IO	6O	L73	W58	ina
2431.	5750	32-21-450	none	VIII	rubbing	basalt	Ke	9K	L145	W97	ina
2432.	5755	Baghdad	none	VIII	weight	haematite	IM	6M	L29	T10	ina
2433.	5757	32-21-432	none	VIII	celt	basalt	IIO	5O	L50	W35	ina
2434.	5761	32-21-462	none	VIII	weight ?	blue gray stone	Og	10O	L57	W35	ina
2435.	5762	32-21-451	none	VIII	rubbing	basalt	Og	10O	D56	none	ina
2436.	5763	Baghdad	none	VIII	weight	basalt	Og	10O	L102	none	ina

15	16	17	18	19
silo				
unknown				
unknown				
unknown				
unknown	headless			
unknown	fragmentary			
unknown				
unknown				
unknown				
unknown				
SW of altar in Room 802	elev. 13.26m	signs of grinding		
in stone plate NE of altar	room 802	ground tip	red pigment	
SE of Altar in Room 802	brazier ?			
NE of altar in Rm 802	with stone phallus	mortar ?		
trial trench				
trial trench				
trial trench				
trial trench				
trial trench				
trial trench				
trial trench	pecked & polished			
trial trench	pecked & polished			
unknown				
trial trench				
room 804				
room 804				
unknown	or bowl ?			
room 810	smooth base			
unknown				
unknown				
unknown	like 5473 more convex			
room 812	damaged & repaired			
room 812	pear-shaped	repaired		
unknown	suspension like 5091			
room 812	like 5098			
room 818	polished			
unknown	polished	flat bottom		
unknown	cracked by burning			
unknown	like 5081			
unknown	edge well polished			
unknown	polished			
unknown	polished			
unknown	elliptical with pointed	ends		
unknown	two heads			
unknown	like 5481			
unknown	like 5481			
unknown	flattened sides			
room 812B	cutting edge used			
unknown	triangular			
unknown	like 5081			
room 818	2 sides flattened			
silo	elliptical			
unknown	weight ?			
unknown				
unknown				
unknown	two ends used			
unknown	like 5485			
unknown	pear shaped			
unknown	polished			
unknown	elliptical	one side flat		
unknown	flattened ends			
unknown				
unknown	oval pebble knotched			
unknown	two ends used			
unknown	like 5091			

(*continues*)

Level VIII   (continued)

1	2	3	4	5	6	7	8	9	11	12	13
2437.	5764	Baghdad	none	VIII	celt	gray stone	dump	dump	L47	W32	ina
2438.	5765	Baghdad	none	VIIIA	palette	basalt	none	8O	D185	T43	ina
2439.	5783	Baghdad	none	VIII	weight	basalt	Me	9M	L101	none	ina
2440.	5810	Baghdad	none	VIII	smoother	purple stone	IK	6K	L44	W20	ina
2441.	5812	32-21-464	none	VIII	ballista	diorite	Qa	7Q	L68	T39	ina
2442.	5818	Baghdad	none	VIII	celt	gray stone	Ka	7K	L42	W28	ina
2443.	5829	Baghdad	none	VIII	celt	basalt	Kc	8K	L75	W42	ina
2444.	5835	Baghdad	none	VIII	macehead	stone	Ka	7K	L58	D76	ina
2445.	5836	Baghdad	none	VIII	maul ?	granite	Ka	7K	L96	T52	ina
2446.	5838	Baghdad	none	VIII	object	marble	Jc	8J	L77	T36	ina
2447.	5850	Baghdad	none	VIII	smoother	gray stone	none	none	L40	W16	none
2448.	5884	Baghdad	none	VIIIBC	celt	green graystone	Kc	9K	L49	W37	ina
2449.	5890	32-21-433	none	VIIIBC	celt ?	green stone	Kc	8K	L110	W51	ina
2450.	5894	Baghdad	none	VIIIBC	celt	brown stone	Me	9M	L60	W33	ina
2451.	5895	32-21-465	none	VIIIBC	ballista	marble	Me	9M	L58	T36	ina
2452.	5899	32-21-452	none	VIII	rubbing	gray stone	IO	6O	D28	T18	ina
2453.	5903	32-21-434	none	VIIIBC	celt	gray stone	IO	6O	L28	W29	ina
2454.	5936	Baghdad	none	VIII	perforator	red stone	dump	dump	L41	T11	ina
2455.	5941	32-21-460	none	VIIIBC	hammer	stone	Me	9M	L56	D30	ina
2456.	5942	32-21-435	none	VIIIBC	celt	gray stone	Mg	10M	L53	W37	ina
2457.	5946	unknown	none	VIIIA	celt	black stone	Ma	7M	L31	T27	ina
2458.	5951	unknown	none	VIIIBC	lid	pink stone	Me	9M	D68	T13	ina
2459.	5971	32-21-453	none	VIIIA	rubbing	basalt ?	Ke	9K	L71	W41	ina
2460.	5972	unknown	none	VIIIC	pebble	gray stone	Ke	9K	L72	W38	T22
2461.	5973	unknown	none	VIIIC	hammer ??	unknown	Ke	9K	L65	W55	T25
2462.	5974	32-21-463	none	VIIIC	pebble	sandstone	Mg	10M	L103	W54	ina
2463.	5975	unknown	none	VIIIA	celt	green stone	IIIM	4M	L225	T12	ina
2464.	5978	32-21-436	none	VIIIC	celt	gray stone	Ke	9K	L48	W26	ina
2465.	6083	32-21-438	none	VIII	celt	serpentine	Q7	7Q	L36	W38	ina
2466.	6095	32-21-470	none	VIIIA	battle axe	stone	none	none	none	none	none
2467.	6097	Baghdad	none	VIIIA	battle axe	basalt	none	none	L93	T60	ina
2468.	2-none	32-21-456	none	VIII	smoother	gray stone	Oc	8O	L58	none	ina
2469.	3-036	33-3-15	none	VIII	macehead	stone	12K	8J	L52	W54	T28
2470.	3-055	33-3-25	none	VIII	buffer	black stone	11H	10K	L60	W22	T4
2471.	3-056	Baghdad	none	VIII	celt	serpentine	dump	dump	L39	W20	T10
2472.	3-065	Baghdad	none	VIII	counter	marble	10K	8M	D19	T5	ina
2473.	3-066	Baghdad	none	VIII	hammer	stone	10K	8M	L42	W40	T25
2474.	3-079	Baghdad	none	VIII	burnisher	black stone	9K	8O	L43	W20	T7
2475.	3-081	Baghdad	none	VIII	celt	slate	10H	10M	L71	W38	T11
2476.	3-093	Baghdad	none	VIII	hammer	gray stone	12L	7J	D105	T50	ina
2477.	3-109	Baghdad	none	VIII	sphere	yellow stone	8J	9Q	D20	ina	ina
2478.	3-135	33-3-61	none	VIII	celt	serpentine	9K	8O	L38	W27	T7
2479.	3-none	33-3-280	none	VIII	battle ax	green granite	9L	7O	L93	W65	T3.2
2480.	3-none	33-3-281	none	VIII	pestle	basalt	none	none	L102	W80	T60
2481.	3-none	33-3-282	none	VIII	pestle	basalt	none	none	L90	W84	T65
	Jewelry										
2482.	1025	31-52-413	none	VIII	bead	blue limestone	L	7M ?	L33	ina	ina
2483.	1028	31-52-372	none	VIII	amulet ?	shell	K	7M ?	L60	W54	ina
2484.	1063	31-52-409	none	VIII	beads	sandstone	e	6J ?	L25	W13	ina
2485.	1082	31-52-410	none	VIII	ring	shell obsidian	g	9M ?	none	none	none
2486.	1106	31-52-285	none	VIII	amulets	steatite ?	none	10M	L14	none	ina
2487.	1146	31-52-411	none	VIII	beads	shell	I3	6M ?	none	none	none
2488.	5479	Baghdad	none	VIII	pendant	obsidian	Oa	7O	L20	W9	T3
2489.	5582	Baghdad	none	VIII	bead	limestone	Ka	7K	L52	T11	ina
2490.	5583	32-21-472	none	VIIIAB	pendant	obsidian	Ma	7M	L34	W8	ina
2491.	5585	32-21-474	none	VIII	amulet	carnelian ?	IO	6O	L30	ina	ina
2492.	5596	32-21-471	none	VIII	pendant	blue gray stone	IK	6K	L63	none	ina
2493.	5601	32-21-476	none	VIIIAB	beads	stone	Ma	7M	L630	ina	ina
2494.	5608	Baghdad	none	VIIIAB	beads	shell	Ma	7M	ina	ina	ina
2495.	5651	32-21-477	none	VIIIAB	bead	bone	Ma ?	8M	L31	D11	ina
2496.	5660	Baghdad	none	VIII	ring	shell	IIO	5O	D24	ina	ina
2497.	5674	Baghdad	none	VIII	pendant	rose quartz	IIK	5K	L24	W16	ina
2498.	5737	Baghdad	none	VIII	beads	stone shell	none	none	ina	ina	ina
2499.	5749	32-21-443	none	VIII	pendant	stone	Ke	9K	L113	W53	ina
2500.	5756	Baghdad	none	VIII ?	pendant	black stone	none	none	L14	D10	ina
2501.	5758	Baghdad	none	VIII	pendant	blgray stone	Oc	8O	L16	W13	ina
2502.	5771	Dropsie	none	VIII	pendant	white stone	Oc	8O	L15	W9	ina

15	16	17	18	19
unknown	polished cutting edge			
room 834	round			
unknown				
unknown	like 5481			
unknown	basalt ?			
unknown	polished			
unknown	almost adze shaped			
unknown	unfinished hole			
unknown				
unknown	blunt edged ballista ?			
unknown	like 5481			
unknown	polished blade			
unknown	end battered in use			
unknown	badly worn			
unknown				
unknown	well polished in use			
unknown	sharp cutting edge			
unknown				
with core and blades ?	elliptical weight ?			
unknown				
unknown				
unknown				
unknown	rectangular surface			
unknown	perforated	weight ?		
unknown	with bitumen	triangular shaped		
unknown	notched on two sides			
unknown				
unknown				
unknown				
unknown				
unknown				
unknown	split in drilling			
unknown				
unknown				
unknown				
unknown	conical indent on top			
unknown				
unknown	badly chipped			
unknown	circular			
unknown	covered with wavy lines			
unknown				
unknown				
unknown				
unknown				
unknown				
unknown				
trial trench				
unknown	torquoise ?			
trial trench				
unknown	top painted			
unknown				
room 812	like 5479			
unknown	incised cross-hatching			
unknown	polished perforated			
room 812	discolored by burning			
room 812	all burned			
room 812B	burned			
unknown	or white stone			
unknown				
unknown	also lapis lazuli			
unknown				
unknown				
unknown				
unknown				

(continues)

Level VIII　(continued)

1	2	3	4	5	6	7	8	9	11	12	13
2503.	5772	32-21-479	none	VIII	beads	shell stone	IIO	5O	ina	ina	ina
2504.	5778	32-21-480	none	VIII	bead	shell	IO	6O	L7	D14	ina
2505.	5779	Baghdad	none	VIIIA	pin	bronze lapis	none	5K	L88	none	ina
2506.	5800	Baghdad	none	VIIIAB	beads	shell paste	none	8O	ina	ina	ina
2507.	5801	32-21-481	none	VIII	beads	stone paste	IIM	5M	ina	ina	ina
2508.	5809	Baghdad	none	VIII	pendant	gray stone	IK	6K	L30	W24	ina
2509.	5857	32-21-371	none	VIIIA	bracelet	bronze	none	9O	D45	none	ina
2510.	5868	32-21-375	none	VIIIBC	bead	gold	Me	9M	L12	D6	ina
2511.	5869	Baghdad	none	VIIIBC	pendant	gold	Me	9M	L29	W19	ina
2512.	5913A	32-21-483	none	VIII	beads	stone bone	Me	9M	ina	ina	ina
2513.	5913B	Baghdad	none	VIII	beads 911	shell quartz	Me	9M	ina	ina	ina
2514.	5920	32-21-487	none	VIII	beads	carnelian	none	none	ina	ina	ina
2515.	5921	Baghdad	none	VIIIA	beads	stone	none	11K ?	ina	ina	ina
2516.	5940	Baghdad	none	VIIIBC	amulet	steatite	Me	9M	L25	W14	ina
2517.	5952	32-21-475	none	VIIIA	amulet	black stone	Me	9M	L16	T10	ina
2518.	5990	unknown	none	VIIIC	pendant	red stone	Ki	11K	L17	D9	ina
2519.	5992	32-21-473	none	VIIIA	pendant	gray stone	Ki	11K	L27	W20	ina
2520.	3-008	Baghdad	none	VIII	bead	limestone	11M	6K	D11	T5	ina
2521.	3-013	33-3-7	none	VIII	pendant	stone	11L	7K	L20	W12	T5
2522.	3-014	Baghdad	none	VIII	bead	obsidian	9K	8O	D17	T3	ina
2523.	3-033	discarded	none	VIII	bead	carnelian	12K	8J	D8	T5	ina
2524.	3-049	33-3-23	none	VIII	pendant	obsidian	11L	7K	L32	T6	ina
2525.	3-050	Baghdad	none	VIII	bead	obsidian	10P	4M	D7	T3	ina
2526.	3-061	33-3-28	none	VIII	button	bone	11J	9K	D17	T7	ina
2527.	3-070	33-3-35	none	VIII	button	buffware	dump	dump	L9	D19	BD17
2528.	3-076	33-3-88	none	VIII	bead	rose quartz	8M	6Q	L15	W9	T6
2529.	3-120	Baghdad	none	VIII	pendant	black stone	11J	9K	L17	W21	T5
2530.	3-129	33-3-58	none	VIII ?	pendant ?	marble	dump	dump	L19	W14	T6
2531.	3-148	33-3-70	none	VIII ?	amulet	marble	dump	dump	L10	W11	T4
2532.	3-186	Baghdad	none	VIII	pendant	gray stone	10J	9M	L18	T8	ina
2533.	3-187	Baghdad	none	VIII	pendant	limestone	10J	9M	L11	W2	T3
	Lithics										
2534.	1-none	31-52-390	none	VIII	arrowhead	obsidian	none	none	L63	W30	T6.4
2535.	1-none	31-52-393	none	VIII	blade	obsidian	M	7M ?	none	none	none
2536.	1-none	31-52-392	none	VIII	blade	obsidian	none	none	L60	W15	T4
2537.	1-none	31-52-392	none	VIII	blade	obsidian	none	none	L92	W23	T5.2
2538.	1-none	31-52-392	none	VIII	blade	obsidian	none	none	L47	W17	T3
2539.	1-none	31-52-392	none	VIII	blade	obsidian	none	none	L47	W17	T3.3
2540.	1-none	31-52-392	none	VIII	blade	obsidian	none	none	L83	W18	T4
2541.	1-none	31-52-392	none	VIII	blade	obsidian	none	none	L33	W15	W3.8
2542.	1-none	31-52-392	none	VIII	blade	obsidian	none	none	L62	W16	T5.5
2543.	1-none	31-52-392	none	VIII	blade	obsidian	none	none	L56	W17	T3.9
2544.	1-none	31-52-392	none	VIII	blade	obsidian	none	none	L47	W23	T3
2545.	1-none	31-52-392	none	VIII	blade	obsidian	none	none	L57	W16	T3
2546.	1-none	31-52-392	none	VIII	blade	obsidian	none	none	L46	W11	T2.8
2547.	1-none	31-52-392	none	VIII	blade	obsidian	none	none	L43	W18	T4.1
2548.	1-none	31-52-392	none	VIII	blade	obsidian	none	none	L60	W15	T2.7
2549.	1-none	31-52-392	none	VIII	blade	obsidian	none	none	L46	W10	T6.7
2550.	1010a	31-52-392	none	VIII	blade	obsidian	M	7M ?	L47	W18	T5.3
2551.	1010b	31-52-392	none	VIII	blade	obsidian	M	7M ?	L49	W13	T4.4
2552.	1010c	31-52-392	none	VIII	blade	obsidian	M	7M ?	L50	W14	T7
2553.	1010d	31-52-392	none	VIII	blade	obsidian	M	7M ?	L43	W15	T3.8
2554.	1010e	31-52-392	none	VIII	blade	obsidian	M	7M ?	L38	W13	T3.1
2555.	1010f	31-52-392	none	VIII	blade	obsidian	M	7M ?	L33	W15	T2.9
2556.	1010g	31-52-392	none	VIII	blade	obsidian	M	7M ?	L35	W13	T3.4
2557.	1016a	31-52-392	none	VIII	blade	obsidian	M	7M ?	L39	W14	T4.3
2558.	1016b	31-52-392	none	VIII	blade	obsidian	M	7M ?	L51	W16	T3.4
2559.	1016c	31-52-392	none	VIII	blade	obsidian	M	7M ?	L48	W14	T4.5
2560.	1016d	31-52-392	none	VIII	blade	obsidian	M	7M ?	L40	W14	T3.7
2561.	1016e	31-52-392	none	VIII	blade	obsidian	M	7M ?	L35	W13	T4.1
2562.	1019b	31-52-392	none	VIII	blade	obsidian	M	7M ?	L25	W13	T4
2563.	1019a	31-52-392	none	VIII	blade	obsidian	M	7M ?	L57	W17	T4.7
2564.	1019c	31-52-392	none	VIII	blade	obsidian	M	7M ?	L51	W19	T3.3
2565.	1019d	31-52-392	none	VIII	blade	obsidian	M	7M ?	L59	W17	T4.5
2566.	1019e	31-52-392	none	VIII	blade	obsidian	M	7M ?	L59	W16	T4.7
2567.	1019f	31-52-392	none	VIII	blade	obsidian	M	7M ?	L50	W16	T5.4
2568.	1056a	31-52-392	none	VIII	blade	obsidian	M	7M ?	L38	W10	T3.6

15	16	17	18	19
unknown				
unknown	square			
room 803	lapis bead at head			
room 818				
unknown				
unknown	unfinished			
room 826	square			
unknown				
unknown				
unknown	also shell ceramic			
unknown	also obsidian stone			
unknown	also agate stone shell			
unknown				
unknown				
unknown	animal head			
unknown				
unknown				
unknown	white	fluted		
unknown				
unknown	pierced at center			
unknown	spheroid			
unknown	polished			
unknown	crudely cut			
unknown	pierced off center			
unknown	pierced			
unknown				
unknown	flat			
unknown	part missing			
unknown	foot shaped			
found with 3-187	incised at top			
found with 3-186	soft	white		
trial trench	blank			
trial trench				
trial trench	striations 38 unused			
trial trench	retouch 54 striations 42			
trial trench	little wear 23 & 24			
trial trench	retouch 43 unused 32			
trial trench	striations	used 38 & 43		
trial trench	striations 38 retouch 44			
trial trench	grinding 45	striations 49		
trial trench	striations retouch 45	& 49		
trial trench	striations 42 retouch 39			
trial trench	slight striations 31, 32			
trial trench	striations	retouch 44 & 44		
trial trench	retouch 57 striations 32			
trial trench	retouch 43 & 49			
trial trench	retouch 63 & 52			
trial trench	use retouch 48 & 53			
trial trench	much use 61	minor use 37		
trial trench	much use 65 unused 54			
trial trench	use striations 43 & 46			
trial trench	little used 38 & 52			
trial trench	little used 39 & 34			
trial trench	little used 29 & 31			
trial trench	minor use 34 & 47			
trial trench	dense striations 36 & 39			
trial trench	dense striations 38	unused 58		
trial trench	striations 43 unused 54			
trial trench	much use 57	some use 52		
trial trench	pointed edge 29			
trial trench	much use 48 & 49			
trial trench	much use striations 47,	44		
trial trench	use striations 40	less use 47		
trial trench	wide striations 40	use 46		
trial trench	wide striations 48	used 44		
trial trench	little used 34 & 48			

(*continues*)

Level VIII   (continued)

1	2	3	4	5	6	7	8	9	11	12	13
2569.	1056b	31-52-392	none	VIII	blade	obsidian	M	7M ?	L27	W13	T2.9
2570.	1056c	31-52-392	none	VIII	blade	obsidian	M	7M ?	L33	W11	T3.7
2571.	1056d	31-52-392	none	VIII	blade	obsidian	M	7M ?	L37	W13	T2.4
2572.	1056e	31-52-392	none	VIII	blade	obsidian	M	7M ?	L28	W13	T2.5
2573.	1056f	31-52-392	none	VIII	blade	obsidian	M	7M ?	L33	W13	T2.6
2574.	1056g	31-52-392	none	VIII	blade	obsidian	M	7M ?	L29	W10	T3.6
2575.	1056h	31-52-392	none	VIII	blade	obsidian	M	7M ?	L28	W10	T2.8
2576.	1147a	31-52-392	none	VIII	blade	obsidian	M	7M ?	L56	W10	T2.7
2577.	1147b	31-52-392	none	VIII	blade	obsidian	M	7M ?	L43	W13	T4.2
2578.	1147c	31-52-392	none	VIII	blade	obsidian	M	7M ?	L48	W10	T3
2579.	1147d	31-52-392	none	VIII	blade	obsidian	M	7M ?	L44	W10	T3.8
2580.	1147e	31-52-392	none	VIII	sickle	obsidian	M	7M ?	L33	W15	T2.7
2581.	1147f	31-52-392	none	VIII	blade	obsidian	M	7M ?	L33	W15	T3.3
2582.	1225	31-52-389	none	VIII	blade	obsidian	K5	6M ?	L92	W23	T6
2583.	1225	31-52-391	none	VIII	blade	obsidian	K5	6M ?	L93	W13	T4.3
2584.	2-none	32-21-404	none	VIII	blade	flint	none	none	L63	W25	T4
2585.	2-none a	32-21-404	none	VIIIBC	sickle	flint	Me	9M	L50	W20	T4.7
2586.	2-none b	32-21-404	none	VIII	blade	flint	Ja	7J	L65	W22	T4.8
2587.	2-none d	32-21-404	none	VIII	blade	flint	Qa	7Q	L68	W18	none
2588.	2-none e	32-21-404	none	VIII	blade	flint	Me	9M	L70	W17	T4.5
2589.	2-none f	32-21-404	none	VIII	blade	flint	none	none	L58	W13	T6
2590.	2-none g	32-21-404	none	VIII	blade	flint	none	none	L77	W22	T5
2591.	2-none h	32-21-404	none	VIIIBC	blade	flint	Me	9M	L64	W24	T7.4
2592.	2-none i	32-21-404	none	VIII	blade	flint	Og	10O	L62	W19	T4.5
2593.	2-none j	32-21-404	none	VIII	blade	flint	Of	9O	L71	W18	T5
2594.	2-none k	32-21-404	none	VIIIBC	blade	flint	Me	9M	L40	W19	T6.2
2595.	2-none l	32-21-404	none	VIII	blade	flint	Kc	8K	L68	W27	T5
2596.	5264	Baghdad	none	VIII A ?	blade	flint	Of	9O	L137	W21	ina
2597.	5265	Baghdad	none	VIII A ?	blade	flint	Of	9O	L93	W21	ina
2598.	5266	Baghdad	none	VIII A ?	blade	flint	Of	9O	L83	W21	ina
2599.	5267	32-21-407	none	VIII A ?	blade	obsidian	Of	9O	L71	W14	T5
2600.	5268	Baghdad	none	VIII A ?	core	flint	Of	9O	L60	none	ina
2601.	5371	Baghdad	none	VIII	arrowhead	obsidian	Mc	9M	L62	W26	ina
2602.	5377	Baghdad	none	VIII	blade	obsidian	Me	9M	L50	none	ina
2603.	5484	32-21-405	none	VIII	core	flint	Oc	8O	L115	W65	T23
2604.	5488	32-21-386	none	VIII	blade	flint	IO	6O	L148	W23	T5.2
2605.	5489	32-21-388	none	VIII	blade	flint	IIO	5O	L112	W60	ina
2606.	5587	32-21-387	none	VIIIAB	blade	flint	Ma	7M	L114	W26	ina
2607.	5589	Baghdad	none	VIIIAB	blade	flint	Ma	7M	L69	W18	ina
2608.	5590	Baghdad	none	VIIIAB	blade	obsidian	Ma	7M	L54	W8	ina
2609.	5591	32-21-408	none	VIIIAB	blade	obsidian	Ma	7M	L41	W11	ina
2610.	5592	Baghdad	none	VIIIAB	blade	obsidian	Ma	7M	L38	W9	ina
2611.	5593	32-21-409	none	VIIIA	blade	obsidian	Ma	7M	L205	W34	ina
2612.	5611	Baghdad	none	VIIIAB	arrowhead	flint	Ma	7M	L33	W25	ina
2613.	5630	32-21-389	none	VIII	blade	flint	IIO	5O	L100	W22	ina
2614.	5637	32-21-383	none	VIII	arrowhead	flint	Kc	8K	L45	W28	ina
2615.	5652	Baghdad	none	VIII	arrowhead	flint	IIO	5O	L39	W26	ina
2616.	5667	32-21-390	none	VIIIAB	blade	calcedony ?	Kc	8K	L92	W22	ina
2617.	5668	32-21-391	none	VIIIAB	blade	flint	Kc	8K	L77	W15	ina
2618.	5669	32-21-384	none	VIII	arrowhead	flint	Oc	8O	L34	W23	T6.2
2619.	5685	Baghdad	none	VIII	blade	flint	Kc	8K	L67	W16	ina
2620.	5705	32-21-392	none	VIII	blade	tan flint	none	8O	L110	W20	ina
2621.	5716	Dropsie	none	VIIIA 6-sub	arrowhead	dark gray	flint	Jc	no plate	L44	W27
2622.	5739	Baghdad	none	VIII	blade	flint	IIM	5M	L141	W31	ina
2623.	5743	32-21-410	none	VIII	blade	obsidian	IJ	6J	L157	W32	ina
2624.	5747	Baghdad	none	VIII	blade	tan flint	Ke	9K	L99	W24	ina
2625.	5748	32-21-411	none	VIII	blade	obsidian	Ke	9K	L61	W10	ina
2626.	5760	32-21-393	none	VIII	blade	flint	Og	10O	L76	W32	T8
2627.	5760 b	32-21-393	none	VIII	blade	flint	Og	10O	L36	W13	T4.5
2628.	5760 c	32-21-393	none	VIII	blade	flint	Og	10O	L46	W18	T5
2629.	5766	unknown	none	VIII	blade	obsidian	Oa	7O	L92	W16	ina
2630.	5767	Baghdad	none	VIII	blade	obsidian	Oa	7O	L70	W13	ina
2631.	5786	32-21-394	none	VIII	blade	gray flint	none	none	L100	W23	T5
2632.	5797	32-21-412	none	VIII	blade	obsidian	dump	dump	L24	W5	T2.3
2633.	5802	Baghdad	none	VIII	blade	gray flint	Ke	9K	L92	W21	ina
2634.	5815	Baghdad	none	VIII	blade	obsidian	Qa	7Q	L51	W13	ina
2635.	5825	Baghdad	none	VIII	blade	obsidian	IIIM	4M	L98	W24	ina

15	16	17	18	19
trial trench	much retouch 40 & 43			
trial trench	unused 41 & 41			
trial trench	little used 39 & 37			
trial trench	unused 47 & 26			
trial trench	backed 66 striations 37			
trial trench	little used 37 & 32			
trial trench	little used 30 & 34			
trial trench	little used 40 & 46			
trial trench	little used 52 & 32			
trial trench	little used 33 & 32			
trial trench	unused 50 & 41			
trial trench	little used 40 & 25			
trial trench	striations 32 unused 24			
trial trench	striations 32 & 39			
trial trench	use striations 32 & 41			
trial trench	44 serrated 27			
trial trench	sheen 39 unused 29			
trial trench	little used 25 & 29			
trial trench	use 47 unused 41			
trial trench	serrated 48 & 41			
trial trench	serrated 41 serrated 41			
trial trench	serrated 31 serrated 43			
trial trench	use 44 unused 31			
trial trench	sheen	serrated 38 & 38		
trial trench	serrated 36 serrated 41			
trial trench	little used 31 & 38			
trial trench	serrated 31 backed 32			
between 9O and 10O				
between 9O and 10O				
between 9O and 10O				
unknown	much use striation 39, 35			
unknown				
unknown	leaf shaped			
unknown				
unknown	11 to 16 mm blades			
unknown	unused 27 retouch 28			
unknown	blunt retouch 42			
room 812	little used 29 & 24			
room 812				
room 812				
room 812	minor use 29 & 33			
unknown				
Room 812	repaired			
room 812				
unknown	minor use 31 & 32			
unknown				
unknown				
silo	minor use 32 & 29			
silo	little used 35 & 29			
unknown				
unknown				
room 830	used 33 & 35			
ina				
unknown				
unknown	little used 26 & 24			
unknown				
unknown	retouch 42 & 48			
unknown	retouch 53 serrated 45			
unknown	serrated 56, 34			
unknown	little used 36 & 32			
unknown				
unknown				
unknown	serrated 38 & 34			
dump	unused 33 & 32			
unknown				
unknown				
unknown				

(continues)

Level VIII   (continued)

1	2	3	4	5	6	7	8	9	11	12	13
2636.	5831	32-21-413	none	VIII	blade	obsidian	Kc	8K	L88	W16	T3.5
2637.	5843	32-21-395	none	VIII	blade	flint	IQ	6Q	L139	W23	T8.2
2638.	5844	Baghdad	none	VIII	blade	flint	IQ	6Q	L84	W20	ina
2639.	5852	Baghdad	none	VIIIAB	blade	flint	Ja	7J	L93	W17	ina
2640.	5860	32-21-414	none	VIII	blade	obsidian	IO	6O	L82	W17	ina
2641.	5861	32-21-415	none	VIIIA	blade	obsidian	IO	6O	L80	W21	ina
2642.	5866	Baghdad	none	VIIIA	blade	obsidian	Ja	7J	L39	W10	ina
2643.	5871	Baghdad	none	VIIIBC	blade	obsidian	Kc	8K	L85	W17	ina
2644.	5872	32-21-396	none	VIIIBC	blade	tan flint	Kc	8K	L77	W17	T4.8
2645.	5873	32-21-427	none	VIIIBC	scraper	obsidian	Kc	8K	L66	W28	T6.5
2646.	5875	32-21-397	none	VIIIBC	blade	tan flint	IK	6K	L117	W20	T4.8
2647.	5876	32-21-416	none	VIIIBC	blade	obsidian	IK	6K	L99	W18	T4.4
2648.	5877	32-21-417	none	VIIIBC	blade	obsidian	IK	6K	L58	W11	T2.6
2649.	5886	Baghdad	none	VIIIBC	blade	tan flint	Me	9M	L112	W18	T3.6
2650.	5887	Baghdad	none	VIIIBC	blade	obsidian	Me	9M	L87	W20	ina
2651.	5888	32-21-398	none	VIIIBC	blade	calcedony ?	Me	9M	L47	W13	T3.6
2652.	5892	32-21-399	none	VIIIBC	blade	tan flint	Me	9M	L87	W21	T5
2653.	5893	32-21-400	none	VIIIBC	blade	tan flint	Me	9M	L54	W11	T4.7
2654.	5896	Baghdad	none	VIIIAB	blade	tan flint	Me	9M	L48	W15	ina
2655.	5897	Baghdad	none	VIIIBC	blade	obsidian	IO	6O	L103	W18	ina
2656.	5898	Baghdad	none	VIIIBC	blade	obsidian	Ka	7K	L92	W21	ina
2657.	5901	32-21-401	none	VIIIB	blade	tan flint	Me	9M	L86	W33	T7.2
2658.	5902	32-21-402	none	VIIIBC	blade	flint	Me	9M	L175	W33	T9.2
2659.	5904	32-21-418	none	VIIIBC	blade	obsidian	Me	9M	L69	W12	T3
2660.	5928	Baghdad	none	VIIIBC	blade	obsidian	Ma	7M	L61	W9	ina
2661.	5929	32-21-420	none	VIIIBC	blade	obsidian	Ma	7M	L46	W8	T2.4
2662.	5930	Baghdad	none	VIIIBC	blade	obsidian	Ma	7M	L51	W15	ina
2663.	5937	32-21-406	none	VIIIBC	core	flint	Me	9M	L140	W66	ina
2664.	5938	Baghdad	none	VIIIA	blade	obsidian	Me	9M	L207	W33	ina
2665.	5939	Baghdad	none	VIIIA	blade	tan flint	Me	9M	L90	W21	ina
2666.	5949	32-21-419	none	VIIIA	blade	obsidian	Me	9M	L102	W20	T2.9
2667.	5950	Baghdad	none	VIIIBC	blade	obsidian	Me	9M	L65	W14	ina
2668.	5959	Dropsie	none	VIIIA	arrowhead	flint	Me	9M	L30	W27	ina
2669.	5960	unknown	none	VIIIA	blade	obsidian	Mg	10M	L120	W18	ina
2670.	5961	32-21-421	none	VIIIA	blade	obsidian	Mg	10M	L116	W15	T3.5
2671.	5962	unknown	none	VIIIA	blade	flint	Mg	10M	L103	W22	ina
2672.	5963	32-21-422	none	VIIIA	blade	obsidian	IIM	5M	L74	W17	ina
2673.	5964	32-21-385	none	VIIIA	arrowhead	obsidian	IIM	5M	L44	W20	T5
2674.	5965	unknown	none	VIIIA	blade	obsidian	Mg	10M	L78	W18	ina
2675.	5968	32-21-425	none	VIIIA	blade	obsidian	Me	9M	L63	W14	T3.1
2676.	5966	unknown	none	VIIIA	blade	obsidian	Mg	10M	L82	W17	ina
2677.	5967	32-21-424	none	VIIIA	blade	obsidian	Me	9M	L77	W14	T3.5
2678.	5969	unknown	none	VIIIA	blade	obsidian	Mg	10M	L46	W10	ina
2679.	5970	unknown	none	VIIIBC	blade	obsidian	Me	9M	L81	W22	ina
2680.	5995	unknown	none	VIIIC	blade	obsidian	Me	9M	L76	W15	ina
2681.	6003	32-21-428	none	VIII	core	obsidian	none	none	L100	W80	T58
2682.	6092	unknown	none	VIIIA	blade	obsidian	M6	6M	L48	W8	ina
2683.	6093	unknown	none	VIIIA	blade	obsidian	M6	6M	L50	W8	ina
2684.	6098	unknown	none	VIIIA	blade	flint	none	none	none	none	none
2685.	2-none	32-21-403	none	VIII	drill	flint	IO	6O	L58	W12	T4.4
2686.	2-none	32-21-423	none	VIII	blade	obsidian	none	none	L63	W13	T3.1
2687.	2-none a	32-21-426	none	VIII	blade	obsidian	Oa	7O	L58	W33	T5.7
2688.	2-none b	32-21-426	none	VIII	blade	obsidian	Me ?	9M	L50	W20	T3.2
2689.	2-none b	32-21-426	none	VIII	blade	obsidian	none	none	L53	W16	T3.7
2690.	2-none c	32-21-426	none	VIII	blade	obsidian	Me	9M	L50	W18	T4.5
2691.	2-none d	32-21-426	none	VIII	blade	obsidian	none	none	L47	W18	T5.5
2692.	2-none e	32-21-426	none	VIII	blade	obsidian	none	none	L33	W16	T3.1
2693.	2-none e	32-21-426	none	VIII	blade	obsidian	none	none	L48	W15	T2.5
2694.	2-none f	32-21-426	none	VIII	blade	obsidian	none	none	L28	W8	T2.3
2695.	2-none g	32-21-426	none	VIII	blade	obsidian	none	none	L47	W22	T5
2696.	2-none i	32-21-426	none	VIII	blade	obsidian	none	none	L68	W15	T4.2
2697.	2-none j	32-21-426	none	VIII	blade	obsidian	IO	6O	L57	W12	T3.4
2698.	2-none k	32-21-426	none	VIII	blade	obsidian	none	none	L59	W12	T4.2
2699.	2-none l	32-21-426	none	VIII	blade	obsidian	IO	6O	L75	W22	T4.6
2700.	2-none l	32-21-426	none	VIII	blade	obsidian	none	none	L45	W6	T2.7
2701.	2-none m	32-21-426	none	VIII	blade	obsidian	none	none	L46	W13	T3.2
2702.	2-none n	32-21-426	none	VIII	blade	obsidian	IK	6K	L63	W19	T5.4

15	16	17	18	19
unknown	used striations 33 & 36			
unknown	unused 44 & 32			
unknown				
unknown				
unknown	missing			
unknown	36 much retouch 55			
unknown				
unknown				
unknown	unused 37 & 35			
unknown	used 28 retouch 31			
unknown	unused 26 & 29			
unknown	striations	used 31 used 30		
unknown	retouch 31 & 30			
unknown	unused 26 & 33			
unknown				
unknown				
unknown	serrated 32 & 30			
unknown	unused 44 & 39			
unknown				
unknown				
unknown				
unknown	retouch 45 & 41			
unknown	unused 47 & 43			
unknown	retouch 36 little	used 29		
unknown				
unknown	minor use 43 & 45			
unknown				
unknown				
unknown				
unknown				
unknown	striations	use 26 use 27		
unknown				
unknown	convex base			
unknown	well chipped			
unknown	minor striations 29 & 29			
unknown				
unknown	well chipped	missing from storage		
unknown				
unknown				
unknown	minor use 35 & 26			
unknown				
unknown	use striations 33 use 37			
unknown				
unknown	edges chipped			
unknown				
unknown	raw lump			
unknown				
unknown				
unknown				
unknown	heavy retouch 75 & 75			
unknown				
unknown	unused 12 & 20			
unknown	unused 18 retouch 27			
unknown	striations 27 unused 22			
unknown	little used 22 & 26			
unknown	use 28 striations 31			
unknown	striations 23 retouch 26			
unknown	striations 19	striations 31		
unknown	striations 31 unused 19			
unknown	retouch 30 & 28			
unknown	striations 33 unused 24			
unknown	striations 25 use 36			
unknown	use 52 little use 38			
unknown	much use 37 & 28			
unknown	striations 44 unused 34			
unknown	striations 21 & 24			
unknown	striations 38 & 27			

(*continues*)

Level VIII (continued)

1	2	3	4	5	6	7	8	9	11	12	13
2703.	2-none p	32-21-426	none	VIII	blade	obsidian	IIO	5O	L88	W20	T4.1
2704.	2-none q	32-21-426	none	VIII	blade	obsidian	none	none	L54	W16	T4.7
2705.	2-none s	32-21-426	none	VIII	blade	obsidian	Mg	10M	L43	W11	T5
2706.	2-none t	32-21-426	none	VIIIBC	blade	obsidian	Mg	10M	L57	W17	T3.5
2707.	2-none u	32-21-426	none	VIII	blade	obsidian	Me	9M	L60	W11	T3.8
2708.	2-none v	32-21-426	none	VIII	blade	obsidian	Mg	10M	L57	W18	T7.3
2709.	2-none w	32-21-426	none	VIII	blade	obsidian	Ma	7M	L63	W18	T4.4
2710.	2-none x	32-21-426	none	VIII	blade	obsidian	none	none	L43	W19	T5.3
2711.	2-none y	32-21-426	none	VIII	blade	obsidian	none	none	L59	W13	T3.6
2712.	2-none z	32-21-426	none	VIII	blade	obsidian	Mg	10M	L47	W15	T3.5
2713.	3-023	Baghdad	none	VIII	blade	obsidian	12K	8J	L90	W22	T5
2714.	3-024	33-3-11	none	VIII	blade	obsidian	12J	9J	L140	W27	T7.6
2715.	3-057	Baghdad	none	VIII	blade	flint	8K	8Q	L104	W26	T7
2716.	3-058	33-3-26	none	VIII	blade	flint	9L	7O	L116	W24	T4.6
2717.	3-068	33-3-33	none	VIII	blade	obsidian	10J	9M	L116	W26	T5.2
2718.	3-075	Baghdad	none	VIII	blade	flint	9L	7O	L113	W24	T6
2719.	3-078	33-3-39	none	VIII	blade	obsidian	8L	7Q	L69	W13	T3
2720.	3-116	Baghdad	none	VIII	core	obsidian	9L	7O	L131	D45	ina
2721.	3-119	Baghdad	none	VIII	blade	flint	12L	7J	L104	W19	T4
	Metal	**item**									
2722.	1659	31-52-407	none	VIIIA	wire	bronze	none	5K	L115	ina	ina
2723.	5619	Baghdad	none	VIIIA	needle	bronze	IM	6M	L81	none	ina
2724.	5632	32-21-367	none	VIIIAB 6sub ?	disc	bronze	Kc	8K	D64	none	ina
2725.	5633	32-21-368	none	VIIIAB	disc	bronze	Kc	8K	D61	none	ina
2726.	5634	32-21-356	none	VIIIA	dagger	bronze	none	9O	L195	W34	T2
2727.	5645	Baghdad	none	VIIIA	needle	bronze	none	9O	L88	none	ina
2728.	5657	32-21-357	none	VIIIAB 6sub ?	arrowhead	bronze	Kc	8K	L66	none	ina
2729.	5659	Baghdad	none	VIII	needle	bronze	IIO	5O	L103	none	ina
2730.	5661	32-21-361	none	VIII	nail	bronze	IIO	5O	L63	none	ina
2731.	5690	Baghdad	none	VIII	needle	bronze	Kc	8K	L129	ina	ina
2732.	5692	Baghdad	none	VIIIB ?	chisel	bronze	Ke	9K	L178	D14	ina
2733.	5693	Baghdad	none	VIIIA	hook	bronze	Ma	7M	L168	T7	ina
2734.	5695	32-21-362	none	VIIIB ?6-sub	needle	bronze	Ke	9K	L107	none	ina
2735.	5699	32-21-359	none	VIIIB ? 6-sub	chisel	bronze	Ke	9K	L121	none	ina
2736.	5701	32-21-369	none	VIIIAB6-sub	hook	bronze	Kc	8K	L102	none	ina
2737.	5702	Baghdad	none	VIIIAB6-sub	hook	bronze	Kc	8K	L53	none	ina
2738.	5717	Baghdad	none	VIIIA	ring	bronze	Jc	8J	D16	none	ina
2739.	5718	32-21-132	none	VIIIA6-sub ?	wire frag	bronze	Jc	8J	D54	T.8	ina
2740.	5733	Baghdad	none	VIIIA 6-sub ?	chisel	bronze	Ja	7J	L120	none	ina
2741.	5734	Baghdad	none	VIIIAB	ring	bronze	Kc	8K	D13	ina	ina
2742.	5746	Baghdad	none	VIII	needle	bronze	Oc	8O	L121	none	ina
2743.	5752	Dropsie	none	VIII	needle	bronze	Me	9M	L113	none	ina
2744.	5753	32-21-363	none	VIII	needle	bronze	Me	9M	L122	none	ina
2745.	5759	Baghdad	none	VIII	implement	bronze	Og	10O	L49	none	ina
2746.	5791	Baghdad	none	VIIIB ?6-sub	sickle	bronze	Ke	9K	L156	W45	ina
2747.	5828	Baghdad	none	VIII	ferrule	bronze	IIIM	4M	L78	D23	ina
2748.	5837	Baghdad	none	VIIIA6-sub	pin needle	bronze	Ja	7J	L112	none	ina
2749.	5839	Baghdad	none	VIIIA6-sub	ring	bronze	Ja	7J	D30	none	ina
2750.	5840	32-21-366	none	VIIIAB	implement	bronze	Ja	7J	L72	none	ina
2751.	5870	32-21-358	none	VIIIBC	chisel	bronze	Kc	8K	L61	W30	ina
2752.	5889	Baghdad	none	VIII	ornament	bronze	Og	10O	D28	none	ina
2753.	5953	unknown	none	VIIIA	object	bronze	Me	9M	L81	none	ina
2754.	5958	unknown	none	VIIIA	sickle	bronze	dump	dump	L84	W20	ina
2755.	5989	unknown	none	VIIIC	implement	bronze	Ki	11K	L41	none	ina
2756.	5996	unknown	none	VIII	chisel	bronze	none	none	L47	W7	ina
2757.	3-001	33-3-1	none	VIII ?	lance head	copper	11L	7K	L93	W14	T4
2758.	3-088	Baghdad	none	VIII	lump	copper	10M	6M	L37	H18	T6
	Potsherd										
2759.	5481	Dropsie	none	VIII	smoother	green grayware	Ob	8O	L38	W17	T3
2760.	5490	Baghdad	none	VIII	smoother	redware	IO	6O	L67	W24	ina
2761.	5491	32-21-350	none	VIII	smoother	buffware	IO	6O	L93	W19	T6
2762.	5594	Baghdad	none	VIII	smoother	buffware	Ma	7M	L47	W18	ina
2763.	5686	Baghdad	none	VIII	spouted	green grayware	Kc	8K	L41	D29	ina
2764.	5719	Baghdad	none	VIIIA 6-sub ?	smoother	grayware	Jc	8J	L35	ina	ina
2765.	6071	32-21-353	none	VIII	smoother	buffware	O9	9O	L57	W20	ina
2766.	3-250	33-3-123	none	VIIIC	2 channel	gray brownware	10K	8M	L410	W700	none
2767.	3-none	33-3-227	none	VIII	tongue	shaped	Qa	7Q	L67	W30	T7
2768.	1658	unknown	none	VIIIA	painted	ceramic	none	5K	none	none	none

15	16	17	18	19
unknown	little used 25 & 27			
unknown	use 37 unused 24			
unknown	little use 37 & 41			
unknown	striations 23 use 29			
unknown	retouch 34 & 28			
unknown	striations 41 retouch 38			
unknown	striations used 31 & 31			
unknown	striations used 45 & 36			
unknown	retouch 26 & 28			
unknown	striations 22 used 34			
unknown				
unknown	used 37 retouch 58			
unknown				
unknown	little used 24 & 29			
unknown	striations 23 striations	retouch 32		
unknown	serrated edge			
unknown	given to donor			
unknown				
unknown				
room 804 with 1658-1662				
unknown	like 5044			
silo ?	balance plate ?			
unknown	balance plate ?			
room 826 silo				
room 826 silo	like 5044			
silo				
unknown				
unknown	flat head			
unknown				
silo	edge badly damaged			
7-8				
silo ?	like 5044			
silo	square end			
silo				
silo				
unknown				
unknown				
unknown				
unknown	flat			
unknown	like 5044			
unknown	like 5044			
unknown	like 5044			
unknown	end is flat & blunt			
silo				
dump ?	crudely made			
silo	like 5020			
silo				
unknown	pointed end			
unknown				
unknown				
unknown	long pointed			
dump				
unknown				
shrine				
unknown	broken in 2 pieces			
unknown	unwrought			
between 7O and 8O				
unknown				
unknown	like 5482			
unknown				
unknown				
unknown				
unknown				
hammam				
unknown				
room 804	with 1659 to 1662			

(continues)

Level VIII   (continued)

1	2	3	4	5	6	7	8	9	11	12	13
	Vessels										
2769.	1018	31-52-405	none	VIII	lid	gray stone	none	none	D82	H13	ina
2770.	1117	31-52-374	none	VIII	jar	dark buffware	i2	10M ?	H72	D75	none
2771.	1133	31-52-373	none	VIII	open bowl	orange redware	l3	7M ?	H52	D115	none
2772.	1135	31-52-376	none	VIII	jar	red brownware	l3	7M ?	H85	D58	none
2773.	1198	31-52-377	none	VIII	funnel	orange redware	Mk4	6M ?	L117	RD76	BD46
2774.	1541	31-52-317	none	VIIIA	bowl	brown ware	Ma	7M	H60	RD85	ina
2775.	1655	31-52-375	none	VIII	small jar	buffware	none	none	H120	D105	none
2776.	1667	unknown	none	VIII	large jar	buffware	none	none	H300	RD380	ina
2777.	5330	32-21-298	none	VIII	jar	green grayware	Mf	9M	H103	RD94	BD40
2778.	5343	32-21-285	none	VIII	strainer	green grayware	Nc	8M	H51	RD118	ina
2779.	5426	unknown	none	VIII	jar	green grayware	Oa	7O	H172	RD123	BD55
2780.	5458	32-21-466	none	VIII	jar	limestone	Oa	7O	H194	D120	ina
2781.	5477	32-21-299	none	VIIIA	2 body jar	brownware	Oa	7O	H48	RD48	D58
2782.	5485	Baghdad	none	VIII	lid	stone	Oc	8O	D80	T18	ina
2783.	5588	32-21-300	none	VIIIAB	small jar	red brownware	Ma	7M	H148	RD105	D156
2784.	5598	32-21-307	none	VIIIA ?	pot	buffware	none	8O	H135	RD120	D178
2785.	5602	Baghdad	none	VIIIA ?	jar	grayware	none	8O	H95	RD49	D90
2786.	5606	Baghdad	none	VIII	jar	buffware	IIO	5O	H225	D222	none
2787.	5613	32-21-301	none	VIII	paint small jar	buff gray ware	Oa	7O	H90	RD71	D96
2788.	5623	32-21-302	none	VIII	small jar	buffware	Ma	7M	H91	RD74	D94
2789.	5624	32-21-303	none	VIIIAB	3 neck jar	buffware	Ma ?	8M	H84	D99	ina
2790.	5626	32-21-291	none	VIII 6-sub ?	cup	red brownware	Kc	8K	H64	RD82	D102
2791.	5628	32-21-292	none	VIII	cup	grayware	Oa	7O	H70	RD67	BD44
2792.	5629	Baghdad	none	VIII	bell-shaped	grayware	Oc	8O	H48	BD72	ina
2793.	5631	32-21-288	none	VIII	open bowl	green grayware	Qa	7Q	H58	RD80	D158
2794.	5636	32-21-293	none	VIII6-sub	cup	green grayware	Kc	8K	H77	RD70	D96
2795.	5638	32-21-304	none	VI/VIII	jar	brown ware	Kc	8K	H47	D81	none
2796.	5639	unknown	none	VIII6-sub ?	pot	buffware	Ka	7K	H115	RD108	D137
2797.	5640	Baghdad	none	VIIIAB	jar	brown ware	Ma ?	8M	H92	D103	ina
2798.	5644	32-21-284	none	VIII	ash tray	brownware	Ma ?	8M	H24	RD65	D79
2799.	5675	Baghdad	none	VIIIAB	Wide flower	redware	Ma ?	8M	H60	D214	ina
2800.	5677	32-21-308	none	VIII 6-sub	pot	buffware	none	9K	H101	D118	ina
2801.	5687	unknown	none	VIII	cup	grayware	Kc	8K	H98	D88	ina
2802.	5691	32-21-294	none	VIII	cup	green grayware	Ke	9K	H75	D57	ina
2803.	5700	32-21-55	none	VIII	pot	green grayware	Ke	9K	H101	RD84	D118
2804.	5703	Baghdad	none	VIII	spouted pot	buffware	none	none	H156	RD125	D193
2805.	5706	32-21-287	none	VIII	recepticle	grayware	IIO	5O	H63	D98	ina
2806.	5725	32-21-289	none	VIII	bowl	green grayware	Ka	7K	H40	D106	ina
2807.	5726	32-21-61	none	VIIIA 6-sub	pot	green grayware	Ja	7J	H67	D75	ina
2808.	5727	32-21-62	none	VIIIA6-sub	pot	green grayware	Ja	7J	H67	D80	ina
2809.	5728	Baghdad	none	VIIIA6-sub	cookingpot	rd brownware	Ja	7J	H156	D180	ina
2810.	5741	Baghdad	none	VIII	Wide flower	redware	IIM	5M	H54	D201	ina
2811.	5751	32-21-295	none	VIII	point cup	green grayware	Ma	7M	H85	RD90	D98
2812.	5769	32-21-309	none	VIII	model bowl	grayware	Oc	9O	H35	D60	ina
2813.	5807	32-21-290	none	VIII	bowl	green grayware	Qa	7Q	H65	RD110	D127
2814.	5808	32-21-296	none	VIIIB ?6-sub	cup	buffware	Ke	9K	H104	D91	ina
2815.	5819	Baghdad	none	VIII	cup	redware	IIIO	4O	H32	D113	ina
2816.	5832	Baghdad	none	VIIIA ?6-sub	cup	green grayware	Ja	7J	H104	D83	ina
2817.	5846	Baghdad	none	VIII	Wide flower	buffware	IQ	6Q	H57	D210	ina
2818.	5867	32-21-311	none	VIIIBC6-sub	jar	stone	Ka	7K	H19	D27	ina
2819.	5879	32-21-310	none	VIIIBC ?6sub	pot	green grayware	Kc	8K	H50	D56	ina
2820.	5900	32-21-297	none	VIIIBC	cup	gray buff	Oe	9O	H50	RD48	D40
2821.	5922	Baghdad	none	VIIIBC	Wide flower	brownware	IO	6O	H53	D216	ina
2822.	5948	Baghdad	none	VIIIBC	bowl	grayware	Mg	10M	H220	D312	ina
2823.	5956	32-21-305	none	VIIIA	small jar	brownware	Mg	10M	H73	D73	ina
2824.	5957	Baghdad	none	VIIIA	jar	ceramic	Pg	10P	H65	D64	RD38
2825.	6009	Baghdad	none	VIIIB	bowl	brownware	M9	9M	H82	D195	ina
2826.	6010	Baghdad	none	VIIIC	bowl	buffware	none	8O	H45	D120	ina
2827.	6011	Baghdad	none	VIIIA	bowl	green grayware	O6	6O	H82	D225	ina
2828.	6012	Baghdad	none	VIIIA	bowl	grayware	M7	7M	H27	D85	ina
2829.	6013	Baghdad	none	VIIIB	bowl	green grayware	O5	5O	H120	D282	ina
2830.	6014	Baghdad	none	VIIIA	pot	buffware	none	8O	H67	D118	ina
2831.	6015	Baghdad	none	VIII	cup	buffware	O8	8O	H112	D103	ina
2832.	6016	Baghdad	none	VIII	pot	buffware	o*	8O	H92	D112	ina
2833.	6018	Baghdad	none	VIIIB	bowl	brownware	none	none	H82	D180	ina
2834.	6019	Baghdad	none	VIIIB	small jar	grayware	M9	9M	H75	D88	ina

15	16	17	18	19
trial trench				
unknown	globular body			
unknown	flat base	quartz grit & chaff	HM	
unknown	flat base	basalt grit HM		
trial trench	quartz & basalt grit HM			
unknown				
room 804	globular			
unknown				
unknown	fine basalt grit	WM		
unknown	like 5017			
unknown	brown paint under rim			
unknown	see 32-21-467			
room 810	like 5425	quartz & basalt grit	HM	
unknown				
unknown	burnished fine basalt &	quartz grit	HM	
unknown	traces of burning	chaff and basalt grit	HM	
room 818	burned HM			
unknown				
unknown	orangy tinge	fine quartz & basalt grit	HM	
unknown	quartz & basalt grit	& chaff	HM	
room 812B	basalt grit & vegetable	HM		
unknown	fine basalt & quartz	grit & chaff	HM	
unknown				
unknown	perforated bottom			
unknown	sand temper WM			
silo	bead rim	sand temper	WM	
unknown	neck broken off	Akkadian		
silo	VI type			
room 812B	like 5588			
room 812B	traces of burning	quartz & basalt	HM	
room 812B	like 5607			
silo	like 5639 VI type	quartz & basalt	WM	
unknown				
unknown	like one from VI			
unknown	sand temper WM			
unknown				
unknown	square	incised herringbone	sand HM	
unknown	sand temper WM			
VI type	punctate under rim			
like 5141 VI type				
unknown				
unknown	sand temper WM			
unknown	traces of burning	quartz & basalt grit	HM	
unknown	bead rim	fine quartz, basalt grit	WM	
silo	VI type			
unknown	like 5607			
silo	VI type			
unknown				
unknown	hole in base			
unknown	sand temper	WM		
unknown	sand temper	WM		
unknown				
unknown				
unknown	basalt grit	HM		
unknown				
unknown	HM			
"room 830" = west of rm 835	WM			
unknown	WM			
unknown	incised	WM		
unknown	HM			
room 834	WM			
unknown				
unknown				
unknown	WM			
unknown	WM			

(*continues*)

Level VIII   (continued)

1	2	3	4	5	6	7	8	9	11	12	13
2835.	6020	Baghdad	none	VIIIB	jar	buffware	M9	9M	H138	D160	ina
2836.	6021	Baghdad	none	VIIIB 6-sub ?	jar	buffware	K8	8K	H90	D100	ina
2837.	6022	Baghdad	none	VIIIA 6-sub ?	pot	buffware	K7	7K	H90	D115	ina
2838.	6023	Baghdad	none	VIIIA	jar	green grayware	none	10M	H370	D465	ina
2839.	6024	Baghdad	none	VIII	storage jar	buffware	M6	6M	H405	D355	ina
2840.	6066	Baghdad	none	VIII	tray	grayware	none	none	L450	W175	ina
2841.	unknown	unknown	none	VIIIA	2 rim bowl	ceramic ?	Oc	8O	none	none	none
2842.	2-none	unknown	none	VIIIAB	2 rim bowl	ceramic	Qa	7Q	none	none	none
2843.	2-none	32-21-352	none	VIII	bricks 57	ceramic	none	none	L52	W27	T12
2844.	2-none	32-21-469	none	VIII	lid	limestone	Oe	9O	D85	none	ina
2845.	3-019	Baghdad	none	VIII	bottle	redware	12M	6J	H182	RD65	D146
2846.	3-021	33-3-10	none	VIII	jar	redware	9L	7O	H12	RD100	D130
2847.	3-039	33-3-17	none	VIII	jar	buffware	12J	9J	H94	RD57	D117
2848.	3-040	discarded	none	VIII	Wide flower	buffware	12L	7J	H63	RD200	ina
2849.	3-047	33-3-21	none	VIII	jar	redware	12P	4J	H73	D95	RD54
2850.	3-067	33-3-32	none	VIII	tumbler	grayware	10K	8M	H41	RD71	ina
2851.	3-073	33-3-37	none	VIII	cup	steatite	9K	8O	H49	RD54	BD28
2852.	3-084	33-3-40	none	VIII	jar top	green grayware	10K	8M	H81	RD155	ina
2853.	3-085	33-3-41	none	VIII	Wide flower	buffware	8M	6Q	H60	RD192	ina
2854.	3-090	33-3-43	none	VIII	bowl	oolite	9P	4O	H51	RD60	ina
2855.	3-125	33-3-55	none	VIII	jar	brownware	10L	7M	H67	RD44	D75
2856.	3-136	33-3-62	none	VIII	jar	buffware	10L	7M	H124	RD73	D103
2857.	3-138	discarded	none	VIII	bowl	ceramic	8J	9Q	H68	RD184	BD42
2858.	3-139	discarded	none	VIII	jar	ceramic	12N	5J	H66	RD42	BD29
2859.	3-140	33-3-64	none	VIII	jar	buffware	9L	7O	H68	RD25	BD22
2860.	3-141	33-3-65	none	VIIIC	laver	grayware	11M	6K	H70	RD88	ina
2861.	3-143	discarded	none	VIII	Wide flower	buffware	8J	9Q	H42	RD172	BD76
2862.	3-144	33-3-68	none	VIII	jar	buffware	12J	9J	H115	RD82	D142
2863.	3-145	discarded	none	VIII	bowl	buffware	12J	9J	H23	RD72	BD31
2864.	3-147	discarded	none	VIII	Wide flower	redware	10M	6M	H68	RD225	BD105
2865.	3-230	33-3-115	none	VIII	bowl	orange redware	8M	6Q	H20	RD62	ina
2866.	3-231	discarded	none	VIII	bowl	buffware	8M	6Q	H11	D33	ina
2867.	3-250	33-3-124	none	VIIIC	laver	redware	10K	8M	H41	D70	ina
2868.	3-none	unknown	none	VIIIC ?	Wide flower	buffware	10H	10M	none	RD240	none
	Spindle	**whorl**									
2869.	1011	31-52-380	none	VIII	whorl	brown ware	m	6K ?	D34	H16	ina
2870.	1012	31-52-378	none	VIII	whorl	buffware	M	7M ?	H19	D28	none
2871.	1049	31-52-379	none	VIII	whorl	buffware	l	6K ?	D35	H13	ina
2872.	5286	Baghdad	none	VIII	whorl	brown ware	Of	9O	L71	none	ina
2873.	5287	32-21-325	none	VIII A ?	whorl	gray ware	Of	9O	D40	T24	ina
2874.	5307	Baghdad	none	VIII A ?	whorl	buffware	Of	9O	D33	T19	ina
2875.	5362	Baghdad	none	VIII	whorl	green grayware	Mb	8M	D55	none	ina
2876.	5363	Dropsie	none	VIII	whorl	bone	Mb	8M	D38	T23	ina
2877.	5364	32-21-326	none	VIII	whorl	buffware	Mb	8M	D37	T17	ina
2878.	5493	Baghdad	none	VIII	whorl	buffware	IIO	5O	D31	T24	ina
2879.	5597	32-21-327	none	VIII	whorl	green grayware	Ma	7M	D29	T16	ina
2880.	5603	32-21-328	none	VIII	whorl	buffware	IO	6O	D40	T26	ina
2881.	5604	32-21-329	none	VIII	whorl	buffware	IIO	5O	D36	H19	ina
2882.	5610	32-21-382	none	VIIIAB	whorl	bone	Ma	7M	D39	T16	ina
2883.	5663	Baghdad	none	VIIIAB 6sub ?	whorl	buffware	Kc	8K	L67	none	ina
2884.	5664	Dropsie	none	VIIIAB	whorl	buffware	Kc	8K	L69	none	ina
2885.	5665	32-21-330	none	VIIIAB	whorl	buffware	Kc	8K	D31	T17	ina
2886.	5680	32-21-378	none	VIII	whorl	bone	none	none	D44	T18	ina
2887.	5681	32-21-331	none	VIII	whorl	gray ware	Oc	8O	D35	T21	ina
2888.	5688	32-21-332	none	VIII	whorl	gray ware	IIO	5O	D37	T21	ina
2889.	5710	Baghdad	none	VIII	whorl	green grayware	Ke	9K	L74	none	ina
2890.	5724	Baghdad	none	VIIIA 6-sub ?	whorl	gray ware	Ja	7J	L49	none	ina
2891.	5740	32-21-333	none	VIII	whorl	buffware	IIM	5M	D25	T14	ina
2892.	5745	Baghdad	none	VIIIA	whorl	buffware	Oc	8O	D30	T19	ina
2893.	5785	32-21-379	none	VIII	whorl	bone	Ka	7K	D45	T21	ina
2894.	5787	32-21-380	none	VIII	whorl	bone	Og	10O	D43	T20	ina
2895.	5788	32-21-381	none	VIII	whorl	bone	Og	10O	D36	T19	ina
2896.	5803	Baghdad	none	VIIIA	whorl	buffware	none	7M	D32	H18	ina
2897.	5806	Baghdad	none	VIII	whorl	buffware	IK	6K	L74	none	ina
2898.	5813	Baghdad	none	VIII	whorl	buffware	Qa	7Q	D38	T23	ina
2899.	5814	32-21-334	none	VIII	whorl	gray ware	Qa	7Q	D35	T24	ina
2900.	5817	32-21-335	none	VIII	whorl	gray ware	Ka	7K	D28	T16	ina

15	16	17	18	19
unknown	WM			
unknown	gray slip	WM		
unknown	WM			
room 841	HM			
unknown				
unknown				
set in floor room 830				
set in floor room 831	subsq c10			
unknown				
unknown				
unknown	gray slip			
unknown	fineware gray slip			
unknown	fine ware			
unknown				
unknown	brownish slip			
unknown	conical	basalt & quartz grit	HM	
unknown				
unknown	quartz & basalt grit	HM		
unknown				
unknown	fragment	fits 3-35		
unknown				
unknown	sand temper	WM		
unknown	ring base			
unknown				
unknown				
loc 8: set in floor of room				
unknown				
unknown	red slip	chaff & basalt grit	HM	
unknown	coarse			
unknown				
unknown	chaff & quartz grit	HM		
unknown				
loc 21: "hammam"	bitumen marks			
stack on floor rm 875	elev. 12.36m	in 5 cm burnt grain		
trial trench	serrated edge			
trial trench				
trial trench	dots on top			
between 9O and 10O	like 5074			
between 9O and 10O	like 5079			
between 9O and 10O				
between 7M and 8M	like 5005			
between 7M and 8M				
unknown				
unknown				
unknown				
unknown				
Room 812	like 5363			
in silo	like 5074			
silo				
silo				
unknown				
unknown				
unknown				
unknown				
unknown				
Room 834				
unknown				
unknown				
unknown				
Room 810				
unknown				
unknown				
unknown				
unknown				

(continues)

Level VIII   (continued)

1	2	3	4	5	6	7	8	9	11	12	13
2901.	5834	32-21-336	none	VIII	whorl	brown ware	Ja	7J	D31	T16	ina
2902.	5841	Baghdad	none	VIIIAB	whorl	buffware	Ja	7J	D38	T20	ina
2903.	5842	32-21-337	none	VIIIAB	whorl	gray ware	Ja	7J	D32	T22	ina
2904.	5851	Baghdad	none	VIII	whorl	buffware	IM	6M	D30	T15	ina
2905.	5853	Baghdad	none	VIII	whorl	buffware	Ja	7J	D33	T18	ina
2906.	5854	32-21-338	none	VIIIAB	whorl	gray ware	Ja	7J	D35	T23	ina
2907.	5856	32-21-339	none	VIIIAB	whorl	buffware	Ja	7J	D21	T15	ina
2908.	5862	32-21-340	none	VIIIA	whorl	brown ware	IO	6O	D29	T14	ina
2909.	5865	32-21-341	none	VIIIA	whorl	brown ware	Ja	7J	D30	T17	ina
2910.	5905	Baghdad	none	VIIIBC	whorl	buffware	Me	9M	D34	T21	ina
2911.	5906	32-21-342	none	VIIIBC	whorl	buffware	Ka	7K	D35	T16	ina
2912.	2-none	32-21-343	none	VIII	whorl	buffware	Me	9M	D40	H17	ina
2913.	2-none	32-21-344	none	VIII	whorl	grayware	Mc	8M	H15	D26	ina
2914.	2-none	32-21-345	none	VIII	whorl	grayware	Me	9M	H17	D33	ina
2915.	3-045	33-3-19	none	VIII	whorl	ceramic	12M	6J	D37	T18	ina
2916.	3-069	33-3-34	none	VIII	whorl	buffware	10J	9M	D34	T21	ina
	Seals	**sealings**									
2917.	1008	31-52-383	none	VIII	impression	clay	j	10M	L55	T26	ina
2918.	1072	31-52-384	none	VIII	impression	clay	Mc	8M	L63	W37	T21
2919.	1099	31-52-385	none	VIII	impression	clay	none	9M	L51	W38	T19
2920.	1660A	31-52-386	none	VIIIA	impression	clay	none	5K	L107	W51	T25
2921.	1660B	Baghdad	none	VIIIA	impression	clay	none	5K	L98	W54	T32
2922.	1660B1	31-52-386	none	VIII	impression	clay	IIK	5K	L115	W52	T30
2923.	1661	31-52-387	none	VIIIA	impression	clay	none	5K	L72	W50	T26
2924.	1662	Dropsie	none	VIIIA	impression	clay	none	5K	L131	W49	T34
2925.	5480	Baghdad	none	VIII	stamp	baked clay	Oa	7O	D47	T23	ina
2926.	5495	32-21-492	none	VIIIA	impression	on potsherd	IIO	6K	L125	W31	none
2927.	5576	Baghdad	none	VIII	stamp	steatite	Oc	8O	L36	W29	T14
2928.	5577	Baghdad	none	VIII	stamp	baked clay	Oc	8O	D32	T15	ina
2929.	5612	32-21-493	none	VIIIAB	impression	clay	Ma	7M	L87	W43	T22
2930.	5642	32-21-494	none	VIIIA	impression	clay	Qe	9Q	L45	W45	T15
2931.	5643	32-21-495	none	VIIIAB	impression	clay	Ma ?	8M	L48	W40	T11
2932.	5713	Baghdad	none	VIII	plaque	bone	dump	dump	L39	W31	ina
2933.	5776	32-21-496	none	VIIIB	impression	clay	Me	9M	L79	W52	T21
2934.	5777	32-21-497	none	VIII	impression	clay	M9	9M	L56	W34	T27
2935.	5784	32-21-498	none	VIIIB	impression	clay	Og	10O	L48	W53	T24
2936.	5789	32-21-499	none	VIII	impression	clay	Og	10O	L93	W55	T
2937.	5790	32-21-500	none	VIII	impression	clay	Og	10O	L36	W27	T
2938.	5811	Baghdad	none	VIII	cylinder	bone	Qa	7Q	L27	T14	ina
2939.	5820	32-21-501	none	VIIIB	impression	clay	Ka	7K	L74	W50	T40
2940.	5821	32-21-502	none	VIIIB	impression	clay	Ka	7K	L59	W53	T23
2941.	5822	32-21-503	none	VIIIB	impression	clay	Ka	7K	L58	none	none
2942.	5823	32-21-517	none	VIIIB	impression	clay	IIK	5K	L65	W52	T21
2943.	5824	Baghdad	none	VIII	impression	clay	IIK	5K	L47	none	none
2944.	5830	32-21-504	none	VIIIB	impression	clay	IIO	5O	L73	W65	T21
2945.	5848	32-21-505	none	VIIIB	impression	clay	Ka	7K	L66	W33	T40
2946.	5859	Baghdad	none	VIII	stamp	red stone	IIK	5K	L25	W25	T13
2947.	5863	32-21-506	none	VIII	impression	clay	IIQ	5Q	L32	W55	T8
2948.	5874	32-21-507	none	VIIIBC	impression	clay	IIM	5M	L41	W35	T24
2949.	5880	32-21-508	none	VIIIBC	impression	clay	IIM	5M	L33	W40	T25
2950.	5881	32-21-509	none	VIIIBC	impression	clay	IIM	5M	L39	W37	T29
2951.	5882	32-21-510	none	VIIIBC	impression	clay	IIM	5M	L43	W44	T24
2952.	5883	32-21-511	none	VIIIBC	impression	clay	IIM	5M	L57	W44	T19
2953.	5885	32-21-512	none	VIII	impression	clay	Me	9M	L47	W40	T19
2954.	5907	32-21-513	none	VIIIBC	impression	clay	IQ	6Q	L49	W22	T30
2955.	5908	32-21-514	none	VIIIBC	impression	clay	IQ	6Q	L30	W30	T15
2956.	5911	32-21-563	none	VIIIBC	impression	clay	IQ	6Q	L30	W30	T7
2957.	5911	Baghdad	none	VIIIBC	impression	clay	IQ	6Q	L70	none	none
2958.	5917	32-21-525	none	VIII	plaque	shell	IIO	5O	L67	W46	T12
2959.	5924	32-21-491	none	VIIIBC	stamp	bone	Ma	7M	L20	W7	ina
2960.	5943	32-21-515	none	VIIIA	impression	clay	Me	9M	L32	W38	T24
2961.	5944	32-21-564	none	VIIIA	impression	clay	Me	9M	L47	W44	T27
2962.	5945	Baghdad	none	VIIIA	impression	clay	Me	9M	L115	none	ina
2963.	5954A-D	32-21-516	none	VIIIA	4 impression	clay	Me	9M	L45+	W38	T16
2964.	5955	Baghdad	none	VIIIA	impression	clay	Me	9M	L62	none	ina
2965.	5991	32-21-490	none	VIIIA	stamp	stone	Ki	11K	D24	T8	ina
2966.	6077	32-21-522	none	VIII	impression	clay	none	9M	L35	W32	T17

15	16	17	18	19
unknown	traces of burning			
unknown				
unknown				
unknown				
unknown				
unknown				
unknown				
unknown				
unknown				
unknown				
unknown				
unknown				
unknown	radiating lines			
unknown	serrated edge			
unknown				
unknown				
unknown	seal 15×15	bale tag	dog under heart	
unknown	Seal 19×21	on jar shoulder	ibex and border	
unknown	Seal 22 Dia	over knot: cover	crude long horn animal	
Room 804	Seal 25 dia	on jar shoulder	ram fish and dog	
Room 804	Seal 14×16	on jar shoulder	crude animal spiked horn	
Room 804	Seal 32+×34	on sack	bull dog snake	
Room 804	Seal 49×30	on jar shoulder	crossed horn beast & snake	
Room 804	Seal 34 dia	long flat:door tag ?	antelope gazelle. dog	(indent on base)
unknown	Seal 47 dia	seal	spoked wheel	stem handled
Room 801	Seal 17×15	on jar cover	short horned ram	
unknown	Seal 36×29	seal	3 antelopes in line	tabloid
unknown	Seal 32 dia	seal	3 animals in wheel	pyramid
Room 812	Seal 25 dia	on jar shoulder	ram dog fish	
unknown	Seal 33 dia	in jar mouth	2 crossed horn antelope	
Room 812B	Seal 19 dia	wall tag ?	2 superimposed animals	
dump	Seal 33×30	seal	horned ram in wavy border	tabloid ?
unknown	Seal 36 dia	on jar cover	bull dog snake	
unknown	Seal 28+×26+	on sack tie	goats bulls and fillers	
unknown	Seal 35+ dia	on sack tie	bull dog snake	
unknown	Seal 30+×29+	on top box ??	big headed lovers & dog	
unknown	Seal 31+×15+	basketry:jar mouth	small animal under snake	
unknown	ina	seal	abstract drillings	cylinder
unknown	Seal 36×32+	in jar mouth	bull dog snake	
unknown	Seal 36×35+	sack ? reeds ?	bull dog snake	
unknown	Seal 36×28+	on sack	bull dog snake	
unknown	Seal 33×22+	too broken to know bull	bull dog snake	
unknown	Seal 13×14+	unknown	horned antelope ?	
unknown	Seal 36×36	on sack	bull dog snake	
unknown	Seal 36×21+	on sack	bull dog snake	
unknown	Seal 25 dia	seal	free form	high hemispheroid
unknown	Seal 21×13	on jar shoulder	horned ram grazing	
unknown	Seal 21×19	too broken to know	horned ram grazing	
unknown	Seal 19+×31+	too broken to know	animal grazing	
unknown	Seal 32+×25+	on jar shoulder	horned beasts wave border	
unknown	Seal 38+×18+	jar shoulder ??	horned beasts wave border	
unknown	Seal 37+×27+	in jar mouth	vulture	horned beast etc
unknown	Seal 30×23	in jar mouth	antelope runs in trees	
unknown	Seal 27+ dia	on jar shoulder	long horned ram	
unknown	Seal 20+×16+	on jar cover	antelope seen in bushes	
unknown	Seal 21+×23+	unknown	horned beasts wave border	
unknown	Seal 36×44	unknown	horned beasts wave border	
none	Seal 67×46	seal	ibexes & birds inverted	tabloid ?
unknown	Seal 7+×20	seal	animal	rectangular
unknown	Seal 27+×26+	in jar mouth	lovers and snake	
unknown	Seal 25+×34+	unclear	2 crossed antelope etc.	
unknown	Seal 33 dia	unknown	horned animal and snake	
unknown	Seal 20+×27+	too broken to know	lions attack bull & snake	
unknown	Seal 25×24	unknown	4 circling dogs	
unknown	Seal 24 dia	seal	abstract scratched	hemispheroid
unknown	Seal 26+×23+	on jar cover	2 horned animals snake	

(continues)

Level VIII   (continued)

1	2	3	4	5	6	7	8	9	11	12	13
2967.	6078	32-21-524	none	VIII	impression	clay	none	9M	L45	W43	T16
2968.	6079	32-21-519	none	VIII	impression	clay	M9	9M	L42	W42	T21
2969.	6096	Baghdad	none	VIII	impression	clay	O10	10O	none	none	none
2970.	2-none	32-21-518	none	VIII	impression	clay	none	none	L59	W40	T23
2971.	2-none	32-21-520	none	VIII	impression	clay	none	none	L53	W43	ina
2972.	2-none	32-21-521	none	VIII	impression	clay	none	none	L51+	W47	T27
2973.	2-none	32-21-523	none	VIII	impression	clay	none	none	L34	W31	T18
2974.	3-003	Baghdad	none	VIII	stamp	marble	11M	8K	D25	T17	ina
2975.	3-005	33-3-2	none	VIII	stamp	bone	dump	dump	L40	W25	T7
2976.	3-006	Baghdad	none	VIII ?	cylinder	paste	11L ?	7J	L31	T7	ina
2977.	3-007	33-3-3	none	VIII	impression	clay	dump	dump	L32	W25	T11
2978.	3-026	33-3-12	none	VIII	impression	clay	12K	8J	L25	W27	T9
2979.	3-032	IM15643	none	VIIIB	impression	clay	12K	8J	L35	W36	ina
2980.	3-062	33-3-29	none	VIII	stamp	steatite	9N	5O	D17	T6	ina
2981.	3-063	33-3-30	none	VIII	stamp	marble	9H	10O	D18	T6	ina
2982.	3-064	33-3-31	none	VIII	stamp	steatite	9H	10O	D19	T6	ina
2983.	3-115	33-3-53	none	VIII	impression	clay	8H	10Q	S22	L30	W30e
2984.	3-121	Baghdad	none	VIII	stamp	bone	8J	9Q	L20	W15	T7
2985.	3-126	33-3-56	none	VIII	stamp ?	clay ? stone ?	11K	8K	L26	W23	T14
2986.	3-127	33-3-57	none	VIII	impression	clay	12K	8J	L26	W23	T8
2987.	3-128	Baghdad	none	VIII ?	stamp	stone	dump	dump	L13	W7	T7
2988.	3-131	Baghdad	none	VIII	stamp	steatite	12K	8J	L18	W17	T9
2989.	3-188	33-3-88	none	VIIIC	impression	clay	10K	8M	L30	W34	ina
2990.	3-188	33-3-88	none	VIIIC	3 impression	clay	10K	8M	ina	ina	ina
2991.	3-188	33-3-88	None	VIIIC	3 impression	clay	10K	8M	L38	W30	none
2992.	3-188	33-3-88	none	VIIIC	17 impression	clay	10K	8M	L38	W30	none
2993.	3-none	33-3-239	none	VIIIC ?	36 impression	clay	10K	8M	L34	W24	none
2994.	3-none	33-3-239	none	VIIIC ?	impression	clay	10K	8M	L34	W24	none
2995.	3-none	33-3-239	none	VIIIC ?	6 impression	clay	10K	8M	L34	W24	none

15	16	17	18	19
unknown	Seal 35×38	in jar mouth	back-to-back dogs & snake	
unknown	Seal 19 dia	on jar neck	quadraped looks at bird	
unknown	Seal 22 dia	unknown	short horned antelope	
unknown	Seal 28×22+	on jar cover	2 horned animals	
unknown	Seal 32 dia	in jar mouth	quadruped and plants	
unknown	Seal 22+×21+	on jar cover	3 dogs in pursuit	
unknown	Seal 25+×30+	on jar shoulder	horned animal wave border	
unknown	Seal 24 dia	seal	angular ibex and snake	high hemispheroid
unknown	Seal 24 ×38	seal	1 figure: human ? gazelle ?	lentoid
well debris	ina	seal	2 gazelles	man holds tree
unknown	Seal 18+×25+	on jar cover	3 horned animals circling	
unknown	Seal 21+ dia	on jar shoulder	animal	
unknown	Seal 35 dia	unknown	bull	dog and snake
unknown	Seal 17 dia	seal	lattice & tree of life	hemispheroid
unknown	Seal 13 dia	seal	1 prancing antelope	lentoid
unknown	Seal 18 dia	seal	sitting man & animals	hemispheroid
unknown	Seal 22+×21+	unclear	4 circling animals:sheep ?	
unknown	Seal 20×15	seal	drilled 'I'	flat hemispheroid
unknown	Seal 25+ dia	unclear	swirl	
unknown	Seal 24 dia	bale tag	criss cross grid	
dump	none	seal	angling lines	irregular bossed
unknown	Seal 18×17	seal	2 animals: lion ? dogs ?	loop handled
loc23 cache	Seal 38+×30	on jar shoulder	4 horned caprids	
over IX "pig"	Seal 38+×30	on sack	4 horned caprids	
over IX "pig"	Seal 38+ ×30	bale tags4	horned caprids	
over IX "pig"	Seal 38+ ×30	pressed on knot	4 horned caprids	
in "hammam"	Seal 34+×24+	? knots:	on sacks ?animals	
in "hammam"	Seal 34+×24+	on basket lid	animals	
in "hammam"	Seal 34+×24+	on basket lid	animals	

Plate 1a.   View of Tepe Gawra Mound in its surroundings. Reproduced by permission of the University of Pennsylvania Museum Archives.

Plate 1b.   View of the White Room of Level XII from the west. Reproduced by permission of the University of Pennsylvania Museum Archives.

Plate 2a. View of sorting bins behind the rooms along the northeastern entranceway, Level XII. Reproduced by permission of the University of Pennsylvania Museum Archives.

Plate 2b. View of room 23 and adjoining walls, Level XIA/B. Reproduced by permission of the University of Pennsylvania Museum Archives.

Plate 2c. View of the oven rooms with *tanur* and oven behind the temple, Level XI/XA. Reproduced by permission of the University of Pennsylvania Museum Archives.

Plate 3a.   View of the deep pit by the kiln from Phase XI, Level XI/XA. Reproduced by permission of the University of Pennsylvania Museum Archives.

Plate 3b.   View into the courtyard 27 door (upper left) from room 29, Phase XI, Level XI/XA, showing stratigraphy of this building. Reproduced by permission of the University of Pennsylvania Museum Archives.

Plate 4a. View of room 27, Phase XI, Level XI/XA. Reproduced by permission of the University of Pennsylvania Museum Archives.

Plate 4b. View of room 15, Phase XIA, Level XIA/B. Reproduced by permission of the University of Pennsylvania Museum Archives.

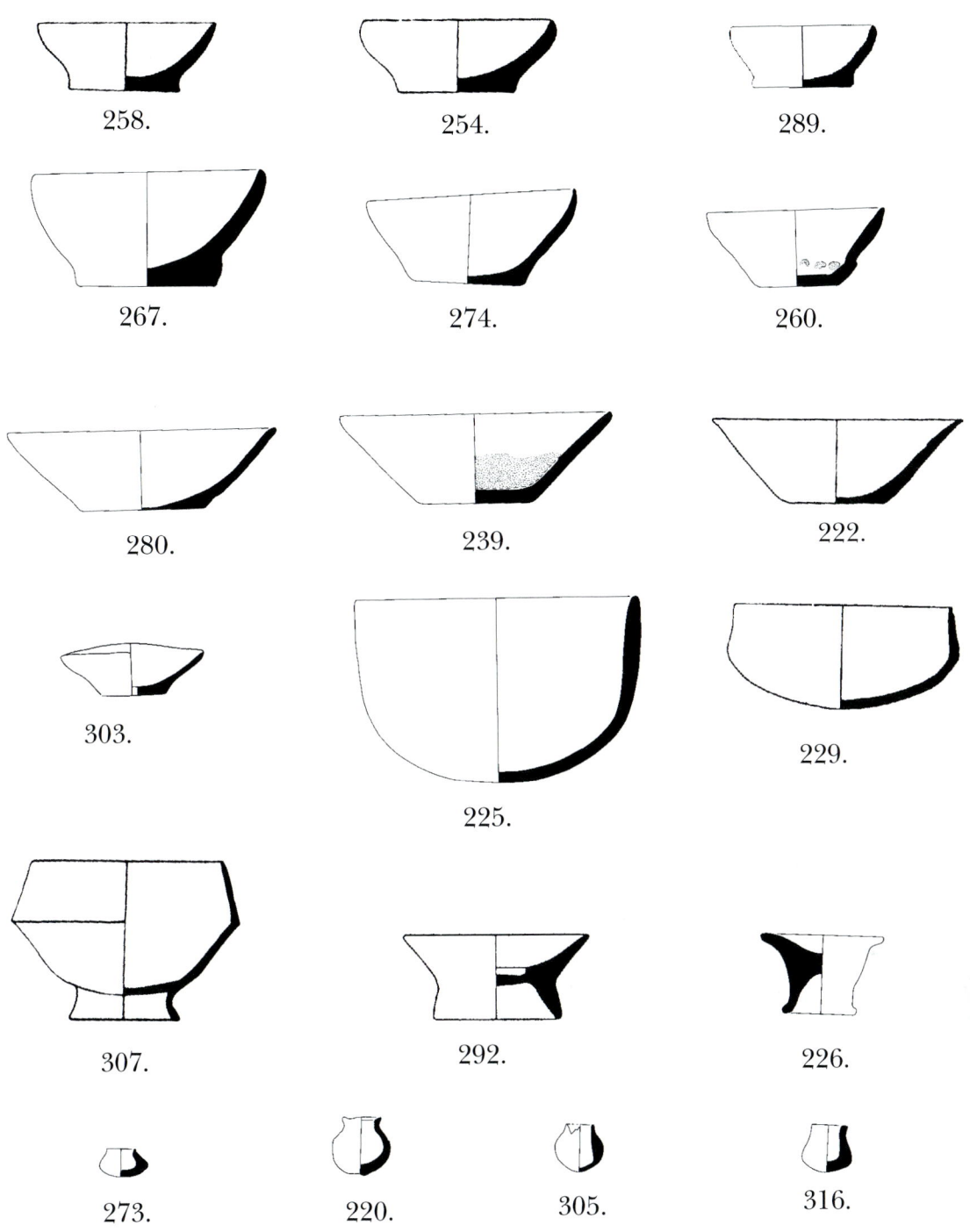

258.

254.

289.

267.

274.

260.

280.

239.

222.

303.

225.

229.

307.

292.

226.

273.

220.

305.

316.

1:5

Plate 5.   Types of plain ware pottery, Level XII.

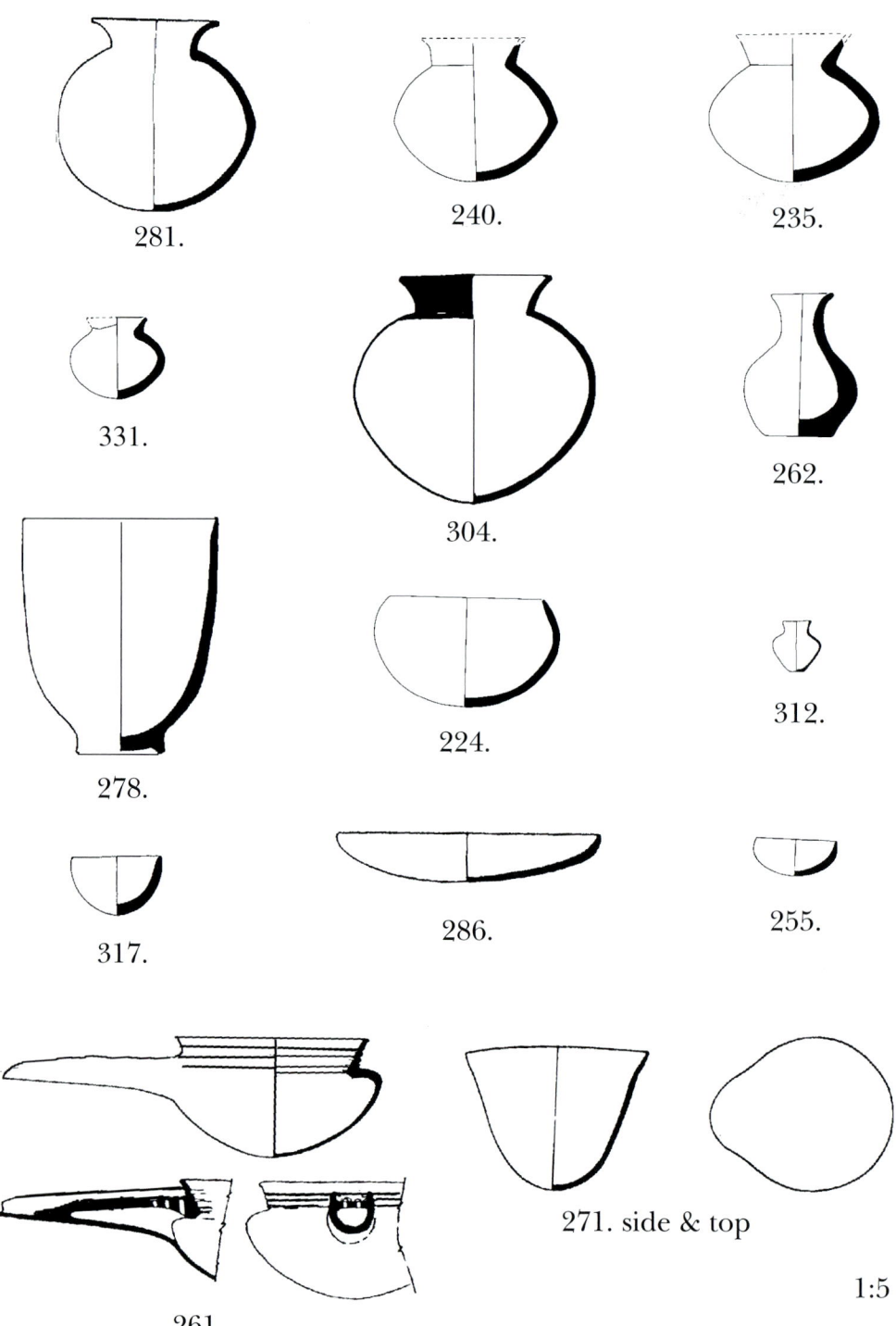

281.

240.

235.

331.

304.

262.

278.

224.

312.

317.

286.

255.

261.

271. side & top

1:5

Plate 6.   Types of jars and tall bowls, Level XII.

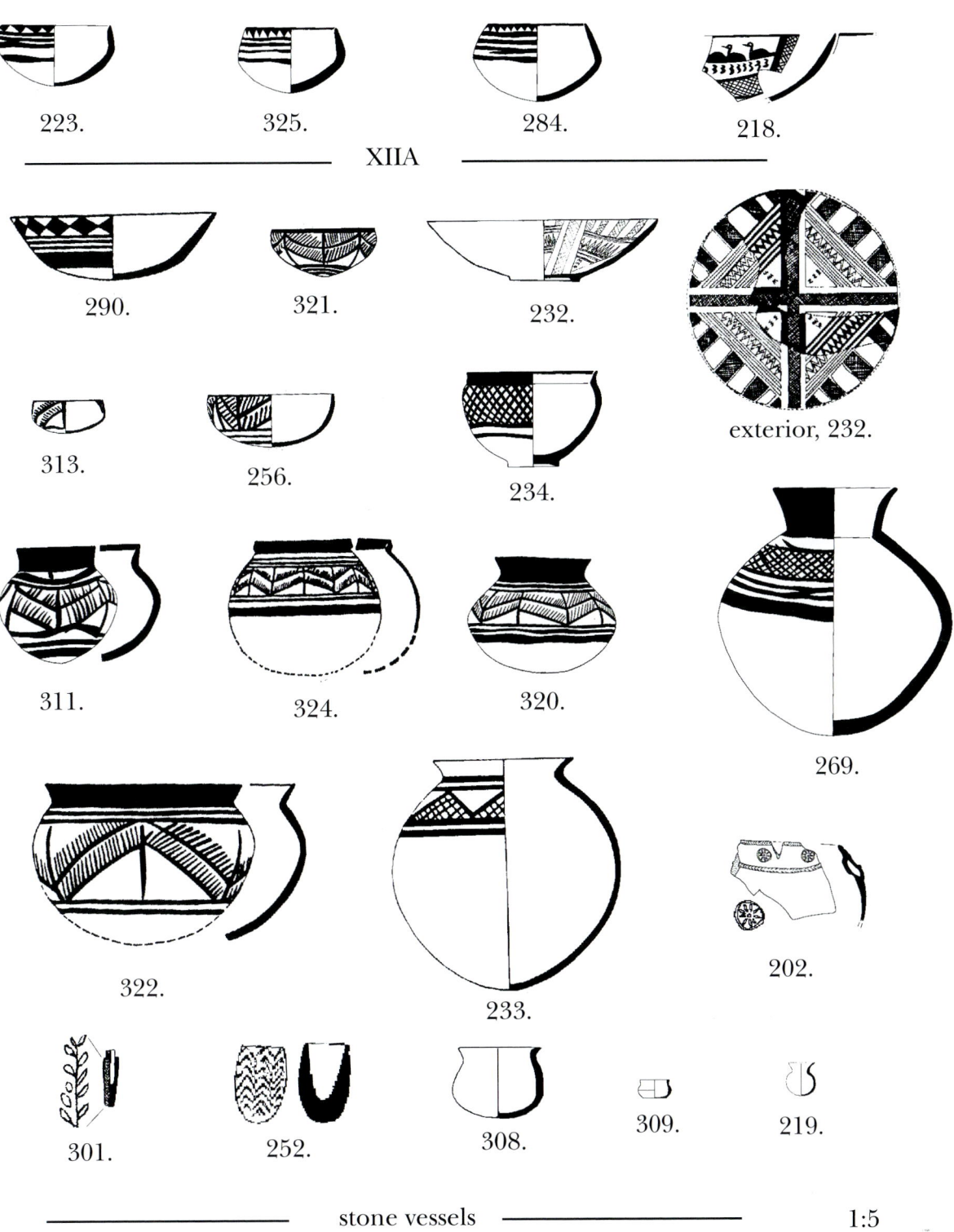

223.   325.   284.   218.

XIIA

290.   321.   232.

exterior, 232.

313.   256.   234.

311.   324.   320.

269.

322.   233.   202.

301.   252.   308.   309.   219.

stone vessels   1:5

Plate 7.   Types of painted, appliqué, and stone vessels, Levels XII and XIIA.

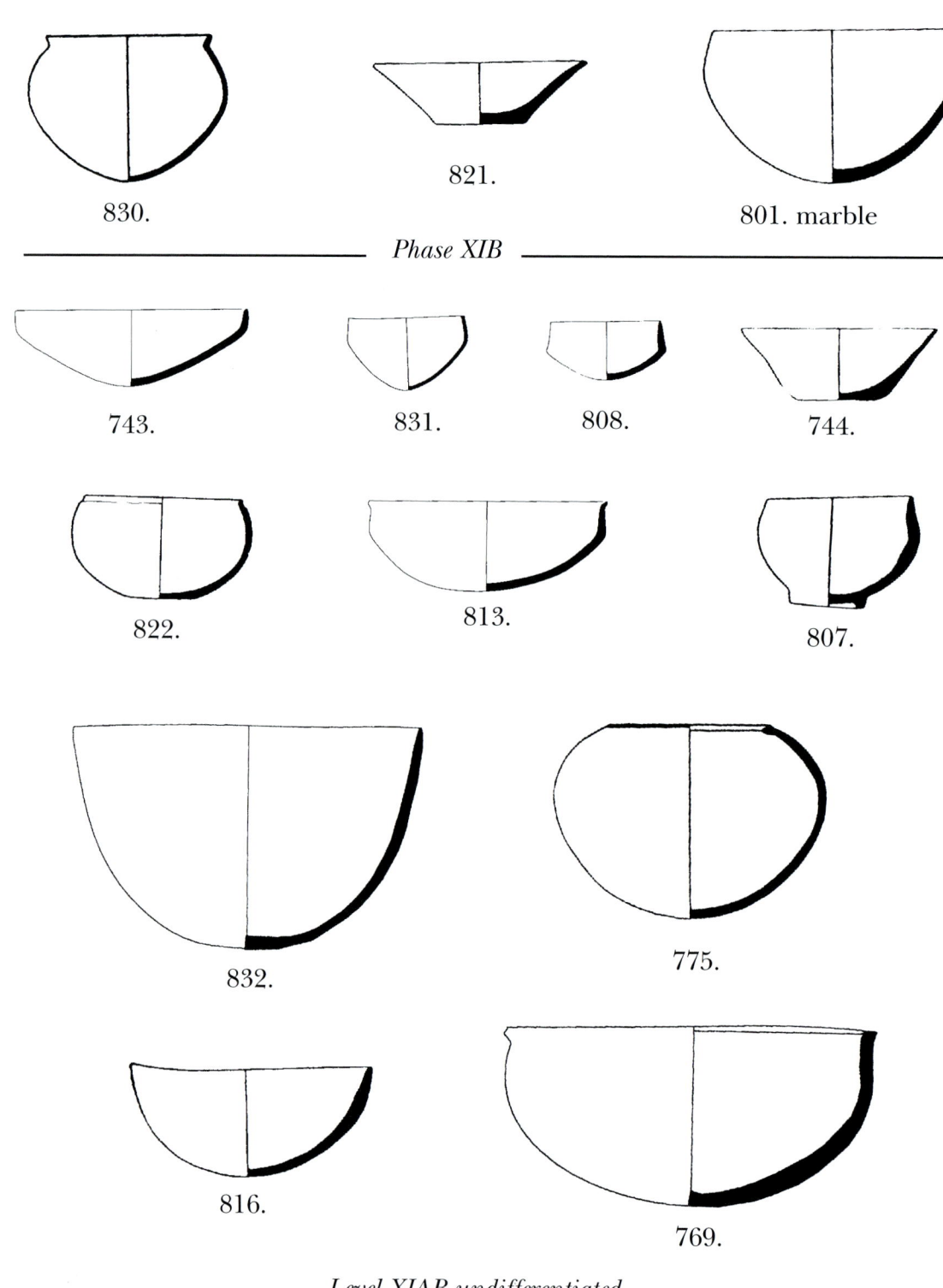

830.

821.

801. marble

Phase XIB

743.

831.

808.

744.

822.

813.

807.

832.

775.

816.

769.

Level XIAB undifferentiated

1:5

Plate 8.   Types of plain ware pottery, Level XIA/B.

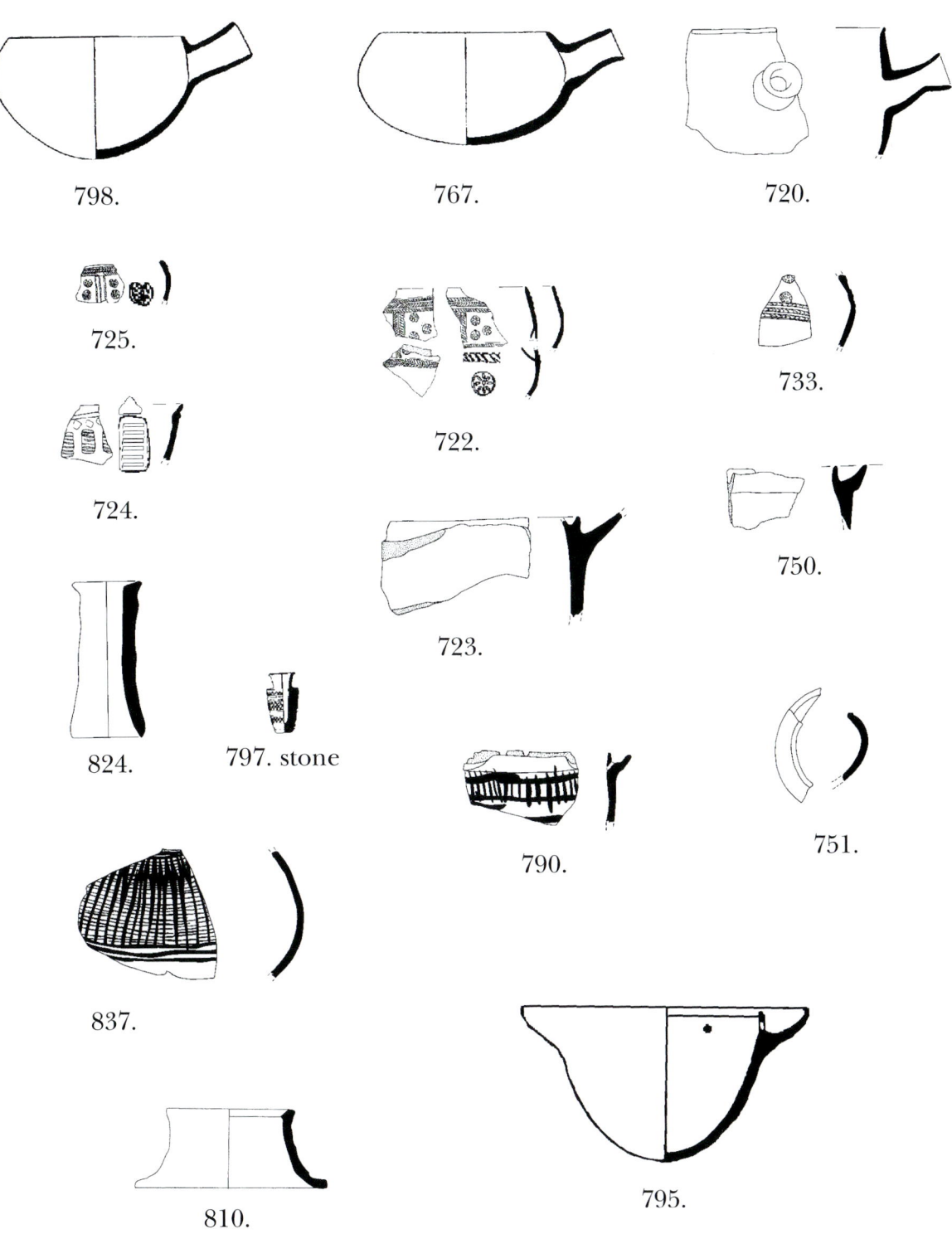

798.

767.

720.

725.

722.

733.

724.

723.

750.

824.

797. stone

790.

751.

837.

810.

795.

Scale 1:5

Plate 9.　Types of bowls and miscellaneous forms, Level XIA/B.

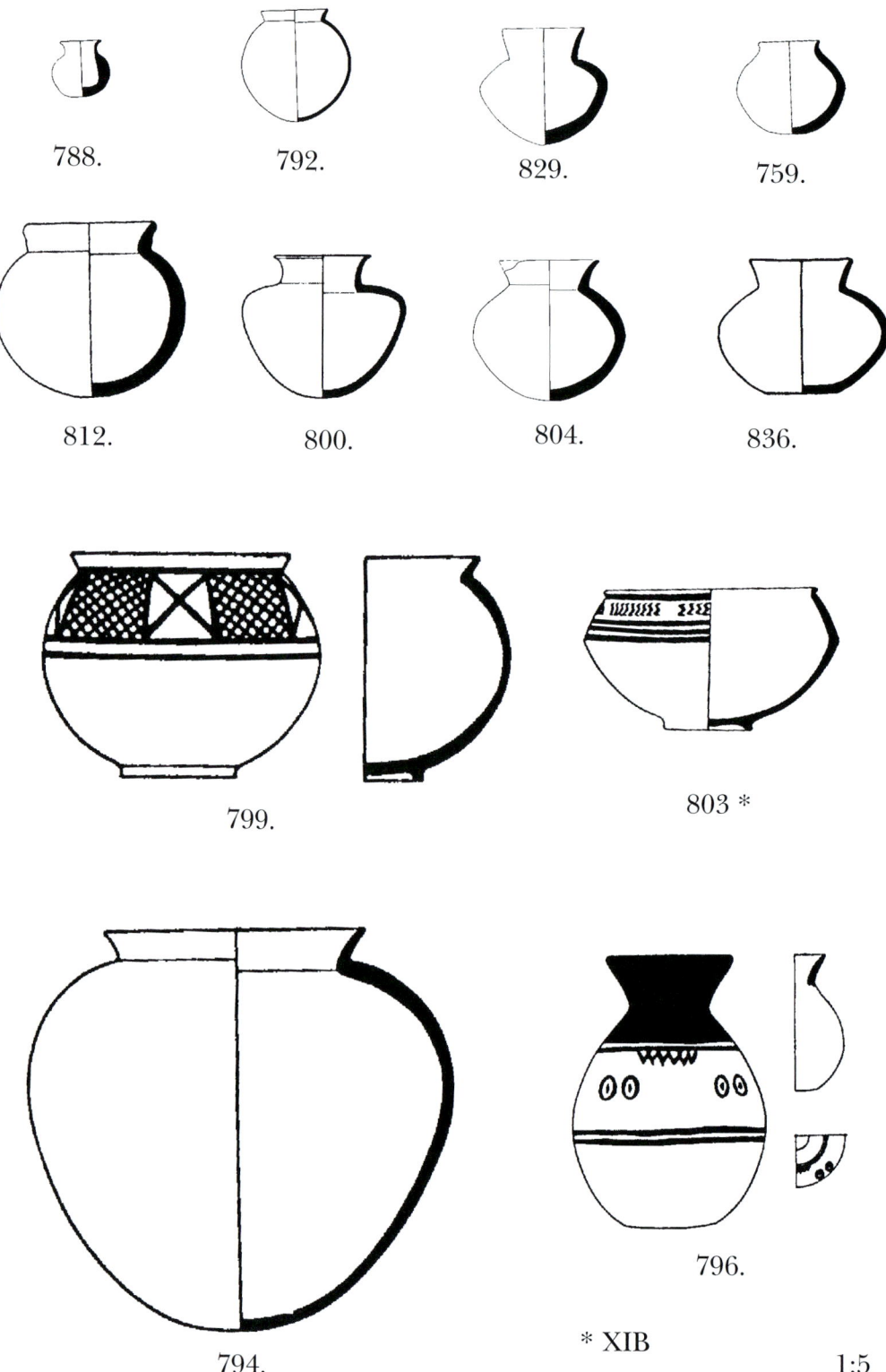

788. 792. 829. 759.

812. 800. 804. 836.

799. 803 *

794. 796.

* XIB

1:5

Plate 10.   Types of jars and tall bowls, Level XIA/B.

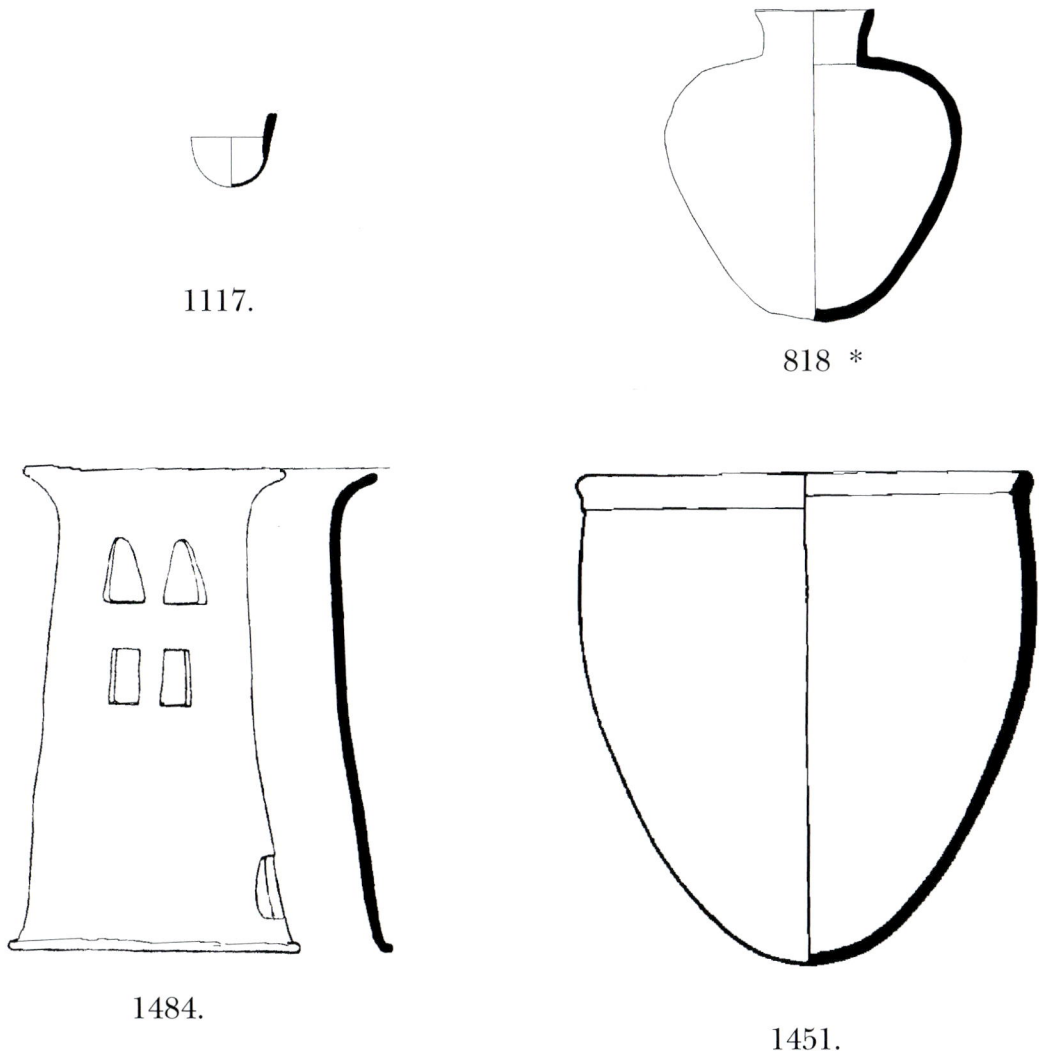

1117.

818 *

1484.

1451.

* from Level XIAB, all others XI

1:10

Plate 11.   Types of miscellaneous forms, Levels XIA/B and XI/XA.

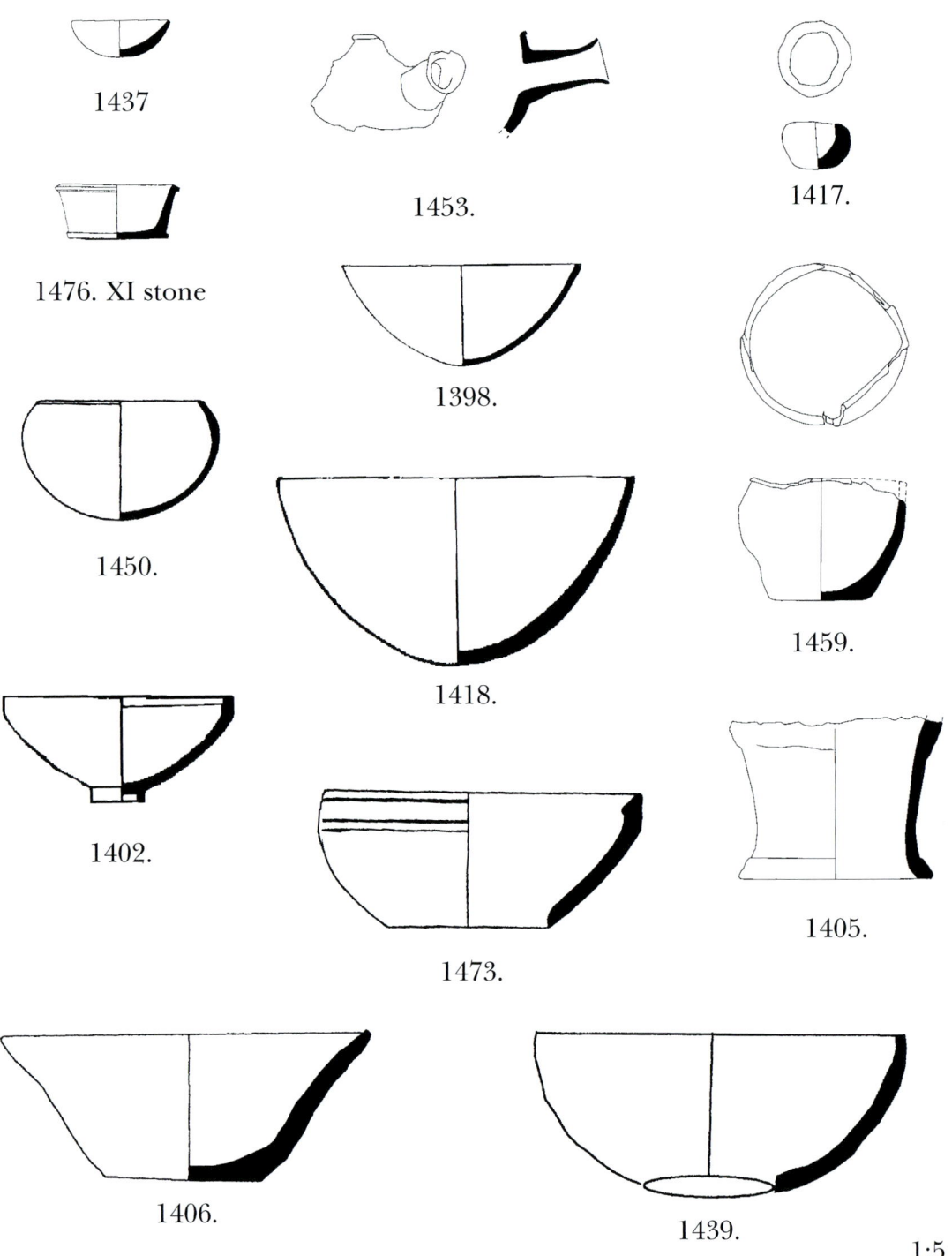

1437

1453.

1417.

1476. XI stone

1398.

1450.

1418.

1459.

1402.

1473.

1405.

1406.

1439.

1:5

Plate 12.   Types of bowls, Phase XI, Level XI/XA.

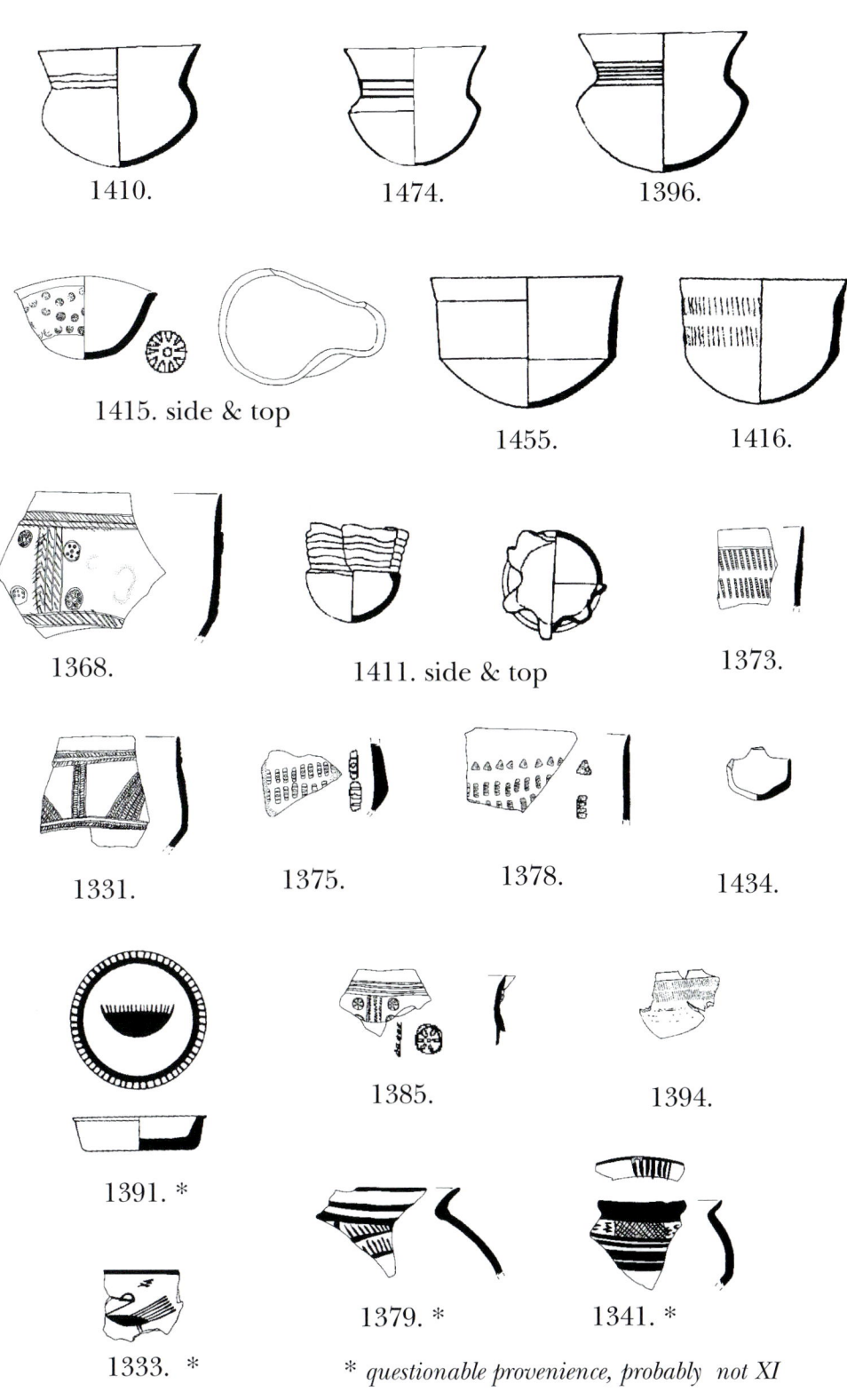

1410.

1474.

1396.

1415. side & top

1455.

1416.

1368.

1411. side & top

1373.

1331.

1375.

1378.

1434.

1391. *

1385.

1394.

1379. *

1341. *

1333. *

* *questionable provenience, probably not XI*

1:5

Plate 13.   Types of cups and small jars, Phase XI, Level XI/XA.

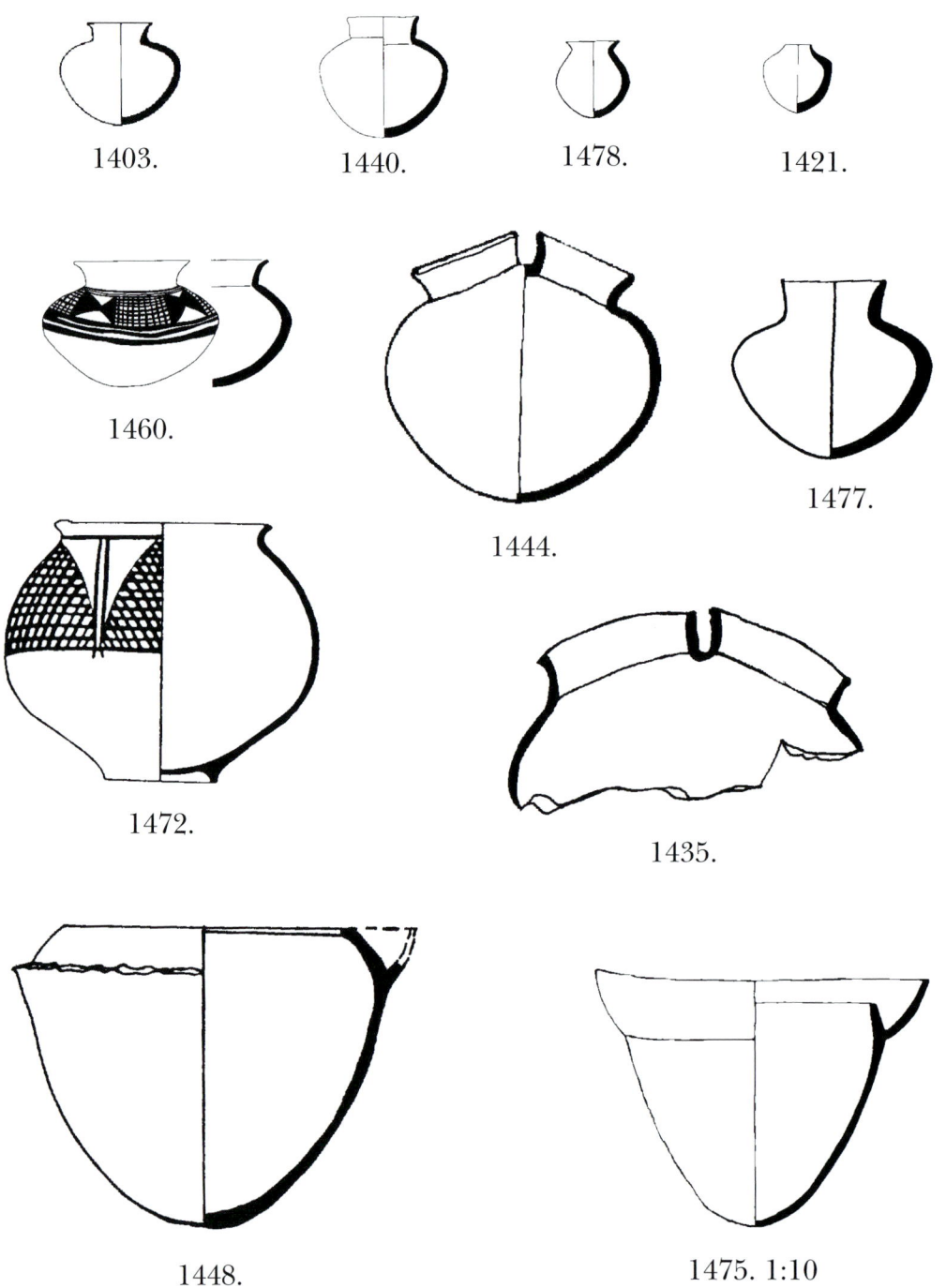

1403.

1440.

1478.

1421.

1460.

1444.

1477.

1472.

1435.

1448.

1475. 1:10

1:5, except 1475

Plate 14.   Types of jars, Phase XI Level XI/XA.

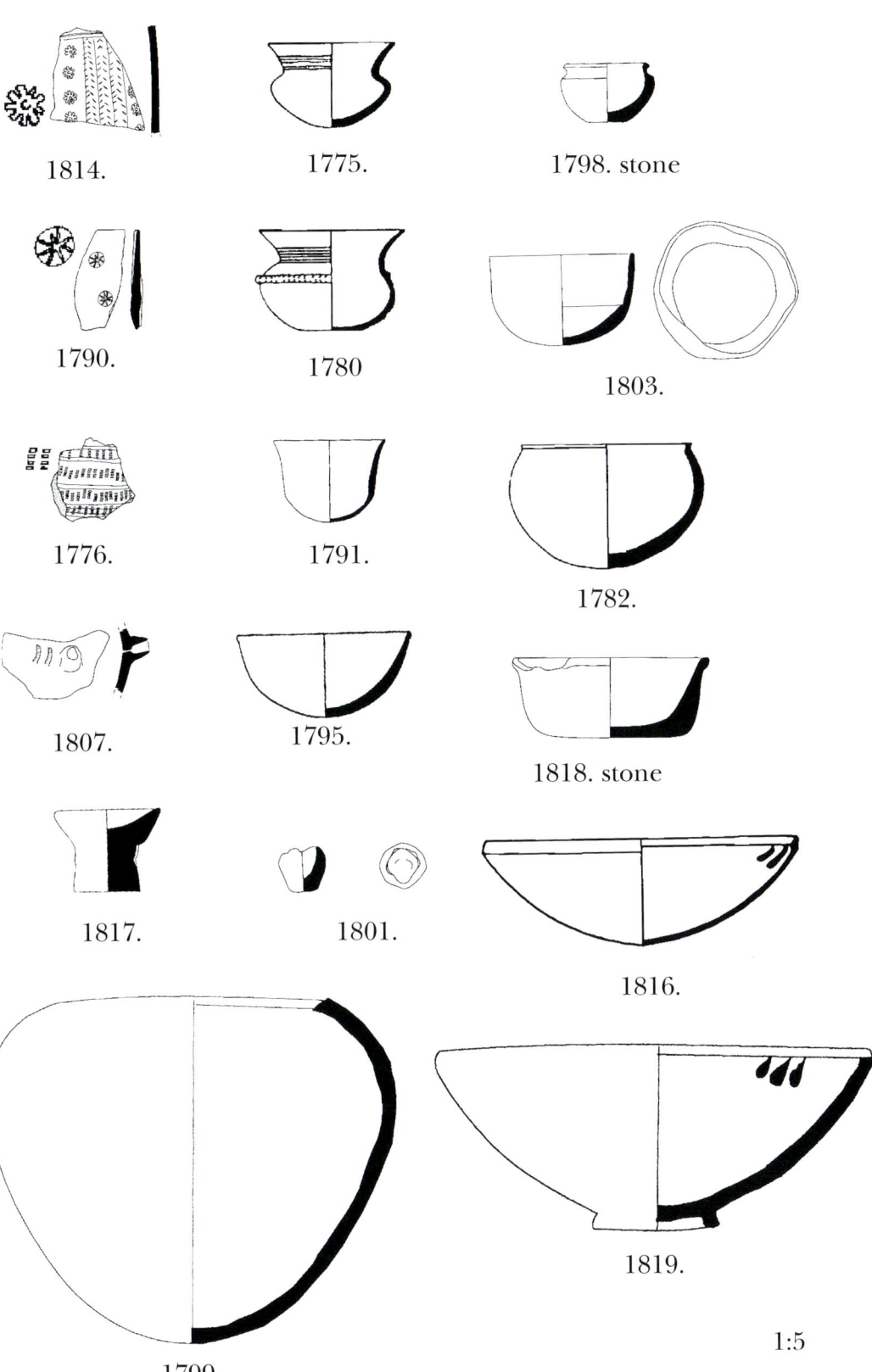

1814.

1775.

1798. stone

1790.

1780

1803.

1776.

1791.

1782.

1807.

1795.

1818. stone

1817.

1801.

1816.

1799.

1819.

1:5

Plate 15.   Types of cups and bowls, Phase XA Level XI/XA.

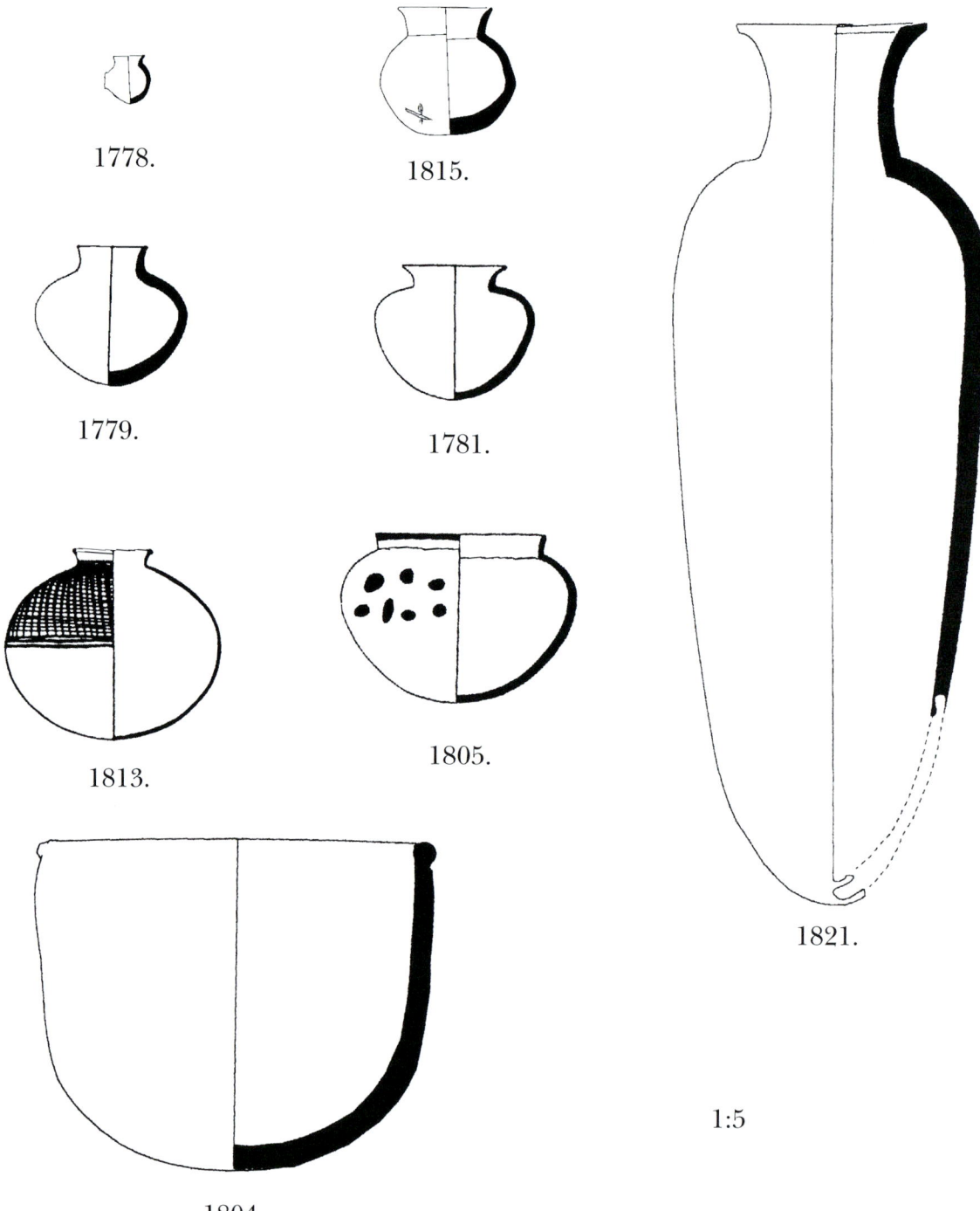

1778.

1815.

1779.

1781.

1813.

1805.

1804.

1821.

1:5

Plate 16.   Types of jars and urns, Phase XA Level XI/XA.

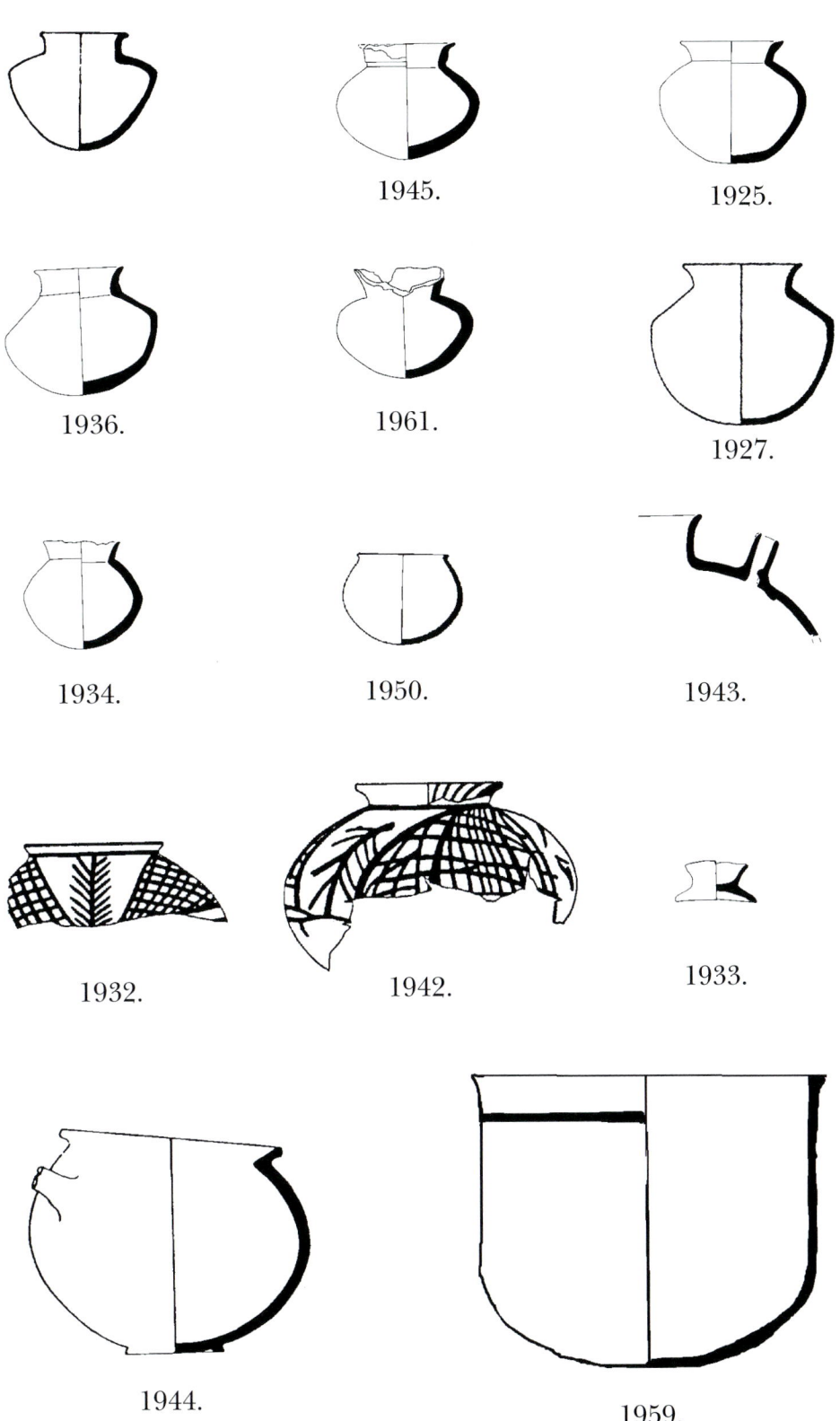

1945.

1925.

1936.

1961.

1927.

1934.

1950.

1943.

1932.

1942.

1933.

1944.

1959.

1:5

Plate 17. Types of jars, Level X.

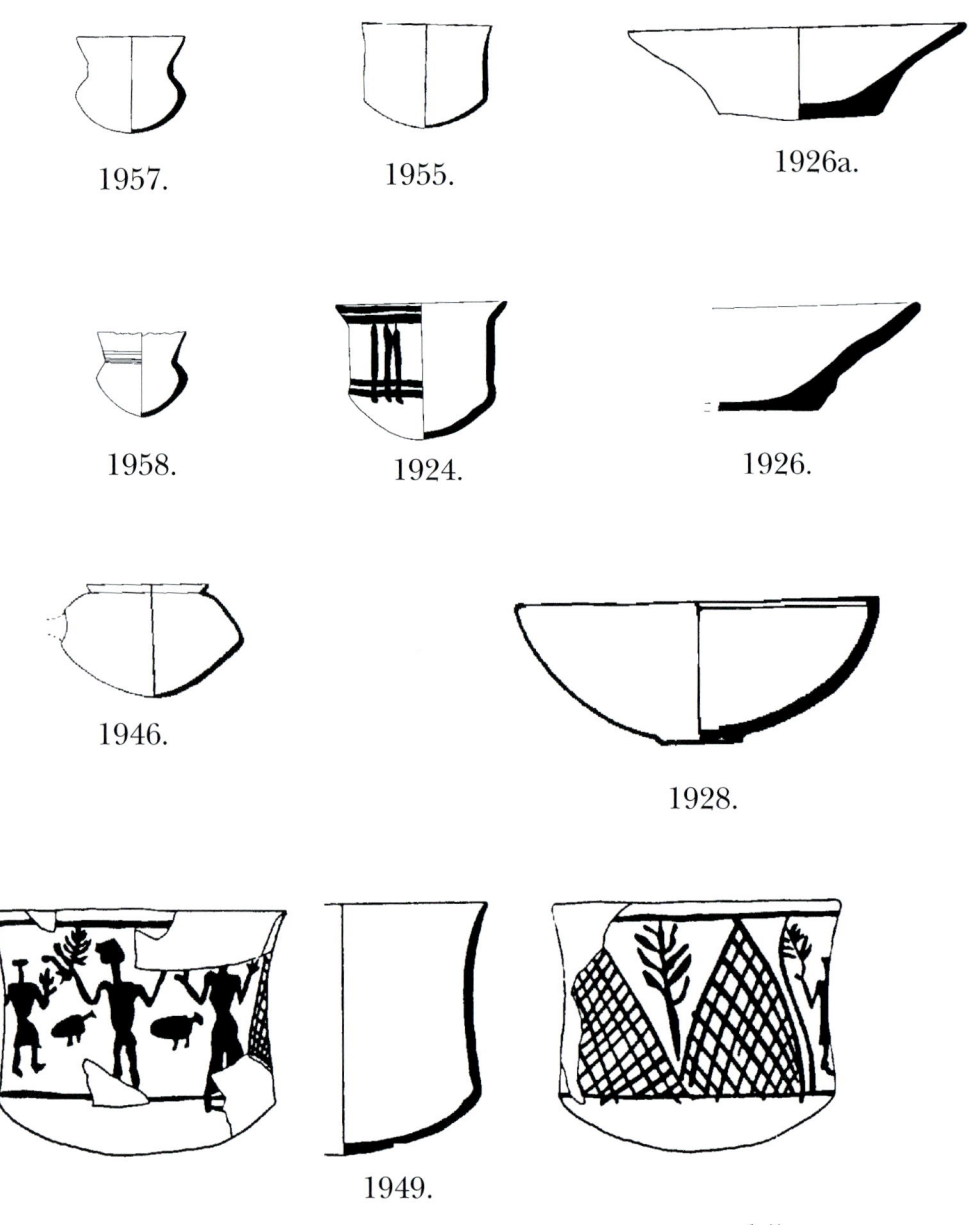

1957.

1955.

1926a.

1958.

1924.

1926.

1946.

1928.

1949.

1:5

Plate 18.   Types of cups and bowls, Level X.

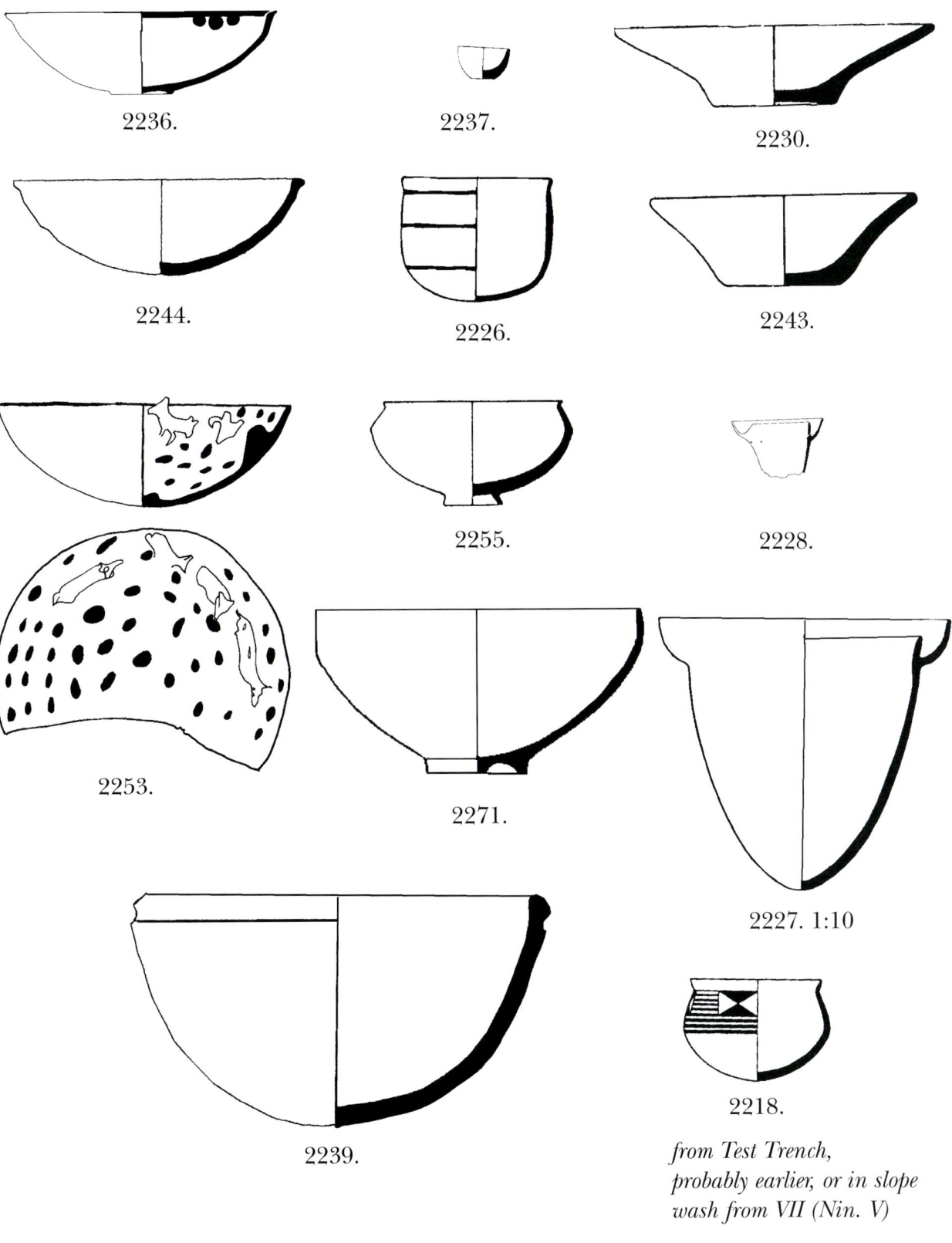

2236.

2237.

2230.

2244.

2226.

2243.

2253.

2255.

2228.

2271.

2227. 1:10

2239.

2218.

from Test Trench,
probably earlier, or in slope
wash from VII (Nin. V)

1:5, except 2227

Plate 19.   Types of bowls, Level IX.

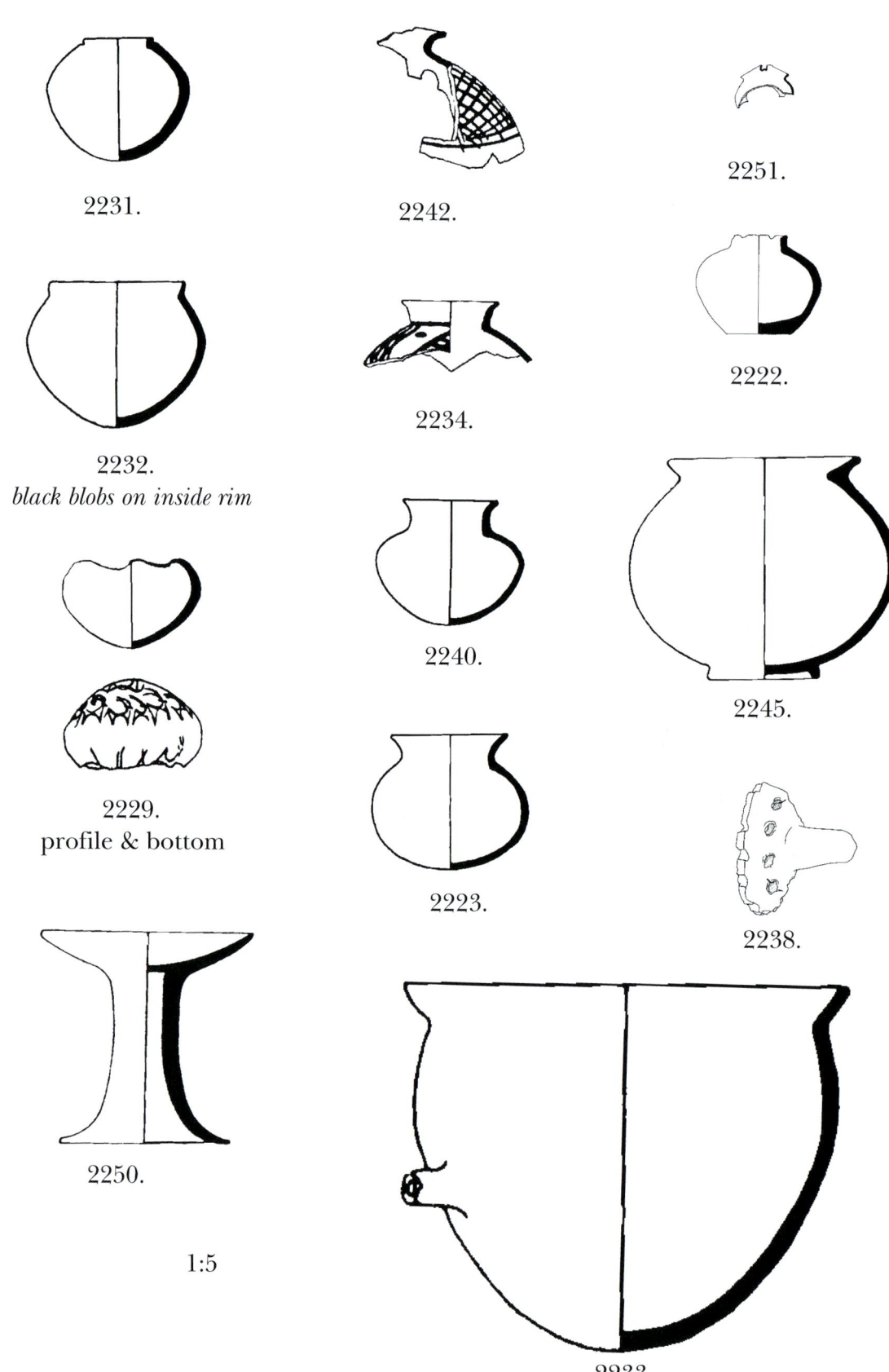

2231.

2242.

2251.

2232.
black blobs on inside rim

2234.

2222.

2229.
profile & bottom

2240.

2245.

2223.

2238.

2250.

1:5

2233.

Plate 20.   Types of jars and miscellaneous forms, Level IX.

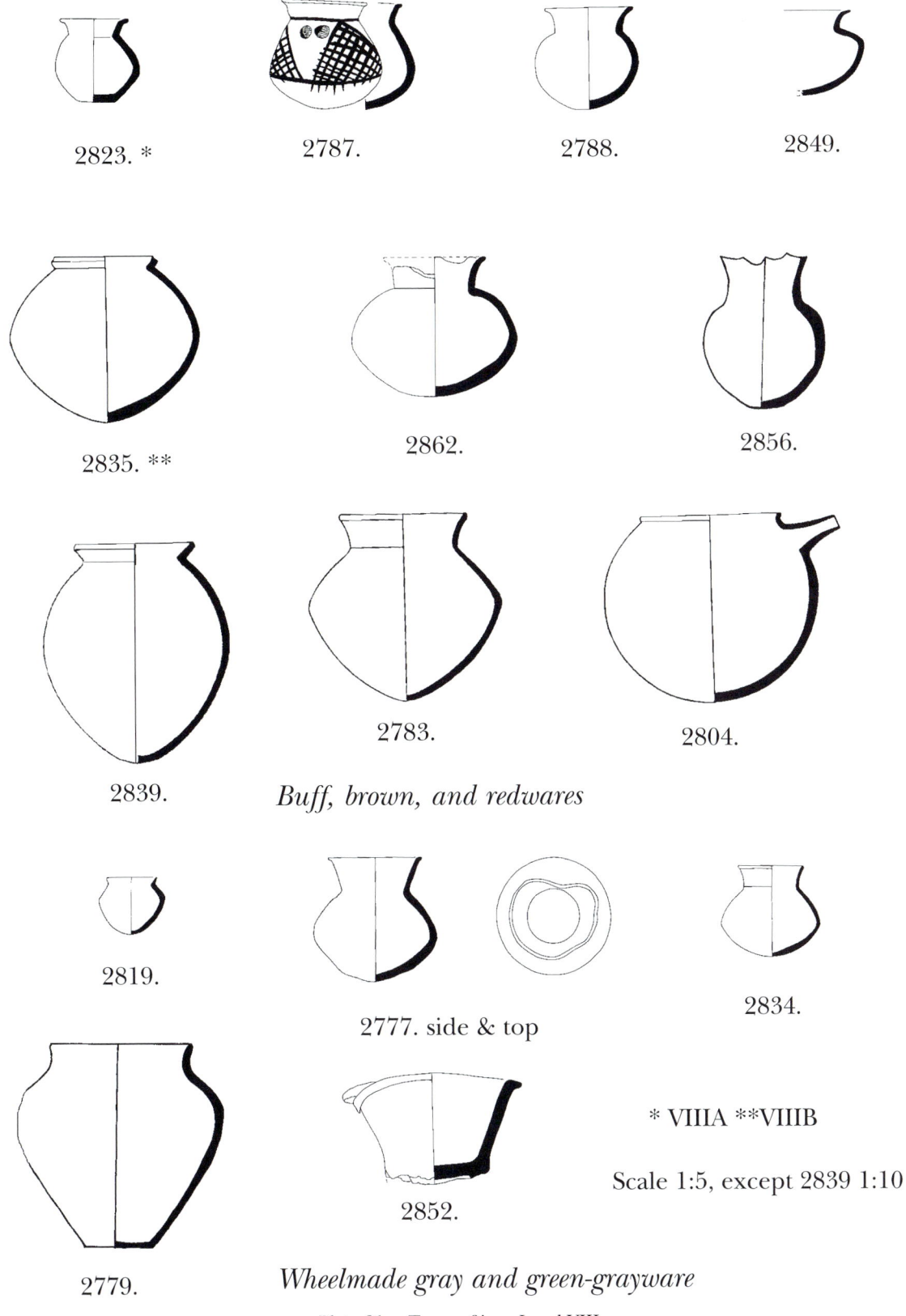

2823. *

2787.

2788.

2849.

2835. **

2862.

2856.

2839.

2783.

2804.

Buff, brown, and redwares

2819.

2777. side & top

2834.

* VIIIA **VIIIB

Scale 1:5, except 2839 1:10

2779.

2852.

Wheelmade gray and green-grayware

Plate 21.   Types of jars, Level VIII.

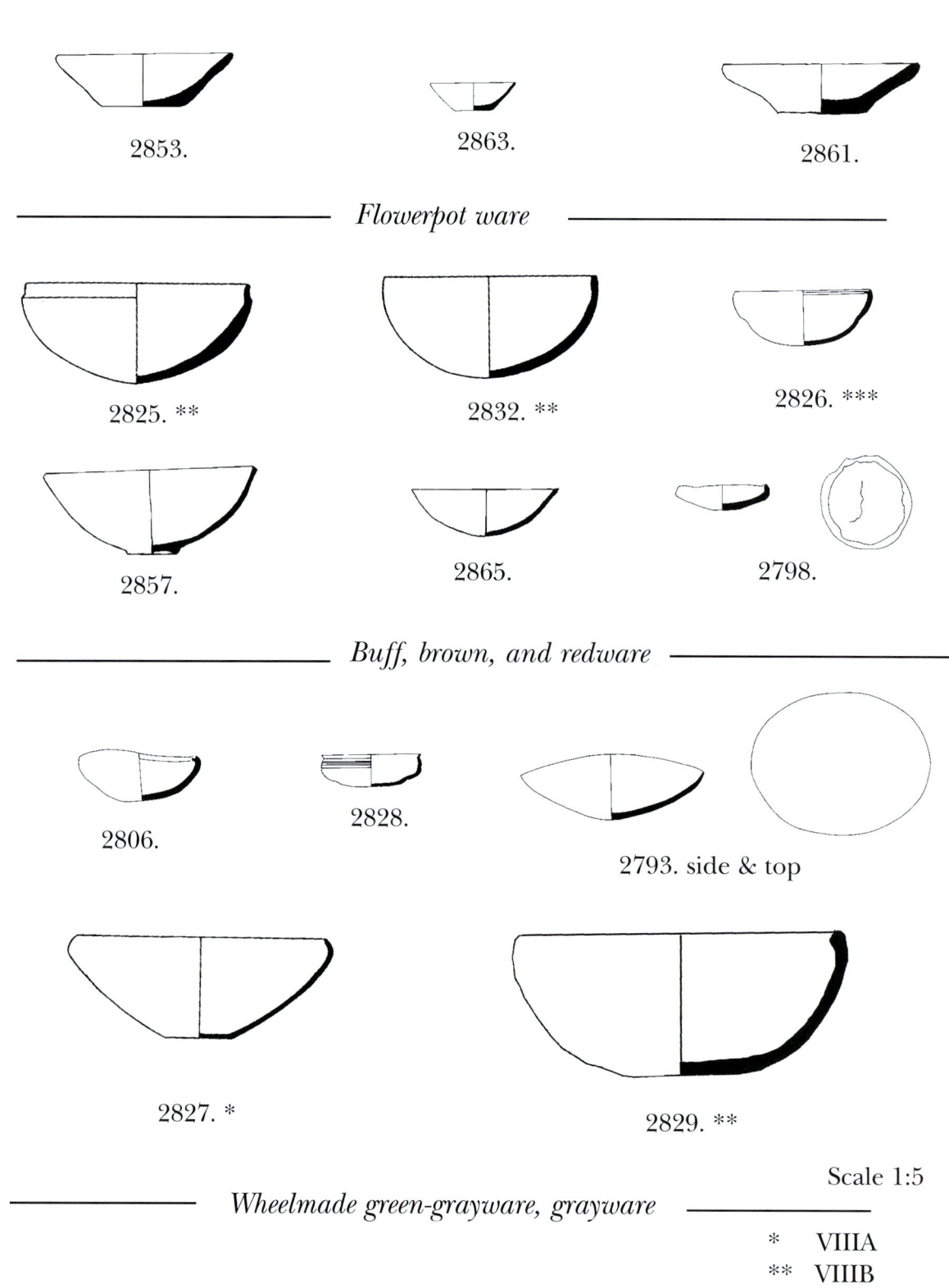

2853.

2863.

2861.

Flowerpot ware

2825. **

2832. **

2826. ***

2857.

2865.

2798.

Buff, brown, and redware

2806.

2828.

2793. side & top

2827. *

2829. **

Scale 1:5

Wheelmade green-grayware, grayware

*   VIIIA
**   VIIIB
*** VIIIC

Plate 22.   Types of bowls, Level VIII.

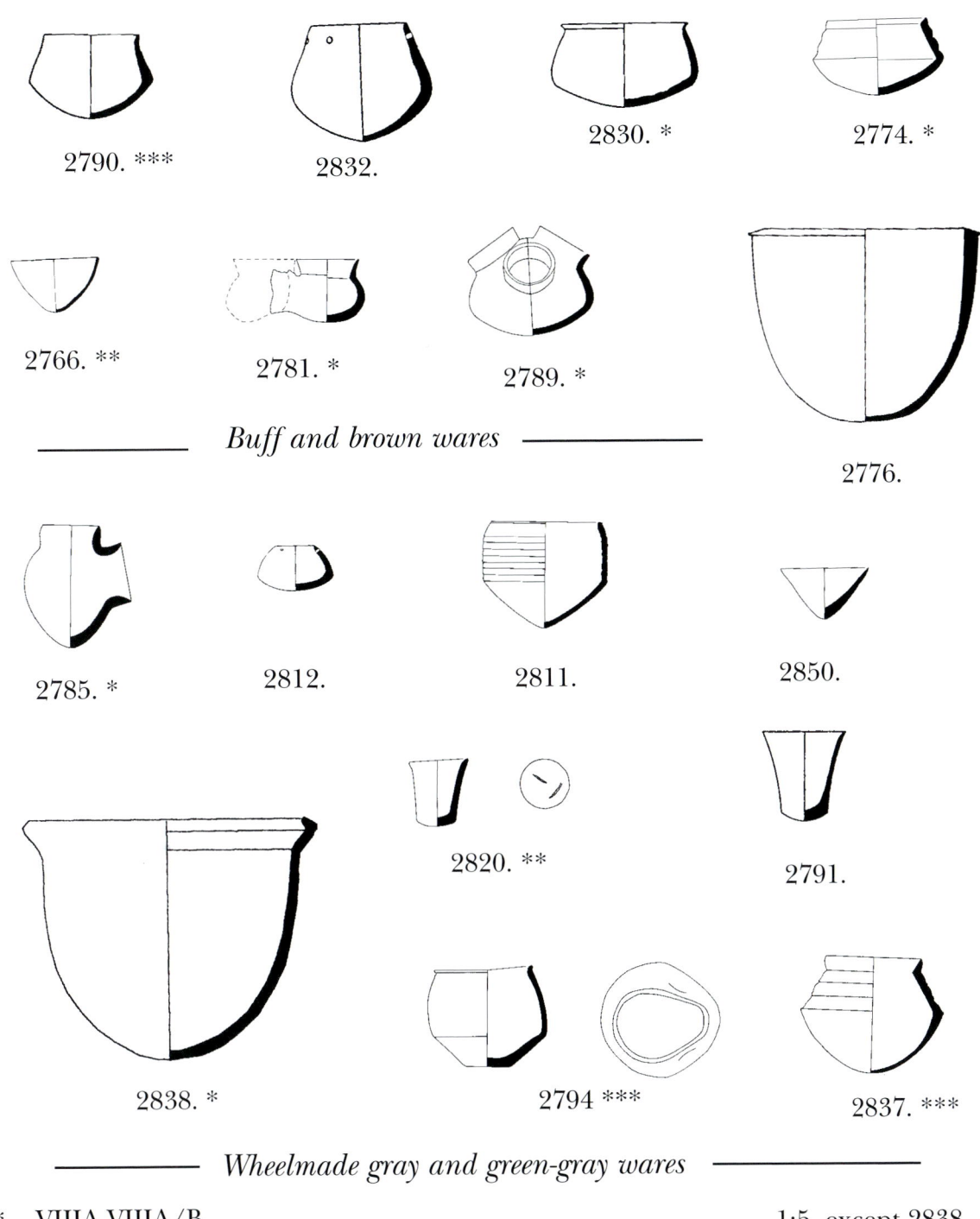

2790. ***

2832.

2830. *

2774. *

2766. **

2781. *

2789. *

Buff and brown wares

2776.

2785. *

2812.

2811.

2850.

2838. *

2820. **

2791.

2794 ***

2837. ***

Wheelmade gray and green-gray wares

*   VIIIA VIIIA/B
**   VIIIB/C, VIIIC
*** sub-VI

1:5, except 2838
and 2776

Plate 23.   Types of cups and urns, Level VIII.

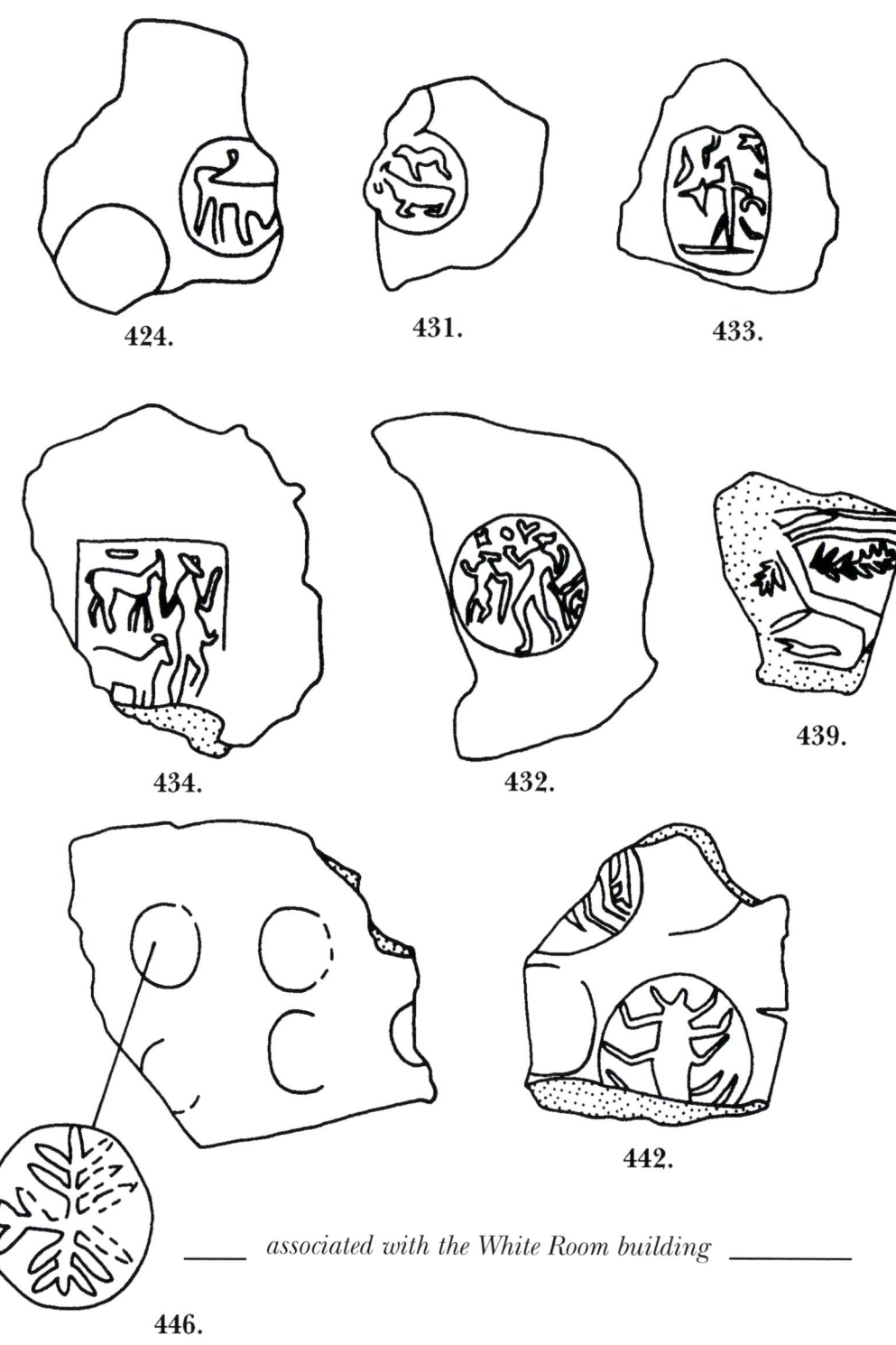

424.

431.

433.

434.

432.

439.

442.

associated with the White Room building

446.

Scale 1:1

Plate 24.   Seals and sealings from Level XII associated with the White Room. All seals drawn in square frame.

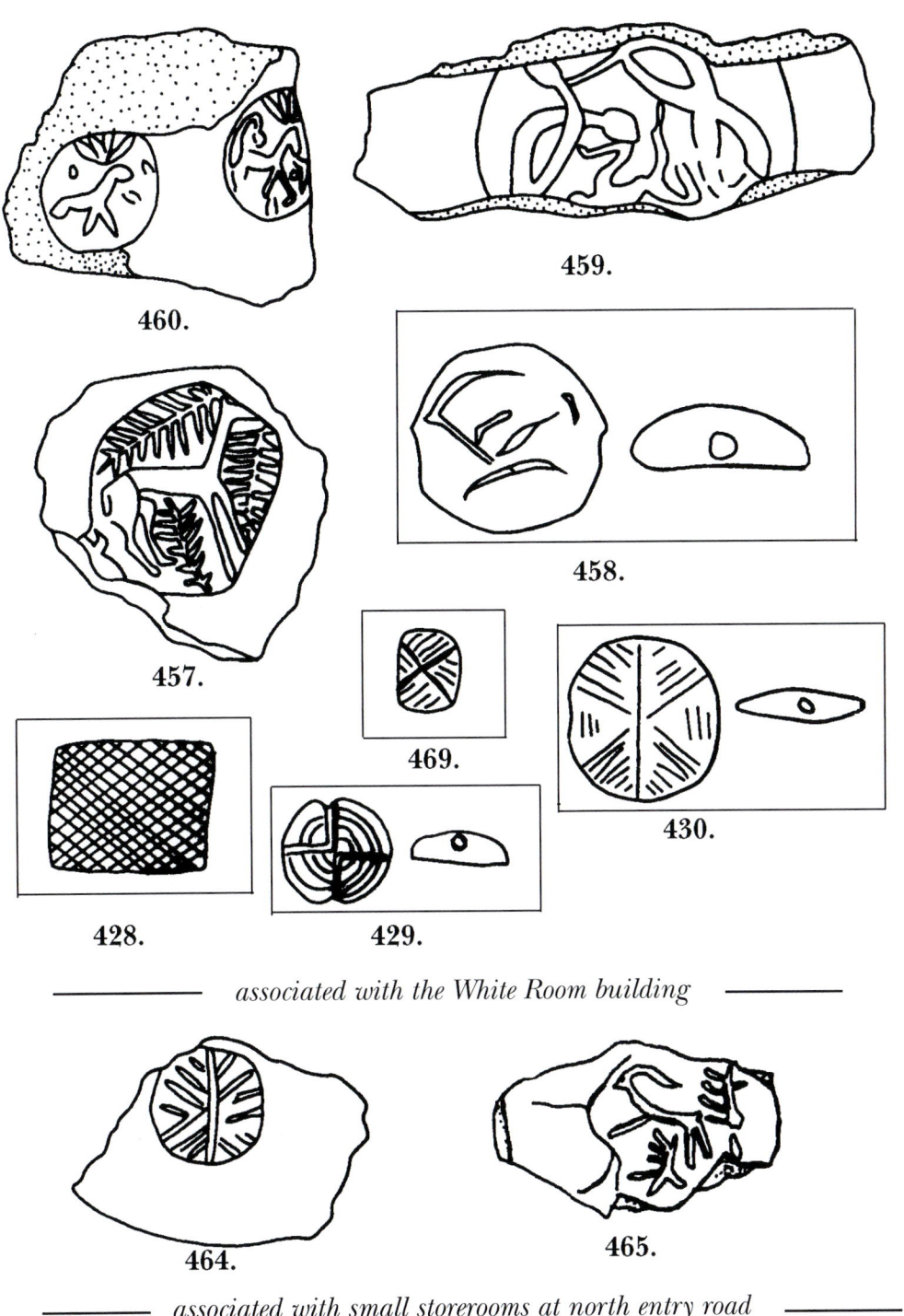

460.

459.

458.

457.

469.

430.

428.

429.

associated with the White Room building

464.

465.

associated with small storerooms at north entry road

Scale 1:1

Plate 25.   Seals and sealings from Level XII associated with the White Room and small storerooms.

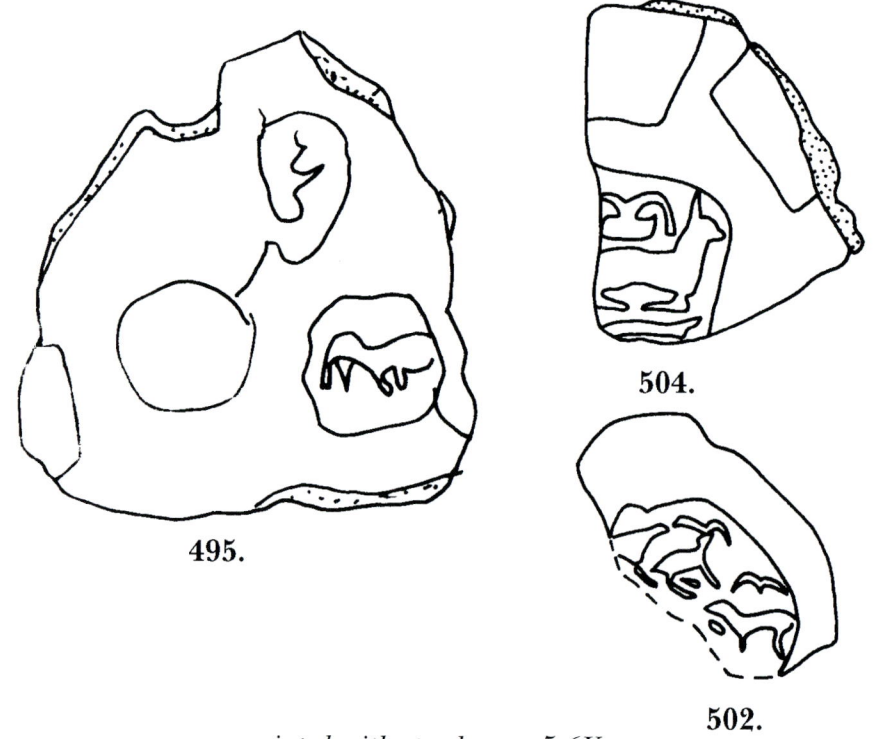

associated with storehouse, 5-6K

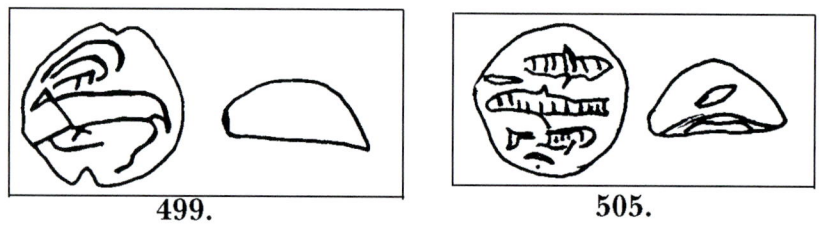

associated with building due south of storehouse

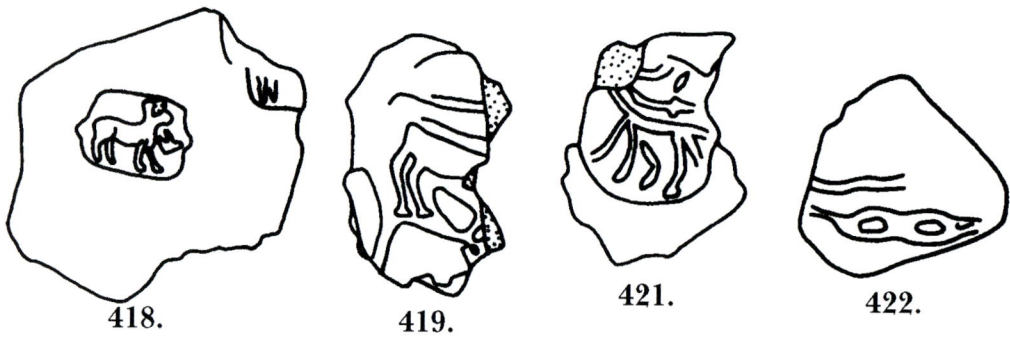

Plate 26. Seals and sealings from Level XII   Scale 1:1

Plate 26.   Seals and sealings from Level XII associated with storehouse and adjoining buildings.

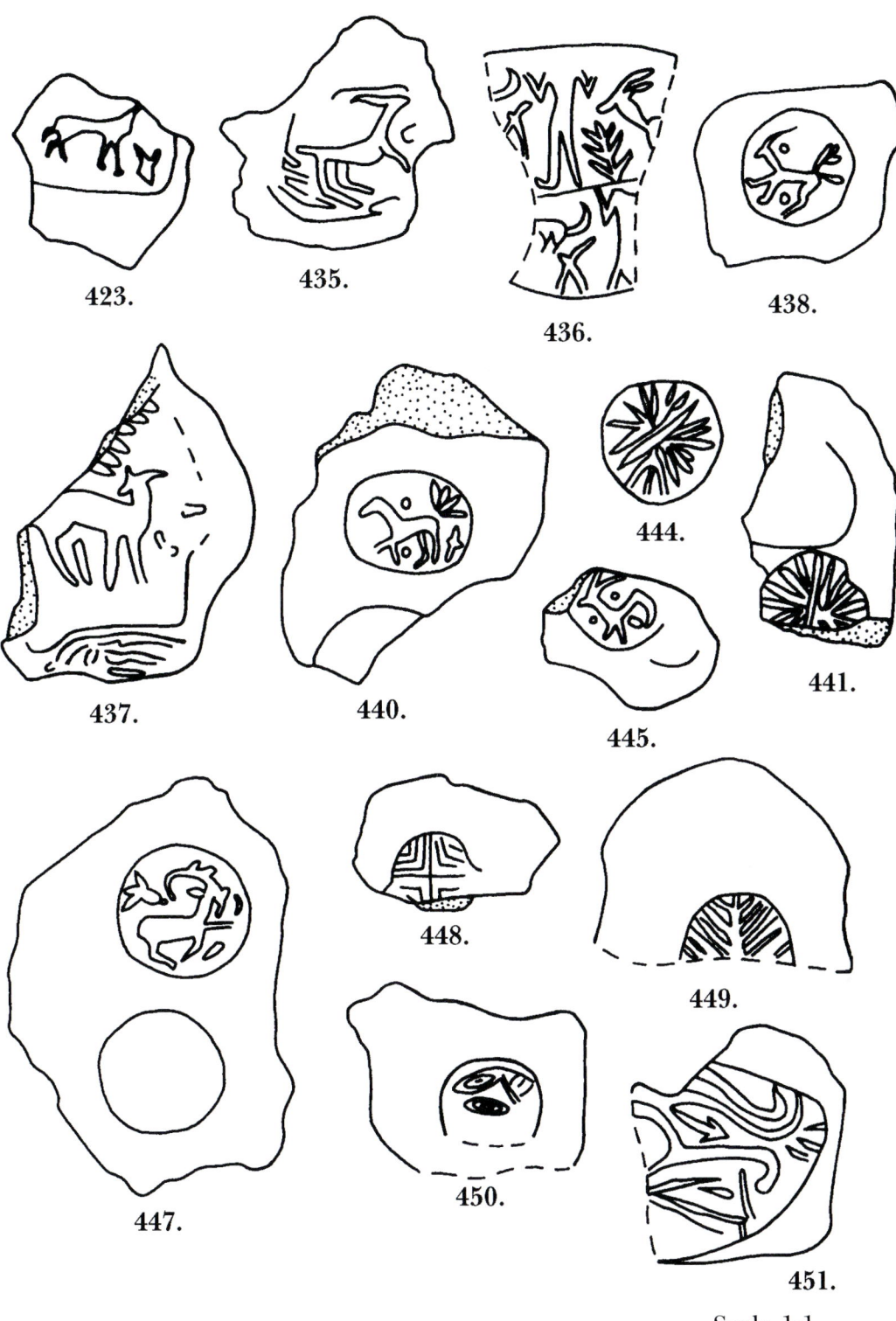

423.

435.

436.

438.

437.

440.

444.

441.

445.

447.

448.

449.

450.

451.

Scale 1:1

Plate 27.   Seals and sealings from Level XII, various proveniences.

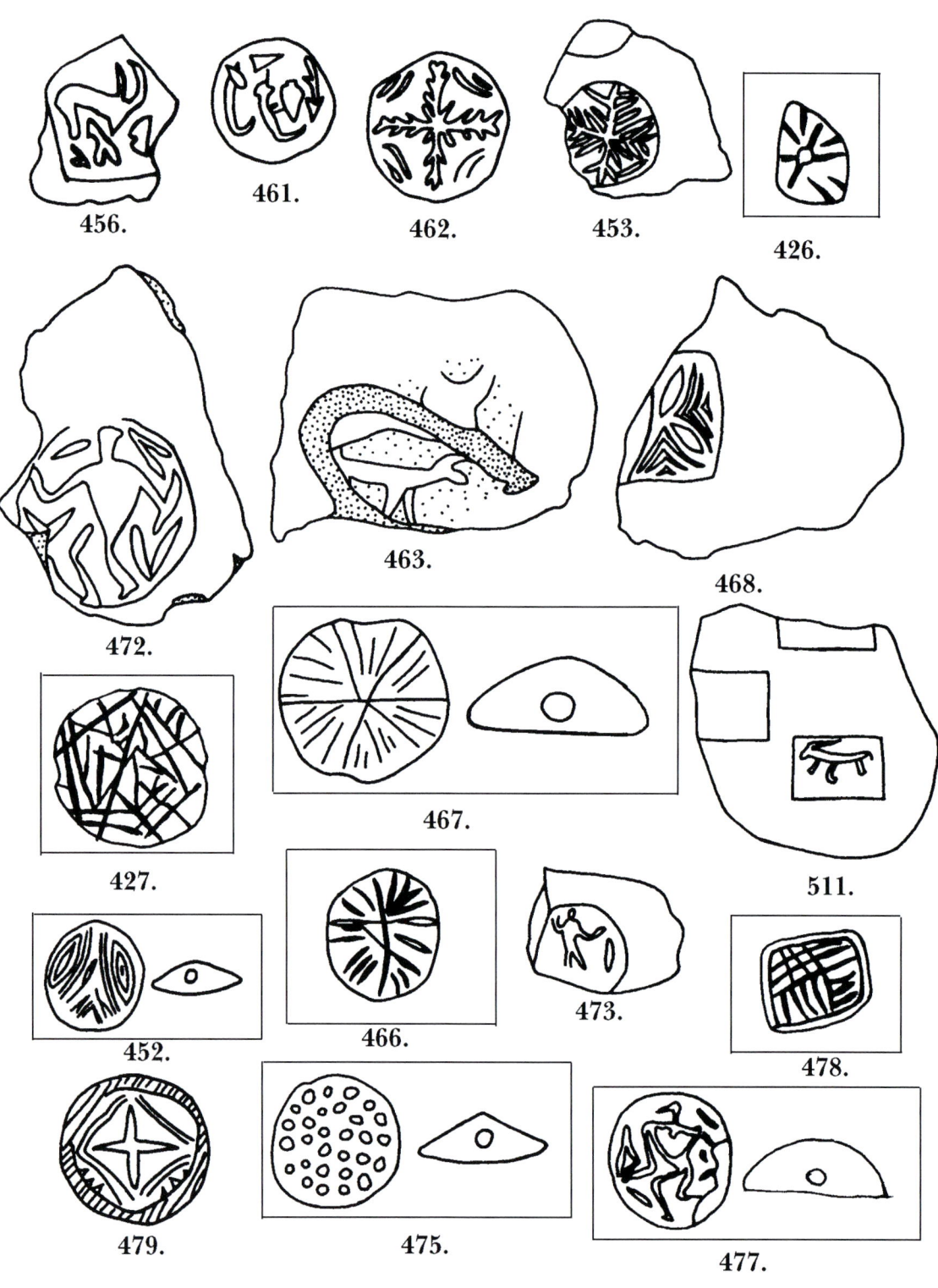

456.

461.

462.

453.

426.

472.

463.

468.

427.

467.

511.

452.

466.

473.

478.

479.

475.

477.

Scale 1:1

Plate 28.   Seals and sealings from Level XII, various proveniences.

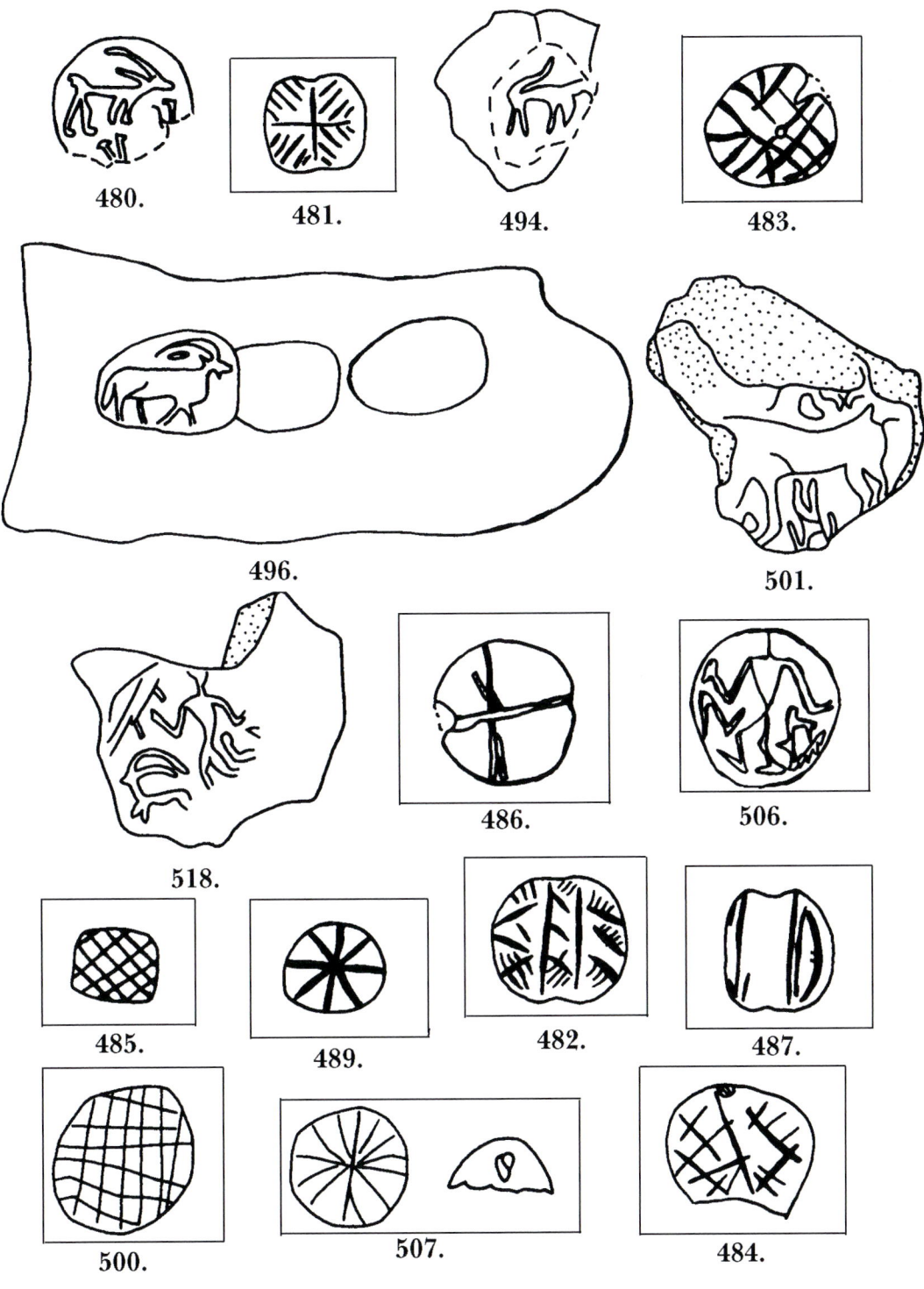

480.

481.

494.

483.

496.

501.

518.

486.

506.

485.

489.

482.

487.

500.

507.

484.

Scale 1:1

Plate 29.   Seals and sealings from Level XII, various proveniences.

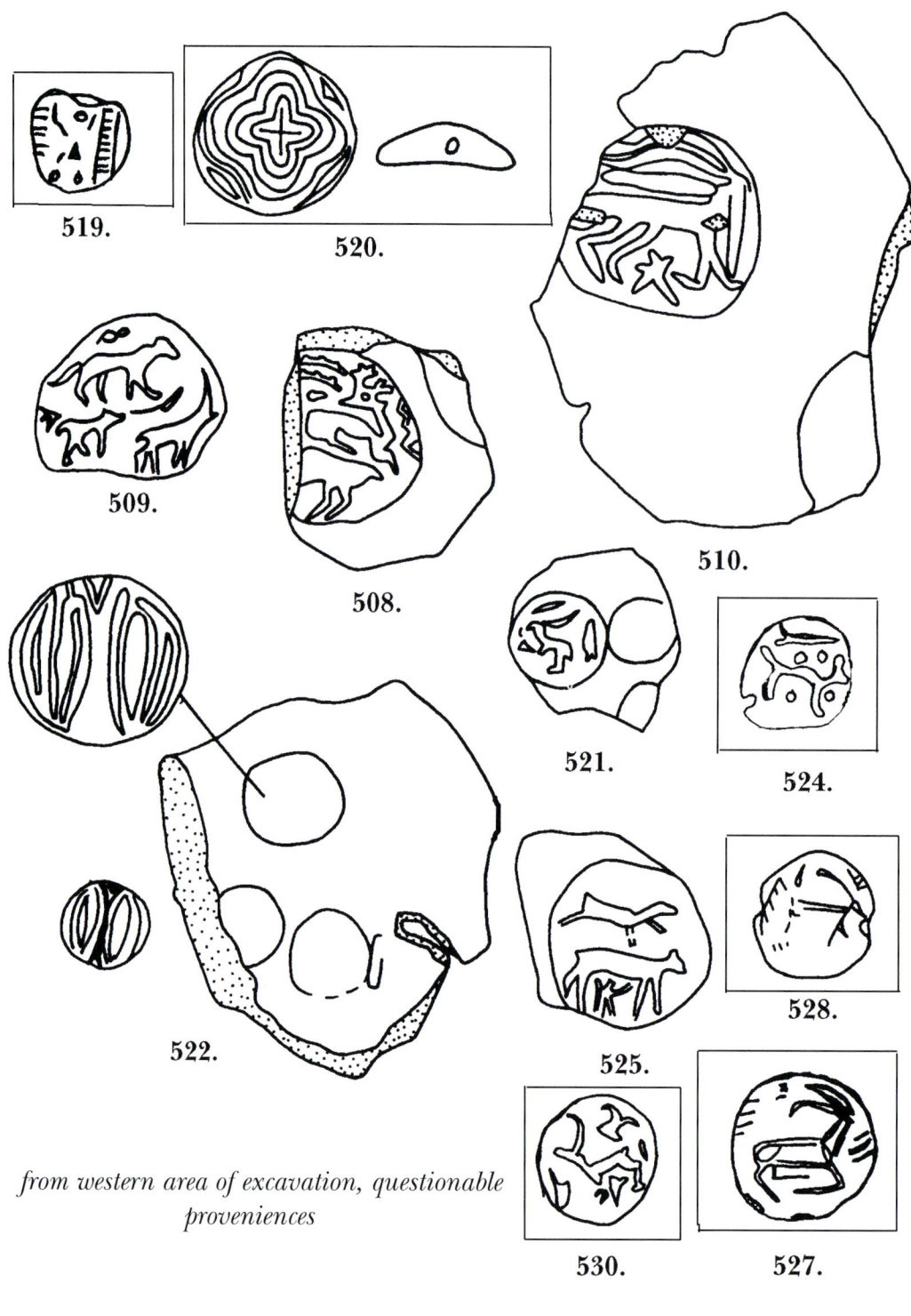

519.

520.

509.

508.

510.

521.

524.

522.

525.

528.

from western area of excavation, questionable proveniences

530.

527.

Scale 1:1

Plate 30. Seals and sealings from Level XII, from the western area of excavation and questionable proveniences.

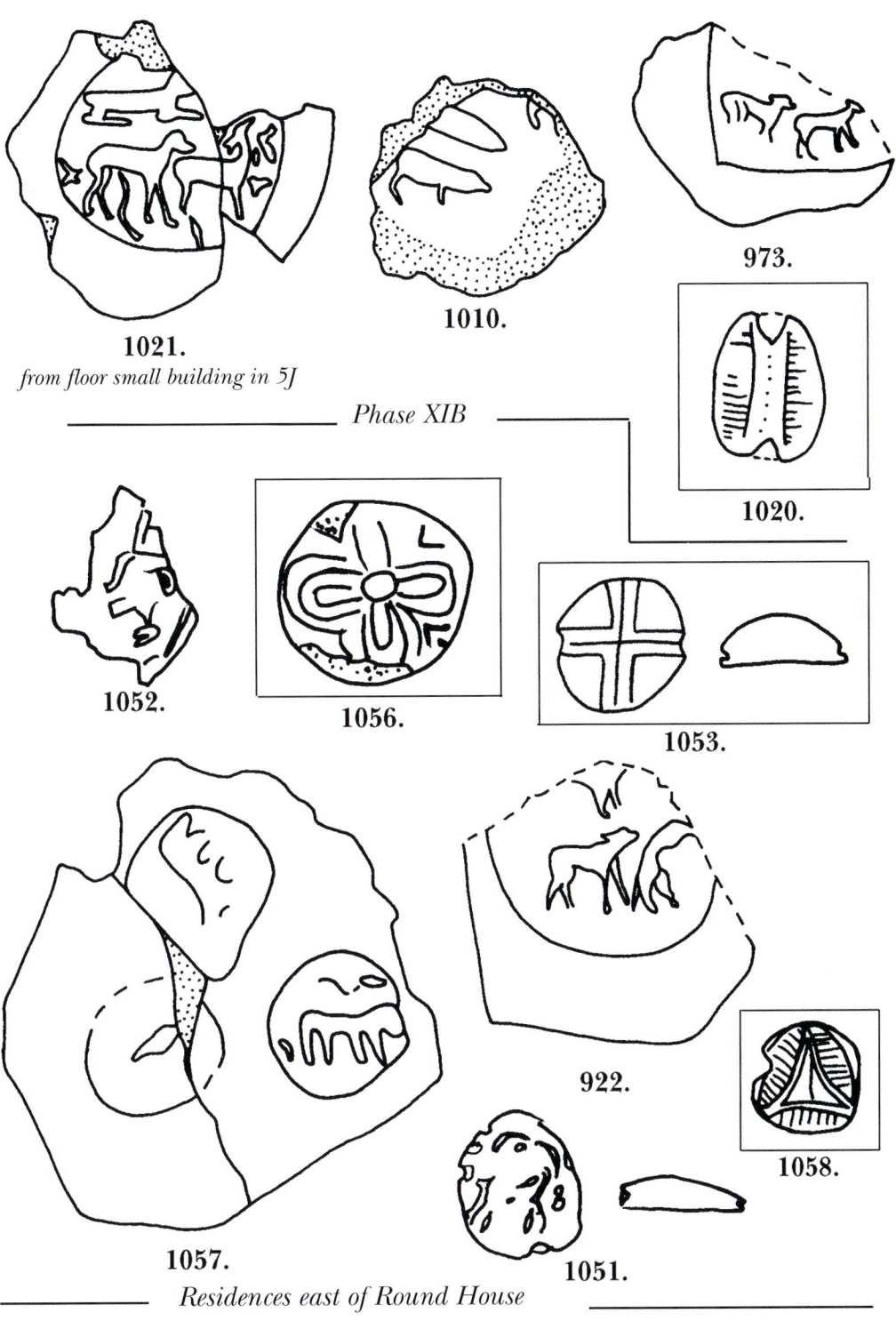

1021.
from floor small building in 5J

1010.

973.

1020.

——————— *Phase XIB* ———————

1052.

1056.

1053.

922.

1057.

1051.

1058.

Residences east of Round House

Scale 1:1

Plate 31.   Seals and sealings from Level XIA/B, Phase XIB and residences East of the Round house.

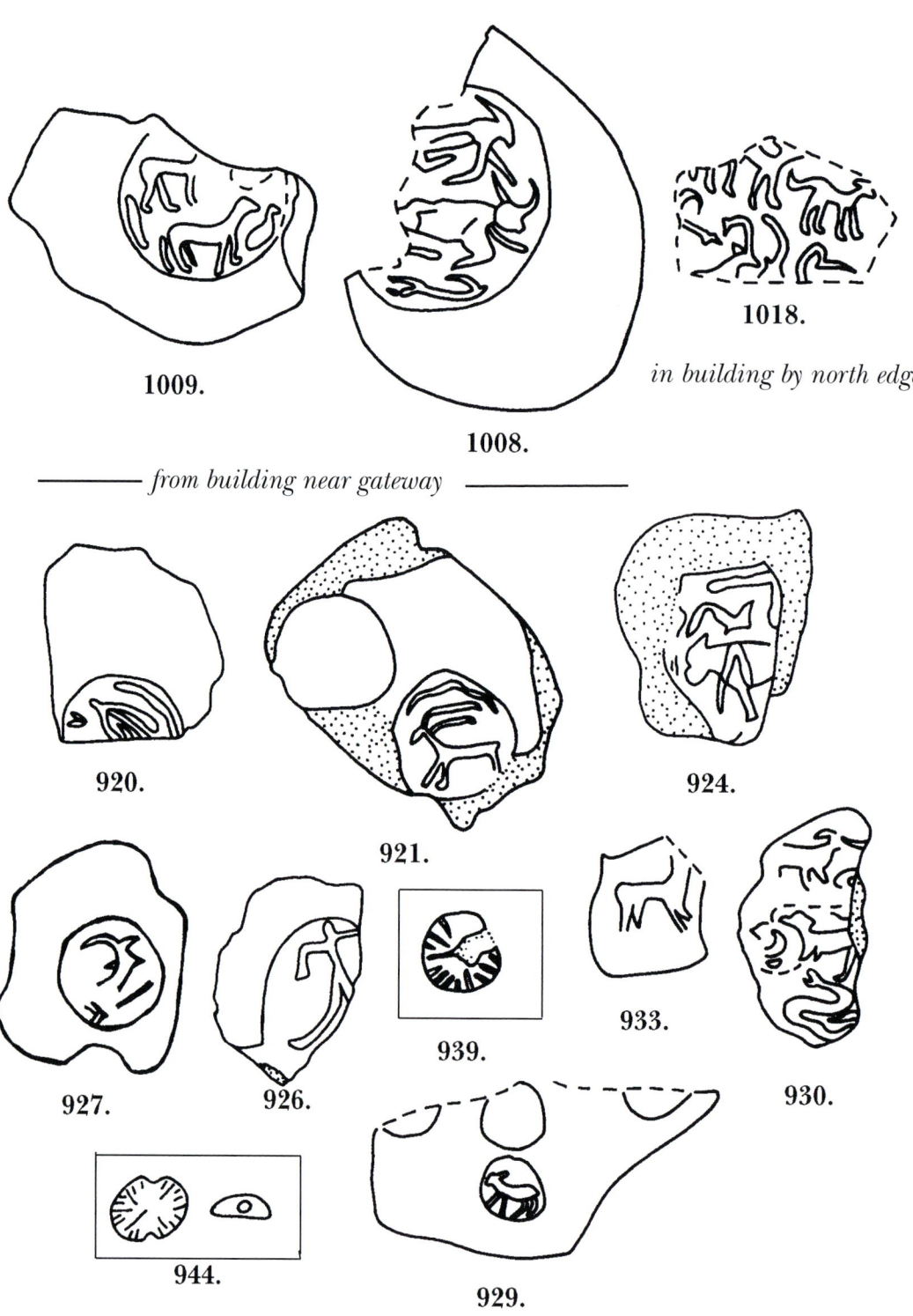

1009.

1008.

1018.

in building by north edge

—————— *from building near gateway* ——————

920.

921.

924.

927.

926.

939.

933.

930.

944.

929.

Scale 1:1

Plate 32. Seals and sealings from Level XIA/B, from the building near the gateway and various proveniences.

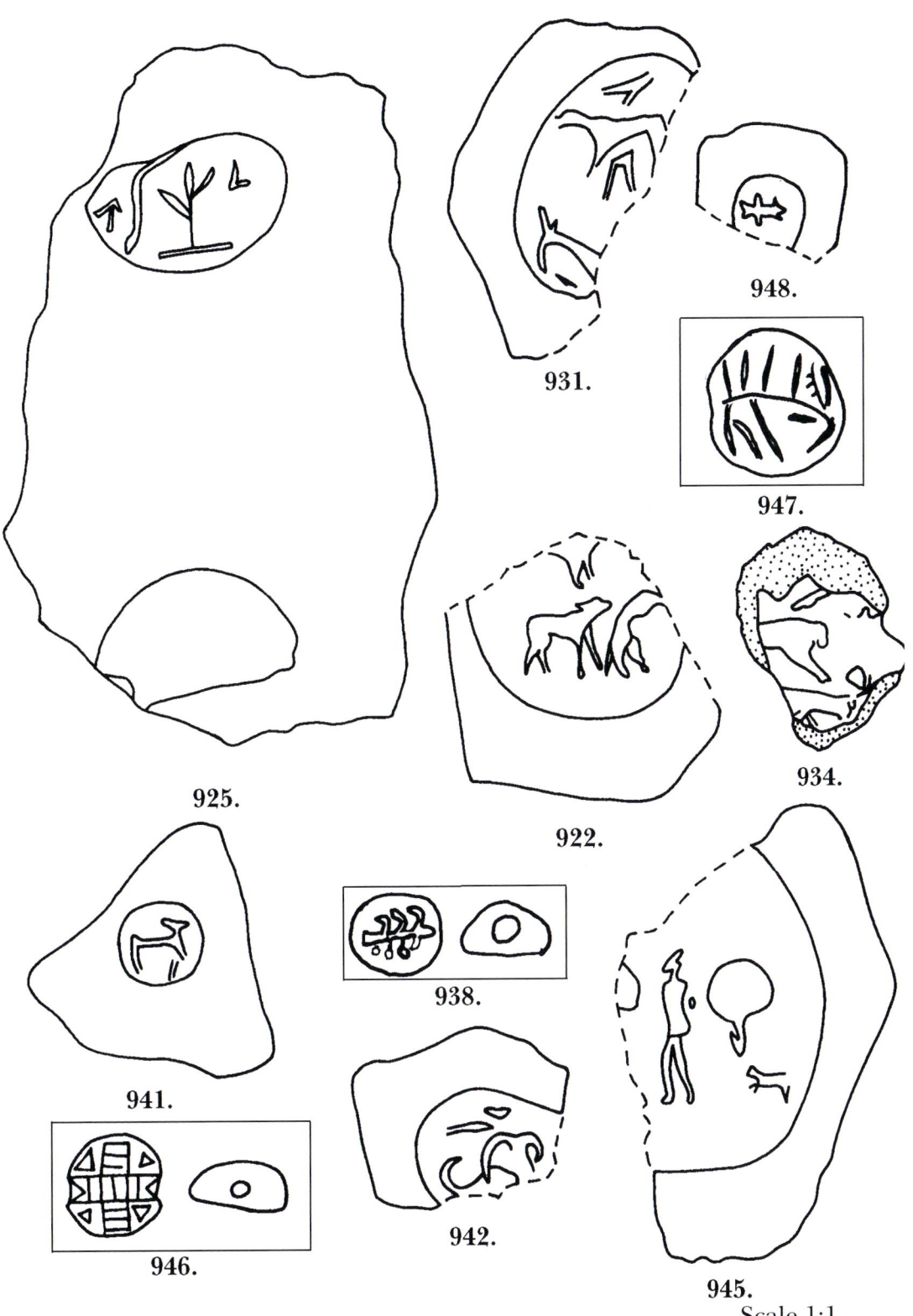

925.

931.

948.

947.

934.

922.

938.

941.

946.

942.

945.

Scale 1:1

Plate 33. Seals and sealings from Level XIA/B, various proveniences.

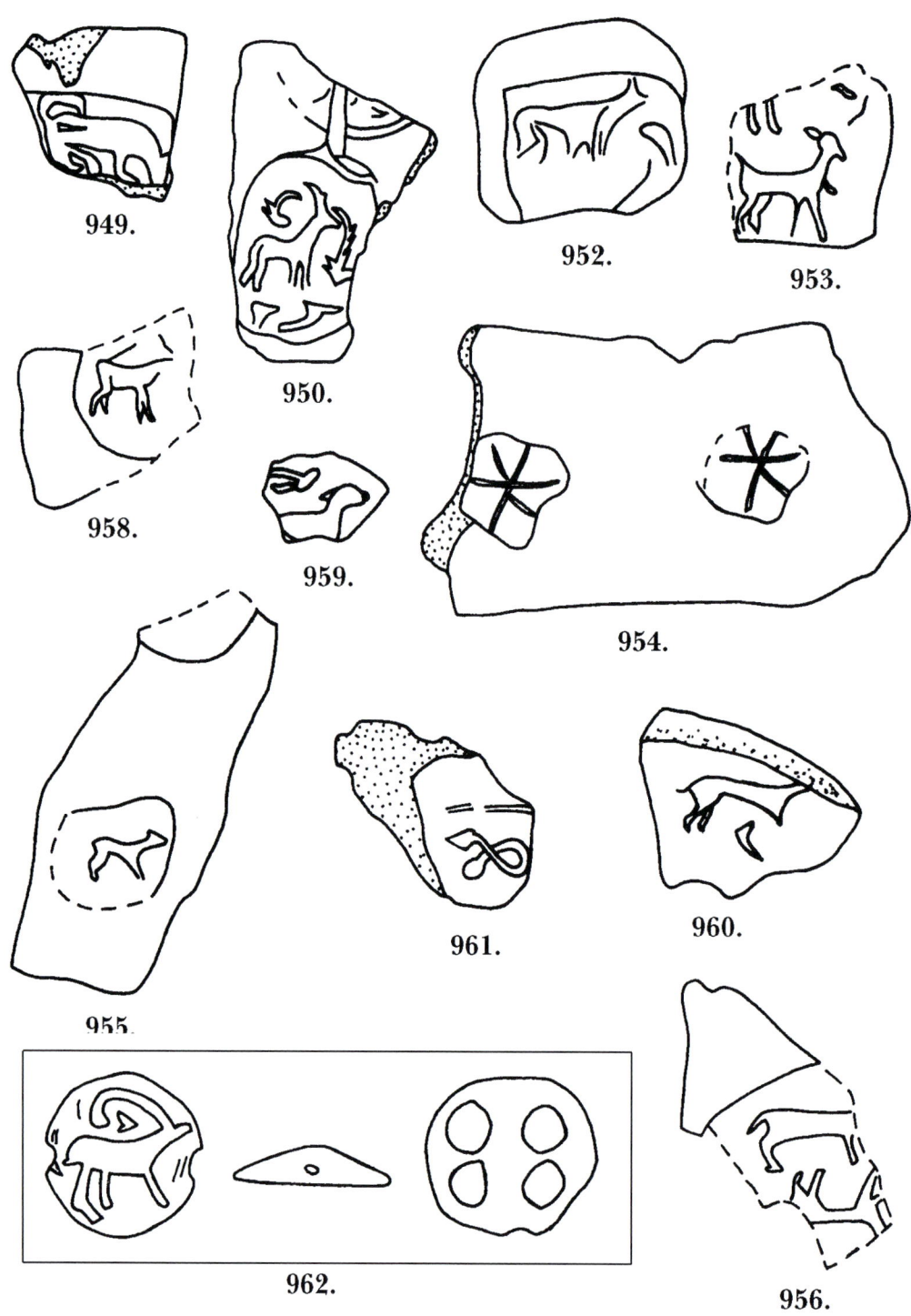

949.

950.

952.

953.

958.

959.

954.

955.

961.

960.

962.

956.

Scale 1:1

Plate 34.   Seals and sealings from Level XIA/B, various proveniences.

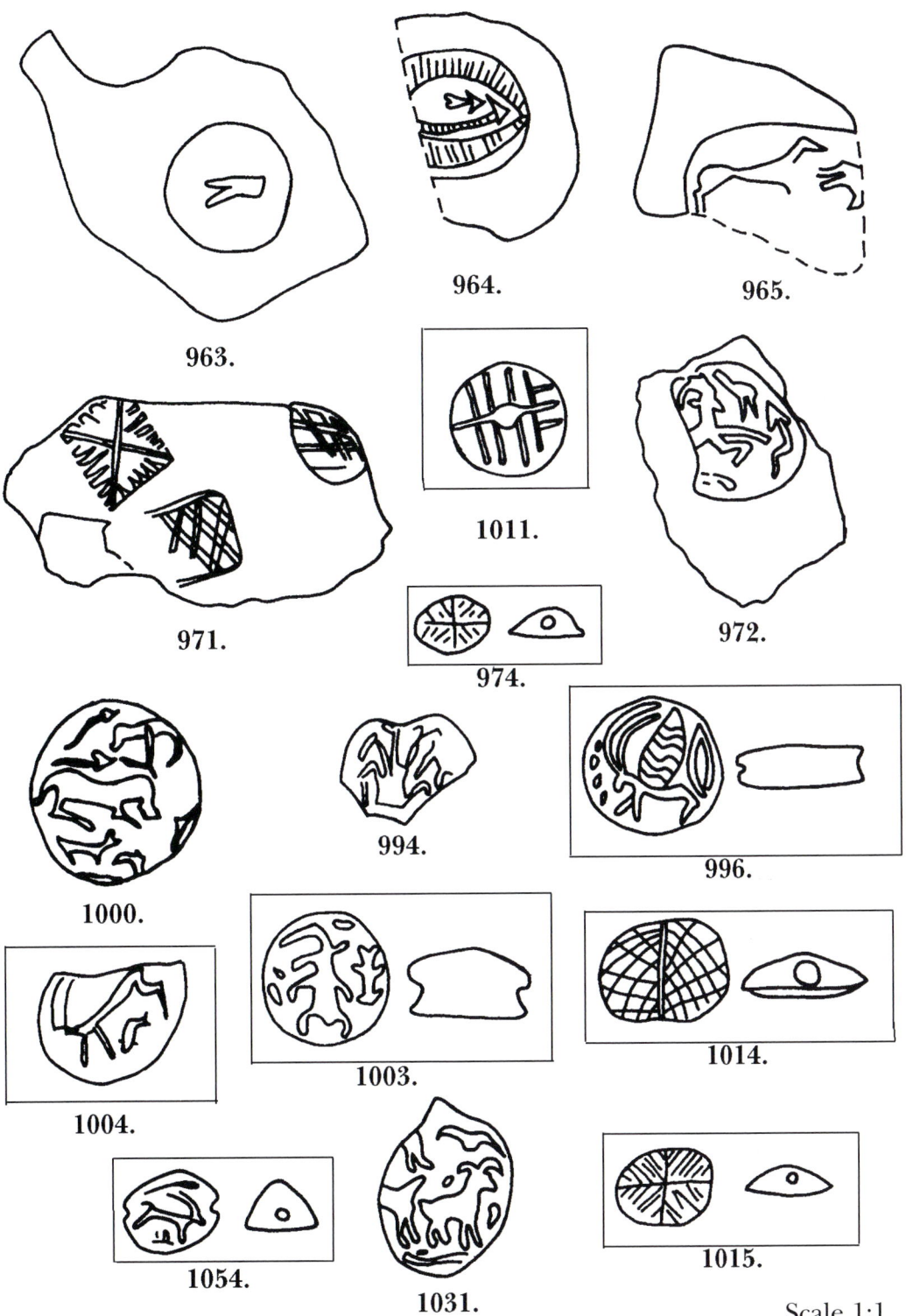

963.

964.

965.

971.

1011.

972.

974.

1000.

994.

996.

1004.

1003.

1014.

1054.

1031.

1015.

Scale 1:1

Plate 35. Seals and sealings from Level XIA/B, various proveniences.

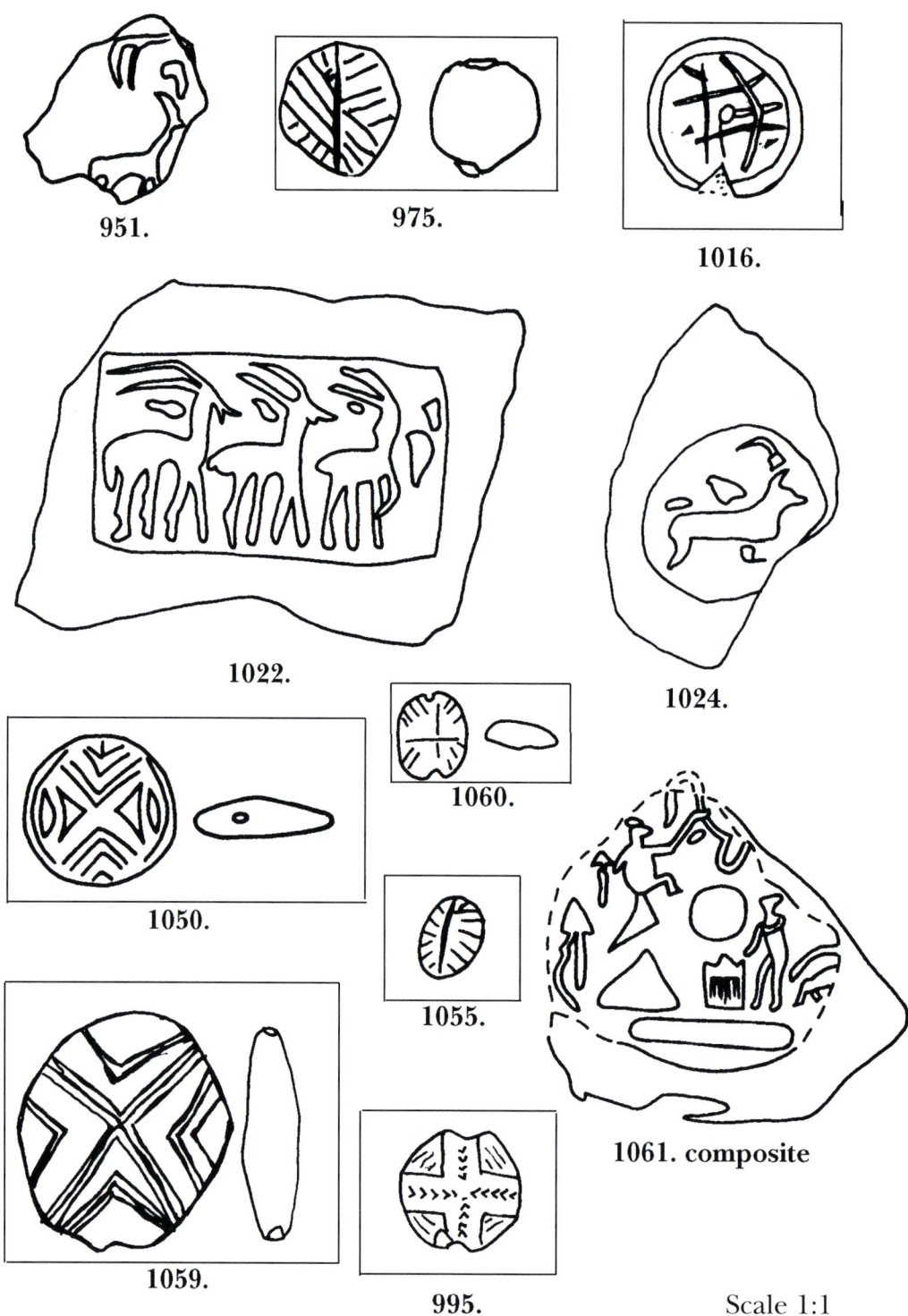

951.

975.

1016.

1022.

1024.

1050.

1060.

1055.

1059.

995.

1061. composite

Scale 1:1

Plate 36.   Seals and sealings from Level XIA/B, various proveniences.

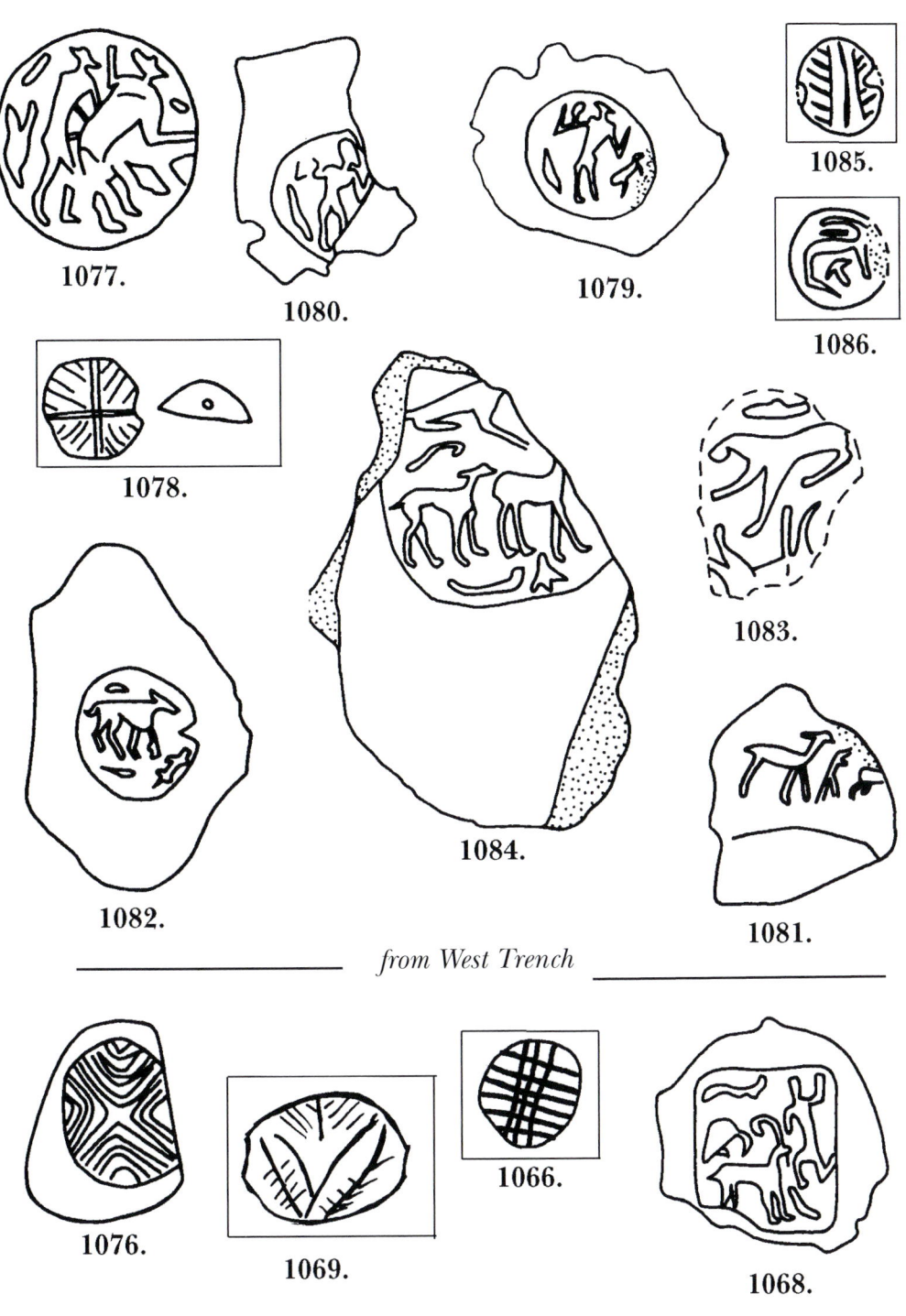

1077.

1080.

1079.

1085.

1086.

1078.

1084.

1083.

1082.

1081.

from West Trench

1076.

1069.

1066.

1068.

Scale 1:1

Plate 37.   Seals and sealings from Level XIA/B, from the West Trench.

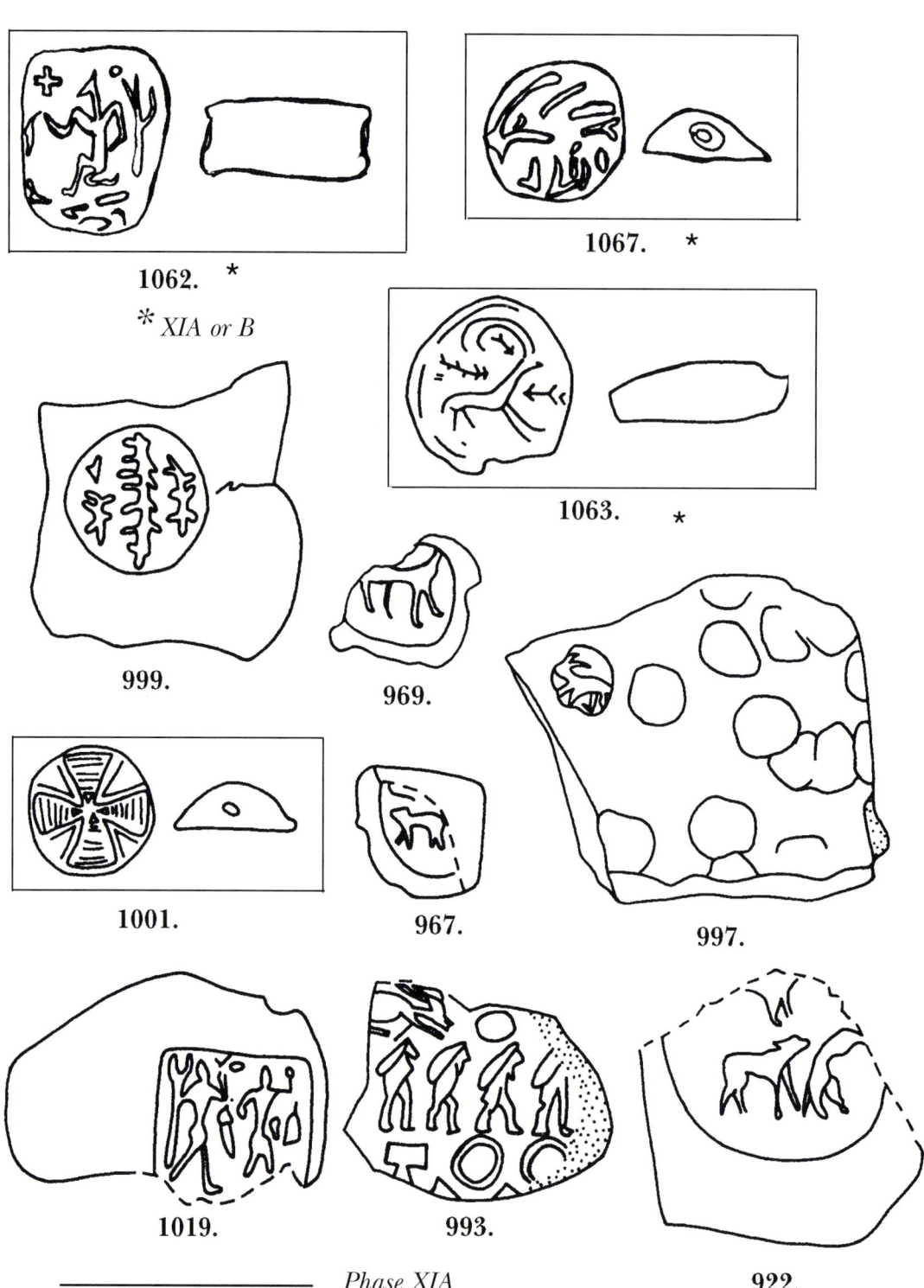

1062. *

* *XIA or B*

1067. *

1063. *

999.

969.

1001.

967.

997.

1019.

993.

—————————— *Phase XIA* —————————— 922.

Scale 1:1

Plate 38.   Seals and sealings from Phase XIA, Level XIA/B.

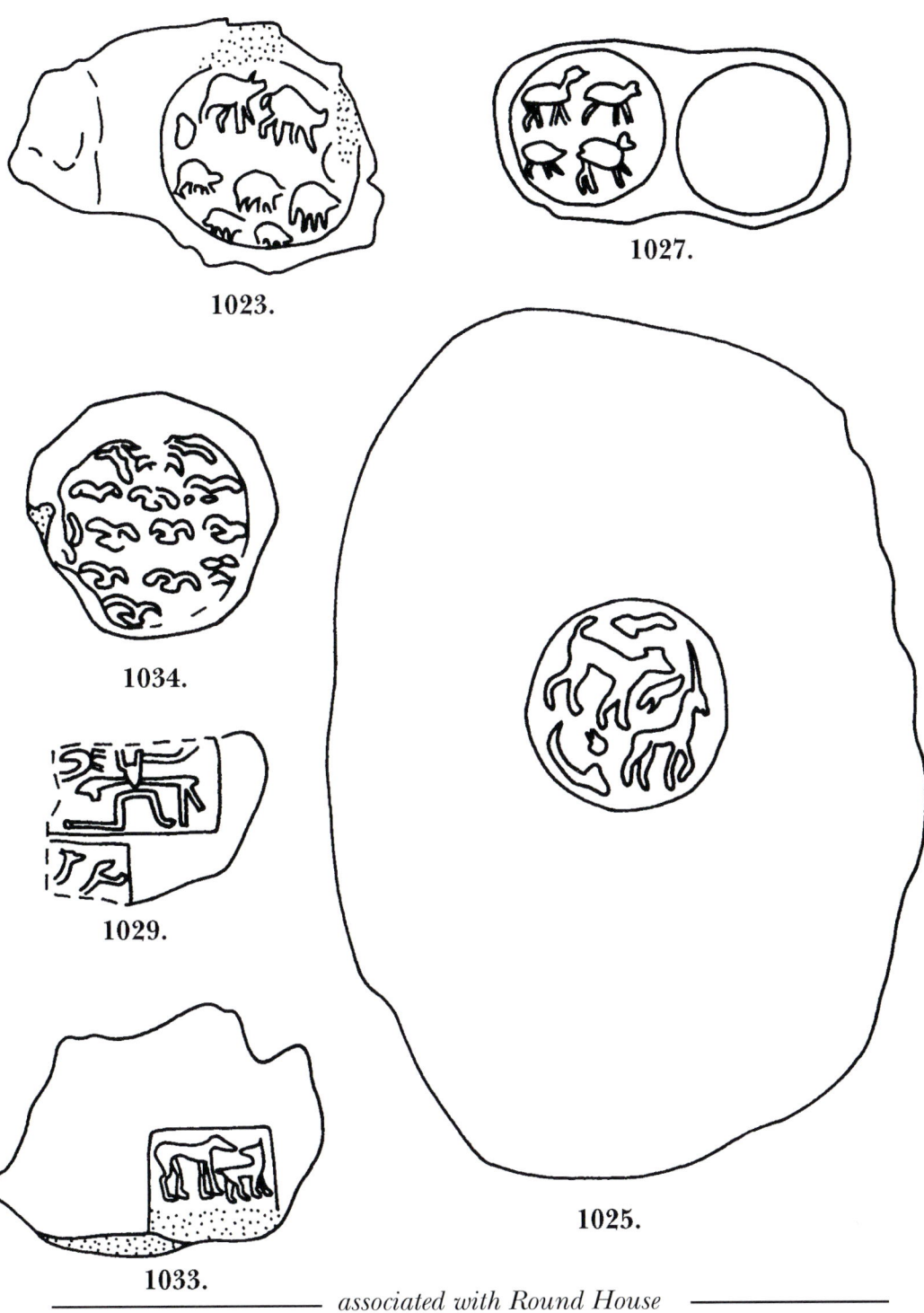

1023.

1027.

1034.

1029.

1025.

1033.

associated with Round House

Scale 1:1

Plate 39.   Seals and sealings from Level XIA/B, associated with the Round house.

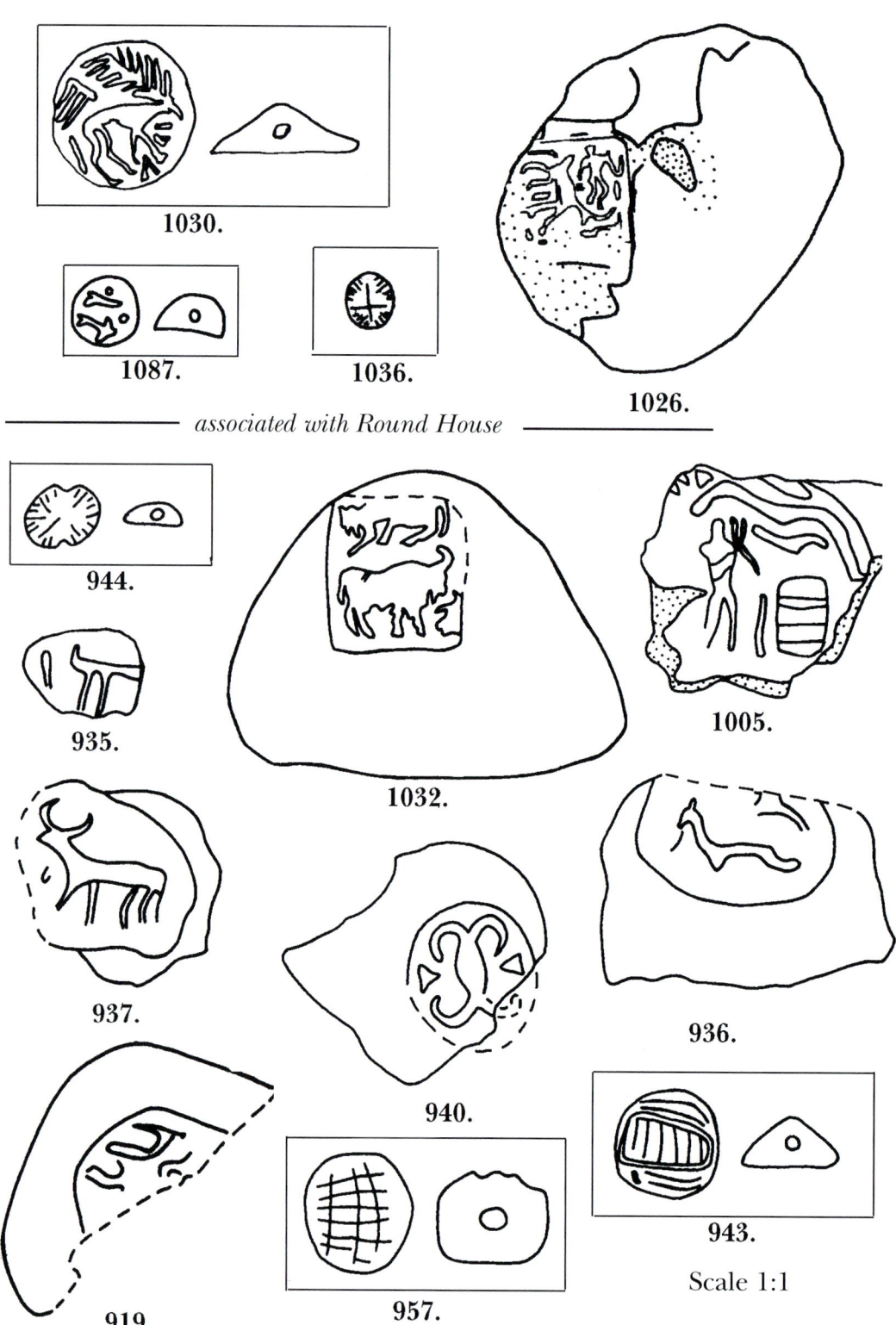

1030.

1087.

1036.

1026.

——————— *associated with Round House* ———————

944.

935.

1032.

1005.

937.

940.

936.

919.

957.

943.

Scale 1:1

Plate 40. Seals and sealings from Level XIA/B, associated with the Round house and various proveniences.

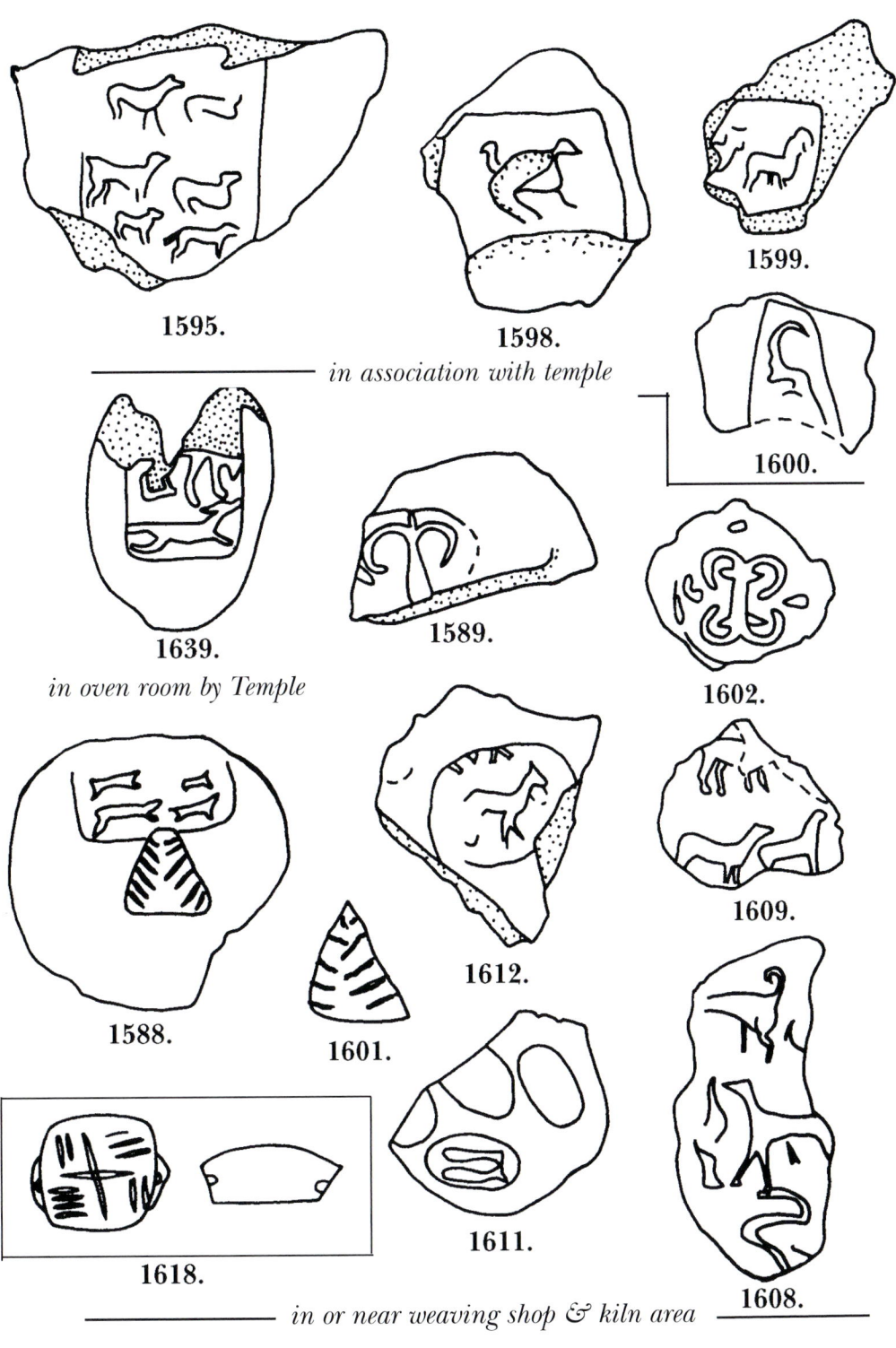

1595.

1598.

1599.

in association with temple

1600.

1639.

in oven room by Temple

1589.

1602.

1588.

1601.

1612.

1609.

1618.

1611.

1608.

in or near weaving shop & kiln area

Scale 1:1

Plate 41. Seals and sealings from Phase XI, Level XI/XA, associated with the temple and weaving shop, kiln Area.

1614. composite

1610.

in association with weaving shop

1660.

1579.

1580.

1623.

1593.

1584.

1626.

1592. *associated with fortress building*

1631.

1630.

1627.

Scale 1:1

Plate 42.   Seals and sealings from Phase XI, Level XI/XA, associated with the weaving shop and fortress.

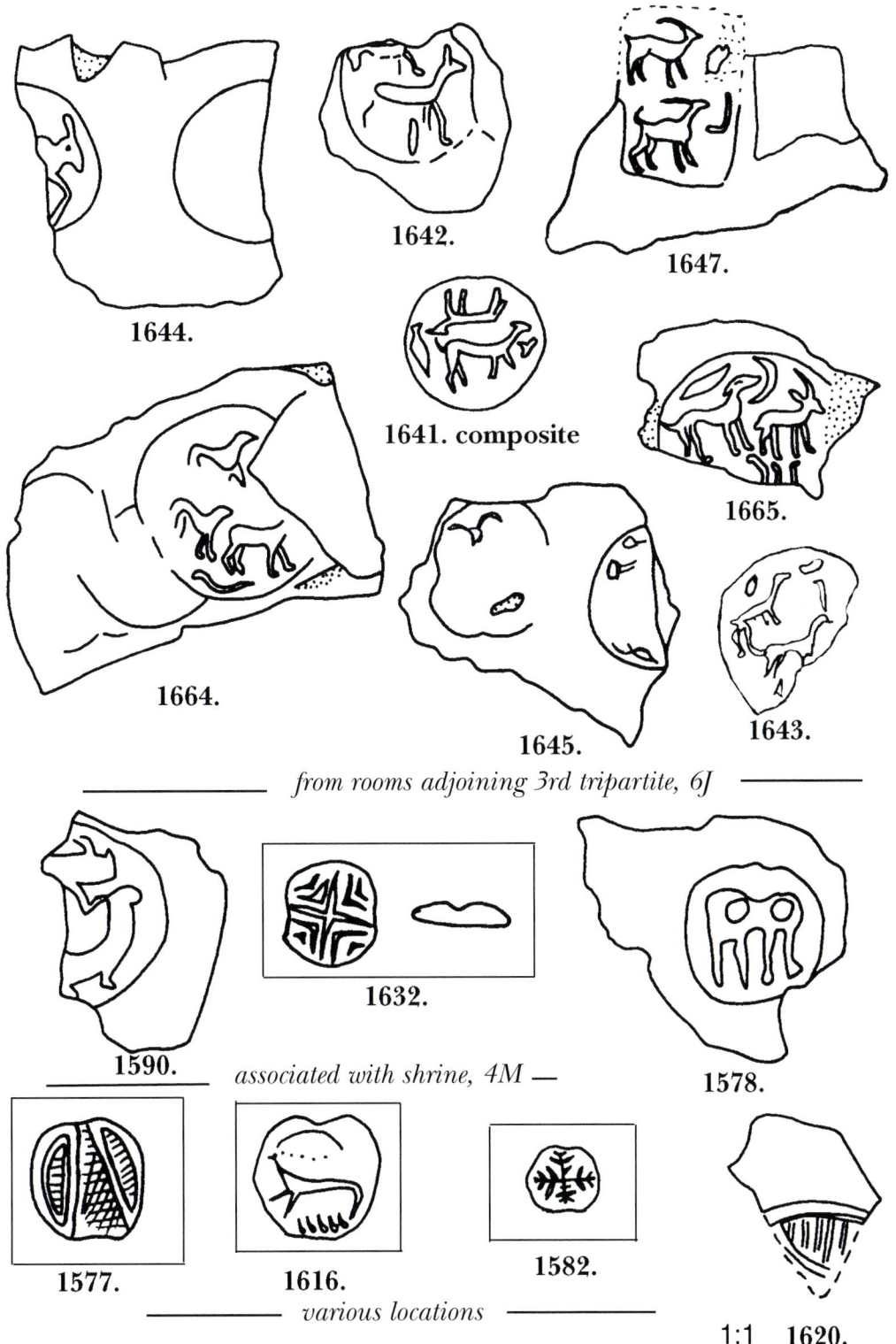

1644.

1642.

1647.

1641. composite

1665.

1664.

1645.

1643.

from rooms adjoining 3rd tripartite, 6J

1590.

1632.

associated with shrine, 4M —

1578.

1577.

1616.

1582.

various locations

1:1   1620.

Plate 43.   Seals and sealings from Phase XI, Level XI/XA, associated with third tripartite building and shrine.

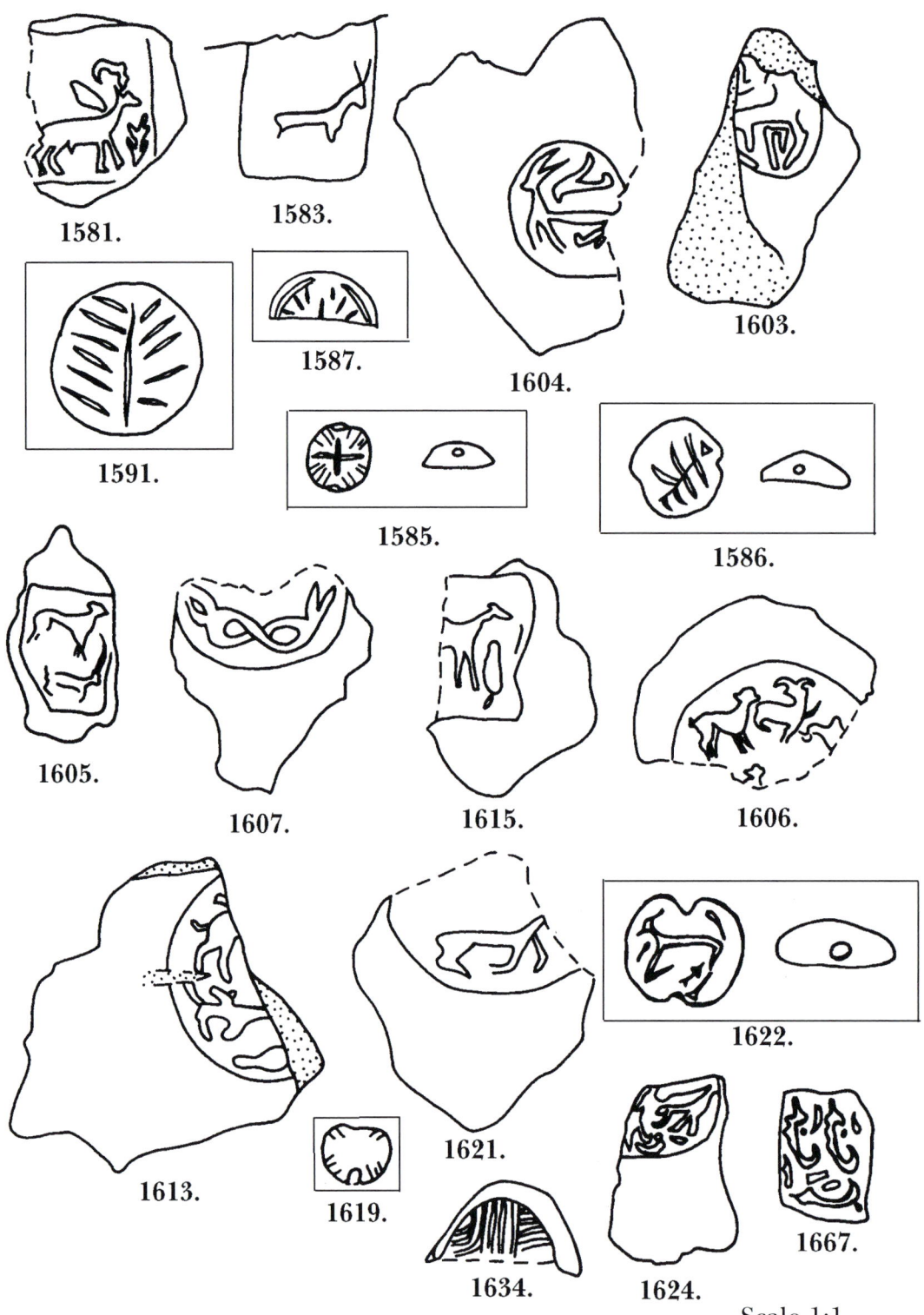

1581.

1583.

1591.

1587.

1604.

1603.

1585.

1586.

1605.

1607.

1615.

1606.

1613.

1619.

1621.

1622.

1634.

1624.

1667.

Scale 1:1

Plate 44.   Seals and sealings from Phase XI, Level XI/XA, unclear proveniences.

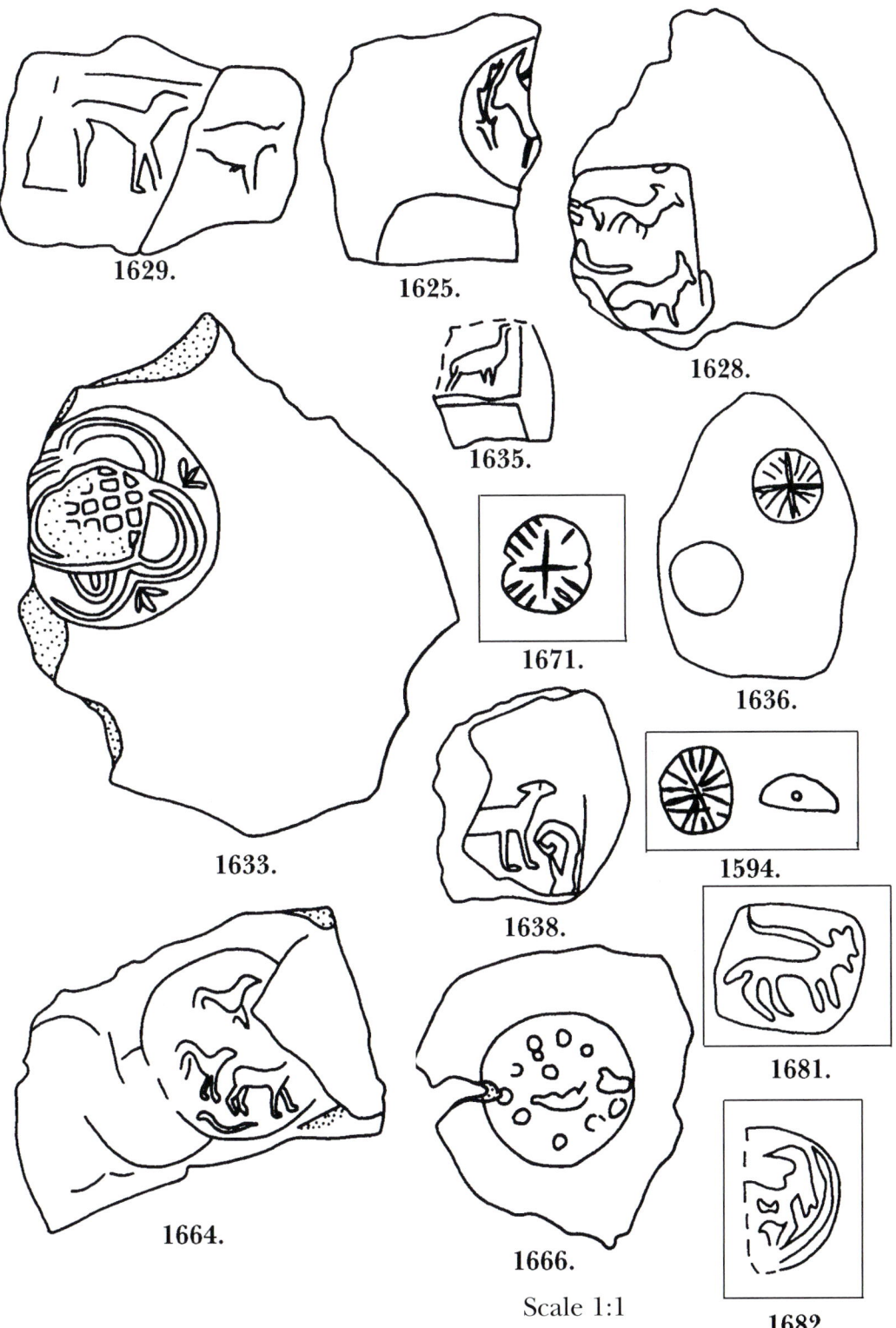

1629.

1625.

1628.

1635.

1671.

1636.

1633.

1594.

1638.

1681.

1664.

1666.

1682.

Scale 1:1

Plate 45.   Seals and sealings from Phase XI, Level XI/XA, unclear proveniences.

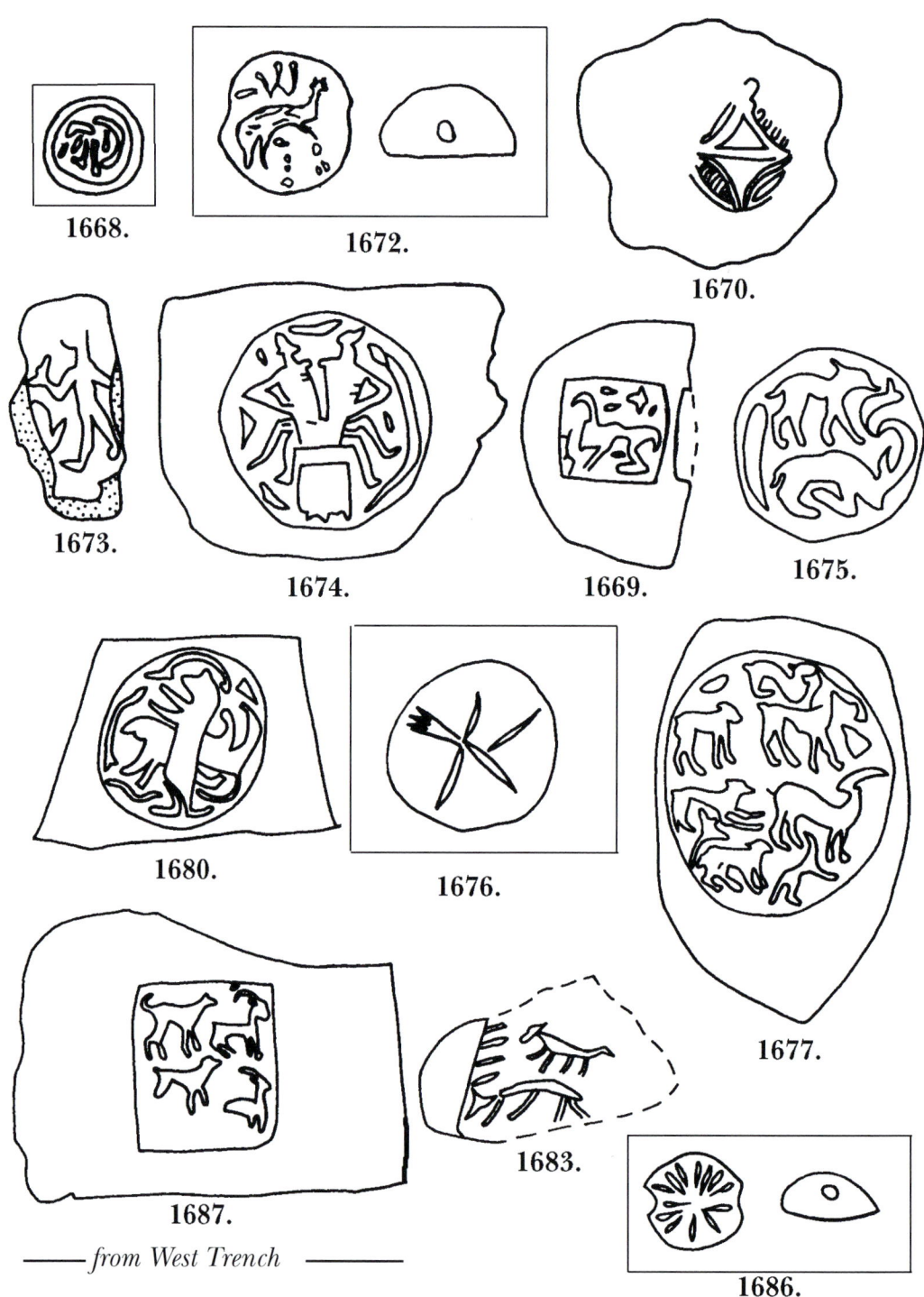

1668.

1672.

1670.

1673.

1674.

1669.

1675.

1680.

1676.

1677.

1687.

1683.

1686.

—— from West Trench ——

Scale 1:1

Plate 46.   Seals and sealings from Phase XI, Level XI/XA, unclear proveniences.

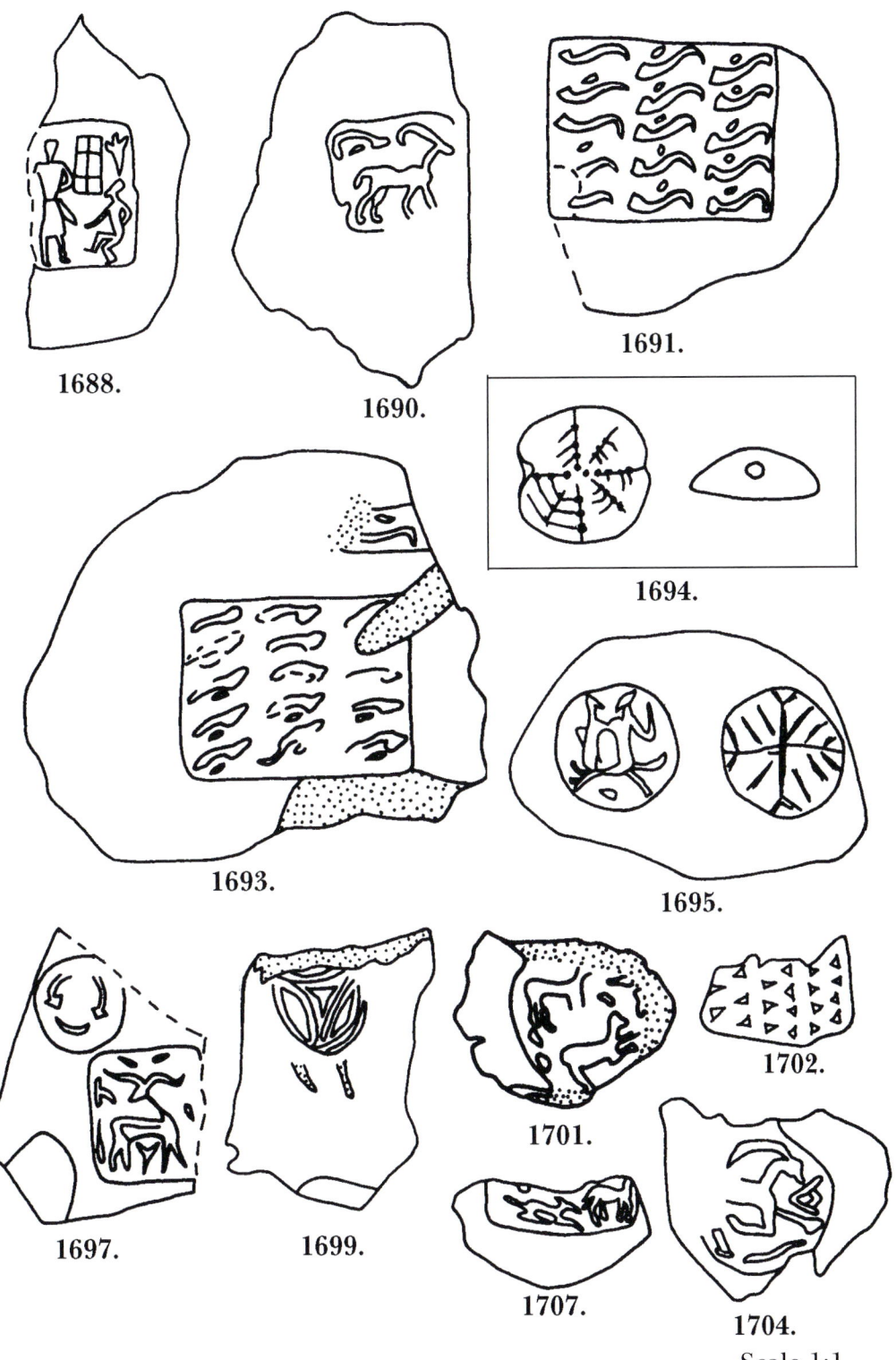

1688.

1690.

1691.

1694.

1693.

1695.

1697.

1699.

1701.

1702.

1707.

1704.

Scale 1:1

Plate 47.   Seals and sealings from Phase XI, Level XI/XA, from the West Trench.

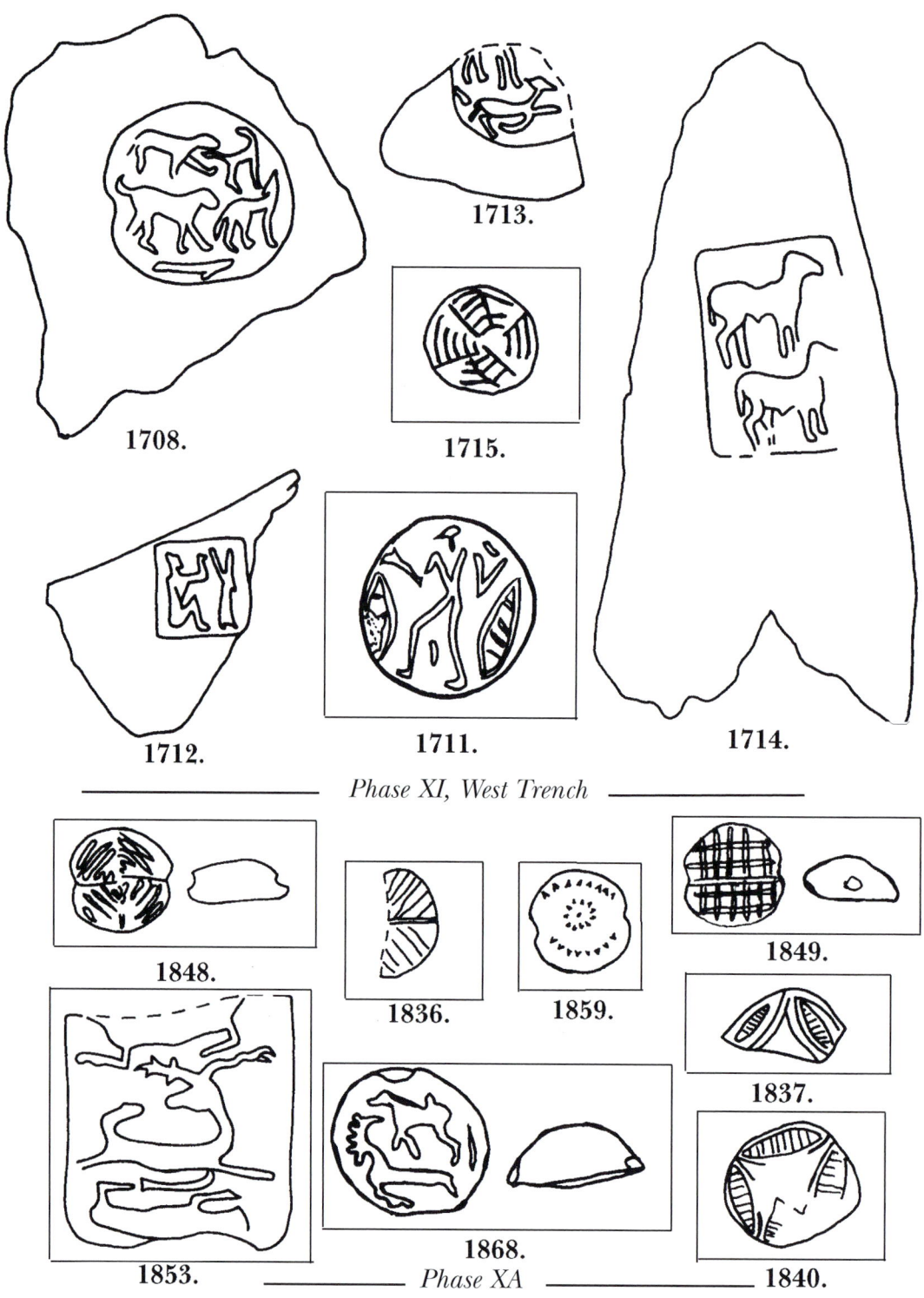

1708.

1713.

1715.

1712.

1711.

1714.

Phase XI, West Trench

1848.

1836.

1859.

1849.

1837.

1853.

1868.

1840.

Phase XA

Scale 1:1

Plate 48.   Seals and sealings from Phases XI and XA, Level XI/XA, from the West Trench and Phase XA.

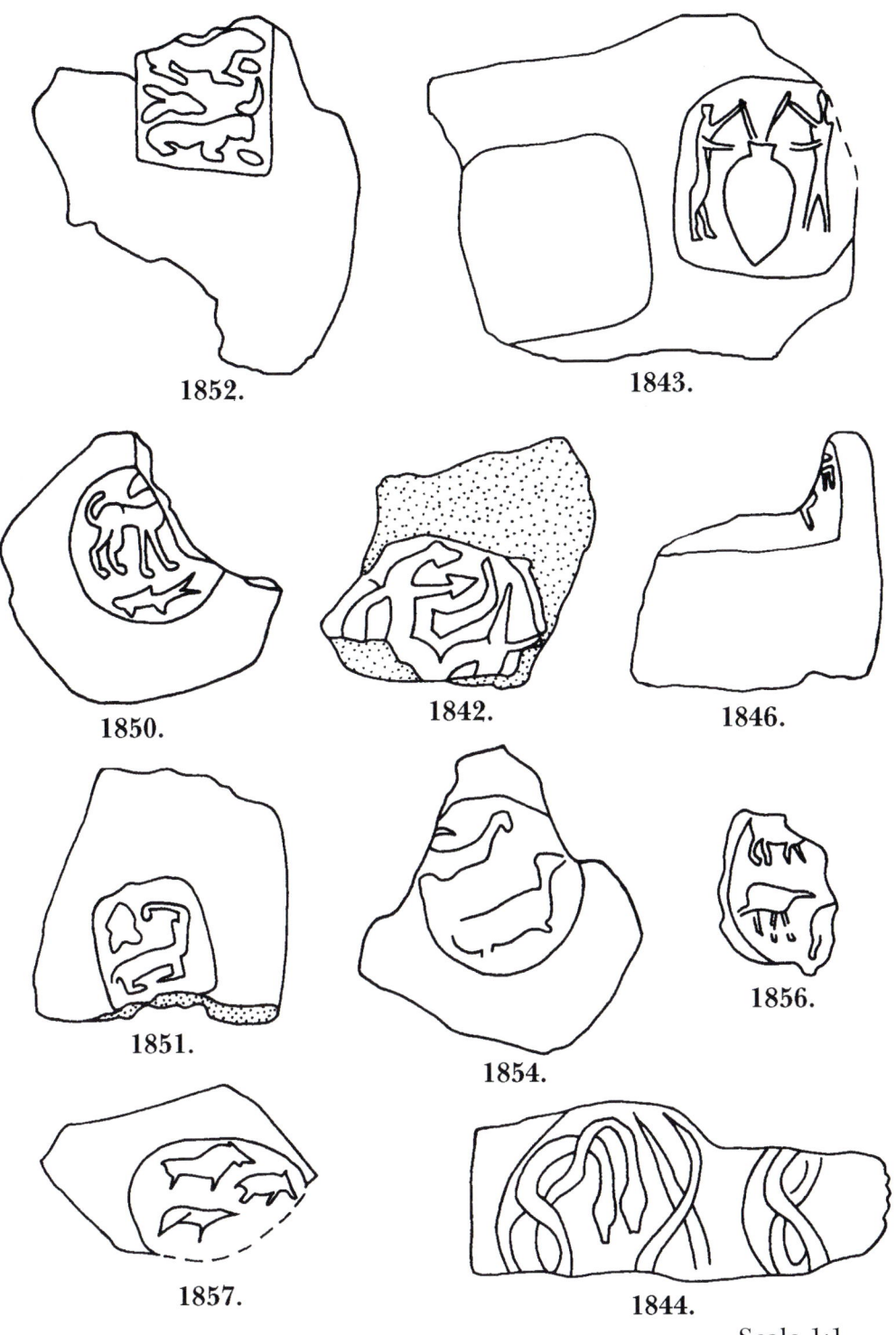

1852.

1843.

1850.

1842.

1846.

1851.

1854.

1856.

1857.

1844.

Scale 1:1

Plate 49. Seals and sealings from Phase XA, Level XI/XA, various proveniences.

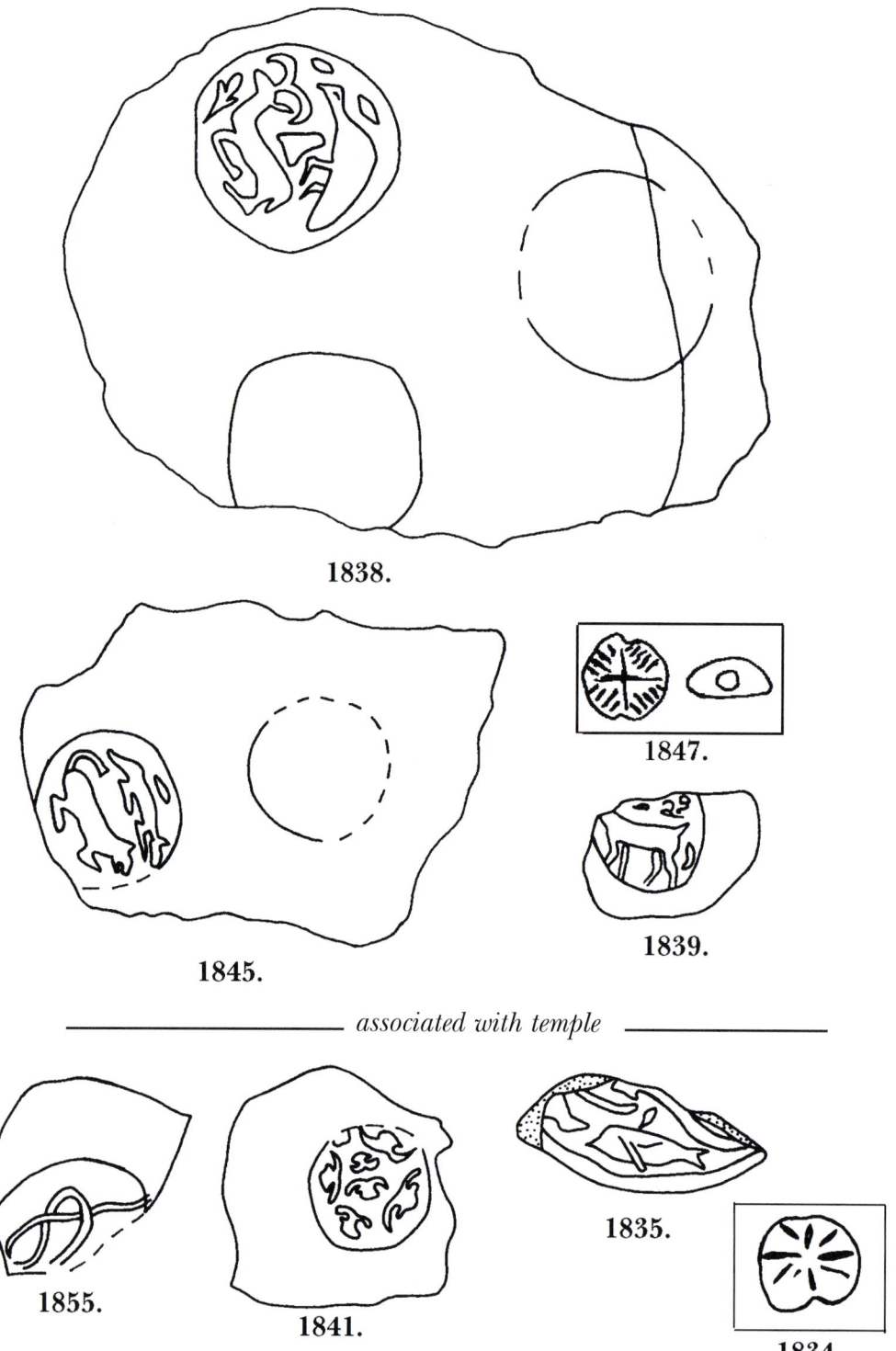

1838.

1845.

1847.

1839.

——————— *associated with temple* ———————

1855.

1841.

1835.

1834.

Plate 50.   Seals and sealings from Phase XA, Level XI/XA, associated with the temple.

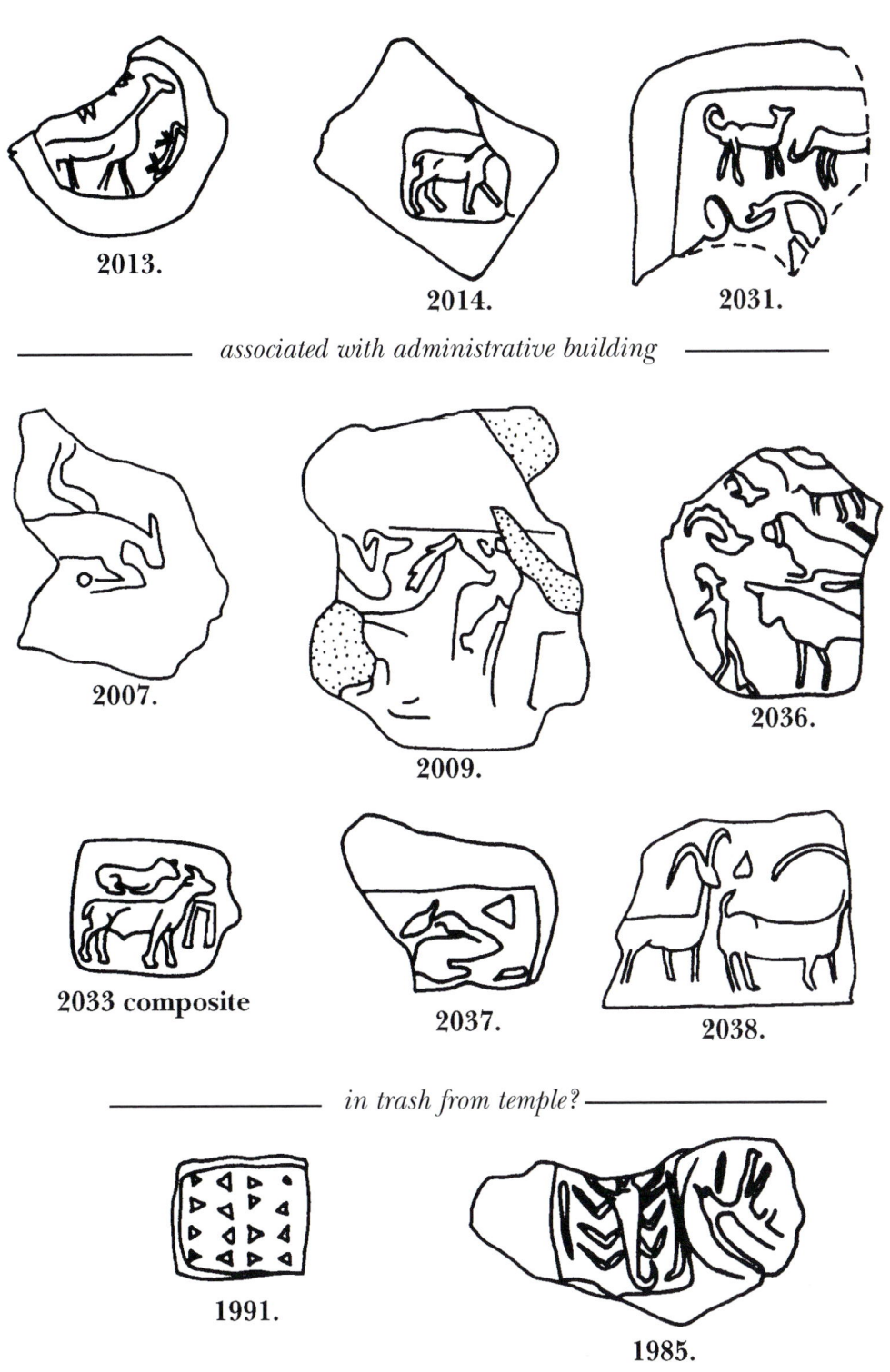

2013.

2014.

2031.

——————— *associated with administrative building* ———————

2007.

2009.

2036.

2033 composite

2037.

2038.

——————— *in trash from temple?* ———————

1991.

1985.

Scale 1:1

Plate 51.   Seals and sealings from Level X, associated with the administrative building and temple.

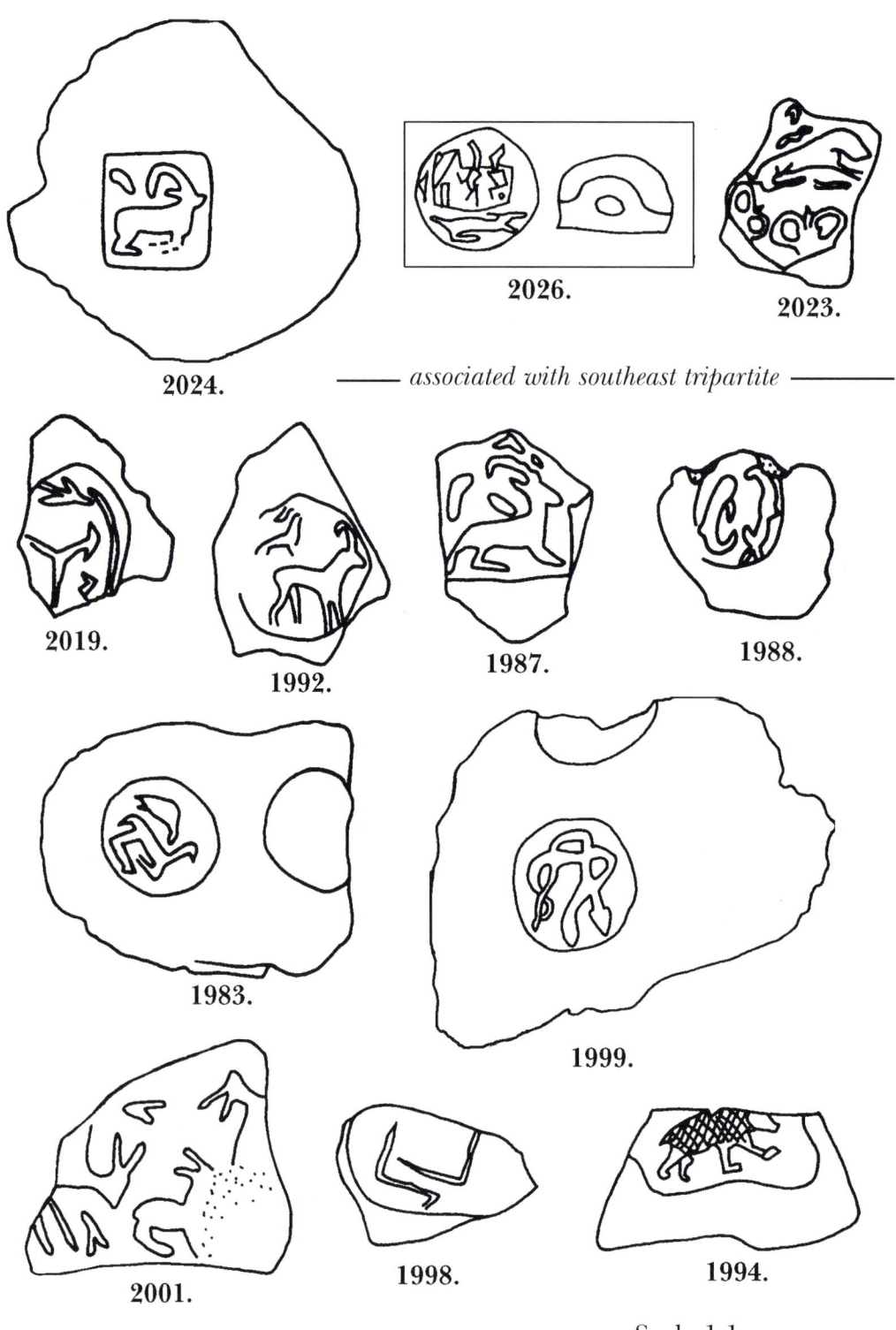

2024.

2026.

2023.

— *associated with southeast tripartite* —

2019.

1992.

1987.

1988.

1983.

1999.

2001.

1998.

1994.

Scale 1:1

Plate 52. Seals and sealings from Level X, associated with the southeast tripartite building and various proveniences.

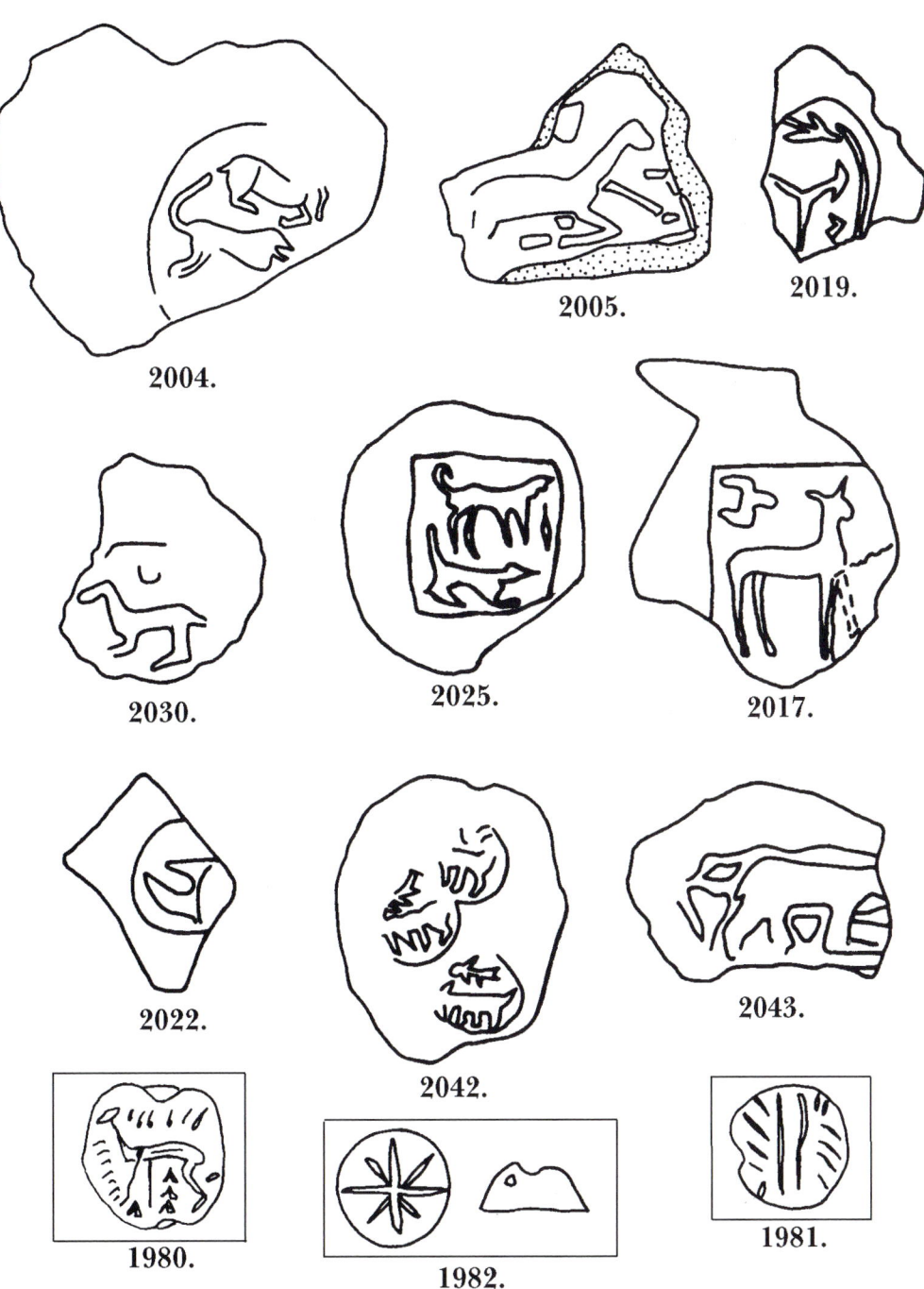

2004.

2005.

2019.

2030.

2025.

2017.

2022.

2042.

2043.

1980.

1982.

1981.

Scale 1:1

Plate 53.   Seals and sealings from Level X, various proveniences.

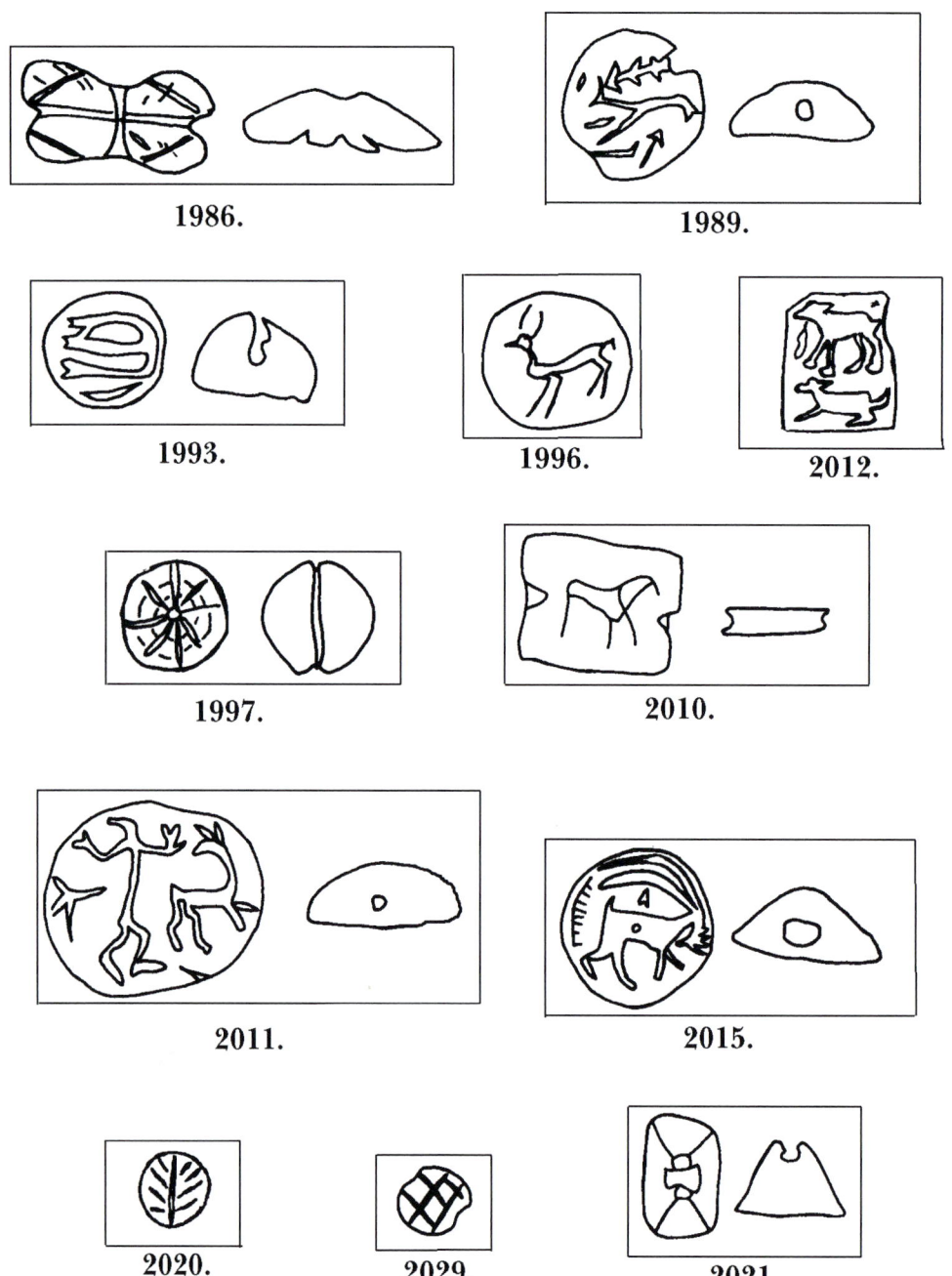

1986.

1989.

1993.

1996.

2012.

1997.

2010.

2011.

2015.

2020.

2029.

2021.

Scale 1:1

Plate 54. Seals and sealings from Level X, various proveniences.

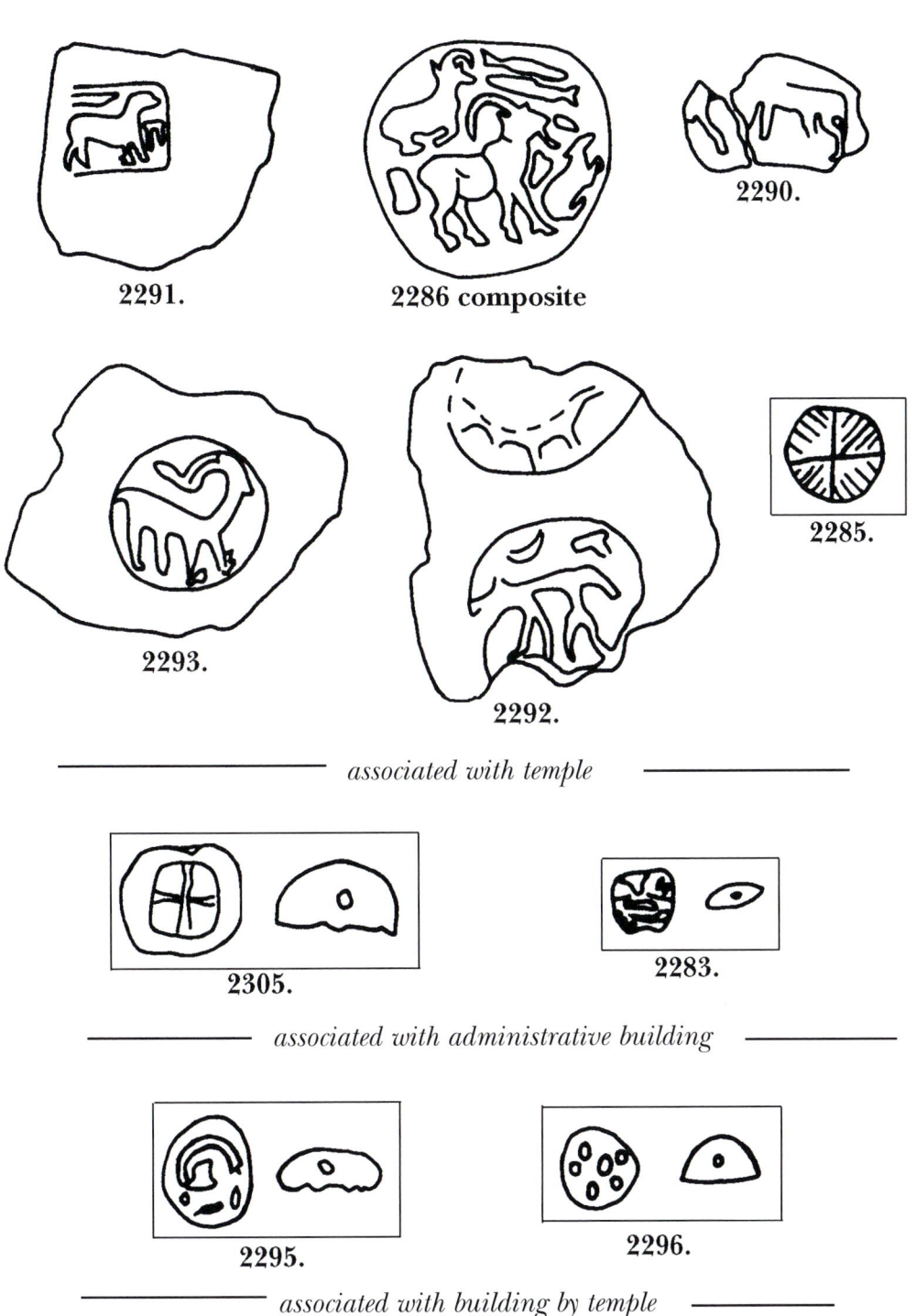

2291.

2286 composite

2290.

2293.

2292.

2285.

associated with temple

2305.

2283.

associated with administrative building

2295.

2296.

associated with building by temple

Scale 1:1

Plate 55.   Seals and sealings from Level IX, associated with the temple and administrative building.

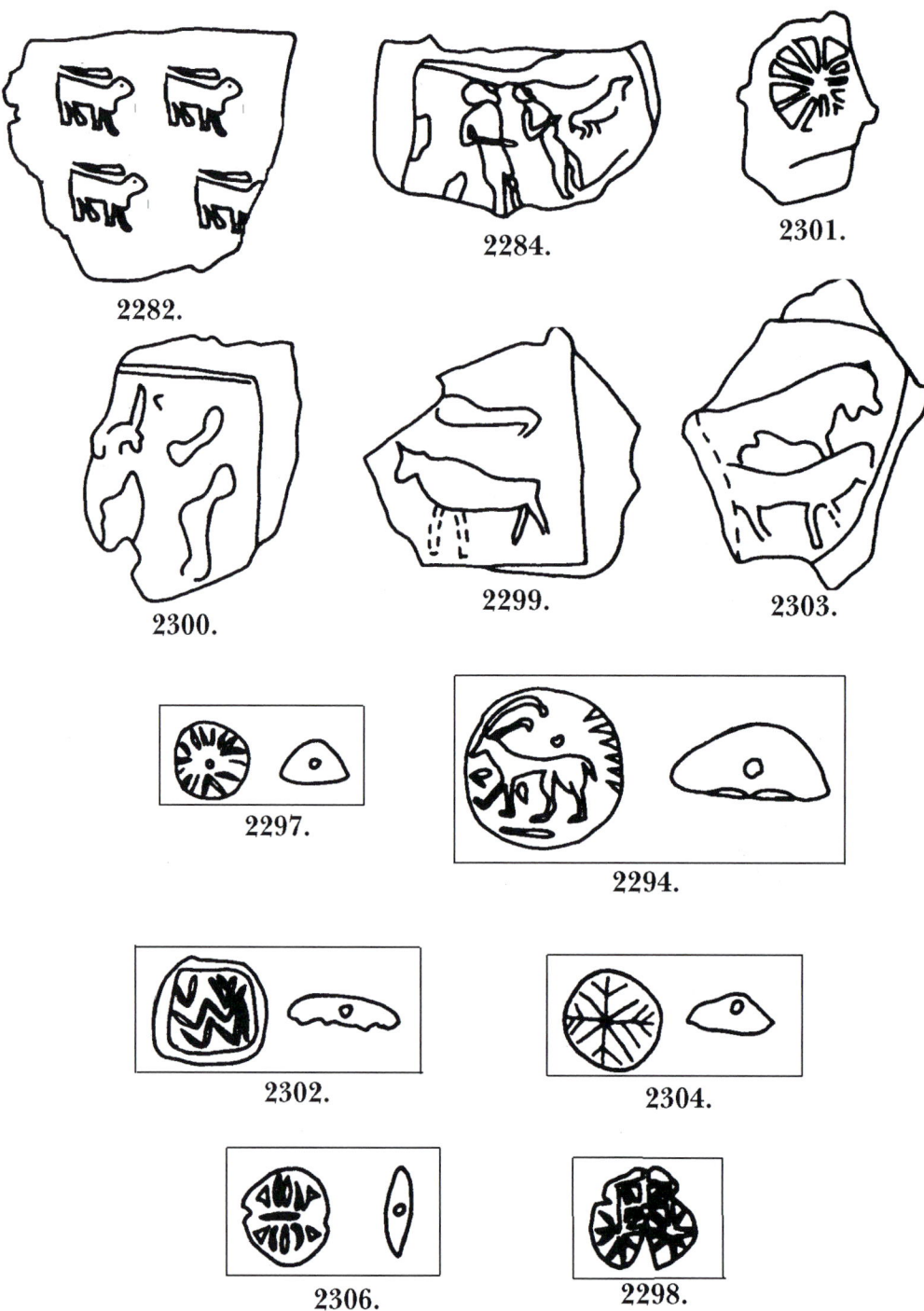

2282.

2284.

2301.

2300.

2299.

2303.

2297.

2294.

2302.

2304.

2306.

2298.

Scale 1:1

Plate 56.   Seals and sealings from Level IX, various proveniences.

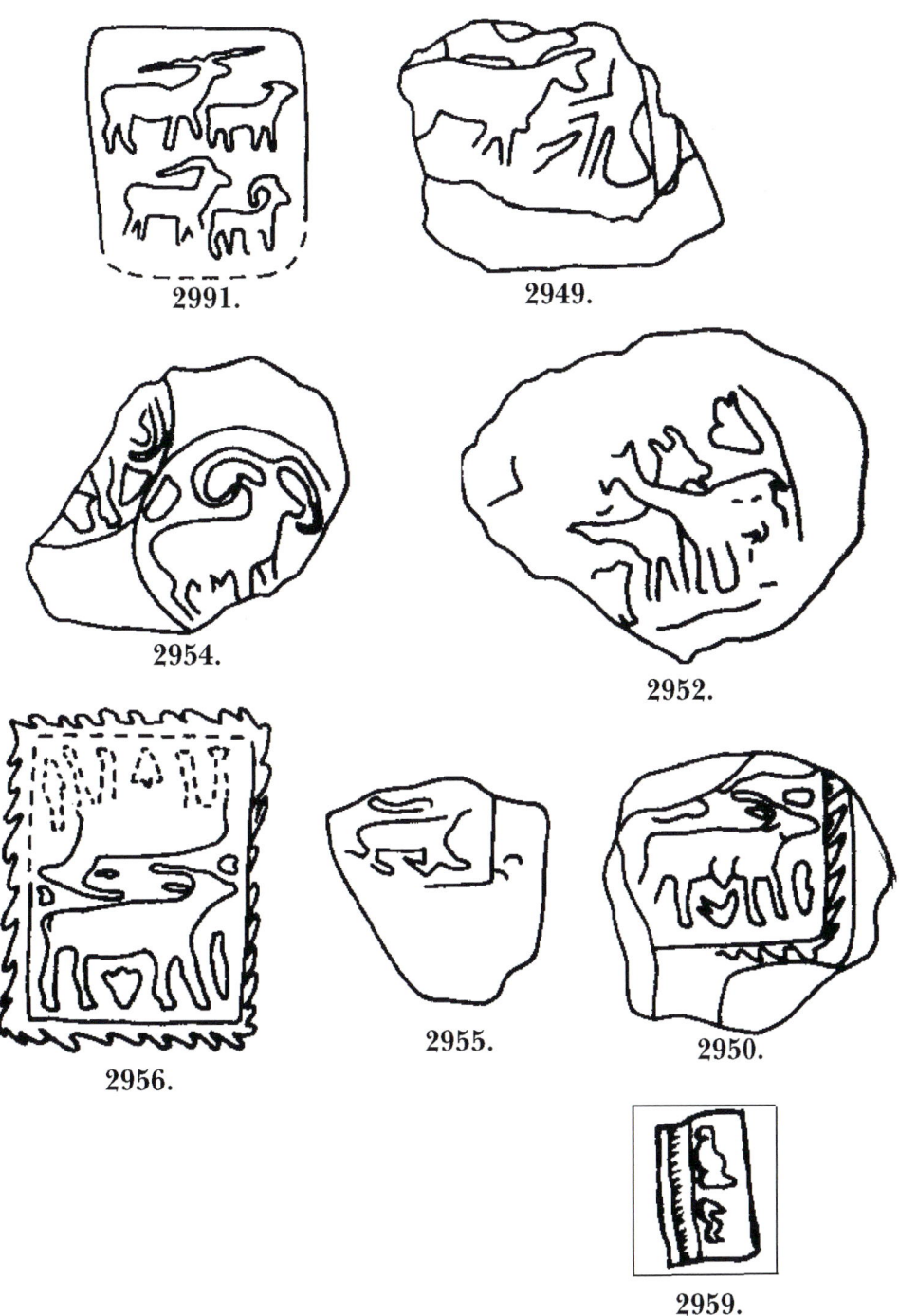

2991.

2949.

2954.

2952.

2956.

2955.

2950.

2959.

Plate 57.   Seals and sealings from Level VIII, Phase C or B.

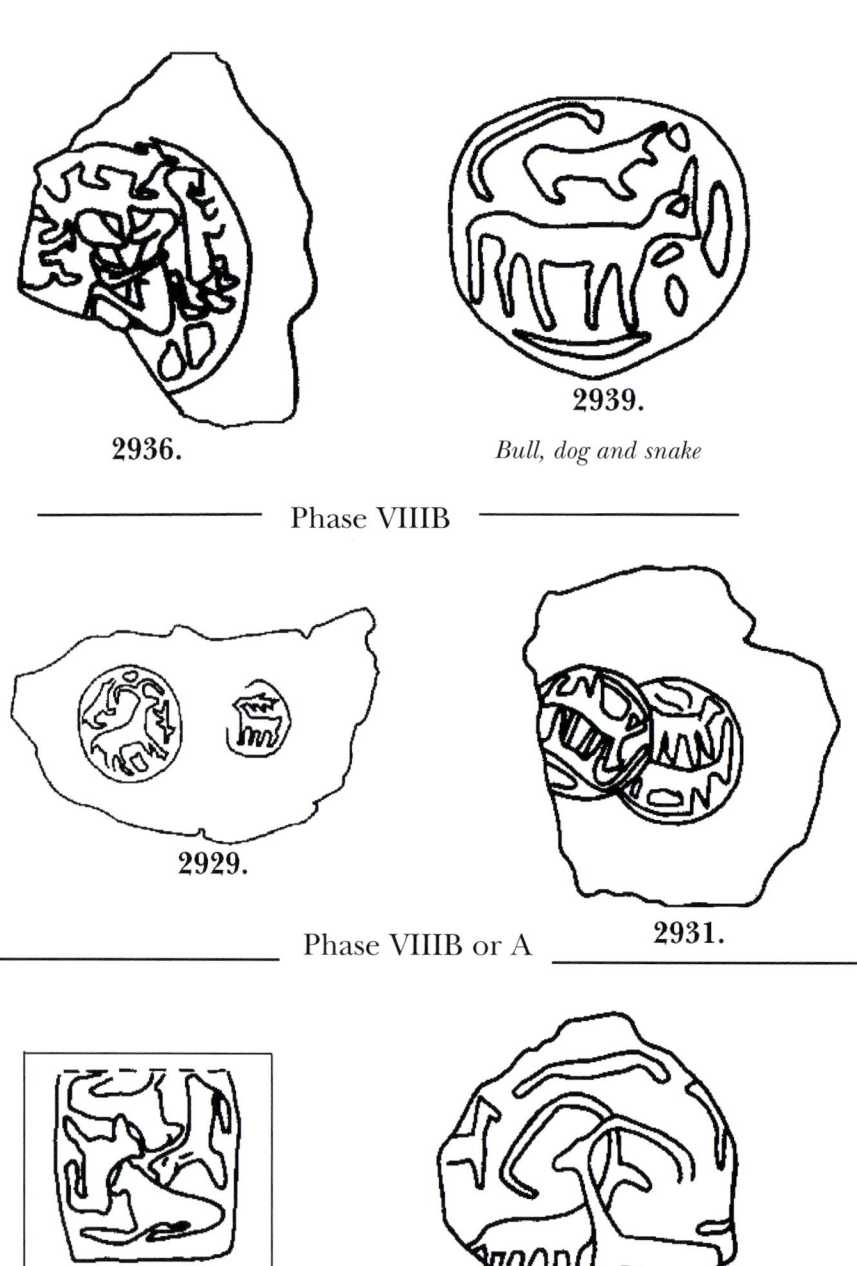

2936.

2939.

Bull, dog and snake

——————— Phase VIIIB ———————

2929.

2931.

——————— Phase VIIIB or A ———————

2964.

2930.

——————— Phase VIIIA ———————

Scale 1:1

Plate 58.   Seals and sealings from Level VIII, Phases VIIIB, VIIIA.

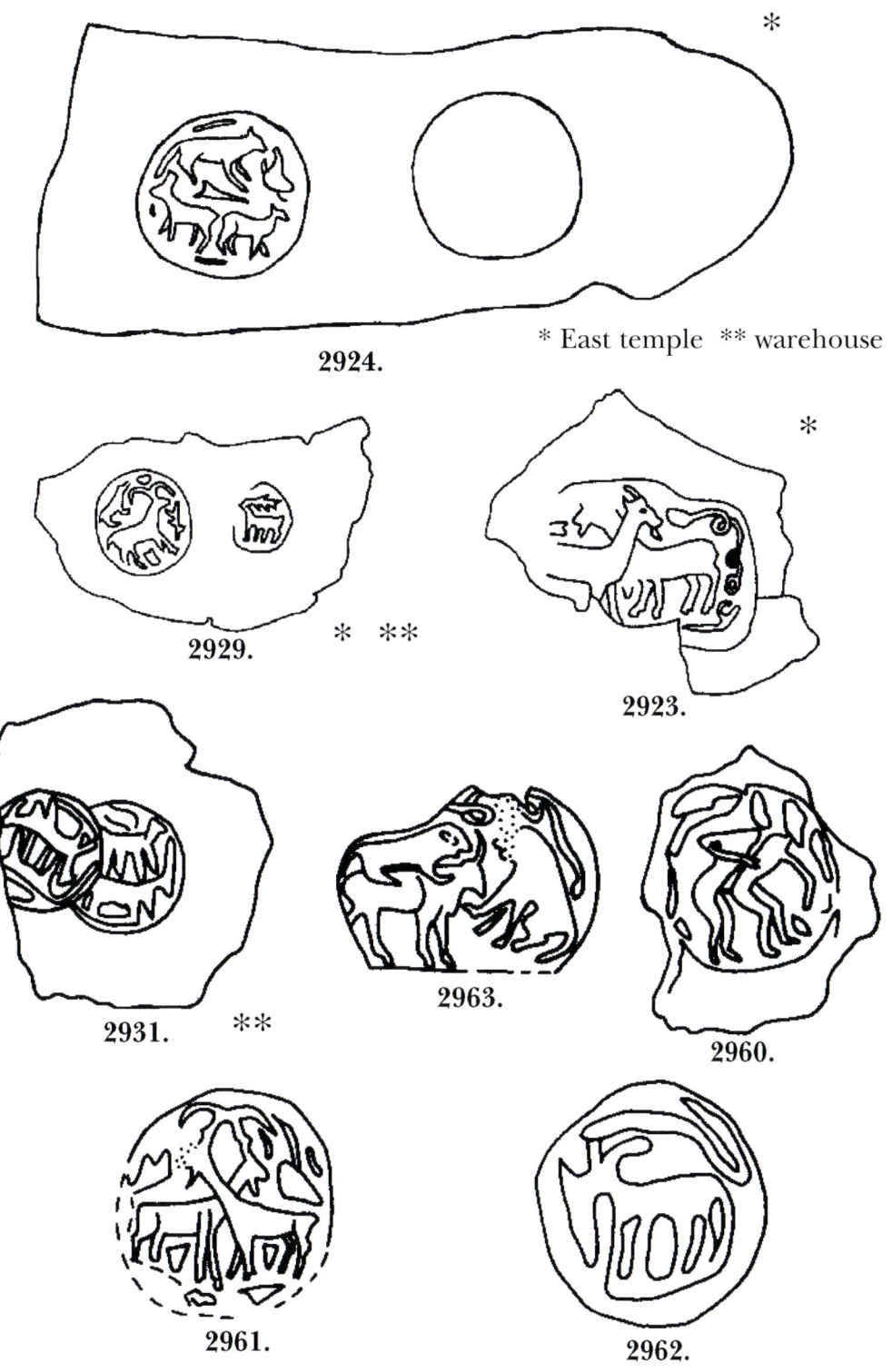

2924.

* East temple ** warehouse

2929.   * **

2923.

2931.   **

2963.

2960.

2961.

2962.

Scale 1:1

Plate 59.   Seals and sealings from Level VIII, Phase VIIIA.

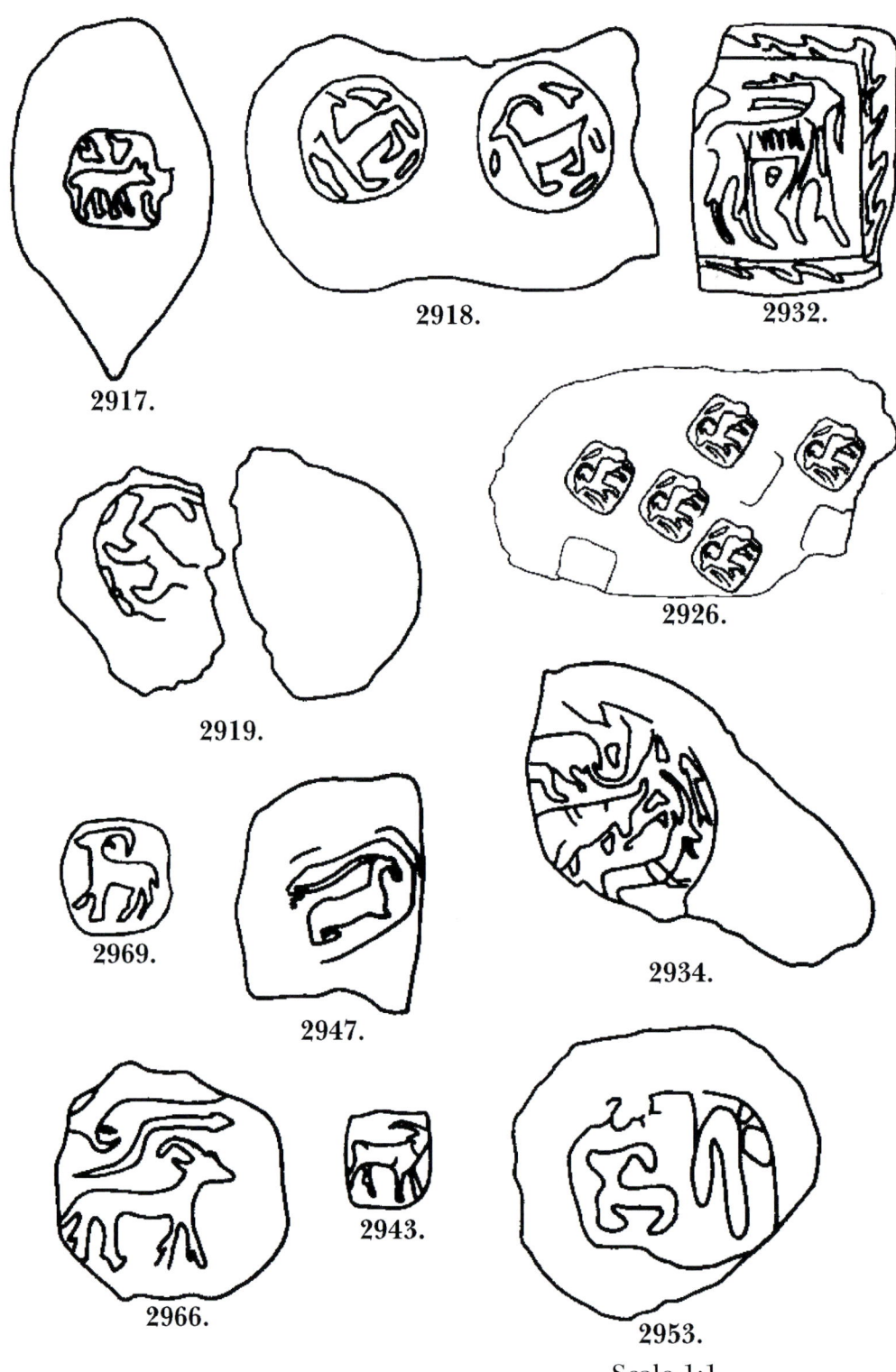

2917.

2918.

2932.

2919.

2926.

2969.

2947.

2934.

2966.

2943.

2953.

Scale 1:1

Plate 60.   Seals and sealings from Level VIII, various proveniences.

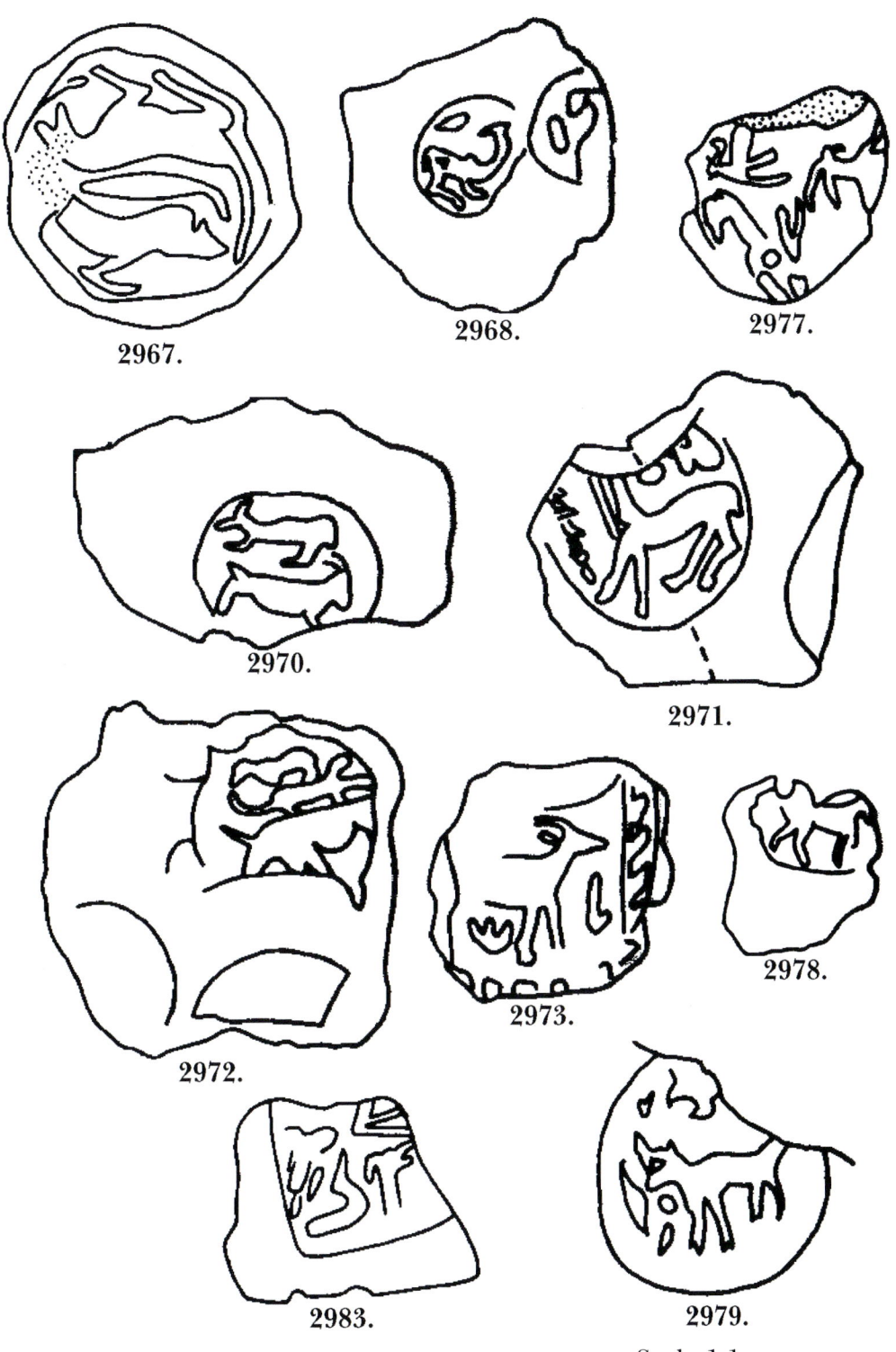

2967.

2968.

2977.

2970.

2971.

2972.

2973.

2978.

2983.

2979.

Scale 1:1

Plate 61.   Seals and sealings from Level VIII, various proveniences.

2974.

2928.

2927.

2946.

2958.

2986.

Scale 1:1

Plate 62. Seals and sealings from Level VIII, various proveniences.

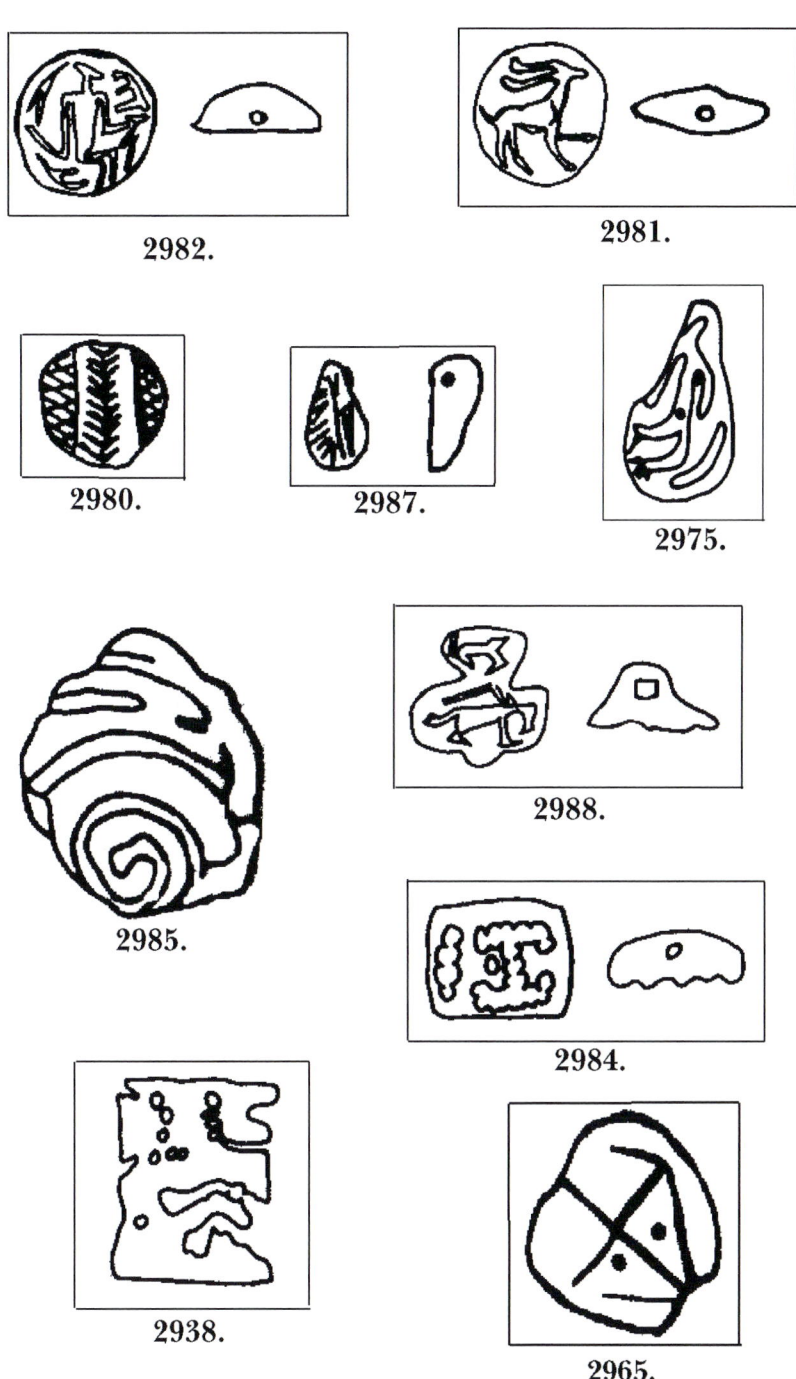

2982.

2981.

2980.

2987.

2975.

2985.

2988.

2984.

2938.

2965.

Scale 1:1

Plate 63.   Seals and sealings from Level VIII, various proveniences.

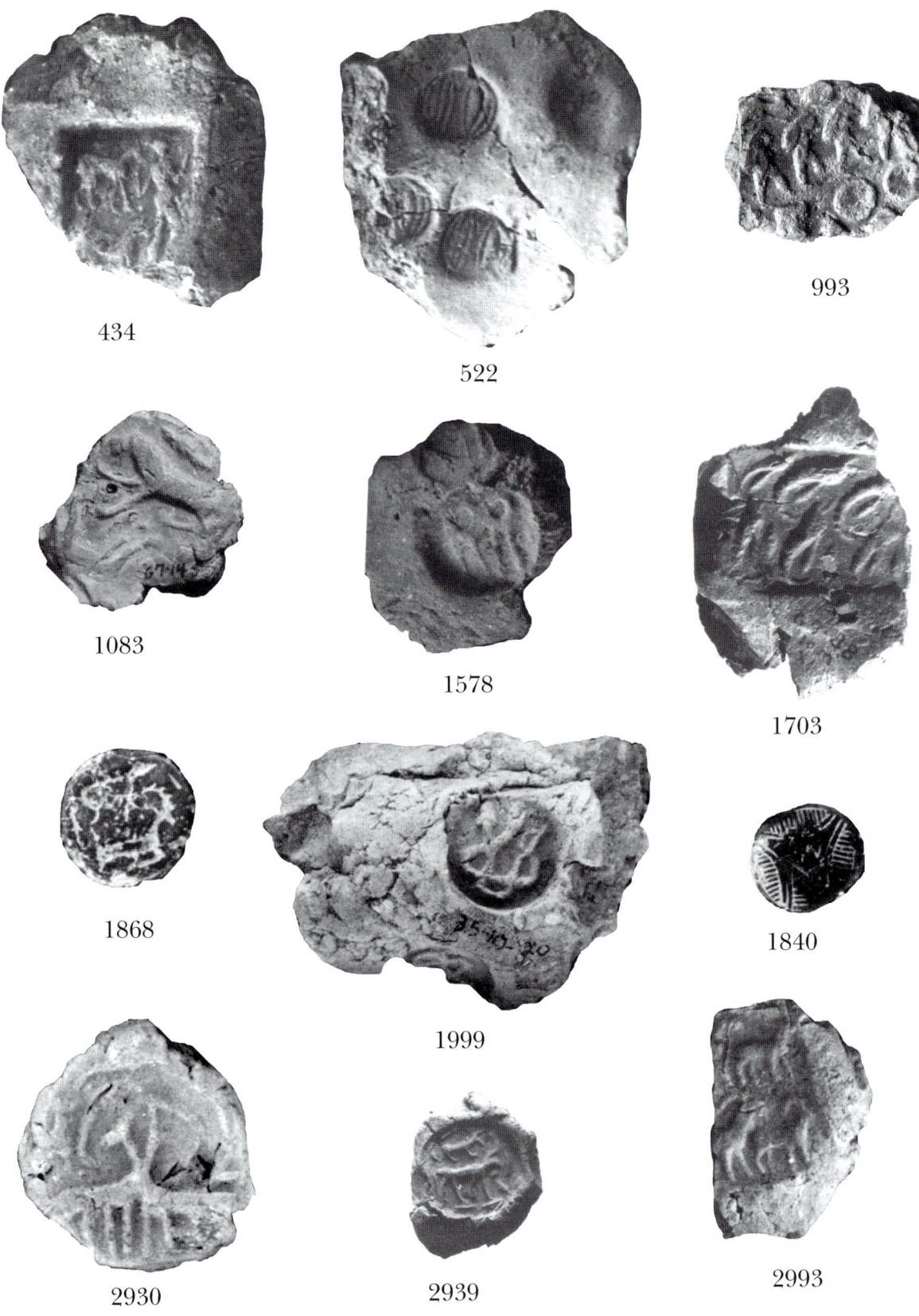

434

522

993

1083

1578

1703

1868

1999

1840

2930

2939

2993

Scale 1:1

Plate 64.   Photograph of various seals and sealings.

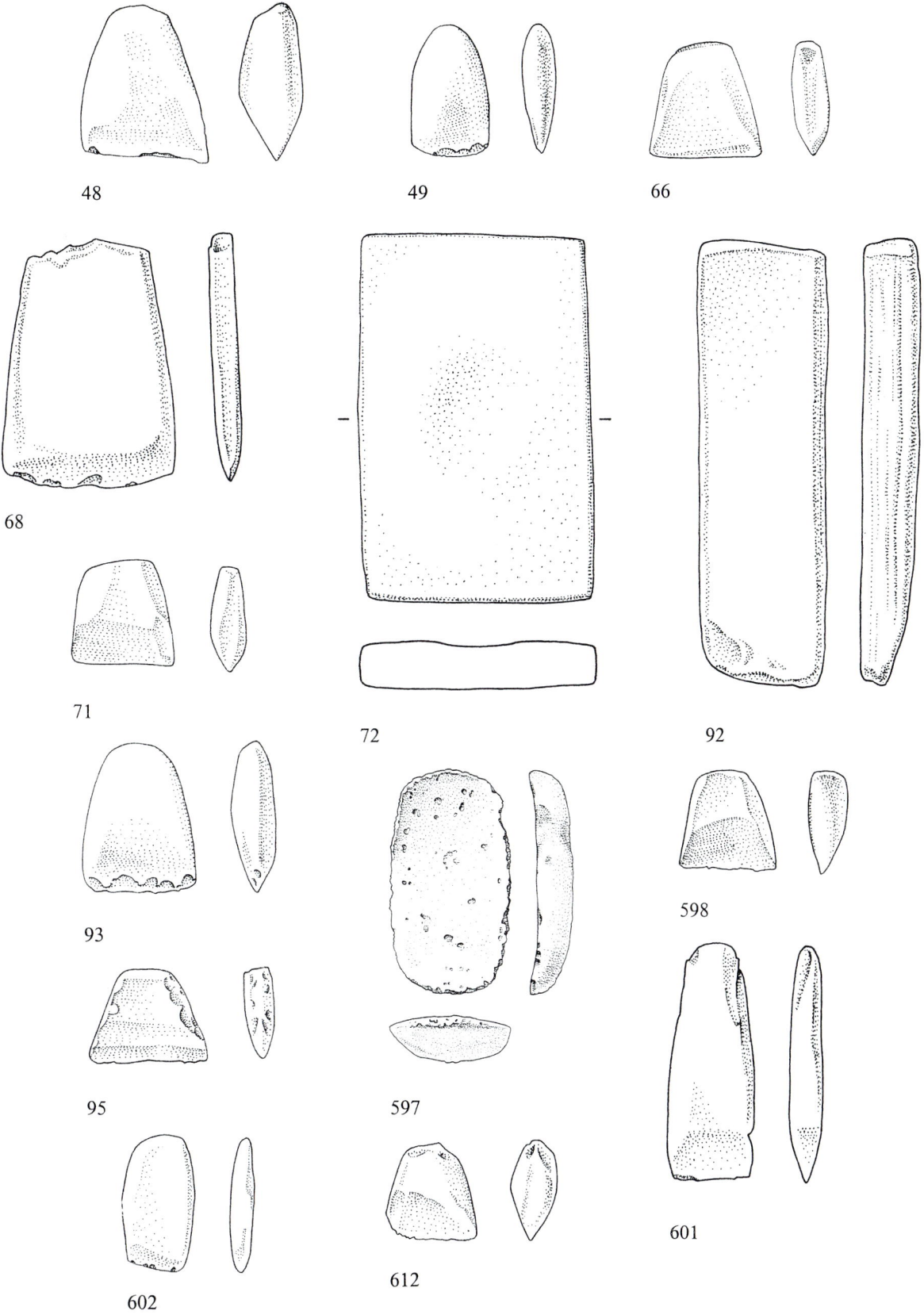

48   49   66

68

71   72   92

93   597   598

95   597   601

602   612   601

1:2
597–1:4

Plate 65.   Ground stone celts, palettes, and grinding stones, Levels XII (48–95), XIA/B (597–612).

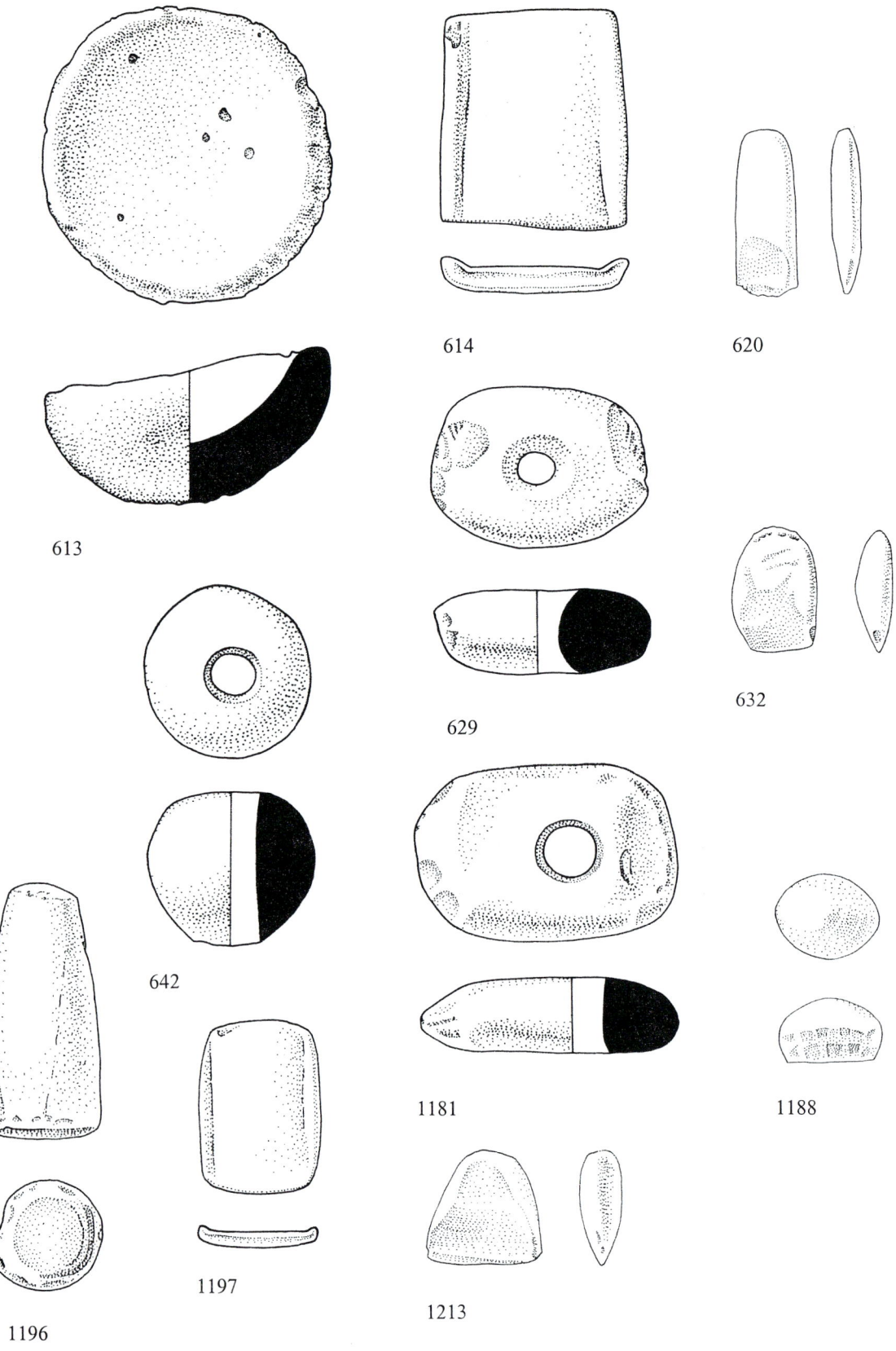

614

620

613

629

632

642

1181

1188

1196

1197

1213

1:2
613–1:4

Plate 66.   Ground stone hammers, maceheads, palettes, ballista, and grinding stones, Levels XIA/B (613– 642) to XI/XA (1181–1213).

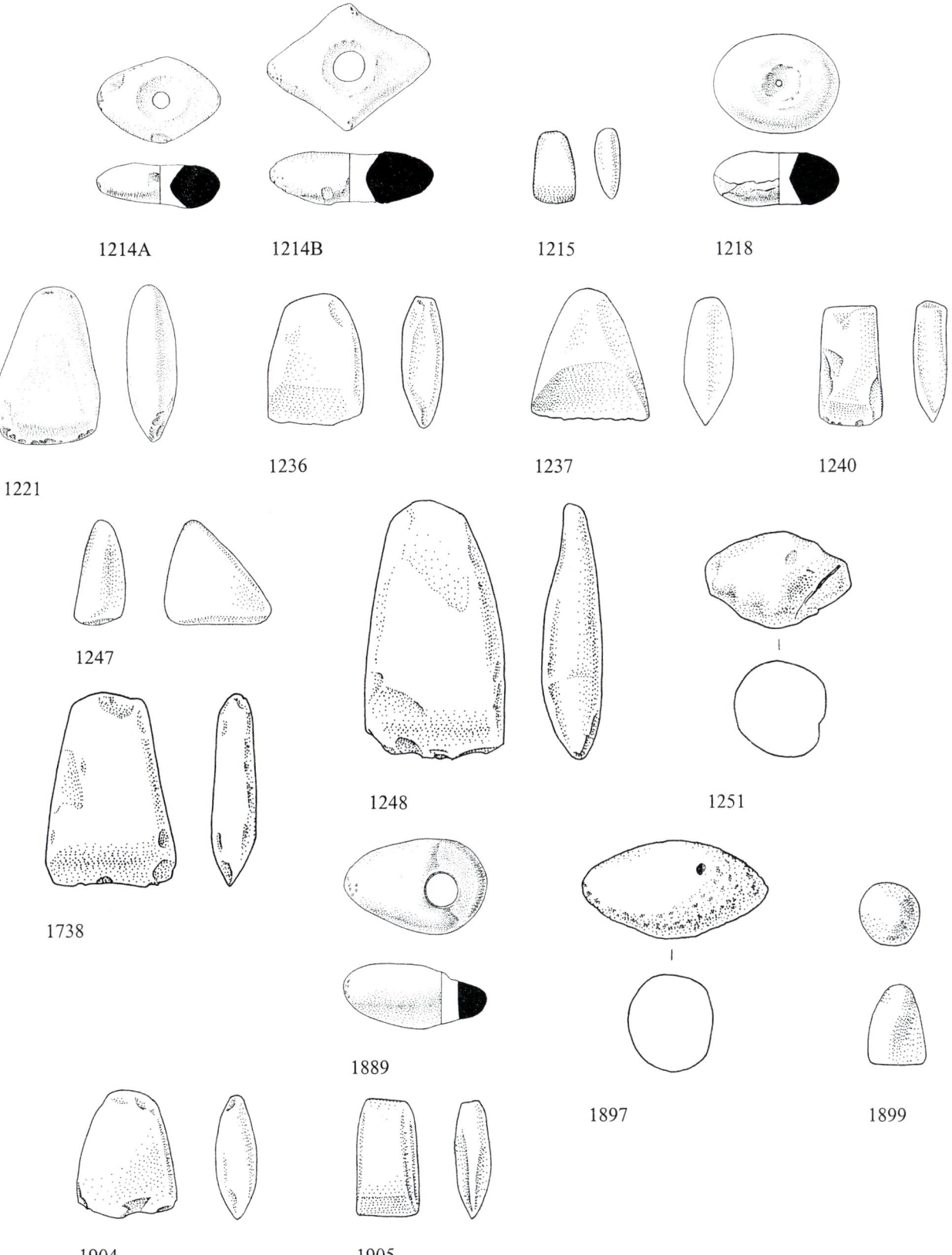

1214A 1214B 1215 1218

1221 1236 1237 1240

1247 1248 1251

1738

1889 1897 1899

1904 1905

1:2
1214, 1218, 1221, 1889–1:4

Plate 67.   Ground stone hammers, celts, and ballista, Levels XI/XA (Phase XI: 1214A–1251, XA: 1738) to X 1889–1905).

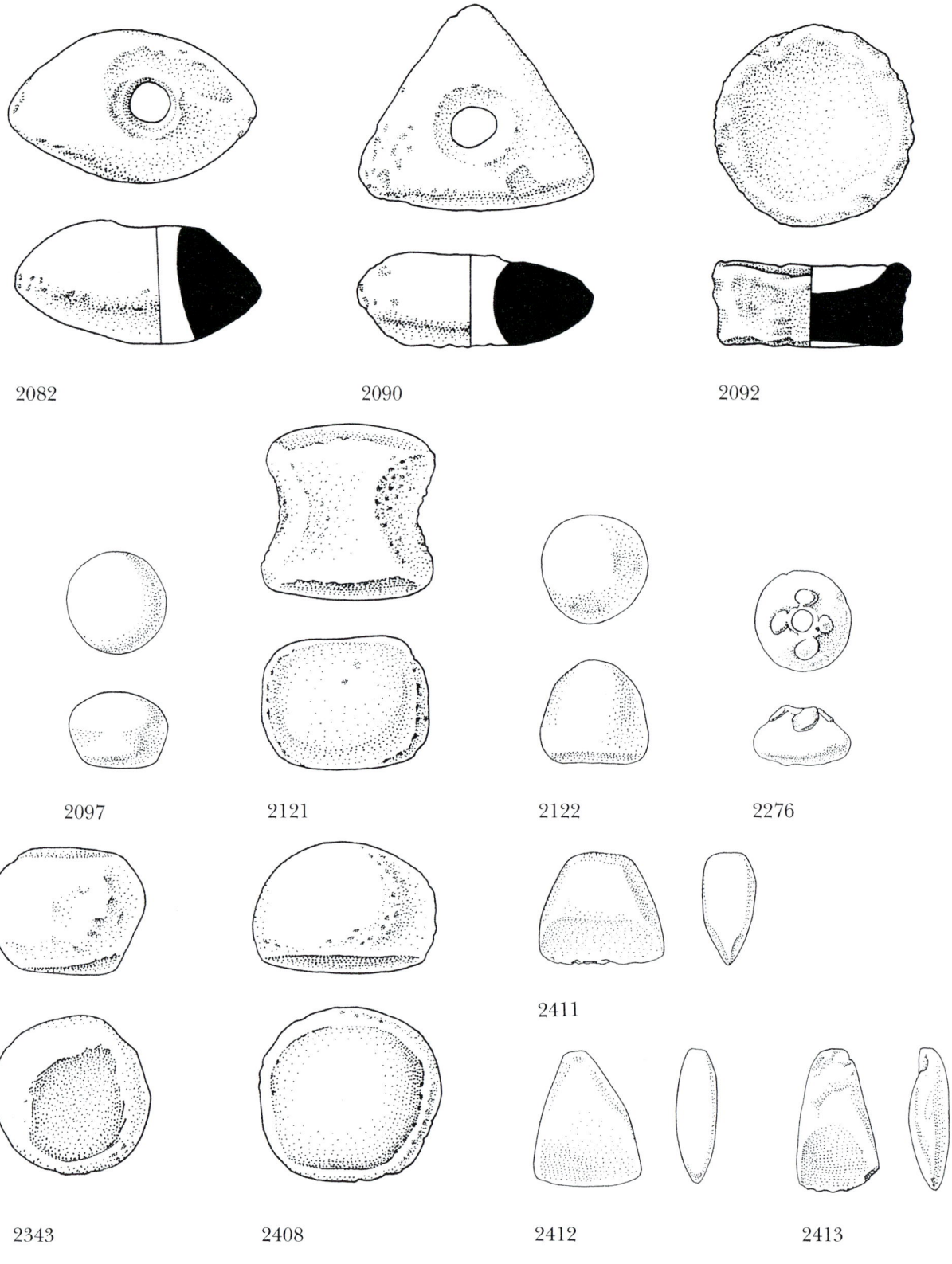

2082

2090

2092

2097

2121

2122

2276

2343

2408

2411

2412

2413

1:2
2092–1:4

Plate 68.   Ground stone celts, hammers, and spheres, Levels IX (2082–2276) to VIII (2411–2413).

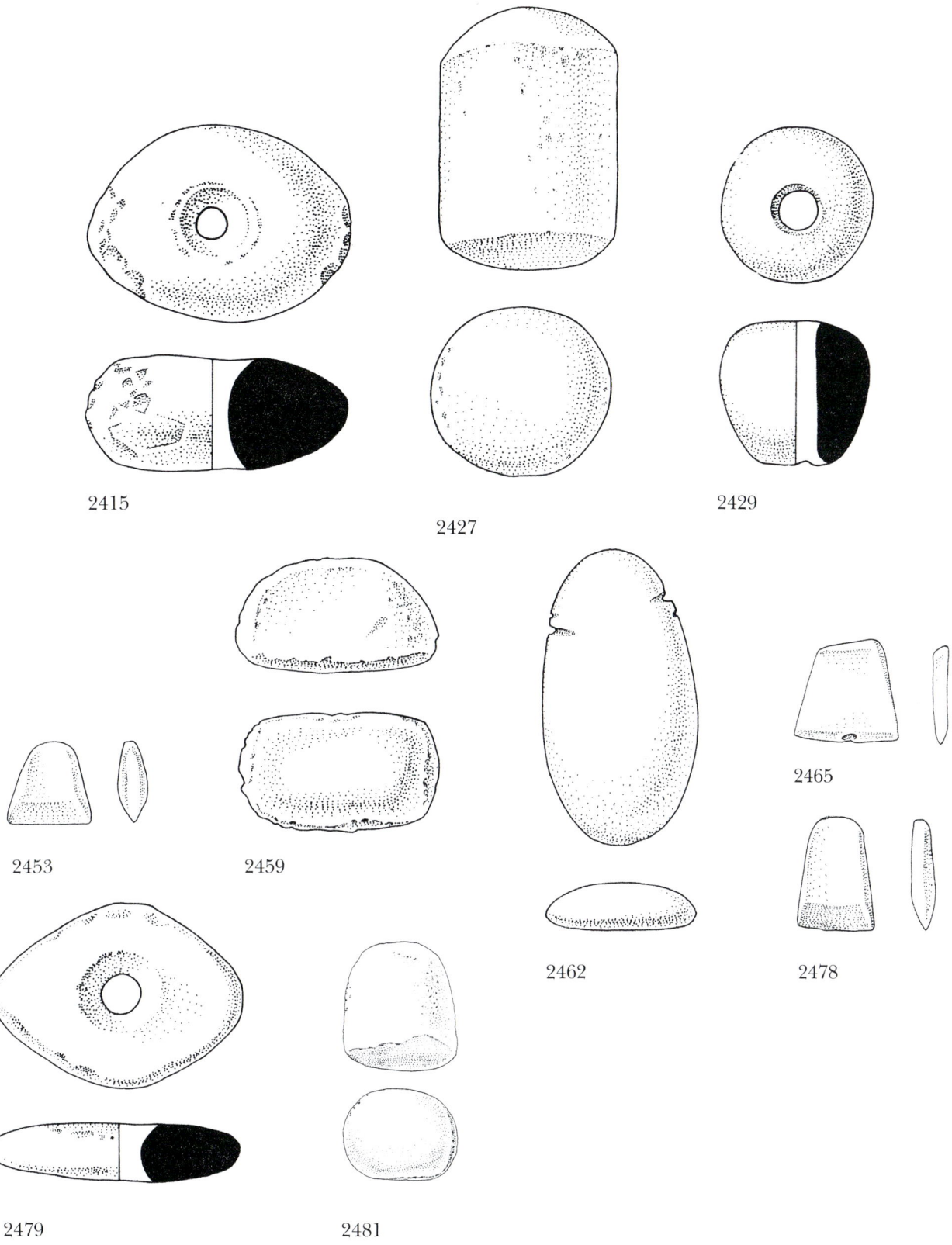

2415

2427

2429

2453

2459

2465

2462

2478

2479

2481

1:2
2481–1:4

Plate 69.   Ground stone hammers and celts, Level VIII.

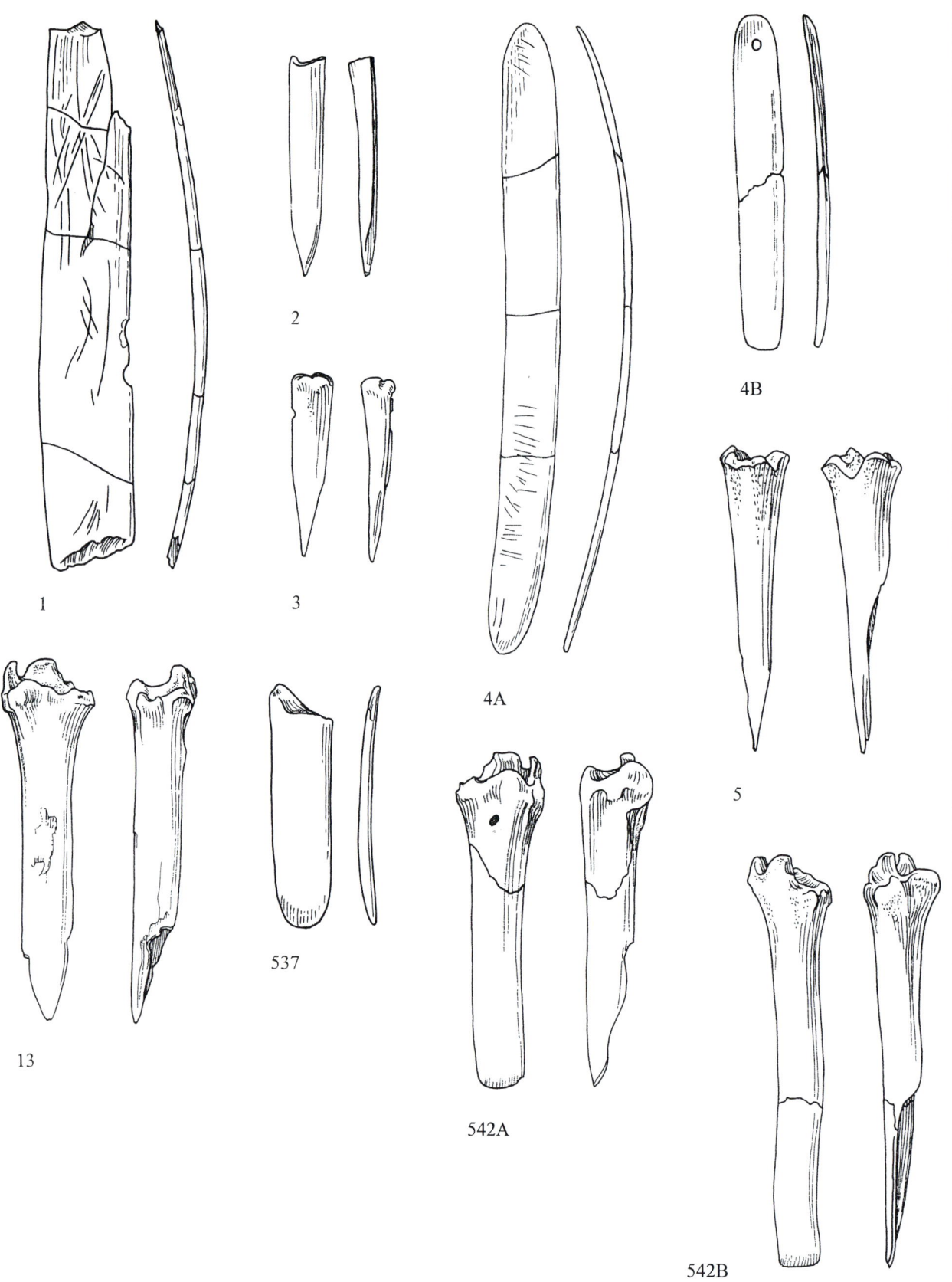

1

2

3

4A

4B

5

13

537

542A

542B

1:2

Plate 70.   Various bone objects, Levels XII (1–13) to XIA/B (537–542B).

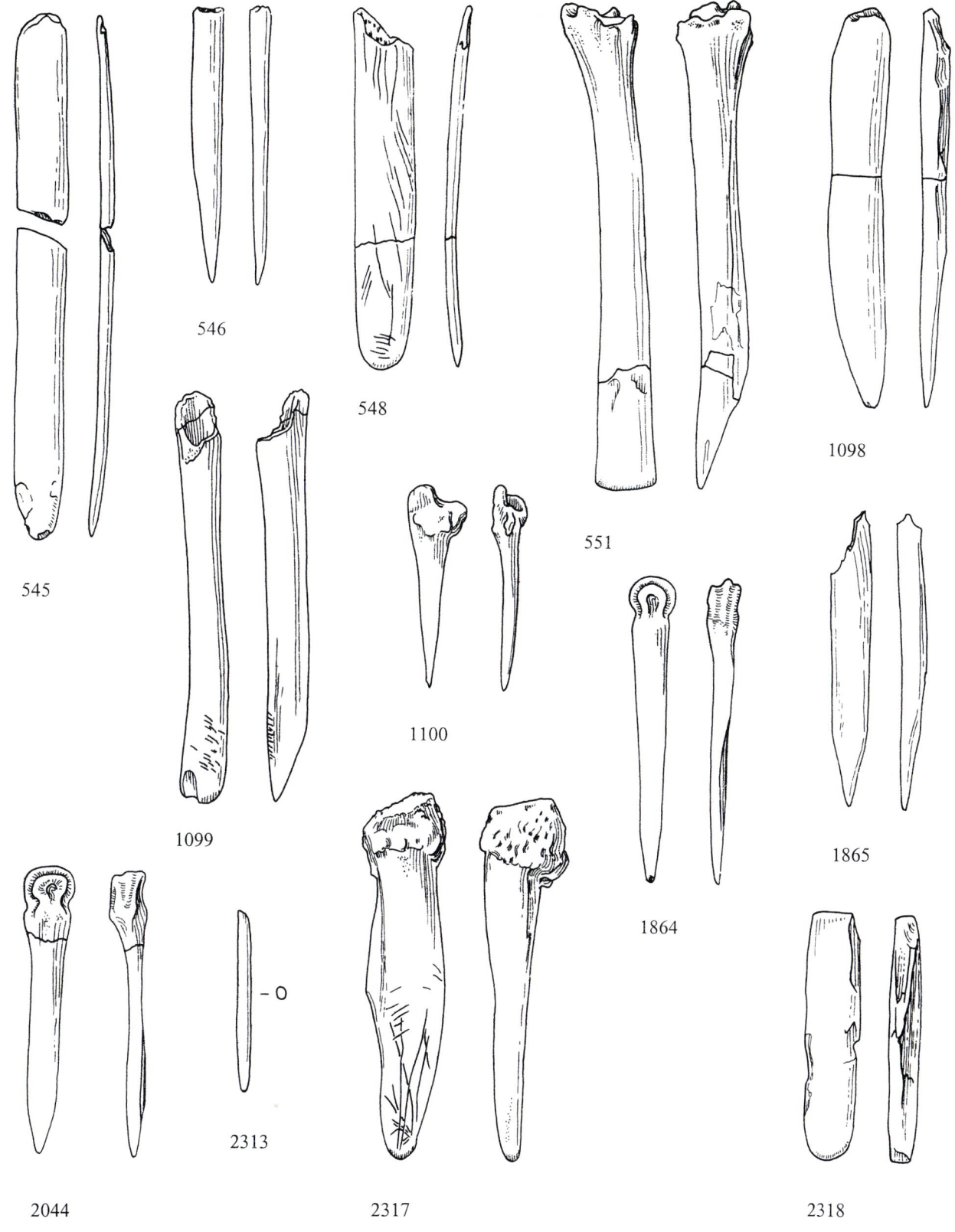

546

548

1098

545

551

1099

1100

1865

1864

2044

2313

2317

2318

1:2

Plate 71. Various bone objects, Levels XIA/B (545–551), XI/XA (1098–1100), X (1864–1865), IX (2044) to VIII (2313–2318).

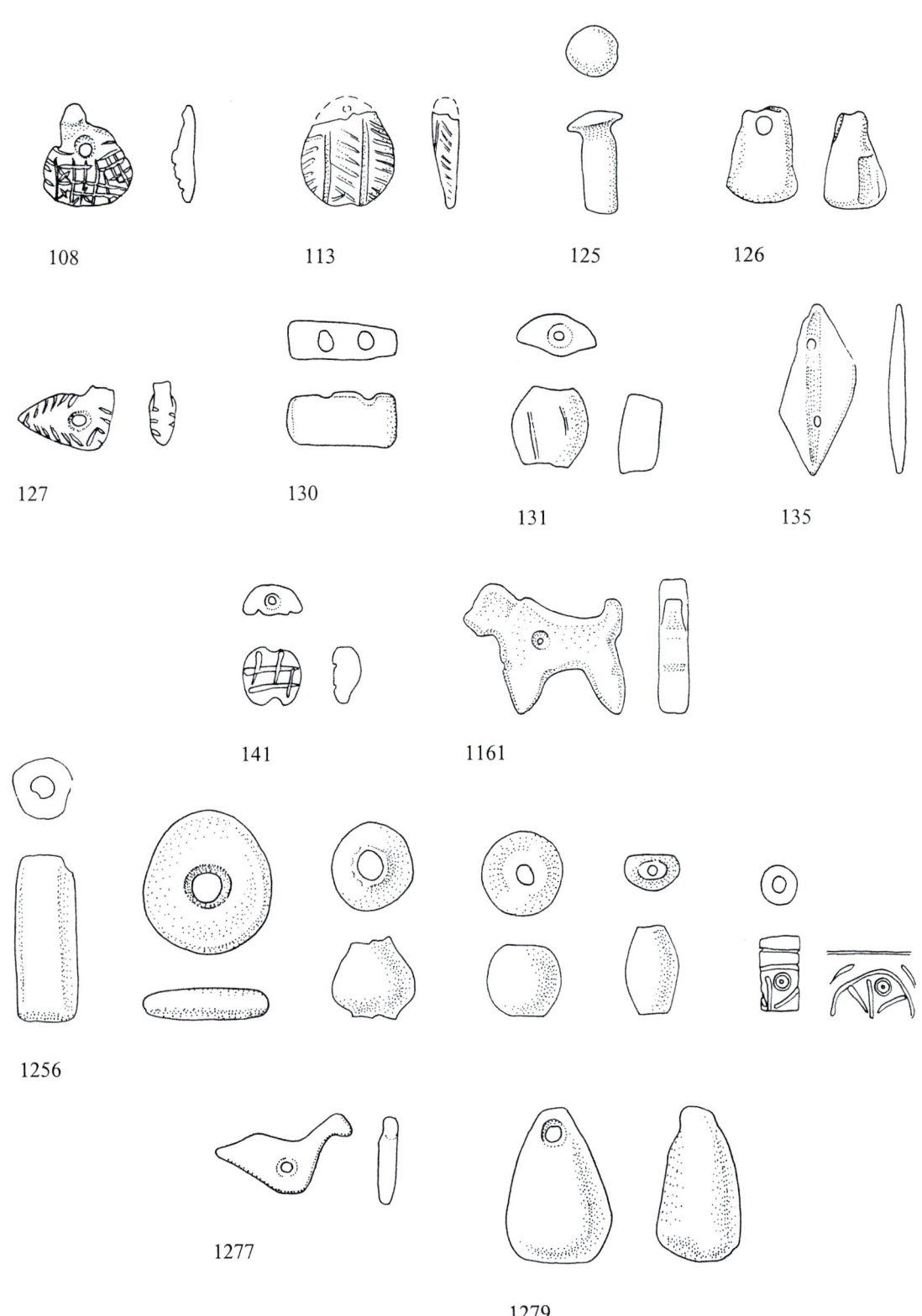

108   113   125   126

127   130   131   135

141   1161

1256

1277   1279

1:1

Plate 72.   Jewelry from various materials, Levels XII (108–141) to XI/XA (1161–1279).

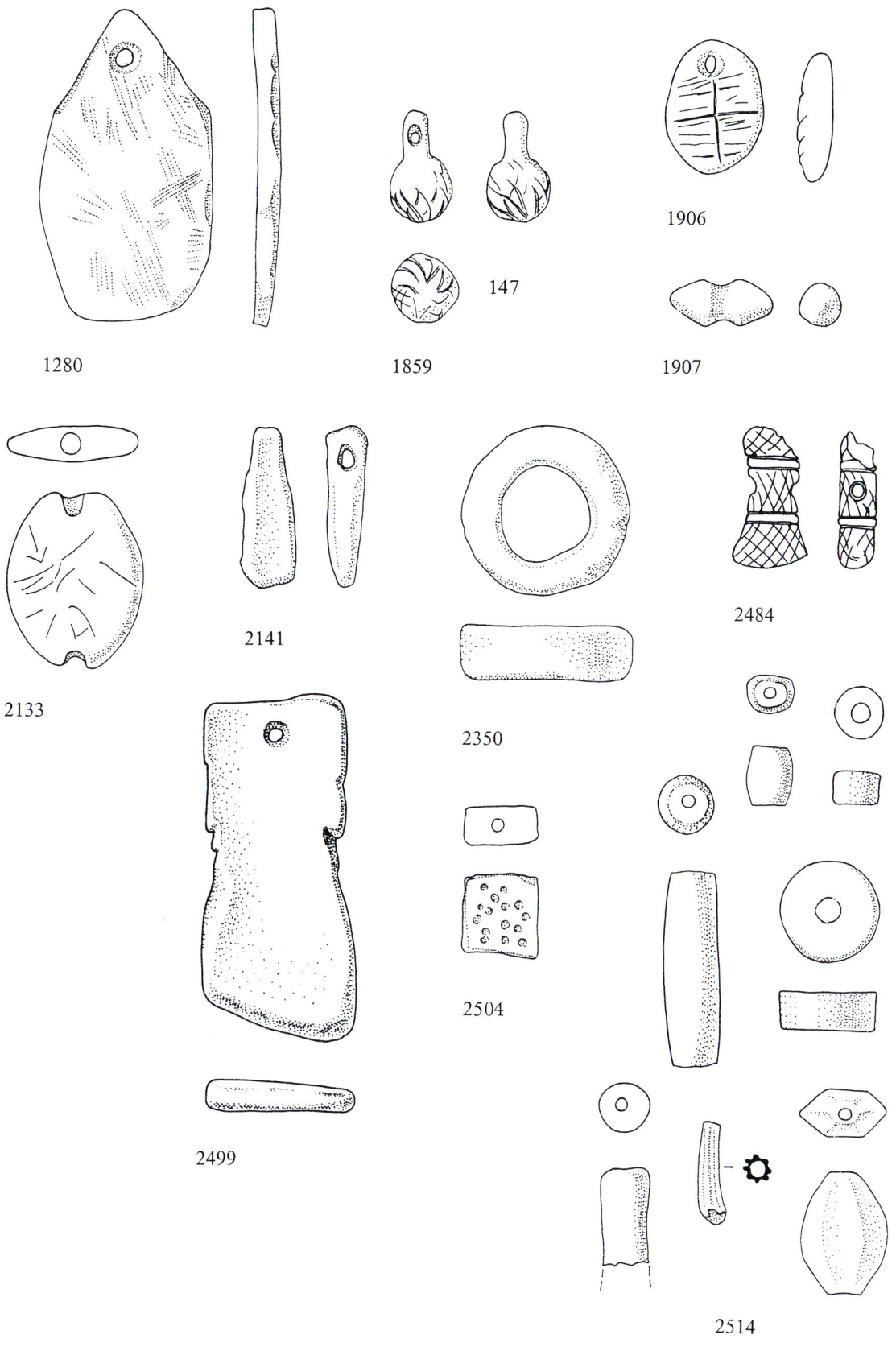

1280   1859   147   1906   1907

2133   2141   2350   2484   2504   2499   2514

1:1

Plate 73.   Jewelry from various materials, Levels XII (147), XI/XA (1280–1859), X (1906–1907), IX (2133–2141), VIII (2350–2514).

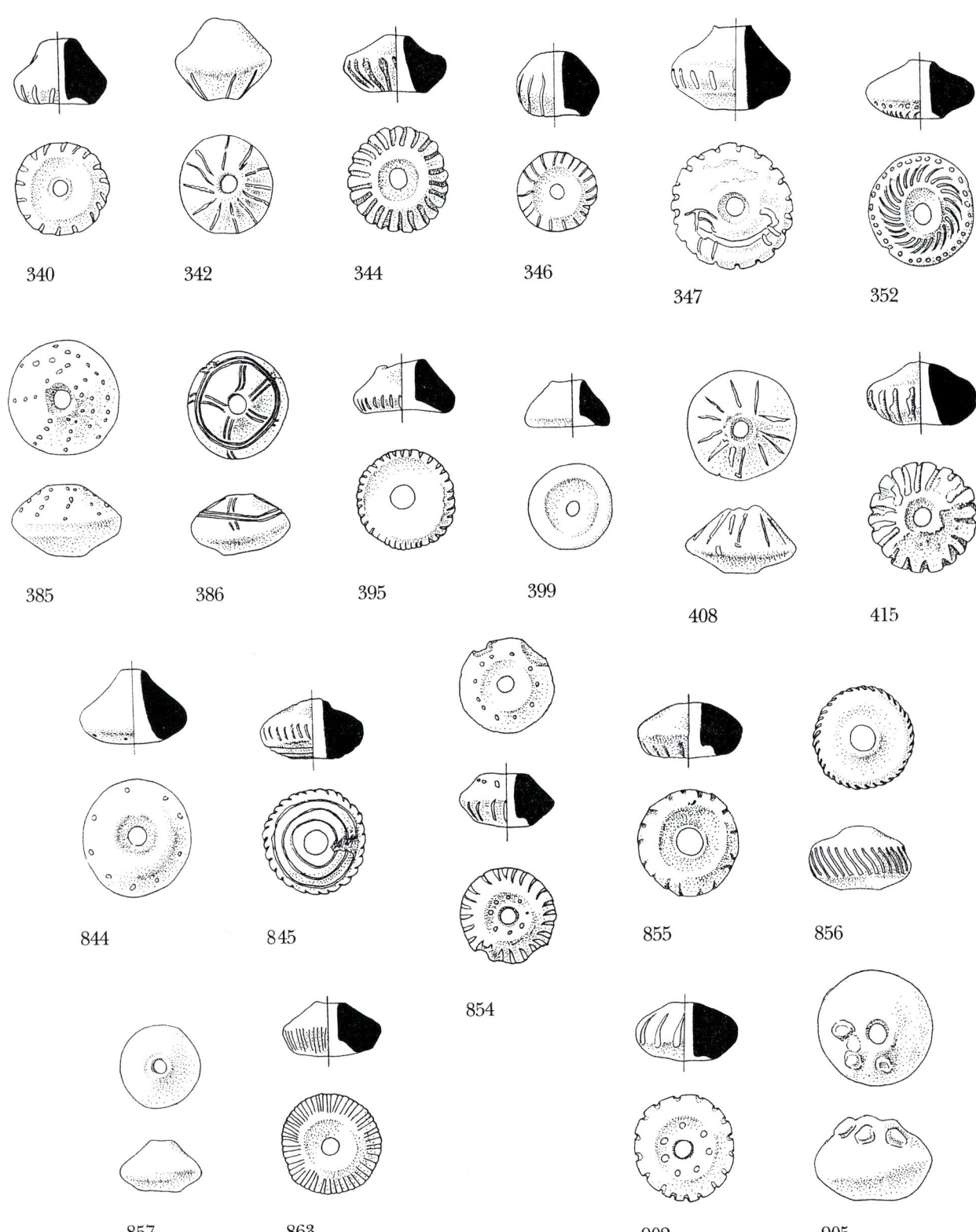

340 342 344 346 347 352

385 386 395 399 408 415

844 845 854 855 856

857 863 902 905

1:2

Plate 74. Spindle whorls, Levels XII (340–415) and XIA/B (844–905).

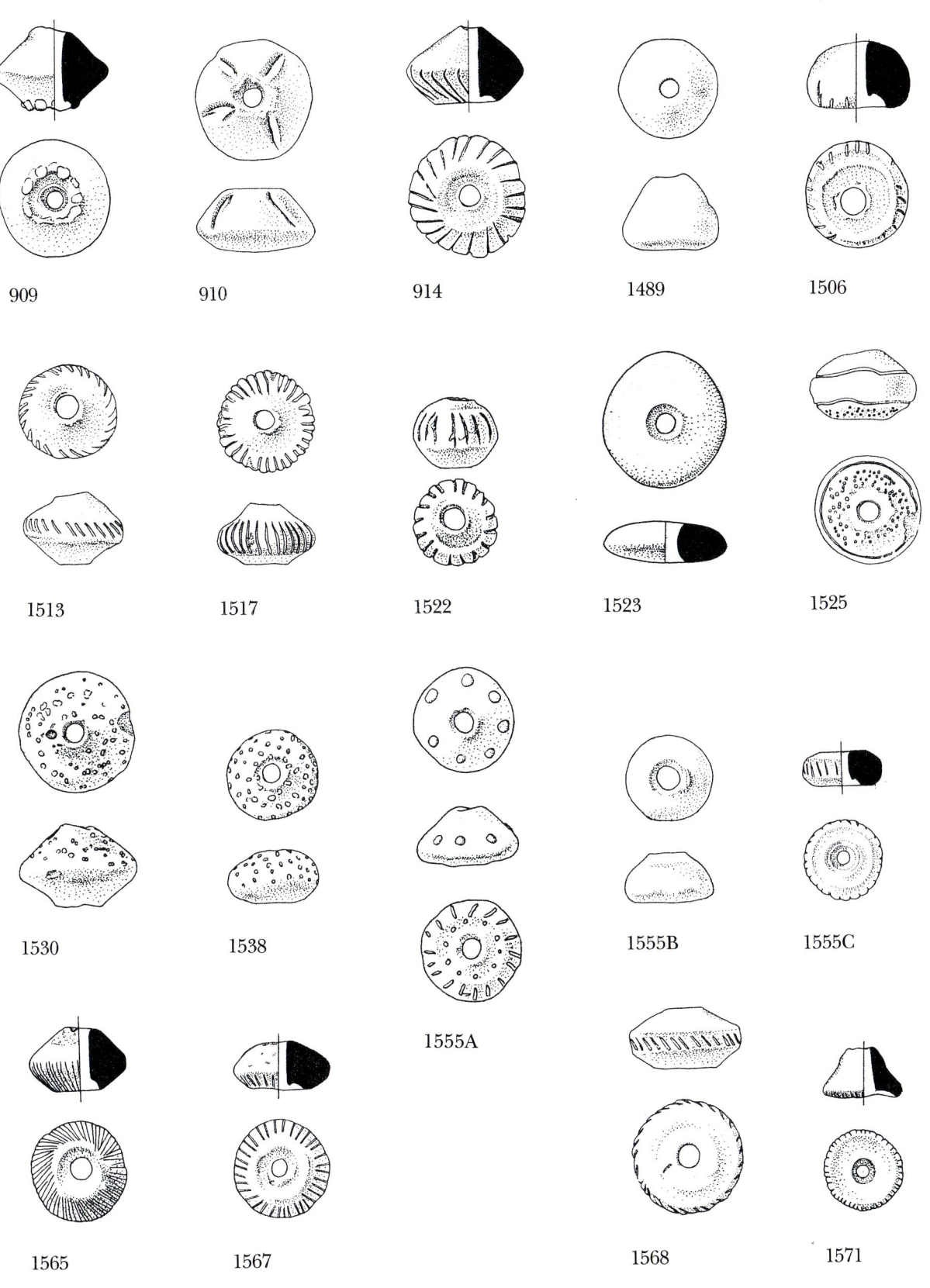

909 910 914 1489 1506

1513 1517 1522 1523 1525

1530 1538 1555A 1555B 1555C

1565 1567 1568 1571

1:2

Plate 75.   Spindle whorls, Levels XIA/B (909–914) to XI/XA (1489–1571).

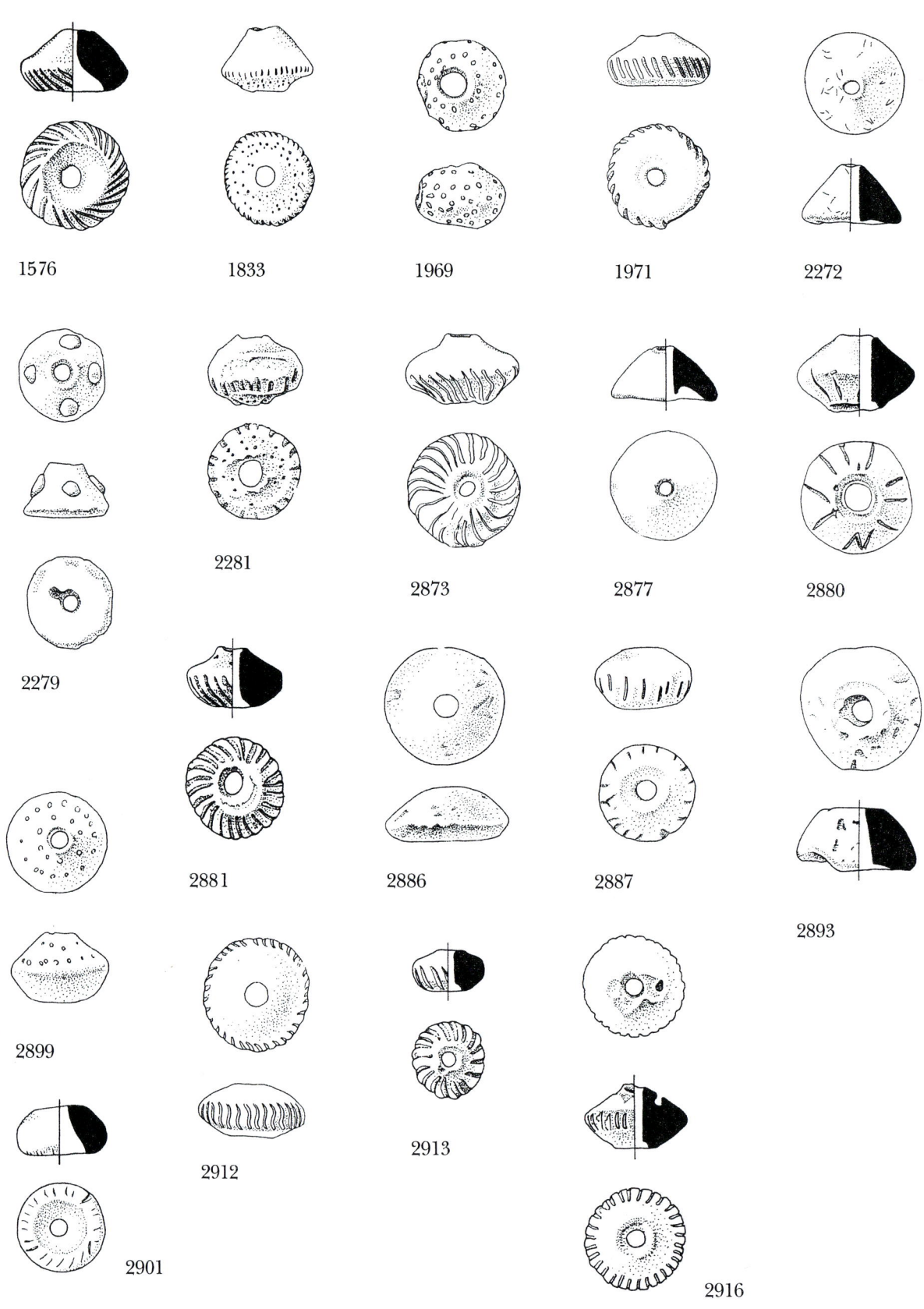

1576   1833   1969   1971   2272

2281   2873   2877   2880

2279   2881   2886   2887   2893

2899   2913   2912   2916   2901

1:2

Plate 76.   Spindle whorls, Levels XI/XA (Phase XI: 1576, Phase XA: 1833), X (1969–1971), IX (2272–2281) to VIII 2873–2916).

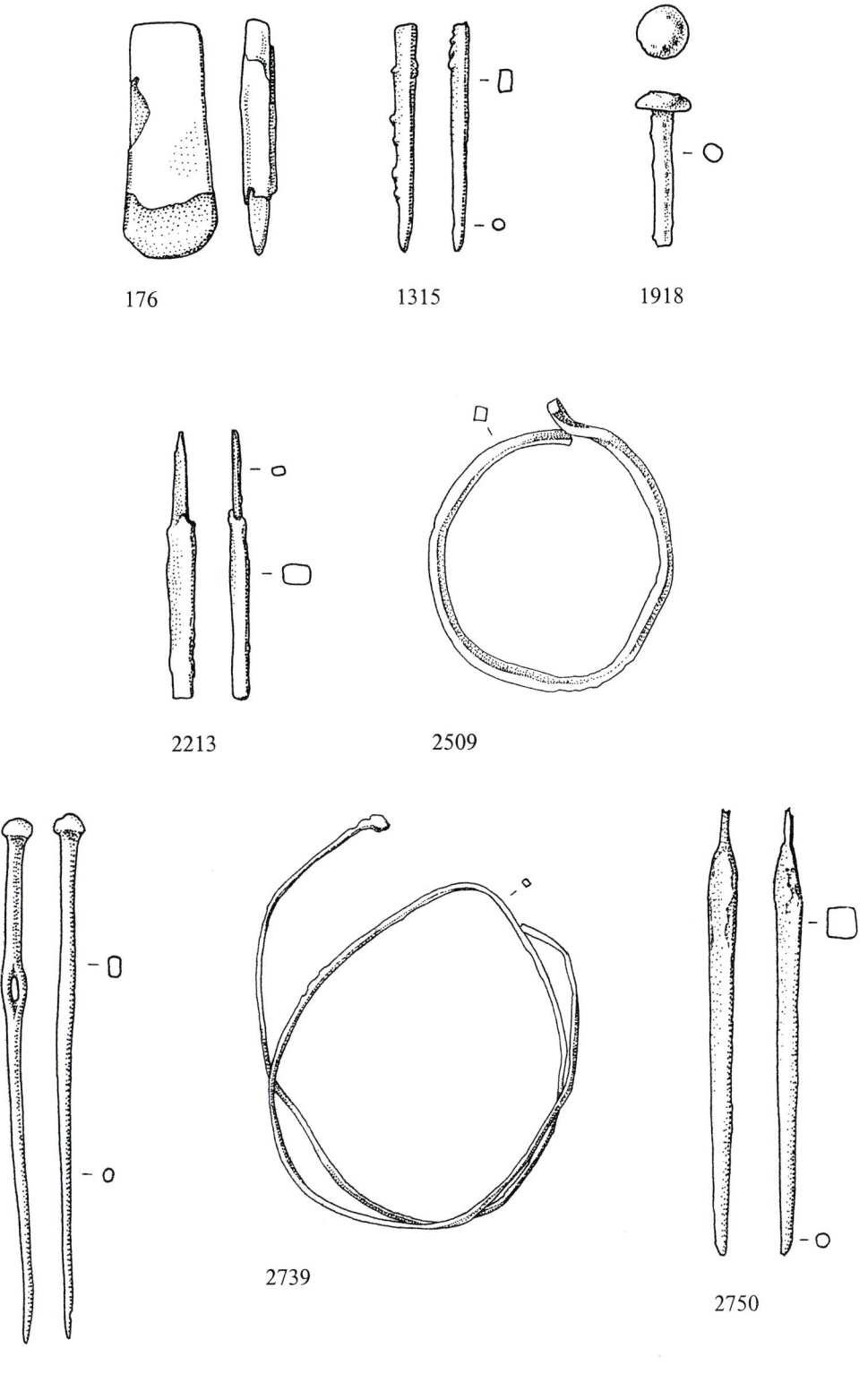

176

1315

1918

2213

2509

2730

2739

2750

1:1

Plate 77.   Metal objects, Levels XII (176), XI/XA (1315), X (1315), IX (2213), and VIII (2509–2750).

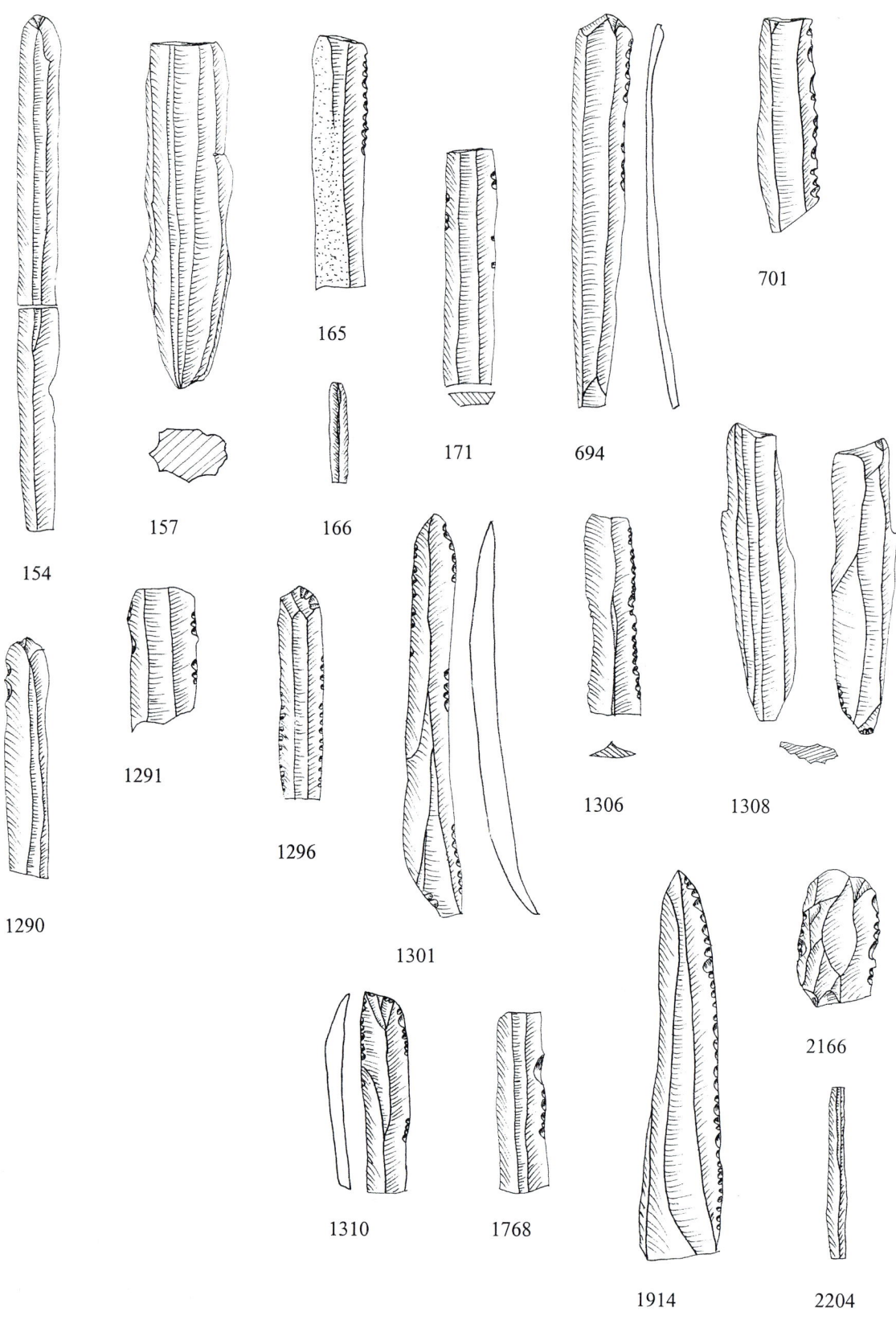

Plate 78.   Lithics, Levels XII (154–171), XIA/B (694–701), XI/XA (1290–1768), X (1914), IX (2204).

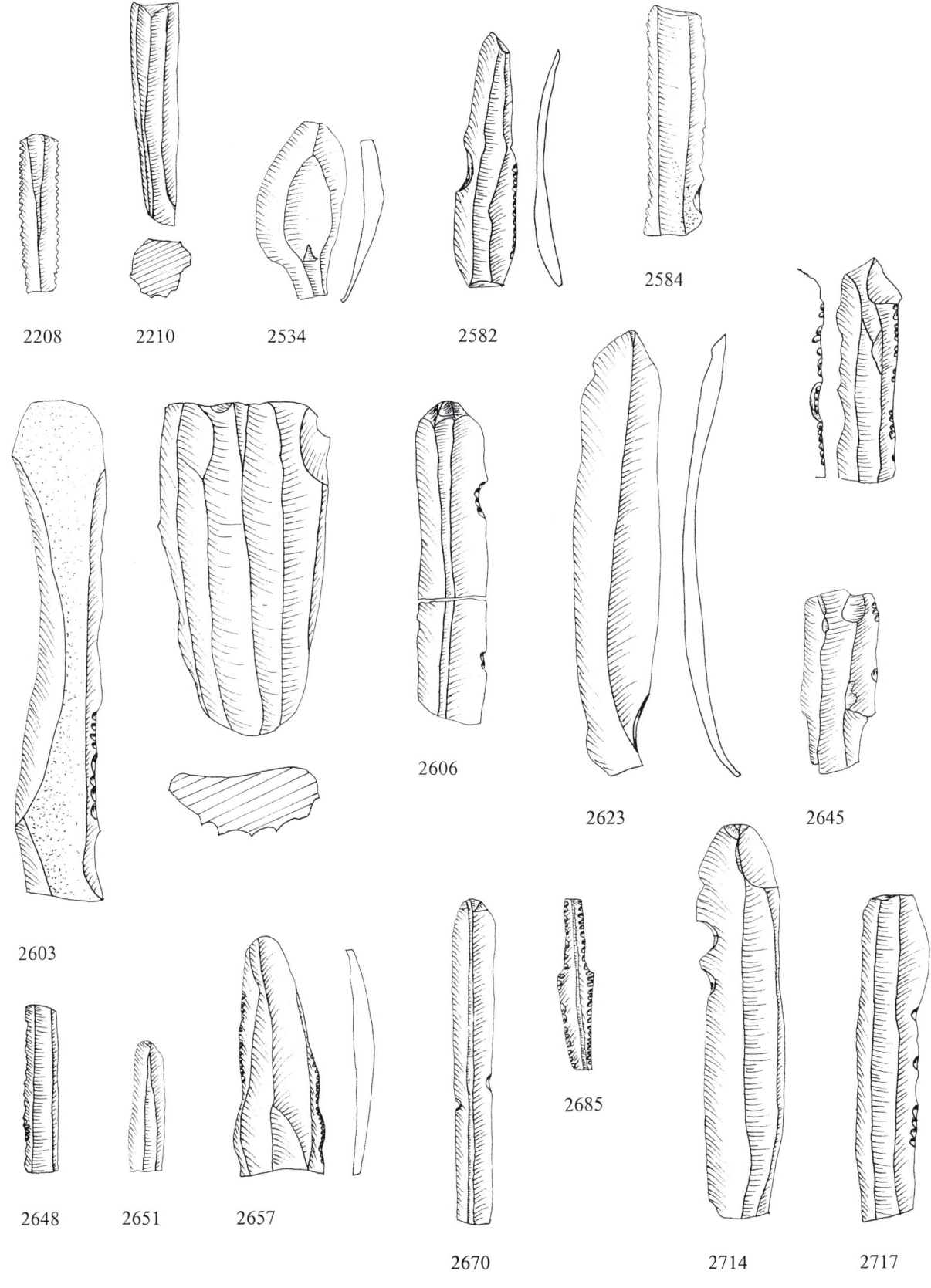

2208

2210

2534

2582

2584

2603

2606

2623

2645

2648

2651

2657

2670

2685

2714

2717

1:2

Plate 79.   Lithics, Levels IX (2208–2210) and VIII (2534–2717).

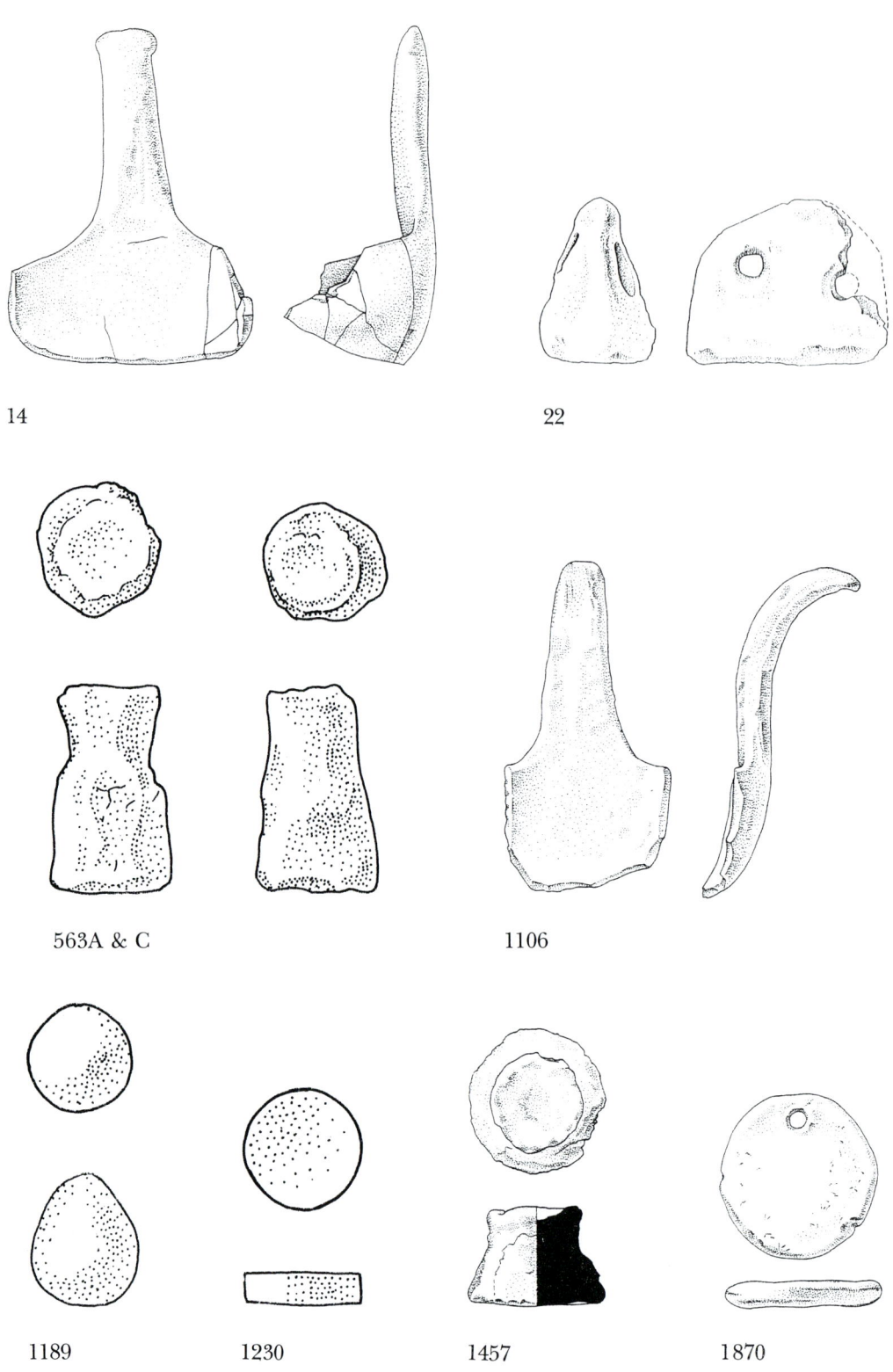

14

22

563A & C

1106

1189   1230   1457   1870

1:4
563, 1189, 1230–1:1

Plate 80.   Clay items, Levels XII (14–22), XIA/B (563), XI/XA (1106–1457) to X (1870).

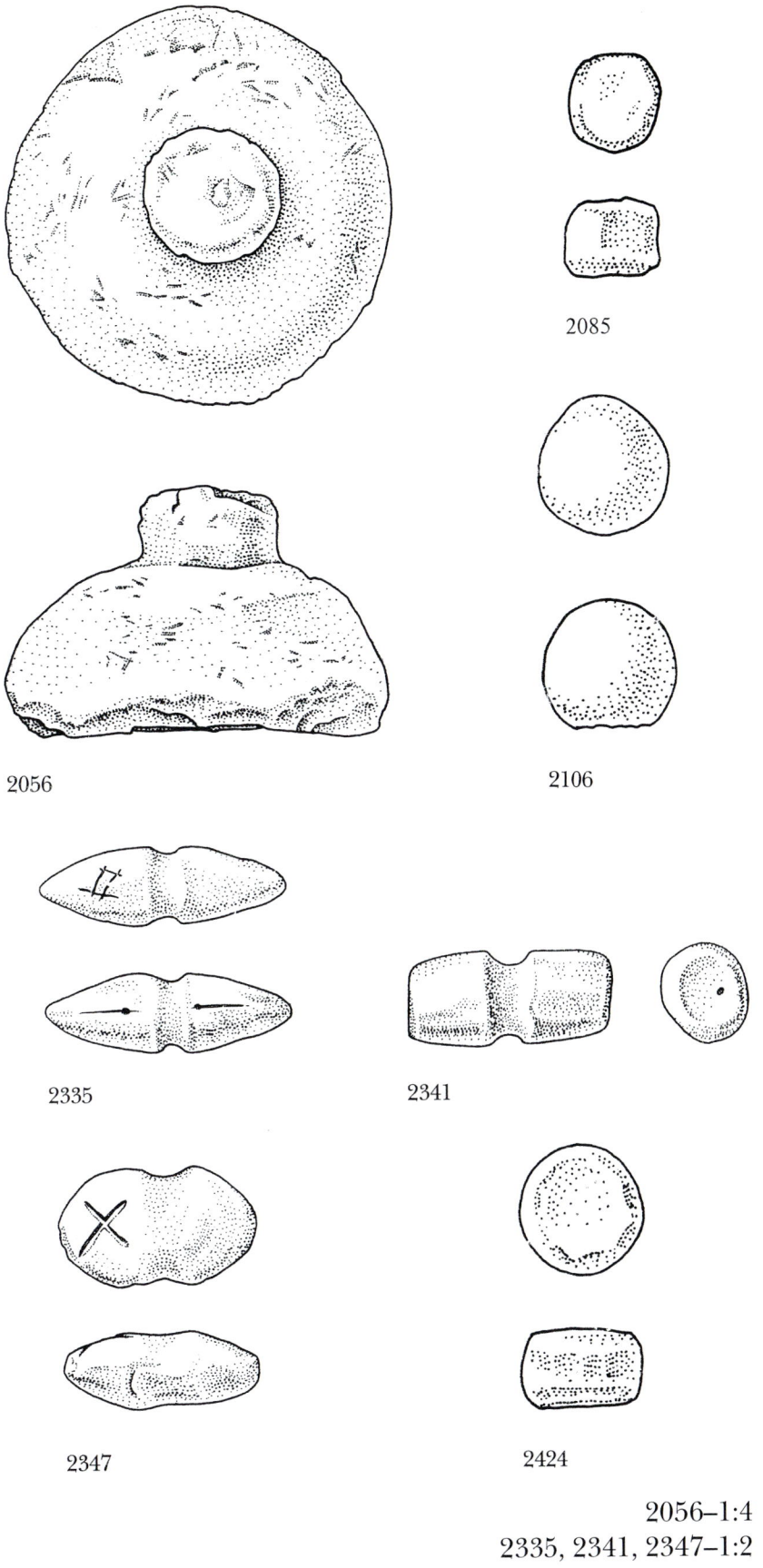

2085

2056

2106

2335

2341

2347

2424

2056–1:4
2335, 2341, 2347–1:2
2085, 2106, 2424–1:1

Plate 81.   Clay items, Levels IX (2056–2106) and VIII 2335–2424).

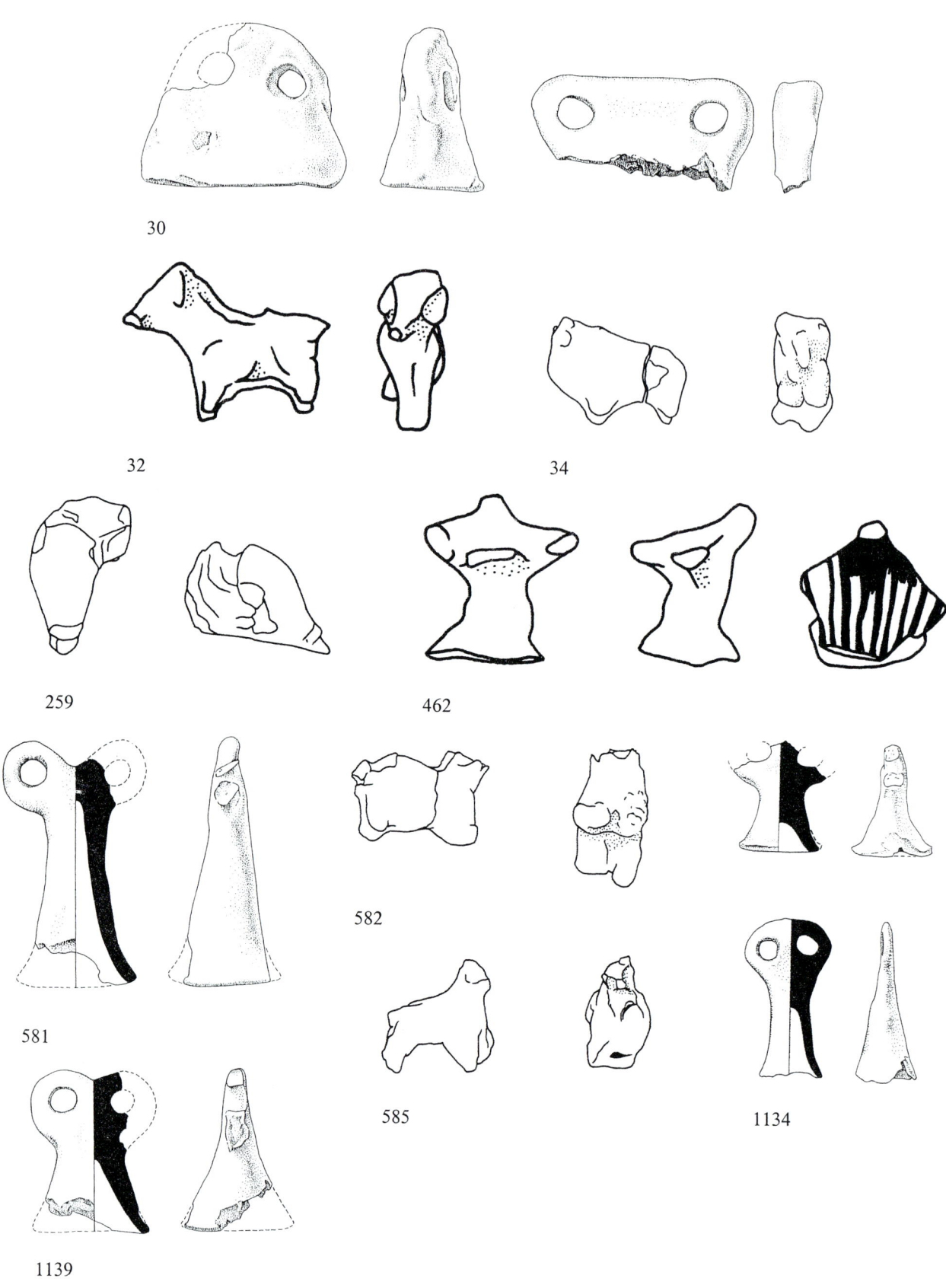

30

32

34

259

462

581

582

585

1134

1139

32, 462–1:1
34, 259, 582, 585–1:2
30, 581, 1134, 1139–1:4

Plate 82.   Figurines, Levels XII (30–34, 259), XIA/B (462–585) to XI/XA 1134–1139).

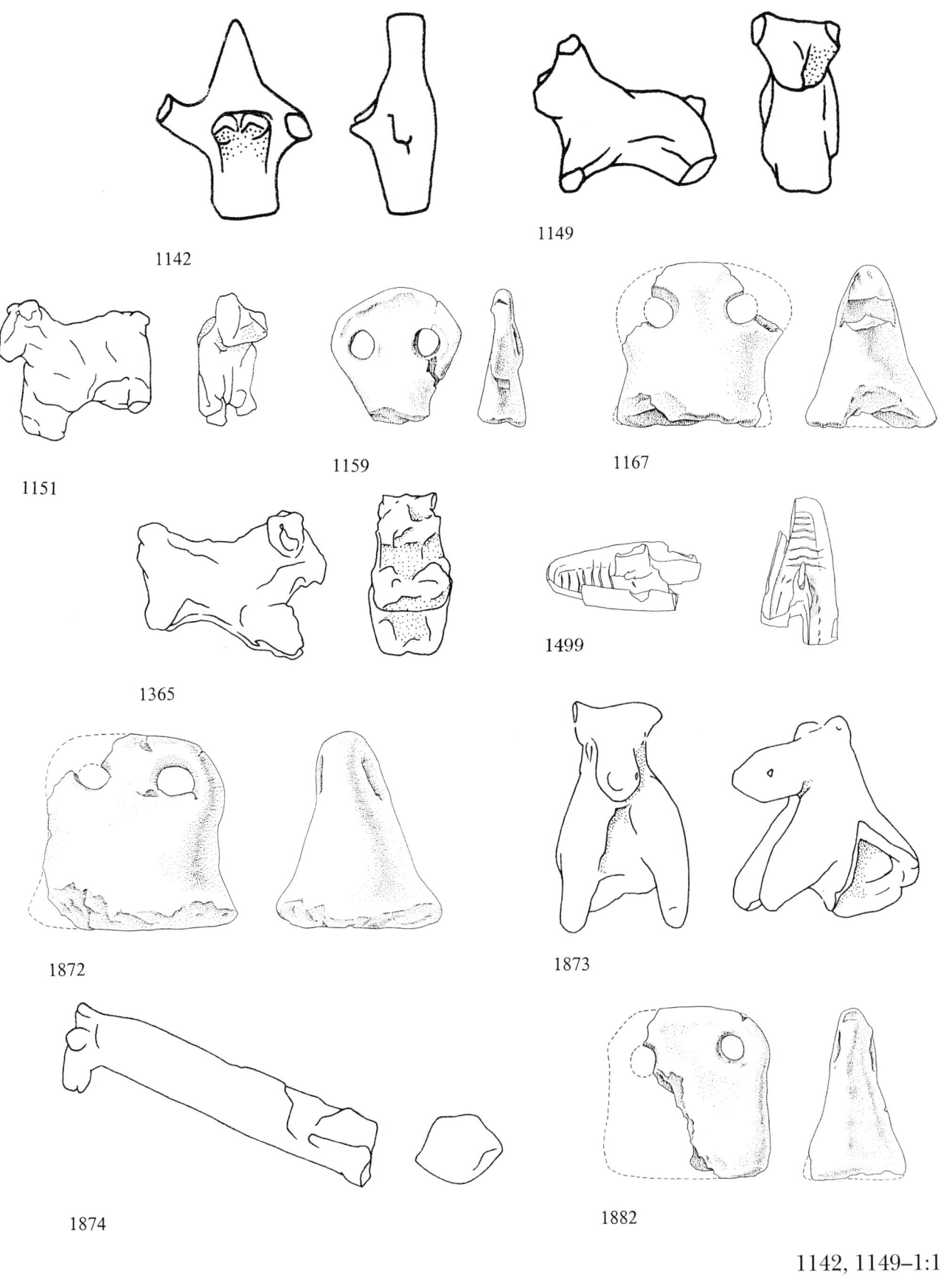

1142

1149

1151

1159

1167

1365

1499

1872

1873

1874

1882

1142, 1149–1:1
1151, 1365, 1873, 1874–1:2
1159, 1167, 1499, 1872, 1882–1:4

Plate 83. Figurines, Levels XI/XA (1142–1499) to X (1872–1882).

1965

2072

2073

2074

2075

2076

2077

2348

2368

2373

2375

2380

1:2
1965, 2075–1:1
2076, 2348–1:4

Plate 84. Figurines, Levels X (1965), IX (2072–2077), and VIII (2348–2380).

Index